# AN INTRODUCTION TO BRAIN AND BEHAVIOR

AN INTRODUCTION TO

# Brain and Behavior

BRYAN KOLB
*University of Lethbridge*
IAN Q. WHISHAW
*University of Lethbridge*

WORTH PUBLISHERS

An Introduction to Brain and Behavior

Printed in the United States of America
ISBN: 0-7167-5169-0
First Printing, 2000

Sponsoring Editor: Jessica Bayne
Marketing Manager: Renee Altier
Developmental Editors: Mary Marshall, Cele Gardner
Project Editor: Tracey Kuehn
Designer: Michael Mendelsohn
Art Director and Cover Designer: Barbara Reingold
Production Manager: Sarah Segal
Illustration Coordinator: Bill Page
Photo Editors: Elyse Rieder, Karen Barr
Supplements and Media Editor: Graig Donini
Illustrations: J/B Woolsey Associates
Composition: TSI Graphics
Printer and Binder: R.R. Donnelley and Sons Co.

Cover art: Charles Yuen, *Jug Boy,* 1994 (oil painting, 48″ × 76″)



Library of Congress Cataloging in Publication Data available upon request.

Worth Publishers
41 Madison Avenue
New York, New York 10010
www.worthpublishers.com

# About the Authors

Bryan Kolb received his Ph.D. from the Pennsylvania State University in 1973. He conducted postdoctoral work at the University of Western Ontario and the Montreal Neurological Institute. He moved to the University of Lethbridge in 1976, where he is currently a Professor of Psychology and Neuroscience. His current research examines how neurons of the cerebral cortex change in response to various factors, including hormones, experience, drugs, neurotrophins, and injury, and how these changes are related to behavior in normal and diseased brains. Kolb is a Killam Fellow (Canada Council), and a Fellow of the Canadian Psychological Association, the American Psychological Association, the American Psychological Society, and the Royal Society of Canada. He is a recipient of the Hebb Prize from CPA, and is a former president of the Canadian Society for Brain, Behavior, and Cognitive Science.

Ian Whishaw received his Ph.D. from the University of Western Ontario in 1971. He moved to the University of Lethbridge in 1970, where he is currently a Professor of Psychology and Neuroscience and holds a Board of Governors Chair in Neuroscience. He has had visiting appointments at the University of Texas, the University of Michigan, Cambridge University, and the University of Strasbourg, France. He is also a Fellow of Clair Hall, Cambridge. His current research examines how the precise details of bodily movements are influenced by injury or disease to the motor systems of rodents and humans. Whishaw is a Fellow of the Canadian Psychological Association, the American Psychological Association, and the Royal Society of Canada. He is a recipient of a bronze medal from the Canadian Humane Society, a recipient of the Ingrid Speaker Medal, and president of NeuroDetective Inc.

*To the first neuron, our ancestors, our families, and students who read this book*

# Contents in Brief

# Contents

# Preface

In the past decades, scientific understanding of the brain and human behavior has grown exponentially. In this book we have tried to communicate the excitement of recent breakthroughs in brain science and some of our own experiences in studying the brain over the past 30 years. We have tackled this story by imagining ourselves as students taking this first brain-science course, and we have tried to make sense of it by structuring the text around the key questions we ask about the brain, both as students and as neuroscientists: Why do we have a brain? How is it organized? How do drugs affect our behavior? How does the brain learn? How does it think? Emphasizing these and other basic questions about the brain will help to make clear our reasons for covering the information we do in this book. For example, if the reader realizes that we are ultimately interested in how the brain understands language or music, the functioning of the ear becomes more relevant because the ear is where auditory information enters the brain. And asking fundamental questions about the brain has another important benefit: It piques students' interest in the subject they are studying and challenges them to join us on the journey of discovery that is brain science.

## Learning Aids That Distinguish This Book

### Scientific Background Provided

We have tried to describe this journey in a way that students just beginning to study the brain and behavior will be able to understand. We have found that this course can sometimes be quite daunting, largely because information from all of the basic sciences is needed to understand brain function. This can be both a surprise and a shock to introductory students, who often come to the course lacking the necessary background. Many books provide their readers with little assistance in acquiring this background, assuming that students can simply jump right into the fray. But often that is not possible or appropriate. This book takes a different approach to dealing with the problem. It provides all the background students require to understand an introduction to brain science. For example, we provide the philosophical background needed to understand modern evolutionary theory, and we offer a short introduction to chemistry before describing the chemical activities of the brain. Similarly, we briefly discuss electricity before exploring the brain's electrical activity. In these ways the student is able to tackle brain science with greater confidence.

### Teaching Through Metaphors, Examples, and Principles

We've tried to develop this book in a style that students will enjoy, for if a textbook is not enjoyed, it has little chance of teaching well. We have heightened student interest in the material they are reading particularly through abundant use of metaphors and examples. We have also facilitated learning by reemphasizing main points, and by distilling out sets of principles about brain function that can serve as frameworks to guide students' thinking. For instance, Chapter 2 contains a discussion of eight key principles explaining how the various parts of the nervous system work together. This set of principles forms the basis of many later discussions in the book. Similarly, Chapter 15 provides a summary of major points extracted from the previous 14 core chapters of the book. Students will find that reading and rereading this summary can help them understand and remember the broader themes and messages of the book. This summary will also help students put the key information in each chapter into a meaningful context.

### Abundant Chapter Pedagogy

In addition to the innovative teaching devices just described, you will find numerous other pedagogical aids in every chapter. For instance, each chapter begins with both an outline and an opening vignette that connects the world of brain and behavior to some concrete experience. Within the chapters there are end-of-section reviews that help students remember the major points, marginal pictures that add visual illustration of concepts, and a marginal glossary that highlights and reinforces the definitions of important terms. Each chapter ends with a chapter summary organized around key questions, a list of additional questions to aid in review and preparation for tests, and a number of provocative questions for further thought that explore interesting implications of chapter content. At the end of every chapter there is also a list of key terms (with the page numbers on which those terms are defined in the book), an annotated list of recommended readings, and a list of on-line sources that can broaden a student's understanding of chapter topics.

### Unique Illustration Program

Our most important learning aid you'll be able to see by simply paging through this book. We have developed an expansive and, we believe, exceptional set of illustrations which, hand in hand with our words, describe and illuminate the world of the brain. In addition, the illustrations in every chapter are consistent and reinforce each other. For example, in every picture we use the same color code for each aspect of the neuron, and we often include an electronmicrograph image to show what a particular structure actually looks like when viewed through a microscope. You will also find these images on our Powerpoint presentations and integrated as labeling exercises in our study guide and testing materials.

## Our Integration of Certain Topics

### Clinical Information

Instructors will find that the placement of some topics is novel relative to traditional treatments. For example, we include brief descriptions of brain diseases close to discussions of basic processes that may involve those diseases. This placement is intended to help the first-time student repeatedly see the close links between what they are learning and real-life problems. The integration of real-life problems, especially behavioral disorders, into every chapter is further accomplished by our many Focus on Disorders boxes. These boxes typically employ interesting case studies to highlight specific disorders that are related to a chapter's content. We cover more than sixty disorders from addiction to Tourette's syndrome (a complete list of these discussions is presented in Table 15-2 on page 586). Our capstone Chapter 15 includes in-depth coverage of schizophrenia and affective disorders, along with a discussion of treatments, causes, and classifications of abnormal behavior.

### The Relationship of the Brain to Behavior

We feature the relationship between the brain and behavior in every chapter. For example, when we first describe how neurons communicate, we also describe how plasticity in connections between neurons can serve as the basis of learning. Later, in the chapter directed to the question of how we learn, we explore how interactions between different parts of the brain enable our more complex behaviors, a topic that is usually reserved for a discussion of cognitive processes.

### Research Methods

Some instructors may be surprised that we have not included a separate chapter on research methods. The reason is that the subject of research methods has also been integrated throughout the book. We believe that research methods are best understood in the context of what they are used for. We've included coverage of more than twenty methods (for a complete list, see Table 15-1 on page 585), many of which are accompanied by an illustration in the text and an animation on the accompanying CD-ROM. For instance, in describing how a neuron works, we explore how scientists record the electrical activity of the neuron. When we discuss how humans think, we examine the techniques of medical imaging that researchers use to see the brain in the act of thinking. And when answering the question of what motivates behavior, we delve into the research methods of producing brain lesions or electrically stimulating the brain. In these ways the uses of a particular method are made more meaningful to students.

## Areas of Emphasis

### Big-Picture Issues

One of the challenges in writing an introductory book on any topic is to decide what to include and what to exclude. We have organized discussions so as to focus on the bigger picture. A prime example is the discussion of general principles of nervous system function contained in Chapter 2. Although such a set of principles may be a bit arbitrary, it nevertheless gives students a useful framework for understanding the brain's activities. Similarly, in later chapters of this text we tackle topics in a more general way than most contemporary books do. For instance, in Chapter 11 we revisit the experiments and ideas of the 1960s as we try to understand why animals behave the way they do, after which we consider behaviors as diverse as drinking and anxiety attacks. Another example of our focus on the larger picture is our discussion of learning and memory, which occurs alongside a discussion of recovery from brain damage. We believe that such a broader focus helps students appreciate the larger problems that behavioral neuroscience is all about. Of course, broadening our focus has required us to leave out some of the details that might be found in other texts. But for us, discussions of larger problems and issues in the study of brain and behavior are more interesting for, and more likely to be remembered by, the student who is new to this field.

### The Relevance of Neuroscience

Throughout this book we have repeatedly emphasized that neuroscience is a human science — that everything in this book is relevant to our lives. Neuroscience helps us understand how we learn, how we develop, and how we can help people who suffer from sometimes deadly and destructive brain and behavioral disorders. We have found that emphasizing the clinical aspects of neuroscience is especially useful in motivating introductory students and in demonstrating to them the relevance of our field. Clinical material helps to make neurobiology particularly relevant to those who are going on to careers in psychology, social work, or other mental-health-related professions, as well as to students pursuing careers in the biological sciences. That is why we have not only integrated clinical information throughout this text and featured it in our Focus on Disorders boxes, but have also expanded upon it in our final chapter (Chapter 15).

### The Biological Basis of Behavior

Another area of emphasis in this book is a focus on questions that relate to the biological basis of behavior. For us, the excitement of neuroscience is in understanding how the brain explains what we do, whether it be talking, sleeping, seeing, or learning.

Readers will therefore find nearly as many illustrations about behavior as there are illustrations about the brain. This emphasis on explaining behavior is another reason why we have included three boxes on neurological disorders in every chapter.

### Evolution, Genetics, and Psychopharmacology

We wanted to make sure that this book reflected the excitement of current neuroscience, as we understand it as active researchers. Therefore, we have given emphasis to coverage of evolution, genetic research, contemporary research methods, and psychopharmacology. We cover the evolution of the brain in depth in Chapters 1 and 2 and return to this perspective in almost every chapter. The foundations of genetic research is introduced in depth in Chapter 3, but we discuss genetics in many other places in the text. You'll find the newest research methods throughout the book, with PET in Chapter 9, fMRI in Chapters 11 and 14, TMS in Chapter 14, and ERP in Chapter 4. We have an entire chapter on drugs and behavior (Chapter 6), but we return to the topic in many chapters, with coverage of drugs and information transfer in Chapter 4, drugs and cellular communication in Chapter 5, drugs and motivation in Chapter 11, drugs and sleep disorders in Chapter 12, and cellular changes with drug use in Chapter 13.

| COVERAGE OF THE EVOLUTION OF THE BRAIN | |
|---|---|
| Evolution of the neuron, the brain, and hominids | Chapter 1 |
| Evolution of the human brain | Chapter 2 |
| Evolution of the synapse | Chapter 5 |
| Evolution of geniculostriate and tectopulvinar pathways | Chapter 8 |
| Evolution of thought and language | Chapter 9 |
| Evolutionary and environmental influences on thought and language | Chapter 11 |
| Evolutionary theories of sleep and dreaming | Chapter 12 |
| Evolution of spacial cognition, language, and sex differences | Chapter 14 |

| COVERAGE OF GENETICS | |
|---|---|
| Genes, cells, and behavior | Chapter 3 |
| Metabotropic receptors and DNA | Chapter 5 |
| Learning and genes | Chapter 5 |
| Genes and drug action | Chapter 6 |
| Genes and development | Chapter 7 |
| Genetics of color vision | Chapter 8 |
| Genetics of sleep disorders | Chapter 12 |

### Current Research

Finally, in this book we emphasize the findings of current research. You will not, however, find a great many citations embedded in the chapter discussions. We feel that numerous citations can sometimes disrupt the flow of a text and distract students from the task of mastering what they read. We have consequently been selective in our citation of the truly massive literature on the brain and behavior. We provide citations to classic works by including the names of the researchers, and sometimes their pictures, and by mentioning where the research was performed. In areas where there is controversy or new breakthroughs, we also include more detailed citations to current papers, citing papers from the year 2000 when possible. A reference list to all of the literature used in developing this text is provided at the end of the book.

## Supplements

A number of student and instructor materials are available to supplement our book.

You'll find the innovative ***Foundations of Behavioral Neuroscience CD-ROM*** inside the back cover of this book. Created by Uri Hasson from the Weizmann Institute in Israel and Yehuda Shavit from Hebrew University of Jerusalem and produced by the Open University of Israel, this CD includes five modules: Research Methods, Neural Communication, Vision, Movement, and the Central Nervous System. References to this CD (and to the book's Web site, described below) appear in the margins of each chapter, pointing to places where the text discussion is enhanced by a video clip or an animation. The CD features rotating 3-D models of the human brain and eye, more than twenty-five video clips, animations of key physiological mechanisms, and interactive examples of new neuroimaging technology. It also includes multiple-choice questions for each chapter of the text.

A **Web site,** found at www.worthpublishers.com/kolb, with material provided by Keith Trujillio of California State University at San Marcos, offers a variety of simulations, video clips, tutorials, and quizzes. It is updated periodically with new links, exercises, and developments in neuroscience. For the instructor, the site offers on-line testing, a syllabus posting service, Web site building service, Powerpoint presentation files, and access to electronic versions of the artwork from the book.

The **Instructor's Manual,** written by Debora Baldwin of the University of Tennessee, Knoxville, contains lecture suggestions, lab activities, and handouts for student projects. Course planning suggestions, ideas for term projects, and a guide to videos and Internet resources are also included.

A battery of more than 2000 test questions is available in a **Test Bank** written by Robert Sainsbury of the University of Calgary. The Test Bank provides true/false, multiple-choice, short-answer, and essay questions, as well as labeling exercises tied to the art in the text. Each question is keyed to a learning objective and page-referenced to the textbook. The Test Bank is also available on a dual-platform CD-ROM, which allows instructors to quickly add, edit, re-format, and re-sequence questions. The CD is also the access point for Diploma On-line Testing, which allows instructors to create and administer secure exams over a network and over the Internet.

The **Student Study Guide,** written by Terry Bazzett of the State University of New York at Geneseo, is a carefully crafted guide with multiple tools for learning and retaining text material. Each chapter includes a review of key conceps, terms, practice tests, short-answer questions, illustrations for labelling and identification, Internet activities, CD-ROM questions, and crossword puzzles.

Other helpful supplements for instructors include the **transparency package**, available as traditional acetates as well as on-line in our Web site. There is also a library of **videos,** including a collection of Scientific American Frontiers segments on the brain and behavior featuring the work of Irene Pepperberg, Steve Pinker, and Linda Bartoshuk, as well as the revised second editions of both ***The Brain*** and ***The Mind*** Video Teaching Modules, updated by Frank Vattano and his colleagues at Colorado State University.

## Acknowledgments

Although as authors our names are on the cover of this book, we did not write the book alone, although we are certainly responsible for any errors. The staff at Worth Publishers and W.H. Freeman, Inc., played a major role, right from the beginning until the end. We especially want to thank Buck Rogers, with whom we originally conceived this book; Susan Brennan for insisting that we write it; and Jessica Bayne, who cheerfully kept us at it and guided ourselves, the editors, the artists, and the photo researchers, Elyse Rieder and Karen Barr, to produce a book that is far more elegant than we had originally imagined. We must also thank the development editors, Janet Tannenbaum and Marjorie Anderson, who challenged every idea and illustration that our early drafts contained, as well as Mary Marshall and Patty Zimmerman, whose job was to make sure that the book read as if there were but a single author. Tracey Kuehn, Cele Gardner, and Sarah Segal ensured that all the details in the book came out right. We would also like to thank John Woolsey and Mike Demaray, who in pursuit of producing the comprehensive and beautiful art program came to Canada to discuss every figure with us in person (and to ski).

Our colleagues, too, played a major role in developing this text. We are especially indebted to those reviewers who provided extensive comments on selected chapters and artwork: Patrick Ament, Central Missouri State University; Trevor Archer, University of Goteborg; Giorgio Ascoli, George Mason University; Brian Auday, Gordon College; Aldo Badiani, University of Michigan; Debora Baldwin, University of Tennessee, Knoxville; Terry Bazzett, SUNY, Geneseo; Kent Berridge, University of Michigan; Gayle Brosnan-Waters, Vanguard University; John Bruno, Ohio State University; Rebecca Chesire, University of Hawaii, Manoa; Paul Currie, Barnard College; Darragh Devine, University of Florida; Shelly Dickinson, Reed College; Sherry Dingman, Marist College; D.L. Dodson, Lebanon Valley College; Betty Dorr, Fort Lewis College; Steven Dworkin, University of North Carolina, Wilmington; Marcia Earhard, Dalhousie University; Thor Eysteinsson, University of Iceland; Gregory Ervin, Brigham Young University; Rick Gilmore, Penn State University; Karen Glendenning, Florida State University; Dennis Goff, Randolph-Macon Women's College; Ed Green, University of Miami; Kenneth Green, California State University, Long Beach; Stuart Hall, University of Montana; Andrew Harver, University of North Carolina, Charlotte; Harold Herzog, Western Carolina University; Jonathan Hess, University of Illinois, Springfield; Theresa Jones, University of Washington; Wesley Jordan, St. Mary's College of Maryland; Stephen Kiefer, Kansas State University; Jeansok Kim, Yale University; Mark Kristal, SUNY, Buffalo; Paul Kulkosky, University of Southern Colorado; Charles Kutscher, Syracuse University; Daniel Leger, University of Nebraska, Lincoln; Michael Markham, Florida International University; Richard Marshall, University of Texas, Austin; William Meil, Indiana University of Pennsylvania; Garrett Milliken, College of Charleston; Daniel Moriarty, University of San Diego; Tony Nunez, Michigan State University; Joseph Porter, Virginia Commonwealth University; Julio Ramirez, Davidson College; Michael Renner, West Chester University; Tony Robertson, Malaspina University College; Robin Roof, Eastern Michigan University; Neil Rowland, University of Florida; Robert Schneider, Metropolitan State College; Katherine Schultz, University of Winnipeg; Susan Sesack, University of Pittsburgh; Fred Shaffer, Truman State University; Cheryl Sisk, Michigan State University; Leslie Skeen, University of Delaware; R.W. Skelton, University of Victoria; Laura Smale, Michigan State University; Robert Spencer, University of Colorado, Boulder; Rodney Swain, University of Wisconsin, Milwaukee; Susan Swithers, Purdue University; Anne Jane Tierney, Colgate University; C. Robin Timmons, Drew University; Keith Trujillo, California State University, San Marcos; Lawrence Wichlinski, Carleton College; Diane Witt, Binghamton University; Xiaojuan Xu, Grand Valley State University; William Yates, University of Pittsburgh; and Mark Zrull, Appalachian State University. We especially want to thank Robert Sainsbury of the University of Calgary, who tried the book out with his students and provided invaluable feedback.

Finally, we must thank our families for putting up with what turned out to be a bigger project than even we bargained for.

*Bryan Kolb and Ian Q. Whishaw*

# AN INTRODUCTION TO Brain and Behavior

CHAPTER

# 1

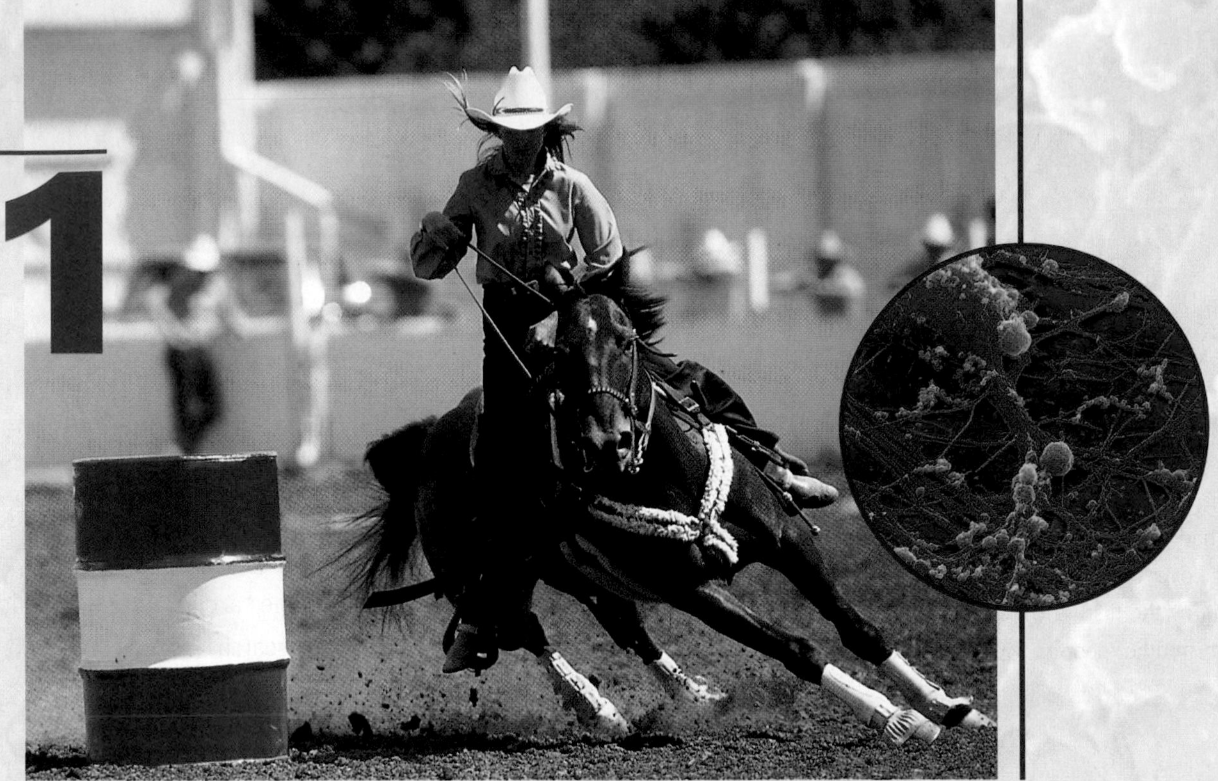

# What Are the Origins of Brain and Behavior?



Crandall/The Image Works

Micrograph: Oliver Meckes/Ottawa/Photo Researchers

Twelve years ago, I survived a serious head injury. In the second it took for my car to crash head-on, my life was permanently changed, and I became another statistic in what has been called "the silent epidemic."

During the next months, my family and I began to understand something of the reality of the experience of head injury. I had begun the painful task of recognizing and accepting my physical, mental, and emotional deficits. I couldn't taste or smell. I couldn't read even the simplest sentence without forgetting the beginning before I got to the end. I had a hair-trigger temper that could ignite instantly into rage over the most trivial incident.

During the first year, I could not take too much stimulation from other people. My brain would simply overload, and I would have to go off into my room to get away. Noise was hard for me to take, and I wanted the place to be kept quiet, which was an impossibility in a small house with three youngsters in it. I remember laying down some impossible rules for all of us. For example, I made rules that everybody had to be in bed by 9:30 PM, that all lights had to be out, and that no noise of any kind was permitted after that time. No TV, radios, or talking was allowed. Eventually the whole family was in an uproar.

Two years after my injury, I wrote a short article: "What Does It Feel Like to Be Brain Damaged?" At that time, I was still intensely focusing on myself and my own struggle. (Every head-injured survivor I have met seems to go through this stage of narcissistic preoccupation, which creates a necessary shield to protect them from the painful realities of the situation until they have a chance to heal.) I had very little sense of anything beyond the material world and could only write about things that could be described in factual terms. I wrote, for example, about my various impairments and how I learned to compensate for them by a variety of methods.

At this point in my life, I began to involve myself with other brain-damaged people. This came about in part after the publication of my article. To my surprise, it was reprinted in many different publications, copied, and handed out to thousands of survivors and families. It brought me an enormous outpouring of letters, phone calls, and personal visits that continue to this day. Many were struggling as I had struggled, with no diagnosis, no planning, no rehabilitation, and most of all, no hope.

The far-ranging effects of head injury on the survivor's life and that of his or her family cannot be overemphasized. In my own case I realize that it was for me the single most significant event of my lifetime. The catastrophic effect of my injury was such that I was shattered and then remolded by the experience, and I emerged from it a profoundly different person with a different set of convictions, values, and priorities. Above all, I have learned that there is no limit to the power of faith, hope, and love. With these, I made the journey out of the shadows into a larger, brighter world than the one I had left behind before my injury. (Linge, 1990)

This description of what it is like to be brain injured was written by Fred Linge, a clinical psychologist with a degree in brain research. (For an explanation of how the brain can be injured in an accident, see "Closed Head Injury" on page 2.) In the years after his injury, Linge made an immense journey. He traveled from a time before the car crash, when he gave less thought to the relation between his brain and his behavior than he did to the way in which he dressed. At the end of the journey, thoughts about his brain and his behavior dominated his life. He became a consultant and advisor to many people who also had suffered brain injury.

Most of you are like Fred Linge before he took that journey. Your brain does its work so efficiently and unobtrusively that you hardly give it any thought. You may be unaware that the human brain has hundreds of parts, each of which participates in certain tasks. You may have no knowledge that the brain changes as you age, as you undergo major life events, and even as you engage in seemingly trivial behaviors, such as reading the words on this page. In learning about the origins of the universe, the world, and human beings, you may have encountered no mention of the brain and its relation to behavior. Yet, if you ever had first-hand experience with brain damage, you, too, would be confronted with the workings of this most wonderful and complex machine.

The purpose of this book is to take you on a journey not unlike the one that Fred Linge took. Through it you, too, will come to understand the link between brain and behavior. Of course, we do not ask that you experience brain damage to undertake this journey. The road that we offer is simply one of information and discovery. Yet, along

## Focus on Disorders

## Closed Head Injury

Closed head injury results from a blow to the head that subjects the brain to a variety of forces. First, the force exerted on the skull at the site of the blow causes bruising (contusion) known as a "coup." Second, the blow may force the brain against the opposite side of the skull, producing an additional bruise called a "countercoup" (see the accompanying illustration). Third, the movement of the brain may cause a twisting or shearing of nerve fibers, causing microscopic lesions. Such lesions may be found throughout the brain, but they are most common in the frontal and temporal lobes. Fourth, the bruises and strains caused by the impact may produce bleeding (hemorrhage). Because the blood is trapped within the skull, it acts as a growing mass (hematoma), which exerts pressure on surrounding brain regions. Finally, like blows to other parts of the body, blows to the brain produce swelling (edema). This swelling, which is a collection of fluid in and around damaged tissue, is another source of pressure on the brain.

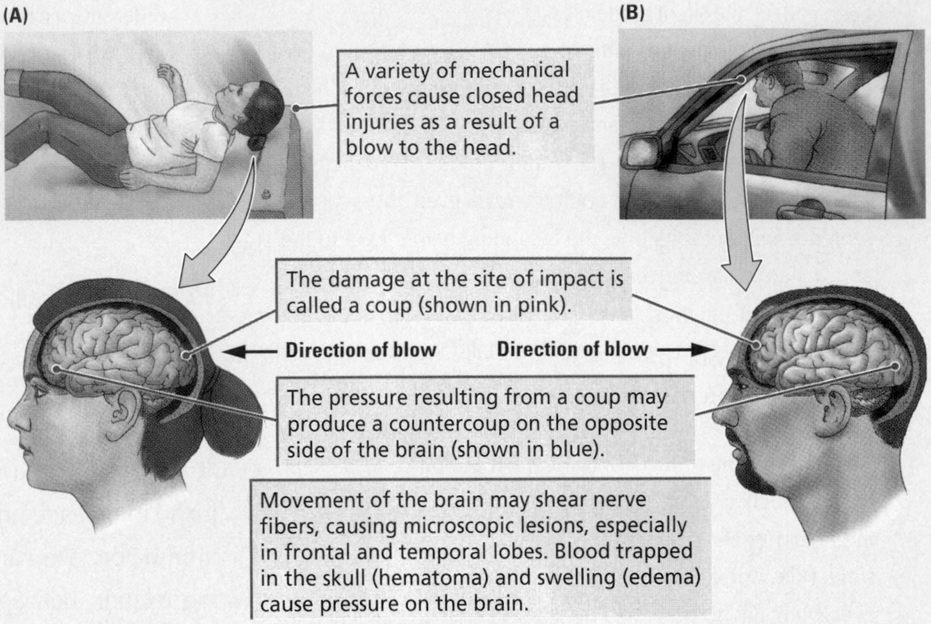

People who sustain closed head injury often lose consciousness because the injury affects fibers in lower parts of the brain that are associated with waking. The severity of coma can indicate the severity of the injury. Closed head injuries resulting from motor vehicle accidents are particularly severe because the head is moving when the blow is struck, thereby increasing the velocity of the impact.

The diffuse effects of closed head injuries make diagnosis very difficult, which is why these kinds of injuries have been collectively called a "silent epidemic." Victims of severe closed head injury can suffer serious repercussions in their everyday lives. Like Fred Linge, many have difficulty returning to their former levels of functioning, including carrying out their previous jobs.

(A)
(B)
A variety of mechanical forces cause closed head injuries as a result of a blow to the head.
The damage at the site of impact is called a coup (shown in pink).
Direction of blow
Direction of blow
The pressure resulting from a coup may produce a countercoup on the opposite side of the brain (shown in blue).
Movement of the brain may shear nerve fibers, causing microscopic lesions, especially in frontal and temporal lobes. Blood trapped in the skull (hematoma) and swelling (edema) cause pressure on the brain.



Shading (pink and blue) indicates regions of the brain most frequently damaged in closed head injury. A blow can produce a contusion both at the site of impact and at the opposite side of the brain owing to compression of the brain against the front **(A)** or back **(B)** of the skull.

it, you will find that much of the evidence that we have about the brain and behavior comes from the study of changes in people who have suffered brain injury. At the same time, we are also learning more and more about how the brain works when we are healthy. This emerging knowledge is changing how we think about ourselves, how we structure education and our social interactions, and how we aid those with brain injury.

In this chapter, we answer the question, What are the origins of brain and behavior? We begin by defining both the brain and behavior and outlining the nervous system's basic structure. We then look at how people through history have viewed the relation between brain and behavior, starting with the mentalistic perspective of Aristotle and progressing to the biological perspective of today. With this background in mind, we explore the evolution of brain and behavior. Here we pay special attention to the evolution of the human species, while still recognizing the many traits that we have in common with other animals. Finally, we look at several matters concerning the study of the brain and behavior in modern humans, including the matter of how our brains acquire the sophisticated skills of human culture. In subsequent chapters, we will further develop many of the ideas introduced here in addition to filling in a great many details about brain anatomy and function and how behavior is organized.

## DEFINING BRAIN AND BEHAVIOR

Brain and behavior differ greatly but are linked. The brain is a physical object, a living tissue, a body organ. Behavior is action, momentarily observable, but fleeting. Yet one is responsible for the other, which is responsible for the other, which is responsible for the other, and so on, and so on. We begin by defining first the brain, then behavior, and finally their interrelation.

### What Is the Brain?

For his postgraduate research, our friend Harvey chose to study the electrical activity that the brain gives off. He said that he wanted to live on as a brain in a bottle after his body died. He expected that his research would allow his bottled brain to communicate with others who could "read" his brain's electrical signals. Harvey failed in his objective, in part because the goal was technically impossible but also because he lacked a full understanding of what "brain" means.

*Brain* is the Anglo-Saxon word for the tissue that is found within the skull, and it is this tissue that Harvey wanted to put into a bottle. Figure 1-1 shows a typical human brain oriented as in the skull of an upright human. The brain has two relatively symmetrical halves called **hemispheres,** one on the left and one on the right. So, just as your body is symmetrical, having two arms and two legs, so is the brain. If you make your right hand into a fist and hold it up, the fist can represent the positions of the brain's hemispheres within the skull, with the thumb pointing toward the front.

The entire outer layer of the brain consists of a folded tissue. The folds are called **gyri** (singular, gyrus). This outer layer is known as the **cerebral cortex** (usually referred to simply as the cortex). The word *cortex,* which means "bark" in Latin, is aptly chosen both because of the cortex's folded appearance and because it covers most of the rest of the brain. The cortex of each hemisphere is divided into four lobes, named after the skull bones beneath which they lie. The **temporal lobe** is located approximately at the same place as the thumb on your upraised fist. Because it points forward, it is a good landmark for identifying which part of the brain is the front. The lobe lying immediately above the temporal lobe is called the **frontal lobe** because it is located at the front of the brain, beneath the frontal bone of the skull. The **parietal lobe** is located behind the frontal lobe, and the **occipital lobe** constitutes the area at the back of each hemisphere.

It is clear that Harvey, who wanted to have his brain bottled after he died, wanted to preserve not just his brain but his self—his consciousness, his thoughts, all of his intelligence. This meaning of the term *brain* refers to something other than the organ found inside the skull. It refers to the brain as that which exerts control over behavior. This meaning of *brain* is what we intend when we talk of someone being "the brain behind the operation" or when we speak of the computer that guides a spacecraft as being the vessel's "brain." The term *brain,* then, signifies both the organ itself and the fact that this organ controls behavior. Could Harvey manage to preserve his control-exerting self inside a bottle? Read on to learn the answer to this question.

On the CD, visit the module on the Central Nervous System. Look at the 3-D view of the human cortex in the section on the overview of the brain for a hands-on view of what this organ looks like.

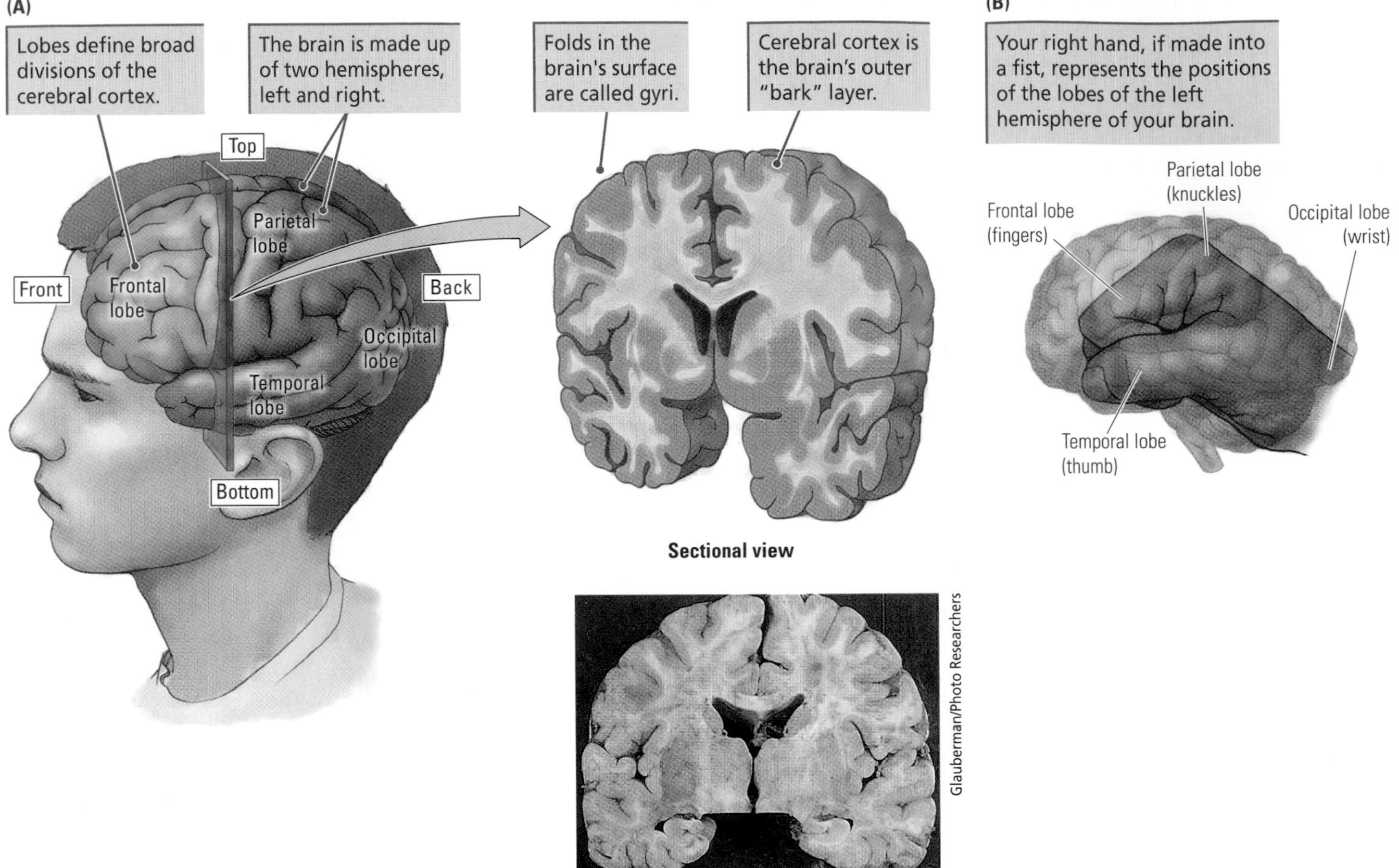
(A)
Lobes define broad divisions of the cerebral cortex.
The brain is made up of two hemispheres, left and right.
Folds in the brain's surface are called gyri.
Cerebral cortex is the brain's outer "bark" layer.
Top
Parietal lobe
Front
Frontal lobe
Back
Occipital lobe
Temporal lobe
Bottom
Sectional view
Glauberman/Photo Researchers
(B)
Your right hand, if made into a fist, represents the positions of the lobes of the left hemisphere of your brain.
Parietal lobe (knuckles)
Frontal lobe (fingers)
Occipital lobe (wrist)
Temporal lobe (thumb)

**Figure 1-1**

**(A)** In this representation of the human brain, showing its orientation in the head, the visible part of the brain is the cerebral cortex (*cortex* means "bark," and the cortex resembles the bark of a tree). The cortex is a thin sheet of tissue that is folded many times so that it fits inside the skull. The folds are called gyri. The brain consists of two symmetrical halves called hemispheres. Each hemisphere is divided into four lobes: frontal, parietal, temporal, and occipital. **(B)** The fist of your hand can serve as a guide to the orientation of the brain and its lobes. The thumb represents the temporal lobe and points forward, the flexed fingers represent the frontal lobe, the knuckles represent the parietal lobe, and the wrist represents the occipital lobe.

## How Is the Nervous System Structured?

Just like every other organ of the body, the brain is composed of cells. These brain cells come in a variety of shapes and sizes. One type of brain cell is the **neuron** (sometimes called nerve cell), which has fibers projecting from it that make contact with other cells. These interconnecting fibers make the brain a sensing, integrating organ that also instructs the body to move.

Most of the connections from the brain to the rest of the body are made through the **spinal cord,** which descends through a canal in the vertebrae (the bones that form the backbone). The spinal cord is in the same orientation as that of the upright arm supporting your fist. The brain and spinal cord, which in mammals such as ourselves are both protected by bones, together make up the **central nervous system** (CNS).

The central nervous system is connected to the rest of the body through **nerve fibers,** as shown in Figure 1-2. To sense what goes on in the world around us and in our own bodies, these nerve fibers are extensively connected to sensory receptors on the body's surface, to internal body organs, and to muscles. All of these nerve fibers radiating out beyond the brain and spinal cord as well as all the neurons outside the brain and spinal cord are referred to as the **peripheral nervous system** (PNS). The central and peripheral nervous systems together make up the whole **nervous system.**

Networks of sensory pathways made up of bundles of nerve fibers and motor pathways also made up of bundles of nerve fibers of the peripheral nervous system are connected to the central nervous system. **Sensory nerves** are those related to specific senses, such as hearing, vision, and touch. They connect receptors for these

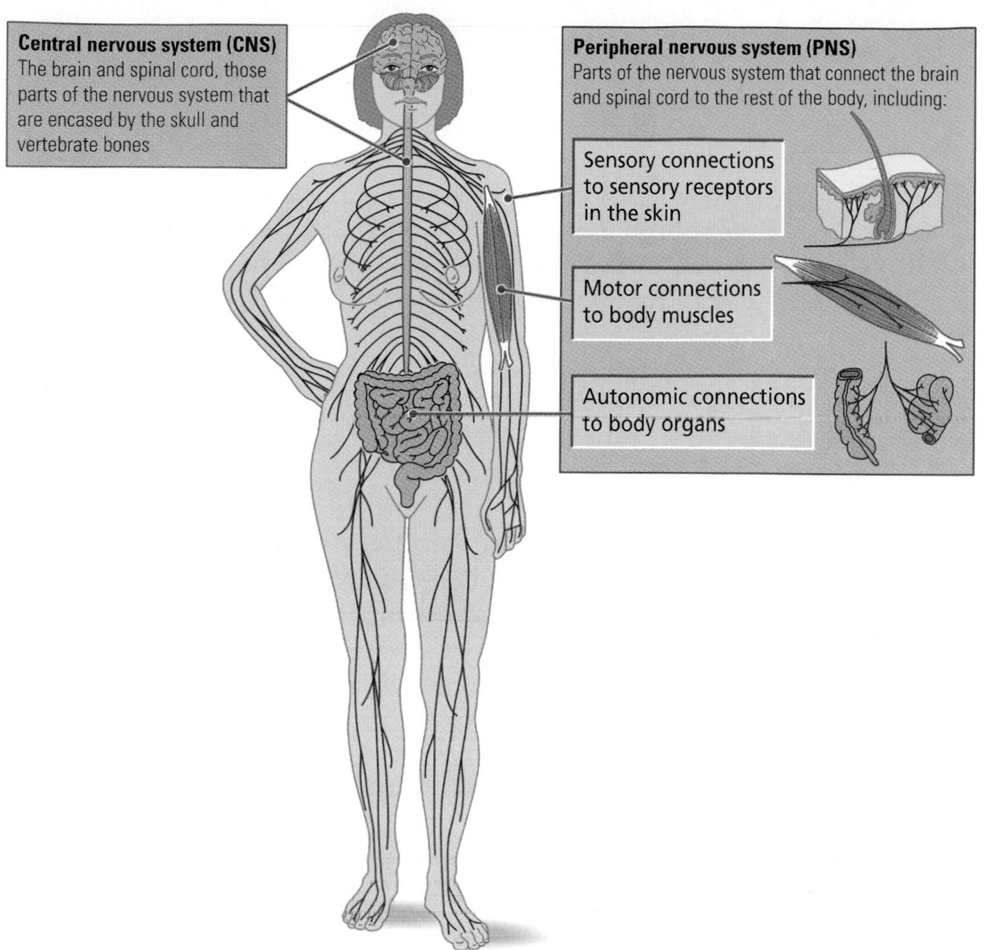
Central nervous system (CNS)
The brain and spinal cord, those parts of the nervous system that are encased by the skull and vertebrate bones
Peripheral nervous system (PNS)
Parts of the nervous system that connect the brain and spinal cord to the rest of the body, including:
Sensory connections to sensory receptors in the skin
Motor connections to body muscles
Autonomic connections to body organs

**Figure 1-2**

The human nervous system receives sensory information and produces behavior. The nervous system consists of the central nervous system (the brain and spinal cord) and the peripheral nervous system (the many neurons that connect the brain and spinal cord to the rest of the body).

senses to sensory-processing areas of the brain. With information from sensory receptors, the brain constructs current images of the world, as well as memories of past events and expectations about the future. In addition, sensory information helps the brain to construct a self-identity, as will be considered shortly. The **motor nerves** connect the brain and spinal cord to the body's muscles. The movements produced by motor pathways include the eye movements that you are using to read this book, the hand movements that you make while turning the pages, and the posture that you maintain as you read.

Motor pathways are also used in the workings of your body's organs, such as the beating of your heart, the contractions of your stomach, and the movement of your diaphragm, which inflates and deflates your lungs. These pathways are part of another subdivision, called the autonomic nervous system, of the nervous system. The **autonomic nervous system** consists of all the neurons that receive messages from or send commands to the various organs of the body, including the heart, digestive system, sex organs, excretory organs, blood vessels, and glands. Your autonomic system allows you, for instance, to feel both hunger before eating and satisfaction after a meal. It also enables you to digest and process food through your digestive tract. The autonomic nervous system, in short, regulates all your bodily functions, as well as the emotional responses associated with your voluntary actions.

Knowing that the nervous system is far more than just a brain, we can return to the question of whether a brain kept alive in a bottle is a brain in the fullest sense of the word. What Harvey wanted to try in the "brain in a bottle experiment" and failed

Plug in the CD to look at how these nerve networks work in our brains. The overview of the brain in the module on the Central Nervous System includes a rotatable, 3-D view of the brain that will help you visualize how all these parts fit together

to consider was whether his brain could sustain intelligent behavior in the absence of the sensations and movements provided by the brain's connections to the rest of the body. We can probably never be really sure of the capacities of a bottled brain. Still, some research suggests that sensations and movements are essential for consciousness.

In one study in the 1920s, Edmond Jacobson wondered what would happen if our muscles completely stopped moving. Jacobson believed that, even when we believe that we are entirely motionless, we still make subliminal movements related to our thoughts. The muscles of the larynx subliminally move when we "think in words," for instance, and we make subliminal movements of our eyes when we imagine a visual scene. So Jacobson had people practice "total" relaxation and later asked them what the experience was like. They reported a condition of "mental emptiness," as if the brain had gone blank.

In another study in the 1950s, Donald O. Hebb and his coworkers investigated the effects of sensory deprivation, as well as lack of movement, by having each subject lie on a bed in a soundproof room and remain completely still. Tubes covered the subjects' arms so that they had no sense of touch, and translucent goggles cut off their vision. The subjects reported that the experience was extremely unpleasant, not just because of the social isolation, but also because they lost their normal focus in this situation. Some subjects even had hallucinations, as if their brains were somehow trying to create the sensory experiences that they suddenly lacked. Most asked to be released from the study before it ended.

These experiments suggest that the brain needs ongoing sensory and motor experience if it is to maintain its intelligent activity. Thus, when we use the term *brain* to mean an intelligent, functioning organ, we should probably refer to a brain that is connected to the rest of the nervous system. It seems very unlikely that a "brain in a bottle" would continue to function in a normal way.

## What Is Behavior?

I. Eibl-Eibesfeldt began his textbook titled *Ethology: The Biology of Behavior*, published in 1970, with the following definition of behavior: "Behavior consists of patterns in time." These patterns can be made up of movements, vocalizations, or changes in appearance, such as the color changes associated with blushing. The expression "patterns in time" can even include thinking. Although we cannot directly observe someone's thoughts, there are techniques for monitoring changes in the brain's electrical and biochemical activity that may be associated with thought. So thinking, too, forms patterns in time.

A simpler definition of **behavior** is any kind of movement in a living organism. Such movements are limited to those that we can somehow see and measure. To distinguish the movements of a living organism from the movements of other things, such as a falling leaf or waves rolling onto the seashore, we can add that the movements of a living organism have both a cause and a function.

For some animals, most movements are inherited ways of responding; but, for others, movements entail both inherited and learned patterns of behavior. If all members of a species display the same behavior under the same circumstances, that species has probably inherited a nervous system designed to produce that behavior automatically. In contrast, if each member of a species displays a somewhat different response in a similar situation, that species has inherited a nervous system that is much more flexible and capable of allowing changes in behavior due to learning.

An example of the difference between a relatively fixed behavior pattern and a more flexible one is seen in the eating behavior of two different animal species—crossbills and roof rats—as illustrated in Figure 1-3. Crossbills are birds with beaks

A crossbill's beak is specifically designed to open pine cones. This behavior is innate.


A baby roof rat must learn from its mother how to eat pine cones. This behavior is learned.

**Figure 1-3** Some animal behaviors are largely innate, whereas others are largely learned. The eating of pine cones by crossbills is an example of an innate behavior made possible by this bird's specially designed beak, the tips of which are crossed, as illustrated by the parrot crossbill on the left. In contrast, *Rattus rattus,* a roof rat that lives in pine trees in Israel, can become an effective pine-cone eater only if it learns the skill from its mother. This learning is a form of cultural transmission.

*Left:* Adapted from *The Beak of the Finch* (p. 183), by J. Weiner, 1995, New York: Vintage. *Right:* Adapted from "Cultural Transmission in the Black Rat: Pinecone Feeding," by J. Terkel, 1995, *Advances in the Study of Behavior, 24,* p. 122.

that seem to be awkwardly crossed at the tips; yet this beak is exquisitely designed to eat certain kinds of pine cones. When eating these pine cones, crossbills use largely fixed behavior patterns that do not require much modification through learning. If a crossbill's beak is changed even slightly by trimming, the bird is no longer able to eat. Roof rats, in contrast, are rodents with sharp incisor teeth that appear to be designed to cut into anything. Roof rats are also effective pine-cone eaters, but they can eat pine cones efficiently only if they are taught to do so by an experienced mother. For roof rats, then, in contrast with crossbills with their relatively fixed action pattern, pine-cone eating is an acquired skill made possible by a flexible nervous system that is open to learning. The behavior described here is limited to pine-cone eating, and we do not intend to imply that all behavior displayed by crossbills is fixed or that all behavior displayed by roof rats is learned. A central goal of research is to distinguish between behaviors that are inherited and those that are learned and to understand how the nervous system produces each type of behavior.

The complexity of behavior varies considerably in different species, largely depending on the degree to which a species is capable of learning and has flexibility in its responses. Generally, animals with smaller, simpler nervous systems have a narrower range of behaviors that they can use to react to a situation. Animals with complex nervous systems have more behavioral options in any given situation. We humans believe that we are the animal species with the most complex nervous system and the greatest capacity for learning new responses. Species that have evolved greater complexity have not thrown away their simpler nervous systems, however. Rather, complexity emerges in part because new nervous system structures are added to old ones. For this reason, although human behavior depends mostly on learning, we, like other species, still possess many inherited ways of responding.

## In Review

The brain consists of two hemispheres, one on the left and one on the right. Each has a folded outer layer called the cortex, which is divided into four lobes: the temporal, the frontal, the parietal, and the occipital. The brain and spinal cord together make up the central nervous system, and all the nerve fibers radiating outward from the spinal cord to other parts of the body compose the peripheral nervous system. Networks of sensory and motor nerves span these two systems. A simple definition of behavior is any kind of movement in a living organism. Although all behaviors have both a cause and a function, behaviors vary in their complexity and the degree to which they depend on learning.

**Mind.** A nonmaterial entity that is proposed to be responsible for intelligence, attention, awareness, and consciousness.

**Mentalism.** Of the mind; an explanation of behavior as a function of the mind.

Link to a timeline on the history of brain research at **www.worthpublishers.com/kolb/chapter1.**

# PERSPECTIVES ON BRAIN AND BEHAVIOR

The central question in the study of brain and behavior is how the two are related. Fred Linge believed that both the behavioral problems that he suffered after his injury and the gradual recovery that he made in the months that followed were in some way related to changes that took place in his brain. This view has not always been generally accepted, however. More than 2000 years ago, Aristotle proposed that something called the mind, soul, or psyche produces behavior. In this section, we explore Aristotle's view and two other influential perspectives on how the brain and behavior are related. Certain older ideas that we will consider are still commonly held by contemporary religions or by people who see them as "common sense." Knowing the origin of these ideas will allow you to see why some of them are useful to the modern science of the brain and behavior, whereas others are not.

## Aristotle and Mind

Aristotle (384–322 BC)

E. Lessing/Art Resource, NY

François Gerard, Psyche and Cupid (1798)

The hypothesis that the mind, soul, or psyche is responsible for behavior can be traced more than 2000 years to ancient Greece. (The terms *mind, soul,* and *psyche* are often used interchangeably.) In classical mythology, Psyche was a maiden who became the wife of the young god Cupid. Venus, Cupid's mother, opposed his marriage to a mortal, and so she harassed Psyche with a number of almost impossible tasks. Psyche performed the tasks with such dedication, intelligence, and compassion that she was made immortal, thus removing Venus's objection to her. The ancient Greek philosopher Aristotle was alluding to this story when he suggested that all human intellectual functions are produced by a person's **psyche**. The psyche, Aristotle argued, was responsible for life, and its departure from the body resulted in death.

Aristotle's account of behavior had no role for the brain, which he thought existed to cool the blood. To Aristotle, the psyche was nonmaterial. To him, the psyche was responsible for human thoughts, perceptions, and emotions and for such processes as imagination, opinion, desire, pleasure, pain, memory, and reason. The psyche was an entity, or "stuff," as philosophers call it, that was independent of the body. Aristotle's view that a nonmaterial psyche governs our behavior was adopted by Christianity in its concept of the soul and has been widely disseminated throughout the Western world.

**Mind** is an Anglo-Saxon word for memory and, when "psyche" was translated into English, it became mind. The philosophical position that a person's mind, or psyche, is responsible for behavior is called **mentalism,** meaning "of the mind." Mentalism is not a scientific perspective. Because the mind is nonmaterial, it cannot be studied with the use of scientific methods. Furthermore, most modern scientists believe that, when we understand how the nervous system produces behavior, it will not be necessary to explain behavior by the actions of a mind. But, despite this scientific rejection of mentalism, terms that are mentalistic—such as *sensation, perception, attention, imagination, emotion, motivation, memory,* and *volition*—are still used in psychology textbooks today. These terms, however, are usually employed as labels for patterns of behavior, not in the Aristotelian sense of being products of some nonmaterial entity totally divorced from any part of the body.

Click on the Web site to read a detailed history of the origins of the mind–body question at **www.worthpublishers.com/kolb/chapter1.**

## Descartes and Dualism

Aristotle's mentalistic explanation of behavior survived almost unquestioned until the 1500s. Then, in his book titled *Treatise on Man,* the first book on brain and behavior, René Descartes (1596–1650), a French physiologist, mathematician, and philosopher, proposed a new explanation of behavior in which the brain played an important role. Descartes placed the seat of the mind in the brain and linked the mind to the body. He saw mind and body as separate but interconnected. In the first sentence of *Treatise on Man,* he stated that people must be composed of both a mind and a body. Descartes wrote:

René Descartes (1596–1650)

> I must first separately describe for you the body [which includes the brain]; then, also separately, the mind; and finally I must show you how these two natures would have to be joined and united to constitute people. . . . (Descartes, 1664, p. 1)

To Descartes, most of the activities of the body, including sensation, motion, digestion, breathing, and sleep, can be explained by the mechanical principles by which the physical body and brain work. The mind, on the other hand, is nonmaterial, separate from the body, and responsible for rational behavior. Figure 1-4, an illustration from Descartes's book, shows how the mind receives information from the body. When a hand touches a ball, for example, the mind learns through the brain that a ball exists, where the ball is located, and what its size and texture are. The mind also directs the body to touch the ball, but again it does so through the brain. The mind can command the brain to make the body carry out a great variety of actions, such as running, changing breathing rate, or throwing the ball across the room. The rational mind, then, depends on the brain both for information and for control of behavior.

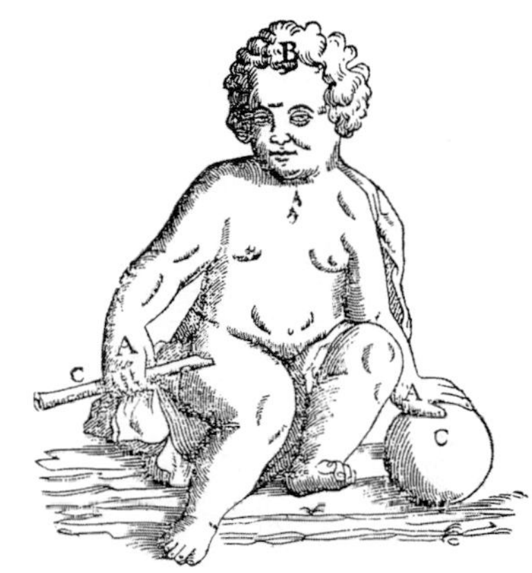


**Figure 1-4**

Descartes proposed that humans have both a mind and a brain. He argued that the pineal body in the brain receives different messages from a hand holding a flute and from a hand touching a ball. The mind, located in the pineal body, interprets these messages and so learns about the flute and ball.

From *Treatise on Man,* by R. Descartes, 1664. Reprint and translation (p. 60), 1972, Cambridge, MA: Harvard University Press.

The age in which Descartes lived was exciting because scientists and engineers were making advances in understanding the universe, in constructing mechanical devices, and in comprehending the functions of the body. Descartes, who dissected animals that he obtained from butcher shops, was recognized to be among the best anatomists of his day. He was also aware of the many new machines being built, including clocks, water wheels, and gears. He saw mechanical gadgets on public display in parks, such as those in the water gardens in Paris. One device caused a hidden statue to approach and spray water when an unsuspecting stroller walked past it. The statue's actions were triggered when the person stepped on a pedal hidden in the sidewalk.

Influenced by these mechanical devices, Descartes proposed that the functions of the body were produced by similar mechanical principles. For example, he used mechanical analogies both in describing how we automatically make decisions about distances and angles on the basis of visual information and in trying to explain why, when we look at an object, we are less aware of what surrounds it. He also considered in detail "mechanical" physiological functions, such as digestion, respiration, and the roles of nerves and muscles.

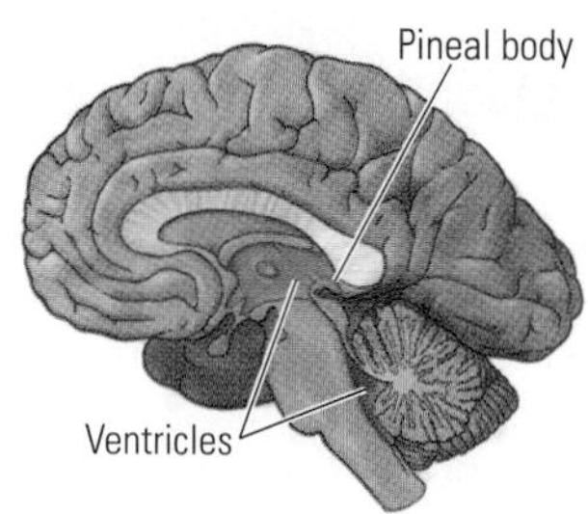


To explain how the mind controls the body, Descartes suggested that the mind resides in a small part of the brain called the **pineal body,** which is located in the center of the brain beside fluid-filled cavities called **ventricles.** According to Descartes, the pineal body directs fluid from the ventricles through nerves and into muscles. When the fluid expands those muscles, the body moves. In Descartes's theory, then, the mind regulates behavior by directing the flow of ventricular fluid to the appropriate muscles. Note that, for Descartes, mind and body were separate entities and the pineal body was only a structure through which the mind works.

Descartes's proposal that an entity called the mind directs a machine called the body was perhaps the most influential idea ever proposed in philosophy or neuroscience. It was the first serious attempt to explain the role of the brain in controlling intelligent behavior. The problem of how a nonmaterial mind and a physical brain might interact has come to be called the **mind–body problem,** and the philosophical position that behavior is controlled by two entities, a mind and a body, is called **dualism.**

**Mind–body problem.** The problem of how to explain how a nonmaterial mind can command a material body.

**Dualism.** A philosophical position that holds that both a nonmaterial mind and the material body contribute to behavior.

Descartes's theory has many problems in its details and logic. With respect to its details, we now know that people who have a damaged pineal body or even no pineal body at all still display normal intelligent behavior. The pineal body has a role in biological rhythms, not in governing all of human behavior. Furthermore, we now know that fluid is not pumped from the brain into muscles when they contract. Placing an arm in a bucket of water and contracting the arm's muscles does not cause the water level in the bucket to rise, as it should if the volume of the muscle increased because fluid had been pumped into it. With respect to its logic, Descartes's theory was also flawed. There is no obvious way that a nonmaterial entity could influence the body, because doing so would require the creation of energy, which would violate the laws of physics.

## Descartes's Legacy

To determine if an organism possesses a mind, Descartes proposed two tests: the language test and the action test. To pass the language test, an organism must use language to describe and reason about things that are not physically present. The action test requires the organism to display behavior that is based on reasoning and is not just an automatic response to a particular situation. Descartes believed that, even if an engineer made a robot that appeared very human, it could be distinguished from a real human because it would fail these two tests. Descartes also assumed that animals are unable to pass the tests. A good deal of experimental work today is directed toward determining if he was right in this assumption. For example, studies of sign language taught to apes are partly intended to find out whether apes can describe and reason about things that are not present and so pass the language test.

Descartes's theory had a number of unfortunate results. On the basis of it, some people argued that young children and the mentally insane must lack human minds because they often fail to reason appropriately. We still use the expression "he's lost his mind" to describe someone who is "mentally ill." Some proponents of this view also reasoned that, if someone lacked a mind, that person was simply a machine and not due normal respect or kindness. Cruel treatment of animals, children, and the mentally ill was justified by Descartes's theory. It is unlikely that Descartes himself intended these interpretations. He was reportedly very kind to his own dog, named Monsieur Grat.

Without being aware of the source of their ideas, some people still hold a very dualistic notion about the mind and the body, including the brain. For instance, people still refer to the "mind's ideals" on the one hand, and the body's "animal instincts" on the other. John M. Harlow used such language to describe his now-famous brain-injured patient Phineas Gage, who lived a century ago. Gage was a 25-year-old dynamite worker who survived an explosion that blasted an iron tamping bar (about a meter long and 3 centimeters wide) through the front of his head (Figure 1-5). Gage had been of average intelligence and very industrious and dependable. He was described as "energetic and persistent in executing all of his plans of operation." But, after the accident, his behavior changed completely. As Harlow wrote:

> The equilibrium or balance, so to speak, between his intellectual faculties and animal propensities seems to have been destroyed. He is fitful, irreverent, indulging at times in the grossest profanity, manifesting but little deference to his fellows, impatient of restraint or advice when it conflicts with his desires, at times perniciously obstinate, yet capricious and vacillating, devising many plans of operation, which are no sooner arranged than they are abandoned in turn for others appearing more feasible. A child in his intellectual capacity and manifestations, he has the animal passions of a strong man. (Blumer and Benson, 1975, p. 153)

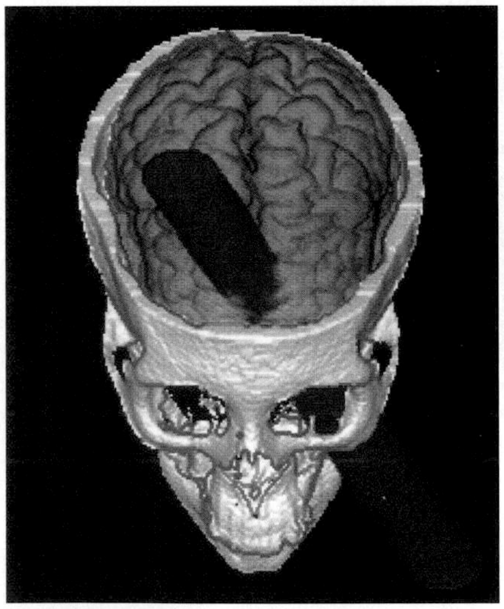

Department of Neurology and Image Analysis Facility, University of Iowa

**Figure 1-5**

When Phineas Gage died in 1861, no autopsy was performed, but his skull was later recovered. Measurements from Gage's skull and modern imaging techniques were used to reconstruct the accident and determine the probable location of the lesion. The frontal cortex of both hemispheres was damaged.

From "The Return of Phineas Gage: Clues About the Brain from the Skull of a Famous Patient," by H. Damasio, T. Grabowski, R. Frank, A. M. Galaburda, and A. R. Damasio, 1994, *Science, 20,* p. 1102.

## Focus on Disorders

### Linking Brain Function to Brain Disease

With the growth of cities in Europe in the 1500s, there were too many mental patients to be accommodated in home care. The mentally ill were placed in hospitals, monasteries, and other buildings that had been converted into asylums. There, patients were little more than prisoners. They lived under appalling conditions and were often chained and placed on public view. They were poorly treated in part because many people at the time accepted Descartes's belief that an entity called the mind controls rational behavior. Having "lost their minds," these patients were considered little more than animals.

Giraudon/Art Resource, NY

Philippe Pinel supervising the unchaining of the insane in La Bicêtre asylum in Paris in 1793.

At the end of the 1700s, the French Revolution brought in a new social order and new attitudes toward freedom, including the idea that all people were equal before the law, even those in asylums. The French physician Philippe Pinel reformed two large asylums in Paris—La Bicêtre and La Salpêtrière. He released many of the patients and greatly improved conditions there for those too ill to leave. Nevertheless, as cities continued to grow, so too did the size of asylums. For example, La Salpêtrière (which was originally a saltpeter factory) was the size of a small city, housing as many as 5000 female patients.

When Jean Charcot came to La Salpêtrière Hospital in the 1860s, he and his staff began to document the symptoms of the patients. Then, when the patients later died, the scientists examined their nervous systems and correlated the abnormalities that they found with the patients' previous behavior. Charcot described the results in his lectures to others in the hospital and published them in his textbooks and journals. Many scientists, attracted by Charcot's approach, visited and studied with him, including Sigmund Freud, the founder of psychoanalysis. They, in turn, began to apply his method in other countries and in other ways. Many of Charcot's coworkers are well known today for the diseases that they identified, many of which were named after them.

The method of relating nervous system abnormalities to behavioral abnormalities contributed greatly to scientific knowledge. It led to the understanding that an intact brain is essential for normal behavior. It also showed that, when the link between symptoms and nervous system pathology is known, patients can be diagnosed and given more intelligent treatment. At the same time, systematic study linking brain pathology to behavioral symptoms contributed to the downfall of Descartes's view that the pineal body was central to the control of behavior.

This description embraces the idea that we humans are composed of both a mind that controls our rational behavior and a body that expresses our animal passions. The description would be more accurate, though perhaps less colorful, without referring to this dualism of mind and body. After all, people are animals, so all of their behaviors are animal behaviors. Some behaviors are "high minded," whereas others are lower, or "animalistic." Furthermore, this appeal to dualism detracts from the most important aspect of Harlow's findings. Because Gage's brain damage was in the frontal lobes, Harlow was providing evidence that the frontal lobes were locations of foresight and planning. "Linking Brain Function to Brain Disease," above, describes the beginnings of the important discovery that particular parts of the brain regulate specific kinds of behaviors.

Link to more research about Charles Darwin on the Web site at **www.worthpublishers.com/kolb/chapter1.**

## Darwin and Materialism

By the middle of the nineteenth century, the beginnings of another theory of the brain and behavior were emerging. This theory was the modern perspective of **materialism**—the idea that rational behavior can be fully explained by the working of the brain and the rest of the nervous system, without any need to refer to a mind that controls our actions. This perspective had its roots in the evolutionary theories of Alfred Russel Wallace and Charles Darwin.

Wallace and Darwin independently arrived at the same conclusion—the idea that all living things are related. Each outlined this view in a paper presented at the Linnaean Society of London in July 1858. Darwin further elaborated on the topic in his book titled *On the Origin of Species by Means of Natural Selection,* published in 1859. This book presented a wealth of supporting detail, which is why Darwin is mentioned more often as the founder of modern evolutionary theory.

Both Darwin and Wallace had looked carefully at the structure of plants and animals and at animal behavior. Despite the diversity of living organisms, they were struck by the number of characteristics common to so many species. For example, the skeleton, muscles, and body parts of humans, monkeys, and other mammals are remarkably similar. These observations led first to the idea that living organisms must be related, an idea widely held even before Wallace and Darwin. But, more importantly, these same observations led to Darwin's explanation of how the great diversity in the biological world could have come from common ancestry. Darwin's principle of natural selection proposes that animals have traits in common because traits are passed from parents to their offspring.

Darwin believed that all organisms, both living and extinct, are descended from some unknown ancestor that lived in the remote past. In Darwin's terms, all living things are said to have **common descent.** As the descendants of that original organism spilled into various habitats over millions of years, they developed different structural and behavioral adaptations that made them suited for specific ways of life. But, at the same time, they retained many similar traits that reveal their relatedness to each other. Brain cells are one such characteristic common to animal species. Brain cells are an adaptation that emerged only once in animal evolution. Consequently, all brain cells that living animals possess are descendants of that first brain cell.

**Natural selection** is Darwin's way of explaining how new species evolve and existing species change over time. A species is a group of organisms that can breed among themselves, but not with members of other species. Individual organisms within any given species vary extensively in their characteristics, with no two members of the species being exactly alike. Some are big, some are small, some are fat, some are fast, some are lightly colored, and some have large teeth. Those individual organisms whose characteristics best help them to survive in their environment are likely to leave more offspring than are less-fit members. This unequal ability of individual members to survive and reproduce leads to a gradual change in a species' population, with characteristics favorable for survival in that particular habitat becoming more prevalent over generations. If some part of a species population then becomes reproductively isolated—say, because it is separated by a physical barrier such as an ocean or a mountain range—that subgroup over time could evolve into a new species, different from the species from which it originated. For example, imagine a chubby primate living in an environment of dense vegetation that is faced with gradual drying of the climate so that its environment eventually becomes a savanna with only scattered trees. Those members of the species that are thinnest and so can run quickly, are lightly colored and so blend with the grass, and have fine teeth, which are better for eating insects, will prosper and so leave the most descendants.

**Materialism.** The philosophical position that holds that behavior can be explained as a function of the nervous system without explanatory recourse to the mind.

**Common descent.** Refers to individual organisms or families that descend from the same ancestor.

**Natural selection.** Differential success in the reproduction of different phenotypes resulting from the interaction of organisms with their environment. Evolution takes place when natural selection causes changes in relative frequencies of alleles in the gene pool.

Neither Darwin nor Wallace understood the basis of the great variation in plant and animal species. The underlying principles of that variation were discovered by another scientist, Gregor Mendel, beginning about 1857, through experiments that he did with pea plants. Mendel deduced that there are heritable factors, which we now call **genes,** related to the various physical traits displayed by the species. Members of a species that have a particular gene or combination of genes will express that trait. If the genes for a trait are passed on to offspring, the offspring also will have the same characteristic. New traits appear because genes combine in new ways, because existing genes change or mutate, or because new genes are formed. Thus, the unequal ability of individual organisms to survive and reproduce is related to the different genes that they inherit and pass on to their offspring. By the same token, similar characteristics within or between species are usually due to similar genes. For instance, genes that produce the nervous system in different kinds of animal species tend to be very similar to one another.

## Darwin's Legacy

Darwin's theory of natural selection has three important implications for the study of the brain and behavior. First, because all animal species are related, so too must be their brains. Darwin himself did not say much about this topic, but contemporary scientists do. Today, brain researchers study a wide range of animals, including slugs, fruit flies, rats, and monkeys, knowing that they can often extend their findings to human beings. Second, because all species of animals are related, so too must be their behavior. Darwin was particularly interested in this subject. In his book titled *On the Expression of the Emotions in Man and Animals,* he argued that emotional expressions are similar in humans and other animals because we inherited these expressions from a common ancestor. Evidence for such inheritance is illustrated in Figure 1-6, which shows that smiling is common to people throughout the world. That people in different parts of the world display the same behavior suggests that the trait is inherited rather than learned. The third implication of Darwin's theory is that both the brain and behavior were built up bit by bit in animals that evolved to greater complexity, as humans obviously did. Later in this chapter, we will trace how the human nervous system evolved from a simple net of nerves, to a spinal cord connected to that net, and finally to a nervous system with a brain that controls behavior.

Evidence that the brain controls behavior is today so strong that the idea has the status of a theory: *the brain theory*. Donald O. Hebb in his influential book titled *The Organization of Behavior,* published in 1949, described the brain theory as follows:

> Modern psychology takes completely for granted that behavior and neural function are perfectly correlated, that one is completely caused by the other. There is no separate soul or life force to stick a finger into the brain now and then and make neural cells do what they would not otherwise. (Hebb, 1949, p. xiii)

J. Tisne/Stone Images

O. Benn/Stone Images

A. Cassidy/Stone Images

J. Greenberg/Visuals Unlimited

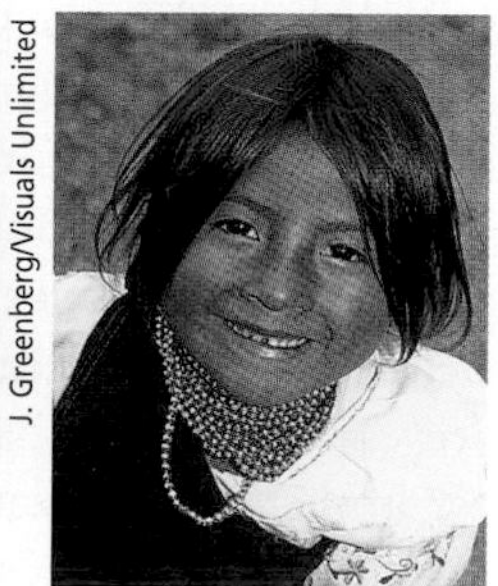

**Figure 1-6**

Darwin proposed that emotional expression is inherited. Part of the evidence supporting this suggestion is the finding that people from all parts of the world use the same emotional expressions that they also recognize in others, as is illustrated by these smiles.

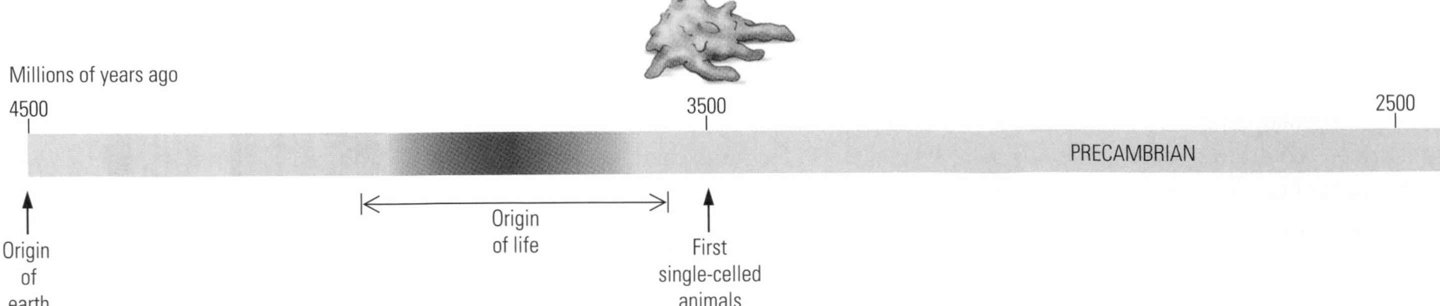


Some people reject the idea that the brain is responsible for behavior, because they think it denies religion. Their thinking, however, is mistaken. The biological explanation of brain and behavior is neutral with respect to religious beliefs. Fred Linge, the brain-injured man described in the beginning of this chapter, has strong religious beliefs, as do the other members of his family. They used their religious strength to aid in his recovery. Yet, despite their religious beliefs, they realized that Linge's brain injury was the cause of his change in behavior and that the process of recovery that his brain underwent was the cause of his restored health. Similarly, there are many behavioral scientists with strong religious beliefs who see no contradiction between those beliefs and their use of the scientific method to examine the relations between the brain and behavior.

## In Review

We have considered three perspectives on how behavior arises. Mentalism is the view that behavior is a product of an intangible entity called the mind, implying that the brain has little importance. Dualism is the notion that the mind acts through the brain to produce language and rational behavior, whereas the brain alone is responsible for the "lower" kinds of actions that we have in common with other animal species. Finally, materialism is the view that all behavior, language and reasoning included, can be fully accounted for by brain function. Materialism is the perspective that guides contemporary research on the brain and behavior.

## THE EVOLUTION OF BRAIN AND BEHAVIOR

The popular interpretation of human evolution is that we are descended from apes. Actually, apes are not our ancestors, although we *are* related to them. To demonstrate the difference, consider the following story. Two people named Joan Campbell were introduced at a party, and their names afforded a good opening for a conversation. Although both belonged to the Campbell lineage (family line), one Joan was not descended from the other. The two women lived in different parts of North America. One was from Texas and the other was from Ontario, and both their families had been in those locations for many generations. But, after comparing family histories, the two Joans discovered that they had ancestors in common. The Texas Campbells were descended from Jeeves Campbell, brother of Matthew Campbell, from whom the Ontario Campbells were descended. Jeeves and Matthew had both boarded the same fur-trading ship when it stopped for water in the Orkney Islands north of Scotland before sailing to North America. The Joan Campbells' **common ancestors,** then, were the mother and father of Jeeves and Matthew

**Common ancestor.** An ancestor from which two or more lineages or family groups arise and so is ancestral to both groups.

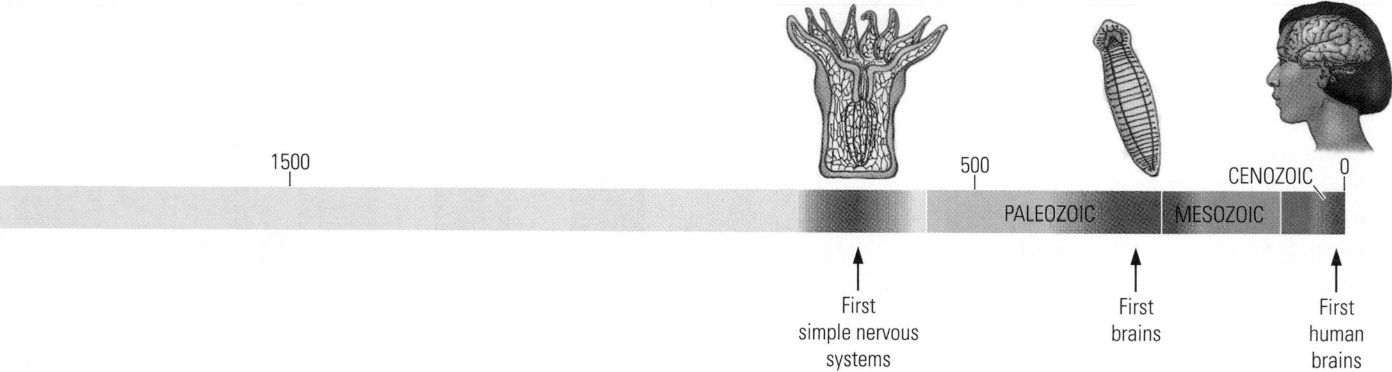


**Figure 1-7**

Relative to the origin of the earth 4500 million years ago, the first single-celled animals 3500 million years ago, the origin of neurons 700 million years ago, and the first brain about 250 million years ago, the appearance of the first human brain within about the past 4 million years is a very recent event.

Campbell. Both the Texas Campbell family line and the Ontario one were descended from this same man and woman. In much the same way, humans and apes are descended from common ancestors. But, unlike the Joan Campbells, we do not know who those distant relatives were. By comparing the characteristics of humans and related animals, however, scientists are tracing our lineage back farther and farther. In this way, they can piece together the story of the origin of the human brain and behavior.

## Origin of Brain Cells and Brains

The brain and brain cells go back a very long time. The earth originated about 4500 million years ago, and the first life forms arose about 3500 million years in the past. About 700 million years ago, animals evolved the first brain cells, and, by 250 million years ago, the first brain had evolved. A humanlike brain, however, first developed only about 3 million to 4 million years ago, and our modern human brain has been around for only the past 100,000 to 200,000 years. As evolutionary history goes, that is a rather short amount of time. Although life evolved very early in the history of our planet, brain cells and the brain are more recent adaptations, and large complex brains, such as ours, evolved only very, very recently. Figure 1-7 shows this evolutionary time line.

## Classification Systems

Since the first appearance of a living organism, the diversity of life on earth has been enormous. Millions of species have evolved, some of which have become extinct. As many as 30 million to 100 million species currently inhabit the planet. Scientists have described only a small number of these species, about 1.5 million. The rest remain to be found, named, and classified.

**Taxonomy,** the branch of biology concerned with naming and classifying species, groups organisms according to their common characteristics and their relationships to one another. As shown in Figure 1-8, the broadest unit of classification is a kingdom, with more subordinate groups being a phylum, class, order, family, genus, and species. We humans belong to the animal kingdom, the chordate phylum, the mammalian class, the primate order, the Hominidae family, the *Homo* genus, and the *sapiens* species. Animals are usually identified with a first and second name, their genus and species name. So we humans are called *Homo sapiens,* meaning "wise humans."

This hierarchy of categories helps us trace the evolutionary history of our human brain and behavior. Brain cells and muscles first evolved in animals; the brain as an organ first evolved in chordates; a large brain with many different functions first evolved in mammals; a brain capable of producing complex tools first evolved in

**Taxonomy.** The branch of biology concerned with naming and classifying the diverse forms of life.

**Figure 1-8**

Taxonomy classifies animals into groups subordinate to more comprehensive groups. (*From bottom to top*) Modern humans are the only surviving species of the genus that included numerous extinct species of humanlike animals. Humans belong to the ape (Hominidae) family, which includes a number of living members, among them chimpanzees. Hominidae are but one of many families of the primate order. The primates are members of the class of mammals, which in turn belongs to the chordate phylum, which in turn belongs to the animal kingdom. A characteristic feature of animals is a nervous system, and in chordates the nervous system includes a brain and spinal cord. A distinctive feature of mammals is a large brain, and, among the mammals, the primates are a particularly large-brained order, with the largest brains being found in humans.

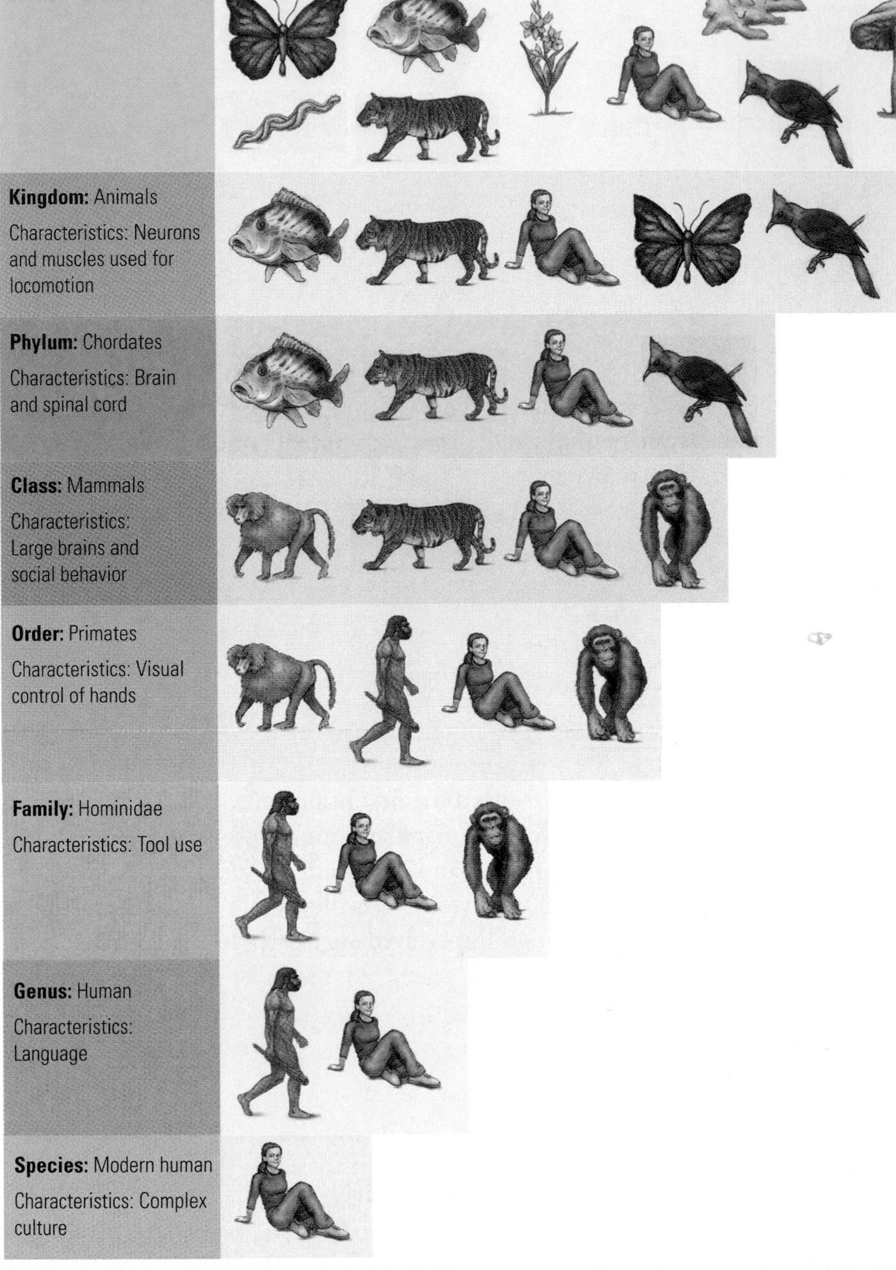

Galápagos woodpecker finch

apes; and a brain capable of language and culture first evolved in *Homo sapiens*. Although the most complex brain and patterns of behavior have evolved in the human lineage, large brains and complex behaviors have also evolved in some other lineages. Some birds, such as the Galápagos woodpecker finch, use simple tools, and dolphins have surprisingly large brains.

## Evolution of Animals with Nervous Systems

**Cladogram.** A phylogenetic tree that branches repeatedly, suggesting a classification of organisms based on the time sequence in which evolutionary branches arise.

A nervous system is not essential for life. In fact, most organisms in both the past and the present have done without one. Of the five major taxonomic kingdoms, only one contains species with nervous systems. Figure 1-9 shows these five kingdoms in a chart called a **cladogram** (from the Greek word *clados,* meaning "branch"). A cladogram displays groups of organisms as branches on a tree in such a way that branch

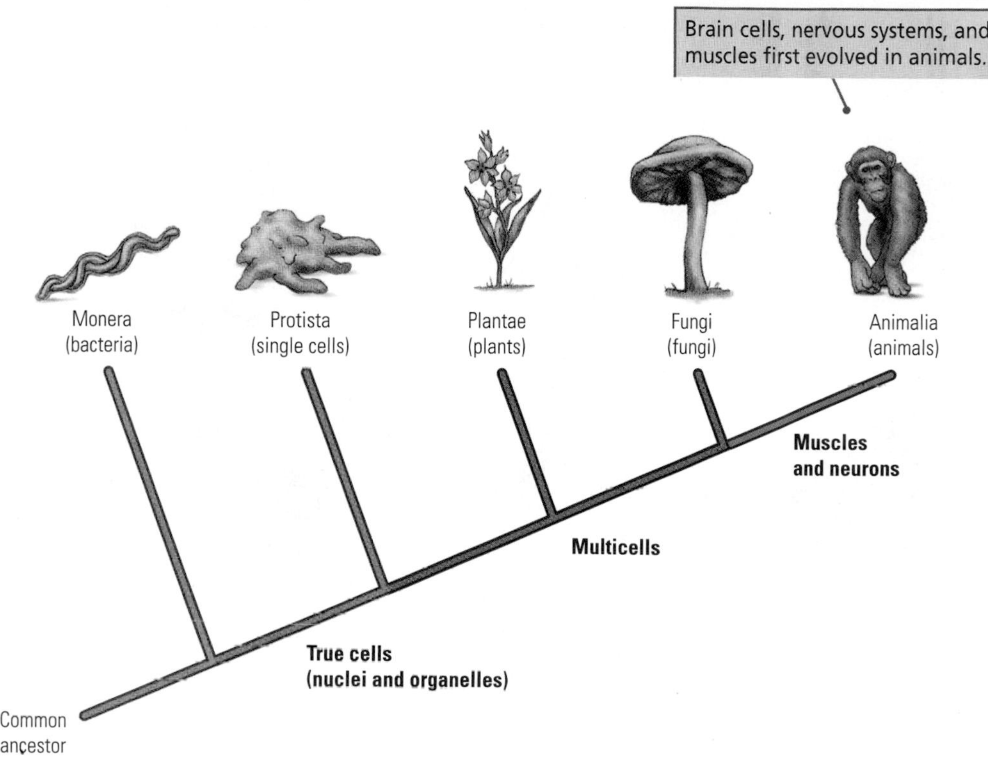


**Figure 1-9**

In this cladogram of the five kingdoms of living organisms, the line connecting the kingdoms represents the sequence in which the kingdoms evolved. Animals are members of the most recently evolved kingdom, and their characteristics include brain cells, nervous systems, and muscles.

order represents how the groups are related. The five kingdoms shown are: Monera (simple cells, such as bacteria), Protista (more complex cells, such as protozoa), Plantae (plants), Fungi, and Animalia (animals). Looking at this chart tells you at a glance how uncommon the nervous system is in the living world: it is found only in animals. You can also see that neurons are associated with muscles, suggesting that the functions of both were to enable movement. This cladogram also reinforces our earlier point that the nervous system is a late evolutionary development. Life first appeared with Monera, and it thrived for millions of years with nothing but single-celled organisms. The first multicellular organisms arose in Plantae and Fungi. Brain cells, nervous systems, and muscles did not appear in Animalia until much later. They are structures that life did without for eons.

Brain cells, nervous systems, and muscles are what give animal species their characteristic feature: the ability to move. This ability has enabled animals to occupy many different biological niches, where they use their movements for food gathering, reproduction, and self-preservation. The animal kingdom contains a great many species. Taxonomists have so far identified about 1 million animal species and organized them into 15 phyla (*phyla* is the plural of *phylum*).

Figure 1-10 shows the evolution of the nervous system in animal phyla. The nervous system in species in older phyla, such as jellyfishes and sea anemones, is extremely simple. It consists of a nerve net, with no structure that resembles a brain. (The net looks a little like a human nervous system from which the brain and spinal cord have been removed). Species in somewhat more recent phyla, such as flatworms, are more complexly structured. These organisms have heads and tails, are **bilaterally symmetrical** (one-half of the body is the mirror image of the other), and are **segmented** (the body is composed of similarly appearing segments). They also have segmented nervous systems that resemble the human nervous system, with sensory and motor neurons projecting from each segment. Bilateral symmetry and segmentation are two important structural features of the human nervous system. For example, just as our body is bilaterally

**Bilateral symmetry.** Refers to organs or parts that are present on both sides of the body and very similar in appearance on each side (For example, the hands are bilaterally symmetrical, whereas the heart is not.)

**Segmentation.** Refers to animals that can be divided into a number of parts that are similar; also refers to the idea that many animals, including vertebrates, are composed of similarly organized body segments.

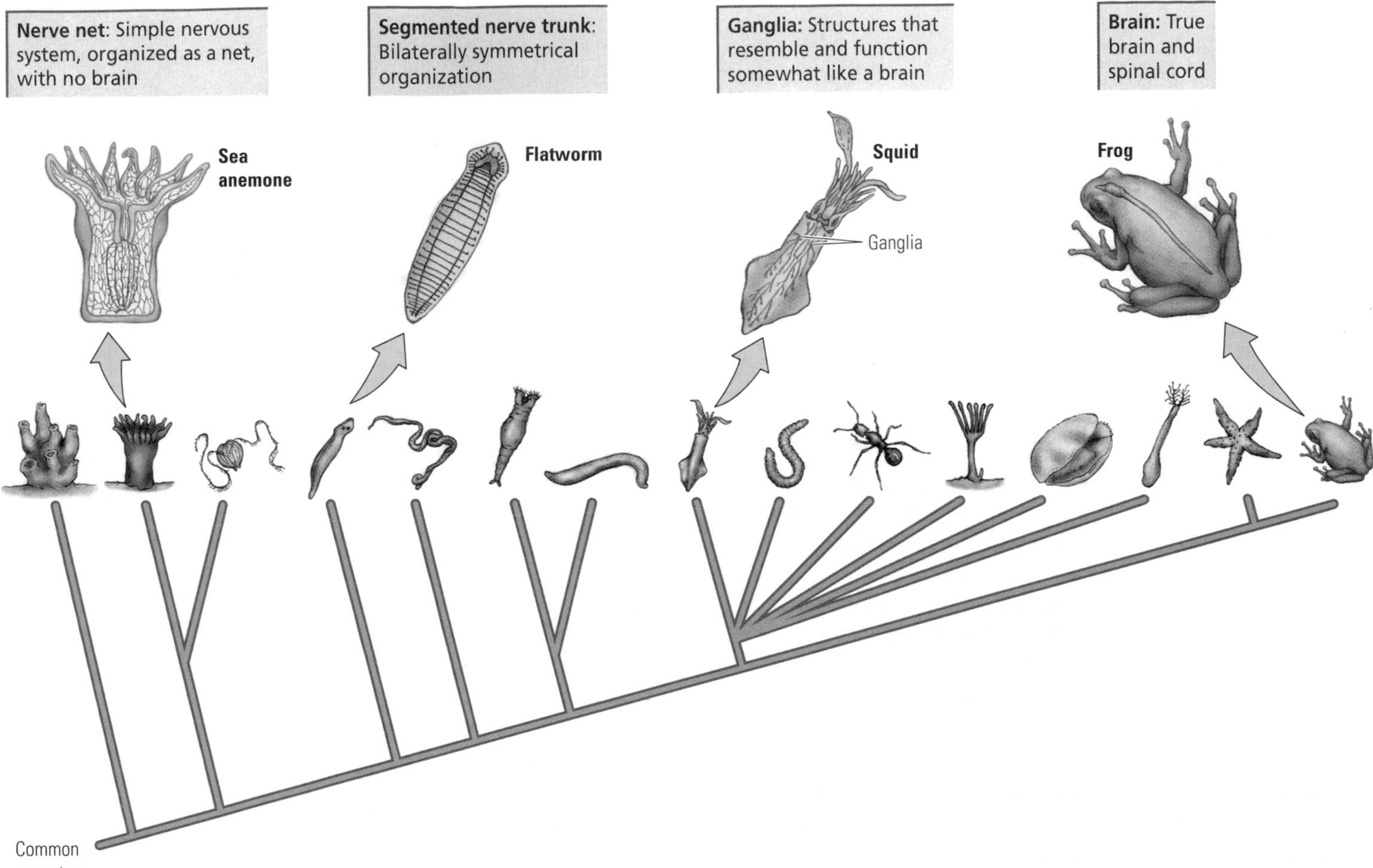
**Nerve net**: Simple nervous system, organized as a net, with no brain
**Segmented nerve trunk**: Bilaterally symmetrical organization
**Ganglia:** Structures that resemble and function somewhat like a brain
**Brain:** True brain and spinal cord
Sea anemone
Flatworm
Squid
Ganglia
Frog
Common ancestor

**Figure 1-10**

This cladogram illustrates the evolutionary relationship of the 15 animal phyla, showing the evolution of the nervous system from a nerve net, to a segmented nervous system, to a nervous system consisting of ganglia and nerve trunks, and finally to a nervous system featuring a brain.

symmetrical, our brain has two bilaterally symmetrical hemispheres. The brain itself evolved by growth in the most anterior (front) segments of the nervous system.

Species in still more recently evolved phyla, such as clams, snails, and octopuses, have an additional feature in their nervous systems: collections of neurons called **ganglia** (singular, *ganglion*), some of which are in the region of the animal's head. Ganglia resemble a brain and function somewhat like one, but, unlike a brain, they are not a central structure coordinating all of the animal's behavior. Only species in one phylum, the **chordates,** have a true spinal cord and brain. Chordates get their name from the **notochord,** a flexible rod that runs the length of the back. In humans, the notochord is present only in an embryo; by birth, it has been replaced by vertebrae that encase the spinal cord.

There are several important differences between the chordate nervous system and the nervous system in older phyla. Whereas the chordate nervous system is located along the back, in other animals the nervous system is located below the gut. In addition, the brain is a central processing structure in the chordate nervous system. It is located in the animal's head (the body part that arrives first as the animal moves). It is also in close proximity to the animal's many sensory-receptor systems, such as those for vision, hearing, taste, and smell. This positioning of the brain makes it quick to receive and respond to sensory information as the animal travels from one place to another.

## The Chordate Nervous System

Although much variation exists in the nervous systems of chordates, the basic pattern of a brain attached to a spinal cord is common to all of them. This pattern is found even in the earliest chordate species. Figure 1-11 shows seven of the nine classes of chordates to which the approximately 38,500 chordate species belong. In each class, the nervous system consists

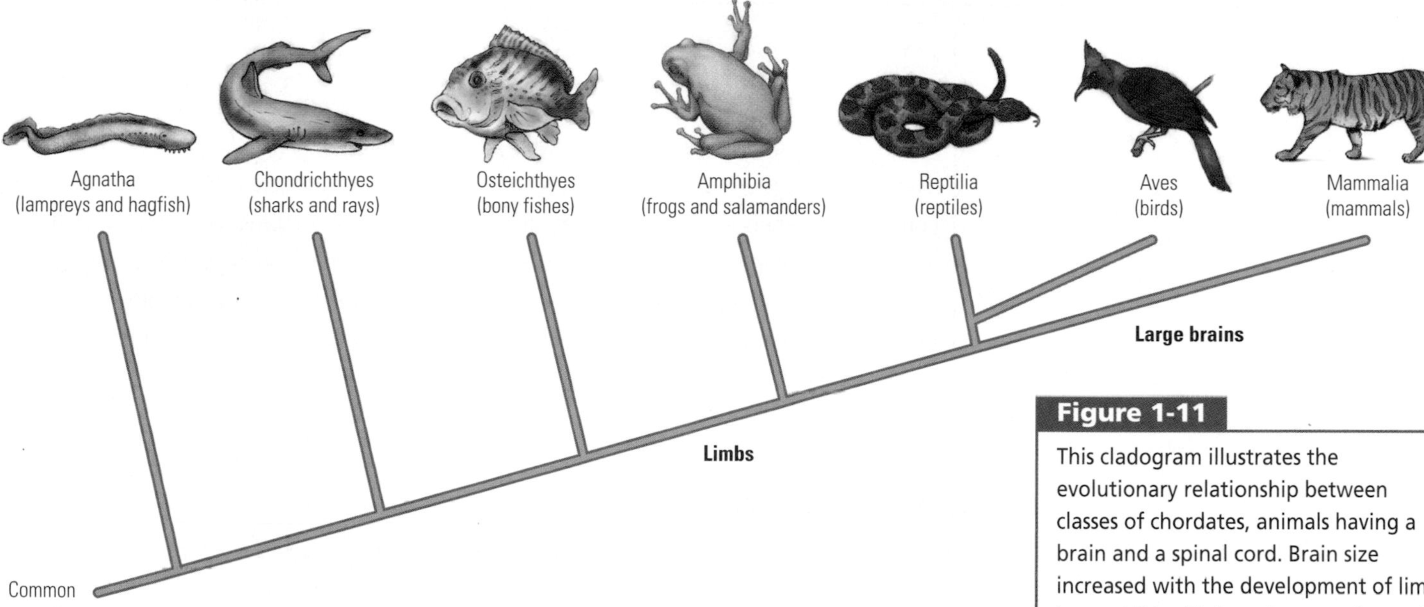


**Figure 1-11**

This cladogram illustrates the evolutionary relationship between classes of chordates, animals having a brain and a spinal cord. Brain size increased with the development of limbs in amphibia. Birds and mammals are the most recently evolved chordates, and large brains are found in both classes.

of a brain and a spinal cord as well as sensory and motor connections, but, in each class, there is an enormous range of brain sizes. Distinguishing features of chordates are limbs for locomotion along with some very large-brained species, especially the birds and mammals.

The relative difference in brain size in different classes of chordates is illustrated in Figure 1-12, which shows representative brains of a fish, an amphibian, a bird, and a mammal (in this case, a human). The **cerebrum,** of which the cerebral cortex is the external structure (described earlier as being folded and covering most of the rest of the brain in humans), is proportionately small and smooth in the earliest-evolved chordate shown in Figure 1-12. In later-evolved chordates with larger brains, the cortex is disproportionately larger and begins to cover other structures. Finally, in large-brained mammals, the cortex is folded. By folding, the cortex is able to greatly increase its size while still fitting into a small skull (just as a folded piece of paper can occupy a small container). Toward the back of the brain, a structure called the **cerebellum** (which means "little brain" in Latin) also has increased in size, taking on the appearance of a little cortex. Figure 1-12 shows the human brain cut longitudinally through its center to illustrate how the cortex has grown to cover the rest of the brain, including the cerebellum. The evolution of more complex behavior in chordates is closely related to the evolution of both the cerebral cortex and the cerebellum. The large differences in brain size that exist in the 4000 species of mammals are due mainly to differences in the size of these two brain regions.

Turn on the CD to view a close-up of the cerebellum in the module on the Central Nervous System in the section on the brainstem and subcortical structures.

**Figure 1-12**

The brains of representative chordates have many structures in common. These side views of the brains of some representative chordates show that the cerebrum and cerebellum account for most of the increase in brain size. The human brain has been cut through the center to illustrate how the cerebral cortex enfolds the rest of the brain. The similar parts of the brain found in these diverse animal species also illustrate that there is a basic brain plan.

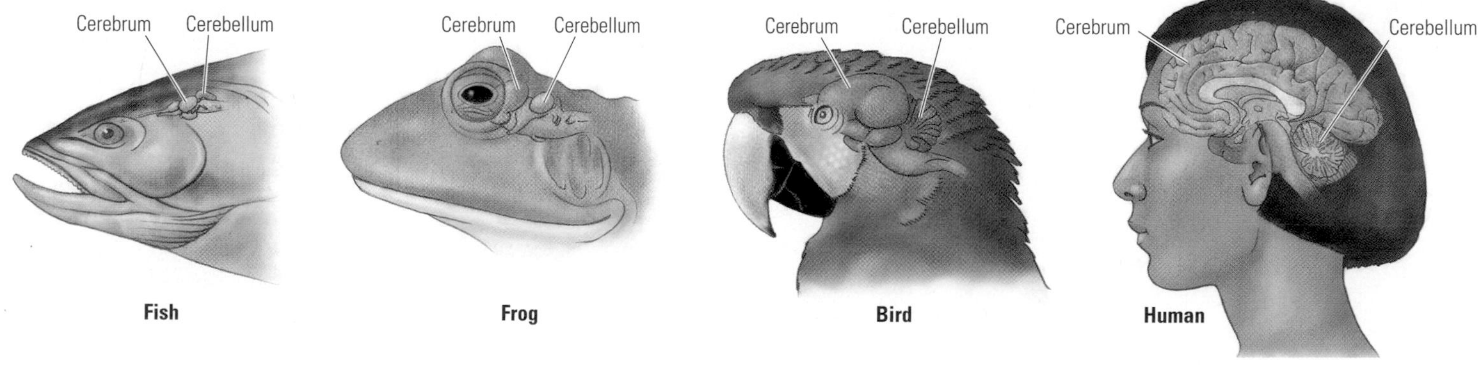

## In Review

Brain cells and the nervous system are relatively recent developments in the evolution of life on this planet. Because they evolved only once in the animal kingdom, a similar basic nervous system pattern exists in all animals. The nervous system did become more complex in certain groups of animals, and this increase in complexity closely parallels increasingly complex behavior. Particular lineages of animals, such as the lineage to which humans belong, are characterized by especially large brains and complex behavior. These evolutionary developments are closely tied to the growth of the cerebral cortex and cerebellum.

# HUMAN EVOLUTION

Although everyone can see similarities among humans, apes, and monkeys, many people once believed that humans are far too different from monkeys and apes to have had a common ancestor with them. These skeptics also reasoned that the absence of a "missing link," or intermediate form of ancestor, further argued against the possibility of common descent. In the past century, however, so many intermediate forms between humans and other apes have been found in the fossil record that entire books are required to describe them. Here we consider only some of the more prominent ancestors that link apes to ourselves.

Visit the Web site for links to a tutorial about human evolution at **www.worthpublishers.com/kolb/chapter1.**

## Humans: Members of the Primate Order

The human relationship to apes and monkeys places us in the *primate order,* a subcategory of mammals that includes not only apes and monkeys, but lemurs, tarsiers, and marmosets as well. In fact, we humans are only 1 of about 275 species in the primate order, some of which are illustrated in Figure 1-13. Primates have excellent vision—including color vision and eyes in the front of the face to enhance depth perception—

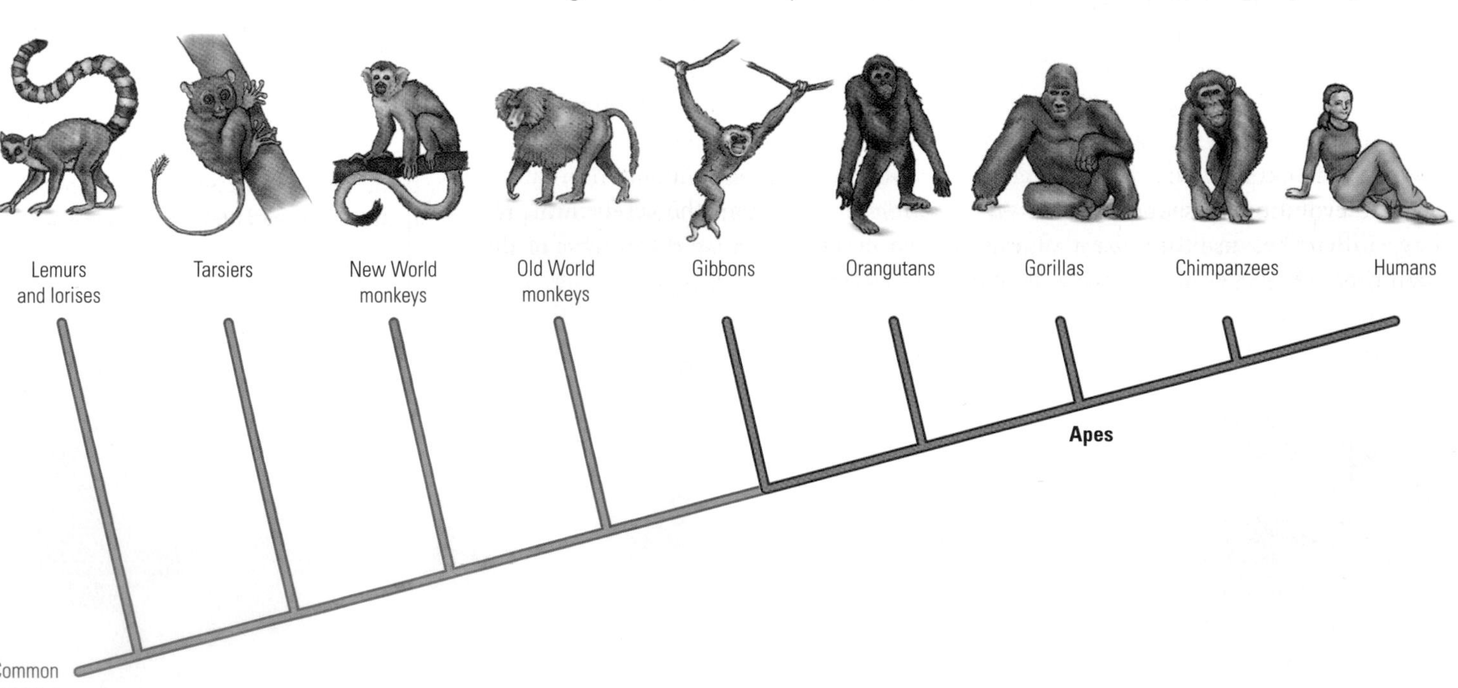


**Figure 1-13** This cladogram illustrates a hypothetical relationship between the members of the primate order. Humans are members of the family of apes. In general, brain size increases across the groupings, with humans having the largest brains.

and they use this excellent vision to deftly guide their hand movements. Female primates usually have only one infant per pregnancy, and they spend a great deal more time caring for their young than most other animals do. Associated with their skillful movements and their highly social nature, primates on average have larger brains than animals in other orders of mammals, such as rodents (mice, rats, beavers, squirrels) and carnivores (wolves, bears, cats, weasels).

**Hominid.** General term referring to primates that walk upright, including all forms of humans, living and extinct.

Humans are members of the suborder apes, which in addition to us includes gibbons, orangutans, gorillas, and chimpanzees. Apes are arboreal animals, with limber shoulder joints that allow them to brachiate (swing from one handhold to another) in trees. Among the apes, we are most closely related to the chimpanzee, having had a common ancestor between 5 million and 10 million years ago. The family to which humans belong is called Hominidae. In the past 5 million years, there have been many **hominids,** or humanlike animals that are members of the Hominidae family. Some extinct hominid species lived at the same time as one another. At present, however, we are the only surviving hominid species.

## *Australopithecus*: Our Distant Ancestor

One of our hominid ancestors is probably ***Australopithecus*** (*Australo* meaning "southern," *pithecus* meaning "ape") or a primate very much like it. A reconstruction of what the animal looked like is shown in Figure 1-14. The name *Australopithecus* was coined by an Australian, Raymond Dart, for the skull of a child that he found in a box of fossilized remains from a limestone quarry near Taung, South Africa, in 1924. (The choice of a name to represent his native land is probably not accidental.) We now know that there were many species of *Australopithecus,* some of which existed at the same time. The skull of the "Taung child" did not belong to the earliest species, which lived about 4 million years ago.

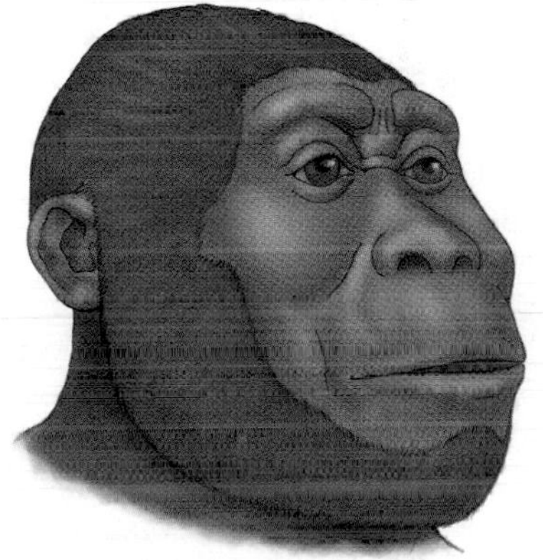

**Figure 1-14**

Reconstruction of *Australopithecus,* one of the oldest known species in the hominid family, to which modern humans belong. *Australopithecus* walked upright with free hands, as do modern humans, but its brain was the size of an ape's, about one-third the size of our brain.

These early australopiths are the first primates to show a distinctly human characteristic: they walked upright. Scientists have deduced their upright posture from the shape of their back, pelvic, knee, and foot bones and from a set of 3.6-million- to 3.8-million-year-old fossilized footprints that a family of them left behind when walking through freshly fallen ash from a volcano. The footprints feature a well-developed arch and a big toe that was more like that of humans than of apes. The most complete *Australopithecus* skeleton yet found is that of a young female, popularly known as "Lucy." This skeleton was 40 percent complete even after having been buried for 3 million years. Lucy was only about 1 meter tall and had a brain about the size of a modern chimpanzee's brain, which is about one-third the size of a modern human brain.

The evolutionary sequence from *Australopithecus* to humans is not known precisely, in part because there were a number of species of *Australopithecus* alive at the same time. One possible lineage is shown in Figure 1-15. A common ancestor gave rise to *Australopithecus,* and one member of this group gave rise to the *Homo* lineage. The last of the australopith species disappeared from the fossil record about 1 million years ago after coexisting with hominids for some time. Also illustrated in Figure 1-15 is the large increase in brain size that evolved in the hominid lineage.

## The First Humans

The oldest fossils to be designated as *Homo,* or human, are those found by Mary and Louis Leakey in the Olduvai Gorge in Tanzania in 1964, dated at about 2 million years. The primates that left these skeletal remains had a strong resemblance to *Australopithecus,* from which they were thought to descend. But Mary Leakey argued that their dental pattern is more similar to that of modern humans than to that of australopiths and, more

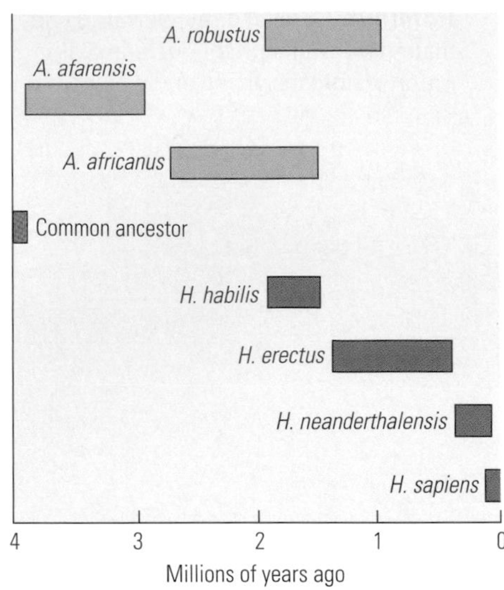


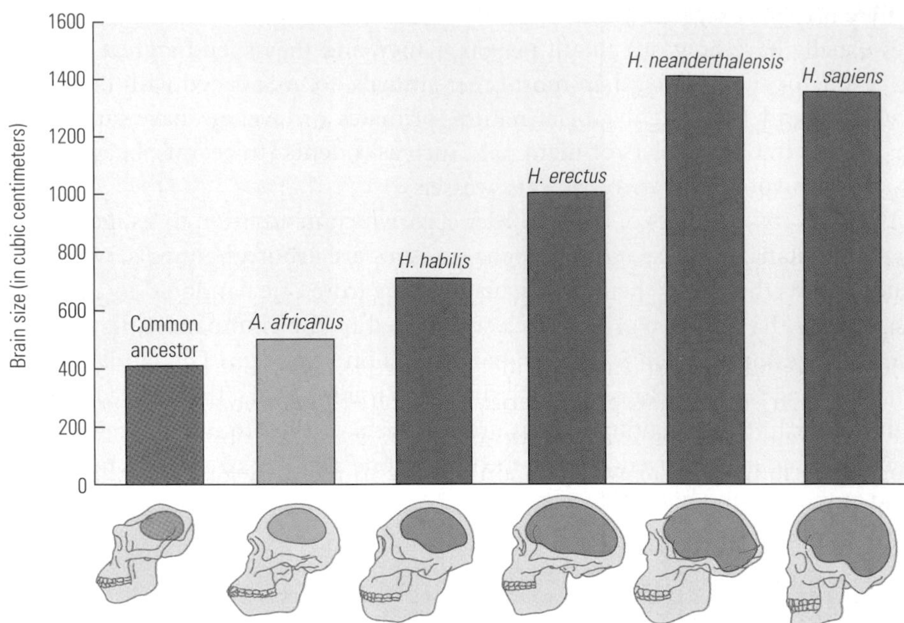


**Figure 1-15**

The origins of humans. The human lineage and a lineage of extinct *Australopithecus* likely arose from a common ancestor about 4 million years ago. Thus the ancestor of the human lineage *Homo* was likely an animal similar to *Australopithecus africanus*. The probable sequence of human evolution was from *Homo habilis* to *Homo erectus* to *Homo sapiens*. Connecting lines are not shown, because a number of species of each group were alive at the same time. *Homo neanderthalensis* is considered a subspecies of *Homo sapiens,* but how closely they were related is unclear. There was a very large increase in brain size in this proposed lineage.

important, that they apparently made simple stone tools, which were found near their bones. The Leakeys named the species ***Homo habilis*** (meaning "handy human") to signify that its members were tool users. Again, the precise relationships in the *Homo* lineage are not known, because there were a number of species of *Homo* alive at the same time.

The first humans whose populations spread beyond Africa migrated into Europe and into Asia. This species was ***Homo erectus*** ("upright human"), so named because of the mistaken notion that its predecessor, *Homo habilis,* had a stooped posture. *Homo erectus* first shows up in the fossil record about 1.6 million years ago and lasts until perhaps as recently as 100,000 to 30,000 years ago. *Homo erectus* has a pivotal position in our evolutionary history. Its brain was bigger than that of any previous hominid, overlapping in size the measurements of present-day human brains. *Homo erectus* also made more sophisticated tools than did *Homo habilis.*

Modern humans, *Homo sapiens,* appeared in Asia and North Africa about 200,000 to 100,000 years ago and in Europe about 40,000 years ago. Most anthropologists think that they migrated from Africa. Until about 60,000 years ago, perhaps even as recently as 30,000 years ago, they coexisted with other hominid species in Africa, Europe, and Asia. For example, in Europe they coexisted with **Neanderthals,** named after Neander, Germany, where the first Neanderthal skulls were found. Neanderthals had brains as large as or larger than those of modern humans, used tools similar to those of early *Homo sapiens,* and possibly had a similar hunting culture. We do not know how *Homo sapiens* completely replaced other human species, such as Neanderthals. *Homo sapiens* may have been more aggressive and killed off competing species. Or they may have been more skilled at toolmaking and so were better at getting food. Or perhaps the various human species interbred so completely that characteristics of all but ourselves simply disappeared.

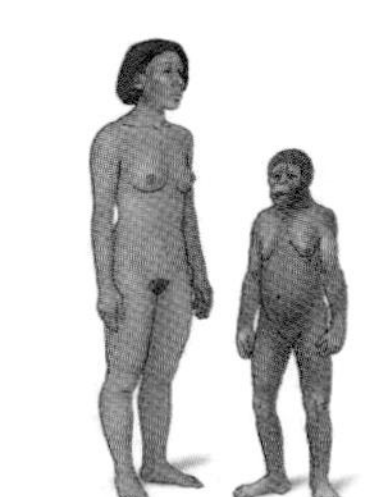


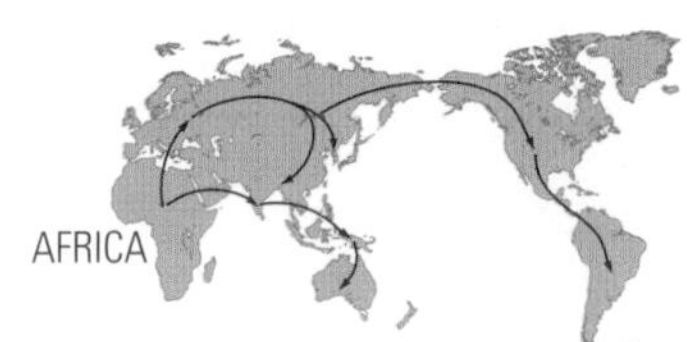


## The Evolution of the Human Brain

Scientists who study the evolution of the brain propose that a relative increase in the size and complexity of the brain in different species is what enabled the evolution of more complex behavior. In this section, we consider the relation between brain size and behavior across different species. We also consider a number of hypotheses about how the human brain became so large.

## BRAIN SIZE AND BEHAVIOR

In his book titled *The Evolution of the Brain and Intelligence,* published in 1973, H. J. Jerison uses the **principle of proper mass** to sum up the relation between increased size of the nervous system and increased complexity of behavior. This principle states that the amount of neural tissue responsible for a particular function is equivalent to the amount of processing that the function requires. So, as behaviors become more complex and require more neural processing, a greater amount of neural tissue must be allocated to them. It follows that species exhibiting more complex behaviors will possess relatively larger brains than those of species whose behaviors are simpler.

**Principle of proper mass.** The idea that complex behavioral functions are produced by a larger brain or brain region than that in which simple behavioral functions are produced; usually used to refer to the idea that the brain size of an animal species is proportional to its behavioral complexity.

Jerison found support for the principle of proper mass by comparing brain size in a wide variety of animal species. Jerison calculated that, as body size increases, the size of the brain increases at about two-thirds the increase in body weight. With the use of this formula, plus an average brain-volume-to-body-weight ratio as a base, it is possible to determine the expected brain size for a mammal of any given weight. This expected brain size is plotted in the diagonal line shown in Figure 1-16, a graph in which body size is on the $x$-axis and brain size on the $y$-axis. The diagonal line represents the expected increase in brain size as body size increases. The polygon surrounding the diagonal line encompasses the brain and body sizes of all mammals. The actual brain and body sizes of a number of representative animals also are plotted on this graph. Animals that lie below the diagonal line have brains that are below average for an animal of that size, whereas animals that lie above the diagonal line have brains that are larger than expected for an animal of that size. Notice that the rat has a brain that is a little smaller and the elephant a brain that is a little larger than expected. Notice also that a modern human is located farther to the upper left than any other animal, indicating a brain that is relatively larger for its body size than that of any other animal.

To further illustrate the relative sizes of brains, Jerison developed a numerical system that eliminates body weight as a factor and adjusts brain sizes according to a

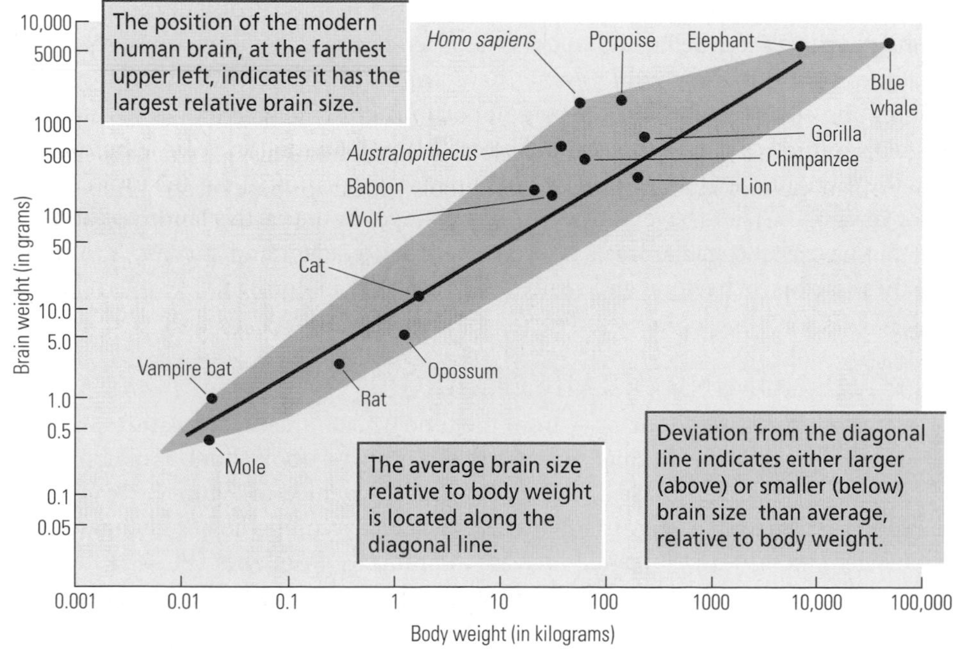


**Figure 1-16**

Brain and body sizes of some common mammals. The axes are in logarithmic units to represent the wide range of body and brain sizes. The polygon includes the brain and body sizes of all mammals. The line through the polygon illustrates the expected increase in brain size as body weight increases. The labeled dots show the brain and body sizes of a number of representative species. Animals that lie above the diagonal line have brain sizes that are larger than would be expected for an animal of that size. Modern humans have the largest brain relative to body size of all mammals.

Adapted from *The Evolution of the Brain and Intelligence* (p. 175), by H. J. Jerison, 1973, New York: Academic Press.

**Encephalization quotient (EQ).** A measure of brain size obtained from the ratio of actual brain size to the expected brain size for an animal of a particular body size.

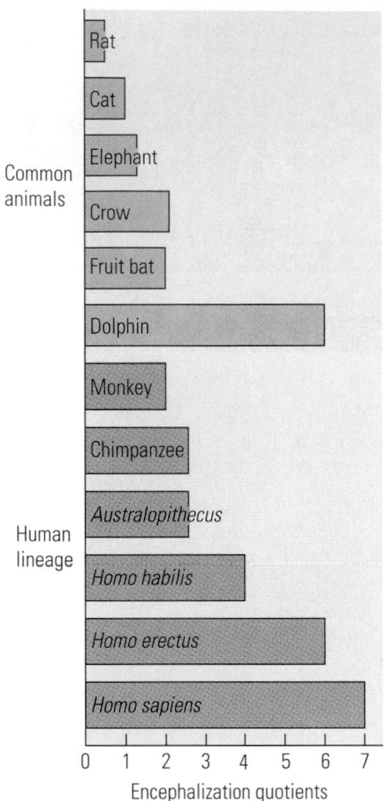


**Figure 1-17**

The EQ (encephalization quotient) of (*top*) some common animals and (*bottom*) members of the human lineage.

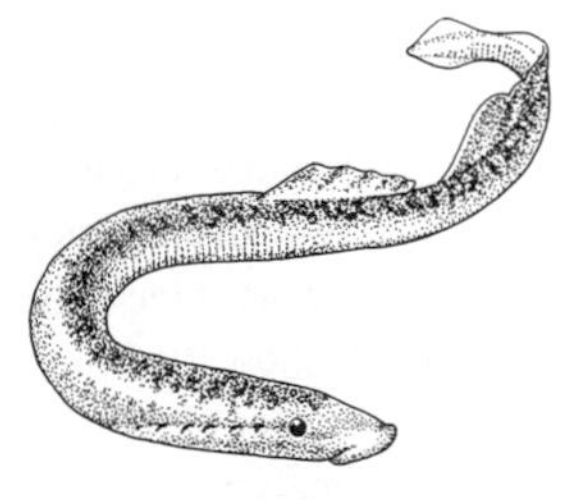


scaling factor. He calls this system an **encephalization quotient (EQ).** Figure 1-17 (top) lists the EQs for several common animals. Notice that a rat has an EQ about one-half that of a cat, which is representative of the average mammal. Interestingly, a crow has an EQ similar to that of a monkey, and a dolphin has a very large EQ indeed. People who study crows would agree that they are intelligent, whereas people who study dolphins, although admitting that they are intelligent social creatures, are still uncertain about the reason for their need of such a large brain. Figure 1-17 (bottom) lists the EQs for a number of species in the human lineage. Clearly, we modern humans are descended from a lineage of large-brained animals, but we have the largest brain.

Underlying the principle of proper mass is the idea that a larger brain is needed for increasingly complex behavior. Although it is not always easy to compare the complexity of behavior in different animal species, there are some fairly obvious examples of more complex behaviors that correlate with greater brain size. These examples are seen as we progress up the chordate ladder from older to more recent groups of animals. For instance, among the older chordates, cyclostomes, such as the lamprey, move by making snakelike, side-to-side body movements, whereas the more recent fish have fins with which to move, in addition to using these lateral movements of the body. Fish, significantly, have relatively larger brains than those of cyclostomes. Fins evolved into limbs in amphibians, and these limbs are used in a more complex way than fins are to enable walking on land. Amphibians, significantly, have relatively larger brains than those of fish. Birds and mammals use their limbs for still more complex movements, both for locomotion and for handling objects. Birds and mammals, significantly, have relatively larger brains than those of amphibians. Being a primate is associated with many other behavioral innovations. Primates engage in complex social and sexual behavior, as well as complex feeding habits, care of their young, defense of their territories, and, in regard to humans, the use of language. Primates, significantly, have relatively larger brains than other mammals do.

Why is there this trend toward greater brain size and behavioral complexity in chordates? Why, in the course of evolutionary history, did animals not retain very simple nervous systems? A number of factors have created relatively constant opportunities and pressures for animals to modify their behavior and thus their nervous systems. For example, because the first animals were relatively simple, they left a wide variety of more complex behaviors available as potential means of gaining a survival advantage. Filling these behavioral niches was often favored through natural selection. In addition, various cataclysmic events have wiped out large numbers of species, changing the environment and offering opportunities for new evolutionary adaptations. For example, a comet that struck the earth about 60 million years ago probably led to the dinosaurs' extinction and opened up new opportunities for the rapid evolution of mammals. There have also been many changes in the earth's landmass and climate that have challenged animals to evolve in order to adapt and survive. As a result of all these factors, behavioral and structural complexity has grown.

## WHY THE HOMINID BRAIN ENLARGED

The evolution of modern humans—from the time when humanlike creatures first appeared until the time when humans like ourselves existed—took about 5 million years. As illustrated by the relative size differences of skulls presented in Figure 1-18, much of this evolution entailed a change in brain size, which was accompanied by changes in behavior. There was a nearly threefold increase in brain size from apes (EQ 2.5) to modern humans (EQ 7.0). What caused this substantial growth of the brain? Most likely, the appearance of each new hominid species was associated with climate changes that produced new environments that isolated populations of existing hominids and produced a rapid selection of traits that were adaptive for the new environment.

The first of these climate changes was triggered about 8 million years ago. Before that time, most of Africa was a rich forest inhabited by monkeys and apes, as well as other animal species. Then a massive tectonic event (a deformation of the earth's crust) produced the Great Rift Valley, which runs from south to north across the African continent. This reshaping of the African landmass left a wet jungle climate to the west and a much drier climate to the east. To the west, the apes continued unchanged in their former habitat, but, in the drier region to the east, apes had to evolve rapidly to adapt to the mixture of tree-covered and grassy regions that formed their new home. An upright posture is an efficient means of rapid locomotion across grass-covered areas. Such an upright posture may have evolved in *Australopithecus* because these animals were forced to spend more time on the ground moving between clumps of trees. In addition, an upright posture may have helped to regulate body temperature by reducing the amount of the body's surface directly exposed to the sun.

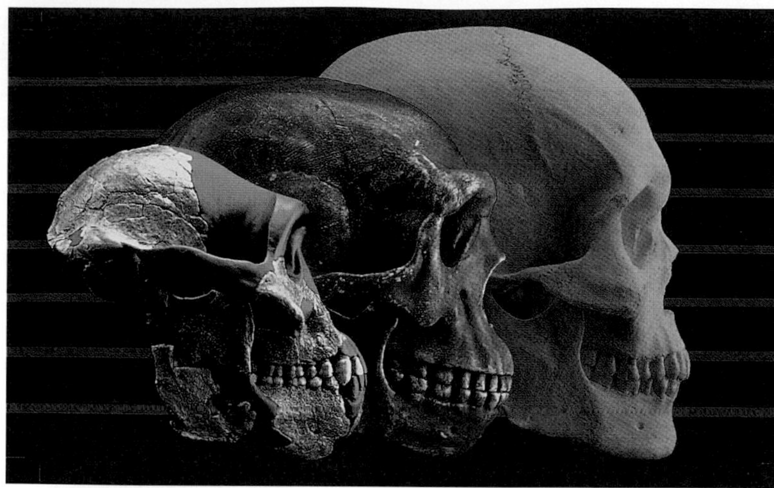

K. O'Farrell/Concepts

**Figure 1-18**

In the course of human evolution, the relative size of the brain increased threefold, as illustrated here by a comparison between *Australopithecus afarensis* (*left*), *Homo erectus* (*center*), and a modern human. The part of the *Australopithecus* skull shown in blue is missing.

From *The Origin of Modern Humans* (p. 165), by R. Lewin, 1998, New York: Scientific American Library.

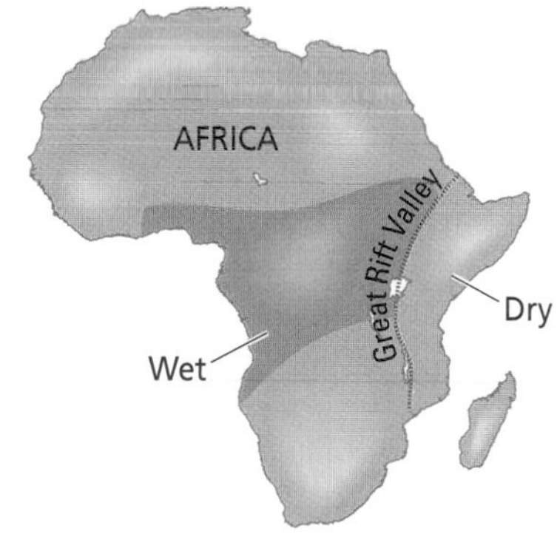


Just before the appearance of *Homo habilis,* the African climate changed again, becoming drier, with increasing amounts of grassland and even fewer trees. Anthropologists speculate that a group of hominids that evolved into *Homo habilis* adapted to this new habitat by becoming scavengers on the dead of the large herds of grazing animals that then roamed the open grasslands. The appearance of *Homo erectus* may have been associated with further change in climate that opened up land bridges into Europe and Asia. At the same time, the new hominids added hunting to their behavioral skills and were constantly upgrading the quality of their tools for killing, skinning, and butchering animals. Archeologists think there were a number of migrations of hominids from Africa into other parts of the world, with modern humans being the last of these migrants. Each of the migrations may have been forced by changes in climate that altered the habitat to which the animals residing there were adapted. In any case, modern humans eventually replaced all other species of hominids everywhere on earth.

At least three factors are thought to be related to the development of a larger brain as our species evolved. The first is the primate life style, which favored a more complex nervous system. The second is the development of a new way of cooling a larger brain mass. And the third is neoteny, a process by which maturation is delayed and an adult retains infant characteristics.

**The Primate Life Style** That the primate life style favors a larger brain can be illustrated by examining how primates forage for food. Foraging is a very important activity for all animals, but some foraging activities are quite simple, whereas others are more complex. Eating grass or vegetation is not an especially difficult task; if there is lots of vegetation, an animal need only munch. Vegetation eaters do not have especially large brains. Among the apes, gorillas, which are mainly vegetation eaters, have relatively small brains. In contrast, apes that eat fruit, such as chimpanzees, have relatively large brains. The relation between fruit foraging and larger brain size can be seen in a study by Katharine Milton (1993), who examined the feeding behavior and brain size of two South American (New World) monkeys that have the same body size—the spider monkey and the howler monkey. As is illustrated in Figure 1-19, the spider monkey obtains 72 percent of its nutrients from eating fruit and has a brain that is twice as large as that of the howler monkey, which obtains only 42 percent of its nutrients from fruit.

What is so special about eating fruit that favors a larger brain? The answer is not that fruit contains a brain-growth factor, although fruit *is* a source of sugar, on which the brain depends for energy. The answer is that foraging for fruit is a difficult, complex activity. Unlike plentiful vegetation within easy reach on the ground, fruit grows on trees, and only on certain trees, in certain seasons. There are many kinds of fruit, some better for eating than others, and many different animals and insects compete for a fruit crop. Moreover, after a fruit crop has been eaten, it takes time for a new crop to grow. Each of these factors poses a challenge for an animal that eats mostly fruit. Good sensory skills, such as color vision, are needed to recognize ripe fruit in a tree, and good motor skills are required to reach and manipulate it. Good spatial skills are needed to navigate to trees that contain fruit. Good memory skills are required to remember where fruit trees are, when the fruit will be ripe, and in which trees the fruit has already been eaten. Fruit eaters have to be prepared to deal with competitors, including members of their own species, who also want the fruit. To keep track of ripening fruit, it also benefits a fruit eater to have friends who can help search. As a result, successful fruit-eating animals tend to have complex social relations and a means of communicating with others of their species. In addition, it is very helpful for a fruit eater to have a parent who can teach fruit-finding skills, so it is useful to be both a good learner and a good teacher. Each of these abilities requires the evolution of new brain areas or more brain cells in existing brain regions. Added up, more brain cells produce a larger brain.

**Figure 1-19**

Katharine Milton examined the feeding behavior and brain size of two South American (New World) monkeys that have the same body size. She found that the spider monkey obtains 72 percent of its nutrients from eating fruit and that it has a brain that is twice the size of that of the howler monkey, which obtains only 42 percent of its nutrients from fruit.

P. A. Souders/Corbis

**Spider monkey diet**

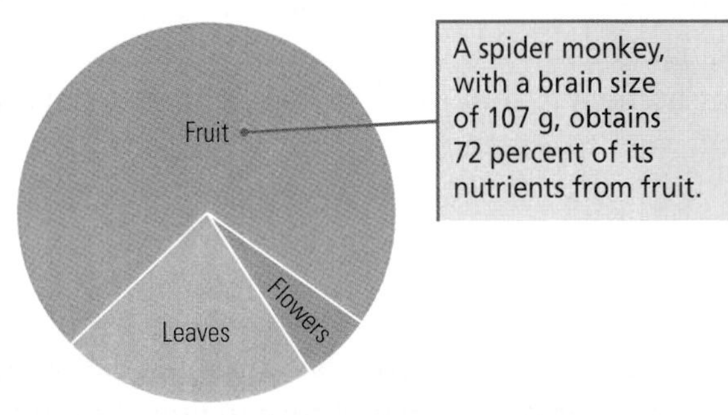
Fruit
Leaves
Flowers
A spider monkey, with a brain size of 107 g, obtains 72 percent of its nutrients from fruit.

K. Schafer/Corbis

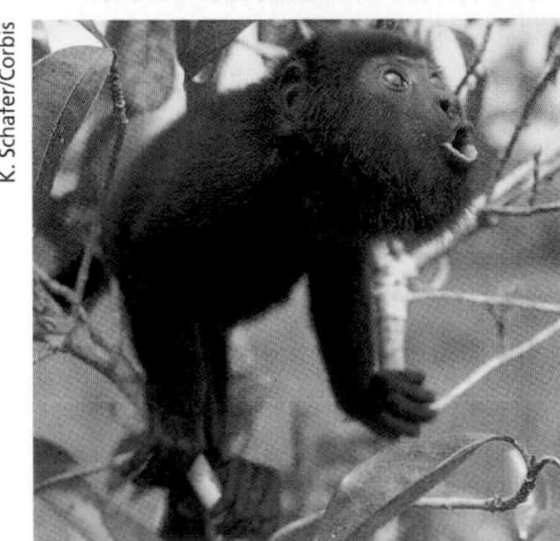

**Howler monkey diet**

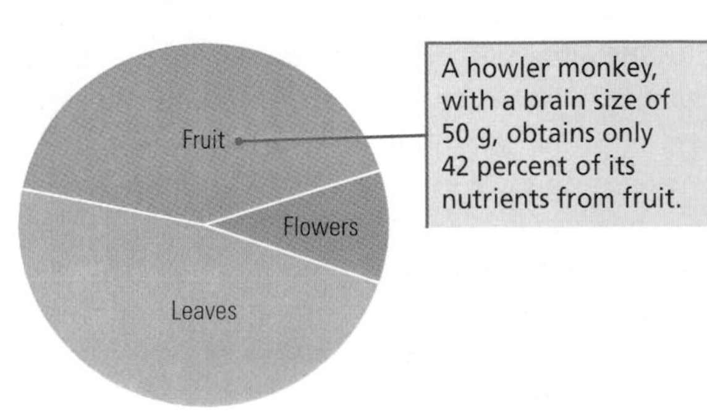
Fruit
Flowers
Leaves
A howler monkey, with a brain size of 50 g, obtains only 42 percent of its nutrients from fruit.

We humans are fruit eaters and we are descended from fruit eaters, so we are descended from animals with large brains. In our evolution, we also exploited and elaborated fruit-eating skills to obtain other temporary and perishable food items as we scavenged, hunted, and gathered. These new food-getting efforts required navigating for long distances, and they required recognition of a variety of food sources. At the same time, they required making tools for digging up food, killing animals, cutting skin, and breaking bones. These tasks also required a good deal of cooperative behavior. The elaboration of all of these skills necessitated new brain areas or more brain cells in existing brain regions. Added up, more brain cells produce an even larger brain.

**Neoteny.** A process in which maturation is delayed, so an adult retains infant characteristics; the idea derived from the observation that newly evolved species resemble the young of their ancestors.

**The Radiator Hypothesis** An event that may have given a special boost to greater brain size in our human ancestors was a new form of brain cooling. Dean Falk (1990), a neuropsychologist who studies brain evolution, came up with this idea from something that her car mechanic told her. He said that, to increase the size of a car's engine, you have to also increase the size of the radiator that cools it. Consequently, Falk proposed the **radiator hypothesis,** the theory that a change in blood flow around the brain increases the rate at which the brain is cooled, thus allowing the brain to become larger.

Why is brain cooling so important? The answer is the tremendous amount of work done by a human brain. Although your brain makes up less than 2 percent of your body, it uses 25 percent of your body's oxygen and 70 percent of its glucose. As a result of all this metabolic activity, your brain generates a great deal of heat and is at risk of overheating under conditions of exercise or heat stress. This risk of overheating, Falk argues, places a limit on how big the brain can be. In animals with less efficient brain-cooling systems than we have, the size limit on the brain is even lower. This more stringent constraint has kept the brain of the chimpanzee at its current size.

Falk speculates that a more efficient brain-cooling mechanism arose in the hominid line between *Australopithecus* and more humanlike species, such as *Homo habilis.* When examining hominid skeletons, Falk noticed that, unlike australopith skulls, *Homo* skulls contain holes through which blood vessels pass. These holes suggest that *Homo* species had a much more widely dispersed blood flow from the brain than did earlier hominids, and this more widely dispersed blood flow would have greatly enhanced brain cooling. The increase in brain cooling, in turn, would have allowed the brain to become larger, which it apparently did in response to evolutionary pressures posed by the new environments exploited by these animals.

**Neoteny** One mechanism through which an increase in brain size could have taken place is through **neoteny,** in which a species' rate of maturation slows down, so juvenile stages of predecessors become the adult features of descendants. Because the head of an infant is large relative to body size, this process would have led to adults with larger skulls and larger brains. Many other features of human anatomy, besides a large brain-size-to-body-size ratio, also link us with the juvenile stages of other primates. These features include a small face, a vaulted cranium, an unrotated big toe, an upright posture, and a primary distribution of hair on the head, armpits, and pubic areas. Figure 1-20 illustrates that the head shape of a baby chimpanzee is more

C. A. Schmidecker/FPG

R. Stacks/Index Stock

**Figure 1-20**

An adult human more closely resembles a juvenile chimpanzee than an adult chimp. The rounder head of the baby chimpanzee compared with the more elongated head of the adult chimpanzee leads to the hypothesis that we humans may be neotenic descendants of our more apelike distant ancestors.

similar to an adult human head shape than it is to the head shape of an adult chimpanzee. We also retain behavioral features of primate infants, including play, exploration, and an intense interest in learning new things. Neoteny is a very common occurrence in the animal world. Domesticated dogs are thought to be neotenic wolves, and sheep are thought to be neotenic goats.

Another aspect of neoteny in relation to human brain development is that a slowing down of human maturation would have allowed more time for brain cells to be produced (McKinney, 1998). Most brain cells in humans develop just before and after birth, so an extended prenatal and neonatal period would have prolonged the stage of life in which brain cells are developing. This, in turn, would have enabled the creation of increased numbers of brain cells.

### In Review

Constant changes in the climate and physical features of the earth have eliminated certain animal species and created new opportunities for other species to emerge. The large human brain evolved in response to a number of pressures and opportunities. They included changes in climate, the appearance of new food resources to exploit, a more widely dispersed blood flow from the brain that enabled better brain cooling, and the retention of certain juvenile physical and behavioral traits.

## STUDYING BRAIN AND BEHAVIOR IN MODERN HUMANS

So far, we have taken an evolutionary approach in exploring the human brain. But because this approach is designed mainly for comparisons *between* species, special care must be taken in extending its principles to comparisons *within* species, especially comparisons within groups of modern humans. We will illustrate the difficulty of within-species comparisons by considering attempts to correlate human brain size with intelligence. Then we will turn to another aspect of studying the brain and behavior in modern humans—the fact that, unlike the behavior of other animal species, so much of modern human behavior is culturally learned.

### Human Brain-Size Comparisons

In comparisons between animal species, larger brain size correlates with more complex behavior. Does the same relation hold true in comparisons between individual members of a single species? For instance, do people with the largest brains display the most complex and intelligent behavior? Stephen Jay Gould (1981), in his book titled *The Mismeasure of Man*, reviewed numerous attempts to correlate human brain size and intelligence. He is critical of this research because its logic and methods leave conclusions completely muddled.

For one thing, it is difficult to determine how to measure the size of a person's brain. If a tape measure is simply placed around a person's head, it is impossible to factor out the thickness of the skull. There is also no agreement about whether volume or weight is a better indicator of brain size. And, no matter which indicator we use, we must consider as well the relation between body size and brain size. For instance, the human brain varies in weight from about 1000 grams to more than 2000 grams, but people also vary in body mass. To what extent should we factor in body mass in deciding if a particular brain is large or small? And how should we measure the mass of the body, given that a person's total weight can fluctuate quite widely? There is also the matter of when in life brain size should be measured, because age and health affect the brain's mass. If we wait until after death to measure a brain, the cause of death, the water content of the brain, and the time after death will all affect the results. And, even if the problems of measurement could be solved, there remains the question of what is causing what. Exposure to a complex environment can promote growth in existing brain cells. So, if larger brains are found to correlate with higher intelligence, does the complex problem solving cause the greater brain mass or does the greater brain mass enable the more complex behavior?

As if these matters were not perplexing enough, there is also the question of what is meant by intelligence. When we compare the behavior of *different* species, we are comparing **species-typical behavior**—in other words, behavior displayed by all members of a species. When we compare behavior *within* a species, however, we are usually comparing how well one individual member performs a certain task in relation to other members. This comparison is a completely different kind of measure. In addition, individual performance on a task is influenced by many factors unrelated to inherent ability, such as interest level, training, motivation, and health. People vary enormously in their individual abilities, depending on the particular task. One person may have superior verbal skills but mediocre spatial abilities, whereas another person may be adept at solving spatial puzzles but struggle with written work, and still another excels at mathematical reasoning but is average in everything else. Which of these people should we consider the most intelligent? Should certain skills get greater weight as measures of intelligence? Clearly, it is difficult to say.

**Species-typical behavior.** A behavior that is characteristic of all members of a species.

Given these questions, it is not surprising that brain size and intelligence within the human species do not seem particularly related to each other. People who virtually everyone agrees are very intelligent have been found to have brains that vary in size from the low end to the high end of the range for our species. For instance, the brilliant physicist Albert Einstein had a brain of average size. Similarly, women have brains that weigh about 10 percent less than men's brains (roughly equivalent to the average difference in female and male body size), but there is little evidence that the two sexes differ in average intelligence.

The lack of correlation between brain size and intelligence within a single species is found not only in humans. For instance, Figure 1-21 plots the average brain size in

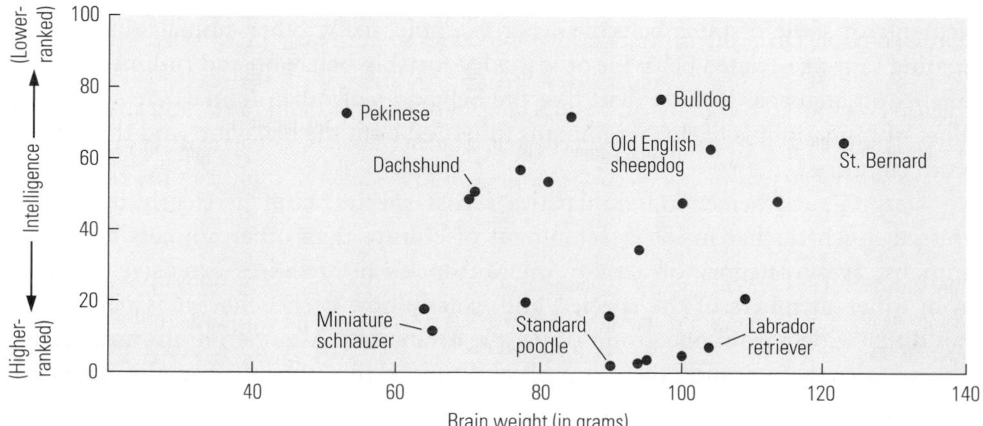


**Figure 1-21**

In a comparison of intelligence rankings and brain size in breeds of dogs—animals that are all members of the same species—the correlation is $r = 0.009$, which indicates no relationship (an $r = 1$ would show a perfect relationship). If your dog does not show well, do not be distressed, because there are a lot of problems in determining dog intelligence.

Intelligence rankings are from *The Intelligence of Dogs,* by S. Coren, 1994, Toronto: The Free Press. Size measures are from "Brain Weight–Body Weight Scaling in Dogs and Cats," by R. T. Bronson, 1979, *Brain, Behavior and Evolution, 16,* 227–236.

different breeds of dogs against each breed's level of intelligence as ranked by dog experts. The brain sizes, which range from less than 50 grams to nearly 130 grams, were not adjusted for the breeds' body sizes, because such adjustments are not made in studies of humans. As you can see, there is no relation at all between the overall size of a breed's brain and that breed's intelligence ranking.

There must be differences of some kind in the brains of individual persons because people differ in behavior and talents. At present, though, we are not yet sure of what structural or functional measures are related to behavioral traits. However, it is very unlikely that gross brain size will provide an accurate or useful measure. Researchers who study this question believe that measures of the relative size and function of particular brain regions will be more helpful. Important, too, will probably be differences in how the various parts of the brain are organized and interrelated.

## Culture

The most remarkable thing about the brains of modern humans is that they have allowed us to develop an extraordinarily rich culture. Human **culture** consists of the complex learned behaviors characteristic of a group of people who pass those behaviors on to one another and from generation to generation. Biologist G. P. Murdock compiled the following list, in alphabetical order, of major categories of behavior that are part of human culture:

> Age-grading, athletic sports, bodily adornment, calendar [use], cleanliness training, community organization, cooking, cooperative labor, cosmology, courtship, dancing, decorative art, divination, division of labor, dream interpretation, education, eschatology, ethics, ethnobotany, etiquette, faith healing, family feasting, fire making, folklore, food taboos, funeral rites, games, gestures, gift giving, government, greetings, hair styles, hospitality, housing, hygiene, incest taboos, inheritance rules, joking, kin groups, kinship nomenclature, language, law, luck, superstitions, magic, marriage, mealtimes, medicine, obstetrics, penal sanctions, personal names, population policy, postnatal care, pregnancy usages, property rights, propitiation of supernatural beings, puberty customs, religious ritual, residence rules, sexual restrictions, soul concepts, status differentiation, surgery, toolmaking, trade, visiting, weaving, and weather control. (Murdock, 1945)

Not all the items in this list are unique to humans. Many other animal species display elements of some of these behaviors. For example, many other animals display age grading (any age-related behavior or status), courtship behavior, and rudimentary elements of language. To the extent that the behaviors of other animals are similar to those of humans, it is likely that humans inherited both the behaviors and the related brain circuitry.

Despite such behavioral similarities across species, humans clearly have progressed much further in the development of culture than other animals have. For humans, every category of activity on Murdock's list requires extensive learning from other members of the species, and exactly how each behavior is performed can differ widely from one group of people to another. A human brain must function adequately to acquire these complex cultural skills. When its functioning is inadequate, a person may be unable to learn even basic elements of culture. "Learning

**Culture.** Behaviors that are learned and passed on from one generation to the next through teaching and learning.

Focus on Disorders

## Learning Disabilities

During the first third of their lives, children expend much energy in learning a society's culture, and acquiring the language skills of their culture is a challenge that we expect them to meet. Yet some people have difficulties in mastering language-related tasks. These difficulties and others that affect performance in school are classified under the "umbrella" of *learning disabilities.*

One of the most common learning disabilities is *dyslexia* (from the Latin *dys,* meaning "poor," and *lexia,* meaning "reading"), an impairment in learning to read. Not surprisingly, children with dyslexia have difficulty learning to write as well as to read. In 1895, James Hinshelwood, an eye surgeon, examined some schoolchildren who were having reading problems, but he could find nothing wrong with their vision. Hinshelwood was the first person to suggest that these children had an impairment in brain areas associated with the use of language.

In more recent times, Norman Geshwind and Albert Galaburda proposed a way in which such an impairment might come about. These researchers were struck by the finding that dyslexia is far more common in boys than in girls. Perhaps, they reasoned, excessive amounts of the hormone testosterone, which produces male physical characteristics early in development, might also produce abnormal development in language areas of the brain. Pursuing this hypothesis, they examined the brains of a small sample of dyslexic people who had died. They found abnormal collections of neurons, or "warts," in the language areas of the left hemisphere. This relation between structural abnormalities in the brain and learning difficulties is further evidence that an intact brain is necessary for normal human functioning.

Disabilities," above, describes how incapacitating it can be to have a brain that has difficulty in learning to read.

Because of vast differences in cultural achievements, the behavior of modern humans is completely unlike that of *Homo sapiens* 100,000 years ago. Granted, simple toolmaking and tool use predate modern humans, but art, such as carvings and paintings, dates back only some 30,000 years, well after the appearance of *Homo sapiens.* Agriculture appears still more recently in human history, about 10,000 to 15,000 years ago. And reading and writing, the foundations of our modern literate and technical societies, were invented only about 7000 years ago. St. Ambrose, who lived in the fourth century, is reported to be the first person who could read silently. So silent reading is an even more recent behavior than writing. Most forms of mathematics, another basis of modern technology, were invented still more recently than reading and writing were. Although most researchers think that the origin of verbal language coincided with the beginning of modern humans, it may have developed much later. If we consider that most of our culture was invented long after our brains evolved into their present form, most of our verbal language skills also could have been learned long after *Homo sapiens* first evolved. It is likely that, when you have completed your college or university curriculum, your vocabulary will be larger and your language will be richer than those of your parents and grandparents.

A remarkable feature of the modern human brain is that it can do so many things for which it was not seemingly designed. The brains of early *Homo sapiens* certainly did not develop to help program computers or travel to distant planets. And yet the brains of modern humans are capable of both these complex tasks and more. Apparently, the things that the human brain did evolve to do contained all the elements necessary for the invention and use of far more sophisticated skills. The human brain is apparently a highly flexible organ that allows the great variety of knowledge and achievements that are part of modern culture.

The acquisition of a complex culture was a gradual, step-by-step process, with one achievement leading to another. The development of language, for instance, must have started when our early ancestors began to use concepts to represent the things important to them in their world. In her book titled *The Chimpanzees of Gombe,* primatologist Jane Goodall described the process by which such concepts might have developed in chimpanzees. She used the development of the concept of "fig" as an example, explaining how a chimp might progress from knowing a fig only as a tangible, here-and-now entity to having a special vocal call that represents this concept symbolically. Goodall writes:

> We can trace a pathway along which representations of . . . a fig become progressively more distant from the fig itself. The value of a fig to a chimpanzee lies in eating it. It is important that he quickly learn to recognize as *fig* the fruit above his head in a tree (which he has already learned to know through taste). He also needs to learn that a certain characteristic odor is representative of *fig,* even though the fig is out of sight. Food calls made by other chimpanzees in the place where he remembers the fig tree to be located may also conjure up a concept of *fig*. Given the chimpanzees' proven learning ability, there does not seem to be any great cognitive leap from these achievements to understanding that some quite new and different stimulus (a symbol) can also be representative of *fig*. Although chimpanzee calls are, for the most part, dictated by emotions, cognitive abilities are sometimes required to interpret them. And the interpretations themselves may be precursors of symbolic thought. (Goodall, 1986, pp. 588–589)

Presumably, in our own distant ancestors, the repeated acquisition of concepts, as well as the education of children in those concepts, gradually led to the acquisition of language and other aspects of a complex culture. The study of the human brain, then, is not just the study of the structure of an organ that evolved thousands of years ago. It is also the study of how that organ acquires sophisticated cultural skills—that is, of how the human brain functions in today's world.

## In Review

Care must be taken in extending principles learned in studying the evolution of the brain and behavior. What is true for comparisons across different species may not be true for comparisons within a single species. For instance, although a larger brain correlates with more complex behavior when comparing different species, brain size and intelligence are not particularly related when looking at individual persons within the species of modern humans. We humans are also distinguished in the animal kingdom by the amount of our behavior that is culturally learned. We have progressed much further in the development of culture than other species have.

## SUMMARY

1. *What is the brain and what is behavior?* Behavior can be defined as any kind of movement in a living organism. As such, a behavior has both a cause and a function. The flexibility and complexity of behavior vary greatly in different species, with human behavior being highly flexible and complex. Located inside the skull, the brain is the organ that exerts control over behavior. The brain seems to need ongoing sensory and motor activity to maintain its intelligent activity.
2. *How is the nervous system structured?* The nervous system is composed of the central nervous system, which includes the brain and the spinal cord, and the peripheral nervous system, through which the brain and spinal cord communicate with sensory receptors and with muscles. The brain and spinal cord communicate not only with the skeletal muscles that enable movement of the body, but also with the body's many internal organs. The nerve pathways taking part in regulating internal bodily functions, including emotional responses, are collectively called the autonomic nervous system.
3. *How have people through history viewed the relation between the brain and behavior?* Aristotle believed that the brain has no role in behavior, but rather that behavior is the product of an intangible entity called the psyche or mind. Descartes modified this theory, proposing that only rational behavior is produced by the mind, whereas other behaviors are produced mechanically by the brain. Finally, Darwin's proposal that all living things are descended from a common ancestor led to the conclusion that the source of *all* behavior is the brain.
4. *How did brain cells and the nervous system evolve?* Brain cells and the nervous system evolved in animals over millions of years. The evolutionary stages through which the brain evolved can be traced though groups of living animals. The nervous system evolved in the animal kingdom and the brain and spinal cord evolved in the chordate phylum. Mammals are a class of chordates characterized by especially large brains.
5. *What species were the early ancestors of modern humans?* One of our early hominid ancestors was probably *Australopithecus* or a primate very much like it, who lived in Africa several million years ago. From an australopith species, more humanlike species likely evolved. Among these species are *Homo habilis* and *Homo erectus*. Modern humans, *Homo sapiens,* did not appear in Asia and North Africa until about 200,000 to 100,000 years ago.
6. *How did the human brain evolve?* The human brain evolved through the sequence of hominid species that are the ancestors of modern humans. Since *Australopithecus,* the brain has increased in size almost threefold. This evolution was stimulated by the natural selection of more complex behavior patterns. It was also made possible by changes in blood circulation that enabled a larger brain to be adequately cooled.
7. *What are some important considerations in studying the brain and behavior of modern humans?* It is important to realize that principles learned in studying the evolution of the brain and behavior may not apply to the brain and behavior within a single species, such as *Homo sapiens*. As animals evolved, a larger brain was associated with more complex behavior, yet, within our species, the most able and intelligent people do not necessarily have the largest brains. In the study of modern humans it is also important to recognize the great extent to which our behavior is not inherent in our nervous systems, but rather is culturally learned.

**neuroscience interactive**

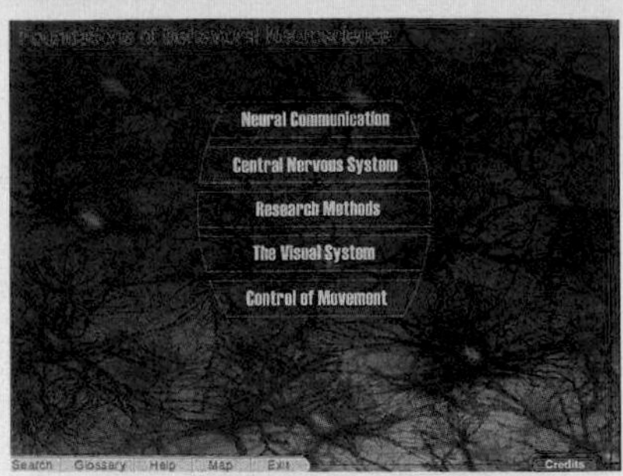


There are many resources available for expanding your learning online:

- **www.worthpublishers.com/kolb/chapter1**

Try some self-tests to reinforce your mastery of the material in Chapter 1. Look at some of the news updates reflecting current research on the brain. You'll also be able to link to other sites which will reinforce what you've learned.

- **http://neurolab.jsc.nasa.gov/timeline.htm**

Review a timeline of important people in the study of the brain from René Descartes to Roger Sperry put together by the Spotlight on Neuroscience, National Aeronautics and Space Administration (NASA).

- **http://serendip.brynmawr.edu/Mind/Table.html**

Visit this site from R. H. Wozniak of Bryn Mawr College to learn more about the philosophical underpinnings of dualism and materialism and to read a detailed history of the origins of the mind–body question and the rise of experimental psychology.

On your CD-ROM you'll be able to quiz yourself on your comprehension of the chapter. You'll be able to begin learning about the anatomy of the brain in the module on the Central Nervous System. This module is composed of a rotatable, three-dimensional brain as well as a number of sections of the brain that you can move through with the click of a mouse. In addition, the Research Methods module contains various CT and MRI images of the brain, including a video clip of a coronal MRI scan.

## KEY TERMS

bilateral symmetry, p. 17
cladogram, p. 16
common ancestor, p. 14
common descent, p. 12
culture, p. 30
dualism, p. 9
encephalization quotient (EQ), p. 24
hominid, p. 21
materialism, p. 12
mentalism, p. 8
mind, p. 8
mind–body problem, p. 9
natural selection, p. 12
neoteny, p. 27
principle of proper mass, p. 23
segmentation, p. 17
species-typical behavior, p. 29
taxonomy, p. 15

## REVIEW QUESTIONS

1. Summarize the ideas of Aristotle, Descartes, and Darwin regarding the relation between the brain and behavior.
2. Trace your own lineage by using the taxonomic system described in this chapter.
3. Can you recall the number of species of living organisms in each taxonomic subgrouping? What do you think accounts for the apparent relation between numbers of species and brain size?
4. We suggested that brain size is one way of accounting for behavioral complexity for interspecies comparisons but not for intraspecies comparisons. Why did we make this distinction?
5. How does culture increase the difficulty of understanding human brain function?

## FOR FURTHER THOUGHT

Darwin's principle of natural selection is based on there being large individual differences within species. There are large individual differences in the brain size of modern humans. Under what conditions could a new human species with a still larger brain evolve?

## RECOMMENDED READING

Campbell, N. A. (1999). *Biology,* 2nd ed. Menlo Park, CA: Benjamin Cummings. This introductory biology textbook provides a comprehensive overview of the structure and function of living organisms.

Coren, S. (1994). *The intelligence of dogs.* Toronto: The Free Press. This very popular book includes a number of tests that are supposed to tell you how smart your dog is. The book also provides comparisons of intelligence for different dog breeds as rated by dog trainers. Check your dog out against other breeds by using easy-to-perform tests. Remember, if your dog is not well trained, it might not do well on the tests.

Darwin, C. (1965). *The expression of the emotions in man and animals.* Chicago: University of Chicago Press. (Original work published 1872) If a dog growls at you, is the dog angry? Darwin thought so. Darwin's only book on psychology is one in which he argues that the expression of emotions is similar in animals, including humans, which suggests the inheritance of emotions from a common ancestor. This view is becoming popular today, but Darwin proposed it more than 100 years ago.

Darwin, C. (1963). *On the origin of species by means of natural selection, or the preservation of favored races in the struggle for life.* New York: New American Library. (Original work published 1859) This book is the most important one ever written in biology. Darwin extensively documents the evidence for his theory of natural selection. The book is an enjoyable account of natural life, and one chapter, titled "Instincts," describes behavior in both wild and domesticated animals.

Goodall, J. (1986). *The chimpanzees of Gombe*. Cambridge, MA: Harvard University Press. Goodall's three-decade-long study of wild chimpanzees, begun in 1960, rates as one of the most scientifically important studies of animal behavior ever undertaken. Learn about chimpanzee family structure and chimpanzee behavior, and look at the beautiful photographs of chimpanzees engaged in various behaviors.

Gould, S. J. (1981). *The mismeasure of man*. New York: Norton. Gould criticizes and repudiates extensive literature of the nineteenth and twentieth centuries that claims that differences in human intelligence and differences in the intelligence of the sexes are due to differences in brain size. The appealing feature of this book is that Gould is highly critical of the methodology of the proponents of the brain-size hypothesis while also giving reasons derived from modern genetics to criticize their position.

Lorenz, K. Z. (1981). *The foundations of ethology*. New York: Springer Verlag. Learn how to study animals and learn how they behave from one of the founders of ethology, the study of animal behavior.

Martin, R. D. (1990). *Primate origins and evolution: A phylogenetic reconstruction.* Princeton, NJ: Princeton University Press. Martin provides a detailed description of the origins and the evolution of primates. This book is an excellent primate reference.

Weiner, J. (1995). *The beak of the finch*. New York: Vintage. This book is a marvelous study of evolution in action. Weiner documents how the populations of Galápagos finches are affected by changes in the availability of certain kinds of food. Careful measurements of the finches' beaks demonstrate that certain beak sizes and shapes are useful when certain kinds of food are available; however, when the appropriate food becomes unavailable, populations of birds with differently shaped beaks become favored.

CHAPTER

# 2

# How Is the Brain Organized?



A. Klehr / Stone Images
Micrograph: Carolina Biological Supply Co. / Phototake

When buying a new car, people first inspect the outside carefully, admiring the flawless finish and perhaps even kicking the tires. Then they open the hood and examine the engine, the part of the car responsible for most of its behavior—and misbehavior. This means gazing at a maze of tubes, wires, boxes, and fluid reservoirs. All most of us can do is gaze, because what we see simply makes no sense, except in the most general way. We know that the engine burns gasoline to make the car move and somehow generates electricity to run the radio and lights. But this tells us nothing about what all the engine's many parts do. What we need is information about how such a system works.

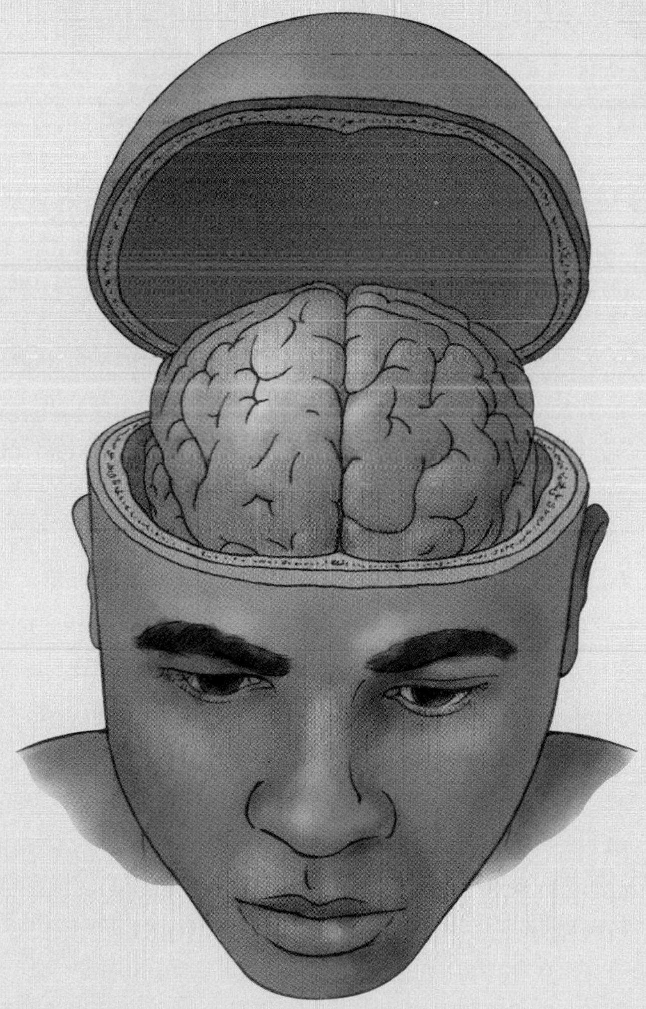

**Figure 2-1**
View of the human brain when the skull is opened. The gyri (bumps) and sulci (cracks) of the cerebral hemispheres are visible, but their appearence gives little information about their function.

In many ways, examining a brain for the first time is similar to looking under the hood of a car. We have a vague sense of what the brain does but no sense of how the parts that we see accomplish these tasks. We may not even be able to identify many of the parts. In fact, at first glance the outside of a brain may look more like a mass of folded tubes divided down the middle than like a structure with many interconnected pieces. See what you can make of the human brain in Figure 2-1. Can you say anything about how it works? At least a car engine has parts with regular shapes that are recognizably similar in different engines. This is not true of mammals' brains, as shown in Figure 2-2. When we compare the brain of a cat with that of a human, for example, we see that there is an enormous difference not just in overall size, but in the relative sizes of parts and in structure. In fact, some parts present in one are totally absent in the other. What is it that all these parts do that makes one animal stalk mice and another read textbooks?

To make matters worse, even for trained research scientists, the arrangement of the brain's parts does not just *seem* random, it really *is* haphazard. The challenge that we face in learning about the brain is to identify some regularities in its organization and to establish a set of principles that can help us understand how the nervous system works. After decades of investigation, we now have a good idea of how the nervous system functions, at least in a general way. That knowledge is the subject of this chapter. But before we turn our attention to the operation manual for the brain and the rest of the nervous system, let us examine what the brain is designed to do. Knowing the brain's functions will make it easier to grasp the rules of how it works.

Perhaps the simplest statement of the brain's functions is that it produces behavior, as seen in Chapter 1. There is more to this statement than is immediately apparent, however. In order for the brain to produce behavior, it must have information about the world, such as information about the objects around us—their size, shape, movement, and so forth. Without such information, the brain cannot know how to orient and direct the body to produce an appropriate response. This is especially true when the response needed is some complex behavior, such as

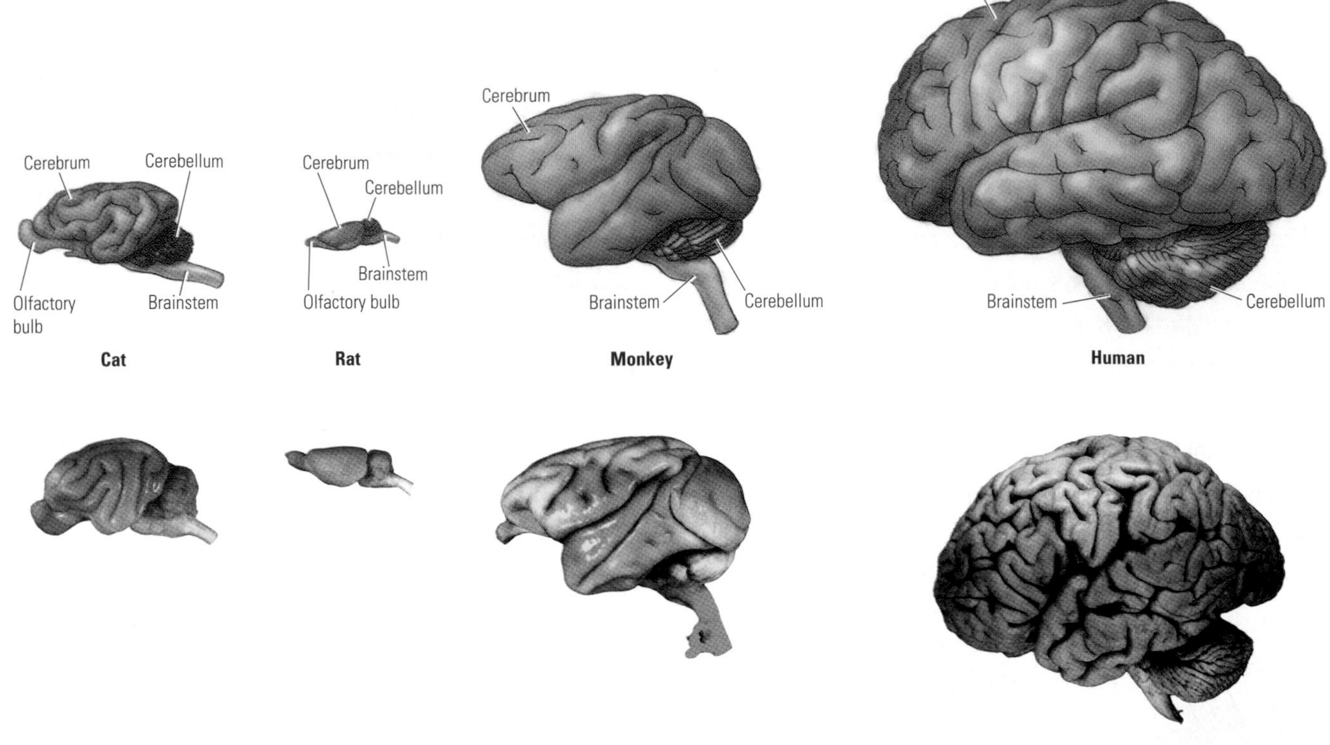


**Figure 2-2**

Inspection of the outside features of the brains of a cat, rat, monkey, and human shows them to differ dramatically in size and in general appearance. The rat brain is smooth, whereas the other brains have furrows in the cerebral cortex. The pattern of furrows differs considerably in the human, the monkey, and the cat. The cat brain and, to some extent, the monkey brain have long folds that appear to run much of the length of the brain, whereas the human brain has a more diffuse pattern. The cerebellum is wrinkled in all species and is located above the brainstem. The brainstem is the route by which information enters and exits the brain. The olfactory bulb, which controls the perception of smells, is relatively larger in cats and rats but is not visible in monkeys and humans, because it is small and lies under the brain.

Photos courtesy of Wally Welker, University of Wisconsin Comparative Mammalian Brain Collection.

catching a ball. To perform complex behaviors, the nervous system has organs designed to receive information from the world and convert this information into biological activity that produces subjective experiences of reality. The brain thus produces what we believe is reality in order for us to move. These subjective experiences of reality are essential to carrying out any complex task.

This view of the brain's primary purpose may seem abstract to you, but it is central to understanding how the brain functions. Consider the task of answering a telephone. The brain directs the body to pick up the receiver when the nervous system responds to vibrating molecules of air by creating the subjective experience of a ring. We perceive this sound and react to it as if it actually existed, when in fact the sound is merely a fabrication of the brain. That fabrication is produced by a chain reaction that takes place when vibrating air molecules hit the eardrum. In the absence of the nervous system, especially the brain, there is no such thing as sound. Rather, there is only the movement of air molecules.

The subjective nature of the experiences that the brain creates can be better understood by comparing the realities of two different kinds of animals. You are probably aware that dogs perceive sounds that humans do not. This difference in perception does not mean that a dog's nervous system is better than ours or that our hearing is poorer. Rather, a dog brain simply creates a different world from that of our brain. Neither subjective experience is "right." The difference in experience is merely due to two different systems for processing physical stimuli. The same differences exist in visual perceptions. Dogs see very little color, whereas our world is rich with color because our brains create a different reality from that of a dog's brain. Such differences in subjective realities exist for good reason: they allow different animals to exploit different features of their environments. Dogs use their hearing to detect the movements of mice in the grass, whereas early humans probably used color for such tasks as identifying ripe fruit in trees. Evolution, then, equipped each species with a view of the world that would help it survive.

These examples show how a brain's sensory experiences help guide an organism's behavior. For this link between sensory processing and behavior to be made, the brain must also have a system for accumulating, integrating, and using knowledge. Whenever the brain collects sensory information, it is essentially creating knowledge about the world, knowledge that can be used to produce more effective behaviors. The knowledge currently being created in one sensory domain can be compared both with past knowledge and with knowledge gathered in other domains.

We can now identify the brain's three primary functions:

1. to produce behavior;
2. to create a sensory reality; and
3. to create knowledge that integrates information from different times and sensory domains and to use that knowledge to guide behavior.

Each of the brain's three functions requires specific machinery. The brain must have systems to create the sensory world, systems to produce behavior, and systems to integrate the two.

In this chapter, we consider the basic structures and functions of those systems. First, we identify the components of the nervous system. Then we look at what those components do. Finally, we look at how the parts work together and at some general principles of brain function. Many of the ideas introduced in this chapter are developed throughout the rest of the book, so you may want to return to this chapter often to reconsider the basic principles as new topics are introduced.

# AN OVERVIEW OF BRAIN STRUCTURE

The place to start our overview of the brain's structure is to "open the hood" by opening the skull and looking at the brain snug in its home. Figure 2-1 shows a brain viewed from this perspective. The features that you see are part of what is called the brain's "gross anatomy," not because they are ugly, but because they constitute a broad overview. Zooming in on the brain's microscopic cells and fibers is largely reserved for Chapter 3, although this section ends with a brief introduction of some terms used for these tiny structures. Those terms are just a few of a great many new terms that you will encounter in this book, which is why we deal with brain terminology in general before moving on to a look at the brain itself. Because many of the words in this chapter will seem foreign to you, they will be accompanied by a pronunciation guide at their first appearance.

## Brain Terminology

There are hundreds, even thousands of brain regions, making the task of mastering brain terminology seem daunting. To make matters worse, many structures have several names, and many terms are often used interchangeably. This peculiar nomenclature arose because research on brain and behavior has spanned several centuries. When the first anatomists began to examine the brain with the primitive tools of their time, they made many erroneous assumptions about how the brain works, and the names that they chose for brain regions are often manifestations of those errors. For

Link to an index listing the roots of neuroanatomical terms at **www.worthpublishers.com/kolb/chapter2.**

**Figure 2-3**

Anatomical terms are used to describe anatomical locations. **(A)** Anatomical directions relative to the head and brain. Because a human is upright, the terms *posterior* and *caudal* (both meaning "tail") refer to a slightly different orientation for the human head compared with the head of a four-legged animal. **(B)** Anatomical directions relative to the body.

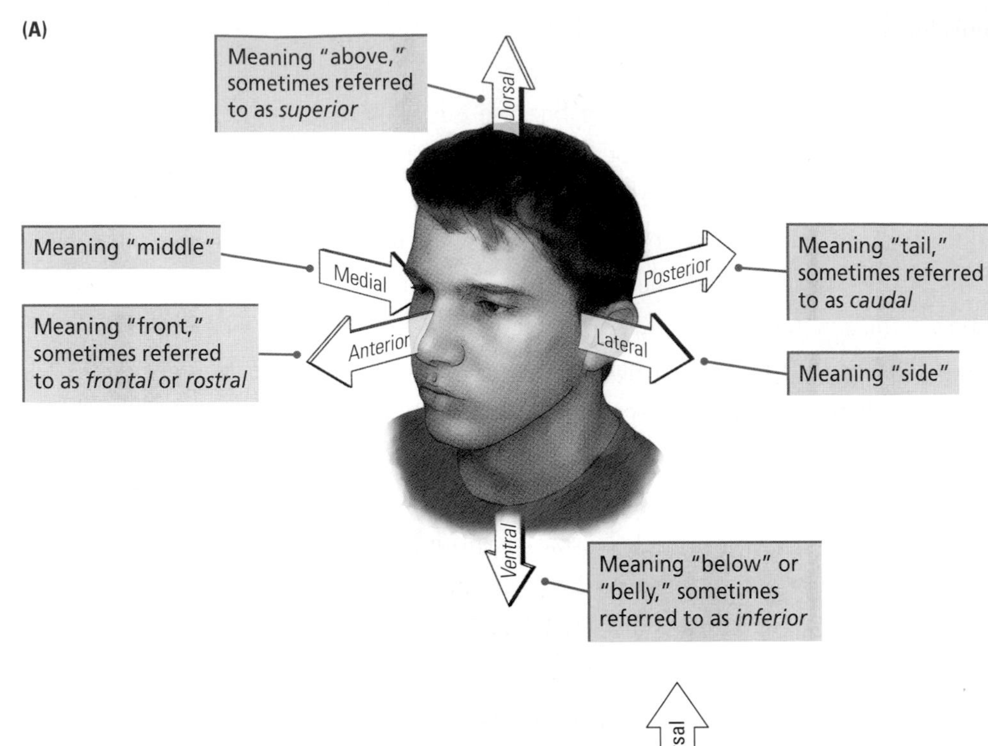


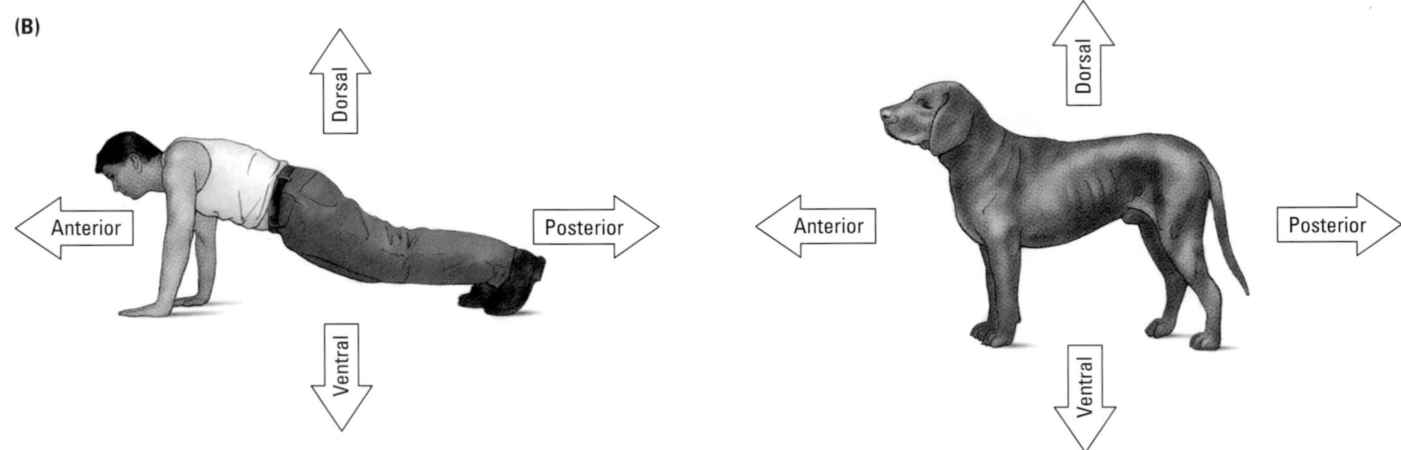


**Figure 2-4**

An afferent nerve carries information into the brain, and an efferent nerve takes information out of the brain and controls movement of a muscle.

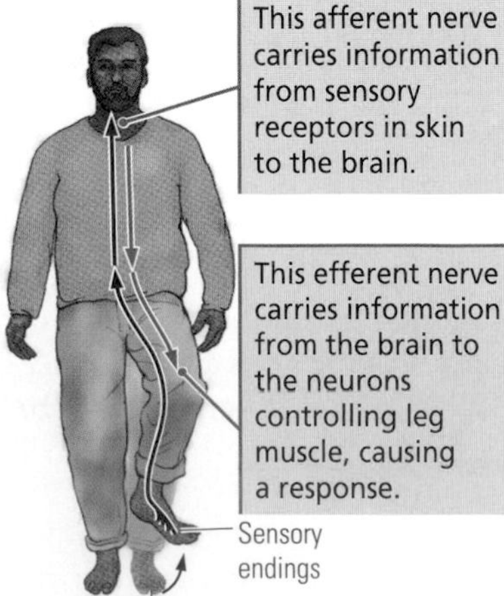

This afferent nerve carries information from sensory receptors in skin to the brain.
This efferent nerve carries information from the brain to the neurons controlling leg muscle, causing a response.
Sensory endings

instance, they named one region of the brain the *gyrus fornicatus* because they thought it had a role in sexual function. In fact, most of this region has nothing to do with sexual function. Another area was named the *red nucleus* because it appears reddish in fresh tissue. This name denotes nothing of the area's potential functions, which turn out to be the control of limb movements.

As time went on, the assumptions and tools of brain research changed, but the naming continued to be haphazard and inconsistent. Early investigators named structures after themselves or objects or ideas. They used different languages, especially Latin, Greek, and English. More recently, investigators have often used numbers or letters, but even this system lacks coherence because the numbers may be Arabic or Roman numerals and are often used in combination with letters, which may be either Greek or Latin. When we look at current brain terminology, then, we see a mixture of all these naming systems.

Despite this sometimes confusing variety, many names do include information about a structure's location in the brain. Table 2-1 summarizes these location-related terms, and Figure 2-3 shows how they relate to body locations. Structures found on the top of the brain or on the top of some structure within the brain are *dorsal*. Structures located toward the bottom of the brain or one of its parts are *ventral.* Structures found toward the middle of the brain are *medial,* whereas those located toward the side are *lateral.* Structures located toward the front of the brain are *anterior,* whereas those located toward the back of the brain are *posterior.* Sometimes the terms *rostral* and *caudal* are used instead of *anterior* and *posterior,* respectively. And, occasionally, the terms *superior* and *inferior* are used to refer to structures that are located dorsally or ventrally (these terms do *not* label structures according to their importance). It is also common to combine terms. For example, a structure may be described as *dorsolateral,* which means that it is located "up and to the side."

**Table 2-1 Orientation Terms for the Brain**

| Term | Meaning with respect to the nervous system |
|---|---|
| Anterior | Located near or toward the front or the head |
| Caudal | Located near or toward the tail |
| Dorsal | On or toward the back or, in reference to brain nuclei, located above |
| Frontal | "Of the front" or, in reference to brain sections, a viewing orientation from the front |
| Inferior | Located below |
| Lateral | Toward the side of the body |
| Medial | Toward the middle; sometimes written as *mesial* |
| Posterior | Located near or toward the tail |
| Rostral | "Toward the beak"; located toward the front |
| Sagittal | Parallel to the length (from front to back) of the skull; used in reference to a plane |
| Superior | Located above |
| Ventral | On or toward the belly or side of the animal in which the belly is located or, in reference to brain nuclei, located below |

You should also learn two terms that describe the direction of information flowing to and from cells in the brain. **Afferent** refers to information coming into the brain or a part of the brain, whereas **efferent** refers to information leaving the brain or one of its parts, meaning that efferent refers to brain signals that trigger some response (Figure 2-4). These words are very similar, but there is an easy way to keep them straight. The letter "a" in *afferent* comes alphabetically before the "e" in *efferent,* and sensory information must come into the brain *before* an outward-flowing signal can trigger a response. Therefore, *afferent* means "incoming" and *efferent* means "outgoing."

On the CD, visit the module on the Central Nervous System to better visualize the various planes of the brain.

## The Brain's Surface Features

Returning to the brain in the open skull, you are now ready to examine its structures more closely. The first thing to notice is that the brain is covered by a tough material known as the **meninges** [*men* ***in*** *jeez* (the accented syllable is in boldface type)], which is a three-layered structure, as illustrated in Figure 2-5. The outer layer is known as the *dura mater* (from Latin, meaning "hard mother"). It is a tough double layer of fibrous tissue enclosing the brain in a kind of loose sack. The middle layer is the *arachnoid* layer (from Greek, meaning "like a spider's web"). It is a very thin sheet of delicate

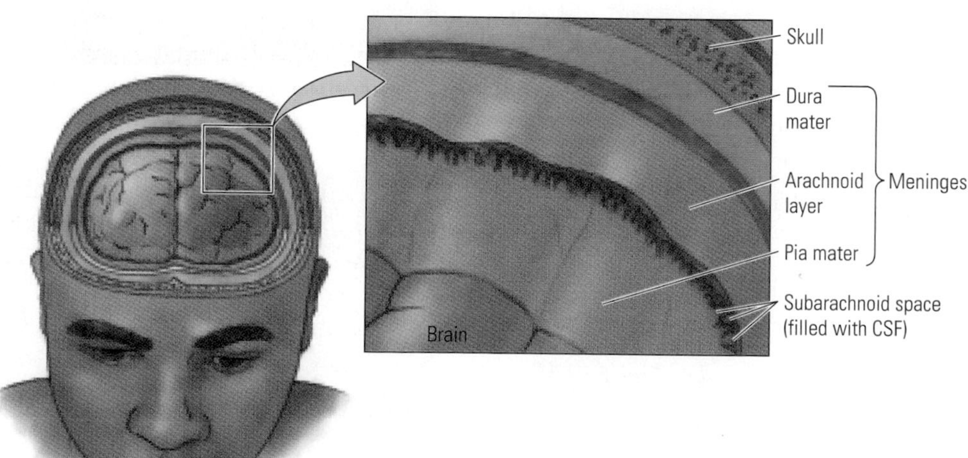


**Figure 2-5**

The brain is covered by thick coverings known as the meninges and is cushioned by a fluid known as the cerebrospinal fluid (CSF).

**Figure 2-6**

In these views of the human brain (from the top, bottom, side, and middle), the locations of the frontal, parietal, occipital, and temporal lobes of the cerebral hemispheres are shown, as are the cerebellum and the three major sulci (the central sulcus, lateral fissure, and longitudinal fissure) of the cerebral hemispheres.

Photos courtesy of Yakolev Collection/AFIP.

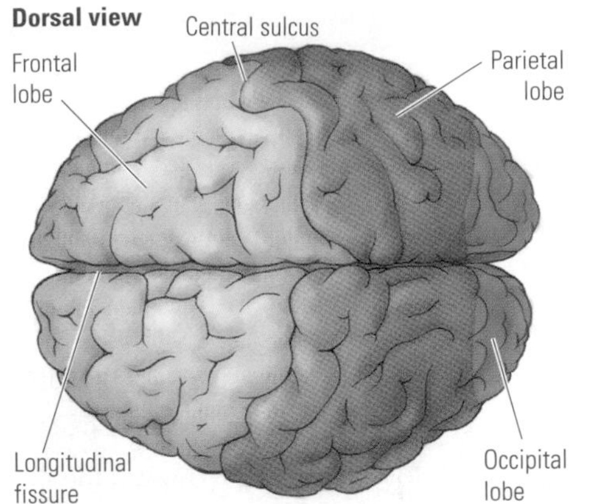


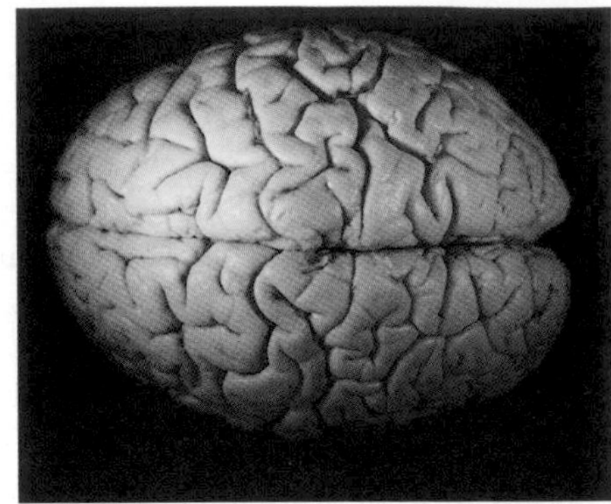

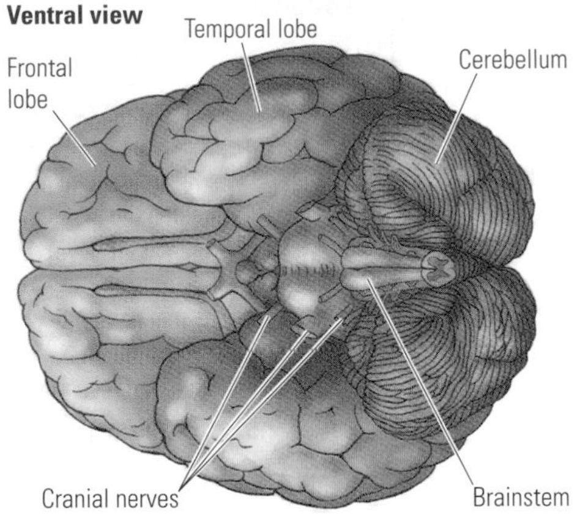


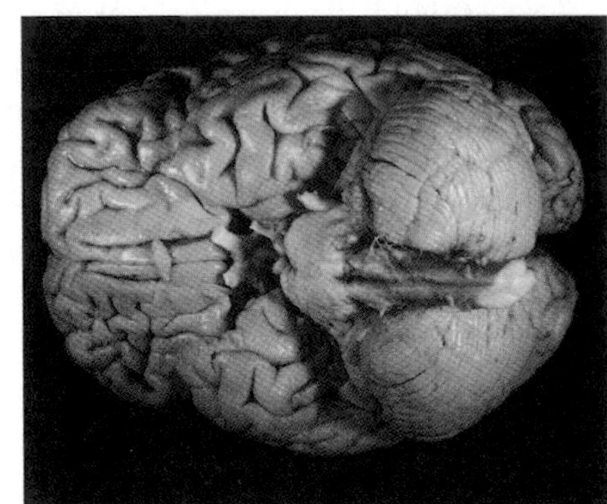

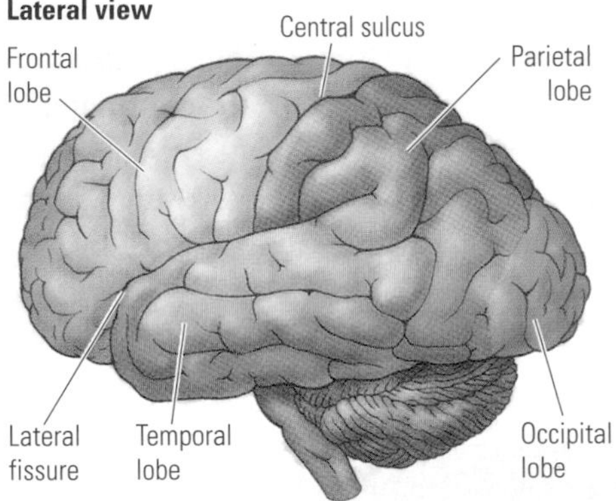


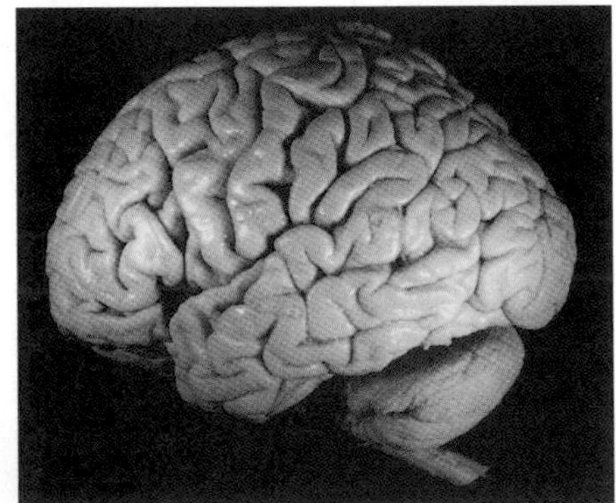

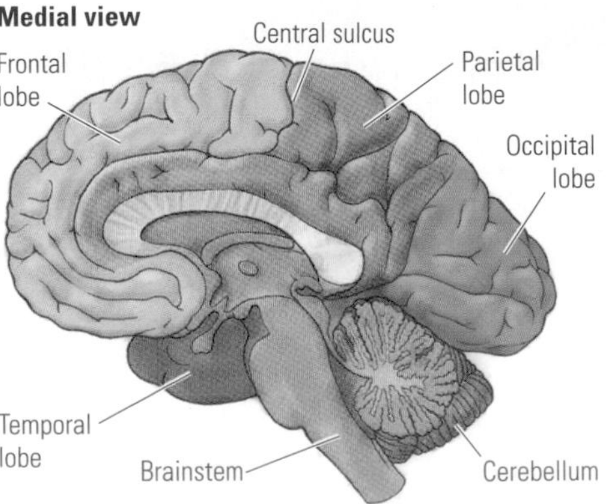


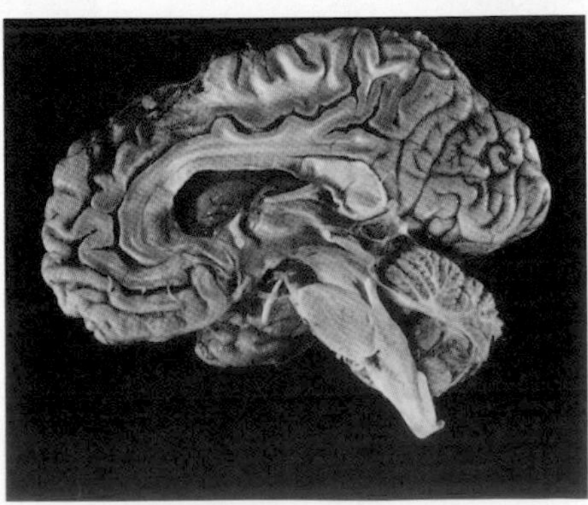

connective tissue that follows the brain's contours. The inner layer is the *pia mater* (from Latin, meaning "soft mother"). It is a moderately tough membrane of connective-tissue fibers that cling to the surface of the brain. Between the arachnoid and pia mater is a fluid, known as **cerebrospinal fluid (CSF),** which is a colorless solution of sodium chloride and other salts. It provides a cushion so that the brain can move or expand slightly without pressing on the skull. (Meningitis is an infection of the meninges. Its symptoms are described in "Meningitis and Encephalitis" on page 46.)

If we remove the meninges, we can now remove the brain from the skull and examine its various parts. As we look at the brain from the top or the side, it appears to have two major parts, each wrinkly in appearance. The larger part is the **cerebrum** [*sa **ree** brum*], which consists of two cerebral hemispheres, the left and the right, and the smaller part is the **cerebellum** [*sair a **bell** um*]. Both the cerebrum and the cerebellum are visible in the brains shown in Figure 2-2. Each of these structures is wrinkled in large-brained animals because its outer surface is made of a relatively thin sheet of tissue, the cortex, that has been pushed together to make it fit into the skull. To see why the cortex is wrinkled, force a piece of writing paper, $8\frac{1}{2}$ by 11 inches, into a cup. The only way is to crinkle the paper up into a ball. Essentially the same crinkling-up has been done to the cortex of the cerebrum and the cerebellum. Like a crinkled piece of paper, much of the cortex is invisible from the surface. All we can see from the surface are bumps and cracks. The bumps are known as **gyri** [*jye rye;* singular: gyrus (*jye russ*)], whereas the cracks are known as **sulci** [***sul** sigh;* singular: sulcus (***sul** kus*)]. Some of the sulci are very deep and so are often called *fissures.* The two best-known fissures are the longitudinal fissure and the lateral fissure, both of which are shown in Figure 2-6, along with the central sulcus.

**Cerebrum.** The major structure of the forebrain, consisting of two equal hemispheres (left and right).

**Cerebellum.** Major structure of the hindbrain specialized for motor coordination; in large-brained animals, it may also have a role in the coordination of other mental processes.

**Brainstem.** Central structures of the brain including the hindbrain, midbrain, thalamus, and hypothalamus.

**Cranial nerve.** One of a set of nerves that control sensory and motor functions of the head; includes senses of smell, vision, audition, taste, and touch on the face and head.

Plug in the CD to examine, locate, and rotate the parts of the brain in the section on the subdivisions of the CNS in the module on the Central Nervous System.

If we now look at the bottom of the brain, we see something completely different. The cerebrum is still the wrinkled part, but now there is also a whitish structure down the middle with little tubes attached. This middle structure is known as the **brainstem,** and the little tubes are **cranial nerves** that run to and from the head.

One final gross feature is obvious: the brain appears to be covered in blood vessels. As in other parts of the body, the brain receives blood through arteries and sends it back through veins to the kidneys and lungs for cleaning and oxygenation. The arteries come up the neck and then wrap around the outside of the brainstem, cerebrum, and cerebellum, finally piercing the brain's surface to get to its inner regions. Figure 2-7 shows the three major arteries that feed blood to the cerebrum—namely, the anterior, middle, and posterior cerebral arteries. Because the brain is very sensitive to loss of blood, a blockage or break in a cerebral artery is likely to lead to the death of the affected region, a condition known as a **stroke** (see "Stroke" on page 48). Because the three cerebral arteries service different parts of the brain, strokes disrupt different brain functions, depending on the artery affected.

**Figure 2-7**

Each of the three major arteries of the cerebral hemispheres—the anterior, middle, and posterior—provides blood to a different region of the cerebrum.

Anterior cerebral artery

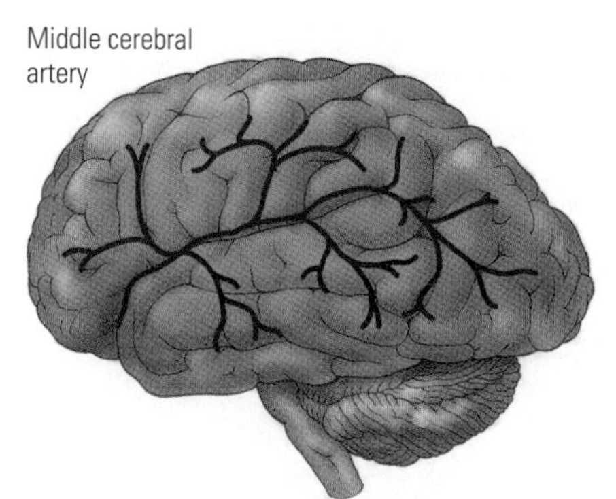


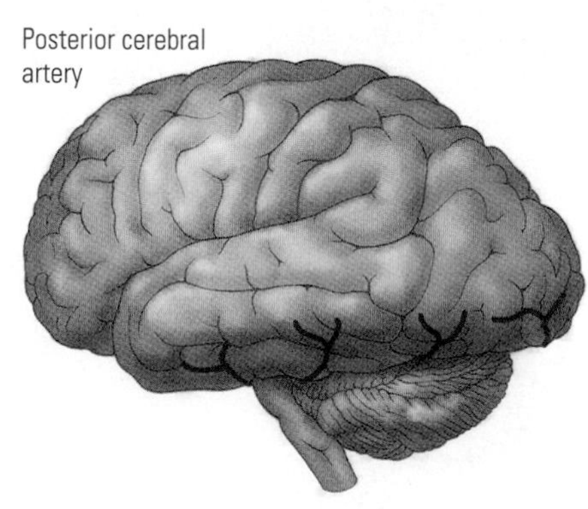

**White matter.** Those areas of the nervous system rich in axons, leading to a white appearance.

**Gray matter.** Those areas of the nervous system composed predominantly of cell bodies, leading to a gray appearance.

**Reticular matter.** Area composed of intermixed cell bodies and axons that produce a mottled gray and white, or netlike, appearance.

## The Brain's Internal Features

The simplest way to examine what is inside something—be it an engine, a pear, or a brain—is to cut it in half. The orientation in which we cut makes a difference in what we see, however. Consider what happens when we slice through a pear held in different orientations. If we cut a pear from side to side, we cut across the core; whereas, if we cut it from top to bottom, we cut parallel to the core. Our impression of what the inside of a pear looks like is clearly influenced by the way in which we slice it. The same is true of the brain.

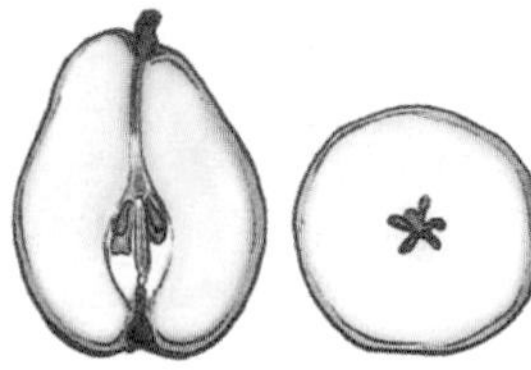

We can begin by cutting the brain in half, slicing it downward through the middle. The result is shown in Figure 2-8. This view of the brain is known as a *frontal section* because we can now see the inside of the brain from the front.

Several features of the brain's interior are immediately apparent. First, it contains four cavities, known as **ventricles** [***ven*** *trik uls*], which are shown in Figure 2-9. Cells that line the ventricles make the cerebrospinal fluid that fills them. The ventricles are connected, so CSF flows from the two lateral ventricles to the ventricles that lie on the brain's midline, eventually flowing into the space between the lower layers of the meninges as well as into the spinal-cord canal. Although the function of the ventricles is not well understood, they are thought to play an important role in maintaining the brain. The CSF may allow certain compounds access to the brain, and it probably helps the brain excrete metabolic wastes. Very likely, too, the CSF produced in the ventricles acts as a kind of shock absorber. The CSF surrounds the brain; so, if there is a blow to the head, this fluid cushions the movement of the brain within the skull.

Look at the CD to examine a three-dimensional model of the ventricular system in the section on subcortical structures in the module on the Central Nervous System.

A second feature apparent in our frontal section of the brain is that the brain's interior is not homogeneous. There are both light and dark regions. These light and dark regions may not seem as distinct as the different parts of a car's engine, but nevertheless they represent different components. The light regions, called **white matter,** are mostly fibers with fatty coverings. The fatty coverings produce the white appearance, much as fat droplets in milk make it appear white. The dark regions, called **gray matter** because of their gray-brown color, are areas where capillary blood vessels and cell bodies predominate. Some regions of the brain have a mottled gray and white, or netlike, appearance. These regions, which have both cell bodies and fibers mixed together, are called **reticular matter** (from the Latin word *rete,* meaning "net").

Another way to cut the brain is from front to back. The result is a side view, called a *sagittal* [***sadj*** *i tal*] section. If we make our cut down the brain's midline, we divide the cerebrum into its two hemispheres. Figure 2-10 shows such a sagittal section.

**Figure 2-8**

This frontal section through the brain shows the internal features. The brain is **(A)** cut and then **(B)** viewed at a slight angle. This section displays regions that are relatively white and gray. The white areas are largely composed of fibers, whereas the gray areas are composed of cell bodies. The large bundle of fibers joining the two areas is the corpus callosum. Each ventricle is a fluid-filled tube.

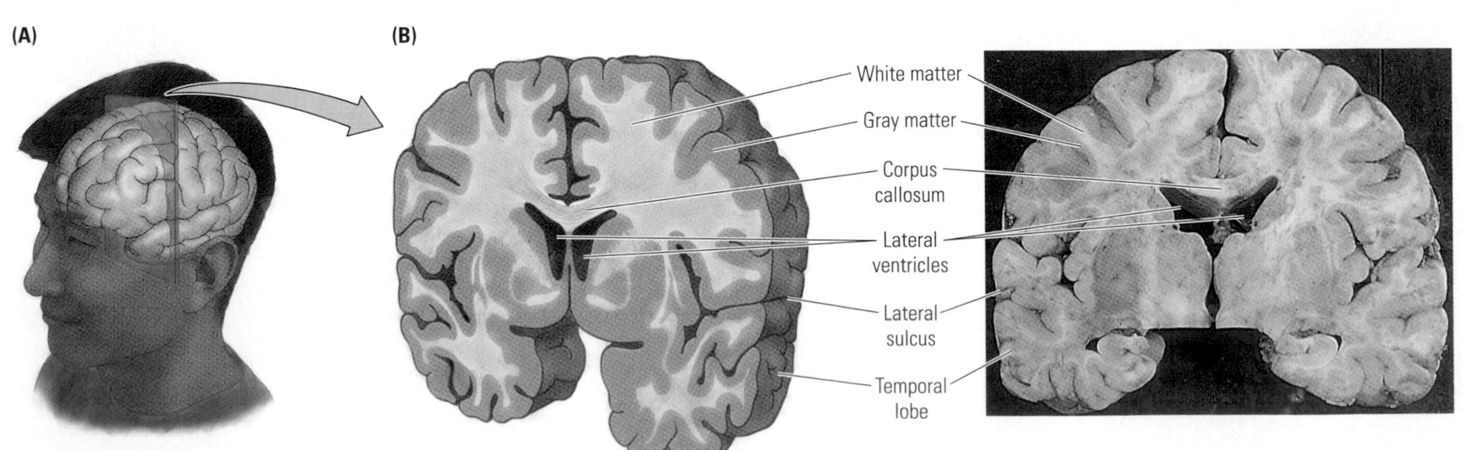

One feature seen from this viewing angle is a long band of white matter that runs much of the length of the cerebral hemispheres. This band is called the **corpus callosum** [*ka* ***loh*** *sum*]. The corpus callosum contains about 200 million fibers that join the two hemispheres and allow communication between them. It is also clear in Figure 2-10 that the cortex covers the cerebral hemispheres above the corpus callosum, whereas below the corpus callosum are various internal structures of the brain. Owing to their location below the cortex, these structures are known as **subcortical regions.**

We can see the internal structures of the brain in much more detail by coloring them with special stains. For example, if we use a dye that selectively stains cell bodies, we can see that the distribution of cells within the gray matter is not homogeneous, as shown in Figure 2-11. In particular, it becomes apparent that the cerebral cortex is composed of layers, each of which contains similarly staining cells. Furthermore, subcortical regions are now seen to be composed of clusters, known as **nuclei,** of similarly stained cells. Although layers and nuclei are very different in appearance, they both form functional units within the brain. Whether a particular brain region has layers or nuclei is largely an accident of evolution.

If you were to compare the two sides of the brain in sagittal section, you would be struck by their symmetry. The brain, in fact, has two of nearly every structure, one on each side. The few structures that are one of a kind are found along the brain's midline. Examples are the third and fourth ventricles and the pineal gland, mentioned in Chapter 1 in reference to Descartes's theory about how the brain works.

**Figure 2-9**

There are two lateral cerebral ventricles, one in each hemisphere, and a third and fourth cerebral ventricle, each of which lies in the midline of the brain.

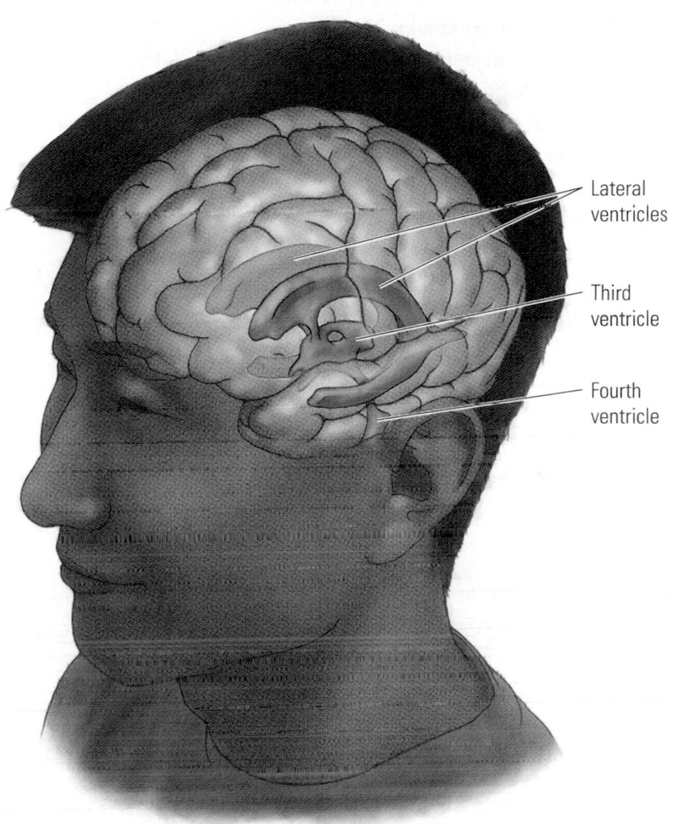


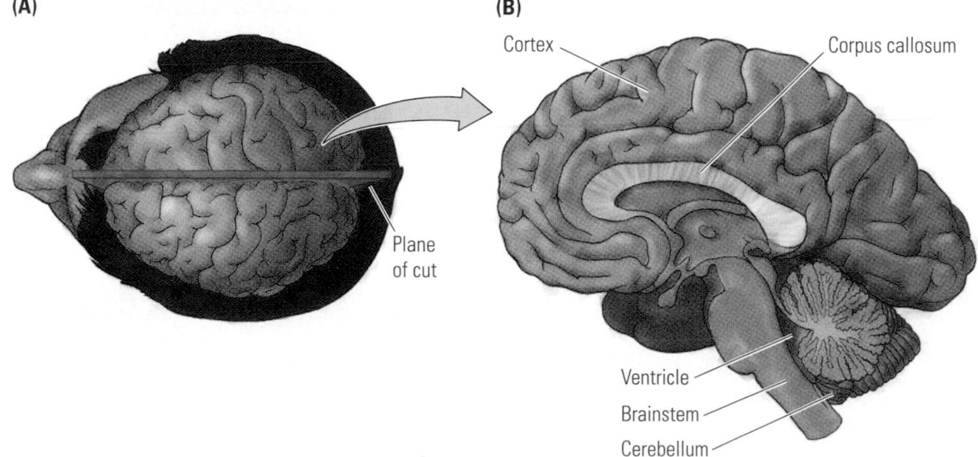


**Figure 2-10**

In this sagittal section through the brain, the brain is **(A)** cut and then **(B)** viewed from the side. This particular plane of cut separates the hemispheres, allowing a view of the midline structures of the brain, including the corpus callosum, which connects the two hemispheres. You can see the subcortical structures (ventricle, brainstem, and cerebellum) that lie below the corpus callosum.

## Microscopic Inspection: Cells and Fibers

Although the parts of a car engine are all large enough to be seen with the naked eye, the fundamental units of the brain—its cells—are so small that they can be viewed only with the aid of a microscope. By using a microscope, we quickly discover that the

**Subcortical regions.** All of the regions of the brain that are located beneath the neocortex; the term is usually used to distinguish regions of the brain that control basic functions from those regions controlling cognitive functions, which are mediated by the neocortex.

**Figure 2-11**

When brain sections are stained, various regions become clearly demarcated. These brain sections from the left hemisphere of a monkey (midline is to the left in each photograph) are stained with **(A)** a selective cell-body stain, known as a Nissl stain, and **(B)** a selective fiber stain, staining for myelin. It is immediately apparent that the two stains reveal a very different picture of the brain. **(C** and **D)** Higher-power micrographs through the Nissl- and myelin-stained sections show different cortical regions. Notice the difference in appearance.

(A)

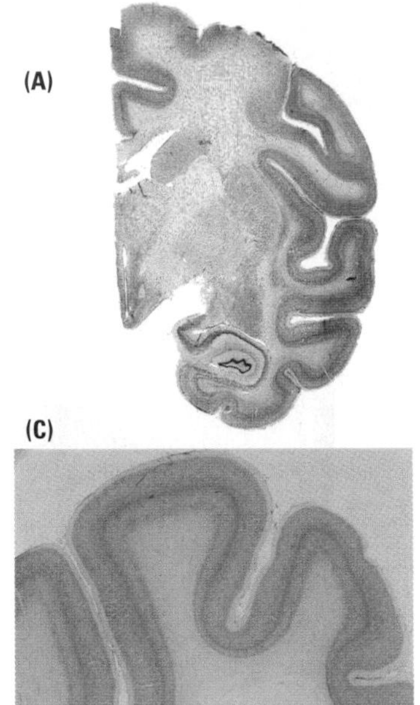

(B)

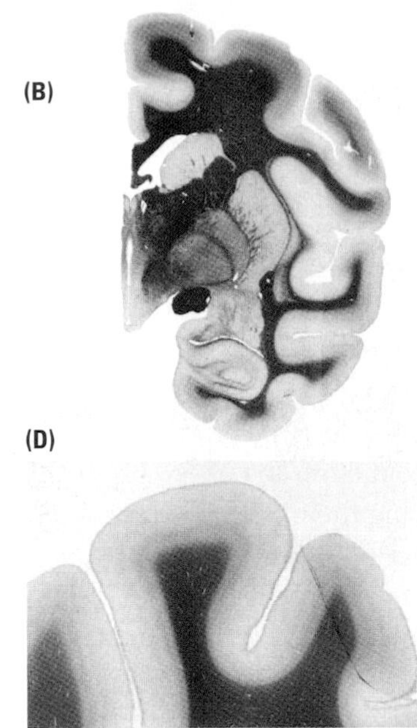

(C)

(D)

**Focus on Disorders**

## Meningitis and Encephalitis

A large number of harmful organisms can invade the linings, or meninges, of the brain, particularly the pia mater and the arachnoid layer, as well as the cerebrospinal fluid between them. Such infections are called *meningitis.* One symptom is inflammation, which, because the skull is solid, places pressure on the brain. This pressure often leads to delirium and, if the infection progresses, to drowsiness, stupor, and even coma.

Meningitis usually begins with severe headache and a stiff neck (known as cervical rigidity). Head retraction is an extreme form of cervical rigidity. Convulsions are a common symptom in children. They indicate that the brain also is affected by the inflammation.

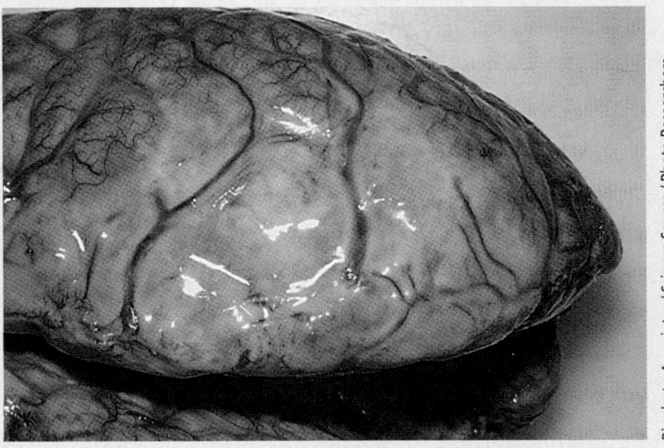

Biophoto Associates / Science Source / Photo Researchers

In this photograph of the right hemisphere of a brain infected with meningitis, there is pus visible over the surface of the brain.

Infection of the brain itself is called *encephalitis.* There are many forms of encephalitis, some of which have great historical significance. In World War I, a form of encephalitis referred to as sleeping sickness (encephalitis lethargica) reached epidemic proportions. The first symptoms were disturbances of sleep. People slept all day and became wakeful, even excited, at night. Subsequently, they showed symptoms of Parkinson's disease, characterized by severe tremors and difficulty in controlling body movements. Many were completely unable to make any voluntary movements, such as walking or even combing their hair. (These patients were immortalized in the movie *Awakenings.*) The cause of these symptoms is death of the brain nucleus known as the substantia nigra (black substance). Other forms of encephalitis may have different effects on the brain. For example, Rasmussen's encephalitis attacks one cerebral hemisphere in children. In most cases, the only effective treatment is a radical one: removal of the entire affected hemisphere. Surprisingly, some young children who lose a hemisphere adapt rather well. They may even complete college, literally with half a brain. But, unfortunately, retardation is a more common outcome of hemispherectomy after encephalitis.

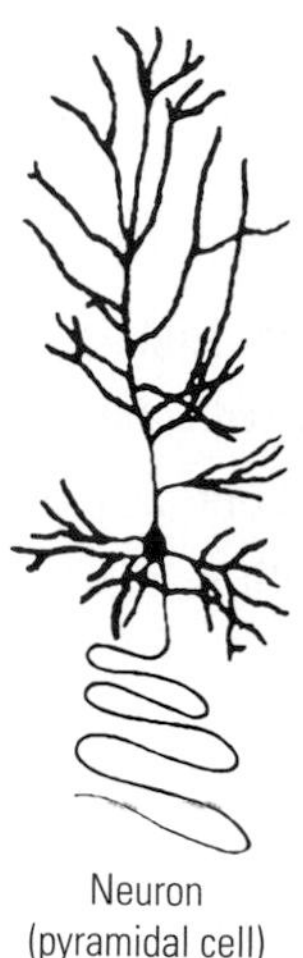

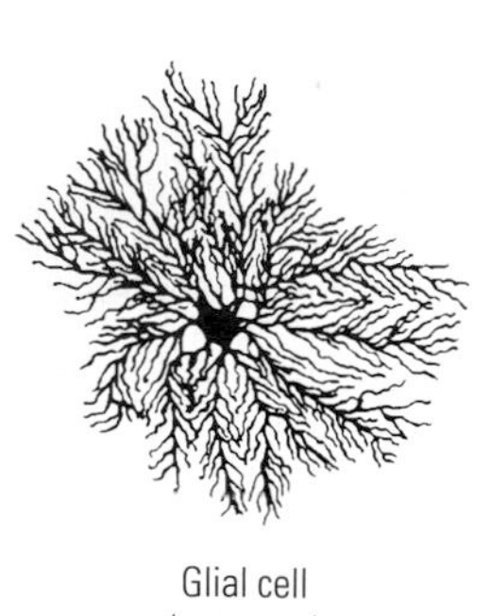


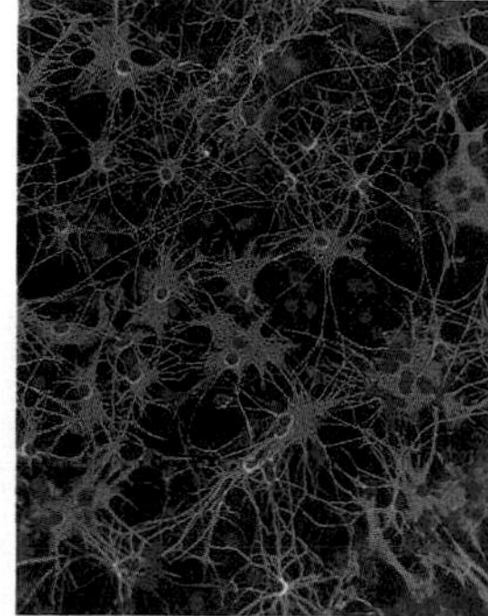

**Figure 2-12**

These examples of a prototypical neuron and glial cell show that both the neuron and the astrocyte have branches emanating from the cell body. This branching organization increases the surface area of the cell membrane. The neuron is a pyramidal cell, so called because the cell body is shaped somewhat like a pyramid; the glial cell is an astrocyte, so called because of its star-shaped appearance.

Photos: *left,* CNRI/ Science Photo Library; *right,* N. Kedesha/ Science Photo Library.

brain has two main types of cells: *neurons* and *glia,* illustrated in Figure 2-12. There are about 80 billion neurons and 100 billion glia in a human brain. Neurons are the cells that carry out the brain's major functions, whereas glia play a supporting role to aid and modulate the neurons' activities. Both neurons and glia come in many forms, each determined by the work done by particular cells. We return to neurons and glia in Chapter 3.

A key feature of neurons is that they are connected to one another by fibers known as *axons.* When axons run along together, much like the wires that run from a car engine to the dashboard, they form a **nerve tract.** By convention, the term *tract* is usually used to refer to collections of nerve fibers found within the brain (or within the brain and spinal cord), whereas bundles of fibers located outside these central structures are typically referred to simply as *nerves.* Thus, the pathway from the eye to the brain is known as the optic nerve, whereas the pathway from the cerebral cortex to the spinal cord is known as the corticospinal tract.

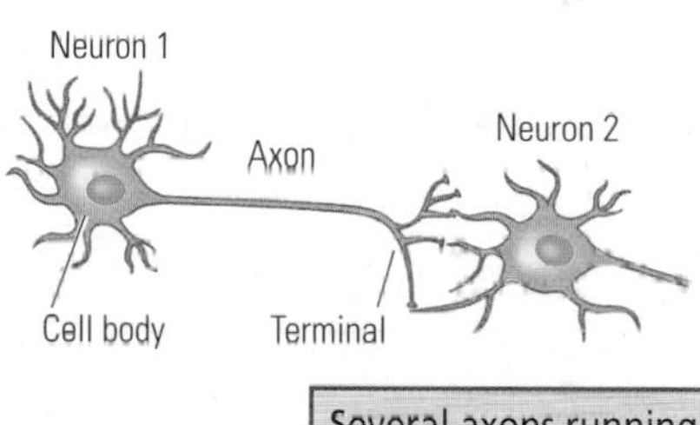


Several axons running together are a nerve (when outside the brain) or a tract (when inside the brain).

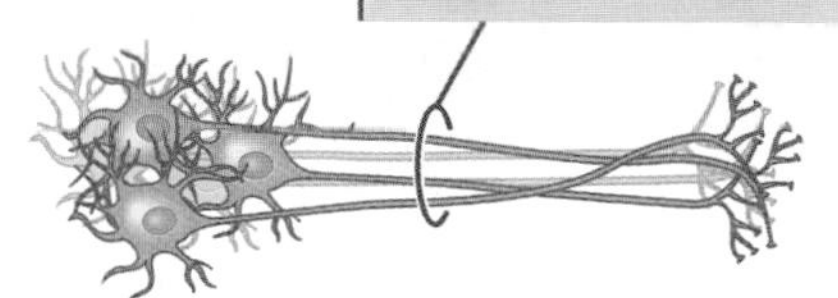

## In Review

We began this chapter by looking at the brain as we would a car engine. Inside the skull and under the meninges, we find two main structures: the cerebral hemispheres and the cerebellum. Both have many gyri and sulci covering their surfaces. At the base of the brain, we see the brainstem, of which the cerebellum is a part. Cutting open the brain, we observe the fluid-filled ventricles, the corpus callosum that connects the two hemispheres, and the cortex and subcortical regions below it. We also see that brain tissue is of three basic types: white matter, gray matter, and reticular matter. The question is how this jumble of parts produces behaviors as complex as human thought.

Focus on Disorders

## Stroke

Stroke is the sudden appearance of neurological symptoms when severe interruption of blood flow to the brain kills brain cells. Stroke is a serious and common illness that occurs approximately every minute in the United States. This rate of occurrence produces about 500,000 new stroke victims in the United States every year.

The effects of stroke are illustrated by the case of Mr. Anderson, an electrical engineer who was 45 years old at the time of his stroke. He and his wife had three children and a comfortable middle-class life style. One Saturday afternoon in early 1998, Mr. Anderson was at a movie theater with his children when he suddenly collapsed. He was rushed to the hospital, where he was diagnosed with a massive stroke of the middle cerebral artery of his left hemisphere. A year after his stroke, Mr. Anderson was still unable to speak, although he could understand simple conversations. He had severe difficulties in moving his right leg, which required him to use a walker. Because he could not move the fingers of his right hand, he had difficulty in feeding himself. It is unlikely that Mr. Anderson will ever return to his old job or be able to drive or to get around on his own. In addition, the lost income and stroke-related medical bills have had a significant effect on the Andersons' standard of living.

The prognosis for many other stroke victims is equally grave. For every ten people who have a stroke, two die, six have varying degrees of disability, and two achieve some neurological recovery but still have a diminished quality of life. The survivors risk suffering further strokes, with the annual rate of recurrence being about 10 percent a year. Strokes, then, have significant consequences, both for the people who have them and for their families. Most stroke survivors require help to perform everyday tasks. Their caregivers are usually female, either a wife or a daughter, and most of them must give up work or other activities to care for the stroke victims. One year after a stroke occurs, half the caregivers develop an emotional illness, primarily depression or anxiety or both.

The hopeful news regarding stroke is that it may now be treatable with a new drug called tissue plasminogen activator (t-PA). The results of clinical trials showed that, when patients were given t-PA within 3 hours of a stroke, the number who made a nearly complete recovery increased by 32 percent, compared with those who were given a placebo (Chiu et al., 1998). In addition, impairments were reduced in the remaining patients who survived the stroke. Other drugs offering an even better outcome will likely become available in the future. These drugs may extend the 3-hour window for administering treatment after a stroke. But, even with the best and fastest medical attention, most stroke victims will still suffer some residual motor, sensory, or cognitive deficit.

## A CLOSER LOOK AT NEUROANATOMY

When we look at the parts of a car engine, we can make some pretty good guesses about what each part does. For example, we can guess that the battery must provide electrical power to run the radio and lights, and, because batteries need to be charged, we can infer that there must be some mechanism for charging them. The same approach can be taken to deduce the functions of the parts of the brain. For example, we can guess that the part of the brain connected to the optic nerve coming from an eye must have something to do with vision. Similarly, we can guess that brain structures connected to the auditory nerve coming from an ear must have something to do with hearing. With these simple observations, we can begin to understand how the brain is organized. The real test of inferences about the brain is analysis of actual brain function. Nevertheless, the place to start is with brain anatomy.

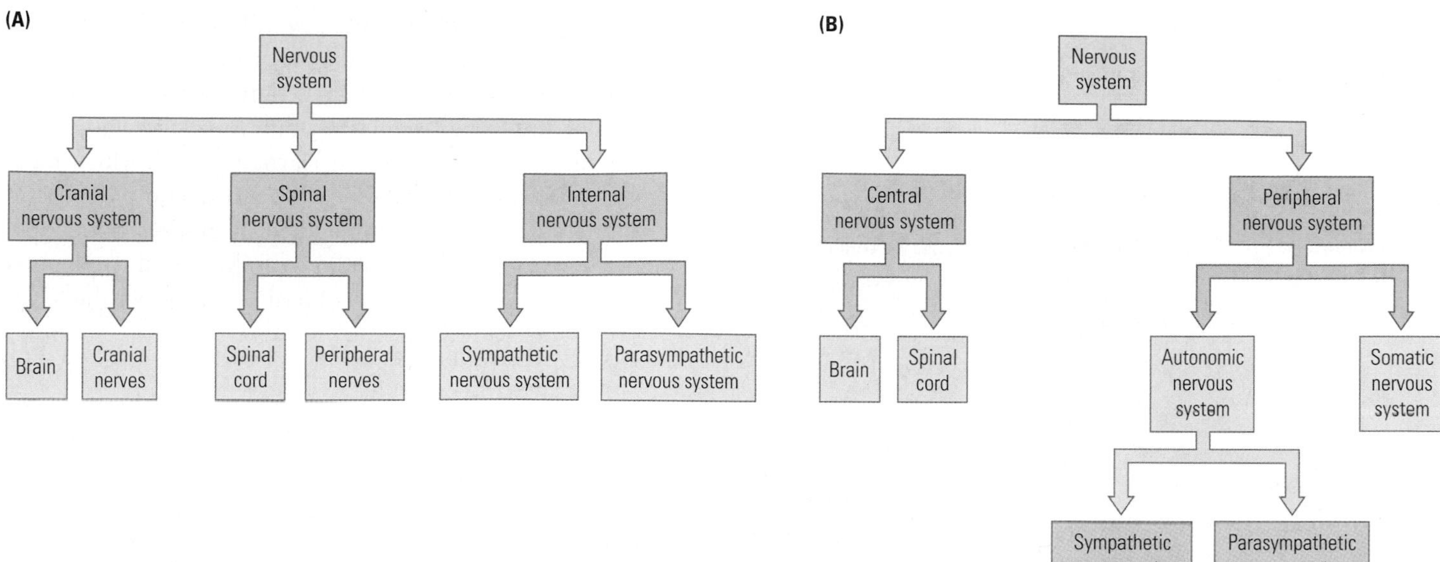


**Figure 2-13**

In a conceptualization of the nervous system, the nervous system can be **(A)** divided into three gross divisions: cranial, spinal, and internal. Each of these divisions can in turn be subdivided into smaller component parts. In a more traditional division of the nervous system, it is **(B)** divided into the central and peripheral nervous systems. Again, each division is subdivided into smaller components. The diagram in **(A)** is based on a practical functional distinction, whereas the diagram in **(B)** is based on a purely anatomical distinction. The internal nervous system **(A)** is equivalent to the autonomic nervous system **(B)**. The peripheral nerves **(A)** are equivalent to the somatic nervous system **(B)**.

One traditional way of categorizing the parts of the nervous system is to group them into two major divisions: the central nervous system (CNS) and the peripheral nervous system (PNS). These two major divisions were introduced in Chapter 1. The CNS consists of the brain and the spinal cord, and the PNS encompasses everything else. This way of dividing up the nervous system is shown in Figure 2-13B.

The CNS–PNS distinction, however, is based more on anatomy than on function. It is not very helpful for investigating how the nervous system actually works. A better approach for a functional analysis is shown in Figure 2-13A, which depicts three major divisions: the cranial, the spinal, and the internal nervous systems. The **cranial nervous system** includes the brain and its connections to parts of the head, such as to the eyes and ears. Because this system can control the other two systems, it can regulate all of behavior. The **spinal nervous system** includes the spinal cord and its connections to and from the body's muscles, as well as its connections from the joints and the skin. This system produces movements of the body (excluding movements of the head and face). It also receives incoming sensory information about such things as touch on the body's surface and the position and movement of limbs. Finally, the **internal nervous system** (also called the autonomic nervous system, discussed in Chapter 1) controls the body's internal organs and is composed of two subdivisions: the sympathetic and the parasympathetic. In the following sections, we explore the anatomy of the human nervous system by using this three-division approach. We begin with the master control center: the cranial nervous system.

## The Cranial Nervous System

The cranial nervous system includes the brain and all of the nerves that connect the brain to the muscles and sensory organs of the head. There are literally thousands of parts to the cranial nervous system. Learning the name of a particular part is pointless without also learning something about its function. In this section, therefore, we focus on the names and functions of the major components of the cranial nervous system. We divide this system into the three subdivisions outlined in Table 2-2: the cranial nerves, the brainstem, and the forebrain.

These three subdivisions introduce a concept known as levels of function. This concept means that something is organized into functional levels, with newer levels partly replicating the work of older ones. A simple example is learning to read. When

**Table 2-2 Anatomical Divisions of the Cranial Nervous System**

| Anatomical divisions | Functional divisions | Principal structures |
|---|---|---|
| Forebrain | Forebrain | Cerebral cortex |
| | | Basal ganglia |
| | | Limbic system |
| Brainstem | Diencephalon | Thalamus |
| | | Hypothalamus |
| | Midbrain | Tectum |
| | | Tegmentum |
| | Hindbrain | Cerebellum |
| | | Pons |
| | | Medulla oblongata |
| | | Reticular formation |
| Cranial nerves | Cranial nerves | 12 cranial nerves |

you began to read in grade 1, you learned simple words and sentences. Then, as you progressed to higher levels, you mastered new, more challenging words and longer, more complicated sentences, but you still retained the simpler skills that you had learned before. Much later, you encountered Shakespeare, with a complexity and subtlety of language unimagined in grade school. Each new level of training added new abilities that overlapped and built on previously acquired skills. Yet all the levels dealt with reading. In much the same way, the brain has functional levels that overlap each other in purpose but allow for a growing complexity of behavior. For instance, the brain has functional levels that control movements. With the addition of each new level, the complexity of movements becomes increasingly refined. We return to this concept of levels of function at the end of this chapter.

## THE CRANIAL NERVES

The cranial nerves are all the nerves that link the brain to various parts of the head, as illustrated in Figure 2-14, as well as to the internal organs. Cranial nerves can have either afferent functions, such as inputs to the brain from the eyes, ears, mouth, and nose, or efferent functions, such as control of the facial muscles, tongue, and eyes. There are 12 pairs of cranial nerves. One set of 12 controls the left side of the head, whereas the other set controls the head's right side. This arrangement makes sense for innervating duplicated parts of the head (such as the eyes), but it is not so clear why separate nerves should control the right and left sides of a singular structure (such as the tongue). Yet this is how the cranial nerves work. If you have ever received novocaine for dental work, you know that usually just one side of your tongue becomes anesthetized because the dentist injects the drug into only one side of your mouth. The rest of the skin and muscles on each side of the head are similarly controlled by cranial nerves located on that side.

We consider many of the cranial nerves in some detail later when we deal with topics such as vision and hearing. For now, you simply need to know that cranial nerves form part of the cranial nervous system, providing inputs to the brain from the head's sensory organs and muscles and controlling head and face movements.

On the CD, visit the module on the Central Nervous System for a detailed, three-dimensional view of the brainstem.

## THE BRAINSTEM

It is now time to look at the brain itself, starting at its base with the region called the brainstem. The brainstem begins where the spinal cord enters the skull and extends upward to the lower areas of the forebrain. The brainstem receives afferent nerves from all of the body's senses, and it sends efferent nerves to control all of the body's movements except the most complex movements of the fingers and toes. The brainstem, then, both produces movements and creates a sensory world. In some animals, such as frogs, the entire brain is largely equivalent to the brainstem of mammals or birds. With this kind of brain, frogs get along quite well, indicating that the brainstem must be a relatively sophisticated piece of machinery. If we had only a brainstem, we would still be able to create a world, but it would be a far simpler world, more like what a frog experiences.

The brainstem can be divided into three regions: the **hindbrain,** the **midbrain,** and the **diencephalon** [*dye en **seff** a lon*], which is also sometimes called the "between brain" because it borders upper parts of the brain. Figure 2-15 illustrates these three

**Hindbrain.** The embryonic part of the brain that contains the brainstem and cerebellum; thought to coordinate movements and support movements of walking and posture.

**Midbrain.** The middle part of the embryonic brain, which, in the adult, contains circuits for hearing and seeing as well as walking.

**Diencephalon.** The part of the brain that contains the hypothalamus, thalamus, and epithalamus; thought to coordinate many basic instinctual behaviors, including temperature regulation, sexual behavior, and eating.

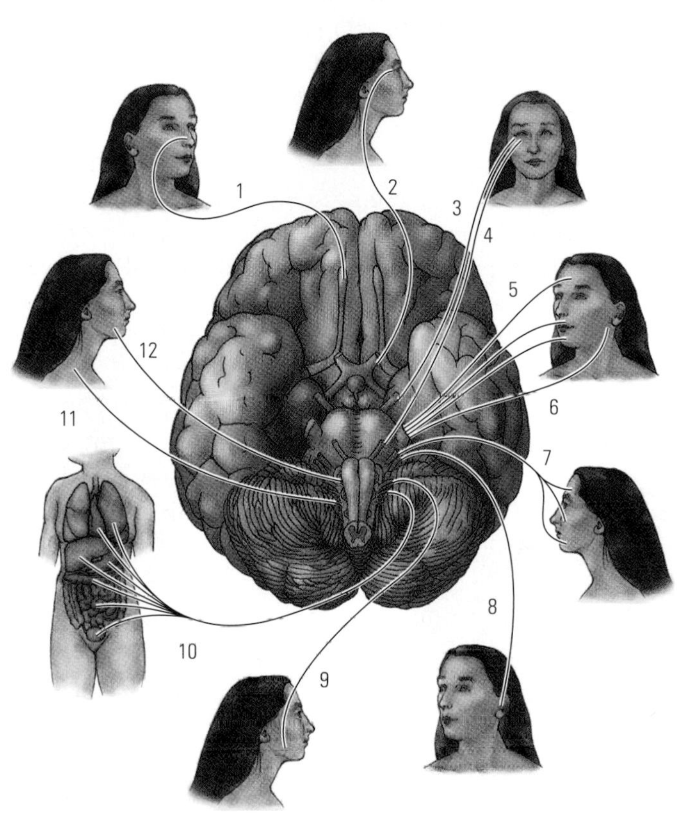


| Cranial nerve | Name | Functions |
|---|---|---|
| 1 | Olfactory | Smell |
| 2 | Optic | Vision |
| 3 | Oculomotor | Eye movement |
| 4 | Trochlear | Eye movement |
| 5 | Trigeminal | Masticatory movements and facial sensation |
| 6 | Abducens | Eye movement |
| 7 | Facial | Facial movement and sensation |
| 8 | Auditory vestibular | Hearing and balance |
| 9 | Glossopharyngeal | Tongue and pharynx movement and sensation |
| 10 | Vagus | Heart, blood vessels, viscera, movement of larynx and pharynx |
| 11 | Spinal accessory | Neck muscles |
| 12 | Hypoglossal | Tongue muscles |

**Figure 2-14**

Each of the 12 pairs of cranial nerves has a different function. A common device for learning the order of the cranial nerves is: On old Olympus's towering top, a Finn and German vainly skip and hop. The first letter of each word (except the last *and*) is, in order, the first letter of the name of each nerve.

brainstem regions, all of which lie under the cerebral hemispheres. As Figure 2-15 shows, the shape of the brainstem can be compared to the lower part of your arm held upright. The hindbrain is long and thick like your forearm, the midbrain is short and compact like your wrist, and the diencephalon at the end is bulbous like your hand forming a fist.

Each of these three major regions of the brainstem performs more than a single task. Each contains various subparts, made up of groupings of nuclei, that serve different purposes. All three regions, in fact, have both sensory and motor functions. However, the hindbrain is especially important in various kinds of motor functions, the midbrain in sensory functions, and the diencephalon in integrative tasks. Here we consider the central functions of these three regions; later chapters will contain more information about them.

**The Hindbrain** The hindbrain, shown in Figure 2-16, controls various types of motor functions ranging from breathing to balance to the control of fine movements, such as those used in dancing. The most distinctive structure in the hindbrain is the cerebellum, which looks much like a cauliflower. Actually, the cerebellum is a separate structure lying above the rest of the hindbrain. In humans, it is one of the largest structures of the brain. As Figure 2-17 illustrates, the size of the cerebellum increases with the physical speed and dexterity of a species. Animals that move slowly (such as a sloth) have rather small cerebellums, whereas animals that can perform rapid, acrobatic movements (such as a hawk or a cat) have very large cerebellums. The cerebellum is apparently important in controlling complex movements.

**Figure 2-15**

This medial view of the brain (*upper left*) shows the brainstem and its relation to the cerebral hemisphere. The shapes and relative sizes of the parts of the brainstem can be imagined to be like a hand and forearm, with the diencephalon being the fist, the midbrain being the wrist, and the hindbrain being the forearm.

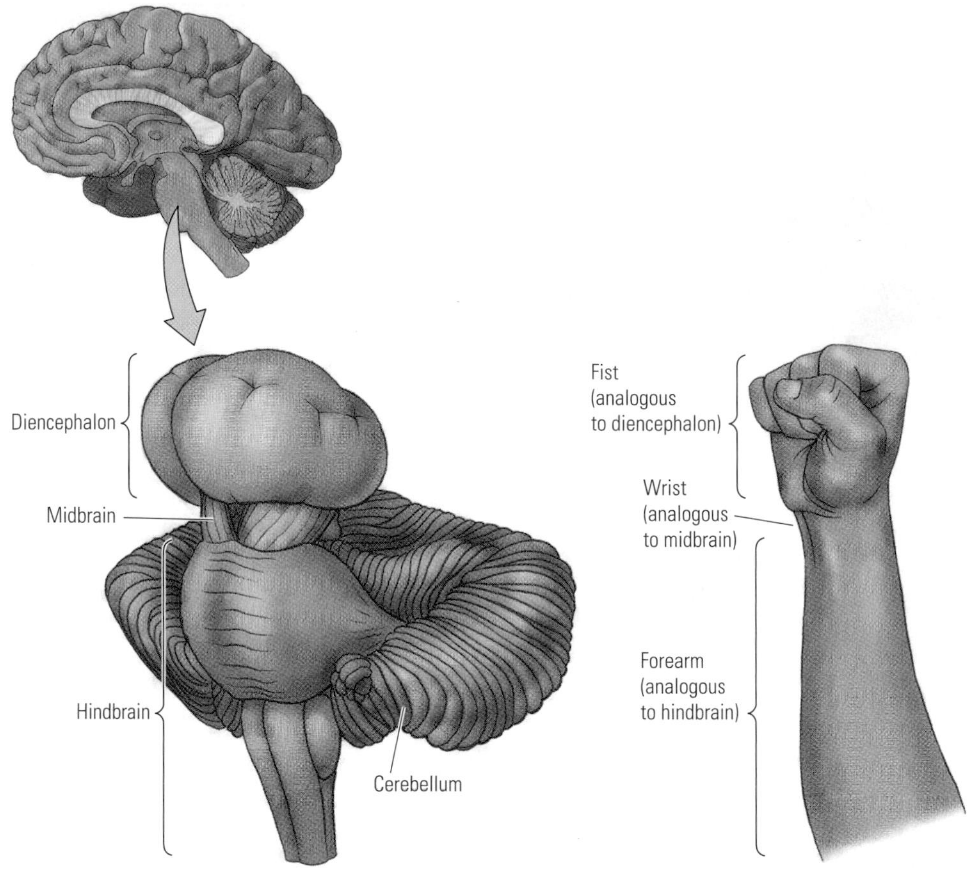


As we look below the cerebellum at the rest of the hindbrain, we find that it is composed of three subparts: the *reticular formation*, the *pons*, and the *medulla*. The **reticular formation** is a mixture of neurons and nerve fibers that gives this structure the mottled appearance from which its name comes (the term *reticular*, as stated earlier, comes from the Latin word for "net"). We can visualize the reticular formation as being formed by a stack of poker chips lying on its side. Each chip has a special function in stimulating the forebrain, such as in awakening from sleep. Not surprisingly,

**Figure 2-16**

The principal structures of the hindbrain are the cerebellum, pons, medulla, and reticular formation.

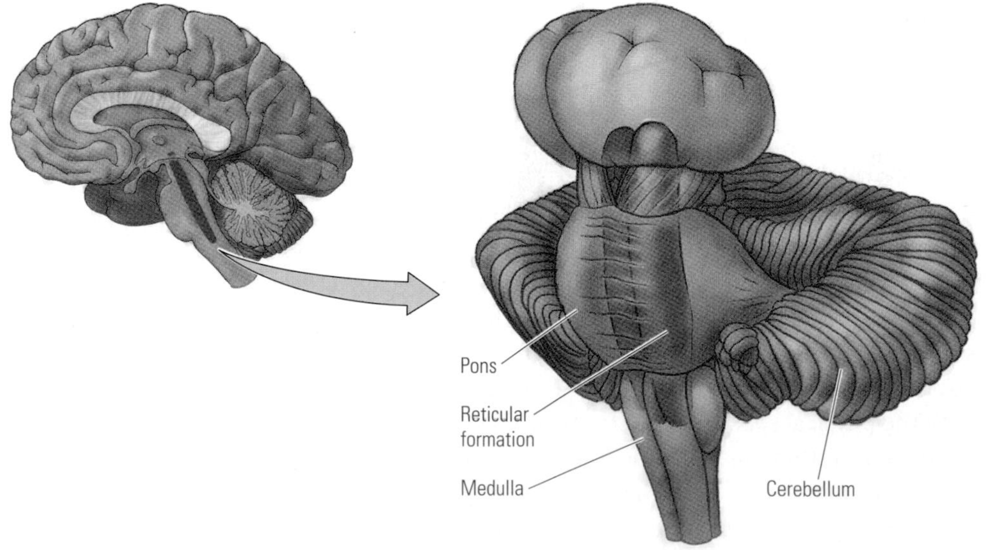


**Reticular formation.** A part of the midbrain in which nuclei and fiber pathways are mixed, producing a netlike appearance; associated with sleep–wake behavior and behavioral arousal.

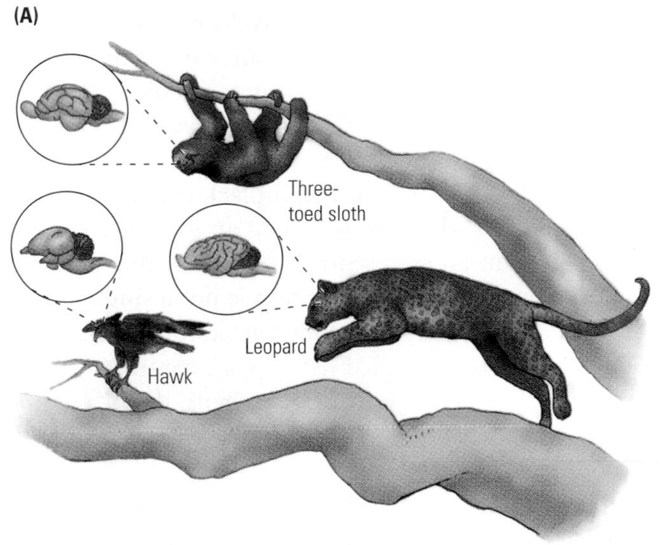


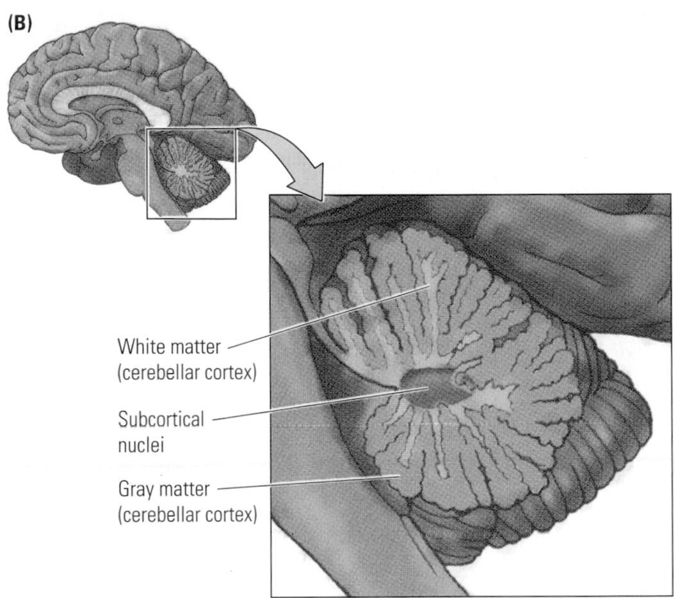


**Figure 2-17**

**(A)** The cerebellum is necessary for fine, coordinated movements such as flight and landing in birds and prey catching in cats. Like the sloth, animals that have slow movements have relatively smaller cerebellums. **(B)** Like the cerebrum, the cerebellum has a cortex, which has gray and white matter, and subcortical nuclei, as shown in this gross structure of the cerebellum.

the reticular formation is sometimes also called the *reticular activating system*. The other two structures in the hindbrain, the pons and medulla, contain substructures that control many vital movements of the body. The pons has nuclei that receive inputs from the cerebellum and provide a key bridge (the word *pons* means "bridge") between the cerebellum and the rest of the brain. The medulla has several nuclei that control such vital functions as the regulation of breathing and the cardiovascular system. For this reason, a blow to the back of the head can kill you—your breathing stops if the control centers in the hindbrain are injured.

**The Midbrain** In the midbrain, shown in Figure 2-18, a specialized structure known as the **tectum** receives a massive amount of information from the eyes and ears. The tectum consists of two principal parts, the *superior* and *inferior colliculi* [*kuh* ***lik*** *yew lee*], which have visual and auditory functions, respectively. The optic nerve sends a large bundle of nerve fibers to the superior colliculus, whereas the inferior colliculus receives much of its input from auditory pathways. But the colliculi

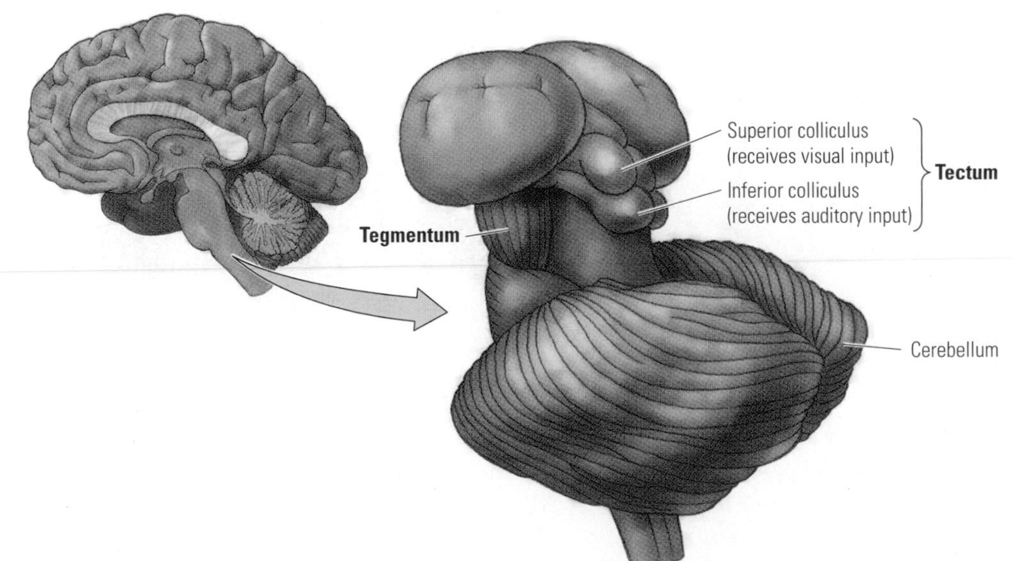


**Figure 2-18**

The major structures of the midbrain are the tectum and tegmentum. The tectum is made up of the superior colliculus, which receives visual input, and the inferior colliculus, which receives auditory input.

**Tectum.** The roof, or area above the ventricle, of the midbrain; its functions are sensory.

**Tegmentum.** The floor, or area below the ventricle, of the midbrain; has motor functions.

**Hypothalamus.** A part of the diencephalon that contains many nuclei associated with temperature regulation, eating and drinking, and sexual behavior.

**Thalamus.** A part of the diencephalon through which all of the sensory system projects to reach the neocortex and then projects, through one region of the neocortex, to relay messages to another region of the forebrain.

function not only to process sensory information. They also produce movements related to sensory inputs, such as turning your head to see the source of a sound. This orienting behavior is not as simple as it may seem. To produce it, the auditory and visual systems must share some sort of common "map" of the external world so that the ears can tell the eyes where to look. If the auditory and visual systems had different maps, it would be impossible to use the two systems together. In fact, the colliculi also have a tactile map. After all, if you want to look at the source of an itch on your leg, your visual and tactile systems need a common representation of where that place is.

Lying below the tectum is the **tegmentum.** The tegmentum is not a single structure but is composed of many nuclei, largely with movement-related functions. It has several nuclei that control eye movements, the so-called *red nucleus,* controlling limb movements, and the *substantia nigra*, connected to the forebrain; both the substantia nigra and the forebrain are especially important in initiating movements.

**The Diencephalon** The diencephalon, shown in Figure 2-19, has more structures than the hindbrain and midbrain have, owing to its role in both motor and sensory functions, as well as their integration. The two principal structures of the diencephalon are the **hypothalamus** and the **thalamus.** The hypothalamus is composed of about 22 small nuclei, as well as fiber systems that pass through it. Attached to the base of the hypothalamus is the pituitary gland. Although comprising only about 0.3 percent of the brain's weight, the hypothalamus takes part in nearly all aspects of behavior, including feeding, sexual behavior, sleeping, temperature regulation, emotional behavior, hormone function, and movement. The hypothalamus is organized more or less similarly in different mammals, largely because the control of feeding, temperature, and so on, is carried out similarly. But there are sex differences in the structures of some parts of the hypothalamus, which are probably due to differences between males and females

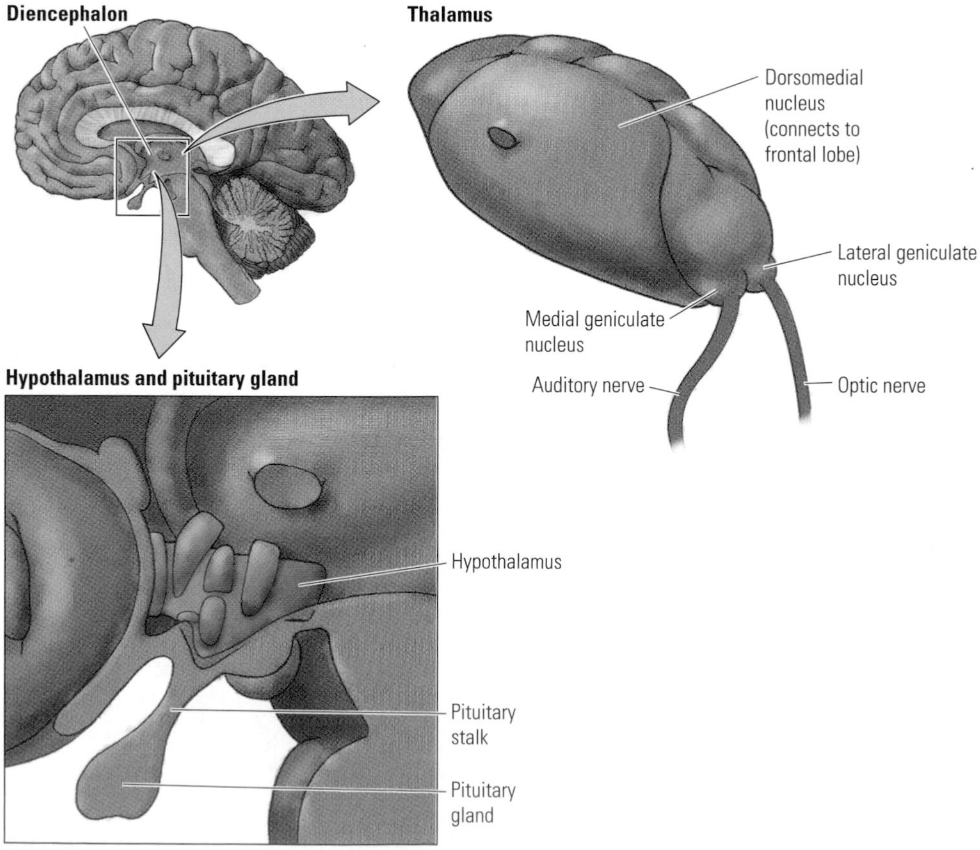

Plug in the CD to examine the hypothalamus and the thalamus in three dimensions in the module on the Central Nervous System in the subsection on subcortical structures.



**Figure 2-19**

The diencephalon is composed of the thalamus, hypothalamus, and associated pituitary gland. The hypothalamus and pituitary are at the base of the brain and lie above the roof of the mouth. The pituitary gland lies adjacent to the optic chiasm, which is the place where the left and right optic nerves (originating from the eyes) cross over. The hypothalamus is composed of many nuclei, each with distinctly different functions. The thalamus lies above the hypothalamus. The connections of only three of the thalamic nuclei are shown, but every thalamic nucleus connects to a discrete region of cortex.

in activities such as sexual behavior and parenting. A critical function of the hypothalamus is to control the body's production of various hormones, which is accomplished by interactions with the pituitary gland.

The other principal structure of the diencephalon is the thalamus, which is much larger than the hypothalamus. Like the hypothalamus, the thalamus contains about 20 nuclei, although the nuclei in the thalamus are much larger than those in the hypothalamus. Perhaps the most distinctive function of the thalamus is to act as a kind of gateway for sensory information traveling to the cerebral cortex. All of the sensory systems send inputs to the thalamus, which then relays this information to the cortex. The optic nerve, for example, sends information through a large bundle of fibers to a region of the thalamus known as the *lateral geniculate nucleus.* In turn, the lateral geniculate nucleus processes some of this information and then sends it to the visual region of the cortex. Analogous regions of the thalamus receive auditory and tactile information, which is subsequently relayed to the respective auditory and tactile cortical regions. Some thalamic regions are not sensory in function. These regions have motor functions or perform some sort of integrative task. An example of a region with an integrative function is the *dorsomedial thalamic nucleus.* It has connections to most of the frontal lobe of the cortex. We return to the thalamic sensory nuclei in Chapters 8 through 10, where we examine how sensory information is processed. Other thalamic regions are considered in Chapters 11 and 13, where we explore motivation and memory.

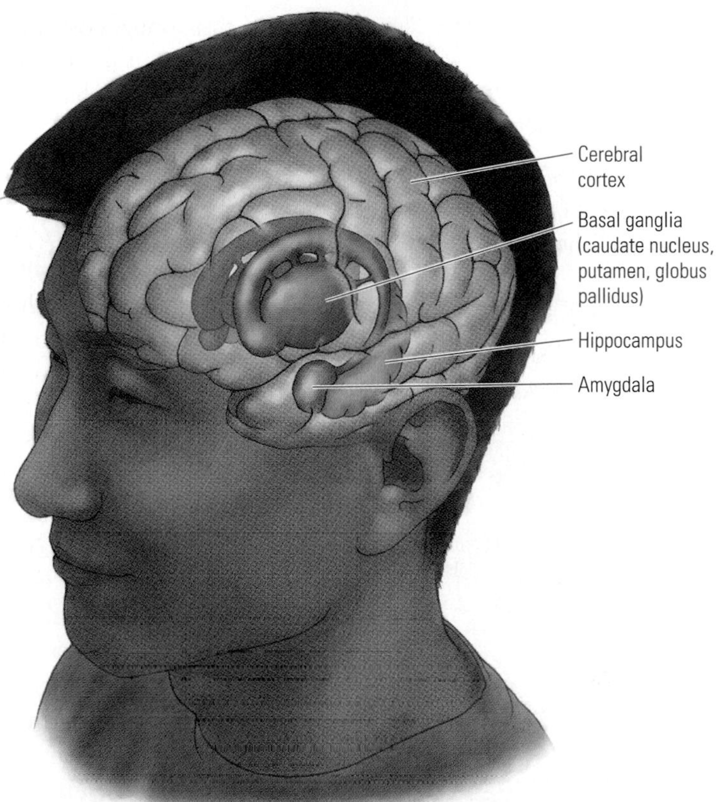


**Figure 2-20**

The major structures of the forebrain include the cerebral cortex, the basal ganglia, and the limbic system of which the amygdala and hippocampus are shown.

## THE FOREBRAIN

The **forebrain,** shown in Figure 2-20, is the largest region of the mammalian brain. Its three principal structures are the **cortex,** the **limbic system,** and the **basal ganglia.** Extending our analogy between the brainstem and your forearm, imagine that the "fist" of the brainstem (the diencephalon) is thrust inside a watermelon. The watermelon represents the forebrain, with the rind being the cortex and the fruit inside being the limbic system and the basal ganglia. By varying the size of the watermelon, we can vary the size of the brain. In a sense, this is what evolution has done. The forebrain varies considerably in size across species.

The three principal structures of the forebrain are the largest parts of the mammalian brain, and each has multiple functions. To summarize these functions briefly, the cortex regulates mental activities such as perception and planning, the basal ganglia control movement, and the limbic system regulates emotions and behaviors that require memory. Because we encounter each of these structures in detail later in this book, they are only briefly presented here.

**The Cortex** There are actually two types of cortex. The first type, called **neocortex,** has six layers of gray matter on top of a layer of white matter. The neocortex is the tissue that is visible when we view the brain from the top or the side, as in two of the views in Figure 2-6. This cortex is unique to mammals, and its primary function is to create a perceptual world. The second type of cortex, sometimes called **limbic cortex,** has three or four layers of gray matter on top of a layer of white matter. This tissue is not easily observed on the outside surface of the human brain, except for where it forms the *cingulate cortex,* which lies just above the corpus callosum (see Figure 2-24).

**Forebrain.** The most anterior part of the embryonic brain; contains the basal ganglia and the neocortex and is therefore thought to coordinate advanced cognitive functions such as thinking, planning, and language.

**Cortex (neocortex).** Newest layer of the forebrain, forming the outer layer or "new bark" and composed of about six layers.

**Limbic system.** Consists of structures that lie between the neocortex and the brainstem and form a hypothetical functional system that controls affective behavior and certain forms of memory; includes the cingulate cortex and hippocampus.

**Basal ganglia.** A group of structures in the forebrain that are located just beneath the neocortex and have connections to the thalamus and to the midbrain; thought to have motor functions that coordinate the movements of the limbs and the body.

Look at the CD for a three-dimensional model of the cortex along with photographs of cortical sections in the module on the Central Nervous System.

Click onto the Web site to see how the cortex looks in other animals at **www.worthpublishers.com/kolb/chapter2.**

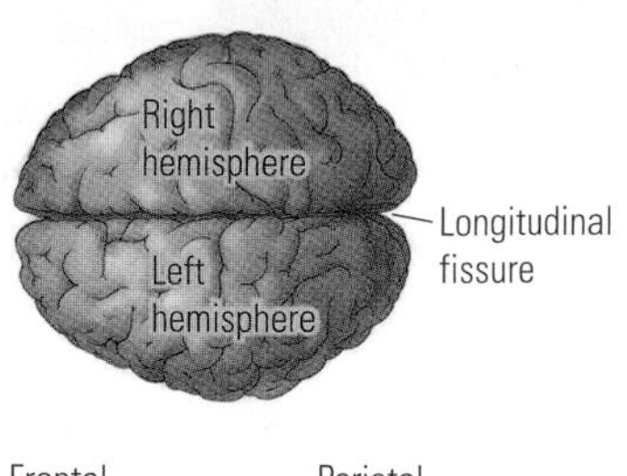


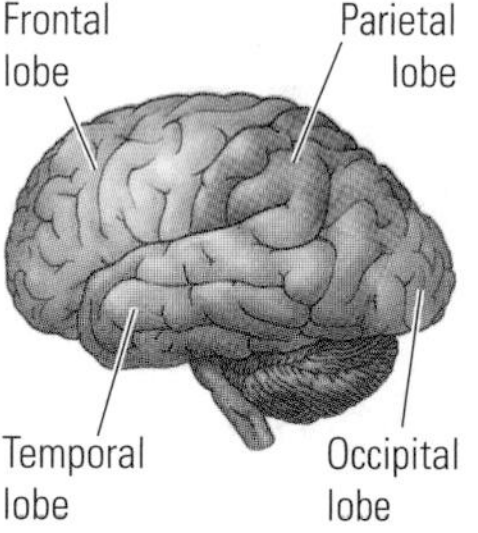


The limbic cortex is more primitive than the neocortex. It is found in the brains of other animals in addition to mammals, especially in birds and reptiles. This cortex is thought to play a role in controlling motivational states. Although anatomical and functional differences exist between the neocortex and the limbic cortex, the distinctions are not critical for most discussions in this book. Therefore, we will usually refer to both types of tissue simply as cortex.

Measured by volume, the cortex makes up most of the forebrain, comprising 80 percent of the brain overall. It is the brain region that has expanded the most during mammalian evolution. The human neocortex has an area as large as 2500 square centimeters but a thickness of only 1.5 to 3.0 millimeters. This area is equivalent to about four pages of this book. (In contrast, a chimpanzee has a cortical area equivalent to about one page.) The pattern of sulci and gyri formed by the folding of the cortex varies across species. Some species, such as rats, have no sulci or gyri, whereas carnivores have gyri that form a longitudinal pattern (look back at Figure 2-2). In humans, the sulci and gyri form a more diffuse pattern.

As Figure 2-6 shows, the human cortex consists of two nearly symmetrical hemispheres, the left and the right, which are separated by the longitudinal fissure. Each hemisphere is subdivided into the four lobes introduced in Chapter 1: the frontal, the temporal, the parietal, and the occipital. These names correspond to the skull bones overlying each hemisphere. Unfortunately, there is little relation between bone location and brain function. As a result, the lobes of the cortex are rather arbitrarily defined regions that include many different functional zones.

Fissures and sulci often establish the boundaries of cortical lobes. For instance, in humans, the central sulcus and lateral fissure form the boundaries of each frontal lobe. They also form the boundaries of each parietal [*pa* ***rye*** *i tul*] lobe, but in this case the lobes lie *behind* the central sulcus, not in front of it (refer again to Figure 2-6). The lateral fissure demarcates each temporal [***tem*** *por ul*] lobe as well, forming its dorsal (top) boundary. The occipital [*ok* ***sip*** *i tul*] lobes are not so clearly separated from the parietal and temporal lobes, because there is no large fissure to mark their boundaries. Traditionally, the occipital lobes are defined on the basis of other anatomical features, which are presented in Chapter 8.

The layers of the cortex have several distinct characteristics. First, different layers have different cell types, as shown in Figure 2-11. Second, the density of the cells varies, ranging from virtually no cells in layer I (the top layer) to very dense cell packing in layer IV. Third, there are other differences in appearance related to the functions of cortical layers in different regions. These visible differences led neuroanatomists of the early twentieth century to make maps of the cortex, like the one in Figure 2-21A.

**Figure 2-21**

**(A)** In his cytoarchitectonic map of the cortex, Brodmann defined areas by the organization and characteristics of the cells. A few numbers are missing from the original sources, including 12 through 16 and 48 through 51. **(B)** This schematic map shows the regions associated with the simplest sensory perceptions of touch, vision, and audition. As we shall see, the areas of the cortex processing sensory information are far greater than these basic areas.

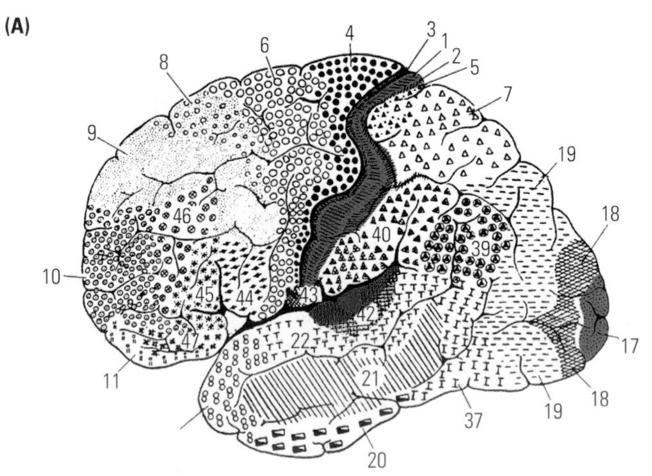


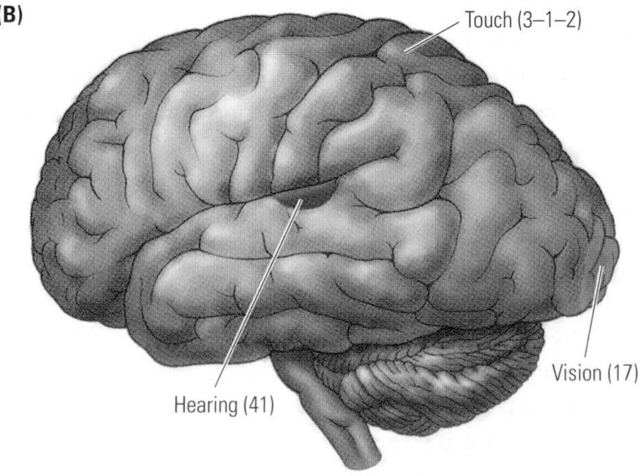

Because these maps are based on cell characteristics, the subject of cytology, they are called **cytoarchitectonic maps.** As the early neuroanatomists suspected, the characteristics of cells in a particular region of the cortex are related to that region's function. For example, sensory regions of the parietal lobe, shown in red in Figure 2-22, have a distinct layer IV, whereas motor regions of the frontal lobe, shown in blue in the same illustration, have a more distinctive layer V. Layer IV is an afferent layer, whereas layer V is an efferent one. It makes sense that a sensory region would have a large input layer, whereas a motor region would have a large output layer. Finally, there are chemical differences in the cells in different regions of the cortex. These differences can be revealed by coloring cortical tissue with stains that have affinities for specific chemicals. Some regions are rich in one chemical, whereas others are rich in another. These differences are presumably related to functional specialization of different areas of the cortex.

There is one significant difference between the organization of the cortex and the organization of other parts of the brain. Unlike most brain structures that connect to only selective brain regions, the cortex is connected to virtually all other parts of the brain. The cortex, in other words, is the ultimate meddler. It takes part in everything. This fact not only makes it difficult to identify specific functions of the cortex, but also complicates our study of the rest of the brain because the cortex's role in other brain regions must always be considered.

To illustrate, consider your perception of clouds. Undoubtedly, you have gazed up at clouds on a summer's day and imagined that they look like familiar shapes. You see in them galleons, elephants, faces, and countless other objects. Although a cloud does not really look exactly like an elephant, you can concoct an image of one if you impose your cortex's imagination on the sensory inputs. This kind of cortical activity is known as *top-down processing* because the top level of the nervous system, the cortex, is influencing how information is processed in lower regions—in this case the midbrain and hindbrain. The cortex influences many things besides the perception of objects. It influences our cravings for foods, our lust for things (or people), and how we interpret the meaning of abstract concepts such as words. The cortex is the ultimate creator of our reality, and one reason that it serves this function is that it is so well connected.

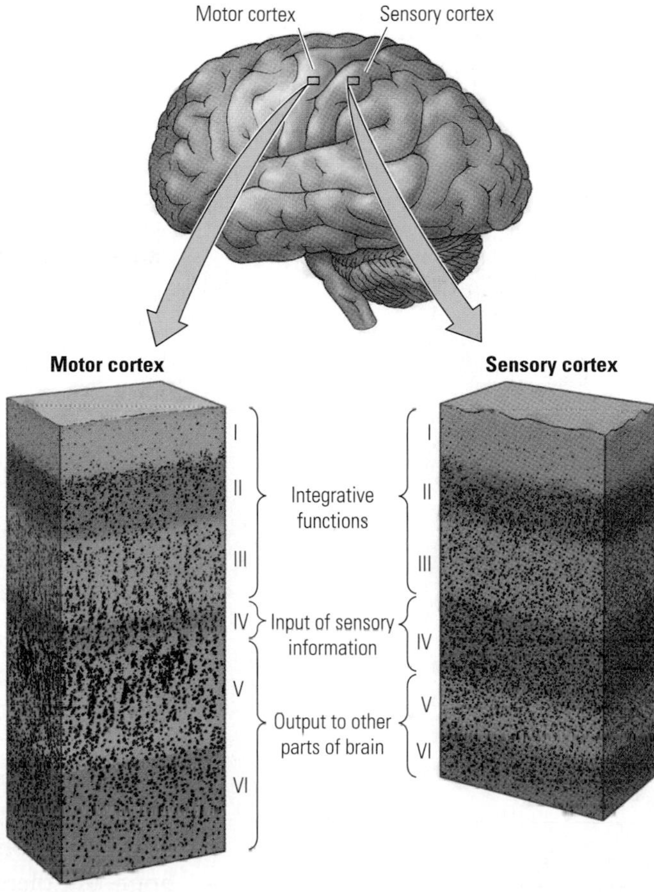


**Figure 2-22**

As this comparison of cortical layers in the sensory and motor cortices shows, layer IV is relatively thick in the sensory cortex and relatively thin in the motor cortex. Afferents go to layer IV (from the thalamus) as well as to layers II and III. Efferents go to other parts of the cortex and to the motor structures.

**The Basal Ganglia** The basal ganglia are a collection of nuclei that lie within the forebrain just below the white matter of the cortex. The three principal structures of the basal ganglia, shown in Figure 2-23 on page 58, are the *caudate nucleus,* the *putamen,* and the *globus pallidus.* Together with the thalamus and two closely associated structures, the *substantia nigra* and *subthalamic nucleus,* the basal ganglia form a system that functions primarily to control certain aspects of movement.

Visit the CD for a three-dimensional model of the basal ganglia in the section on subcortical structures in the module on the Central Nervous System.

We can observe the functions of the basal ganglia by analyzing the behavior of people who have one of the many diseases that interfere with the normal functioning of these nuclei. For instance, people afflicted with Parkinson's disease, one of the most common disorders of movement in the elderly, take short, shuffling steps, have bent posture, and often require a walker to get around. Many have an almost continual tremor of the hands and sometimes of the head as well. (We return to this disorder in Chapter 10.) Another example of a disorder of the basal ganglia is Tourette's syndrome, characterized by various forms of tics, involuntary noises (including curse

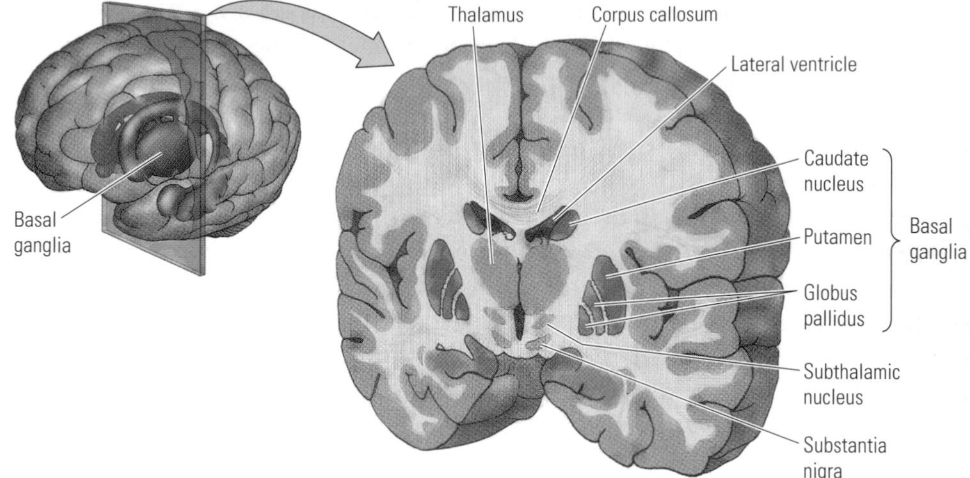


**Figure 2-23** This frontal section of the cerebral hemispheres shows the basal ganglia relative to the surrounding structures. Two associated structures, the substantia nigra and subthalamic nucleus, also are illustrated.

words and animal sounds), and odd, involuntary movements of the body, especially of the face and head. Neither Parkinson's disease nor Tourette's syndrome is a disorder of *producing* movements, as in paralysis. Rather they are disorders of *controlling* movements. The basal ganglia, therefore, must play a role in the control and coordination of movement patterns, not in activating the muscles.

**The Limbic System** In the 1930s, psychiatry was dominated by the theories of Sigmund Freud, who emphasized sexuality and emotion in understanding human behavior. At the time, regions controlling these behaviors had not been identified in the brain, but there was a group of brain structures, collectively called the limbic system, that as yet had no known function. It was a simple step to thinking that perhaps the limbic system played a central role in sexuality and emotion. One sign that this hypothesis might be right came from James Papez, who discovered that people with rabies had infections of limbic structures, and one of the symptoms of rabies is emotional blunting. We now know that such a simple view of the limbic system is inaccurate. In fact, the limbic system is not a unitary system at all, and, although some limbic structures have roles in emotion and sexual behaviors, limbic structures serve other functions, too, including memory.

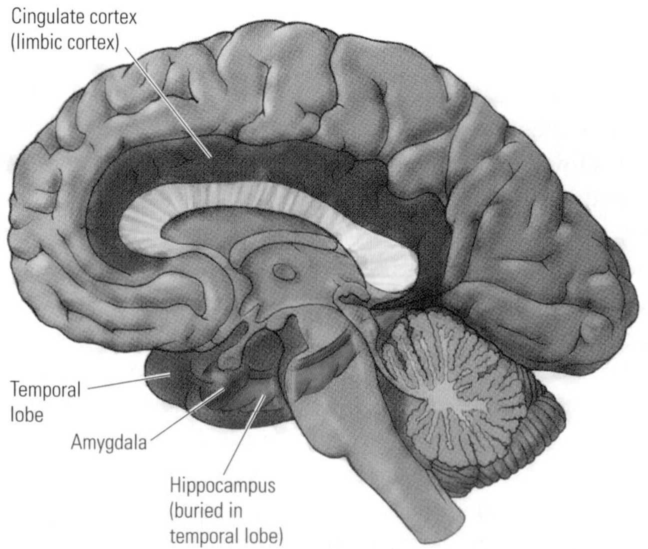


**Figure 2-24** This medial view of the right hemisphere illustrates the principal structures of the limbic system, including the cingulate cortex, the hippocampus, and the amygdala.

The principal structures of the limbic system are shown in Figure 2-24. They include the *amygdala* [*a* **mig** *da la*], the *hippocampus,* and the *cingulate cortex,* which lies in the cingulate gyrus. Removal of the amygdala produces truly startling changes in emotional behavior. For example, a cat with the amygdala removed will wander through a colony of monkeys, completely undisturbed by their hooting and threats. No self-respecting cat would normally be caught anywhere near such bedlam. The hippocampus, the cingulate cortex, and associated structures have roles in certain memory functions, as well as in the control of navigation in space.

**The Olfactory System** At the very front of the brain are the *olfactory bulbs,* the organs responsible for our sense of smell. The olfactory system is unique among the senses, as Figure 2-25 shows, because it is almost entirely a forebrain structure. Unlike the other sensory systems, which send most of their inputs from the sensory receptors to the midbrain and thalamus, the olfactory bulb sends most of its inputs to a specialized region of the cortex lying on the bottom of the brain. This region is known as the *pyriform cortex.* Compared with the olfactory bulbs of animals such as rats and dogs, which depend more heavily on the sense of smell than we do, the human olfactory bulb is relatively small. Because the sense of smell tends to be less important in humans than the senses of vision, hearing, and touch, we will not consider the olfactory system in any detail.

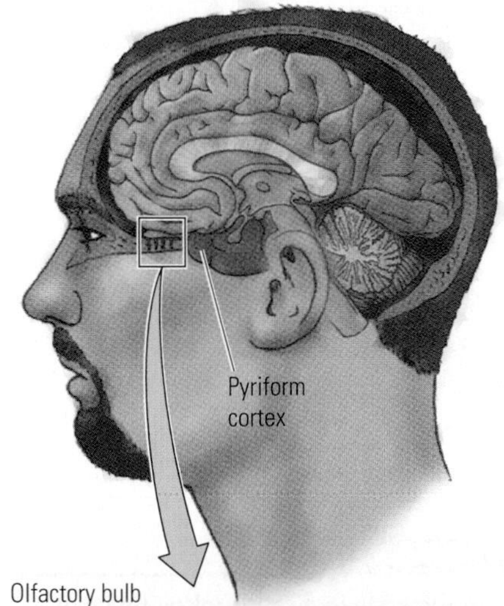


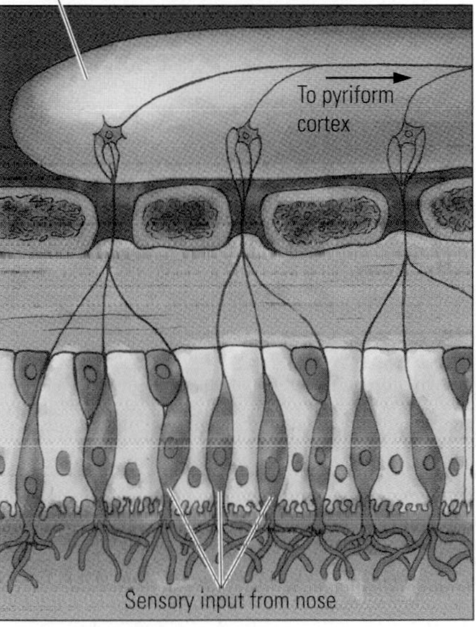


**Figure 2-25**

The olfactory bulb lies at the base of the human brain and is connected to receptor cells that lie in the nasal cavity. Although relatively small in humans, the olfactory bulb is larger in animals, such as rats or cats, that rely more heavily on the sense of smell.

## The Spinal Nervous System

Although producing movements of the body is one of the functions of the brain, it is ultimately the spinal nervous system that controls these movements. To understand how important the spinal nervous system is, think of the old saying "running around like a chicken with its head cut off." This saying refers to the spinal nervous system at work. When a chicken's head is lopped off to provide dinner for the farmer's family, the chicken is still capable of running around the barnyard until it collapses from loss of blood. The chicken accomplishes this feat with its spinal nervous system, because that system can act independently of the brain.

You can demonstrate movement controlled by the spinal nervous system in your own body by tapping your patellar tendon, just below your kneecap (the patella), as shown in Figure 2-26 on page 60. Your lower leg kicks out and, try as you might, it is very hard to prevent the movement from occurring. Your brain, in other words, has trouble inhibiting the spinal nervous system reaction. This type of automatic movement is known as a *spinal reflex,* a topic we return to in Chapter 10.

The spinal nervous system is composed of both the spinal cord, which lies inside the bony spinal column, and the nerves running to and from the skin, joints, and muscles. As Figure 2-27 shows (see page 60), the spinal column is made up of a series of small bones called **vertebrae** that are categorized into five groups: the *cervical, thoracic, lumbar, sacral,* and *coccygeal.* You can think of each vertebra (the singular of *vertebrae*) within these five groups as a very short segment of the spinal column. The spinal cord within each vertebra functions as that segment's "minibrain."

This arrangement of having so many minibrains within the spinal column may seem a bit odd, but it has a long evolutionary history. Think of a simple animal, such as a worm, which evolved long before humans did. A worm's body is a tube divided into segments. Within that tube is another tube, this one of neurons, which also is segmented. Each of the worm's nervous system segments receives fibers from sensory receptors in the part of the body adjacent to it, and that nervous system segment sends fibers back to the muscles in that body part. Each segment, therefore, works

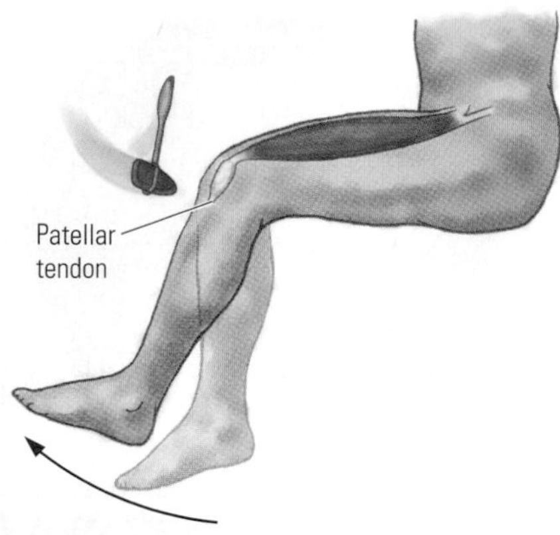


**Figure 2-26**

In the knee-jerk reflex (also known as the patellar reflex), when the patellar tendon is struck lightly, the lower leg flexes out "reflexively."

relatively independently, although fibers interconnect the segments and coordinate their activities. As vertebrates evolved a spinal column, this segmental organization was maintained. The vertebrae correspond to the segments of the worm's nerve tube, and the nerves running in and out of a vertebra's section of the spinal cord send information to and from muscles and sensory receptors at that particular level of the body.

A complication arises in animals that have limbs. The limbs may originate at one segment level, but they extend past other segments of the spinal column. Your shoulders, for example, may begin at C3 (cervical segment 3), but your arms hang down well past the sacral segments. So, unlike the worm, which has nerve-tube segments that connect to body segments directly adjacent to them, human body segments appear to be in a strange patchwork pattern, as shown in Figure 2-27B.

Regardless of their complex pattern, however, the segments of our bodies still correspond to segments of the spinal cord. Each of these body segments is called a **dermatome** (meaning "skin cut"). A dermatome has both a sensory nerve, which sends information from the skin, joints, and muscles to the spinal cord, and a motor nerve, which controls the movements of the muscles in that particular segment of the body. These sensory and motor nerves are known as **peripheral nerves,** and they are functionally equivalent to the cranial nerves of the head. Whereas the cranial nerves receive information from sensory receptors in the eyes, ears, facial skin, and so forth, the peripheral nerves receive information from sensory receptors in the rest of the

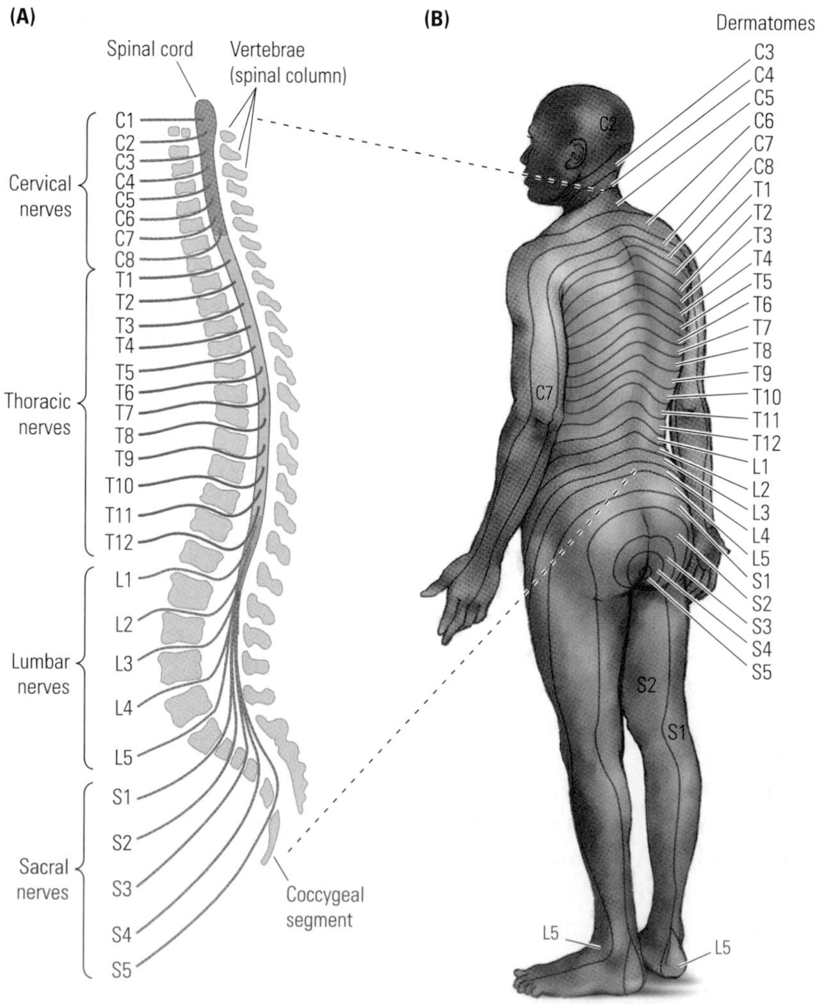


**Figure 2-27**

**(A)** The spinal column showing the vertebrae is illustrated in this saggital view. There are five segments: cervical (C), thoracic (T) , lumbar (L), sacral (S), and coccygeal. **(B)** Each spinal segment corresponds to a region of body surface (dermatome) that is identified by the segment number (examples are C5 and L2).

**Dermatome.** Area of the skin supplied with afferent nerve fibers by a single spinal-cord dorsal root.

body. Similarly, whereas the cranial nerves move the muscles of the eyes, tongue, and face, the peripheral nerves move the muscles of the limbs and trunk. Like the cranial nervous system, the spinal nervous system is also two sided. The left side of the spinal cord controls the left side of the body, and the right side of the spinal cord controls the body's right side.

You are now ready to look inside the spinal cord to see how it is structured. Figure 2-28 shows a cross section of it. Look first at the fibers entering the spinal cord's dorsal side (in the body of a normally upright animal such as a human, the dorsal side means the back, as illustrated in Figure 2-3). These dorsal fibers carry information from the body's sensory receptors. The fibers collect together as they enter a spinal-cord segment, and this collection of fibers is called a *dorsal root.* Fibers leaving the spinal cord's ventral side (*ventral* here means the front) carry information from the spinal cord to the muscles. They, too, bundle together as they exit the spinal cord and so form a *ventral root.* As you can see in the cross section at the top of the drawing in Figure 2-28, the outer part of the spinal cord consists of white matter, or tracts. These tracts are arranged so that, with few exceptions, the dorsal tracts are sensory and the ventral tracts are motor. The inner part of the cord, which has a butterfly shape, is gray matter. It is composed largely of cell bodies.

Go to the CD and find the spinal cord area of the Central Nervous System module. There you can see various sections of the spinal cord as well as a rotatable model of a spinal cord.

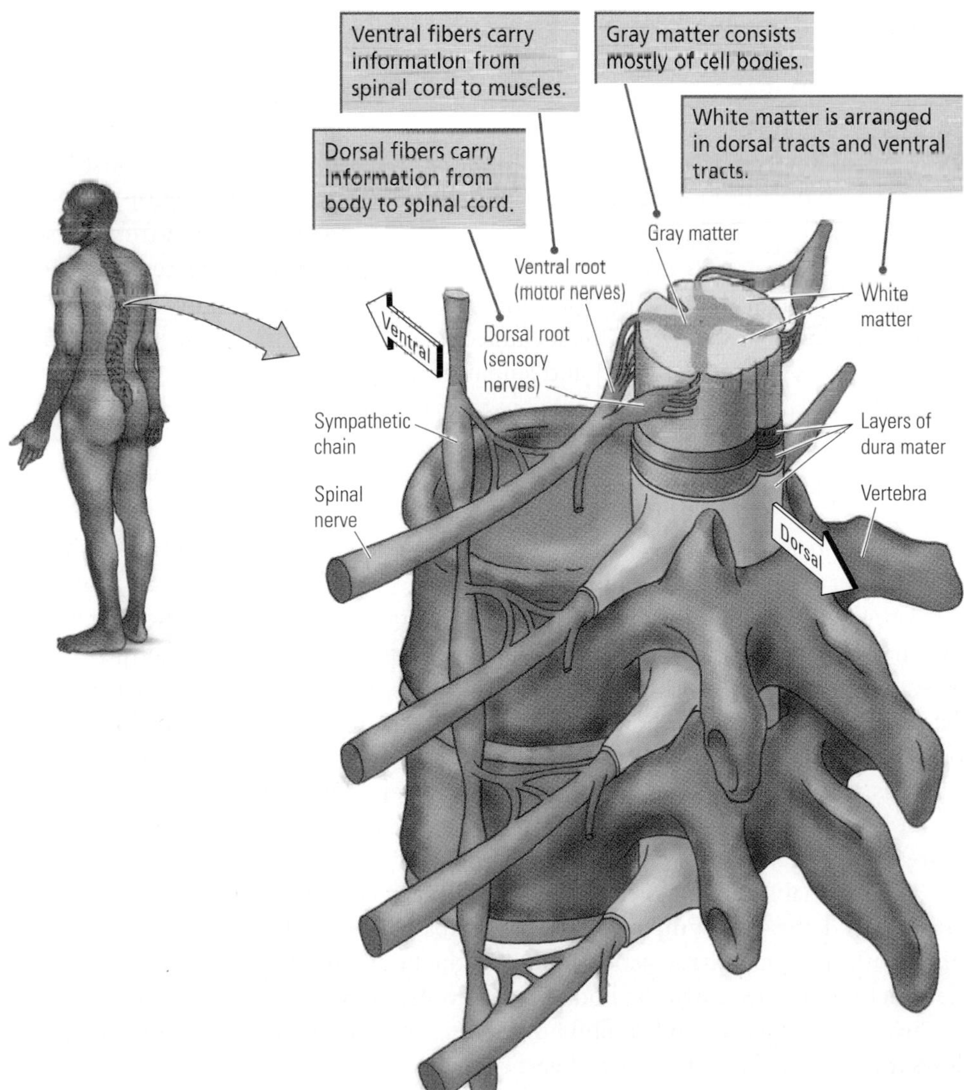


## Figure 2-28

The spinal cord runs inside the vertebral column. Part of the internal nervous system (the sympathetic nerve chain) lies outside the spinal column. The gray matter is made up largely of cell bodies, whereas the white matter is made up of fiber tracts that ascend and descend to and from the brain, respectively. Note that dorsal is in front in this diagram so that you can imagine that the skin and muscles of the back have been removed to allow this view of the spinal cord and vertebral column. Below, a photo shows the exposed spinal column.

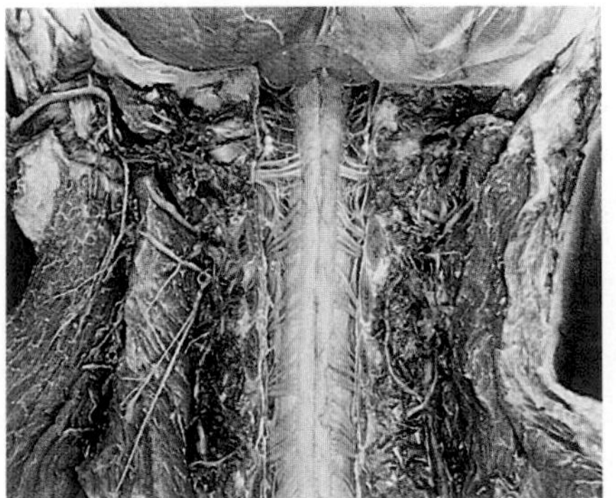

Bassett/Visuals Unlimited

The observation that the dorsal side of the spinal cord is sensory and the ventral side is motor is known as the **law of Bell and Magendie,** one of the nervous system's very few laws. The Bell and Magendie law, combined with an understanding of the spinal cord's segmental organization, enables neurologists to make quite accurate inferences about the location of spinal-cord damage or disease on the basis of changes in sensation or movement that patients experience. For instance, if a person experiences numbness in the fingers of the left hand but can still move the hand fairly normally, one or more of the dorsal nerves in spinal-cord segments C7 and C8 must be damaged. In contrast, if sensation in the hand is normal but the person cannot move the fingers, the ventral roots of the same segments must be damaged. The topic of diagnosing spinal-cord injury or disease is further discussed in "Magendie, Bell, and Bell's Palsy."

So far we have emphasized the segmental organization of the spinal cord, but the spinal cord must also somehow coordinate inputs and outputs across different segments. For example, many body movements require the coordination of muscles that are controlled by different segments, just as many sensory experiences require the coordination of sensory inputs to different parts of the spinal cord. How is this coordination of spinal-cord activities accomplished? The answer is that the spinal-cord segments are interconnected in such a way that adjacent segments can operate together to form rather complex coordinated movements.

The integration of spinal-cord activities does not require the brain's participation, which is why the headless chicken can run around in a reasonably coordinated way. Still, there must be a close working relation between the brain (and therefore the cranial nervous system) and the spinal nervous system. Otherwise, how could we consciously plan and execute our voluntary actions? Somehow information must be relayed back and forth between the cranial and the spinal systems. Examples of this sharing of information are numerous. For instance, tactile information from sensory nerves in the skin travels not just to the spinal cord, but also to the cerebral cortex through the thalamus. Similarly, the cerebral cortex and other brain structures can control movements because of their connections to the ventral roots of the spinal cord. So, even though the cranial and spinal nervous systems can function independently, the two are intimately connected in their functions.

## The Internal Nervous System

The internal nervous system (which, as mentioned earlier, is another term for the autonomic nervous system) is a hidden partner in controlling behavior. Even without our conscious awareness, it stays on the job to keep the heart beating, the liver releasing glucose, the pupils of the eyes adjusting to light, and so forth. Without the internal nervous system, life would quickly cease, because the internal nervous system is in charge of regulating all the body's internal organs and glands. Although it is possible to learn to exert some conscious control over some of the internal nervous system's activities, such conscious interference is unnecessary. One important reason is that the internal nervous system must keep working during sleep, a time when conscious awareness is off-duty.

The internal nervous system is composed of two opposing subsystems: the **sympathetic** and the **parasympathetic.** These subsystems work in opposition to each other, with the sympathetic acting to arouse the body for action and the parasympathetic acting to quiet down the body. For example, the sympathetic system stimulates the heart to beat faster and inhibits digestion, whereas the parasympathetic system slows the heartbeat and stimulates digestion.

Focus on Disorders

## Magendie, Bell, and Bell's Palsy

François Magendie, a volatile and committed French experimental physiologist, reported in a three-page paper in 1822 that he had succeeded in cutting the dorsal and ventral roots of puppies, animals in which the roots are sufficiently segregated to allow such surgery. Magendie found that cutting the dorsal roots caused loss of sensation, whereas cutting the ventral roots caused loss of movement. Eleven years earlier, however, a Scotsman named Charles Bell also had proposed functions for these nerve roots based on anatomical information and the results of somewhat inconclusive experiments on rabbits. Although Bell's findings were not identical with Magendie's, they were similar enough to ignite a controversy. Bell hotly disputed Magendie's claim to the discovery of dorsal and ventral root functions. As a result, the principle of sensory and motor segregation in the nervous system has been given both researchers' names: the law of Bell and Magendie.

Magendie's conclusive experiment on puppies was considered extremely important because it enabled neurologists for the first time to localize nervous system damage from the symptoms that a patient displays. Bell went on to describe an example of such localized motor-nerve dysfunction, which still bears his name—Bell's palsy. Bell's palsy is a facial paralysis that occurs when the motor part of the facial nerve on one side of the head becomes inflamed (see the accompanying photograph). The onset of Bell's palsy is typically sudden. Often the stricken person wakes up in the morning and is shocked to discover that the face is paralyzed on one side. He or she cannot open the mouth on that side of the head or completely close the eye on that side. Most people fully recover from Bell's palsy, although it may take several months. But, in rare instances, such as that of Jean Chretien, the Prime Minister of Canada, paralysis of the mouth is permanent.

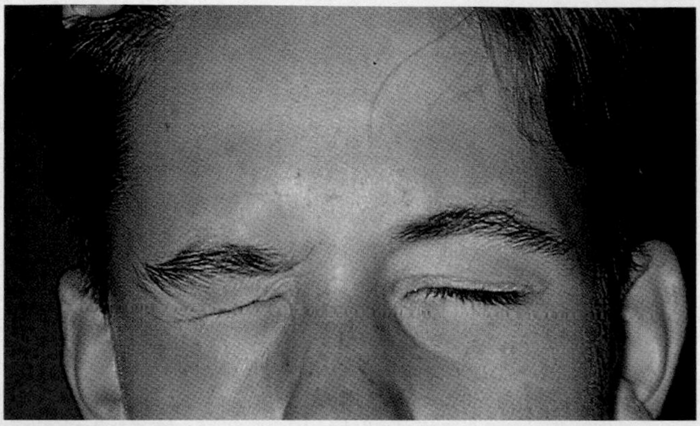

Dr. P. Marazzi / Science Photo Library/ Photo Researchers

A young man suffering from Bell's palsy, a paralysis of the facial nerve that causes weakness over one side of the face. He was photographed during an involuntary tic (a nervous reaction) that affects the right side of the face, causing his right eye to close tightly.

The internal nervous system is connected to the rest of the nervous system, especially to the spinal nervous system. In fact, activation of the sympathetic system starts in the thoracic and lumbar spinal-cord regions. But the spinal nerves do not directly control the target organs. Rather, the spinal cord is connected to *autonomic control centers,* which are collections of cells called ganglia. It is the ganglia that actually control the organs. The sympathetic system ganglia are located near the spinal cord, forming a chain that runs parallel to the cord, as illustrated in Figure 2-29 on page 64. The parasympathetic system also is connected to the spinal cord—in this case, to the sacral region. But an even larger part of it derives from three cranial nerves: the *vagus nerve,* which controls most of the internal organs, and the *facial* and *oculomotor nerves,* which control salivation and pupil dilation, respectively. In contrast with the sympathetic system, the parasympathetic system connects with ganglia that are near the target organs, as shown in Figure 2-29.

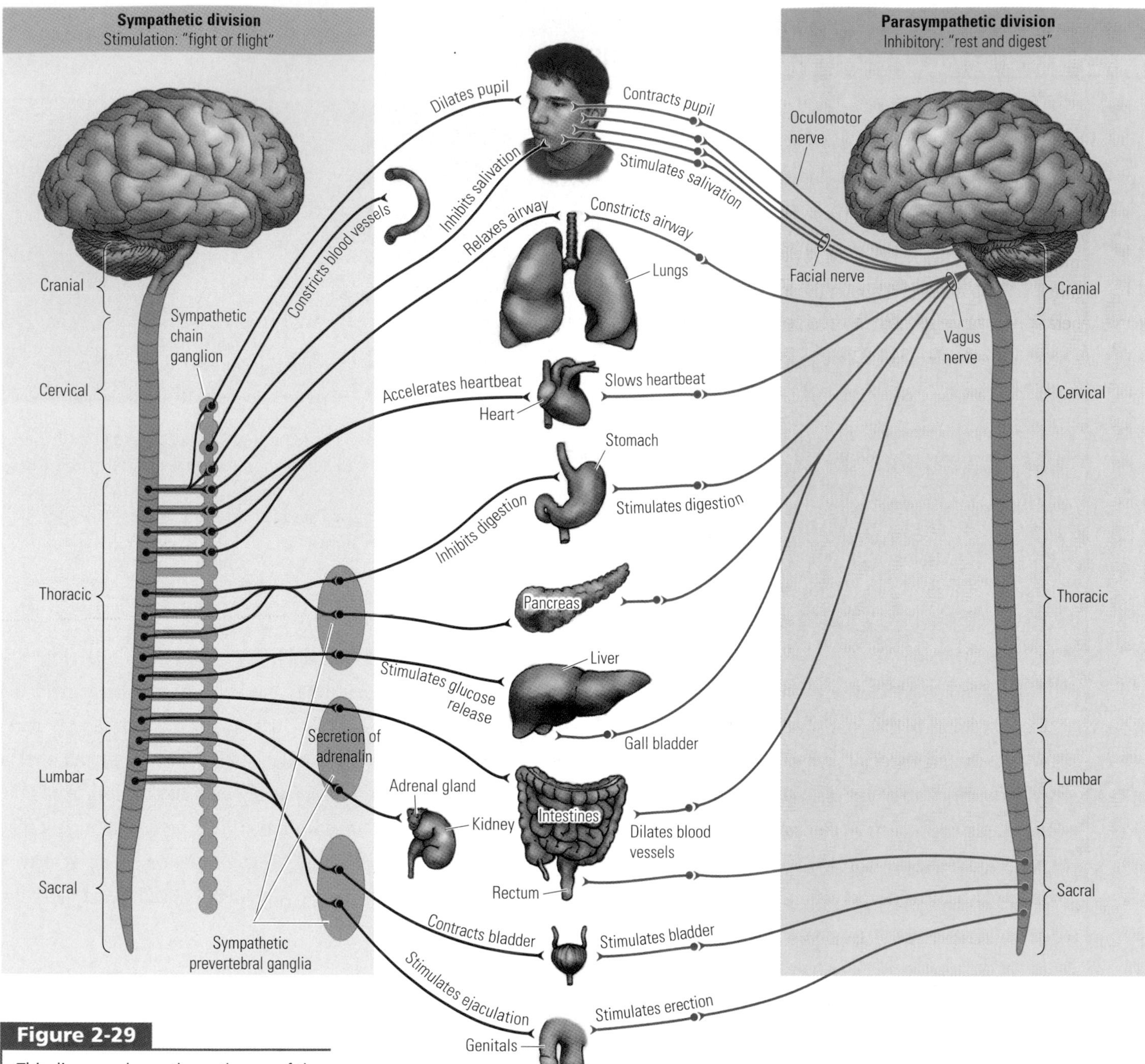


**Figure 2-29**

This diagram shows the pathways of the internal nervous system, also called the autonomic nervous system. The internal nervous system consists of two parts, the sympathetic and the parasympathetic, that exert opposing effects on the organs that they innervate. All of the autonomic fibers "stop" en route from the spinal cord to their target organs. For the sympathetic system, the fibers "stop" near the spinal cord in the celiac ganglion. For the parasympathetic system, the fibers "stop" on individual parasympathetic ganglia that are found near the target organs.

## In Review

We began the chapter by taking a general look at the anatomy of the nervous system and then, in this section, we started to make some guesses about what different nervous system structures might do. Traditional discussions of the nervous system distinguish between the central nervous system, which consists of the brain and spinal cord, and the peripheral nervous system, which encompasses everything else. An alternative categorization is based more on function and divides the nervous system into the cranial nervous system (which includes the brain and its connections to parts of the head), the spinal nervous system (which includes the spinal cord and its connections to and from the body's muscles, joints, and skin), and the internal nervous system (which controls the body's internal organs). Each of these sections of the nervous system can be subdivided into large subsections that are functionally distinct, such as the forebrain and hindbrain of the cranial nervous system. Similarly, within each of the subsections, we find more functional subregions, such as the limbic system and the basal ganglia of the forebrain. Finally, each of these functional systems can be further divided into areas that have their own unique functions, such as the caudate nucleus, putamen, and globus pallidus of the basal ganglia. The process of learning the anatomy of the nervous system is to work from the general to the more specific in each part of the nervous system and, in each case, to remember to associate structure with function.

## THE FUNCTIONAL ORGANIZATION OF THE BRAIN

Knowing the parts of a car engine is the place to start in understanding how an engine works. But knowing the parts, unfortunately, is not enough. You also need some principles concerning how the parts work together. For example, even though you know which part the carburetor is, you will not understand its function until you grasp the principle of air and fuel mixing and igniting in the cylinders. Similarly, although you now know the basic parts of the nervous system, you need some general principles to help you understand how these different parts work together. Table 2-3 lists eight such principles, which form the basis for many discussions later in this book. You should spend the time needed to understand these principles fully before moving on to the next chapters.

### Principle 1: The Sequence of Brain Processing Is "In → Integrate → Out"

The parts of the brain make a great many connections with one another. Recall, for example, the meddling cerebral cortex that appears to be connected to everything. This connectivity of the brain is the key to its functioning. The points of connection, known as *synapses,* allow cells in different brain regions to influence one another. Chapter 5 explains the organization of the synapse. The key point here is that most

**Table 2-3 Principles of Brain Functioning**

1. Information is processed in a sequence of "in → integrate → out."
2. There is a functional division between sensory and motor throughout the nervous system.
3. Inputs and outputs to the brain are crossed.
4. There is both symmetry and asymmetry in brain anatomy and function.
5. The nervous system operates by a juxtaposition of excitation and inhibition.
6. The nervous system has multiple levels of function.
7. The nervous system operates as a series of systems arranged both in parallel and hierarchically.
8. Functions in the brain are both localized in specific regions and distributed.

neurons have afferent (incoming) connections with tens or sometimes hundreds of thousands of other neurons, as well as efferent (outgoing) connections to many other cells.

Figure 2-30 shows how these multiple connections enable neurons to integrate information, creating new information. The inputs to a neuron at any given moment are "summed up," and the neuron sends out signals to other neurons that incorporate this summation. The summation is more than just a matter of adding up equally weighted inputs. Some inputs have a greater influence than others on the receiving neuron, and the simultaneous occurrence of certain inputs may have effects that far exceed their simple sum. The summation of information, then, allows that information to be transformed in some way before being passed on to other neurons. This transformation makes the summation process partly one of creating new information.

For an animation of how neurons integrate information, go to the section on neural integration in the CD module on Neural Communication.

Figure 2-31 gives a simple example of the creation of new information in the brain. This example begins with receptor cells that are located in the eyes' retinas and are maximally responsive to light of a particular wavelength: red, green, or blue. Now imagine a brain with neurons that receive inputs from one or more of these color-sensitive receptors. A neuron can receive inputs from only one receptor type, from two receptor types, or from all three receptor types. A neuron receiving input from green-type receptor cells would "know" only about green and would forward only green information. In contrast, a neuron receiving input from both green- and red-type receptors would "know" about two colors and would forward a very different message, as would a neuron receiving input from all three receptor types. Both neurons with more than one kind of input would sum the information that they get. In a sense, they would *create* new information that did not previously exist. Such a neuron

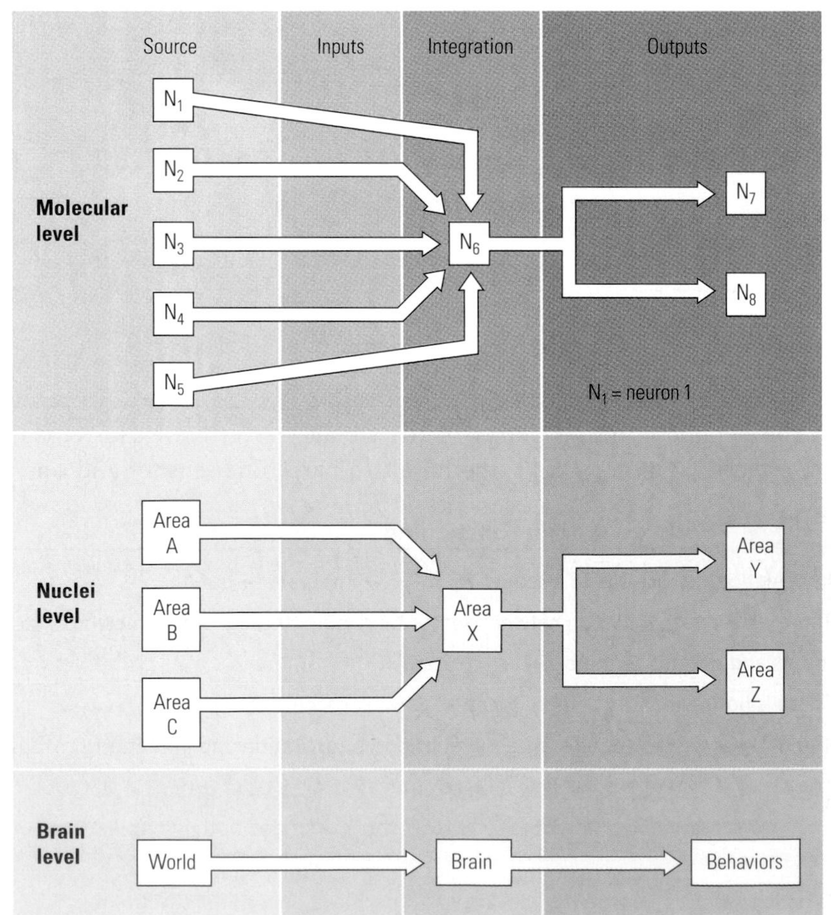


**Figure 2-30**

The neuron and the brain are devices for gathering, integrating, and sending information. At the cellular level, each of neurons 1 through 5 sends some message to neuron 6, which essentially now "knows" what neurons 1 through 5 signaled. This "knowledge" is a form of integration. The output from neuron 6 is sent to neurons 7 and 8, whose activity is affected by the "knowledge" of neuron 6. Similarly, three neural areas, A through C, send their signals to area X, which can combine (integrate) the information from areas A through C. The integrated information is then sent to areas Y and Z. A similar concept can be applied at the level of the brain as well. The world provides information to the brain, which produces behavior.

might know that an object is both green *and* red, whereas the inputs coming from each receptor contain information about one color only. This creation of new information is what is meant by the "integration operation" of the brain.

The same principle holds for the functioning of a nucleus within the brain or of a layer of brain tissue, as illustrated in Figure 2-30. In regard to a nucleus, the inputs to each neuron in a nucleus are not identical, so there are internal connections between the neurons. These internal connections are known as intrinsic connections. Several areas of the nucleus might each send different information to another area, which integrates that information and sends a combined message along to several other areas. This process is much like the summation of information in a single neuron, but, in this case, the summation takes place in a collection of neurons. As a result of the summation, the output of all of the cells in the nucleus is changed. Once again, there is integration.

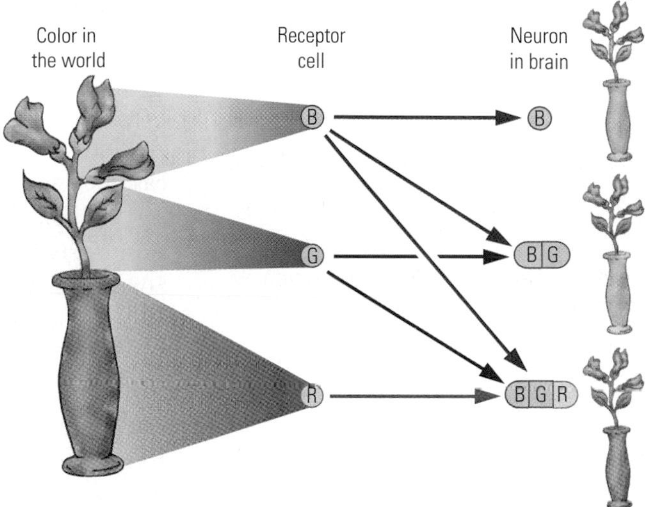


**Figure 2-31**

Input and output cells differ with respect to their knowledge about the world. Receptor cells B (blue), G (green), and R (red) each code information about one hue in the world. Neurons B, B/G, and B/G/R receive this information and alter it to send a new message that we understand to be color.

The logical extension of this discussion is to view the entire brain as an organ that receives inputs, creates information, and expresses thoughts about the world, as illustrated in Figure 2-30. To the animal whose brain is engaged in this process, the creation of information from inputs represents reality. The bigger the brain, the more complex the reality that can be created and, subsequently, the more complex the thoughts that can be expressed. The emergence of thought that enables consciousness may be the brain's ultimate form of integration.

## Principle 2: Sensory and Motor Divisions Exist Throughout the Nervous System

You learned earlier that the spinal cord has separate sensory and motor structures, described in the Bell and Magendie law. This segregation of sensory and motor functions exists throughout the nervous system. However, distinctions between motor and sensory functions become more subtle in places such as the forebrain.

### SENSORY AND MOTOR DIVISIONS AT THE PERIPHERY

The peripheral nerves going to and from the spinal cord can be divided into sensory and motor parts, as shown in Figure 2-28. In addition, the cranial nerves, too, have sensory and motor functions, although they are arranged somewhat differently from those in the peripheral nerves. Some of the cranial nerves are exclusively sensory; some are exclusively motor; and some have two parts, one sensory and one motor, much like the sensory and motor branches of peripheral nerves.

### SENSORY AND MOTOR DIVISIONS IN THE BRAIN

The hindbrain and midbrain are essentially extensions of the spinal cord; they developed as simple animals evolved a brain at the anterior end of the body. It makes sense, therefore, that, in these lower brainstem regions, there should be a division between structures having sensory functions and those having motor functions, with sensory structures located dorsally and motor ones ventrally. Recall that an important function of the midbrain is to orient the body to stimuli. This orientation requires both sensory input and motor output. The midbrain's colliculi, which are located dorsally, are the sensory component, whereas the tegmentum, which is ventral (below the colliculi), is a motor structure that plays a role in controlling various types of movements, including orienting ones. Both these midbrain structures are illustrated in Figure 2-18.

Distinct sensory and motor nuclei are present in the thalamus, too, although they are no longer located dorsally. Because all sensory information reaches the forebrain through the thalamus, it is not surprising to find separate nuclei associated with vision, hearing, and touch. Separate thalamic nuclei also control movements. Other nuclei have neither sensory nor motor functions. They have connections to cortical areas, such as the frontal lobe, that perform more integrative tasks.

Finally, sensory and motor functions are divided in the cortex as well. This division exists in two ways. First, there are separate sensory and motor cortical regions. Some primarily process a particular sensory input, such as vision, hearing, or touch. Others control detailed movements of discrete body parts, such as the fingers. Second, the entire cortex can be viewed as being organized around the sensory and motor distinction. For instance, layer IV of the cortex always receives sensory inputs, whereas layers V and VI always send motor outputs, as shown in Figure 2-22. Layers I, II, and III are integrative, providing a connection between sensory and motor operations.

## Principle 3: The Brain's Circuits Are Crossed

A most peculiar organizational feature of the brain is that its inputs and outputs are "crossed." Each of its halves receives sensory stimulation from the *opposite* (called *contralateral*) side of the body and controls muscles on the opposite side as well. Examples of this crossed organization are shown in Figure 2-32. Crossed organization explains why people with strokes in the left cerebral hemisphere may have difficulty in sensing stimulation to the right side of the body or in moving body parts on the right side. The opposite is true of people with strokes in the right cerebral hemisphere.

In humans, who have forward-facing eyes, the visual system is crossed in a more complex fashion than in animals with eyes on the sides of their head. This complexity is required because, if two eyes are facing forward instead of sideward, they inevitably see much the same thing, except on the far sides of the field of vision. The problem with this arrangement is that, to see an object, information about it must go to the same place in the brain. Duplicate information cannot be sent to two different places. Figure 2-32 (right) shows how the brain solves this problem by dividing each eye's visual field into a left half and a right half. The information that either eye receives from the left half of its visual field is sent to the right side of the brain, and the information that either eye receives from the right half of its visual field is sent to the left side of the brain. The visual system is still crossed, but in a more complicated way than are systems for other parts of the body.

For an animation and illustration of how the visual system is crossed, go to the section on the optic chiasm in the Visual System module on the CD.

One difficulty with a crossed nervous system is that the two sides of the world must be joined together somehow. This joining is accomplished by having numerous connections between the left and right sides of the brain. The most prominent connecting cable is the corpus callosum, shown in Figure 2-8. As stated earlier, the corpus callosum connects the left and right cerebral hemispheres with about 200 million fibers.

## Principle 4: The Brain Is Both Symmetrical and Asymmetrical

You know that the brain has two halves, the left and the right hemispheres, which look like mirror images of each other. Although these two halves are symmetrical in many ways, they also have some asymmetrical features. This asymmetrical organization is essential for certain tasks. Consider speaking. If a language zone existed in both hemispheres, each connected to one side of the mouth, we would have the strange ability to talk out of both sides of the mouth at once. This would not make talking

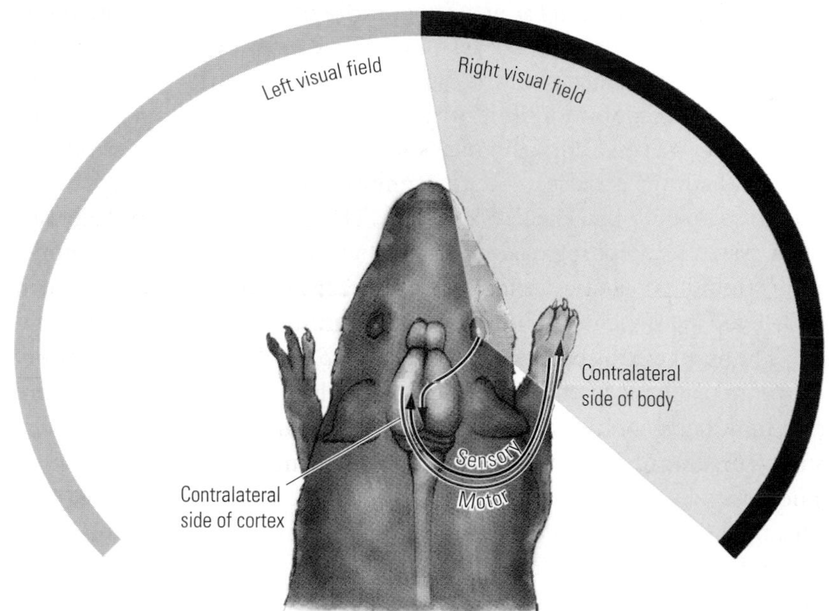


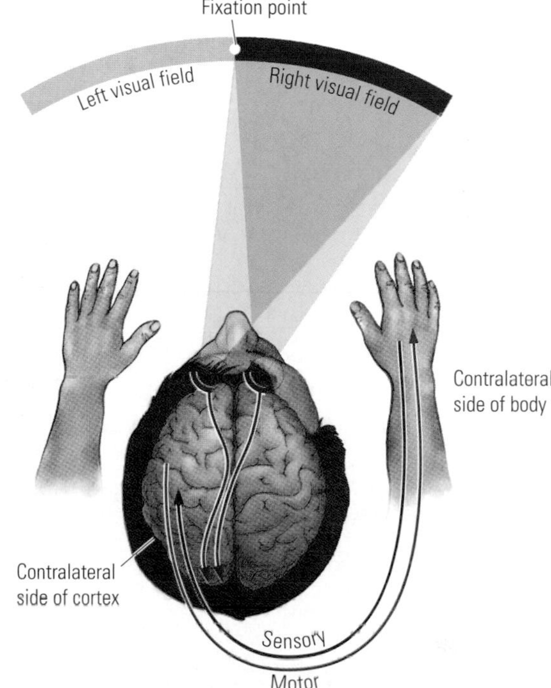


**Figure 2-32**

(*Left*) This schematic representation of a rat's brain from a dorsal view shows the projection of visual and somatosensory input to contralateral (opposite-side) areas of the cortex and the crossed projection of the motor cortex to the contralateral side of the body. The eyes of the rat are laterally placed, such that most of the input from each eye travels to the opposite hemisphere. (*Right*) In the human head, the two eyes are frontally placed. As a result, the visual input is split in two so that input from the right side of the world as seen by both eyes goes to the left hemisphere and input from the left side of the world as seen by both eyes goes to the right hemisphere. The somatosensory input of both rats and humans is completely crossed, so that information coming from the right paw or hand goes to the left hemisphere. Note that although the diagram as drawn shows activity as going directly to and from the brain, there are connectors en route.

easy, to say the least. One solution is to locate control of the mouth on one side of the brain only. Organizing the brain in this way would allow us to speak with a single voice. A similar problem arises in controlling the body's movement in space. We would not want the left and the right hemispheres each trying to take us to a different place. Again, the problem can be solved if a single brain area controls this sort of spatial processing.

In fact, processes such as language and spatial navigation *are* localized on only one side of the brain. Language is usually on the left side, and spatial functions are usually on the right. This asymmetrical organization is not unique to humans. Birds have developed a solution to producing song by locating the control of singing in one hemisphere. Curiously, like human language, bird song also is usually located on the brain's left side. Why this similarity exists is not completely clear. But the key point is that, in many species, the brain has both symmetrical and asymmetrical organization.

## Principle 5: The Nervous System Works Through Excitation and Inhibition

Imagine that, while you are reading this page, the telephone rings. You stop reading, get up, walk to the telephone, pick it up, and talk to a friend who convinces you that going to a movie would be more fun than reading. To carry out this series of actions, not only must your brain produce certain behaviors, it must also stop other behaviors. When you were walking and talking, for example, you were not engaged in reading. To walk and talk, you had to first stop reading. Producing behavior, then, requires both initiating some actions and inhibiting others.

In talking about the nervous system, we refer to the initiation of an activity as **excitation** and the stoppage of an activity as **inhibition.** The juxtaposition of excitation and inhibition is a key principle of nervous system functioning. Recall, for example, that the sympathetic and parasympathetic systems produce opposite actions. The sympathetic system excites the heart, whereas the parasympathetic inhibits it. This general principle of excitation and inhibition is central to how the nervous system works.

The same principle can be seen in the activity of individual neurons. Neurons can pass on information to other neurons either by being active or by being silent. That is, they can be "on" or "off." Some neurons in the brain function primarily to excite other neurons, whereas others function to inhibit other neurons. These excitatory and inhibitory effects are produced by various chemicals that turn the neurons on or off.

Just as individual neurons can act to excite or inhibit other neurons, brain nuclei (or layers) can do the same to other nuclei (or layers). These actions are especially obvious in the motor systems. Inhibiting reading and initiating walking to the telephone, for example, result from the on and off actions of specific motor-system nuclei.

Now imagine that one of the nuclei that normally inhibits some type of movement is injured. The injury will result in an inability to inhibit that particular response. This symptom can be seen in people with frontal-lobe injury. Such people are often unable to inhibit behaviors, such as talking at inappropriate times or using certain words, such as curse words. In contrast, people with injury to the speech zones of the left hemisphere may be unable to talk at all, because the injury is in an area that normally initiates the behavior of speech. These contrasting symptoms lead to an important conclusion: brain injury can produce either a loss of behavior or a release of behavior. Behavior is lost when the damage prevents excitatory instructions; behavior is released when the damage prevents inhibitory instructions.

## Principle 6: The Central Nervous System Has Multiple Levels of Function

You have seen that similar sensory and motor functions are carried out in various parts of the brain and spinal cord. But why are multiple areas with overlapping functions needed? After all, it would seem simpler to put all the controls for a certain function in a single place. Why bother with duplication?

The answer is that the mammalian brain is a product of evolution in which it changed according to the "descent with modification" rule. As the brain evolved, new areas were added, but old ones were retained. As a result, there was a problem of where to put the new regions. The simplest solution was to add them on top of the existing brain. We can see this solution in the evolution from primitive vertebrates to amphibians to mammals. For instance, primitive vertebrates, such as fish, make only whole-body movements to swim, movements that are controlled by the spinal cord and hindbrain. Amphibians developed legs and corresponding neural control areas in the brainstem. Mammals later developed new capacities with their limbs, such as independent limb movements and fine digit movements. These movements, too, required new control areas, which were added in the forebrain. We therefore find three distinct areas of motor control in mammals: the spinal cord, the brainstem, and the forebrain.

At the beginning of the twentieth century, John Hughlings-Jackson suggested that the addition of new brain structures in the course of evolution could be viewed as adding new levels of nervous system control. The lowest level is the spinal cord, the next level is the brainstem, and the highest level is the forebrain. These levels are not autonomous, however. To move the arms, the brainstem must use circuits in the spinal cord. Similarly, to make independent movements of the arms and fingers, such as in tying a shoelace, the cortex must use circuits in both the brainstem and the spinal cord. Each new level offers a refinement and elaboration of the motor control provided by one or more lower levels.

For more about the evolution of the brain, go to the Web site for a connection to the National Museum of Health and Medicine for photographs of brains from all sorts of creatures and discussion of brain evolution.

We can observe the operation of functional levels in the behavior of people with brain injuries. Someone whose spinal cord is disconnected from the brain cannot voluntarily move a limb because the brain has no way to control the movement. But the limb can still move automatically to withdraw from a noxious stimulus because the circuits for moving the muscles are still intact in the spinal cord. Similarly, if the forebrain is not functioning but the brainstem is still connected to the spinal cord, a person can still move, but the movements are relatively simple: there is limited limb use and no digit control.

The principle of multiple levels of function can also be applied to the cortex in mammals, which evolved by adding new areas, mostly sensory-processing ones. The newer areas essentially added new levels of control that provide more and more abstract analysis of inputs. Consider the recognition of an object, such as a car. The simplest level of analysis recognizes the features of this object such as its size, shape, and color. A higher level of analysis recognizes this object as a car. And an even higher level of analysis recognizes it as Susan's car with a dent in the fender. Probably the highest levels are cortical regions that substitute one or more words for the object (Honda Civic, for instance) and can think about the car in its absence.

When we consider the brain as a structure composed of multiple levels of function, it is clear that these levels must be extensively interconnected to integrate their processing and create unified perceptions or movements. The nature of this connectivity in the brain leads to the next principle of brain function: the brain has both parallel and hierarchical circuitry.

## Principle 7: Brain Systems Are Organized Both Hierarchically and in Parallel

The brain and spinal cord are two semiautonomous nervous systems organized into functional levels, and, even within a single level, more than one area may take part in a given function. How then, with these different systems and levels, do we eventually obtain a unified conscious experience? Why, when we look at Susan's car, do we not have the sense that one part of the brain is processing features such as shape while another part is processing color? Or why, when we tie our shoelaces, are we not aware that different levels of motor control are at work to move our arms and fingers and coordinate their actions? These questions are part of what is called the "binding problem." It focuses on how the brain ties together its various activities into a whole. The solution to the problem must somehow be related to the ways in which the parts of the nervous system are connected.

There are two alternative possibilities for wiring the nervous system: serial or parallel circuits. A *serial circuit* hooks up in a series all the regions concerned with a given function. Consider Susan's car again. In a serial system, the information from the eyes would go first to a region (or regions) that performs the simplest analysis—for example, the detection of specific properties, such as color and shape. This information would then be passed on to another region that sums up the information and identifies a car. The information would next proceed to another region that compares this car with stored images and identifies it as Susan's car. Notice how the perceptual process entails the flow of information sequentially through the circuit. Because the regions in the chain range from simple to complex, this serial type of system is usually called a simple hierarchical model. It is illustrated in Figure 2-33A on page 72.

In the 1960s and 1970s, neuropsychologists proposed models of **hierarchical organization** to help in understanding how the brain might produce complex behaviors. One difficulty with such models, however, is that functionally related structures in the brain are not always linked serially. Although the brain has many serial connections, many expected connections are missing. For example, within the visual system, one group of cortical areas is not connected with what appears to be a parallel group of areas.

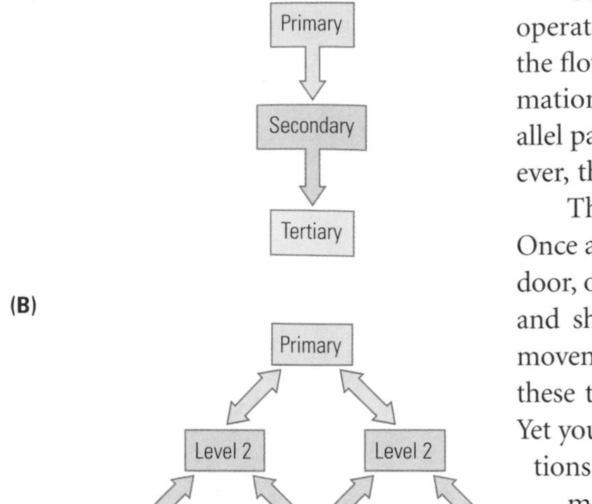


**Figure 2-33**

**(A)** This simple serial hierarchical model of cortical processing is similar to that first proposed by A. R. Luria. In Luria's scheme, information was conceptualized as being organized into three levels: primary, secondary, and tertiary. **(B)** In Daniel Felleman and David van Essen's distributed hierarchical model, there are multiple levels in each of several processing streams. Areas at each level are interconnected with one another.

One solution to this problem is to imagine multiple hierarchical systems that operate in parallel to one another but are also interconnected. Figure 2-33B illustrates the flow of information in such a distributed hierarchical model. If you trace the information flow from the primary area to levels 2, 3, and 4, you can see that there are parallel pathways. These multiple parallel pathways are also connected to each other. However, the connections are more selective than those that exist in a purely serial circuit.

The visual system provides a good example of such parallel hierarchical pathways. Once again we return to Susan's car—this time to one of its doors. As we look at the car door, one set of visual pathways processes information about its nature, such as its color and shape, while another set of pathways processes information about door-related movements, such as those required to open the door. It may surprise you to learn that these two systems are independent of each other, with no connections between them. Yet your perception when you pull the door open is not one of two different representations—the door's size, shape, and color, on the one hand, and the opening movements, on the other. When you open the door, you have the impression of unity in your conscious experience. Interestingly, the brain is organized into multiple parallel pathways in all of its subsystems. Yet our conscious experiences are always unified. We will return to this conundrum (and the binding problem) at the end of this book. For now, keep in mind that your common-sense impressions of how the brain works may not always be right.

## Principle 8: Functions in the Brain Are Both Localized and Distributed

In our consideration of brain organization, we have so far assumed that functions can be localized in specific parts of the brain. This assumption makes intuitive sense, but it turns out to be controversial. One of the great debates in the history of brain research has been about what aspects of different functions are actually localized in specific brain regions.

Perhaps the fundamental problem is that of defining a function. Consider language, for example. Language includes the comprehension of spoken words, written words, signed words (as in American Sign Language), and even touched words (as in Braille). Language also includes processes of producing words, both orally and in writing, as well as constructing whole linguistic compositions, such as stories, poems, songs, and essays. Because the function that we call language has many aspects, it is not surprising that they reside in widely separated areas of the brain. We see evidence of this widespread distribution in language-related brain injuries. People with injuries in different locations may selectively lose the abilities to produce words, understand words, read words, write words, and so forth. Specific language-related abilities, therefore, are found in specific locations, but language itself is distributed throughout a wide region of the brain.

Memory provides another example of this same pattern. Memories can be extremely rich in detail and can include sensory material, feelings, words, and much more. Like language, then, memory is not located in just one brain region. Rather, it is distributed throughout a vast area of the brain.

Because many functions are both localized and distributed in the brain, damage to a small brain region produces only *focal symptoms*. Massive brain damage is required to completely remove some function. For instance, a relatively small injury could impair some aspect of language functioning, but it would take a very widespread injury to completely remove all language abilities. In fact, one of the characteristics of dementing diseases, such as Alzheimer's, is that people can have widespread deterioration of the cortex yet maintain remarkably normal language functions until late stages of the disease.

## In Review

Knowing the parts of a car engine or a brain, and some general notions of what they might do, was only the beginning. The next step was to learn some principles concerning how the parts work together. We have identified eight such principles that will allow us to proceed to a closer look, in the chapters that follow, at how the brain produces behavior. You will benefit from reviewing each of these principles with an eye toward understanding the general concept being addressed, rather than simply memorizing the statement itself. For example, as you think about the principle stating that the nervous system works through excitation and inhibition, think about the balance created by this principle's application and what this balance means for the functioning brain. What would happen, say, if you could not inhibit behavior? When we encounter the rules that govern the operation of neurons in the next four chapters, you will want to revisit the inhibition–excitation principle and again think about how it can relate to the way in which individual cells work to produce behavior.

## SUMMARY

1. *What are some of the larger external and internal features of the brain?* Under the tough, protective meninges that covers the brain lie its two major structures—the larger cerebrum, divided into two hemispheres, and the smaller cerebellum. Both structures are covered with gyri (bumps) and sulci (cracks), some of which are so deep that they are called fissures. At the base of the brain, where it joins the spinal cord, the brainstem is visible, as are the cranial nerves that run to the head. Cutting the brain in half reveals the fluid-filled ventricles inside it, as well as the white matter, gray matter, and reticular matter that make up its tissue. Also apparent is the corpus callosum, which joins the two hemispheres and the subcortical regions below the cerebral cortex.
2. *How can the nervous system be divided for functional analysis?* The nervous system is composed of subsystems that function semiautonomously. These subsystems are the cranial, spinal, and internal nervous systems. The cranial nervous system includes the brain and the cranial nerves, which link the brain to various parts of the head. The spinal nervous system consists of the spinal cord and the peripheral nerves that enter and leave it, going to and from muscles, skin, and joints in the body. The internal nervous system, which controls the body's internal organs, is also called the autonomic nervous system. It has two parts, the sympathetic and parasympathetic divisions. They work in opposition to each other, one arousing the body for action and the other calming the body down.
3. *What are the basic structures and functions of the lower part of the brain, called the brainstem?* The brainstem consists of three regions: the hindbrain, the midbrain, and the diencephalon. The cerebellum is important in controlling complex movements. Three other structures are the reticular formation (which serves to activate the forebrain), the pons (which provides a bridge from the cerebellum to the rest of the brain), and the medulla (which controls such vital functions as breathing). In the midbrain, the tectum processes information from the eyes and ears and produces movements related to these sensory inputs. Below it lies the tegmentum, which consists of many nuclei, largely with movement-related functions. Finally, the diencephalon consists of two main structures: the thalamus and the hypothalamus.

4. *What are some important structures in the upper part of the brain, called the forebrain?* The forebrain is the largest region of the brain. Its outer surface is the cortex. Sulci, especially deep ones called fissures, form the boundaries of the four lobes on each cerebral hemisphere: the frontal, the parietal, the temporal, and the occipital. The cells of the cortex form distinctive layers based on their specialized functions. Interconnections exist between these layers and virtually all other parts of the brain. These extensive connections to other brain regions are essential to the cortex with its directing role in top-down processing. The basal ganglia, lying just below the white matter of the cortex, are another important part of the forebrain that primarily play a role in movement. Also important in the forebrain is the limbic system. The part of the limbic system called the amygdala regulates emotional behavior, whereas the hippocampus and the cingulate cortex both have roles in memory and in navigating the body in space.
5. *How does the spinal nervous system work?* The spinal nervous system has sensory input from the skin, muscles, and joints of the body. It also has efferent connections to the skeletal muscles, which makes it responsible for controlling the body's movements. The spinal cord functions as a kind of minibrain for the nerves that enter and leave a particular spinal segment. Each segment works relatively independently, although fibers interconnect them and coordinate their activities. According to the law of Bell and Magendie, nerves entering a segment's dorsal side carry information from sensory receptors in the body, whereas nerves leaving a segment's ventral side carry information to the muscles.
6. *What are some basic principles related to the functional organization of the brain?* One principle is that the sequence of processing within the brain is "in → integrate → out," in which the term *integrate* refers to the creation of new information as cells, nuclei, and brain layers sum the inputs that they receive from different sources. A second principle is that sensory and motor functions are separated throughout the nervous system, not just in the spinal system but in the brain as well. A third principle is that the organization of the brain is *crossed,* meaning that the right hemisphere is connected to the left side of the body, whereas the left hemisphere is connected to the body's right side. Fourth is the principle that the brain, though largely symmetrical, also has asymmetrical organization appropriate for certain tasks, and fifth is the principle that the nervous system works through a combination of excitatory and inhibitory signals. The sixth principle is that the nervous system has multiple levels of function. Tasks are often duplicated in these multiple levels, which range from older, more primitive ones to higher levels that evolved more recently. Two final principles are that brain circuits are organized both hierarchically and in parallel and that functions are both localized and distributed in the brain.

## KEY TERMS

basal ganglia, p. 55
brainstem, p. 43
cerebellum, p. 43
cerebrum, p. 43
cortex (neocortex), p. 55
cranial nerve, p. 43
dermatome, p. 60
diencephalon, p. 50
forebrain, p. 55
gray matter, p. 44
hindbrain, p. 50
hypothalamus, p. 54
limbic system, p. 55
midbrain, p. 50
reticular formation, p. 52
reticular matter, p. 44
subcortical regions, p. 45
tectum, p. 53
tegmentum, p. 54
thalamus, p. 54
white matter, p. 44

## REVIEW QUESTIONS

1. What are the three primary functions of the brain?
2. What features of the brain are visible from the outside?
3. Contrast the anatomical and functional divisions of the nervous system.
4. Expand the Bell and Magendie law to include the entire nervous system.
5. In what sense is the nervous system crossed?
6. In what sense is the activity of the nervous system a summation of excitatory and inhibitory processes?
7. What does it mean to say that the nervous system is organized into levels?

## FOR FURTHER THOUGHT

In the course of studying the effects of the removal of the entire cerebral cortex on the behavior of dogs, Franz Goltz noticed that the dogs were still able to walk, smell, bark, sleep, withdraw from pain, and eat. He concluded that functions must not be localized in the brain, reasoning that only widely distributed functions could explain how the dogs still performed all these behaviors despite so much lost brain tissue. On the basis of the principles introduced in this chapter, how would you explain why the dogs behaved so normally in spite of having lost about one-quarter of the brain?

## RECOMMENDED READING


Diamond, M. C., Scheibel, A. B., & Elson, L. M. (1985). *The human brain coloring book.* New York: Barnes & Noble. Although a coloring book might seem an odd way to learn neuroanatomy, many students find this book to be a painless way to study the relations between brain structures.

Jerison, H. J. (1991). *Brain size and the evolution of mind.* New York: American Museum of Natural History. What is the mind and why do we have language? These questions and many more are discussed by the leading expert in brain evolution. This monograph is a fascinating introduction to the issues surrounding why the brain grew larger in the primate evolutionary branch and what advantage a large brain might confer in creating a richer sensory world.

Heimer, L. (1995). *The human brain and spinal cord: Functional neuroanatomy and dissection guide* (2nd ed.). New York: Springer Verlag. If coloring books aren't your thing, then Heimer's dissection guide to the human brain will provide a more traditional, and sophisticated, guide to human brain anatomy.

Luria, A. R. (1973). *The working brain.* Harmondsworth, England: Penguin. Luria was a Russian neurologist who studied thousands of patients over a long career. He wrote a series of books outlining how the human brain functions, of which *The Working Brain* is the most accessible. In fact, this book is really the first human neuropsychology book. Although many of the details of Luria's ideas are now outdated, his general framework for how the brain is organized is substantially correct.

Zeki, S. (1993). *A vision of the brain.* London: Blackwell Scientific. Humans are visual creatures. Zeki's book uses the visual system as a way of introducing the reader to how the brain is organized. It is entertaining and introduces the reader to Zeki's ideas about how the brain functions.


### neuroscience interactive

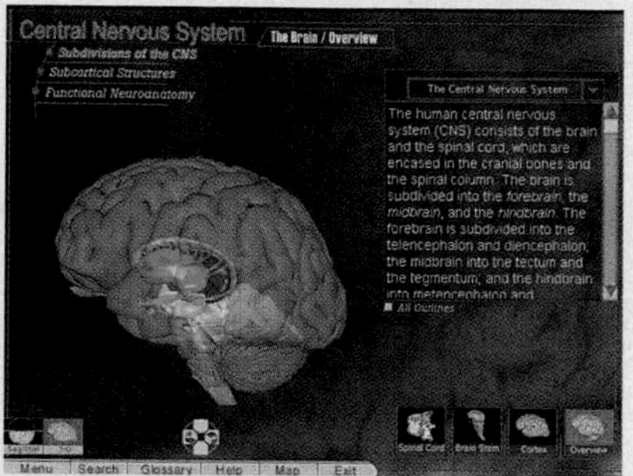


There are many resources available for expanding your learning on line:

■ **www.worthpublishers.com/kolb/chapter2**
Try some self-tests to reinforce your mastery of the material in Chapter 2. Look at some of the news updates reflecting current research on the brain. You'll also be able to link to some other sites which will reinforce what you've learned.

■ **www.neurophys.wisc.edu/brain**
Link to brain atlases that include photographs, stained sections, and movie clips from humans, monkeys, and even a dolphin. Note the differences among the brains (the increasing complexity as you move from mouse to human) as well as the similarities (try to find brain nuclei that are the same across species).

■ **www.williamcalvin.com/1990s/1998SciAmer.htm**
Read an article about the theory of brain evolution from *Scientific American.*

On your CD-ROM you'll be able to quiz yourself on your comprehension of Chapter 2. An entire module devoted to the Central Nervous System includes a rotatable, three-dimensional brain and many sections of the brain you can move through with the click of a mouse. In addition, the Research Methods module includes various CT and MRI images of the brain, including a video clip of a coronal MRI scan.

CHAPTER

# 3

# What Are the Units of Brain Function?



Tom Sanders / The Stock Market
Micrograph: Dr. Dennis Kunkel/Phototake

In the search for how a nervous system produces behaviors, robots may help provide answers. Robots, after all, engage in goal-oriented actions, just as animals do. A computer must guide and coordinate those actions, doing much the same work as a nervous system does. Barbara Webb's little robot, shown in Figure 3-1, illustrates this interesting use of electronic technology. Although far more cumbersome than nature's model, this robot is designed to mimic a female cricket that listens for and travels to the source of a male's chirping song. These behaviors are not as simple as they may seem. In approaching a male, a female cricket must avoid open, well-lit places where a predator could easily detect her. In addition, a female cricket must often choose between competing males, sometimes preferring the male that makes the longest chirps. All these behaviors must be "wired into" a successful cricket robot, making sure that one behavior does not interfere with another. In simulating cricket behavior in a robot, Webb is duplicating the rules of a cricket's nervous system.

Do not be surprised that we begin this chapter by comparing a cricket's nervous system to a robot's computer-driven parts. In their attempts to explain behavior, scientists, like philosophers, frequently search for analogies among the things they know. In earlier times, the nervous system was compared to simpler mechanical devices, such as a water pump or a clock. Today's comparison to computerized robots is just a modern version. But this analogy is one that may also help us to learn more. Researchers such as Webb switch back and forth between studying the nervous system and the behaviors that it enables and writing computer programs designed to simulate those behaviors. When the animal under study and the computerized robot respond in exactly the same way, the researchers can be fairly sure that they understand how part of the nervous system works.

This chapter explores how the nervous system works by investigating the units from which it is built. These units are cells, the basic building blocks of life. Our bodies are composed of many kinds of cells, but the ones of interest to us in this book are the neurons and glia that make up the nervous system. These nervous system cells allow us to respond to stimuli in the environment, process that information, and act. There are different types of neurons and glia, each distinctive in its structure and function. Just as we can explore the function of a robot by examining its overall structure, so we can investigate the overall structure of a cell as a source of insight into its work.

This chapter also investigates the internal structures of cells, the so-called organelles inside cells that perform various tasks. If you think of a cell as nature's microscopic robot, the organelles become the miniaturized components that allow the cell to do its job. Learning about these components is essential to understanding not only how a single cell works but also how the brain produces behavior.

Robert P. Carr / Bruce Coleman Inc. (animal); Barbara Webb (model)

**Figure 3-1**
Robotic and real crickets differ in many physical attributes. The rules obtained from the study of crickets can be programmed into robots to be tested. This robot, which is constructed from Lego blocks, wires, and a motor, follows the rules used by a female cricket to travel to the source of a chirping sound made by a male cricket.
From "A Cricket Robot," by B. Webb, 1996, *Scientific American, 214*(12), p. 99.

Genes intimately participate in the production of behavior. Genes located in the chromosomes of each cell determine the proteins that a particular cell will make and consequently the functions that the cell will serve. Ultimately, the genes of female and male crickets determine their behavior. Think of the challenge of programming into a robot all the instructions needed to carry out its every task. Yet a cell, nature's tiny robot, contains all the instructions that it requires packed away in its chromosomes. At the end of this chapter, you will learn a little about how genes function and how their workings can go awry, sometimes with devastating consequences for behavior. Many of the neurological disorders described in this book are caused by errors that occur as genetic information is passed from parent to child, which is why we explore the process of genetic transmission in this chapter.

## THE CELLS OF THE NERVOUS SYSTEM

Link to articles about robotics at the Web site at **www.worthpublishers.com/kolb/chapter3.**

If Barbara Webb's little robot mysteriously arrived in a box on your doorstep, you might examine its structure carefully to guess what it is designed to do. The robot's wheels imply that it is meant to move, and the gears next to the wheels suggest that it can vary its speed or perhaps change directions by varying the speed of one wheel relative to the other. The robot's many exposed wires show that it is not intended to go into water. And, because this robot has no lights or cameras, you can infer that it is not meant to see. The structure of the robot suggests its function. So it is with cells.

But there is a problem in examining the cells of the nervous system for insights into their function. Nervous system cells are very small, are packed tightly together, and have the consistency of jelly. To see a brain cell, you must first isolate it from surrounding cells, stain it to make it visible, and then magnify it by using a microscope. Anatomists have developed ways of removing most of the water from the brain by soaking it in formaldehyde, after which the brain can be cut into thin slices to be stained with various dyes that either color its cells completely or color some of the cells' components. Now the cells can be placed under a microscope for viewing.

Visit the CD to learn about different ways to look at the brain. In the module on Research Methods, you'll find a section on histology which includes samples of six common stains for brain sections.

There is still, however, the problem of making sense of what you see. Different brain samples can yield different images, and different people can interpret those images in different ways. So began a controversy over how the brain is structured between two great scientists of the late nineteenth and early twentieth centuries. One was the Italian Camillo Golgi and the other the Spaniard Santiago Ramón y Cajal. Both men were awarded the Nobel Prize for medicine in 1906.

Imagine that you are Camillo Golgi hard at work in your laboratory staining and examining cells of the nervous system. You immerse a thin slice of brain tissue in a solution containing silver nitrate and other chemicals, a technique used at the time to produce black-and-white photographic prints, producing a microscopic image that looks something like the one in Figure 3-2. The image is beautiful and intriguing, but what do you make of it? To Golgi, this structure suggested that the nervous system is composed of a network of interconnected fibers. He thought that information, like water running through pipes, somehow flowed around this nerve net and produced behavior. His theory was not implausible, given what he saw.

**Figure 3-2**

These human pyramidal cells are stained by using the Golgi technique.

Biophoto Associates / Science Source / Photo Researchers

But Santiago Ramón y Cajal came to a different conclusion. He studied the brain tissue of chick embryos because he assumed that their nervous systems would be simpler and easier to understand. Figure 3-3 shows one of the images that he obtained from an embryo. Cajal concluded that the nervous system is made up of discrete cells that begin life with a rather simple structure, which becomes more complex with age. In adulthood, these cells consist of a main body with extensions projecting from it. The structure looks something like a radish, with branches coming out of the top and roots coming out of the bottom.

Cajal's belief that these complexly shaped cells are the functional units of the nervous system is now universally accepted. Today, we refer to these nervous system cells as *neurons,* a name that comes from the Greek word for "nerve." The idea proposed by Cajal, that neurons are the units of brain function, is called the **neuron hypothesis.**

Figure 3-3 shows the three basic parts of a neuron. The neuron's core region is called the **cell body.** Most of a neuron's branching extensions are called **dendrites** (Latin for "branch"), but the main "root" is called the **axon** (Greek for "axle"). A neuron has only one axon, but most neurons have many dendrites. Some small neurons have so many dendrites that they look like a garden hedge.

**Figure 3-3**

A neuron consists of three parts: dendrites, cell body, and axon. The dendrites gather information from other neurons, the cell body integrates the information, and the axon sends the information to other neurons. Note that, although there is only one axon, it may have branches called collaterals.

Adapted from *Histologie du système nerveux de l'homme et des vertebres,* by S. Ramón y Cajal, 1909–1911, Paris: Maloine.

As stated earlier, the nervous system is composed not only of neurons, but also of cells called glia (the name comes from the Greek word for "glue"). The neurons are the functional units that enable us to receive information, process it, and produce actions. The glia help the neurons out, tying them together (some *do* act as glue) and providing support. In the human nervous system, there are about 100 billion neurons and perhaps 10 times as many glial cells. No, no one has counted them all. Scientists have estimated the total number by counting the cells in a small sample of brain tissue and then multiplying by the brain's volume (Figure 3-4).

Explaining how 100 billion cells cooperate, make connections, and produce behavior is not an easy matter. But, fortunately, the examination of how one cell works can be a source of insight that can be generalized to other cells. Brain cells really are like robots built to a common plan, depending on their particular type. In this section, you will learn to recognize some of the different types of neurons and glial cells in your body. You will also see how their specialized structures contribute to their functions.

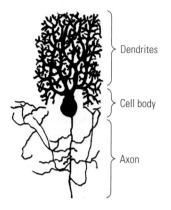

Click on the Web site to read more about the history of the neuron hypothesis at **www.worthpublishers.com/kolb/chapter3.**

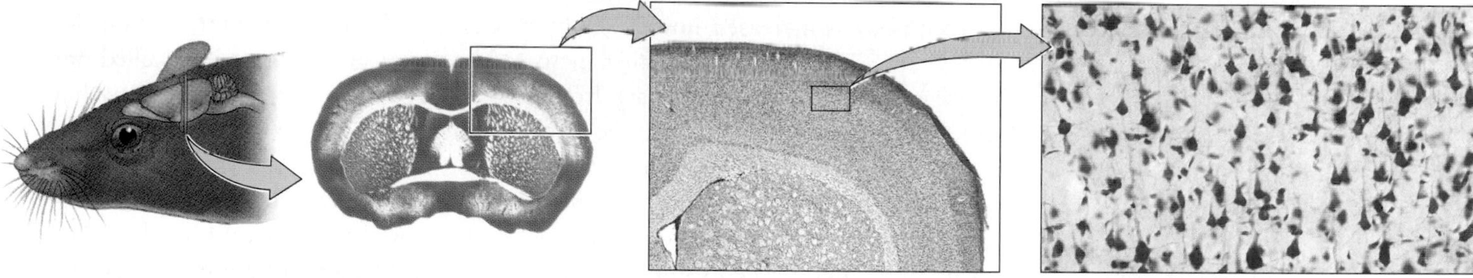

**Figure 3-4**

How are cells counted? We first obtain a thin slice of brain tissue from a rat. Then we select a region of the cortex for cell counting. By counting the number of cells in this part of the tissue and multiplying that number by the volume of the cortex, we can estimate the number of cells in the cortex. The cells in this example are stained with Cresyl violet, which adheres to protein molecules in the cell body and gives the cell body a blue color.

## Neurons

As the information-processing units of the brain, neurons must do many things. They must acquire information from sensory receptors, pass that information on to other neurons, and make muscles move to produce behaviors. They must also hold the instructions for how we behave—that is, they must encode memories—and they have to produce our thoughts and emotions as well. At the same time, they must regulate all the many body processes to which we seldom give a thought, such as breathing, heartbeat, body temperature, and the sleep–wake cycle. This is a tall order but apparently easily accomplished by things as small as neurons.

Some scientists think that a specific function is sometimes assigned to a single neuron. For example, Fernando Nottebohm and his colleagues (1994) studied how birds produce songs and believe that a single neuron may be responsible for each note sung. Most scientists, however, think that neurons work together in groups of many hundreds to many thousands to produce some aspect of behavior. According to this view, the loss of a neuron or two would be no more noticeable than the loss of one or

**Neuron hypothesis.** The idea that the neuron is the basic unit of behavior.

two voices from a cheering crowd of people. It is the crowd that produces the overall action, not each individual person. In much the same way, although we say that neurons are the information-processing units of the brain, we really mean that large teams of neurons serve this function.

Visit the Web site to watch a movie on a neuron in action at **www.worthpublishers.com/kolb/chapter3**.

It is also somewhat inaccurate to speak of *the* structure of a particular neuron, as if that structure never changed. If fresh brain tissue were kept alive in a dish of salty water and viewed occasionally through a microscope, the neurons would reveal themselves to be surprisingly active in both producing new dendrite branches and losing old ones. In fact, if you could watch neurons over a long period of time—say, years—they would appear, like living plants, to be continuously growing and shrinking and changing their shape. The neurons in our brains are similarly changing from day to day and from year to year. For some neurons, these physical changes result from coding and storing our experiences and memories. Neural changes of all kinds are possible because of a special property that neurons possess. Even in a mature, fully grown neuron, the cell's genetic blueprints can be "reopened," allowing the neuron to alter its structure, produce new chemicals, or modify its activities in other ways.

Another important property of neurons is their longevity. Most neurons in our bodies are never replaced; rather, they survive with us throughout our lives. This survival is fortunate because neurons have much less ability than other cells to replace themselves when seriously injured. For example, if the brain or spinal cord is damaged, most lost neurons are not replaced. For most of the twentieth century, the idea that the human brain cannot gain new neurons after birth was dogma. Recently, a lot of exceptions to this dogma have been reported. It is now correct to say that most of your neurons are with you for life and, if you lose some through injury, it is not yet possible to replace them all.

## BASIC NEURON STRUCTURE AND FUNCTION

Figure 3-5 displays the external features of neurons in more detail. The surface area of the cell body is increased immensely by extensions of the cell membrane into dendrites. The dendritic area is further increased by many small protrusions called **dendritic spines.** A neuron may have from 1 to 20 dendrites, each of which may have from one to many branches, and the spines on the branches may number in the many thousands. Because dendrites collect information from other cells, their surface area indicates how much information the neuron can gather. Each neuron also has a single axon. It begins at an expansion of the cell body known as the **axon hillock** (hillock means "little hill"). The axon may have branches called **axon collaterals,** which usually emerge from it at right angles. Toward its end, the axon may divide into a number of smaller branches called **teleodendria** (end branches). At the end of each teleodendrion is a knob called an **end foot** or **terminal button.** The end foot is very close to a dendritic spine of another neuron, although it does not touch it (see Figure 3-5C). This "almost connection," which includes the surfaces of the end foot and the neighboring dendritic spine as well as the space between them, is called a **synapse.**

Plug in the CD to see more about synapses in the module on Neural Communication in the section on the structure of a neuron.

Chapter 4 describes how a neuron works in some detail, but here we will simply draw some generalizations about its function by examining its shape. A neuron has a cell wall within which are enclosed its contents. The dendrites and axon are fluid-filled extensions of the cell body. Imagine looking at a river system from an airplane. You see many small streams merging to make creeks, which join to form tributaries, which join to form the main river channel. As the river reaches its delta, it breaks up into a number of smaller channels again before discharging its contents into the sea. The shape of a neuron is somewhat similar to such a river system, and the neuron works in a broadly similar way. It collects information from many different sources on its dendrites, channels that information onto its axon, and then sends the information

Turn on the CD to view an animation of neural integration in the module on Neural Communication.

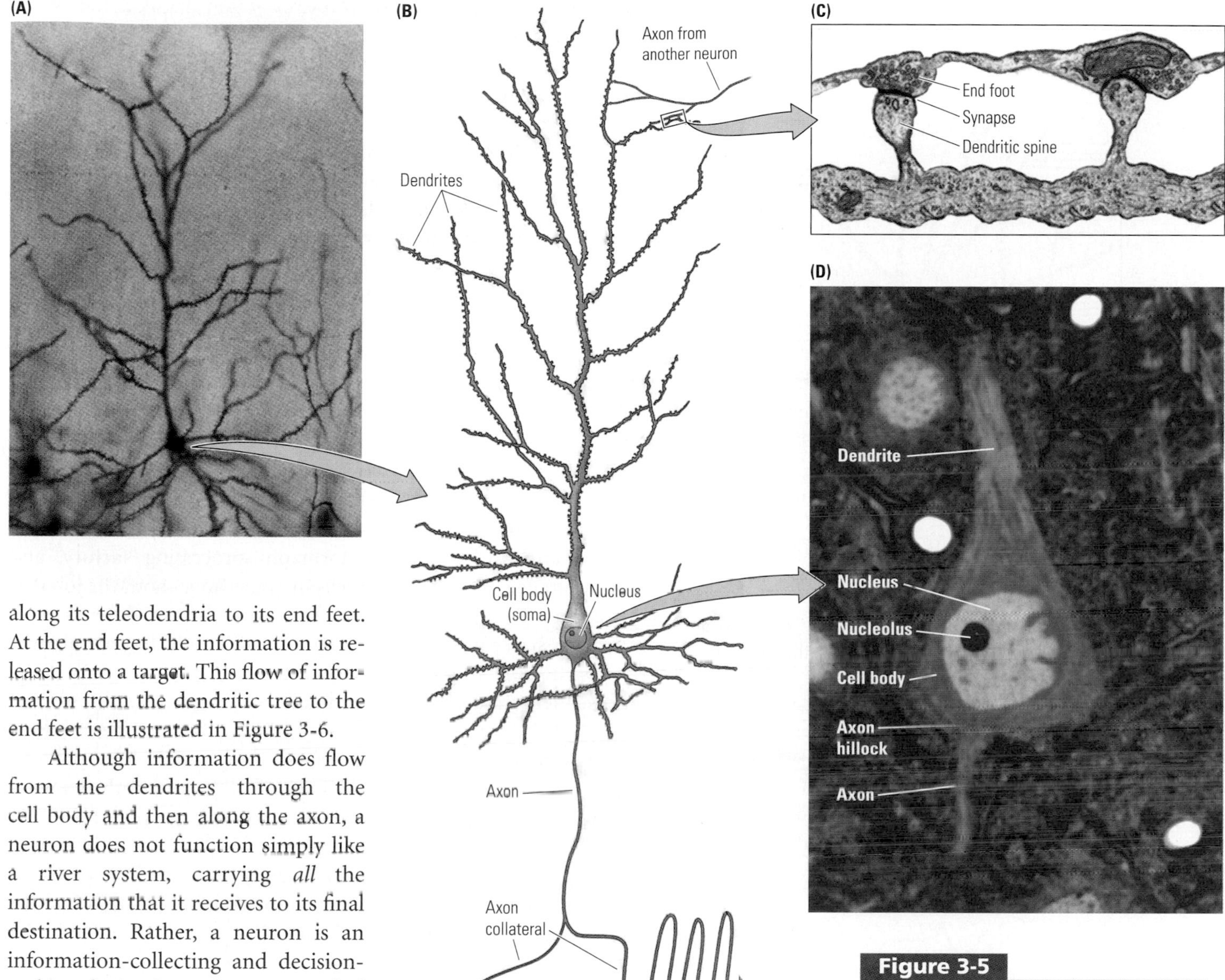


along its teleodendria to its end feet. At the end feet, the information is released onto a target. This flow of information from the dendritic tree to the end feet is illustrated in Figure 3-6.

Although information does flow from the dendrites through the cell body and then along the axon, a neuron does not function simply like a river system, carrying *all* the information that it receives to its final destination. Rather, a neuron is an information-collecting and decision-making device. It receives a great deal of information on its hundreds to thousands of dendritic spines, but it has only one axon, so the message that it sends must be an averaged, or summary, response to all the incoming information. Because it produces a summary response, a neuron is also a computational device. It is like an instructor who listens to comments from all of the students in her class about a recently administered examination and then decides to make the next examination a little different. It is also like a river system blocked by dams that can be opened to allow more water flow at some times and less at others. Chapter 4 will describe in detail how these decision-making processes take place.

**Figure 3-5** The major parts of a neuron. **(A)** A typical neuron that is stained by using the Golgi technique, showing some of its major physical features, including the dendrites and cell body. **(B)** A drawing of the neuron illustrating the location of some of its dendrites, the cell body, and the axon. **(C)** An electron micrographic image of the contacts between an axon from another neuron and a dendrite, illustrating the synapse formed by the opposition of the end foot of the axon and the dendritic spine of the dendrite. **(D)** A high-power light-microscopic view of the cell body, illustrating the nucleus and the nucleolus. Note that the different stains highlight different aspects of the neuron.

## TYPES OF NEURONS

The nervous system contains an array of neurons of different shapes and sizes, some of which appear quite simple and others very complex. With a little practice in looking into a microscope, you can quickly learn to recognize some neuron types by their

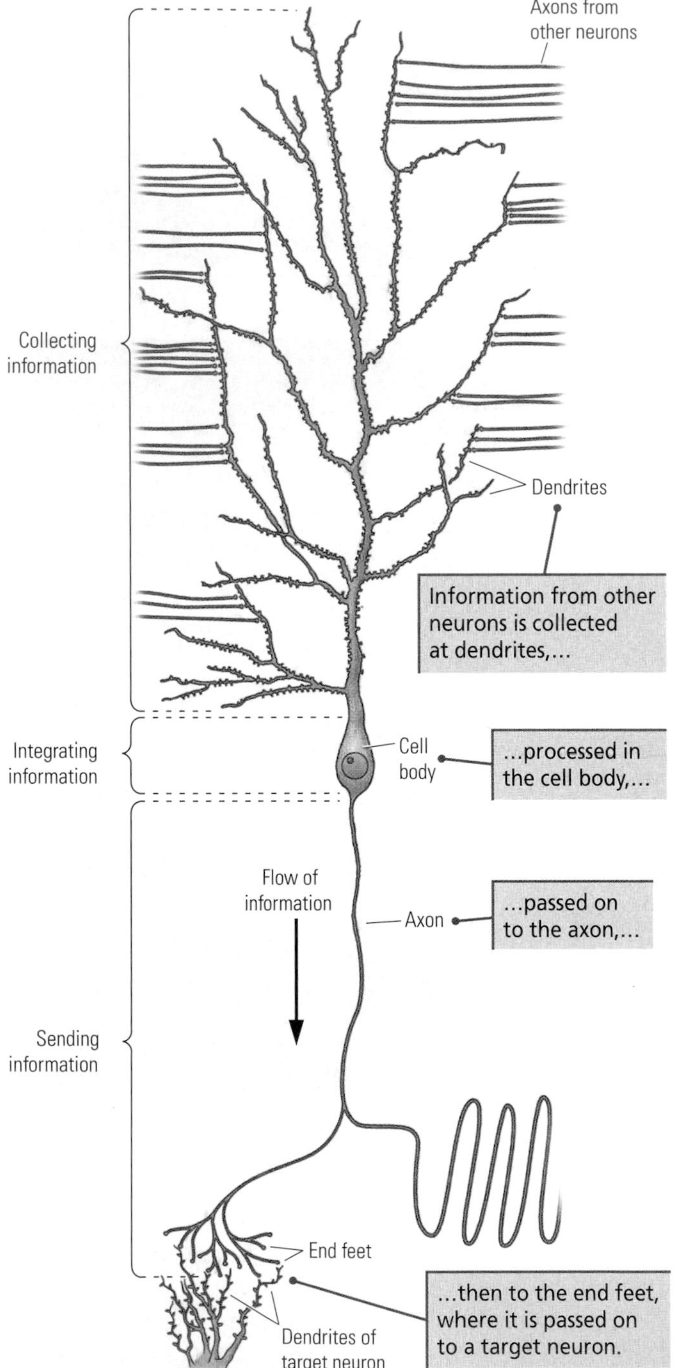
Axons from other neurons
Collecting information
Dendrites
Information from other neurons is collected at dendrites,...
Integrating information
Cell body
...processed in the cell body,...
Flow of information
Axon
...passed on to the axon,...
Sending information
End feet
Dendrites of target neuron
...then to the end feet, where it is passed on to a target neuron.

**Figure 3-6**

In this schematic representation of information flow in a neuron, information from other neurons is collected on dendrites, processed at the cell body, and then sent through the axon to the dendrites of other neurons.

features. Figure 3-7 shows the relative sizes and shapes of some representative kinds of neurons. The simplest is called a **bipolar neuron.** It has a single short dendrite on one side of its cell body and a single short axon on the other side. A more complicated neuron is a **sensory neuron.** It has its dendrite connected directly to its axon, so its cell body sits to one side of this long pathway. **Interneurons** include association cells, pyramidal cells, and Purkinje cells. An association cell, also called a **stellate cell** (meaning a cell that is star shaped), is characteristically small, with many dendrites extending from the cell body. Its axon is difficult to see among the maze of dendrites. A **pyramidal cell** has a long axon, a pyramidal-shaped cell body, and two sets of dendrites, one of which projects from the apex of the cell body and the other from the cell body's side. A **Purkinje cell** (named for its discoverer) is a distinctive kind of pyramidal cell with extremely branched dendrites that form a fan shape. Finally, a **motor neuron** has an extensive network of dendrites, a large cell body, and a long axon that goes to a muscle.

You may wonder if there is any sense to all the many different kinds of neurons that are packed into the nervous system. There is. Neurons are "workers" in an information-processing "factory," and the appearance of each neuron tells us something about the job that it must do. For instance, one of the most obvious differences in neurons is size, particularly the size of the cell body. In general, neurons with large cell bodies have extensions that are very long, whereas neurons with small cell bodies have short extensions. The long extensions carry information to distant parts of the nervous system, whereas the short extensions are engaged in local processing. The size of the cell body therefore is in accord with the work that it must do in providing nutrients and other supplies for its axons and dendrites.

Neurons are also structured differently because of their specialized tasks. Some neurons are designed to bring information into the brain from sensory receptors, others to process it within the brain, and still others to carry it out of the brain to the body's various muscles. On the basis of these three major functions, neurons are categorized into three major groups: *sensory neurons, interneurons* (also called association cells because they associate sensory and motor activity), and *motor neurons.* A major difference between animals with small brains and animals with large brains is that large-brained animals have more interneurons.

By looking at different kinds of neurons with these three major functions in mind, you can see how they are structured to perform their various roles. Sensory neurons are designed to be efficient relay cells. A bipolar cell, for example, is a type of sensory neuron. Bipolar cells are found in the eye's light-receptor region, called the retina. The dendrites of bipolar cells collect information from the retina's photoreceptors and pass it along their axons to other neurons that carry it to the brain. The very simple structure of a bipolar cell is all that is needed to serve the relay function in this location. In other parts of the nervous system, other sensory neurons have much longer dendrites and axons. For instance, a sensory neuron carrying information from the body surface has its single long dendrite connected to a similarly long axon. This long, joined fiber efficiently serves as an information "highway" across large distances. For example, the tips of the dendrites of some sensory neurons are located in your big toe, whereas the target of their axons is at the base of your brain. These sensory neurons send information over a distance as large as 2 meters.

Interneurons, a group that comprises all the neurons between sensory and motor neurons, have a wide range of structures that conform to their functions. For example, the interneurons called stellate cells receive incoming sensory information in a number of brain structures. Their bushy dendrites suggest that they collect information from many sources, which they must pass on to nearby neurons, because the axon on a stellate cell is not very long (the axon seems "lost" among the dendrites). Pyramidal cells are the most distinctive of the interneurons found in the neocortex. From the neocortex, they send information to other nervous system structures. For example, some of your neocortex's pyramidal cells have axons that descend to your spinal cord, a distance as large as a meter, depending on your height. Purkinje cells are the most distinctive interneurons found in the brain's cerebellum. The Purkinje cell's bushy dendrites suggest that it collects information from a wide variety of other neurons, and its large cell body indicates that it sends the information to a distant target. Purkinje cells are, in fact, the output neurons for the cerebellum.

The basic function of motor neurons can be seen in their structure, too. As the nervous system's final pathway to enabling movement, motor neurons have cell bodies that are located in the spinal cord. Their long axons extend to muscles, which they stimulate to contract. The bushy dendritic trees of motor neurons collect information from many other cells.

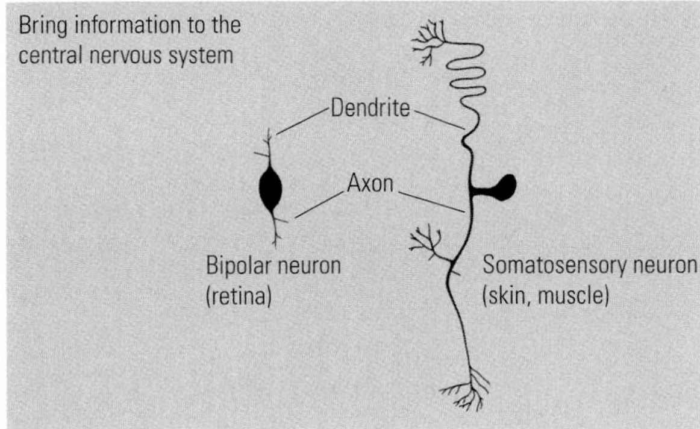


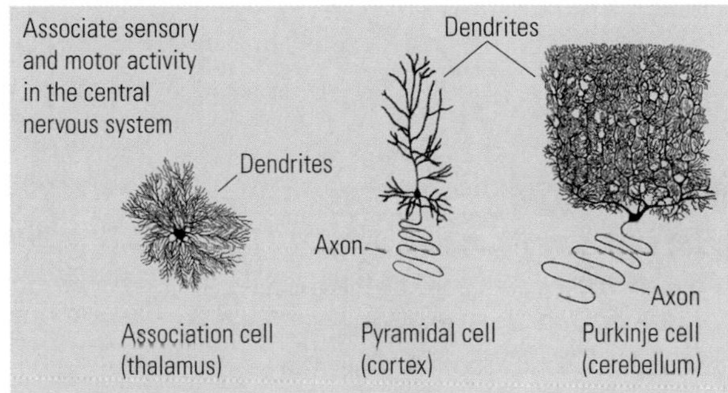


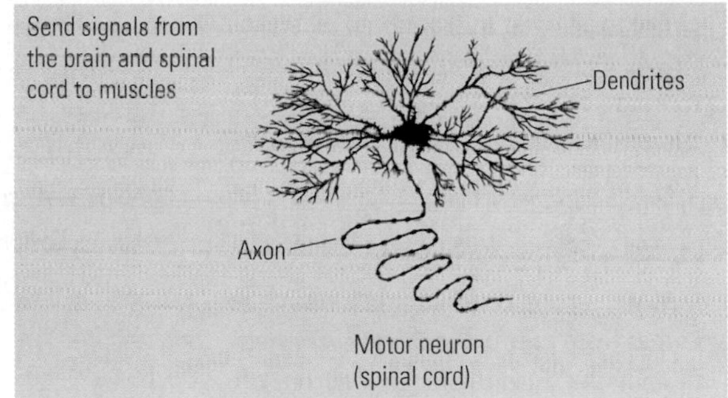


**Figure 3-7**

Examples of some nervous system cells (not to scale): **(A)** sensory neurons, **(B)** interneurons, and **(C)** motor neurons. Note that the appearance of the different kinds of neurons is distinctive; the appearance of each kind of neuron is due to its function. A sensory neuron collects information from a source and passes it on to an interneuron. The many branches of interneurons suggest that they collect information from many sources. Motor neurons are distinctively large and collect information from many sources; they pass this information on to command muscles to move.

## COMMUNICATING ACROSS SYNAPSES

Subsequent chapters will present a detailed account of how neurons communicate, but a brief summary of communication between neurons will be useful here. Neurons must communicate with each other to pass along information, but, as you know, a tiny gap separates an axon's end foot from another neuron's dendritic spine. Until the 1950s, scientists were not aware that these gaps existed. They thought that end feet and dendritic spines were directly connected. Two discoveries changed this view. First, when synapses were examined with an electron microscope, it was clear that end feet come close to, but do not contact, dendritic spines. Second, neurons were also found to contain chemicals in their end feet, which suggested that they use chemical messages to communicate.

The large number of dendritic spines on neurons suggests that each neuron has many synaptic connections with other neurons. The number of connections may be from hundreds to a hundred thousand, depending on the particular neuron. And this transfer of information is not just one-way communication. Most neurons send axon collaterals back to the neurons from which they receive signals. A close look at the neuron in Figure 3-3 on page 79 reveals many axon collaterals coming off the main axon. These collaterals target the cells from which the neuron receives connections. The process of sending information back to a source is called *feedback,* and feedback allows a neuron to say, "Yes, I got the message," or perhaps, "Say that again."

Most connections made between neurons are with immediate neighbors. The information processing takes place in a local area. Within this area, some cells also send or receive information to or from more distant locations. The majority of cells, however, communicate locally. Chapter 5 deals with communication between neurons in greater detail.

## THE LANGUAGE OF NEURONS: EXCITATION AND INHIBITION

Neurons are in constant communication with each other, but what is the nature of the messages they send? The biochemical explanation will be presented in Chapter 4. Here, an introduction to the basic language of neurons will suffice. Neurons either *excite* other neurons (turn them on) or *inhibit* other neurons (turn them off). In other words, neurons send "yes" or "no" signals to each other; the "yes" signals are the excitatory signals, and the "no" signals are the inhibitory signals. Each neuron receives thousands of these excitatory and inhibitory signals every second.

What does a neuron do with the thousands of "yes" or "no" signals that it receives? Its response to all those inputs is democratic. It *sums* the inputs. A neuron is spurred into action only if its excitatory inputs exceed its inhibitory inputs. If the reverse is true and inhibitory inputs exceed excitatory inputs, the neuron does not act.

We can apply this simple principle of neuron action to the workings of a robot, such as the little cricket robot described at the beginning of this chapter. Suppose we could insert a neuron between the microphone for sound detection on each side of this robot and the motor on the *opposite* side. Figure 3-8A shows how the two neurons would be connected. It would take only two rules to make the robot seek out a chirping male cricket. Rule 1 is that, each time a microphone detects a male cricket's song, an excitatory message is sent to the opposite wheel's motor, activating it. This rule ensures that the robot turns toward the cricket each time it hears a chirp. Rule 2 ensures that the robot travels in the right direction. It says that the message sent should be proportional to the intensity of the sound. This rule means that, if the chirp is coming from the robot's left side, it will be detected as being louder by the microphone on the left, which will make the right wheel turn a little faster, swinging the robot to the left. The opposite would happen if the sound came from the right. If the sound comes from straight ahead, both microphones will detect it equally, and the robot will move directly forward.

To make the robot act more like a real cricket requires more neurons. Figure 3-8B shows how we could mimic the idea of sensory and motor neurons. The robot now has two sound-detecting sensory neurons receiving input from its microphones. When activated, each of these sensory neurons excites a motor neuron that turns on

**Figure 3-8**

**(A)** Excitatory inputs from the chirping of a male cricket are heard by the cricket robot through its microphones, and the sounds turn the robot's wheels. The robot will orient to the cricket because the microphone that hears the loudest chirp (the closest microphone) will turn its wheel, located on the opposite side, more quickly than the wheel attached to the other microphone can be turned. **(B)** In a slightly more complex cricket robot that will not travel in the light, the sensory neurons from the speaker excite motor neurons, but inhibitory input also comes from photoreceptors that, when illuminated, turn the motor neurons off.

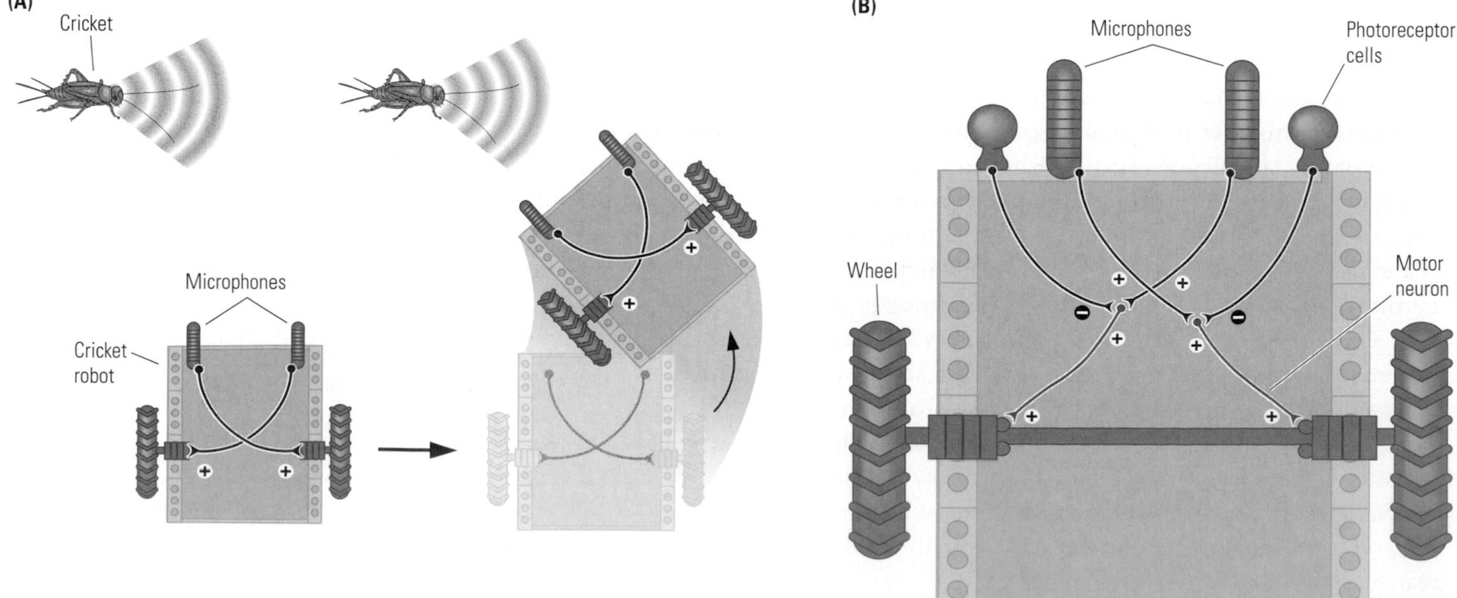

one of the two wheel motors. But there are also sensory neurons coming from photoreceptors that detect light. These light-detecting sensory neurons, when activated, inhibit the motor neurons leading to the wheels and so prevent the robot from moving toward a male until it is dark and "safe." This arrangement might give the robot some interesting properties. For example, at dusk there might be a conflict between excitatory signals from sound and weak inhibitory signals from the dim light. The robot might make small "intention" movements that orient it to the male while not actually searching for it. A researcher might want to examine the behavior of a real female cricket to see if it acts in the same way under these conditions.

If this arrangement sounds relatively complex, bear in mind that it contains only six neurons and each has only one connection with another neuron. We have not even placed interneurons in the robot. Imagine how infinitely more complex a human nervous system is with its hundred billion neurons, most of which are interneurons, each with its thousands of connections. Still, this simple example serves a valuable purpose. It shows the great versatility of function possible from using neurons along with the dual principles of excitation and inhibition. From the simple yes-or-no language of neurons emerges enormous possibilities for behavior.

## Glial Cells

Imagine how much more efficient you could make a small robot if you had components dedicated to supporting your simulated neurons. Some of these components could attach the "neurons" to the appropriate parts of the robot, whereas others could insulate the "neurons" to prevent them from short-circuiting each other. These insulating components might also increase the speed with which messages traveled along the robot's wired pathways. Still other auxiliary components could lubricate moving parts, whereas others could function to eliminate debris, keeping your robot clean and shiny. Do auxiliary components that could do all this sound too good to be true? Not really. All these functions are served by glial cells in your nervous system.

**Glial cells** are often described as the support cells of the nervous system. Although they do not transmit information themselves, they help neurons carry out this task. Unlike neurons, which form only in the first few years of life, glial cells are constantly replacing themselves. (Uncontrolled growth of glial cells can result in brain tumors; see "Brain Tumors" on page 86). Table 3-1 lists the five major classes of glial cells. Each has a characteristic structure and function. We begin by exploring ependymal cells.

### EPENDYMAL CELLS

On the walls of the ventricles, or cavities, inside your brain are **ependymal cells,** one of the glial-cell classes. Ependymal cells produce and secrete the cerebrospinal fluid that fills the ventricles. This fluid, which is constantly being formed, flows through the ventricles toward the base of the brain, where it is absorbed into the blood vessels. Cerebrospinal fluid serves several purposes. It acts as a shock absorber when the brain is jarred; it provides a medium through which waste products are eliminated; it may play a role in brain cooling; and it may be a source of nutrients for certain parts of the brain located adjacent to the ventricles.

**Table 3-1** Types of Glial Cells

| Type | Appearance | Features and function |
|---|---|---|
| Ependymal cell | | Small, ovoid; secretes cerebrospinal fluid (CSF) |
| Astrocyte | | Star-shaped, symmetrical; nutritive and support function |
| Microglial cell | | Small, mesodermally derived; defensive function |
| Oligodendroglial cell | | Asymmetrical; forms myelin around axons in brain and spinal cord |
| Schwann cell | | Asymmetrical; wraps around peripheral nerves to form myelin |

Focus on Disorders

## Brain Tumors

R. J. was a 19-year-old college sophomore. One day while she was watching a movie in a neuropsychology class, she collapsed on the floor and began twitching, displaying symptoms of a brain seizure. The instructor helped her to the university clinic, where she recovered, except for a severe headache. She reported that she had suffered from severe headaches on a number of previous occasions. A computer tomographic (CT) scan of her brain a few days later showed that she had a tumor over her left frontal lobe. She underwent surgery to have the tumor removed and returned to classes after an uneventful recovery. She successfully completed her studies, finished law school, and has been practicing law for more than 15 years without any further symptoms.

A *tumor* is a mass of new tissue that persists and grows independently of surrounding structures. No region of the body is immune to tumors, but the brain is a common site of them. Brain tumors do not grow from neurons; instead, they grow from glia or other supporting cells. The rate of growth depends on the type of cell undergoing uncontrolled growth. Some tumors are benign and not likely to recur after removal (such as R. J.'s tumor), whereas other tumors are malignant, likely to progress, and apt to recur after removal. Both kinds of tumors can pose a risk to life if they develop in sites from which they are difficult to remove.

The first symptoms of a brain tumor are usually due to increased pressure on surrounding brain structures. These symptoms can include headaches, vomiting, mental dullness, and changes in sensory and motor abilities. They can also include seizures like R. J.'s. Many symptoms depend on the precise location of the tumor.

There are three major types of brain tumors based on how they originate. *Gliomas* are tumors that arise from glial cells. They constitute roughly half of all brain tumors. Gliomas that arise from astrocytes are usually slow growing, not very malignant, and relatively easy to treat. In contrast, gliomas that arise from blast or germinal cells (precursor cells that grow into glial cells) are much more malignant, grow more quickly, and often recur after treatment. *Meningiomas* are a second type of brain tumor, the type that R. J. had. They attach to the meninges, or covering of the brain, and so grow entirely outside the brain, as shown in the accompanying photograph. These tumors are usually well encapsulated, and, if they are located in places that are accessible, recovery after surgery is good. A third type of brain tumor is the *metatastic tumor,* which becomes established by a transfer of tumor cells from one region of the body to another (this transfer of disease from one organ to another is what the term *metatastic* means). Typically, metatastic tumors are present in multiple locations, making treatment difficult. Symptoms of the condition often first appear when the tumor cells reach the brain.

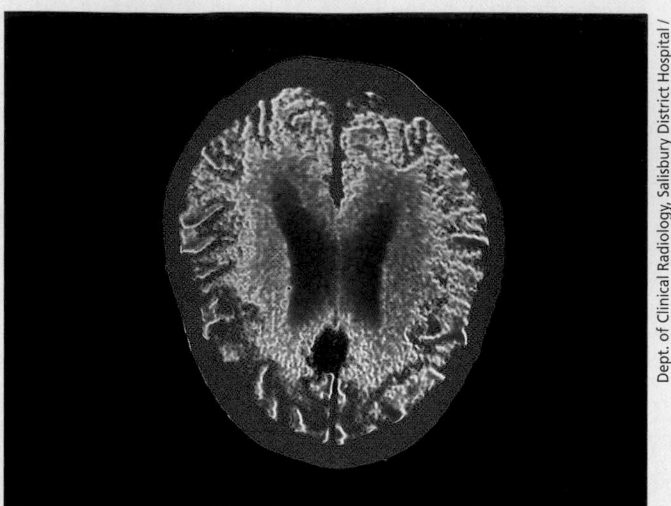

Dept. of Clinical Radiology, Salisbury District Hospital / Science Photo Library / Photo Researchers

The red area in this colored CT scan is a meningioma, a noncancerous tumor arising from the arachnoid membrane covering the brain. A meningioma may grow large enough to compress the brain but usually does not invade brain tissue.

Treatment for a brain tumor is usually surgery, which also is one of the main means of diagnosing the type of tumor. If possible, the entire tumor is removed. Radiotherapy (treatment with X rays) is useful for destroying developing tumor cells. Chemotherapy, although common for treating tumors in other parts of the body, is less successful in the treatment of brain tumors because it is difficult to get the chemicals across the blood–brain barrier.

As cerebrospinal fluid flows through the ventricles, it passes through some narrow passages, especially the fourth ventricle, which runs through the brainstem. If the fourth ventricle is fully or partly blocked, the flow of cerebrospinal fluid is restricted. Because the fluid is continuously being produced, this blockage causes a buildup of pressure that begins to expand the ventricles, which in turn push on the surrounding brain. If such a blockage occurs in a newborn infant, before the skull bones are fused, the pressure on the brain is conveyed to the skull and the baby's head consequently swells. This condition, called **hydrocephalus** (literally, water brain), can cause severe mental retardation and even death. To treat it, doctors insert one end of a tube, called a shunt, into the blocked ventricle and the other end into a vein. The shunt allows the cerebrospinal fluid to drain into the bloodstream.

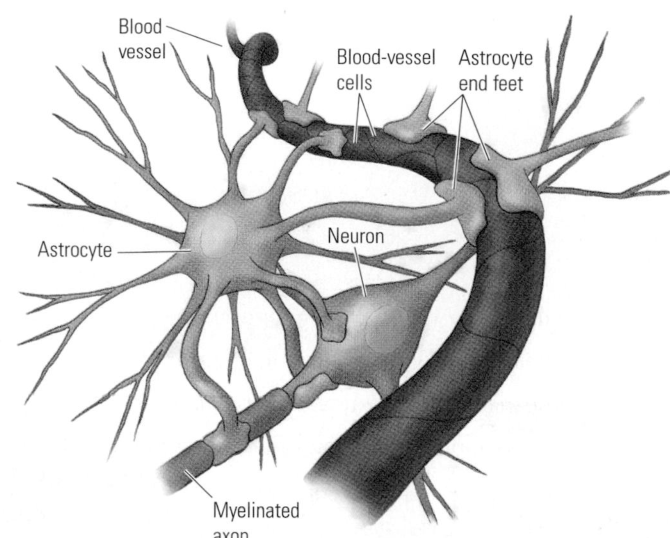


**Figure 3-9**

Astrocytes have processes that can attach both to neurons and to blood vessels. They provide support between different structures in the brain, they stimulate the cells on blood vessels to form tight junctions and so form the blood–brain barrier, and they transport chemicals excreted by neurons to blood vessels.

## ASTROGLIA

**Astrocytes** (star-shaped glia), also called *astroglia,* provide structural support within the central nervous system. Their extensions attach to blood vessels and to the brain's lining, thus creating scaffolding that holds neurons in place. These same extensions provide pathways for the movement of certain nutrients between blood vessels and neurons. Astroglia also secrete chemicals that keep neurons healthy and help them heal if injured. At the same time, astroglia play an important role in forming a protective barrier between blood vessels and the brain, called the **blood–brain barrier.**

As shown in Figure 3-9, the end feet of astrocytes attach to the cells of blood vessels, causing the blood-vessel cells to bind tightly together. This tight binding prevents an array of substances, including many toxic ones, from entering the brain through the blood-vessel walls. The molecules (smallest units) of these substances are too large to pass between the blood-vessel cells unless the blood–brain barrier is somehow injured. But the downside to the blood–brain barrier is that many kinds of useful drugs, including antibacterial drugs such as penicillin, cannot pass through to the brain either. As a result, brain infections are very difficult to treat.

Yet another important function of astroglia is to enable increased brain activity. When you engage a part of your brain for some behavior, the brain cells of that area require more oxygen and glucose. In response, the blood vessels of the area dilate, allowing greater oxygen- and glucose-carrying blood flow. But what triggers the blood vessels to dilate? This is where the astrocytes come in. They convey signals from the neurons to the blood vessels, stimulating them to expand and so provide more oxygen.

Astroglia also contribute to the process of healing damaged brain tissue. If the brain is injured by a blow to the head or by some sharp object, astroglia form a scar to seal off the damaged area. Although the scar tissue is beneficial in healing the injury, it can unfortunately act as a barrier to the regrowth of the damaged neurons. Some experimental approaches to repairing brain tissue seek to get the axons and dendrites of central nervous system neurons to grow around or through a glial scar.

## MICROGLIA

**Microglia** are small glial cells scattered throughout normal brain tissue. Unlike other glial cells, which originate in the brain, microglia originate in the blood and migrate into the brain. Microglia monitor the health of brain tissue. When brain cells are damaged, microglia invade the area to provide growth factors that aid in

**Hydrocephalus.** A condition in which the flow of ventricular fluid is blocked, causing a buildup of pressure in the brain and swelling of the head that can result in retardation.

**Blood–brain barrier.** A barrier formed by tight junctions of capillaries, preventing the passage of most substances from the blood into the brain.

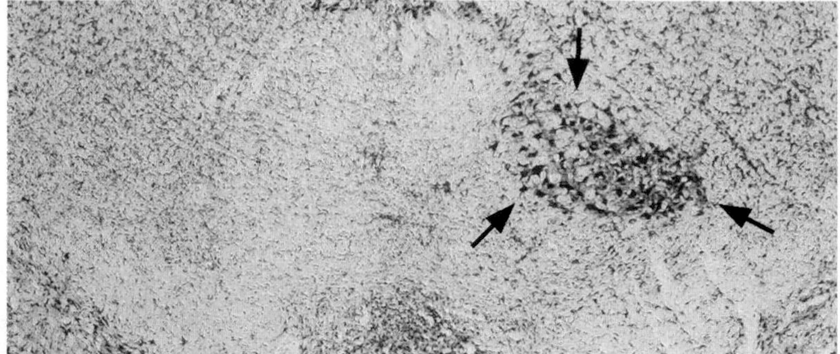

(A) 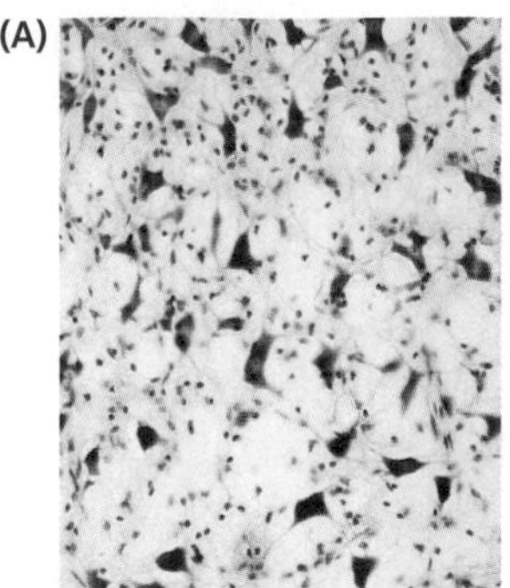

(B) 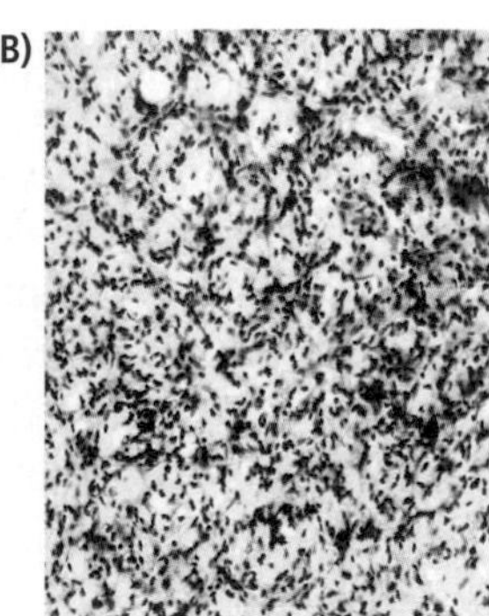

**Figure 3-10**

The arrows in the micrograph at left indicate a brain area called the red nucleus in a rat. **(A)** Cresyl violet–stained neurons in the red nucleus. **(B)** Appearance of the tissue after the cells have been killed with a neurotoxin, leaving only microglia.

repair. If tissue is dead, microglia engulf cell debris to remove it, a process called **phagocytosis.** Damage to the brain can be detected in a postmortem examination because, as illustrated in Figure 3-10, microglia will be left where neurons were once located.

## OLIGODENDROGLIA AND SCHWANN CELLS

Two kinds of glial cells provide **myelin,** or "insulation," to the axons of neurons: oligodendroglia and Schwann cells. Like the rubber insulation on electrical wires, myelin prevents adjacent neurons from short-circuiting each other's activity. The **oligodendroglia,** or glia with few branches (the prefix *oligo* means "few," referring to the fact that these glia have few branches in comparison with astroglia, which have many branches), provide myelin to axons in the brain and spinal cord. Oliogendroglia send out large flat branches that enclose and separate adjacent axons. **Schwann cells** provide myelin to axons in the peripheral nervous system. Each Schwann cell wraps itself repeatedly around a part of an axon, forming a structure somewhat like a bead on a string. Between two oligodendroglia or two Schwann cells is a small exposed segment of the axon called a **node of Ranvier.** Thus, the myelin produces a banded pattern of exposed and insulated axon. In addition to the myelination that Schwann cells and oligodendroglia provide to axons, they contribute to a neuron's nutrition and function. They absorb chemicals that the neuron releases and release chemicals that the neuron absorbs.

The functions of myelin and the nodes of Ranvier will be discussed in detail later. For the present, it is sufficient to know that myelin plays an important role in speeding up the flow of information along a neuron. Neurons that are heavily myelinated are able to send information much faster than neurons having little or no myelin. Most neurons that must send messages over long distances, including sensory and motor neurons, are heavily myelinated. If myelin is damaged, a neuron may be unable to send any messages over its axons. In **multiple sclerosis,** myelin is damaged and the functions of the neurons whose axons it encases are disrupted. "Multiple Sclerosis," on page 89, describes the symptoms of the disease.

## GLIAL CELLS AND NEURON REPAIR

When you receive a deep cut on your body, such as on your arm or leg, the axons connecting your spinal cord to muscles and sensory receptors may be cut as well. Severed motor-neuron axons will render you unable to move the affected part of your body, whereas severed sensory fibers will result in loss of sensation from that body part. When both movement and sensation are gone, the condition is called **paralysis.** Over a period of weeks to months after motor and sensory axons were severed, movement and sensation return. The human body can repair this kind of nerve damage, and so the paralysis is not permanent.

**Myelin.** The glial coating that surrounds axons in the central and peripheral nervous system.

**Paralysis.** The loss of sensation and movement due to nervous system injury.

Focus on Disorders

## Multiple Sclerosis

One day J. O., an accountant, noticed a slight cloudiness in her right eye that did not go away when she wiped the eye. The area of cloudiness grew over the next few days. Her optometrist suggested that she see a neurologist, who diagnosed optic neuritis, a symptom that could be a flag for multiple sclerosis (MS). The eye cleared over the next few months, and J. O. had no further symptoms until after the birth of her first child 3 years later. She felt a tingling in her right hand that spread up her arm, until gradually she lost movement in the arm. Movement was restored 5 months later. Then 2½ years later, after her second child was born, she felt a tingling in her left big toe that spread along the sole of her foot and then up to her leg, eventually leading again to loss of movement. J. O. received corticosteroid treatment, which helped, but the condition rebounded when she stopped treatment. Then it subsided and eventually disappeared.

Since then, J. O. has had no major outbreaks of motor impairment, but she still feels occasional tingling in her trunk, some weakness in her left leg, and brief periods of tingling and numbness in different body parts that last a couple of weeks before clearing. The feeling is very similar to the numbness in the face after a dentist gives a local anesthetic. Although she suffers no depression, J. O. reports enormous fatigue, takes daily long naps, and is ready for bed early in the evening. Her sister and a female cousin have experienced similar symptoms. One of J. O.'s grandmothers was confined to a wheelchair, although the source of her problem was not known. J. O. occasionally wears a brace to support her left knee and sometimes wears a collar to support her neck. She makes every effort to reduce stress to a minimum, but otherwise she lives a normal life that includes exercise and even vigorous sports such as water skiing.

J. O.'s extremely strange symptoms, which are often difficult to diagnose, are typical of multiple sclerosis. The first symptoms usually appear in adulthood, and their onset is quite sudden and swift. These initial symptoms may be loss of sensation in the face, limbs, or body or loss of control over movements or loss of both sensation and control. Motor symptoms usually appear first in the hands or feet. Often there is remission of early symptoms, after which they may not appear again for years. In some of its forms, however, the disease may progress rapidly over a period of just a few years until the person is reduced to bed care. In cases in which the disease is fatal, the average age of death is between 65 and 84.

Although we do not yet understand what causes multiple sclerosis, we do know that it is characterized by a loss of myelin, both on pathways bringing sensory information to the brain and on pathways taking commands to muscles. This loss of myelin occurs in patches, and scarring is frequently left in the affected areas. Computer tomographic scans on both J. O. and her sister revealed scarring in the spinal cord, a condition that helped confirm an MS diagnosis for them. Eventually, a hard plaque may form in the affected areas, which is why the disease is called sclerosis (from the Greek word meaning "hardness"). Associated with the loss of myelin is impairment in neuron function, causing patients to have the symptoms of sensory loss and difficulty in moving. Fatigue, pain, and depression are common related symptoms. Bladder dysfunction, constipation, and sexual dysfunction all complicate the condition. MS greatly affects a person's emotional, social, and vocational functioning. As yet, it has no cure.

Both microglia and Schwann cells play a part in repairing damage to the peripheral nervous system. When a peripheral nervous system axon is cut, the portion still attached to the cell body dies. Microglia remove all the debris left by the dying axon. Meanwhile, the Schwann cells that provided its myelin first shrink and then divide, forming numerous smaller glial cells along the path that the axon formerly took. The neuron then sends out axon sprouts that search for and follow the path made by the Schwann cells. Eventually, one sprout reaches the intended target, and this sprout becomes the new axon, whereas all other sprouts retract. The Schwann cells envelop the new axon, forming new myelin and restoring normal function, as shown in Figure 3-11. In the peripheral nervous system, then, Schwann cells serve as signposts to guide axons to their appropriate end points. Axons can get lost, however, as sometimes happens after surgeons reattach a severed limb. If axons destined to innervate one finger end up innervating another finger instead, the wrong finger will move when a message is sent along that neuron.

Unfortunately, glial cells are not able to help neurons in the central nervous system regrow. When the central nervous system is damaged, as happens, for example, when the spinal cord is cut, function does not return, even though the distance that damaged fibers must bridge is short. That recovery should take place in the peripheral nervous system but not in the central nervous system is both a puzzle and a challenge in attempts to help people with brain and spinal-cord injury. The absence of recovery after spinal-cord injury is especially frustrating, because the spinal cord contains many axon pathways, just like those found in the peripheral nervous system. So why do axons regrow in the peripheral nervous system but not in the spinal cord and brain?

A number of factors appear to be implicated. First, as already stated, astroglia form a scar to seal off a damaged area of the central nervous system, but, in doing so, they create a barrier to regrowing axons. Second, the oligodendroglia of the central nervous system do not appear to divide and provide the same signposts for regrowing axons as do Schwann cells in the peripheral nervous system. In fact, the oligodendroglia that provide the myelin of any remaining neurons may actively repel regrowing axons with an antigrowth agent called NOGO. This repellent is probably useful under normal circumstances because it prevents the random regrowth of axons; however, in injury, it acts as a deterrent to repair.

**(A)**

When a peripheral axon is cut, the portion still attached to the cell body dies.

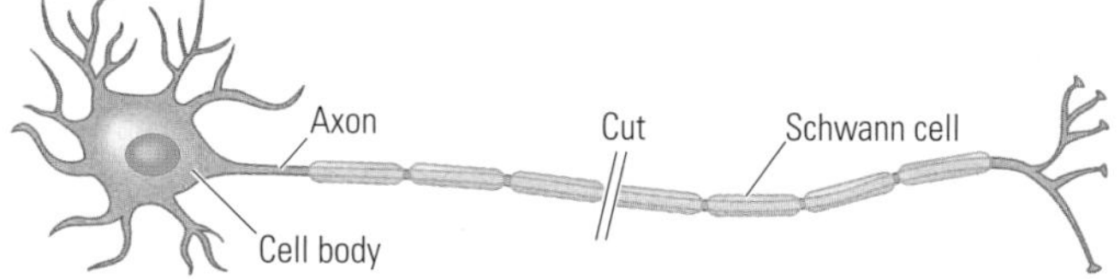


**(B)**

Schwann cells first shrink and then divide, forming glial cells along the axon's former path.

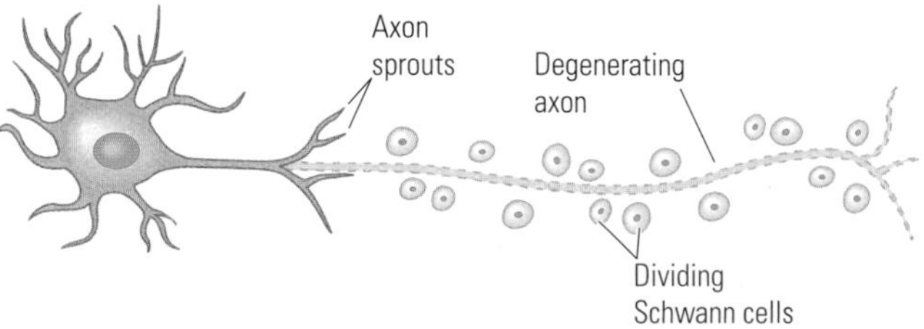


**(C)**

The neuron sends out axon sprouts, one of which finds the Schwann-cell path and becomes a new axon.

**(D)**

Schwann cells envelop it, forming new myelin.

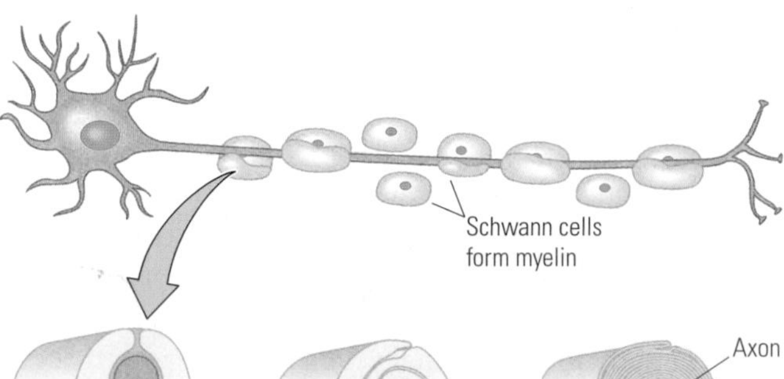


**Figure 3-11**

Schwann cells aid the regrowth of axons in the peripheral nervous system. **(A)** A peripheral nerve, such as that projecting from the spinal cord to a muscle, is wrapped in myelin by Schwann cells. **(B)** After a cut, the axon dies from the cut back to the cell body, and the Schwann cells divide and produce new cells. **(C)** Sprouts form from the cell body and, when one sprout finds the Schwann cells, it follows the path that they make to the original target. **(D)** Schwann cells then wrap around the axon to form new myelin on the axon.

Researchers investigating how to encourage the regrowth of central nervous system neurons have focused on all these factors. For instance, in attempts to circumvent glial barriers, they have placed tubes across an injured area, trying to get axons to regrow through them. They have also inserted immature glial cells into injured areas to facilitate axon regrowth, and they have used chemicals to block NOGO. Some success has been obtained with each of these techniques, but none is as yet sufficiently successful to be used as a treatment for people with spinal-cord injury.

## In Review

There are two types of nervous system cells: neurons and glia. The three types of neurons are sensory neurons, interneurons, and motor neurons. They are the information-conducting units of the nervous system and either excite or inhibit each other through their connecting synapses. The five types of glial cells are ependymal cells, astroglia, microglia, oligodendroglia, and Schwann cells. Their function is to nourish, insulate, support, and repair neurons.

# THE INTERNAL STRUCTURE OF A CELL

What is it about the structure of neurons that gives them their remarkable ability to receive, process, store, and send a seemingly limitless amount of information? To answer this question, we must look inside a neuron to see what its components are. Fortunately, the internal features of a neuron can be colored with stains and examined under a light microscope or, if they are very small, under an electron microscope. Just as we can take apart a robot to see how its pieces work, we can take apart a cell to understand how its pieces function.

Because a cell is so small, it is sometimes hard to imagine that it, too, has components. Yet packed inside a cell is a whole system of interrelated parts that do the cell's work. This feature is as true of neurons as it is of any other cell type. A cell is a miniature "factory" of work centers, which manufacture and transport the proteins that are the cell's products. To a large extent, the characteristics of cells are determined by their proteins. Time and again, when we ask how a cell performs a certain function, the answer lies in the structure of a certain protein.

The smallest unit of a protein, or any other chemical substance, is known as a molecule. Molecules, and the even smaller atoms of which they are made up, are the basic units of a cell factory's inputs and outputs. Our journey into the interior of a cell will therefore begin with a look at these basic components. You may be familiar with basic chemistry; so, if you understand the structure of water and you know what a salt is and what ions are, this section will serve as a brief review.

## Elements and Atoms

Of the earth's 92 natural **elements,** substances that cannot be broken down into other substances, 10 account for most of a cell's composition. These 10 elements are listed in Table 3-2. Three of them—oxygen, carbon, and hydrogen—account for 96 percent of the cell, with the other 7 elements constituting most of the remaining 4 percent. Cells also contain many other elements, but these elements, although important, are present in extremely small quantities.

Scientists represent each element with a symbol, many of which are simply the first one or two letters of the element's English name. Examples are the symbols O for oxygen, C for carbon, and H for hydrogen. Other symbols, however, come from the element's Latin name: K, for instance, is the symbol for potassium, called *kalium* in Latin, and Na is the symbol for sodium, in Latin called *natrium.*

An **atom** is the smallest quantity of an element that retains the properties of that element. An atom has a nucleus that contains **neutrons** and **protons.** The neutrons are neutral in charge, but the protons carry a positive charge (+). Atoms are surrounded by orbiting particles called **electrons,** each of which carries a negative charge (–). The basic structures of a cell's most common atoms are shown in the right-hand column of Table 3-2.

**Table 3-2 Chemical Composition of the Brain**

| Name of element | Symbol | % weight | Nucleus and electrons |
|---|---|---|---|
| Hydrogen | H | 9.5 |  |
| Carbon | C | 18.5 | 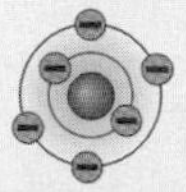 |
| Oxygen | O | 65 | 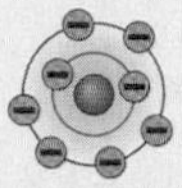 |
| Nitrogen | N | 3.5 | 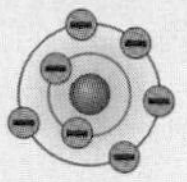 |
| Calcium | Ca | 1.5 | 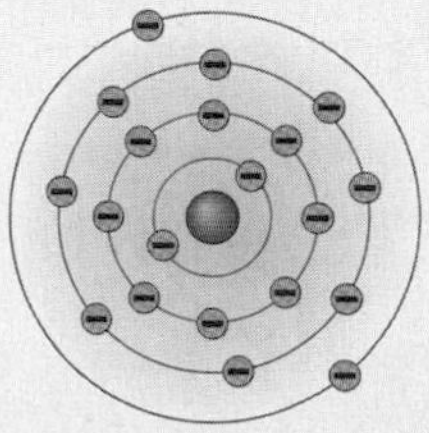 |
| Phosphorus | P | 1.0 | 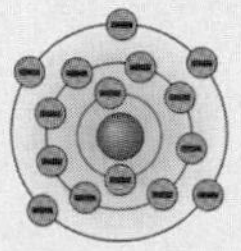 |
| Potassium | K | 0.4 | 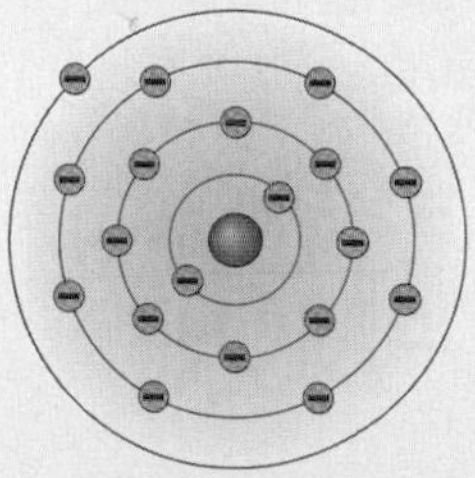 |
| Sulfur | S | 0.2 | 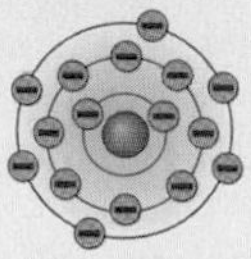 |
| Sodium | Na | 0.2 | 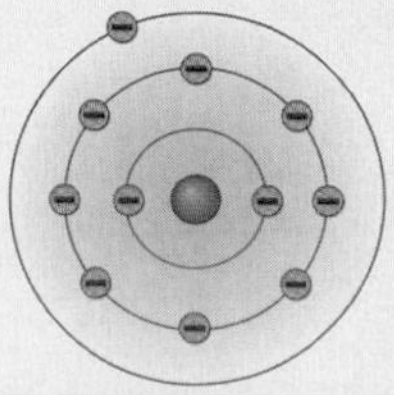 |
| Chlorine | Cl | 0.2 | 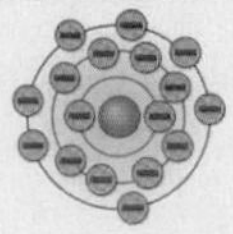 |

Ordinarily an atom has an equal number of positive and negative charges, but elements that are chemically reactive can lose or gain one or more electrons. When an atom gives up an electron, it becomes positively charged; when it takes on an electron, it becomes negatively charged. In either case, it is now called an **ion.** An ion that is formed by losing one electron is represented by the element's symbol and a plus sign. For example, $K^+$ represents a potassium ion, and $Na^+$ represents a sodium ion. An ion formed by losing two electrons is represented by the element's symbol followed by two positive charges ($Ca^{2+}$ for a calcium ion). Some of the other ions that are important for cell function have gained electrons rather than lost them. Such an ion is represented by the element's symbol followed by a negative sign (for example, $Cl^-$ representing an ion of chlorine, called a chloride ion).

## Molecules

When atoms become bound together, they form a molecule of a substance. A **molecule** is the smallest unit of a substance that contains all that substance's properties. For example, a water molecule is the smallest unit of water that still retains the properties of water. Breaking down water any further would divide it into its two component gases—hydrogen and oxygen.

A substance can be represented by atomic symbols that specify the substance's formula. For example, $H_2O$, the formula for water, indicates that a water molecule is a union of two hydrogen atoms and one oxygen atom. Similarly, NaCl, the formula for table salt, shows that this substance consists of one sodium atom and one chlorine atom, whereas KCl, the formula for potassium chloride, another kind of salt, says that this substance is composed of one potassium atom and one chlorine atom.

Atoms join together in different ways to form different kinds of substances. Salts are substances that break into their constituent ions in water. When salts such as NaCl and KCl are formed, the sodium or potassium atom gives up an electron to the chlorine atom. Therefore these salts are actually composed of negatively and positively charged ions tightly held together by their electrical attraction. In contrast, the atoms that constitute a water molecule are held together by *shared* electrons.

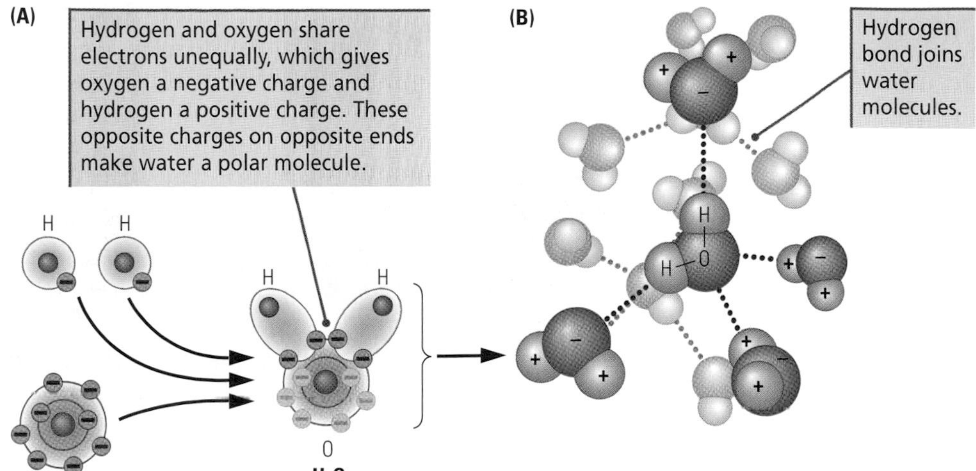

(A)
Hydrogen and oxygen share electrons unequally, which gives oxygen a negative charge and hydrogen a positive charge. These opposite charges on opposite ends make water a polar molecule.
H
H
H
H
O
O
$H_2O$
(B)
Hydrogen bond joins water molecules.


## Figure 3-12

**(A)** In bonding to oxygen (O), two hydrogen atoms (H) share electrons with one oxygen atom. The resulting molecule is polar. Each hydrogen carries a positive charge (+) because it shares an electron with oxygen. Oxygen is negatively charged, having gained a share of the electrons. **(B)** The charged regions of a polar water molecule are attracted to oppositely charged parts of neighboring molecules. Each water molecule can hydrogen-bond to a maximum of four partners.

As you can see in Figure 3-12, the electrons provided by the H atoms spend some of their time orbiting the O atom. In this particular case, the electron sharing is not equal. The shared electrons spend more time orbiting the O than they do the H. This gives the oxygen region of the molecule a slight negative charge and leaves the hydrogen regions with a slight positive charge. Water, therefore, is a **polar molecule,** meaning that it has opposite charges on opposite ends (just as the earth does at the North and South Poles).

Because water molecules are polar, they are electrically attracted to each other. A slightly positively charged hydrogen of one molecule is attracted to the slightly negatively charged oxygen of a nearby molecule. This attracting force is called a **hydrogen bond.** Each water molecule can form hydrogen bonds with a maximum of four neighbors. Hydrogen bonding gives water some interesting properties, such as high surface tension (small insects can walk across water), strong cohesion (water runs down window panes in relatively large droplets), and a high boiling point (the temperature at which water's hydrogen bonds are finally broken). The attraction of water molecules for each other is also described by the term **hydrophilic,** or water loving (from Greek *hydro,* meaning "water," and *philic,* meaning "love"). Other polar molecules also are hydrophilic—that is, they, too, are attracted to water molecules.

Salts are a completely different matter. As noted earlier, salts are compounds that come apart in water. An example is sodium chloride, or table salt. As already stated, NaCl is formed when sodium atoms give up electrons to chlorine atoms and the resulting positively and negatively charged ions ($Na^+$ and $Cl^-$) join together to form a crystal because of their electrical attraction. Salt cannot retain its crystal shape

The nucleus contains neutrons and protons.

Outer orbit contains 7 electrons

Chlorine atom (Cl)

The outer orbit gains an electron.

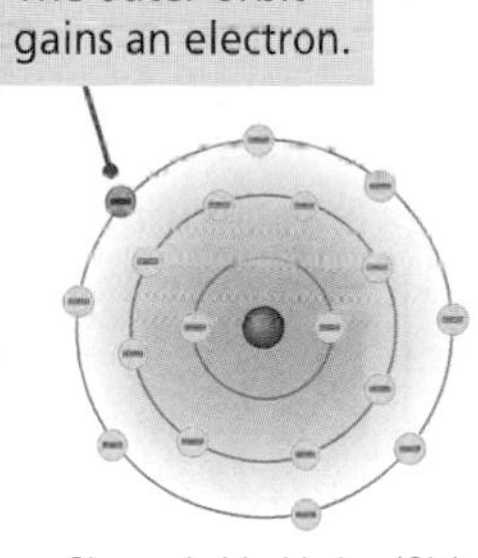

Charged chloride ion ($Cl^-$)

Outer orbit contains 1 electron

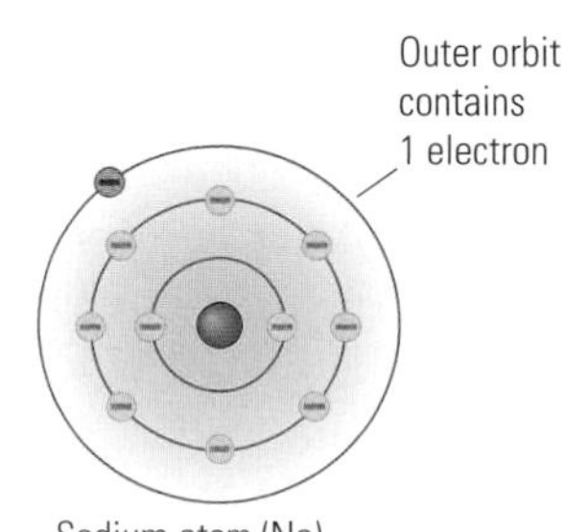

Sodium atom (Na)

The outer orbit disappears because it lost its only electron.

Charged sodium ion ($Na^+$)

**Hydrophilic.** Refers to a substance that binds weakly to polar water molecules.

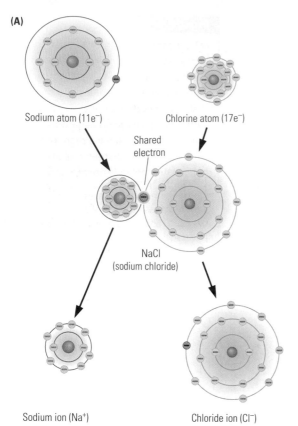

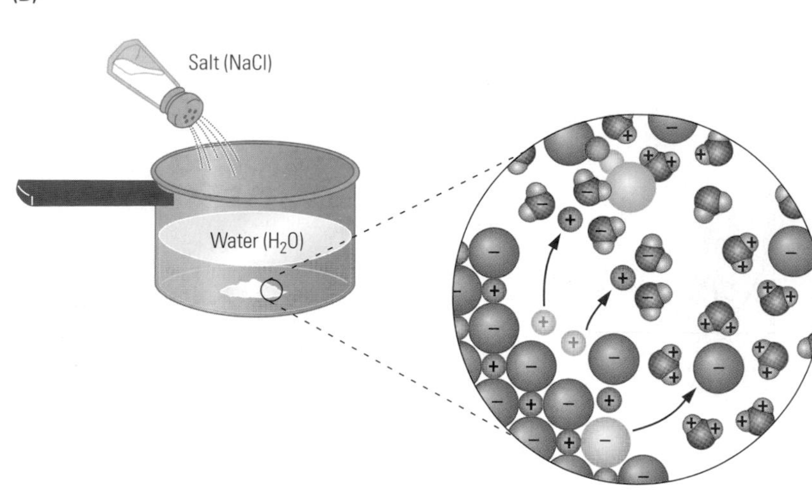


in water, however. As shown in Figure 3-13, the polar water molecules muscle their way between the $Na^+$ and $Cl^-$ ions, surrounding and separating them. We refer to this process as **dissolving,** and the result is salty water. Sodium chloride is one of the dissolved salts found in the fluid that exists inside and outside of cells. Many other salts, such as KCl (potassium chloride) and $CaCl_2$ (calcium chloride) are found there, too.

Water, salts, and ions play a prominent part in the cell's functions, and we will come across these substances again throughout the next few chapters.

**Figure 3-13**

**(A)** Table salt is formed by the joining of sodium and chlorine, which share an electron. If they are separated, the sodium ion is short one electron and so carries a positive charge ($Na^+$), whereas the chloride gains an electron and so has a negative charge ($Cl^-$). **(B)** Because water molecules are weakly bonded, they can surround $Na^+$ ions and $Cl^-$ ions, thus dissolving the salt. The positive part of the water molecule is attracted to the negative $Cl^-$ ion, and the negative part of the water molecule is attracted to the positive $Na^+$ ion.

**Cell membrane.** Two layers of phospholipid molecules that surround the cell, separating its contents from the extracellular fluid; membranes that surround components inside the cell also are bilayer.

## The Parts of a Cell

Earlier, we compared a cell to a miniature factory, with work centers that cooperate to make and ship the cell's products, proteins. We can now carry this analogy even further as we start to investigate the internal parts of a cell and how they function. Figure 3-14 illustrates many of the parts of a cell. Just as a factory has an outer wall that separates it from the rest of the world and gives it some security from unwanted intruders, a cell has an outer **cell membrane** that separates it from its surroundings and allows it to regulate what enters and leaves its domain. The cell membrane surrounds the cell body of a neuron, the dendrites and their spines, and the axon and its terminals and so forms a boundary around a continuous intracellular compartment. Very few substances can enter or leave a cell because the cell membrane serves as an almost impenetrable barrier. For substances to cross the cell membrane, the cell has to make proteins, which, when embedded in the cell membrane, can facilitate the transport of substances across the cell membrane. The proteins serve as the factory's gates. Furthermore, one of the main functions of the cell factory is making its own proteins.

Within the cell are other membranes that divide the cell into compartments, similar to the work areas that the inner walls of a factory create. In each of these compartments, the cell concentrates chemicals that are needed, while keeping out unneeded ones. Prominent among the membranes inside a cell is the **nuclear membrane,** which surrounds the cell's **nucleus.** The nucleus is like the executive office of a factory. It is here that the blueprints for the cell's proteins are stored, copied, and sent to the factory floor. The factory floor is analogous to a part of the cell called the **endoplasmic reticulum** (ER). The ER is an extension of the nuclear membrane and is where the cell's protein products are assembled in accord with the nucleus's "blueprint" instructions. When those products are finished, they have to be packed and sent

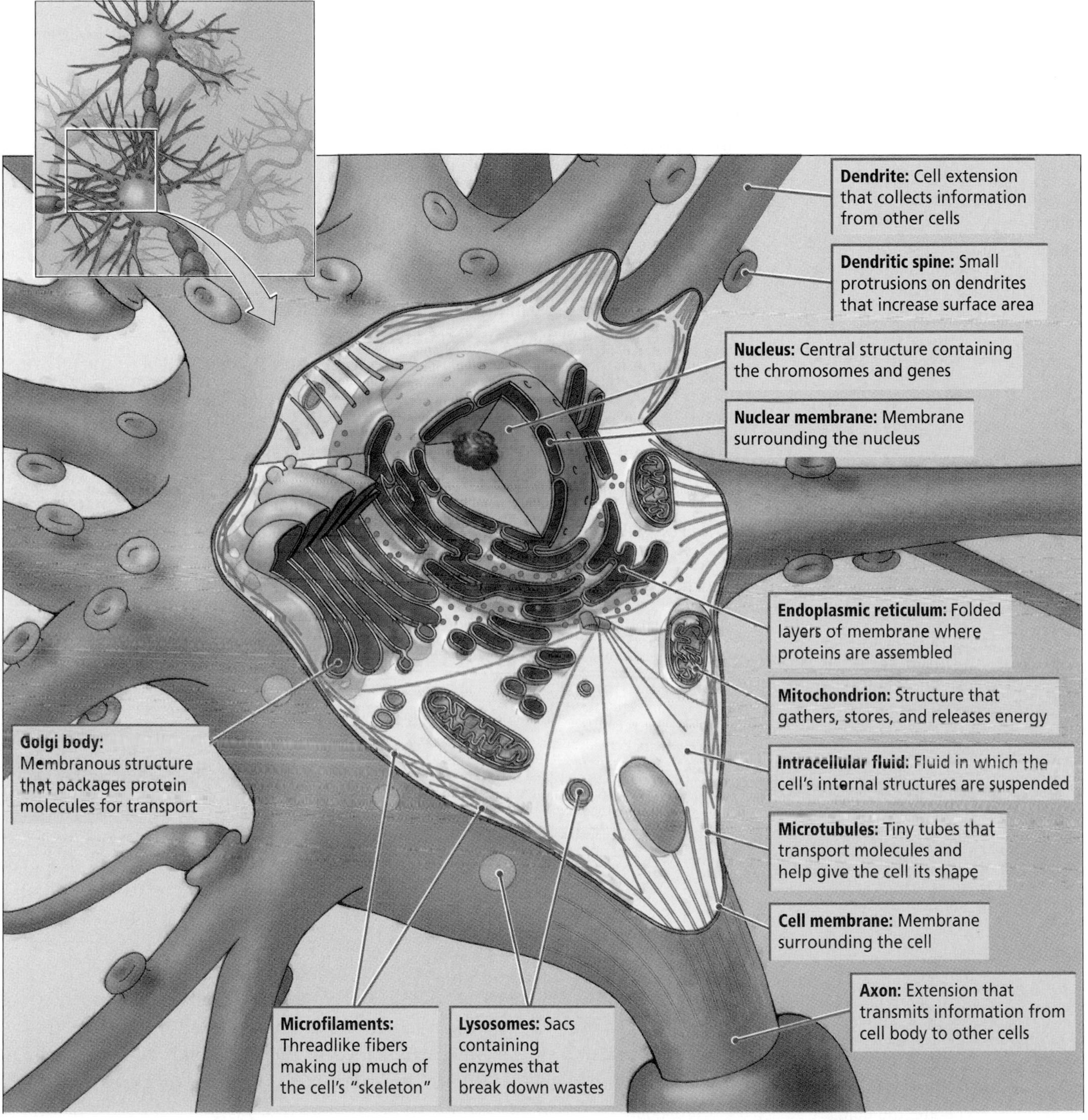
Dendrite: Cell extension that collects information from other cells
Dendritic spine: Small protrusions on dendrites that increase surface area
Nucleus: Central structure containing the chromosomes and genes
Nuclear membrane: Membrane surrounding the nucleus
Endoplasmic reticulum: Folded layers of membrane where proteins are assembled
Mitochondrion: Structure that gathers, stores, and releases energy
Intracellular fluid: Fluid in which the cell's internal structures are suspended
Microtubules: Tiny tubes that transport molecules and help give the cell its shape
Cell membrane: Membrane surrounding the cell
Axon: Extension that transmits information from cell body to other cells
Golgi body: Membranous structure that packages protein molecules for transport
Microfilaments: Threadlike fibers making up much of the cell's "skeleton"
Lysosomes: Sacs containing enzymes that break down wastes

**Figure 3-14**

A typical cell consists of a nucleus, a number of membranes that enclose organelles in the cell (including the nucleus, lysosomes, and the endoplasmic reticulum), and Golgi bodies. It has an internal tubule system to provide motility, support, and material transport. Mitochondria provide energy. Many of the structures and organelles are found in the dendrites and axon of a neuron.

to their future users. Parts of the cell called the **Golgi bodies** provide the packaging rooms where the proteins are wrapped, addressed, and shipped. Other cell components are called **tubules,** of which there are a number of kinds. Some tubules provide structure to the cell, others are contractile and aid in the cell's movements, and still others create the transportation network that carries the cell's products to their destinations, much as a factory's interior system of trucks and forklifts delivers its goods. Two other important parts of the cell factory are the **mitochondria** and **lysosomes.** The mitochondria are the cell's power plants that supply its energy needs, whereas the lysosomes are sacklike vesicles that are the transportation vehicles for incoming supplies and for the movement and storage of wastes. Interestingly, more lysosomes are found in old cells than in young ones. Cells apparently have trouble disposing of their garbage, just as we do.

## THE CELL MEMBRANE: BARRIER AND GATEKEEPER

With this overview of the cell's internal structure in mind, we can look at its parts in more detail, beginning with the cell membrane. Although the neurons and glia of the brain appear to be tightly packed together, they, like all cells, are separated by **extracellular fluid.** This fluid is composed mainly of water with dissolved salts and many other chemical substances. Fluid is found inside a cell as well. It, too, is made up mainly of water with dissolved salts and other chemicals. The important point is that the concentrations of substances inside and outside the cell are different. The inner fluid of a cell is known as the **intracellular fluid.**

Look at the CD for more details on the internal structure of a neuron in the module on Neural Communication.

The cell membrane that encases a cell separates the intracellular from the extracellular fluid and so allows the cell to function as an independent unit. The structure of the membrane that allows it to separate two fluid environments is shown in Figure 3-15. In addition to being a barrier, the cell membrane also regulates the movement of substances into and out of the cell. One of these substances is water. If too much water entered a cell, the cell could burst, and if too much water left a cell, the cell could shrivel. The cell membrane helps ensure that neither will happen. The cell membrane also regulates the concentration of salts and other chemicals on its inner and outer sides. This regulation is important because, if the concentrations of chemicals within a cell become unbalanced, the cell will not function normally.

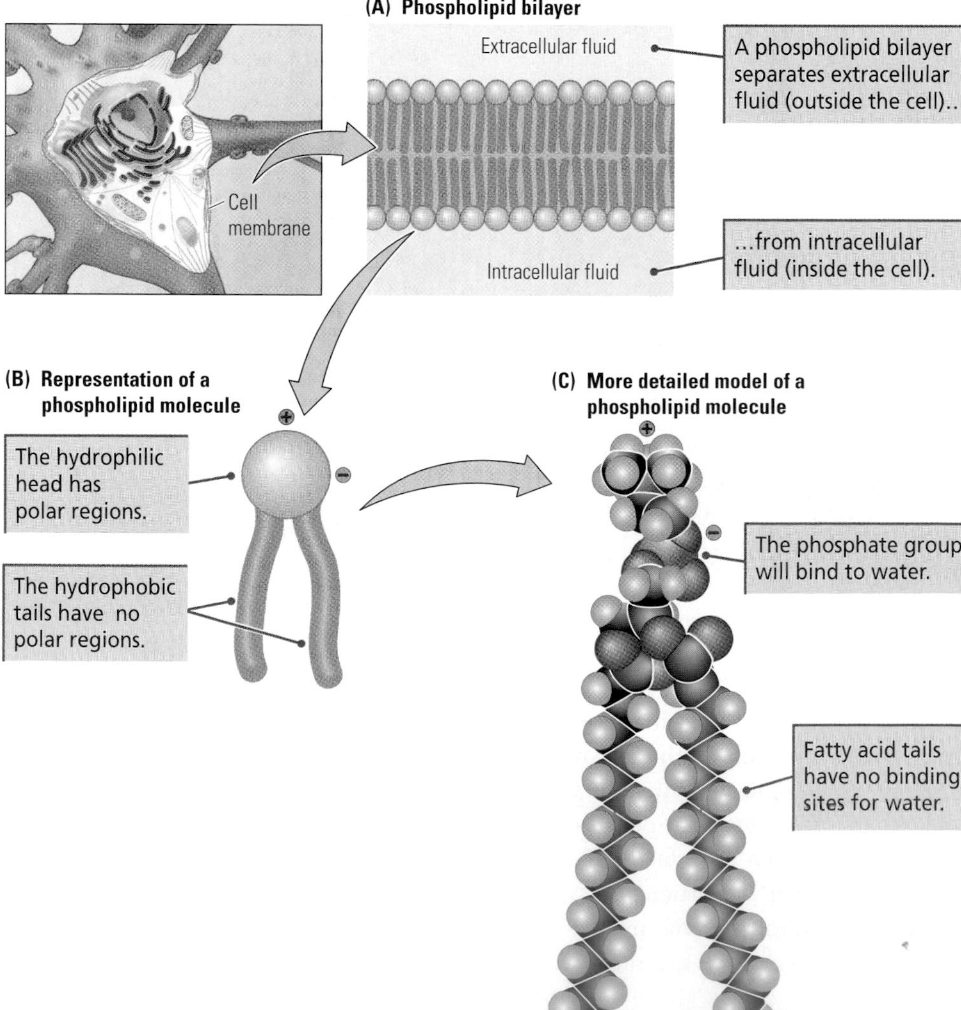
Cell membrane
(A) Phospholipid bilayer
Extracellular fluid
A phospholipid bilayer separates extracellular fluid (outside the cell)...
Intracellular fluid
...from intracellular fluid (inside the cell).
(B) Representation of a phospholipid molecule
The hydrophilic head has polar regions.
The hydrophobic tails have no polar regions.
(C) More detailed model of a phospholipid molecule
The phosphate group will bind to water.
Fatty acid tails have no binding sites for water.

**Figure 3-15**

The cell membrane separates the fluid outside a cell from the fluid within the cell. **(A)** The membrane is composed of a bilayer (two layers) of phospholipid cells in which the tails of the phospholipids face inward and the heads face outward. **(B)** This conventional representation of a phospholipid molecule illustrates its head and tail regions. **(C)** This space-fllling model of a phospholipid molecule shows that the head has polar regions (positive and negative poles) and so is hydrophilic and that the tail has no polar regions and so is hydrophobic.

What properties of a cell membrane allow it to regulate water and salt concentrations within the cell? One is the fact that a cell membrane is composed of a special kind of molecule called a **phospholipid.** This name comes from the molecule's structure. The molecule has a "head" that contains the element phosphorus (P) bound to some other atoms, and it has two "tails" that are lipids, or fats. The head is polar, with a slight positive charge in one location and a slight negative charge in another. The tails consist of hydrogen and carbon atoms that are tightly bound to each other in such a way that there are no polar regions. Figure 3-15C shows a model of this molecule.

The polar head and the nonpolar tails of a phospholipid molecule are the underlying reasons that it can form membranes. The head is hydrophilic and so is attracted to polar water molecules. The nonpolar tails have no such attraction for water. They are **hydrophobic,** or water hating (the suffix *phobic* comes from the Greek word *phobia,* meaning "fear"). Quite literally, then, the head of a phospholipid loves water and the tails hate it. If phospholipid molecules are poured onto the surface of water, they stand on their heads with their tails in the air. You can confirm the behavior of fat molecules by pouring olive oil into water. The oil forms a bilayer (two-layer) bubble, with molecules of the oil having their heads on the outside and inside of the bubble pointing toward the water and their tails pointing inward toward each other. This arrangement puts the heads in contact with water both on the inside and on the outside of the bubble, while the tails stay dry, an arrangement that is much like that of a cell.

The cell membrane is flexible while still forming a remarkable barrier to a wide variety of substances. It is impenetrable to intracellular and extracellular water because polar water molecules cannot pass through the hydrophobic tails of the membrane. Ions in the extracellular and intracellular fluid also cannot penetrate this membrane, because they carry charges and thus cannot pass the phospholipid heads. In fact, only a few small molecules, such as oxygen ($O_2$), can pass through a phospholipid bilayer.

If cell membranes are such effective barriers to substances, there must be some mechanisms to carry needed materials into and out of cells. The cell factory, in other words, must have doors of some kind to receive its supplies, dispose of its wastes, and ship its products. Proteins that are embedded in the cell membrane serve as the gates and transportation systems that allow substances to cross the cell membrane. These mechanisms for crossing the cell membrane will be described a little later. First, we will consider how proteins are manufactured by the cell and how they are transported within the cell.

**Hydrophobic.** Refers to a substance containing no polar regions that will not bind with polar water molecules.

**Gene.** A segment of DNA that encodes a protein.

**Chromosome.** A double-helix structure containing the DNA of an organism's genes.

For animations of the membrane potential, look in the module on Neural Communication on your CD.

## THE NUCLEUS: SITE OF GENE TRANSCRIPTION

In our factory analogy, the nucleus is described as the cell's executive office where the blueprints for making proteins are stored, copied, and sent to the factory floor. These blueprints are called **genes,** and they are encoded in the chemical structure of the nucleus's **chromosomes.** (The name *chromosome* means "colored bodies," referring to the fact that chromosomes can be readily stained with certain dyes.) The chromosomes are like a book of blueprints for making a complex building, whereas a gene is like one page of the book containing the plan for a door or a corridor between rooms. Each chromosome is a body with a double-helix structure and containing thousands of genes. The location of the chromosomes in the nucleus of the cell, the appearance of a chromosome, and the structure of the DNA in a chromosome are shown in Figure 3-16.

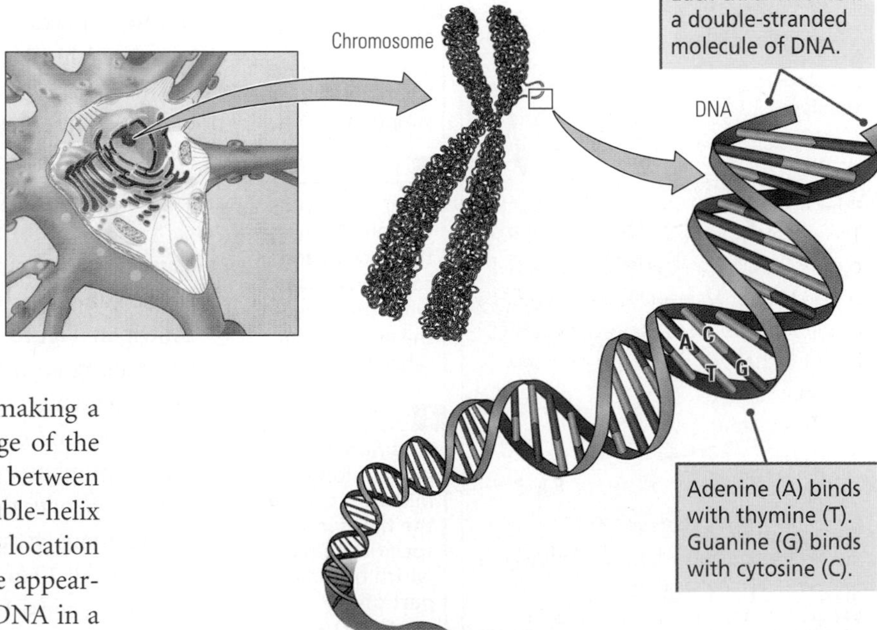
Chromosome
Each chromosome is a double-stranded molecule of DNA.
DNA
A
C
T
G
Adenine (A) binds with thymine (T). Guanine (G) binds with cytosine (C).

**Figure 3-16**

The cell nucleus contains chromosomes, each of which contains many genes. A chromosome is made up of two strands of DNA bound to each other by their nucleotide bases. The nucleotide base adenine (A) binds with thymine (T), and the nucleotide base guanine (G) binds with cytosine (C).

**Transcription.** The transfer of information from a DNA molecule to an RNA molecule.

**Messenger RNA (mRNA).** A type of RNA synthesized from DNA; attaches to ribosomes to specify the sequences of amino acids that form proteins.

**Translation.** The transfer of information from an RNA molecule into a polypeptide, in which the "language" of nucleic acids is translated into that of amino acids.

A human somatic cell has 23 pairs of chromosomes, or 46 in all (in contrast, a reproductive cell does not have paired chromosomes). Each chromosome is a double-stranded molecule of **deoxyribonucleic acid (DNA).** The two strands of a DNA molecule coil around each other, as shown in Figure 3-16. Each strand possesses a variable sequence of four **nucleotide bases: adenine (A), thymine (T), guanine (G),** and **cytosine (C).** Adenine on one strand always pairs with thymine on the other, whereas guanine on one strand always pairs with cytosine on the other. The two strands of the DNA helix are bonded together by the attraction that these paired bases have for one another.

Now you are ready to understand exactly what a gene is. A gene is simply a segment of a DNA strand that encodes the synthesis of a particular protein molecule. The code is contained in the sequence of the nucleotide bases, much as a sequence of letters spells out a word. The sequence of bases "spells out" the particular order in which amino acids, the building blocks of proteins, should be assembled to construct a certain kind of protein.

To initiate the process of producing a protein, the appropriate gene segment of the DNA strands first unwinds. The exposed sequence of nucleotide bases on one of the DNA strands then serves as a template on which a complementary strand of **ribonucleic acid (RNA)** is constructed from free-floating nucleotides. This process, called **transcription,** is shown at the top of Figure 3-17. (To transcribe means "to copy," as one would copy in writing a piece of typed text.) The RNA produced through transcription is much like a single strand of DNA except that the base **uracil** (**U,** which also is attracted to adenine) takes the place of thymine. The strand of RNA is called **messenger RNA (mRNA)** because it carries the genetic code out of the nucleus to the part of the cellular factory where proteins are manufactured. This protein-manufacturing center is the endoplasmic reticulum.

**Figure 3-17**

The flow of information in a cell is from DNA to mRNA to protein (peptide chain).

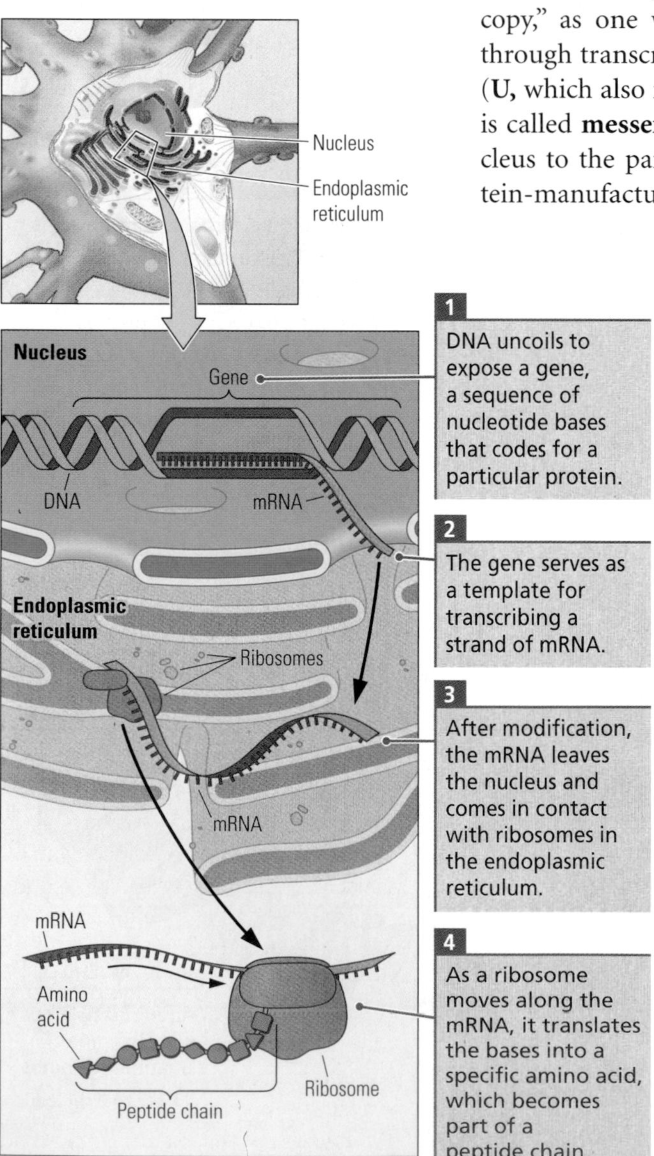

Nucleus
Endoplasmic reticulum
Nucleus
Gene
DNA
mRNA
Endoplasmic reticulum
Ribosomes
mRNA
mRNA
Amino acid
Peptide chain
Ribosome
1
DNA uncoils to expose a gene, a sequence of nucleotide bases that codes for a particular protein.
2
The gene serves as a template for transcribing a strand of mRNA.
3
After modification, the mRNA leaves the nucleus and comes in contact with ribosomes in the endoplasmic reticulum.
4
As a ribosome moves along the mRNA, it translates the bases into a specific amino acid, which becomes part of a peptide chain.

## THE ENDOPLASMIC RETICULUM: SITE OF PROTEIN SYNTHESIS

Figure 3-17 shows that the endoplasmic reticulum consists of membranous sheets that are folded to form numerous channels. A distinguishing feature of the ER is that it may be studded with **ribosomes,** structures that play a vital role in the building of proteins. When an mRNA molecule reaches the ER, it passes through a ribosome, where its genetic code is "read." In this process, called **translation,** a particular sequence of nucleotide bases in the mRNA is translated into a particular sequence of **amino acids.** (To translate means to convert one language into another, in contrast with transcription, in which the language remains the same.) **Transfer RNA (tRNA)** assists in translation. **Proteins** are just long chains of amino acids, folded up to form specific shapes.

The flow of the information contained in the genetic code is conceptually quite simple: a DNA strand is transcribed into an mRNA strand, and the mRNA strand is translated into a **polypepide.** As shown in Figure 3-18, each group of three consecutive nucleotide bases along an mRNA molecule encodes one particular amino acid. These sequences of three bases are called **codons**. For example, the base sequence uracil, guanine, guanine (UGG) encodes the amino acid tryptophan (Trp), whereas the base sequence uracil, uracil, uracil (UUU) encodes the amino acid phenylalanine (Phe).

Humans require 20 different amino acids for the synthesis of proteins. All 20 of them are structurally similar, as illustrated in Figure 3-19. Each consists of a central carbon atom (C) bound to a hydrogen atom (H), an *amino group* ($NH^{3+}$), a *carboxyl group* ($COO^-$), and

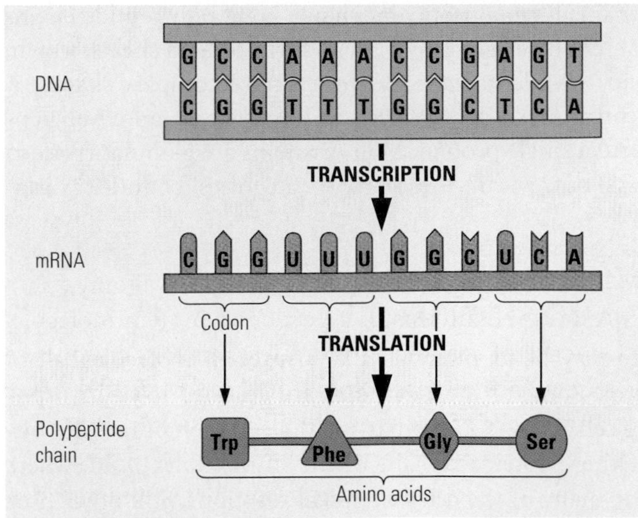


**Figure 3-18**

In the synthesis of a protein (see Figure 3-17), a strand of DNA is transcribed into mRNA. Each sequence of three bases in the mRNA encodes one amino acid and is translated to form the amino acid. The amino acids are linked together to form a polypeptide chain. The amino acids in this illustration are tryptophan (Trp), phenylalanine (Phe), glycine (Gly), and serine (Ser).

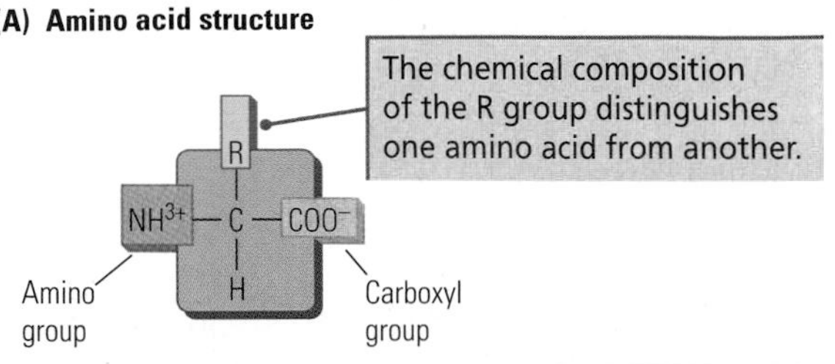


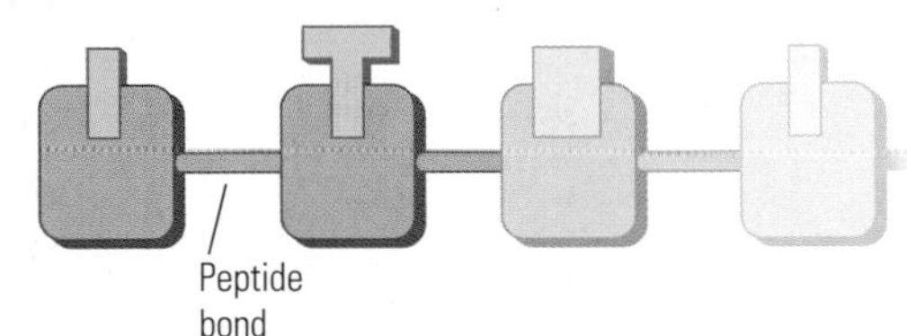


**Figure 3-19**

**(A)** Each amino acid consists of a central carbon atom (C) attached to an amine group ($NH^{3+}$), a carboxyl group ($COO^-$), and a side chain (R). **(B)** The amino acids are linked by peptide bonds to form a polypeptide chain.

a *side chain* (represented by the letter R). The side chain, which varies in chemical composition from one amino acid to another, is what helps to give different protein molecules their distinctive biochemical properties. Amino acids are linked together by a special bond called a *peptide bond.* A chain of amino acids is called a *polypeptide chain* (meaning "many peptides"). Just as a remarkable number of words can be made from the 26 letters of our alphabet, a remarkable number of peptide chains can be made from the 20 different amino acids. These amino acids can form 400 (20 × 20) different dipeptides (two-peptide combinations), 8000 (20 × 20 × 20) different tripeptides (three-peptide combinations), and an almost countless number of polypeptides.

A polypeptide chain and a protein are related, but they are not the same thing. The relation is somewhat analogous to that between a ribbon and a bow of a particular size and shape that can be made from the ribbon. As Figure 3-20 shows, a protein

**Protein.** An organic molecule whose folded and twisted shape is determined by its sequence of amino acids. A protein can comprise several polypeptides.

**Polypeptide.** A molecule in which a number of amino acids are connected by peptide bonds.

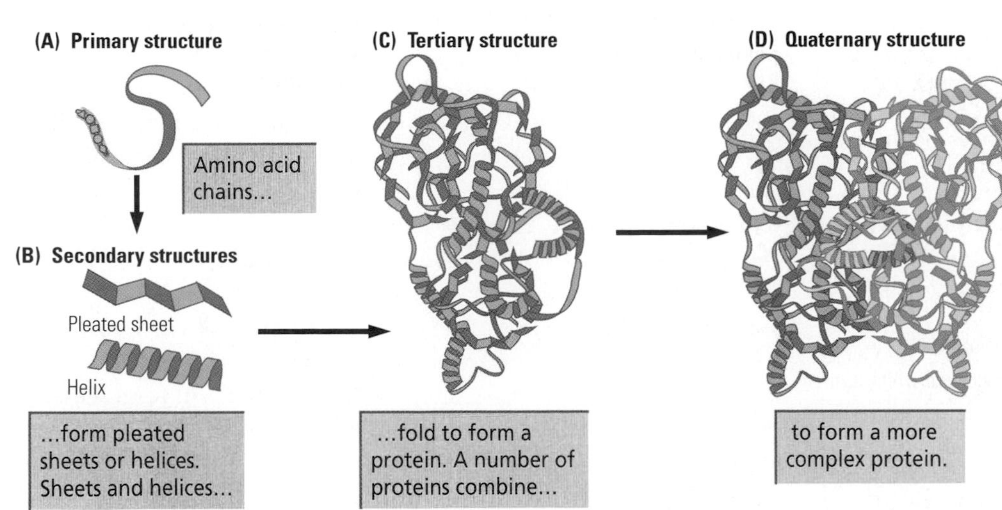


**Figure 3-20**

A protein can have as many as four levels of structure. **(A)** The primary structure consists of the chain of amino acids (that is, the polypeptide chain). **(B)** The secondary structure is a helix or pleated sheet formed by the primary chain. **(C)** The tertiary structure emerges when pleated sheets or helices or both fold to form a three-dimensional shape. **(D)** The quaternary structure also is three-dimensional and consists of two or more polypeptides. Whether a polypeptide chain forms a pleated sheet or a helix and what three-dimensional shape is ultimately formed are determined by the sequence of amino acids in the primary structure.

is formed when polypeptide chains form a particular shape. Long polypeptide chains have a strong tendency to twist into a helix (a spiral) or to form pleated sheets, which, in turn, have a strong tendency to fold together to form more complex shapes. A folded-up polypeptide chain constitutes a protein. In addition, two or more polypeptide chains may combine to form a single protein. Many proteins are globular (round) in shape and others are fibrous, but, within these broad categories, countless variations are possible.

## GOLGI BODIES AND MICROTUBULES: PROTEIN PACKAGING AND SHIPMENT

Within any one neuron, there may be as many as 10,000 protein molecules, all of which the cell has manufactured. Some of these proteins are destined to be incorporated into the structure of the cell. They become part of the cell membrane, the nucleus, the ER, and so forth. Other proteins remain in the intracellular fluid, where they act as enzymes, facilitating many of the cell's chemical reactions. Still other proteins are excreted by the cell as hormones or messenger molecules. How does the cell manage to get all these different proteins to the right destinations? The answer lies in cell components that package, label, and ship proteins. These components operate much like a postal service.

To reach their appropriate destinations, the protein molecules that have been synthesized in the cell must first be wrapped in membranes and given labels that indicate where they are to go. This wrapping and labeling takes place in organelles called *Golgi bodies.* The work of the Golgi bodies is illustrated in Figure 3-21. The packaged proteins are then loaded onto motor molecules that "walk" along one of the many tubules radiating through the cell, thus carrying the protein to its destination.

If a protein is destined to remain within the cell, it is unloaded into the intracellular fluid. If it is intended to be incorporated into the cell membrane, it is carried to the membrane, where it inserts itself. Suppose that a particular protein is destined to be excreted at the cell membrane. In this process, called **exocytosis,** the membrane in which the protein is wrapped first fuses with the membrane of the cell. Now the protein inside the "wrapper membrane" can be expelled into the extracellular fluid. Many excreted proteins travel to other cells to induce chemical reactions and so serve as messenger molecules.

**Figure 3-21**

The steps in exporting a protein consist of packaging, transport, and function at destination.

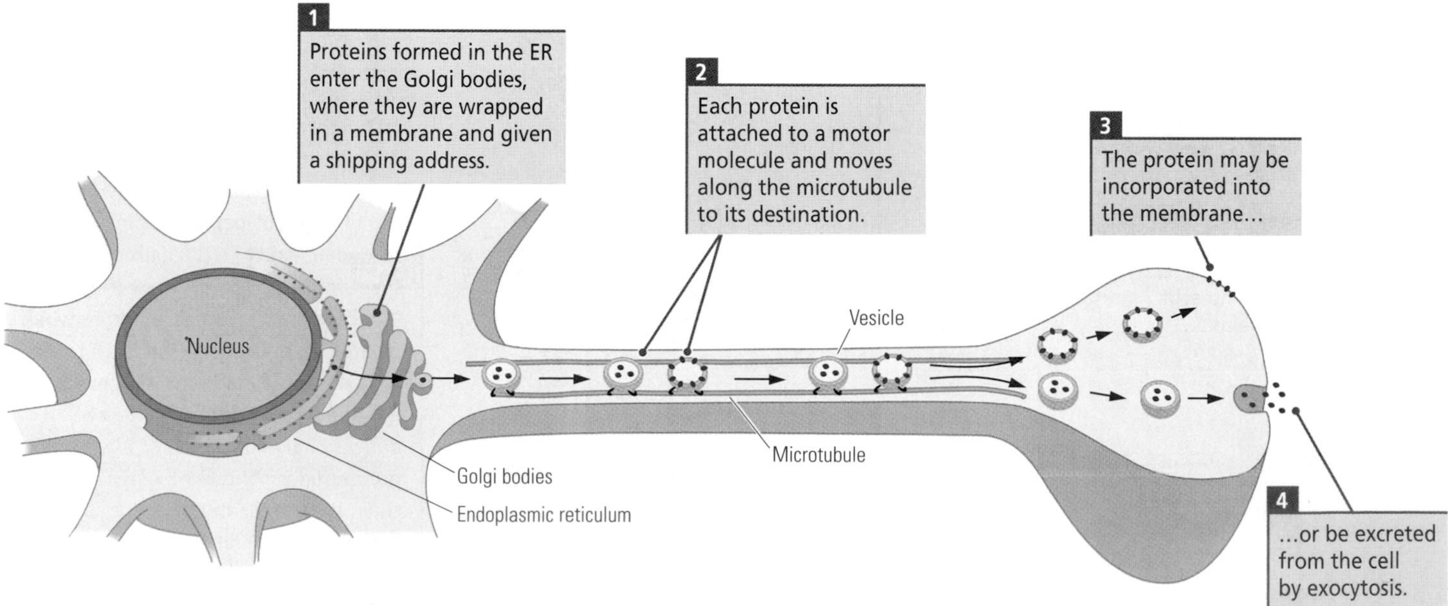

1
Proteins formed in the ER enter the Golgi bodies, where they are wrapped in a membrane and given a shipping address.
2
Each protein is attached to a motor molecule and moves along the microtubule to its destination.
3
The protein may be incorporated into the membrane...
4
...or be excreted from the cell by exocytosis.
Nucleus
Vesicle
Microtubule
Golgi bodies
Endoplasmic reticulum

## THE CELL MEMBRANE REVISITED: CHANNELS, GATES, AND PUMPS

Knowing something about the structure of proteins will help you to understand other ways that substances can travel across what would otherwise be an impermeable cell membrane. As already mentioned, some of the proteins that cells manufacture are carried to the cell membrane, where they become embedded. These membrane proteins play a number of important roles, one of which is transporting substances across the membrane. We will consider how three such membrane proteins work. In each case, notice how the function of the particular protein is an emergent property of its shape.

An important feature of protein molecules is that they can *change* shape. This changing of shape is done in a number of ways. For instance, some protein molecules change shape when other chemicals bind to them. The protein molecule is analogous to the lock in a door. When a key of the appropriate size and shape is inserted into the lock and turned, the locking device changes shape and becomes activated. An example of a shape-changing protein is the enzyme hexokinase, illustrated in Figure 3-22. The surface of this protein molecule has a groove, called a **receptor,** which is analogous to a keyhole. When another molecule—in this case, glucose—enters the receptor area, it induces a slight change in the shape of the protein, causing the hexokinase to embrace the glucose. Either small molecules or other proteins can bind to the receptors of proteins and cause the proteins to change their shapes. The changes in shape may then allow the proteins to serve some new functions.

Other types of changes in a protein's shape enable substances to cross the cell membrane. Some membrane proteins become shaped in such a way that they create **channels** through which substances can pass. Different-sized channels in different proteins allow different substances to pass. Figure 3-23A illustrates a protein with a particular shape forming a small channel in the cell membrane that is large enough for potassium ($K^+$) ions to pass through it. Other protein molecules allow sodium ions or chloride ions to pass through the cell membrane.

Other membrane proteins regulate the passage of substances across the cell membrane by changing their shapes in response to some trigger, as the protein hexokinase does. Figure 3-23B shows a protein molecule that acts as a **gate** in this way. The protein allows the passage of substances when its shape leaves the gate open and prevents

**Channel.** An opening in a protein that is embedded in the cell membrane and allows the passage of ions through the cell membrane.

**Gate.** A protein that is embedded in a neural or glial membrane and allows substances to pass through the membrane on some occasions but not on others.

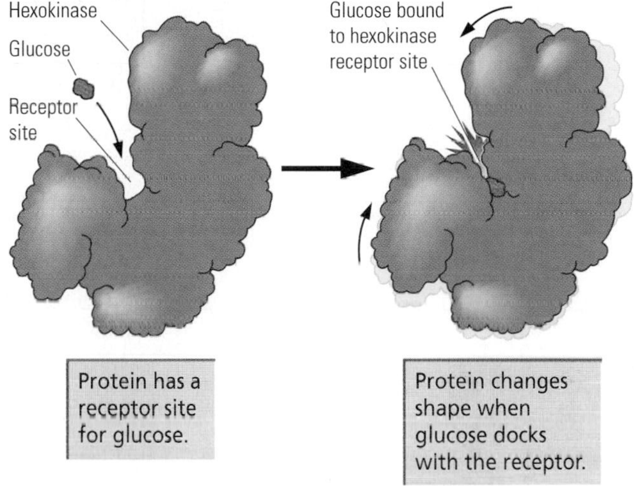


Protein has a receptor site for glucose.

**Figure 3-22**

Hexokinase (purple) changes shape when a glucose molecule (orange) binds to its receptor.

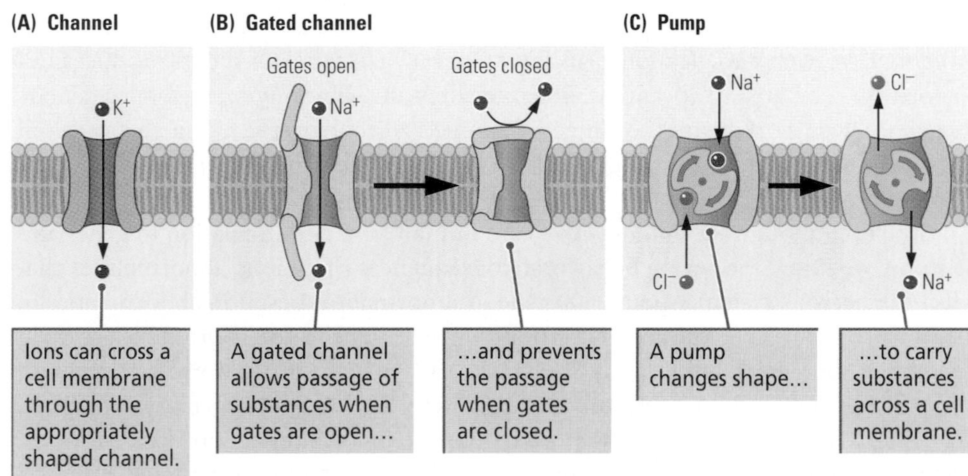

(A) Channel
(B) Gated channel
(C) Pump
K+
Gates open
Gates closed
Na+
Na+
Cl−
Cl−
Na+
Ions can cross a cell membrane through the appropriately shaped channel.
A gated channel allows passage of substances when gates are open...
...and prevents the passage when gates are closed.
A pump changes shape...
...to carry substances across a cell membrane.

**Figure 3-23**

Transmembrane proteins form channels that allow substances to enter and exit the cell: **(A)** a channel that allows passage of potassium ions; **(B)** a gated channel that, in one conformation, allows the passage of sodium ions, whereas, in another conformation, it blocks their passage; **(C)** a pump that, when it changes shape, carries an ion across the membrane.

**Pump.** A protein, in the cell membrane, that actively transports a substance across the membrane.

the passage of substances when its shape leaves the gate closed. Changes in the shape of a protein can also allow it to act as a **pump.** Figure 3-23C shows a protein that changes its shape to carry ("pump") substances across the membrane.

Channels, gates, and pumps all play an important role in allowing substances to enter and leave a cell. This passage of substances is critical to explaining how neurons send messages. Chapter 4 explores the topic of neuron communication in detail.

### In Review

Cells contain elements that combine to form molecules that are in turn organized together to make up the constituent parts of the cell, including the cell membrane, the nucleus, the endoplasmic reticulum, Golgi bodies, tubules, and vesicles. Important products of the cell are proteins, which serve many functions including acting as channels, gates, and pumps to allow substances to cross the cell membrane. Simply put, the sequence of events in building a protein is: DNA makes mRNA and mRNA makes protein. When formed, the protein molecules are wrapped by the Golgi bodies and are transported to their designated sites of use by microtubules.

## GENES, CELLS, AND BEHAVIOR

Genes are the blueprints for proteins, proteins are essential to the function of cells, and cells produce behavior. That sequence of connections sounds simple enough. But exactly how one connection leads to another is one of the big challenges for future research; so, if you choose a career in neuroscience, you will most likely be working out this relation. As already mentioned, genes are chromosome segments that encode proteins, and proteins serve as enzymes, channels, gates, and pumps. This knowledge does not tell you much about the ultimate structure and function of a cell, because so many genes and proteins take part. The eventual function of a cell is an emergent property of all its many constituent parts. Similarly, knowing that behaviors result from the actions of neurons does not tell you much about the ultimate form that behaviors will take, because so many neurons participate in them. Your behavior is a property of the action of all your billions of neurons. The challenge for future research is to be able to explain how genes, proteins, cells, and behavior are related.

Understanding the contributions of genes alone is a tremendous challenge. Humans have an estimated 100,000 genes, about half of which contribute to building the brain. If we knew what proteins all of these genes encode and what functions those proteins have, our understanding of how the brain is constructed and produces behavior would be greatly advanced. This understanding is a long-term goal of genetic research. Those working on the Human Genome Project have the human genome (all the genes in our species) catalogued, but identifying the function of every gene will take a long time.

For the latest update on the Human Genome Project, look at the current news feature at **www.worthpublishers.com/kolb/chapter3.**

Still, even though we cannot yet explain human behavior in relation to genes and neurons, we know the severe behavioral consequences of genetic abnormalities that affect the nervous system. About 2000 genetic abnormalities result in abnormalities in the brain and in behavior. For example, an error in a gene could produce a protein that should be a $K^+$ channel but will not allow $K^+$ to pass, it could produce a pump that will not pump, or it could produce a protein that the transportation system of the cell refuses to transport. If there are about 10,000 different proteins in a cell, a genetic mutation that results in an abnormality of any one protein could have a beneficial effect, it could have little noticeable effect, or it could have severe consequences. Studying genetic abnormalities is one source of insight into how genes, neurons, and behaviors are linked. Such studies may also help us to reduce the negative effects of these abnormalities, perhaps someday even eliminating them completely. For example, just as the replacement of a malfunctioning part of a robot restores the function of the robot, the identification and replacement of an abnormal gene could provide a cure for the brain and the behavioral abnormalities that it produces. Genetic research, then, promises to have a revolutionary effect not only on the study of the brain and behavior, but also on the search for new ways to treat genetic disorders. For these reasons, we will focus on human genetics in the rest of this chapter.

To learn more about genetics, you'll find links and tutorials on the Web site at **www.worthpublishers.com/kolb/chapter3.**

## Chromosomes and Genes

As stated earlier, the nucleus of each human somatic cell contains 23 pairs of chromosomes, or 46 in all. One set of 23 chromosomes comes from the mother, and the other set comes from the father. The chromosomes are numbered from 1 to 23, with chromosome 1 being the largest and chromosome 22 being almost the smallest (chromosome 21 is the smallest; Figure 3-24). The chromosomes numbered from 1 to 22 are called **autosomes,** and they contain the genes that contribute to most of our physical appearance and behavioral functions. The 23rd pair of chromosomes comprises the **sex chromosomes,** which eventually produce our physical and behavioral sexual characteristics. There are two types of sex chromosomes, referred to as X and Y because of their appearance. Female mammals have two X chromosomes, whereas males have an X and a Y.

Because your chromosomes are "matched" pairs, a cell contains two copies of every gene, one inherited from your mother, the other from your father. These two matching copies of a gene are called **alleles.** The term "matching" here does not necessarily mean identical. The nucleotide sequences in a pair of alleles may be either identical or different. If they are identical, the two alleles are called **homozygous** (*homo* means "the same"). If they are different, the two alleles are called **heterozygous** (*hetero* means "different"). The nucleotide sequence that is most common in a population is called the **wild-type** allele, whereas a less frequently occurring sequence is called a **mutation.** Mutant genes often determine genetic disorders.

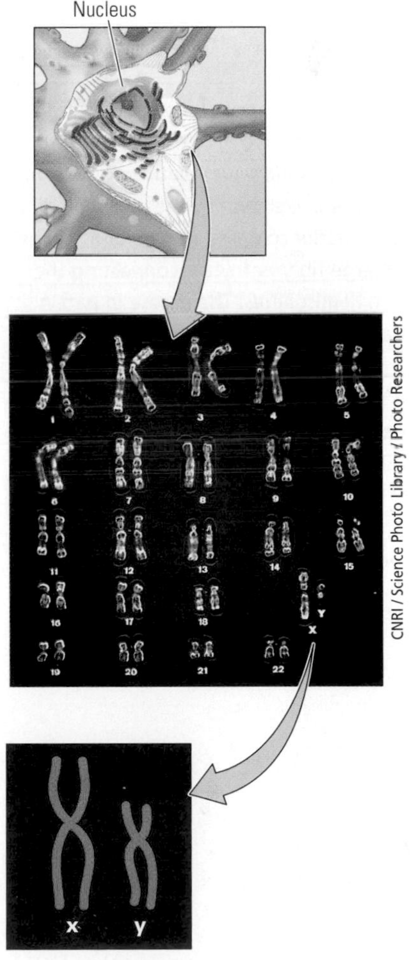


**Figure 3-24**

The human nucleus contains 46 chromosomes, 23 derived from the father and 23 derived from the mother. A person's sex is determined by the sex chromosomes.

## Genotype and Phenotype

The actions of genes give rise to what we call physical or behavioral *traits,* but these actions are not always straightforward. For a variety of reasons, some genes are not expressed as traits or they may be expressed only incompletely. For instance, the actions of a protein manufactured by one gene may be suppressed or modified by other genes. The proteins and genes that contribute to human skin color provide a good example. The color expressed depends on the precise complement of a number of different genes. In addition, environmental factors may modify gene expression. In regard to skin color, exposure to sunlight is often a factor modifying genetic influences.

Because genes and expressed traits can be so different, scientists distinguish between genotype and phenotype (the prefix *pheno* comes from the Greek word meaning "show"). **Genotype** refers to the full set of all the genes that an organism possesses, whereas **phenotype** refers to the appearance of an organism that results from the interaction of genes with one another and with the environment.

The extent of phenotypic variation, given the same genotype, can be dramatic. For example, in some strains of genetically identical mice, certain mice develop a brain with no corpus callosum, the large band of fibers that connects the two hemispheres

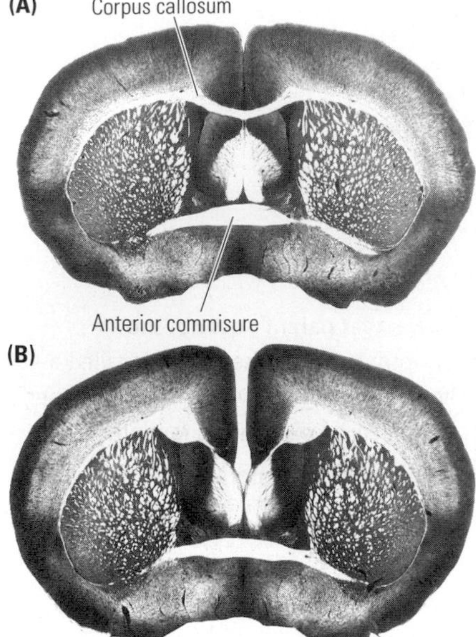


**Figure 3-25**

Both of these coronal sections through the brains of two genetically identical mice are in the same relative position in the brain, as shown by the presence of the anterior commissure, one of a number of large fiber pathways connecting the two hemispheres. The mouse in part A has a corpus callosum, whereas the mouse in part B does not. Despite their genetic identity, other factors determine each mouse's phenotype.

Adapted from "Defects of the Fetal Forebrain in Acallosal Mice," by D. Wahlsten and H. W. Ozaki, in *Callosal Agenesis* (p. 126), edited by M. Lassonde and M. A. Jeeves, 1994, New York: Plenum Press.

(Figure 3-25). The absence of a corpus callosum has a genetic cause, but something happens in the development of the brain that determines whether the trait is expressed in a particular mouse's phenotype. Although the precise causal factors are not known, they affect the embryo at about the time at which the corpus callosum should form. This example illustrates the importance of distinguishing between genotype and phenotype. Having identical genes does not mean that those genes will be identically expressed. By the same token, even if we knew everything about the structure and function of our own genes, it would be impossible to predict how much of our behavior is due to our genotype, because so much of our behavior is phenotypical.

## Dominant and Recessive Genes

If both alleles in a pair of genes are the same (homozygous), the two encode the same protein, but if the two alleles in a pair are different (heterozygous), they encode two different proteins. There are three possible outcomes of the heterozygous condition when the proteins express a physical or behavioral trait: only the allele from the mother may be expressed; only the allele from the father may be expressed; or both alleles may be expressed simultaneously. A member of a gene pair that is expressed as a trait is called a **dominant** allele; an unexpressed allele is called a **recessive** allele. Alleles can vary considerably in their dominance, however. Some exhibit complete dominance, in which only their own trait is expressed in the phenotype. Others exhibit incomplete dominance, in which the expression of their own trait is only partial. And still others exhibit codominance, in which both their own trait and that of the other allele in the pair are expressed completely.

The concept of dominant and recessive alleles was first introduced by Gregor Mendel, a nineteenth-century monk who studied pea plants in his monastery garden, as mentioned in Chapter 1. Mendel showed that organisms possess discrete units of heredity, which we now call genes. Each gene makes an independent contribution to what the offspring of two parents inherit, even though that contribution may not always be visible in the offspring's phenotype. When paired with a dominant allele, a recessive allele often is not expressed. Still, it can be passed on to future generations and influence their phenotypes when not masked by the influence of some dominant trait.

## Genetic Mutations

The mechanism for reproducing genes and passing them on to offspring is not infallible. Errors can arise in the nucleotide sequence when reproductive cells make gene copies. The new versions of the genes are mutations. The number of potential genetic mutations is enormous. A mutation may consist of something as small as a change in a single nucleotide base. Because the average gene has more than 1200 nucleotide bases, an enormous number of mutations can potentially occur on a single gene. For example, the *BRCA1* gene, found on chromosome 17, predisposes women to breast cancer, and more than 100 different mutations have already been found on this gene.

A change in a nucleotide or the addition of a nucleotide in a gene sequence can be either beneficial or disruptive. An example of a mutation that is both causes sickle-cell anemia, a condition in which blood cells have an abnormal shape. The sickle-shaped blood cells offer some protection against malaria, but they also have poor oxygen-carrying capacity, thus weakening the person who possesses them. Other genetic mutations are more purely beneficial in their results, and still others are seemingly neutral to the functioning of the organism that carries them. Most mutations, however, have a negative effect. If not lethal, they produce in their carriers debilitating physical and behavioral abnormalities.

A mutation may have a specific effect on one particular trait or it can have widespread effects. The ability of a gene to affect an organism in many ways is called **pleiotropy** (from the Greek word *pleion,* meaning "more"). Most mutant genes responsible for hereditary disorders in humans cause multiple symptoms. The abnormal protein produced by the gene takes part in many different chemical reactions, and so the affected person may have an abnormal appearance as well as abnormal function.

## Mendel's Principles Apply to Genetic Disorders

Some disorders caused by mutant genes clearly illustrate Mendel's principles of dominant and recessive alleles. One of them, called **Tay-Sachs disease,** is caused by a dysfunctional protein that acts as an enzyme known as HexA (hexosaminidase A), which fails to break down a class of lipids (fats) in the brain. Symptoms usually appear a few months after birth. The baby begins to suffer seizures, blindness, and degenerating motor and mental abilities. Inevitably, the child dies within a few years. The Tay-Sachs mutation appears in high frequency among certain ethnic groups, such as Jews of European origin and French Canadians.

Figure 3-26A shows that the dysfunctional Tay-Sachs enzyme is caused by a recessive allele, which means that two copies of the allele (one from both the mother *and* the father) are needed for the disorder to develop. Distinctive inheritance patterns result from a recessive allele. A baby can inherit Tay-Sachs disease only when both parents carry the recessive Tay-Sachs allele. Because both parents have survived to adulthood, they must also both possess a corresponding normal allele for that particular gene pair. The egg and sperm cells produced by this man and woman will therefore contain a copy of one or the other of these two alleles. Which allele is passed on is determined completely by chance.

This situation gives rise to three different potential gene combinations in any child produced by two Tay-Sachs carriers. The child may have two normal alleles, in which case he or she will be spared the disorder. The child may have one normal and

**Figure 3-26**

**(A)** The gene for Tay-Sachs disease is recessive. Each parent has two copies of a gene that encodes the production of an enzyme. If one parent has a mutant allele, that parent does not show symptoms of the disease but is called a carrier. Mating (×) with a normal partner, whose chromosomes are randomly assorted to the offspring, produces a 50 percent chance that the offspring will be normal and a 50 percent chance that they will be carriers. If two parents are carriers, the offspring have a 25 percent chance of developing Tay-Sachs disease, a 50 percent chance of being carriers, and a 25 percent chance of being normal noncarriers. **(B)** The gene for Huntington's disease is dominant. A person with the Huntington allele will develop the disease. If this person mates with a normal partner, offspring have a 50 percent chance of developing Huntington's disease and a 50 percent chance of being normal. If both parents are carriers, both will develop the disease. Their offspring have a 75 percent chance of developing the disease and a 25 percent chance of being normal.

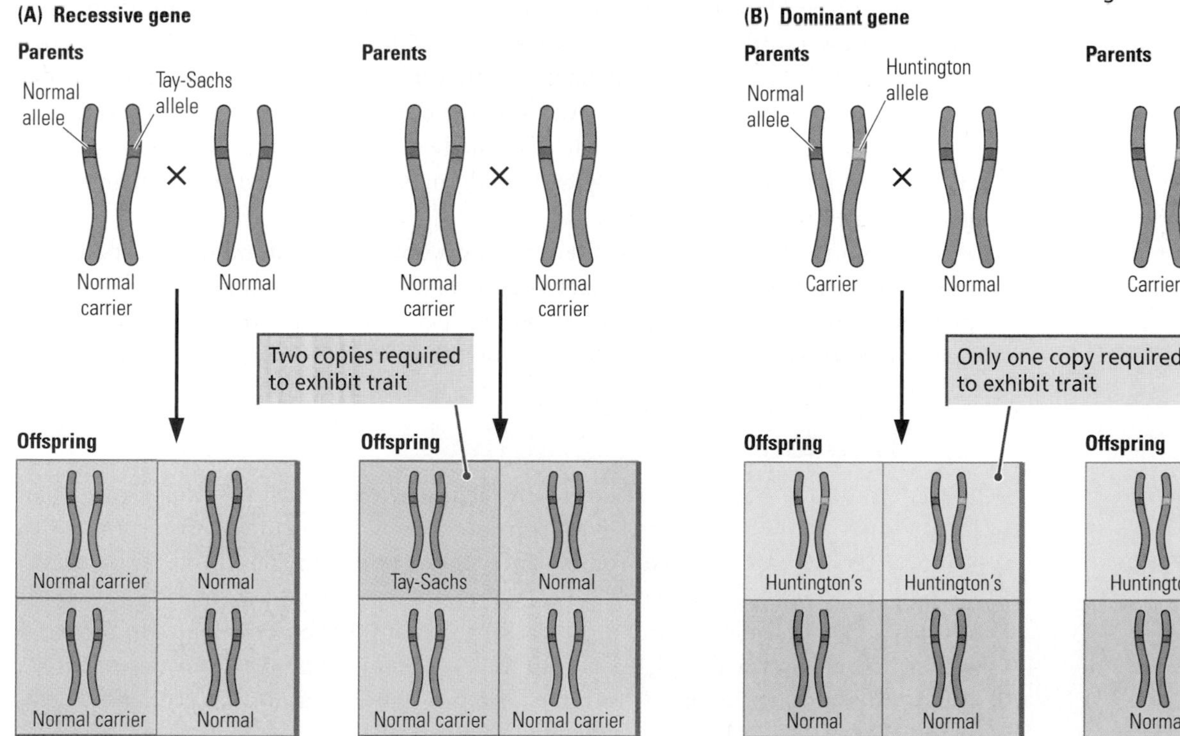

one Tay-Sachs allele, in which case he or she, like the parents, will be a carrier of the disorder. Or the child may have two Tay-Sachs alleles, in which case he or she will have Tay-Sachs disease. Figure 3-26 shows that the chance of a child of two carriers being normal is 25 percent, the chance of being a carrier is 50 percent, and the chance of having Tay-Sachs disease is 25 percent as well. If only one of the parents is a Tay-Sachs carrier and the other is normal, then any of their children has a 50-50 chance of being either normal or a carrier. Such a couple has no chance of conceiving a baby with Tay-Sachs disease.

Fortunately, there is a way of determining whether a person is a carrier of the recessive Tay-Sachs allele. This allele operates independently of the dominant allele, just as Mendel described. As a result, it still produces the defective HexA enzyme, so the person who carries it has a higher-than-normal lipid accumulation in the brain. Because this person also has a normal allele that produces a functional enzyme, the abnormal lipid accumulation is not enough to cause Tay-Sachs disease. The condition can, however, be detected with a blood test. People found to be carriers can then make informed decisions about conceiving children. If they avoid having children with another Tay-Sachs carrier, none of their children will have the disorder, although some will probably be carriers.

The one normal allele that a carrier of Tay-Sachs possesses produces enough functional enzyme to enable the brain to operate in a satisfactory way. This would *not* be the case if the normal allele were recessive, however, as happens with a genetic disorder called **Huntington's chorea.** In Huntington's chorea, a protein known as huntingtin builds up in nervous system cells. This protein causes the death of brain cells, especially cells in the basal ganglia and the cortex, as discussed further in "Huntington's Chorea." Symptoms can begin anytime from infancy to old age, but they most often start in midlife. These symptoms include abnormal involuntary movements, which is why the disorder is called chorea (Greek *chorea,* meaning "dance"). Other symptoms are memory loss and eventually a complete deterioration of behavior, followed by death. The Huntington allele is dominant to a normal allele, so only one defective allele is needed to cause the disorder.

Figure 3-26B illustrates the inheritance patterns associated with a dominant allele that produces a disorder, such as Huntington's chorea. If one of a child's parents has the defective allele, that child will have a 50 percent chance of inheriting the disorder, too. If both parents have the defective allele, the chance of inheriting it increases to 75 percent. Because the Huntington allele is usually not expressed until midlife, after the people who possess it have already had children, it can be passed from generation to generation even though it is lethal.

As with the Tay-Sachs allele, there is now a test for determining if a person possesses the allele that causes Huntington's chorea. If a person is found to have the allele, he or she can elect not to produce children. A decision not to have children in this case will reduce the incidence of the Huntington allele in the human gene pool.

## Chromosome Abnormalities

Genetic disorders are not caused only by single defective alleles. Some disorders are caused by aberrations in a part of a chromosome or even an entire chromosome. One such condition is **Down's syndrome,** which affects approximately 1 of every 700 children. Down's syndrome is usually the result of an extra copy of chromosome 21. One of the parents (usually the mother) passes on two of these chromosomes to the child, rather than the normal single chromosome. Combining these two chromosomes with one from the other parent yields three chromosomes, an abnormal number called a trisomy.

Focus on Disorders

## Huntington's Chorea

Woody Guthrie was born in Oklahoma on July 14, 1912, and grew up to be a great songwriter and entertainer. (His best-known song is "This Land Is Your Land.") After marrying and having three children, he was caught up in the great midwestern drought of the 1930s and moved to California with thousands of other farmers. There his protest songs made him a spokesman for farm workers. Along with other entertainers, including Pete Seeger, Lee Hayes, and Leadbelly, he became one of the founders of American folk music. Bob Dylan, who gave his first concert wearing Woody Guthrie's suit, was instrumental in reviving Woody's popularity in the 1960s.

Photofest

Woody Guthrie.

Woody was described as always being a little odd, but in the 1950s his odd behavior began to disrupt his life. He started having trouble playing his guitar and remembering his songs, and he was in and out of hospitals. He died in 1967 after struggling with the symptoms of what was eventually diagnosed as Huntingon's chorea. His mother died of a similar condition, although her illness had never been diagnosed. Two of Guthrie's five children, produced in two marriages, developed the same disease. His second wife, Marjorie, became active in promoting the study of Huntington's chorea. Arlo Guthrie, his son, has become a singer and songwriter in his own right.

Huntington's chorea is a devastating disorder. It is characterized by memory impairments, abnormal uncontrollable movements, and marked changes in personality, eventually leading to virtually total loss of normal behavioral and emotional and intellectual functioning. Fortunately, it is a relatively rare disease, with an incidence of only 5 to 10 victims in 100,000 people. It is most common in people of European origin.

The symptoms of Huntington's chorea result from the degeneration of neurons in the basal ganglia and cortex. Those symptoms can appear at any age but usually start in midlife. In 1983, the gene responsible for Huntington's chorea was located on chromosome 4, and 10 years later its abnormality was identified as an expanded region characterized by many repeats of the codon CAG. (Normal people have fewer than 30 CAG repeats.) The CAG nucleotide sequence encodes the amino acid glutamine. As a result, the protein produced by the defective Huntington gene contains many repeats of glutamine in its polypeptide chain. As the number of repeats increases beyond 30, the onset of the disease comes earlier and earlier. Thus the disease can begin from very early to very late in life, depending on the number of repeats. The area of CAG repeats is also prone to expansion in transmission from the father, when it can double or even triple in size. In inheritance from the mother, the area of repeats remains stable. Typically, non-Europeans have fewer CAG repeats than do Europeans, which accounts for their decreased susceptibility to Huntington's chorea.

Despite our current insights into the causes of Huntington's chorea, there are still many unanswered questions about it. One such question is why symptoms take so long to develop even with many CAG repeats. Another is why the abnormal Huntington protein causes cell death only in certain regions of the brain. As yet, we also know little about how the progress of the disease might be stopped.

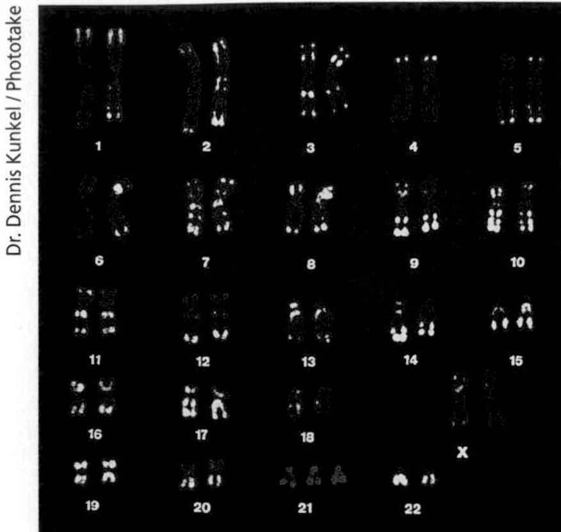


Dr. Dennis Kunkel / Phototake

Ron Batzdorf / Everett Collection

**Figure 3-27**

(*Top*) Down's syndrome is also known as trisomy 21, to indicate that it is caused by an extra copy (a trisomy, or abnormal number) of chromosome 21. (*Bottom*) Chris Burke, who has Down's syndrome, played a leading role on the television series *Life Goes On* in the 1990s.

**Genetic engineering.** An application of genetics directed toward changing physical or behavioral traits by changing genes.

**Cloning.** The creation of an identical twin from the DNA of a donor animal.

Although chromosome 21 is the smallest human chromosome, its trisomy severely alters a person's phenotype. As illustrated in Figure 3-27, people with Down's syndrome have characteristic facial features and short stature. They also have heart defects, susceptibility to respiratory infections, and mental retardation. They are prone to developing leukemia and Alzheimer's disease. Although people with Down's syndrome usually have a much shorter-than-normal life span, some live to middle age or beyond. Improved education for children with Down's syndrome shows that they can learn to compensate greatly for their mental handicap.

## Genetic Engineering

Enormous advances have been made in understanding the structure and function of genes. Still, there remains a huge gap between understanding genes and understanding how genes produce behavior. Despite this gap, geneticists have invented a number of methods to influence the traits that genes express. The most recent of these methods is called **genetic engineering,** but other methods have preceded it.

Probably the oldest means of influencing genetic traits is selective breeding. Beginning with the domestication of wolves more than 12,000 years ago, about 20 species of animals have been domesticated by selectively breeding males and females that display particular traits. For instance, the selective breeding of dogs has produced breeds that can run fast, haul heavy loads, retrieve prey, dig for burrowing animals, climb rocky cliffs in search of sea birds, herd sheep and cattle, or sit on an owner's lap and cuddle. Although selective breeding is an effective way to alter gene expression, at present little is known about the basis of the genetic alterations that are obtained in this way.

Maintaining spontaneous mutations is another method of affecting genetic traits. By using this method, researchers create whole populations of animals possessing some unusual trait that originally arose as an unexpected mutation in only one or a few individual animals. In laboratory colonies of mice, for example, large numbers of spontaneous mutations have been discovered and maintained. There are strains of mice that have abnormal movements, such as reeling, staggering, and jumping. Some have diseases of the immune system; others have sensory deficits and are blind or cannot hear. Many of these genetic abnormalities can also be found in humans. As a result, the neural and genetic bases of the altered behavior in the mice can be studied systematically to develop treatments for human disorders.

More direct approaches to manipulating the expression of genetic traits are to alter early embryonic development. One of these approaches is **cloning,** or producing genetically identical organisms. To clone an animal, scientists allow a fertilized egg to replicate a number of times and then implant the identical cells into the uterus of a female. Because all of the individual animals that develop from these cells are genetically the same, such clones can be used to study the relative influences of heredity and environment. Dolly, a female sheep and the first mammal to be cloned (Figure 3-28), opened up a new technology in which identical animals can be produced. If such animals are genetically engineered to produce medicines in their milk, those medicines can be easily extracted from the milk to treat human diseases (Coleman, 1999). It is also possible to produce **chimeric animals,** which have genes from two different species. A cell from one species is introduced into the early embryonic stage of a different species. The resulting animal has cells with genes from both parent species and behaviors that are a product of those gene combinations. Psychologists interested in behavior can find that a chimeric animal displays an interesting mix of the behaviors of the parent species. For example, chickens that have received Japanese quail cells in early embryogenesis display some aspects of quail crowing behavior rather than chicken crowing behavior, thus providing evidence for the genetic basis of some bird vocalization (Balaban et al., 1988). The chimeric preparation provides an investigative tool for studying the neural basis of crowing because quail neurons can be distinguished from chicken neurons when examined under a microscope.

Genetic engineering, derived from DNA research, is the most direct avenue for the study of gene expression. In its simplest form, genetic engineering entails either removing a gene from a genome or adding a gene to it. In so-called **transgenic animals,** usually mice, a gene added to the genome is passed along and expressed in subsequent generations. One application of genetic engineering is in the study and treatment of human genetic disorders. For instance, researchers have introduced into a line of mice the human gene that causes Huntington's chorea (Lione et al., 1999). The mice express the Huntington gene and display symptoms similar to those of human Huntington's chorea. This mouse line is being used to study potential therapies for this disorder in humans. So-called **knockout technology** can be used to inactivate a gene so that a line of mice fails to express it (Mayford & Kandel, 1999). That line of mice can then be used to study possible therapies for human disorders caused by the loss of a single protein due to a mutant gene. Remarkably interesting knockout animals can be produced. For example, a knockout mouse may be prepared that will grow up with a superior memory or with no memory or a mouse may be allowed to grow up quite normally and the gene is then knocked out in adulthood. It is potentially possible to knock out genes that are related to certain kinds of memory, such as emotional memory, social memory, or spatial memory. Such technology provides a useful way of investigating the neural basis of memory. So genetic research is directed not only toward finding cures for genetic abnormalities in brain and behavior, but also toward studying normal brain function.

AP Photo / John Chadwick

**Figure 3-28**

Dolly (*at right*) was the first mammal to be artificially cloned from an adult somatic cell. In 1996, a team of researchers in Scotland implanted a nucleus from a mammary-gland cell of an adult sheep into another ewe's unfertilized egg, from which the nucleus had been removed. Once the nucleus had been induced to begin dividing, the embryo was implanted into a third sheep's uterus. Dolly, a clone of the donor of the original mammary cell, subsequently produced a lamb (*at left*) from an egg fertilized in the traditional manner.

## In Review

Our 46 chromosomes each contain thousands of genes, and each gene contains the code for one protein. The genes that we receive from our mothers and fathers may include slightly different versions (alleles) of particular genes, which will be expressed in slightly different proteins. The proteins are the building blocks of cells, forming the cells' various organelles as well as the channels, pumps, neurotransmitters, and receptors that are central to the cells' functions. Abnormalities in a gene, caused by mutations, can result in an abnormally formed protein that, in turn, results in the abnormal function of cells. The abnormal function of cells can result in neurological disorders such as Tay-Sachs disease and Huntington's chorea. Genetic engineering is a new science in which the genome of an animal is altered. Cloned animals have the identical genetic composition of a parent or sibling; transgenic animals contain new or altered genes; and knockouts have genomes from which a gene has been deleted. The study of alterations in the nervous systems or in the behavior of animals produced by these manipulations can be a source of insight into how genes produce proteins and how proteins contribute to the structure and function of the nervous system.

**Transgenic animal.** An animal that has artificially received a new gene.

**Knockout technology.** A method in genetics in which a gene is deleted from a chromosome or its expression is blocked.

**neuroscience interactive**

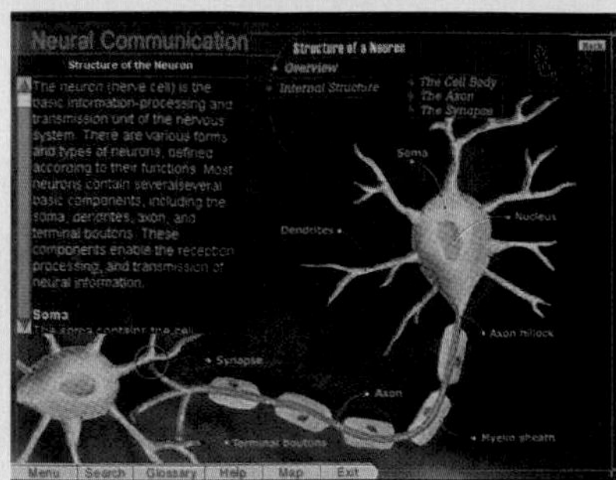


There are many resources available for expanding your learning on line:

- **www.worthpublishers.com/kolb/chapter3**

Try some self-tests to reinforce your mastery of the material. Look at some of the news updates reflecting current research on the brain. You'll also be able to link to other sites which will reinforce what you've learned.

- **http://neurowww.neur.cwru.edu/teach/movies.htm**

Link to a video of neurons in action from the National Institutes of Health.

- **http://vector.cshl.org/dnaftb/**

Review genetics at this Web site from the Cold Spring Harbor Laboratory.

On your CD-ROM you'll be able to quiz yourself on your comprehension of the chapter. You'll also be able to begin learning about the cells of the nervous system in the module on Neural Communication. This module includes animations and detailed drawings of the neuron. In addition, the Research Methods module includes a video clip of neurons and glia as well as a detailed overview of various histological techniques.

## SUMMARY

1. *What kinds of cells are found in the nervous system?* The nervous system is composed of two kinds of cells: neurons, which transmit information, and glia, which are support cells. The three types of neurons are sensory neurons (which send information from the body's sensory receptors), motor neurons (which send commands enabling muscles to move), and interneurons (which link sensory and motor activities). Glial cells also can be grouped by their structure and function. Ependymal cells produce cerebrospinal fluid; astroglia structurally support neurons, help to form the blood–brain barrier, and seal off damaged brain tissue; microglia aid in the repair of brain cells; and oligodendroglia and Schwann cells provide myelin to axons in the central and peripheral nervous systems, respectively.
2. *What is the basic external structure of a neuron?* A neuron is composed of three basic parts: a cell body, or soma; branching extensions called dendrites designed to receive information; and a single axon that passes information along to other cells. A dendrite's area is greatly increased by numerous dendritic spines; an axon may have branches called axon collaterals, which are further divided into teleodendria, each ending at a terminal button. The "almost connection" between a terminal button and the dendritic spine of another neuron is known as a synapse.
3. *How is a cell internally structured?* A cell is surrounded by a cell membrane that protects the cell and regulates what enters and leaves it. Within the cell are a number of compartments, also enclosed in membranes. These compartments include the nucleus (which contains the cell's chromosomes and genes), the endoplasmic reticulum (where proteins are manufactured), the mitochondria (where energy is gathered and stored), the Golgi bodies (where protein molecules are packaged for transport), and lysosomes (which break down wastes). A cell also contains a system of tubules that aid cell movements, provide structural support, and act as highways for transporting substances.
4. *Why are proteins important to cells?* The nucleus of a cell contains chromosomes, which are long chains of genes, each of which carries the code for manufacturing a certain protein that is necessary for the cell's structure and function. Proteins perform many different tasks by virtue of their many different shapes. Some act as enzymes to facilitate chemical reactions; others serve as membrane channels, gates, and pumps; and still others are exported from the cell that made them for use in other parts of the body. To a large extent, the work of cells is carried out by proteins.
5. *How do genes work?* A gene is a segment of a DNA molecule and is made up of a sequence of nucleotide bases. Through a process called transcription, a copy of a gene is produced in a strand of mRNA. The mRNA then travels to the endoplasmic reticulum, where it passes through a ribosome and is translated into a sequence of amino acids. The resulting chain of amino acids is called a polypeptide. Polypeptides fold and combine to form protein molecules with distinctive shapes that are used for specific purposes in the body.
6. *What do we inherit genetically from our parents?* From each parent, we inherit one of each of the chromosomes in our 23 chromosome pairs. Because chromosomes are "matched" pairs, a cell contains two copies (alleles) of every gene, one from the mother and one from the father. Sometimes alleles are homozygous (the same), and sometimes they are heterozygous (different). An allele may be dominant and expressed as a trait, recessive and not expressed, or codominant, in which case both it and the other allele in the pair are expressed. One allele of each gene is designated the wild type, or most common one in a population, whereas the other alleles of that gene are called mutations. A person might inherit any of these alleles from a parent, depending on that parent's genotype.

7. *What is the relation between genes, cells, and behavior?* Comprehending the links between genes, cells, and behavior is the ultimate goal of future research, but as yet these links are only poorly understood. The structure and function of a cell are properties of all its many genes and proteins, just as behavior is a property of the actions of billions of nerve cells. It will take years to learn how such a complex system works. In the meantime, the study of genetic abnormalities is a potential source of insight into the relation among gene, neurons, and behavior.
8. *What causes genetic abnormalities?* Genes can potentially undergo many mutations, in which their codes are altered by one or more changes in the nucleotide sequence. Most mutations are harmful and may produce abnormalities in nervous system structure and behavioral function. Examples are Tay-Sachs disease and Huntington's chorea. Genetic research seeks to prevent the expression of such abnormalities and to find cures for those that are expressed.

## KEY TERMS

blood–brain barrier, p. 87
cell membrane, p. 94
channel, p. 101
chromosome, p. 97
cloning, p. 108
gate, p. 101
gene, p. 97
genetic engineering, p. 108
hydrocephalus, p. 87
hydrophilic, p. 93
hydrophobic, p. 97
knockout technology, p. 109
messenger RNA (mRNA), p. 98
myelin, p. 88
neuron hypothesis, p. 79
paralysis, p. 88
polypeptide, p. 99
protein, p. 99
pump, p. 102
transcription, p. 98
transgenic animal, p. 109
translation, p. 98

## REVIEW QUESTIONS

1. Describe five kinds of neurons and five kinds of glia and their functions.
2. Describe the functions of the different parts of a cell.
3. Why can so many nervous system diseases be due to faulty genes?

## FOR FURTHER THOUGHT

People often compare the "machine of the day" to the nervous system. Why can we never understand our nervous system by comparing it to a computer and how it works?

## RECOMMENDED READING

Alberts, B., Bray, D., Lewis, J., Raff, M., Roberts, K., & Watson, J.D. (1983). *Molecular biology of the cell* (3rd ed.). New York: Garland. This standard text provides a comprehensive description of the cells and cell function in living organisms.

Levitan, I. B., & Kaczmarek, L. K. (1997). *The neuron: Cell and molecular biology* (2nd ed). Oxford: Oxford University Press. An extremely readable text describing the function of the neuron. Although the coverage is comprehensive, the text is enjoyable to read and is accompanied by numerous illustrations that assist in explanation.

CHAPTER

# 4

# How Do Neurons Convey Information?



Mason Morfit / FPG International / PictureQuest
Micrograph: Dr. David Scott/Phototake

Figure 4-1 is perhaps the most reproduced drawing in behavioral neuroscience. Taken from René Descartes's book titled *Treatise on Man,* it illustrates the first serious attempt to explain how information travels through the nervous system. Descartes proposed that the carrier of information is cerebrospinal fluid flowing through nerve tubes. When the fire in Figure 4-1 burns the man's toe, it stretches the skin, which tugs on a nerve tube leading to the brain. In response to the tug, a valve in a ventricle of the brain opens and cerebrospinal fluid flows down the tube and fills the leg muscles, causing them to contract and pull the toe back from the fire. The flow of fluid through other tubes to other muscles of the body (not shown here) causes the head to turn toward the painful stimulus and the hands to rub the injured toe.

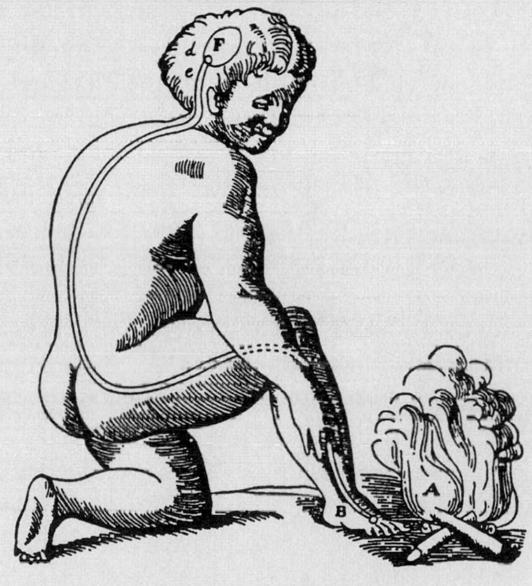

**Figure 4-1**
In Descartes's concept of how the nervous system conveys information, heat from a flame causes skin on the foot to stretch, and this stretching pulls a nerve tube going to the brain. The pull opens a valve in the brain's ventricle. The fluid in the ventricle flows through the nerve tube to fill the muscles of the leg, causing the foot to withdraw. Tubes to other muscles (not shown) cause the eyes and head to turn to look at the burn and cause the hand and body to bend to protect the foot.
From Descartes, 1664.

Descartes's theory was inaccurate, as discussed in Chapter 1. Even at the time that his book appeared, this theory did not receive much support. It was clear from the examination of nerves that they were not tubes, and the idea that muscles fill with fluid as they contract proved to be equally wrong. If an arm muscle is contracted when the arm is held in a tub of water, the water level in the tub does not rise, as it should if the mass of the muscle were increasing owing to an influx of fluid.

Still, Descartes's theory was remarkable for its time because it considered the three basic processes that underlie a behavioral response:

1. Detecting a sensory stimulus and sending a message to the brain
2. Deciding, by using the brain, what response should be made
3. Sending a response from the brain to command muscles to move

Descartes was trying to explain the very same things that we want to explain today. If it is not stretched skin tugging on a nerve tube that initiates the message, the message must still be initiated in some other way. If it is not the opening of valves to initiate the flow of cerebrospinal fluid to convey the information, the flow of information must still be sent by some other means. If it is not the filling of muscles with fluid that produces movements, some other mechanism must still cause muscles to contract. What all these other mechanisms are is the subject of this chapter. We will examine how information gets from the environment to neurons, how neurons conduct the information throughout the nervous system, and how neurons ultimately activate muscles to produce movement.

## ELECTRICITY AND NEURONS

The first hints about how the nervous system conveys its messages came in the second half of the eighteenth century with the discovery of electricity. By following the clue that electricity was in some way implicated in neural messages, scientists eventually provided an accurate answer to the three questions to be examined in this chapter.

### What Is Electricity?

Link to an introductory review of electricity at the Web site at **www.worthpublishers.com/kolb/chapter4.**

**Negative pole:** more electrons
**Positive pole:** fewer electrons
**Current:** flow of electrons from negative to positive pole
**Electrical potential:** *difference* in electrical charge (measured in volts) between negative and positive poles

**Electricity** is a flow of electrons from a body that contains a higher charge (more electrons) to a body that contains a lower charge (fewer electrons). The body with the higher electrical charge is called the **negative pole,** because electrons are negatively charged and this body has more of them. The body with the lower electrical charge is called the **positive pole.** Electricity is measured in **volts,** which describe the *difference* in **electrical potential** between the two poles. The term *potential* is used here because the electrons on the negative pole have the potential to flow to the positive pole. The negatively charged electrons are attracted to the positive pole because opposite charges are attracted to each other. A flow of electrons is called a **current.** If you look at a battery, you will see that one of its poles is marked "−" for negative and the other "+" for positive. These two poles are separated by an **insulator,** a substance through which electrons cannot flow. Therefore, a current of electrons flows from the negative (−) to the positive (+) pole only if the two poles are connected by a conducting medium, such as a wire. If a wire from each pole is brought into contact with tissue, the current will flow from the wire connected to the negative pole into the tissue and then from the tissue into the wire connected to the positive pole. Such wires are called **electrodes.**

Electrons can accumulate on many substances, including ourselves, which is why you sometimes get a shock from touching a metal object after walking on a carpet. From the carpet, you accumulate relatively loose electrons, which give you a greater negative charge than that of objects around you. In short, you become a negative pole. Electrons normally leave your body as you walk around, because the earth acts as a positive pole. If you are wearing rubber-soled shoes, however, you retain an electrical potential because the soles of the shoes act as an insulator. If you then touch a metal object, such as a water fountain, electrons that are equally distributed on your body suddenly rush through the contact area of your fingertips. In fact, if you watch your fingertips just before they touch the water fountain, you will see a small lightning bolt as the electrons are transferred. These electrons leaving your fingertips give you the shock.

Combing your hair is another way to accumulate electrons. If you then hold a piece of paper near the comb, the paper will bend in the comb's direction. The negative charges on the comb have pushed the negative charges on the front side of the paper to the back side of the paper, leaving the front side of the paper positively charged. Because unlike charges attract, the paper bends toward the comb.

### Early Clues to Electrical Activity in the Nervous System

In 1731, Stephen Gray performed a similar experiment. He rubbed a rod with a piece of cloth to accumulate electrons on the rod. Then he touched the charged rod to the feet of a boy suspended on a rope and brought a metal foil to the boy's nose. The foil bent on approaching the boy's nose, being attracted to it, and, as the foil and nose touched, electricity passed from the rod, through the boy, to the foil. Yet the boy was completely unaware that the electricity had passed through his body. Gray speculated that electricity might be the messenger in the nervous system. Although this conclusion was not precisely correct, two other lines of evidence suggested that electrical activity was somehow implicated in the nervous system's flow of information. One of these lines of evidence consisted of the results of electrical-stimulation studies, the other of the results of electrical-recording studies.

**Electrical stimulation.** The flow of electrical current from the tip of an electrode through brain tissue that results in changes in the electrical activity of the tissue.

## ELECTRICAL-STIMULATION STUDIES

Electrical-stimulation studies began in the eighteenth century when an Italian scientist, Luigi Galvani, observed that frogs' legs hanging on a wire in a market twitched during a lightning storm. He surmised that sparks of electricity from the storm were activating the muscles. Investigating this possibility, he found that, if an electrical current is applied to a dissected nerve, the muscle to which the nerve is connected contracts. Galvani concluded that the electricity flowed along the nerve to the muscle. He was wrong in this conclusion, but his experiment was pointing scientists in the right direction.

Many other researchers have used Galvani's technique of electrically stimulating the nervous system to produce muscle contraction. This technique requires an **electrical stimulator,** which is a device like a battery that can deliver an electrical current. Figure 4-2A illustrates an electrical stimulator. This stimulator transforms the 120-volt current from a wall socket into a current ranging from 2 to 10 volts, which will not damage cells. Timers allow the stimulator to deliver either a single pulse of current lasting about 1/100 of a second or a series of these brief pulses. Wire leads connected to the stimulator's negative and positive poles carry the electrical current. One lead is attached to a stimulating electrode, which is usually a wire (or a specially constructed glass tube) insulated except for the tip that comes in contact with the cells to be stimulated. The lead (also called the reference) attached to the positive pole is placed on some other part of the body. When the stimulator is on, the flow of electricity out of the tip of the electrode onto the cells is enough to produce a physiological response.

In the mid-nineteenth century, two Prussian scientists, Gustave Theodor Fritsch and Eduard Hitzig, demonstrated a link between electrical stimulation of the brain and muscle contraction, causing movement. They studied several animal species, including rabbits and dogs, and may even have stimulated the brain of a person, whom they were treating for head injuries on a Prussian battlefield. They observed

Visit the CD and find the area on electrical stimulation in the module on Research Methods. You'll see a model of an electrical stimulator and a video clip of the self-stimulation of a rat.

**Figure 4-2**

**(A)** A stimulator is a source of electrical current. Current leaves the stimulator through a wire lead (red) that attaches to an electrode. From the uninsulated tip of the electrode, the current enters the tissue and, in doing so, stimulates it. A second lead (green) is connected to a reference electrode, which contacts a relatively large surface area to which current from the site of stimulation can flow. Because the surface area of the reference electrode is large, the electrical current is spread out and therefore does not excite the tissue here. **(B)** A voltmeter records electrical current. If a charge under the recording electrode (red) is high relative to the reference electrode (green), current flows from the uninsulated tip of the recording electrode through the voltmeter, deflecting its recording needle, and into the reference electrode.

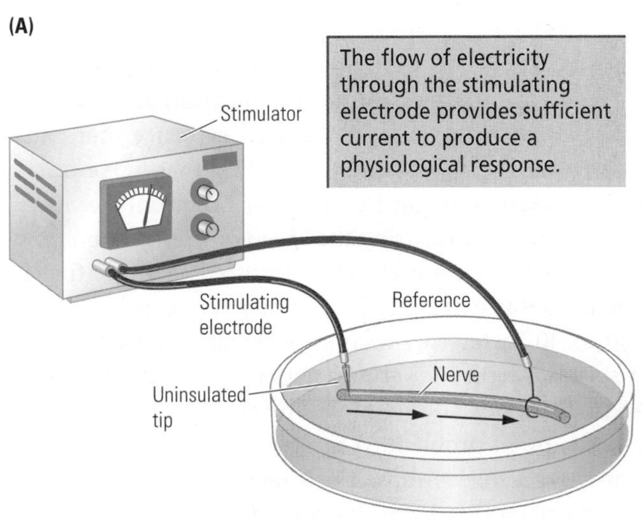
(A)
Stimulator
The flow of electricity through the stimulating electrode provides sufficient current to produce a physiological response.
Stimulating electrode
Reference
Nerve
Uninsulated tip

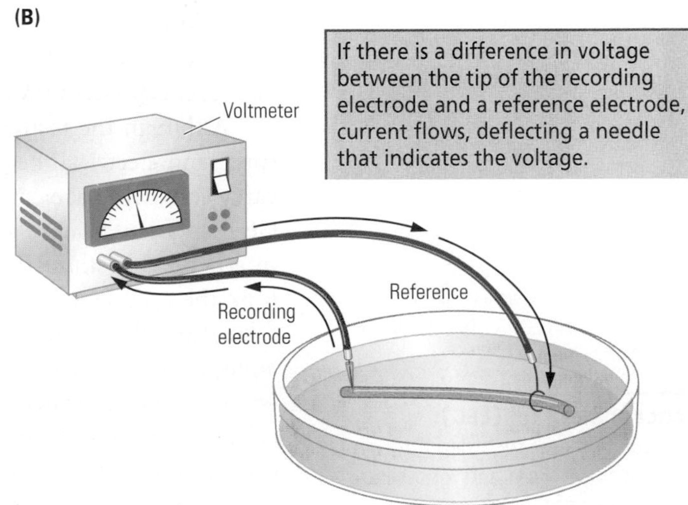
(B)
Voltmeter
If there is a difference in voltage between the tip of the recording electrode and a reference electrode, current flows, deflecting a needle that indicates the voltage.
Recording electrode
Reference

movements of the arms and legs in response to the stimulation of the neocortex. In 1874, R. Bartholow, a Cincinnati physician, wrote the first report describing the effects of human brain stimulation. His patient, Mary Rafferty, had a skull defect that exposed part of her neocortex. Bartholow stimulated her exposed neocortex to examine the effects. In one of his observations he wrote:

> Passed an insulated needle into the left posterior lobe so that the non-insulated portion rested entirely in the substance of the brain. The reference was placed in contact with the dura mater. When the circuit was closed, muscular contraction in the right upper and lower extremities ensued. Faint but visible contraction of the left eyelid, and dilation of the pupils, also ensued. Mary complained of a very strong and unpleasant feeling of tingling in both right extremities, especially in the right arm, which she seized with the opposite hand and rubbed vigorously. Notwithstanding the very evident pain from which she suffered, she smiled as if much amused. (Bartholow, 1874)

Wilder Penfield (1891–1976)

Bartholow's report was not well received. An uproar after its publication forced him to leave Cincinnati. Nevertheless, he had demonstrated that the brain of a conscious person could be stimulated electrically to produce movement of the body.

In the twentieth century, brain stimulation became a standard part of many neurosurgical procedures. In particular, after the method had been perfected in experimental animal studies, Wilder Penfield, a neurosurgeon at the Montreal Neurological Institute, used electrical stimulation to map the neocortex of surgery patients in the 1950s. The maps that he produced allowed him to determine the function of various neocortical regions and so to minimize the removal of undamaged tissue. Penfield especially wanted to locate language areas in the neocortex to be able to spare them during surgery.

## ELECTRICAL-RECORDING STUDIES

Click on the CD and find the EEG section in the module on Research Methods. Investigate a model of an EEG and view EEG recordings.

Another line of evidence that the flow of information in the brain is partly electrical in nature came from the results of recording experiments with the use of a **voltmeter,** a device that measures the flow of electricity. A voltmeter, which is illustrated in Figure 4-2B, has one wire connected to a recording electrode and a second connected to a reference electrode, much as an electrical stimulator does. Any difference in voltage between the tip of the recording electrode and the reference causes a current to flow through the voltmeter, deflecting a needle that indicates the voltage. Richard Caton, a Scottish physician who lived in the late nineteenth and early twentieth centuries, was the first person to attempt to measure the electrical currents of the brain with a sensitive voltmeter. He reported that, when he placed electrodes on the skull, he could detect fluctuations in his voltmeter recordings. This type of brain recording, called an **electroencephalogram (EEG)**, is now a standard way of measuring brain activity.

Hermann von Helmholtz (1821–1894)

Although the results of electrical-recording studies provided evidence that neurons send electrical messages, there was a problem with concluding that nerve tracts carry conventional electrical currents. Hermann von Helmholtz, a nineteenth-century German scientist, developed a procedure for measuring the speed of information flow in a nerve. He stimulated a nerve leading to a muscle and measured the time that it took the muscle to contract. The time was extremely long. The nerve conducted information at the rate of only 30 to 40 meters per second, whereas electricity flows along a wire at the much faster speed of light ($3 \times 10^8$ meters per second). The flow of electricity in the nervous system, then, was not identical with the flow of electricity along a wire. In addition, there was another problem. When two electrodes are placed on the brain, the electrical current flows between those electrodes. So how do muscles that are a considerable distance away from the electrodes come to move? The answer

**Electroencephalogram (EEG).** Electrical activity that is recorded through the skull or from the brain and represents graded potentials of many neurons.

**Figure 4-3**

A wave in water does not entail the forward movement of the water. The stimulus (a stone) changes the height of the surface of the water, and these height differences indicate differences in pressure.

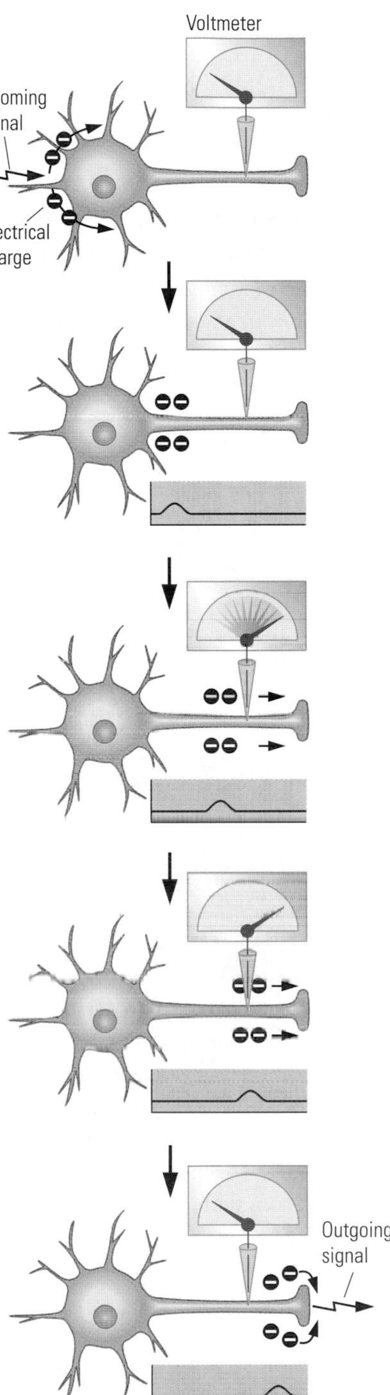


**Figure 4-4**

Neurons can convey information as a wave. Here a wave induced by the stimulation of a neuron travels from the source of a signal on the cell body down the axon to its terminal. A voltmeter recording from the axon detects the passage of the wave.

did not seem to be through conventional electrical impulses. But, if conventional electrical impulses are not the means, how do nerves convey information?

To explain the electrical signals of a neuron, Julius Bernstein suggested in 1886 that the neuron's electrical charge has a chemical basis. This suggestion led to the idea that modifications of a neuron's charge travel along the axon as a wave. Successive waves constitute the message that the neuron conveys. Notice that it is not the *charge* but the *wave* that travels along the axon. To understand the difference, consider other kinds of waves. If you drop a stone into a pool of water, the contact made by the stone hitting the water produces a wave that travels away from the site of impact, as shown in Figure 4-3. The water itself does not move away from the site of impact. Only the change in pressure moves, creating the wave effect. Similarly, when you speak, you induce pressure waves in air molecules, and these waves carry the "sound" of your voice to a listener. If you flick a towel, a wave travels to the other end of the towel. Just as waves through the air send a spoken message, waves of chemical change travel along an axon to deliver a neuron's message.

## Modern Tools for Measuring a Neuron's Electrical Activity

Because we do not feel waves traveling around our bodies, the waves that carry the nervous system's messages must be very small and restricted to the surface of neurons. Still, we can measure such waves and determine how they are produced by using electrical-stimulation and -recording techniques. If an electrode connected to a voltmeter is placed on a single axon, the electrode can detect a change in electrical charge on that axon's membrane as the wave passes. It is also possible to initiate such a wave by electrically stimulating the neuron. Detecting a wave as it moves along an axon is illustrated in Figure 4-4. As simple as this process may sound in concept, it is technically difficult to carry out. The procedure requires a neuron large enough to record, a recording device sufficiently sensitive to detect a very small electrical impulse, and an electrode small enough to place on the surface of a single neuron. The discovery of the giant axon of the squid, the invention of the oscilloscope, and the development of microelectrodes met all these requirements.

## THE GIANT AXON OF THE SQUID

The neurons of most animals, including humans, are very tiny, on the order of 1 to 20 micrometers (μm) in diameter (1 μm = one-one thousandth of a millimeter). An object of this size is too small to be seen by the eye and too small to perform experiments on easily. To measure a neuron's electrical charge requires a much larger neuron.

Link to the CD and find the section on the membrane potential in the module on Neural Communication. You'll view the output from an oscilloscope used for neural recording. Note the oscilloscope changes in electrical potential when the cell is stimulated.

The British zoologist J. Z. Young, when dissecting the North Atlantic squid, *Loligo*, noticed that it has truly giant axons that are as much as a millimeter (1000 micrometers) in diameter. Figure 4-5 illustrates the North Atlantic squid and the giant axons leading to its body wall, or mantle, which contracts to propel the squid through the water. This squid itself is not giant. It is only about a foot long. But these particular axons are giant as axons go. Each is formed by the fusion of many smaller axons into a single large one. Because larger axons send messages faster than smaller axons do, these giant axons allow the squid to jet propel away from predators.

In 1936, Young suggested to Alan Hodgkin and Andrew Huxley, two neuroscientists at Cambridge University in England, that these axons were large enough to be used for electrical-recording studies. A giant axon could be dissected out of the squid and kept functional in a bath of liquid that approximates body fluids. In this way, Hodgkin and Huxley could easily study the neuron's electrical activity.

Andrew Huxley (b. 1917)

Alan Hodgkin (1914–1988)

## THE OSCILLOSCOPE

Hodgkin and Huxley's experiments with the giant squid axon were made possible by the invention of the **oscilloscope.** You are familiar with one form of oscilloscope, a television set. An oscilloscope can also be used as a sensitive voltmeter to measure the very small and rapid changes in electrical currents that come from an axon.

A brief overview of how an oscilloscope works is helpful for understanding its uses in this kind of study. The important component of an oscilloscope is its vacuum

(A)

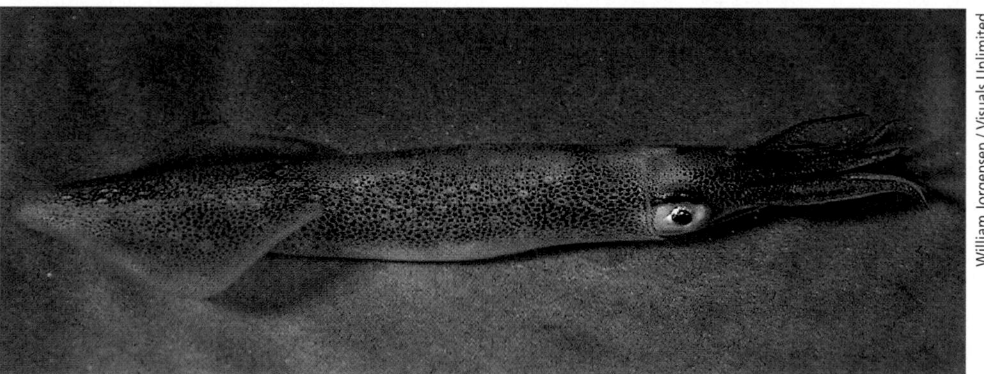


(B)

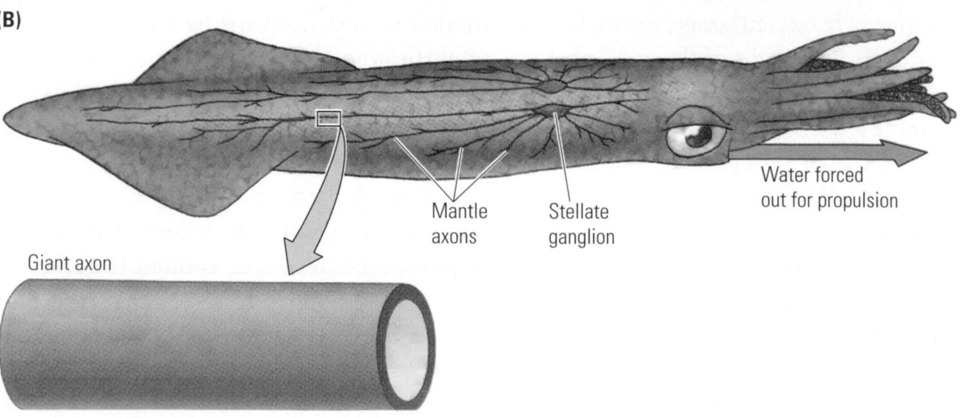


**Figure 4-5**

**(A)** The squid, *Loligo,* propels itself both with fins and with contractions of the mantle, which squirts water for propulsion. **(B)** The stellate ganglion projects axons to the mantle to contract it. These giant axons consist of many smaller axons that are fused together to produce a single axon that rapidly conveys a message instructing the mantle to contract.

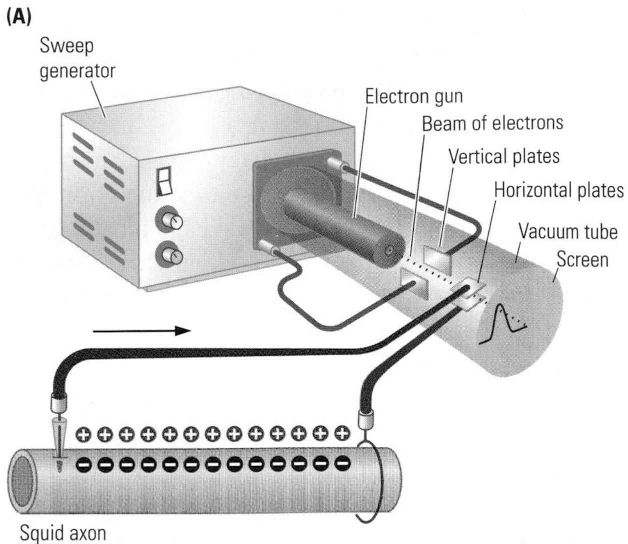


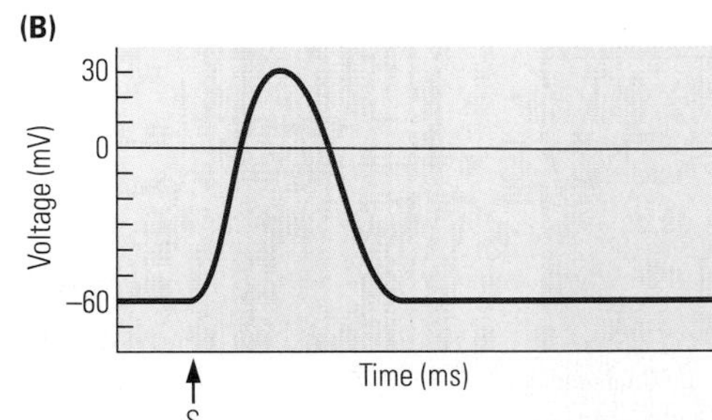


**Figure 4-6**

**(A)** The principal parts of an oscilloscope include: a vacuum tube, which contains an electron gun that emits a beam of electrons toward a screen; horizontal plates, which are connected to a sweep generator that controls a charge on the plates that moves the beam of electrons in the horizontal plane; and vertical plates, which can be connected to an axon from which recordings are made. Changes in electrical current across the membrane deflect the electron beam in the vertical plane. **(B)** In this graphic representation of a recording of voltage change, the horizontal axis measures time in milliseconds (ms) and the vertical axis measures voltage in millivolts (mV). The graph illustrates a change in voltage (from −60 to +30) recorded from the axon. (S stands for stimulation.)

tube, a glass tube from which air is removed. In the tube, a beam of electrons, or negatively charged particles, is projected onto the tube's phosphorus-painted face. When the electrons hit the paint, the phosphorus glows momentarily. Moving the beam of electrons around leaves a visible trace on the screen that lasts a second or so. The movement of the electron beam is produced by changing the charge on two pairs of metal plates. The members of each pair are positioned opposite one another on the inner surface of the tube, as shown in Figure 4-6. Changing the charges on the vertical pair of plates, located on the tube's sides, pushes the electron beam away from the negative pole toward the positive pole. This leaves a horizontal line on the screen. One metal plate of the horizontal pair is located at the top of the tube; the other is located at the bottom. One of these horizontal plates is connected to the recording electrode and the other to the ground electrode. Any electrical change between these two electrodes drives the beam of electrons up and down, leaving a vertical line on the screen.

To visualize how recordings are made with an oscilloscope, imagine aiming a hose at a brick wall. The spray of water is analogous to the beam of electrons. Moving the hose horizontally leaves a horizontal line of water on the wall, whereas moving the hose vertically leaves a vertical line. The water line on the wall is analogous to the phosphorus line traced by the oscilloscope's electron beam. If you move the hose horizontally at a constant rate across the wall and then block the water temporarily and start again, each horizontal sweep provides a measure of time. Now imagine that someone bumps your arm as you make a horizontal sweep. There will be a vertical deflection of the trace as it sweeps horizontally across the wall. The time during which the trace is deflected away from the horizontal baseline indicates how long the bump lasted, and the height of the deflection indicates the size of the bump.

An oscilloscope operates in a very similar way. The charge on the horizontal poles is controlled by a timer, whereas the vertical poles are connected to the preparation from which the recording is being made. A vertical deflection of the horizontally moving trace indicates a change in electrical activity on the preparation. Measuring the duration of this deflection tells how long the electrical change lasts, whereas measuring the size of the deflection tells the change's magnitude. The advantage of using an oscilloscope instead of a voltmeter with a mechanical needle is that an oscilloscope can record extremely small and rapid events, such as those that take place in an axon. The scales used when recording from an axon are *milliseconds* (1 ms = one-one thousandth of a second) and *millivolts* (1 mV = one-one thousandth of a volt).

Link to the CD and find the area on microelectrodes in the Research Methods module. You'll see a model and a video clip demonstrating how microelectrodes are used.

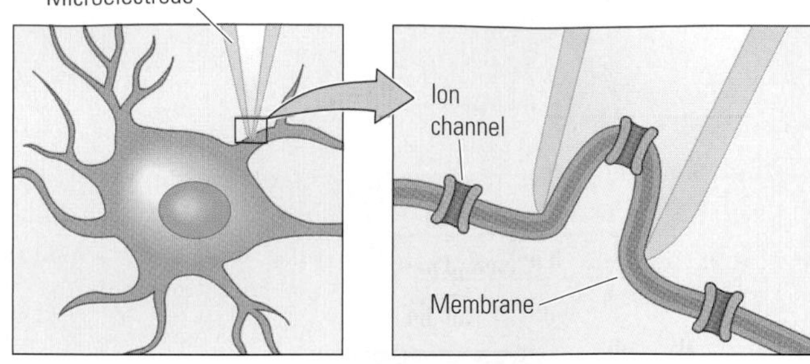


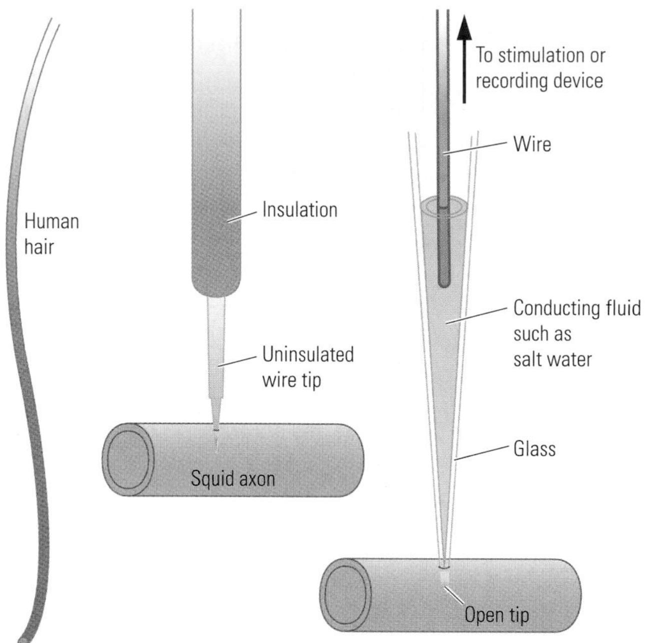


**Figure 4-7**

(*Top*) One way to use a microelectrode is to record from only a small piece of an axon. Here, a small piece has been pulled up into the electrode through suction. (*Bottom*) A squid axon is about the size of a human hair (*left*) but is larger than the tip of either a wire (*middle*) or a glass (*right*) microelectrode. The tip of the wire electrode is etched to a thickness of about a micrometer, and all of the wire except the tip is insulated. The glass tube is heated and pulled so that it has a sharp tip about a micrometer in size. The tube is filled with salt water to act as a conducting medium. Both types of electrodes can be placed on an axon or into it.

### MICROELECTRODES

The final ingredient needed to measure a neuron's electrical activity is a set of electrodes small enough to be placed on or into an axon. Such electrodes, called *microelectrodes,* can also be used to deliver an electrical current to a single neuron. One way to make a microelectrode is to etch the tip of a piece of thin wire to a fine point and insulate the rest of the wire. The very tiny tip is what is placed on or into the neuron, as illustrated in Figure 4-7, which shows such a microelectrode inserted into a squid axon. Microelectrodes can also be made from a thin glass tube. If the middle of the tube is heated while the ends of the tube are pulled, the middle stretches as it turns molten, and eventually breaks, producing two pieces of glass tubing, each tapered to a very fine tip. The tip of a glass microelectrode can be as small as 1 micrometer (one-one thousandth of a millimeter), even though it still remains hollow. When the glass tube is then filled with salty water, which provides the medium through which an electrical current can travel, it acts as an electrode. Figure 4-7 also shows a glass microelectrode containing a salt solution. A wire placed in the salt solution connects the electrode to an oscilloscope.

Microelectrodes are used to record from an axon in a number of different ways. Placing the tip of a microelectrode on an axon provides an extracellular measure of the electrical current from a very small part of the axon. If a second microelectrode is used as the ground, one tip can be placed on the surface of the axon and the other inserted into the axon. This technique provides a measure of voltage across the cell membrane. A still more refined use of a microelectrode is to place its tip on the axon and apply a little back suction until the tip becomes sealed to a patch of the axon. This technique is analogous to placing a soda straw against a piece of plastic wrapping and sucking back to grasp the plastic. This method allows a recording to be made only from the small patch of axon that is clamped.

Using the giant axon of the squid, an oscilloscope, and microelectrodes, Hodgkin and Huxley recorded the electrical voltage on an axon's membrane and explained a nerve impulse. The basis of this electrical activity is the movement of intracellular and extracellular ions, which carry positive and negative charges. So to understand Hodgkin and Huxley's results, you first need to understand the principles underlying the movement of ions.

## How the Movement of Ions Creates Electrical Charges

**Examples of positive ions (cations):**
Sodium ($Na^+$), Potassium ($K^+$)

**Examples of negative ions (anions):**
Chloride ($Cl^-$), Many proteins

As you learned in Chapter 3, the intracellular and extracellular fluid of a neuron is filled with various kinds of charged ions, including positively charged $Na^+$ (sodium) and $K^+$ (potassium) ions, and negatively charged $Cl^-$ (chloride) ions. These fluids also contain numerous negatively charged protein molecules. Positively charged ions are called *cations,* and negatively charged ions are called *anions* ($A^-$ for short), a term that we will use for negatively charged protein molecules, too.

Three factors influence the movement of ions into and out of cells: *diffusion, concentration,* and *charge.* Diffusion results from the fact that all molecules have an intrinsic kinetic energy called thermal motion or heat. Because molecules move constantly, they spontaneously tend to spread out from where they are more concentrated to where they are less concentrated. This spreading out is **diffusion.** Requiring no work, diffusion results from the random motion of molecules as they spontaneously move and bounce off one another, until they gradually disperse in a solution. When diffusion is complete, there is dynamic equilibrium, with an equal number of molecules everywhere. Smoke from a fire gradually diffuses into the air of a room, until every bit of air contains the same number of smoke molecules. Dye poured into water diffuses in the same way—from its point of contact to every part of the water in the container. As you learned in Chapter 3, when salts are placed in water, they fall to the bottom of the container and dissolve into ions surrounded by water molecules. Carried by the random motion of the water molecules, the ions diffuse throughout the solution, until every part of the container has exactly the same concentration.

**Concentration gradient** is a term that describes the relative differences in concentration of a substance between two spatial locations. As illustrated in Figure 4-8A, if a little ink is placed in water, the dye will start out concentrated at the site of first contact and then spread away from that site. In this way, the ink diffuses down a gradient from a point of high concentration to points of low concentration until it is equally distributed. At that point, all of the water in the container is colored equally. A similar process takes place when a salt solution is placed into water. The concentration of the salt solution is initially high in the location where it enters the water, but it then diffuses from that location to other points in the container until its ions are in equilibrium. You are familiar with other kinds of gradients. For example, a car parked on a hill will roll down the grade if it is taken out of gear.

Because ions carry an electrical charge, their movement can be described by either a concentration gradient or a **voltage gradient.** The ions move down a voltage gradient from an area of high charge to an area of lower charge, just as they move down a concentration gradient from an area of high concentration to an area of lower concentration. Figure 4-8B illustrates this process. It shows that, when salt is dissolved in water, its diffusion can be described as either movement down a concentration gradient (for sodium and chloride) or movement down a voltage gradient (for the positive and negative charges). In a container such as a beaker, which allows unimpeded movement of ions, the positive and negative charges balance one another, and so there is no voltage difference.

**Diffusion.** The movement of ions from an area of high concentration to an area of low concentration through random motion.

**Concentration gradient.** The difference in the concentration of a substance between two regions of a container that allows the flow of the substance from an area of high concentration to an area of low concentration.

Click on the CD and find the membrane potential section in the module on Neural Communication. You'll watch an animation of how electrical and concentration gradients mediate ionic movement through the membrane. Note the changes on the oscilloscope as ions flow into and out of the cell.

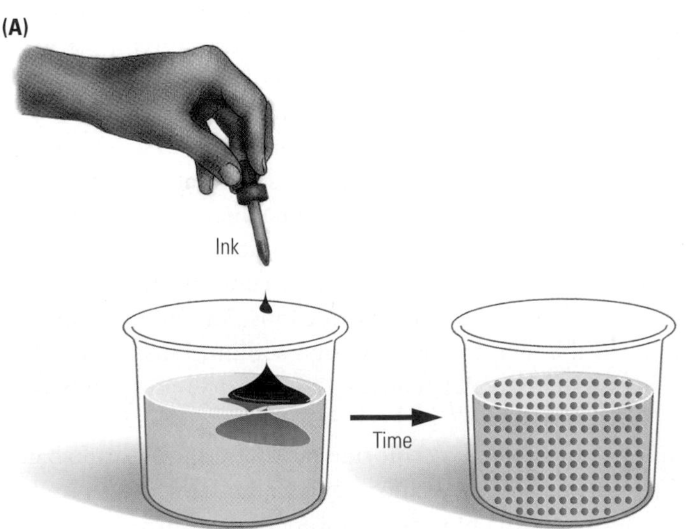


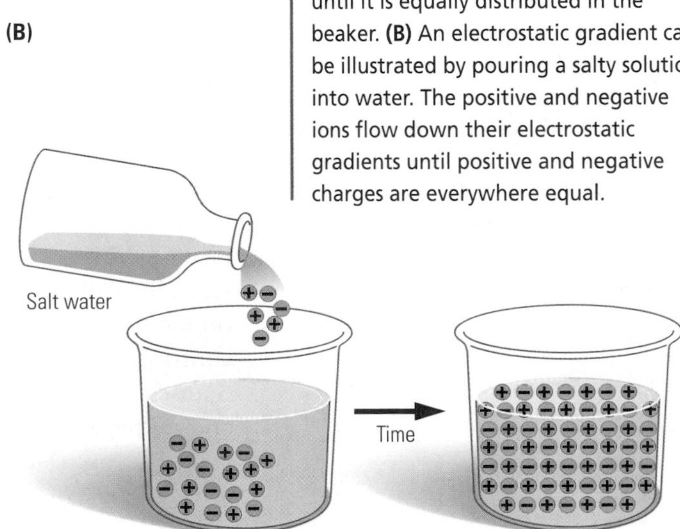


**Figure 4-8**

**(A)** A concentration gradient can be illustrated by dropping a small amount of ink in a beaker of water. The ink will flow away from the initial point of contact, where it has a high concentration, into areas of low concentration until it is equally distributed in the beaker. **(B)** An electrostatic gradient can be illustrated by pouring a salty solution into water. The positive and negative ions flow down their electrostatic gradients until positive and negative charges are everywhere equal.

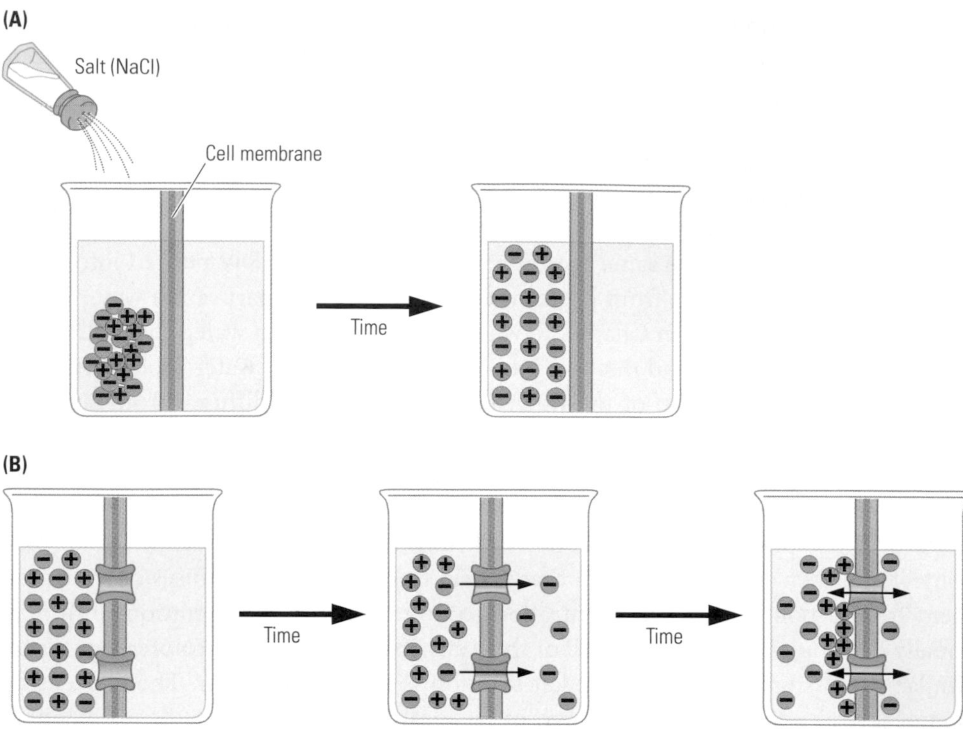


**Figure 4-9**

**(A)** When salt is placed into a container of water, which in this example is divided into two parts by a barrier, the salt dissolves. Positive and negative ions distribute themselves through half of the container but cannot cross the barrier. **(B)** If the barrier has a hole through which $Cl^-$ can pass but $Na^+$ cannot pass, $Cl^-$ will diffuse from the side of high concentration through the hole in the barrier. However, $Cl^-$ will not be equally distributed on the two sides of the container, because the negative chloride ions will be attracted back to the positive sodium ions. Thus, half of the container will be positively charged and the other half will be negatively charged, and the voltage difference will be greatest across the membrane.

The lack of an impediment is not the case in intracellular and extracellular fluid, because the semipermeable cell membrane acts as a partial barrier to the movement of ions between a cell's interior and exterior. As described in Chapter 3, a cell membrane is composed of a phospholipid bilayer, with its hydrophobic tails pointing inward toward each other and its hydrophilic heads pointing outward. This membrane is impermeable to salty solutions because the salt ions, which are surrounded by water molecules, will not pass through the membrane's hydrophobic tails.

An imaginary experiment will help to illustrate how a cell membrane influences the movement of ions in this way. Figure 4-9A shows a container of water that is divided in half by a membrane. If we place a few grains of salt (NaCl) in one half of the container, the salt dissolves and the ions diffuse down their concentration gradient until the water in that side of the container is in equilibrium. In this side of the container, there is no longer a concentration gradient for either sodium or chloride ions, because the water everywhere is equally salty. There are no concentration gradients for these ions on the other side of the container either, because the membrane prevents the ions from entering that side. But there *are* concentration gradients for both sodium and chloride ions *across* the membrane—that is, from one side of it to the other.

In Chapter 3, you learned that protein molecules are embedded in a cell membrane and that some of these protein molecules form channels that act as pores to allow certain kinds of ions to pass through. Returning to our imaginary experiment, we place a chloride channel in the membrane that divides the container of water. Chloride ions will now cross the membrane and move down their concentration gradient on the side of the container that previously had no chloride ions. The sodium ions, in contrast, will not be able to cross the membrane. Although sodium ions are smaller than chloride ions, sodium ions have a greater tendency to stick to water molecules and so they are bulkier.

If the only factor affecting the movement of chloride ions were the chloride concentration gradient, the efflux (outward flow) of chloride from the salty to the unsalty side of the container would continue until chloride ions were in equilibrium on both sides. But this is not what actually happens. Because the chloride ions carry a negative charge, they are attracted back toward the positively charged sodium ions (opposite charges attract). Consequently, the concentration of chloride ions remains higher in the first side of the container than in the second side, as illustrated in Figure 4-9B. The efflux of chloride ions down the chloride concentration gradient is counteracted by the influx (inward flow) of chloride ions down the chloride voltage gradient. At some point, an equilibrium is reached in which the concentration gradient of chloride ions is balanced by the voltage gradient of chloride ions. In brief:

concentration gradient = voltage gradient

At this equilibrium, there is a disproportionate concentration of the ions on the two sides of the membrane, so a voltage across the membrane exists. The first side of the container is positively charged because some chloride ions have left, leaving a preponderance of positive ($Na^+$) charges. The second side of the container is negatively charged because some chloride ions ($Cl^-$) have entered that chamber where no ions were before. The charge is highest on the surface of the membrane, the point at which positive and negative ions accumulate to balance each other. This example is much the same as what happens in a real cell, which will be described in the next section.

## In Review

Even several hundred years ago, the results of studies suggested that electrical activity was somehow implicated in the nervous system's flow of information. But it was not until the mid-twentieth century that scientists solved all the technical problems in measuring the changes in electrical charge that travel like a wave along an axon's membrane. Their solutions included recording from the giant axons of the North Atlantic squid, using an oscilloscope to measure small changes in voltage, and obtaining microelectrodes small enough to place on or into an axon. The electrical activity of axons entails the flow of charged particles called ions. Ions move both down a concentration gradient (from an area of relatively high concentration to an area of lower concentration) and down a voltage gradient (from an area of relatively high charge to an area of lower charge). The flow of ions in the nervous system is also affected by ion channels in cell membranes, which may be either open (facilitating ion movement) or closed (impeding that movement).

# THE ELECTRICAL ACTIVITY OF A MEMBRANE

With this imaginary experiment in mind, you are now ready to delve inside the nervous system to see how the movement of ions across real neural membranes creates electrical activity. We will consider five aspects of the membrane's electrical activity: the resting potential, graded potentials, the action potential, the nerve impulse, and saltatory conduction. In doing so, we will also investigate the role that ion channels play in these processes. By the end of this section, you will understand how all of these events are related—how all enable an axon to convey information.

## The Resting Potential

An undisturbed axon has a difference in electrical charge across its membrane, called resting potential. Figure 4-10D graphs the voltage difference recorded when one microelectrode is placed on the outer surface of an axon's membrane and another is

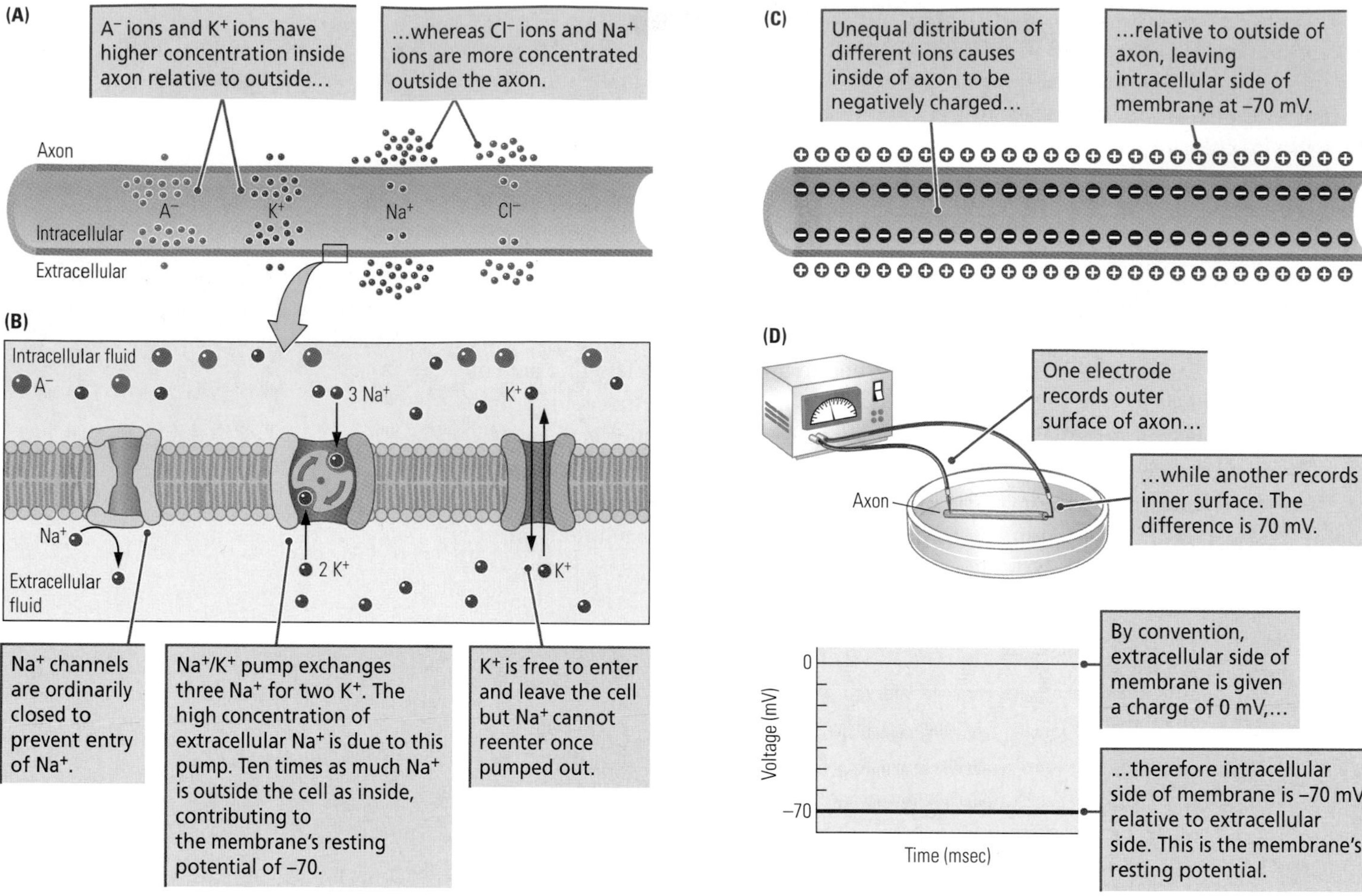
(A)
A⁻ ions and K⁺ ions have higher concentration inside axon relative to outside...
...whereas Cl⁻ ions and Na⁺ ions are more concentrated outside the axon.
Axon
A⁻
K⁺
Na⁺
Cl⁻
Intracellular
Extracellular
(B)
Intracellular fluid
A⁻
3 Na⁺
K⁺
Na⁺
2 K⁺
K⁺
Extracellular fluid
Na⁺ channels are ordinarily closed to prevent entry of Na⁺.
Na⁺/K⁺ pump exchanges three Na⁺ for two K⁺. The high concentration of extracellular Na⁺ is due to this pump. Ten times as much Na⁺ is outside the cell as inside, contributing to the membrane's resting potential of –70.
K⁺ is free to enter and leave the cell but Na⁺ cannot reenter once pumped out.
(C)
Unequal distribution of different ions causes inside of axon to be negatively charged...
...relative to outside of axon, leaving intracellular side of membrane at –70 mV.
(D)
One electrode records outer surface of axon...
...while another records inner surface. The difference is 70 mV.
Axon
0
–70
Voltage (mV)
Time (msec)
By convention, extracellular side of membrane is given a charge of 0 mV,...
...therefore intracellular side of membrane is –70 mV relative to extracellular side. This is the membrane's resting potential.

**Figure 4-10**

**(A)** The relative concentrations of ions on the intracellular and extracellular sides of an axon's cell membrane produce an electrical charge. Protein ($A^-$) ions and potassium ($K^+$) ions have higher concentrations on the intracellular side of the membrane relative to the extracellular side, and $Cl^-$ ions and $Na^+$ ions have higher relative concentrations on the extracellular side. **(B)** Closed gates prevent $Na^+$ ions from entering the axon, and a sodium/potassium pump pumps out sodium ions in exchange for potassium ions. The potassium ions are free to reexit the cell. **(C)** The summed ionic charges across the membrane illustrate that the intracellular side of the membrane is negative relative to the extracellular side. **(D)** In this graph of the resting potential of the axon's membrane, the intracellular side of the membrane is −70 millivolts relative to the extracellular side of the membrane.

placed on its inner surface. The difference is about 70 millivolts. Although the charge on the extracellular side of the membrane is actually positive, by convention the extracellular side of the membrane is given a charge of zero. Therefore, the inside of the membrane is −70 millivolts *relative* to the extracellular side. If we were to continue to record for a long period of time, the charge across the membrane would remain much the same. This charge, however, has the potential to change, given certain changes in the membrane. Because the charge is currently stable but is a store of *potential* energy, it is called the membrane's **resting potential.** The term *potential* here is used in the same way as we might use it in talking about the financial potential of someone who has money in the bank—that person can spend that money at some future time. The resting potential is a store of energy that can be used at a later time. The resting potential is not identical on every axon. It can vary from −40 to −90 millivolts on axons of different animal species.

Four charged particles take part in producing the resting potential: sodium ions ($Na^+$), chloride ions ($Cl^-$), potassium ions ($K^+$), and large protein anions ($A^-$). As Figure 4-10A shows, these charged particles are distributed unequally across the axon's membrane, with more protein anions and $K^+$ ions in the intracellular fluid, and more $Cl^-$ and $Na^+$ ions in the extracellular fluid. Let us consider how the unequal concentrations arise and how each contributes to the membrane's resting potential.

Large protein anions are manufactured inside cells. Because there are no membrane channels through which they can leave the cell, they remain in the intracellular fluid and their charge contributes to the negative charge on the intracellular side of the cell membrane. The negative charge of protein anions alone is sufficient to produce a transmembrane voltage. Because most cells in the body manufacture these large negatively charged protein molecules, most cells have a charge across the cell membrane.

To balance the negative charge of the large protein anions in the intracellular fluid, cells accumulate positively charged potassium ions ($K^+$) to the extent that there are about 20 times as many potassium ions inside the cell as outside it. Potassium ions cross the cell membrane through open potassium ion channels. With this very high concentration of potassium ions inside the cell, however, an efflux of $K^+$ ions also is produced, owing to the potassium ion concentration gradient across the membrane. In other words, some potassium ions leave the cell because the internal concentration of $K^+$ ions is much higher than the external $K^+$ concentration. The efflux of even a very small number of $K^+$ ions is enough to contribute to the charge across the membrane, with the intracellular side of the membrane being negatively charged relative to the extracellular side.

**Resting potential.** The voltage across the cell membrane produced by a greater negative charge on the intracellular side relative to the extracellular side in the absence of stimulation.

Visit the CD and find the animation on membrane potential in the module on Neural Communication.

You may be wondering if you read this last sentence correctly. If there are 20 times as many positively charged potassium ions on the inside of the cell as on the outside, why should the inside of the membrane have a *negative* charge? Should not all of those $K^+$ ions in the intracellular fluid give the inside of the cell a positive charge instead? No, because you are forgetting the negatively charged protein anions. Think of it this way. If there were no restriction on the number of potassium ions that could accumulate on the intracellular side of the membrane, the positive charges on the intracellular potassium ions would exactly match the negative charges on the intracellular protein anions, and there would be no charge across the membrane at all. But there *is* a limit on the number of $K^+$ ions that accumulate inside the cell because, when the intracellular potassium ion concentration becomes higher than the extracellular concentration, potassium ions start moving out of the cell down their concentration gradient. The equilibrium of the potassium voltage gradient and the potassium concentration gradient results in some potassium ions remaining outside the cell. Only a few potassium ions staying outside the cell are needed to leave a negative charge on the intracellular side of the membrane. As a result, potassium ions contribute to the charge across the membrane.

But what about the other two ions that take part in producing the resting potential—sodium ($Na^+$) and chloride ($Cl^-$)? If positively charged sodium ions were free to move across the membrane, they could diffuse into the cell and reduce the transmembrane charge produced by the unequal distribution of potassium ions. This diffusion would not happen rapidly. Although a cell membrane does have sodium ion channels, they are ordinarily closed, blocking the entry of most sodium ions. Still, given enough time, sufficient sodium could leak into the cell to reduce its membrane potential to zero. What prevents this from occurring?

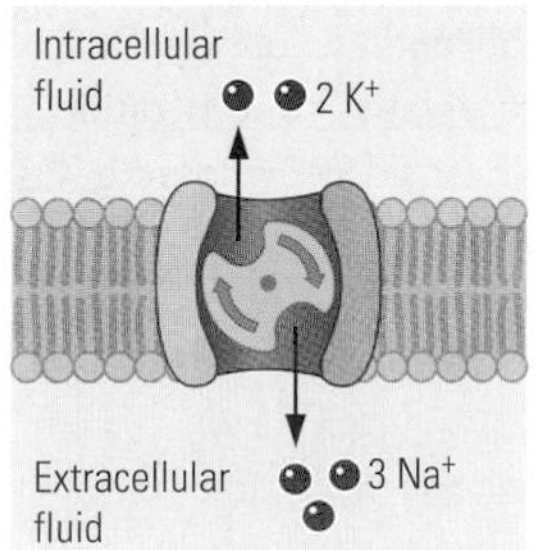

Sodium/potassium pump

The high concentration of sodium outside the cell is caused by the action of a *sodium/potassium pump.* This pump is a complex protein molecule embedded in the cell membrane. With each pumping action, a membrane's many thousands of pumps continually exchange three intracellular $Na^+$ ions for two $K^+$ ions. The $K^+$ ions are free to leave the cell through open potassium channels, but closed sodium channels prevent reentry of the $Na^+$ ions. Consequently, there are about 10 times as many sodium ions on the extracellular side of the axon membrane as there are on the membrane's intracellular side.

Now consider the chloride ions. Unlike sodium ions, $Cl^-$ ions move in and out of the cell through open chloride channels in the membrane. The equilibrium at which the chloride concentration gradient equals the chloride voltage gradient is approximately the membrane's resting potential, so chloride ions ordinarily make little contribution to the resting potential of the membrane. At this equilibrium point, there are about 12 times as many $Cl^-$ ions outside the cell as inside it.

As summarized in Figure 4-10C, this unequal distribution of ions leaves a neuron's intracellular fluid negatively charged relative to the outside of the cell. Two structures of the cell membrane contribute to this resting potential. First, because the membrane is semipermeable, it keeps large negatively charged protein molecules inside the cell, keeps out positively charged $Na^+$ ions, and allows $K^+$ and $Cl^-$ ions to pass more freely. Second, the membrane has a $Na^+/K^+$ pump that extrudes $Na^+$. The summed charges of the unequally distributed ions leaves the intracellular side of the membrane at −70 millivolts relative to the extracellular side. This is the membrane's resting potential.

## Graded Potentials

The resting potential provides an energy store that can be expended if the membrane's barrier to ion movement is suddenly removed. This store is somewhat like the water in a dam—small amounts of water can be released from the dam by opening gates for irrigation or electrical generation. More specifically, if the barrier to the influx of sodium ions is suddenly taken away, sodium ions will flow across the membrane and reduce the size of the transmembrane voltage. Alternatively, if the barrier to the flow of sodium ions is suddenly improved (further reducing the leakage of sodium into the cell), the voltage across the membrane will increase. Slight changes in the voltage of an axon's membrane, called **graded potentials,** are relatively small voltage fluctuations that are usually restricted to the vicinity on the axon where they are produced. Just as a small wave produced in the middle of a large, smooth pond decays before traveling much distance, graded potentials produced on a membrane decay before traveling very far.

**Figure 4-11**

**(A)** Stimulation (S) that increases membrane voltage produces a hyperpolarizing graded potential. Hyperpolarization results from the opening of channels to produce an inward flow of $Cl^-$ ions or an outward flow of $K^+$ ions or both. **(B)** Stimulation that decreases the membrane voltage produces a depolarizing graded potential. Depolarization results from the opening of sodium channels to allow an inward flow of $Na^+$ ions.

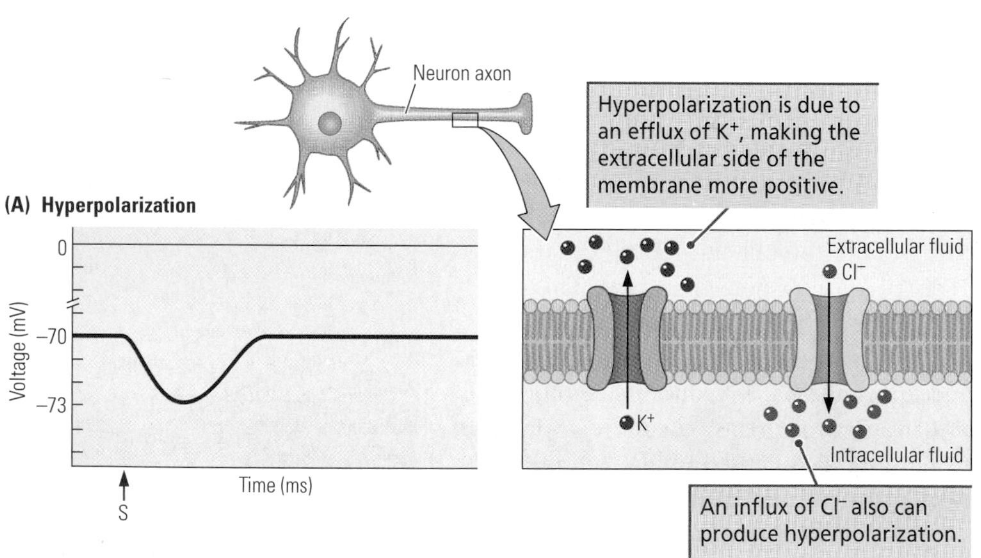
Neuron axon
Hyperpolarization is due to an efflux of K+, making the extracellular side of the membrane more positive.
(A) Hyperpolarization
0
-70
-73
Voltage (mV)
Time (ms)
S
Extracellular fluid
Cl−
K+
Intracellular fluid
An influx of Cl− also can produce hyperpolarization.

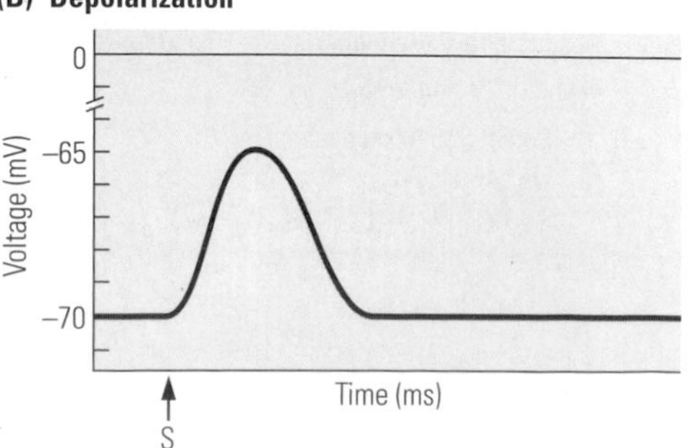
(B) Depolarization
0
-65
-70
Voltage (mV)
Time (ms)
S

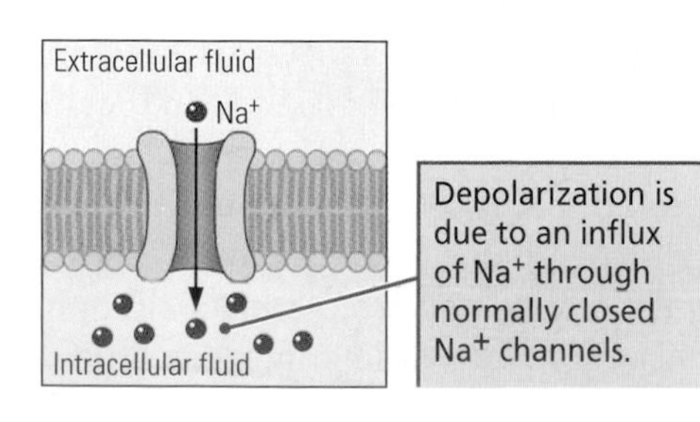
Extracellular fluid
Na+
Intracellular fluid
Depolarization is due to an influx of Na+ through normally closed Na+ channels.

There is no reason for an isolated axon to undergo a spontaneous change in charge. For a graded potential to arise, an axon must be somehow stimulated. Stimulating the axon electrically through a microelectrode is one way to alter its membrane's voltage and produce a graded potential. If the current applied to the membrane is negative, the membrane potential becomes more negative by a few millivolts (it increases its charge). As illustrated in Figure 4-11A, it may suddenly change from a resting potential of −70 millivolts to a new, slightly higher potential of −73 millivolts. This change is called **hyperpolarization** to indicate that the polarity of the membrane becomes larger. Conversely, if the current applied to the membrane is positive, the membrane potential becomes more positive by a few millivolts (it decreases its charge). As illustrated in Figure 4-11B, it may suddenly change from a resting potential of −70 millivolts to a new, slightly lower potential of −65 millivolts. This change is called **depolarization** because the polarity of the membrane becomes smaller. Such sudden changes are usually brief, lasting only milliseconds.

What are the bases of these changes in the membrane's polarity? The answer is that electrical stimulation influences membrane channels and the opening and closing of various channels cause the membrane potential to change. For the membrane to become hyperpolarized, the extracellular side must become more positive, which can be accomplished with an efflux of $K^+$ ions (or an influx of $Cl^-$ ions). The removal of intracellular $Na^+$ ions through increased activity of sodium/potassium pumps would not be a cause of hyperpolarization, because it would not be rapid enough. Evidence that potassium channels have a role in hyperpolarization comes from the fact that the chemical *tetraethylammonium* (TEA), which blocks potassium channels, also blocks hyperpolarization. But, if potassium channels are ordinarily open, how can a greater than normal efflux of $K^+$ ions take place? Apparently, even though potassium channels are open, there is still some resistance to the outward flow of potassium ions. The reduction of this resistance enables hyperpolarization.

Depolarization, on the other hand, is due to the influx of sodium ions and is produced by the opening of normally closed sodium channels. The involvement of sodium channels in depolarization is indicated by the fact that the chemical *tetrodotoxin,* which blocks sodium channels, also blocks depolarization. The puffer fish, which is considered a delicacy in certain countries, especially Japan, secretes this potentially deadly poison, so skill is required to prepare this fish for dinner. The fish is lethal to the guests of careless cooks because its toxin impedes the electrical activity of neurons.

**Graded potentials.** Hyperpolarization of a neural membrane or depolarization of the membrane.

**Hyperpolarization.** An increase in the electrical charge across a membrane, usually due to the inward flow of chloride ions or the outward flow of potassium ions.

**Depolarization.** A decrease in the electrical charge across a membrane, usually due to the inward flow of sodium ions.

**Action potential.** A large, brief, reversing change in the voltage of a neuron.

**Threshold potential.** The voltage level of a neural membrane at which an action potential is triggered by the opening of $Na^+$ and $K^+$ voltage-sensitive channels; about −50 millivolts.

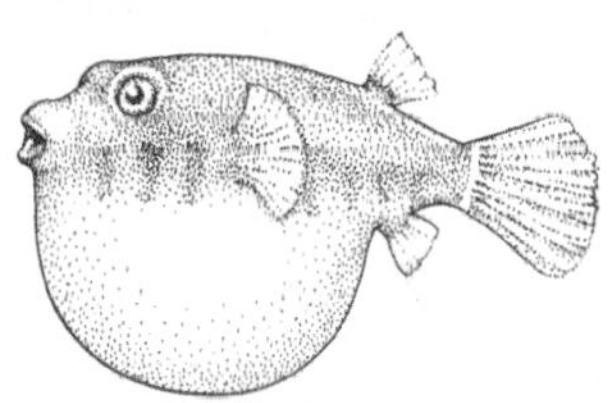

Puffer fish

## The Action Potential

An **action potential** is a brief but extremely large change in the polarity of an axon's membrane lasting about 1 millisecond. Figure 4-12A and B show that, during this time, the voltage across the membrane suddenly reverses, making the intracellular side positive relative to the extracellular side, and then abruptly reverses again, after which the resting potential is restored. Because the duration of the action potential is so brief, many action potentials can occur within a second, as illustrated in Figure 4-12C.

This rapid change in the polarity of the membrane occurs when electrical stimulation causes the membrane's potential to drop to about −50 millivolts. This voltage level is called the **threshold potential** because, at it, the membrane undergoes a remarkable change without any further contribution from the stimulation. The voltage of the membrane suddenly drops to zero and then continues to become more positive until the charge on the inside of the membrane is as great as +30 millivolts—a total voltage change of 100 millivolts. Then, almost as quickly, the membrane potential

**Figure 4-12**

In these representations of an action potential, the scale of the horizontal axis is changed **(A)** to illustrate the phases of the action potential, **(B)** to illustrate that each action potential is a discrete event, and **(C)** to illustrate that a membrane can produce many action potentials in a short period of time.

(A)

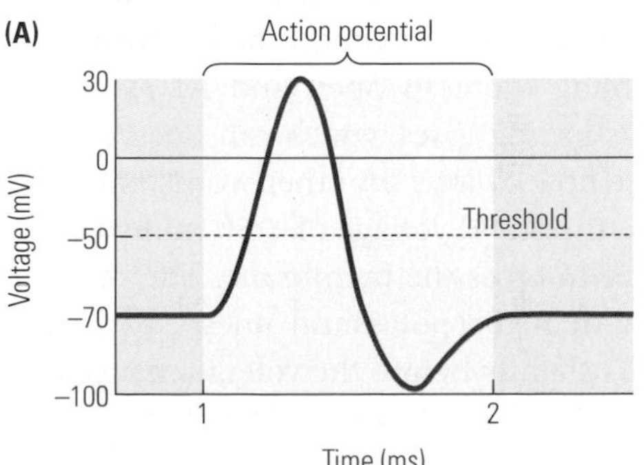


(B)

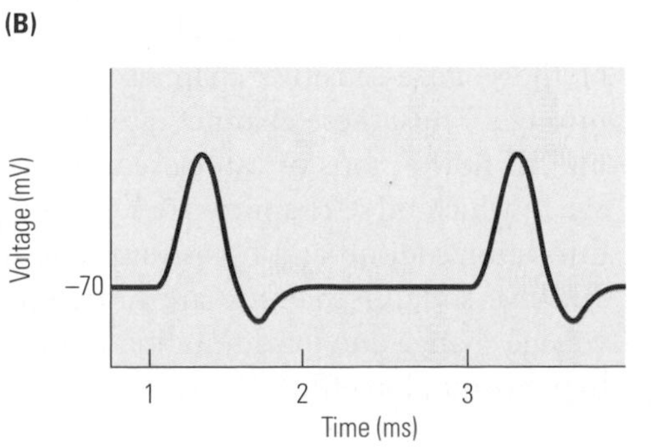


(C)

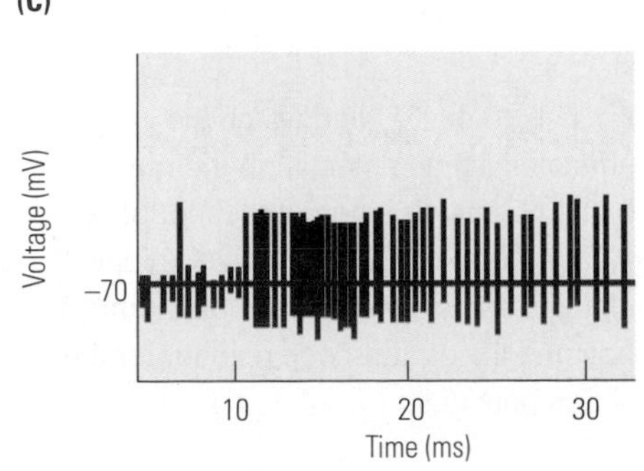

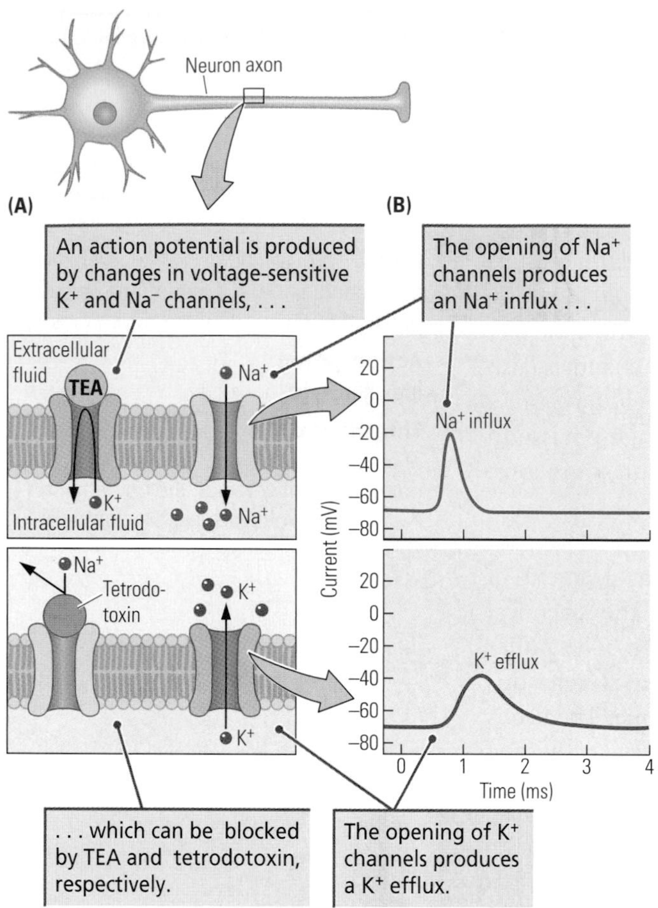

Neuron axon
(A)
An action potential is produced by changes in voltage-sensitive $K^+$ and $Na^-$ channels, . . .
Extracellular fluid
TEA
$Na^+$
$K^+$
Intracellular fluid
$Na^+$
$Na^+$
Tetrodo-toxin
$K^+$
$K^+$
. . . which can be blocked by TEA and tetrodotoxin, respectively.
(B)
The opening of $Na^+$ channels produces an $Na^+$ influx . . .
$Na^+$ influx
$K^+$ efflux
Current (mV)
20
0
−20
−40
−60
−80
0
1
2
3
4
Time (ms)
The opening of $K^+$ channels produces a $K^+$ efflux.

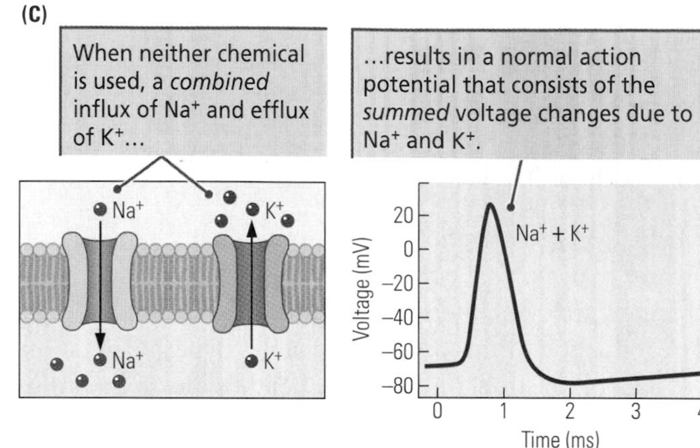

(C)
When neither chemical is used, a *combined* influx of $Na^+$ and efflux of $K^+$...
...results in a normal action potential that consists of the *summed* voltage changes due to $Na^+$ and $K^+$.
$Na^+$
$K^+$
$Na^+$
$K^+$
$Na^+ + K^+$
Voltage (mV)
20
0
−20
−40
−60
−80
0
1
2
3
4
Time (ms)

reverses again, returning through its resting potential and becoming slightly hyperpolarized—a reversal of a little more than 100 millivolts. After this second reversal, the membrane slowly returns to its resting potential.

The changes in voltage that produce an action potential are due to a brief influx of sodium ions and a brief efflux of potassium ions. In the laboratory, if an axon's membrane is stimulated to produce an action potential while the solution surrounding the axon contains TEA (to block potassium channels), a somewhat smaller than normal action potential due entirely to a sodium influx is recorded. Similarly, if an axon's membrane is stimulated to produce an action potential while the solution surrounding the axon contains tetrodotoxin (to block sodium channels), a slightly different action potential due entirely to the efflux of potassium is recorded. As Figure 4-13 illustrates, these results show that the action potential on an axon normally consists of the summed voltage changes caused by the flow of both sodium and potassium ions.

**Figure 4-13**

Experiments demonstrate that the action potential on an axon is due to an inward flow of sodium ions and an outward flow of potassium ions. **(A)** The separate contributions of sodium and potassium channels can be demonstrated by blocking potassium channels with tetraethylammonium (TEA) and sodium channels with tetrodotoxin. **(B)** Sodium channels open first, allowing an influx of $Na^+$ ions, and potassium channels open slightly later, allowing an efflux of $K^+$ ions. **(C)** The combined influx of sodium and efflux of potassium is responsible for the action potential.

Link to the CD and watch the animated action potential in the membrane potential section of the module on Neural Communication. Note the ionic changes associated with this phenomenon and the oscilloscope readout for the action potential.

## THE ROLE OF VOLTAGE-SENSITIVE ION CHANNELS

What are the cellular mechanisms that underlie the action potential? There are many different kinds of sodium and potassium channels in the membrane of a neuron. So the answer to this question lies in the behavior of a class of ion channels that are sensitive to the membrane's voltage. These are called voltage-sensitive sodium channels and voltage-sensitive potassium channels. **Voltage-sensitive channels** are closed when an axon's membrane is at its resting potential, so ions cannot pass through them. Then, when the membrane changes to reach the threshold voltage, the configuration of the voltage-sensitive channels alters, enabling them to open and let ions pass through. Thus, these channels are described as having gates, which can open to permit the flow of ions or can close to restrict the flow of ions. In other words, the voltage to which these channels are sensitive is the threshold voltage of −50 millivolts. At this point, sodium and potassium ions are free to cross the membrane. The voltage-sensitive sodium channels are more sensitive than the potassium ones, and so the voltage change due to sodium ion influx occurs slightly before the voltage change due to potassium ion efflux.

## ACTION POTENTIALS AND REFRACTORY PERIODS

Although action potentials can occur as many as hundreds of times a second, there is an upper limit to their frequency. If the axon membrane is stimulated during the depolarizing or repolarizing phases of the action potential, another action potential will not occur. The axon in these phases is described as **absolutely refractory.** If, on the other hand, the axon membrane is stimulated during the hyperpolarization phase, another action potential can be induced, but the intensity of stimulation must be higher than that which initiated the first action potential. During this phase, the membrane is described as **relatively refractory.** Because of refractory periods, there is about a 5-millisecond limit on how frequently action potentials can occur. In other words, an axon can produce action potentials at a maximum rate of about 200 per second.

Refractory periods are due to the way that gates of the voltage-sensitive sodium and potassium channels open and close. The sodium channels have two gates and the potassium channels have one gate. Figure 4-14 illustrates the position of these gates before, during, and after the various phases of the action potential. During the resting potential, gate 1 of the sodium channel depicted in Figure 4-14 is closed and only gate 2 is open. At the threshold level of stimulation, gate 1 becomes open also. Gate 2, however, closes very quickly after gate 1 opens. This sequence produces a brief period during which both gates are open followed by a brief period during which gate 2 is closed. When gate 2 is closed, the membrane cannot be changed by further stimulation. That is the time when the axon membrane is absolutely refractory. Both of the sodium gates are eventually restored to their resting potential positions, with gate 1 closed and gate 2 open. But, because the potassium channels close more slowly than the sodium channels do, the hyperpolarization produced by a continuing efflux of potassium ions makes the membrane relatively refractory for a period of time after the action potential has occurred. The refractory periods have very practical uses in conducting information, as you will see when we consider the nerve impulse.

A lever-activated toilet provides an analogy for some of the changes in polarity that take place during an action potential. Pushing the lever slightly produces a slight flow of water, which stops when the lever is released. This activity is analogous to a

**Voltage-sensitive channel.** In a membrane, a protein channel that opens or closes only at certain membrane voltages.

**Absolutely refractory.** Refers to the period in an action potential during which a new action potential cannot be elicited, because of the closing of gate 2 of voltage-sensitive sodium channels.

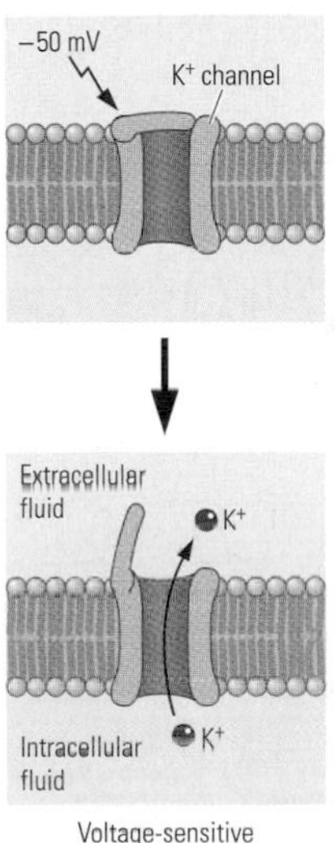

Voltage-sensitive potassium channel

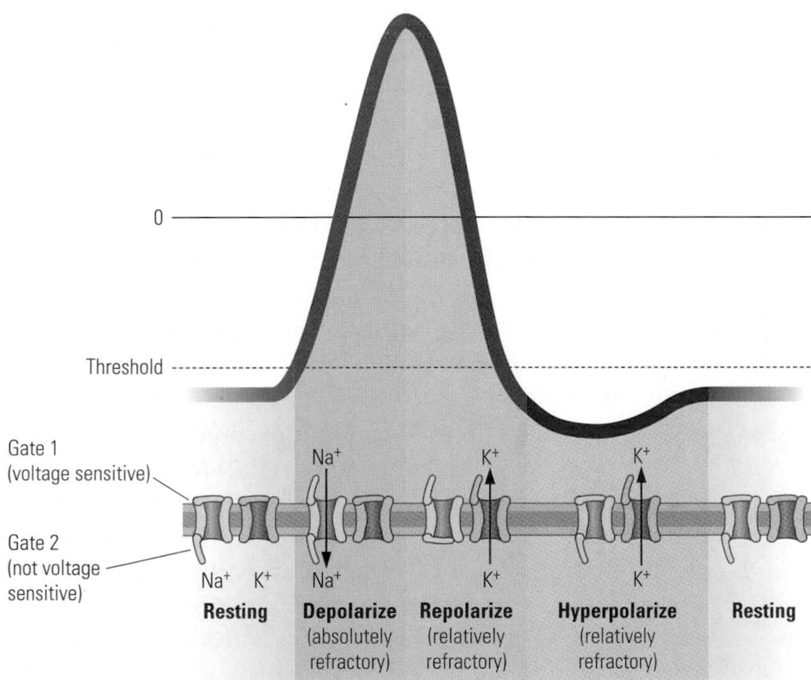


**Figure 4-14**

Changes in voltage-sensitive sodium and potassium channels are responsible for the phases of the action potential. The opening of gate 1 of the sodium channels initiates depolarization, and the closing of gate 2 ends depolarization. The potassium channel gate opens more slowly and contributes to repolarization and hyperpolarization. Restoration of the initial condition of the gates is associated with restoration of the resting potential. The membrane is absolutely refractory once gate 2 of the sodium channels closes and relatively refractory until the resting membrane potential is restored.

graded potential. A harder lever press brings the toilet to threshold and initiates flushing, a response that is out of all proportion to the lever press. This activity is analogous to the action potential. During the flush, the toilet is absolutely refractory, meaning that another flush cannot be induced at this time. During the refilling of the bowl, in contrast, the toilet is relatively refractory, meaning that reflushing is possible but harder to bring about. Only after the cycle is over, and the toilet is once again "resting," can the usual flush be produced again.

**Figure 4-15**

A nerve impulse is the flow of action potentials along an axon. When voltage-sensitive $Na^+$ channels and $K^+$ channels are opened, the voltage change spreads to adjacent sites of the membrane, inducing voltage-sensitive gates to open at adjacent locations along the axon's length. Because gates are briefly inactivated as the action potential is completed, the impulse cannot travel back in the direction from which it has come. Here, the voltage changes are shown only in one direction and on one side of the membrane.

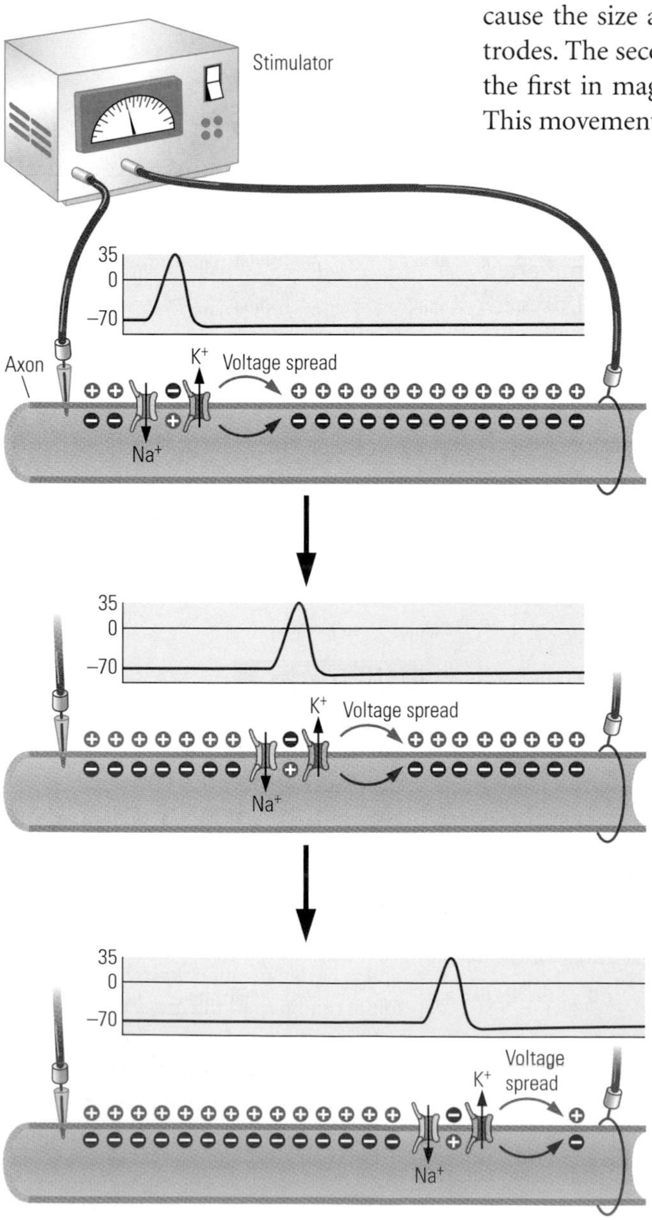

## The Nerve Impulse

Suppose you place two recording electrodes at a distance from each other on an axon's membrane and then electrically stimulate an area adjacent to one of these electrodes. That electrode would immediately record an action potential. This recording would very soon be followed by a similar recording on the second electrode, however. Apparently, an action potential has arisen near this electrode also, even though this second electrode is some distance from the original point of stimulation. Is this second action potential simply an echo of the first that passes down the axon? No, it cannot be, because the size and shape of the action potential are exactly the same at the two electrodes. The second is not just a faint, degraded version of the first; instead, it is equal to the first in magnitude. Somehow the full action potential has moved along the axon. This movement of an action potential along an axon is called a **nerve impulse.**

Why does an action potential move? Why does it not remain where it starts? Remember that the voltage change during an action potential is 100 millivolts, which is far beyond the 20-millivolt change needed to bring the membrane to the threshold level of −50 millivolts. Consequently, the voltage change on the part of the membrane at which an action potential first occurs is large enough to bring adjacent parts of the membrane to a threshold of −50 millivolts. When the membrane of an adjacent part of the axon reaches −50 millivolts, the voltage-sensitive channels at that location pop open to produce an action potential there as well. This second occurrence, in turn, induces a change in the voltage of the membrane still farther along the axon, and so on, and so on, down the axon's length. Figure 4-15 illustrates this process by which a nerve impulse travels along an axon. The nerve impulse occurs because each action potential propagates another action potential on an adjacent part of the axon membrane. The word *propagate* means to "give birth," and that is exactly what happens. Each successive action potential gives birth to another down the length of the axon.

Several factors ensure that a single nerve impulse of a constant size travels down the axon. One factor is the existence of voltage-sensitive channels that produce refractory periods. Although an action potential can travel in either direction on an axon, refractory periods prevent it from reversing direction and returning to the point from which it has come. Thus refractory periods create a single, discrete impulse that travels in one direction. The repeated expenditure of energy as a nerve impulse travels also is an important factor. An action potential depends on energy expended at the site where it occurs, and the same amount of energy is expended at every site along the membrane where an action potential is propagated. As a result, all the action potentials generated as a nerve impulse travels are of the same magnitude. There is no such thing as a dissipated or weaker action potential. Simply stated, an action potential is either generated completely or it is not generated at all, which means that a nerve impulse always maintains a constant size.

**Nerve impulse.** The propagation of an action potential on the membrane of an axon.

To summarize the action of a nerve impulse, another analogy may help. Think of the voltage-sensitive channels along the axon as a series of dominoes. When one domino falls, it knocks over its neighbor, and so on down the line. The "wave" cannot return the way that it has come until the dominoes are set back up again. There is also no decrement in the size of the falling action. The last domino travels exactly the same distance and falls just as hard as did the first one. Essentially the same things happen when voltage-sensitive channels open. The opening of one channel triggers its neighbor to open, just as one domino knocks over the next. When gate 2 on a voltage-sensitive sodium channel closes, that channel is inactivated, much as a domino is temporarily inactivated after it has fallen over. Both channel and domino must be restored to their original positions before they can work again. Finally, the channel-opening response does not grow any weaker as it moves along the axon. The last channel opens exactly like the first, just as the domino action stays constant until the end of the line. Because of this behavior of voltage-sensitive channels, a single nerve impulse of constant size moves in one direction along an axon.

The domino effect

## Saltatory Conduction and Myelin Sheaths

Because the giant axons of squid are so large, they can send nerve impulses very quickly, much as a large-diameter pipe can deliver a lot of water at a rapid rate. But large axons take up a substantial amount of space, so a squid cannot accommodate many of them or its body would become too bulky. For us mammals, with our repertoires of complex behaviors, giant axons are out of the question. Our axons must be extremely slender because our complex behaviors require a great many of them. Our largest axons are only about 30 micrometers wide, so the speed with which they convey information should not be especially fast. And yet most mammals are far from sluggish creatures. We often process information and generate responses with impressive speed. How do we manage to do so if our axons are so thin? The mammalian nervous system has evolved a solution that has nothing to do with axon size.

Glial cells play a role in speeding nerve impulses in the mammalian nervous system. Schwann cells in the peripheral nervous system and oligodendroglia in the central nervous system wrap around each axon, insulating it except for a small region between each glial cell (Figure 4-16). As described in Chapter 3, this insulation

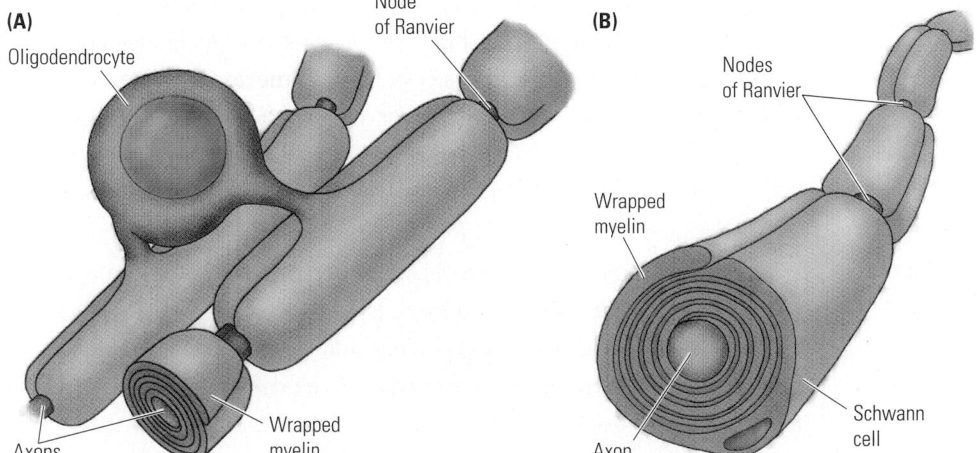


**Figure 4-16**

An axon is myelinated by **(A)** oligodendroglia in the central nervous system and **(B)** Schwann cells in the peripheral nervous system. Each glial cell is separated by a node of Ranvier, at which location there is no myelin.

**Saltatory conduction.** The propagation of an action potential at successive nodes of Ranvier; saltatory means "jumping" or "dancing."

Click on the CD and find the action potential area in the module on Neural Communication. Watch the animation on the role of the myelin sheath in conducting an action potential and note the role of the nodes of Ranvier in this process.

**Figure 4-17**

**(A)** Nodes of Ranvier have no myelin and are rich in voltage-sensitive channels. **(B)** In saltatory conduction, the action potential jumps from node to node.

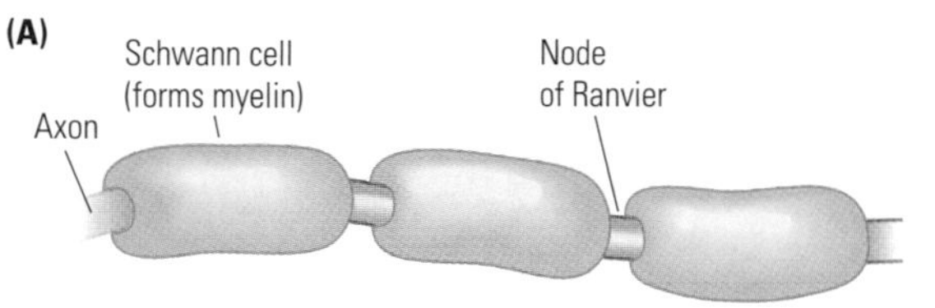


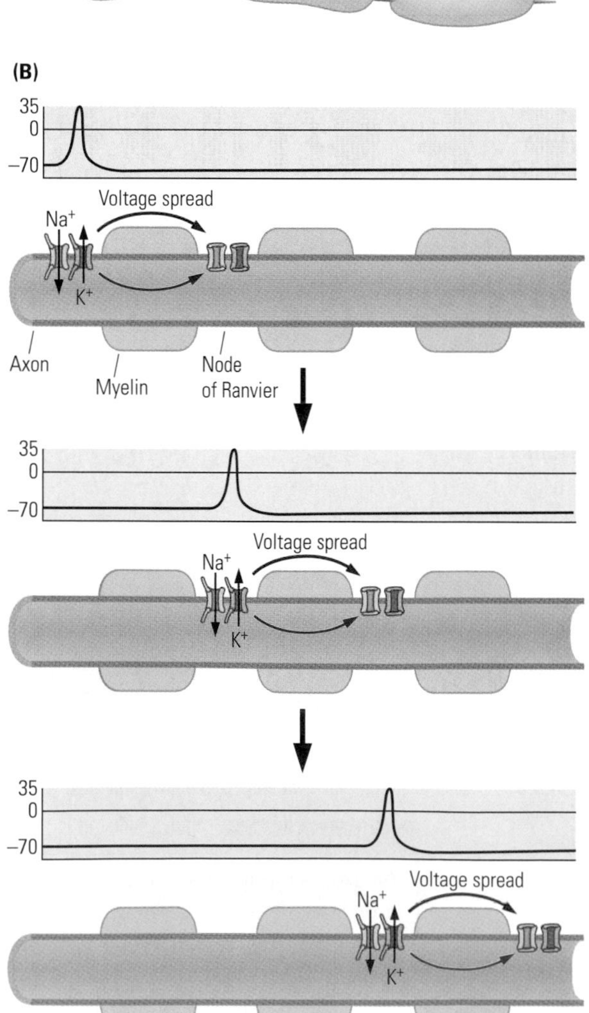


is referred to as myelin or as a myelin sheath, and insulated axons are said to be myelinated. Action potentials cannot occur where myelin is wrapped around an axon. For one thing, the myelin creates a barrier to the flow of ionic currents. For another, regions of an axon that lie under myelin have few channels through which ions can flow, and, as you know, such channels are essential to generating an action potential. But axons are not totally encased in myelin. The nodes of Ranvier, which are the unmyelinated parts of the axon between successive glial cells, are richly endowed with voltage-sensitive channels. These tiny gaps in the myelin sheath are sufficiently close to each other that an action potential occurring at one of them can trigger voltage-sensitive gates to open at an adjacent one. In this way, an action potential jumps from node to node, as shown in Figure 4-17. This mode of conduction is called **saltatory conduction** (from the Latin verb *saltare,* meaning "to dance").

Jumping from node to node greatly speeds the rate at which an action potential can travel along an axon. On larger myelinated mammalian axons, the nerve impulse can travel at a rate as high as 120 meters per second, compared with only about 30 meters per second on smaller uninsulated axons. Think of how a "wave" of consecutively standing spectators travels around a football stadium. As one person rises, the adjacent person rises, producing the wave effect. This wave is like conduction along an uninsulated axon. Now think of how much faster the wave would complete its circuit around the field if only spectators in the corners rose to produce it, which is analogous to a nerve impulse that travels by jumping from one node of Ranvier to another. The quick reactions of which humans and other mammals are capable are due in part to this saltatory conduction in their nervous systems.

## In Review

If microelectrodes connected to a voltmeter are placed on either side of an axon membrane, a voltage difference of about 70 millivolts is recorded. This voltage difference is due to the unequal distribution of ions on the two sides of the membrane. The membrane prevents the efflux of large negatively charged protein anions, and it pumps positively charged sodium ions out of the cell. Although potassium ions and chloride ions are relatively free to move across the membrane through their respective channels, the equilibrium at which their concentration gradient matches their voltage gradient contributes to a transmembrane charge. Some sodium and potassium channels that are sensitive to the membrane's voltage open when the membrane is electrically stimulated, allowing a brief free flow of ions across the membrane. That flow of ions is responsible for a brief reversal of the charge on the membrane, called the action potential. The voltage change associated with an action potential is sufficiently large to bring adjacent parts of the axon membrane to the threshold for producing another action potential. In this way, the action potential is propagated along the length of an axon as a nerve impulse. Along a myelinated axon, a nerve impulse travels by saltatory conduction, in which the action potential jumps from one node of Ranvier (tiny gap in the myelin) to the next node. This mode of conduction greatly increases the speed at which a nerve impulse travels.

## HOW NEURONS INTEGRATE INFORMATION

So far, we have focused simply on nerve impulses as they travel along axons. A neuron is more than just an axon connected to microelectrodes by some curious scientist who stimulates it with electrical current. A neuron has an extensive dendritic tree covered with synaptic spines, and, through these spines, it can have more than 50,000 connections to other neurons. Nerve impulses traveling to each of these synapses from other neurons bombard the receiving neuron with all manner of inputs. In addition, a neuron has a cell body between its dendritic tree and its axon, and this cell body, too, can receive connections from many other neurons. How does this enormous array of inputs and the presence of a cell body result in producing a nerve impulse?

In the 1960s, John C. Eccles and his students performed experiments that helped to answer this question. Rather than record from the giant axon of a squid, these researchers recorded from the cell bodies of large motor neurons in the vertebrate spinal cord. They did so by refining the stimulating and recording techniques developed previously for the study of squid axons. A spinal-cord motor neuron has a very extensive dendritic tree with as many as 20 main branches that subdivide numerous times. The dendrites are also covered with many dendritic spines. Motor neurons receive input from multiple sources, including the skin, the joints, the muscles, and the brain, which is why they are ideal for studying how a neuron responds to diverse inputs. Each motor neuron sends its axon directly to a muscle, as you would expect for neurons that produce all of our movements. "Myasthenia Gravis," on page 134, discusses what happens when muscle receptors lose their sensitivity to motor-neuron messages.

**Excitatory postsynaptic potential (EPSP).** A brief depolarization of a neuron membrane in response to stimulation from a terminal of another neuron, making the neuron more likely to produce an action potential.

**Inhibitory postsynaptic potential (IPSP).** A brief hyperpolarization of a neuron membrane in response to stimulation from a terminal of another neuron, making the neuron less likely to produce an action potential.

John C. Eccles (1903–1997)

### Excitatory and Inhibitory Postsynaptic Potentials

To study the activity of motor neurons, Eccles inserted a microelectrode into a vertebrate spinal cord until the tip was located in or right beside a motor neuron's cell body. He then placed stimulating electrodes on the axons of sensory fibers entering the spinal cord. By teasing apart the fibers of the incoming sensory nerves, he was able to stimulate one fiber at a time. A diagram of the experimental arrangement is illustrated in Figure 4-18. He found that stimulating some of the fibers depolarized (reduced the charge) on the membrane of the motor neuron to which these fibers were connected—a form of graded potential described earlier. This type of graded potential is called an **excitatory postsynaptic potential (EPSP)** because, in reducing the charge on the membrane toward the threshold level, it increases the probability that an action potential will occur. In contrast, when Eccles stimulated other incoming sensory fibers, they hyperpolarized (increased the charge) on the receiving motor-neuron membrane. This type of graded potential is called an **inhibitory postsynaptic potential (IPSP)** because, by increasing the charge on the membrane away from the threshold level, it decreases the probability that an action potential will result. Both EPSPs and IPSPs last only a few milliseconds, after which they decay and the neuron's resting potential is restored.

EPSPs and IPSPs are produced in the same way that graded potentials are produced on squid axons. EPSPs are associated with the opening of sodium channels, which allows an influx of $Na^+$ ions. IPSPs are associated with the opening of potassium channels, which allows an efflux of $K^+$ ions (or with the opening of chloride channels, which allows an influx of $Cl^-$ ions). Although the size of a graded potential is proportional to the intensity of the stimulation, an action potential is not

**Figure 4-18**

In the experimental arrangement used by Eccles to demonstrate how input onto neurons influences the excitability of a neuron, a recording is made from a motor neuron while either an excitatory or an inhibitory input is delivered. Stimulation (S) of the excitatory pathway produces a membrane depolarization called an EPSP (excitatory postsynaptic potential). Stimulation of the inhibitory pathway produces a membrane hyperpolarization called an IPSP (inhibitory postsynaptic potential).

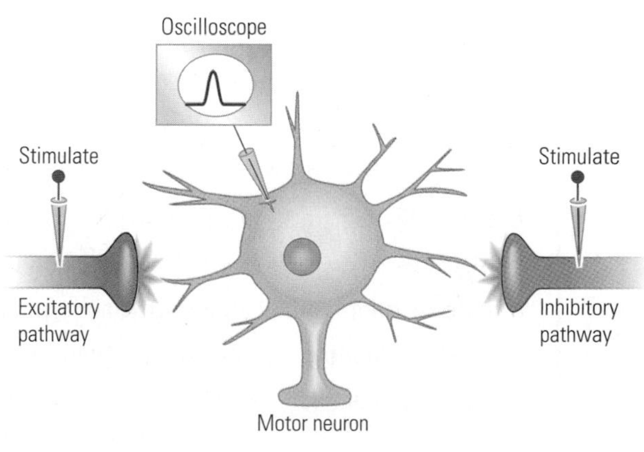


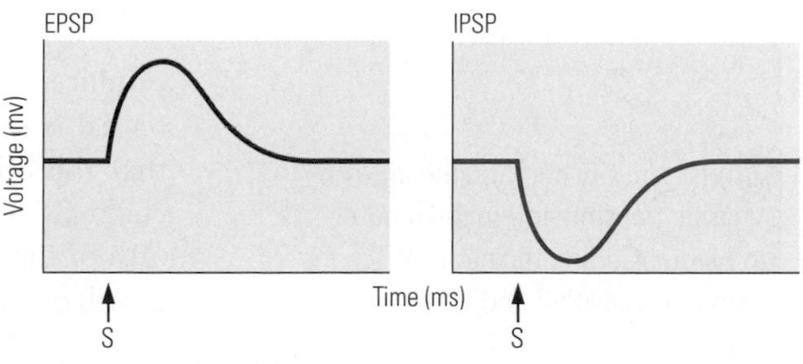

Focus on Disorders

## Myasthenia Gravis

R. J. was 22 years old in 1941 when she discovered something wrong with her eyelid. It drooped. She consulted her physician, but he was unable to explain her condition or give her any help. In the course of the next few years, she experienced some difficulty in swallowing, general weakness in her limbs, and a terrible feeling of fatigue. Many of the symptoms would disappear for days and then suddenly reappear. She also noted that, if she got a good night's sleep, she felt better but, if she performed physical work or became stressed, the symptoms got worse. She had been in a car accident and then had had her first baby about a year before the symptoms began; so she wondered if these events had something to do with her problems. About 3 years after the symptoms first appeared, she was finally diagnosed with myasthenia gravis, a condition that affects the communication between motor neurons and muscles. A specialist suggested that she undergo a new treatment in which the thymus gland is removed. She underwent the surgery and, within the next 5 years, all of her symptoms gradually disappeared. She has been symptom free for more than 50 years.

In myasthenia gravis, the end-plate receptors of muscles are insensitive to the chemical messages passed from axon terminals. Consequently, the muscles do not respond to the commands from motor neurons. Myasthenia gravis is relatively rare, with a prevalence of 14/100,000, and the disorder is more common in women than in men. The age of onset is usually in the 30s to 40s for women and after age 50 for men. In about 10 percent of cases, the condition is limited to the eye muscles, whereas, in the remaining patients, the condition gets worse, with about a third of patients dying from the disease or from complications such as respiratory infections.

Why is removal of the thymus gland sometimes an effective treatment for myasthenia gravis? The thymus gland takes part in producing antibodies to foreign material and viruses that enter the body. In myasthenia gravis, the thymus may start to make antibodies to the end-plate receptors on muscles. Blocked by these antibodies, the receptors can no longer produce a normal response to acetylcholine, the chemical transmitter at the muscle synapse, so the muscle cannot move in response to the signal. Disorders in which the immune system makes antibodies to a person's own body are called *autoimmune diseases.*

1 2 3 4

Courtesy of Y. Harati, M.D./ Baylor College of Medicine, Houston, Texas

This patient with myasthenia gravis was asked to look up, which is recorded in photo 1. Her eyelids quickly became fatigued and drooped, as in photos 2 and 3. Photo 4 shows her eyelids back at normal after a few minutes of rest.

In the past 50 years, myasthenia gravis has gone from being a poorly understood syndrome of fatigue to a well-understood condition. The condition has now been modeled almost completely in animals. A variety of treatments besides removal of the thymus include thyroid removal and drug treatments, such as those that increase the release of acetylcholine at muscle receptors. As a result, most patients today live out their normal life spans. Myasthenia gravis is now a model disease for studying other autoimmune diseases.

produced on the membrane of the motor neuron's cell body even when a graded potential is strongly excitatory. The reason that the action potential is not produced is that the cell-body membrane of most neurons does not contain voltage-sensitive channels. The electrical stimulation to the neuron must reach the axon hillock, the area of the cell where the axon begins. This area is rich in voltage-sensitive channels, as will be discussed shortly.

Visit the CD and find the area on synaptic transmission in the module on Neural Communication. Watch the animations of EPSP and IPSP.

## Summation of Inputs

Remember that a motor neuron has thousands of dendritic spines, allowing for a large number of inputs to its membrane, both EPSPs and IPSPs. How do the incoming EPSPs and IPSPs interact? For example, what happens if there are two EPSPs in succession? Does it matter if the time between them is increased or decreased? And what is the result when an EPSP and an IPSP arrive together? Answers to questions such as these provide an understanding of how the thousands of inputs to a neuron influence its activities.

If one excitatory pulse of stimulation is delivered and is followed some time later by a second excitatory pulse, one EPSP is recorded and, after a delay, a second identical EPSP is recorded, as shown in Figure 4-19 on page 136. These two EPSPs are independent and do not interact. If the delay between them is shortened so that the two occur in rapid succession, however, a single large EPSP is produced, as also shown in Figure 4-19. Here the two excitatory pulses are added together (summated) to produce a larger depolarization of the membrane than either would induce alone. This relation between two EPSPs occurring closely together in time is called **temporal summation.** Figure 4-19 also illustrates that very similar results are obtained with IPSPs. Therefore, temporal summation is a property of both EPSPs and IPSPs.

Now let us use two recording electrodes to see the effects of spatial relations on the summation of inputs. What happens when the inputs to the cell body's membrane are close together spatially, and what happens when the inputs are spatially farther apart? Figure 4-20 (see page 136) illustrates these two situations. If two EPSPs occur at the same time but on widely separated parts of the membrane (as in Figure 4-20A), they do not influence each other. If two EPSPs occurring close together in time are also close together in location, however, they add to form a larger EPSP. This form of summation is called **spatial summation** to indicate that two separate inputs occurring very close to each other in space summate. Similarly, if two IPSPs are produced at the same time, they summate if they occur at approximately the same place on the cell-body membrane but not if they are widely separated. What about an EPSP and an IPSP that occur close together in both time and space? Do they summate also? Yes, they do. Summation is a property of both EPSPs and IPSPs in any combination.

The interactions between EPSPs and IPSPs are understandable when you consider that it is the influx and efflux of ions that are being summated. The influx of sodium ions accompanying one EPSP is added to the influx of sodium ions accompanying a second EPSP if the two occur close together in time and space. If the two influxes of sodium ions are remote either in time or in space or in both, no summation is possible. The same thing is true regarding effluxes of potassium ions. When they occur close together in time and space, they summate; when they are far apart in either of these ways or in both of them, there is no summation. The pattern is identical for an EPSP and an IPSP. The influx of sodium ions associated with the EPSP is added to the efflux of potassium ions associated with the IPSP, and the difference between them is recorded as long as they are spatially and temporally close together. If, on the other hand, they are widely separated in time or space or both, they do not interact and there is no summation.

A neuron with thousands of inputs responds no differently from one with only a few inputs. It democratically sums up all of its inputs that are close together in time and space. The cell-body membrane, therefore, always indicates the summed influences of many inputs. Because of this temporal and spatial summation, a neuron can be said to analyze its inputs before deciding what to do. The ultimate decision is made at the axon hillock.

**Temporal summation.** Graded potentials that occur at approximately the same time on a membrane are added together (summate).

**Spatial summation.** Graded potentials that occur at approximately the same location on a membrane are added together (summate).

Link to the CD and find the area on neural integration in the module on Neural Communication. Watch the animation on the process of spatial and temporal summation.

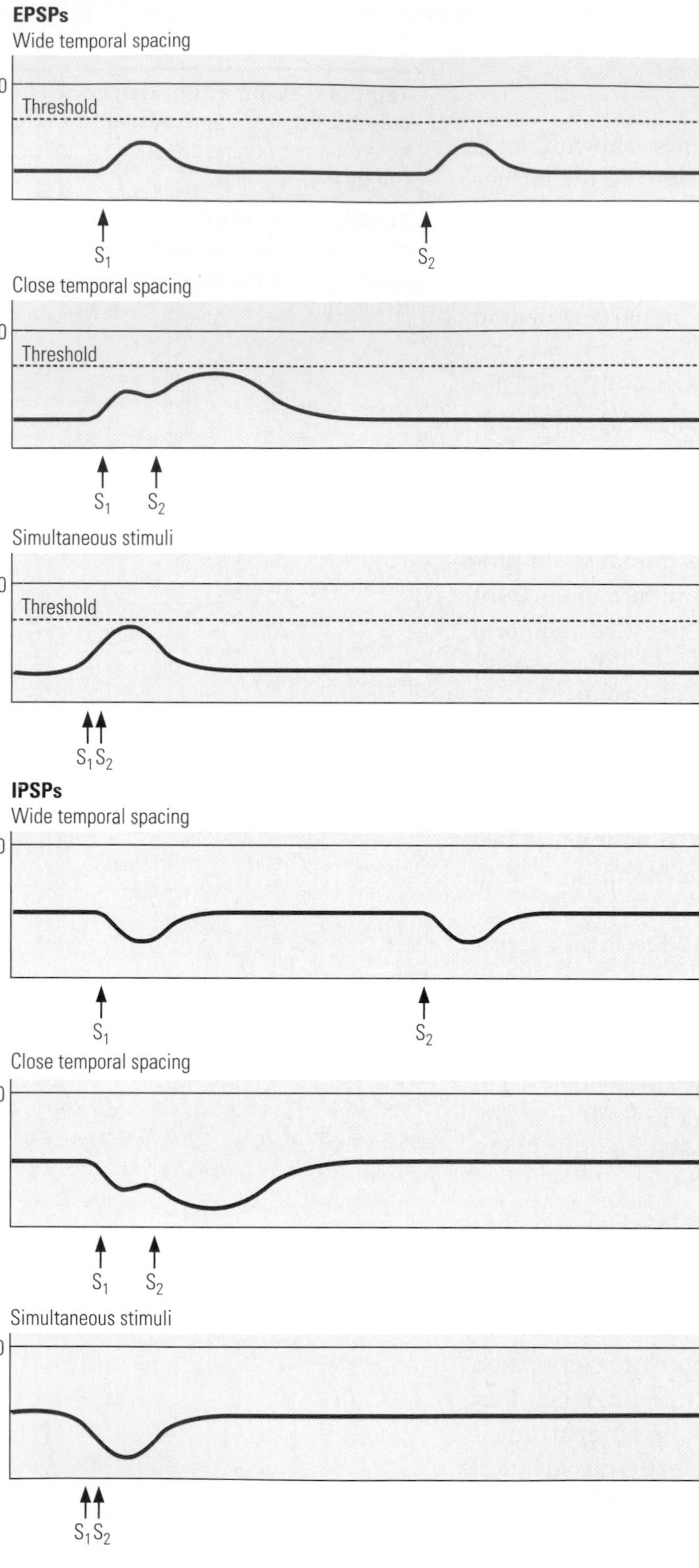

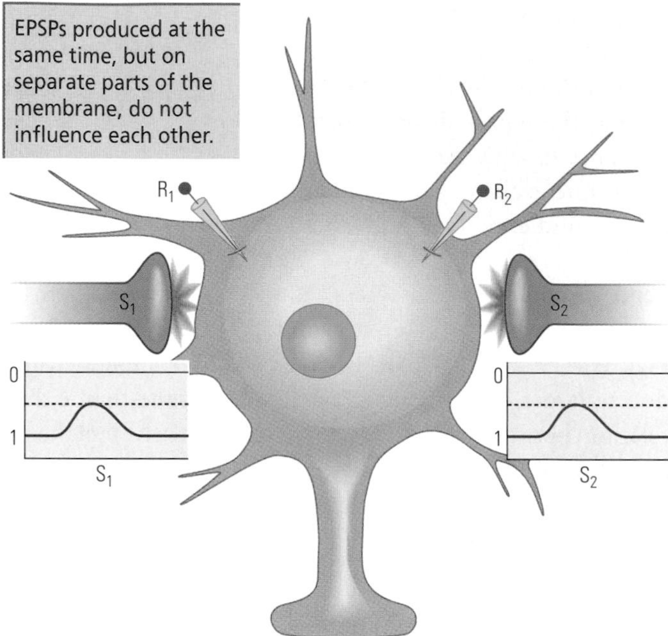


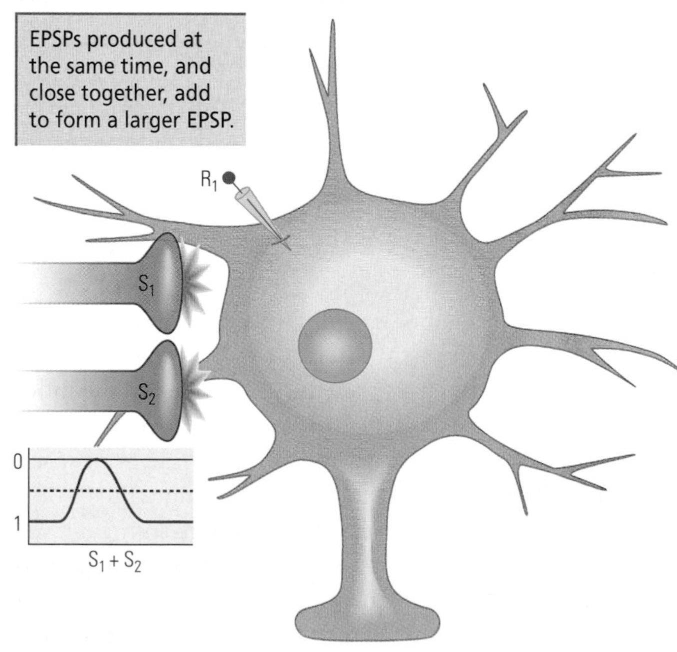


**Figure 4-19**

Temporal summation is a property of both ESPSs and ISPSs. (*Top*) Two pulses of stimulation ($S_1$ and $S_2$) separated in time produce two EPSPs that are similar in size. If the two pulses of stimulation are given in close temporal spacing, they partly add. If given at the same time, the EPSPs sum as one large EPSP. (*Bottom*) Two pulses of stimulation ($S_1$ and $S_2$) separated in time produce two IPSPs that are similar in size. If the two pulses of stimulation are given in close temporal proximity, they partly add. If given at the same time, the IPSPs sum as one large IPSP.

**Figure 4-20**

Examples of spatial summation on a schematic neuron. **(A)** Two excitatory pulses of stimulation ($S_1$ and $S_2$) delivered to widely separated parts of the neuron membrane produce two separate EPSPs recorded by two different recording electrodes ($R_1$ and $R_2$). The two EPSPs are similar in size but do not interact. **(B)** In contrast, two excitatory inputs in close proximity on the neuron membrane summate to produce a large EPSP at recording site $R_1$.

## The Axon Hillock

Figure 4-21 shows the location of the axon hillock on a neuron. The axon hillock is rich in voltage-sensitive channels. These channels, like those on the squid axon, open at a particular membrane voltage. The actual threshold voltage varies with the type of neuron, but, to keep things simple, we will stay with a threshold level of −50 millivolts. To produce an action potential, the summed IPSPs and EPSPs on the cell-body membrane must depolarize the membrane at the axon hillock to −50 millivolts. If that threshold voltage is only briefly obtained, just one or a few action potentials may occur. If the threshold level is maintained for a longer period, however, action potentials will follow each other in rapid succession, just as quickly as the gates on the voltage-sensitive channels can recover. Each action potential is then repeatedly propagated to produce a nerve impulse that travels down the length of the axon.

Do all graded potentials equally influence the voltage-sensitive channels at the axon hillock? Not necessarily. Remember that neurons have extensive dendritic trees. EPSPs and IPSPs on the distant branches of dendrites may have less influence than that of EPSPs and IPSPs that are closer to the axon hillock. Inputs close to the axon hillock are usually much more dynamic in their influence than those occurring some distance away, which usually have a modulating effect. As in all democracies, some inputs have more of a say than others.

To summarize the relation between EPSPs, IPSPs, and action potentials, imagine a brick that is standing on end a few inches away from a wall. It can be tilted back and forth over quite a wide range. If it is tilted too far in one direction, it falls against the wall, whereas, if it is tilted too far in the other direction, it topples over completely. Movements toward the wall are like IPSPs (inhibitory inputs). No matter how much these inputs summate, the brick never falls. Movements away from the wall are like EPSPs (excitatory inputs). If their sum reaches some threshold point, the brick topples over. With sufficient excitation, then, the brick falls, which is equivalent to an action potential.

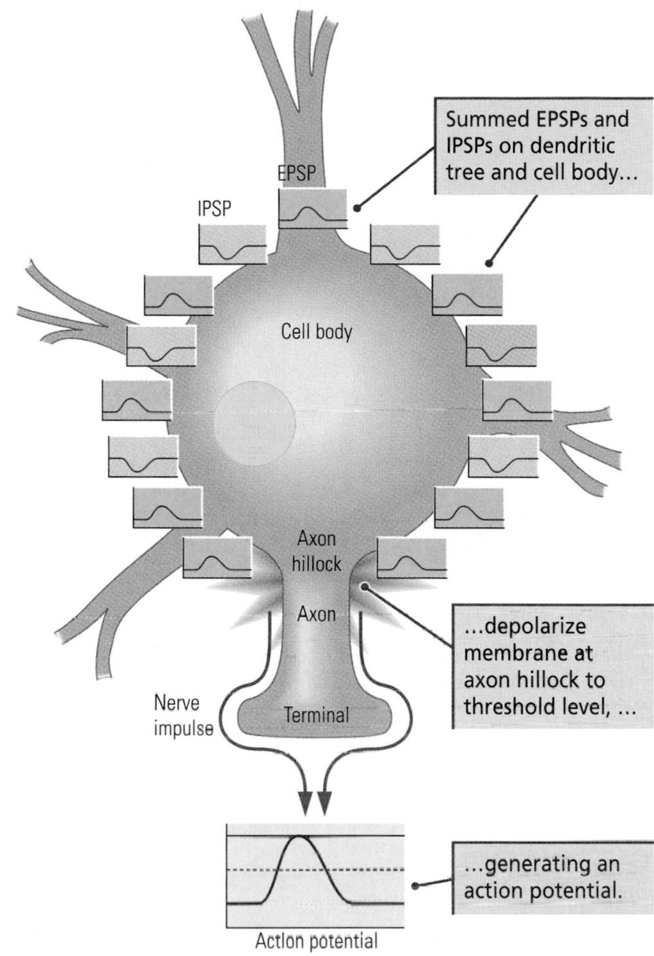
Summed EPSPs and IPSPs on dendritic tree and cell body...
EPSP
IPSP
Cell body
Axon hillock
Axon
Nerve impulse
Terminal
...depolarize membrane at axon hillock to threshold level, ...
...generating an action potential.
Action potential

**Figure 4-21**

If the sum of EPSPs and IPSPs on the dendritic tree and cell body of a neuron changes the membrane to threshold level at the axon hillock, it results in an action potential that flows down the axon membrane as a nerve impulse.

## In Review

Graded potentials are produced on a neuron's cell body and dendrites by stimulation at synapses. Graded potentials that decrease the charge on the cell membrane, moving it toward the threshold level, are called excitatory postsynaptic potentials because they increase the likelihood that an action potential will occur. Graded potentials that increase the charge on the cell membrane, moving it away from the threshold level, are called inhibitory postsynaptic potentials because they decrease the likelihood that an action potential will result. EPSPs and IPSPs that occur close together in time and space are added together, or summated. In this way, a neuron integrates information that it receives from other neurons. If summated inputs are sufficiently excitatory to bring the axon hillock to a threshold level, an action potential is triggered, which is then propagated again and again as it travels along the cell's axon as a nerve impulse.

# INTO THE NERVOUS SYSTEM AND BACK OUT

The nervous system allows us to respond to sensory stimuli by detecting sensory stimuli in the environment and sending messages about them to the brain. The brain then interprets the information, triggering responses that contract muscles and cause movements of the body. Until now, we have been dealing with only the middle of this process—how neurons convey information to each other, integrate that information, and generate action potentials. We have still not explored the beginning and end of the journey into the nervous system and back out. We have yet to explain how a sensory stimulus initiates a nerve impulse or how a nerve impulse produces a muscular contraction. In this section, we fill in those missing pieces. You will learn that ion channels are again important but that these channels are different from those described so far. You will first see how they differ as we examine the production of action potentials by sensory stimuli.

## How Sensory Stimuli Produce Action Potentials

In Descartes's theory of how sensations are produced, a sensory stimulus applied to the skin stretches the skin, which tugs on a cord that leads to the brain. We now know that this theory is correct only in its broadest outline. A stimulus to the skin does initiate a message in the body that does travel to the brain through a cord of sorts. But that cord is nothing like what Descartes envisioned. The "cord" by which messages are sent is an interconnected set of neural fibers on which nerve impulses travel. But how exactly does a sensory stimulus initiate a nerve impulse?

We receive information about the world through tactile sensations (body senses), auditory sensations (hearing), visual sensations (vision), and chemical sensations (taste and olfaction). Each of these sensory modalities has one or more separate functions. For example, the body senses include touch, pressure, joint sense, pain, and temperature. Receptors for audition and balance are actually modified touch receptors. The visual system has receptors for different colors, as well as for light and dark. And taste and olfactory senses are sensitive to many chemical compounds. To process all of these different kinds of sensory inputs requires a remarkable array of different sensory receptors. But one thing that these diverse receptors have in common is the presence of ion channels on their cell membranes. When a sensory stimulus activates these ion channels, it initiates the chain of events that produces a nerve impulse.

Let us take touch as an example. Each hair on the human body is very sensitive to touch, allowing us to detect an even very slight displacement of it. You can demonstrate this sensitivity to yourself by selecting a single hair on your arm and bending it. If you are patient and precise in your experimentation, you will discover that some hairs are sensitive to displacement in one direction only, whereas others respond to displacement in any direction. What enables this very fine-tuned sensitivity?

The dendrites of sensory neurons are specialized to conduct nerve impulses, and one of these dendrites is wrapped around the base of each hair on your body, as shown in Figure 4-22. When a hair is mechanically displaced, the dendrite around it is stretched. This stretching initiates the opening of a series of **stretch-sensitive channels** in the dendrite's membrane, and their opening eventually produces a nerve impulse. ("Ah," you might say, "doesn't this response to stretching mean that Descartes was right?" No, not quite, because Descartes had no concept of microscopic channels and ions or of electrical charges.) When the stretch-sensitive channels open, they allow an influx of $Na^+$ ions that is sufficient to depolarize the dendrite to its threshold level. At threshold, the voltage-sensitive sodium and potassium channels open to initiate the nerve impulse.

**Stretch-sensitive channel.** On a membrane, a channel that is activated to allow the passage of ions in response to stretching of the membrane; initiates nerve impulses on tactile sensory neurons.

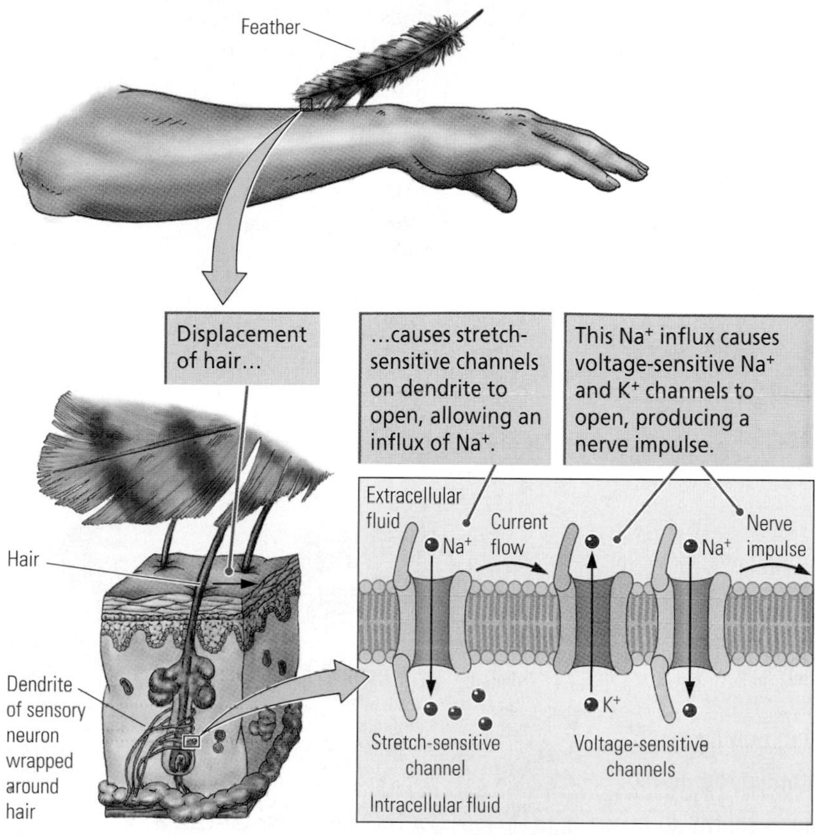
Feather
Displacement of hair...
...causes stretch-sensitive channels on dendrite to open, allowing an influx of Na+.
This Na+ influx causes voltage-sensitive Na+ and K+ channels to open, producing a nerve impulse.
Extracellular fluid
Na+
Current flow
Na+
Nerve impulse
Hair
Dendrite of sensory neuron wrapped around hair
K+
Stretch-sensitive channel
Voltage-sensitive channels
Intracellular fluid

**Figure 4-22**

A hair's touch receptor is activated by a feather. The dendrite of a sensory neuron is wrapped around the hair so that, when the hair is displaced, the dendrite stretches. Stretch-sensitive sodium channels on the dendrite are opened by stretching, thus depolarizing the dendrite membrane to threshold, at which point voltage-sensitive channels open. The opening of the voltage-sensitive channels produces an action potential that is conducted along the dendrite as a nerve impulse.

Other kinds of sensory receptors have similar mechanisms for changing the energy of a sensory stimulus into nervous system activity. The receptors for hearing and balance also have hairs that, when displaced, likewise activate stretch-sensitive channels. In the visual system, light particles strike chemicals in the receptors in the eye, and the resulting chemical change activates ion channels in the membranes of relay neurons. An odorous molecule in the air lands on an olfactory receptor and fits itself into a specially shaped compartment, thereby opening chemical-sensitive ion channels. When tissue is damaged, injured cells release a chemical called bradykinin that activates bradykinin-sensitive channels on a pain nerve. In later chapters, we will consider the details of how sensory receptors change energy from the external world into action potentials. The point here is that, in all our sensory systems, ion channels begin the process of information conduction.

## How Nerve Impulses Produce Movement

What about the end of the journey into the nervous system and back out? How, after sensory information has traveled to the brain and been interpreted, is a behavioral response that includes the contraction of muscles generated? Behavior, after all, is movement, and, for movement to occur, muscles must contract. If Descartes's idea that it is a flow of liquid that "pumps up" muscles is wrong, how, then, does the nervous system produce muscular contractions?

You know that motor neurons send nerve impulses to muscles through their axons. If the motor neurons fail to work, movement becomes impossible and muscles atrophy, as occurs in Lou Gehrig's disease (see "Lou Gehrig's Disease" on page 140). The motor-neuron axons, in turn, generate action potentials in muscle cells, which are instrumental in making the muscle contract. So the question is, How does an action potential on a motor-neuron axon produce an action potential on a muscle?

Focus on Disorders

## Lou Gehrig's Disease

Lou Gehrig played baseball for the New York Yankees from 1923 until 1939. During his playing career, he was a member of numerous World Series championship teams, set a host of individual records, some of which still stand today, and was immensely popular with the fans, who knew him as the "Iron Man." His record of 2130 consecutive games was untouched until 1990, when Cal Ripkin, Jr., played his 2131st consecutive game.

Lou Gehrig's problems began in 1938, when he seemed to start losing his strength. In 1939, he played only eight games and then retired from baseball. Eldon Auker, a pitcher for the Detroit Tigers, described Lou's physical decline this way: "Lou seemed to be losing his power. His walking and running appeared to slow. His swing was not as strong as it had been in past years." Eldon was describing not the symptoms of normal aging but the symptoms of amyotrophic lateral sclerosis (called ALS for short), a diagnosis shortly to be pronounced by Lou's physician. ALS was first described by Jean-Martin Charcot in 1869, but, after Lou Gehrig developed the condition, it became known as Lou Gehrig's disease. Lou Gehrig died in 1941 at the age of 38.

Baseball Hall of Fame Library, Cooperstown, N.Y.

Lou Gehrig jumping over the bat of Yankee teammate Joe DiMaggio.

ALS affects about 6 of every 100,000 people and strikes most commonly between the ages of 50 and 75, although its onset can be as early as the teenage years. About 10 percent of victims have a family history of the disorder, whereas the rest do not. The disease begins with general weakness, at first in the throat or upper chest and in the arms and legs. Gradually, walking becomes difficult and falling becomes more common. The patient may lose use of the hands and legs, have trouble swallowing, and have difficulty speaking. The disease does not usually affect any of the sensory systems, cognitive functions, bowel or bladder control, or even sexual function. Death is usually within 5 years of diagnosis.

ALS is due primarily to the death of motor neurons, which connect the rest of the nervous system to muscles, allowing movement. Neurons in the brain that connect primarily with motor neurons also can be affected. The technical term for the disorder, amyotrophic lateral sclerosis, describes its consequences on both muscles (*amyotrophic* means "muscle weakness") and the spinal cord (*lateral sclerosis* means "hardening of the lateral spinal cord," where motor neurons are located). There are several theories about why motor neurons suddenly start to die in ALS victims. Perhaps this cell death is caused by the death of microtubules that carry proteins down the motor-neuron axons or perhaps by a buildup of toxic chemicals within the motor neurons or by toxic chemicals released from other neurons. No one knows for sure. At the present time, there is no cure for ALS, although some newly developed drugs appear to slow its progression and offer some hope for future treatments.

The axon of each motor neuron makes one or a few connections (synapses) with its target muscle, as shown in Figure 4-23. These connections are similar to those that neurons make with each other. The part of the muscle membrane that is contacted by the axon terminal is a specialized area called an **end plate.** The axon terminal releases a chemical onto the end plate. ("Ah," you might say, "doesn't that mean that Descartes was correct about liquid playing a part?" No, not quite, because Descartes had no notion that the "liquid" is instead minuscule amounts of chemical transmitters.) The chemical transmitter that is released onto muscles is **acetylcholine.** This transmitter does not enter the muscle but rather attaches, or binds, to **transmitter-sensitive channels** on the end plate. When these channels open in response to the acetylcholine, they allow a flow of ions across the muscle membrane sufficient to depolarize the muscle membrane to the threshold for its action potential. At threshold, adjacent voltage-sensitive channels open. They, in turn, produce an action potential on the muscle fiber, which is the basis for muscular contraction.

The transmitter-sensitive channels on muscle end plates are somewhat different from the channels on axons and dendrites. A single end-plate channel is larger than two sodium and two potassium channels combined. When the transmitter-sensitive channels open, they allow both sodium ions and potassium ions to flow through the same pore. The number of channels that open depends on the amount of transmitter released. Therefore, to generate a sufficient depolarization on the end plate to activate neighboring voltage-sensitive channels requires the release of an appropriate amount of transmitter.

Notice how a wide range of neural events can be explained by the actions of membrane channels. Some channels are responsible for generating the transmembrane charge. Other channels mediate graded potentials. Still others are responsible for the action potential. Sensory stimuli activate channels on neurons to initiate a nerve impulse, and the nerve impulse eventually activates channels on motor neurons to produce muscle contractions. These various channels and their different functions probably evolved over a long period of time in the same way that new species of animals and their behaviors evolved. So far, not all the different channels that neural membranes possess have been described. You will learn about some additional channels in subsequent chapters.

(A)

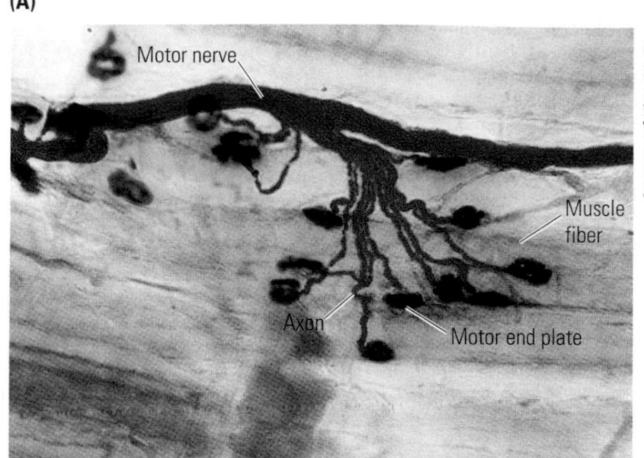


(B)

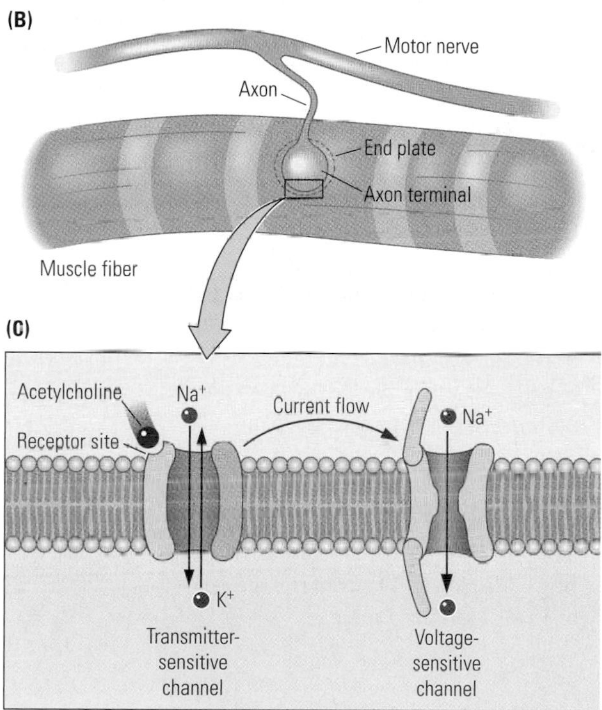


**Figure 4-23**

**(A)** In this microscopic view of a motor neuron axon connecting to muscle end plates, the dark patches are end plates and the axon terminals are not visible. **(B)** Each axon has a terminal that ends on an end plate. **(C)** The neurotransmitter acetylcholine attaches to receptor sites on transmitter-sensitive end-plate channels, opening them. The large channels allow the simultaneous influx of sodium ions and efflux of potassium ions, generating a current that is sufficient to activate voltage-sensitive channels. The opening of voltage-sensitive channels produces the action potential on the muscle, causing it to contract.

## In Review

The way in which a sensory stimulus initiates a nerve impulse is surprisingly similar for all our sensory systems. The membrane of a receptor cell contains a mechanism for transducing sensory energy into changes in ion channels. These changes in ion channels, in turn, allow ion flow to alter the voltage of the membrane to the point that voltage-sensitive channels open, initiating a nerve impulse. Muscle contraction also depends on ion channels. The axon terminal of a motor neuron releases a chemical transmitter, acetylcholine, onto the end plate of a muscle-cell membrane. Transmitter-sensitive channels on the end plate open in response to the acetylcholine, and the subsequent flow of ions depolarizes the muscle membrane to the threshold for its action potential. This depolarization, in turn, activates neighboring voltage-sensitive channels, producing an action potential on the muscle fiber, which brings about contraction of the muscle.

**Acetylcholine.** The first neurotransmitter discovered in the peripheral and central nervous system; also the neurotransmitter that activates skeletal muscles.

**Transmitter-sensitive channel.** A receptor complex that has both a receptor site for a chemical and a pore through which ions can flow.

# USING ELECTRICAL ACTIVITY TO STUDY BRAIN FUNCTION

Our description of how a sensory stimulus initiates a flow of information in the nervous system that eventually results in some behavioral response should not mislead you into thinking that neurons are active only when something in the environment triggers them. Results of brain-wave recording studies show that electrical activity is always going on in the brain. The nervous system is electrically active during vigorous exercise, during rest, during daydreaming and sleep, and even during anesthesia. In each case, moreover, it is active in a different way. The various electrical patterns associated with different kinds of behaviors are sufficiently distinctive to allow some fairly accurate assessments of what a person is doing at any given time. The ability to read the brain's electrical recordings has not progressed to the point at which we can tell what someone is thinking, however. But we can tell whether someone is awake or asleep and whether the brain is working normally. As a result, measures of brain activity have become very important for studying the function of various brain regions, for medical diagnosis, and for monitoring the effectiveness of therapies used to treat brain disorders. Three major techniques for studying the brain's electrical activity are: (1) single-cell recordings, (2) electroencephalograms (EEGs), and (3) event-related potentials (ERPs). This section describes and gives examples of each of them.

## Single-Cell Recordings

While recording the activity of single neurons in a region of the rat brain called the subiculum, James Ranck (1973) noticed that the action potentials of one especially interesting neuron had a remarkable relation to the rat's behavior, summarized in Figure 4-24. Whenever the rat faced in a particular direction, the neuron vigorously fired—that is, it generated an action potential. When the rat turned somewhat away from this direction, the neuron fired more slowly. And when the rat faced in the direction opposite the neuron's favored direction, the neuron did not fire at all. Ranck called this type of neuron a **head-direction cell.** In studying it further, he found that it displays still more remarkable behavior. If a rat is taken to another room, the neuron maintains its directional selectivity. Even when the rat is picked up and pointed in different directions, the neuron still behaves just as it does when the rat turns by itself.

**Figure 4-24**

A rat's head-direction cells are located in the subiculum, a part of the limbic system. These cells fire when the rat faces in a given direction. The firing rate of a single cell decreases as the rat is displaced from the cell's preferred direction, which in this case is when the rat is facing the bottom of the page. Each of the eight traces of neural activity shows the cell's relative rate of firing when the rat is placed in the direction indicated by the corresponding arrow. Head-direction cells help inform the rat about its location in space.

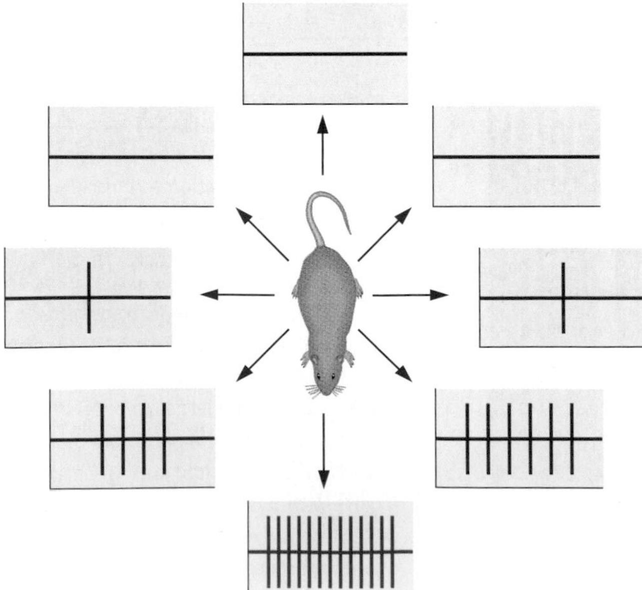

Who would have predicted that a neuron in the brain would behave in such a way? This discovery serves as an excellent example of the power of single-cell recording techniques to provide information about how different regions of the brain work. We humans also have head-direction cells that tell us where we are in relation to some reference point, such as home. We can keep track of both our active and our passive movements to maintain a "sense of direction" no matter how many times we turn or are turned. The region of the human brain in which head-direction cells are found presumably regulates this sense of direction.

The technique of single-cell recording has come a long way since the pioneering experiments of Hodgkin and Huxley. It is now possible to record the activity of single neurons in freely moving mammals by permanently implanting microelectrodes into the brain. Nevertheless, the basic recording procedure has not changed that much. Small, insulated wire microelectrodes, with their uninsulated tips filed to a fine point, are preferred to glass microelectrodes. An oscilloscope is still used to visualize the behavior of the cell, but, in addition, the cell's activity is played into a loudspeaker so that cell firing can be heard as a beep or pop. Ranck's cell went "beep beep beep" extremely rapidly when the rat pointed in the preferred direction, and it was silent when the rat turned completely away. Today, too, the massive amount of information obtained during cell recordings is stored and analyzed on a computer.

Many hundreds of single-cell recording studies have been conducted to discover the types of stimuli that cause neurons to fire. Neurons fire in response to stimuli as simple as lights or tones and to stimuli as complex as the face of a particular person or the sound of a particular voice. Single neurons have also been found to have a wide range of firing patterns. For example, they may discharge in proportion to the intensity of a stimulus, fire rhythmically with it, or fire when the stimulus starts or stops. Remarkably, single cells also communicate by becoming silent. The cells in the pathway between the eye and the brain, for example, have a very high discharge rate when an animal is in the dark. Many of these cells decrease their rate of firing in response to light.

You will encounter other examples of the link between behavior and single-cell activity in later chapters of this book. It is impossible to fully understand how a region of the brain works without understanding what the individual cells in that region are doing, and this knowledge is acquired through the use of single-cell recording techniques. Such studies must usually be done with animals, because only in exceptional circumstances, such as brain surgery or as a treatment for disease, is it possible to implant electrodes into the brain of a person for the purposes of recording single-cell activity.

Hans Berger (1873–1941)

## EEG Recordings

In the early 1930s, Hans Berger discovered that electrical activity of the brain could be recorded simply by placing electrodes onto the skull. This form of brain electrical activity is popularly known as "brain waves." Recording this electrical activity produces an electroencephalogram, or EEG (*electroencephalogram* literally means "electrical record from the head"). EEGs reveal some remarkable features of the brain's electrical activity. First, the brain's electrical activity is never silent even when a person is asleep or anesthetized. Second, an EEG recorded from the cortex has a large number of patterns, some of which are extremely rhythmical. Third, an EEG changes as behavior changes.

The EEGs in Figure 4-25 illustrate these three features of human brain waves. When a person is aroused, excited, or even just alert, the EEG pattern has a low amplitude (the height of the brain waves) and a fast frequency (the number of brain waves per second), as shown in Figure 4-25A. This pattern is typical of an EEG taken from anywhere on the skull of an alert subject, not only a human subject, but other animals, too. In contrast, when a person is calm and relaxing quietly, especially with eyes closed, the rhythmical brain waves shown in Figure 4-25B often emerge. These waves, known as **alpha rhythms,** are extremely rhythmical, with a frequency of approximately 11 cycles per second and an amplitude that waxes and wanes as the pattern is generated. In humans, alpha rhythms are recorded in the region of the visual cortex, which lies at the back of the head. If a relaxed person is disturbed or opens his or her eyes, the alpha rhythms abruptly stop.

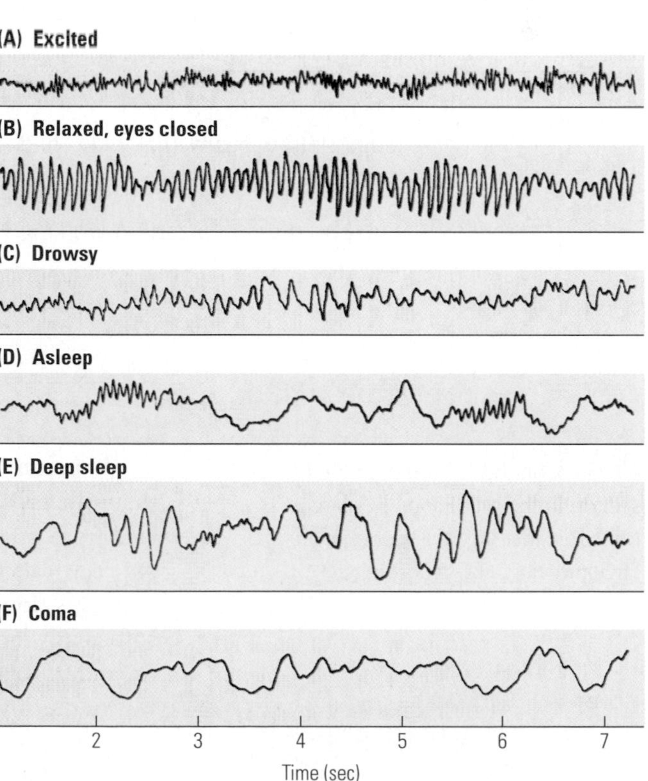


**Figure 4-25**

These characteristic EEGs recorded during various behavioral states in humans show **(A)** the brain-wave pattern in an awake, excited person; **(B)** the alpha rhythm associated with relaxation with the eyes closed; **(C)** the slowing in frequency and increase in amplitude associated with a drowsy condition; **(D)** the slow high-amplitude waves associated with sleep; **(E)** the larger slow waves associated with deep sleep; and **(F)** the further slowing of EEG waves associated with coma.

Adapted from *Epilepsy and the Functional Anatomy of the Human Brain* (p. 12), by W. Penfield & H. H. Jasper, 1954, Boston: Little, Brown.

Focus on Disorders

## Epilepsy

J. D. worked as a disc jockey for a radio station. In his off-hours, he also played recorded music at parties with a sound system that he had purchased. One evening he had his sound system set up on the back of a truck at a rugby field to provide music for a jovial and raucous rugby party. Between musical sets, he was master of ceremonies and made introductions, told jokes, and exchanged toasts and jugs of beer with the partyers. At about one o'clock in the morning, he suddenly began making unusual jerky motions, after which he collapsed in a coma. He was rushed to a hospital emergency room, where he gradually recovered. The attending physician noted that he was not drunk and released him to his friends with the recommendation that he undergo a series of neurological tests the next day.

Subsequent brain scans indicated no abnormal brain patterns. When given an EEG recording test, however, during which a strobe light was flashed before his eyes, he displayed a series of abnormal spike-and-wave patterns characteristic of epilepsy. He was given a prescription for Dilantin and advised to refrain from drinking. He was also required to give up his driver's license because of the possibility that a similar attack while driving could cause an accident. When the radio station heard that J. D. had suffered an epileptic seizure, they dismissed him on the improbable grounds that he posed a fire hazard in working with electrical equipment. After 3 months of uneventful drug treatment,

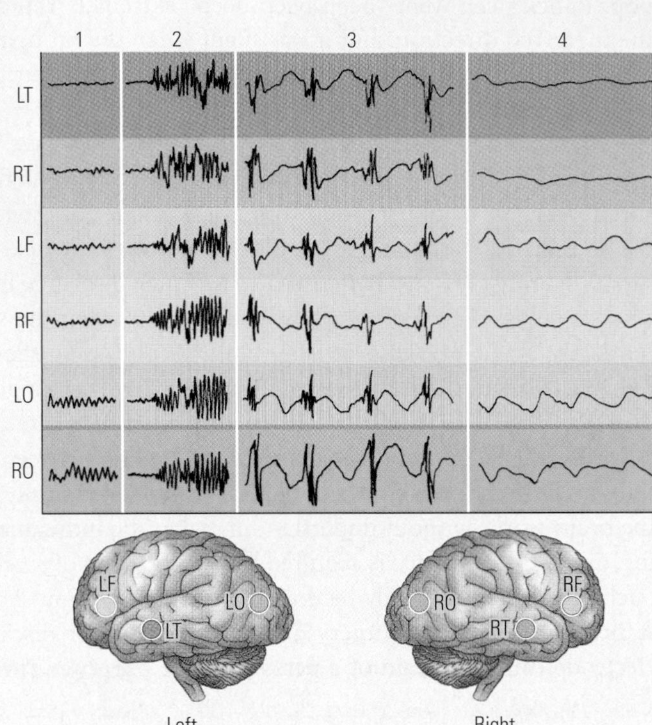


Examples of EEG patterns recorded during a grand mal seizure. Abbreviations: LT and RT, left and right temporal; LF and RF, left and right frontal; LO and RO, left and right occipital. Color dots on the hemispheres indicate the approximate recording sites and are coded to the recordings. Numbers refer to stages of the seizure: (1) normal record before the attack; (2) onset of the attack; (3) clonic phase in which the person makes rhythmic movements in time with the large abnormal discharges; and (4) period of coma after the seizure ends.

Adapted from *Fundamentals of Human Neuropsychology* (p. 80), by B. Kolb & I. Q. Whishaw, 1980, San Francisco: W. H. Freeman and Company.

Click on the CD and find the EEG section in the module on Research Methods. Investigate a model of an EEG and view EEG recordings.

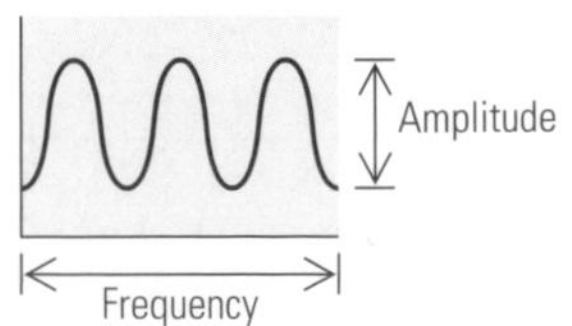


Not everyone displays alpha rhythms, and some people display them much better than others. You can buy a little voltmeter for monitoring your own alpha rhythms. A lead from one pole of the voltmeter is attached to the skull with a paste that conducts an electrical current, and the ground wire is pasted to the ear lobe. You can then relax with eyes closed, trying to make the voltmeter "beep." Each wave of the alpha rhythm, if sufficiently large, produces a beep. Many people can quickly learn to turn alpha waves on and off by using this procedure. Beeping EEG voltmeters were once promoted as a way of quickly learning how to obtain a state of transcendental meditation.

An EEG is a sensitive indicator of other behaviors, too, not just of arousal and relaxation. Figure 4-25C–E illustrates the EEG changes that occur as a person goes from drowsiness to sleep and finally into deep sleep. The EEG rhythms become slower

he was taken off medication and his driver's license was restored. He also successfully sued the radio station for back pay and the return of his job. In the past 10 years, he has not had another epileptic attack.

Epileptic seizures are caused by abnormal brain activity, in which neurons begin to fire synchronously and then, after a course of discharge, stop firing completely. Like a flame put to paper, the abnormal activity often spreads to adjacent brain areas. The abnormal discharges are often accompanied by abnormal movements, suggesting that the discharges are driving those movements. Loss of consciousness and loss of movement are usually associated with cessation of electrical activity in the affected area of the brain. Epileptic seizures can last for seconds to minutes. Synchronous events can often be the trigger to start an epileptic attack and, for that reason, a strobe light is often used as part of diagnosis.

Epileptic seizures are very common. One person in 20 will experience at least one seizure in his or her lifetime. The prevalence of multiple seizures is much lower, about 1 in 200. Sometimes epileptic seizures are symptomatic seizures—that is, they can be linked to a specific cause, such as infection, trauma, tumors, or other events that cause damage to a part of the brain. Other seizures, however, called idiopathic (related to the individual person), appear to arise spontaneously in the absence of other brain diseases. Their cause is poorly understood.

Three symptoms are found in many kinds of epilepsy. First, the victim often has a warning or aura of an impending seizure, which may take the form of a sensation, such as odors or sounds, or may simply be a "feeling" that the seizure is about to occur. Second, the victim may lose consciousness and later have amnesia for the seizure, being unaware that it ever happened. Third, the seizure is often accompanied by abnormal movements such as repeated chewing or shaking, twitches that start in a limb and spread across the body, and, in some cases, a total loss of muscle tone and postural support, causing the person to collapse. Seizures may be categorized according to the severity of these symptoms. In *petit mal* (from the French for "little bad") *seizures,* there is usually a brief loss of awareness and small or brief abnormal movements. In contrast, *grand mal* ("big bad") *seizures* entail severe abnormalities of movement, collapse, and loss of consciousness.

An epileptic seizure is usually confirmed by EEG recordings that reveal large, rhythmical, abnormal brain-wave patterns that often have the appearance of spikes and waves. When this abnormal rhythmical activity stops, the EEG may simply be a flat line before recovering its normal pattern over a period of minutes. The treatment of choice for epilepsy is diphenylhydantoin (Dilantin), a form of anesthetic drug given in low doses. If seizures occur repeatedly and cannot be controlled by drug treatment, surgery may be performed. The goal of surgery is to remove damaged or scarred tissue that serves as the focal point of a seizure. Removing this small area of abnormal brain prevents the seizure from starting and spreading to other brain regions.

in frequency and larger in amplitude. Still slower waves occur during anesthesia, after brain trauma, or when a person is in a coma (illustrated in Figure 4-25F). If the brain dies (brain death), the EEG becomes a flat line. These distinctive brain-wave patterns make the EEG a reliable tool for monitoring sleep stages, estimating the depth of anesthesia, evaluating the severity of head injury, and searching for other brain abnormalities. For example, an EEG is routinely used to evaluate epilepsy and its distinctive EEG patterns. The brief periods of unconsciousness and involuntary movements that characterize epileptic seizures are associated with very abnormal spike-and-wave patterns in the EEG (see"Epilepsy," above, for a fuller description). The important point here is that EEG recording provides both a useful research tool and a useful way of diagnosing brain abnormalities.

Michael Rosenfeld / Stone Images

1 Electrodes are attached to the skull, corresponding to specific areas of the brain...

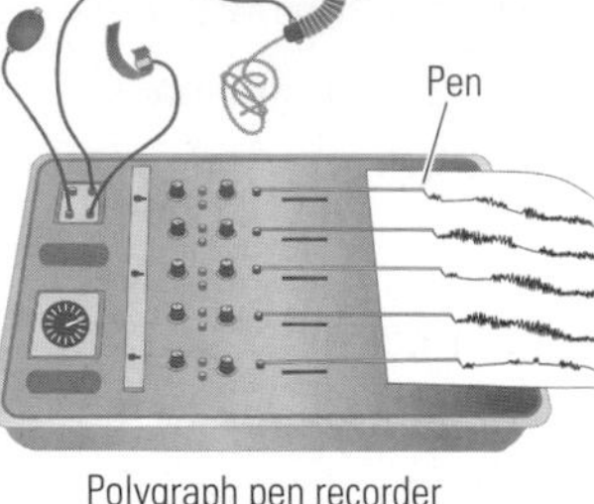


2 ...polygraph electrodes are connected to magnets, which are connected to pens...

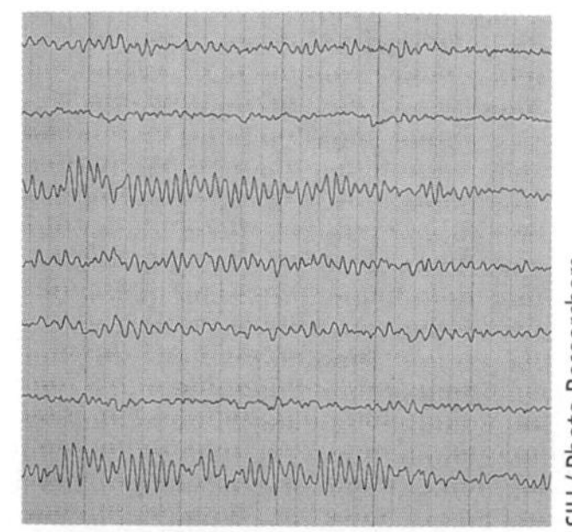
SIU / Photo Researchers

3 ...that produce a paper record of electrical activity in the brain. This record indicates a relaxed person.

What produces an EEG? An EEG is a measure of graded potentials. It measures the summed graded potentials from many thousands of neurons. Neurons of the neocortex provide an especially good source of EEG waves because these cells are lined up in layers and have a propensity to produce graded potentials in a rhythmical fashion.

EEG waves are usually recorded with a special kind of oscilloscope called a polygraph (meaning "many graphs"). Each channel on a polygraph is equivalent to one oscilloscope. Instead of measuring electrical activity with a beam of electrons, the polygraph electrodes are connected to magnets, which are in turn connected to pens. A motor pulls a long sheet of paper at a constant rate beneath the pens, allowing the patterns of electrical activity to be written on the paper. Because the graded potentials being measured have quite low frequencies, the pens can keep up with the EEG record. To read this record, the experimenter simply observes its changing patterns.

Recently, computers have been programmed to read EEG waves. Many channels of EEG activity are "fed" into the computer, and the computer then matches active areas with specific regions of the brain. The computer can display a representation of the brain on the screen, with changes in color representing brain activity. Because the EEG is recorded on-line, as a subject is engaged in some behavior or problem-solving activity, the computer display can show an on-line display of brain activity. The computer-assisted analysis is useful for finding how the brain processes sensory information, solves problems, and makes decisions. It is also useful in clinical diagnosis—for example, for charting the progress of abnormal electrical activity associated with epilepsy.

There are also miniaturized computer-based polygraphs about the size of an audiocassette recorder, which can be worn on a belt. They store the EEG record of a freely moving person for later replay on a chart polygraph or computer. One possible future use of miniaturized EEG recording devices is to enable brain-wave patterns to control the cursor on a computer. This technology would be very helpful to people who are paralyzed. If they could learn to control their EEGs sufficiently to command a cursor, they would be able to use the computer to communicate with others.

## Event-Related Potentials

**Event-related potential (ERP).** A change in the slow-wave activity of the brain in response to a sensory stimulus.

**Event-related potentials (ERPs)**, are brief changes in an EEG signal in response to a discrete sensory stimulus. ERPs are largely the graded potentials on dendrites that a sensory stimulus triggers. You might think that they should be easy to detect, but they are not. The problem is that ERPs are mixed in with so many other electrical signals in the brain that they are difficult to spot just by visually inspecting an EEG record. One way to detect ERPs is to produce the stimulus repeatedly and average the recorded responses. Averaging tends to cancel out any irregular and unrelated electrical activity, leaving in the EEG record only the potentials that the stimulus event generated.

An analogy will help to clarify this procedure. Imagine throwing a small stone into a lake of choppy water. Although the stone produces a splash, that splash is hard to see among all of the water's ripples and waves. This splash made by a stone is analogous to an event-related potential caused by a sensory stimulus. Like the splash surrounded by choppy water, the ERP is hard to detect because of all the other electrical activity around it. A solution is to throw a number of stones exactly the same size, always hitting the same spot in the water and producing the same splash over and over. If a computer is then used to calculate an average of the water's activity, random wave movements will tend to average each other out, and you will see the splashes produced by the stones as clearly as if a single stone had been thrown into a pool of calm water.

Figure 4-26 (top) shows an ERP record that results when a person hears a tone. Notice that the EEG record is very irregular when the tone is first presented. But, after averaging over 100 stimulus presentations, a distinctive wave pattern appears. This ERP pattern consists of a number of negative (N) and positive (P) waves that occur over a period of a few hundred milliseconds after the stimulus. The waves are numbered in relation to the time at which they occur. For instance, $N_1$ is a negative wave occurring about 100 milliseconds after the stimulus, whereas $P_2$ is a positive wave occurring about 200 milliseconds after the stimulus. Not all of the waves are unique to this particular stimulus. Some are common to any auditory stimulus that might be presented. Other waves, however, correspond to important differences in this specific tone. ERPs to spoken words even contain distinctive peaks and patterns that differentiate such similar words as "cat" and "rat."

There are many practical reasons for using ERPs to study the brain. One advantage is that the technique is noninvasive, because electrodes are placed on the surface of the skull, not into the brain. Therefore, ERPs can be used to study humans, including college students—the most frequently used subjects. Another advantage of using ERPs is their cost. In comparison with other brain-analyzing techniques, such as brain scans, this method is very inexpensive. Additionally, with modern ERP technology, it is possible to record ERPs from many brain areas simultaneously, by pasting an array of electrodes (sometimes more than 100) onto different parts of the skull. Because certain brain areas respond only to certain kinds of sensory stimuli (for example, auditory areas respond to sounds and visual areas to sights), the relative responses at different locations can be used to map brain function.

Figure 4-27 shows a multiple-recording method that uses 64 electrodes simultaneously to detect ERPs at many cortical sites. Computerized averaging techniques reduce the masses of information obtained to simpler comparisons between electrode sites. For example, if the focus of interest is $P_2$, a computer record can display a graph of the skull on which only the amplitude of $P_2$ is shown. A computer can also convert the averages at different sites into a color code, creating a graphic representation showing the brain regions that are most responsive. In Figure 4-27, the subject is viewing a picture of a rat that appears repeatedly in the same place on a computer screen. The $P_2$ recorded on the posterior right side of the head is larger than $P_2$ occurring anywhere else, meaning that this region is a "hot spot" for processing the visual stimulus. Presumably, for this particular subject, the right

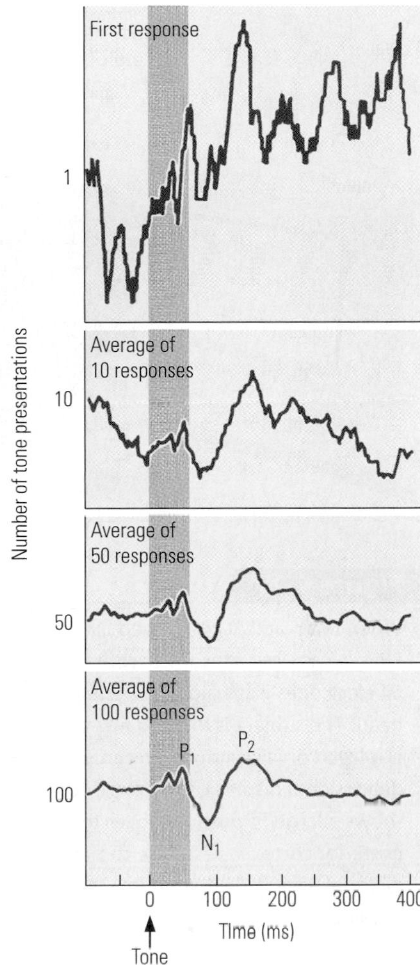


**Figure 4-26**

In this illustration of the averaging process for an auditory ERP, a tone is presented at time "0," and the EEG activity in response to the tone is recorded. After many EEG responses to successive presentations of the tone, the averaged wave sequence develops a distinctive shape. This distinctive shape is extremely clear after averaging 100 responses. Positive ($P_1$ and $P_2$) and negative ($N_1$) waves that occur at different times after the stimulus are used for analysis.

Electrodes attached to the scalp of research subject are connected to...

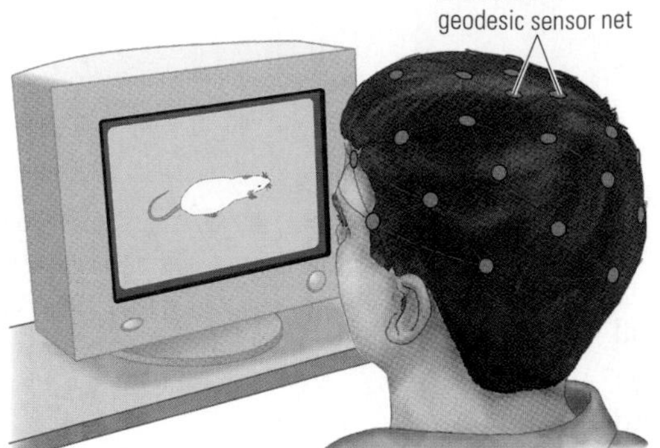


...computer display of electrical activity, showing a large positive ($P_2$) wave at posterior right side of the head.

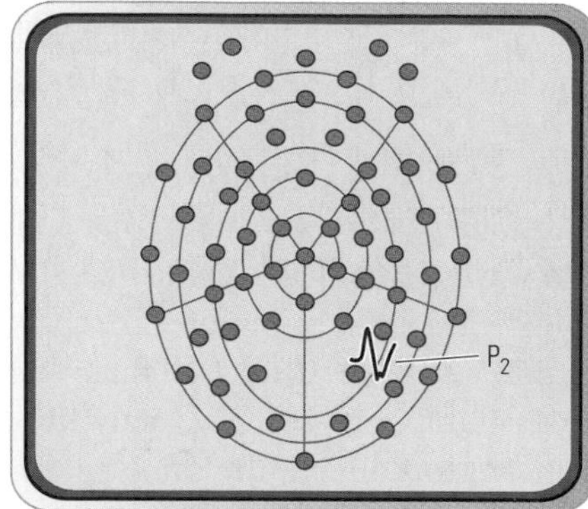


This electrical activity can be converted into a color representation showing the hot spot for the visual stimulus.

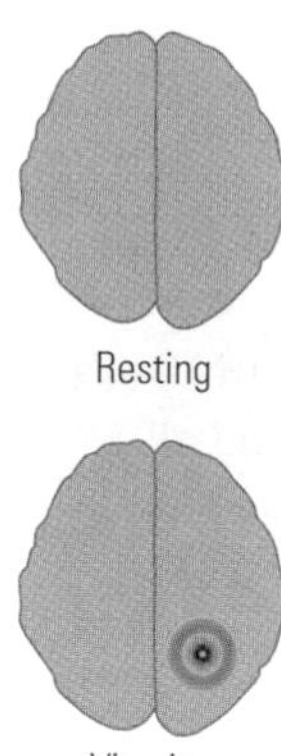


**Figure 4-27**

When brain activity is imaged by using ERPs, a geodesic sensor net containing 64 electrodes is placed on the subject's head. The subject is looking at a rat displayed on a computer screen. A two-dimensional display of the electrode sites shows a large $P_2$ potential over the right posterior cortex in response to the pictorial display. The brain image obtained with a computer transformation of the ERPs is shown in the resting condition and 200 milliseconds after stimulation in the viewing condition.

posterior part of the brain is central in decoding the picture of the rat 200 milliseconds after it is presented. In this way, ERPs can be used not only to detect which areas of the brain are processing particular stimuli, but also to study the order in which different regions play a role. This second use of ERPs is important because, as information travels through the brain, we want to know the route that it takes on its journey.

Many other interesting questions can be investigated with the use of ERPs. For instance, they can be used to study how children learn and process information differently as they mature. They can also be used to examine how a person with a brain injury compensates for the impairment by using other, undamaged regions of the brain. ERPs can even help reveal which brain areas are most sensitive to the aging process and therefore contribute most to declines in behavioral functions among the elderly. All are questions that can be addressed with this simple, inexpensive research method.

## In Review

There are three major techniques for studying the brain's electrical activity. One of them is the single-cell recording technique in which readings are taken from a single neuron. Many hundreds of such studies have been conducted to determine what the firing patterns of particular neurons are and what stimuli trigger them to fire. The electrical activity of the brain can also be recorded simply by placing electrodes onto the skull and obtaining an electroencephalogram, or EEG. EEGs show that the brain's electrical activity never ceases, even under anesthesia, that this activity can be extremely rhythmical, and that different patterns of brain waves are often associated with different behaviors. Finally, researchers can study the brief changes in an EEG in response to a discrete sensory stimulus, such as a tone or a flash of light. These event-related potentials, or ERPs, allow scientists to determine which areas of the brain are processing various kinds of stimuli and in which order those areas come into play.

## SUMMARY

1. *What two kinds of studies provided early clues that electrical activity was somehow implicated in the nervous system's flow of information?* The two kinds of studies that provided these early clues were electrical-stimulation studies and electrical-recording studies. The results of early electrical-stimulation studies, which date as far back as the eighteenth century, showed that stimulating a nerve with electrical current sometimes induces the contraction of a muscle. The results of early electrical-recording studies, in which the brain's electrical current was measured with a voltmeter, showed that electrical activity is continually occurring within the nervous system.
2. *What technical problems had to be overcome to measure the electrical activity of a single neuron?* To measure the electrical activity of a single neuron, researchers first had to find neurons with large enough axons to study. They also had to develop both a recording device sufficiently sensitive to detect very small electrical impulses and an electrode tiny enough to be placed on or into a neuron. These problems were overcome with the study of the giant axons of squid, the invention of the oscilloscope, and the development of microelectrodes.
3. *How is the electrical activity of neurons generated?* The electrical activity of neurons is generated by the flow of electrically charged particles called ions across the cell membrane. These ions flow both down a concentration gradient (from an area of relatively high concentration to an area of lower concentration) and down a voltage gradient (from an area of relatively high voltage to an area of lower voltage). The distribution of ions is also affected by the opening and closing of ion channels in neural membranes.
4. *What are graded potentials and how do they change the resting potential of a neuron's membrane?* In an undisturbed neuron, the intracellular side of the membrane has an electrical charge of about −70 millivolts relative to the extracellular side. This charge, called the resting potential, is due to an unequal distribution of ions on the membrane's two sides. Large negatively charged protein anions are too big to leave the neuron, and the cell membrane actively pumps out positively charged sodium ions. In addition, unequal distributions of potassium ions and chloride ions contribute to the resting potential. Then, when the neuron is stimulated, ion channels in the membrane are affected, which in turn changes the distribution of ions, suddenly increasing or decreasing the transmembrane voltage by a small amount. A slight increase in the voltage is called hyperpolarization, whereas a slight decrease is called depolarization. Both conditions are known as graded potentials.
5. *What is an action potential and how is it related to a nerve impulse?* An action potential is a brief but large change in the polarity of an axon's membrane that is triggered when the transmembrane voltage drops to a threshold level of about −50 millivolts. The transmembrane voltage suddenly reverses (with the intracellular side becoming positive relative to the extracellular side) and then abruptly reverses again, after which the resting potential is restored. These reversals are due to the behavior of sodium and potassium channels that are sensitive to the membrane's voltage, called voltage-sensitive channels. When an action potential is triggered at the axon hillock, it can propagate along the axon. This movement of an action potential along an axon is called a nerve impulse. Nerve impulses travel more rapidly on myelinated axons because the action potentials jump between the nodes separating the glial cells that form the axon's myelin.
6. *How do neurons integrate information?* The inputs to neurons from other cells can produce both excitatory postsynaptic potentials (EPSPs) and inhibitory

**neuroscience interactive**

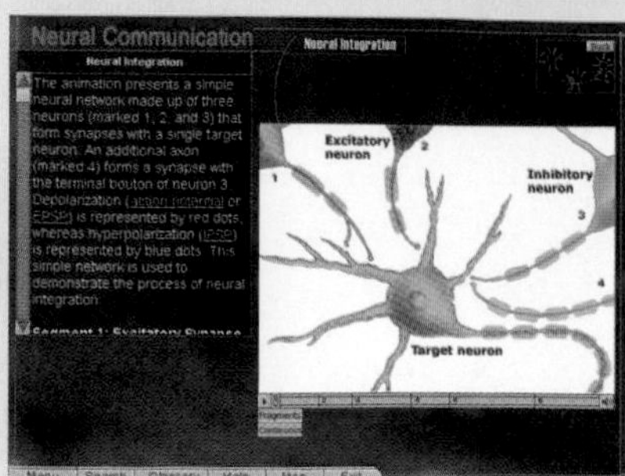


There are many resources available for expanding your learning on line:

- **www.worthpublishers.com/kolb/chapter4**

Try some self-tests to reinforce your mastery of the material. Look at some of the news updates reflecting current research on the brain. You'll also be able to link to other sites which will reinforce what you've learned.

- **www.efa.org**

Learn more about epilepsy at the Web site for the Epilepsy Foundation of America.

- **www.myasthenia.org**

Investigate myasthenia gravis at the Myasthenia Gravis Foundation of America.

On your CD-ROM you'll be able to quiz yourself on your comprehension of the chapter. You'll also be able to learn more about how information is conveyed between neurons in the module on Neural Communication. This module includes animations of many processes, including the membrane potential and the action potential. In addition, the Research Methods module has an overview of many of the different technologies covered in this chapter, including the EEG, electrical stimulation, and microelectrodes.

postsynaptic potentials (IPSPs). These EPSPs and IPSPs are summed both temporally and spatially, which integrates the incoming information. If the resulting sum moves the voltage of the membrane at the axon hillock to the threshold level, an action potential will be produced on the axon of the neuron.

7. *How do nerve impulses travel into the nervous system and back out?* Sensory-receptor cells in the body contain mechanisms for transducing sensory energy into changes in ion channels. These changes, in turn, alter the transmembrane voltage to the point at which voltage-sensitive channels open, triggering an action potential and a nerve impulse. After traveling through the nervous system and being processed by the brain, nerve impulses may produce the muscular contractions that enable behavioral responses. Ion channels again come into play at this end of the pathway because the chemical transmitter released at the axon terminal of a motor neuron activates channels on the end plate of a muscle-cell membrane. The subsequent flow of ions depolarizes the muscle-cell membrane to the threshold for its action potential. This depolarization, in turn, activates voltage-sensitive channels, producing an action potential on the muscle fiber.
8. *What are some of the techniques for studying the brain's electrical activity?* There are three main techniques for studying the electrical activity of the brain. One is by recording action potentials from single neurons in the brain. Another is by obtaining electroencephalogram (EEG) tracings of the graded potentials of brain cells, usually recorded from the surface of the scalp. The third is by recording event-related potentials (ERPs) also from the scalp. ERPs show the brief changes in an EEG signal in response to some particular sensory stimulus.

## KEY TERMS

absolutely refractory, p. 129
acetylcholine, p. 141
action potential, p. 127
concentration gradient, p. 121
depolarization, p. 126
diffusion, p. 121
electrical stimulation, p. 115
electroencephalogram (EEG), p. 116
event-related potential (ERP), p. 146
excitatory postsynaptic potential (EPSP), p. 133
graded potential, p. 126
hyperpolarization, p. 126
inhibitory postsynaptic potential (IPSP), p. 133
nerve impulse, p. 130
resting potential, p. 124
saltatory conduction, p. 132
spatial summation, p. 135
stretch-sensitive channel, p. 138
temporal summation, p. 135
threshold potential, p. 127
transmitter-sensitive channel, p. 141
voltage-sensitive channel, p. 128

## REVIEW QUESTIONS

1. Explain the contribution of the membrane, channels, and four types of ions to a cell's resting potential.
2. The transduction of sensory energy into neural activity at a sensory receptor, the nerve impulse, and the activation of a muscle can all be explained by a common principle. Explain that principle.
3. Three techniques for monitoring brain activity measure electrical activity of the brain. Describe these techniques.

## FOR FURTHER THOUGHT

The brain is in a constant state of electrical activity, which requires a substantial amount of energy to sustain. Why do you suppose this constant electrical activity is needed?

## RECOMMENDED READING

Posner, M. I., & Raichle, M. E. (1994). *Images of mind.* New York: W. H. Freeman and Company. This book will introduce you to the new field of imaging psychology. For the past 300 years, scientists have studied people with brain injuries to obtain insights into the relationship between the brain and human behavior. This book describes how computerized electroencephalographic recordings (EEGs), computerized axial tomographic (CAT) scans, positron emission tomographic (PET) scans, magnetic resonance imaging (MRI), and functional MRI allow neuropsychologists to look at the structure and function of the living brain.

Valenstein, E. S. (1973). *Brain control.* New York: Wiley. When scientists discovered that they could implant stimulating electrodes into the brains of animals to elicit behavior and to generate what seemed to be pleasure or pain, it was not long before psychiatrists experimented with the same techniques in humans in an attempt to control human brain disease. A renowned scientist, Valenstein writes about the application of brain-control techniques to humans in an engaging and insightful manner, bringing his own scientific knowledge to bear on the procedures and the ethics of this field.

CHAPTER

5

# How Do Neurons Communicate?



Patrisha Thomson/Stone
Micrograph: Dr. Dennis Kunkel/Phototake

The sea bird called the puffin (genus *Fratercula,* which is Latin for "little brother") exhibits remarkable behavior during its breeding season. It digs a burrow as deep as 4 feet into the earth, in which to lay its single egg. While on the ground, the puffin is relatively inactive, sitting on its egg or in front of its burrow. But, after the egg hatches, the puffin begins a period of Herculean labors. It must fly constantly back and forth between its burrow and its fishing ground to feed its ravenous young. It fishes by diving underwater and propelling itself by flapping its short stubby wings as if it were flying. One by one it catches as many as 30 small fish, all of which it holds in its beak to be carried back to its chick (Figure 5-1). The chick may eat as many as 2000 fish in its first 40 days of life. When flying to its fishing ground, the puffin exerts a great deal of effort to maintain its momentum. It also expends much energy as it "flies" through the water, because the water, although it supports the puffin's body, imposes greater resistance to movement than air does.

To meet its nutrient and oxygen needs during its various behaviors, the puffin's heart rate changes to match its energy expenditure. The heart beats slowly on land and increases greatly in flight. When the puffin dives beneath the surface of the water, however, its heart stops beating. This response is called **diving bradycardia** (*brady* meaning "slow"; *cardia* meaning "heart"). Bradycardia is a strategy for conserving oxygen under water, because the circulatory system expends no energy when the heart ceases pumping.

Your heart rate varies in the same way as the puffin's to meet your energy needs, slowing when you are at rest and increasing when you are active. Even exciting or relaxing thoughts can cause your heart to increase or decrease its rate of beating. And, yes, like the puffin and all other diving animals, when you submerge your head in water, you, too, display diving bradycardia. What regulates all this turning up, down, and off of heartbeat as behavior requires?

Because the heart has no knowledge about how quickly it should beat, it must be told to adjust its rate of beating. These commands consist of at least two different messages: an excitatory message that says "speed up" and an inhibitory message that says "slow down." What is important to our understanding of how neurons interact is that it was an experiment designed to study how heart rate is controlled that yielded an answer to the question of how neurons communicate with one another. In this chapter, we explore that answer in some detail. First, we consider the chemical signals that neurons use to inhibit or excite each other. Then, we examine the function of excitatory and inhibitory synapses and excitatory and inhibitory receptors. Finally, we investigate the changes that synapses undergo during learning.

Kevin Schafer

**Figure 5-1**
A puffin is returning with food for its chick. Its heart rate varies to match its energy needs, slowing down on land, increasing during flight, and stopping completely when the puffin dives below the surface of the water to fish.

Otto Loewi (1873–1961)

## A CHEMICAL MESSAGE

In 1921, Otto Loewi conducted a now well-known experiment on the control of heart rate, the design of which came to him in a dream. One night, having fallen asleep while reading a short novel, he awoke suddenly and completely, with the idea fully formed. He scribbled the plan of the experiment on a scrap of paper and went back to sleep. The next morning, he could not decipher what he had written, yet he felt it was important. All day he went about in a distracted manner, looking occasionally at his notes, but wholly mystified about their meaning. That night he again awoke, vividly recalling the ideas in his previous night's dream. Fortunately, he still remembered them the next morning. Loewi immediately set up and successfully performed the experiment.

Loewi's experiment involved electrically stimulating a frog's vagus nerve, which leads from the brain to the heart, while at the same time channeling the fluid in which the stimulated heart had been immersed to a second heart that was not electrically stimulated, as shown in Figure 5-2. The fluid traveled from one container to the other through a tube. Loewi recorded the rate of beating of both hearts. The electrical stimulation decreased the rate of beating of the first heart, but, more important, the fluid transferred from the first to the second container slowed the rate of beating of the second heart, too. Clearly, a message about the speed at which to beat was somehow carried in the fluid.

But where did the message originally come from? The only way in which it could have gotten into the fluid was by a chemical released from the vagus nerve. This chemical must have dissolved into the fluid in sufficient quantity to influence the second heart. The experiment therefore demonstrated that the vagus nerve contains a

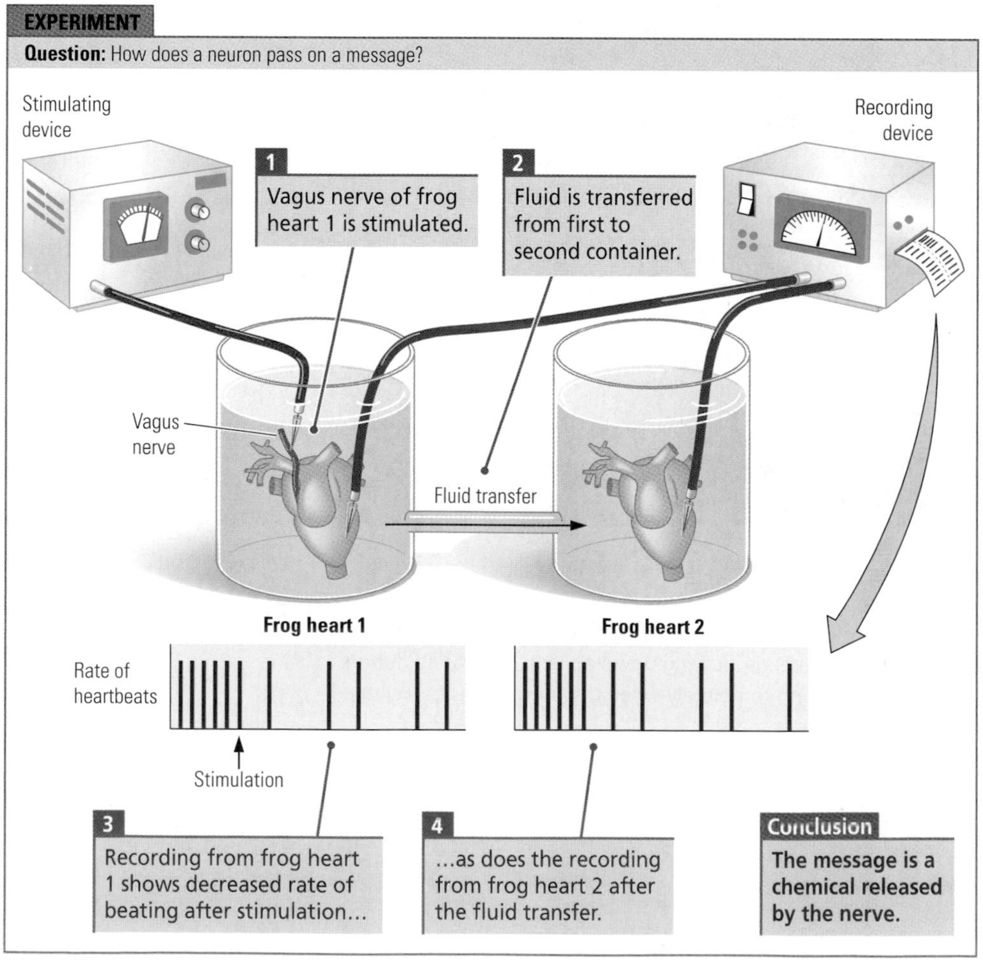

EXPERIMENT

**Question:** How does a neuron pass on a message?

Stimulating device

Recording device

1 Vagus nerve of frog heart 1 is stimulated.

2 Fluid is transferred from first to second container.

Vagus nerve

Fluid transfer

**Frog heart 1**

**Frog heart 2**

Rate of heartbeats

Stimulation

3 Recording from frog heart 1 shows decreased rate of beating after stimulation…

4 …as does the recording from frog heart 2 after the fluid transfer.

**Conclusion**

**The message is a chemical released by the nerve.**

**Figure 5-2**

Otto Loewi's 1921 experiment demonstrating the involvement of a neurochemical in controlling heart rate. He electronically stimulated the vagus nerve going to a frog heart that was maintained in a salt bath. The heart decreased its rate of beating. Fluid from the bath was transferred to a second bath containing a second heart. The electrical recording from the second heart shows that its rate of beating also decreased. This experiment demonstrates that a chemical released from the vagus nerve of the first heart can reduce the rate of beating of the second heart. Follow the main steps in the experiment to arrive at the conclusion that neurotransmission is chemical.

chemical that tells the heart to slow its rate of beating. Loewi subsequently identified that chemical as acetylcholine (ACh).

In further experiments, Loewi stimulated another nerve, called the accelerator nerve, and obtained a speeding-up of heart rate. Moreover, the fluid that bathed the accelerated heart increased the rate of beating of a second heart that was not electrically stimulated. Loewi identified the chemical that carried the message to speed up heart rate as **epinephrine** (EP). Together, these complementary experiments showed that chemicals from the vagus nerve and the accelerator nerve modulate heart rate, with one inhibiting the heart and the other exciting it.

Chemicals that are released by a neuron onto a target are now referred to as **chemical neurotransmitters.** Neurons that contain a chemical neurotransmitter of a certain type are named after that neurotransmitter. For example, neurons with terminals that release ACh are called acetylcholine neurons, whereas neurons that release EP are called epinephrine neurons. This naming of neurons by their chemical neurotransmitters helps to tell us whether those particular neurons have excitatory or inhibitory effects on other cells. It also helps to tell us something about the behavior in which the neuron is engaged.

In the next section, we will look at the structure of a synapse, the site where chemical communication by means of a neurotransmitter takes place. We will also examine the mechanisms that allow the release of a neurotransmitter into a synapse, as well as the types of synapses that exist in the brain. You will learn how a group of neurons, all of which use a specific neurotransmitter, can form a system that mediates a certain aspect of behavior. Damage to such a system results in neurological disorders such as Parkinson's disease (described in "Parkinson's Disease" on page 156).

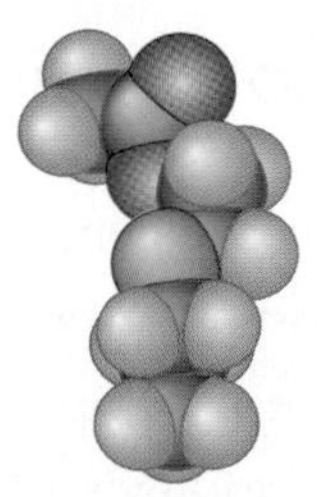
Acetylcholine (ACh)

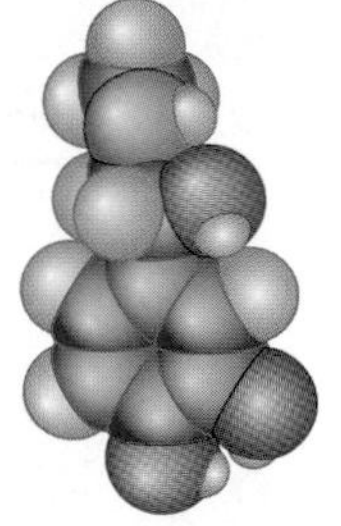
Epinephrine (EP)

## The Structure of Synapses

Otto Loewi's discovery about the regulation of heart rate was the first of two important findings that provided the foundation for our current understanding of how neurons communicate. The second had to wait for the invention of the electron microscope, which enabled scientists to see the structure of a synapse.

The electron microscope uses some of the principles of both an oscilloscope and a light microscope. As Figure 5-3 shows, it works by projecting a beam of electrons through a very thin slice of tissue that is being examined. The varying structure of the tissue scatters the beam of electrons and, when these electrons strike a phosphorus-coated screen, they leave an image, or shadow, of the tissue. The resolution of an electron microscope is much higher than that of a light microscope because electron waves are smaller than those of light and so there is much less scatter of the beam when it strikes the tissue. If the tissue is stained with substances that reflect electrons, very fine details of structure can be observed.

**Figure 5-3**

In a light microscope, light is reflected through the specimen and into the eye of the viewer. In an electron microscope, an electron beam is directed through the specimen and onto a reflectant surface, where the viewer sees the image. Because electrons scatter less than do light particles, an electron microscope can show finer details than a light microscope can show. Whereas a light microscope can be used to see the general features of a cell, an electron microscope can be used to examine the details of a cell's organelles.

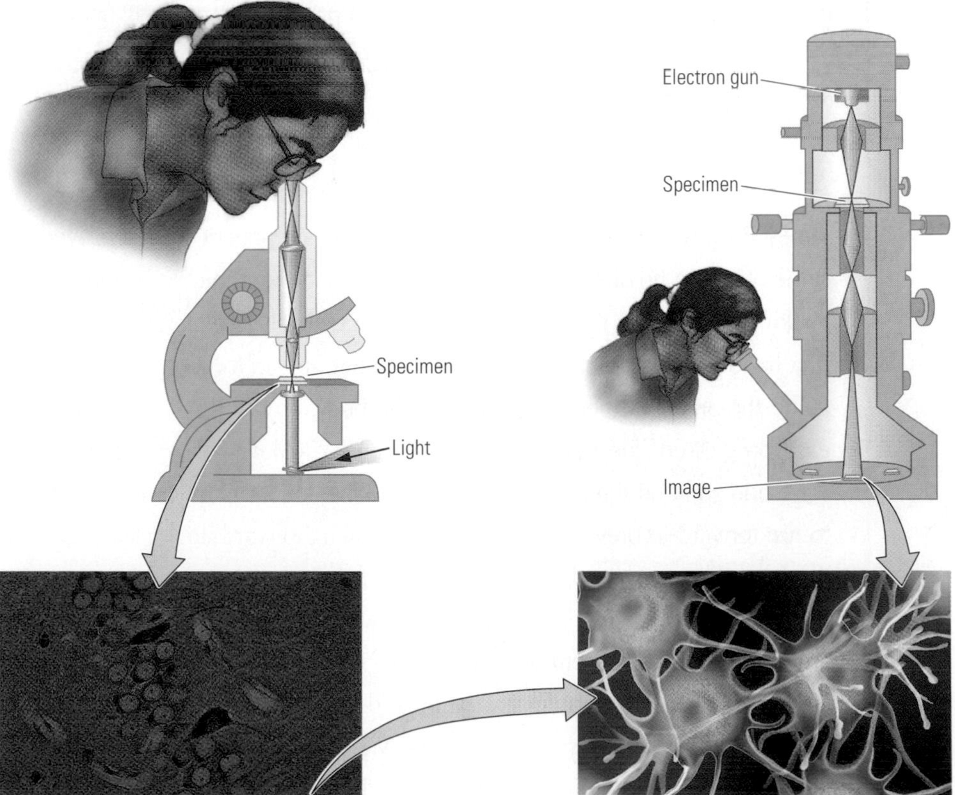


R. Roseman/Custom Medical Stock

Superstock

Focus on Disorders

## Parkinson's Disease

Case VI: The gentleman who is the subject of [this case] is seventy-two years of age. He has led a life of temperance, and has never been exposed to any particular situation or circumstance which he can conceive likely to have occasioned, or disposed to this complaint: which he rather seems to regard as incidental on his advanced age, than as an object of medical attention. He however recollects that about twenty years ago he was troubled by lumbago, which was severe and lasted some time. About eleven or twelve, or perhaps more, years ago, he first perceived weakness in the left hand and arm, and soon after found the trembling to commence. In about three years afterwards the right arm became affected in a similar manner: and soon afterwards the convulsive motions affected the whole body and began to interrupt speech. In about three years from that time the legs became affected. Of late years the action of the bowels had been very much retarded. (James Parkinson, 1817/1989)

In his 1817 essay from which this case study is taken, James Parkinson reported similar symptoms in six patients, some of whom he observed only in the streets near his clinic. Shaking was usually the first symptom, and it typically began in a hand. Over a number of years, the shaking spread to include the arm and then other parts of the body. As the disease progressed, the patients had a propensity to lean forward and walk on the forepart of their feet. They also tended to run forward to prevent themselves from falling forward. In the later stages of the disease, patients had difficulty eating and swallowing. Being unable to swallow, they drooled, and their bowel movements slowed as well. Eventually, the patients lost all muscular control and were unable to sleep, because of the disruptive tremors. More than 50 years after James Parkinson first described this debilitating set of symptoms, Jean Charcot named them Parkinson's disease in recognition of the accuracy of Parkinson's observations.

Three major findings have helped researchers understand the neural basis of Parkinson's disease. The first came in 1919 when C. Tréatikoff studied the brains of nine Parkinson patients on autopsy and found that an area of the midbrain called the substantia nigra (meaning "dark substance") had degenerated. In the brain of one patient who had experienced symptoms of Parkinson's disease on one side of the body only, the substantia nigra had degenerated on the side opposite that of the symptoms. These observations clearly implicated the substantia nigra in the disorder.

The other two major findings about the neural basis of Parkinson's disease came almost half a century later when methods for analyzing the brain for neurotransmitters had been developed. One was the discovery that a single neurotransmitter, dopamine, was related to the disorder, and the other was that axons containing dopamine connect the substantia nigra to the basal ganglia. In 1960, when examining the brains of six Parkinson patients during autopsies, H. Ehringer and O. Hornykiewicz observed that, in the basal ganglia, the dopamine level was reduced to less than 10 percent of normal. Confirming the role of dopamine in this disorder, U. Ungerstedt found in 1971 that injecting a neurotoxin called 6-hydroxydopamine into rats selectively destroyed neurons containing dopamine and produced the symptoms of Parkinson's disease as well.

The results of these studies and many others, including anatomical ones, show that the substantia nigra contains dopamine neurons and that the axons of these neurons project to the basal ganglia. The death of these dopamine neurons and the loss of the neurotransmitter dopamine from their terminals create the symptoms of Parkinson's disease. Researchers do not yet know exactly why dopamine neurons start to die in the substantia nigra of patients who have the idiopathic form of Parkinson's disease (*idiopathic* refers to a condition related to the individual person, not to some external cause such as a neurotoxin). Discovering why idiopathic Parkinsonism arises is an important area of ongoing research.

The first good electron micrographs, made in the 1950s, revealed many of the structures of a synapse. In the center of the micrograph in Figure 5-4 is a typical **chemical synapse.** The synapse is in color and its parts are labeled. The upper part of the synapse is the axon and terminal; the lower part is the dendrite. Note the round granular substances in the terminal, which are vesicles containing the neurotransmitter. The dark band of material just inside the dendrite provides the receptors for the neurotransmitter. The terminal and the dendrite are separated by a small space.

The drawing in Figure 5-4 illustrates the three main parts of the synapse: the axon terminal, the membrane encasing the tip of an adjacent dendritic spine, and the very small space separating these two structures. That tiny space is called the **synaptic cleft.** The membrane on the tip of the dendritic spine is known as the **postsynaptic membrane.** It contains many substances that are revealed in micrographs as patches of dark material. Much of this material consists of protein receptor molecules that receive chemical messages. Micrographs also reveal some dark patches on the **presynaptic membrane,** the membrane of the axon terminal, although these patches are harder to see. Here, too, the patches are protein molecules, which in this case serve largely as channels and pumps, as well as receptor sites. Within the axon terminal are many specialized structures, including both mitochondria (the organelles that supply the cell's energy needs) and what appear to be round granules. The round granules are **synaptic vesicles** that contain the chemical neurotransmitter. Some axon terminals have larger compartments, called **storage granules,** which hold a number of synaptic vesicles. In the micrograph, you can also see that this centrally located synapse is sandwiched by many surrounding structures, including glial cells, other axons and dendritic processes, and other synapses.

Chemical synapses are not the only kind of synapses in the nervous system. A second type is the **electrical synapse,** which is rare in mammals but is found in other animals. An

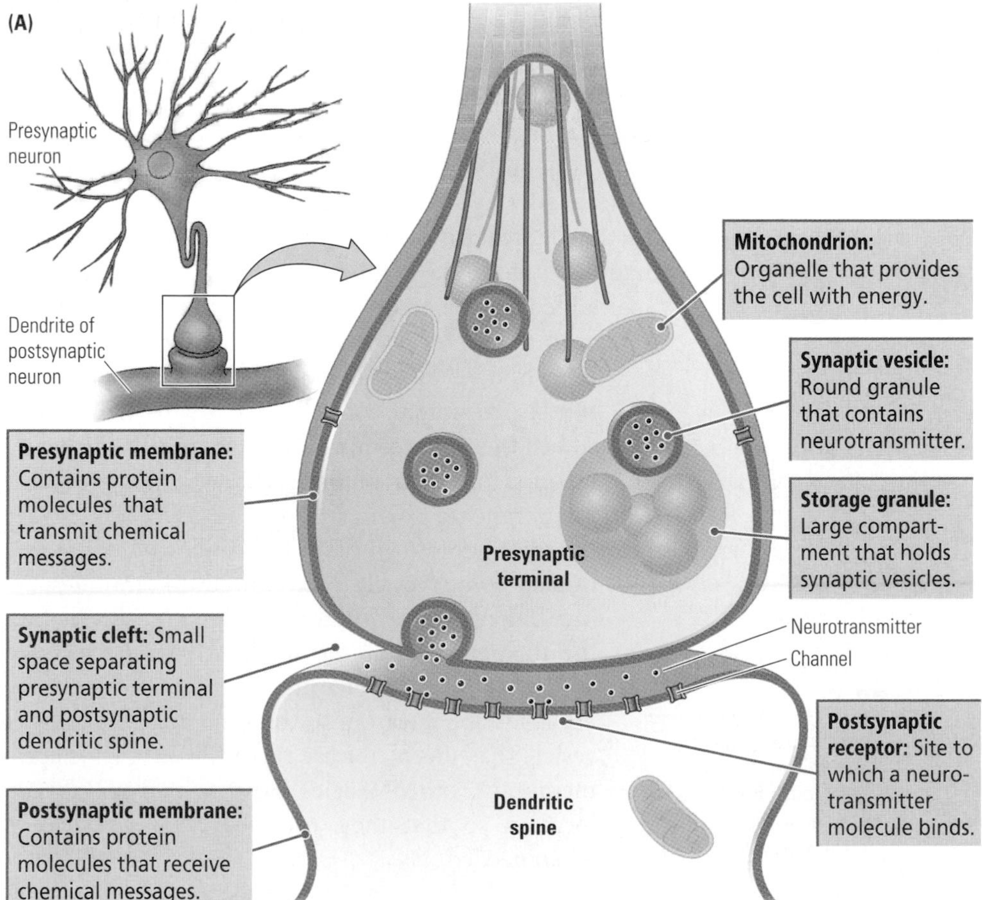
(A)
Presynaptic neuron
Dendrite of postsynaptic neuron
Presynaptic membrane: Contains protein molecules that transmit chemical messages.
Synaptic cleft: Small space separating presynaptic terminal and postsynaptic dendritic spine.
Postsynaptic membrane: Contains protein molecules that receive chemical messages.
Presynaptic terminal
Dendritic spine
Mitochondrion: Organelle that provides the cell with energy.
Synaptic vesicle: Round granule that contains neurotransmitter.
Storage granule: Large compartment that holds synaptic vesicles.
Neurotransmitter
Channel
Postsynaptic receptor: Site to which a neurotransmitter molecule binds.

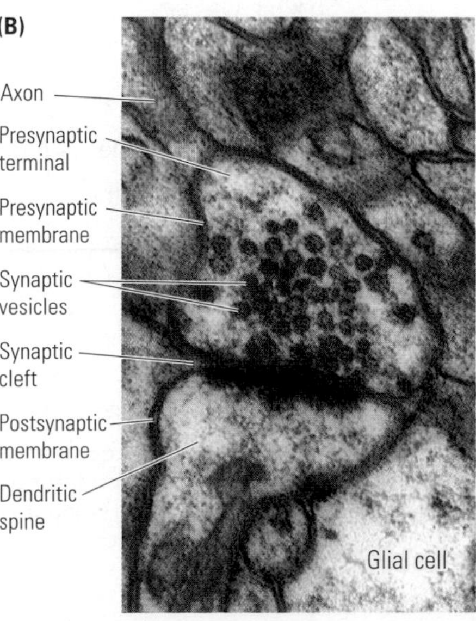
(B)
Axon
Presynaptic terminal
Presynaptic membrane
Synaptic vesicles
Synaptic cleft
Postsynaptic membrane
Dendritic spine
Glial cell
Courtesy Jeffrey Klein

**Figure 5-4**

**(A)** The parts of this synapse are characteristic of most synapses. The neurotransmitter, contained in vesicles, is released from storage granules and travels to the presynaptic membrane where it is expelled into the synaptic cleft through the process of exocytosis. The neurotransmitter then crosses the cleft and binds to receptors (proteins) on the postsynaptic membrane. **(B)** An electron photomicrograph of a synapse in which an axon terminal connects with a dendritic spine. Surrounding the centrally located synapse are other synapses, glial cells, axons, and dendrites. Within the terminal, round vesicles containing neurotransmitters are visible. The dark material on the postsynaptic side of the synapse includes receptors and substances related to receptor function.

electrical synapse has a fused presynaptic and postsynaptic membrane that allows an action potential to pass directly from one neuron to the next. This mechanism prevents the brief delay in information flow—on the order of about 5 milliseconds per synapse—of chemical transmission. For example, the crayfish has electrical synapses to activate its tail flick, a response that allows it to escape quickly from a predator.

Why, if chemical synapses transmit messages more slowly, do mammals depend on them almost exclusively? There must be some benefits that outweigh the drawback of slowed communication. Probably the greatest benefit is the flexibility that chemical synapses allow in controlling whether a message is passed from one neuron to the next. This benefit is discussed later in this chapter.

**Figure 5-5**

Synaptic transmission generally consists of four steps. (1) Synthesis: Using chemical building blocks imported into the axon terminal, a neurotransmitter is synthesized and packaged in vesicles. (2) Release: In response to an action potential, the transmitter is released across the presynaptic membrane by exocytosis. (3) Receptor action: The transmitter crosses the synaptic cleft and binds with a receptor on the postsynaptic membrane. (4) Inactivation: After use, the transmitter is either taken back into the terminal or inactivated in the synaptic cleft.



## Stages in Neurotransmitter Function

The process of transmitting information across a synapse includes four basic steps.

1. The transmitter molecules must be synthesized and stored in the axon terminal.
2. The transmitter must be transported to the presynaptic membrane and released in response to an action potential.
3. The transmitter must interact with the receptors on the membrane of the target cell located on the other side of the synapse.
4. The transmitter must somehow be inactivated or it would continue to work indefinitely.

These steps are illustrated in Figure 5-5. Each requires further explanation.

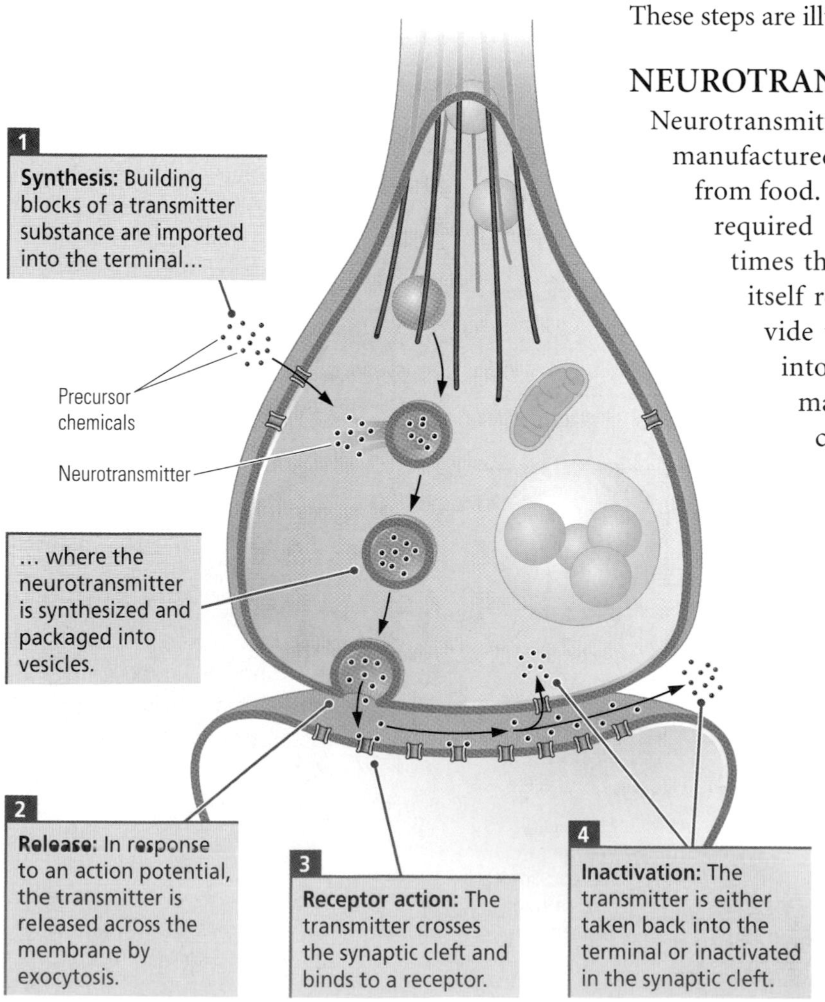

### NEUROTRANSMITTER SYNTHESIS AND STORAGE

Neurotransmitters are manufactured in two general ways. Some are manufactured in the axon terminal from building blocks derived from food. Transporter proteins in the cell membrane absorb the required precursor chemicals from the blood supply. (Sometimes these transporter proteins absorb the neurotransmitter itself ready-made.) Mitochondria in the axon terminal provide the energy needed to synthesize precursor chemicals into the neurotransmitter. Other neurotransmitters are manufactured in the cell body according to instructions contained in the neuron's DNA. Molecules of these transmitters are packaged in membranes on the Golgi bodies and transported on microtubules to the axon terminal.

In the axon terminal, neurotransmitters manufactured in either of these ways are wrapped in a membrane to form synaptic vesicles, which can usually be found in three locations within the terminal. Some vesicles are stored in granules, as mentioned earlier. Other vesicles are attached to the filaments in the terminal, and still others are attached to the presynaptic membrane, where they are ready for release into the synaptic cleft. After a vesicle has been released from the presynaptic membrane, other vesicles move to that membrane location so that they, too, are ready for release when needed.

## THE RELEASE OF THE NEUROTRANSMITTER

What exactly triggers the release of a synaptic vesicle and the spewing of its neurotransmitter into the synaptic cleft? The answer is, an action potential. When an action potential is propagated on the presynaptic membrane, the voltage changes on the membrane set the release process in motion. Calcium ions ($Ca^{2+}$) play an important role in the process. The presynaptic membrane is rich in voltage-sensitive calcium channels, and the surrounding extracellular fluid is rich in $Ca^{2+}$. As illustrated in Figure 5-6, the arrival of the action potential opens these voltage-sensitive calcium channels, allowing an influx of calcium ions into the axon terminal.

Next, the incoming $Ca^{2+}$ binds to a chemical called **calmodulin,** and the resulting complex takes part in two chemical actions: one reaction releases vesicles bound to the presynaptic membrane, and the other releases vesicles bound to filaments in the axon terminal. The vesicles released from the presynaptic membrane empty their contents into the synaptic cleft through the process of exocytosis, described in Chapter 3. The vesicles that were formerly bound to the filaments are then transported to the presynaptic membrane to replace the vesicles that just emptied their contents.

Link to your CD and find the area on synaptic transmission in the Neural Communication module to better visualize the structure and function of the axon terminal. Watch the animation and note how the internal components work as a unit to release neurotransmitter substances into the synapse.

## THE ACTIVATION OF RECEPTOR SITES

After the neurotransmitter has been released from vesicles on the presynaptic membrane, it diffuses across the synaptic cleft and binds to specialized protein molecules embedded in the postsynaptic membrane. These protein molecules are called

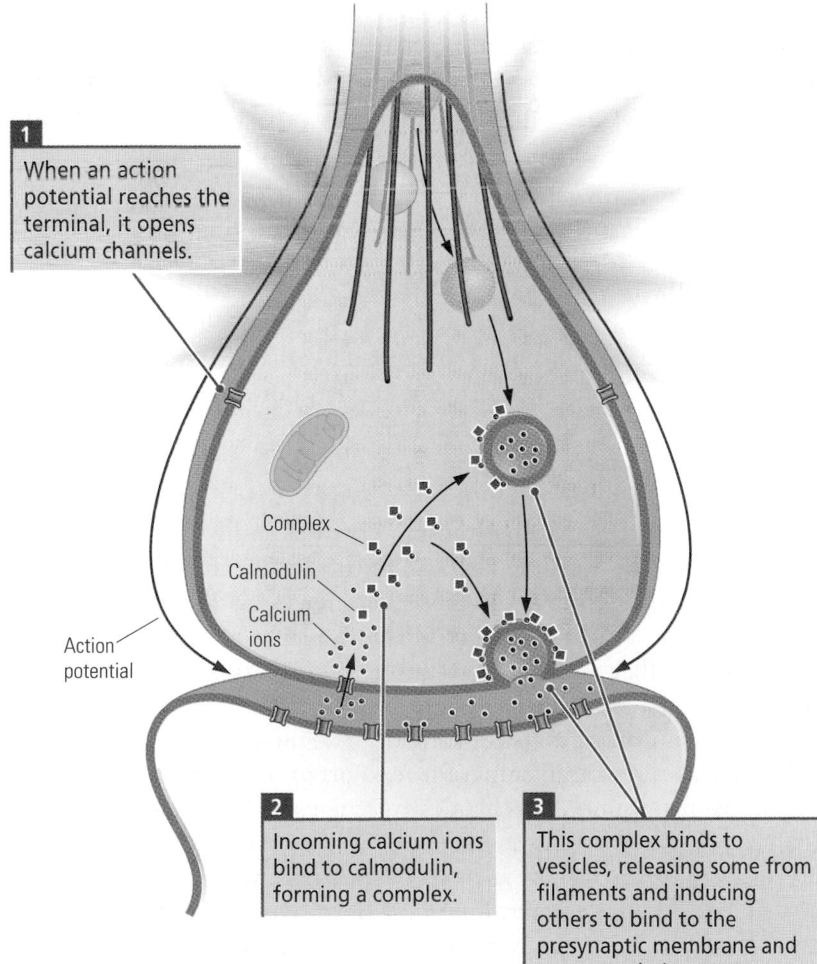
1
When an action potential reaches the terminal, it opens calcium channels.
Complex
Calmodulin
Calcium ions
Action potential
2
Incoming calcium ions bind to calmodulin, forming a complex.
3
This complex binds to vesicles, releasing some from filaments and inducing others to bind to the presynaptic membrane and to empty their contents.

**Figure 5-6**

When an action potential reaches an axon terminal, it opens voltage-sensitive calcium channels. The extracellular fluid adjacent to the synapse has a high concentration of calcium ions that then flow into the terminal. The calcium ions bind to synaptic vesicles in the free vesicle pool, inducing these vesicles to bind to the presynaptic membrane and expel their contents into the synaptic cleft. Calcium ions also bind to vesicles that are bound to filaments, which frees these vesicles so that they are available for release.

**Transmitter-activated receptor.** In the membrane of a cell, a receptor that has a binding site for a neurotransmitter.

**Transporter.** A protein molecule that pumps substances across a membrane.

**transmitter-activated receptors** (or just *receptors,* for short), because they receive the transmitter substance. The postsynaptic cell may be affected in one of three ways, depending on the type of neurotransmitter and the kind of receptors on the postsynaptic membrane. First, the transmitter may depolarize the postsynaptic membrane and so have an excitatory action on the postsynaptic cell; second, the transmitter may hyperpolarize the postsynaptic membrane and so have an inhibitory action on the postsynaptic cell; or, third, the transmitter may initiate other chemical reactions. The types of receptors that mediate these three effects will be described later in this chapter.

In addition to interacting with the postsynaptic membrane's receptors, a neurotransmitter may also interact with receptors on the presynaptic membrane. That is, it may have an influence on the cell that just released it. The presynaptic receptors that a neurotransmitter may activate are called **autoreceptors** (self-receptors) to indicate that they receive messages from their own axon terminals.

Bernard Katz (b. 1911)

How much neurotransmitter is needed to send a message? In the 1950s, Bernard Katz and his colleagues provided an answer. Recording electrical activity from the postsynaptic membranes of muscles, they detected small spontaneous depolarizations. They called these depolarizations **miniature postsynaptic potentials.** The potentials varied in size, but the sizes appeared to be multiples of the smallest potential. The researchers concluded that the smallest potential is produced by releasing the contents of just one synaptic vesicle. They called this amount of neurotransmitter a **quantum.** To produce a postsynaptic potential that is large enough to propagate an action potential requires the simultaneous release of many quanta.

The results of subsequent experiments showed that the number of quanta released from the presynaptic membrane in response to a single action potential depends on two factors: (1) the amount of $Ca^{2+}$ that enters the axon terminal in response to the action potential and (2) the number of vesicles that are docked at the membrane, waiting to be released. Keep these two factors in mind, because they will become relevant when we consider synaptic activity during learning.

## THE DEACTIVATION OF THE NEUROTRANSMITTER

Chemical transmission would not be a very effective messenger system if a neurotransmitter lingered within the synaptic cleft, continuing to occupy and stimulate receptors. If this happened, the postsynaptic cell could not respond to other messages sent by the presynaptic neuron. Therefore, after a neurotransmitter has done its work, it must be removed quickly from receptor sites and from the synaptic cleft.

This removal of a neurotransmitter is done in at least four ways. First, some of the neurotransmitter simply diffuses away from the synaptic cleft and is no longer available to bind to receptors. Second, the transmitter is inactivated or degraded by enzymes that are present in the synaptic cleft. Third, the transmitter may be taken back into the presynaptic axon terminal for subsequent reuse, or the by-products of degradation by enzymes may be taken back into the terminal to be used again in the cell. The protein molecule that accomplishes this reuptake is a membrane pump called a **transporter.** Fourth, some neurotransmitters are taken up by neighboring glial cells, which may contain enzymes that further degrade those transmitters. Potentially, the glial cells can also store a transmitter for reexport to the axon terminal.

Interestingly, an axon terminal has chemical mechanisms that enable it to respond to the frequency of its own use. If the terminal is very active, the amount of neurotransmitter made and stored there increases. If the terminal is not often used, however, enzymes located within the terminal may break down excess transmitter. The by-products of this breakdown are then reused or excreted from the cell.

## Types of Synapses

So far we have considered a generic synapse, with features that most synapses possess. There actually is a wide range of synapses, each with a relatively specialized location, structure, and function. Figure 5-7 shows a number of different kinds of synapses.

If you think back to Chapter 4, you will realize that you have already encountered two different kinds of synapses. One is the kind in which the axon terminal of a neuron ends on a dendrite or dendritic spine of another neuron. This kind of synapse, called an **axodendritic synapse,** is the kind shown in Figure 5-4. The other kind of synapse with which you are already familiar is an **axomuscular synapse,** in which an axon synapses with a muscle.

The other types of synapses include the **axosomatic synapse,** in which an axon terminal ends on a cell body; the **axoaxonic synapse,** in which an axon terminal ends on another axon; and the **axosynaptic synapse,** in which an axon terminal ends on another synapse—that is, a synapse between some other axon and its target. There are also axon terminals that have no specific targets but instead secrete their transmitter chemicals nonspecifically into the extracellular fluid. These synapses are called **axoextracellular synapses.** In addition, there is the **axosecretory synapse,** in which an axon terminal synapses with a tiny blood vessel called a capillary and secretes its transmitter directly into the blood. Finally, synapses are not limited to axon terminals. Dendrites also may send messages to other dendrites through **dendrodendritic synapses.**

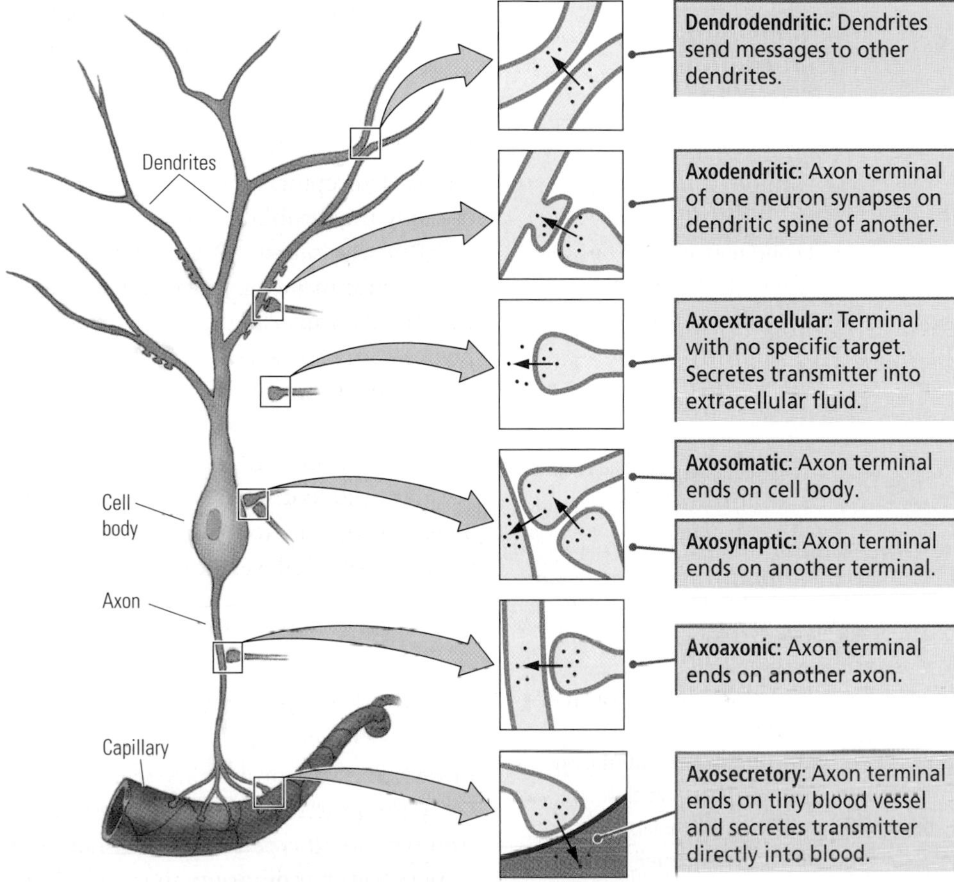
Dendrites
Cell body
Axon
Capillary
**Dendrodendritic:** Dendrites send messages to other dendrites.
**Axodendritic:** Axon terminal of one neuron synapses on dendritic spine of another.
**Axoextracellular:** Terminal with no specific target. Secretes transmitter into extracellular fluid.
**Axosomatic:** Axon terminal ends on cell body.
**Axosynaptic:** Axon terminal ends on another terminal.
**Axoaxonic:** Axon terminal ends on another axon.
**Axosecretory:** Axon terminal ends on tiny blood vessel and secretes transmitter directly into blood.

**Figure 5-7**

Synapses in the central nervous system are of various types. An axon terminal can end on a dendrite, on another axon terminal, on any cell body, or on an axon. It may also end on a blood capillary or end freely in extracellular space. Dendrites may also make synaptic connections with each other.

This wide range of synaptic types makes synapses a very versatile chemical delivery system. Synapses can deliver chemical transmitters to highly specific sites or to more diffuse locales. Through connections to the dendrites, cell body, or axon of a neuron, chemical transmitters can directly control the actions of that neuron. Through axosynaptic connections, they can also provide exquisite control over another neuron's input onto a cell. And, by excreting transmitters into extracellular fluid or into the blood, axoextracellular and axosecretory synapses can modulate the function of large areas of tissue or even of the entire body. In fact, many of the hormones that circulate in your blood and have widespread influences on your body are transmitters secreted by neurons.

## The Evolution of a Complex Neural Transmission System

If you consider all the biochemical steps required to get a message across a synapse, as well as the many different kinds of synapses that exist in the body, you may wonder why such a complex communication system ever developed. The answer must be that this arrangement makes up for its complexity by allowing the nervous system to be flexible about the behavior that it produces. Puffins, after all, sometimes fish energetically and other times sit quietly to incubate an egg. These very different behaviors are governed by the various ways in which messages sent across synapses are regulated. In the following sections, you will see that there are also great varieties of neurotransmitters and receptor sites. They, too, add versatility to neural transmission, further increasing the flexibility of behavior.

But why *chemical* transmitters in this complex communication system? Why not some other messenger with equal potential for flexibility? If you think about the behaviors of simple single-celled creatures, the start of the strategy of using chemical secretions for messages is not that hard to imagine. The first primitive cells secreted digestive juices onto bacteria to prepare them for ingestion. These digestive juices were probably expelled from the cell body through the process of exocytosis, in which a vacuole or vesicle attaches itself to the cell membrane and then opens into the extracellular fluid to discharge its contents. The mechanism of exocytosis for digestion parallels the use of exocytosis to release a neurotransmitter. Quite possibly the digestive processes of a cell were long ago co-opted for processes of communication.

Visit the CD and find the area on synaptic transmission in the Neural Communication module. Go to the sections on excitatory and inhibitory synapses to learn more about type I and type II synapses.

## Excitatory and Inhibitory Messages

Despite all the different kinds of synapses, in the end, they convey only two types of messages: excitatory or inhibitory. That is to say, a neurotransmitter either increases or decreases the probability that the cell with which it comes in contact will produce an action potential. In keeping with this dual message system, synapses can be divided into type I and type II. **Type I synapses** are excitatory in their actions, whereas **type II synapses** are inhibitory.

**Figure 5-8**

Type I synapses are found on the spines and dendritic shafts of the neuron, and type II synapses are found on the neuron's cell body. The structural features of type I and type II synapses differ in the shape of vesicles, in the density of material on the presynaptic membrane, in cleft size, and in the size of the postsynaptic active zone. Type I synapses are usually excitatory, and type II synapses inhibitory.

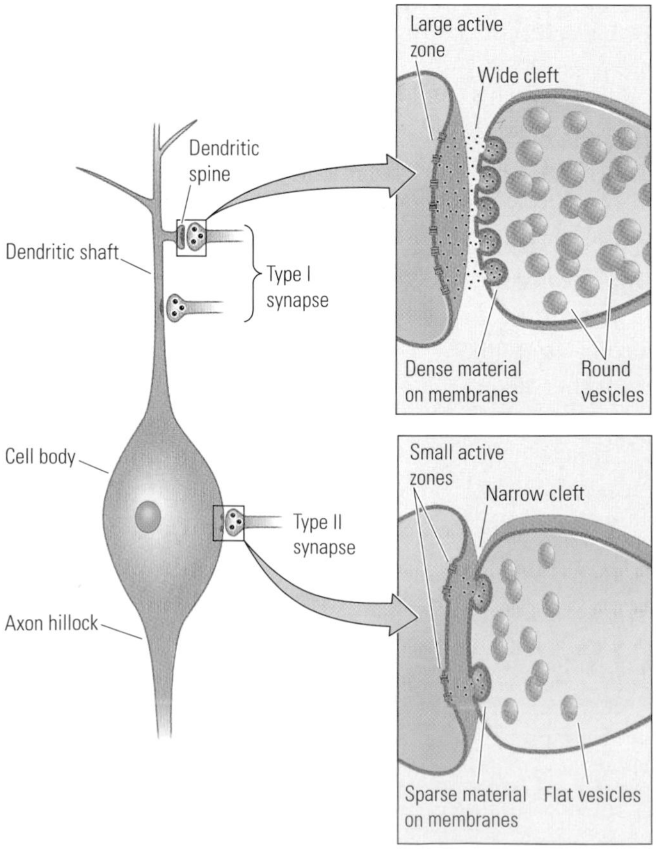

These two types of synapses vary both in location and in appearance. As shown in Figure 5-8, type I synapses are typically located on the shafts or the spines of dendrites, whereas type II synapses are typically located on a cell body. In addition, type I synapses have round synaptic vesicles, whereas the vesicles of type II synapses are flattened. The material on the presynaptic and postsynaptic membranes is denser in a type I synapse than it is in a type II, and the type I cleft is wider. Finally, the active zone on a type I synapse is larger than that on a type II synapse.

The different locations of type I and type II synapses divide a neuron into two zones: an excitatory dendritic tree and an inhibitory cell body. With this arrangement, you can think of excitatory and inhibitory messages as interacting in two ways. First, you can picture excitation coming in over the dendrites and spreading to the axon hillock, where it may trigger an action potential that travels down the length of the axon. If the message is to be stopped, it is best stopped by applying inhibition close to the axon hillock, the origin of the action potential. This model of excitatory–inhibitory interaction is viewed from an inhibitory perspective. Inhibition is a blocking of excitation—essentially a "cut 'em off at the pass" strategy. Another way to conceptualize how these two kinds of messages interact is to picture excitatory stimulation overcoming inhibition. If the cell body is normally in an inhibited state, the only way for an action potential to be generated at the axon hillock is for the cell body's inhibition to be reduced. This is an "open the gates" strategy. The excitatory message is like a racehorse ready to run down the track, but first the inhibition of the starting gate must be removed.

The English neurologist John Hughlings-Jackson recognized the role of inhibition and its removal in human neurological disorders. Many such disorders are characterized by symptoms that seem to be "released" when a normal inhibitory influence is lost. Hughlings-Jackson termed this process "release of function." An example is an involuntary movement, such as a tremor, called a **dyskinesia** (from the Greek *dys*, meaning "disordered," and *kinesia*, meaning "movement"). Later in this chapter, other examples of released behavior will be described.

John Hughlings-Jackson (1835–1911)

## In Review

Chemical transmission is the principal form of communication between neurons. When an action potential is propagated on an axon terminal, a chemical transmitter is released from the presynaptic membrane into the synaptic cleft. There the transmitter diffuses across the cleft and occupies receptors on the postsynaptic membrane, after which the transmitter is deactivated. The nervous system has evolved various kinds of synapses, including those between axon terminals and dendrites, cell bodies, muscles, other axons, and even other synapses, as well as those that release their chemical transmitters into extracellular fluid or into the blood and those that connect dendrites to other dendrites. Together, these different types of synapses increase the flexibility of behaviors. Even though synapses vary in both structure and location, they all do one of only two things: either excite target cells or inhibit them.

# THE KINDS OF NEUROTRANSMITTERS

In the 1920s, after Otto Loewi's discovery that excitatory and inhibitory chemicals control the heart's rate of beating, many researchers thought that the brain must work in much the same way. They assumed that there must be excitatory and inhibitory brain cells and that epinephrine and acetylcholine were the transmitters through which these neurons worked. At that time, they could never have imagined what we know today: the human brain employs as many as 100 neurotransmitters to control our highly complex and adaptable behaviors. Although we are now certain of only about 50 substances that act as transmitters, we are in the midst of a research revolution in this field. Few scientists are willing to put an upper limit on the eventual number of transmitters that will be found. In this section, you will learn how these neurotransmitters are identified and examine the categories of those currently known.

**Figure 5-9** The four criteria for determining whether a chemical is a neurotransmitter are summed up in this diagram.

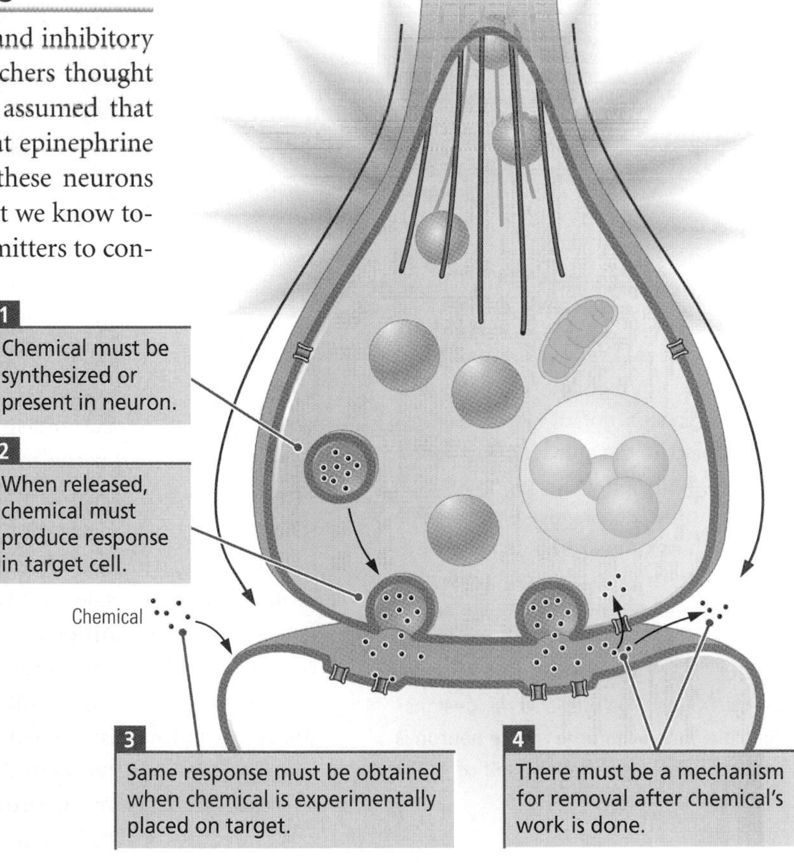
1
Chemical must be synthesized or present in neuron.
2
When released, chemical must produce response in target cell.
Chemical
3
Same response must be obtained when chemical is experimentally placed on target.
4
There must be a mechanism for removal after chemical's work is done.

## Identifying Neurotransmitters

Figure 5-9 shows four criteria for identifying neurotransmitters:

1. The chemical must be synthesized in the neuron or otherwise be present in it.
2. When the neuron is active, the chemical must be released and produce a response in some target cell.

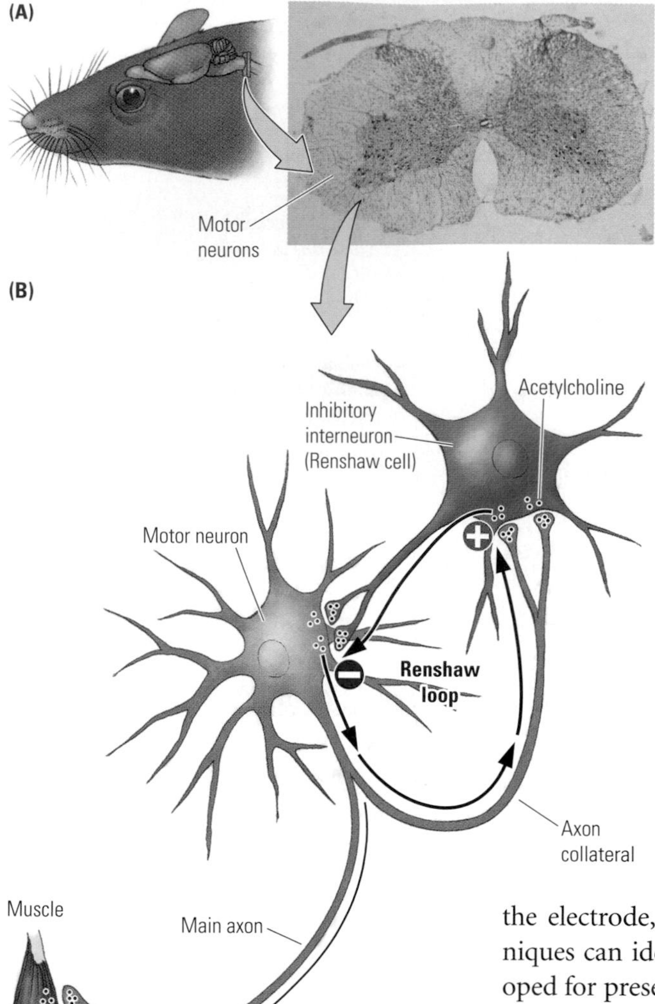


**Figure 5-10**

The Renshaw loop is a circular set of connections. **(A)** Cresyl violet–stained cross section of the spinal cord of a rat showing the location of motor neurons that project to the muscles of the forelimb. **(B)** A diagrammatic representation of a motor neuron involved in a Renshaw loop with its main axon going to a muscle and its axon collateral remaining in the spinal cord to synapse with an interneuron there. The terminals of both the main axon and the collateral contain acetylcholine. The plus and minus signs indicate that, when the motor neuron is highly excited, it can turn itself off through the Renshaw loop.

3. The same response must be obtained when the chemical is experimentally placed on the target.
4. There must be a mechanism for removing the chemical from its site of action after its work is done.

By systematically applying these criteria, researchers can determine which of the many thousands of chemical molecules that exist in every neuron is a neurotransmitter.

The criteria for identifying a neurotransmitter are fairly easy to apply when examining the peripheral nervous system, especially at an accessible nerve–muscle junction, where there is only one main neurotransmitter, acetylcholine. But identifying chemical transmitters in the central nervous system is not so easy. In the brain and spinal cord, thousands of synapses are packed around every neuron, preventing easy access to a single synapse and its activities. Consequently, for many of the substances thought to be central nervous system neurotransmitters, the four criteria needed as proof have been met only to varying degrees. A chemical that is suspected of being a neurotransmitter but has not yet been shown to meet all the criteria for one is called a *putative* (supposed) *transmitter.*

Researchers trying to identify new CNS neurotransmitters use microelectrodes to stimulate and record from single neurons. A glass microelectrode can be filled with the chemical being studied so that, when a current is passed through the electrode, the chemical is ejected into or onto the neuron. New staining techniques can identify specific chemicals inside the cell. Methods have also been developed for preserving nervous system tissue in a saline bath while experiments are performed to determine how the neurons in the tissue communicate. The use of slices of tissue simplifies the investigation by allowing the researcher to view a single neuron through a microscope while stimulating it or recording from it.

Acetylcholine was the first substance identified as a neurotransmitter in the central nervous system. This identification was greatly facilitated by a logical argument that predicted its presence even before experimental proof was gathered. All the motor-neuron axons leaving the spinal cord contain acetylcholine, and each of these axons has an axon collateral within the spinal cord that synapses on a nearby interneuron that is part of the central nervous system. The interneuron, in turn, synapses back on the motor neuron's cell body. This circular set of connections, called a *Renshaw loop* after the researcher who first described it, is shown in Figure 5-10. Because the main axon to the muscle releases acetylcholine, investigators suspected that its axon collateral also might release acetylcholine. It seemed unlikely that two terminals of the same axon would use different transmitters. Knowing what chemical to look for made it easier to find and obtain the required proof that acetylcholine was in fact a neurotransmitter in this location, too. Incidentally, the loop made by the axon collateral and the interneuron in the spinal cord forms a feedback circuit that enables the motor neuron to inhibit itself and not become overexcited if it receives a great many excitatory inputs from other parts of the central nervous system. Follow the positive and negative signs in Figure 5-10 to see how the Renshaw loop works.

Today the term "neurotransmitter" is used more broadly than it was when researchers first started trying to identify these chemicals. The term applies not only to substances that carry a message from one neuron to another by influencing the voltage on the postsynaptic membrane, but also to chemicals that have little effect on membrane voltage but instead induce effects such as changing the structure of a synapse. Furthermore, not only do neurotransmitters communicate in the orthodox fashion by delivering a message from the presynaptic side of a synapse to the postsynaptic side, but they can send messages in the opposite direction as well. To make matters even more complex, different kinds of neurotransmitters can coexist within the same synapse, complicating the question of what exactly each contributes in relaying a message. To find out, researchers have to apply various transmitter "cocktails" to the postsynaptic membrane. There is the added complication that some transmitters are gases that act so differently from a classic neurotransmitter such as acetylcholine that it is hard to compare the two. Because neurotransmitters are so diverse and work in such an array of ways, the definition of what a transmitter is and the criteria used to identify one have become increasingly flexible in recent years.

**Small-molecule transmitters.** A class of neurotransmitters that are manufactured in the synapse from products derived from the diet.

Visit the Web site to link to current research on neurotransmitters at **www.worthpublishers.com/kolb**.

## Neurotransmitter Classification

Some order can be imposed on the diversity of neurotransmitters by classifying them into three groups on the basis of their composition: (1) small-molecule transmitters, (2) peptide transmitters (also called neuropeptides), and (3) transmitter gases. Here we look briefly at the major characteristics of each group and list some of the neurotransmitters that the groups include.

### SMALL-MOLECULE TRANSMITTERS

The first transmitters to be identified were **small-molecule transmitters**, one of which is acetylcholine. As the name of this category suggests, these transmitters are made up of small molecules. Typically, they are synthesized and packaged for use in axon terminals. When a small-molecule transmitter has been released from an axon terminal, it can be quickly replaced at the presynaptic membrane. Compared with other transmitters, these transmitters act relatively quickly.

Small-molecule transmitters or their main components are derived from the food that we eat. Therefore, their level and activity in the body can be influenced by diet. This fact is important in the design of drugs that affect the nervous system. Many of the neuroactive drugs are designed to reach the brain in the same way that small-molecule transmitters or their precursor chemicals do.

Table 5-1 lists some of the best-known and most extensively studied small-molecule transmitters. In addition to acetylcholine, this list includes four amines (an amine is a chemical that contains an amine [NH] in its chemical structure) and four amino acids. A few other substances are sometimes also classified as small-molecule transmitters. In the future, researchers are likely to find additional ones as well.

Figure 5-11 illustrates how a small-molecule transmitter is made and destroyed. The example used is acetylcholine, the transmitter present at the junction of neurons and muscles, including the heart. Acetylcholine is made up of two parts, **choline** and **acetate.** Choline is a substance obtained from the breakdown of fats, such as egg yolk, and acetate is a compound found in such substances as vinegar. One enzyme, acetyl coenzyme A (acetyl CoA), carries acetate to the site where the transmitter is synthesized, and a second enzyme, choline acetyltransferase (ChAT), transfers acetate to choline to

**Figure 5-11**

This diagrammatic representation shows how the neurotransmitter acetylcholine is synthesized and broken down. Within the cell, acetate combines with choline to produce acetylcholine. The enzymes acetyl coenzyme A (acetyl CoA) and choline acetyltransferase (ChAT) are catalysts in the reactions that combine the molecules. Outside the cell, the enzyme acetylcholinesterase (AChE) takes the molecules apart again.

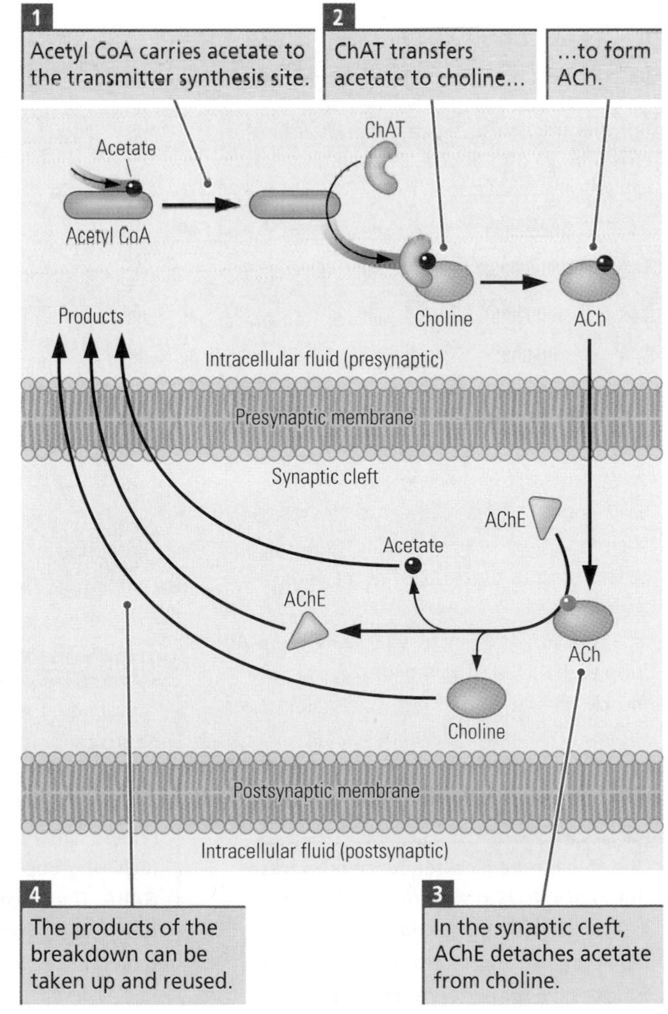
1
Acetyl CoA carries acetate to the transmitter synthesis site.
2
ChAT transfers acetate to choline...
...to form ACh.
Acetate
Acetyl CoA
ChAT
Choline
ACh
Products
Intracellular fluid (presynaptic)
Presynaptic membrane
Synaptic cleft
AChE
Acetate
AChE
ACh
Choline
Postsynaptic membrane
Intracellular fluid (postsynaptic)
4
The products of the breakdown can be taken up and reused.
3
In the synaptic cleft, AChE detaches acetate from choline.

**Table 5-1 Small-Molecule Neurotransmitters**

| Transmitter | Abbreviation |
|---|---|
| Acetylcholine | ACh |
| **Amines** | |
| Dopamine | DA |
| Norepinephrine | NE |
| Epinephrine | EP |
| Serotonin | 5-HT |
| **Amino acids** | |
| Glutamate | Glu |
| Gamma-aminobutyric acid | GABA |
| Glycine | Gly |
| Histamine | H |

form acetylcholine (ACh). After ACh has been released into the synaptic cleft and diffuses to receptor sites on the postsynaptic membrane, a third enzyme, called acetylcholinesterase (AChE), reverses the process of synthesis, detaching acetate from choline. The products of the breakdown can then be taken back into the axon terminal for reuse.

Some of the amines and amino acids included in Table 5-1 are synthesized by the same biochemical pathway and so are considered related to one another. They are grouped together in Table 5-1. One such grouping consists of the amines **dopamine, norepinephrine,** and **epinephrine** (which, as you already know, is the excitatory transmitter at the heart). Figure 5-12 shows that epinephrine is the third transmitter produced by a single biochemical sequence. The precursor chemical is tyrosine, an amino acid that is abundant in food. The enzyme tyrosine hydroxylase changes tyrosine into L-dopa, which is sequentially converted by other enzymes into dopamine, norepinephrine, and, finally, epinephrine.

An interesting fact about this biochemical sequence is that the enzyme tyrosine hydroxylase is in limited supply; consequently, so is the rate at which dopamine, norepinephrine, and epinephrine can be produced, regardless of how much tyrosine is present or ingested. This **rate-limiting factor** can be bypassed by orally ingesting L-dopa, which is why L-dopa is a medication used in the treatment of Parkinson's disease, as described in "Awakening with L-Dopa" on page 168.

Two of the amino acid transmitters, **glutamate** and **gamma-aminobutyric acid (GABA)**, also are closely related, because GABA is formed by a simple modification of glutamate, as shown in Figure 5-13. These two transmitters are considered the workhorses of the nervous system because so many synapses use them. In the forebrain and cerebellum, glutamate is the main excitatory transmitter and GABA is the main inhibitory transmitter. (The amino acid glycine is a much more common inhibitory transmitter in the brainstem and spinal cord). Interestingly, glutamate is widely distributed in neurons, but it becomes a neurotransmitter only if it is appropriately packaged in vesicles in the axon terminal.

## PEPTIDE TRANSMITTERS

More than 50 short chains of amino acids form the families of the neuropeptide transmitters listed in Table 5-2. As you learned in Chapter 3, amino acid chains are connected by peptide bonds, which accounts for the name of this class of neurotransmitters. **Neuropeptide transmitters** are made from instructions contained in the cell's DNA. Although in some neurons these transmitters are made in the axon terminal, most are assembled on the neuron's ribosomes, packaged in a membrane by Golgi bodies, and transported by the microtubules to the axon terminals. The entire process of synthesis and transport is relatively slow, compared with that of other

**Dopamine.** A chemical neurotransmitter released by dopamine neurons.

**Glutamate.** An amino acid neurotransmitter that excites neurons.

**Gamma-aminobutyric acid (GABA).** An amino acid neurotransmitter that inhibits neurons.

**Neuropeptides.** A class of chemical neurotransmitters, manufactured with instructions from the cell's DNA; thus a neuropeptide consists of a chain of amino acids that act as a neurotransmitter.

Tyrosine hydroxylase
↓ Enzyme 1
L-Dopa
↓ Enzyme 2
Dopamine
↓ Enzyme 3
Norepinephrine
↓ Enzyme 4
Epinephrine

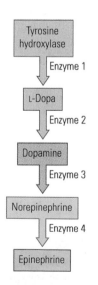

**Figure 5-12**

A single biochemical sequence produces three of the classical neurotransmitters—dopamine, norepinephrine, and epinephrine. A different enzyme (1–4) is responsible for each synthetic step.

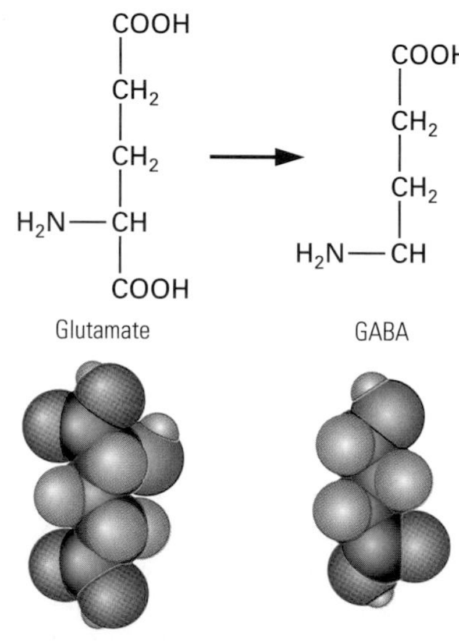


**Figure 5-13**

Glutamate, the major excitatory neurotransmitter in the brain, and GABA, the major inhibitory neurotransmitter in the brain, are related. The removal of the carboxyl (COOH) group from glutamate produces GABA. The space-filling models of the two neurotransmitters show that their shapes are different, thus allowing them to bind to different receptors.

types of nerotransmitters. Consequently, these transmitters are not replaced quickly.

Peptides have an enormous range of functions in the nervous system, as might be expected from the large number of them that exist there. Peptides serve as hormones, are active in responses to stress, have a role in allowing a mother to bond to her infant, probably contribute to learning, help to regulate eating and drinking, and help to regulate pleasure and pain. For example, opium, obtained from seeds of the poppy flower, has long been known to produce both euphoria and pain reduction. Opium and its related synthetic chemicals, such as morphine, appear to mimic the actions of three peptides: **met-enkephalin, leu-enkephalin,** and **beta-endorphin.** (The term *enkephalin* derives from the phrase "in the cephalon," meaning "in the brain or head," whereas the term *endorphin* is a shortened form of "endogenous morphine.") A part of the amino acid chain in each of these three peptide transmitters is structurally similar to the others, as shown in Figure 5-14. Presumably, opium mimics this part of the chain. The discovery of these naturally occurring opium-like peptides suggested that one or more of them might take part in the management of pain. Opioid peptides, however, appear to have a number of locations and functions in the brain, so they may not be just pain-specific transmitters.

Unlike small-molecule transmitters, peptide transmitters do not bind to ion channels, so they have no direct effects on the voltage of the postsynaptic membrane. Instead, peptide transmitters activate receptors that indirectly influence cell structure and function. Because peptides are amino acid chains that are degraded by digestive processes, they generally cannot be taken orally as drugs, as the small-molecule transmitters can.

**Table 5-2 Peptide Neurotransmitters**

| Family | Example |
|---|---|
| Opioids | Enkephaline, dynorphin |
| Neurohypophyseals | Vasopressin, oxytocin |
| Secretins | Gastric inhibitory peptide, growth-hormone-releasing peptide |
| Insulins | Insulin, insulin growth factors |
| Gastrins | Gastrin, cholecystokinin |
| Somatostatins | Pancreatic polypeptides |

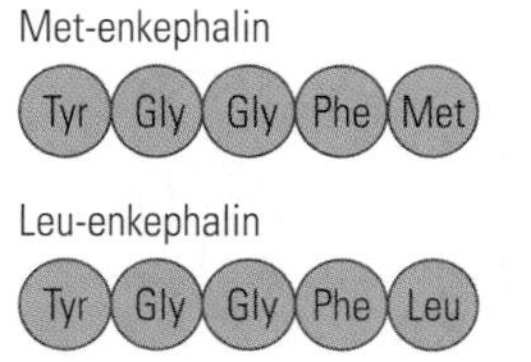


**Figure 5-14**

Chains of amino acids that act as neurotransmitters are called neuropeptides. The ones above are similar in structure; their function is mimicked by opium.

## TRANSMITTER GASES

The gases **nitric oxide** (NO) and **carbon monoxide** (CO) are the most unusual neurotransmitters identified. As soluble gases, they are neither stored in nor released from synaptic vesicles; instead, they are synthesized as needed. After synthesis, each gas diffuses away from the site at which it was made, easily crossing the cell membrane and immediately becoming active.

Nitric oxide is a particularly important neurotransmitter because it serves as a messenger in many parts of the body. It controls the muscles in intestinal walls, and it dilates blood vessels in brain regions that are in active use (allowing these regions to receive more blood). Because it also dilates blood vessels in the sexual organs, NO is active in producing penile erections. Unlike classical neurotransmitters, nitric oxide is produced in many regions of a neuron, including the dendrites.

**Nitric oxide (NO).** A gas that acts as a chemical neurotransmitter in many cells.

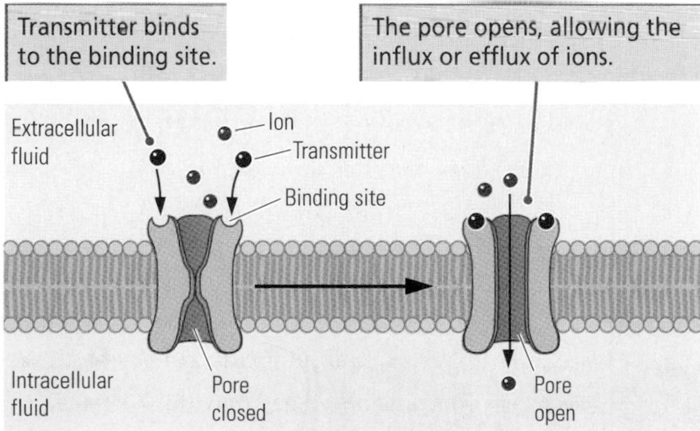


**Figure 5-15**

Ionotropic receptors are proteins that consist of two functional parts: a binding site and a pore. When a transmitter binds to the binding site, the shape of the receptor changes, either opening the pore or closing it. In the example shown here, when the transmitter binds to the binding site, the pore opens and ions are able to flow through it.

# The Types of Receptors for Neurotransmitters

When a neurotransmitter is released from a synapse, it crosses the synaptic cleft and binds to a receptor. What happens next depends on the kind of receptor. There are two general classes of receptors: ionotropic receptors and metabotropic receptors. Each has a different effect on the postsynaptic membrane.

**Ionotropic receptors** allow the movement of ions across a membrane (the suffix *tropic* in the word *ionotropic* means "to move toward"). As Figure 5-15 illustrates, an ionotropic receptor has two parts: (1) a binding site for a neurotransmitter and (2) a pore or channel. When the neurotransmitter attaches to the binding site, the receptor

## Awakening with L-Dopa

Focus on Disorders

> He was started on L-dopa in March 1969. The dose was slowly raised to 4.0 mg a day over a period of three weeks without *apparently* producing any effect. I first discovered that Mr. E. was responding to L-dopa by accident, chancing to go past his room at an unaccustomed time and hearing regular footsteps inside the room. I went in and found Mr. E., who had been chair bound since 1966, walking up and down his room, swinging his arms with considerable vigor, and showing erectness of posture and a brightness of expression completely new to him. When I asked him about the effect, he said with some embarrassment: "Yes! I felt the L-dopa beginning to work three days ago—it was like a wave of energy and strength sweeping through me. I found I could stand and walk by myself, and that I could do everything I needed for myself—but I was afraid that you would see how well I was and discharge me from the hospital." (Sacks, 1976)

In this case history, neurologist Oliver Sacks describes administering L-dopa to a patient who had acquired Parkinson's disease as a result of getting severe influenza in the 1920s. This form of the disorder is called postencephalitic Parkinsonism. The relation between the influenza and symptoms of Parkinsonism suggests that the flu virus entered the brain and selectively attacked dopamine neurons in the substantia nigra. L-Dopa, by being able to increase the amount of dopamine in remaining dopamine synapses, was able to relieve the patient's symptoms.

The use of L-dopa to treat Parkinson's disease began in 1961, when two groups of investigators led by O. Hornykiewicz and A. Barbeau quite independently tried giving it to Parkinson patients. They knew that L-dopa is a chemical that is turned into dopamine at dopamine synapses, but they did not know if it could relieve the symptoms of Parkinsonism. The L-dopa turned out to have a dramatic effect in reducing the muscular rigidity that the patients suffered, although it did not relieve their tremors. Since then, L-dopa has become a standard treatment for Parkinson's disease. Its effects have been improved by administering drugs that prevent L-dopa from being broken down before it gets to dopamine neurons in the brain.

L-Dopa is not a cure for Parkinson's disease. The disorder still progresses during treatment. As more and more dopamine synapses are lost, the treatment becomes less and less effective and eventually begins to produce involuntary movements called dyskinesia. When these side effects eventually become severe, the L-dopa treatment must be discontinued.

Everett Collection, Inc.

The movie *Awakenings* gives a very accurate rendition of the L-dopa trials conducted by Oliver Sacks and described in his book of the same title.

**Ionotropic receptor.** A receptor that has two parts: a binding site for a neurotransmitter and a pore that regulates ion flow.

**Metabotropic receptor.** This receptor is linked to a G protein and can affect other receptors or act with second messengers to affect other cellular processes.

changes its shape, either opening the pore and allowing ions to flow through it or closing the pore and blocking the flow of ions. Because the binding of the transmitter to the receptor is quickly followed by a single step (the opening or closing of the receptor pore) that affects the flow of ions, ionotropic receptors bring about very rapid changes in membrane voltage.

Structurally, ionotropic receptors are similar to voltage-sensitive channels, discussed in Chapter 4. They are composed of a number of membrane-spanning subunits that

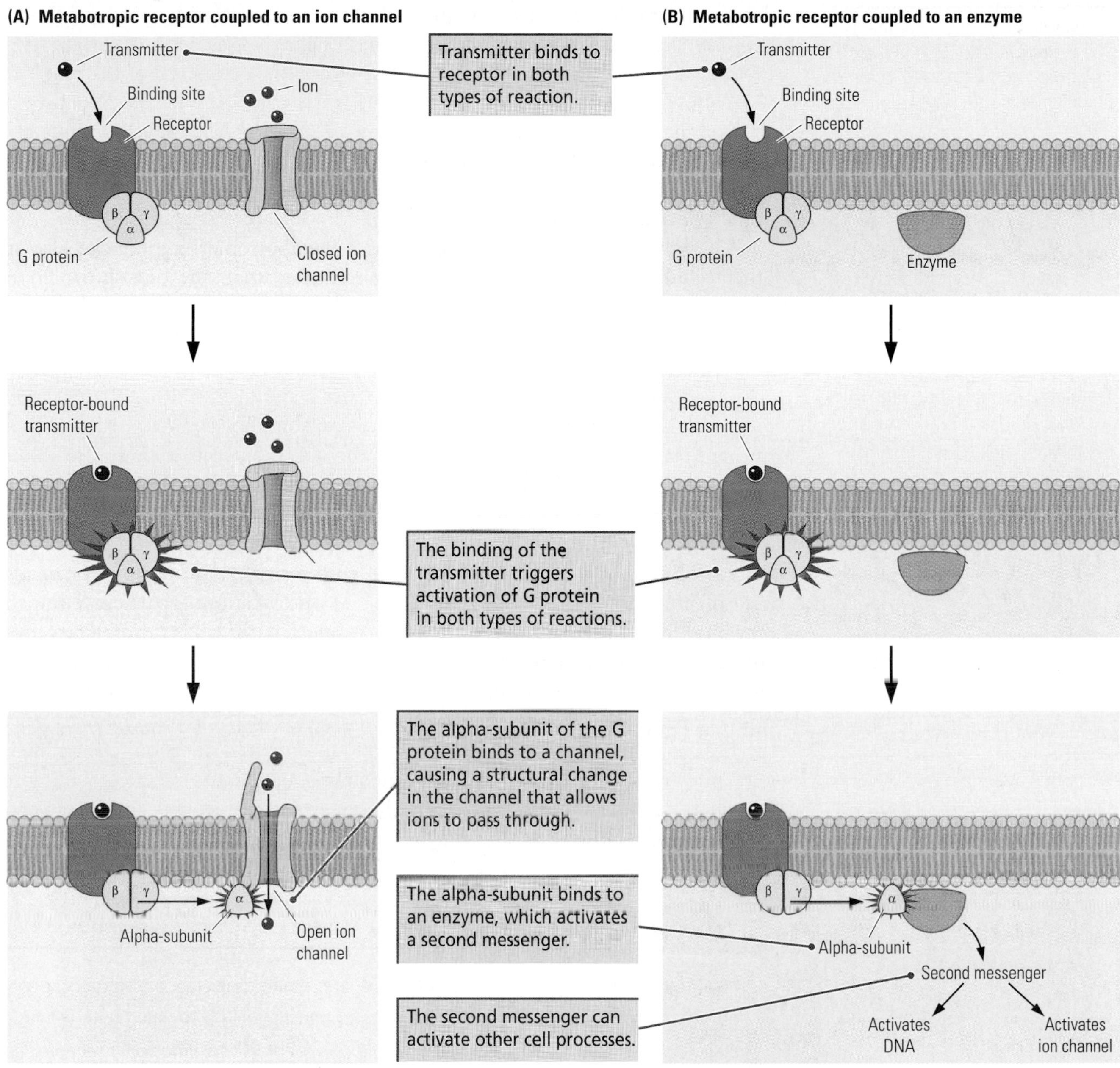
(A) Metabotropic receptor coupled to an ion channel
(B) Metabotropic receptor coupled to an enzyme
Transmitter
Binding site
Receptor
Ion
G protein
Closed ion channel
Enzyme
Transmitter binds to receptor in both types of reaction.
Receptor-bound transmitter
The binding of the transmitter triggers activation of G protein in both types of reactions.
The alpha-subunit of the G protein binds to a channel, causing a structural change in the channel that allows ions to pass through.
Alpha-subunit
Open ion channel
The alpha-subunit binds to an enzyme, which activates a second messenger.
The second messenger can activate other cell processes.
Second messenger
Activates DNA
Activates ion channel

form petals around the pore, which lies in the center. Within the pore is a shape-changing segment that allows the pore to open or close, which regulates the flow of ions through the pore.

In contrast with an ionotropic receptor, a **metabotropic receptor** lacks its own pore through which ions can flow, although it does have a binding site for a neurotransmitter. Through a series of steps, metabotropic receptors produce changes in nearby ion channels or they bring about changes in the cell's metabolic activity (that is, in activity that requires an expenditure of energy, which is what the term *metabolic* means).

Figure 5-16A shows the first of these two effects. The metabotropic receptor consists of a single protein, which spans the cell membrane. The receptor is associated with one of a family of proteins called **guanyl nucleotide-binding proteins,** or **G proteins** for short. A G protein consists of three subunits: alpha, beta, and gamma. The alpha-subunit

**Figure 5-16**

**(A)** A metabotropic receptor coupled to an ion channel has a binding site and an attached G protein. When a neurotransmitter binds to the binding site, the alpha-subunit of the G protein detaches from the receptor and attaches to the ion channel. In response the channel changes its conformation, allowing ions to flow through its pore. **(B)** A metabotropic receptor coupled to an enzyme also has a binding site and an attached G protein. When a neurotransmitter binds to the binding site, the alpha-subunit of the G protein detaches and attaches to the enzyme. The enzyme in turn activates a compound called a second messenger. The second messenger, through a series of biochemical steps, can activate ion channels or activate other cell processes, including the production of new proteins.

**Second messenger.** A chemical that is activated by a neurotransmitter (the first messenger) and carries a message to initiate some biochemical process.

Click on your CD and find the section on the membrane potential in the module on Neural Communication. Review ionic flow across the cell membrane. Imagine this flow being associated with ionotropic receptor stimulation to induce action potentials and neural signals.

detaches from the other two subunits when a neurotransmitter binds to the G protein's associated metabotropic receptor. The detached alpha-subunit can then bind to other proteins within the cell membrane or within the cytoplasm of the cell. If the alpha-subunit binds to a nearby ion channel in the membrane, the structure of the channel changes, modifying the flow of ions through it. If the channel is already open, it may be closed by the alpha-subunit or, if already closed, it may become open. This change in the channel and the flow of ions across the membrane influence the membrane's electrical potential.

The binding of a neurotransmitter to a metabotropic receptor can also trigger other cellular reactions that are more complicated than the one shown in Figure 5-16A. These other reactions are summarized in Figure 5-16B. They all begin when the detached alpha-subunit binds to an enzyme, which in turn activates another chemical called a **second messenger** (the neurotransmitter is the first messenger). A second messenger, as the name implies, carries a message to other structures within the cell. It can bind to a membrane channel, causing the channel to change its structure and thus alter ion flow through the membrane. It can initiate a reaction that causes protein molecules within the cell to become incorporated into the cell membrane, resulting in the formation of new ion channels; or it can send a message to the cell's DNA instructing it to initiate the production of a new protein.

No one neurotransmitter is associated with a single kind of receptor or a single kind of influence on the postsynaptic cell. At one location, a particular transmitter may bind to an ionotropic receptor and have an excitatory effect on the target cell. At another location, the same transmitter may bind to a metabotropic receptor and have an inhibitory effect. For example, acetylcholine has an excitatory effect on skeletal muscles, where it activates an ionotropic receptor, but it has an inhibitory effect on the heart, where it activates a metabotropic receptor. In addition, each transmitter may bind with a number of different kinds of ionotropic or metabotropic receptors. Elsewhere in the nervous system, acetylcholine, for example, may activate a variety of either type of receptor.

## In Review

The three main classes of neurotransmitters are: small-molecule transmitters, peptide transmitters, and transmitter gases. Each class of transmitter is associated with ionotropic (excitatory) and metabotropic (mainly inhibitory) receptors. An ionotropic receptor contains a pore or channel that can be opened or closed to regulate the flow of ions through it. This, in turn, brings about voltage changes on the cell membrane. Metabotropic receptors activate second messengers to indirectly produce changes in the function and structure of the cell. The more than 100 neurotransmitters used in the nervous system are each associated with many different ionotropic and metabotropic receptors.

## NEUROTRANSMITTER SYSTEMS

When researchers began to study neurotransmitters, they thought that any given neuron would contain only one transmitter at all its axon terminals. This belief was called Dale's law, after its originator. New methods of staining neurochemicals, however, have revealed that Dale's law is an oversimplification. A single neuron may use one transmitter at one synapse and a different transmitter at another synapse, as David

Sulzer (1998) and his coworkers have shown. Moreover, different transmitters may coexist in the same terminal or in the same synapse. For example, peptides have been found to coexist in terminals with small-molecule transmitters, and more than one small-molecule transmitter may be found in a single synapse. In some cases, more than one transmitter may even be packaged within a single vesicle.

All this complexity makes for a bewildering number of combinations of neurotransmitters and the receptors for them. What are the functions of so many combinations? We do not have a complete answer. Very likely, however, this large number of combinations is critically related to the many different kinds of behavior of which humans are capable.

Fortunately, the complexity of neurotransmission can be simplified by concentrating on the dominant transmitter located within any given axon terminal. The neuron and its dominant transmitter can then be related to a behavioral function. In this section, we consider some of the links between neurotransmitters and behavior. We begin by exploring the two parts of the peripheral nervous system: the skeletal motor system and the autonomic system. Afterward, we investigate neurotransmission in the central nervous system.

**Cholinergic neuron.** A neuron that contains acetylcholine in its synapses.

## Neurotransmission in the Skeletal Motor System

The brain and spinal cord contain neurons that send their axons to the body's skeletal muscles (the muscles attached to bones). These muscles include those of the eyes and face, the trunk, the limbs, and the fingers and toes. The neurons of the skeletal motor system are sometimes referred to as the final common path for movement because, without them, movement would not be possible. These neurons are also called **cholinergic neurons** because acetylcholine is their main neurotransmitter. (The term *cholinergic* applies to any neuron that uses acetylcholine as its main transmitter.) At a muscle, cholinergic neurons are excitatory and produce muscular contractions.

Not only does a single neurotransmitter serve as the workhorse for the skeletal motor system, so does a single kind of receptor. The receptor on all skeletal muscles is an ionotropic, transmitter-activated channel called a **nicotinic ACh receptor** (nAChr). When ACh binds to this receptor, the receptor's pore opens to permit ion flow, thus depolarizing the muscle fiber. The pore of a nicotinic receptor is large and permits the simultaneous efflux of potassium ions and influx of sodium ions. Nicotine, a chemical contained in cigarette smoke, activates a nicotinic ACh receptor in the same way that ACh does, which is how this type of receptor got its name. In other words, the molecular structure of nicotine is sufficiently similar to that of acetylcholine that nicotine fits into an acetylcholine receptor "slot."

Although acetylcholine is the primary neurotransmitter at skeletal muscles, other neurotransmitters also are found in these cholinergic axon terminals and are released onto the muscle along with acetylcholine. One of these other transmitters is a neuropeptide called **calcitonin-gene-related peptide** (CGRP), which acts through second messengers to increase the force with which a muscle contracts.

## Neurotransmission in the Autonomic Nervous System

In Chapter 2, you learned that the autonomic nervous system has two divisions: the sympathetic and the parasympathetic (see Figure 2-29). They work in complementary fashion to regulate the body's internal environment, preparing it for action or calming it down. The sympathetic division is responsible for producing what is called the

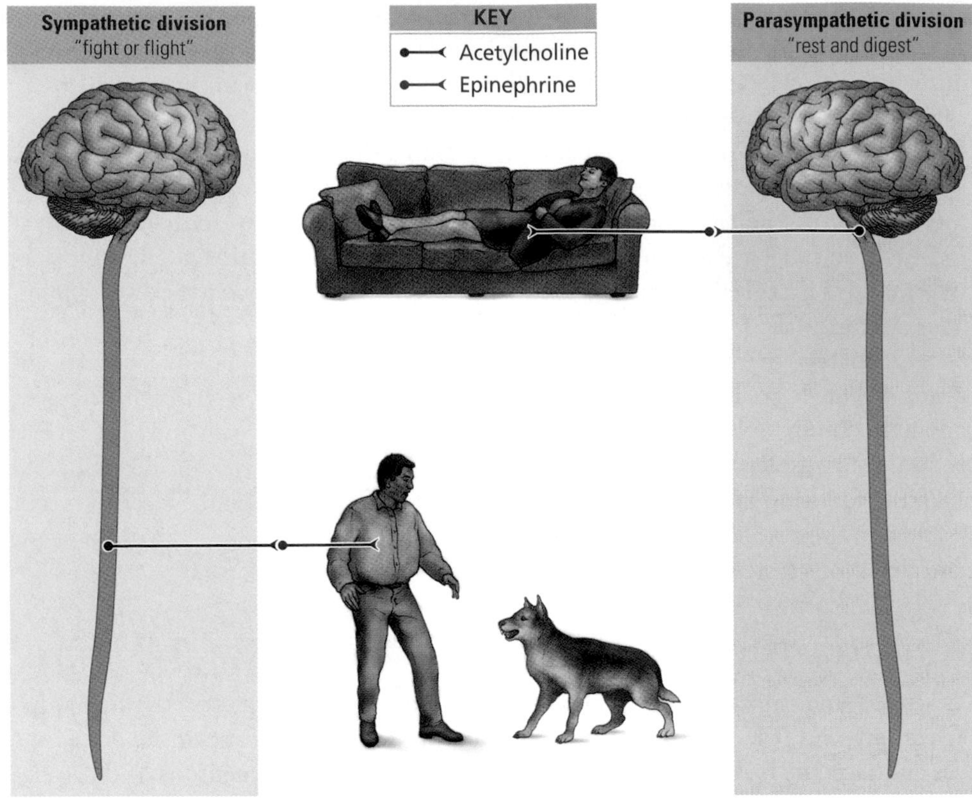


**Figure 5-17**

The autonomic nervous system is made up of the sympathetic division, which prepares the body for fight or flight, and the parasympathetic system, which prepares the body to rest and digest. All the neurons leaving the spinal cord have acetylcholine as a neurotransmitter. In the sympathetic system, these acetylcholine neurons activate epinephrine neurons, which turn on organs required for fight or flight and turn off organs used to rest and digest. In the parasympathetic nervous system, the acetylcholine neurons of the spinal cord activate other acetylcholine neurons, which turn off organs used for fight or flight and turn on organs used to rest and digest.

*fight-or-flight response.* In this response, heart rate is turned up, digestive functions are turned down, and the body is made ready to run away or to fight. The parasympathetic division is responsible for producing an essentially opposite reaction called the *rest-and-digest response.* Here digestive functions are turned up, heart rate is turned down, and the body is made ready to lie back and digest dinner.

Figure 5-17 shows the neurochemical organization of the autonomic nervous system's sympathetic and parasympathetic divisions. The parasympathetic neurons are cholinergic, whereas the sympathetic neurons are **adrenergic,** meaning that they contain the chemical transmitter adrenaline, which is another name for epinephrine. Cholinergic neurons in the spinal cord, in turn, control both the sympathetic and the parasympathetic neurons. In other words, cholinergic neurons in the spinal cord synapse with adrenergic neurons to prepare the body's organs for fight or flight; they also synapse with other cholinergic neurons to prepare the body's organs to rest and digest.

Whether cholinergic synapses or andrenergic synapses are excitatory or inhibitory on a particular body organ depends on the receptors of that organ. Epinephrine turns up heart rate and turns down digestive functions because its receptors on the heart and the digestive organs are different. Epinephrine receptors on the heart are excitatory, whereas epinephrine receptors on the gut are inhibitory. Similarly, acetylcholine turns down heart rate and turns up digestive functions because its receptors on these organs are different. Acetylcholine receptors on the heart are inhibitory, whereas those on the gut are excitatory. The ability of neurotransmitters to be excitatory in one location and inhibitory in another allows the sympathetic and parasympathetic divisions to form a complementary system for regulating the body's internal environment.

**Adrenergic neuron.** A neuron containing epinephrine; the term *adrenergic* derives from the term *adrenaline.*

## Neurotransmission in the Central Nervous System

Some neurotransmitters in the central nervous system have very specific functions. For instance, a variety of chemical transmitters specifically prepare female white-tail deer for the fall mating season. Then, come winter, a different set of biochemicals takes on the new specific function of facilitating the development of the fetus in the mother deer. The mother gives birth in the spring and is subjected to yet another set of biochemicals with highly specific functions, such as the chemical influence that enables her to recognize her own fawn and another one that enables her to nurse. The transmitters in these very specific functions are usually neuropeptides.

In contrast, other neurotransmitters in the central nervous system have more general functions, helping an organism carry out routine daily tasks. These more general functions are mainly the work of small-molecule transmitters. For example, the small-molecule transmitters GABA and glutamate are the most common neurotransmitters in the brain, with GABA having an inhibitory effect and glutamate an excitatory one.

In addition, each of four small-molecule transmitters—acetylcholine, dopamine, norepinephrine, and serotonin—participates in its own general system, the purpose of which seems to be to ensure that neurons in wide areas of the brain act in concert by being stimulated with the same neurotransmitter. For example, Figure 5-18 shows a cross section of a rat brain that is stained for the enzyme acetylcholinesterase, which breaks down ACh. The darkly stained areas of the neocortex have high acetylcholinesterase concentrations, indicating the presence of cholinergic terminals. These terminals, which are clearly located throughout the neocortex, belong to neurons that are clustered in a rather small area just in front of the hypothalamus. There also are high concentrations of ACh in the basal ganglia and basal forebrain, which renders these structures very dark in Figure 5-18. An anatomical organization such as this one, in which a few neurons send axons to widespread brain regions, suggests that these neurons play a role in synchronizing activity throughout the brain. These general-purpose systems are commonly called **ascending activating systems.** They can be envisioned as something like the power supply to a house, in which a branch of the power line goes to each room of the house but the electrical appliance powered in each room differs, depending on the room.

Referred to by the transmitters that their neurons contain, the four ascending activating systems are the cholinergic, dopaminergic, noradrenergic, and serotonergic

**Ascending activating system.** A group of neurons, each of which contains a common neurotransmitter, that have their cell bodies located in a nucleus in the basal forebrain or brainstem and their axons distributed to a wide region of the brain.

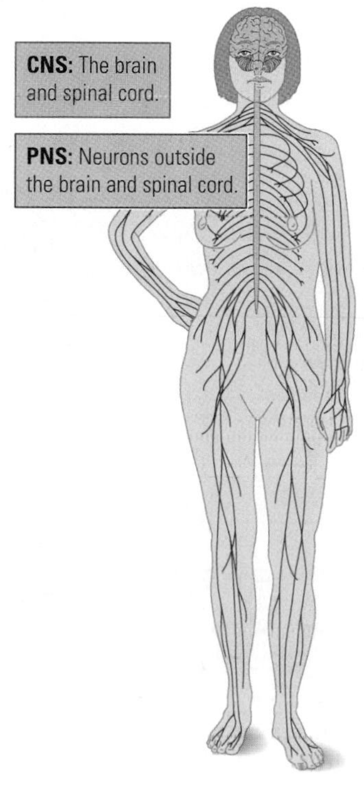


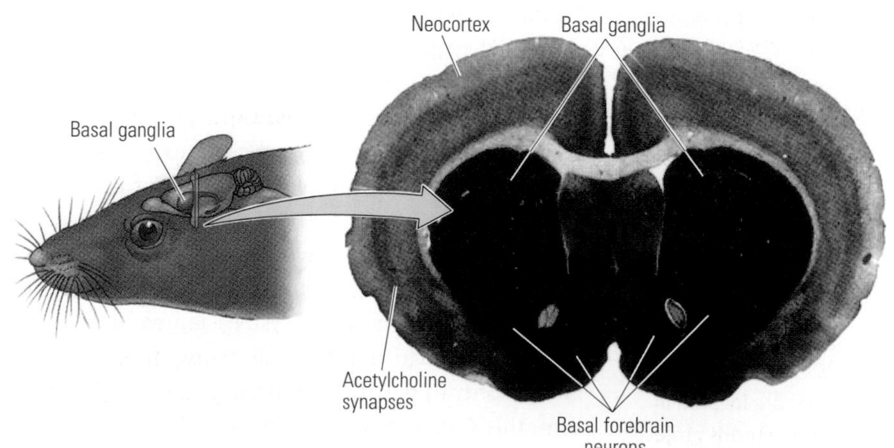


**Figure 5-18**

This micrograph shows the localization of acetylcholinesterase, the enzyme that breaks down acetylcholine, in the brain of a rat. The drawing (*left*) shows the location at which the transverse section (*right*) was taken. The cholinergic neurons of the basal forebrain are located in the lower part of the section, adjacent to the two white circles, which comprise fibers in the anterior commissure. The basal forebrain neurons project to the neocortex, and the darkly stained bands in the cortex show areas that are rich in cholinergic synapses. The dark central parts of the section are the basal ganglia, which also are rich in cholinergic neurons.

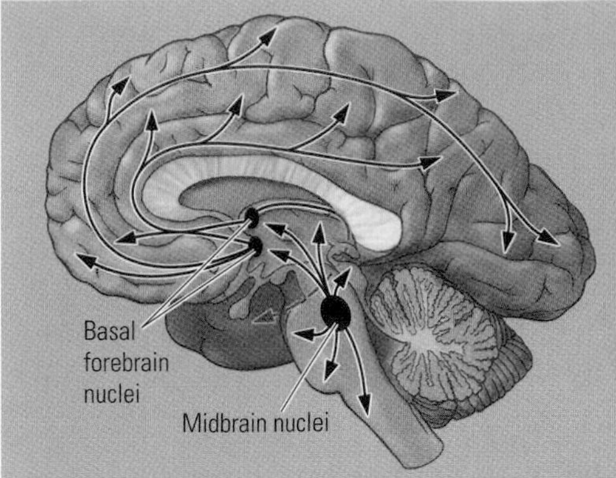


**Cholinergic system**
(acetylcholine): Active in maintaining waking electroencephalographic (EEG) patterns of the neocortex. Thought to play a role in memory by maintaining neuron excitability. Death of acetylcholine neurons and decrease in acetylcholine in the neocortex are thought to be related to Alzheimer's disease.

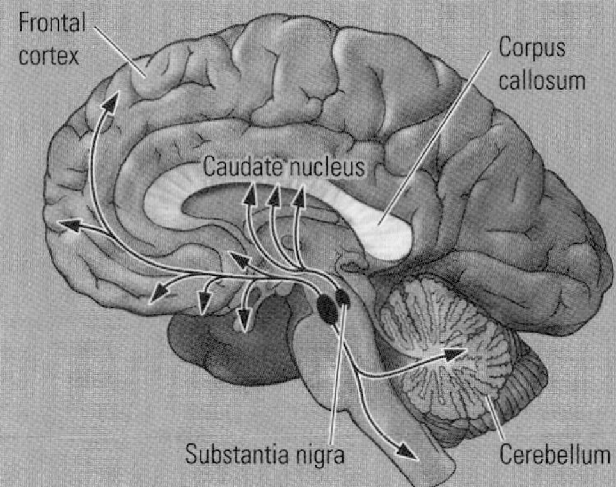


**Dopaminergic system**
(dopamine): Active in maintaining normal motor behavior. Loss of dopamine is related to Parkinson's disease, in which muscles are rigid and movements are difficult to make. Increases in dopamine activity may be related to schizophrenia.

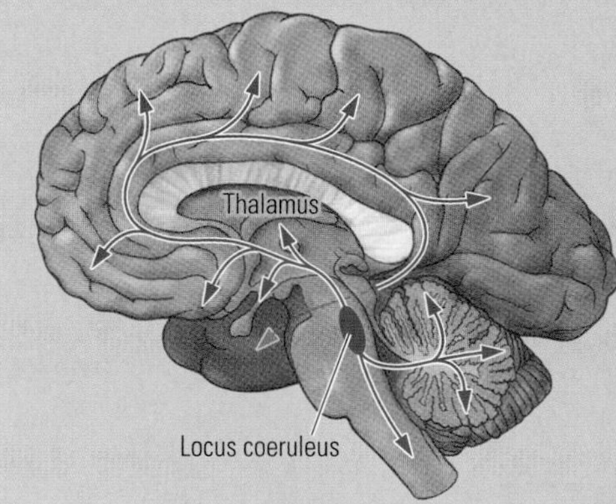


**Noradrenergic system**
(norepinephrine): Active in maintaining emotional tone. Decreases in norepinephrine activity are thought to be related to depression, whereas increases in it are thought to be related to mania (overexcited behavior).

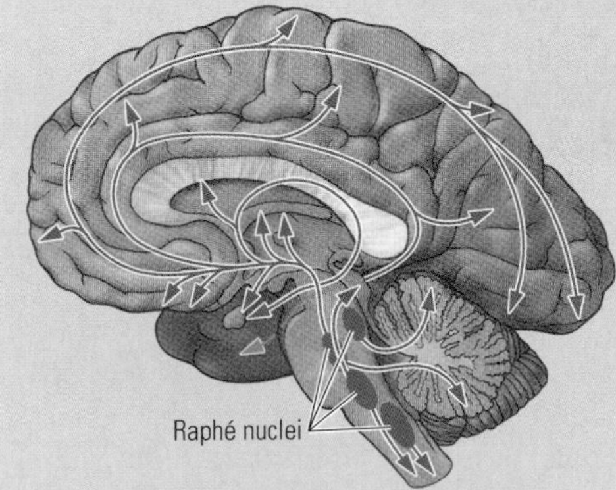


**Serotonergic system**
(serotonin): Active in maintaining waking EEG patterns. Increases in serotonin activity are related to obsessive-compulsive disorder, tics, and schizophrenia. Decreases in serotonin activity are related to depression.

**Figure 5-19**

For all four major nonspecific ascending systems, the cell bodies are located in nuclei (large round circles) in the brainstem. The axons of these neurons project diffusely to the forebrain, cerebellum, and spinal cord, where they synapse with most neurons of the target structure. Each system has been associated with one or more behaviors or nervous system diseases.

systems. Figure 5-19 shows the location of neurons in each of these four systems, with arrow shafts indicating the pathways of axons and arrow tips indicating axon terminals. The four ascending activating systems are similarly organized in that the cell bodies of their neurons are clustered together in only a few nuclei in or near the brainstem, whereas the axons of the neurons are widely distributed in the forebrain, brainstem, and spinal cord.

Figure 5-19 summarizes the behavioral functions as well as the brain disorders in which each of the four ascending activating systems has been implicated. The ascending cholinergic system contributes to the EEG activity of the cortex and hippocampus in an alert, mentally active person, and so seems to play a role in normal wakeful behavior. People who suffer from Alzheimer's disease, which starts with minor forgetfulness and progresses to major memory dysfunction, show a loss of these cholinergic neurons at autopsy. One treatment strategy currently being pursued for Alzheimer's is to develop drugs that stimulate the cholinergic system to enhance behavioral alertness. The brain abnormalities associated with Alzheimer's disease are not limited to the cholinergic neurons, however. There is also extensive damage to the neocortex and other brain regions. As a result, it is not yet clear what role the cholinergic neurons play in the progress of the disorder. Perhaps their death causes degeneration in the cortex or perhaps the cause-and-effect relation is the other way around, with cortical degeneration being the cause of cholinergic cell death. Then, too, it may be that the loss of cholinergic neurons is just one of many neural symptoms of Alzheimer's disease.

One function of the ascending dopaminergic system is involvement in motor behavior. If dopamine neurons in the brain are lost, the result is a condition of extreme rigidity, in which opposing muscles are contracted, making it difficult for an affected person to move. Patients also show rhythmic tremors of the limbs. This condition, called Parkinson's disease, is discussed in "Focus on Disorders" throughout this chapter. Although Parkinson's disease usually arises for no known cause, it can also be triggered by the ingestion of certain drugs, as described in "The Case of the Frozen Addict" on page 175. Those drugs may act as selective poisons, or neurotoxins, that kill the dopamine neurons. Another function of the dopaminergic system is involvement in reward or pleasure, inasmuch as many drugs that people abuse seem to act by stimulating this system. In addition, this system has a role in a condition called schizophrenia, one of the most common and debilitating psychiatric disorders. One explanation of schizophrenia is that the dopaminergic system is overactive.

Focus on Disorders

## The Case of the Frozen Addict

> Patient 1: During the first 4 days of July 1982, a 42-year-old man used 4½ grams of a "new synthetic heroin." The substance was injected intravenously three or four times daily and caused a burning sensation at the site of injection. The immediate effects were different from heroin, producing an unusual "spacey" high as well as transient visual distortions and hallucinations. Two days after the final injection, he awoke to find that he was "frozen" and could move only in "slow motion." He had to "think through each movement" to carry it out. He was described as stiff, slow, nearly mute, and catatonic during repeated emergency room visits from July 9 to July 11. He was admitted to a psychiatric service on July 15, 1982, with a diagnosis of "catatonic schizophrenia" and was transferred to our neurobehavioral unit the next day. (Ballard et al., 1985, p. 949)

This patient was one of seven young adults who were hospitalized at about the same time in California. All the patients showed symptoms of severe Parkinson's disease, which is extremely unusual in people their age. The symptoms, which had appeared very suddenly after drug injection, were similar to those displayed by patients who have had Parkinson's disease for many years. All appeared to have injected a synthetic heroin that was being sold on the streets in the summer of 1982. What was the link between the heroin and the Parkinson's symptoms?

An investigation by J. William Langston and his colleagues (1992) found that the heroin contained a contaminant called MPTP (1-methyl-4-phenyl-1,2,3,6-tetrahydropyridine). The contaminant resulted from poor preparation of the heroin during its synthesis. The results of experimental studies in rodents showed that MPTP was not itself responsible for the patients' symptoms, but it was metabolized into $MPP^+$ (1-methyl-4-phenylpyridinium), which is a neurotoxin. In one autopsy of a suspected case of MPTP poisoning, the victim suffered a selective loss of dopamine neurons in the substantia nigra, with the rest of the brain being normal. Injection of MPTP into monkeys produced symptoms similar to those produced in humans and a similar selective loss of dopamine neurons in the substantia nigra. Thus, the combined clinical and experimental evidence indicates that Parkinson's disease can be induced by a toxin that selectively kills dopamine neurons in this part of the brain.

Is there any hope of a cure for this selective cell destruction? In 1988, Patient 1 was taken to University Hospital in Lund, Sweden, to receive an experimental treatment. The treatment consisted of implanting into the caudate and putamen of his brain dopamine neurons taken from human fetal brains. Extensive work with rodents and nonhuman primates had demonstrated that fetal neurons, which have not yet developed dendrites and axons, can survive transplantation and grow into mature neurons that can secrete neurotransmitters. The patient had no serious postoperative complications. Twenty-four months after the surgery, he was much improved and could function much more independently. He could dress and feed himself, visit the bathroom with help, and make trips outside his home. He also responded much better to the medication that he received. The transplantation of fetal neurons to treat Parkinson's disease continues to be an area of active research.

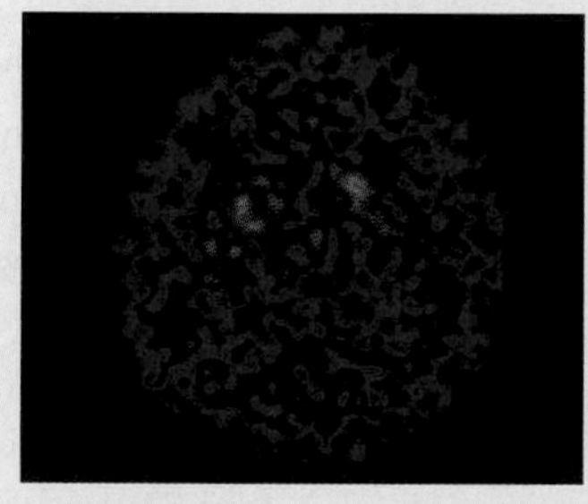

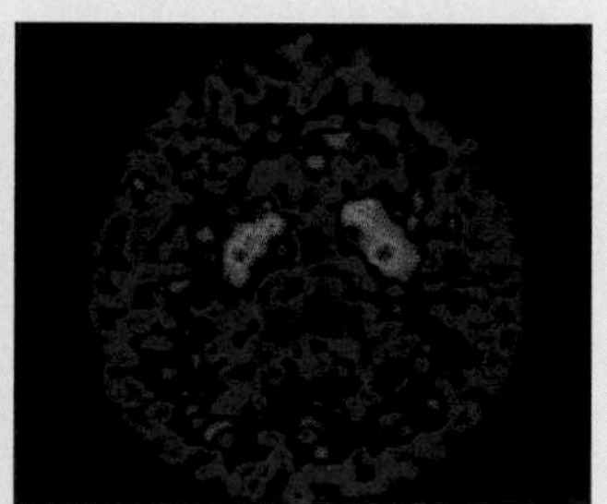

Dr. Hakan Widner, M.D., PhD., Lord University, Sweden

**Positron emission tomographic images of Patient 1's brain comparing levels of fluoro-dopa (a weakly radioactive form of L-dopa) before the implantation of fetal dopamine neurons (*left*) and 12 months after this operation (*right*). The increased size of the red and gold area indicates that transplanted dopamine neurons are present and producing dopamine in the patient's brain.**

From "Bilateral Fetal Mesencephalic Grafting in Two Patients with Parkinsonism Induced by 1-Methyl-4-phenyl-1,2,3,6-tetrahydropyradine (MPTP)," by H. Widner, J. Tetrud, S. Rehngrona, B. Snow, P. Brundin, B. Gustavii, A. Bjorklund, O. Lindvall, and W. J. Langston, 1992, *New England Journal of Medicine, 327,* p. 151.

Learn more about Parkinson's disease at the Web site (**www.worthpublishers.com/kolb/chapter5**) with links to current research and foundations devoted to investigating this disorder.

Behaviors and disorders related to the noradrenergic ascending system have been very difficult to identify. Some of the symptoms of depression may be related to decreases in the activity of noradrenergic neurons, whereas some of the symptoms of manic behavior (excessive excitability) may be related to increases in the activity of these same neurons.

The serotonergic ascending system has a role in producing a waking EEG in the forebrain, as does the cholinergic system. But behavioral functions for serotonin are not well understood. It may be that some of the symptoms of depression are related to decreases in the activity of serotonin neurons. Consequently, there may be two forms of depression, one related to norepinephrine and the other related to serotonin. Some research suggests that some of the symptoms of schizophrenia also may be related to serotonin, which, again, implies that there may be different forms of schizophrenia.

### In Review

Although axon terminals can contain more than one kind of neurotransmitter, neurons are usually identified by the principal neurotransmitter in their terminals. Many neurotransmitters take part in rather specific behaviors that may occur only once each month or year, whereas other neurotransmitters take part in behavioral functions that occur continuously. Neurons containing a specific neurotransmitter may be organized into functional systems that mediate some aspect of behavior. For instance, acetylcholine is the main neurotransmitter in the skeletal motor system, and acetylcholine and epinephrine are the main neurotransmitters in the autonomic system. The central nervous system contains not only widely dispersed glutamate (excitatory) and GABA (inhibitory) neurons, but also systems of neurons that have acetylcholine, norepinephrine, dopamine, or serotonin as their neurotransmitter. These systems are associated both with specific aspects of behavior and with specific kinds of neurological disorders.

## THE ROLE OF SYNAPSES IN LEARNING AND MEMORY

Clearly, synapses are very versatile in structure and function, but are they also capable of change? The question of change asks about the *plasticity* of synapses. Can the experiences that an organism has as it functions in the world bring about long-lasting alterations in synapses? If such change is possible, synapses provide a potential site for the neural processes of learning. After all, learning is usually defined as a relatively permanent change in behavior as a result of experience. That change in behavior must somehow be linked to a change in the structure and function of the nervous system. Does the synapse lie at the heart of this nervous system change?

Donald O. Hebb (1904–1985)

In 1949, Donald O. Hebb, in his book titled *The Organization of Behavior,* suggested that learning is mediated by structural changes in synapses. He was not the first person to make this suggestion, but the change that he envisioned was novel. According to Hebb, "When an axon of cell A is near enough to excite a cell B and repeatedly or persistently takes part in firing it, some growth process or metabolic change takes place in one or both cells such that A's efficiency, as one of the cells firing B, is increased" (Hebb, 1949, p. 62).

When Hebb proposed this idea, there were no methods available to test it. But through the years, as such methods have been developed, Hebb's proposal has been supported. Learning does often require the joint firing of two neurons, which increases the efficiency with which their synapse functions. This increased efficiency provides the structural basis for new behavior. A synapse that undergoes this kind of change is commonly called a **Hebb synapse.**

In the following sections, you will discover that synapses are capable of change and mediate a number of different kinds of learning, including habituation, sensitization, and associative learning. We will explore three different ways that synapses can be altered in response to an organism's experiences. First, they can change in the release of a neurotransmitter; second, they can grow new synaptic connections; and, third, they can modify their structures. We will also see that channels and receptors, structures critical to the action potential and neurotransmitter release, can also participate in learning.

**Hebb synapse.** A synapse that can change with use so that learning takes place.

**Habituation.** A form of learning in which a response to a stimulus weakens with repeated stimulus presentations.

## Learning and Changes in Neurotransmitter Release

The marine snail *Aplysia californica,* shown in Figure 5-20, is slightly larger than a softball and has no shell. When threatened, it defensively withdraws its more vulnerable body parts—the gill (through which it extracts oxygen from the water) and the siphon (a spout above the gill used to expel seawater and waste). Some of the roughly 20,000 neurons that mediate the snail's behaviors are quite accessible to researchers, and circuits with very few synapses can be isolated for study. This makes *Aplysia* extremely useful for experiments on learning. By touching or shocking the animal's appendages, researchers can produce a number of enduring changes in its defensive responses. These behavioral changes can then be used to study underlying changes in the nervous system. Eric Kandel (1976) and many other neuroscientists have conducted just such studies to try to explain the neurological basis of simple kinds of learning.

Jeff Rotman

**Figure 5-20**

The sea snail *Aplysia californica.*

### NEUROTRANSMITTER RELEASE AND HABITUATION

**Habituation** is a simple form of learning in which the strength of a response to a certain stimulus becomes weaker with repeated presentations of that stimulus. For example, if you are accustomed to living in the country and then move to a city, you might at first find the sounds of traffic and people extremely loud and annoying. With time, however, you stop noticing most of the noise. You have habituated to it. Similar habituation develops with our other senses. When you first put on an item of clothing, such as a shoe, you "feel" it on your body, but very shortly it is as if the shoe is no longer there. The reason? Habituation. You have not become insensitive to sensations, however. When people talk to you on a city street, you still hear them; when someone steps on your foot, you still feel the pressure. It is the customary, "background" sensations that your brain has learned to screen out.

*Aplysia* also displays habituation. One example is habituation to waves in the shallow tidal zone in which it lives. These snails are constantly buffeted by the flow of waves against their bodies, and they learn that waves are just the background "noise" of daily life. They do not flinch and withdraw every time a wave passes over them. They habituate to this stimulus. But a sea snail that is habituated to waves is not insensitive to other touch sensations. If the snail is touched with a novel object, it responds by withdrawing its siphon and gill. The animal's reaction to repeated presentations of the same novel stimulus forms the basis for studying its habituation response.

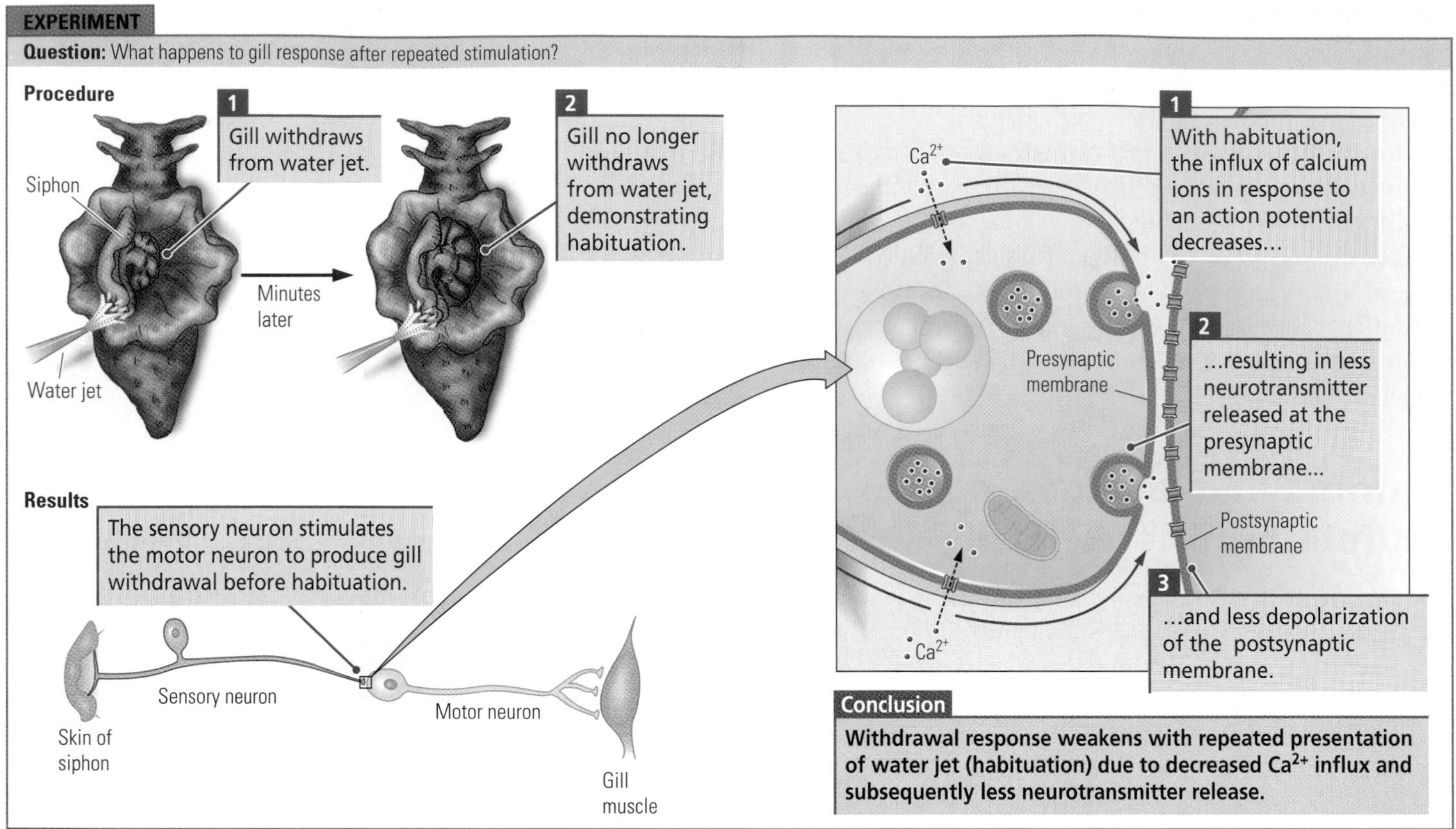
EXPERIMENT
Question: What happens to gill response after repeated stimulation?
Procedure
1
Gill withdraws from water jet.
Siphon
Water jet
Minutes later
2
Gill no longer withdraws from water jet, demonstrating habituation.
Results
The sensory neuron stimulates the motor neuron to produce gill withdrawal before habituation.
Sensory neuron
Skin of siphon
Motor neuron
Gill muscle
Ca2+
1
With habituation, the influx of calcium ions in response to an action potential decreases...
Presynaptic membrane
2
...resulting in less neurotransmitter released at the presynaptic membrane...
Postsynaptic membrane
3
...and less depolarization of the postsynaptic membrane.
Conclusion
Withdrawal response weakens with repeated presentation of water jet (habituation) due to decreased Ca2+ influx and subsequently less neurotransmitter release.

**Figure 5-21**

The neural basis of habituation. A jet of water is sprayed on the siphon of *Aplysia* while movement of the gill is recorded. The gill withdrawal response weakens with repeated presentations of the water jet. As a result, a sensory neuron from the skin of the siphon forms a connection with a motor neuron that contracts the gill muscle. Recordings from the sensory neuron and motor neuron after habituation show that neither has lost its sensitivity to electrical stimulation. Measures of transmitter release at the sensory–motor synapse show that less neurotransmitter is released after habituation. This decrease in neurotransmitter occurs because calcium channels have become less responsive to the voltage changes associated with action potentials, causing a reduction in the influx of calcium needed to release neurotransmitter.

The procedure section of Figure 5-21 shows the experimental setup for studying the withdrawal response of *Aplysia* to a light jet of water. If the jet of water is presented as many as 10 times, the withdrawal response is weaker some minutes later when the animal is again tested with the water jet. The decrement in the strength of the withdrawal is habituation. This habituation can last as long as 30 minutes. What is its neural basis?

The results section of Figure 5-21 starts by showing a simple representation of the pathway that mediates *Aplysia's* gill-withdrawal response. For purposes of illustration, only one sensory neuron, one motor neuron, and one synapse are shown, even though, in actuality, about 300 neurons may take part in this response. The jet of water stimulates the sensory neuron, which in turn stimulates the motor neuron that is responsible for the gill withdrawal. But exactly where do the changes associated with habituation take place? In the sensory neuron? In the motor neuron? Or in the synapse between the two?

Habituation is *not* a result of an inability of either the sensory or the motor neuron to produce action potentials. In response to direct electrical stimulation, both the sensory neuron and the motor neuron retain the ability to generate action potentials even after habituation. Electrical recordings from the motor neuron show that, accompanying the development of habituation, the excitatory postsynaptic potentials in the motor neuron become smaller. The most likely way that these EPSPs (excitatory postsynaptic potentials) decrease in size is that the motor neuron is receiving less neurotransmitter across the synapse. And, if less neurotransmitter is being received, then the changes accompanying habituation must be taking place in the presynaptic axon terminal of the sensory neuron.

Kandel and his coworkers measured neurotransmitter output from a sensory neuron and verified that less of it is in fact released from a habituated neuron than from a nonhabituated one. Recall that the release of a neurotransmitter in response to an action potential requires an influx of calcium ions across the presynaptic membrane. As habituation takes place, that calcium ion influx decreases in response to the voltage changes associated with an action potential. Presumably, with repeated use, calcium channels become less responsive to voltage changes and more resistant to the passage of calcium ions. Why this happens is not yet known. At any rate, the neural basis of habituation lies in the presynaptic part of the synapse. Its mechanism, which is summarized in the right-hand close-up of Figure 5-21, is a reduced sensitivity of calcium channels and a consequent decrease in the release of a neurotransmitter. This reduced sensitivity of calcium channels in response to voltage changes produces habituation, a form of learning and memory about an organism's experiences.

**Sensitization.** A process by which the response to a stimulus increases with repeated presentations of that stimulus.

## NEUROTRANSMITTER RELEASE AND SENSITIZATION

*Aplysia* is capable of other forms of learning as well. One is **sensitization,** an enhanced response to some stimulus. Sensitization is the opposite of habituation. The organism becomes hyperresponsive to a stimulus rather than accustomed to it. For instance, a sprinter crouched in her starting blocks is often hyperresponsive to the starter's gun; its firing triggers in her a very rapid reaction. The stressful, competitive context in which the race takes place helps to sensitize her to this sound. Sensitization occurs in other contexts, too. Sudden and novel forms of stimulation often heighten our general awareness and result in larger-than-normal responses to all kinds of stimulation. If you are suddenly startled by a loud noise, you become much more responsive to other stimuli in your surroundings, including some of those to which you had previously become habituated.

The same thing happens to *Aplysia.* Sudden novel stimuli can heighten a snail's responsiveness to familiar stimulation. For example, if the snail is attacked by a predator, it becomes acutely aware of other changes in its environment and hyperresponds to them. In a laboratory, a small electric shock to the tail mimics a predatory attack and is effective in producing this kind of sensitization, which is illustrated in the procedure section of Figure 5-22. In fact, a single electric shock to the tail of *Aplysia* enhances its gill-withdrawal response for a period that lasts from minutes to hours.

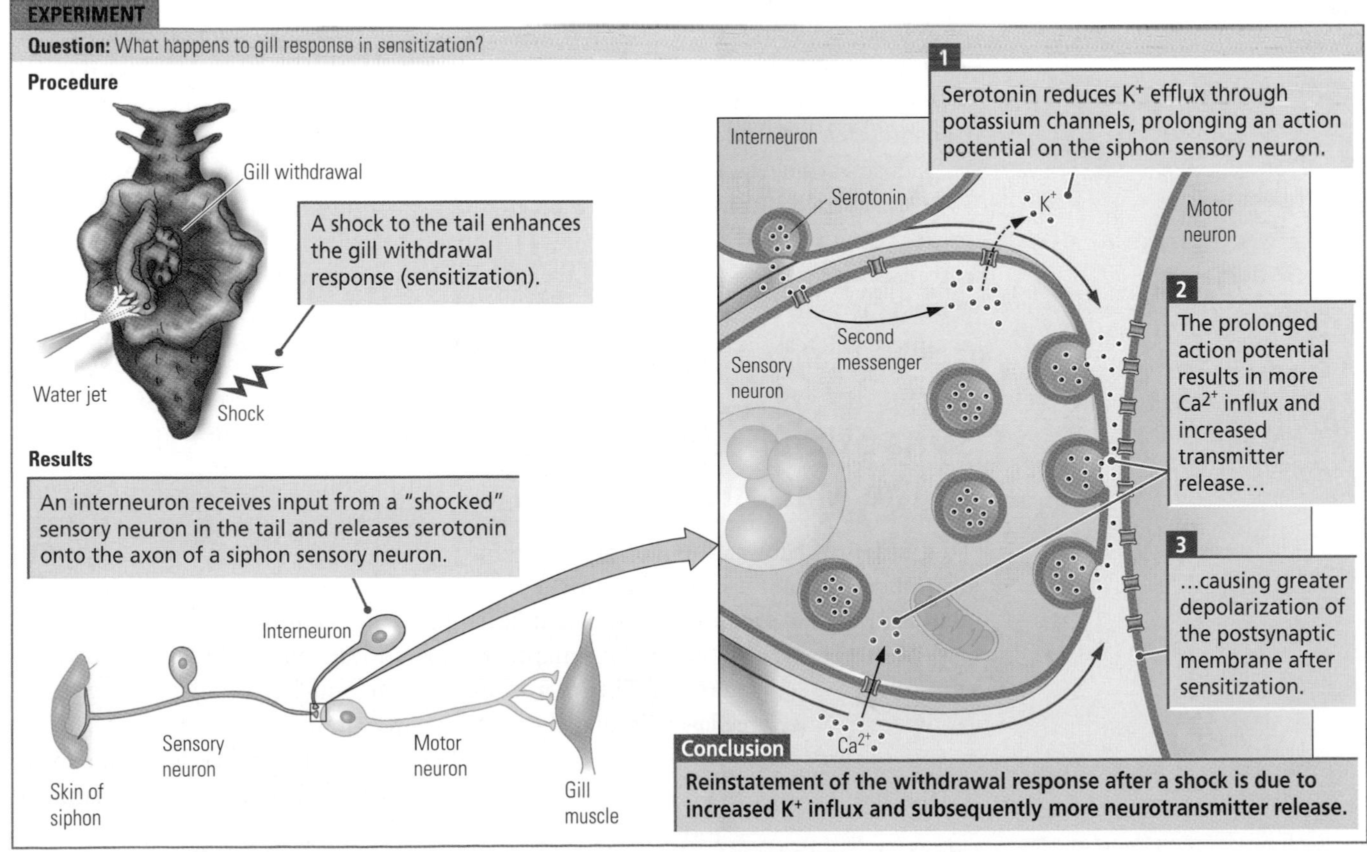

EXPERIMENT
Question: What happens to gill response in sensitization?
Procedure
Gill withdrawal
A shock to the tail enhances the gill withdrawal response (sensitization).
Water jet
Shock
Results
An interneuron receives input from a "shocked" sensory neuron in the tail and releases serotonin onto the axon of a siphon sensory neuron.
Interneuron
Sensory neuron
Motor neuron
Skin of siphon
Gill muscle
1
Serotonin reduces K+ efflux through potassium channels, prolonging an action potential on the siphon sensory neuron.
Interneuron
Serotonin
K+
Motor neuron
Second messenger
Sensory neuron
2
The prolonged action potential results in more Ca2+ influx and increased transmitter release...
3
...causing greater depolarization of the postsynaptic membrane after sensitization.
Ca2+
Conclusion
Reinstatement of the withdrawal response after a shock is due to increased K+ influx and subsequently more neurotransmitter release.


**Figure 5-22**

The neural basis of sensitization. A shock is delivered to the tail of *Aplysia* before the siphon is stimulated with a jet of water, resulting in an enhanced gill-withdrawal response. As a result, a serotonin interneuron that makes a presynaptic connection with the sensory neuron releases serotonin. Serotonin reduces $K^+$ efflux through potassium channels, thus prolonging the action potential. The prolonged action potential results in a greater calcium influx and therefore increased release of transmitter.

In addition to studying the neurological basis of habituation, Kandel and his coworkers studied the neurological basis of sensitization. In this case, the neural circuits are a little more complex than those taking part in habituation. To simplify the picture, the results section of Figure 5-22 shows only one of each kind of neuron. An interneuron that receives input from a sensory neuron in the tail (and so carries information about the shock) makes an axoaxonic synapse with a siphon sensory neuron. The interneuron contains the neurotransmitter serotonin in its axon terminal. Consequently, in response to a tail shock, the tail sensory neuron activates the interneuron, which in turn releases serotonin onto the axon of the siphon sensory neuron. Information from the siphon still comes through the siphon sensory neuron to activate the motor neuron leading to the gill muscle. This last link you already know about from the discussion of habituation.

Now let us see what happens at the molecular level. The serotonin released from the interneuron binds to a metabotropic serotonin receptor on the axon of the siphon sensory neuron. This binding causes second messengers to be activated in the sensory neuron. Specifically, the serotonin receptor is coupled though its G protein to the enzyme adenyl cyclase. This enzyme increases the concentration of the second messenger cyclic adenosine monophosphate (cAMP) in the presynaptic membrane of the siphon sensory neuron, the membrane that forms one side of a synapse with the motor neuron leading to the gill. Through a number of chemical steps, cAMP attaches a phosphate ($PO_4$) to potassium ($K^+$) channels, and the phosphate renders the $K^+$ channels relatively unresponsive. The close-up of the results section of Figure 5-22, on the right, sums up the result. In response to an action potential traveling down the axon of the siphon sensory neuron (such as one generated by a touch to the siphon), the $K^+$channels on that neuron are slower to open. Consequently, potassium ions cannot repolarize the membrane as quickly as is normal, so the action potential lasts a little longer than it usually would. The longer-lasting action potential prolongs the inflow of $Ca^{2+}$ into the membrane. In turn, the increased concentration of $Ca^{2+}$ results in more neurotransmitter being released from the sensory synapse onto the motor neuron that leads to the gill muscle, which produces a larger-than-normal gill-withdrawal response. The gill withdrawal may also be enhanced by the fact that the second messenger cAMP may mobilize more synaptic vesicles, making more neurotransmitter ready for release into the sensory– motor synapse.

Sensitization, then, is the opposite of habituation at the transmitter level as well as at the behavioral level. In sensitization, more calcium influx results in more transmitter being released, whereas, in habituation, less calcium influx results in less neurotransmitter being released. The structural basis of memory in these two forms of learning is different, however. In sensitization, the change takes place in potassium channels, whereas, in habituation, the change takes place in calcium channels.

## Synaptic Change with Learning in the Mammalian Brain

The studies of habituation and sensitization in *Aplysia* show that changes in synapses do underlie simple forms of learning. In this section, we look at experiments that demonstrate that synapses participate in learning in the mammalian brain.

We begin our exploration of synaptic change in learning in the forebrain structure called the hippocampus. The hippocampus of mammals is relatively simple cortex that has only three layers, rather than the six layers in the neocortex. The neurons in one of these layers are packed closely together to form a bandlike line. This linear arrangement of the neurons aligns their dendrites and cell bodies, and so summed

EPSPs from many of them—sums known as **field potentials**—can be recorded quite easily with extracellular electrodes. Both the relatively simple circuitry of the hippocampus and the ease of recording large field potentials there make the hippocampus a very popular structure for studying the neural basis of learning.

In 1973, Timothy Bliss and Terje Lomo demonstrated that repeated electrical stimulation of the *perforant pathway* entering the hippocampus produces a progressive increase in the size of the field potentials recorded from hippocampal cells. This enhancement in the size of the field potentials lasts for a number of hours to a number of days or even weeks. Bliss and Lomo called it **long-term enhancement** (LTE). Long-term enhancement can be obtained at many synapses of the nervous system, but the hippocampus, because of its simple structure, continues to be a favorite location for LTE studies. The fact that LTEs last for days or months suggests two things. First, some change must have taken place at the synapse that allowed the field potential to become larger. Second, the change in the synapse might be related to the kinds of learning that we experience each day.

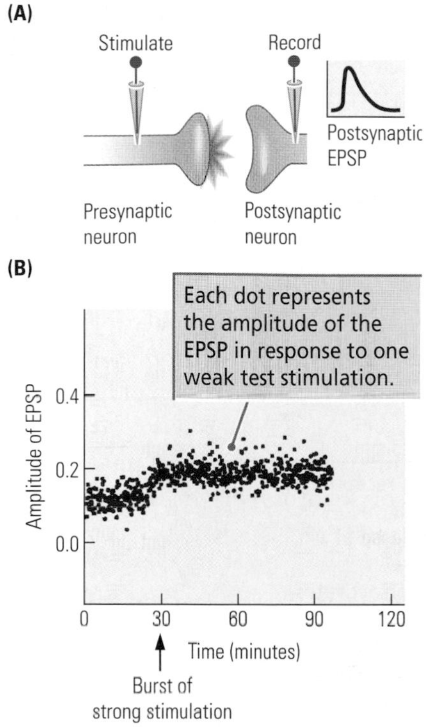

**Figure 5-23**

**(A)** In this experimental setup for demonstrating long-term enhancement, the presynaptic neuron is stimulated with a test pulse and the EPSP is recorded from the postsynaptic neuron. **(B)** Each test pulse of stimulation produces an EPSP, the amplitude of which is indicated by a dot on a graph. After a period of intense stimulation, the amplitude of the EPSP produced by the test pulse increases.

Because LTE can be recorded at many different locations in the brain, Figure 5-23A illustrates the experimental procedure for a typical synapse. The presynaptic neuron is stimulated electrically while the electrical activity produced by the stimulation is recorded from the postsynaptic neuron. The insert in Figure 5-23A shows the excitatory postsynaptic potential produced by a single pulse of electrical stimulation. In a typical experiment, a number of test stimuli are given to estimate the size of the induced EPSP. Then a strong burst of stimulation, consisting of a few hundred pulses of electrical current per second, is administered. Then the test pulse is given again. Figure 5-23B illustrates the fact that the amplitude of the EPSP has increased and remains larger for as long as 90 minutes after the high-frequency burst of stimulation. The high burst of stimulation has produced a long-lasting change in the response of the postsynaptic neuron. In other words, LTE has occurred. In order for the EPSP to increase in size, more neurotransmitter must be released from the presynaptic membrane or the postsynaptic membrane has to become more sensitive to the same amount of transmitter. So the question is, What is the mechanism that enables this change?

To examine the possible synaptic changes underlying LTE, we will turn to the results of some experiments in which glutamate is the chemical transmitter at the terminals of the neurons being stimulated. Glutamate acts on two different types of glutamate receptors located on the postsynaptic membrane, called *N*-methyl-D-aspartate (NMDA) and alpha-amino-3-hydroxy-5-methylisoazole-4-proprionic acid (AMPA) receptors. As Figure 5-24A shows, AMPA receptors ordinarily mediate the responses produced when glutamate is released from a presynaptic membrane. NMDA receptors usually do not respond to glutamate, because their pores are blocked by magnesium ions ($Mg^{2+}$) .

Under appropriate circumstances, however, NMDA receptors can open to allow the passage of calcium ions. For them to open requires two events to take place at approxi-

**Long-term enhancement (LTE).** A change in the amplitude of an excitatory postsynaptic potential that lasts for hours to days in response to stimulation of a synapse; may play a part in learning. Sometimes referred to as long-term or long-lasting potentiation (LTP or LLP).

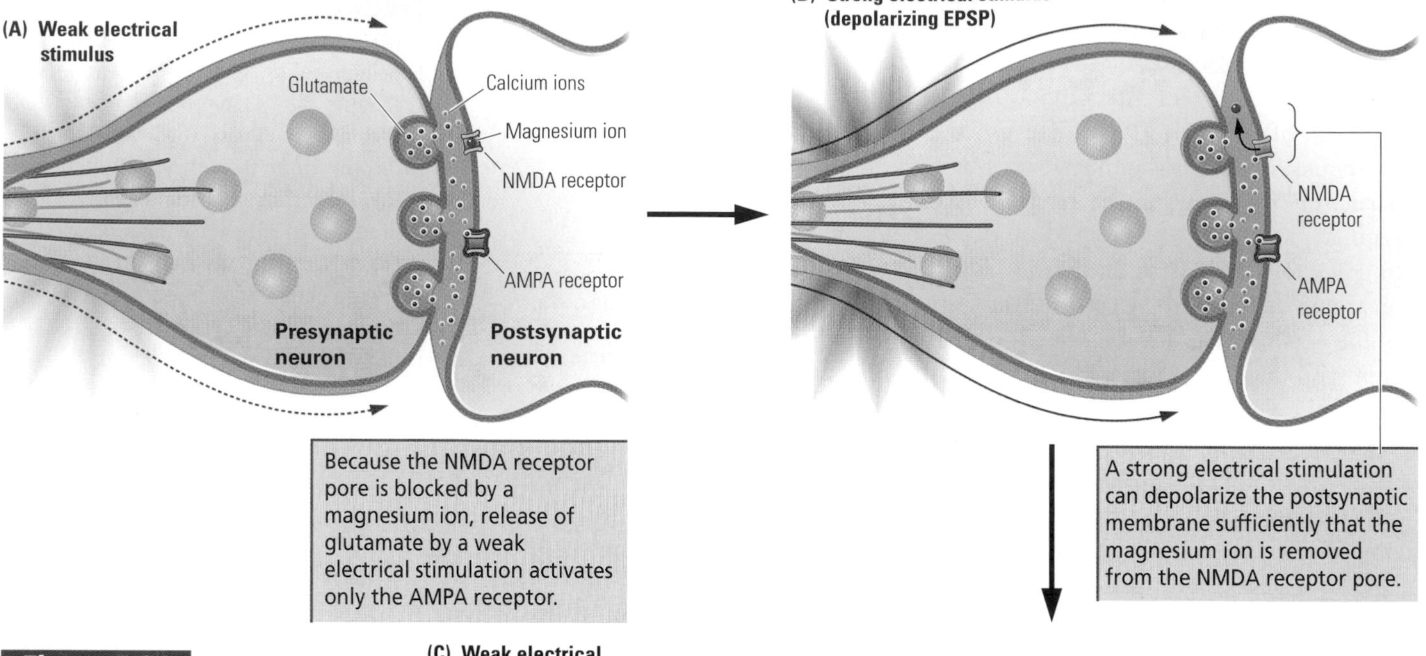

(A) Weak electrical stimulus
Glutamate
Calcium ions
Magnesium ion
NMDA receptor
AMPA receptor
Presynaptic neuron
Postsynaptic neuron
Because the NMDA receptor pore is blocked by a magnesium ion, release of glutamate by a weak electrical stimulation activates only the AMPA receptor.
(B) Strong electrical stimulus (depolarizing EPSP)
NMDA receptor
AMPA receptor
A strong electrical stimulation can depolarize the postsynaptic membrane sufficiently that the magnesium ion is removed from the NMDA receptor pore.

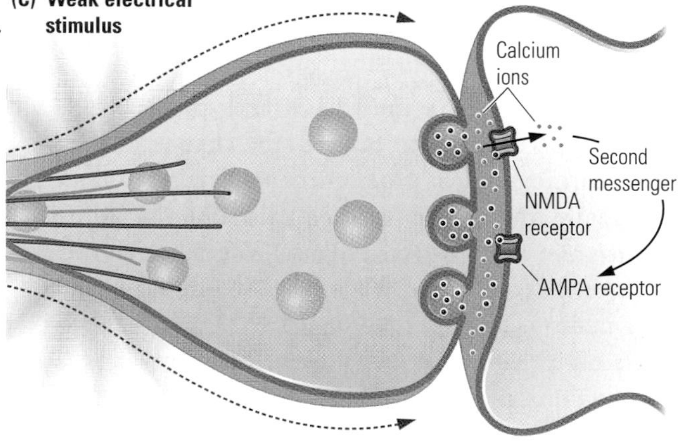

(C) Weak electrical stimulus
Calcium ions
Second messenger
NMDA receptor
AMPA receptor
Now glutamate, released by weak stimulation, can activate the NMDA receptor to allow $Ca^{2+}$ influx, which, through a second messenger, increases the function or number of AMPA receptors, or both.

**Figure 5-24**

The synaptic change that underlies LTE. **(A)** A weak electrical stimulus (test stimulus) releases glutamate from the presynaptic terminal, and the glutamate binds to the AMPA receptor. The NMDA receptor is insensitive to glutamate and is blocked by a magnesium ion. **(B)** An intense burst of strong stimulation is sufficient to depolarize the postsynaptic membrane to the point at which the magnesium block is removed from the NMDA receptor. **(C)** Now, in response to a test stimulus, glutamate binds to the NMDA receptor, and the receptor pore opens to allow the influx of calcium ions. Calcium ions, acting through second messengers, produce a number of changes that include an increase in the responsiveness of AMPA receptors to glutamate, the formation of new AMPA receptors, and even retrograde messages to the presynaptic terminal to enhance glutamate release.

**Doubly gated channel.** A membrane channel containing a pore that opens to allow entry of calcium into the cell only when the membrane is depolarized and is stimulated by the appropriate neurotransmitter.

mately the same time, which is why NMDA receptors are called **doubly gated channels.** The two required events are illustrated in Figure 5-24B and C. First, as shown in Figure 5-24B, the postsynaptic membrane must be depolarized by strong electrical stimulation. When the membrane is depolarized, the $Mg^{2+}$ ion is displaced from the pore. Second, as shown in Figure 5-24C, the NMDA receptors must be activated by glutamate from the presynaptic membrane. If these two changes take place at roughly the same time, $Ca^{2+}$ ions are able to enter the postsynaptic neuron through the NMDA receptor pore. This entry of $Ca^{2+}$ into the cell initiates the cascade of events associated with the long-lasting increase in the size of the field potential, which is long-term enhancement.

What happens when $Ca^{2+}$ enters a postsynaptic neuron? There are three proposals. The first has calcium acting through a second messenger to improve current flow through the AMPA receptor. The second has calcium acting through a second messenger to stimulate the formation of new AMPA receptors. In both cases, the same amount of neurotransmitter therefore produces a larger field potential because of a change in the AMPA receptors. The third proposal is a little more complex. In this case, $Ca^{2+}$ is suggested to trigger the production of a substance called **retrograde plasticity factor.** Retrograde plasticity factor diffuses back into the presynaptic membrane and reacts with second messengers there. One of the functions of the presynaptic second messengers is to enhance the release of glutamate in response to presynaptic stimulation. Accordingly, this increase in the release of glutamate results in LTE. The results of some experiments suggest that retrograde plasticity factor may be the gaseous transmitter NO.

The novel part of this story is that hippocampal NMDA receptors thus mediate a change that in every way meets the criteria of a Hebb synapse. The synapse changes with use. The familiar part of the story is that calcium ions take part, just as in learning in *Aplysia*.

**Associative learning.** A form of learning in which two or more unrelated stimuli become associated with each other to elicit a behavioral response.

## Long-Term Enhancement and Associative Learning

**Associative learning** involves learning associations between stimuli, such as learning that A goes with B. This form of learning is very common. Learning that a certain telephone number goes with a certain person, that a certain odor goes with a certain food, or that a certain sound goes with a certain musical instrument are all everyday examples of associative learning. Your learning that NMDA receptors take part in mammalian learning is another example of associative learning.

The NMDA receptor change just described is not associative, because one stimulus is not linked with another. There was only the initial strong electrical stimulation—no pairing of this stimulation with another stimulus. But this mechanism may mediate associative learning. Remember that the NMDA receptor is doubly gated. In order for calcium ions to pass through its pore, the magnesium block must be removed by depolarization of the membrane, and then glutamate must bind to the receptor. If one of the two stimuli in the associative pair depolarized the membrane and the other released glutamate, then that would provide the basis for associative learning.

The demonstration of LTE occurring at a synapse when a weak stimulus is paired with a stronger one provides a model for how associations might be learned between two different events that take place together in time. But is this neural change actually related to learning in an organism's natural environment? And, if this change does underlie real-life associative learning, what are the natural equivalents of the weak and the strong stimulation?

The strong source of stimulation comes from an interesting feature of the action potentials produced by certain neurons. When these neurons fire, the nerve impulse travels not only down the axon, but also back up the dendritic tree. This dendritic action potential creates a depolarization of the postsynaptic membrane that is adequate to remove the $Mg^{2+}$ block in NMDA receptors. When the $Mg^{2+}$ blocks are removed, the release of glutamate into any synapse on the dendrite can activate NMDA receptors and thus produce LTE. This is where the weak stimulation comes in. The weak stimulation is any environmental event that triggers glutamate-releasing activity into a synapse at the same time as the postsynaptic membrane is being depolarized. Initially, this transmitter input onto the dendritic tree of the postsynaptic neuron would not be strong enough to produce LTE. With repeated pairing of the glutamate release and a depolarization of the postsynaptic membrane caused by dendritic action potentials, however, LTE could eventually occur. Potentially, then, if one behavioral event causes the hippocampal cells to discharge at the same time as some other event causes the release of glutamate onto those cells' dendrites, LTE would result in response to the second event.

A specific example will help you see how this process relates to associative learning. Suppose that, as a rat walks around, a hippocampal cell fires when the rat reaches a certain location. The stimulus that produces this firing may be the sight of a particular object, such as a red light. The signal about the light would presumably be carried by the visual system to the neocortex and then from the visual neocortex to the hippocampal cell. Now suppose that, during an excursion to this place where the light is located, the rat encounters a novel object—say, a tasty piece of food. Input concerning that food could be carried from the taste area of the neocortex to the same hippocampal cell that fires in response to the light. As a result, the taste and odor input associated with the food would arrive at the cell at the time that it is firing in response to the light. Because the cell is firing, the $Mg^{2+}$ block is removed, so LTE can take place. Subsequently, the sight of the red light will fire this hippocampal cell, but so will the odor of this particular food. The hippocampal cell, in other words, stores an association between the food and the light.

You may be wondering how this association could be useful to a rat, or even yourself. Let us use the rat as an example. If the rat were to smell the odor of this food on the snout of another rat that had eaten it, the hippocampal cell would discharge. Because the discharge of this cell is also associated with a particular light and location in the environment, the rat might know (or think) that, if it goes to that location, it will once again find food there. Jeff Galef and his coworkers (1990) in fact demonstrated that a rat that smells the odor of a particular food on the breath of a demonstrator rat will go to the appropriate location to obtain some of the food. This example of the social transmission of food-related information is an excellent example of associative learning. Although this behavior can be disrupted by brain lesions in the hippocampus, it has not yet been demonstrated that learning this food-and-place association is mediated by LTE in synapses, because it is technically difficult to locate the appropriate synapses and record from them in a freely moving animal.

## Learning and the Formation or Loss of Synapses

When we view pictures of neurons, dendrites, and synapses, they are inanimate and static, but living neurons are not like this. Living neurons are constantly changing. Maria Fischer and her coworkers (1998) video-recorded the behavior of living hippocampal neurons that were maintained in a culture. They labeled the neurons with a green fluorescent dye that binds to actin, a contractile protein that is found in the cell and is responsible for dendritic movement. As the dye bound to the actin, each neuron could be seen to have numerous fluorescent protuberances. Many were filopodia—small fingerlike extensions that continuously projected from and retracted back into the dendrites. These filopodia are presumed to be precursors of dendritic spines. Other protuberances were clearly dendrites with well-developed heads and narrow shafts. These dendrites were continuously changing their size, shape, and length over periods of seconds. A cultured neuron in a dish has no axon connections, and the absence of such connections may have contributed to much of the dendritic movement observed. Nevertheless, the results of the experiment show that dendrites and their spines can be formed or lost or change their shape rapidly enough to be responsible for the neural changes associated with learning.

The neural changes associated with learning must be long-lasting enough to account for a relatively permanent change in an organism's behavior. The changes at synapses described in the preceding sections develop quite quickly, but they do not last indefinitely, as memories often do. How, then, can synapses be responsible for the relatively permanent changes in behavior that we call long-term memory and learning?

If the procedures that produce habituation and sensitization or associative learning are repeated a number of times, the behavioral changes that result, instead of lasting for hours or days, can last for months. In other words, a brief period of training produces learning that lasts only a short time, whereas a longer period of training produces more enduring learning. You can probably think of instances in

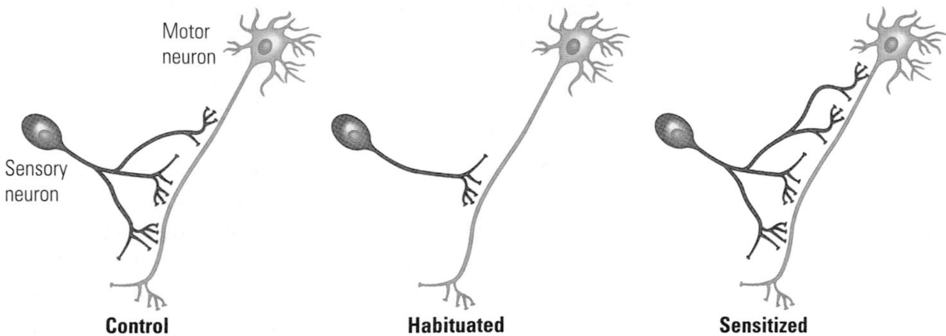


**Figure 5-25**

Habituation and sensitization in *Aplysia* can be accompanied by structural changes in the sensory neuron in which the number of synapses with the motor neuron decline as a result of habituation and increase as a result of sensitization. These structural changes may underlie enduring memories.

your own life. If you cram for an exam the night before, you usually forget the material quickly; but, if you study a little each day for a week, your learning tends to endure. What underlies this more persistent form of learning? It seems that the basis of it would be more than just a change in the release of a neurotransmitter, and, whatever the change is, it must be a relatively permanent one.

Craig Bailey and Mary Chen (1989) have helped to answer this question. They found that the number and size of sensory synapses and the amount of transmitter that they contain are changed in well-trained habituated and sensitized *Aplysia.* The number and size of synapses are decreased in habituated animals and increased in sensitized animals, as shown in Figure 5-25. Apparently, the synaptic events associated with habituation and sensitization can also trigger processes in the sensory cell that result in the loss or formation of new synapses. A mechanism through which these processes can take place begins with calcium ions. These calcium ions can mobilize second messengers to send instructions to nuclear DNA. The nuclear DNA, in turn, can initiate changes that result in the increase or decrease of various structural aspects of the synapse, including the number of synapses.

The second messenger cAMP probably plays an important role in carrying these instructions to nuclear DNA. The evidence for cAMP's involvement comes from studies of fruit flies. In the fruit fly *Drosophila,* two genetic mutations can occur that produce the same learning deficiency. One mutation, called *dunce,* produces a lack of the enzymes needed to degrade cAMP, so the fruit fly has abnormally high levels of cAMP. These high levels of cAMP, which are outside the normal range for *Drosophila* neurons, render the cAMP second messenger inoperative. The other mutation, called *rutabaga,* also renders the cAMP second messenger inoperative, but it does so by producing levels of cAMP so low that they, too, are outside the normal range for *Drosophila* neurons. Significantly, fruit flies with either of these two mutations are impaired in their ability to acquire habituated and sensitized responses. It seems that new synapses are required in these types of learning and that the second messenger cAMP is needed to carry instructions to form them. Figure 5-26 summarizes the findings of this research.

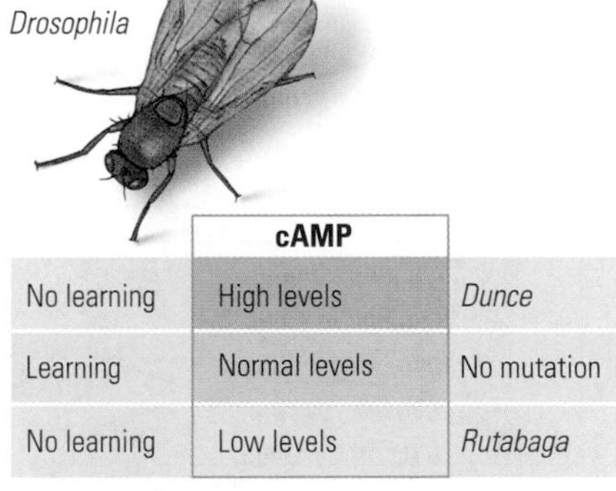


| | cAMP | |
|---|---|---|
| No learning | High levels | *Dunce* |
| Learning | Normal levels | No mutation |
| No learning | Low levels | *Rutabaga* |

**Figure 5-26**

Two genetic mutations can disrupt learning in the fruit fly *Drosophila.* The mutation *dunce* increases the amount of the second messenger cAMP, moving it above the concentration range at which it can be regulated. The mutation *rutabaga* decreases the amount of the second messenger cAMP, moving it below the concentration range at which it can be regulated.

To confirm that the growth and loss of synapses underlie relatively permanent changes in behavior requires not only studies of fruit flies and sea snails, but also studies of mammalian brains. Such studies are difficult to do, however. There are many more neurons and connections in a mammalian brain than in a snail ganglion, and it is almost impossible to know where a learning-related change may take place. Even in a simplified experimental condition that uses the hippocampus and a known pathway, there are far too many synaptic connections to be certain of which synapse or synapses are changing to mediate learning. But many of these methodological difficulties can be overcome if the experiment is conducted in a dish, as the following experiment was.

The German researchers Florian Engert and Tobias Bonhoffer (1999) took slices of the hippocampus from the brains of rats and maintained them in a culture for 2 to 4 weeks before beginning their study. When hippocampal slices are initially cultured, there is a large increase in the number of dendritic spines on certain neurons, but,

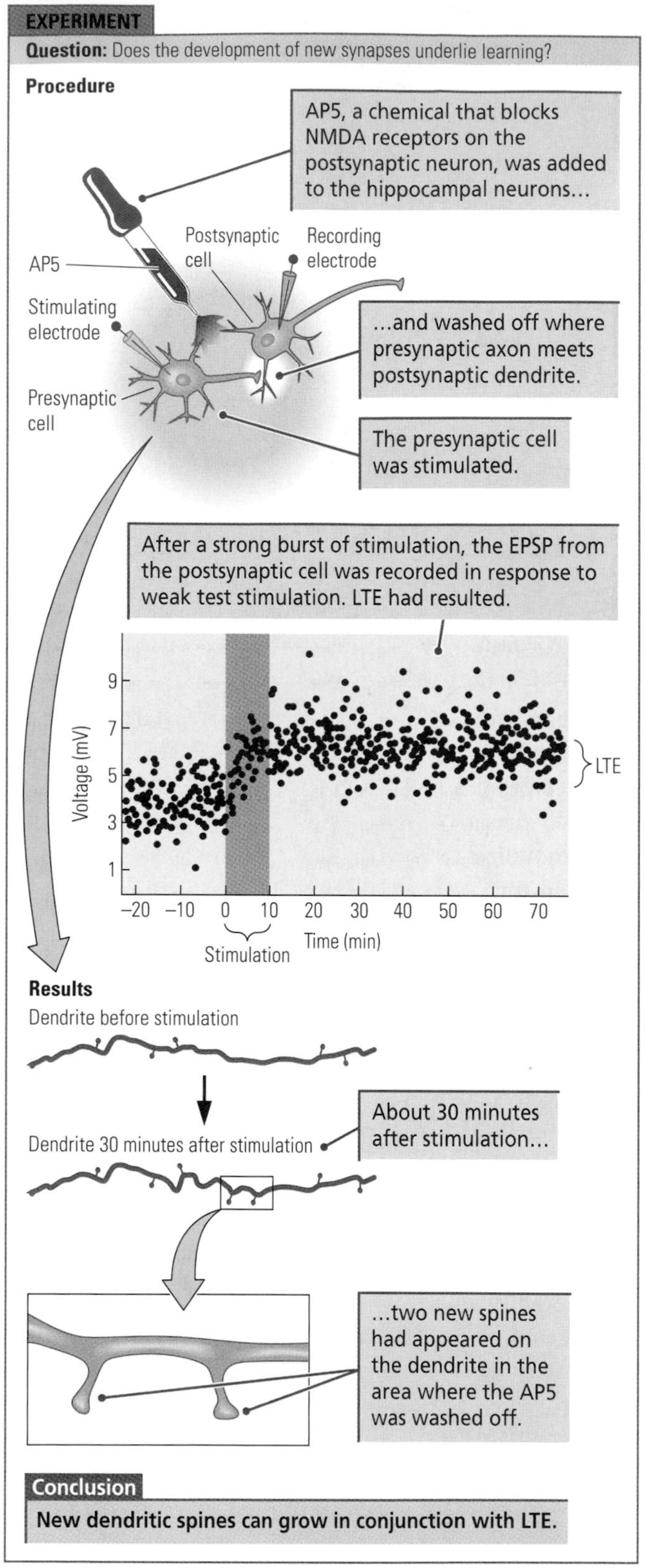

**EXPERIMENT**

**Question:** Does the development of new synapses underlie learning?

**Procedure**

AP5, a chemical that blocks NMDA receptors on the postsynaptic neuron, was added to the hippocampal neurons...

AP5

Postsynaptic cell

Recording electrode

Stimulating electrode

Presynaptic cell

...and washed off where presynaptic axon meets postsynaptic dendrite.

The presynaptic cell was stimulated.

After a strong burst of stimulation, the EPSP from the postsynaptic cell was recorded in response to weak test stimulation. LTE had resulted.

Voltage (mV)

LTE

Stimulation

Time (min)

**Results**

Dendrite before stimulation

Dendrite 30 minutes after stimulation

About 30 minutes after stimulation...

...two new spines had appeared on the dendrite in the area where the AP5 was washed off.

**Conclusion**

**New dendritic spines can grow in conjunction with LTE.**

**Figure 5-27**

To demonstrate the formation of new synapses in the mammalian hippocampus, a slice of hippocampus is maintained in a dish. A recording electrode is placed in a presynaptic neuron and a stimulating electrode is placed in a postsynaptic neuron. A fluorescent dye is injected into the postsynaptic neuron through the recording electrode so that the neuron can be visualized through a microscope. A chemical that blocks receptors on the postsynaptic neuron (AP5) is placed over the preparation but is washed away from the zone in which the presynaptic and postsynaptic neurons have synapses. A weak test stimulation of the presynaptic neuron produces low-amplitude EPSPs in the postsynaptic neuron. After an intense burst of stimulation, the test stimulus produces a larger EPSP. Each dot represents the size of an EPSP in response to a single test stimulus. About 30 minutes after LTE, two new dendritic spines appear on the dendrite of the postsynaptic neuron. The finding that new dendritic spines grow in conjunction with LTE suggests that they support long-term changes in interneuron communication and may provide the neural substrate for new learning in behaving animals.

after 2 weeks of incubation, the neurons become stabilized. The experimental setup is illustrated in Figure 5-27. A glass microelectrode was inserted into a hippocampal neuron. Through the electrode, the fluorescent molecule calcein was injected into the cell to color it green. The cell was also stimulated through this electrode, which sufficiently depolarized the cell membrane to remove the $Mg^{2+}$ block from NMDA receptors. A drug called AP5 (2-amino-5-phosphonovaleric acid), which blocks NMDA receptors, was then added to the bath surrounding the neuron, and a second microelectrode was inserted into the axons of other neurons that had synapsed with the first cell. Next, the area of the dendrite adjacent to the second stimulating electrode was washed to remove AP5 from just this region of the postsynaptic neuron. The axons were then stimulated electrically, and the EPSPs produced by that stimulation were recorded from the postsynaptic cell.

Structural changes on the stimulated dendrite were observed with the use of a *confocal microscope.* A confocal microscope is similar to a light microscope except that the light that shines through the tissue comes from a laser. Light from a laser does not scatter, so a small object can be viewed clearly. In addition, changing the focal point of the laser makes it possible to see through the dendrite and then reconstruct a three-dimensional picture of it. The fluorescent molecule calcein that was injected into the neuron makes its dendrites readily observable through the confocal microscope.

The graph in Figure 5-27 shows the changes in the size of the EPSPs recorded from the postsynaptic neuron. First, a number of test stimuli are given to determine the size of the EPSP, followed by 10 minutes of electrical stimulation. Then, EPSPs with a larger amplitude, indicating that LTE has occurred, are recorded in response to test stimuli. The results section of Figure 5-27 shows that, about 30 minutes after stimulation, two new spines appeared on the dendrite. No spines appeared on other parts of the neuron that were still subject to the AP5 block. Consequently, this experiment demonstrates that new dendritic spines can grow in conjunction with LTE. In this experiment, it was not possible to see the axon terminals, but presumably new terminals arose to connect the stimulated axons to the new dendritic spines, thus forming new synapses. Note that the new synapses appeared about 30 minutes after LTE, so these new connections were not required for LTE. The new synapses, however, are probably required for LTE to endure.

Learn more about the confocal microscope in the Research Methods section on your CD. You'll see a diagram of the apparatus and video clips of cells taken with a confocal microscope.

## In Review

Are synapses required for learning? The answer is, Yes, in a number of different ways. In *Aplysia,* changes in synaptic function can mediate two forms of learning: habituation and sensitization. Presynaptic voltage-sensitive calcium channels mediate habituation by becoming less sensitive with use. Presynaptic serotonin metabotropic receptors can change the sensitivity of potassium channels and so increase $Ca^{2+}$ influx to mediate sensitization. At the same time, these same receptors can produce fewer or more synapses to provide a structural basis for long-term habituation and sensitization. Mammals provide an example of synaptic change related to associative learning. Here learning occurs only if certain events take place at the same time. Clearly, many changes in the synapses of neurons can mediate learning. Because learning can have a structural basis, measurements of different structures within a synapse can be a source of insight into the relations between synaptic change and behavioral experience. Figure 5-28 summarizes the areas of a synapse that can be measured and related to behavior.

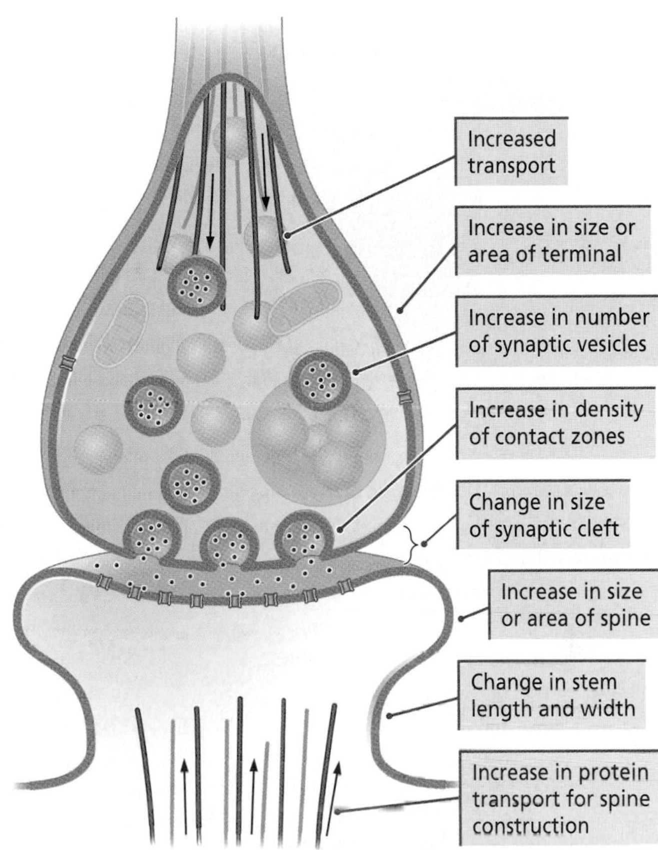


**Figure 5-28**

A summary of locations on a synapse where changes may subserve learning.

## SUMMARY

1. *What early experiments provided the key to understanding how neurons communicate with each other?* In the 1920s, Otto Loewi suspected that nerves secrete a chemical onto the heart, which regulates its rate of beating. His subsequent experiments showed that acetylcholine slows heart rate, whereas epinephrine increases it. This observation provided the key to understanding the basis of chemical neurotransmission.
2. *What is the basic structure of a synapse that connects one neuron to another neuron?* A synapse between two neurons consists of the first neuron's axon terminal (which is surrounded by a presynaptic membrane), a synaptic cleft (a tiny gap between the two neurons), and a postsynaptic membrane on the second neuron. Systems for manufacturing the chemical neurotransmitter used in communicating between the two neurons are located in the first neuron's axon terminal or cell body, whereas systems for storing the neurotransmitter are in its axon terminal. Receptor systems on which that neurotransmitter acts are located on the postsynaptic membrane.
3. *What are the major stages in the function of a neurotransmitter?* There are four major stages in neurotransmitter function: (1) synthesis and storage of the neurotransmitter, (2) its release from the axon terminal, (3) action of the neurotransmitter on postsynaptic receptors, and (4) processes for inactivating the neurotransmitter. After its manufacture, the neurotransmitter is wrapped in a membrane to form synaptic vesicles, which become attached to the presynaptic membrane of the axon terminal. When an action potential is propagated on the presynaptic membrane, voltage changes set in motion the release of the neurotransmitter. Exocytosis of the contents of one synaptic vesicle releases a quantum of neurotransmitter into the synaptic cleft. This quantum produces a miniature postsynaptic potential on the postsynaptic membrane. To generate an action potential on the postsynaptic cell requires the simultaneous release of many

**neuroscience interactive**

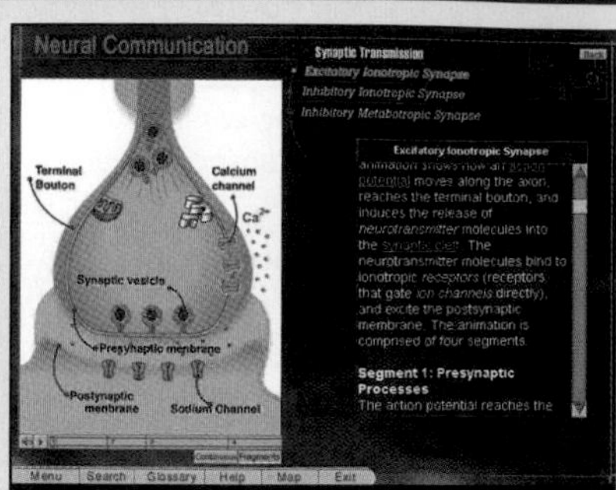


There are many resources available for expanding your learning on-line:

■ **www.worthpublishers.com/kolb/chapter5**

Try some self-tests to reinforce your mastery of the material. Look at some of the news updates reflecting current research on the brain. You'll also be able to link to other sites which will reinforce what you've learned.

■ **www.pdf.org**

Link to this site to learn more about Parkinson's disease and current research to find a cure.

On your CD-ROM you'll be able to quiz yourself on your comprehension of the chapter. The module on Neural Communication also provides important reinforcement of what you've learned. In addition, the Research Methods module includes coverage of some of the technological techniques referred to in this chapter, including the confocal microscope.

quanta of transmitter. After a transmitter has done its work, it is inactivated by such processes as diffusion out of the synaptic cleft, breakdown by enzymes, and uptake of the transmitter or its components into the axon terminal (or sometimes into glial cells).

4. *What are the three major types of neurotransmitters, and in what kinds of synapses do they participate?* There may be as many as 100 neurotransmitters, including small-molecule transmitters, neuropeptides, and gases. Neurons containing these transmitters make a variety of connections with various parts of other neurons, as well as with blood vessels and extracellular fluid. Functionally, neurons can be both excitatory and inhibitory, and they can participate in local circuits or general brain systems. Excitatory synapses, known as type I, are usually located on a dendritic tree, whereas inhibitory synapses, known as type II, are usually located on a cell body.
5. *What are the two general classes of receptors for neurotransmitters?* Most neurotransmitters act on one of two receptors: ionotropic or metabotropic. An ionotropic receptor contains a pore that can be opened or closed to regulate the flow of ions through it, thereby producing voltage changes on the cell membrane. Metabotropic receptors activate second messengers to indirectly produce changes in the function and structure of the cell. Each of the numerous neurotransmitters used in the nervous system is associated with many different ionotropic and metabotropic receptors.
6. *What are some of the systems into which neurons that employ the same principal neurotransmitter are organized, and how are these systems related to behavior?* Systems of neurons that employ the same principal neurotransmitter govern various aspects of behavior. For instance, the skeletal motor system controls movement of the skeletal muscles, whereas the autonomic system controls the body's internal organs. Acetylcholine is the main neurotransmitter in the skeletal motor system, and acetylcholine and epinephrine are the main transmitters in the autonomic system. The central nervous system contains not only widely dispersed glutamate and GABA neurons, but also systems of neurons that have either acetylcholine, norepinephrine, dopamine, or serotonin as their main neurotransmitter. These systems ensure that wide areas of the brain act in concert, and each is associated with its own behavioral functions and disorders.
7. *How do changes in synapses effect learning?* Changes in synapses underlie learning and memory. In habituation, a form of learning in which a response becomes weaker as a result of repeated stimulation, calcium channels become less responsive to an action potential and, consequently, less neurotransmitter is released when an action potential is propagated. In sensitization, a form of learning in which a response becomes stronger as a result of stimulation, changes in potassium channels prolong the duration of the action potential, resulting in an increased influx of calcium ions and, consequently, a greater release of a neurotransmitter. With repeated training, new synapses can develop, and both these kinds of learning can become relatively permanent.
8. *What structural changes in synapses may be related to learning?* In *Aplysia*, in response to repeated sessions of habituation, the number of synapses connecting the sensory neurons and the motor neurons decreases. Similarly, in response to repeated sessions of sensitization, the number of synapses connecting the sensory and the motor neurons increases. Presumably, these changes in synapse number are related to long-term learning. The results of experiments using the mammalian hippocampus show that the number of synapses can change rapidly in cultured preparations. Within about 30 minutes of inducing LTE, new dendritic spines appear, suggesting that new synapses are formed during LTE. Possibly the formation of new synapses can similarly be responsible for new learning.

## KEY TERMS

adrenergic neuron, p. 172
ascending activating system, p. 173
associative learning, p. 183
cholinergic neuron, p. 171
dopamine, p. 166
doubly gated channel, p. 182
gamma-aminobutyric acid (GABA), p. 166
glutamate, p. 166
habituation, p. 177
Hebb synapse, p. 177
ionotropic receptor, p. 167
long-term enhancement (LTE), p. 181
metabotropic receptor, p. 169
neuropeptides, p. 166
nitric oxide (NO), p. 167
second messenger, p. 170
sensitization, p. 179
small-molecule transmitters, p. 165
transmitter-activated receptor, p. 160
transporter, p. 160

## REVIEW QUESTIONS

1. Explain the way in which neurotransmitters are synthesized, stored, released, and broken down.
2. How many kinds of neurotransmitters are there? Describe some problems in proving that a chemical found in a neuron is a neurotransmitter.
3. Describe the differences in function between the two main kinds of transmitter-activated receptors.
4. Describe an example of the organization of a neurotransmitter system.
5. What mechanisms are the same and what mechanisms are different in the various kinds of learning discussed in this chapter?

## FOR FURTHER THOUGHT

Can you speculate about how synaptic systems in the brain have origins that parallel the evolution of species? Why could such a relation be important?

## RECOMMENDED READING

Cooper, J. R., Bloom, F. E., & Roth, R. H. (1991). *The biochemical basis of neuropharmacology.* New York: Oxford University Press. If you would like a readable and up-to-date account of the chemical systems in the brain, this is a good reference. The book describes the various kinds of brain neurotransmitters and the kinds of synapses and chemical systems in which they are found.

CHAPTER

# 6

# How Do Drugs and Hormones Influence Behavior?



Natsuko Utsumi / Liaison
Micrograph: Dr. Dennis Kunkel / Phototake

Japanese and Chinese fishermen are credited with discovering that seaweed can be used as a medicine. They may have observed that flies die after alighting on seaweed washed up on the shore, so they tried rubbing seaweed onto the skin as an insect repellent. It worked. They also found that, when eaten, seaweed kills intestinal worms, so they used extracts from it to treat worms in children. These folk remedies led scientists to analyze the chemical composition of the seaweed *Chondria armata* and identify two chemically similar insecticidal compounds in it: domoic acid and kainic acid. Purified doses of these acids were given to large numbers of children as a treatment for worms, with no reported side effects. Physicians therefore concluded that these substances weren't toxic to humans. Unfortunately, they were wrong.

Domoic acid

Kainic acid

On November 22, 1987, two people in Moncton, New Brunswick, Canada, were hospitalized after suffering from gastroenteritis and mental confusion. Soon more reports of the illness came from Quebec, and, by December 9, five people had died. In all, more than 200 cases of this mysterious disorder were reported. The severity of symptoms varied greatly, but the worst cases included marked confusion and memory loss. For some of those who survived, the memory impairments were permanent. Autopsies revealed extensive cell loss in the hippocampus, amygdala, and surrounding cortex and in the thalamus (Hynie & Todd, 1990).

The only experience common to the victims was to have eaten mussels. To find out whether the mussels were responsible, scientists injected mussel extracts into mice. Soon after, the mice started scratching behind one ear and then convulsed and died. Apparently, the mussels did contain a toxin, but the curious scratching behavior indicated that the toxin was unlike any other known shellfish poison. Chemical analysis of the mussels showed that they contained large amounts of domoic acid. Investigators were surprised. How did the mussels become contaminated with domoic acid, and why was it suddenly acting like a poison in humans?

To answer the first question, the investigators traced the mussels. They found that they came from two Prince Edward Island cultured-mussel farms. Cultured-mussel farming began in 1975 and by the 1980s had grown into a large, successful industry, producing as much as 3.2 million pounds of mussels annually. Mussel farmers release mussel sperm and eggs into the water, where the resulting zygotes attach themselves to long ropes suspended there. The mussels feed by siphoning from 2 to 6 liters of water per hour to extract small sea organisms called phytoplankton. More than 90 percent of the phytoplankton that the Prince Edward Island mussels consumed were single-cell diatoms called *Nitzschia pungens,* shown in Figure 6-1. When analyzed, the diatoms were found to contain domoic acid. Because there had been no evidence of domoic acid in diatoms before 1987, a search for the origins of the contamination began. Apparently, a dry climate in 1987 produced a buildup of domoic acid–containing seaweed in the streams and along the shoreline. By feeding on seaweed, the diatoms had accumulated large quantities of domoic acid, which was then passed on to the mussels as they fed on the diatoms.

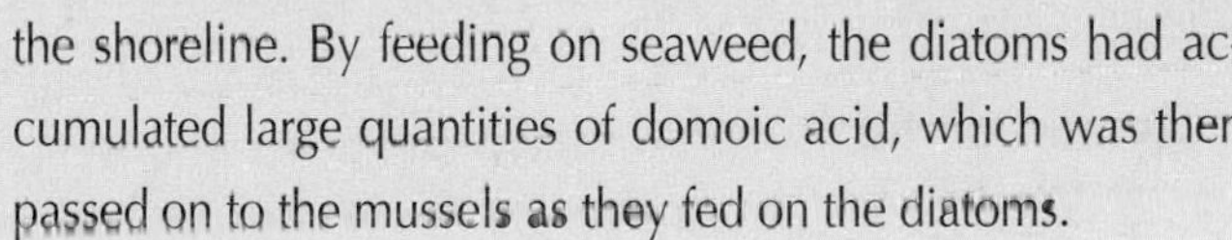

But the discovery that domoic acid was the toxic agent in this episode only partly solved the mystery with which investigators were confronted. Remember that domoic acid had been thought to be harmless. It had been widely used to rid children of worms. How had it now

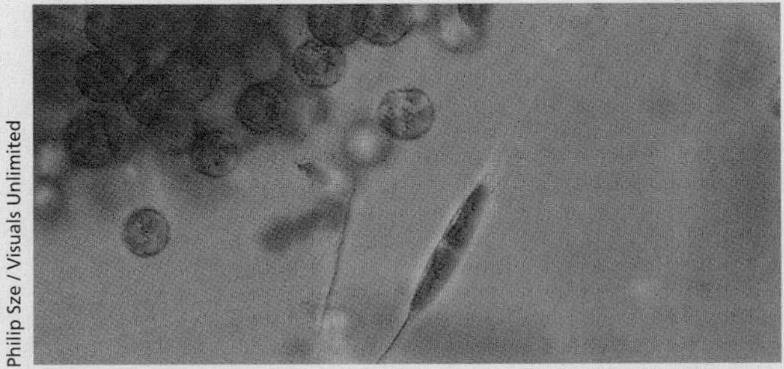
Philip Sze / Visuals Unlimited

**Figure 6-1**
Diatoms have a variety of shapes and sizes. They are ubiquitous in the ocean and common in fresh water, where they are frequently present in great numbers. *Nitzschia pungens*, shown here, is a diatom that can accumulate domoic acid.

resulted in sickness, brain damage, and death? And why were only some people affected? Certainly more than 200 people had eaten the contaminated mussels. These two questions will be answered in the following sections, where domoic acid poisoning is used to illustrate some of the principles of drug action. Many of those principles also apply to the action of hormones, which are drugs that we make in our own bodies. Hormones are the topic of the last section of this chapter. Before we begin to tell how drugs produce their effects on the brain, we must make an admission. The sheer number of neurotransmitters, receptors, and possible sites of drug action is astounding. The science of drug research has made important advances, but we do not know everything there is to know about any drug.

## PRINCIPLES OF DRUG ACTION

A **drug** is a chemical compound that is administered to bring about some desired change in the body. Drugs are usually used to diagnose, treat, or prevent illness, to relieve pain and suffering, or to improve some adverse physiological condition. The kinds of drugs that we will be concerned with in this chapter are **psychoactive drugs**—those substances that act to alter mood, thought, or behavior and that are used to manage neuropsychological illness. Many psychoactive drugs are also *abused substances.* That is, they are taken for nonmedical reasons to the point at which they impair the user's functioning and may produce addiction. Some psychoactive drugs can also act as toxins, producing sickness, brain damage, or death.

In this chapter you will learn that the effects of many drugs depend on how they are taken, in what quantities, and under what circumstances. We begin by looking at the major ways that psychoactive drugs are administered, what routes they take to reach the central nervous system, and how they are eliminated from the body. We then consider how drugs act on neurons and why different people may respond differently to the same dose of a drug.

### How Psychoactive Drugs Get into the Nervous System

To be effective, a psychoactive drug has to reach its nervous system target. The way that a drug enters and passes through the body to reach that target is called its *route of administration.* Many drugs are administered orally because it is a natural and safe way to consume a substance. Drugs can also be inhaled into the lungs, administered through rectal suppositories, absorbed from patches applied to the skin, or injected into the bloodstream, into a muscle, or even into the brain. Figure 6-2 illustrates the various routes of drug administration.

These different routes pose different barriers between the drug and its target. Taking a drug by mouth is easy and convenient, but not all drugs can pass the barriers of the digestive-tract contents and walls. Generally, there are fewer barriers between a drug and its target if the drug is inhaled rather than swallowed, and fewer still if it is injected into the blood. The fewest obstacles are encountered if a psychoactive drug is injected directly into the brain. Figure 6-2 also summarizes the characteristics of drugs that allow them to pass through various barriers to reach their targets.

Let us look more closely at the barriers that an orally taken drug must pass to get to the brain. To reach the bloodstream, an ingested drug must first be absorbed through the lining of the stomach or small intestine. If the drug is liquid, it is absorbed more readily. Drugs taken in solid form are not absorbed unless they can be dissolved by the stomach's gastric juices. In either form, liquid or solid, absorption is

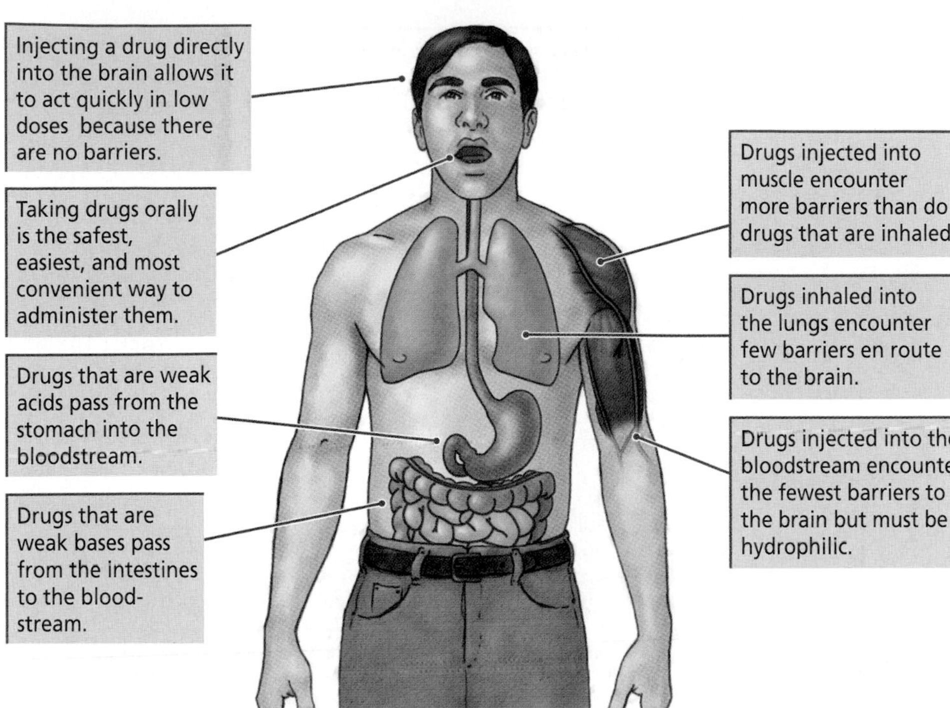

Injecting a drug directly into the brain allows it to act quickly in low doses because there are no barriers.
Taking drugs orally is the safest, easiest, and most convenient way to administer them.
Drugs that are weak acids pass from the stomach into the bloodstream.
Drugs that are weak bases pass from the intestines to the bloodstream.
Drugs injected into muscle encounter more barriers than do drugs that are inhaled.
Drugs inhaled into the lungs encounter few barriers en route to the brain.
Drugs injected into the bloodstream encounter the fewest barriers to the brain but must be hydrophilic.

**Figure 6-2**

There are a number of routes of administration of drugs. Injecting drugs onto their targets in the brain is not practical. Taking drugs by mouth is easy and convenient, but the drugs may not pass from the gut into the bloodstream. Drugs are absorbed more slowly when injected into muscles than when inhaled and are absorbed more slowly when inhaled than when injected into the bloodstream.

affected by the physical and chemical properties of the drug, as well as by the presence of other stomach or intestinal contents. In general, if a drug is a weak acid, such as alcohol, it is readily absorbed across the stomach lining. If it is a weak base, it cannot be absorbed until it passes through the stomach and into the intestine—a process that may destroy it.

After it has been absorbed by the stomach or intestine, the drug must next enter the bloodstream. This part of the journey requires additional properties. Because blood has a high water concentration, a drug must be hydrophilic to be carried in the blood. A hydrophobic substance will be blocked from entering the bloodstream. If it makes its way into the blood, a drug is then diluted by the approximately 6 liters of blood that circulate through an adult person's body.

To reach its target, a drug must also travel from the blood into the extracellular fluid, which requires that molecules of the drug be small enough to pass through the pores of capillaries, the tiny vessels that carry blood to the body's cells. And, even if the drug makes this passage, it may encounter still other obstacles. For one thing, the extracellular fluid's roughly 35 liters of water dilute it even further. For another, the drug is at risk of being modified or destroyed by various metabolic processes taking place in cells.

At the brain, the passage of drugs across capillaries is much more difficult because of the **blood–brain barrier.** It is not that the brain is deficient in capillaries. The brain has a rich capillary network. In fact, none of its neurons is farther than about 50 micrometers (μm, one-millionth of a meter) away from a capillary. But capillaries to the brain are impermeable to many substances, which is what creates the blood–brain barrier.

Figure 6-3 shows the structure of brain capillaries and why they are impermeable to many substances. As you can see, like all capillaries, brain capillaries are composed of a single layer of **endothelial cells.** In most parts of the body, the walls of capillary endothelial cells are not fused together, so substances can pass through the clefts between the cells. In contrast, in the brain (at least in most parts of it), endothelial cell walls are fused to form **tight junctions,** so molecules of most substances cannot squeeze between them.

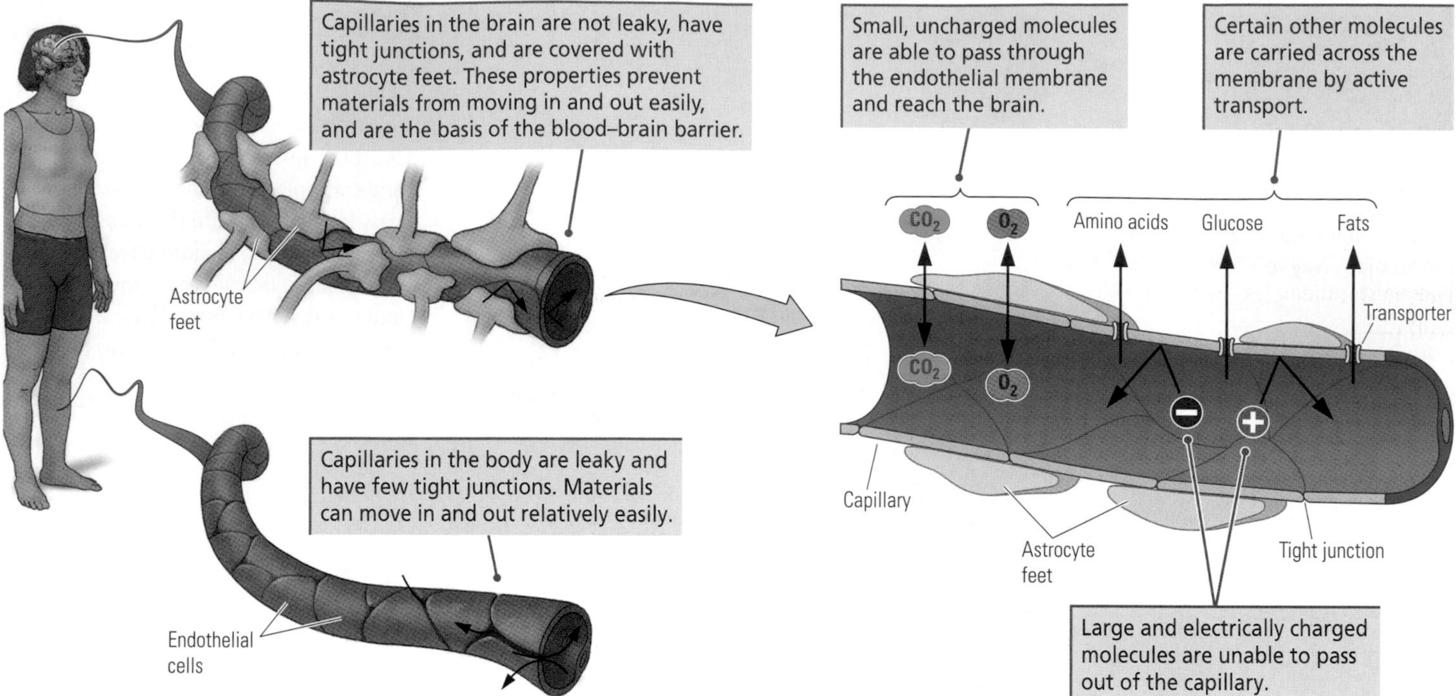

Capillaries in the brain are not leaky, have tight junctions, and are covered with astrocyte feet. These properties prevent materials from moving in and out easily, and are the basis of the blood–brain barrier.
Astrocyte feet
Capillaries in the body are leaky and have few tight junctions. Materials can move in and out relatively easily.
Endothelial cells
Small, uncharged molecules are able to pass through the endothelial membrane and reach the brain.
Certain other molecules are carried across the membrane by active transport.
$CO_2$
$O_2$
Amino acids
Glucose
Fats
Transporter
Capillary
Astrocyte feet
Tight junction
Large and electrically charged molecules are unable to pass out of the capillary.

**Figure 6-3**

Capillaries in most of the body allow for the passage of substances between capillary cell walls, but those in the brain have tight junctions and are lined by astrocytes. Some substances, such as oxygen and carbon dioxide, perfuse through brain capillary walls, whereas other substances, such as amino acids, glucose, and fats, must be transported across the walls. Most other substances, especially large charged molecules, are unable to cross the blood–brain barrier.

Figure 6-3 also shows that the endothelial cells of a brain capillary are surrounded by the end feet of astrocyte glial cells, which are attached to the capillary wall and cover about 80 percent of it. The glial end feet play only minor roles in the blood–brain barrier. The glial cells provide a route for the exchange of food and waste between capillaries and the brain's extracellular fluid and from there to other cells. They may also play a role in maintaining the tight junctions between endothelial cells and in making capillaries dilate to increase blood flow to areas of the brain in which neurons are very active.

You may wonder why endothelial cells form tight junctions only in *most* parts of the brain, not in *all* of it. The cells of capillary walls in a few brain regions lack tight junctions, and so these regions, shown in Figure 6-4, lack a blood–brain barrier. One is the **pituitary** of the hypothalamus, which allows the passage of hormones into the pituitary gland. Another is the **area postrema** of the lower brainstem. The absence of a blood–brain barrier here allows toxic substances in the blood to trigger a vomiting response. The **pineal gland** also lacks a blood–brain barrier, enabling hormones to reach it and modulate the day–night cycles that this structure controls.

The rest of the brain needs certain substances to carry out its work, and these substances must be able to cross the blood–brain barrier. For instance, oxygen, glucose, and amino acids (the building blocks of proteins) must routinely travel from the blood to brain cells, just as carbon dioxide and other waste products must routinely be excreted from brain cells into the blood. There are two ways that molecules of these substances cross the blood–brain barrier. First, small molecules such as oxygen and carbon dioxide, which are not ionized and so are fat soluble, can pass right through the endothelial membrane. Second, molecules of glucose, amino acids, and other food components can be carried across the membrane by **active-transport systems.** An active-transport system is a pump, such as the sodium/potassium pump, that is specialized for the transport of a particular substance. When a substance has passed from the capillaries into the brain's extracellular fluid, it can move readily into neurons and glia.

But the blood–brain barrier halts more substances than it lets through. In most cases, the barrier is beneficial. For example, because the electrical activity of neurons depends on certain extracellular concentrations of ions, it is important that ionic substances not cross the blood–brain barrier and upset the brain's electrical activity. It is also important that neurochemicals from the rest of the body not pass into the brain and disrupt the communication between neurons. In addition, the blood–brain barrier protects the brain from many circulating hormones and from various toxic and infectious substances. Injury or disease can sometimes rupture the blood–brain barrier, thereby letting pathogens through. For the most part, however, the brain is very well protected from substances potentially harmful to its functioning.

The blood–brain barrier has special relevance for understanding drug actions on the nervous system. A drug can reach the brain only if its molecules are small and not ionized, enabling them to pass through endothelial cell membranes, or if the drug has a chemical structure that allows it to be carried across the membrane by an active-transport system. Because very few drugs are small or have the correct chemical structure, very few can gain access to the central nervous system. For example, the neurotransmitter dopamine, although a small molecule, is unable to cross the blood–brain barrier because of its chemical composition. Therefore it cannot be used as a drug for Parkinson's disease, even though, once in the brain, it could be very effective. In contrast, L-dopa, the precursor from which dopamine is made, has a slightly different chemical makeup, crosses the blood–brain barrier through an active-transport system, and so can be used to treat Parkinson's disease. Because the blood–brain barrier works so well, it is extremely difficult to find new drugs to use as treatments for brain diseases.

To summarize, drugs that can make the entire trip from the mouth to the brain have some special chemical properties. The most effective ones are small in size, weak acids, water and fat soluble, potent in small amounts, and not easily degraded. **Domoic acid** is such a drug. Because it is a weak acid, it is easily absorbed through the stomach. It is potent in small amounts, so it survives dilution in the bloodstream and in the extracellular fluid. Finally, it is a small molecule that is similar in structure to those of food substances that are transported across the blood–brain barrier and so it, too, is transported.

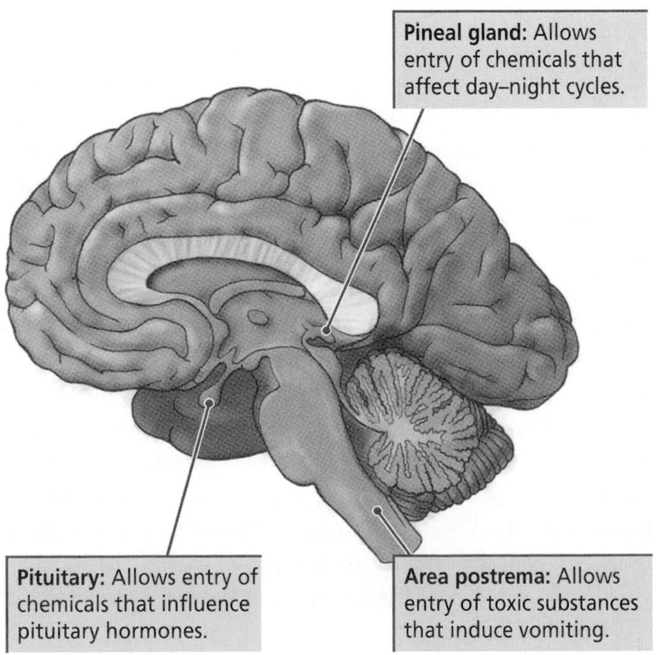
**Pineal gland:** Allows entry of chemicals that affect day–night cycles.
**Pituitary:** Allows entry of chemicals that influence pituitary hormones.
**Area postrema:** Allows entry of toxic substances that induce vomiting.

**Figure 6-4**

The following three sites in the brain have no blood-brain barrier: the medial eminence (pituitary), which is a target for many blood-borne hormones, the pineal gland, which is a target for hormones that affect behavioral rhythms, and the area postrema, which initiates vomiting in response to noxious substances.

Considering the many obstacles that psychoactive drugs encounter on their journey from the mouth to the brain, it is clear why inhaling a drug or injecting it into the bloodstream has advantages. These alternative routes of administration bypass the obstacle of the stomach. In fact, with each obstacle eliminated on the route to the brain, the dosage of a drug can be reduced by a factor of 10 without reducing the effects of the drug. For example, 1 milligram (1000 micrograms) of amphetamine, a psychomotor stimulant, produces a noticeable behavioral change when ingested orally. However, if inhaled into the lungs or injected into the blood, thereby circumventing the stomach, 100 micrograms (1000 micrograms ÷ 10) of the drug produces the same results. Similarly, if amphetamine is injected into the cerebrospinal fluid, thus bypassing both the stomach *and* the blood, 10 micrograms is enough to produce an identical outcome, as is 1 microgram if dilution in the cerebrospinal fluid is skirted also and the drug is injected directly onto target neurons. These numbers are well known to users of illicit drugs. Drugs that can be inhaled or injected intravenously are much cheaper to use because the doses required are less than those needed for drugs taken by mouth.

After a drug has been administered, the body soon begins to remove it. Drugs are metabolized throughout the body, including in the kidneys, liver, and bile. They are excreted in urine, feces, sweat, breast milk, and exhaled air. Drugs that are developed for therapeutic purposes are usually designed not only to increase their chances of reaching their targets but also to enhance their survival in the body.

There are some substances that, if ingested, the body has trouble removing. Such substances are potentially dangerous because, if large doses of them are taken, they can build up in the body and become poisonous. For instance, certain metals, such as mercury, are not easily eliminated from the body; when they accumulate there, they can produce severe neurological conditions. Interestingly, when researchers studied the medical histories of patients with severe domoic acid poisoning, they found that all the patients had preexisting kidney problems. This finding suggests that the kidneys play an important role in eliminating domoic acid. Because these patients had kidneys that did not function normally, domoic acid reached toxic levels in their bodies.

## Individual Differences in Response to Drugs

There are vast individual differences in responses to drugs due to differences in age, sex, body size, and other factors that affect sensitivity to a particular substance. For instance, large people are generally less sensitive to a drug than smaller people are, because of greater dilution of the drug in their body fluids. Females are about twice as sensitive to drugs as males. This difference is due in part to their relatively smaller body size, but it is also due to hormonal differences between females and males. Old people may be twice as sensitive to drugs as young people are. The elderly often have less-effective barriers to drug absorption as well as less-effective processes for metabolizing and eliminating drugs from their bodies.

Individual differences in sensitivity to domoic acid were observed among people who ate toxic mussels. Only 1 in 1000 became ill, and only some of those who were ill suffered severe memory impairments, with even fewer dying. The three patients with memory impairments were men age 69, 71, and 84. All of those who died were men older than 68. Apparently, domoic acid is either more readily absorbed or more poorly excreted, or both, in older men. Subsequent studies of mice confirmed the greater sensitivity of older animals to the toxic effects of domoic acid.

## Drugs and Synapses

Drugs have their effects by initiating chemical reactions in the body or by influencing the body's ongoing chemical activities. As you know, many chemical reactions take place in the nervous system's neurons, especially at synapses. Most drugs that have psychoactive effects do so by influencing these chemical reactions at synapses. So, to understand how drugs work, we must explore the ways in which they modify synaptic actions.

Figure 6-5 summarizes the seven major steps in neurotransmission at a synapse. Synthesis of the neurotransmitter can take place in the cell body, the axon, or the terminal. The neurotransmitter is then stored in storage granules or in vesicles until it is released from the terminal's presynaptic membrane. The amount of transmitter released into the synapse is regulated in relation to previous experience. When released, the transmitter acts on a receptor embedded in the postsynaptic membrane. It is then either destroyed or taken back up into the terminal from which it came for reuse. The synapse also has mechanisms for degrading excess neurotransmitter and removing unneeded by-products from the synapse.

Link to your CD and find the area on synaptic transmission in the Neural Communication module. Review the processes of excitatory synaptic function and consider drugs that act as agonists, such as those that affect acetylcholine.

Each of these steps in neurotransmission includes a chemical reaction that a drug can potentially influence in one of two ways: either by increasing the effectiveness of neurotransmission or by diminishing it. Drugs that increase the effectiveness of neurotransmission are called **agonists,** whereas those that decrease its effectiveness are called **antagonists.** Agonists and antagonists can work in a variety of ways, but their end results are always the same. For example, drugs that stimulate the release of the neuro-

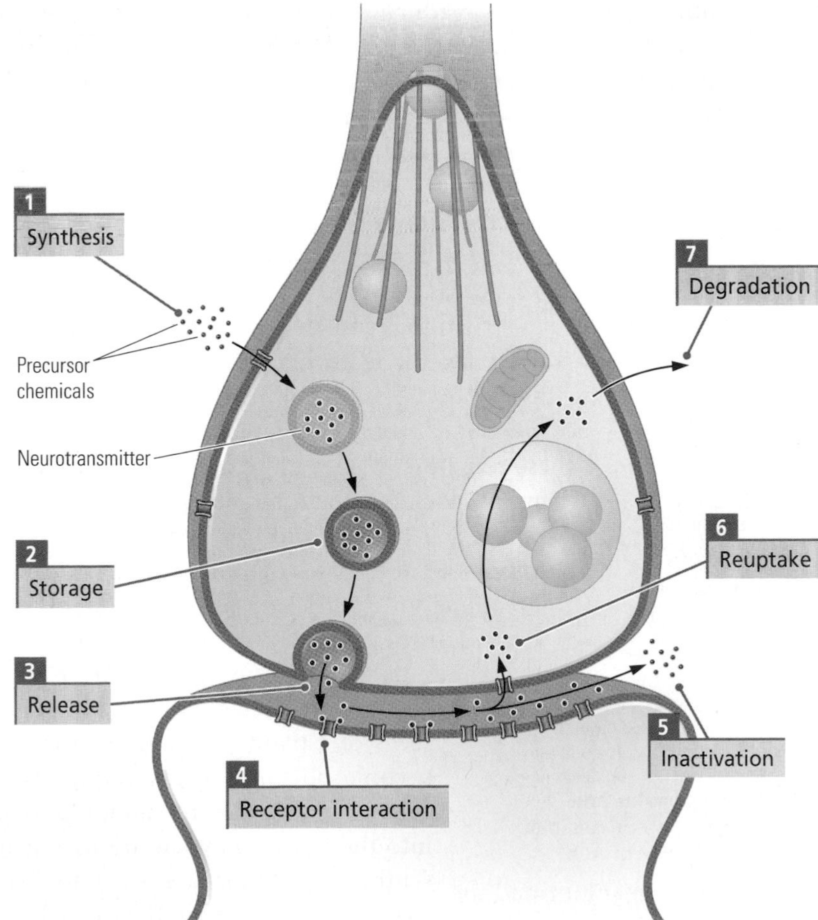


**Figure 6-5**

Seven major processes that a drug can modify to influence synaptic transmission. In principle, a drug can enhance or block a chemical process at each site, resulting in reduced or enhanced synaptic transmission.

transmitter dopamine, that block the reuptake of this transmitter, or that block its inactivation are all considered dopamine agonists because they all increase the amount of dopamine available in the synapse. Conversely, drugs that block the synthesis of dopamine or its release from the presynaptic membrane or that block dopamine receptors or speed up its inactivation are all considered dopamine antagonists because they all decrease the biochemical effect of this transmitter in the synapse.

## An Acetylcholine Synapse: Examples of Drug Action

Using the acetylcholine synapse between motor neurons and muscles as an example, Figure 6-6 shows how several drugs and toxins affect neurotransmission. Some of these drugs will be new to you, but you have probably heard of others. Knowing their effects at the synapse will allow you to understand the behavioral effects that they produce.

Figure 6-6 shows two toxins that influence the release of acetylcholine from the axon terminal: black widow spider venom and botulin toxin. **Black widow spider venom** is an agonist because it promotes the release of acetylcholine—an excess amount of it. For the insects that are the prey of black widow spiders, the excitation caused by this excess acetylcholine at neuromuscular synapses is sufficient to paralyze and kill them. A black widow spider bite does not contain enough toxin to similarly affect a human. **Botulin toxin** is the poisonous agent in tainted foods, such as canned goods that have been improperly processed. It acts as an antagonist because it blocks the release of acetylcholine. The effects of botulin toxin can last from weeks to months. A severe case of poisoning from it can result in paralysis of both movement and breathing and so cause death. It might surprise you to know that, despite being a poison, botulin toxin has medical uses. If injected into a muscle, it can selectively paralyze that muscle. This selective action makes it useful in blocking excessive and enduring muscular twitches or contractions. It is also used cosmetically to paralyze facial muscles that cause facial wrinkling.

Figure 6-6 also shows two drugs that act on receptors for acetylcholine: nicotine and curare. **Nicotine,** a chemical contained in cigarette smoke, acts as an agonist to stimulate cholinergic receptors. Its molecular structure is similar enough to that of acetylcholine to allow it to fit into the receptors' binding sites. **Curare** acts as an antagonist by occupying cholinergic receptors and so preventing acetylcholine from binding to them. When curare binds to these receptors, it does not cause them to function; instead, it simply blocks them. After being introduced into the body, curare acts quickly, and it is cleared from the body in a few minutes. Large doses of it, however, arrest movement and breathing for a sufficient period of time to result in death. Early European explorers of South America discovered that the Indians along the Amazon River killed small animals by using arrows coated with curare prepared from the seeds of a plant. The hunters themselves did not become poisoned when eating the animals, because ingested curare cannot pass from the gut into the body. Many curare-like drugs have been synthesized. Some are used to briefly paralyze large animals so that they can be examined or

**Figure 6-6**

This example of how drugs affect the cholinergic synapse shows how agonists increase the effect of acetylcholine on the postsynaptic receptor and how antagonists decrease its effect. Note the many different ways that drugs affect acetylcholine transmission: by acting on synthesis, by affecting release, by affecting binding to the postsynaptic receptor, and by affecting inactivation.

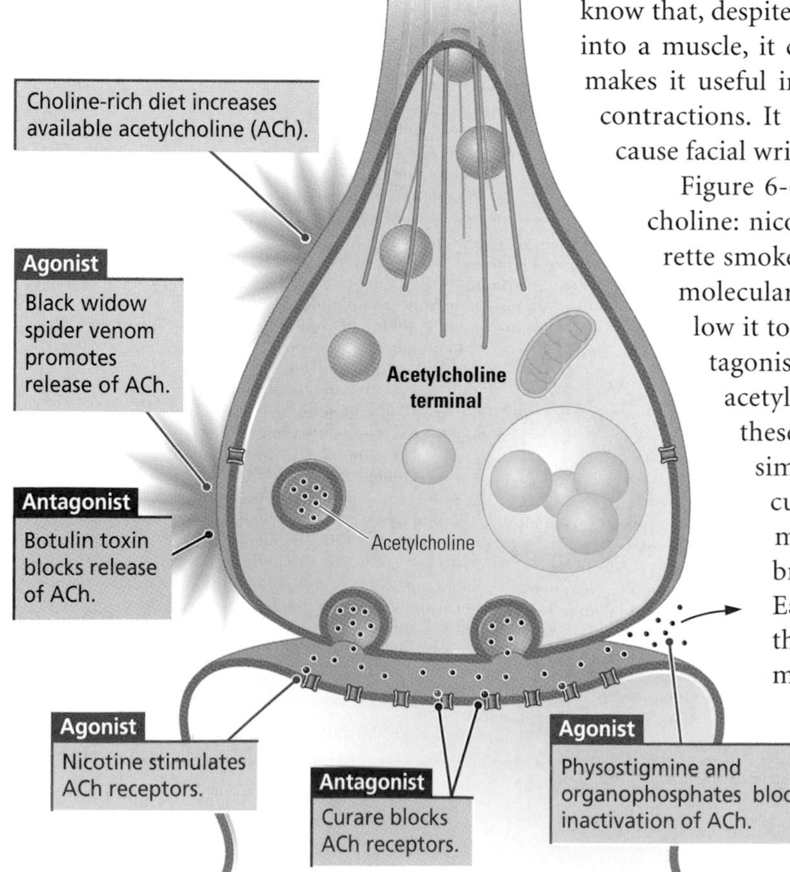
Choline-rich diet increases available acetylcholine (ACh).
Agonist
Black widow spider venom promotes release of ACh.
Acetylcholine terminal
Antagonist
Botulin toxin blocks release of ACh.
Acetylcholine
Agonist
Nicotine stimulates ACh receptors.
Antagonist
Curare blocks ACh receptors.
Agonist
Physostigmine and organophosphates block inactivation of ACh.

tagged for identification. You have probably seen this use of these drugs in wildlife programs on television. Skeletal muscles are more sensitive to curare-like drugs than are respiratory muscles, so an appropriate dose will paralyze an animal's movement but still allow it to breathe.

A fifth drug action shown in Figure 6-6 is that of **physostigmine,** a drug that inhibits cholinesterase, which is the enzyme that breaks down acetylcholine. Physostigmine therefore acts as an agonist to increase the amount of acetylcholine available in the synapse. Physostigmine is obtained from an African bean and was used as a poison by native peoples in Africa. Large doses of physostigmine can be toxic because they produce excessive excitation of the neuromuscular synapse and so disrupt movement and breathing. In small doses, however, physostigmine is used to treat myasthenia gravis, a condition of muscular weakness in which muscle receptors are less than normally responsive to acetylcholine. The action of physostigmine is short lived, lasting only a few minutes or, at most, a half hour. But another class of compounds called **organophosphates** bind irreversibly to acetylcholinesterase and consequently are extremely toxic. Many insecticides are organophosphates. Organophosphates are also used in chemical warfare.

Many hundreds of other drugs can act on acetylcholine neuromuscular synapses, and thousands of additional substances can act on other kinds of synapses. A few that are neurotoxins are listed in Table 6-1. Despite their varied effects, all these substances act as either agonists or antagonists. If you understand the opposing actions of agonists and antagonists, you will also understand how some drugs can be used as antidotes for poisoning by other drugs.

If a drug or toxin that is ingested affects neuromuscular synapses, will it also affect acetylcholine synapses in the brain? That depends on whether the substance can cross the blood–brain barrier. Some of the drugs that act on acetylcholine synapses at the muscles can also act on acetylcholine synapses in the brain. For example, physostigmine and nicotine can readily pass the blood–brain barrier and affect the brain, whereas curare cannot. Thus, whether a cholinergic agonist or antagonist has psychoactive action depends on the size and structure of its molecules, which determine whether that substance can manage to reach the brain.

**Table 6-1 Some Neurotoxins, Their Sources, and Their Actions**

| Substance | Origin | Action |
|---|---|---|
| Tetrodotoxin | Puffer fish | Blocks membrane permeability to $Na^+$ ions |
| Magnesium | Natural element | Blocks $Ca^{2+}$ channels |
| Reserpine | Tree | Destroys storage granules |
| Colchicine | Crocus plant | Blocks microtubules |
| Caffeine | Coffee bean | Blocks adenosine receptors, blocks $Ca^{2+}$ channels |
| Spider venom | Black widow spider | Stimulates ACh release |
| Botulin toxin | Food poisoning | Blocks ACh release |
| Curare | Plant berry | Blocks ACh receptors |
| Rabies virus | Infected animal | Blocks ACh receptors |
| Ibotenic acid | Mushroom | Similar to domoic acid |
| Strychnine | Plant | Blocks glycine |
| Apamin | Bees and wasps | Blocks $Ca^{2+}$ channels |

## In Review

Psychoactive drugs are substances that produce changes in behavior by acting on the nervous system. These drugs encounter various barriers between their entry into the body and their action at a central nervous system target. One of the most important of these obstacles is the blood–brain barrier, which generally allows only substances needed for nourishing the brain to pass from the capillaries into the central nervous system. Most drugs that have psychoactive effects do so by crossing the blood–brain barrier and influencing chemical reactions at brain synapses. Drugs that influence communication between neurons do so by acting either as agonists or as antagonists to neurotransmission—that is, by either increasing or decreasing the effectiveness of neurotransmission. There are, however, great individual differences in people's responses to drugs due to differences in age, sex, body size, and other factors that affect sensitivity to a particular substance.

## THE CLASSIFICATION OF PSYCHOACTIVE DRUGS

It is difficult to devise a classification system for the many thousands of psychoactive drugs. Classifications based on a drug's chemical structure have not been very successful, because drugs having similar structures can have quite different effects, whereas drugs having different structures can have very similar effects. Classification schemes based on receptors in the brain also have been problematic, because a single drug can act on many different receptors. The same problem arises with classification systems based on the neurotransmitter that a drug affects, because many drugs act on many different transmitters. The classification used in this book, summarized in Table 6-2, is based on the most pronounced psychoactive effect that a drug produces. That classification divides drugs into seven classes, with each class containing from a few to many thousands of different chemicals in its subcategories.

Visit the Web site at **www.worthpublishers.com/kolb/chapter6** to learn more about the variety of psychoactive drugs.

**Table 6-2 Classification of Psychoactive Drugs**

I. Sedative hypnotics and antianxiety agents
   - Barbiturates (anesthetic agents), alcohol
   - Benzodiazepines: diazepam (Valium)

II. Antipsychotic agents
   - Phenothiazines: chlorpromazine
   - Butyrophenones: haloperidol

III. Antidepressants
   - Monoamine oxydase (MAO) inhibitors
   - Tricyclic antidepressants: imipramine (Tofranil)
   - Atypical antidepressants: fluoxetine (Prozac)

IV. Mood stabilizers
   - Lithium

V. Narcotic analgesics
   - Morphine, codeine, heroin

VI. Psychomotor stimulants
   - Cocaine, amphetamine, caffeine, nicotine

VII. Psychedelics and hallucinogens
   - Anticholinergics: atropine
   - Noradrenergics: mescaline
   - Serotonergics: LSD (lysergic acid diethylamide), psilocybin
   - Tetrahydrocannabinol: marijuana

Drugs that are used to treat neuropsychological illnesses are listed again in Table 6-3, along with the dates that they were discovered and the names of their discoverers. You may be surprised to know that their therapeutic actions were originally discovered by accident. Subsequently, scientists and pharmaceutical companies developed many forms of each drug in an effort to increase its effectiveness and reduce its side effects. At the same time, experimental researchers attempted to explain each drug's action on the nervous system. Those drug actions are what we examine here, as we consider some of the classes of drugs given in Table 6-2.

**Table 6-3 Drugs Used for the Treatment of Mental Illness**

| Illness | Drug class | Representative drug | Common trade name | Discoverer |
|---|---|---|---|---|
| Schizophrenia | Phenothiazines | Chlorpromazine | Largactile<br>Thorazine | Jean Delay and Pierre Deniker (France), 1952 |
| | Butyrophenone | Haloperidol | Haldol | Paul Janssen (Belgium), 1957 |
| Depression | Monoamine oxidase (MAO) inhibitors | Iproniazid | Marsilid | Nathan S. Kline and J. C. Saunders (United States), 1956 |
| | Tricyclic antidepressants | Imipramine | Tofranil | Roland Kuhn (Switzerland), 1957 |
| | Selective serotonin reuptake inhibitors | Fluoxetine | Prozac | Eli Lilly Company, 1986 |
| Bipolar disorder | | Lithium (metallic element) | | John Cade (Australia), 1949 |
| Anxiety disorders | Benzodiazepines | Chlordiazepoxide | Librium<br>Valium | Leo Sternbach (Poland), 1940 |
| | | Meprobamate | Miltown<br>Equanil | Frank Berger and William Bradley (Czechoslovakia), 1946 |

## Sedative Hypnotics and Antianxiety Agents

The effects of sedative hypnotics and antianxiety agents differ, depending on their dose. At low doses they reduce anxiety, at medium doses they sedate, and at high doses they produce anesthesia or coma. At very high doses they can kill (Figure 6-7).

The most common members of this diverse group of drugs are alcohol, barbiturates, and benzodiazepines. Alcohol is well known to most people because it is so widely consumed. Its potentially devastating effects on fetuses are explored in "Fetal Alcohol Syndrome" on page 202. **Barbiturates** are a type of drug sometimes prescribed as a sleeping medication, but they are now mainly used to induce anesthesia before surgery. **Benzodiazepines** are also known as **minor tranquilizers** or **antianxiety agents.** An example is the widely prescribed drug Valium. Benzodiazepines are often given to people who are having trouble coping with some major life stress, such as a traumatic accident or a death in the family. Whereas both alcohol and barbiturates can produce sleep, anesthesia, and coma at doses only slightly higher than those that produce sedation, the dose of benzodiazepines that produces sleep and anesthesia is substantially higher than that which is needed to relieve anxiety.

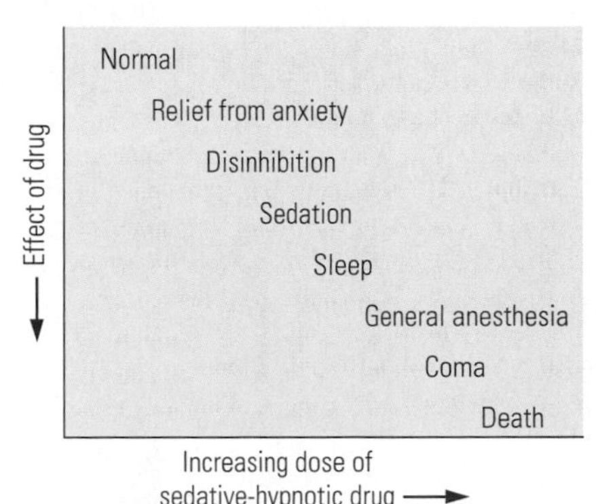


**Figure 6-7** This continuum of behavioral sedation shows how increasing doses of sedative-hypnotic drugs affect behavior, from low doses reducing anxiety to very high doses resulting in death.

A characteristic feature of sedative hypnotics is that they cause weaker and weaker responses in the user who takes repeated doses. A larger dose is then required to maintain the drug's initial effect. This lessening of response to a drug over time is called **tolerance. Cross-tolerance** develops when the tolerance developed for one drug is carried over to a different drug. Cross-tolerance suggests that the two drugs are similar in their actions on the nervous system. Alcohol, barbiturates, and benzodiazepines show cross-tolerance, suggesting that they affect a common nervous system target. This common

**Antianxiety agent.** A type of drug that reduces anxiety; benzodiazepines and sedative-hypnotic agents are of this type.

**Cross-tolerance.** A form of tolerance in which the response to a novel drug is reduced because of tolerance developed in response to a related drug.

Focus on Disorders

## Fetal Alcohol Syndrome

The expression *fetal alcohol syndrome* (FAS) was coined in 1973 to describe a pattern of physical malformation and mental retardation observed in children born of alcoholic mothers. Children with FAS may have abnormal facial features, such as unusually wide spacing between the eyes. They also have a range of brain abnormalities, from small brains with abnormal gyri to abnormal clusters of cells and misaligned cells in the cortex. Related to these brain abnormalities are certain behavioral symptoms that FAS children tend to have in common. They display varying degrees of learning disability and lowered intelligence test scores, as well as hyperactivity and other social problems.

Identification of FAS stimulated widespread interest in the effects of alcohol consumption by pregnant women. The offspring of approximately 6 percent of alcoholic mothers suffer from pronounced FAS. The incidence of it in different geographic regions varies widely, depending largely on the pattern and degree of alcohol abuse in those locations. In major cities, the incidence of FAS is about 1 in 700 births. Its incidence increases to as many as 1 in 8 births on one Native American reservation in Canada.

FAS is not an all-or-none syndrome. Alcohol-induced abnormalities can vary from hardly noticeable physical and psychological effects to the complete FAS syndrome. The severity of effects is thought to be related to when, how much, and how frequently alcohol is consumed. Apparently, the effects are worse if alcohol consumption occurs in the first 3 months of pregnancy, which, unfortunately, may be a time when many women do not yet realize that they are pregnant. Severe FAS is also more likely to coincide with binge drinking, which produces high blood-alcohol levels. Other factors related to a more severe outcome are poor nutritional health of the mother and the mother's use of other drugs, including the nicotine in cigarettes.

A major question raised by FAS is how much alcohol is too much to drink during pregnancy. The answer to this question is complex, because the effects of alcohol on a fetus depend on so many factors. To be completely safe, it is best not to drink at all in the months preceding pregnancy and during it. This conclusion is supported by findings that as little as one drink of alcohol per day during pregnancy can lead to a decrease in intelligence test scores of children.

Fetal alcohol syndrome in both its full-blown and milder forms has important lessons for us. Alcohol is a widely used drug. When taken in moderation, it is thought to have some health benefits; yet it does pose risks, although those risks are completely avoidable if alcohol is used appropriately. A major problem is that women who are most at risk for bearing FAS babies are poor and not well educated, with alcohol-consumption problems that predate pregnancy and little access to prenatal care. It is often difficult to inform these women about the dangers that alcohol poses to a fetus and to encourage them to abstain from drinking while they are pregnant.

George Steinmetz

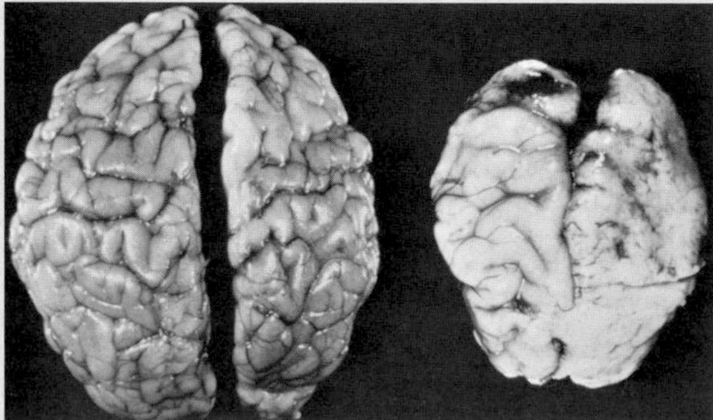

University of Washington, School of Medicine

Children who suffer from fetal alcohol syndrome do not merely *look* abnormal; their brains are underdeveloped and many are severely retarded. The brain of a child who suffered from fetal alcohol syndrome (*lower right*) lacks the convolutions characteristic of the brain of a normal child (*lower left*).

target is now known to be the receptor sites for the major inhibitory neurotransmitter GABA. Neurons that contain GABA are widely distributed in the nervous system and function to inhibit the activity of other neurons.

One of the receptors affected by GABA is the **$GABA_A$** receptor. As illustrated in Figure 6-8, this receptor contains a chloride channel, and excitation of the receptor produces an influx of $Cl^-$ ions. Remember that an influx of $Cl^-$ ions increases the concentration of negative charges on the inside of the cell membrane, depolarizing it and making it less likely to propagate an action potential. The inhibitory effect of GABA, therefore, is to decrease a neuron's rate of firing.

The $GABA_A$ receptor is a complex molecule that has not only a binding site for GABA but also two other binding sites. One of these two binding sites accepts alcohol and barbiturates (the sedative-hypnotic site), whereas the other site accepts benzodiazepines (the antianxiety site). Drugs binding to the sedative-hypnotic site directly increase the influx of chloride ions and so act like GABA. Consequently, the higher the dose of these drugs, the greater their inhibitory effect on neurons. The effect of antianxiety drugs is different. Excitation of the antianxiety site enhances the binding of GABA to its receptor site, which means that the availability of GABA determines the potency of an antianxiety drug. Because GABA is very quickly reabsorbed by the neurons that secrete it and by surrounding glial cells, GABA concentrations are never excessive, making it hard to overdose on antianxiety drugs.

Scientists do not know what natural substances bind to the $GABA_A$ receptor binding sites other than GABA. A. Leslie Morrow and her coworkers (1999) suggest that a natural brain steroid called allopregnanolone may bind to the sedative-hypnotic site. Allopregnanolone is produced by activation of the pituitary. One mechanism by which alcohol may have its effects is by facilitating the production of allopregnanolone, which in turn activates the sedative-hypnotic site of the $GABA_A$ receptor, thus producing sedation. An explanation of the less potent effect of alcohol on human males than on females is that females have higher levels of allopregnanolone, thus making them more sensitive to the effects of alcohol and causing them to drink less and to be less likely to become alcoholic.

Because of their different actions on the $GABA_A$ receptor, sedative-hypnotic and antianxiety drugs should never be taken together. A sedative hypnotic acts like GABA, but, unlike GABA, it is not quickly absorbed by surrounding cells. Thus, by remaining on the site, its effects are enhanced by an antianxiety drug. The cumulative action of the two drugs will therefore exceed the individual action of either one. Even small combined doses of antianxiety and sedative-hypnotic drugs can produce coma or death.

Link to your CD and find the area on synaptic transmission in the Neural Communication module. Review the process of inhibitory synaptic function and consider drugs, like GABA, that act as antagonists in the central nervous system.

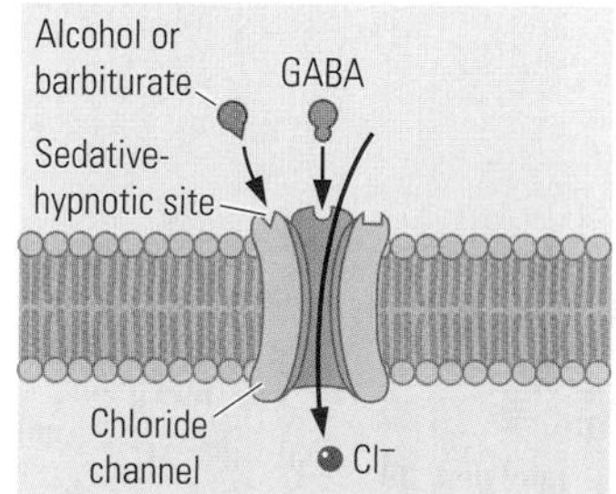


Binding of sedative-hypnotic drugs (such as alcohol or barbiturates) acts like GABA, causing increased chloride conductance.

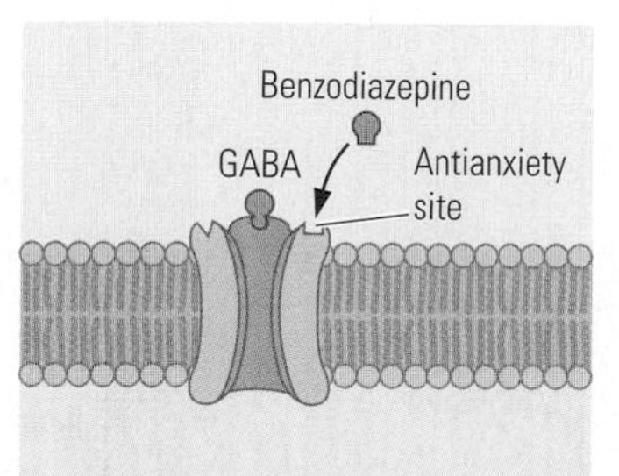


Binding of antianxiety drugs (benzodiazepines) enhances binding effects of GABA.

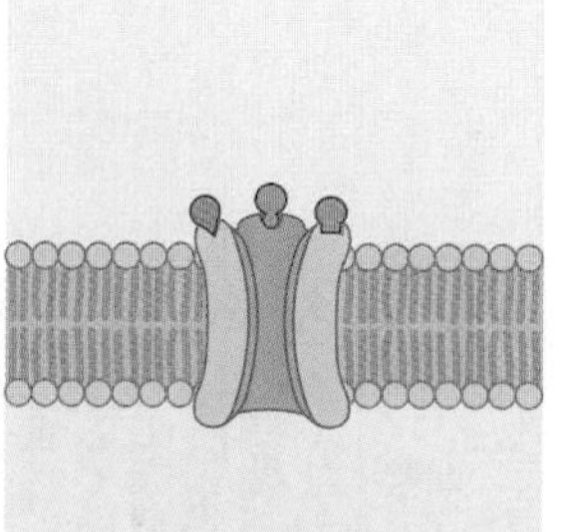

Because of their different actions, these drugs should never be taken together. Combined doses can cause coma or death.

**Figure 6-8**

Sedative hypnotics bind to the $GABA_A$ receptor, which contains a chloride channel. By binding to one of the sites (the sedative-hypnotic site) on the $GABA_A$ molecule, barbiturates and alcohol mimic the effects of GABA. By binding to a different site (the antianxiety site) on the molecule, benzodiazepines enhance the action of GABA. Note that sedative hypnotics, antianxiety agents, and GABA each have different binding sites.

## Antipsychotic Agents

The term *psychosis* refers to a number of neuropsychological conditions, such as schizophrenia, that are characterized by hallucinations or delusions. (An example of delusions is described in "Drug-Induced Psychosis" on page 224.) Drugs used to treat psychosis are known as antipsychotic agents, also called **major tranquilizers** or **neuroleptics.** The use of antipsychotic agents has greatly reduced the number of patients held in mental institutions, as Figure 6-9 shows. Improving the functioning of schizophrenics has been an important achievement because the incidence of schizophrenia is high, about 1 in every 100 people.

Although major tranquilizers have been widely used for nearly 50 years, their therapeutic actions are still not understood. They have an immediate effect in reducing motor activity, and so they alleviate the excessive agitation of some schizophrenic patients. In fact, one of their negative side effects can be to produce symptoms reminiscent of Parkinson's disease, in which control over movement is impaired. With prolonged use, they can cause *dyskinesia* (involuntary movements). This condition includes rhythmical movements of the mouth, hands, and other body parts. The effects are usually reversible if the person stops taking the drug.

At least part of the action of antipsychotic drugs is to block one kind of dopamine receptor, called the **$D_2$ receptor.** This action of antipsychotic drugs has led to the **dopamine hypothesis of schizophrenia.** It holds that some forms of schizophrenia may be related to excessive dopamine activity, which antipsychotic drugs control. Other support for the dopamine hypothesis comes from the "schizophrenia-like" symptoms of chronic users of amphetamine, a stimulant drug. As Figure 6-10 shows, amphetamine is a dopamine agonist that fosters the release of dopamine from the presynaptic membrane of dopamine synapses and blocks the reuptake of dopamine from the synaptic cleft. If amphetamine causes schizophrenia-like symptoms by increasing dopamine activity, perhaps naturally occurring schizophrenia is related to excessive dopamine action, too.

Even though such drug effects suggest that the dopamine hypothesis of schizophrenia may have merit, experimental studies have been unable to find dopamine-

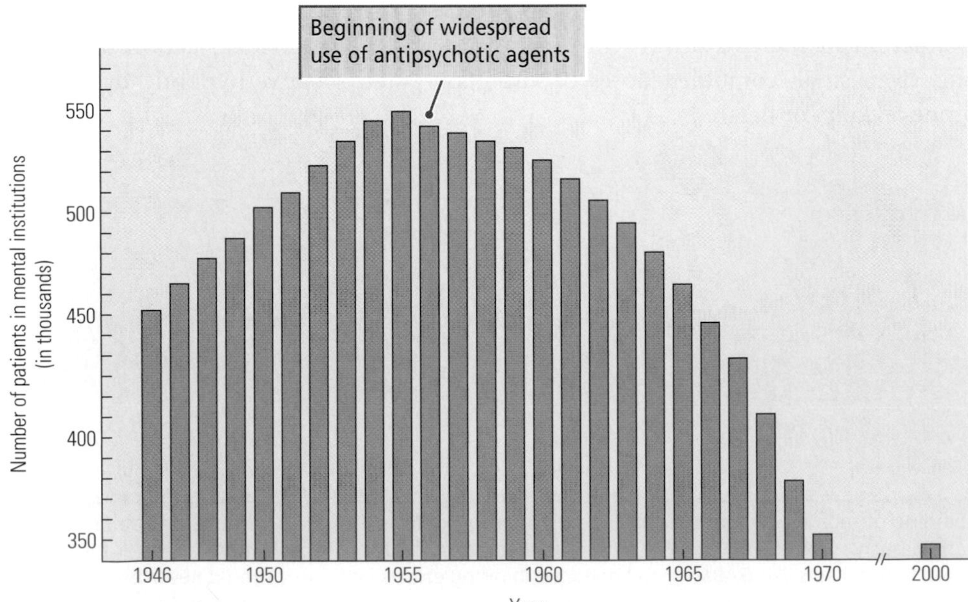


**Figure 6-9**

Number of resident patients in state and municipal mental hospitals in the United States from 1946 to the present. Note the dramatic decrease in the total patient population that began after 1955, when the therapeutic use of psychoactive drugs began.

Adapted from *A Primer of Drug Action* (p. 276), by R. M. Julien, 1995, New York: W. H. Freeman and Company.

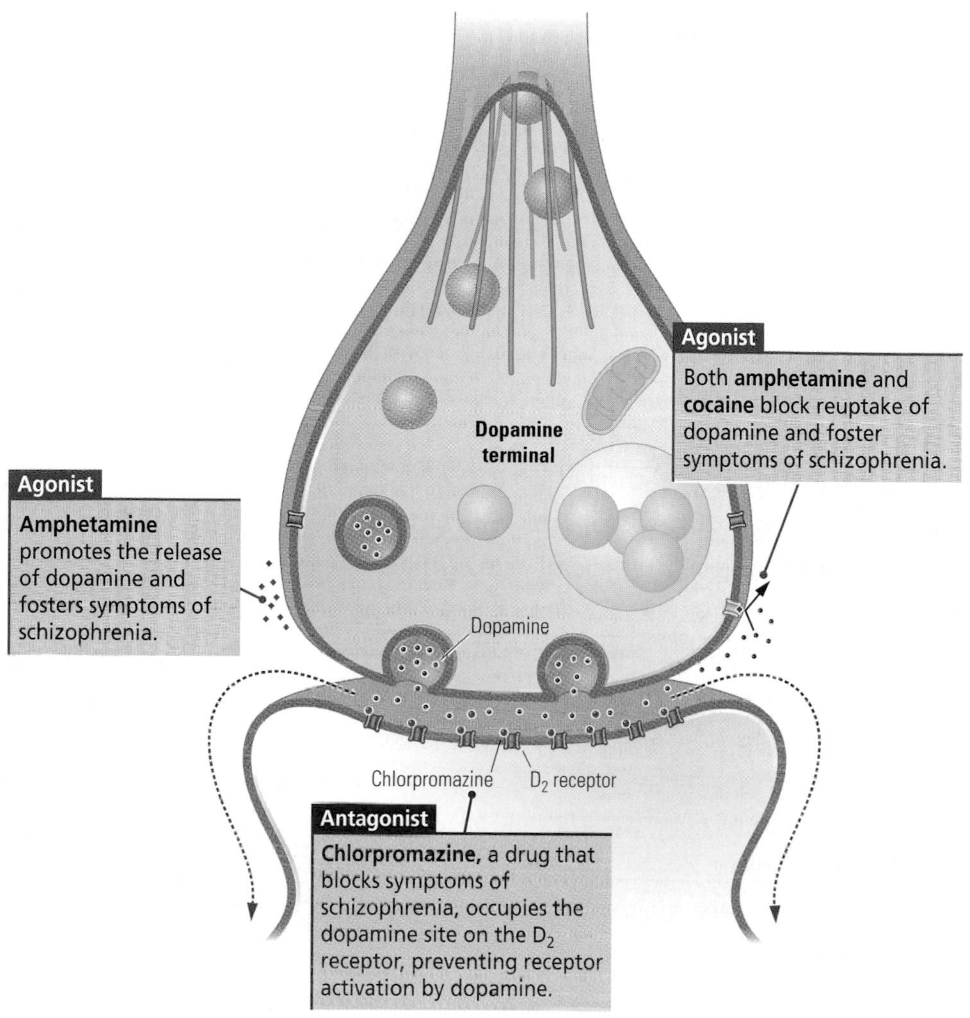
Agonist
Both **amphetamine** and **cocaine** block reuptake of dopamine and foster symptoms of schizophrenia.
Dopamine terminal
Agonist
**Amphetamine** promotes the release of dopamine and fosters symptoms of schizophrenia.
Dopamine
Chlorpromazine
$D_2$ receptor
Antagonist
**Chlorpromazine,** a drug that blocks symptoms of schizophrenia, occupies the dopamine site on the $D_2$ receptor, preventing receptor activation by dopamine.

**Figure 6-10**

Chlorpromazine blocks $D_2$ dopamine receptors, and the stimulant drug amphetamine causes the release of dopamine from the axon terminal. Both cocaine and amphetamine block the transporter that takes dopamine back into the terminal. The fact that chlorpromazine can lessen schizophrenic symptoms while abuse of amphetamine or cocaine can produce them suggests that excessive activity at the dopamine receptor is related to schizophrenia.

related differences between normal people and schizophrenics. Compared with the brains of normal subjects, the brains of patients with schizophrenia do not contain a greater number of dopamine synapses, do not release more dopamine from presynaptic membranes, and do not possess more $D_2$ receptors for dopamine. Consequently, the cause of schizophrenia and the mechanism by which antipsychotic agents work currently remain unclear.

## Antidepressants

Depression is a very common psychological disorder. At any given time, about 5 percent of the adult population suffers from it, and in the course of a lifetime, 30 percent may experience at least one episode of depression. The symptoms of this disorder are discussed in "Depression" on page 206. Most people recover from depression within a year of its onset, but, if the illness is left untreated, the incidence of suicide is high. Two different types of drugs have antidepressant effects: the **monoamine oxidase inhibitors (MAO inhibitors)** and the **tricyclic antidepressants.** The so-called **second-generation antidepressants,** which include fluoxetine (Prozac), are similar to the tricyclic antidepressants.

Click on the Web site at **www.worthpublishers.com/kolb/chapter6** to read more about current events and controversies about antidepressants.

Focus on Disorders

## Depression

P. H. was a 53-year-old high school teacher who, although popular with his students, was obtaining less and less satisfaction from his work. His marriage was also foundering because he was becoming apathetic and no longer wanted to socialize or go on holidays with his wife. He was having great difficulty getting up in the morning and arriving at school on time. He eventually consulted a physician with a complaint of severe chest pains, which he thought signified that he was about to have a heart attack. He informed his doctor that a heart attack would be a welcome relief because it would end his problems. The physician concluded that P. H. was suffering from depression and referred him to a psychiatrist. The psychiatrist arranged for P. H. to come in once a week for counseling and gave him a prescription for a monoamine oxidase (MAO) inhibitor, a kind of antidepressant drug. The psychiatrist informed P. H. that many foods contain tyramine, a chemical that can raise blood pressure to dangerous levels, and, because the action of this chemical increases when taking a MAO inhibitor, he should avoid foods that contain tyramine. The psychiatrist gave him a list of foods to be avoided and especially warned him against eating cheese or drinking wine. This was standard advice given to patients for whom MAO inhibitors were prescribed. A few days later, P. H. opened a bottle of wine, took a two-pound block of cheese out of the refrigerator, and began to consume them. That evening he suffered a massive left-hemisphere stroke that left him unable to speak or to walk. It seemed clear that P. H. had attempted to commit suicide. Because of their dangers, MAO inhibitors are now seldom prescribed.

Depression is a condition that affects about 6 percent of adults and is much more common in women than in men. Approximately 64 percent of severely depressed people recover within 6 months, many without treatment. Depression is characterized by a wide range of symptoms, including emotional ones (such as feelings of emptiness and despair), motivational ones (such as lack of drive and initiative), behavioral ones (such as withdrawal from usual activities), and cognitive ones (such as considering oneself inadequate and inferior). Depressed people may also experience changes in appetite, disturbances of sleep, sexual problems, and various aches and pains, including headaches.

Since the 1950s, depression has been treated with antidepressant drugs, a variety of behavioral therapies, and electroconvulsive therapy (ECT), a treatment in which electrical current is passed briefly through one hemisphere of the brain. Of the drug treatments available, tricyclic antidepressants, including the second-generation versions, are now favored because they are safer and more effective than MAO inhibitors.

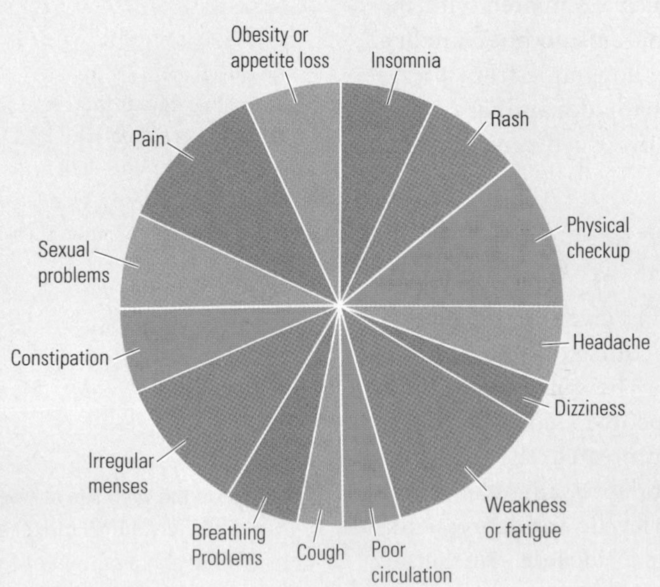

Depression is often detected when patients go to a physician complaining about one of the many somatic symptoms that often accompany the disorder. The most common complaints made by these patients are weakness, pain, and irregular menses.

Graph adapted from *Abnormal Psychology* (p. 264), by R. J. Comer, 1992, New York: W. H. Freeman and Company.

Antidepressants are thought to act by improving chemical transmission in serotonin, noradrenaline, histamine, and acetylcholine receptors and perhaps in dopamine receptors, too. Figure 6-11 shows their action at a serotonin synapse, the synapse on which most research is focused. As you can see, MAO inhibitors and the tricyclic and second-generation antidepressants have different mechanisms of action in increasing the availability of serotonin. Monoamine oxidase is an enzyme that breaks down serotonin within the axon terminal. The inhibition of MAO with an MAO inhibitor therefore provides more serotonin for release with each action potential. The tricyclic antidepressants and the second-generation antidepressants block the transporter that takes serotonin back into the axon terminal. The second-generation antidepressants are thought to be especially selective in blocking serotonin uptake, and, consequently, some are also called **selective serotonin uptake blockers.** Because the transporter is blocked, serotonin remains in the synaptic cleft for a longer period, thus prolonging its action on postsynaptic receptors.

There is, however, a significant problem in understanding how antidepressants function. Although these drugs begin to affect synapses very quickly, their antidepressant actions take weeks to develop. No one is sure why. Additionally, about 20 percent of patients with depression fail to respond to antidepressant drugs, and others cannot tolerate the side effects of these medications. Side effects can include increased anxiety, sexual dysfunction, sedation, dry mouth, blurred vision, and memory impairments. Although many people hoped that the second-generation antidepressants would produce fewer side effects than do the tricyclic antidepressants, that hope has not been fully realized. In fact, it is unclear how selective antidepressants are in their action on the brain. Even advertisements for Prozac, one of the more selective antidepressant compounds, suggest that this drug can be used to treat not only

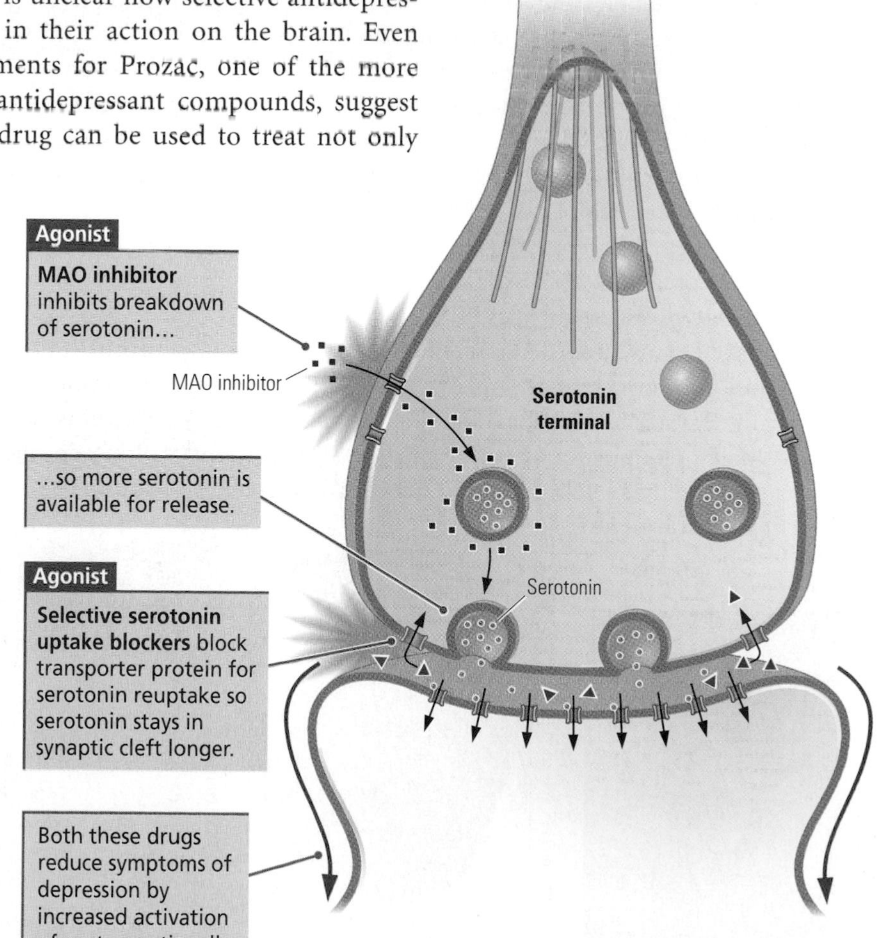
Agonist
MAO inhibitor inhibits breakdown of serotonin...
MAO inhibitor
Serotonin terminal
...so more serotonin is available for release.
Agonist
Selective serotonin uptake blockers block transporter protein for serotonin reuptake so serotonin stays in synaptic cleft longer.
Serotonin
Both these drugs reduce symptoms of depression by increased activation of postsynaptic cells.

**Figure 6-11**

Different antidepressant drugs act on the serotonin synapse in different ways to increase the availability of serotonin. MAO inhibitors block MAO, an enzyme that breaks down serotonin within the terminal. Selective serotonin reuptake blockers block the transporter protein that takes serotonin back up into the terminal after use. Thus, both types of drugs result in increased levels of serotonin available to act on serotonin receptors.

depression but also obsessive-compulsive disorder. The major symptoms of obsessive-compulsive disorder are obsessive thoughts and behaviors, such as ideas that people cannot get out of their heads and ritual-like actions that they keep endlessly performing. Although obsessive-compulsive disorder is related to guilt and anxiety, as is depression, it is usually classified as a separate condition from depression.

## Narcotic Analgesics

The term **narcotic analgesics** describes a group of drugs that have sleep-inducing (narcotic) and pain-relieving (analgesic) properties. Many of these drugs are derived from **opium,** an extract of the seeds of the opium poppy, *Papaver somniferum*, which is shown in Figure 6-12. Opium has been used for thousands of years to produce euphoria, analgesia, sleep, and relief from diarrhea and coughing.

In 1805, the German chemist Friedrich Sertürner synthesized two pure substances from the poppy plant, codeine and morphine. **Codeine** is often included in cough medicine and in pain relievers such as aspirin (although not in the United States). **Morphine,** which was named after Morpheus, the Greek god of dreams, is a very powerful pain reliever. Despite decades of research, no other drug has been found that exceeds morphine's effectiveness as an analgesic. Opium antagonists such as **nalorphine** and **naloxone** block the actions of morphine and so are useful in treating morphine overdoses. **Heroin,** another opiate drug, is synthesized from morphine. It is more fat soluble than morphine and penetrates the blood–brain barrier more quickly, allowing it to produce very rapid relief from pain. Although heroin is a legal drug in some countries, it is illegal in others, including the United States.

What are the effects of opiate drugs on the central nervous system? Candace Pert and Solomon Snyder provided an important answer to this question by injecting radioactive opiates into the brain and identifying special receptors to which the opiates bound. But what were these receptors doing in the brain? Opiates, such as morphine, after all, are not naturally occurring brain chemicals. This question was answered by the Scottish pharmacologists John Hughes and Hans Kosterlitz, who identified two short peptides that had opioid properties and appeared to be neurotransmitters. They called these opiate-like transmitters **endorphins,** an abridgement of the phrase *en*-*d*ogenous m*orphin*elike substances.

We now know that there are endorphin-containing neurons in many brain regions and that morphine is similar enough to endorphins to mimic their action in the brain. Researchers have extensively studied whether endorphins can be used to relieve pain. The answer is so far mixed. Although endorphins do alleviate pain, they are difficult to deliver to the brain. Consequently, morphine remains a preferred pain treatment.

**Figure 6-12**

Opium is obtained from the seeds of the opium poppy. Morphine is extracted from opium, and heroin in turn is synthesized from morphine.

Eye Ubiquitous/Corbis

National Archives

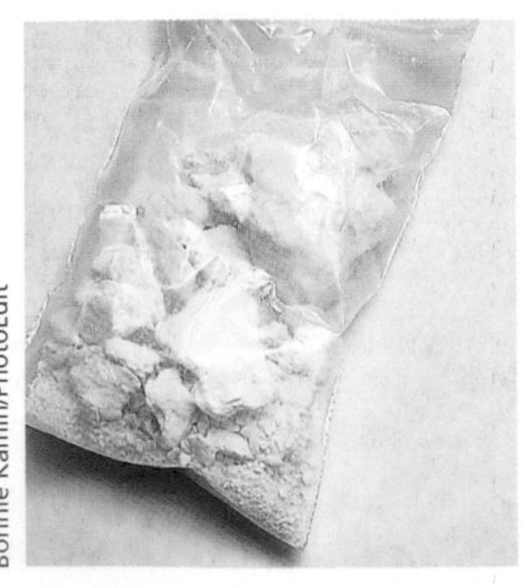

Bonnie Kamin/PhotoEdit

## Stimulants

Stimulants are a diverse group of drugs that increase the activity of neurons in a number of ways. They are subdivided into four groups: behavioral stimulants, convulsants, general stimulants, and psychedelic drugs.

Behavioral stimulants are drugs that increase motor behavior as well as elevate a person's mood and level of alertness. Two examples are cocaine and amphetamine. **Cocaine** is extracted from the Peruvian coca shrub, shown in Figure 6-13. It can be taken either by sniffing (snorting) or by injection. Many cocaine users do not like to inject cocaine intravenously, so they sniff a highly concentrated form of it called "crack." Crack is chemically altered so that it vaporizes at low temperatures, and the vapors are inhaled. The indigenous people of Peru discovered cocaine in coca leaves, which they chewed. **Amphetamine** is a synthetic compound that was discovered in attempts to synthesize the neurotransmitter epinephrine. Both amphetamine and cocaine are dopamine agonists that act by blocking the dopamine transporter, leaving more dopamine available in the synaptic cleft. Amphetamine also stimulates the release of dopamine from presynaptic membranes. Both these mechanisms increase the amount of dopamine available in synapses to stimulate dopamine receptors.

Gregory G. Dimijian/Photo Researchers

Timothy Ross/The Image Works

Tek Image/Science Photo Library/Photo Researchers

**Figure 6-13**

Cocaine is obtained from the leaves of the coca plant. Crack cocaine is a chemically altered form of cocaine that vaporizes when heated.

Cocaine was originally popularized as an antidepressant by the Viennese psychoanalyst Sigmund Freud. In an 1884 paper titled "In Praise of Coca," Freud concluded: "The main use of coca will undoubtedly remain that which the Indians have made of it for centuries: it is of value in all cases where the primary aim is to increase the physical capacity of the body for a given short period of time and to hold strength in reserve to meet further demands—especially when outward circumstances exclude the possibility of obtaining the rest and nourishment normally necessary for great exertion." Freud also recommended that cocaine could be used as a local anesthetic.

Sigmund Freud (1856–1939)

Cocaine was once widely used in soft drinks and wine mixtures, which were promoted as invigorating tonics. It is the origin of the trade name Coca-Cola, because this soft drink once contained cocaine, as suggested by the advertisement in Figure 6-14. The addictive properties of cocaine soon

Granger Collection

**Figure 6-14**

Cocaine was once used as an ingredient to spice a number of beverages, including Coca-Cola.

became apparent, however. Freud had recommended cocaine to a close friend who, in an attempt to relieve excruciating pain after the amputation of his thumb, had become addicted to morphine. The euphoric effects of cocaine helped the friend withdraw from the morphine, but soon he required larger and larger doses of cocaine. Eventually, he experienced euphoric episodes followed by a sudden crash after each injection. He continued to use larger and larger doses and eventually became schizophrenic. Similar experiences by others led to an escalating negative view of cocaine use. Cocaine proved to be valuable as a local anesthetic, however, and many derivatives, such as Novocaine, are used for this purpose today.

Amphetamine was first used as a treatment for asthma. A form of amphetamine, Benzedrine, was sold in inhalers as a nonprescription drug through the 1940s. Soon people discovered that they could open the container and ingest its contents to obtain an energizing effect. In 1937, an article in the *Journal of the American Medical Association* reported that Benzedrine tablets improved performance on mental-efficiency tests. This information was quickly disseminated among students, who began to use the drug as an aid to study for examinations. Amphetamine was widely used in World War II to help keep troops and pilots alert and to improve the productivity of wartime workers. It was also used as a weight-loss aid. In the 1960s, drug users discovered that they could obtain an immediate pleasurable "rush," often described as a whole-body orgasm, by intravenous injection of amphetamine. People who took amphetamine in this way, called "speed freaks," would inject the drug every few hours for days, remaining in a wide-awake, excited state without eating. They would then crash in exhaustion and hunger and, after a few days of recovery, would begin the cycle again. One explanation for repeated injections was to prevent the depressive crash that occurred when the drug wore off.

General stimulants are drugs that cause a general increase in the metabolic activity of cells. Caffeine is a widely used example. Caffeine inhibits an enzyme that ordinarily breaks down **cyclic adenosine monophosphate** (cAMP). The resulting increase in cAMP leads to an increase in glucose production within cells, thus making available more energy and allowing higher rates of cellular activity.

The final class of stimulants consists of **psychedelic drugs;** they alter sensory perception and cognitive processes. There are four major types of psychedelics. One consists of acetylcholine psychedelics, which either block or facilitate transmission at acetylcholine synapses in the brain. A second is made up of norepinephrine psychedelics. This type includes **mescaline,** obtained from the peyote cactus, which is legal for use by Native Americans for religious practices. A third type of psychedelic drug is tetrahydrocannabinol, or THC for short. THC is the active ingredient in marijuana, which is obtained from the hemp plant *Cannabis sativa*. There is growing evidence that cannabis acts on endogenous THC receptors called the CB1 and CB2 receptors. They are thought by scientists to be the receptors for an endogenous neurotransmitter called anandamide. Surprisingly, a number of lines of research suggest that anandamide plays a role in enhancing forgetting. The idea is that anandamide prevents memory systems of the brain from being overwhelmed by the information to which the brain is exposed each day. Thus, THC may have a detrimental effect on memory. The fourth and last type in this drug category consists of the serotonin psychedelics. They include both **lysergic acid diethylamide** (LSD) and **psilocybin** (obtained from a certain mushroom). These substances may stimulate postsynaptic receptors of serotonin synapses or they may block the activity of serotonin neurons through serotonin autoreceptors. In addition, these drugs may stimulate other transmitter systems, including norepinephrine receptors.

## In Review

Classifying psychoactive drugs by their principal effects yields seven major categories: sedative hypnotics and antianxiety agents, antipsychotic agents, antidepressants, mood stabilizers, narcotic analgesics, psychomotor stimulants, and stimulants that have psychedelic and hallucinogenic effects. Researchers are still learning how these drugs act on the nervous system. We now know that sedative hypnotics and antianxiety agents, including alcohol, barbiturates, and benzodiazepines, all affect receptor sites for the neurotransmitter GABA. Although the therapeutic actions of antianxiety agents are still not understood, one of those actions is to block a certain kind of dopamine receptor. Antidepressants, including the tricyclics and MAO inhibitors, are thought to act by improving chemical transmission in serotonin, noradrenaline, histamine, and acetylcholine receptors. The narcotic analgesics derived from opium have their effects by binding to special receptors for naturally occurring brain chemicals called endorphins. Cocaine and amphetamine are examples of psychomotor stimulants that act as dopamine agonists, making more dopamine available in synapses. As scientists continue to study the actions of psychoactive drugs, they will also learn much more about neuropsychological disorders and possible treatments of them.

# DRUGS, EXPERIENCE, CONTEXT, AND GENES

Many behaviors trigger very predictable results. When you strike the same key of a piano repeatedly, you hear the same note each time. When you flick a light switch over and over again, the same bulb goes on exactly as before. This kind of cause-and-effect consistency leads some people to assume that a drug will produce the same results every time it is taken. That assumption is incorrect, however, for several reasons. For one thing, the effect of a drug may change from one administration to another because the drug is taken in different contexts with different accompanying behaviors, which cause the brain to respond to it differently. In addition, the actions of a drug on one person may be quite different from its actions on someone else. The reason is that experience and the influence of genes also determine drug reactions. Finally, with repeated use, the effect of a drug can be dramatically different from the effect obtained with the first use. The reason is that many drugs produce an enduring change in the brain that, in time, can be quite substantial and can alter what subsequent doses do. In the following sections, we will consider a number of ways in which repeated use of drugs changes the brain and behavior.

## Tolerance

Two college freshman roommates, B. C. and A. S., went to a party, then to a bar, and by 3 AM were in a restaurant ordering pizza. A. S. decided that he wanted to watch the chef make his pizza, and off he went to the kitchen. A long and heated argument ensued involving A. S., the chef, and the manager. The two roommates then got into A. S.'s car and were leaving the parking lot when a police officer, called by the manager, drove up and stopped them. A. S. failed a breathalyzer test, which measures body alcohol content, and was taken into custody; but, surprisingly, B. C. passed the test, even though he had consumed the same amount of alcohol as A. S. had. Why this difference in their responses to the drinking bout?

The reason for the difference could be that B. C. had developed greater tolerance for alcohol than A. S. had. In one study, Isbell and coworkers (1955) showed how such tolerance comes about. These researchers gave subjects enough alcohol daily in a 13-week period to keep them in a constant state of intoxication. Yet they found that the subjects did not stay drunk for 3 months straight. When the experiment began, all the subjects showed rapidly rising levels of blood alcohol and behavioral signs of intoxication, as shown in Figure 6-15. Between the 12th and 20th days of alcohol consumption, however, blood alcohol and the signs of intoxication fell to very low levels, even though the subjects maintained a constant alcohol intake. Interestingly, too, although blood-alcohol levels and signs of intoxication fluctuated in subsequent days of the study, one did not always correspond with the other. A relatively high blood-alcohol level was sometimes associated with a low outward appearance of being drunk. Why?

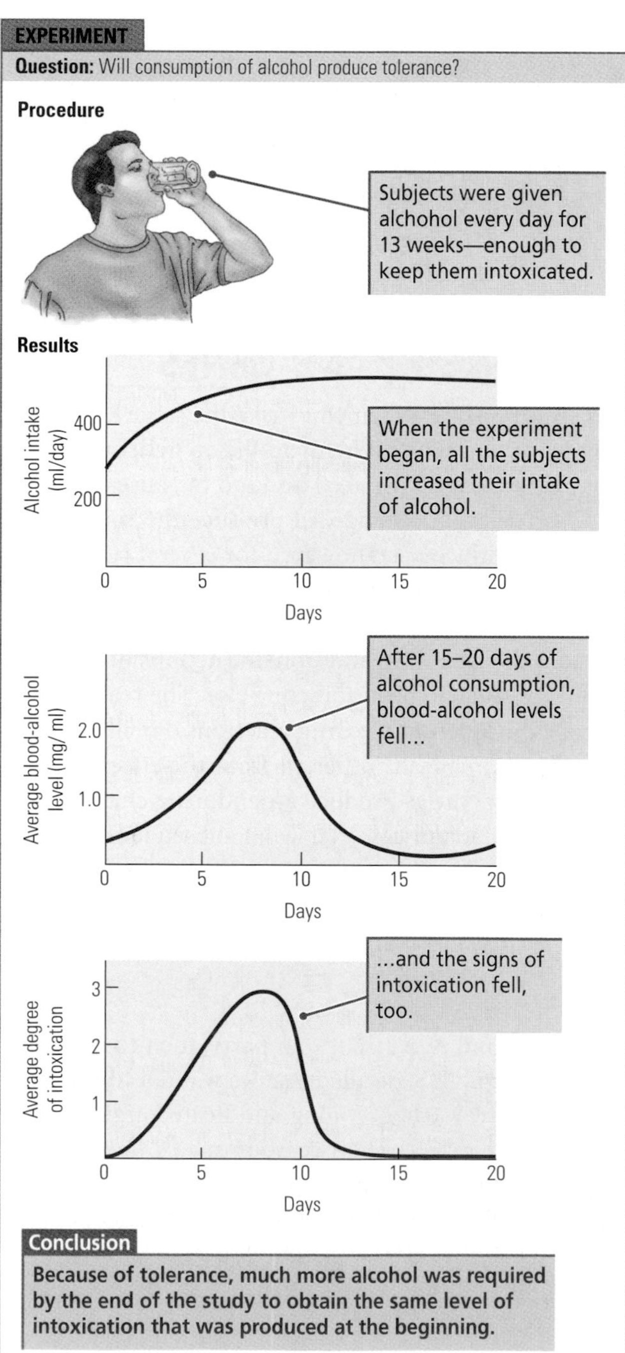

EXPERIMENT
Question: Will consumption of alcohol produce tolerance?
Procedure
Subjects were given alchohol every day for 13 weeks—enough to keep them intoxicated.
Results
Alcohol intake (ml/day)
400
200
When the experiment began, all the subjects increased their intake of alcohol.
0
5
10
15
20
Days
Average blood-alcohol level (mg/ ml)
2.0
1.0
After 15–20 days of alcohol consumption, blood-alcohol levels fell...
Average degree of intoxication
3
2
1
...and the signs of intoxication fell, too.
Conclusion
Because of tolerance, much more alcohol was required by the end of the study to obtain the same level of intoxication that was produced at the beginning.


**Figure 6-15**

Relative changes in intoxication, blood-alcohol level, and alcohol intake in subjects after 20 days of steady drinking document the development of tolerance to alcohol. Note that, as alcohol intake increases initially, so do blood-alcohol levels and the degree of intoxication. With continued consumption, blood-alcohol levels and behavioral intoxication decrease, owing .to tolerance.

Adapted from "An Experimental Study of the Etiology of 'Rum Fits' and Delirium Tremens," by H. Isbell, H. F. Fraser, A. Winkler, R. E. Belleville, and A. J. Eisenman, 1955, *Quarterly Journal of Studies on Alcohol, 16,* 1–21.

These results were likely the products of three different kinds of tolerance—metabolic tolerance, cellular tolerance, and learned tolerance. In the development of **metabolic tolerance,** the number of enzymes needed to break down alcohol in the liver, blood, and brain increases. As a result, any alcohol that is consumed is metabolized more quickly, and so blood-alcohol levels are reduced. In the development of **cellular tolerance,** the activities of brain cells adjust to minimize the effects of alcohol present in the blood. This kind of tolerance can help explain why the behavioral signs of intoxication may be very low despite a relatively high blood-alcohol level. **Learned tolerance,** too, can help explain a drop in the outward signs of intoxication. As people learn to cope with the daily demands of living while under the influence of alcohol, they may no longer appear to be drunk.

That learning plays a role in tolerance to alcohol may seem surprising to you, but this role has been confirmed in many studies. For instance, Wenger and his coworkers (1981) trained rats to walk on a narrow conveyor belt to avoid electric shock to their feet from a grid over which the belt slid. One group of rats received alcohol after training in walking the belt, whereas another group received alcohol before training. A third group received training only, and a fourth group alcohol only. After several days of exposure to their respective conditions, all groups were given alcohol before a walking test. The rats that had received alcohol before training performed well, whereas those that had received training and alcohol separately performed just as poorly as those that had never had alcohol before or those that had not been trained. Apparently, animals can acquire the motor skills needed to balance on a narrow belt despite alcohol intoxication. Over time, in other words, they can learn to compensate for being drunk.

The results of these experiments are relevant to our story of A. S. and B. C. A. S. came from a large city and worked for long hours assisting his father with his plumbing business. He seldom attended parties and so was unaccustomed to alcohol. B. C., in contrast, came from a small town, where he was the acclaimed local pool shark. He was accustomed to "sipping a beer" both while waiting to play and during play, which he did often. B. C.'s body, then, was prepared to metabolize alcohol, and his experience in drinking while engaging in a skilled sport had prepared him to display controlled behavior under the influence of alcohol. Enhanced metabolism and controlled behavior are manifestations of tolerance to alcohol.

Tolerance can develop not only to alcohol but also to many other drugs, such as barbiturates, amphetamine, and narcotics. In humans, for instance, a dose of 100 milligrams of morphine is sufficient to cause profound sedation and even death in some first-time users, but those who have developed tolerance to this drug have been known to take 4000 milligrams of the drug without adverse effects. Similarly, long-time users of amphetamine may take doses 100 or more times as great as the doses that they initially took to produce the same behavioral effect. In other words, with repeated administration of a drug, the effect produced by that drug may progressively diminish owing to tolerance.

## Sensitization

Exposure to the same drug more than once does not always result in the development of tolerance. Sometimes people show the opposite reaction, *increasing* their responses with subsequent doses taken. This increased responsiveness to successive equal doses of a drug is called **sensitization.** Whereas tolerance generally develops with constantly repeated use of a certain drug, sensitization is much more likely to develop with occasional use.

**Metabolic tolerance.** Reduced sensitivity to a substance that results from the increased ability of cells to metabolize the substance.

**Cellular tolerance.** A change that takes place in a cell in which the activity of the cell adjusts to the excitatory or inhibitory effects of a drug.

**Sensitization.** Increased behavioral response to the same dose of a drug.

To demonstrate sensitization, Terry Robinson and Jill Becker (1986) isolated rats in observation boxes and recorded their reactions to an injection of amphetamine, especially reactions such as increases in sniffing, rearing, and walking, which are typical rat responses to this drug. Every 3 or 4 days, the investigators repeated the procedure. The results are given in Figure 6-16 (left). They show that the behavior of the rats was more vigorous each time they received the drug. This increased response on successive tests was not due to the animals becoming "comfortable" with the test situation. Control animals that received no drug did not display a similar escalation in sniffing, rearing, and walking. Moreover, the sensitization to amphetamine was enduring. Even when two injections of amphetamine were separated by months, the animals still showed an increased response to the drug.

Remember that amphetamine is a dopamine agonist and acts both by stimulating the release of dopamine from the axon terminals of dopamine neurons and by blocking the reuptake of dopamine into those terminals. Which of these two actions might underlie sensitization to amphetamine? One possibility is that sensitization is due to the release of dopamine. Perhaps with each successive dose of amphetamine, more dopamine is released, causing a progressively increasing behavioral response to the drug.

This explanation was confirmed by another experiment on rats, some of which had been sensitized to amphetamine and others of which had never been given the drug (Casteñeda et al., 1988). The basal ganglia, which are rich in dopamine synapses, were removed from the brain of each rat and placed in a fluid-filled container. Then the tissue was treated with amphetamine. An analysis of the fluid that bathed the tissue showed that the basal ganglia from sensitized rats released more dopamine than did the basal ganglia of nonsensitized rats. This increased release of dopamine can explain sensitization to amphetamine.

Sensitization also develops to drugs with depressant effects, such as the major tranquilizer Flupentixol, which is a dopamine antagonist that blocks dopamine receptors. Figure 6-16 (right) shows the effect of Flupentixol on the swimming behavior of rats in another study (Whishaw et al., 1989). The researchers trained the rats to swim a short distance to a platform in a swimming pool. When the rats were able to reach the platform within 1 to 2 seconds, they were given an injection of Flupentixol. On the first few swims after the injection of the drug, the rats swam normally, but then they began to slow down. After about 12 swims, they simply sank when placed in the water and had to be removed to prevent them from drowning. This effect was not just the result of administering 12 successive swimming trials on the same day. If the rats were injected with the drug and given only one trial each day for 12 days, the same results were obtained. On the first few days, the rats swam normally, but thereafter they began to slow down until, by the 12th day, they sank when placed into the water. Sensitization to the drug depended on the number of swims, regardless of the spacing between swims or the number of drug injections. Presumably, Flupentixol blocks dopamine synapses in the brain more effectively after sensitization in a way that accounts for these results.

Sensitization can be very selective with respect to the behavior affected, and it is detected only if tests are always given under the same conditions. For example, if rats are given amphetamine in their home cage on a number of occasions before a sensitization experiment starts, their behavior in the test situation does not reveal their previous drug experience. Sensitization develops as if the animals were receiving the drug for the first time. Furthermore, sensitization is difficult to achieve in an animal that is tested in its home cage. Fraioli and coworkers (1999) gave amphetamine to two groups of rats and recorded the rats' behavioral responses to successive injections.

**EXPERIMENT**

**Question:** Does the injection of a drug always produce the same behavior?

**Procedure #1**

In the Robinson and Becker study, animals were given periodic injections of the same dose of amphetamine. Then the researchers measured the number of times the rat reared in its cage.

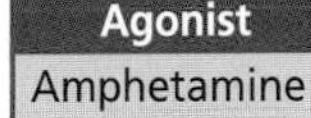


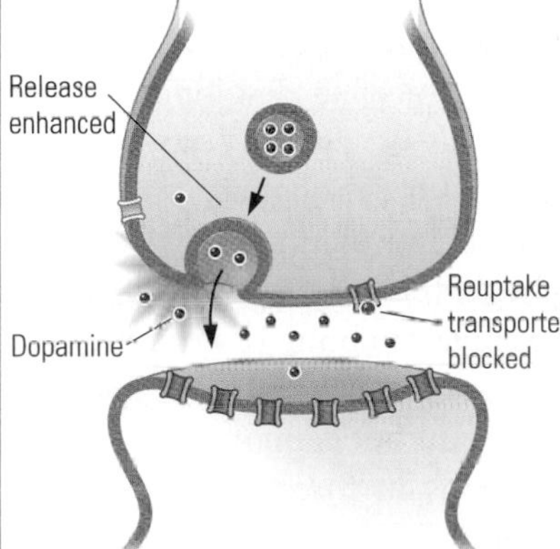


**Results #1**

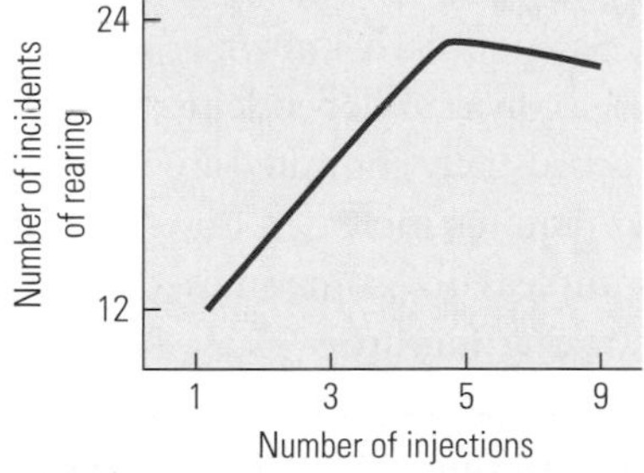


**Conclusion #1**

**Sensitization, as indicated by increased rearing, develops with periodic repeated injections.**

**Procedure #2**

In the Whishaw study, animals were given different numbers of swims after being injected with Flupentixol. Then the researchers measured their speed to escape to a platform in a swimming pool.

**Antagonist**

Flupentixol

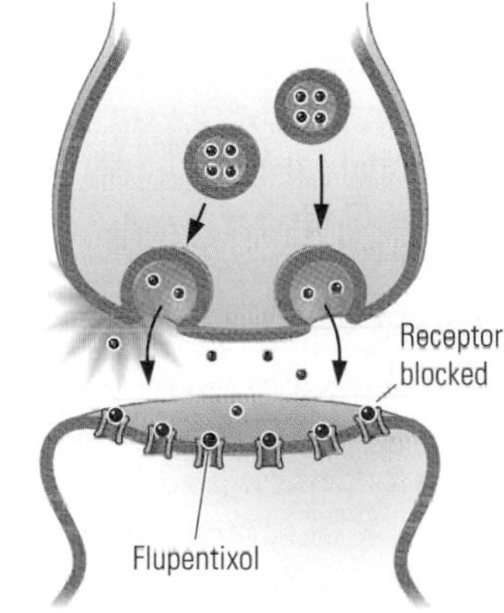


**Results #2**

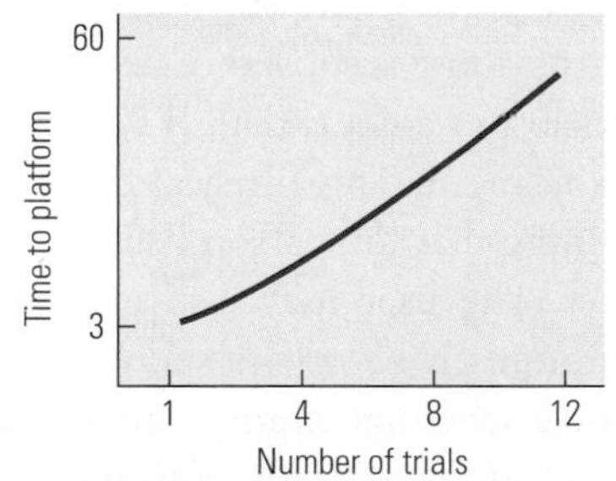


**Conclusion #2**

**Sensitization is also dependent on the occurrence of the behavior. The number of swims, not the spacing of swims or the treatment, causes an increase in the time it takes for the rat to reach the platform.**

**Figure 6-16**

Experimental studies demonstrate two examples of sensitization. (*Left*) Amphetamine stimulates dopamine release and blocks reuptake. Each injection of the same dose of the drug given to rats produces a greater effect, as measured by an increase in the number of behaviors such as rearing. (*Right*) Flupentixol blocks dopamine receptors. The rat swims slower and slower in each trial until it can no longer escape from the swimming pool.

*Left:* Adapted from "Enduring Changes in Brain and Behavior Produced by Chronic Amphetamine Administration: A Review and Evaluation of Animal Models of Amphetamine Psychosis," by T. E. Robinson and J. B. Becker, 1986, *Brain Research Reviews, 397,* 157–198. *Right:* Adapted from "Training-Dependent Decay in Performance Produced by the Neuroleptic *cis(Z)*-Flupentixol on Spatial Navigation by Rats in a Swimming Pool," by I. Q. Whishaw, G. Mittelman, and J. L. Evenden, 1989, *Pharmacology, Biochemistry, and Behavior, 32,* 211–220.

One group of rats lived in the test apparatus; so, for that group, home was the test box. The other group of rats was taken out of its normal home cage and placed in the test box for each day's experimentation. The "home" group showed no sensitization to amphetamine, whereas the "out" group displayed robust sensitization. At least part of the explanation of the "home–out" effect is that the animals are used to engaging in a certain repertoire of behaviors in their home environment, and it is difficult to get them to change that behavior even in response to a drug. When animals are placed in novel environments and receive spaced injections of a drug, however, their response to the drug may increase, showing sensitization to it. Presumably, humans, too, show sensitization to a drug when they periodically take it in novel circumstances.

## Addiction and Dependence

B. G. started smoking when she was 13 years old. Now a university lecturer, she has one child and is aware that smoking is not good for her own health or for the health of her family. She has quit smoking many times but always resumes the habit. Recently, she used a nicotine patch taped to her skin, which provides nicotine without the smoke. After successfully abstaining from cigarettes for more than 6 months with this treatment, she began to smoke again. Because the university where she works has a no-smoking policy, she has to leave the campus and stand across the street from the building in which she works to smoke. Her voice has developed a rasping sound, and she has an almost chronic "cold." She says that she used to enjoy smoking but does not any more. Concern about quitting dominates her thoughts.

Visit the Web site at **www.worthpublishers.com/kolb/chapter6** to learn more about substance abuse and addiction.

B. G. has a drug problem. She is one of approximately 25 to 35 percent of North Americans who smoke. Most smokers begin the habit when they are between the ages of 15 and 35, and each consumes an average of about 18 cigarettes a day. Like B. G., most smokers realize that smoking is a health hazard, have experienced unpleasant side effects from it, and have attempted to quit but cannot. B. G. is exceptional only in her occupation. Most smokers work at jobs in forestry, fishing, construction, and mining rather than teaching and medicine.

**Substance abuse** is a pattern of drug use in which people rely on a drug chronically and excessively, allowing it to occupy a central place in their lives. A more advanced state of drug abuse is **substance dependence,** also popularly known as **addiction.** People who are substance dependent have developed a **physical dependence** on a drug in addition to abusing it. This physical dependence is usually indicated by tolerance to the drug, meaning that the person using the drug requires increased doses to obtain the desired effect. The user may also experience unpleasant, sometimes dangerous **withdrawal symptoms** if he or she suddenly stops taking the drug. These symptoms can include muscle aches and cramps, anxiety attacks, sweating, nausea, and, for some drugs, even convulsions and death. Withdrawal symptoms can begin within hours of the last dose of a drug and tend to intensify over several days before they subside. B. G., although she is an abuser of the drug nicotine, is not physically dependent on it. She smokes approximately the same number of cigarettes each day (she has not developed tolerance to nicotine) and she does not get sick if she is deprived of cigarettes (she does not suffer symptoms of withdrawal from nicotine).

**Substance abuse.** Use of a drug for the psychological and behavioral changes that it produces aside from its therapeutic effects.

**Substance dependence.** Desire for a drug manifested by frequently taking the drug.

**Addiction.** Development of a physical dependence on a drug in addition to abusing it; often associated with tolerance and unpleasant, sometimes dangerous withdrawal symptoms on cessation of drug use.

**Physical dependence.** Indicated by the display of withdrawal symptoms on cessation of drug use.

**Withdrawal symptoms.** Behaviors displayed by a user when drug use ends.

**Psychomotor activation.** Increased behavioral and cognitive activity.

Many different kinds of drugs are abused or cause addiction, including sedative hypnotics, antianxiety agents, narcotics, and stimulants. Drugs that are abused have a common property: they produce **psychomotor activation** in some part of their dose range. That is, at certain levels of consumption, these drugs make the user feel energetic and in control. This common effect has led to the hypothesis that abused drugs may all act on the same target in the brain. One proposed target is dopamine neurons, because their stimulation is associated with psychomotor activity.

Three lines of evidence support a central role for dopamine in drug abuse. First, animals will press a bar for electrical stimulation of the dopamine system in the brain, and they will no longer press it if the dopamine system is blocked or damaged. This finding suggests that the release of dopamine is somehow desirable. Second, abused drugs seem to cause the release of dopamine or to prolong its availability in synaptic clefts. Even drugs that have no primary action on dopamine synapses have been found to increase dopamine. Apparently, when activated, many brain regions that contain no dopamine neurons themselves may stimulate dopamine neurons elsewhere in the brain. Third, drugs that block dopamine receptors or decrease the availability of dopamine at dopamine receptors are not substances that people abuse. For example, even though major tranquilizers are widely available for treating psychosis, they are not abused drugs.

## Explaining Drug Abuse

Why do people become addicted to drugs? Historically, one explanation is the **dependency hypothesis.** According to this hypothesis, habitual users of a drug experience psychological or physiological withdrawal symptoms when the effects of the drug wear off. They feel anxious, insecure, or just plain sick in the absence of the drug, and so they take the drug again to alleviate those symptoms. In this way, they get "hooked" on the drug. Although this hypothesis may account for part of drug-taking behavior, it has shortcomings as a general explanation. For example, an addict may abstain from a drug for months, long after any withdrawal symptoms have abated, and yet still be drawn back to using the drug. In addition, some drugs, such as the tricyclic antidepressants, produce withdrawal symptoms when discontinued, but these drugs are not abused.

Researchers currently see addiction as being a series of stages. The first stage is the activation of *pleasure* by the consequences of drug taking. Using the drug produces in the person a positive subjective sensation. In other words, the user *likes* the experience. In the second stage, pleasure is linked through *associative learning* with mental representations of the objects, acts, places, and events related to taking the drug. This associative learning may be achieved through **classical** (also called **Pavlovian**) **conditioning.** You may recall from your introductory psychology course that classical conditioning consists of learning to associate some formerly neutral stimulus (such as the sound of a bell) with a stimulus (such as food in the mouth) that elicits some involuntary response (such as salivation). The pairing of the two stimuli continues until the formerly neutral stimulus is alone able to trigger the involuntary reaction. In drug use, the sight of the drug and the drug-taking context and equipment are repeatedly paired with administering the drug, which produces a pleasurable reaction. If you are a cat owner, you may have noticed that, when your cat wants to be petted, she may rub against your hand. She has been classically conditioned to associate the pleasure that she gets from petting with your hand. Soon the visual cues alone are enough to elicit pleasure. The third stage is attributing **incentive salience** to the cues associated with drug use. In other words, those cues become highly desired and sought-after incentives in their own right. Stimuli that signal the availability of these incentives also become attractive. For instance, acts that led to the drug-taking situation in the past become attractive, as do acts that the drug taker predicts will lead again to the drug. Drug users may even begin to collect objects that remind them of the drug, such as pipe collecting by pipe smokers or bottle-opener collecting by drinkers. In this sequence of events, then, a number of repetitions of the drug-taking behavior lead from liking that act to seeking it out or wanting it, regardless of its current consequences.

**Incentive salience.** Refers to cues that, after having been associated with drug use, become sought out.

**Incentive-sensitization theory.** A theory that holds that, when a drug has been used in association with certain cues, the cues themselves will elicit desire for the drug.

A number of findings are in keeping with this view of drug addiction. For one thing, there is ample evidence that abused drugs initially have a pleasurable effect. There is also evidence that a habitual user continues to use his or her drug even though taking it no longer produces any pleasure. Street addicts using heroin sometimes report that they are miserable, that their lives are in ruins, and that the drug is not even great anymore, but they still want it. Furthermore, desire for the drug is often greatest just when the addicted person is maximally high on the drug, not when he or she is withdrawing from it, as the dependency hypothesis would predict.

To account for all the facts about drug abuse and addiction, Robinson and Berridge (1993) proposed the **incentive-sensitization theory.** This perspective is also called the *wanting-and-liking theory* because, according to this theory, wanting and liking a drug are affected differently, as is illustrated in Figure 6-17. Robinson and Berridge define *wanting* as equivalent to craving for a drug, whereas *liking* is defined as the pleasure that drug taking produces. The road to drug dependency begins with the initial trying out of the drug. At this time, the user may experience only a mild degree of wanting and liking the substance, because positive reactions may be mixed with some unpleasant side effects. With repeated use, liking the drug may decline from its initial level, but wanting the drug increases. Now the user may also begin to show tolerance to the drug's unpleasant effects and so may begin to increase the dosage to increase liking. Eventually, the drug produces very little liking, but wanting comes to dominate the drug user's behavior. This is because the user has become conditioned to all of the cues associated with drug taking, including needles and other drug paraphernalia, as well as drug-taking friends and locations. According to Robinson and Berridge, encounters with these cues, rather than expected pleasure from the drug, initiates wanting.

How can the wanting-and-liking theory explain B. G.'s behavior toward smoking? B. G. reports that her most successful period of abstinence from cigarettes coincided with moving to a new town. She stopped smoking for 6 months and, during that time, felt as if she were free and in command of her life again. The wanting-and-liking theory would argue that her ability to quit at this time was increased because she was separated from the many cues that had previously been associated with smoking. Then one night after going out to dinner, B. G. and a few of her new colleagues went to a bar, where some of them began to smoke. B. G. reported that her desire for a cigarette became overpowering. Before the evening was over, she bought a package of cigarettes and smoked more than half of it. On leaving the bar, she left the remaining cigarettes on the table, intending that this episode would be only a one-time lapse. Shortly thereafter, however, she resumed smoking. The wanting-and-liking theory suggests that her craving for a cigarette was strongly conditioned to certain social cues that she encountered again on her visit to the bar, which is why the wanting suddenly became overwhelming.

**Figure 6-17**

According to the incentive-sensitization theory of drug addiction, a drug when first used produces a moderate amount of wanting and liking. With repeated use, tolerance for liking develops, and consequently the expression of liking decreases. In contrast the system that mediates wanting sensitizes, and wanting the drug increases. Wanting is associated with the cues encountered in a typical situation in which the drug is used.

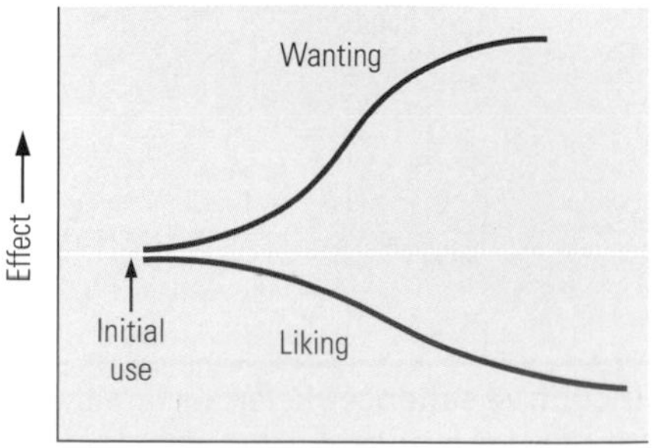

Peter Dokus/Stone

The neural basis for liking and wanting are not completely understood. Robinson and Berridge believe that liking may be due to the activity of opioid neurons, whereas wanting may be due to activity in a part of the dopamine system. In these dopamine pathways, called the **mesolimbic dopamine system,** the axons of dopamine neurons in the midbrain project to the nucleus accumbens, the frontal cortex, and the limbic system, as shown in Figure 6-18. When cues that have previously been associated with drug taking are encountered, this dopamine system becomes active, producing the subjective experience of wanting. That desire for the drug is not a conscious act. Rather, the craving derives from unconsciously acquired associations between drug taking and various cues related to it.

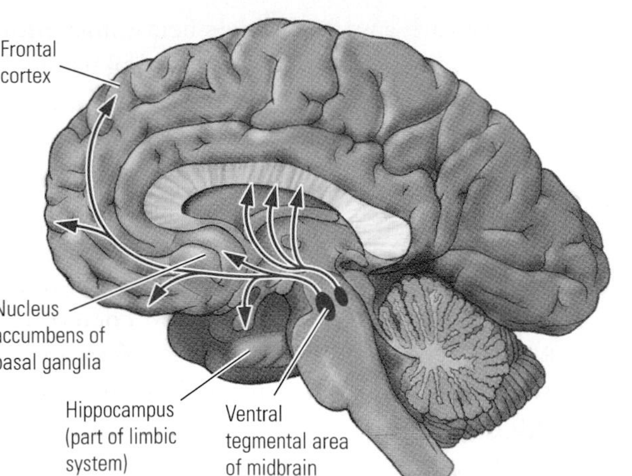


**Figure 6-18**

The dopamine hypothesis of addiction proposes that the mesencephalic dopamine system plays a role in drug craving. The dopamine neurons in the ventral tegmental area of the midbrain project to the nucleus accumbens of the basal ganglia, to the limbic system including the hippocampus, and to the frontal cortex, suggesting that these areas of the brain may be related to addiction.

We can extend the wanting-and-liking explanation of drug addiction to many other life situations. Cues related to sexual activity, food, and even sports can all induce a state of wanting, sometimes in the absence of liking. For example, we frequently eat when prompted by the cue of other people eating, even though we may not be hungry and derive little pleasure from eating at that time. It is interesting that country music is dominated by songs about the opposing forces of wanting and liking.

## Behavior on Drugs

> Ellen is a healthy, attractive, and intelligent nineteen-year-old university freshman. In her high school health class, she learned about the sexual transmission of HIV and other diseases. More recently, in her college orientation, senior students presented a seminar about the dangers of having unprotected sex and provided the freshmen in her residence with free condoms and safe-sex literature. It is certain that Ellen knows the facts about unprotected sex and is cognizant of the dangers associated with this behavior. Indeed, she holds negative attitudes toward having unprotected sex, does not intend to have unprotected sex, and has always practiced safe-sex behavior: She and her former boyfriend were always careful to use latex condoms when having intercourse. At a homecoming party in her residence, Ellen has a great time, drinking and dancing with her friends, and meeting new people. She is particularly taken with Brad, a sophomore at her college, and the two of them decide to go back to her room to order a pizza. One thing leads to another, and Ellen and Brad have sex without using a condom. The next morning, Ellen wakes up, dismayed and surprised at her behavior, and very concerned that she might be pregnant, or may have contracted a sexually transmitted disease. Even worse, she is terrified that she might have contracted AIDS. (MacDonald et al., 1998)

What happened to Ellen? What is it about drugs, especially alcohol, that make people do things that they would not ordinarily do? Ellen is not alone in engaging in risky behavior under the influence of alcohol. Alcohol is associated with many harmful behaviors that are costly both to individual persons and to society. These behaviors include not only unprotected sexual activity but also drinking and driving, date rape, spousal or child abuse, and other forms of aggression and crime.

An early and still widely held explanation of the effects of alcohol is the **disinhibition theory.** It holds that alcohol has a selective depressant effect on the cortex, the region of the brain that controls judgment, while sparing subcortical structures, those areas of the brain responsible for more primitive instincts. Stated differently, alcohol presumably depresses learned inhibitions based on reasoning and judgment, while releasing the "beast" within. This theory often excuses alcohol-related behavior with such statements as, "She was too drunk to know better," or "The boys had a few too many and got carried away." Does such disinhibition explain Ellen's behavior? Not really. Ellen had used alcohol in the past and managed to practice "safe sex" despite the effects of the drug. The disinhibition theory cannot explain why her behavior was different on this occasion. If alcohol is a disinhibitor, why is it not *always* so?

Craig MacAndrew and Robert Edgerton have questioned the disinhibition theory along just these lines in their book titled *Drunken Comportment.* They cite many instances in which behavior under the influence of alcohol changes from one context to another. People who engage in polite social activity at home when consuming alcohol may become unruly and aggressive when drinking in a bar. Even their behavior at the bar may be inconsistent. For example, while drinking one night at a bar, Joe becomes obnoxious and gets into a fight; but on another occasion he is charming and witty, even preventing a fight between two friends, whereas on a third occasion he becomes depressed and only worries about his problems. McAndrew and Edgerton also cite examples of cultures in which people are *dis*inhibited when sober only to become inhibited after consuming alcohol and cultures in which people are inhibited when sober and become *more* inhibited when drinking. How can all these differences in alcohol's effects be explained?

MacAndrew and Edgerton suggest that behavior under the effects of alcohol represents **time out** from the rules of daily life that would normally apply. This time out takes into consideration learned behavior that is specific to the culture, group, and setting. Time out can help explain Ellen's decision to sleep with Brad. In our culture, alcohol is used to facilitate social interactions, so behavior while intoxicated represents time out from more conservative rules regarding dating. But time-out theory has more difficulty explaining Ellen's lapse in judgment regarding safe sex. Ellen had never practiced unsafe sex before and had never made it a part of her time-out social activities. So why did she engage in it with Brad?

Tara MacDonald

Tara MacDonald and her coworkers (1998) suggest that alcohol myopia can explain alcohol-related lapses in judgment, such as that displayed by Ellen. **Alcohol myopia** (nearsightedness) is the tendency for people under the influence of alcohol to respond to a restricted set of immediate and prominent cues while ignoring more remote cues and potential consequences. Immediate and prominent cues are very strong and obvious ones that are close at hand. If there is a fight, the person with alcohol myopia will be quicker than normal to throw a punch because the cue of the fight is so strong and immediate. Similarly, if there is a raucous party, the myopic drinker will be more eager than usual to join in because the immediate cue of boisterous fun dominates the person's view. In regard to Ellen and Brad, once they arrived at Ellen's room, the sexual cues of the moment were far more immediate than concerns about long-term safety. As a result, Ellen responded to those immediate cues and behaved in a way that she normally would not. Such alcohol myopia can explain many other lapses in judgment that lead to risky behavior, including aggression, date rape, and reckless driving under the effects of alcohol.

**Alcohol myopia.** The behavior displayed after imbibing alcohol in which local and immediate cues become prominent.

## Why Doesn't Everyone Abuse Drugs?

Observing that some people are more prone to drug abuse and dependence than other people are, scientists have wondered if this difference might be genetically based. Three lines of evidence suggest a genetic contribution. First, the results of twin studies show that, if one of two twins abuses alcohol, the other is more likely to abuse it if those twins are identical (have the same genetic makeup) than if they are fraternal (have only some of their genes in common). Second, the results of studies of people adopted shortly after birth reveal that they are more likely to abuse alcohol if their biological parents were alcoholic, even though they have had almost no contact with those parents. Third, although most animals do not care for alcohol, selective breeding of mice, rats, and monkeys can produce strains that consume large quantities of it.

There are problems with all these lines of evidence, however. Perhaps identical twins show greater concordance for alcohol abuse because they are exposed to more similar environments than fraternal twins are. And perhaps the link between alcoholism in adoptees and their biological parents has to do with nervous system changes due to prebirth exposure to the drug. Finally, the fact that animals can be selectively bred for alcohol consumption does not mean that human alcoholics have a similar genetic makeup. The evidence for a genetic basis of alcohol abuse will become compelling only when a gene or set of genes related to alcoholism is found.

Another avenue of research into individual differences associated with drug abuse has been to search for personality traits that drug abusers tend to have in common. One such trait is unusual risk taking. Consider Bruno Gouvy, the Frenchman shown in Figure 6-19. He was the first person to jump out of a helicopter and surf the sky on a snowboard. He also set a world speed record on a monoski and was the first person to snowboard down Mont Blanc, the highest peak in Europe. He set a windsurfing record across the Mediterranean Sea and a free-fall speed record after jumping out of a plane. In an attempt to snowboard down three major peaks in one day, he hit black ice and fell 3000 feet to his death. Do people who love high-risk activities have a genetic predisposition toward risk-taking behavior that will also lead them to experiment with drugs (Comings et al., 1996)?

In an attempt to find out if certain behavioral traits are related to drug abuse, Pierre Piazza and his coworkers (1989) gave rats an opportunity to self-administer amphetamine. Some rats were very quick to become amphetamine "junkies," giving themselves very large doses of it, whereas other rats avoided the drug. By examining the behavior of the rats in advance of the drug-taking opportunity, the researchers were able to identify behavioral characteristics associated with becoming an amphetamine junkie. In particular, those rats that ran around the most when placed in an open area, and so seemed less cautious and self-restrained than other rats, were also the most likely to become addicted. Perhaps, the researchers concluded, such behavioral traits make some rats more prone to drug use.

Although research on the characteristics that might influence becoming a drug user continues, there is as yet no unequivocal evidence to suggest that a specific gene determines substance abuse. Nor is there unequivocal evidence that differences in the dopamine system make some people more prone to drug abuse than others. And, even if a particular substance-abuse gene or genes could be found, that genetic factor would not provide a full explanation of drug addiction. Identical twins have all their genes in common, and yet, when one becomes a drug abuser, the other does not necessarily become one, too. Clearly, learning also plays an important role in developing drug abuse and addiction.

**Figure 6-19**

Bruno Gouvy was a French adventurer who was killed while attempting to make a steep snowboard descent.

Redneck/Liaison

**Glutamate analogue.** A drug tht acts like glutamate on glutamate receptors.

## Can Drugs Cause Brain Damage?

Table 6-1 shows that many substances produced by plants and animals can act as neurotoxins, causing damage to neurons. Given the widespread use of psychoactive drugs in our society, it is important to ask whether these substances can do the same. In this section, we both examine the evidence that commonly used psychoactive drugs can act as neurotoxins and investigate the processes by which they might have toxic effects.

### THE DOMOIC ACID STORY

Let us first consider how domoic acid acts as a toxin on the nervous system. The chemical structure of domoic acid is similar to that of the neurotransmitter glutamate. Because of its structural similarity to glutamate, domoic acid is referred to as a **glutamate analogue.** It is also a glutamate agonist because, like glutamate, it binds to glutamate receptors and affects them in the same way. As described in Chapter 5, each neurotransmitter can attach to a number of different types of receptors. Glutamate has three kinds of receptors and domoic acid acts to stimulate one of them, the **kainate receptor,** so named because the chemical substance kainate binds very potently to it. Domoic acid, it turns out, binds to the kainate receptor even more potently than kainate itself. (Because receptors are usually named for the compound that most potently binds to them, had domoic acid been discovered earlier, the kainate receptor would have been called the domoic receptor.)

The distribution of the different glutamate receptor subtypes in the brain varies from region to region. Kainate receptors are especially numerous in the hippocampus. If domoic acid reaches these receptors in high enough concentrations, it overexcites the receptors, initiating a series of biochemical reactions that results in the death of the postsynaptic neuron. Consequently, domoic acid is more toxic to the hippocampus than it is to other brain regions. Figure 6-20 shows a section through the brain of a rat that has been given an injection of domoic acid. The brain is colored with a silver stain that accumulates in damaged neurons. Tissue in the hippocampus exhibits the greatest amount of damage, although there is also sparse damage elsewhere in the brain.

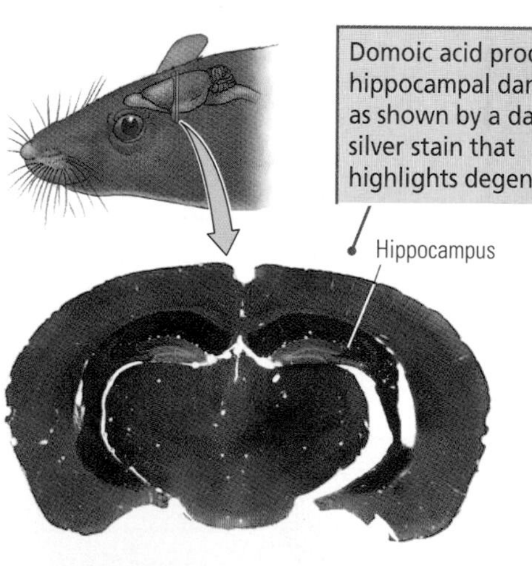

Domoic acid produces hippocampal damage, as shown by a dark silver stain that highlights degeneration.
Hippocampus

**Figure 6-20**

In this micrograph, the darkly stained regions, which are mainly in the hippocampus, are areas that have been damaged by domoic acid. Note, however, that damage is not restricted to the hippocampus but can be seen to a lesser extent in many other brain regions. Micrograph from NeuroScience Associates.

It may seem surprising that a chemical that mimics a neurotransmitter can cause memory problems and brain damage. To understand how domoic acid can act as a neurotoxin requires that we temporarily turn to a different story, that of monosodium glutamate (MSG). The plot of this second story eventually links up with the plot of the domoic acid story.

In the late 1960s, there were many reports that monosodium glutamate, a salty-tasting, flavor-enhancing food additive, produced headaches in some people. In the process of investigating why this happened, scientists placed large doses of monosodium glutamate on cultured neurons and noticed that the neurons died. Subsequently, they injected monosodium glutamate into the brains of experimental animals, where it also produced neuron death. These findings raised the question of whether large doses of the neurotransmitter glutamate, which monosodium glutamate resembles structurally, might also be toxic to neurons. It turned out that it is. This finding suggested that a large dose of *any* substance that acts like glutamate might be toxic.

Now the toxic action of domoic acid can be explained. Domoic acid in large quantities excessively stimulates the glutamate receptors of certain brain cells, which is not to say that people should totally avoid all substances, such as domoic acid and MSG, that are similar in chemical structure to glutamate. Only very large doses of these substances are harmful, just as glutamate itself is not harmful except in large doses. Glutamate, in fact, is an essential chemical in the body. Recent findings show that we even have taste-bud receptors for glutamate in our mouths, in addition to our receptors for sweet, salty, bitter, and sour. The taste-bud receptor for glutamate is called **mGluR4,** and its function is most likely to encourage us to eat foods containing glutamate. Clearly, glutamate in doses typically found in food is required by the body and is not toxic. Only excessive doses of glutamate cause harm.

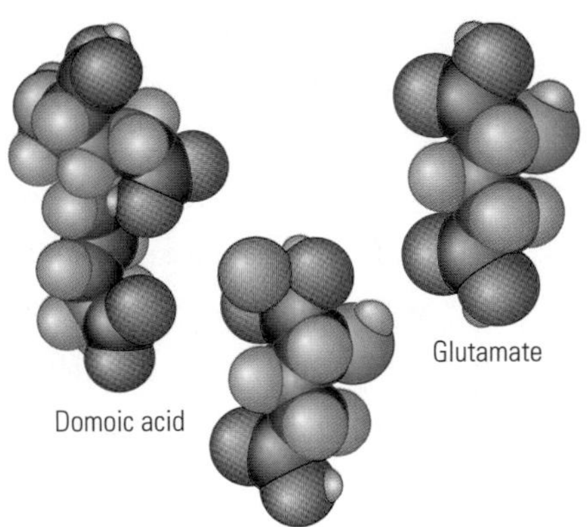


## THE POTENTIAL HARMFULNESS OF RECREATIONAL DRUGS

What about the many recreational drugs that affect the nervous system? Are any of them potentially harmful? The answer is not always easy to determine, as Una McCann and her coworkers (1997) found in their review of studies. For one thing, there is the problem of sorting out the effects of the drug itself from the effects of other factors related to taking the drug. For instance, although chronic alcohol use can be associated with damage to the thalamus and limbic system, producing severe memory disorders, it is not the alcohol itself that seems to cause this damage, but rather related complications of alcohol abuse, including vitamin deficiencies due to poor diet. For example, not only do alcoholics obtain reduced amounts of thiamine (vitamin $B_1$) in their diets, but alcohol also interferes with the absorption of thiamine by the intestine. Thiamine plays a vital role in maintaining cell-membrane structure. Similarly, there are many reports of people who suffer some severe psychiatric disorder subsequent to their abuse of certain recreational drugs, but, in most cases, it is difficult to determine whether the drug initiated the condition or just aggravated an existing problem. It is also hard to determine exactly whether the drug itself or some contaminant in the drug is related to a harmful outcome. For example, cases of Parkinson's disease that developed after the use of synthetic heroin, described in Chapter 5, were caused by a contaminant (MPTP) rather than by the heroin itself. A number of cases of chronic use of marijuana have been associated with psychotic attacks, as "Drug-Induced Psychosis" on page 224 describes. But the marijuana plant contains at least 400 chemicals, 60 or more of which are structurally related to its active ingredient tetrahydrocannabinol. Clearly, it is almost impossible to determine whether the psychotic attacks are related to THC or to some other ingredient contained in marijuana.

Perhaps the best evidence that a recreational drug can cause brain damage comes from the study of **MDMA,** also called "ecstasy," a widely used synthetic amphetamine. Although MDMA is structurally related to amphetamine, it produces hallucinogenic effects, giving it the name "hallucinogenic amphetamine." The results of animal studies show that doses of MDMA approximating those taken by human users result in the degeneration of very fine serotonergic nerve terminals. In rodents, these terminals regrow within a few months after drug use is stopped, but, in monkeys, the terminal loss may be permanent, as shown in Figure 6-21. At present, no clear behavioral effects have been associated with this form of brain damage. But researchers still want to know if use of MDMA in humans is associated with the same loss of serotonergic terminals as it is in rodents and monkeys. Answering this question is complicated by the fact that many MDMA users have also used other drugs. In addition, the types of anatomical analysis used with other animals cannot

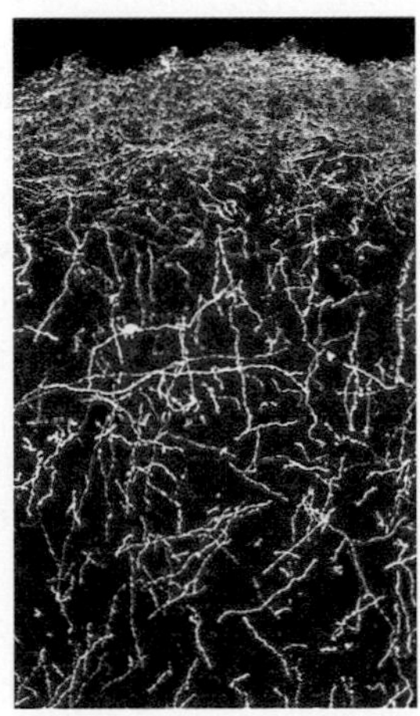

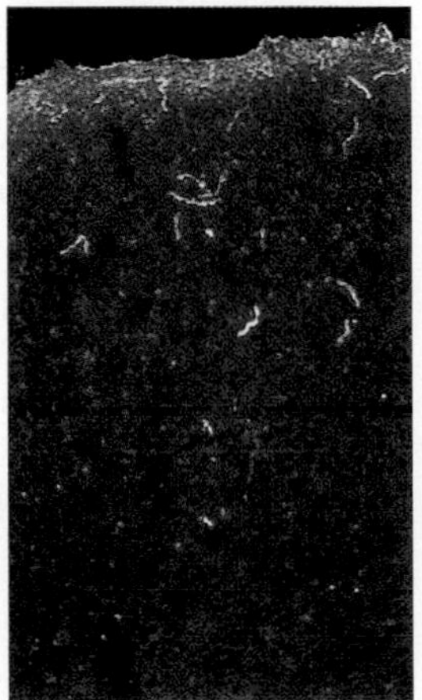

**Figure 6-21**

Treatment with MDMA changes the density of serotonin axons in the neocortex of a squirrel monkey: (*left*) normal monkey; (*right*) monkey 18 months after treatment.

From "Long-Lasting Effects of Recreational Drugs of Abuse on the Central Nervous System," by U. D. McCann, K. A. Lowe, and G. A. Ricaurte, 1997, *The Neurologist, 3,* p. 401.

Focus on Disorders

## Drug-Induced Psychosis

R. B. S. was a 29-year-old pilot who flew small freight aircraft into coastal communities in the Pacific Northwest. He was a heavy marijuana smoker and for years had been selectively breeding a particularly potent strain of marijuana in anticipation of the day when marijuana would become legalized. One evening, he felt that he was experiencing a sudden revelation. He was convinced that he was no longer in control of his life but, instead, was being manipulated by a small computer that had been implanted into his brain when he was 7 years old. He shared this information with a close friend, who urged him to consult a doctor. R. B. S. did so, and the doctor told him that it was unlikely that he had a computer implanted in his brain. But R. B. S. insisted that he had undergone the surgery when he participated in an experiment at a local university. He also claimed that all the other children who participated in the experiment had been murdered. The doctor called the psychology department at the university and confirmed that an experiment in which children took part had in fact been conducted years before, but the records of the study had long since been destroyed. R. B. S. believed that this information completely vindicated his story. R. B. S.'s delusion of the "brain computer" and the murdered children persisted and cost him his pilot's license. The delusion appeared to be completely compartmentalized in his mind. When asked why he could no longer fly, he would intently recount the story of the implant and the murders, saying that his assertion of its truth had lost him the medical certification needed for a license. Then he would happily discuss other topics in a normal way.

R. B. S. was suffering from a mild focal psychosis, a condition in which a person loses contact with reality. In some cases, this loss of contact is so severe and the capacity to respond to the environment is so impaired and distorted that the person can no longer function. People in a state of psychosis may have hallucinations (false sensory perceptions) or delusions (false beliefs), or they may withdraw into a private world that is almost totally isolated from people and events around them. A variety of drugs can produce psychosis, including LSD, amphetamine, cocaine, and, as shown by this case, marijuana. The most common form of psychosis is symptomatic of schizophrenia, a disorder in which many aspects of a person's life that had formerly been adaptive deteriorate into a welter of distorted perceptions and disturbed thoughts.

The marijuana that R. B. S. used so heavily comes from the hemp plant *Cannabis sativa*, which is perhaps the oldest

be used with humans. There is some evidence that MDMA use is associated with memory impairments, but again it is difficult to attribute the deficits specifically to MDMA.

The finding that MDMA can be toxic to neurons has led to investigations into whether amphetamine also is toxic. The results of studies in rodents have shown that high doses of amphetamine can result in the loss of dopamine terminals, but again no behavioral deficits have been associated with this loss. Whether humans using amphetamine show similar neuron damage is not known. The drug doses used in the rodent studies are typically higher than those taken by human amphetamine users, so the implications of the rodent studies are open to question.

The psychoactive actions of cocaine are similar to those of amphetamine, and its possible deleterious effects have been subjected to intense investigation. The results of many studies show that cocaine use is related to blockage of cerebral blood flow and other changes in blood circulation. However, whether cocaine causes these abnormalities or aggravates preexisting conditions is not clear.

cultivated nonfood plant. The active ingredient in this plant is delta-9-tetrahydrocannabinol (THC). At low doses, THC has mild sedative-hypnotic effects, similar to those of alcohol, whereas at higher doses, it produces euphoria and hallucinations. Because there is little cross-tolerance between THC and other drugs, it seems that THC has its own brain receptor. THC may mimic a naturally occurring substance called anandamide, which acts on a THC receptor that naturally inhibits adenyl cyclase, part of one of the second-messenger systems.

Did marijuana cause R. B. S.'s delusion? His heavy use of it certainly raised the suspicion that the drug may have had some influence on his condition. R. B. S.'s doctor found a number of reports of similar conditions linked to marijuana. Although there is no evidence that marijuana use produces brain damage, there is evidence that it exacerbates the symptoms of schizophrenic patients. But, because various forms of schizophrenia are quite common (1 in 100 people), it is possible that R. B. S.'s delusions might have eventually occurred anyway, even if he had not used marijuana. Furthermore, marijuana contains about 400 compounds besides THC, any of which could have triggered his psychotic symptoms.

Marijuana has a number of beneficial effects. They include alleviating the nausea and vomiting associated with chemotherapy in cancer patients, controlling the brain seizures symptomatic of epilepsy, reducing intraocular pressure in patients with glaucoma, and relieving the symptoms of some movement disorders. However, marijuana's effects in altering psychological functioning will likely prevent its legalization.

Phil Schermeister/Stone

Marijuana is made from the leaves of the hemp plant *Cannabis sativa*. The plant is an annual herb that reaches a height of between 3 and 15 feet. It is grown in a wide range of altitudes, climates, and soils.

Phencyclidine (PCP), or "angel dust," is an NMDA receptor blocker that was originally developed as an anesthetic. Its use was discontinued after about half of treated patients were found to display psychotic symptoms for as long as a week after coming out of anesthesia. PCP users report perceptual changes and slurring of speech after small doses, with high doses producing perceptual disorders and hallucinations. Some of the symptoms can last for weeks. The mechanisms by which PCP produces enduring behavioral changes are unknown, but John Olney and his colleagues (1971) reported that, after rats are given a related drug (MK-801), they undergo abnormal changes in neurons, as well as loss of neurons. This finding suggests that the altered behavior of PCP users may be related to neuron damage.

But some drugs that produce altered perceptual experiences and changes in mood do not appear linked to brain damage. For instance, LSD, a drug believed to act on serotonergic neurons, produces hallucinations but does not seem to cause enduring brain changes in rats. Similarly, although opiates produce mood changes, the results of long-term studies of opiate users have not revealed persistent cognitive impairments or brain damage.

## In Review

Behavior may change in a number of ways with the repeated use of a drug. These changes include tolerance, in which a behavioral response decreases; sensitization, in which a behavioral response increases; and addiction, in which the desire to use a drug increases as a function of experience with it. Today, many researchers believe that it is not so much avoidance of withdrawal symptoms that keeps people using a drug as it is a set of powerful learned incentives associated with drug taking. Individual differences in experience and genetic makeup, as well as the context in which a drug is taken, influence that drug's effects on behavior. The behavior of acting in disinhibited ways while under the influence of alcohol can often be explained by the concepts of time out and alcohol myopia. Scientists are still investigating the potential deleterious effects on the brain of different psychoactive drugs. So far, their findings have been mixed, with some drugs producing brain damage and others apparently not.

## HORMONES

**Hormones,** which are chemical messengers produced by **endocrine glands,** have effects on the body by traveling through the bloodstream to various target cells. In 1849, Swedish scientist A. A. Berthold performed the first experiment to demonstrate the existence and function of hormones. Berthold removed the testes of a rooster and found that the rooster no longer crowed; nor did it engage in sexual or aggressive behavior. Berthold then reimplanted one testis in the rooster's body cavity. The rooster began crowing and displaying normal sexual and aggressive behavior again. The reimplanted testis did not establish any nerve connections, so Berthold concluded that it must release a chemical into the rooster's circulatory system to influence the animal's behavior. That chemical, we now know, is the hormone **testosterone.** The effect that Berthold produced by reimplanting the testis can be mimicked by administering testosterone to a castrated rooster, or capon. The hormone is sufficient to make the capon behave like a rooster with testes.

Normal rooster

Rooster who has had gonads removed

Until recently, there was little reason to associate hormones with drugs, except in the most indirect way. But now hormones, like other drugs, are used to treat or prevent disease. People take hormones as a replacement therapy because they have lost glands that produce those hormones. They also take hormones, especially the sex hormones, to counteract the effects of aging, and they take them to increase physical strength and endurance to gain an advantage in sports.

Hormones fall into three main groups. One group maintains a relatively constant internal environment in the body, a condition referred to as **homeostasis.** (The term *homeostasis* comes from the Greek words *homeo,* meaning "the same place," and *stasis,* meaning "standing.") These hormones control sugar levels in the blood and the absorption of sugar by cells. They also control the concentration of water in blood and cells, as well as the levels of sodium, potassium, and calcium in the body, and they play a role in a variety of digestive functions. A second group of hormones controls **reproductive functions.** They instruct the body to develop into a male or female, influence sexual behavior and the conception of children, and, in women, control the menstrual cycle, the birth of babies, and breast feeding. The third group of hormones, the **stress hormones,** is activated in emergency situations. They prepare the body to respond to and cope with challenges.

## The Hierarchical Control of Hormones

Figure 6-22 shows that the control and action of hormones are organized into a four-level hierarchy consisting of the brain, the pituitary gland, the endocrine glands, and the target cells affected by the hormones. The brain, mainly the hypothalamus, produces **releasing factors** that instruct the pituitary gland to produce pituitary hormones. The pituitary hormones, in turn, influence the endocrine glands to release appropriate hormones into the bloodstream. These hormones then act on various targets in the body, also providing feedback about the need for more or less hormone.

Although many questions remain about how hormones produce complex behavior, they appear to do so by targeting the brain and activating neurons there. Testosterone's influence on a rooster illustrates some of the ways that this hormone produces male behaviors. Testosterone may have neurotransmitter-like effects on the brain cells that it targets, but it also enters the neurons taking part in crowing, male sexual behavior, and aggression. In these neurons, it is transported into the cell nucleus, where it activates genes. The genes, in turn, trigger the synthesis of proteins needed for cellular processes that produce the rooster's male behaviors. Sensory stimuli also are needed to elicit these behaviors: the rooster crows only at certain times, it is interested in sexual activity only if in the presence of hens, and it is aggressive only when it encounters another rooster. These sensory stimuli serve as signals to the endocrine system.

In addition to influencing behavior, testosterone also initiates changes in the size and appearance of the body. In a rooster, for example, testosterone produces the animal's distinctive plumage and crest, and it activates other sex-related organs. This diversity of testosterone's functions makes it clear why the body uses hormones as messengers. Their targets are so widespread that the best possible way of reaching all of them is to travel by the bloodstream, which goes everywhere in the body.

**Figure 6-22**

The control of hormones is hierarchical. **(A)** In response to sensory stimuli and cognitive activity, the brain influences the activity of the hypothalamus. The hypothalamus produces releasing factors that enter the anterior pituitary through veins and the posterior pituitary through axons. **(B)** On instructions from the releasing hormones, the pituitary releases pituitary hormones into the bloodstream and these hormones target endocrine glands. **(C)** In response to pituitary hormones, the endocrine glands release their own hormones into the bloodstream. Endocrine hormones target wide areas of the body, including the brain.

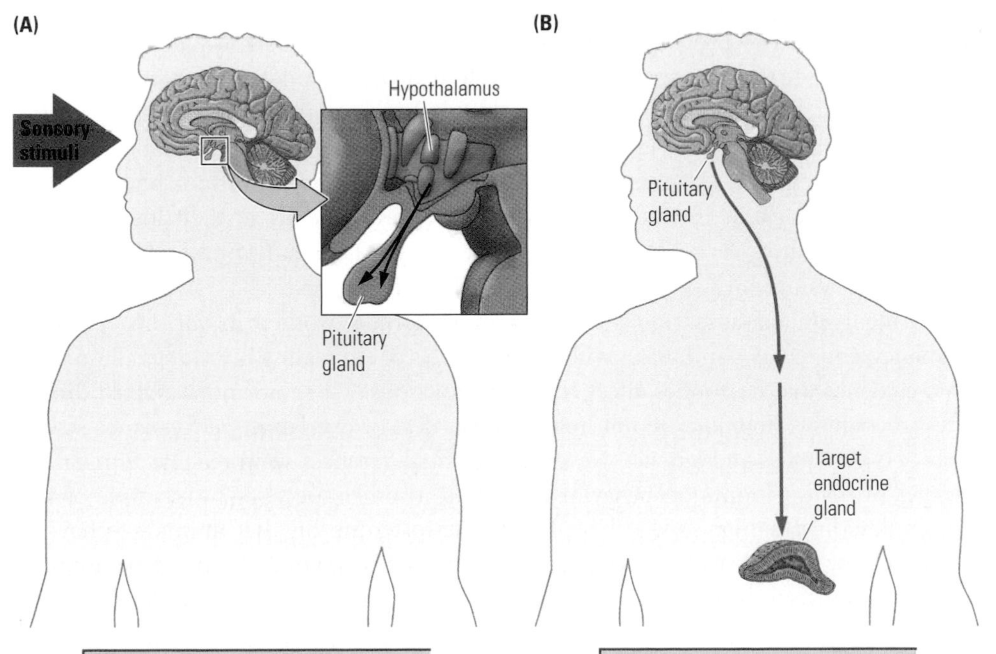


(A) In response to sensory stimuli, the hypothalamus secretes releasing factors into the pituitary gland...

(B) ...which cause the pituitary to release hormones to stimulate the target endocrine gland.

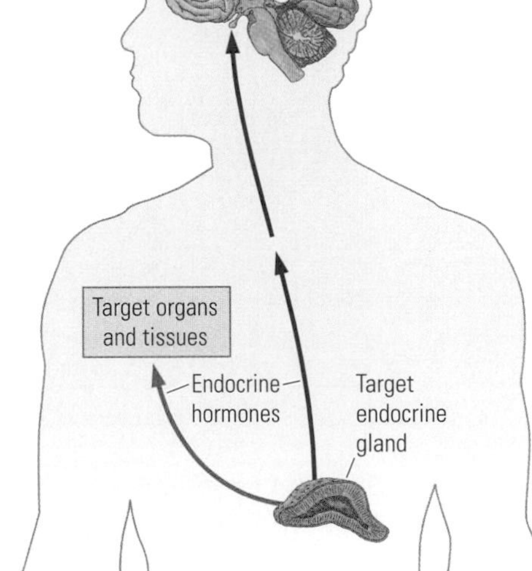


(C) In response to pituitary hormones, the endocrine glands release their own hormones that stimulate target organs, including the brain. In response, the hypothalamus and the pituitary decrease hormone production.

## Homeostatic Hormones

The internal environment of our bodies needs to stay relatively constant in order for us to function. An appropriate balance of sugars, proteins, carbohydrates, salts, and water is required in the bloodstream, in the extracellular compartments of the muscles, in the brain and other body structures, and within all body cells. This constancy, or homeostasis, of the internal environment must be maintained regardless of a person's age, activities, or state. As children or adults, at rest or in strenuous work, when we have overeaten or when we are hungry, a relatively constant internal environment is needed for survival. This makes the homeostatic hormones essential to life itself.

Insulin is an example of a homeostatic hormone. The normal concentration of glucose in the bloodstream varies between 80 and 130 milligrams per 100 milliliters of blood. One group of cells in the pancreas releases insulin, which causes blood sugar to fall by instructing the liver to start storing glucose rather than releasing it and by instructing cells to increase their uptake of glucose. The resulting decrease in glucose then stimulates the pancreatic cells to stop producing insulin. The disorder called diabetes mellitus is caused by a failure of these pancreatic cells to secrete insulin, resulting in a rise in blood-glucose levels and a failure of cells of the body to take up that glucose.

## Reproductive Hormones

We are prepared for reproductive roles by the hormones that give us our sexual appearance and allow us to engage in sex-related behaviors. These sex hormones begin to act on us even before we are born and continue their actions throughout our lives. For males, sex hormones produce the male body and male behaviors. For females, they play a somewhat lesser role in producing the female body, but they control menstrual cycles, regulate many facets of pregnancy and birth, and stimulate milk production for breast-feeding babies.

Hormones also contribute to sex differences in cognitive behavior. Three lines of evidence, summarized by Elizabeth Hamson and Doreen Kimura (1992), support this conclusion. First, the results of spatial and verbal tests given to females and males in many different settings and cultures show that males tend to excel in the spatial tasks and females in the verbal ones. Second, the results of similar tests given to female subjects in the course of the menstrual cycle show fluctuations in test scores with various phases of the cycle. During the phase in which estradiol and progesterone are at their lowest levels, women do comparatively better on spatial tasks, whereas, during the phase when levels of these hormones are high, women do comparatively better on verbal tasks. Third, tests comparing premenopausal and postmenopausal women, women in various stages of pregnancy, and females and males with varying levels of circulating hormones all provide some evidence that hormones affect cognitive functions. These hormone-related differences in cognitive function are not huge. A great deal of overlap in performance scores exists between males and females. Nevertheless, the differences seem reliable. Similar influences of sex hormones on behavior are found in other species. The example of the rooster described earlier shows the effects of testosterone on that animal's behavior. There are now a number of studies that demonstrate that motor skills in female humans and other animals improve at estrus, a time when progesterone levels are high.

## Stress Hormones

**Stress,** a term borrowed from engineering, results from the action of a stressor, an agent that exerts a force and produces a stress response in the recipient. Applied to humans and other animals, **stressors** are events that have an arousing effect on us and

**stress responses** are behavioral and physiological processes that we use to cope with those events. Surprisingly, the response to stress is the same whether the stressor is an exciting event, a sad event, or a frightening event. Robert Sapolsky (1992) uses the vivid image of a hungry lion chasing down a zebra to illustrate this point. The chase for the two animals elicits very different emotional reactions, but their physiological stress responses are the same. Both are in a state of high arousal and are expending maximal energy.

The stress response begins when the brain perceives a stressor—some factor that triggers arousal. The response consists of two separate biochemical sequences, one fast and the other slow. Figure 6-23 shows that the hormone controlling the fast response is **epinephrine,** a chemical very similar to the neurotransmitter noradrenaline, whereas the hormone controlling the slow response is **cortisol.** The epinephrine response causes the "adrenaline" surge that we feel when we are frightened or before an athletic competition or some other important performance. The epinephrine pathway prepares the body for a sudden burst of activity. The cortisol pathway is activated more slowly, in minutes to hours. It prepares the body for longer-lasting adaptations, such as the restoration of cells and tissues after energy expenditure.

Cortisol has a wide range of functions, which include turning off all bodily systems not immediately required to deal with a stressor. For example, cortisol turns off insulin so that the liver starts releasing glucose, thus temporarily producing a homeostatic imbalance. It also shuts down reproductive functions and it inhibits the immune system. In this way, the body's energy supplies can be concentrated on dealing with the stress.

**Figure 6-23**

The stress response activates one of two pathways. In the slow-acting pathway: (1) the hypothalamus releases corticotropin-releasing hormone (CRH) through veins into the anterior pituitary; (2) the pituitary releases adrenocorticotropic-releasing hormone (ACTH) into the bloodstream; (3) cortisol is released by the cortex of the adrenal gland into the circulatory system; and (4) cortisol activates body cells, endocrine glands, and the brain to reduce and control the stressor. In the fast-acting pathway: (1) the brain signals the spinal cord; (2) the sympathetic system of the spinal cord is activated; (3) epinephrine is released from the medulla of the adrenal gland; and (4) epinephrine activates body cells, endocrine glands, and the brain to reduce and control the stressor.

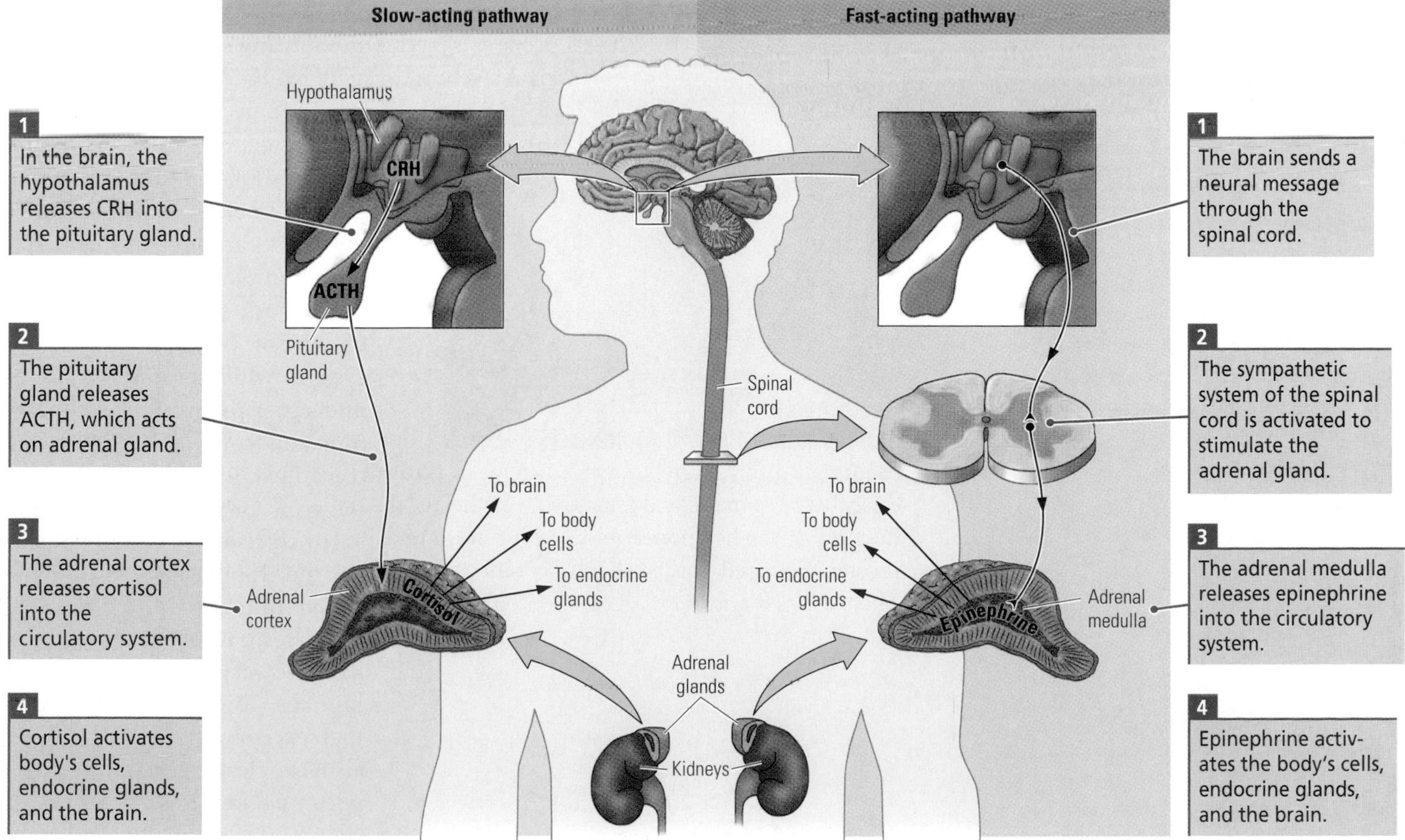

Slow-acting pathway
Fast-acting pathway
1 In the brain, the hypothalamus releases CRH into the pituitary gland.
2 The pituitary gland releases ACTH, which acts on adrenal gland.
3 The adrenal cortex releases cortisol into the circulatory system.
4 Cortisol activates body's cells, endocrine glands, and the brain.
1 The brain sends a neural message through the spinal cord.
2 The sympathetic system of the spinal cord is activated to stimulate the adrenal gland.
3 The adrenal medulla releases epinephrine into the circulatory system.
4 Epinephrine activates the body's cells, endocrine glands, and the brain.
Hypothalamus
CRH
ACTH
Pituitary gland
Spinal cord
To brain
To body cells
To endocrine glands
Adrenal cortex
Cortisol
Adrenal medulla
Epinephrine
Adrenal glands
Kidneys

Cortisol is hydrophobic, but it travels in the bloodstream by attaching itself to a protein. When it leaves the blood, it sheds this protein, penetrates the membranes of cells, and induces gene transcription in the cells' DNA, resulting in the synthesis of new protein molecules. The newly made proteins contribute to mobilizing the body's resources and restoring the damage caused by both the stressor and the stress response.

## Ending a Stress Response

Normally, stressors are short-acting events. The body mobilizes its resources, deals with the challenge, and then shuts off the stress response. Just as the brain is responsible for turning on the stress reaction, it is also responsible for turning it off. When it detects that the stressor is over, it instructs the hypothalamus to shut down the stress response.

Robert Sapolsky argues that the hippocampus plays an important role in turning off the stress response. The hippocampus contains a high density of cortisol receptors, and it has axons that project to the hypothalamus. Consequently, the hippocampus is well suited to detecting cortisol in the blood and instructing the hypothalamus to reduce blood-cortisol levels.

There may, however, be a more insidious relation between the hippocampus and blood-cortisol levels. When Sapolsky and his coworkers observed wild-born vervet monkeys that had become agricultural pests in Kenya and had therefore been trapped and caged, they found that some of the monkeys became sick and died of a syndrome that appeared to be related to stress. The animals that died seemed to have been subordinate ones housed with particularly aggressive dominant monkeys. Autopsies showed high rates of gastric ulcers, enlarged adrenal glands, and pronounced hippocampal degeneration. The hippocampal damage may have been due to prolonged high cortisol levels produced by the unremitting stress of being caged with the aggressive monkeys. Cortisol levels are usually regulated by the hippocampus, but, if these levels remain elevated because a stress-inducing situation continues, the high cortisol levels eventually damage the hippocampus. The damaged hippocampus is then unable to do its work of reducing the level of cortisol. This sets up a vicious cycle in which the hippocampus undergoes progressive degeneration and cortisol levels are not controlled. The circular relation between prolonged stress, elevated cortisol levels, and damage to the hippocampus is illustrated in Figure 6-24. Because stress-response circuits in monkeys are very similar to those in humans, the possibility exists that excessive stress in humans also can lead to damaged hippocampal neurons.

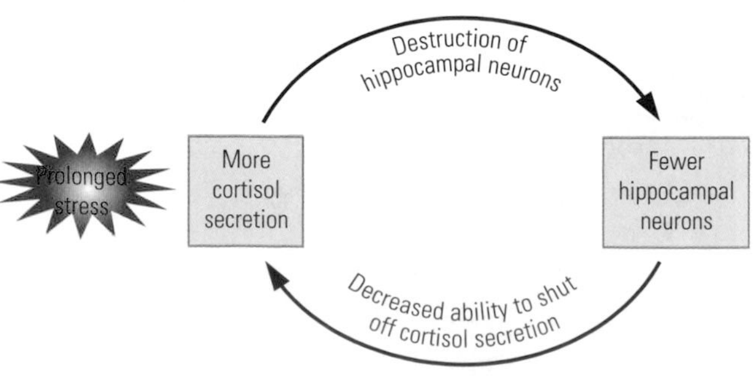


**Figure 6-24** When stress is unrelieved, excessive release of cortisol causes damage to neurons in the hippocampus. The damaged neurons are unable to signal the adrenal gland to shut off the production of cortisol, resulting in enhanced secretion of cortisol and further damage to hippocampal neurons.

## In Review

Endocrine glands produce hormones and distribute them through the bloodstream to targets throughout the body. Hormones are hierarchically controlled by sensory experiences, the brain, the pituitary gland, and the endocrine glands that secrete them. Hormones can be classified into three groups: homeostatic hormones, which regulate body nutrients and metabolic processes; reproductive hormones, which regulate sexual behavior, pregnancy, and child bearing; and stress hormones, which regulate the body's responses to challenging events. Because these hormones often have such widespread targets, traveling through the bloodstream is an effective way for them to deliver their chemical messages.

## SUMMARY

1. *How do drugs enter the body, reach their target, and leave the body?* Drugs, which are chemicals taken to bring about some desired change in the body, are administered in a number of ways, including by mouth, by inhalation, and by injection. To reach a target in the nervous system, a drug must pass a through a number of barriers, including those posed by the digestive system, capillaries of the blood system, the blood–brain barrier, and the cell membranes. Drugs are diluted by the fluids of the body as they pass through these successive barriers until they reach their target cells. Drugs produce their effects by acting on receptors or chemical processes in the nervous system, especially on processes of neural transmission at synapses. They act either as agonists to stimulate neurons or as antagonists to depress neurons. Drugs are metabolized in the body and are excreted through feces, urine, sweat glands, and breath.
2. *How do individual people respond to drugs?* A drug does not have a uniform action on every person. Many physical differences, including differences in body weight, sex, age, and genetic background, influence the effects of a given drug.
3. *How are drugs classified?* Psychoactive drugs are classified into seven groups according to their major behavioral effects: sedative hypnotics and antianxiety agents, antipsychotic agents, antidepressants, mood stabilizers, narcotic analgesics, psychomotor stimulants, and stimulants that have psychedelic and hallucinogenic effects. Each group of drugs contains many natural or synthetic drugs or both, and they may produce their actions in different ways.
4. *How does the repeated use of drugs and their use in different contexts affect behavior?* A common misperception of drugs is that they have relatively specific and constant actions. The body and brain rapidly become tolerant to many drugs, and so the dose must be increased to produce the same effect. Alternatively, people may also become sensitized to a drug, and so the same dose produces increasingly greater effects. Learning also plays an important role in what people do when they are under the influence of a drug.
5. *Why do people become addicted to drugs?* Addiction develops in a number of stages as a result of repeated drug taking. Initially, the drug-taking act produces pleasure or liking. With repeated use of the drug, however, the act of taking it becomes conditioned to associated objects, events, and places. Eventually, those cues acquire incentive salience, causing the drug user to seek them out, which leads to

**neuroscience interactive**

NOFAS.org

There are many resources available for expanding your learning on line:

- **www.worthpublishers.com/kolb/chapter6**
  Try some self-tests to reinforce your mastery of the material. Look at some of the news updates reflecting current research on the brain. You'll also be able to link to other sites which will reinforce what you've learned.

- **www.nofas.org**
  Link to this site to learn more about fetal alchohol syndrome.

- **www.niaaa.nih.gov**
  Investigate the state of the research on alchohol abuse at this branch of the National Institutes of Health.

On your CD-ROM you'll be able to quiz yourself on your comprehension of the chapter. The module on Neural Communication also provides important review on the basics of synaptic communication.

more drug taking. The subjective experience associated with prominent cues and drug seeking is wanting the drug. As addiction proceeds, the subjective experience of liking decreases while that of wanting increases.

6. *Does the effect of a drug depend on the drug-taking situation?* The influence of drugs on behavior varies widely with the situation and as a person learns appropriate drug-related behaviors. Some drugs, such as alcohol, can produce myopia such that a person's behavior is primarily influenced by prominent cues in the environment. These cues may encourage the person to behave in ways that he or she would not normally behave.
7. *Can the repeated use of drugs produce brain damage?* The use of alcohol can be associated with damage to the thalamus and hypothalamus, but the cause of the damage is poor nutrition rather than the direct actions of alcohol. Cocaine can harm the brain's circulation, producing brain damage by reduced blood flow or by bleeding into neural tissue. The drug "ecstasy," or MDMA, can result in the loss of fine axon collaterals of serotonin neurons. Marijuana and LSD are associated with psychotic behavior, but it is not clear whether this behavior is due to the direct effects of the drugs or to the aggravation of preexisting conditions.
8. *What are hormones?* Hormones are substances that are produced by glands in the body and circulate in the bloodstream to affect a wide variety of targets. Homeostatic hormones regulate the balance of sugars, proteins, carbohydrates, salts, and other substances in the body. Reproductive hormones regulate the physical features and behaviors associated with reproduction and the care of offspring. Stress hormones regulate the body's ability to cope with arousing and challenging situations. Hormones are under the hierarchical control of sensory events, the brain, the pituitary gland, and the endocrine glands, which all interact to regulate hormone levels.

## KEY TERMS

addiction, p. 216
alcohol myopia, p. 220
antianxiety agent, p. 201
cellular tolerance, p. 213
cross-tolerance, p. 201
glutamate analogue, p. 222
incentive salience, p. 217
incentive-sensitization theory, p. 218
metabolic tolerance, p. 213
physical dependence, p. 216
psychomotor activation, p. 216
sensitization, p. 213
substance abuse, p. 216
substance dependence, p. 216
withdrawal symptoms, p. 216

## REVIEW QUESTIONS

1. What problems are encountered in making a psychoactive drug a "magic bullet" targeting the central nervous system?
2. Describe how the blood–brain barrier works.
3. Describe the seven categories of drugs.
4. Distinguish between the dependency hypothesis and the wanting-and-liking theory of drug addiction.
5. Distinguish between the disinhibition, time-out, and alcohol-myopia explanations of behavior under the effects of drugs.
6. Describe the hierarchical control of hormones.
7. Describe the relation among stress, cortisol, and the hippocampus.

## FOR FURTHER THOUGHT

A traditional view of drugs is that they cause people to do certain things. Discuss contemporary views of how drugs can influence our behavior.

Because many drugs work by affecting the function of synapses, the effect that they produce must be similar to some naturally produced behavior. Discuss this idea in relation to a drug of your choice.

## RECOMMENDED READING

Becker, J. B., Breedlove, S. M., & Crews, D. (2000). *Behavioral endocrinology*. Cambridge, MA: MIT Press. A book consisting of a number of chapters on hormones, each written by an expert.

Cooper, J. R., Bloom, F. E., & Roth, R. H. (1996). *The biochemical basis of neuropharmacology*. New York: Oxford University Press. A summary of how synapses respond to drugs. Consists of a general description of how synapses work and summarizes the structure and function of a number of different neurochemical synapses.

Feldman, R. S., Meyer, J. S., & Quenzer, L. F. (1997). *Principles of neuropsychopharmacology*. Sunderland, MA: Sinauer. A comprehensive but advanced book about how various drugs affect the nervous system. An outstanding reference on contemporary neuropsychopharmacology.

Julien, R. M. (2001). *A primer of drug action*. New York: Worth. As the name suggests, this book is an extremely readable introduction to how drugs affect the nervous system and produce changes in behavior, mood, and cognitive function.

Sapolsky, R. M. (1994). *Why zebras don't get ulcers*. New York: W. H. Freeman and Company. A readable popular summary of everything you would like to know about stress. The theme of the book is that stress affects the brain and contributes to a great many medical conditions—including heart disease, depression, sexual and reproductive problems, and hormonal disorders—to aging, and to death; finally, of course, it affects zebras.

CHAPTER

7

# How Does the Brain Develop?



Myrleen F. Cate/Photo Network/Picture Quest
Micrograph: Oliver Meckes/Ottawa/Photo Researchers

A monarch butterfly begins life as a fertilized egg and develops into a caterpillar. After a time, the caterpillar spins a cocoon, inside of which it lives as it undergoes a process that transforms it into a butterfly. The stages of development in the life cycle of a monarch butterfly are collectively called metamorphosis and are shown in Figure 7-1. Consider how formidable this insect's development is. First, the egg must develop a body, including a nervous system. This nervous system has to produce caterpillar-like movements and control the animal's feeding apparatus, which is designed for munching leaves. Then, during metamorphosis, the original nervous system has to be reconstructed to control the flight, feeding, and reproductive behaviors of a butterfly. The addition of flying behavior is remarkable because it requires the use of entirely different muscles from those used in crawling. Furthermore, adult monarch butterflies fly very long distances in their annual migration and must navigate to the correct geographical location. In contrast, the caterpillar's main challenge is to find an appropriate food source as it crawls slowly around in a limited area. It seems that a caterpillar would need a major overhaul of its brain to control the completely reconfigured body and brand-new behaviors that go with being a butterfly.

We humans do not metamorphose into a different life form in the course of our development, but the developmental problems that we face are similar to those of the monarch. We also begin life as a fertilized egg that develops a body and a nervous system. When we are born, however, we are not able to fend for ourselves. Human offspring are virtually helpless for an extended period of time. The behavioral demands on the brain of a newborn include relatively simple actions such as searching for and recognizing a nipple with which to feed and signaling hunger or discomfort to caregivers. But soon a human infant undergoes an enormous transformation. The child's brain becomes able to control a variety of new behaviors such as crawling and, later, walking, eating solid foods, using tools, and learning a language. At school age, the child's brain becomes able to formulate complex ideas, solve challenging problems, and remember large quantities of information. And changes in a person's nervous system do not end with graduation from college. As the adult brain begins to age in the third decade of life, it starts to lose cells and grows few new ones. The loss forces the middle-aged brain to reconstruct some of its parts to forestall the effects of aging. Brain development, then, is a continuous process that is central to our functioning. Changes in the brain allow us to adapt to the environment throughout our life cycle.

This chapter answers many questions about the development of the human brain. How did your brain manage to develop from a single embryonic cell into an organ made up of billions of cells? This question parallels one asked in Chapter 1—namely, how did the brain evolve from a small and simple organ into a large and

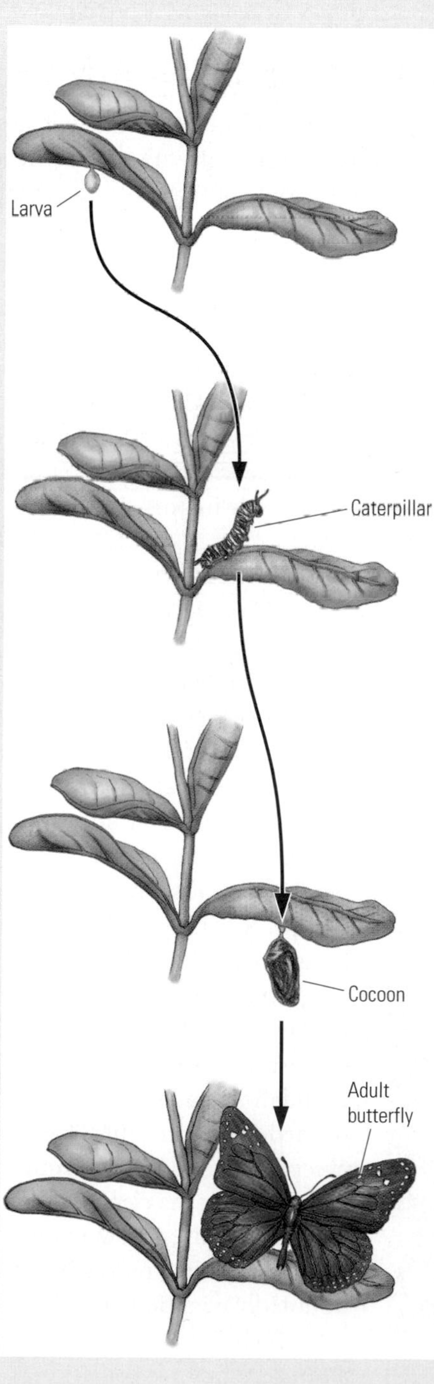


**Figure 7-1**
In metamorphosis, the nervous system of the monarch butterfly must undergo significant changes as the insect develops from a larva into a caterpillar into a butterfly.

highly complex one? When we consider that there are many kinds of neurons and glia and that they must be located in specific nuclei, layers, and so on, we are left wondering how all this complicated architecture is accomplished. Is there a blueprint of some sort and, if so, where does it come from and how is it read? Is there any relation between brain development and behavioral development? And how do our experiences influence the development of the brain? You will soon learn that the brain's development is affected by many factors, some of which can lead to abnormalities. When you become aware of how many influences on brain development there are, you may wonder how so many people end up with a normal brain.

## PERSPECTIVES ON BRAIN DEVELOPMENT

To begin to understand how the brain is constructed, we start with an analogy of building a house. Do not take this analogy too literally. It is used here simply as a way of introducing the topic of brain development and some important principles related to it.

### Mr. Higgins Builds a House

Mr. Higgins finds a picture of his dream house in a magazine and decides to build it himself. The house has a basement, which contains the furnace, a hot-water tank, and other essential machinery. The first floor accommodates a kitchen, a bathroom, and a general living area. The second story contains a master bedroom and Mr. Higgins's den. The den is extremely important, because it is here that Mr. Higgins will work as a mystery book writer.

Mr. Higgins quickly discovers that houses do not just materialize; they go through several stages of development. First, Mr. Higgins orders a blueprint. The blueprint outlines the house's structure and ensures that everyone taking part in its construction is building the same house. The construction process begins with the laying of a concrete foundation. At this point, however, Mr. Higgins starts to realize that the blueprint is not as detailed as it first appeared. It specifies where the walls and pipes and plugs will be, but it does not always say exactly what materials to use where. Thus, the choice of a particular kind of plywood or a particular type of nail or screw is often more or less random within certain limitations. Similarly, the blueprint specifies that there should be connections between certain circuits in the power box and certain fixtures or plugs, but it does not detail the precise route that the connecting wires should take. Mr. Higgins also finds that the blueprint does not specify the precise order in which tasks should be done. He knows that the foundation has to be finished first, the subfloor next, and the walls framed after that. But what comes then is largely left to his discretion, except where a certain sequence is required to make something work (for example, the electrical wiring must be installed before the walls are closed in.) Given how many options are open to him in building the house, Mr. Higgins realizes that his version of the building will undoubtedly be different from anyone else's.

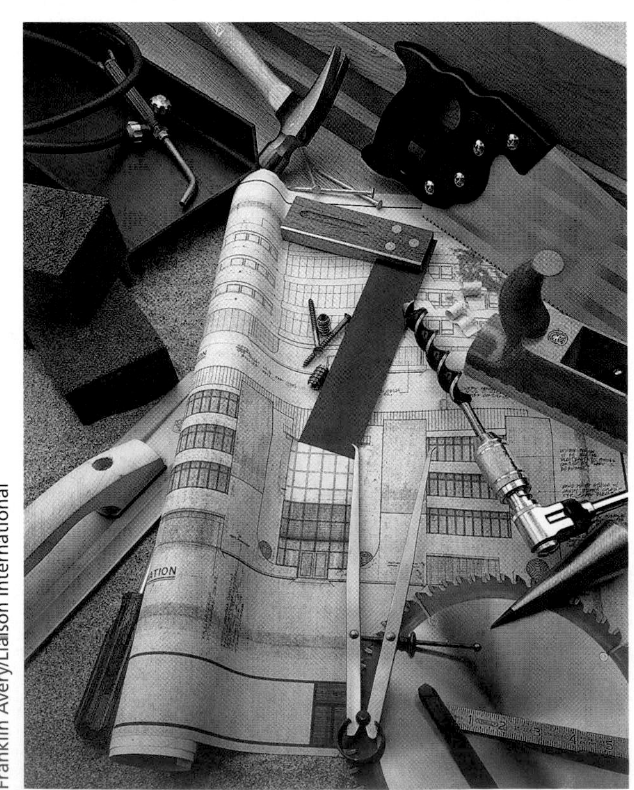

Franklin Avery/Liaison International

Much the same problems are encountered in building a brain. Like a house, a brain is constructed in levels, each one with a different function. And, just as house plans are written in the form of a blueprint, the plans for a brain are encoded in genes. As Mr. Higgins learned, architects do not specify every detail in a blueprint; nor do genes include every instruction for how a brain is assembled and wired. The process of building a brain is just too complex to be encoded entirely and precisely in genes. For this reason, the fate of billions of brain cells is left partly open, especially when it comes to the massive undertaking of forming appropriate connections between cells.

If the structure and fate of each brain cell are not specified in advance, what factors do control brain development? Many factors are at work, including special molecules, such as hormones. Brain development is also influenced by the experiences that people have both in the womb and after they are born. We return to these influences later in this chapter, after examining the major stages in brain development. But first we explore how scientists go about studying the interconnected processes of brain and behavioral development.

## Linking Brain and Behavioral Development

In the course of development, changes take place both in the brain and in behavior. Scientists assume that these two lines of development are closely linked. As the brain develops, neurons become more and more intricately connected, and these increasingly complex interconnections underlie increased behavioral complexity.

We can study the relation between brain and behavioral development in three basic ways. First, we can look at the structural development of the nervous system and correlate it with the emergence of specific behaviors. For example, we can link the development of certain brain structures to the development of, say, grasping or crawling in infants. As the brain structures develop, their functions emerge; these functions are manifested in behaviors that we can observe.

Structures that develop quickly exhibit their functions sooner than structures that develop more slowly. Because the human brain continues to develop well into adolescence, you should not be surprised that some behavioral abilities emerge rather late in development. For example, the frontal lobes continue to develop well into adolescence, reaching maturity at about 16 years of age. It follows that certain behaviors controlled by the frontal lobes also are slow to develop.

Perhaps the best example is the ability to understand the nuances of social interaction, which is a function of the frontal lobes. One way to test a person's understanding of social interaction is illustrated in Figure 7-2. The person looks at a cartoon scene and is asked to mimic the facial expression appropriate for the face that is blank. Adults have no difficulty with this task, but children are very poor at producing the right expression. The ability does not emerge until midadolescence. It is not that children have trouble producing facial expressions; they do so spontaneously at a very early age. What they lack is an adultlike ability to interpret what a particular social interaction means, because brain structures that play an important role in this ability are very late to mature. Children therefore make many social gaffes and are often unable to grasp all the nuances of a social situation. Behaviors that seem simple to us, such as a wink or a flirtatious look, are incomprehensible to children. Children, then, are not miniature adults who simply need to learn the "rules" of adult behavior. The brain of a child is very different from that of an adult, and the brains of children at different ages are really not comparable either.

**Figure 7-2**

This task of social perception is one that children have great difficulty in accomplishing. The task is to mimic the facial expression that is most appropriate for the blank in the drawing.

Adapted from "Developmental Changes in the Recognition and Comprehensional Expression: Implications for Frontal Lobe Function," by B. Kolb, B. Wilson, and L. Taylor, 1992, *Brain and Cognition, 20*, p. 77.

The second way to examine the relation between brain and behavioral development is to turn our sequence of observations around. First we scrutinize behavior for the emergence of new abilities, and then we make inferences about underlying neural maturation. For example, as language emerges in the young child, we expect to find corresponding changes in neural structures that control language. In fact, this is what we do find. At birth, children do not speak, and even extensive speech training would not enable them to do so. The neural structures that control speech are not yet mature enough. As language emerges, we can conclude that the speech-related structures in the brain are undergoing the necessary maturation. The same reasoning can be applied to frontal-lobe development. As frontal-lobe structures mature in adolescence, we look for related changes in behavior, but we can also do the reverse: because we observe new abilities emerging in the teenage years, we infer that they must be controlled by late-maturing neural structures.

The third way to study the relation between brain and behavioral development is to identify and study factors that influence both. From this perspective, the mere emergence of a certain fully developed brain structure is not enough; we must also know the events that shape how that structure functions and produce certain kinds of behaviors. Some of the events that influence brain function are sensory experience, injuries, and the actions of hormones and abnormal genes. Logically, if behavior is influenced by one of these experiences, then structures in the brain that are changed by that experience are responsible for the behavioral outcomes. For example, we might study how the abnormal secretion of a hormone affects both a certain brain structure and a certain behavior. We can then infer that, because the observed behavioral abnormality results from the abnormal functioning of the brain structure, that structure must normally play some role in controlling the behavior.

By applying each of these three approaches to the study of brain and behavioral development, we can shed much light on the nature of brain organization and function. We begin by considering the anatomical development of the child's brain. We then explore the behavioral correlates of brain development. Finally, we explore some factors that influence the development of both the brain and behavior.

### In Review

Brain development can be approached from three different perspectives. First, the structural development can be studied and correlated with the emergence of behavior. Second, behavioral development can be analyzed and predictions can be made about what underlying circuitry must be emerging. Finally, those factors that influence brain and behavioral development, such as an injury to the brain, can be studied. In this last approach, the idea is that events that alter behavioral development should similarly alter structural development.

## THE DEVELOPMENT OF THE CHILD'S BRAIN

Some 2000 years ago the Roman philosopher Seneca proposed that a human embryo was a miniature person. According to him, the task of development was simply to grow bigger. This idea, known as *preformation*, was so appealing that, until fairly recently, it was widely believed to be true. In fact, even with the development of the microscope, the appeal of preformation was so strong that biologists claimed to be able to see microscopic horses in horse semen.

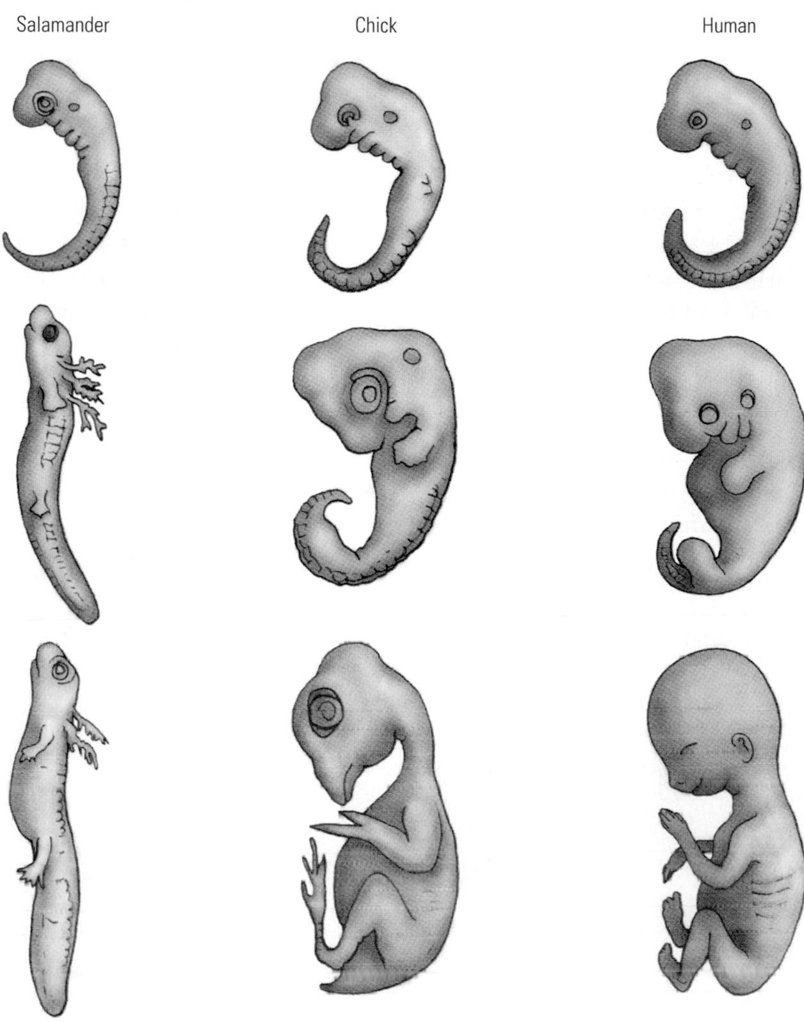


**Figure 7-3**

The similarity of embryos of different species is striking in the earliest stages of development, as these salamander, chick, and human embryos show. This similarity led to the conclusion that embryos are not miniature versions of adults.

By the middle of the nineteenth century, the idea of preformation began to wane as people realized that embryos looked nothing like the adults that they become. In fact, it was obvious that embryos of different species more closely resembled one another than their respective parents. Figure 7-3 shows the striking similarity in the early embryos of species as diverse as salamanders, chickens, and humans. Early in development, all species have a similar-looking primitive head, which is a region with bumps or folds, and all possess a tail. It is only as the embryo develops that it acquires the distinctive characteristics of its species. The similarity of young embryos is so great that many nineteenth-century biologists saw it as evidence for Darwin's view that vertebrates arose from a common ancestor millions of years ago.

Although nervous systems are not shown in Figure 7-3, embryos are structurally similar in their nervous systems as well as in their bodies. Figure 7-4 reveals that the nervous system of a young vertebrate embryo always has three regions: the forebrain, the brainstem (with the midbrain and hindbrain clearly visible), and the remaining neural tube, which forms the spinal cord. Where do these three regions come from? We can answer this question by tracing events as the embryo matures.

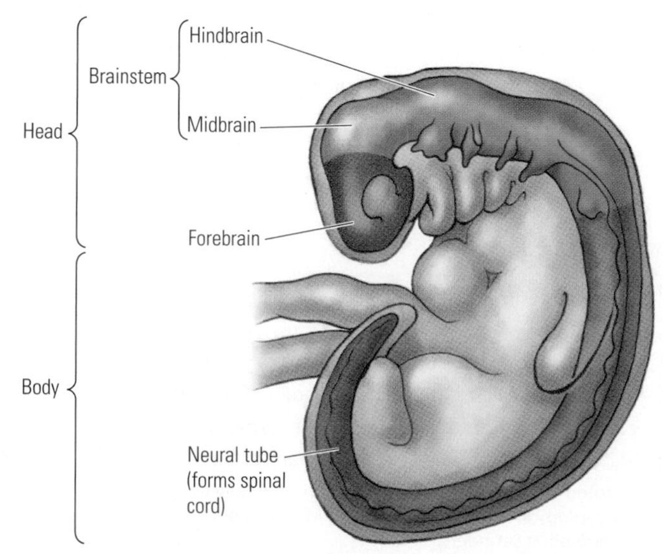


**Figure 7-4**

The basic human brain regions of the forebrain, the midbrain, and the hindbrain are visible at about 28 days, as is the remaining neural tube, which will form the spinal cord.

**Neural plate.** The thickened region of the ectodermal layer that gives rise to the neural tube.

**Neural tube.** A structure in the early stage of brain development from which the brain and spinal cord develop.

Visit the Web site at **www.worthpublishers.com/kolb/chapter7** to link to visual tours of human fetal development.

## The Gross Development of the Human Nervous System

At the time an egg is fertilized by a sperm, a human zygote consists of just a single cell. But this cell soon begins to divide; by the 15th day, the embryo resembles a fried egg. It is made of several sheets of cells with a raised area in the middle, as shown in Figure 7-5. The raised area is called the *primitive body*. By 3 weeks after conception, there is primitive neural tissue, known as the **neural plate,** which is part of the outermost layer of embryonic cells. The neural plate first folds to form a groove, called the *neural groove*, as illustrated in Figure 7-6. The neural groove then curls to form the **neural tube,** much as a flat sheet of paper can be curled to make a cylinder. Micrographs of the neural tube closing in a mouse embryo can be seen in Figure 7-7. The cells that form the neural tube can be thought of as the "nursery" for the rest of the nervous system. The open region in the center of the tube remains open and becomes the brain's ventricles and the spinal canal.

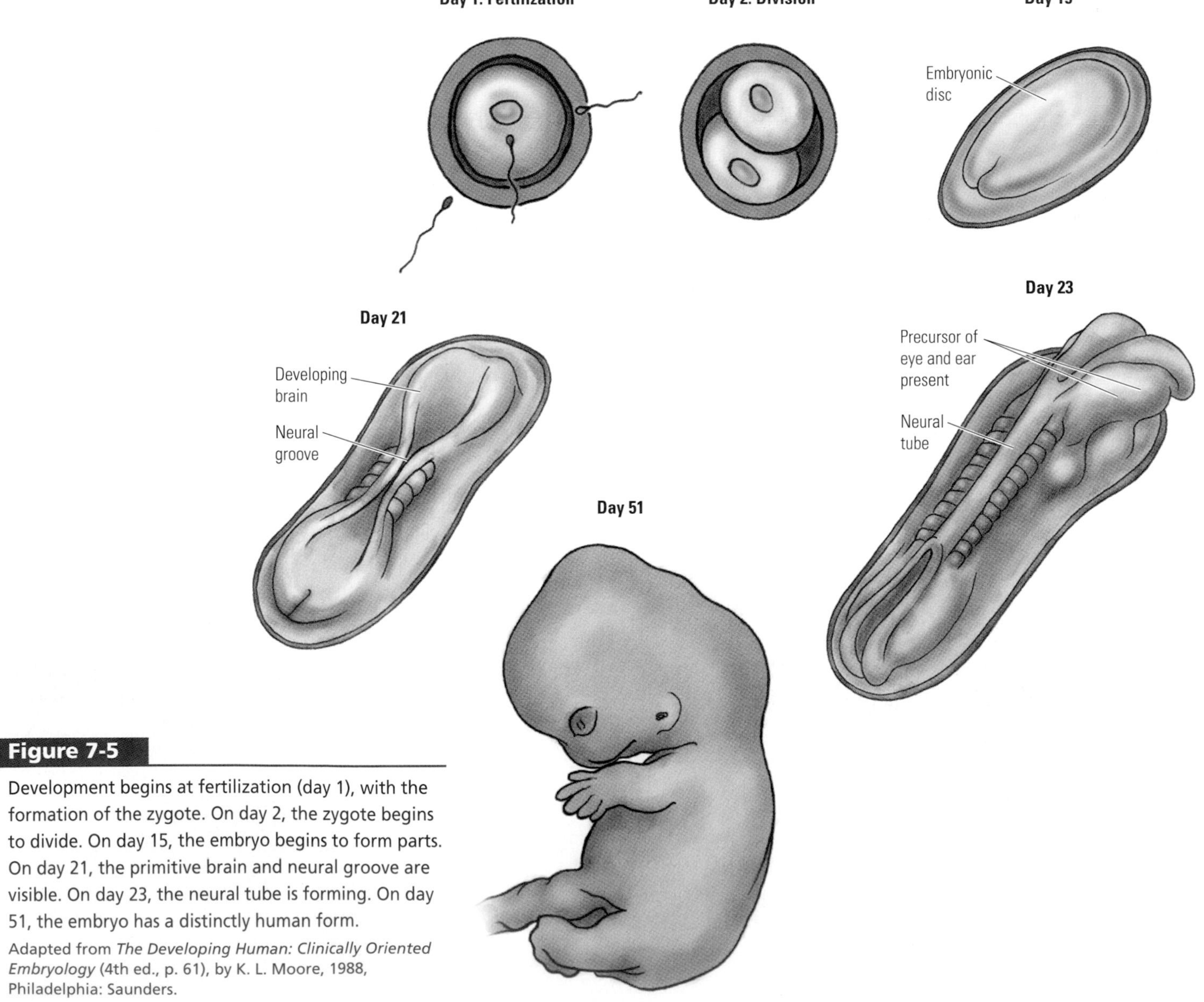


**Figure 7-5**

Development begins at fertilization (day 1), with the formation of the zygote. On day 2, the zygote begins to divide. On day 15, the embryo begins to form parts. On day 21, the primitive brain and neural groove are visible. On day 23, the neural tube is forming. On day 51, the embryo has a distinctly human form.

Adapted from *The Developing Human: Clinically Oriented Embryology* (4th ed., p. 61), by K. L. Moore, 1988, Philadelphia: Saunders.

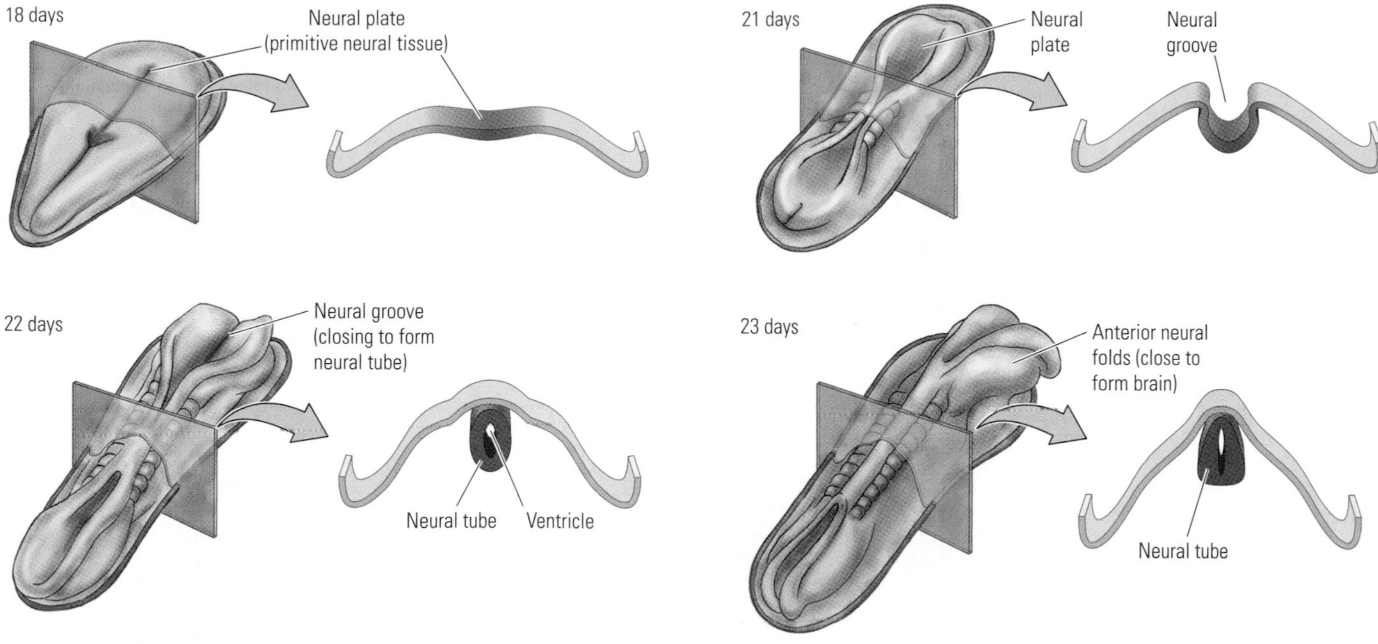


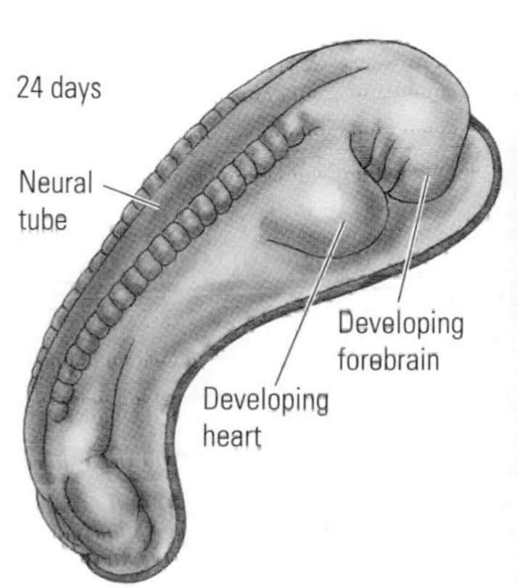


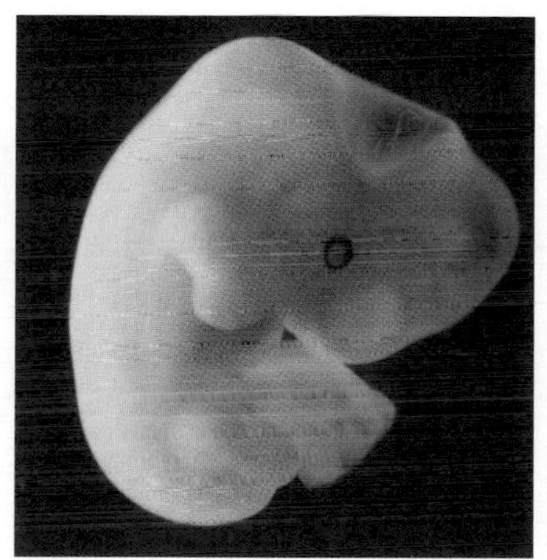


**Figure 7-6**

In the formation of the neural tube, the precursor of the nervous system, a long depression (the neural groove) is first formed in the neural plate. The neural plate collapses inward, forming a tube along the length of the dorsal surface of the embryo. The embryo is shown in a photograph at 24 days.

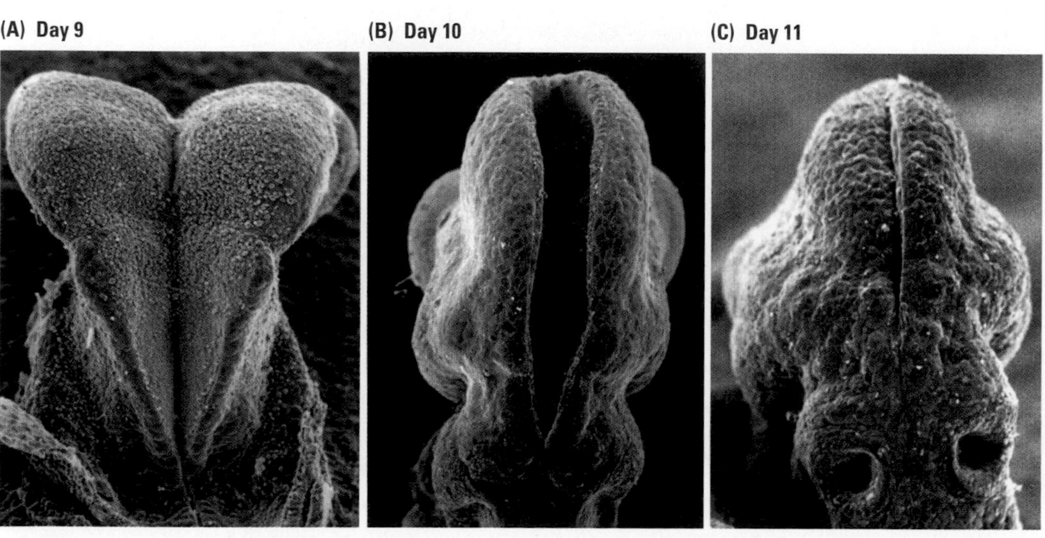


**Figure 7-7**

Scanning electron micrographs show the closing of the neural tube in a mouse embryo.

Reproduced with the permission of Dr. R. E. Poelman, Laboratory of Anatomy, University of Leyden.

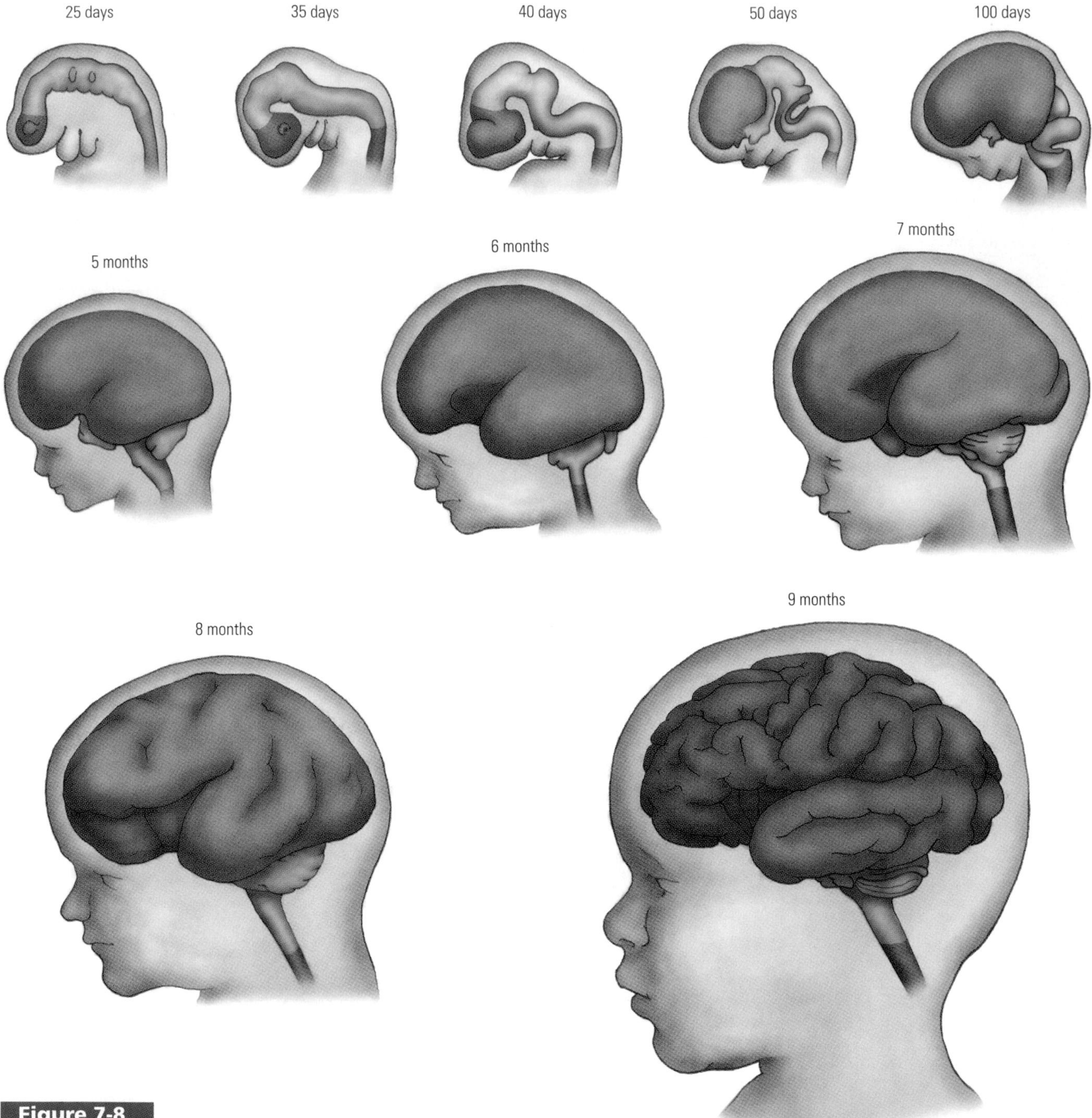


**Figure 7-8**

In prenatal development, the human brain undergoes a series of embryonic and fetal stages. Refer to Figure 7-4 for identification of the various parts of the nervous system.

Adapted from "The Development of the Brain," by W. M. Cowan, 1979, *Scientific American, 241*(3), p. 116.

The body and the nervous system change rapidly in the next 3 weeks of development. By 7 weeks (or 49 days), the embryo begins to resemble a miniature person, as can be seen in Figure 7-5. Figure 7-8 shows that the brain looks distinctly human by about 100 days after conception, but it does not begin to form gyri and sulci until about 7 months. By the end of the 9th month, the brain has the gross appearance of the adult human brain, even though its cellular structure is different.

Another developmental process, shown in Figure 7-9, is sexual development. Although the genitals begin to form in the 7th week after conception, they appear identical in the two sexes at this early stage. There is not yet any *sexual dimorphism*, or

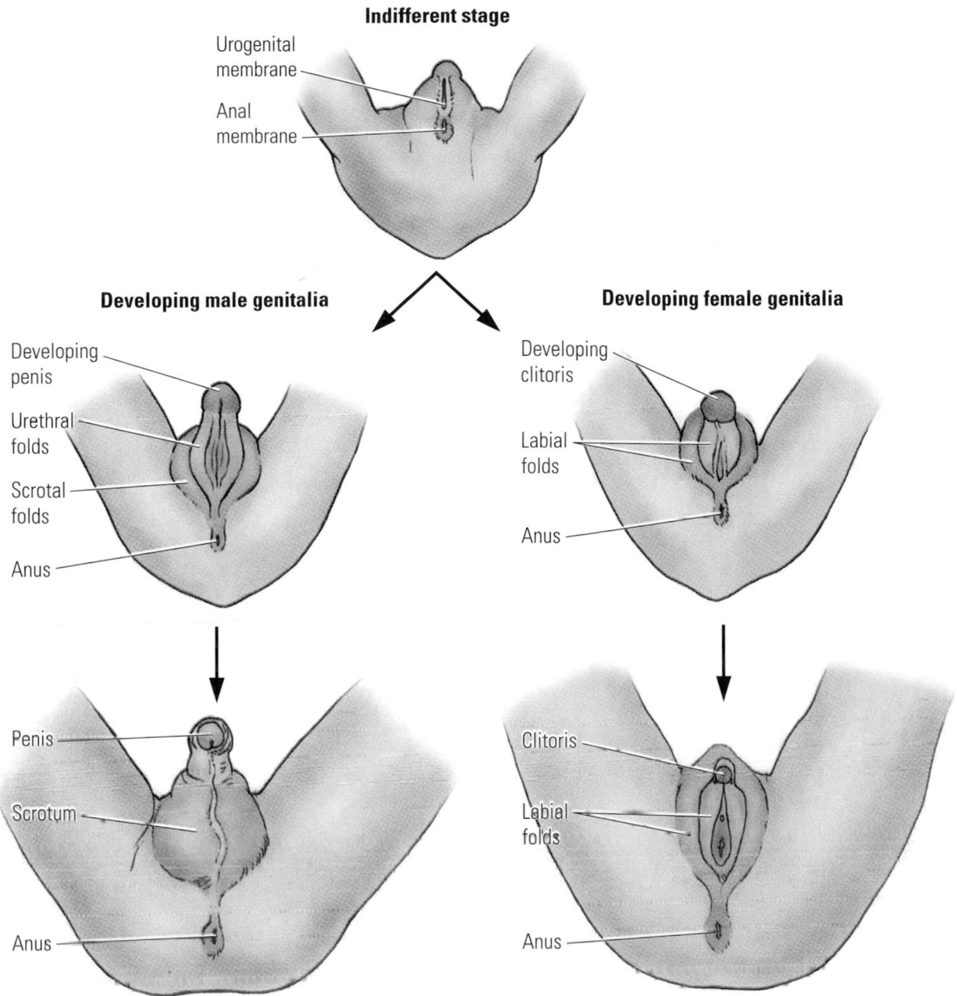


**Figure 7-9**

Sexual differentiation in the human infant. Early in development (indifferent stage), the human male and female embryos are identical. In response to testosterone in male embryos, the genitalia begin to develop into the male structure at about 60 days. In the absence of testosterone, the female structure emerges. Parallel changes take place in the brain in response to the absence or presence of testosterone.

structural difference between the two sexes. Then, about 60 days after conception, male and female genitals start to become distinguishable. But what does this sexual differentiation have to do with brain development? The answer is that sexual differentiation is stimulated by the presence of the hormone testosterone in male embryos. Testosterone changes the genetic activity of certain cells, most obviously those that form the genitals. However, genital cells are not the only cells influenced by testosterone. The brain also has cells that respond to this hormone, so certain regions of the embryonic brain also may begin to show sexual dimorphism, beginning about 60 days after conception.

## The Origins of Neurons and Glia

The cells lining the neural tube, the nursery for the brain, are known as **neural stem cells.** A stem cell is a cell with an extensive capacity for self-renewal. It divides and produces two stem cells, which both can divide again. In adulthood, one stem cell dies after division, leaving a constant number of dividing stem cells. In an adult, the neural stem cells line the ventricles and thus form what is called the **ventricular zone.**

If lining the ventricles were all that stem cells did throughout the decades of a human life, they would seem like odd kinds of cells to possess. But stem cells also have

**Neural stem cells.** Cells that give rise to all neurons in the nervous system.

**Ventricular zone.** The zone surrounding the ventricles in which stem cells reside.

**Figure 7-10**

Cells in the brain begin as multipotential stem cells, which become precursor cells, which become blasts, which finally develop into specialized neurons or glia.

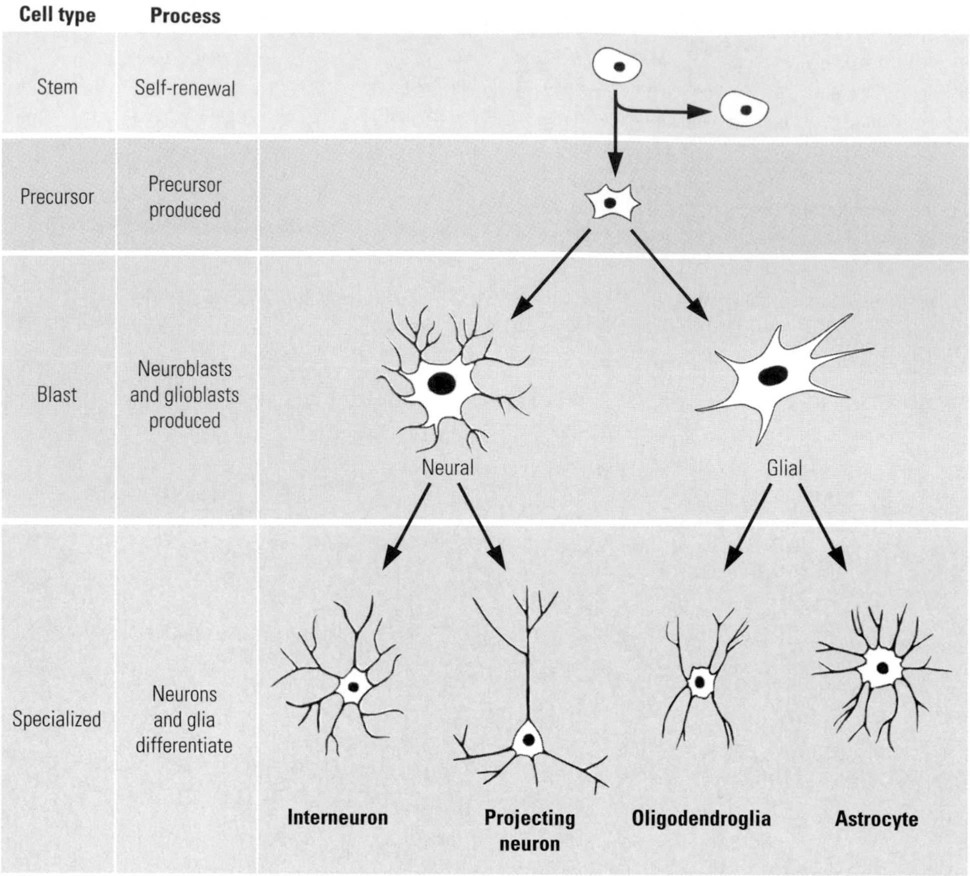


another function: they give rise to so-called **progenitor** (precursor) **cells.** These progenitor cells also can divide and, as shown in Figure 7-10, they eventually produce nondividing cells known as **neuroblasts** and **glioblasts.** In turn, neuroblasts and glioblasts become neurons and glia when they mature. Neural stem cells, then, are the cells that give rise to all the many specialized cells of the brain and spinal cord.

Sam Weiss and his colleagues (1996) discovered that stem cells remain capable of producing neurons and glia not just into early adulthood, but even in an aging brain. This discovery is important because it implies that neurons that die in an adult brain should be replaceable. We do not yet know how to instruct stem cells to carry out this replacement process, however. Consequently, injury to central nervous system tissue usually remains permanent.

An important question in the study of brain development is how cells are generated to form stem cells, progenitor cells, neuro- and glioblasts, and finally neurons and glia. In other words, how does a cell "know" to become a neuron rather than a skin cell? Recall that each human cell has 23 chromosome pairs containing the approximately 100,000 genes of the human genome. In each cell, certain genes are "turned on" by a signal, and those genes then produce a particular cell type. "Turned on" means that a formerly dormant gene becomes activated, which results in the cell making a specific kind of protein. You can easily imagine that certain types of proteins are needed to produce skin cells, whereas other types of proteins are needed for neurons. The specific signals for turning on genes are largely unknown, but these signals are probably chemical. Thus, the chemical environment of a cell in the brain is different from that of a cell forming skin, and so different genes in these cells are activated, producing different proteins and different cell types. The different chemical environments needed to trigger this cellular differentiation could be caused by the activity of other

**Progenitor cell.** A cell that is derived from a stem cell and acts as a precursor cell that migrates and produces a neuron or a glial cell.

**Neuroblast.** A progenitor cell that gives rise to all the different types of neurons.

**Glioblast.** A progenitor cell that gives rise to different types of glial cells.

neighboring cells or by chemicals, such as hormones, that are transported in the bloodstream.

You can see that the differentiation of stem cells into neurons must require a series of signals and the resulting activation of genes. A chemical signal must induce the stem cells to produce progenitor cells, and then another chemical signal must induce the progenitor cells to produce either neuroblasts or glioblasts. Finally, a chemical signal, or perhaps even a set of signals, must induce the genes to make a neuron or a particular type of neuron.

One class of compounds that signal cells to develop in particular ways comprises so-called **neurotrophic factors.** By removing stem cells from the brain of an animal and placing those cells in solutions that keep them alive, researchers can study how neurotrophic factors function. When one compound, known as *epidermal growth factor* (EGF), is added to the cell culture, it stimulates stem cells to produce progenitor cells. Another compound, *basic fibroblast growth factor* (bFGF), stimulates progenitor cells to produce neuroblasts. At this point, the destiny of a given neuroblast is not predetermined. A neuroblast can become any type of neuron if it receives the right chemical signal. The body relies on a "general-purpose neuron" that, when exposed to certain neurotrophic factors, matures into the specific type of cell that the nervous system requires in a particular location. This process makes brain development simpler than it would be if each different kind of cell, and the number of cells of each type, had to be precisely specified in an organism's genes. In the same way, building a house from "all-purpose" two-by-fours that can be cut to any length as needed is easier than specifying in a blueprint a precise number of precut pieces of lumber that can be used only in a certain location.

**Neurotrophic factors.** A class of compounds that act to support growth and differentiation in developing neurons and may act to keep certain neurons alive in adulthood.

## The Growth and Development of Neurons

In humans, approximately $10^9$ cells are needed to form just the cortex of a single hemisphere. To produce such a large number of cells, about 250,000 neurons must be born per minute at the peak of brain development. But, as Table 7-1 shows, this rapid formation of neurons and glia is just the first step in the growth of a brain. These cells must travel to their correct locations (a process called *migration*), they must differentiate into the right type of neuron or glial cell, and the neurons must grow dendrites and axons and subsequently form synapses. It may surprise you to learn that the brain must also prune back unnecessary cells and connections, sculpting itself according to the experiences and needs of the particular person. In the following subsections, we will consider each of these stages in brain development. We will focus our attention on the development of the cerebral cortex because more is known about cortical development than about the development of any other area of the human brain. However, the developmental principles derived from our examination of the cortex apply to other brain regions as well.

| Table 7-1 The Stages of Brain Development |
|---|
| 1. Cell birth (neurogenesis; gliogenesis) |
| 2. Cell migration |
| 3. Cell differentiation |
| 4. Cell maturation (dendrite and axon growth) |
| 5. Synaptogenesis (formation of synapses) |
| 6. Cell death and synaptic pruning |
| 7. Myelogenesis (formation of myelin) |

**Figure 7-11**

The major developmental events in the ontogenesis of the human cerebral cortex. The cortex begins to form at about 6 weeks, with neurogenesis largely complete by 20 weeks. Neural migration begins at about 8 weeks and is largely complete by about 29 weeks. Neuron maturation, including axon and dendrite growth, begins at about 20 weeks and continues until well after birth. Both brain and body weight grow rapidly, and in parallel, during the prenatal period.

Adapted from "Pathogenesis of Late-Acquired Leptomeningeal Heterotopias and Secondary Cortical Alterations: A Golgi Study," by M. Marin-Padilla, in *Dyslexia and Development: Neurobiological Aspects of Extraordinary Brains* (p. 66), edited by A. M. Galaburda, 1993, Cambridge, MA: Harvard University Press.

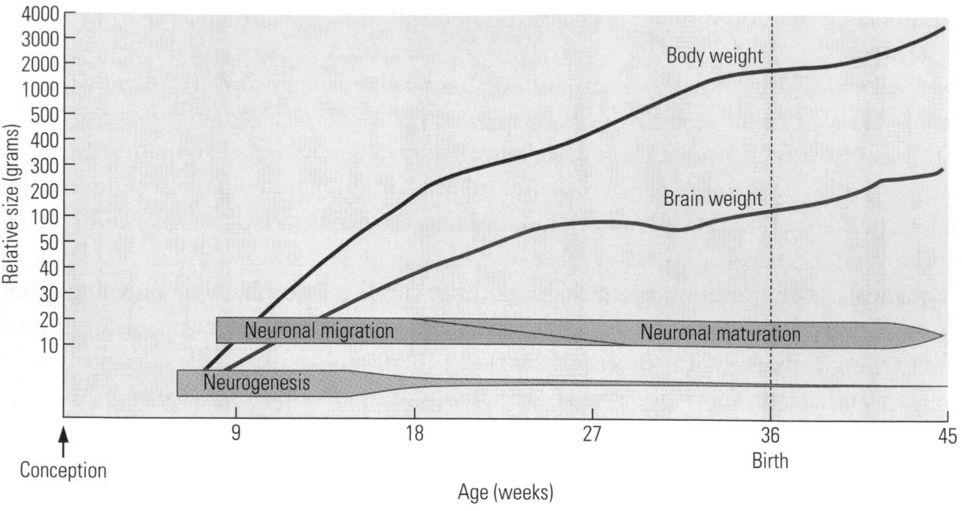


## NEURAL GENERATION, MIGRATION, AND DIFFERENTIATION

In humans, as in other vertebrates, the brain begins as part of the neural tube, the part that contains the cells from which the brain will form. Figure 7-11 shows that the generation of the cells that will eventually form the cortex begins about 7 weeks after conception and is largely complete by 20 weeks. In other words, the process of forming neurons (called *neurogenesis*) is largely finished by about 5 months of gestation, approximately the time at which prematurely born infants have some chance of surviving.

During the next 4 months, until full-term birth, the brain is especially delicate and is extremely vulnerable to injury or trauma, including asphyxia, as explained in "Cerebral Palsy" on page 248. Apparently, the brain can more easily cope with injury during the time of neuron generation than it can during the time of cell migration or differentiation. One reason may be that, when neurogenesis has stopped, it is very hard to start it again. If neurogenesis is still progressing, it may be possible to make more neurons to replace injured ones or perhaps existing neurons can be allocated differently. The same is true in supplying the lumber for a house. If some of the lumber is damaged during milling, it is possible to make more to replace the damaged pieces. But if the lumber is damaged in transit or on site, it is not so easy to replace, especially if the mill is closed. Replacement is even more difficult if the lumber has already has been cut to size for a specific use.

Cell migration begins shortly after the first neurons are generated, but it continues for about 6 weeks after neurogenesis is complete. At this point, the process of cell differentiation, in which neuroblasts become specific types of neurons, begins. Cell differentiation is essentially complete at birth, although neuron maturation, which includes the growth of dendrites, axons, and synapses, goes on for years and, in some parts of the brain, may continue into adulthood.

As you learned in Chapter 2, the cortex is organized into various areas that are distinctly different from each other in their cellular makeup. How is this arrangement of differentiated areas created during development? Pasko Rakic and his colleagues have been finding answers to this question for the past 30 years. Apparently, the ventricular zone contains a primitive map of the cortex that predisposes cells formed in a certain ventricular region to migrate to a certain cortical location. For example, one region of the ventricular zone may produce cells destined to migrate to the visual cortex, whereas another region produces cells destined to migrate to the frontal lobes.

But how do the cells know where these different parts of the cortex are located? This problem is solved by having a road of sorts for the cells to follow. The road is made up of cells known as **radial glial cells;** a radial glial cell has a fiber that extends from the ventricular zone to the surface of the cortex, as illustrated in Figure 7-12. The cells from a given region of the ventricular zone need only follow the glial road and they will end up in the right location. The advantage of this system is that, as the brain grows, the glial fibers stretch but they still go to the same place. Figure 7-12 also shows a cell that is migrating perpendicularly to the radial glial fibers. Although most cortical neurons follow the radial glial fibers, a small number of neurons appear to migrate by seeking some type of chemical signal. We do not yet know why these cells function in this different way.

**Radial glial cells.** Cells that form miniature "highways" that provide pathways for migrating neurons to follow to their appropriate destinations.

Perhaps the most obvious characteristic of the cortex is its layered appearance, also discussed in Chapter 2. The layers develop from the inside out, much like adding layers to a ball. The neurons of layer VI, which is the innermost layer, migrate to their locations first, followed by those destined for layer V, and so on. In this way, successive waves of neurons pass earlier-arriving neurons to assume progressively more exterior positions in the cortex. The formation of the cortex is a bit like building the ground floor of a house first, then the second floor, and so on, until you reach the roof. The materials needed to build higher floors must pass through lower floors to get to their destinations.

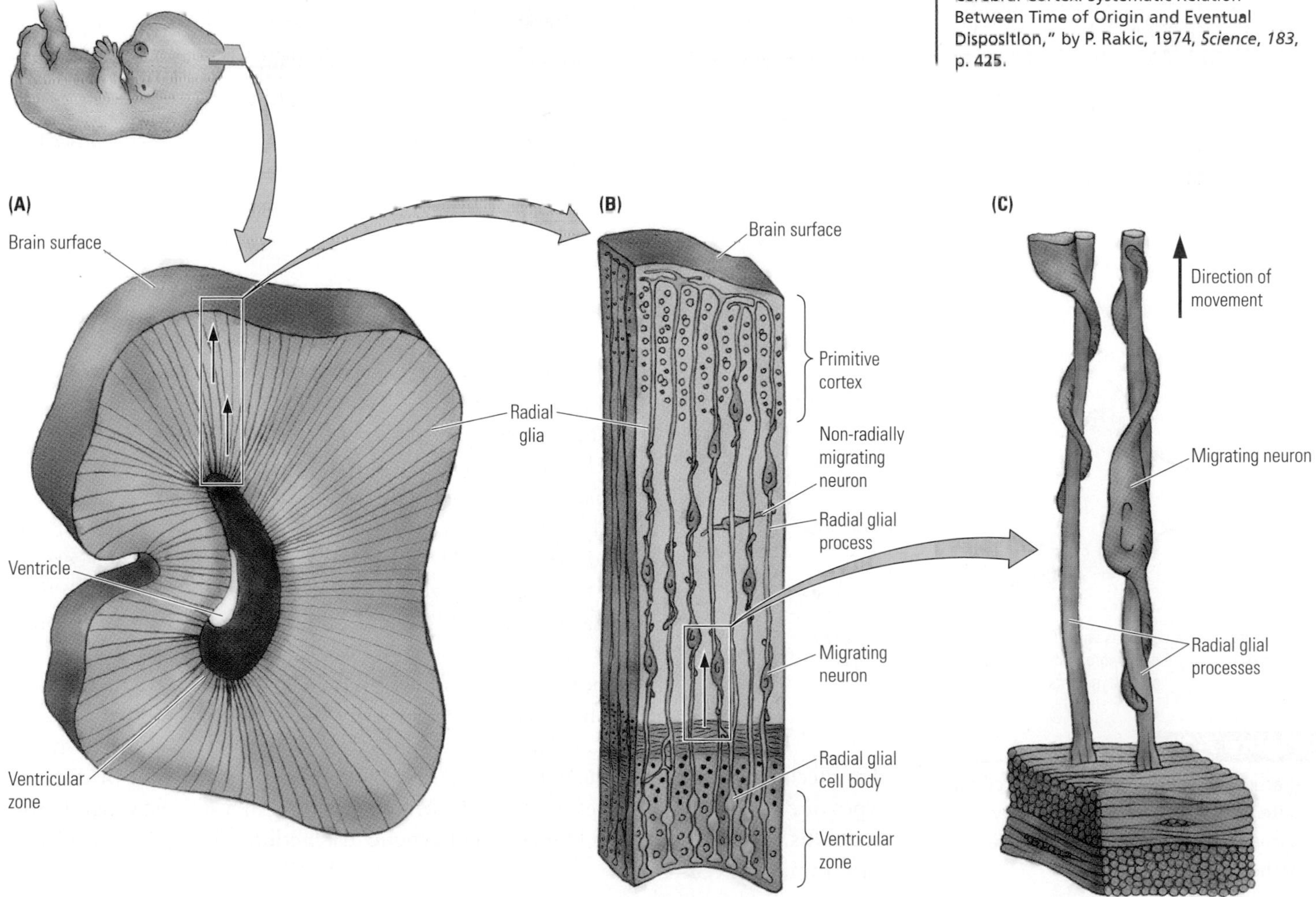


**Figure 7-12**

**(A)** The map for the cortex is hypothesized to be represented in the ventricular zone. **(B)** Radial glial fibers extend from the ventricular zone to the cortical surface. **(C)** Neurons migrate along the radial glial fibers, which take them from the protomap in the ventricular zone to the respective region in the cortex.

Adapted from "Neurons in Rhesus Monkey Cerebral Cortex: Systematic Relation Between Time of Origin and Eventual Disposition," by P. Rakic, 1974, *Science, 183*, p. 425.

Focus on Disorders

## Cerebral Palsy

We first encountered Patsy when she took our introductory course on brain and behavior. She walked with a peculiar shuffle; her handwriting was almost illegible; and her speech was at times almost unintelligible. She got an A in the course. Patsy had cerebral palsy.

It was William Little, an English physician, who first noticed in 1853 that difficult or abnormal births could lead to later motor difficulties in children. The disorder that Little described was cerebral palsy, although it has also been called Little's disease. Cerebral palsy is relatively common worldwide, with an incidence estimated to be 1.5 in every 1000 births. Among surviving babies who weigh less than 2.5 kilograms at birth, the incidence is much higher—about 10 in every 1000.

The most common cause of cerebral palsy is birth injury, especially due to anoxia, a lack of oxygen. Anoxia may result from a defect in the placenta, the organ that allows oxygen and nutrients to pass from mother to child, or it may be caused by an entanglement of the umbilical cord during birth, which may reduce the oxygen supply to the infant. Other causes include infections, hydrocephalus, seizures, and prematurity. All produce a defect in the immature brain either before, during, or just after birth.

Most children with cerebral palsy appear normal in the first few months of life but, as the nervous system develops, the motor disturbances become progressively more noticeable. The most common symptom, which afflicts about half of those affected, is spasticity, or exaggerated contraction of muscles when they are stretched. Not surprisingly, spasticity often interferes with other motor functions. For example, people with cerebral palsy may have an odd gait, sometimes dragging one foot. A second common symptom is dyskinesia, or involuntary extraneous movements. Examples are tremors and uncontrollable jerky twists, called athetoid movements, which often occur during activities such as walking. A third common symptom is rigidity, or resistance to passive movement. For example, the patient's fingers may resist being moved passively by an examiner, even though the person is able to move the fingers voluntarily. In addition to these motor symptoms, people with cerebral palsy are at risk for retardation, although many of them, Patsy included, function at a high intellectual level and earn college and postgraduate degrees.

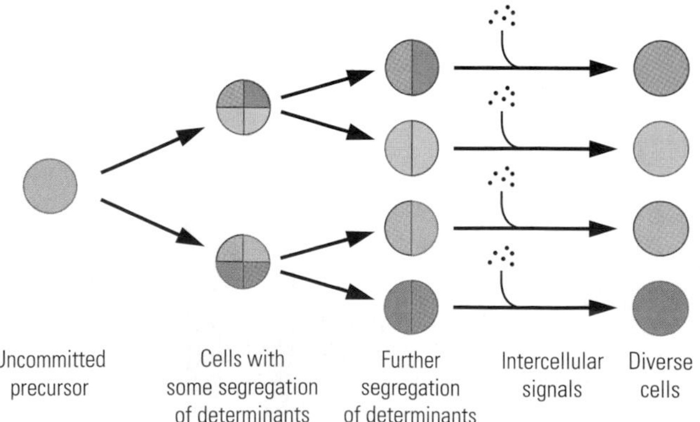


**Figure 7-13**

Precursor cells have an unlimited cell-fate potential but, as they develop, they become increasingly committed to a particular cell type.

One thing that facilitates the building of a house is that each new story has a blueprint-specified dimension, such as 8 feet high. But how do neurons determine how thick a cortical layer should be? This is a tough question, especially when you consider that the layers of the cortex are not all the same thickness. Probably the answer is partly related to timing. Cells that are destined to be located in a certain layer are generated at a certain time in the ventricular zone, and so they migrate together in that particular time frame. The mechanisms that govern this timing are not yet understood, however. In addition, there are likely some local environmental signals—chemicals produced by other cells—that also influence the way in which cells form layers in the cortex. These signals progressively restrict the choice of traits that a cell can express, as illustrated in Figure 7-13. Thus, the emergence of distinct types of cells in the brain does not result from the unfolding of a specific genetic program. Instead, it is due to the interaction of genetic instructions, timing, and local signals from other cells.

## NEURAL MATURATION

After neurons have migrated to their final destinations and differentiated into specific neuron types, they must begin the process of growing dendrites to provide the surface area for synapses with other cells. They must also extend their axons to appropriate targets to initiate the formation of other synapses. These processes are part of neural maturation.

Two events take place in the development of a dendrite: dendritic *arborization* (branching) and the growth of dendritic spines. As illustrated in Figure 7-14, dendrites begin as individual processes protruding from the cell body. Later, they develop increasingly complex extensions that look much like the branches of trees visible in winter; that is, they undergo arborization. The dendritic branches then begin to form spines, which are the location of most synapses on the dendrites.

Although dendritic development begins prenatally in humans, it continues for a long time after birth, as Figure 7-14 shows. Dendritic growth proceeds at a relatively slow rate, on the order of micrometers per day. This rate contrasts with that for the development of axons, which grow on the order of a millimeter per day. The disparate developmental rates of axons and dendrites are important because the faster-growing axon can contact its target cell before the dendrites of that cell are completely formed. In this way, the axon may play a role in dendritic differentiation.

The development of an axon presents a significant "engineering" problem because the axon must find its way through a complex cellular terrain to make appropriate connections that may be millimeters or even centimeters away. Such a task could not possibly be specified in a rigid genetic program. Rather, the formation of axonic connections is guided by various molecules that attract or repel the developing axon.

Santiago Ramón y Cajal in the early twentieth century was the first to describe this developmental process. He called the growing tips of axons **growth cones.** Figure 7-15 shows that, as these growth cones extend, they send out shoots that are similar to fingers reaching out to find a pen on a cluttered desk. When one shoot, known as a **filopod** (plural, *filopodia*), reaches an appropriate target, the others follow. The growth cones are responsive to two types of cues. One cue consists of a variety of cell-manufactured molecules that either lie on the cell surface or are secreted into the space between cells. Some of these molecules provide a surface to which the

**Growth cone.** The growing tip of an axon.

**Filopod.** A process at the end of a developing axon that reaches out to search for a potential target.

Click on your CD to review the structure of dendrites. Find the area on the structure of a neuron in the module on Neural Communication.

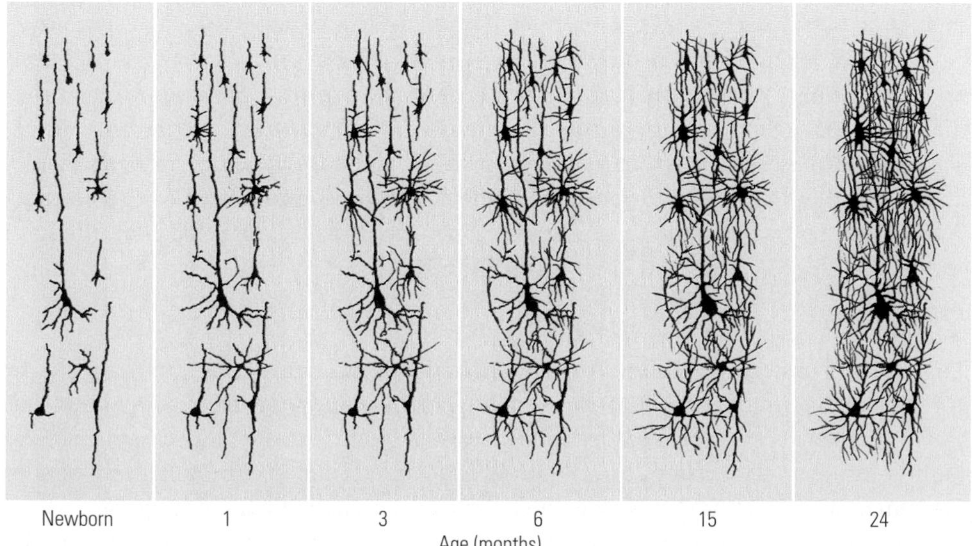


**Figure 7-14**

In postnatal differentiation of the human cerebral cortex around Broca's area, the neurons begin with simple dendritic fields, which become progressively more complex until a child reaches about 2 years of age.

Adapted from *Biological Foundations of Language* (pp. 160–161), by E. Lenneberg, 1967, New York: Wiley.

(A)

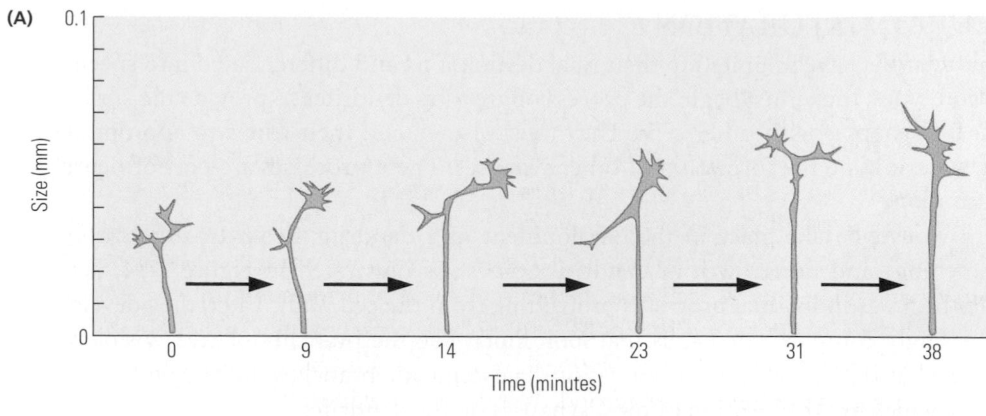


(B)

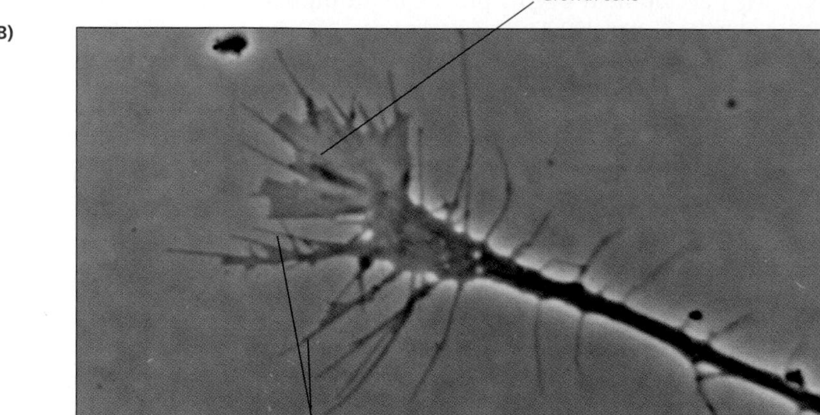


**Figure 7-15**

At the tip of this axon growing in culture is a growth cone that sends out filopodia seeking specific molecules that will guide axon direction. At top are drawings showing the growth in the axon tip over time. The growth cone is at the end of the axon.

growth cones can adhere and are thus called **cell-adhesion molecules** (CAMs), whereas others serve to attract or repel the growth cones. The second cue to which growth cones respond is chemicals, known as **tropic molecules,** that are produced by the targets being sought by the axons. (*Tropic* molecules, which guide axons, should not be confused with the *trophic* molecules that support the growth of neurons and their processes.) These tropic molecules essentially tell growth cones to "come over here." They likely also tell other growth cones seeking different targets to "keep away." Although Ramón y Cajal predicted the presence of tropic molecules more than 100 years ago, they have proved difficult to find. Only one group of tropic molecules, known as **netrins** (from Sanskrit meaning "to guide"), has so far been identified. Given the enormous number of connections in the brain and the great complexity in wiring them, it seems likely that many other types of tropic molecules are still to be found.

## SYNAPTIC DEVELOPMENT

The number of synapses in the human cerebral cortex is staggering, on the order of $10^{14}$. This huge number could not possibly be determined by a genetic program that assigns each synapse a specific location. Instead, it is more likely that only the general outlines of neural connections in the brain are predetermined. The vast array of specific synaptic contacts is then guided into place by a variety of cues and signals.

In humans, simple synaptic contacts exist in the fifth gestational month. By the seventh gestational month, synaptic development on the deepest cortical neurons is extensive. After birth, the number of synapses increases rapidly. In the visual cortex,

**Cell-adhesion molecule (CAM).** A chemical to which specific cells can adhere, thus aiding in migration.

**Tropic molecule.** A signaling molecule that attracts or repels growth cones.

**Netrins.** A class of tropic molecules.

synaptic density almost doubles between age 2 months and age 4 months and then continues to increase until age 1 year.

**Neural Darwinism.** The idea that the process of cell death and synaptic pruning is not random but is the outcome of competition between neurons for connections and metabolic resources.

## CELL DEATH AND SYNAPTIC PRUNING

Perhaps the most surprising events in vertebrate brain development are cell death and synaptic pruning. These terms mean that there is first an overproduction of neurons and synapses and then a subsequent loss of them. For example, as already stated, the number of synapses in the visual cortex increases rapidly after birth, reaches a peak at about 1 year, and begins to decline as the brain apparently prunes out unnecessary or incorrect synapses. The graph in Figure 7-16 plots this rise and fall in synaptic density. Pasko Rakic estimated that, at the peak of synapse loss in humans, as many as 100,000 synapses may be lost per second. We can only wonder what the behavioral consequence of this rapid synaptic loss might be. It is probably no coincidence that children seem to change moods and behaviors quickly.

How does the brain accomplish this elimination of neurons? The simplest explanation is competition, sometimes referred to as **neural Darwinism.** Charles Darwin believed that the key to evolution was the production of variation in the traits that a species possesses. Certain traits can then be selected by the environment for their favorableness in aiding survival. According to a Darwinian perspective, then, more animals are born than can survive to adulthood, and environmental pressures "weed out" the less fit ones. Similar pressures cause neural Darwinism.

But what exactly is causing this weeding out of cells in the brain? It turns out that, when neurons form synapses, they become somewhat dependent on their targets for survival. In fact, if deprived of synaptic targets, they eventually die. This neuron death occurs because target cells produce signaling molecules—the neurotrophic factors that we encountered earlier—that are absorbed by the axon terminals and function to regulate neuronal survival. If many neurons are competing for a limited amount of a neurotrophic factor, only some of those neurons can survive. The death of neurons deprived of a neurotrophic factor is different from the cell death caused by injury or disease. It seems that, when neurons are deprived of a neurotrophic factor,

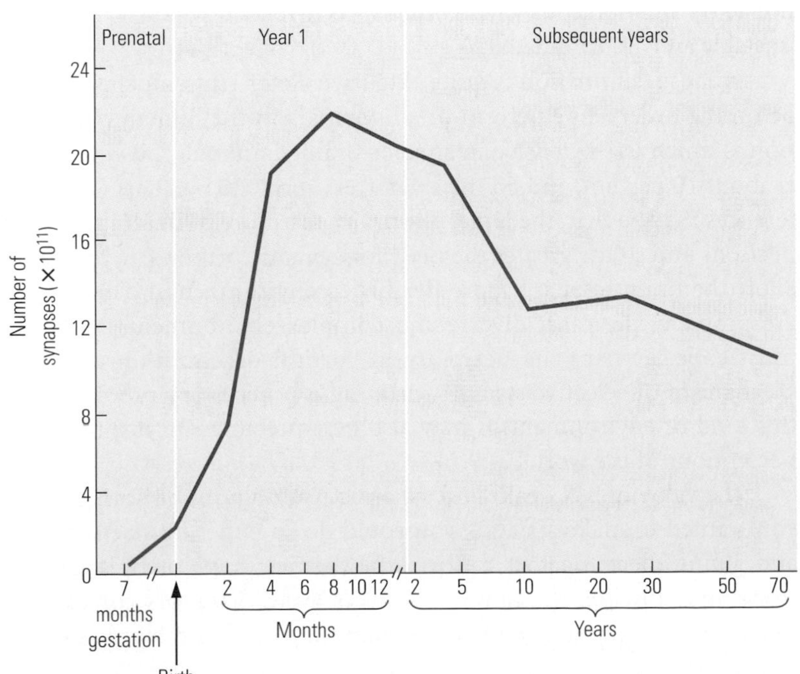


**Figure 7-16**

This estimate of the total number of synapses in the human visual cortex as a function of age shows that the synapse number rises rapidly, peaking at about 1 year. Then the number declines until about 10 years of age, at which point synapse number levels off until early adulthood, when it begins to drop again.

Adapted from "Synaptogenesis in Human Cerebral Cortex," by P. R. Huttenlocher, in *Human Behavior and the Developing Brain* (p. 142), edited by G. Dawson and K. W. Fischer, 1994, New York: Guilford Press.

**Apoptosis.** Cell death that is genetically programmed.

certain genes are "turned on" that result in a message for the cell to die. This process is called **apoptosis.**

Apoptosis accounts for the death of overabundant neurons, but it does not account for the pruning of synapses from cells that survive. In 1976, the French neurobiologist Jean-Pierre Changeux proposed a theory for synapse loss that also is based on competition. According to Changeux, synapses persist into adulthood only if they have become members of functional neural networks. If they have not, they are eventually eliminated from the brain.

Richard Tees Janet Werker

An example will help explain this mechanism of synaptic pruning. Consider neural input to the midbrain from the eyes and ears. The visual input goes to the superior colliculus, and the auditory input goes to the inferior colliculus. Some errant axons from the auditory system will likely end up in the visual midbrain and form synapses with the same cells as those connected to axons coming from the visual pathway. However, the auditory axons are not part of functional networks in this location. Whereas inputs from an eye are apt to be active at the same time as one another, inputs from an ear are unlikely to be active along with the visual ones. The presence of simultaneous electrical activity in a set of visually related synapses leads to the formation of a neural circuit comprising those synapses. In contrast, the errant auditory inputs, because they are not active at the same time as the visual inputs, become unstable and are eventually eliminated. We can speculate that factors such as hormones, drugs, and experience would influence the formation of active neural circuits and thus influence the processes of synapse stabilization and pruning. In fact, as you will see shortly, experience can have truly massive effects on the organization of the nervous system.

In addition to outright errors in synapse formation that give rise to synaptic pruning, more subtle changes in neural circuits may trigger the same process. An instance of this accounts for the findings of Janet Werker and Richard Tees (1992), who studied the ability of infants to discriminate speech sounds taken from widely disparate languages, such as English, Hindi (from India), and Salish (a Native American language). Their results showed that young infants can discriminate speech sounds of different languages without previous experience, but their ability to do so declines over the first year of life. One explanation of this declining ability is that synapses encoding speech sounds not normally encountered in the infant's daily environment are not active simultaneously with other speech-related synapses. As a result, they become unstable and are eliminated.

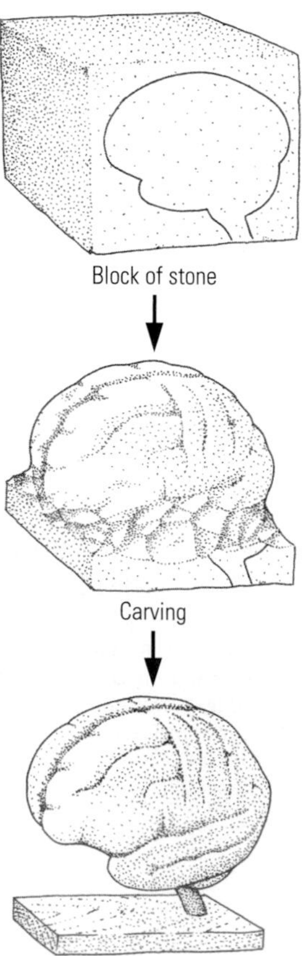


Synapse elimination is quite extensive. Peter Huttenlocher (1994) estimated it to be on the order of 42 percent of all synapses in the human cortex. Synapse elimination is much less extensive in smaller-brained animals, however. In the rat cortex, it is about 10 percent, and, in the cat cortex, about 30 percent. The reason for these differences may be that, the larger the brain, the more difficult it is to make precise connections and so the greater the need for synaptic pruning. Synaptic pruning may also allow the brain to adapt more flexibly to environmental demands. Human cultures are probably the most diverse and complex environments with which any animal must cope. Perhaps the flexibility in cortical organization that is achieved by the mechanism of selective synaptic pruning is a necessary precondition for developing this kind of environment. It may also be a precursor to disputes related to different perceptions of the world.

The value of cell death and synaptic pruning can be seen through an analogy. If you wanted to make a statue, you could do so either by starting with grains of sand and gluing them together to form the desired shape or by starting with a block of stone and chiseling the unwanted pieces away. Sculptors consider the second route much easier. They start with more than they need and eliminate the excess. So does the brain. It makes too many neurons and too many connections and then gets rid of the unessential ones. The "chisel" in the brain could be of several forms, including a genetic signal, experience, reproductive hormones, and stress.

## Glial Development

The birth of astrocytes and oligodendrocytes begins after most neurons are born and continues throughout life. As you know from Chapter 3, oligodendroglia form the myelin that surrounds axons in the spinal cord and brain. Although axons can function before they are encased by myelin, normal adult function is attained only after myelination is complete. Consequently, myelination is useful as a rough index of cerebral maturation.

In the early 1920s, Paul Flechsig noticed that myelination of the cortex begins just after birth and continues until nearly 18 years of age. He also noticed that some cortical regions were myelinated by age 3 to 4 years, whereas others showed virtually no myelination at that time. Figure 7-17 shows one of Flechsig's maps of the brain, with areas shaded according to the age at which myelination takes place. Flechsig hypothesized that the earliest-maturing areas control relatively simple movements or sensory analyses, whereas the late-myelinating areas control the highest mental functions.

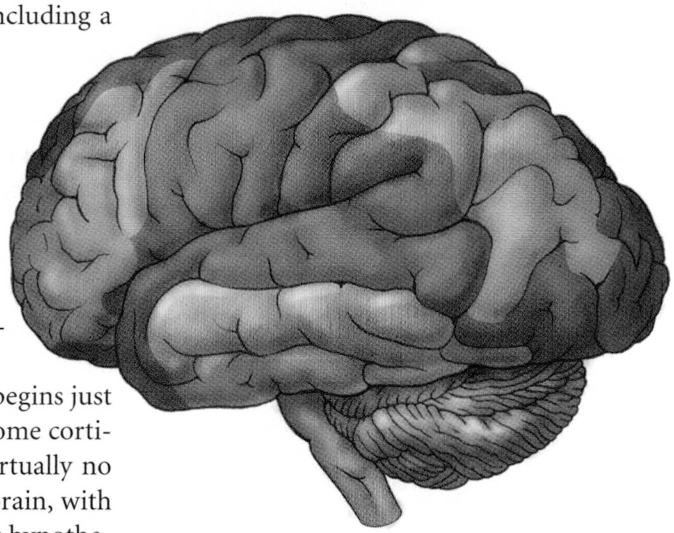

**Figure 7-17**

A map of how myelination progresses in the human cortex, based on Flechsig's research. The light-colored zones are very late to myelinate, which led Flechsig to propose that they are qualitatively different in function from those that mature earlier.

### In Review

Brain development begins with the growth of the first neural stem cell in the third week of embryonic development. The nervous system begins as a sheet of cells that folds to become a tube, known as the neural tube. Brain formation then proceeds rapidly; by about 100 days after conception, the brain begins to look human in form. The neurons and glia of the brain develop through a series of seven stages: birth, migration, differentiation, maturation, synaptic formation, death, and myelination. Neurons begin to process information before they are completely mature, but their activity is much simpler than it will be with full maturation. Behavioral development is therefore constrained by the maturation of brain cells. For example, although infants and children are capable of complex movements, it is not until the completion of myelin formation in adolescence that adult levels of coordination and fine motor control are reached. By studying how the nervous system develops and matures, we are able to make predictions about when behaviors will emerge. Conversely, by studying the stages of behavioral development, we can make predictions about developments taking place in the brain.

# CORRELATING BEHAVIOR WITH BRAIN DEVELOPMENT

It is reasonable to assume that, as a particular brain area matures, a person exhibits behaviors corresponding to that particular mature brain structure. The strongest advocate of this view has been Eric Lenneberg, who, in 1967, published a seminal book titled *Biological Foundations of Language*. A principal theme of this book is that children's acquisition of language is tied to the development of the critical language areas in the cerebral cortex. This idea immediately stimulated debate over the merits of correlating brain and behavioral development. Now, 30-some years later, the relation between brain development and behavior is widely accepted, although the influence of experience and learning on behavior is still considered critical. Psychologists believe that behaviors cannot emerge until the neural machinery for them has developed, but, when that machinery is in place, related behaviors develop quickly and are shaped significantly by experience. The new behaviors then alter brain structure by the processes of neural Darwinism presented earlier. Researchers have studied these interacting changes in the brain and behavior, especially in regard to the emergence of motor skills, language, and problem solving in children. We will explore each of these topics separately.

## Motor Behaviors

Link to the Web site at **www.worthpublishers.com/kolb/chapter7** to see some more examples of motor development during childhood.

The development of locomotion in human infants is easy to observe. At first, babies are unable to move about independently but, eventually, they learn to crawl and then to walk. Other motor skills develop in less obvious but no less systematic ways. For example, Tom Twitchell studied and described the development of the ability to reach for and grasp objects. This development progresses in a series of stages, illustrated in Figure 7-18. Shortly after birth, an infant is capable of flexing the joints of an arm in such a way that he or she could scoop something toward the body, but, at this age, infants do not seem to direct their arm movements toward any specific thing. Then, between 1 and 3 months of age, a baby begins to orient a hand toward an object that the hand has touched and gropes to hold that object. For example, if the baby's hand touches a stick, the fingers will flex to grasp it. At this stage, however, all the fingers flex together. Between 8 and 11 months, infants' grasping becomes more sophisticated as the "pincer grasp," which uses the index finger and the thumb, develops. The pincer grasp is a significant development because it allows babies to make the very precise finger movements needed to manipulate small objects. What we see, then, is a sequence in the development of grasping: first scooping, then grasping with all of the fingers, and then grasping by using independent finger movements.

2 months

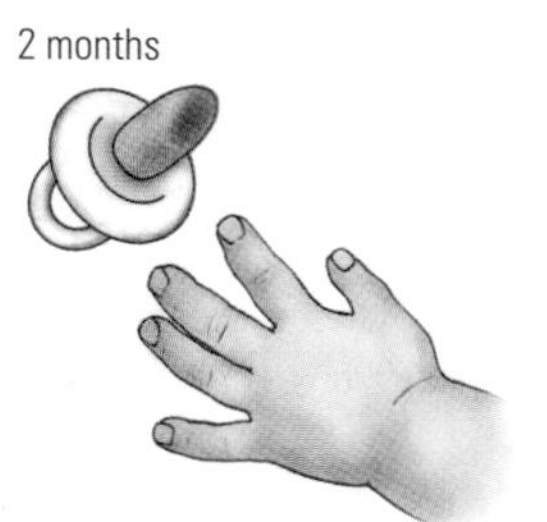

Orients hand toward an object and gropes to hold it.

4 months

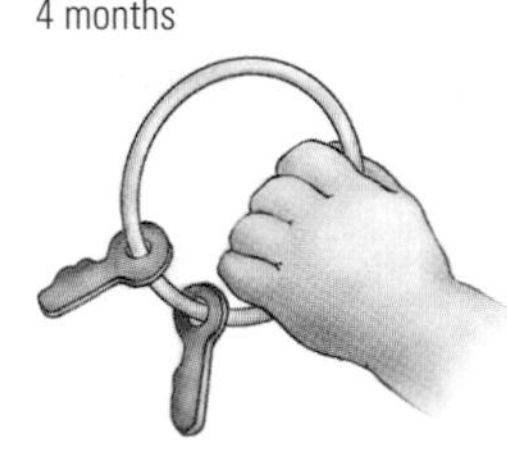

Grasps appropriately shaped object with entire hand.

10 months

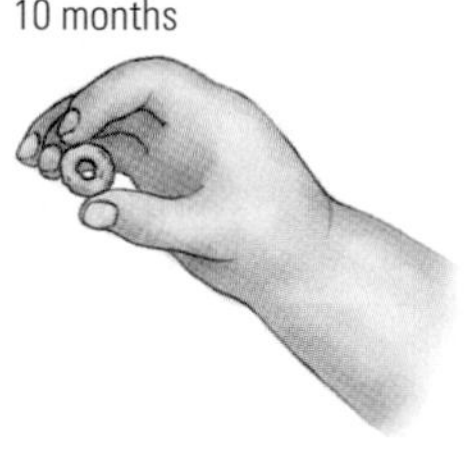

Uses pincer grasp with thumb and index finger opposed.

**Figure 7-18** Development of the grasping response of infants.

Adapted from "The Automatic Grasping Response of Infants," by T. E. Twitchell, 1965, *Neuropsychologia*, 3, p. 251.

If the development of increasingly well-coordinated grasping depends on the emergence of certain neural machinery, anatomical changes in the brain should accompany the emergence of these behaviors. Probably many such changes take place, especially in the development of dendritic arborizations. However, a correlation between myelin formation and the ability to grasp has been found. In particular, a group of axons from motor-cortex neurons becomes myelinated at about the same time that reaching and grasping with the whole hand develop. Similarly, another group of motor-cortex neurons, which are known to control finger movements, becomes myelinated at about the time that the pincer grasp develops.

We can now make a simple prediction. If specific motor-cortex neurons are essential for adultlike grasping movements to emerge, removal of those neurons should make an adult's grasping ability similar to that of a young infant, which is in fact what happens. One of the classic symptoms of damage to the motor cortex is the permanent loss of the pincer grasp.

Visit the CD to review myelination of axons and how this process affects neural transmission. Find the area on the conduction of the action potential in the module on Neural Communication.

## Language Development

The acquisition of speech follows a gradual series of developments that has usually progressed quite far by the age of 3 or 4. According to Lenneberg, children reach certain important speech milestones in a fixed sequence and at relatively constant chronological ages. These milestones are summarized in Table 7-2.

**Table 7-2 Postnatal Development of Basic Language Functions**

| Approximate age | Basic social and language functions |
|---|---|
| Birth | Comforted by sound of human voice; most common utterances are discomfort and hunger cries |
| 6 weeks | Responds to human voice and makes cooing and pleasure noises; cries to gain assistance |
| 2 months | Begins to distinguish different speech sounds; cooing becomes more guttural or "throaty" |
| 3 months | Orients head to voices; makes a vocal response to others' speech; begins babbling, or chanting various syllabic sounds in a rhythmic fashion |
| 4 months | Begins to vary pitch of vocalizations; imitates tones |
| 6 months | Begins to imitate sounds made by others |
| 9 months | Begins to convey meaning through intonation, using patterns that resemble adult intonations |
| 12 months | Starts to develop a vocabulary; a 12-month-old may have a 5–10-word vocabulary that will double in the next 6 months |
| 24 months | Vocabulary expands rapidly and can be approximately 200–300 words; names most common everyday objects; most utterances are single words |
| 36 months | Has 900–1000-word vocabulary; 3- to 4-word simply constructed sentences (subject and verb); can follow two-step commands |
| 4 years | Has a vocabulary of more than 1500 words; asks numerous questions; sentences become more complex |
| 5 years | Typically has a vocabulary of approximately 1500–2200 words; discusses feelings; the average 5- to 7-year-old has acquired a slow but fluent ability to read; handwriting also likely to be slow |
| 6 years | Speaks with a vocabulary of about 2600 words; understands 20,000–24,000 words; uses all parts of speech |
| Adult | Has 50,000+ word vocabulary by 12 years old |

Adapted from "Development of the Child's Brain and Behavior," by B. Kolb and B. Fantie, in *Handbook of Clinical Child Neuropsychology* (2nd ed., p. 29), edited by C. R. Reynolds and E. Fletcher-Janzen, 1997, New York: Plenum.

Although there is a general parallel between language development and the development of motor capacities, language development depends on more than just the ability to make controlled movements of the mouth, lips, and tongue. Precise movements of the muscles controlling these body parts develop well before children can speak. Furthermore, even when children have sufficient motor skill to articulate most words, their vocabulary does not rocket ahead, but rather progresses gradually. A small proportion of children (about 1 percent) have normal intelligence and normal motor-skill development, and yet their speech acquisition is markedly delayed. Such children may not begin to speak in phrases until after age 4, despite an apparently normal environment and the absence of any obvious neurological signs of brain damage. Because the timing of the onset of speech appears to be so universal in the remaining 99 percent of children across all cultures, it seems likely that there is something different in the brain maturation of a child with late language acquisition. But it is hard to specify what that difference is. Because language onset is usually between ages 1 and 2 and language acquisition is largely complete by age 12, the best strategy is to consider how the cortex is different before and after these two age milestones.

By 2 years of age, cell division and migration are complete in the language zones of the cerebral cortex. The major changes that take place between the ages of 2 and 12 are in the interconnections of neurons and the myelination of the speech zones. The changes in dendritic complexity in these areas are among the most impressive in the brain. As illustrated in Figure 7-14, the axons and dendrites of the speech zone called Broca's area are simple at birth but become dramatically more dense between 15 and 24 months of age. This development correlates with an equally dramatic change in language ability, given that this age is when a baby's vocabulary starts to expand rapidly. We can therefore infer that language development may be constrained, at least in part, by the maturation of language areas in the cortex. Individual differences in the speed of language acquisition may be accounted for by differences in this neural development. Children with early language abilities may have early maturation of the speech zones, whereas children with delayed language onset may have later speech-zone maturation.

## The Development of Problem-Solving Ability

The first person to try to identify stages of cognitive development was the Swiss psychologist Jean Piaget. He realized that the behavior of children could be used to make inferences about their understanding of the world. For example, a baby who lifts a cloth to retrieve a hidden toy is showing an understanding that objects continue to exist even when out of sight. This understanding, called the concept of *object permanence*, is revealed by the behavior of the infant in the upper photographs of Figure 7-19. An absence of understanding also can be seen in children's behavior, as shown by the actions of the 5-year-old girl in the lower photographs of Figure 7-19. She was shown two beakers with identical volumes of liquid in each, and then watched as one beaker's liquid was poured into a skinnier beaker. When asked which beaker contained more

Doug Goodman/Monkmeyer

Courtesy Don and Sandy Hockenbury

**Figure 7-19** Stages of cognitive development. (*Top*) The infant illustrates that she understands that things continue to exist when they are out of sight. (*Bottom*) This girl does not yet understand the principle of conservation of volume. Beakers with identical volumes but different shapes seem to hold different amounts.

**Table 7-3 Piaget's Stages of Cognitive Development**

| Typical age range | Description of the stage | Developmental phenomena |
|---|---|---|
| Birth to 18–24 months | *Stage I: Sensorimotor* Experiences the world through senses and actions (looking, touching, mouthing) | Object permanence<br>Stranger anxiety |
| About 2–6 years | *Stage II: Preoperational* Represents things with words and images but lacks logical reasoning | Pretend play<br>Egocentrism<br>Language development |
| About 7–11 years | *Stage III: Concrete operational* Thinks logically about concrete events; grasps concrete analogies and performs arithmetical operations | Conservation<br>Mathematical transformations |
| About 12+ years | *Stage IV: Formal operational* Reasons abstractly | Abstract logic<br>Potential for mature moral reasoning |

liquid, she pointed to the taller, skinnier beaker, not understanding that the amount of liquid remains constant despite the difference in appearance. An understanding of this principle, called *conservation of liquid volume*, is not displayed until about age 7.

By studying children engaged in such tasks, Piaget concluded that cognitive development is a continuous process. Children's strategies for exploring the world, and their understanding of it, are constantly changing. These changes are not simply the result of acquiring specific pieces of new knowledge. Rather, at certain points in development, fundamental changes take place in the organization of a child's strategies for learning about the world, and with these changes come new understandings.

Piaget identified four major stages of cognitive development, which are summarized in Table 7-3. Stage I is the sensorimotor period, from birth to about 18 to 24 months of age. During this time, babies learn to differentiate themselves from the external world, they come to realize that objects exist even when out of sight, and they gain some understanding of cause-and-effect relations. Next is stage II, the preoperational period, from age 2 to 6 years. This stage is when children become able to form mental representations of things in their world and to represent those things in words and drawings. Stage III is the period of concrete operations, from age 7 to 11 years. At this stage, children are able to mentally manipulate concrete ideas such as volumes of liquid and dimensions of objects. Finally, stage IV is the period of formal operations, which is reached after age 11. The child is now able to reason in the abstract, not just in concrete terms.

If we take Piaget's stages as rough approximations of qualitative changes that take place in children's thinking as they grow older, we can ask what changes in the brain might underlie them. One place to look for brain changes is in the relative rate of brain growth. After birth, the brain does not grow uniformly; rather, it tends to increase its mass during irregularly occurring periods commonly called **growth spurts.** In his analysis of brain-to-body-weight ratios, Herman Epstein found consistent spurts in brain growth between 3 and 10 months (accounting for an increase of 30 percent in brain weight by the age of 1½ years) as well as from the ages of 2 to 4, 6 to 8, 10 to 12, and 14 to 16+ years. The increments in brain weight were from about 5 to 10 percent in each of these 2-year periods. The brain growth takes place without a concurrent increase in the number of neurons, so it is most likely due to the growth of glial cells and synapses. Although synapses themselves would be unlikely to add much weight to the brain, the growth of synapses is accompanied by increased metabolic demands, which cause neurons to become larger, new blood vessels to form, and new astrocytes to be produced.

**Growth spurt.** A sudden growth in development that lasts for a finite time.

We would expect such an increase in the complexity of the cortex to generate more complex behaviors, so we might predict that there would be significant, perhaps qualitative, changes in cognitive function during each of the growth spurts. The first four brain-growth spurts coincide nicely with the four main stages of cognitive development described by Piaget. This correspondence suggests that there may be significant alterations in neural functioning with the onset of each of Piaget's stages. At the same time, differences in the rate of brain development or perhaps in the rate at which specific groups of neurons mature may account for individual differences in the age at which the various cognitive advances that Piaget identified emerge. Although Piaget did not identify a fifth stage of cognitive development in later adolescence, the presence of a growth spurt then implies that there may, in fact, be one.

One difficulty in linking brain-growth spurts to cognitive development is that growth spurts are superficial measures of changes taking place in the brain. We need to know what neural events are contributing to brain growth and just where they are taking place. A way to find this out is to observe children's attempts to solve specific problems that are diagnostic of damage to discrete brain regions in adults. If children perform a particular task poorly, then whatever brain region regulates the performance of that task in adults must not yet be mature in children. Similarly, if children can perform one task but not another, the tasks apparently require different brain structures and these structures mature at different rates.

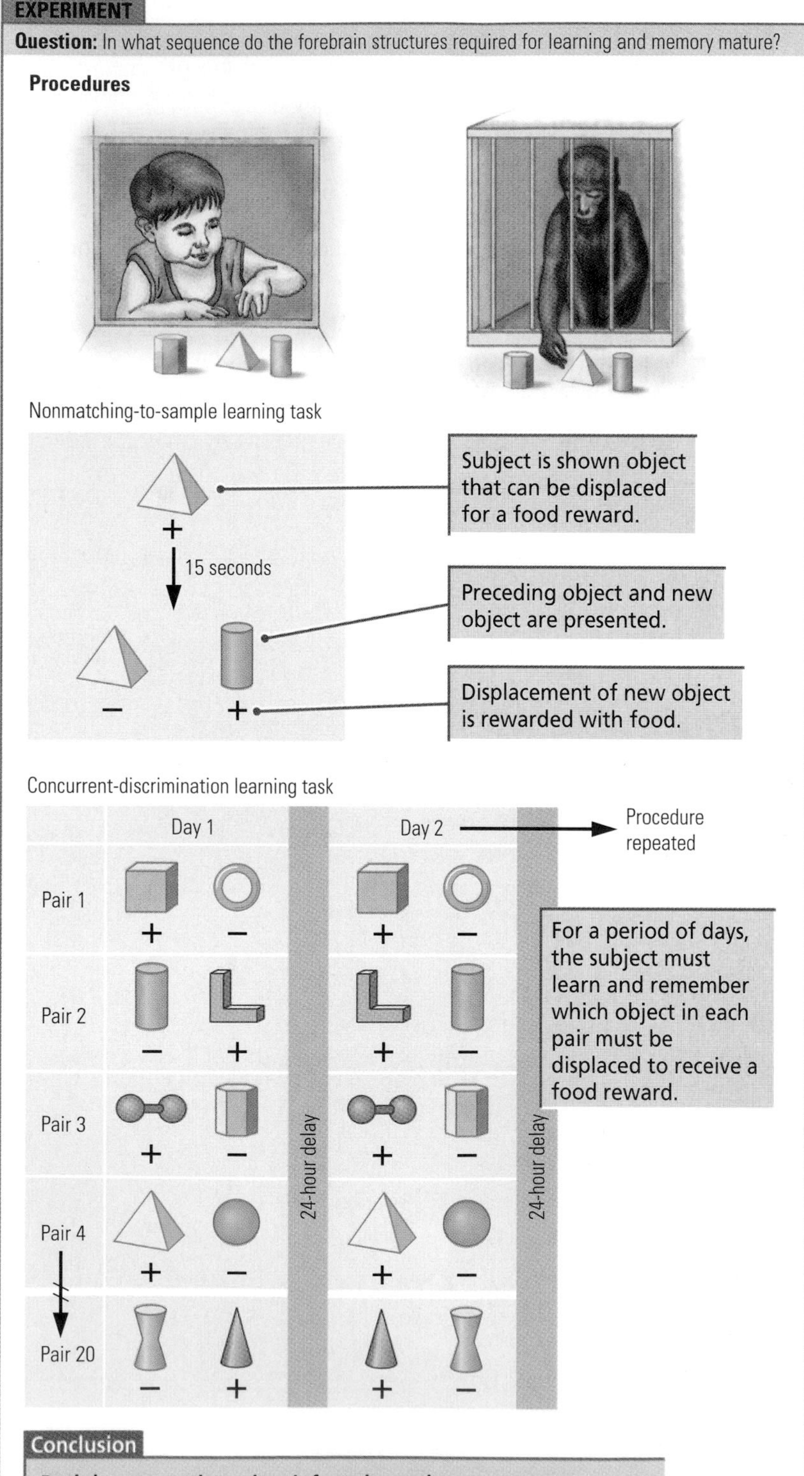
EXPERIMENT
Question: In what sequence do the forebrain structures required for learning and memory mature?
Procedures
Nonmatching-to-sample learning task
Subject is shown object that can be displaced for a food reward.
15 seconds
Preceding object and new object are presented.
Displacement of new object is rewarded with food.
Concurrent-discrimination learning task
Day 1
Day 2
Procedure repeated
Pair 1
Pair 2
Pair 3
Pair 4
Pair 20
24-hour delay
24-hour delay
For a period of days, the subject must learn and remember which object in each pair must be displaced to receive a food reward.
Conclusion
Both human and monkey infants learn the concurrent-discrimination task at a younger age than the nonmatching-to-sample task, implying that the neural structures underlying the former task mature sooner than those underlying the latter.

**Figure 7-20**

An experiment designed to show the order in which forebrain structures involved in learning and memory mature. In these versions of the Wisconsin General Test Apparatus, the subject's task is to displace an object to reveal a food reward. The nonmatching-to-sample task requires maturation of the temporal lobes, while the concurrent-discrimination task requires maturation of the basal ganglia. Both human and monkey infants learn the concurrent task at a younger age than the matching task, implying that the neural structures underlying the former type of learning mature sooner than those underlying the latter.

Adapted from "Object Recognition Versus Object Discrimination: Comparison Between Human Infants and Infant Monkeys," by W. H. Overman, J. Bachevalier, M. Turner, and A. Peuster, 1992, *Behavioral Neuroscience, 106*, p. 18.

Bill Overman and Jocelyn Bachevalier used this logic to study the development of forebrain structures required for learning and memory in young children and monkeys. Figure 7-20 shows the tests that they presented to their subjects. The first task was simply to learn to displace an object to obtain a food reward. When the subjects had learned this task, they were trained in two more tasks that are believed to measure the functioning of the temporal lobes and the basal ganglia, respectively. In the first of these two additional tasks, the subjects were shown an object, which they could displace to receive a food reward. After a brief (15-second) delay, two objects were presented: the first object and a novel object. The subjects then had to displace the novel object to obtain the food reward. This task, called *nonmatching to sample*, is thought to measure object recognition, which is a function of the temporal lobes. The subject can find the food only by recognizing the original object and *not* choosing it. In the second of the two additional tasks, the subjects were presented with a pair of objects and had to learn that one object in that pair was always associated with a food reward, whereas the other object was never rewarded. The task was made more difficult by sequentially giving the subjects 20 different object pairs. Each day, they were presented with one trial per pair. This task, called *concurrent discrimination*, is thought to measure trial-and-error learning of specific object information, which is a function of the basal ganglia.

Bill Overman

Adults easily solve both tasks, but they say that the concurrent task is more difficult because it requires remembering far more information than the nonmatching-to-sample task. The key question developmentally is whether there is a difference in the age at which children (or monkeys) can solve these two tasks. It turns out that children can solve the concurrent task by about 12 months of age, but not until about 18 months of age can they solve what most adults believe to be the easier task. These results imply that the basal ganglia, which is the critical area for the concurrent-discrimination task, mature more quickly than the temporal lobe, which is the critical region for the nonmatching-to-sample task.

## In Review

As children develop, increasingly mature behaviors emerge in a predictable sequence. This behavioral development is probably related to neural changes in the brain. For example, as the cortex and basal ganglia develop, different motor abilities and cognitive capacities emerge. As you will see in the next section, these developing behaviors are shaped not only by the emergence of brain structures but also by the experiences that each person has.

## BRAIN DEVELOPMENT AND THE ENVIRONMENT

**Brain plasticity** refers to the lifelong changes in the structure of the brain that accompany experience. This term suggests that the brain is pliable, like plastic, and can be molded into different forms, at least at the microscopic level. Brains exposed to different environmental experiences are molded in different ways. Culture is part of the human environment, so culture helps to mold the human brain. We would therefore expect people in different cultures to acquire differences in brain structure that would have a lifelong effect on their behavior.

**Brain plasticity.** The capacity of the brain to change in response to chemicals, activity, or experience.

The brain is plastic not only in response to external events but also in response to events within a person's body, including the effects of hormones, injury, and abnormal genes. The developing brain early in life is especially responsive to these internal factors, which in turn alter the way that the brain reacts to external experiences. In this section, we explore a whole range of environmental influences on brain development, including both external and internal ones. We start with the question of exactly how experience manages to alter brain structure.

## Experience and Cortical Organization

Researchers can study the effects of experience on the brain and behavior by placing laboratory animals in different environments and observing the results. In one of the earliest such studies, Donald Hebb took one group of young laboratory rats home and let them grow up in his kitchen. A control group grew up in standard laboratory cages at McGill University. The "home rats" had many experiences that the caged rats did not, including being chased with a broom by Hebb's less-than-enthusiastic wife. Subsequently, Hebb gave all the rats a rat-specific "intelligence test" that consisted of learning to solve a series of mazes, collectively known as *Hebb-Williams mazes*. An example of a Hebb-Williams maze is shown in Figure 7-21. The home rats performed far better on these tasks than the caged rats did. Hebb therefore concluded that intelligence must be influenced by experience.

On the basis of his research, Hebb reasoned that people reared in stimulating environments would maximize their intellectual development, whereas people raised in impoverished environments would not reach their intellectual potential. Although this seems to be a logical conclusion, there is a problem in defining what stimulating and impoverished environments are. People living in slums with little education are not in what we would normally call an enriched setting, but that does not necessarily mean that the environment offers no cognitive stimulation or challenge. Certainly, people raised in this setting would be better adapted for survival in a slum than people raised in upper-class homes. Does this make them more intelligent in a certain way? Perhaps. In contrast, slum dwellers are not likely to be well adapted for college life, which was probably closer to what Hebb had in mind when he referred to such an environment as limiting intellectual potential. Indeed, it was Hebb's logic that led to the development of preschool television programs such as *Sesame Street*, which tried to provide a form of enrichment for children who would otherwise have little preschool exposure to reading.

**Figure 7-21**

In this version of the Hebb-Williams maze, a rat is placed in the start box (S) and must learn to find the food in the goal box (G). The walls of the maze can be moved to create new problems. Rats raised in complex environments solve such mazes much more quickly than do rats raised in standard laboratory cages.

The idea that early experience can change later behavior seems sensible enough, but we are left with the question of why experience should make such a difference. One reason is that experience changes the structure of neurons in the brain, especially in the cortex. Neurons in the brains of animals raised in complex environments, such as the environment shown in Figure 7-22, are larger and have more synapses than do those of animals reared in barren cages. Presumably, the increased number of synapses results from increased sensory processing in a complex and stimulating environment. There are also more (and larger) astrocytes in the brains of animals raised in complex settings.

Although complex-rearing studies do not address the effects of human culture directly, it is easy to make predictions about human development on the basis of their findings. We know that experience can modify the brain, so we can predict that different experiences might modify the brain differently, which seems to be the case in language development. Recall that exposure to different languages in infancy alters a child's subsequent ability to dis-

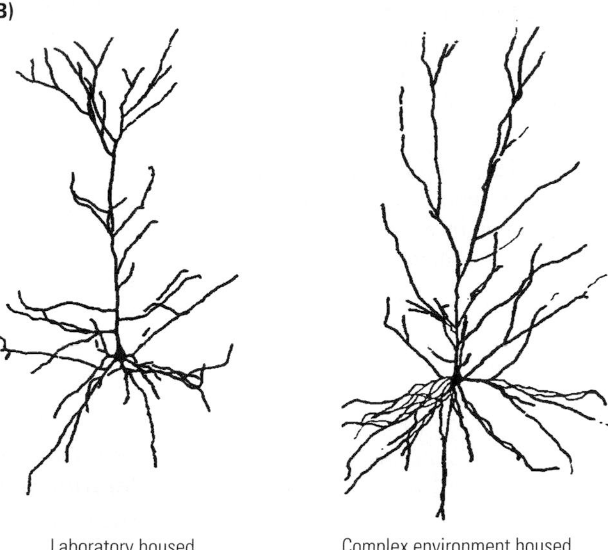


**Figure 7-22**

**(A)** A complex housing environment for a group of about six rats. The animals have an opportunity to move about and to interact with toys that are changed weekly. **(B)** Representative neurons from the parietal cortex of a laboratory-housed rat and of a complex-environment-housed rat. The neuron from the rat raised in the enriched environment is more complex and has about 25 percent more dendritic space for synapses.

criminate language-specific speech sounds. A similar process is likely to occur for music. People exposed to Western music since childhood usually find Eastern music peculiar, even nonmusical, on first encountering it when they are adults. Presumably, cells in the language- and music-analysis systems of the auditory cortex are altered by early experience and lose much of their plasticity in adulthood.

This loss of plasticity does not mean that the human brain becomes fixed and unchangeable in adulthood, however. There is little doubt that the brains of adults are influenced by exposure to new environments and experiences, although probably more slowly and less extensively than the brains of children are. Animal studies have shown plasticity in the adult brain. In fact, there is evidence that the brain is affected by experience well into old age, which is good news for those of us who are no longer children.

## Experience and Neural Connectivity

If experience can influence the structure of the cerebral cortex after a person is born, can it also do so prenatally? It can. This prenatal influence of experience is very clearly illustrated in studies of the developing visual system.

Consider the problem of connecting the eyes to the rest of the visual system. The problem can be understood with a simple analogy. Imagine that students in a large lecture hall are each viewing the front of the room (the visual field) through a small

**Chemoaffinity hypothesis.** The idea that cells or their axons and dendrites are drawn toward a signaling chemical that indicates the correct direction in which to go.

**Amblyopia.** A condition in which vision in one eye is reduced as a result of disuse; usually caused by a failure of the two eyes to point in the same direction.

cardboard tube, such as that for a paper-towel roll. If each student looks directly ahead, he or she will each see only a small bit of the visual field. This is essentially how the photoreceptors in the eyes act. Each of these cells sees only a small bit of the visual field. The problem is to put all the bits together to form a complete picture. To do so, receptors that see adjacent views (analogous to students sitting side by side) must send their information to adjacent regions in the various parts of the brain's visual system, such as the midbrain. How do they accomplish this feat?

Roger Sperry suggested that specific molecules exist in different cells in the various regions of the midbrain, giving each cell a distinctive chemical identity. Each cell, in other words, has an identifiable biochemical label. This idea is called the **chemoaffinity hypothesis.** Presumably, incoming axons seek out a specific chemical, such as the tropic factors discussed earlier, and consequently land in the correct general region of the midbrain. Many experiments have shown this process to take place. But the problem is that chemical affinity "directs" incoming axons to only the general location in which they need to be. To return to our two adjacent retinal cells, how do they now place themselves in the *precisely* correct position?

This fine-tuning of placement is believed to be activity dependent. Because adjacent receptors tend to be activated at the same time, they tend to form synapses on the same neurons in the midbrain, after chemoaffinity has drawn them to a general midbrain region. This process is shown in Figure 7-23. Neurons A and G are unlikely to be activated by the same stimulus and so they seldom fire synchronously. Neurons A and B, in contrast, are apt to be activated by the same stimuli, as are B and C. Through this simultaneous activity, cells eventually line up correctly in the connections that they form.

Now consider what happens to axons coming from different eyes. Although the inputs from the two eyes may be active simultaneously, the activity of cells in the same eye are more likely to be active together than are cells in different eyes. The net effect is that inputs from the two eyes tend to organize themselves into bands, or columns, that represent the same region of space in each of the eyes, as shown in Figure 7-24. The formation of these segregated bands therefore depends on the patterns of coinciding electrical activity on the incoming axons.

The importance of coinciding electrical activity and the formation of neural columns in the brain are demonstrated beautifully in a clever experiment by Martha Constantine-Paton. She knew that, because the optic nerves of frogs are completely crossed, the optic tectum on each side has input from only one eye. She wondered what would happen if a third eye were transplanted in the embryonic frog head. Probably this eye would send connections to one of the tecta, which would now have to accommodate to the new input. This accommodation is exactly what happened, as shown in Figure 7-25.

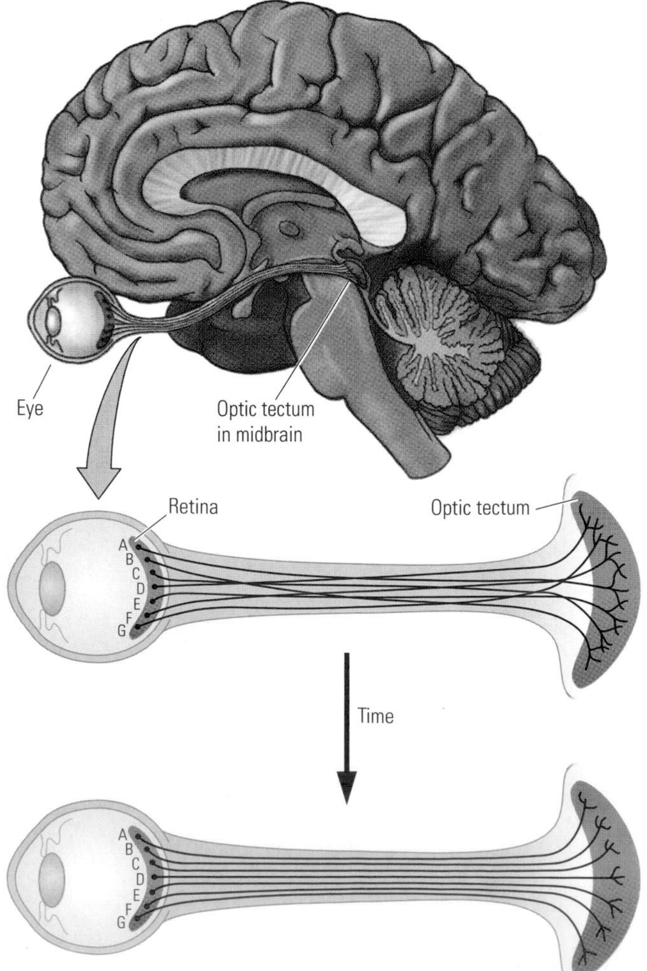


**Figure 7-23**

Experience has a role in organizing connections in the brain. Various neurons (labeled A–G) project from the retina to the tectum. The activities of adjacent neurons (for example, C and D) are more likely to coincide than the activities of neurons that are far apart (for example, A and G). As a result, the adjacent neurons are more likely to establish permanent synapses on the same tectal neurons. Axons grow to the approximate location in the tectum by using chemical signals (*top*), but there is a lack of precision. The connections are made more precise by the correlated activity.

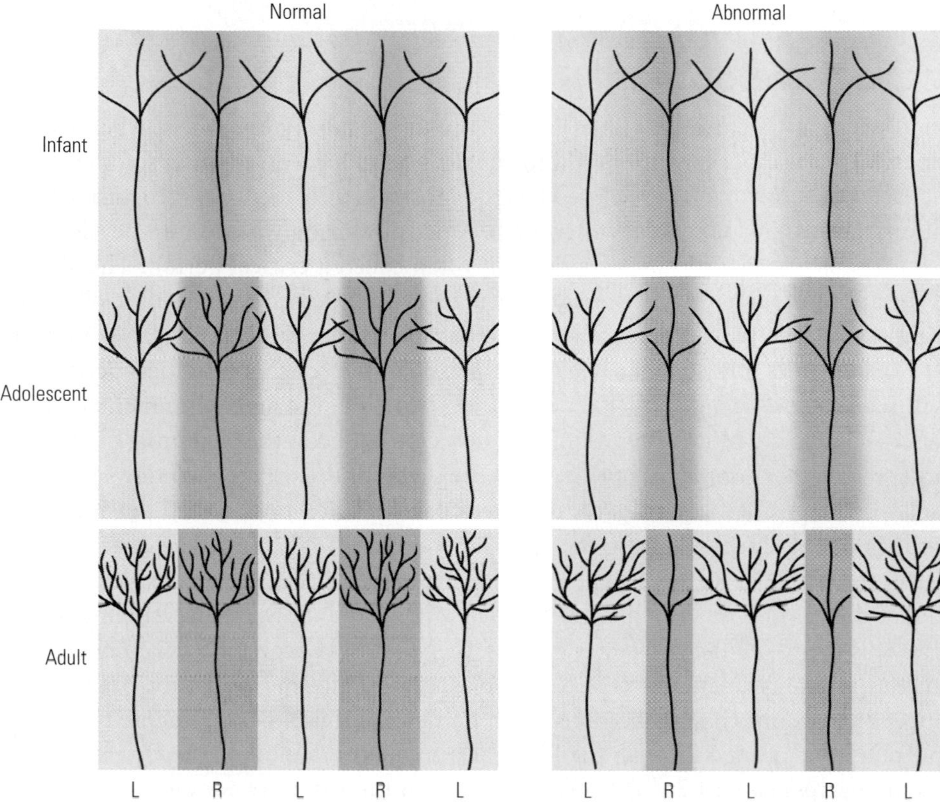


**Figure 7-24**

In the postnatal development of ocular dominance columns in the cat, axons enter the cortex where they grow large terminal arborizations. In infancy, the projections of both eyes overlap (L, left eye; R, right eye). In adulthood, a nonoverlapping pattern of terminal arborizations from each of the eyes is normal. If one eyelid of a kitten is sewn shut during a critical week of development, the terminations from that eye retract and those from the open eye expand.

The new eye sent connections to one of the tecta, which produced competition with one of the ungrafted eyes sending axons there. This competition resulted in the formation of one neural column for each eye. We can only imagine what this frog made of the world with its three eyes.

To summarize, the details of neural connections are modified by experience. An organism's genetic blueprint is vague regarding exactly which connections in the brain go to exactly which neurons. It is experience that fine-tunes neural connectivity. If experience is abnormal, such as would happen if one eye were covered during development, then the connections will not be guided appropriately by experience. In fact, this is exactly what happens to children who have a "lazy eye." The visual input from the lazy eye does not contribute to the fine-tuning of connections as it should, so the details of those connections do not develop normally. The result is a loss of sharpness in vision known as **amblyopia.**

**Figure 7-25**

**(A)** The third eye of this three-eyed frog was grafted into the frog embryo.
**(B)** The third eye forms connections with one optic tectum, in this case the right. Because the connections of the third eye are shared with another eye, these two eyes compete for synaptic space. This competition leads to the formation of alternating bands of connections.

**(A)**

From Martha Constantine-Paton and Margaret I. Law, "Eye Specific Termination Bands in Tecta of Three-Eyed Frogs," *Science,* November 10, 1978, vol. 202, pp. 639–641. ©1978 by the American Association for the Advancement of Science.

**(B)**

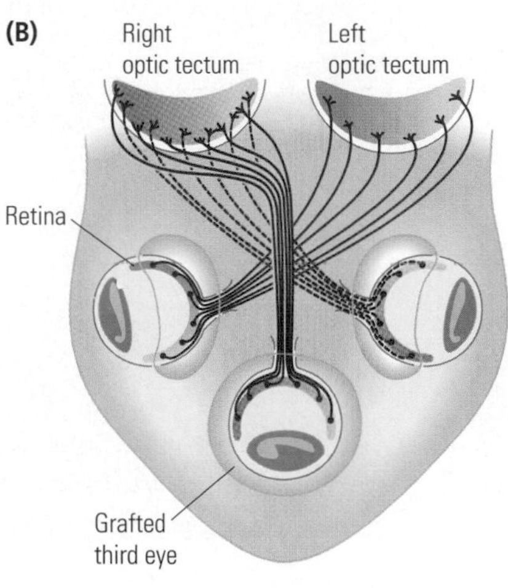

**Critical period.** A period in development during which some event has a long-lasting influence on the brain; often referred to as a sensitive period.

**Imprinting.** The process in which an animal is predisposed to learning an attachment to objects or animals at a critical period in development.

## Critical Periods for Experience and Brain Development

There seem to be particular times in the course of brain development when specific experiences are especially important for normal development. In kittens, for example, the effect of suturing one eye closed has the most disruptive effect on cortical organization between 30 and 60 days after birth. A period during which brain development is most sensitive to a specific experience is often called a **critical period.** The absence of the appropriate sensory experience during a critical period may result in abnormal brain development, leading to abnormal behavior that endures even into adulthood.

Richard Tees offered an analogy to help explain the concept of critical periods. He pictured the developing animal as a little train traveling past an environmental setting, perhaps the Rocky Mountains. All the windows are closed at the beginning of the journey (prenatal development), but, at particular stages of the trip, the windows in certain cars open, exposing the occupants (different parts of the brain) to the outside world. Some windows open to expose the brain to specific sounds, others to certain smells, others to particular sights, and so on. This exposure affects the brain's development and, in the absence of any exposure through an open window, that development is severely disturbed. As the journey continues, the windows become harder to open until, finally, they are permanently closed. This closure does not mean that the brain can no longer change, but changes become much harder to induce. Now, imagine two different trains, one headed through the Rocky Mountains and another, the Orient Express, traveling across eastern Europe. The "views" from the windows are very different, and the effects on the brain are correspondingly different. In other words, not only is the brain altered by the experiences that it has during a critical period, but the particular kinds of experiences encountered matter, too.

**Figure 7-26**

The ethologist Konrad Lorenz is being followed by goslings that imprinted on him. Because he was the first "object" that the geese experienced after hatching, he became their "mother."

Thomas D. McAvoy/*Time Magazine*

An extensively studied behavior that relates to the concept of critical periods is imprinting. In **imprinting,** an animal learns, during a critical period, to restrict its social preferences to a specific class of objects, usually the members of its own species. In birds, such as chickens or waterfowl, the critical period for imprinting is often shortly after hatching. Normally, the first moving object that a young hatchling sees is one of its parents or a sibling, so the hatchling's brain appropriately imprints to its own species. This appropriate imprinting is not inevitable, however. Konrad Lorenz demonstrated that, if the first animal or object that baby goslings encounter is a human, the goslings imprint to the human as though it were their mother. Figure 7-26 shows a flock of goslings that imprinted to Lorenz and followed him about wherever he went. This incorrect imprinting has long-term consequences for the hatchlings, which will often direct their subsequent sexual behavior inappropriately toward humans. For instance, a Barbary dove that had become imprinted to Lorenz directed its courtship toward his hand and even tried to copulate with the hand if it were held in a certain orientation. Interestingly, birds inappropriately imprint not just to humans, but to inanimate objects, too, especially if they are moving. Chickens have been induced to imprint to a milk bottle sitting on the back of a toy train that was moving around a track. But the brain is not entirely "clueless" when it comes to selecting a target to which to imprint. Given a choice, young chicks choose a real chicken to which to imprint over any other stimulus.

The fact that imprinting is rapid and has permanent behavioral consequences suggests that, during imprinting, the brain makes a rapid change of some kind, probably a structural change, given the permanence of the new behavior. Gabriel Horn and his colleagues at Cambridge University tried to identify this change in the brains of chicks during imprinting. Apparently, the change takes place in a specific region of the forebrain, known as the IMHV. The results of electron microscopic studies show that the synapses in this region enlarge with imprinting. Imprinting, then, seems to be a good model for studying brain plasticity during development, in part because the changes are rapid, are related to specific experience, and are localized.

## Abnormal Experience and Brain Development

If complex experiences can stimulate brain growth and influence later behavior, it seems likely that severely restricted experiences might retard both brain growth and behavior. To study the effects of such restrictions, Donald Hebb and his colleagues placed Scottish terriers in a dark environment with as little stimulation as possible and compared their behavior with that of dogs raised in a normal environment. When the dogs raised in the impoverished environment were later removed from that environment, their actions were very unusual. They showed virtually no reaction to people or other dogs, and they appeared to have lost their sense of pain. Even sticking pins in them produced no response. When given a dog version of the Hebb-Williams intelligence test for rats, these dogs performed very poorly and were unable to learn some tasks that dogs raised in more stimulating settings could learn easily.

The results of subsequent studies have shown that depriving young animals specifically of visual input or even of maternal contact has devastating consequences for their behavioral development and, presumably, for the development of the brain. For instance, Austin Riesen and his colleagues extensively studied animals raised in the dark and found that, even though the animals' eyes still work, they may be functionally blind after early visual deprivation. The absence of visual stimulation results in an atrophy of dendrites on cortical neurons, which is essentially the opposite of the results observed in the brains of animals raised in complex and stimulating environments.

Not only does the absence of specific sensory inputs adversely affect brain development, so do more complex kinds of abnormal experiences. This can be seen in the retarded intellectual development of children raised in dreadful circumstances in Romanian orphanages, as described in "Romanian Orphans" on page 266. In the 1950s, Harry Harlow began the first systematic laboratory studies of analogous deprivation in laboratory animals. Harlow showed that infant monkeys raised without maternal (or paternal) contact have grossly abnormal intellectual and social behaviors in adulthood. Harlow separated baby monkeys from their mothers shortly after birth and raised them in individual cages. Perhaps the most stunning effect was that, in adulthood, these animals were totally unable to establish normal relations with other animals. Unfortunately, Harlow did not analyze the brains of the deprived monkeys. We would predict atrophy of cortical neurons, especially in the frontal-lobe regions known to be related to normal social behavior.

The importance of the environment in brain development cannot be overemphasized. Children exposed to impoverished environments or to abuse or neglect can be expected to be at a serious disadvantage later in life. Although it is often thought that children can succeed in school and in life *if they really want to*, it is clear that abnormal developmental experiences can alter the brain irrevocably. As a society, we cannot be complacent about the environments to which our children are exposed.

Focus on Disorders

## Romanian Orphans

In the 1970s, the Communist regime then governing Romania outlawed all forms of birth control and abortion. The natural result was thousands of unwanted pregnancies. More than 100,000 unwanted children were placed in orphanages where the conditions were appalling. Children had virtually no environmental stimulation. In most instances, they were confined to cots. There were few, if any, playthings and virtually no personal interaction with caregivers. Bathing often consisted of being hosed down with cold water. After the Communist government fell and the outside world was able to intervene, hundreds of these children were rescued and placed in adoptive homes throughout the world, especially in the United States, Canada, and the United Kingdom.

There have now been several studies of the fate of these severely deprived children (see Ames, 1997; Rutter et al., 1998). When the children arrived in their new homes, they were in a poor physical state. They were malnourished; they had chronic respiratory and intestinal infections; and they were severely developmentally impaired. A British study by Michael Rutter and his colleagues found them to be two standard deviations below age-matched children for weight, height, and head circumference. Assessments with the use of scales of motor and cognitive development showed most of the children to be in the retarded range.

The improvement in these children in the first 2 years after placement in their adoptive homes was nothing short of spectacular. Average height and weight became nearly normal, although head circumference remained below normal. (Head circumference can be taken as a very rough measure of brain size.) Many of the children were now in the normal range of motor and cognitive development. A significant number, however, were still considered retarded. Why were there individual differences in recovery from the past deprivation?

The key factor in predicting recovery was age at adoption. Those children adopted before 6 months of age did significantly better than those adopted later. In a Canadian study by Elenor Ames, Romanian orphans who were adopted before 4 months of age had an average Stanford-Binet IQ of 98 when tested at 4½ years of age. In comparison, age-matched Canadian controls had an average IQ of 109, whereas Romanian children adopted at a median age of 19 months had an average IQ of only 90. Brain-imaging studies showed the children adopted at an older age to have smaller-than-normal brains. Although there are no formal

## Hormones and Brain Development

The determination of sex is largely genetic. In mammals, the Y chromosome present in males controls the process by which an undifferentiated primitive gonad develops into testes, as illustrated in Figure 7-9. The testes subsequently secrete testosterone, which stimulates the development of male reproductive organs and, during puberty, the growth of male secondary sexual characteristics.

Gonadal hormones also influence the development of neurons. Testosterone is released in males during a brief period in the course of brain development, and it subsequently acts to alter the brain, much as it alters the sex organs. This process is called **masculinization.** Just as testosterone does not affect all body organs, it does not affect all regions of the brain. It does, however, affect many brain regions and in many different ways. For instance, it affects the number of neurons formed in certain brain areas, reduces the number of neurons that die, increases cell growth, increases or reduces dendritic branching, increases or reduces synaptic growth, and regulates the activity of synapses. As a result of these effects due to exposure to testosterone, a male brain and a female brain are not the same.

**Masculinization.** A process by which exposure to androgens alters the brain, rendering it "malelike."

studies of large groups of these children as they approach adolescence, anecdotal reports of individual children who were adopted at an older age and are now adolescents indicate continuing problems. Some of these youngsters have significant learning disabilities in school, suffer from hyperactivity, and have not developed normal patterns of social interaction.

The inescapable conclusion emerging from the Romanian orphanage experience is that the brain may be able to recover from a brief period of extreme deprivation in early infancy, but periods longer than 6 months produce significant abnormalities in brain development that cannot be completely repaired. This conclusion is supported by the case study of an American girl named Genie, who experienced severe social and experiential deprivation as well as chronic malnutrition at the hands of her psychotic father (see Curtis, 1978). She was discovered at the age of 13, after having spent much of her life in a closed room, during which time she was punished for making any noise. After her rescue, she, too, showed rapid growth and cognitive development, although her language development remained severely retarded.

To summarize, studies of the Romanian orphans, of orphans from other highly impoverished settings, and of cases such as that of Genie make it clear that the developing brain requires stimulation for normal development. Although the brain may be able to catch up after a short period of deprivation, more than a few months of severe deprivation results in a smaller-than-normal brain and associated behavioral abnormalities, especially in cognitive and social skills.

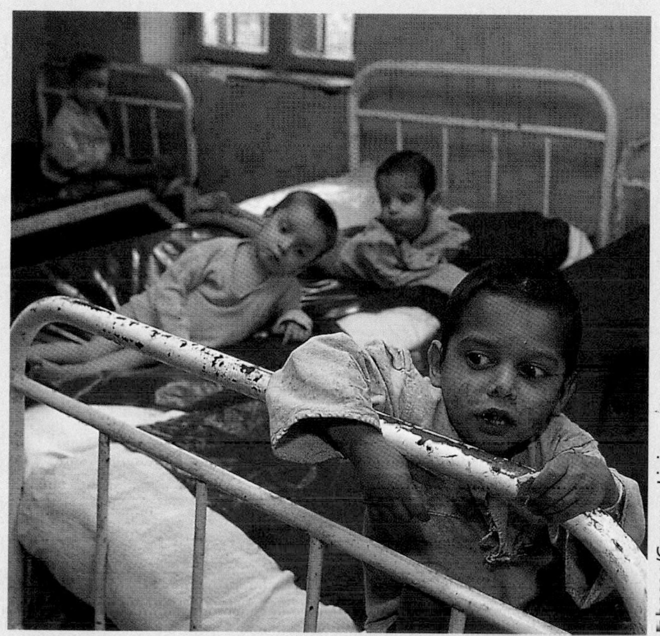

Johnson/Gamma-Liaison

**The situation depicted in this photo was not unusual for Romanian orphans in the 1970s and 1980s: children were housed and clothed, but had no other forms of stimulation, either from caregivers or an enriched environment. Studies on this population have shown that the lack of stimulation has hampered normal brain development.**

It was once believed that testosterone's effects on brain development were not all that important, because this hormone was thought to primarily influence regions of the brain regarding sexual behavior, not regions of "higher" functions. We now know that this belief is false. Testosterone changes the structure of cells in many regions of the cortex, with diverse behavioral consequences that include influences on cognitive processes.

Consider one example. Jocelyn Bachevalier trained infant male and female monkeys in the concurrent-discrimination task described earlier, in which the subject has to learn which of two objects in a series of object pairs conceals a food reward. In addition, Bachevalier trained the animals in another task, known as *object-reversal learning*. The task here is to learn that one particular object always conceals a food reward, whereas another object never does. After this pattern has been learned, the reward contingencies are reversed so that the particular object that has always been rewarded is now never rewarded, whereas the formerly unrewarded object now conceals the reward. When this new pattern has been learned, the contingencies are reversed again, and so on, for five reversals. Bachevalier found that 2½-month-old male monkeys were superior to female monkeys on the object-reversal task, but females did better on the concurrent task. Apparently, the different brain areas required for these two tasks matured at different rates in the male and female monkeys. Bachevalier later tested additional male monkeys whose testes had been removed at birth and so were no longer exposed to testosterone. These animals performed like females on the tasks, implying that testosterone was influencing the rate of brain development in areas related to certain cognitive behaviors.

Bachevalier and her colleague Bill Overman then repeated the experiment, this time using as their subjects children from 15 to 30 months old. The results were the same: boys were superior at the object-reversal task and girls were superior at the concurrent task. There were no such male–female differences in performance among older children (32–55 months of age). Presumably, by this older age, the brain regions required for each task had matured in both boys and girls. At the earlier age, however, gonadal hormones seemed to be influencing the rate of maturation in certain regions of the brain, just as they had in the baby monkeys.

Although the biggest effects of gonadal hormones may be during early development, their role is by no means finished at the end of childhood. Gonadal hormones (including both testosterone and estrogen, the latter of which is produced in large quantities by the ovaries in females) continue to influence the structure of the brain throughout an animal's life. In fact, removal of the ovaries in middle-aged laboratory rats leads to marked growth of dendrites and the production of more glial cells in the cortex. This finding of widespread neural change in the cortex associated with loss of estrogen has implications for the treatment of postmenopausal women.

Gonadal hormones also affect how the brain responds to events in the environment. For instance, among rats housed in complex environments, males show more dendritic growth in neurons of the visual cortex than do females (see Juraska, 1990). In contrast, females housed in this setting show more dendritic growth in the frontal cortex than do males. Apparently, the same experience can affect the male and female brain differently owing to the mediating influence of gonadal hormones. This finding means that, as females and males develop, their brains continue to become more and more different from each other. It is much like coming to a fork in a road. Once having chosen to go down one path, your direction of travel is forever changed as the roads diverge and become increasingly farther apart.

To summarize, gonadal hormones alter the basic development of neurons, shape the nature of experience-dependent changes in the brain, and influence the structure of neurons throughout our lifetime. These effects of sex hormones need to be considered by those who believe that behavioral differences between males and females are solely the result of environmental experiences. In part, it is true that environmental factors exert a major influence. But one reason that they do may be that male and female brains are different to start with, and even the same events, when experienced by structurally different brains, may lead to different effects on the brain. In our view, the important task is not to deny the presence of sex differences in brain organization and function, but rather to understand the degree to which those neurological differences contribute to observed differences in behavior.

## Injury and Brain Development

If the brain is damaged in the course of development, is it irrevocably altered? In the 1930s, Donald Hebb studied children with major birth-related injuries to the frontal lobes and found that such children had severe and permanent behavioral abnormalities in adulthood. He concluded that severe brain damage early in life can alter the subsequent development of the rest of the brain, leading to chronic behavioral disorders.

To what extent have other studies confirmed Hebb's conclusion? There are few anatomical studies of humans with early brain injuries, but we can make some general predictions from the study of laboratory animals. In general, early brain injuries do produce abnormal brains, especially at certain critical periods of development. For humans, the worst time appears to be during the last half of the intrauterine period and the first couple of months after birth. Rats that suffer injuries at a comparative time have significantly smaller brains than normal, and their cortical neurons show a generalized atrophy relative to normal brains, as illustrated in Figure 7-27. Behaviorally, these animals appear cognitively retarded, deficient in a wide range of skills.

The effect of injury to the developing brain is not always devastating, however. For example, we have known for more than 100 years that children with brain injuries in the first couple of years after birth almost never have the severe language disturbances common to adults with equivalent injuries. Animal studies help explain why. Whereas damage to the brain in the period comparable to the last few months of gestation in humans produces widespread cortical atrophy, damage at a time roughly comparable to age 6 months to 2 years in humans actually produces more dendritic development, as also seen in Figure 7-27. Furthermore, these animals show dramatic recovery of functions, implying that the brain has a capacity during development to compensate for injury.

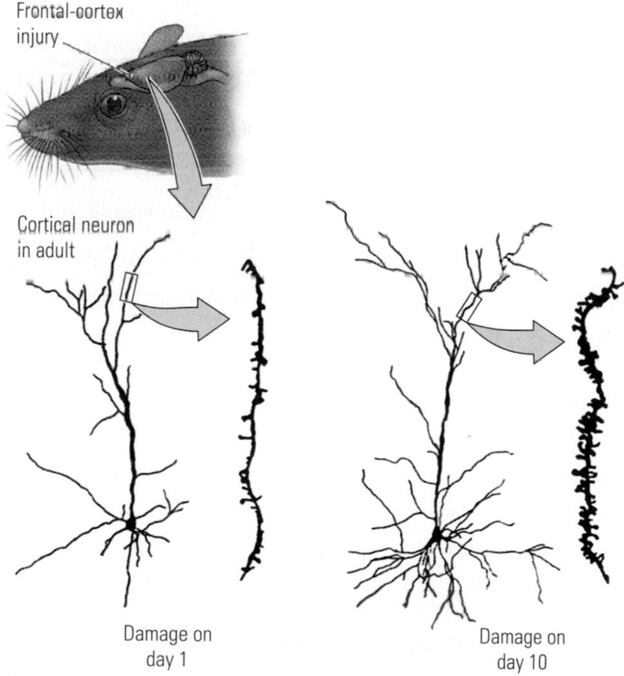


**Figure 7-27**

Cortical injury at different times in the course of development has different anatomical and behavioral consequences. In the rat, damage to the frontal cortex on the day of birth leads to the development of cortical neurons with simple dendritic fields and a sparce growth of spines. In contrast, damage to the frontal cortex at 10 days of age leads to the development of cortical neurons with expanded dendritic fields and denser spines than normal.

Adapted from "Possible Anatomical Basis of Recovery of Function After Neonatal Frontal Lesions in Rats," by B. Kolb and R. Gibb, 1993, *Behavioral Neuroscience*, *107*, p. 808.

## Other Kinds of Abnormal Brain Development

The nervous system need not be damaged by external forces for it to develop abnormally. For instance, many genetic abnormalities are believed to result in abnormalities in the development and, ultimately, the structure of the brain. You may have heard of *spina bifida*, a condition in which the genetic blueprint goes awry and the neural tube does not close completely, leading to an incompletely formed spinal cord. After birth,

**Anencephaly.** Failure of the forebrain to develop.

children with spina bifida usually have serious motor problems because of this spinal-cord abnormality. But imagine what would happen if some genetic abnormality caused the front end of the neural tube not to close properly. Because the front end of the neural tube forms the brain, this failure would result in gross abnormalities in brain development. Such a condition exists and is known as **anencephaly.** Infants affected by this condition die soon after birth.

Abnormal brain development can be much subtler than anencephaly. For example, if cells do not migrate to their correct locations and these mispositioned cells do not subsequently die, they can disrupt brain function and may lead to disorders ranging from seizures to schizophrenia (see "Schizophrenia" below). There are also a variety of conditions in which neurons fail to differentiate normally. In certain cases, the

Focus on Disorders

## Schizophrenia

When Mrs. T. was 16 years old, she began to experience her first symptom of schizophrenia: a profound feeling that people were staring at her. These bouts of self-consciousness soon forced her to end her public piano performances. Her self-consciousness led to withdrawal, then to fearful delusions that others were speaking about her behind her back, and finally to suspicions that they were plotting to harm her. At first Mrs. T.'s illness was intermittent, and the return of her intelligence, warmth, and ambition between episodes allowed her to complete several years of college, to marry, and to rear three children. She had to enter a hospital for the first time at age 28, after the birth of her third child, when she began to hallucinate.

Now, at 45, Mrs. T. is never entirely well. She has seen dinosaurs on the street and live animals in her refrigerator. While hallucinating, she speaks and writes in an incoherent, but almost poetic way. At other times, she is more lucid, but even then the voices she hears sometimes lead her to do dangerous things, such as driving very fast down the highway in the middle of the night, dressed only in a nightgown. . . . At other times and without any apparent stimulus, Mrs. T. has bizarre visual hallucinations. For example, she saw cherubs in the grocery store. These experiences leave her preoccupied, confused, and frightened, unable to perform such everyday tasks as cooking or playing the piano. (Gershon & Rieder, 1992, p. 127)

Schizophrenia is obviously an extraordinary disorder, with symptoms that are hard to generalize. It has always been easier to identify schizophrenic behavior than to define what schizophrenia is. Perhaps the one universally accepted criterion for diagnosing schizophrenia is the absence of other neurological disturbances or affective disorders that could cause a person to lose touch with reality. This is a definition by default. Other authors have emphasized the presence of bizarre hallucinations and disturbances of thought, much like those displayed by Mrs. T. However, the symptoms of schizophrenia are heterogeneous, suggesting that the biological abnormalities vary from person to person.

In 1913, Emil Kraepelin first proposed that schizophrenia follows a progressively deteriorating course with a dismal final outcome. This opinion about the disorder was dominant through most of the twentieth century. Today, however, a consensus is emerging that this view is probably incorrect. Most patients appear to stay at a fairly stable level after the first few years of displaying schizophrenic symptoms, with little evidence of a decline in neuropsychological functioning. The symptoms come and go, much as for Mrs. T., but the severity is relatively constant after the first few episodes.

neurons fail to produce long dendrites or spines. As a result, connectivity in the brain is abnormal, leading to retardation. The opposite condition also is possible: neurons continue to make dendrites and form connections with other cells to the point at which these neurons become extraordinarily large. The functional consequences of all the newly formed connections can be devastating. Excitatory synapses in the wrong location effectively short-circuit a neuron's function.

One curious consequence of abnormal brain development is that the behavioral effects may emerge only as the brain matures and the maturing regions begin to play a greater role in behavior. This consequence is especially true of frontal-lobe injuries. The frontal lobes continue to develop into adolescence, and often not until adolescence do the effects of frontal-lobe abnormalities begin to be noticed. Schizophrenia

To learn more about abnormal brain development, visit the Web site at **www.worthpublishers.com/kolb/chapter7.**

Numerous studies have investigated the brains of schizophrenics, both in autopsies and in MRI and CT scans. Although the results vary, most agree that schizophrenics have brains that are lighter than normal and that have enlarged ventricles. There are also suggestions that schizophrenics have both smaller frontal lobes (or at least a reduction in the number of neurons in the prefrontal cortex) and thinner parahippocampal gyri. One of the most interesting discoveries is that of Joyce Kovelman and Arnold Scheibel (1984), who found abnormalities in the orientation of neurons in the hippocampi of schizophrenics. Rather than the consistently parallel orientation of neurons in this region characteristic of normal brains, the schizophrenics had a more haphazard organization, as shown in the accompanying drawing.

There is increasing evidence that the abnormalities observed in schizophrenic brains are associated with disturbances of brain development. William Bunney and his colleagues (1997) suggest that at least a subgroup of schizophrenics experience either environmental insults or some type of abnormal gene activity in the fourth to sixth month of fetal development. These events are thought to result in abnormal cortical development, particularly in the frontal lobes. Later in adolescence, as the frontal lobes complete development, the person begins to experience symptoms of this abnormal prior development.

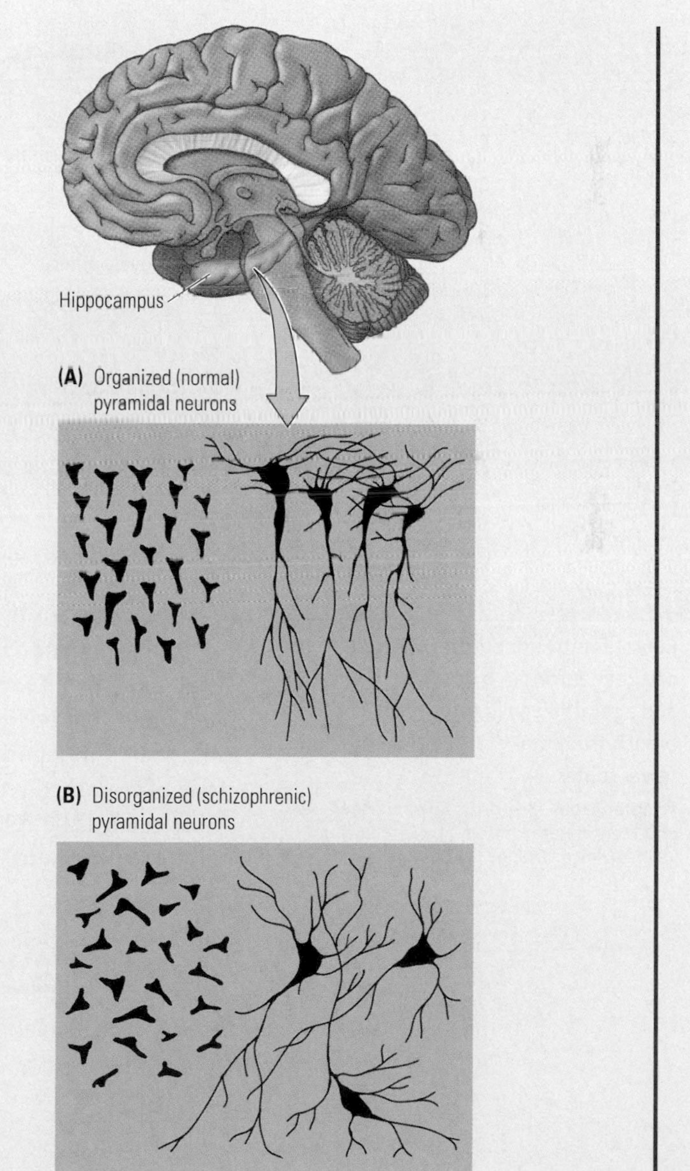


Examples of pyramidal cell orientation from the hippocampus of **(A)** a normal brain and **(B)** a schizophrenic brain. In the schizophrenic brain these pyramidal neurons are much more disorganized.

Adapted from "A Neurohistologic Correlate of Schizophrenia," by J. A. Kovelman and A. B. Scheibel, 1984, *Biological Psychiatry, 19*, p. 1613.

is a disease that is characterized by slow development, usually not becoming obvious until late adolescence. The schizophrenic brain has many abnormalities, some of which are in the frontal lobes.

## Mental Retardation

Mental retardation refers to an impairment in cognitive functioning that accompanies abnormal brain development. Mental retardation may range in severity from mild, allowing an almost normal life style, to severe, requiring constant care. As summarized in Table 7-4, mental retardation can result from chronic malnutrition, genetic abnormalities such as Down's syndrome, hormonal abnormalities, brain injury, or neurological disease. Different causes produce different abnormalities in brain organization, but the critical similarity across all types of retardation is that the brain is not normal.

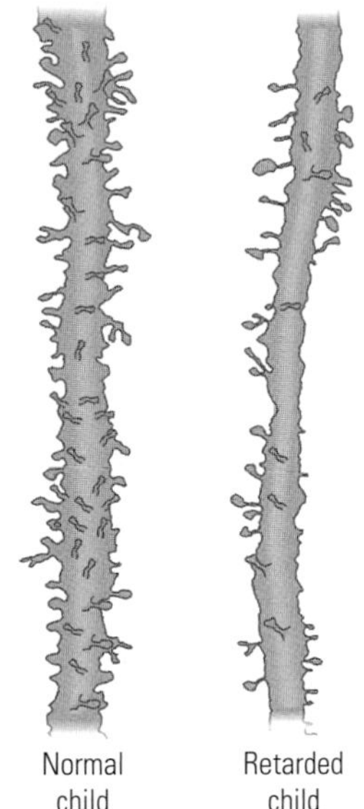


**Figure 7-28** Representative dendritic branches from cortical neurons in a normal child (*left*) and a retarded child (*right*). The dendritic branch from the retarded child has fewer spines.

Adapted from "Dendritic Spine 'Dysgenesis' and Mental Retardation," by D. P. Purpura, 1974, *Science*, *186*, p. 1127.

**Table 7-4 Causes of Mental Retardation**

| Cause | Example mechanism | Example condition |
|---|---|---|
| Genetic abnormality | Error of metabolism<br>Chromosomal abnormality | Phenylketonuria (PKU)<br>Down's syndrome |
| Abnormal embryonic development | Exposure to a toxin | Fetal alcohol syndrome |
| Prenatal disease | Infection | Rubella (also called German measles) |
| Birth trauma | Anoxia (oxygen deprivation) | Cerebral palsy |
| Malnutrition | Abnormal brain development | Kwashiorkor |
| Environmental abnormality | Sensory deprivation | Children in orphanages |

A study by Dominique Purpura provides an example of one of the few systematic investigations of the brains of retarded children. Purpura used Golgi stain to examine neurons of children who had died from accident or disease unrelated to the nervous system. When he examined the brains of children with various forms of retardation, he found that the dendrites were stunted in growth and the spines were very sparse, as illustrated in Figure 7-28. The simple structure of these neurons was probably indicative of a marked reduction in the number of connections in the brain, which presumably caused the retardation. Variation in both the nature and the extent of neuronal abnormality in different children would lead to different behavioral syndromes.

### In Review

The brain is plastic during its development and can therefore be molded by experience into different forms, at least at the microscopic level. The sensitivity of the brain to experience varies with time, however. There are critical periods in the course of development when different parts of the brain are particularly sensitive to different experiences. Not only is the brain plastic in response to external events, but it is changed by internal events as well, including the effects of hormones, injury, and abnormal genes. If experiences are abnormal, then the brain's development is abnormal, possibly leading to disorders such as mental retardation or schizophrenia.

## HOW DO ANY OF US DEVELOP A NORMAL BRAIN?

When we look at the complexity of the brain, the less-than-precise process of brain development, and the large number of factors that can influence it, we are left marveling at how so many of us end up with brains that pass for "normal." After all, we must all have had neurons that migrated to wrong locations, made incorrect connections, and were exposed to viruses or other harmful substances. If the brain were as fragile as it might seem, it would be almost impossible to end up with a normal brain.

Apparently, animals have evolved a substantial capacity to repair minor abnormalities in brain development. Most people have developed in the range that we call "normal" because the human brain's plasticity and regenerative powers are successful in overcoming minor developmental deviations. Recall that one stage in brain development consists of cell death and synaptic pruning. By initially overproducing neurons and synapses, the brain has the capacity to correct any errors that might have arisen accidentally.

These same plastic properties of the brain later allow us to cope with the ravages of aging. Neurons are dying throughout our lifetimes and, by age 50, we ought to be able to see significant effects of all of this cell loss, especially considering the cumulative results of exposure to environmental toxins, drugs, closed head injuries, and so on. But this is not what happens. Although teenagers may not believe it, very few 50-year-olds are demented. By most criteria, the 50-year-old who has been intellectually active throughout adulthood is likely to be much wiser than the 18-year-old whose brain has lost relatively few neurons. Clearly, we must have some mechanism to compensate for loss and minor injury to our brain cells. This capacity for plasticity and change is one of the most important characteristics of the human brain, not only during development but through the rest of life as well. We return to this idea in Chapter 13.

## SUMMARY

1. *What are the stages of neural development?* The process of brain maturation is long, lasting until 16 or 18 years of age. Neurons, the elementary components of the brain, are born, develop a neuronal phenotype, migrate, and, as their processes elaborate, establish connections with other neurons. Because the brain contains such a large number of cells, and an even larger number of connections, the brain produces more neurons and connections than it needs and then prunes back to a stable adult level.
2. *How does behavior develop?* The infant and child go through stages of behavioral development that are similar in children across all cultural spectrums. For example, as infants develop, motor behaviors emerge in a predictable sequence. Infants first make clumsy movements towards objects but they are poorly directed. By about 4 months, the motor system has matured sufficiently so that the infant can grasp objects with the whole hand, and by around 11 months children are able to make pincer grasps to pick up objects like pencils. Other motor behaviors emerge over the ensuing months and years, such as walking, throwing, catching, and so on. Similarly, cognitive behaviors emerge through a series of stages in which children acquire principles that allow them to solve problems. Researchers such as Jean Piaget have identified and characterized four or more distinct stages of cognitive development, each of which can be identified by special behavioral tests.
3. *How do behavioral and neural maturation relate to one another?* The emergence of behaviors is correlated with the development of the neural systems that produce the behaviors. Behavioral and cognitive capacities follow a similar sequence of development from the rudimentary to the complex. The relationship between

**neuroscience interactive**

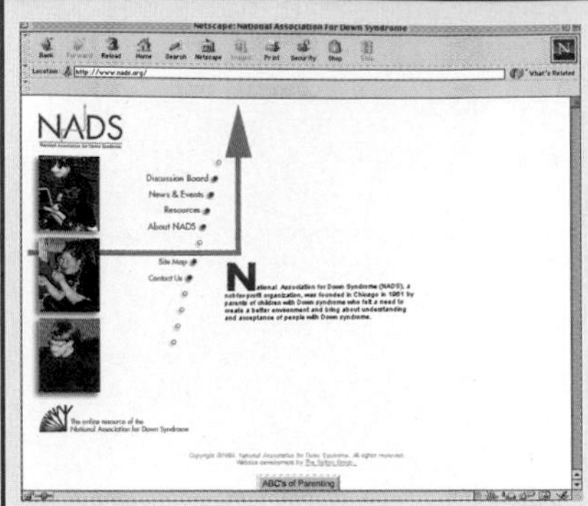

There are many resources available for expanding your learning on line:

■ **www.worthpublishers.com/kolb/chapter7**
Try some self-tests to reinforce your mastery of the material. Look at some of the news updates reflecting current research on the brain. You'll also be able to link to other sites which will reinforce what you've learned.

■ **www.embryo.mc.duke.edu**
Link here to see a remarkable collection of human embryos through magnetic resonance microscopy.

■ **www.nads.org**
Investigate current research about Down's syndrome at the National Association for Down's Syndrome.

■ **www.ucpa.org**
Learn more about cerebral palsy at the home page of United Cerebral Palsy.

On your CD-ROM you'll be able to quiz yourself on your comprehension of the chapter. The module on Neural Communication also provides important review on the neural structure.

brain structure and function can be inferred by matching the developmental timetables of brain anatomy and physiology with that of behavior. For example, motor behaviors emerge in synchrony with the maturation of motor circuits in the cerebral cortex, basal ganglia, and cerebellum, as well as in the connections from these areas to the spinal cord. Similar correlations between behavioral emergence and neuronal development can be seen in the development of other behaviors, including cognitive behaviors. For example, different types of memory abilities emerge as circuits in the frontal and temporal lobes mature.

4. *What factors influence neural maturation?* The brain is modifiable during its development and the structure of neurons and their connections can be molded by various factors throughout the period of development. These factors include external events, gonadal hormones, and injury. The sensitivity of the brain to these factors varies with time as there are periods during the course of development when different brain regions are particularly sensitive to different events. If experiences are abnormal, then the brain's development is abnormal, as well, and can lead to disorders such as retardation.
5. *How sensitive is the developing brain to injury?* Perturbations of the brain during development, such as from anoxia, trauma, or toxins can significantly alter brain development and result in severe behavioral abnormalities including retardation and cerebral palsy. The brain does have a substantial capacity to repair or correct minor abnormalities, however, allowing most people to develop a normal behavioral repertoire.

## KEY TERMS

amblyopia, p. 263
anencephaly, p. 270
apoptosis, p. 252
brain plasticity, p. 259
cell-adhesion molecule (CAM), p. 250
chemoaffinity hypothesis, p. 262
critical period, p. 264
filopod, p. 249
glioblast, p. 244
growth cone, p. 249
growth spurt, p. 257
imprinting, p. 264
masculinization, p. 266
netrins, p. 250
neural Darwinism, p. 251
neural plate, p. 240
neural stem cells, p. 243
neural tube, p. 240
neuroblast, p. 244
neurotrophic factors, p. 245
progenitor cells, p. 244
radial glial cells, p. 247
tropic molecules, p. 250
ventricular zone, p. 243

## REVIEW QUESTIONS

1. Describe the gross development of the nervous system. Summarize and explain the steps in brain development.
2. What roles do different factors such as molecules, genetics, and experience play in development?
3. How does behavioral development relate to neural development?
4. How does experience affect brain development?

## FOR FURTHER THOUGHT

1. Experience plays an important role in brain development. How might an interaction between sex and environment account for behavioral differences in adulthood?

2. How can the principles of behavioral development help to explain why each brain is unique?

## RECOMMENDED READING

Edelman, G. M. (1987). *Neural Darwinism: The theory of neuronal group selection*. New York: Basic Books. You have heard of Darwinism and the idea of survival of the fittest. Edelman applies this Darwinian concept to the nervous system's shedding of neurons in the course of development and throughout a person's lifetime. Although not universally accepted, the ideas in the book are amusing to read.

Greenough, W. T., & Chang, F. F. (1988). Plasticity of synapse structure and pattern in the cerebral cortex. In A. Peters and E. G. Jones (Eds.), *Cerebral cortex: Vol. 7. Development and maturation of the cerebral cortex* (pp. 391–440). New York: Plenum. Greenough is one of the world leaders in the study of experience-dependent change in the nervous system. This chapter not only provides a nice historical review, but also lays out seminal ideas on the developmental plasticity of the nervous system.

Hebb, D. O. (1949). *The organization of behavior*. New York: Wiley. Although 1949 may seem like a long time ago for a book to be still relevant today, Hebb's book may be the most important single volume on brain and behavior. It was the first serious attempt to outline a neuropsychological theory of how the brain could produce behavior and, especially, thought. Development is an important theme in the book because Hebb believed that experience plays an essential role in developing the cognitive and neural structures necessary for adulthood. This book is mandatory reading for any student going on to graduate school in behavioral neuroscience.

Michel, G. F., & Moore, C. L. (1995). *Developmental psychobiology*. Cambridge, MA: MIT Press. Most neural development books are thin on behavioral development, but this book strikes a nice balance in its analysis of both brain and behavioral development.

Purves, D., & Lichtman, J. W. (1985). *Principles of neural development*. Sunderland, MA: Sinauer. Although not primarily about the development of the cortex, the book provides sufficient background to enable a thorough understanding of the principles that guide nervous system development.

CHAPTER

# 8

# How Do We See the World?

Born in a small English town in 1940, D. B. had an uneventful childhood medically until he began to experience headaches at about age 14. These headaches were migraines, described in "D. B., Karl Lashley, and Migraines" on page 278. Before each headache, D. B. received a warning: the sensation of an oval-shaped area containing a flashing light that appeared just to the left of center in his field of vision. In the next few minutes, the oval enlarged, and, after about 15 minutes, the flashing light vanished and the region of the oval was blind. D. B. described the oval as an opaque white area surrounded by a rim of color. A headache on the right side of his head followed. The headache could persist for as long as 48 hours, but usually D. B. fell asleep before that much time elapsed. When he awakened, the headache was gone and his vision was normal again.

D. B.'s attacks continued at intervals of about 6 weeks for 10 years. After one attack, he did not totally regain his vision but was left with a small blind spot. During some attacks, he also began to experience occasional loss of skin sensation along the left side of his body. Like his visual symptoms, these symptoms disappeared once the headache was gone.

When D. B. was 26 years old, a neurologist found a collection of abnormal blood vessels at the back of his right occipital lobe. These blood vessels were causing the migraine attacks. (In case you suffer from migraines, we hasten to point out that this cause is unusual.) By the time D. B. was 30, the migraines became more severe and began to interfere with his family and social life, as well as his job. Because no drug treatment was effective, D. B. had the malformed blood vessels surgically removed in 1973. The operation relieved his pain and generally improved his life, but a part of his right occipital lobe was deprived of blood and died. As a result, D. B. became blind in the left half of his field of vision. In other words, as he looks at the world through either eye, he is unable to see anything to the left of the midline.

D. B. came to the attention of Lawrence Weizkrantz, a world-renowned visual neuroscientist at Oxford University, who made a remarkable discovery about D. B.'s blindness. He found that, although D. B. could not identify objects in his blind area, he could very accurately "guess" if a light had blinked on there. He could even say where the light that he did not "see" was located. Apparently, even though D. B. could not consciously perceive a light in his blind region, his brain knew when a light had blinked and *where* it had appeared. This phenomenon is referred to as *blindsight.* D. B.'s brain, in other words, knew more than he was consciously aware of.

You may be surprised to learn that what applies to D. B. also applies to you. You are consciously aware of only part of the visual information that your brain is processing. This is an important principle of how the human visual system works, which Weizkrantz was able to detect because of D. B.'s injury. Vision is not unique in this regard. We are also unaware of much of the processing that takes place in other sensory pathways, such as those of hearing and touch. But vision is the focus of this chapter. The ability to lose conscious visual perception while retaining unconscious vision leads to this chapter's major question: How do we "see" the world?

The function of the visual system is to convert light energy into neural activity that has meaning for us. In this chapter, we explore how this happens. We begin with a description of what it really means to experience sensory information transmitted by our environment. Then in an overview of the visual system's anatomy, we consider the anatomical structure of the eyes, the connections between the eyes and the brain, and the sections of the brain that process visual information. Next we focus on how neurons respond to visual input, enabling the brain to distinguish different features, such as color and shape. Finally, we explore the culmination of the visual system—to *understand* what we see. How do we process light energy in such a way as to grasp the meaning of written words or to see the beauty in a painting by Monet?

Focus on Disorders

## D. B., Karl Lashley, and Migraines

D. B. and Karl Lashley have several things in common. One is that they are both well known among neuroscientists. D. B. is a well-studied patient in visual neuroscience, and Karl Lashley was a pioneer of research in this field. Both D. B. and Lashley also suffered severe migraines. The term *migraine* (which derives from a Greek word meaning "half of the skull") refers to recurrent attacks of headache that are usually localized to one side of the head; that vary in severity, frequency, and duration; and that are often accompanied by nausea and vomiting. Migraine is perhaps the most common of all neurological disorders, afflicting some 5 to 20 percent of the population at some time in their lives.

Karl Lashley

Both D. B. and Karl Lashley suffered from classic migraine, which is preceded by an aura that usually lasts for 20 to 40 minutes. Lashley carefully described his visual aura, which turned out to be common to many migraine sufferers. The aura began as a spot of flashing light and then slowly enlarged. Lashley had no sight in the flashing (scintillating) area; and, as that area enlarged, he could detect lines of different orientations in it. The results of blood-flow studies have shown that, during such an aura, there is a reduction of blood flow in the posterior occipital cortex, and this reduction spreads at a rate of about 2 millimeters per minute. The aura may gradually expand to fill an entire side of the person's field of vision, but rarely, if ever, does it cross over to the opposite side. When a visual aura is at its maximum, the person can see nothing on that side of the world. Vision then returns, although most people feel dizzy and often nauseated for a while. Although D. B. and Lashley had visual auras, auras may also be auditory or tactile, and, in some cases, they may result in an inability to move or to talk. After the aura passes, most people suffer a severe headache that results from a dilation of cerebral blood vessels. The headache is usually on one side of the head, just as the aura is on one side of the field of vision. Left untreated, migraine headaches may last for hours or even days.

**X** = Fixation point

Novastock/Stock Connection/PictureQuest

The development of a migraine scotoma as described by Karl Lashley. A person looking at the small "x" first sees a small patch of lines, as shown in the photograph at the far left. Information in the world is not visible at that location. The striped area continues to grow outward, leaving a white area where the stripes had been. Within 15 to 20 minutes, the visual field is almost completely blocked by the scotoma. Normal vision returns shortly thereafter.

## THE NATURE OF SENSORY EXPERIENCE

As we look at the world, we naturally assume that what we see is what is really "out there." Indeed, cameras and videos reinforce this impression by seeming to re-create the very same visual world that we experience first hand. But there is a problem. Our version of the world, whether we see it directly or reproduced on film, is always a creation of the brain. What we see is not a faithful reproduction of what is "out there" but rather a construction of reality that the brain manufactures.

## Sensory Experience and Sensory Reality

Dogs provide a good example of the difference between the world that is "out there" and our perception of it. Dogs have very limited capacity to distinguish colors; they likely see very little color. Yet dogs have an olfactory system that smells in "Technicolor" compared with our simple "black and white" version of smell. Which system offers a correct analysis of the world? Neither. The brain of a human and that of a dog each create a set of sensory experiences that is merely one of many different versions of "reality." These sensory experiences are not genuine reproductions of the world; rather, they exist only in the mind of the perceiver.

In fact, the version of the world that we experience is not even constant in our own minds. For instance, as dusk falls, there is a shift in our color perception such that red now appears black even as green remains green. You can observe this color shift in the petals of a red rose and its green leaves. As light fails, the red rose becomes blackish, but the green leaves stay green. It is not that red has suddenly vanished from the external world. Rather, it is that your visual system can no longer create this color as light levels drop. But add light—say, by shining a flashlight on the rose—and the petals will immediately look red again.

The mind creates not just the visual world but the world of the other senses, too. Consider hearing. There is an old philosophical question about whether a tree falling in the forest makes a sound if no one is there to hear it. The answer is no. A falling tree makes sound waves but no sound. Sound does not exist without a brain to create it. The only reason that we experience sound is that the information from the ear goes to a region of the brain that converts the neural activity into what we then perceive to be sound. The brain might just as well convert that neural activity into some other subjective sensation. For instance, imagine that the ear was connected to the visual system. The sound of the tree falling would now become a visual experience rather than an auditory one, because the visual system would not know that the information came from the ear. It is hard to imagine just what the noise of a tree falling would "look" like, but we would not experience sound. Sound is the product of the particular auditory processing system that we possess. Without that system, there is no sound as we know it.

If the sensory world is merely a creation of the brain, it follows that different brains might create different sensory experiences, even among members of the same species. To demonstrate this fact, consider the color red. We perceive red because there are cells in our eyes that are activated by certain wavelengths of light that we call red or green. (How this works will be explained shortly.) If we did not have these cells, we could not experience red. In fact, about 5 percent of all human males lack the cells. They are therefore red-green color-blind and cannot tell these two colors apart.

Color blindness is just one extreme of normal human variation in color perception. More subtle variations also exist. For instance, Joris Winderickx and her colleagues (1992) asked men who were not red-green color-blind to mix red and green lights together to match a series of yellow lights (in the mixing of colors of light, red and green make yellow). The men varied in the amounts of red versus green that they used to match the different yellows, but these variations were consistent for each man. Some of the men required relatively more red to match the yellows, whereas others required relatively more green. We could say that the second group, compared with the first, had a slightly rosier view of the world to begin with. Winderickx found that there are two forms of the receptor cell that detects red; about 60 percent of men have one form, whereas 40 percent have the other. The difference between these two forms is small but significant and results from a small difference in the gene that encodes the red-detecting cell. The Winderickx study provided the first evidence that normal variation in our mental world is traceable to normal variation in our genes.

## Analyzing Sensory Information

Let us return to D. B. to make another point about sensory experiences. D. B. was not consciously aware of the presence of a light in his blind area, yet he could indicate where the light was. Clearly, the brain must process visual information in multiple ways. Some ways allow us to consciously analyze visual stimuli, whereas others process information unconsciously.

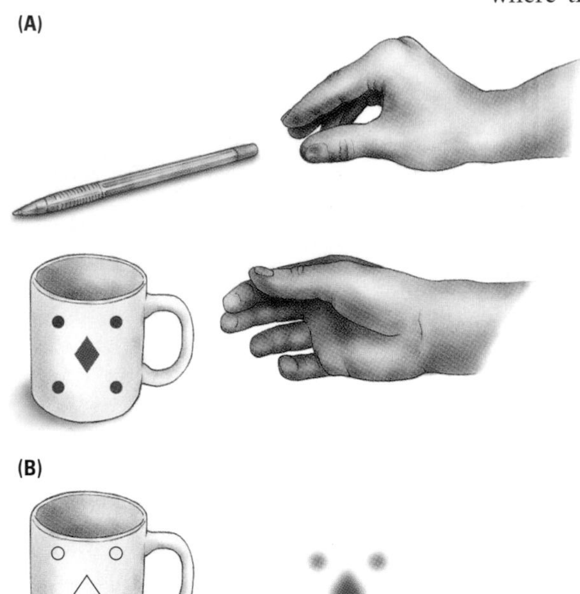


To prove to yourself that your brain does some of both, imagine yourself seated at a desk writing an essay for a course that you are taking. As you work, you engage in many behaviors that require vision. You read books and write notes, you type on a computer, and you reach for and drink from a mug of coffee. What exactly are you doing when you make these visually guided movements? For instance, what happens when you reach for your pen or your coffee mug? Before reading further, reach for objects of different sizes and shapes around you and observe what you do. First, your eyes orient to the object. Then, as your hand moves toward it, your fingers form the appropriate shape long before they get to the object. When you reach for a pen, your thumb and index finger assume a position as if to pinch the pen. When you reach for a mug, your hand is oriented vertically so that your fingers can grasp the handle. These movements are illustrated in Figure 8-1A. You did not consciously think about this finger and hand positioning. It just happened. Your reaching for the pen or the mug was conscious, but the shaping of your hand for the particular object was not. Although both are guided by visual information, different regions of the brain and different kinds of processing are required.

**Figure 8-1**

**(A)** An illustration of the automatic hand posture that forms as you reach for a pen or a mug. Although you may consciously decide to reach for an object, your hand forms the appropriate posture without your conscious command to do so.
**(B)** The mug in part **(A)** can be broken into two distinct representations, one that has only shape and another that has only color. Note that the color representation has only a fuzzy pattern, whereas the shape representation has only shades of gray. These representations are meant to mimic the type of analysis that goes on in two different brain regions as the mug is being analyzed. The mug does not actually exist in the brain as we perceive it.

There is more. Consider your coffee mug. It has a shape and it has a color pattern. Yet you are not consciously aware of each of these attributes separately, as depicted in Figure 8-1B. Instead, you perceive the patterned mug to be a single object. It may therefore surprise you to learn that your brain produces this unified perception after analyzing color separately from shape, each in a different location. Consequently, it is possible to have brain damage that allows a person to see the color of an object but to have no idea of what the object is, because its shape is indecipherable. Conversely, a person with other brain damage might see the shape of an object clearly but have no clue to its color. The brain essentially dissects the object, analyzes the various parts separately, and then produces what appears to be a unified sensation of the whole. Yet there is no "picture" of the entire object in one place in the brain. So how, then, do we perceive a single object if we have only multiple visions of it with which to work? We will return to this fascinating question later.

### In Review

To summarize, we have identified two key points about sensory experience. First, our sensory world is entirely a creation of the brain. Different species and, to a lesser extent, different individual members of a species have different perceptions of what the world is really like. Neither is right or wrong; both are imaginary. Second, the brain does not analyze sensory information as though it were a uniform thing. Rather, when sensory information enters the brain, it is dissected and passed to specialized regions that analyze particular characteristics. We only have the impression that we experience a unified sensory world. This is one of the puzzles of how the brain works. Before returning to that puzzle, we must first identify how the visual system breaks down visual stimuli.

## THE ANATOMY OF THE VISUAL SYSTEM

Vision is our primary sensory experience. Far more of the human brain is used for vision than for any of our other senses. Understanding the organization of the visual system is therefore a key to understanding human brain function. To build this understanding, we begin by following the routes by which visual information travels to the brain and within it. This exercise is a bit like following a road to discover where it goes. The first step is to consider what the visual system analyzes—namely, light.

### Light: The Stimulus for Vision

Light is electromagnetic energy. Simply put, it is electromagnetic energy that we see. This energy comes either directly from something that produces it, such as a lamp or the sun, or indirectly from a light source after being reflected off one or more objects. In either case, light energy travels from the outside world, through the pupil, and into the eye, where it strikes a light-sensitive surface on the back of the eye called the **retina.** From this stimulation of receptors on the retina, we start the process of creating a visual world.

A useful way to represent light is as a continuously moving wave. Not all light waves are the same length, however. Figure 8-2 shows that, within the visible range of electromagnetic energy, the wavelength varies from about 400 nanometers (violet) to 700 nanometers (red). (A nanometer, abbreviated nm, is one-billionth of a meter.) The range of visible light is constrained not by the properties of light waves, but rather by the properties of our visual receptors. If we had receptors that could detect light in the ultraviolet or infrared range, we would see additional colors. In fact, bees can detect light in the ultraviolet range and so have a broader range of color perception than we do.

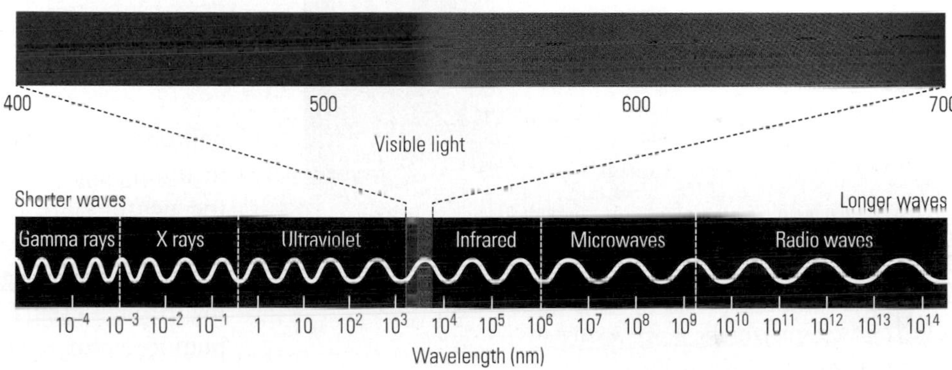


**Figure 8-2**

The part of the electromagnetic spectrum that is visible to the human eye is restricted to a narrow range.

### The Eye

How do the cells of the retina absorb light energy and initiate the processes leading to vision? To answer this question, we first consider the structure of the eye as a whole so that you can understand how it is designed to capture and focus light. Only then do we consider the photoreceptors.

The eye has several functionally distinct parts, shown in Figure 8-3. They include the *sclera* (the white part that forms the eyeball), the *cornea* (the clear outer covering of the eye), the *iris* (which opens and closes to allow more or less light in), the *lens* (which focuses light), and the *retina* (where light energy initiates neural activity). When light enters the eye by traveling through the hole in the iris called the *pupil,* it is bent slightly by the cornea and then more so by the lens. The shape of the lens adjusts to bend the light to greater or lesser degrees so that near and far images can be focused on the retina. When images are not properly focused on the retina, we require a corrective lens, as discussed in "Optical Errors of Refraction and Visual Illuminance" on page 283.

Figure 8-3 also includes a photograph of the retina. As you can see, the retina is composed of photoreceptors and a layer of neurons connected to them. Although the

**Retina.** The neurons and photoreceptor cells at the back of the eye.

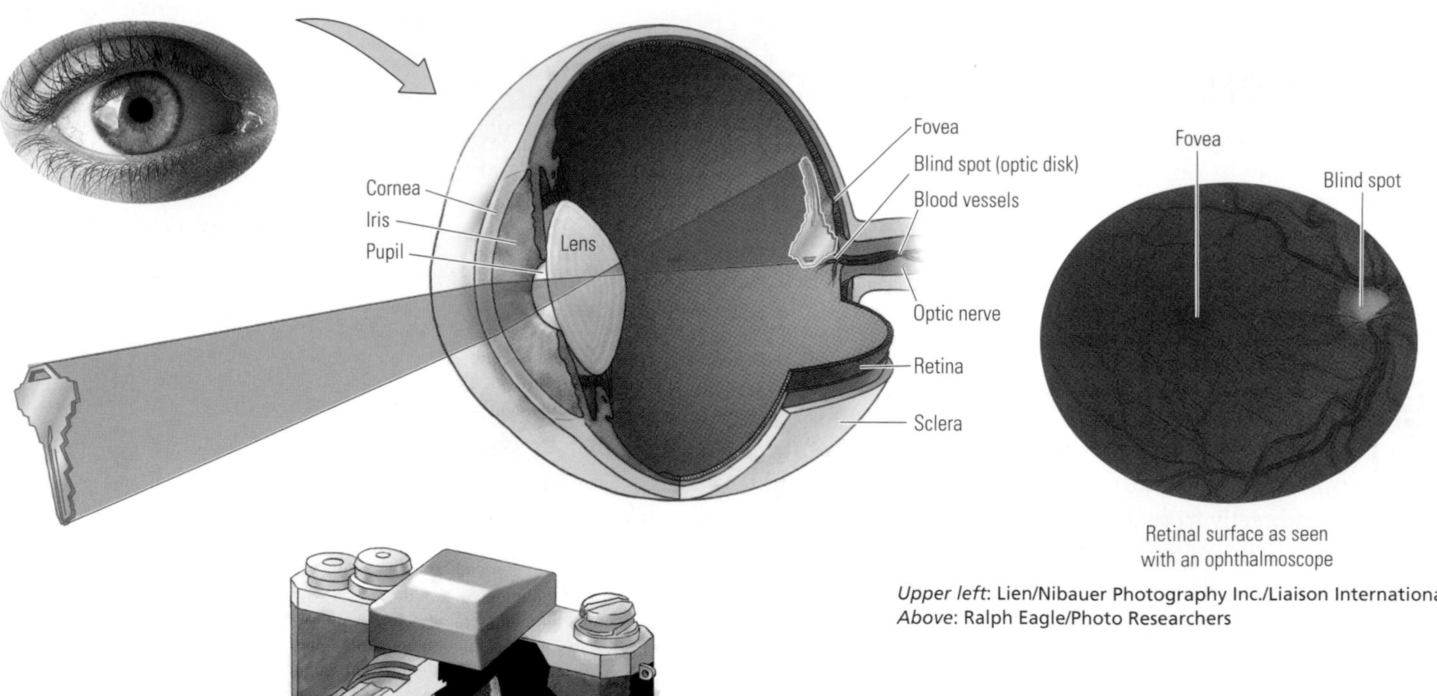


*Upper left*: Lien/Nibauer Photography Inc./Liaison International
*Above*: Ralph Eagle/Photo Researchers

**Figure 8-3**

Light rays are focused by the cornea and lens of the eye and by the lens of a camera so that they land on the receptive surface—namely, the retina and film, respectively. The image of the key is inverted by the optics in both the eye and the camera. The optic nerve conveys information from the eye to the brain. The fovea is the region of best vision and is characterized by the densest receptor distribution. The region in the eye where the blood vessels enter and the axons of the ganglion cells leave, called the optic disc, has no receptors and thus forms a blind spot. Note that there are few blood vessels around the fovea in the photograph of the retina at far right.

**Blind spot.** The region of the retina where the axons forming the optic nerve leave the eye and blood vessels enter; this region has no photoreceptors and is thus "blind."

neurons are in front of the photoreceptors, they do not prevent incoming light from being absorbed by those receptors, because the neurons are transparent and the photoreceptors are extremely sensitive to light. (In contrast, the neurons in the retina are insensitive to light, so they are unaffected by the light passing through them.) Together, the neurons of the retina and the photoreceptor cells perform some amazing functions. They translate light into action potentials, discriminate wavelengths so that we can see colors, work in a range of light intensities from very bright to very dim, and provide visual precision sufficient for us to see a human hair lying on the page of this book.

As in a camera, the image of objects that is projected onto the retina is upside down and backward. This flip-flopped orientation poses no problem for the brain. Remember that the brain is *creating* the outside world, so it does not really care how the image is oriented initially. In fact, the brain can make adjustments regardless of the orientation of the images that it receives. For instance, if you were to put on glasses that invert visual images and kept those glasses on for several days, the world would suddenly appear right side up again because your brain would correct the distortion. Curiously, when you removed the glasses, the world would temporarily seem upside down once more, because your brain at first would be unaware that you had tricked it another time. Eventually, though, your brain would solve this puzzle, too, and the world would flip back in the right orientation.

To learn more about how the eye is structured, try this experiment. Stand with your head over a tabletop and hold a pencil in your hand. Close one eye. Stare at the edge of the tabletop straight below you. Now hold the pencil in a horizontal position and move it along the edge of the table, with the eraser on the table. Beginning at a point approximately below your nose, move the pencil slowly along the table in the direction of the open eye. When you have moved the pencil about 6 inches, the eraser will vanish. You have found your **blind spot.** The blind spot is a small area of the retina that is also known as the *optic disc.* As shown in Figure 8-3, the optic disc is the area where blood vessels enter and exit the eye and where fibers leading from retinal

## Optical Errors of Refraction and Visual Illuminance

The eye, like a camera, works correctly only when sufficient light passes through the lens and is focused on the receptor surface—namely, the retina of the eye or the film in the camera. If the focal point of the light is slightly in front of or behind the receptor surface, a refractive error results and objects appear blurry. Too little light entering the eye or the camera produces a problem of visual illuminance, and it is hard to see any image at all.

In the eye, refractive errors are of two basic types. The most common one in young people (afflicting about 50 percent of the population) is an inability to bring distant objects into clear focus. This condition is known as *myopia* (nearsightedness). Myopia is most commonly caused by the eyeball being too long, although it can also be caused by the front of the cornea being too curved. In either case, the focal point of light falls short of the retina. *Hyperopia* refers to the less common condition in which people are unable to focus on near objects, either because the eyeball is too short or because the lens is too flat and does not adequately refract the light. In either case, the focal point of light falls beyond the retina.

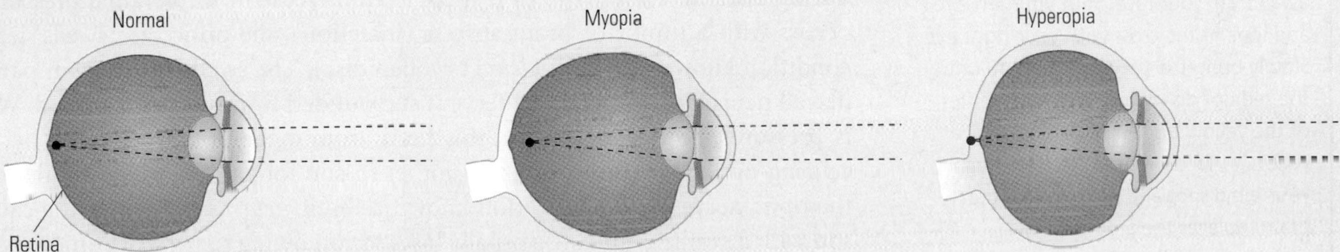


As people age, most begin to develop difficulty in focusing on near objects. This is a result of the lens losing its elasticity and consequently becoming unable to refract light from near objects correctly. The condition is a form of hyperopia called *presbyopia* (old sightedness). Presbyopia is so common that it is rare to find people older than 50 who do not need glasses to see up close, especially for reading. Fortunately, this error and other errors of refraction can be cured by corrective lenses.

There is an additional complication to the aging eye that cannot be cured by corrective lenses. As we age, the eye's lens and cornea allow less light through, and so less light strikes the retina—a problem of visual illuminance. Don Kline (1994) estimated that, between ages 20 and 40, there is a drop of 50 percent in visual illuminance in dim lighting and a further drop of 50 percent over every 20 additional years. As a result, it becomes increasingly difficult to see in dim light, especially at night. Corrective lenses do not compensate for this reduced visual illuminance; the only solution is to increase lighting. The condition is especially problematic in driving at night. Not surprisingly, statistics show a marked drop in the number of people driving at night in each successive decade after age 40.

**These photographs represent the drop in visual illuminance that occurs between age 20 *(left)* and age 60 *(right)*.**

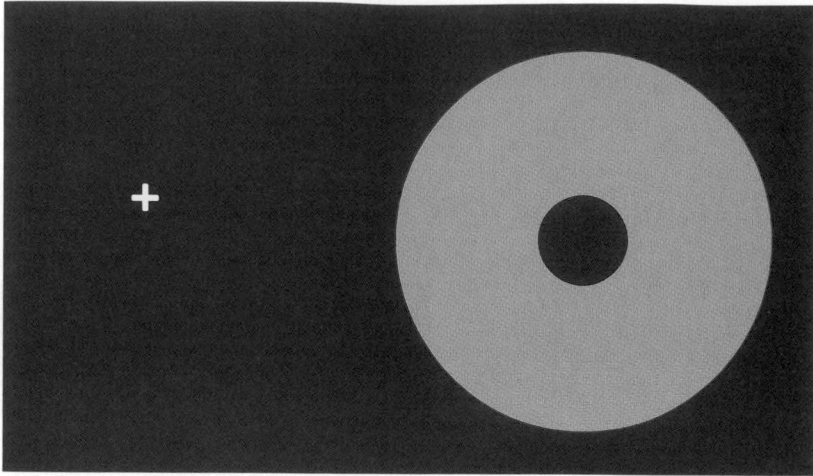


**Figure 8-4**

To test for your blind spot, hold the book about 30 centimeters (about 12 inches) away from your face. Shut your left eye and look at the cross with your right eye. Slowly bring the page toward you until the red dot disappears from the center of the yellow disc and is replaced by a yellow surface. The red spot is now in your blind spot and not visible. Your brain replaces the area with the surrounding yellow. Turn the book upside down to test the other eye.

neurons form the optic nerve that goes to the brain. There are therefore no photoreceptors in this part of the retina, so you cannot see with it. Figure 8-4 shows another way of demonstrating the blind spot.

Fortunately, your visual system solves the blind-spot problem by locating the optic disc in a different location in each of your eyes. Using both eyes together, you can see the whole visual world. People with blindness in one eye have a greater problem, however, because the sightless eye cannot compensate for the blind spot in the functioning eye. Still, the visual system compensates for the blind spot in several other ways, so people who are blind in one eye have no sense of a hole in their field of vision.

The optic disc that produces a blind spot is of particular importance in neurology. It allows neurologists to indirectly view the condition of the optic nerve that lies behind it, while providing a window onto events within the brain. This is why physicians spend so much time looking into our eyes during physical examinations. If there is an increase in intracranial pressure, such as occurs with a tumor or brain abscess (infection), the optic disc swells, leading to a condition known as *papilloedema* (swollen disc). The swelling occurs in part because, like all neural tissue, the optic nerve is surrounded by cerebrospinal fluid. When there is pressure inside the cranium, this fluid around the optic nerve can be displaced, causing swelling at the optic disc. Another reason for papilloedema is inflammation of the optic nerve itself, a condition known as *optic neuritis.* Whatever the cause, a person with a swollen optic disc usually loses vision owing to pressure on the optic nerve. If the swelling is due to optic neuritis, probably the most common neurological visual disorder, the prognosis for recovery is good.

Now try another experiment to learn about a second important region of the retina, this one lying at the center of it. Focus on the left edge of the writing on this page. The words will be clearly legible. Now, while holding your eyes still, try to read the words on the right side of the page. It will be very difficult and likely impossible, even though you can see that there are words there. The lesson here is that our vision is better in the center of the world than at the margins. This difference in visual ability is partly due to the fact that the photoreceptors are more densely packed at the center of the retina, in a region known as the **fovea.** Figure 8-5 shows that, at the fovea, the surface of the retina is depressed; this depression is formed because many of the fibers of the optic nerve skirt the fovea to facilitate light access to its receptors.

Visit the area on the eye in the module on the Visual System on your CD. Rotate the three-dimensional model to better understand the anatomy of the eye and the structure of the retina.

## The Photoreceptors

The retina contains two types of photoreceptor cells, **rods** and **cones.** Both function to convert light energy into neural activity. When light strikes a photoreceptor, it triggers a series of chemical reactions that lead to a change in membrane potential. This change in membrane potential, in turn, leads to a change in the release of neurotransmitter onto nearby neurons.

Rods and cones differ in many ways. As you can see in Figure 8-6, they are structurally different. Rods are longer than cones and cylindrically shaped at one end, whereas cones have an end that is tapered. Rods, which are more numerous than cones, are sensitive to dim light and are used mainly for night vision. Cones do not respond to dim light, but they are highly responsive in bright light. Cones mediate both color vision and our ability to see fine detail. Rods and cones are not evenly distrib-

**Fovea.** The region at the center of the retina that is specialized for high acuity; its receptive fields are at the center of the eye's visual field.

**Rod.** A photoreceptor specialized for functioning at low light levels.

**Cone.** A photoreceptor specialized for color and high visual acuity.

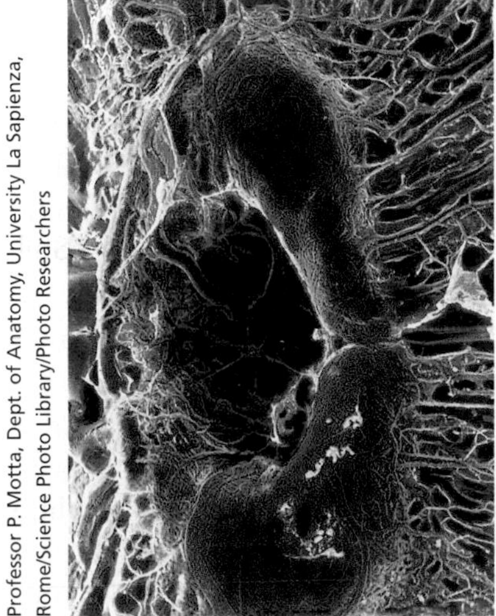


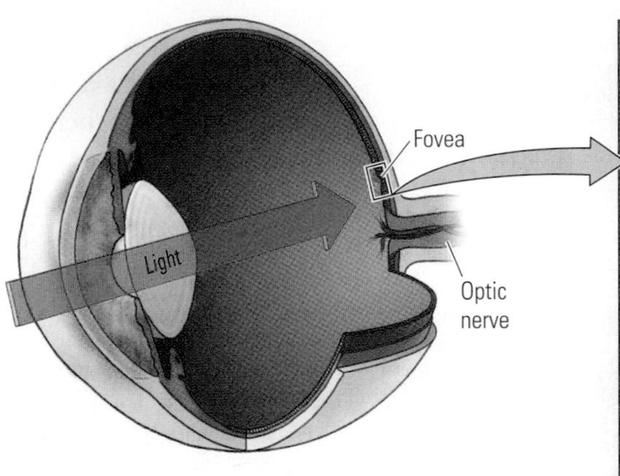


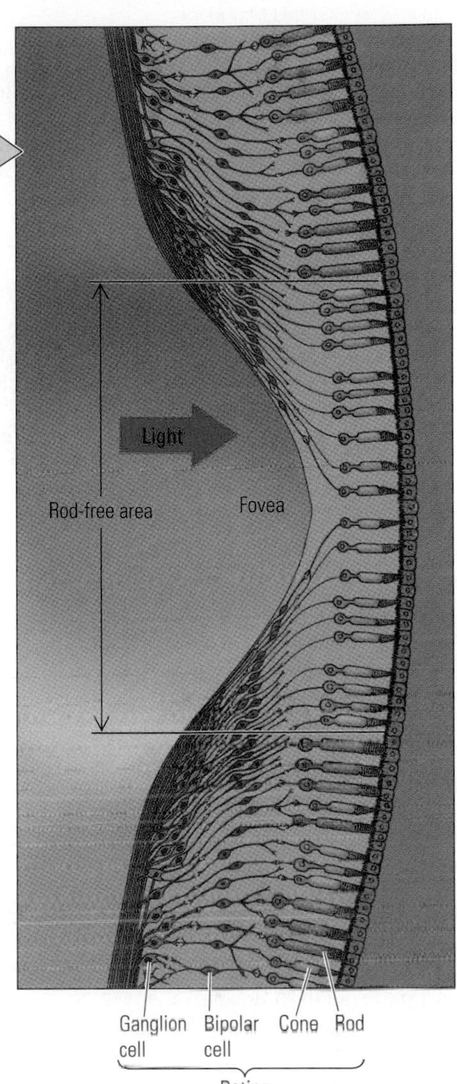


**Figure 8-5**

This cross section through the retina shows the distribution of cones and rods. The fovea (shown in the scanning electron micrograph at left) is rod-free, but the density of rods increases from the fovea to the periphery.

uted over the retina. The fovea has only cones; but, at either side of the fovea, the density of cones drops dramatically, which is why our vision is not so sharp at the edges of our visual field, as demonstrated earlier. A final difference between rods and cones is in their light-absorbing pigments. Although rods and cones both have pigments that absorb light, all rods have the same pigment, whereas cones have three different pigment types. Any given cone has one of these three cone pigments. Therefore four different pigments form the basis of our vision (one type in the rods and three types in the cones).

**Figure 8-6**

Rods and cones are both tubelike in shape (as the scanning electron micrograph, below right, shows), but they differ in structure, especially in the outer segment. Rods are especially sensitive to light but do not discriminate wavelengths. Cones are especially sensitive to particular wavelengths.

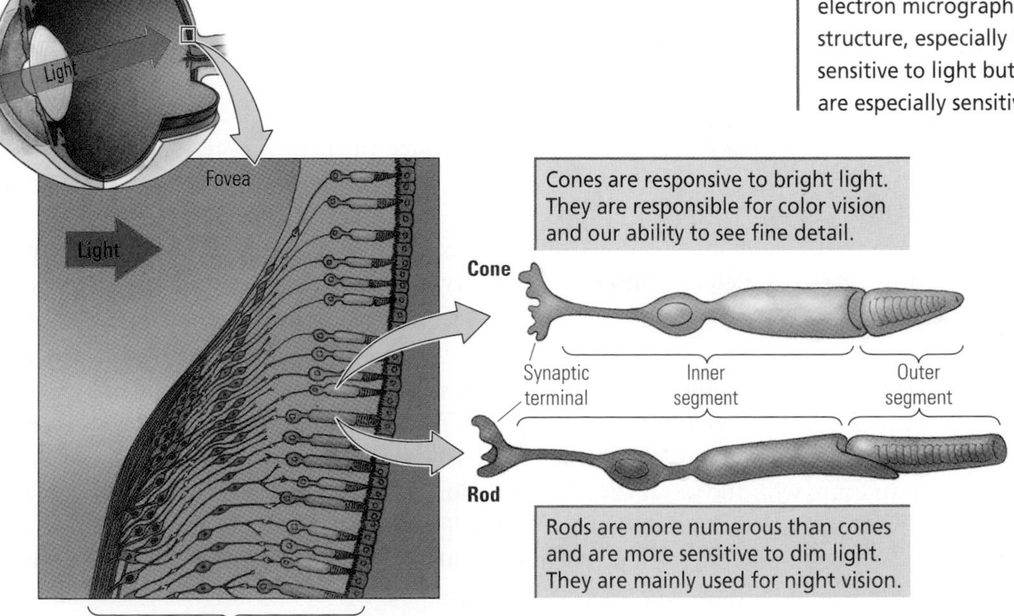


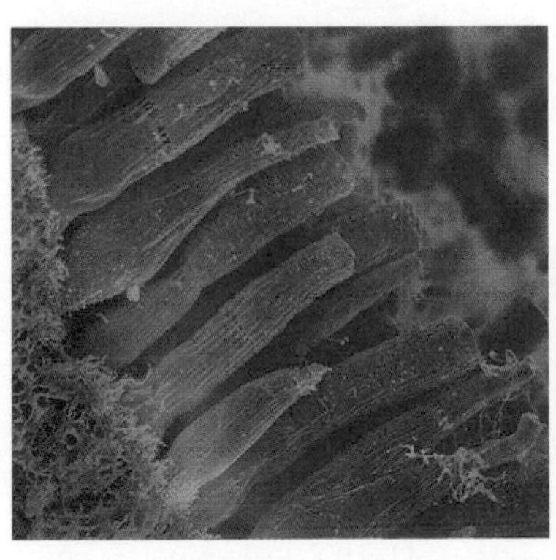

The three types of cones are called "blue," "green," and "red." These names loosely refer to the frequencies of light to which each cone is maximally sensitive (the peak sensitivities are 419, 531, and 559 nm respectively).

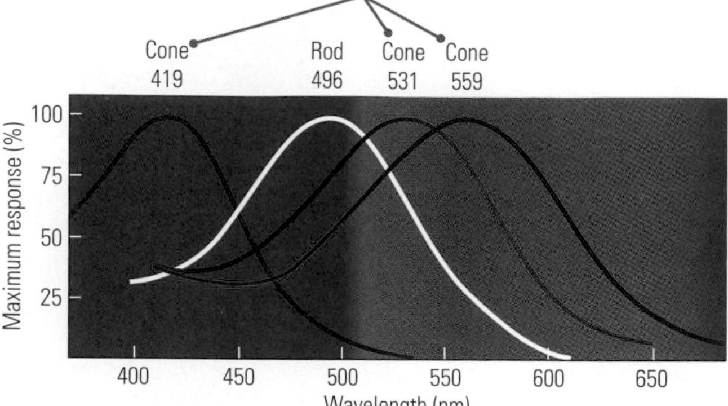


**Figure 8-7**

The wavelengths to which different types of cones are maximally responsive. Note that each cone type is responsive to a broad range of wavelengths but is most sensitive to a relatively narrow range.

The three types of cone pigments absorb light over a range of frequencies, but their maximum absorptions are at about 419, 531, and 559 nanometers, respectively. The small range of wavelengths to which each of the cone pigments is maximally responsive is shown in Figure 8-7. Cones that contain these pigments are called "blue," "green," and "red," loosely referring to colors in their range of peak sensitivity. Note, however, that if you were to look at lights with wavelengths of 419, 531, and 559 nanometers, they would not appear blue, green, and red but rather violet, blue green, and yellow green. Remember, though, that you are looking at the lights with all three cone types and that each cone pigment is responsive to light across a range of frequencies, not just to its frequency of maximum absorption. So the terms blue, green, and red cones are not that far off the mark. But perhaps it would be more accurate to describe these three cone types as short, middle, and long wavelength, referring to the relative length of light waves at which their sensitivities peak. This distinction may seem foreign if you do not think of color in terms of wavelength.

Not only does the presence of three different cone receptors contribute to our perception of color, so does the relative number and distribution of cone types across the retina. As Figure 8-8 shows, the three cone types are distributed more or less randomly across the retina, making our ability to perceive different colors fairly constant across the visual field. Although there are approximately equal numbers of red and green cones, there are fewer blue cones, which means that we are not as sensitive to blue.

Other species that have color vision similar to that of humans also have three types of cones, with three color pigments. But, because of slight variations in these pigments, the exact frequencies of maximum absorption differ among different species. For humans, the exact frequencies are not identical with the numbers given earlier, which were an average across mammals. They are actually 426 and 530 nanometers for the blue and green cones, respectively, and 552 or 557 nanometers for the red cone. There are two peak sensitivity levels given for red because humans, as stated earlier, have two variants of the red cone. The difference in these two red cones appears minuscule, but recall that it does make a functional difference.

This functional difference between the two human variants of red cone becomes especially apparent in some women. The gene for the red cone is carried on the X chromosome. Because males have only one X chromosome, they have only one of these genes and so only one type of red cone. The situation is more complicated for women. Although most women have only one type of red cone, some have both, with the result that they are more sensitive than the rest of us to color differences at the red end of the spectrum. Their color receptors create a world with a richer range of red experiences. However, these women also have to contend with peculiar-seeming color coordination by others.

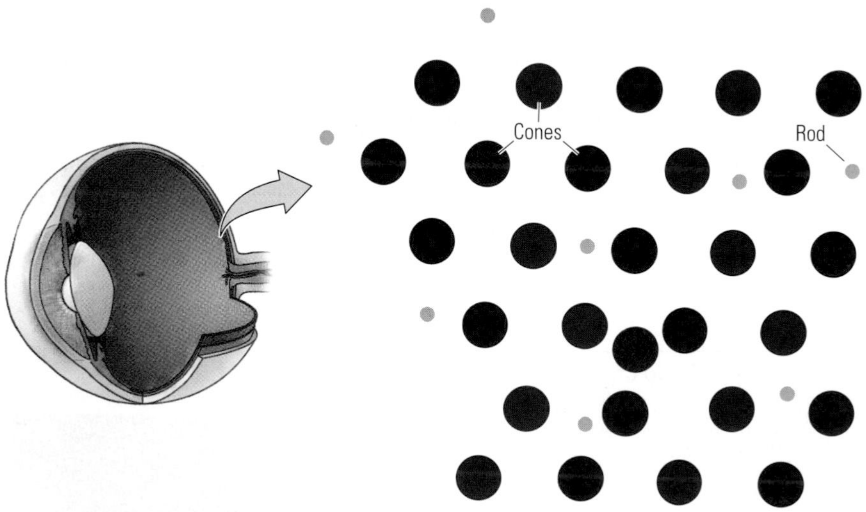

**Figure 8-8**

The retinal receptors form a mosaic of rods and three types of cones. This diagram represents the distribution near the fovea, where the cones outnumber the rods. There are fewer blue cones than red and green cones.

## Retinal Neurons

Figure 8-9 shows that the photoreceptors in the retina are connected to two layers of retinal neurons. In the procession from the rods and cones toward the brain, the first layer contains three types of cells: *bipolar cells, horizontal cells,* and *amacrine cells.* The bipolar cells receive input from the photoreceptors and in turn induce action potentials in cells of the second neural layer, which are called **retinal ganglion cells.** The axons of the ganglion cells collect in a bundle at the optic disc and leave the eye to form the optic nerve. The other two cell types in the first neural layer are essentially linkage cells. The horizontal cells link photoreceptors with bipolar cells, whereas the amacrine cells link bipolar cells with ganglion cells.

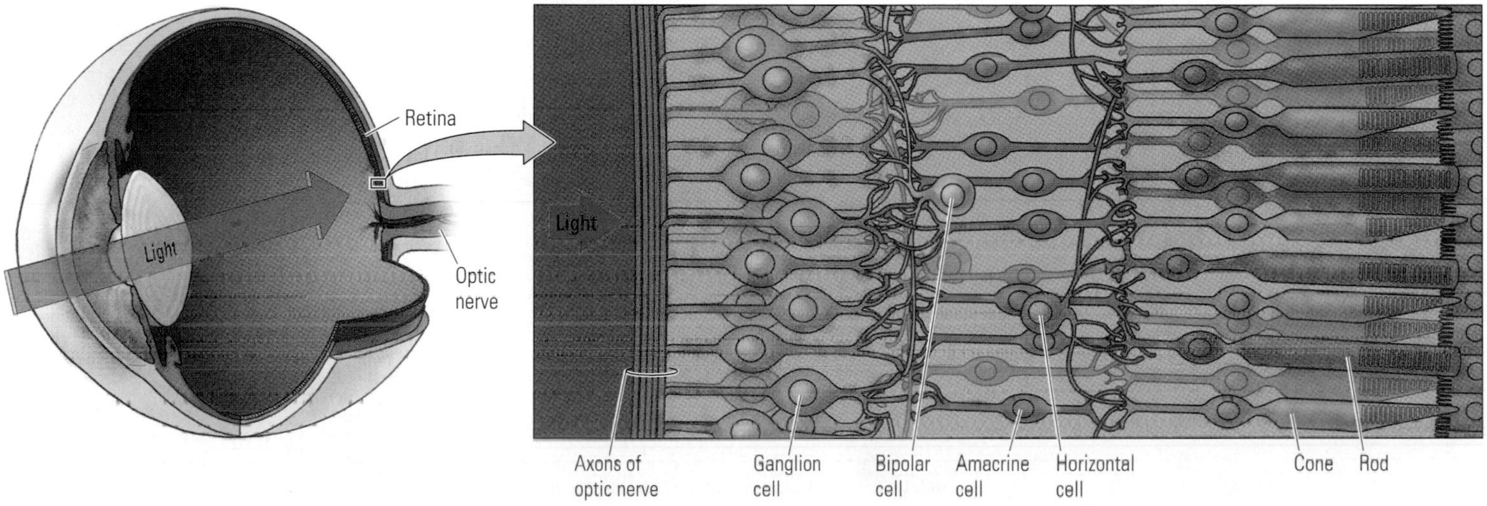


**Figure 8-9**

The enlargement of the retina at the right shows the positions of the three retinal layers. There are four types of neurons in the retina: the horizontal, bipolar, amacrine, and ganglion cells. Notice that light must pass through all of the neuron layers to reach the receptors.

Retinal ganglion cells are not all the same in regard to the cells to which they connect. They fall into two major categories, which in the primate retina are called **M** and **P cells** (see Figure 8-10). The designations M and P derive from the distinctly different populations of cells in the visual thalamus to which these two classes of ganglion cells send their axons. One of these populations consists of **magnocellular cells** (hence M), whereas the other consists of **parvocellular cells** (hence P). The M cells and the magnocellular cells, which are larger (*magno* means "large" in Latin), receive their input primarily from rods and so are sensitive to light but not to color. The P cells and the parvocellular cells, which are smaller (*parvo* means "small" in Latin), receive their input primarily from cones and so are sensitive to color. The M cells are found throughout the retina, including the periphery, where we are sensitive to movement but not to color or fine details. The P cells are found largely in the region of the fovea, where we are sensitive to color and fine details. A distinction between the two categories of ganglion cells is maintained throughout the visual pathways, as you will see in the next section, where we follow the ganglion cell axons into the brain.

## Visual Pathways

Imagine leaving your house and finding yourself on an unfamiliar road. Because the road is not on any map, the only way to find out where it goes is to follow it. You soon discover that the road divides in two, so you must follow each branch sequentially to figure out its end point. Suppose you learn that one branch goes to a city, whereas the other goes to a national park. By knowing the end point of each branch, you can conclude something about their respective functions—namely, that one branch carries people to work, whereas the other carries them to play. The same strategy can be used

**Retinal ganglion cells.** The cells of the retina that give rise to the optic nerve.

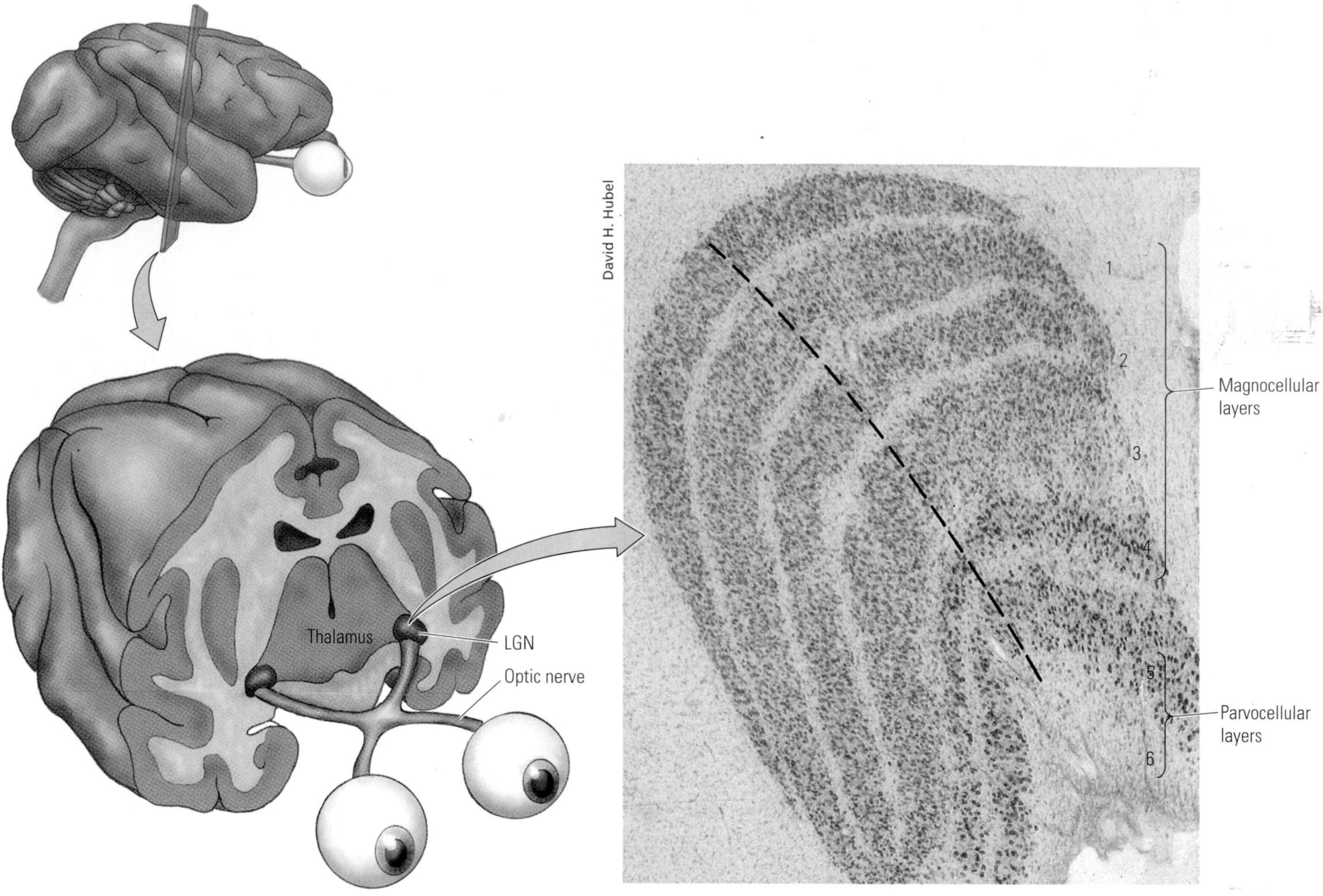


**Figure 8-10**

The optic nerves connect with the lateral geniculate nucleus (LGN) of the thalamus. The thalamus has six layers, including four magnocellular layers and two parvocellular layers.

**Optic chiasm.** The junction of the two optic nerves at which the axons from the nasal (inside) halves of the retinas cross to the opposite side of the brain.

**Geniculostriate system.** A system consisting of projections from the retina to the lateral geniculate nucleus to the visual cortex.

**Striate cortex.** The primary visual cortex in the occipital lobe; it has a striped appearance when stained, which gives it this name.

**Tectopulvinar system.** A system consisting of projections from the retina to the superior colliculus to the pulvinar (thalamus) to the parietal and temporal visual areas.

to follow the paths of the visual system. The retinal ganglion cells form the optic nerve, which is the road into the brain. This road travels to several places, each with a different function. By finding out where the branches go, we can begin to guess what the brain is doing with the visual input and how the brain creates our visual world.

Let us begin with the optic nerves, one exiting from each eye. As you know, they are formed by the axons of ganglion cells leaving the retina. Just before entering the brain, the optic nerves partly cross, forming the **optic chiasm** (from the Greek letter χ, which is pronounced *ki*). Figure 8-11 shows that about half the fibers from each eye cross in such a way that half of each retina is represented on each side of the brain. The left half of each retina goes to the left side of the brain, whereas the right half of each retina goes to the brain's right side. Because the light that falls on the right half of the retina actually comes from the left side of the visual field, information from the left visual field goes to the brain's right hemisphere, whereas information from the right visual field goes to the left hemisphere.

Having entered the brain, the axons of the ganglion cells separate, forming two distinct pathways, illustrated in Figure 8-12. All the axons of the P ganglion cells and some of the M ganglion cells form a pathway called the **geniculostriate system.** This pathway goes from the retina to the lateral geniculate nucleus (LGN) of the thalamus and then to layer IV of the primary visual cortex, which is in the occipital lobe. As Figure 8-13 shows (see page 290), the primary visual cortex appears to have a broad stripe across it in layer IV and so is known as **striate cortex.** The term *geniculostriate* therefore means a bridge between the thalamus (geniculate) and the striate cortex.

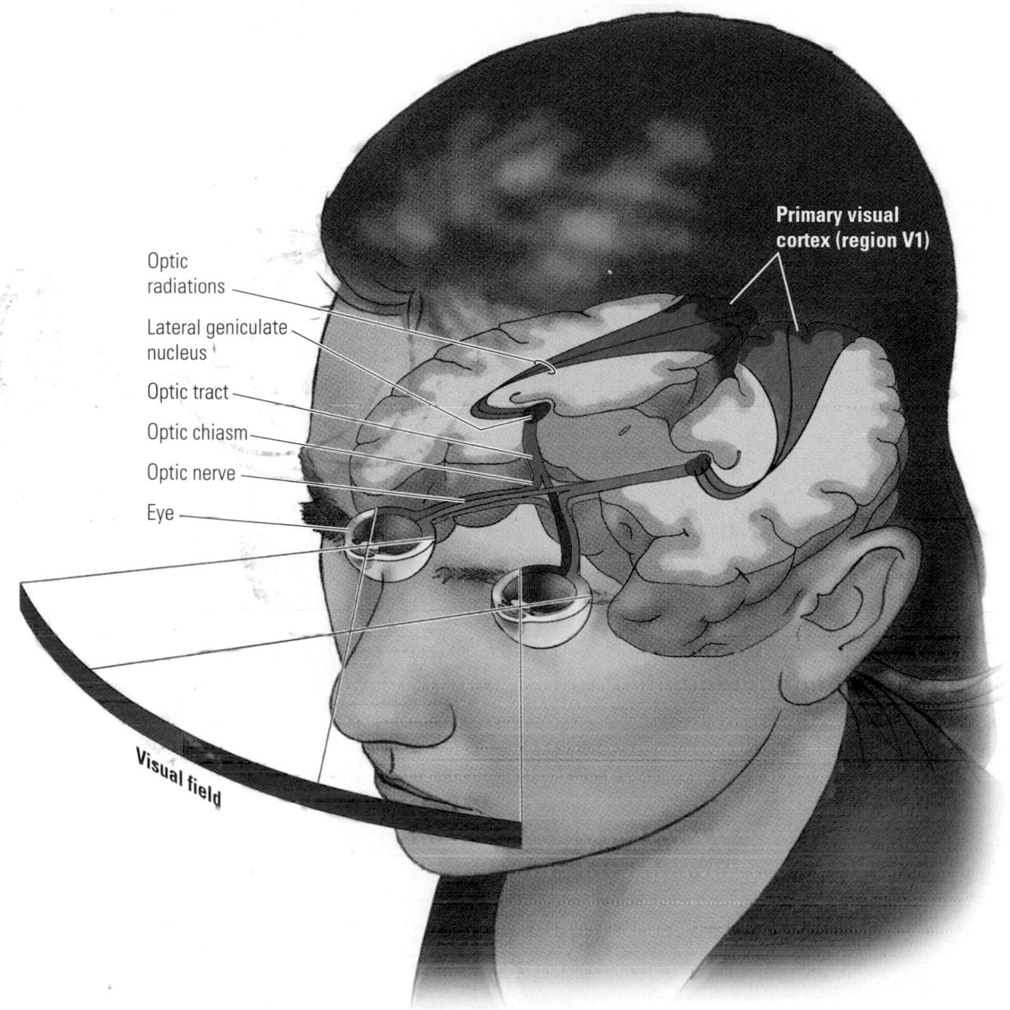


**Figure 8-11**

This horizontal slice through the brain shows the visual pathway from each eye to region V1 of each hemisphere. Information from the blue side of the visual field goes to the two left halves of the retinas and ends up in the left hemisphere. Information from the red side of the visual field hits the right halves of the retinas and travels to the right side of the brain.

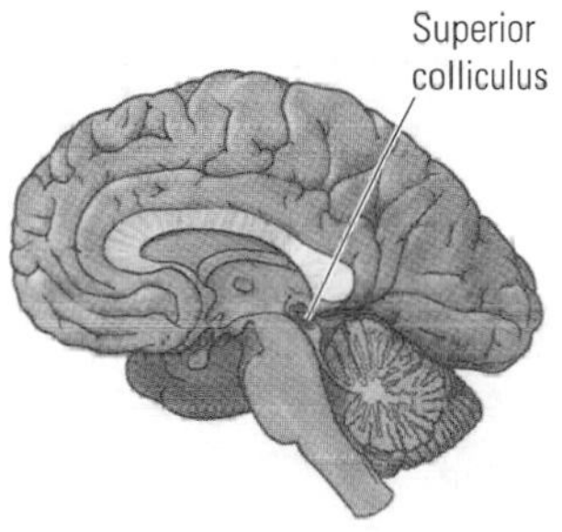


From the striate cortex, the axon pathway now splits, with one route going to vision-related regions of the parietal lobe and another route going to vision-related regions of the temporal lobe.

The second pathway leading from the eye is formed by the axons of the remaining M ganglion cells. These cells send their axons to the superior colliculus, which is located in the tectum of the midbrain (see Chapter 2). The superior colliculus sends connections to a region of the thalamus known as the **pulvinar.** This pathway is therefore known as the **tectopulvinar system** because it goes from the eye through the tectum to the pulvinar. The pulvinar has two main divisions: the medial and the lateral. The medial pulvinar sends connections to the parietal lobe, whereas the lateral pulvinar sends connections to the temporal lobe.

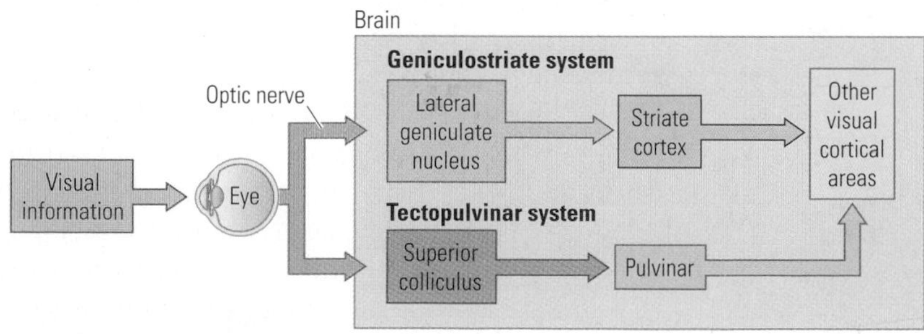


**Figure 8-12**

The flow of visual information into the brain. The optic nerve has two principal branches, one that goes to the lateral geniculate nucleus of the thalamus and another that goes to the superior colliculus. The LGN projects to the occipital cortex, which then projects to the other visual regions in the parietal and temporal cortex, respectively. The superior colliculus projects to the pulvinar, which then projects to the parietal and temporal regions. The route through the lateral geniculate nucleus to the striate cortex is referred to as the geniculostriate system, whereas the flow of information through the colliculus of the tectum to the pulvinar is referred to as the tectopulvinar system.

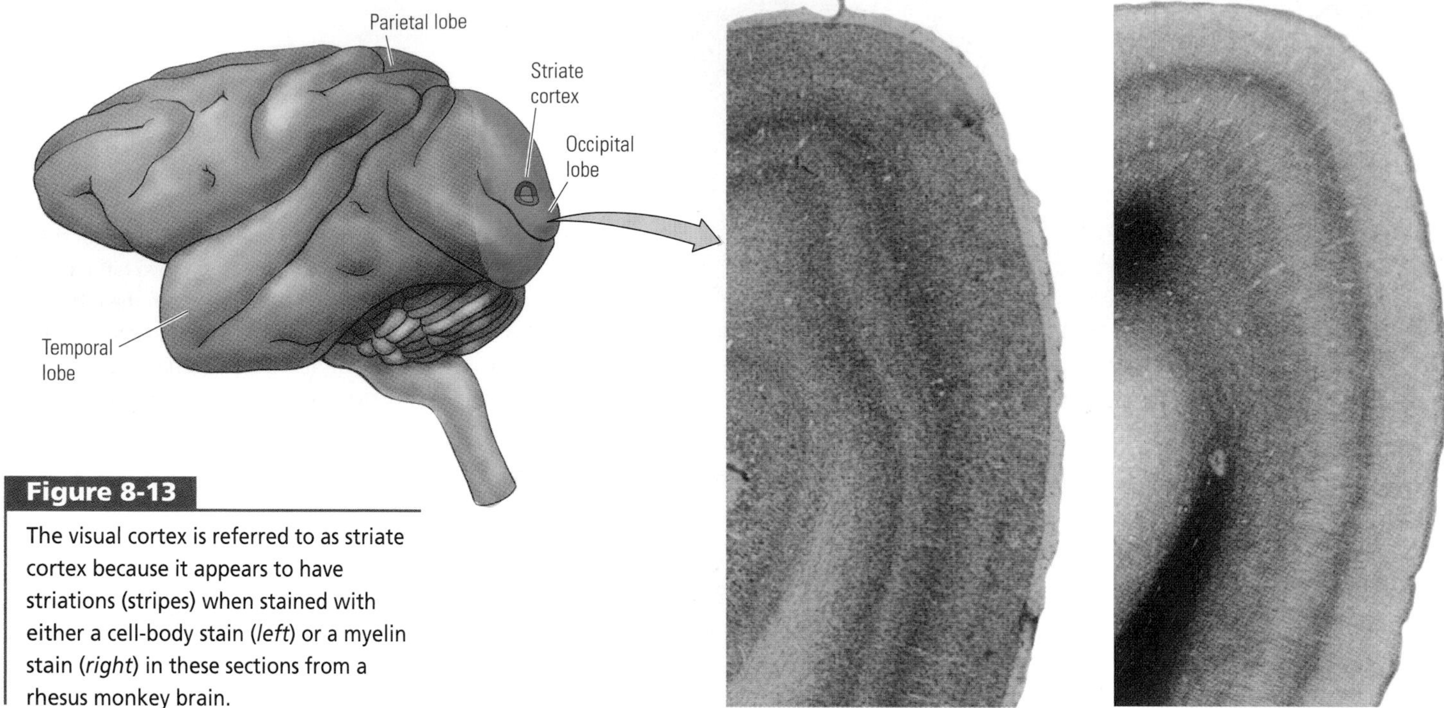


**Figure 8-13**

The visual cortex is referred to as striate cortex because it appears to have striations (stripes) when stained with either a cell-body stain (*left*) or a myelin stain (*right*) in these sections from a rhesus monkey brain.

To summarize, there are two principal pathways into the visual brain—namely, the geniculostriate and tectopulvinar systems. Each of these pathways eventually travels through the thalamus, where each divides again to go either to the parietal or the temporal lobe. Our next task is to determine the respective roles of the parietal lobe and the temporal lobe in creating our visual world.

## The Dorsal and Ventral Streams

Identification of the temporal- and parietal-lobe pathways led researchers on a search for the possible functions of each. One way to examine these functions is to ask why evolution would produce two different destinations for the pathways in the brain. The answer is that each route must create visual knowledge for a different purpose. David Milner and Mel Goodale (1995) proposed that these two purposes are to identify what a stimulus is (the "what" function) and to use visual information to control movement (the "how" function).

This "what" versus "how" distinction came from an analysis of where visual information goes when it leaves the striate cortex. Figure 8-14 shows the two distinct visual pathways that originate in the striate cortex, one progressing to the temporal lobe and the other to the parietal lobe. The pathway to the temporal lobe has become known as the **ventral stream,** whereas the pathway to the parietal lobe has become known as the **dorsal stream.** To understand how these two streams function, we need to return to the details of how the visual input from the eyes contributes to them. Although both the geniculostriate and the tectopulvinar systems contribute to the dorsal and ventral streams, for simplicity here we will consider only the role of the geniculostriate system.

**Figure 8-14**

Visual information travels from the occipital visual areas to the parietal and temporal lobes, forming the dorsal and ventral streams, respectively.

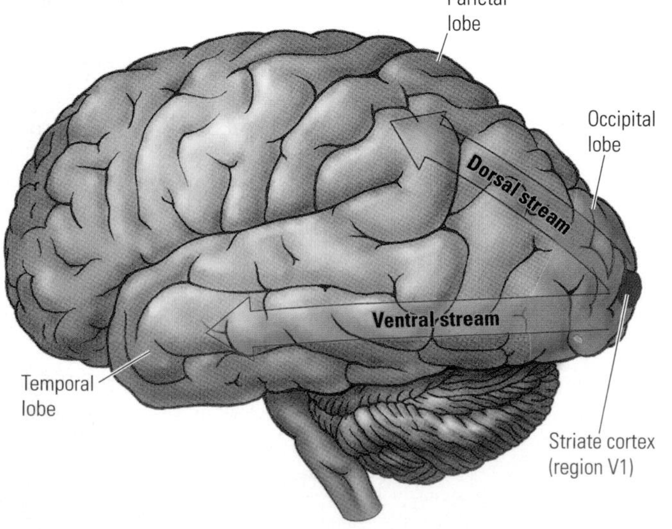

## THE GENICULOSTRIATE PATHWAY

The retinal ganglion-cell fibers from the two eyes distribute their connections to the two lateral geniculate nuclei (left and right) in what at first glance appears to be an unusual arrangement. As seen in Figure 8-11, the fibers from the left half of each retina go to the left LGN, whereas those from the right half of each retina go to the right LGN. But the fibers from each eye do not go to exactly the same place in the LGN. Each LGN has six layers, and the projections from the two eyes go to different layers, as illustrated in Figures 8-10 and 8-15. Layers 2, 3, and 5 receive fibers from the ipsilateral eye (that is, the eye on the same side), whereas layers 1, 4, and 6 receive fibers from the contralateral eye (that is, the eye on the opposite side). This arrangement provides a way to combine the information from the two eyes and to segregate the information from the P and M ganglion cells. Axons from the P cells go only to layers 1 through 4 (referred to as the parvocellular layers), whereas axons from the M cells go only to layers 5 and 6 (referred to as the magnocellular layers). Because the P ganglion cells are responsive to color and fine detail, layers 1 through 4 of the LGN must be processing information about color and form. In contrast, the M cells mostly process information about movement, so layers 5 and 6 must deal with movement.

Let us now see where these LGN cells send their connections in the cortex. But, before we continue, you should be aware that just as there are six layers of the LGN (numbered 1–6), there are also six layers of the striate cortex (numbered I–VI). That there happen to be six layers in each of these locations is an accident of evolution found in all primate brains.

You learned in Chapter 2 that layer IV is the main afferent (incoming) layer of the cortex. Layer IV of the visual cortex has several sublayers, two of which are known as IVCα and IVCβ. Layers 1 through 4 of the LGN go to IVCβ, and LGN layers 5 and 6

Link to the area on the optic chiasm in the module on the Visual System on your CD to investigate the visual pathways to the LGN.

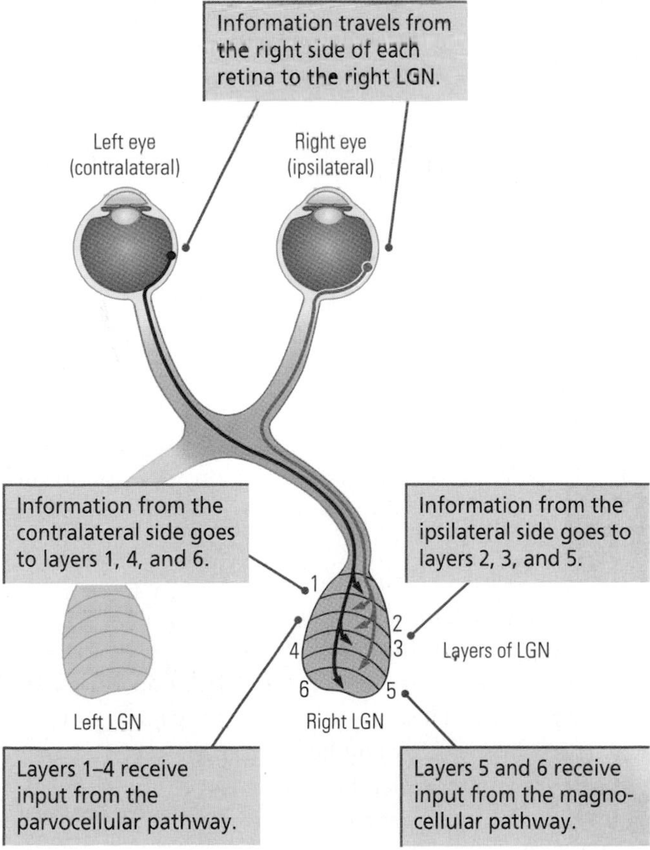
Information travels from the right side of each retina to the right LGN.
Left eye (contralateral)
Right eye (ipsilateral)
Information from the contralateral side goes to layers 1, 4, and 6.
Information from the ipsilateral side goes to layers 2, 3, and 5.
1
2
3
4
5
6
Layers of LGN
Left LGN
Right LGN
Layers 1–4 receive input from the parvocellular pathway.
Layers 5 and 6 receive input from the magnocellular pathway.

**Figure 8-15**

Information travels from the right side of each retina to the right LGN. Information from the same side (the ipsilateral eye) goes to layers 2, 3, and 5, whereas information from the opposite side (the contralateral eye) goes to layers 1, 4, and 6. Layers 1 through 4 receive input from the parvocellular pathway; layers 5 and 6 receive input from the magnocellular pathway.

**Figure 8-16**

Information travels from the lateral geniculate nucleus to layer IV of cortical visual area 1. Layers 1 through 4 project to layer IVCβ; layers 5 and 6 project to layer IVCα. Information from the two eyes is segregated by layers in the LGN, and the LGN maintains this segregation in its projections to the cortex. Information from each eye travels to adjacent columns in cortical layer V1. In a horizontal plane through V1 (*top right*), there is a zebralike effect of alternating columns in the cortex. These columns are referred to as ocular dominance columns.

Photo from "Functional architecture of macaque monkey visual cortex," Figure 23, by D.H. Hubel and T.N. Weisel, 1977, *Proceedings of the Royal Society of London B, 198*, pp. 1–59.

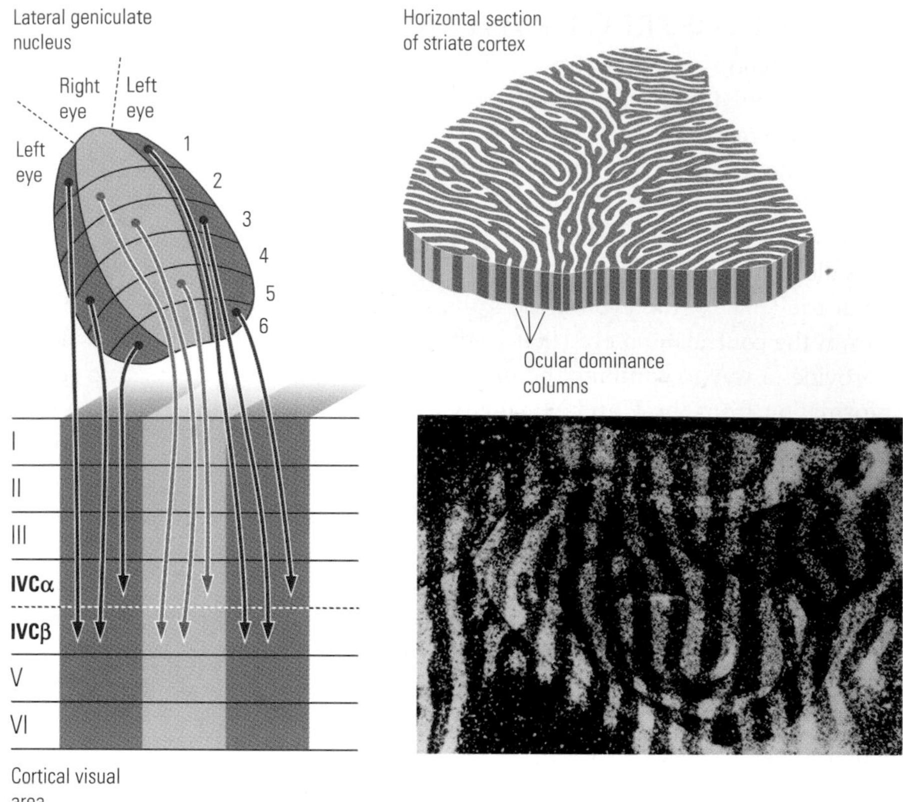


go to IVCα. As a result, a distinction between the P and M functions continues in the cortex. As illustrated in Figure 8-16, the two eyes also remain separated in the cortex, but through a different mechanism. The input from the ipsilaterally connected LGN cells (that is, layers 2, 3, and 5) and the input from the contralaterally connected LGN cells (layers 1, 4, and 6) go to adjacent strips of cortex. These strips, which are about 0.5 millimeter across, are known as **cortical columns.** We return to the concept of cortical columns shortly.

In summary, the P and M ganglion cells of the retina send separate pathways to the thalamus, and this segregation remains in the striate cortex. The left and right eyes also send separate pathways to the thalamus, and these pathways, too, remain segregated in the striate cortex. Let us now look at how visual information proceeds from the striate cortex through the rest of the occipital lobe to the dorsal and ventral streams.

Go to the CD and find the primary visual cortex area in the Visual System module to see the visual connections to the occipital cortex. Notice in particular how the cortex is layered in this region and how this layering parallels that seen in the LGN.

## THE OCCIPITAL CORTEX

As shown in Figure 8-17, the occipital lobe is composed of at least six different visual regions, known as V1, V2, V3, V3A, V4, and V5. Region V1 is the striate cortex, which, as already mentioned, is sometimes also referred to as the **primary visual cortex.** The remaining visual areas of the occipital lobe are called the **extrastriate cortex** or the **secondary visual cortex.** Because each of these occipital regions has a unique structure (cytoarchitecture) and has unique inputs and outputs, we can infer that each must be doing something different from the others.

You already know that a remarkable feature of region V1 is its distinct layers, which extend throughout V1. These seemingly homogeneous layers are deceiving, however. When Margaret Wong-Riley and her colleagues (1993) stained the cortex for the enzyme cytochrome oxidase, which has a role in cell metabolism, they were surprised to find an unexpected heterogeneity in region V1. So they sectioned the V1 layers in such a way that each cortical layer was in one plane of section. This is much like

**Cortical column.** Unit of cortical organization that represents a vertically organized functional unit.

**Primary visual cortex.** The striate cortex; it receives input from the lateral geniculate nucleus.

**Extrastriate (secondary) cortex.** Visual cortical areas outside the striate cortex.

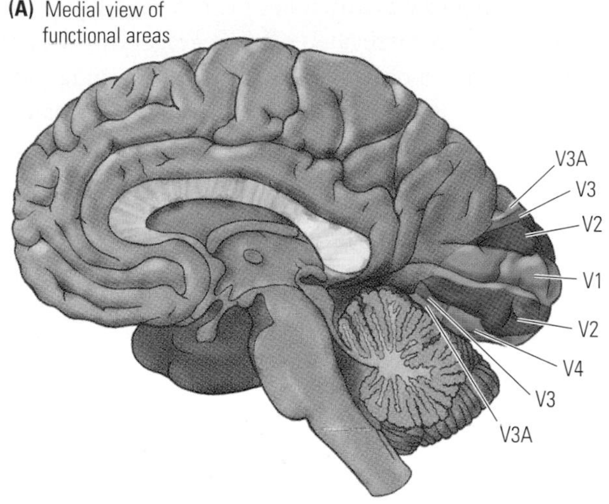


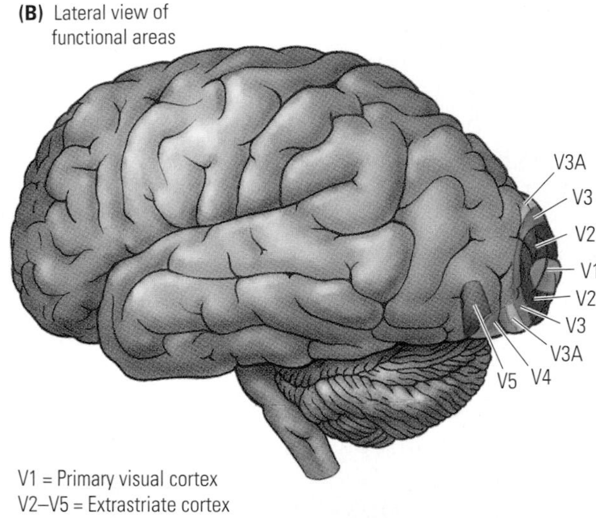


**Figure 8-17**

The visual regions of the occipital lobe.

peeling off the layers of an onion and laying them flat on a table. The surface of each flattened layer can then be viewed from above. As Figure 8-18 illustrates, the heterogeneous cytochrome staining now appeared like random blobs in the layers of V1. In fact, these darkened regions have become known as **blobs**, and the less-dark regions separating them have become known as *interblobs*. Blobs and interblobs serve different functions. Neurons in the blobs take part in color perception, whereas neurons in the interblobs participate in form and motion perception. So within region V1, input that arrives in the parvo- and magnocellular pathways of the geniculostriate system is segregated into three separate types of information: color, form, and movement.

**Blob.** A region in the visual cortex that contains color-sensitive neurons, as revealed by staining for cytochrome oxidase.

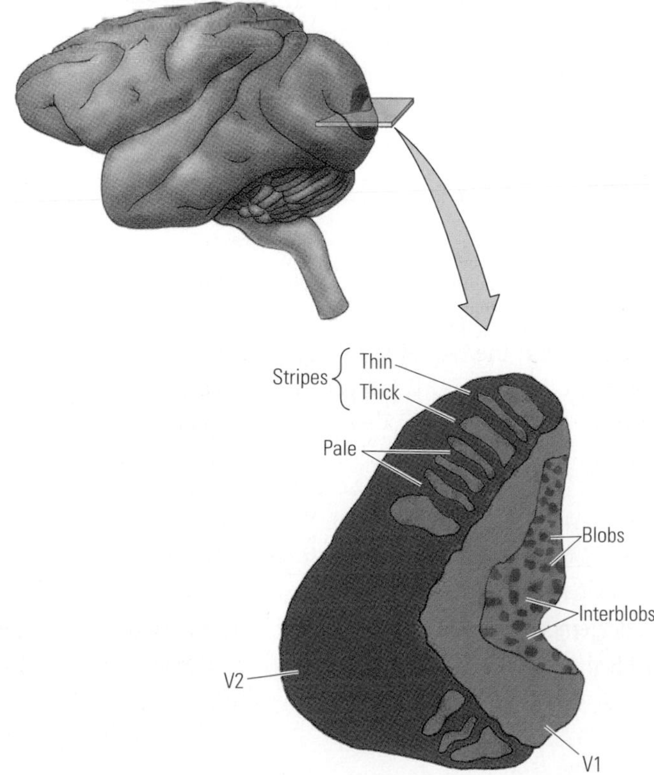


**Figure 8-18**

The blobs in region V1 and the stripes in region V2 are illustrated in this flattened section through the visual cortex. The blobs and stripes can be visualized by using a special stain for cytochrome oxidase, which is a marker for mitochondria.

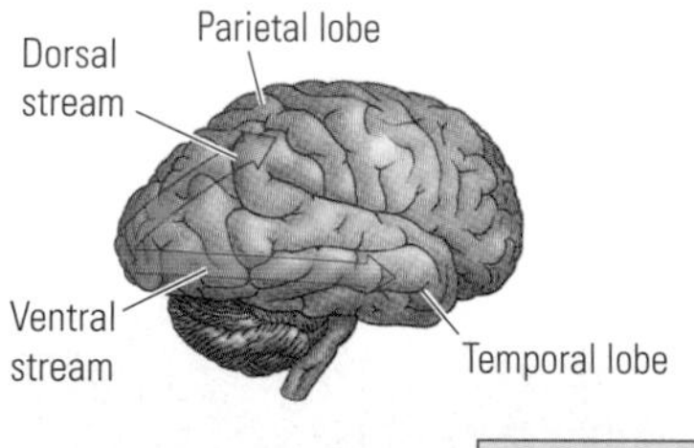


This information is then sent to region V2, which lies next to region V1. Here the color, form, and movement inputs remain segregated. This segregation can again be seen through the pattern of cytochrome oxidase staining, but the staining pattern is different from that in region V1. Figure 8-19 shows that region V2 has a pattern of thick and thin stripes that are intermixed with pale zones. The thick stripes receive input from the movement-sensitive neurons in region V1; the thin stripes receive input from V1's color-sensitive neurons; and the pale zones receive input from V1's form-sensitive neurons.

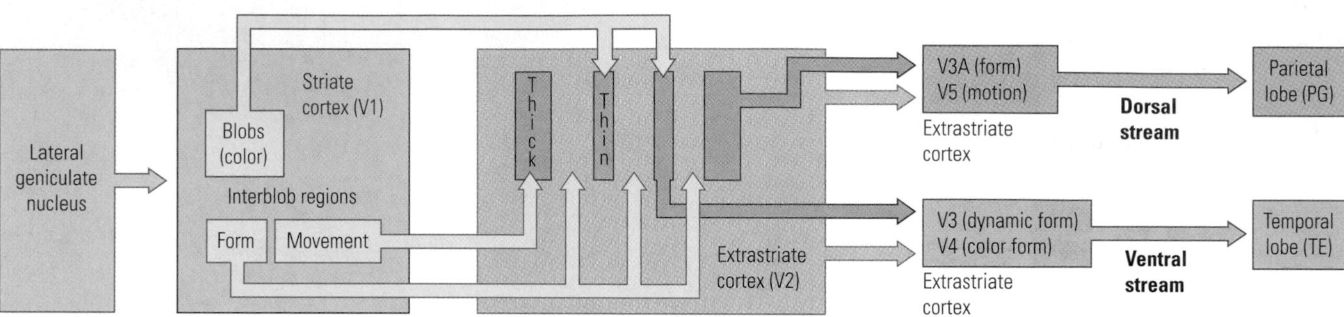


**Figure 8-19**

Both the dorsal and the ventral visual streams originate in region V1 and travel through region V2 to the other occipital areas and finally to the parietal or temporal lobe. The dorsal stream, which controls visual action, begins in V1 and flows to the parietal cortex, ending in an area of the parietal lobe referred to as PG. The ventral stream, which controls object recognition, begins in V1 and flows to the temporal cortex, ending in an area of the temporal lobe referred to as TE. The flow of information from the subregions of V1 (blobs and interblobs) is to the thick, thin, and pale zones of V2. Information in the thin and pale zones goes to V3 and V4 to form the ventral stream. That in the thick and pale zones goes to V3A and V5 to form the dorsal stream.

As also shown in Figure 8-19, these pathways proceed from region V2 to the other occipital visual regions and then to the parietal and temporal lobes, forming the dorsal and ventral streams. Although many parietal and temporal regions take part, the major regions are region G in the parietal lobe (thus called region PG) and region E in the temporal lobe (thus called region TE). Within the dorsal and ventral streams, the function of the visual pathways becomes far more complex than simply those of color, form, and movement. In these two streams, the color, form, and movement information is put together to produce a rich, unified visual world made up of complex objects, such as faces and paintings, and complex visual-motor skills, such as catching a ball. The functions of the dorsal and ventral streams are therefore complicated, but they can be thought of as consisting of "how" versus "what." "How" is action to be visually guided toward objects, whereas "what" identifies what an object is.

## In Review

Vision begins when photoreceptors in the retina at the back of the eye convert light energy into neural activity in neighboring ganglion cells, the axons of which form the optic nerve leading to the brain. P ganglion cells receive input mostly from cones and carry information about color and fine detail, whereas M ganglion cells receive input from rods and carry information about light but not color. Visual input takes two routes into the brain. One route is the geniculostriate pathway, which travels through the lateral geniculate nucleus of the thalamus to layer IV of the striate cortex in the occipital lobe. The other route is the tectopulvinar pathway, which goes from the tectum of the midbrain to the pulvinar of the thalamus and then to visual cortical areas. Both the geniculostriate and the tectopulvinar systems contribute to the dorsal and ventral streams that project to the parietal and temporal lobes, respectively. The dorsal stream to the parietal lobe is concerned with the visual guidance of movements, whereas the ventral stream to the temporal lobe is concerned with the perception of objects.

## LOCATION IN THE VISUAL WORLD

One kind of visual information that we have not yet considered is location. As we move around, we go from place to place, and objects are found in specific locations. Indeed, if we had no sense of location, the world would be a bewildering mass of visual information. Our next task is to look at how the brain constructs a spatial map from this complex array of visual input.

Visit the CD and find the area on the optic chiasm in the module on the Visual System to better understand the concept of visual fields.

The coding of location begins in the retina and is maintained throughout all the visual pathways. To understand how this spatial coding is accomplished, you need to look at your visual world as seen by your two eyes. Imagine looking at a large red and blue wall that has a black cross on which to focus your gaze, like the one in Figure 8-20. All of what you can see of the wall without moving your head is called your **visual field.** The visual field can be divided into two halves by drawing a vertical line down the middle of the black cross. These two halves are called the left and right visual fields, respectively. Now recall from Figure 8-11 that the left half of each retina looks at the right side of the visual field, whereas the right half of each retina looks at the visual field's left side. This means that input from the right visual field goes to the left hemisphere, whereas input from the left visual field goes to the right hemisphere. It is therefore rather easy for the brain to determine whether visual information is located to the left or right of center. If input goes to the left hemisphere, the source must be in the right visual field; if input goes to the right hemisphere, the source must be in the left visual field. This arrangement tells you nothing about the precise location of an object in the left or right side of the visual field, however. To understand how precise spatial localization is accomplished, we must return to the retinal ganglion cells.

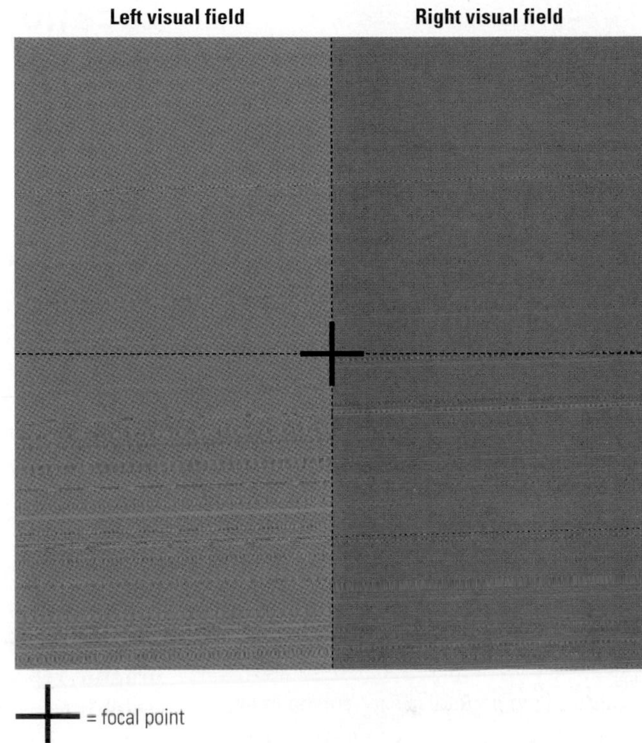


**Figure 8-20**

The visual field is the world seen by the two eyes. If we focus on the cross at the center of the figure, the information at the left of the cross forms the left visual field (red) and travels to the right hemisphere. The information at the right of the cross forms the right visual field (blue) and travels to the left hemisphere. The visual field can be broken horizontally as well so that information above the focal point is in the upper visual field and that below the focal point is in the lower visual field.

### Coding Location in the Retina

If you look again at Figure 8-9, you can see that each retinal ganglion cell receives input through bipolar cells from several photoreceptors. In the 1950s, Stephen Kuffler, a pioneer in studying the physiology of the visual system, made an important discovery about how these photoreceptors and ganglion cells are linked. By shining small spots of light on the receptors, he found that each ganglion cell responded to stimulation on just a small circular patch of the retina. This patch became known as the ganglion cell's receptive field. A ganglion cell's **receptive field** is therefore the region of the retina on which it is possible to influence that cell's firing. Stated differently, the receptive field represents the outer world as seen by a single cell. Each ganglion cell sees only a small bit of the world, much as you would if you looked through a narrow cardboard tube. The visual field is composed of thousands of such receptive fields.

Now let us consider how receptive fields enable the visual system to interpret the location of objects. Imagine that the retina is flattened like a piece of paper. When a tiny light is shone on different parts of the retina, different ganglion cells respond. For example, when a light is shone on the top-left corner of the flattened retina, a particular ganglion cell responds because that light is in its receptive field. Similarly, when a light is shone on the top-right corner, a different ganglion cell responds. By using this information, we can identify the location of a light on the retina by knowing which ganglion cell is activated. We can also interpret the location of the light in the outside world because we know where the light must come from to hit a particular place on

**Visual field.** The region of the visual world that is seen by the eyes.

**Receptive field.** The region of the visual world that stimulates a receptor cell or neuron.

the retina. For example, light from above hits the bottom of the retina after passing through the eye's lens, whereas light from below hits the top of the retina. (Refer to Figure 8-3 to see why this is so.) Information at the top of the visual field will stimulate ganglion cells on the bottom of the retina, whereas information at the bottom of the field will stimulate ganglion cells on the top of the retina.

## Location in the Lateral Geniculate Nucleus and Cortical Region V1

Link to the CD and find the area on the higher-order visual cortex in the module on the Visual System to investigate the location and anatomy of the LGN.

Now consider the connection from the ganglion cells to the lateral geniculate nucleus. In contrast with the retina, the LGN is not a flat sheet; rather, it is a three-dimensional structure in the brain. We can compare it to a stack of cards, with each card representing a layer of cells. Figure 8-21 shows how the connections from the retina to the LGN can represent location. A retinal ganglion cell that responds to light in the top-left corner of the retina connects to the left side of the first card. A retinal ganglion cell that responds to light in the bottom-right corner of the retina connects to the right side of the last card. In this way, the location of left–right and top–bottom information is maintained in the LGN.

Like the ganglion cells, each of the LGN cells has a receptive field, which is the region of the retina that influences its activity. If two adjacent retinal ganglion cells synapse on a single LGN cell, the receptive field of that LGN cell will be the sum of the two ganglion cells' receptive fields. As a result, the receptive fields of LGN cells can be bigger than those of retinal ganglion cells.

The LGN projection to the striate cortex (region V1) also maintains spatial information. As each LGN cell representing a particular place projects to region V1, a **topographic representation** (or topographic map) is produced in the cortex. This topographic representation, illustrated in Figure 8-22, is essentially a map of the visual

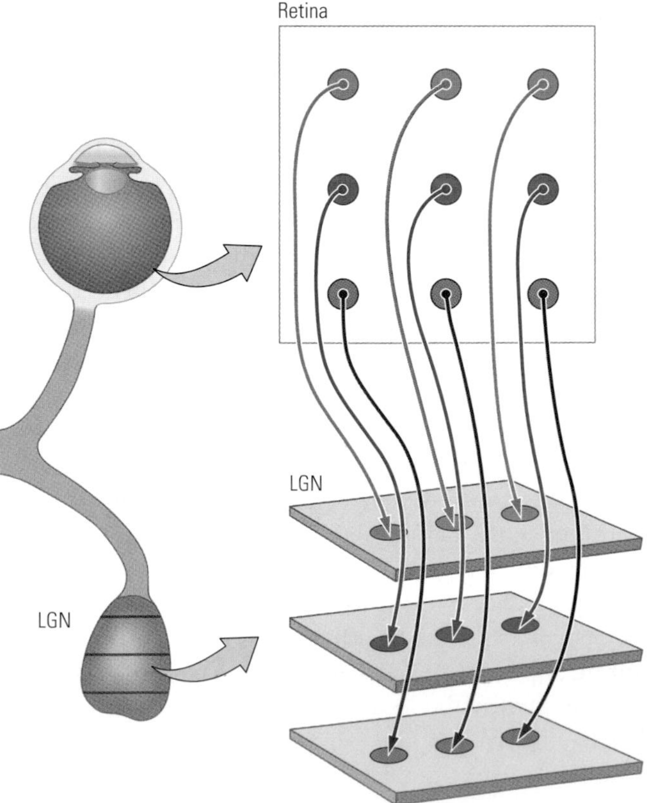


**Figure 8-21**

The information from a visual field retains its spatial relationship when it is sent to the lateral geniculate nucleus. In this example, information at the top of the visual field goes to the top of the LGN and information from the bottom of the visual field goes to the bottom of the LGN. Similarly, information from the left or right goes to the left or right of the LGN, respectively.

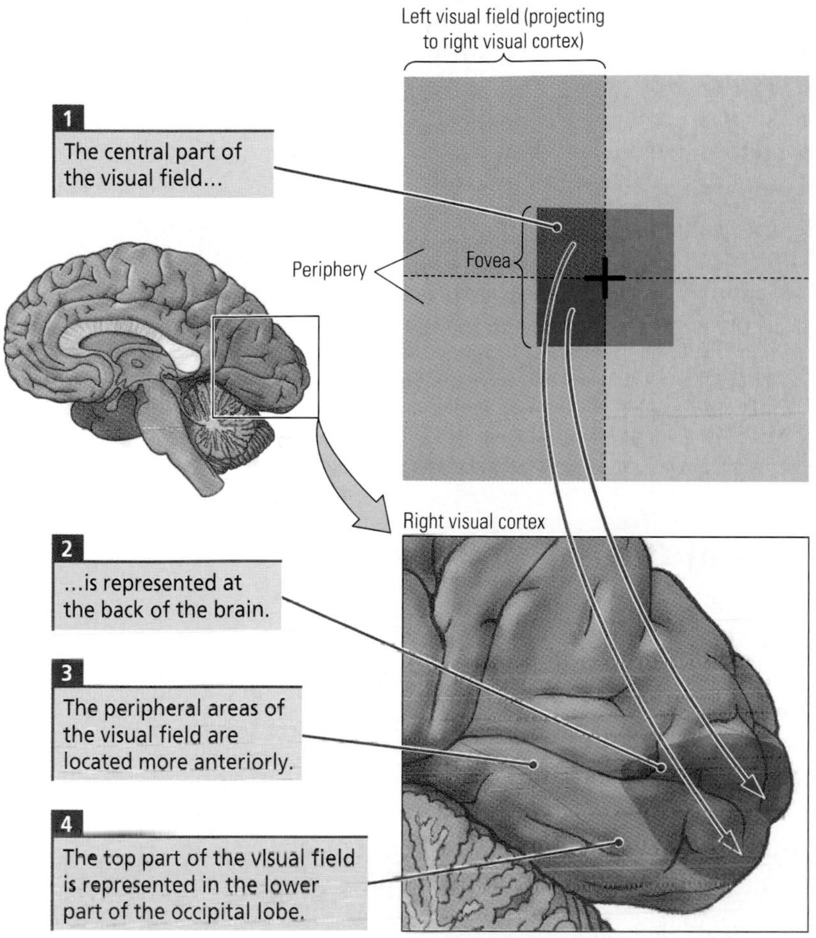

Left visual field (projecting to right visual cortex)
1
The central part of the visual field...
Periphery
Fovea
Right visual cortex
2
...is represented at the back of the brain.
3
The peripheral areas of the visual field are located more anteriorly.
4
The top part of the visual field is represented in the lower part of the occipital lobe.

**Figure 8-22**

The topographic organization of the visual cortex (V1) in the right occipital lobe. The area of left central vision (the fovea) is represented at the back of the brain, whereas the more peripheral areas are represented more anteriorly. The fovea also occupies a disproportionately large part of the cortex, which is why visual acuity is best in the central part of the visual field.

world. The central part of the visual field is represented at the back of the brain, whereas the peripheral part is represented more anteriorly. The upper part of the visual field is represented at the bottom of region V1, whereas the lower part of the visual field is represented at the top of V1. The other regions of the visual cortex (such as V3, V4, and V5) also have topographical maps similar to that of V1. The V1 neurons must project to the other regions in an orderly manner, just as the LGN neurons project to region V1 in an orderly way.

Within each visual cortical area, each neuron has a receptive field, which corresponds to the part of the retina to which the neuron is connected. As a rule of thumb, the cells in the cortex have much larger receptive fields than those of retinal ganglion cells. This increase in receptive-field size means that the receptive field of a cortical neuron must be composed of the receptive fields of many retinal ganglion cells, as illustrated in Figure 8-23.

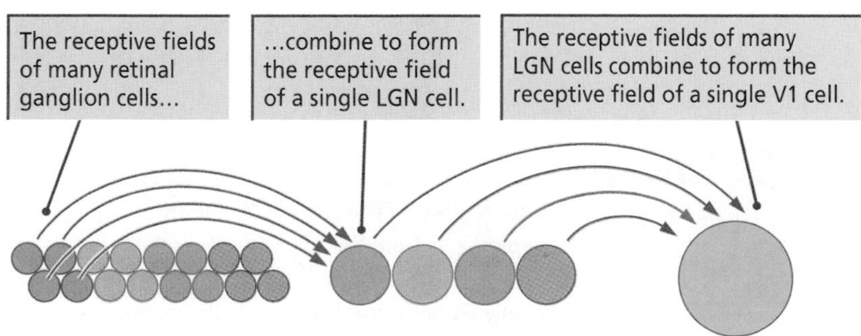

The receptive fields of many retinal ganglion cells...
...combine to form the receptive field of a single LGN cell.
The receptive fields of many LGN cells combine to form the receptive field of a single V1 cell.

**Figure 8-23**

The receptive fields of V1 neurons are constructed from those of lateral geniculate cells, which, in turn, are constructed from those of ganglion cells. The receptive fields of retinal ganglion cells, LGN cells, and V1 cells are illustrated by the circles. The receptive fields of the ganglion cells are small. The receptive fields of the LGN cells are the summation of the fields of four ganglion cells. The receptive field of the V1 cell is the sum of the four LGN cells.

There is one additional wrinkle to the organization of topographic maps. Jerison's principle of proper mass (see Chapter 1) states that the amount of neural tissue responsible for a particular function is equivalent to the amount of neural processing required for that function. Although in Chapter 1 Jerison's principle applied to overall brain size, it can be extended to regions within the brain as well. The visual cortex provides some good examples. You can see in Figure 8-22 that not all parts of the visual field are equally represented in region V1. The small central part of the visual field that is seen by the fovea is represented by a larger area in the cortex than the visual field's periphery, even though the periphery is a much larger part of the visual field. In accord with Jerison's principle, we would predict that there is more processing of foveal information in region V1 than there is of peripheral information. This prediction makes intuitive sense because we can see more clearly in the center of the visual field than at the periphery. In other words, sensory areas that have more cortical representation provide a more detailed creation of the external world.

## The Visual Corpus Callosum

The creation of topographic maps based on the receptive fields of neurons is an effective way for the brain to code the location of objects. But if the left visual field is represented in the right cerebral hemisphere and the right visual field is represented in the left cerebral hemisphere, how are the two halves of the visual field ultimately bound together to make a unified representation of the world? After all, we have the subjective impression not of two independent visual fields, but rather of a single, continuous field of vision. The answer to how this unity is accomplished lies in the corpus callosum, which binds the two sides of the visual field at the midline.

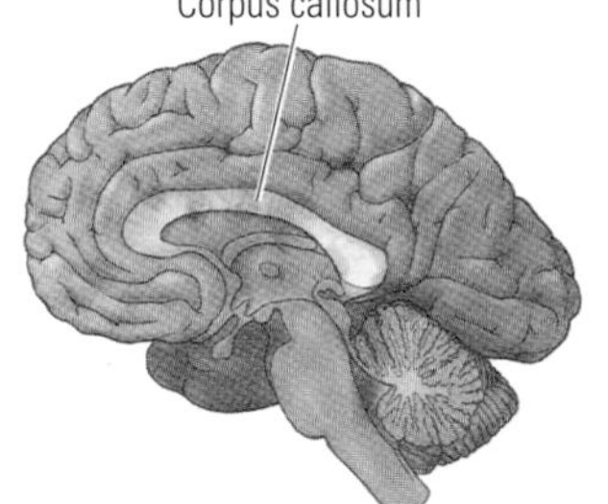
Corpus callosum

Until the 1950s, the function of the corpus callosum was largely a mystery. Physicians had occasionally cut it to control severe epilepsy, as described in "Epilepsy" on page 144, or to reach a very deep tumor, but patients did not appear to be much affected by this surgery. The corpus callosum clearly linked the two hemispheres of the brain, but exactly which parts were connected was not yet known.

We now realize that the corpus callosum connects only certain brain structures. Whereas much of the frontal lobes have callosal connections, the occipital lobes have almost none, as shown in Figure 8-24. If you think about it, there is no reason for a neuron in the visual cortex that is "looking at" one place in the visual field to be concerned with what another neuron in the opposite hemisphere is "looking at" in another part of the visual field. Cells that lie along the midline of the visual field are an exception, however. These cells would be "looking at" adjacent places in the field of vision, one slightly to the left of center and one slightly to the right. If there were connections between such cells, we could combine their receptive fields to form fields that crossed the midline, thus zipping the two visual fields together. This is exactly what happens. Cortical cells with receptive fields that lie along the midline of your field of vision are connected to one another through the corpus callosum so that their receptive fields overlap the midline. The two fields become one.

Most of the two frontal lobes have corpus callosum connections...
Parietal lobe
...whereas the occipital lobes have almost no connections.
Frontal lobe
Occipital lobe
Temporal lobe

**Figure 8-24**

The darker areas indicate regions of the cortex of a rhesus monkey that receive projections from the opposite hemisphere by means of the corpus callosum. Most of the occipital lobe has no such connections. The only visual connections are in the medial part of the visual field, which sews the two visual fields together.

## In Review

The brain is able to determine the location of a particular stimulus because each neuron of the visual system connects to only a small part of the retina, known as that neuron's receptive field. Each receptive field, in turn, receives input from only a small part of the visual field, so which part of the retina is stimulated effectively pinpoints exactly where the light source is positioned in the environment. This method of detecting location is maintained at different levels in the visual system, from the ganglion cells of the retina to the neurons of the LGN in the thalamus to the neurons of the primary visual cortex. Inputs to different parts of cortical region V1 from different parts of the retina essentially form a topographic map of the visual world within the brain. Because cells with receptive fields that lie along the midline of the field of vision are connected by the corpus callosum, the two sides of the visual world are bound together in the middle.

## NEURAL ACTIVITY

The pathways of the visual system are made up of individual cells. By studying how these cells behave when their receptive fields are stimulated, we can begin to understand how the brain processes different features of the visual world besides just the locations of light. To illustrate, we will examine how neurons from the retina to the temporal cortex respond to shapes and colors. We will then briefly consider how neurons in the dorsal stream behave.

Go to the area on the primary visual cortex in the module on the Visual System on your CD to learn more about how shape is perceived within the cortex.

**(A)** Baseline (12 per second)

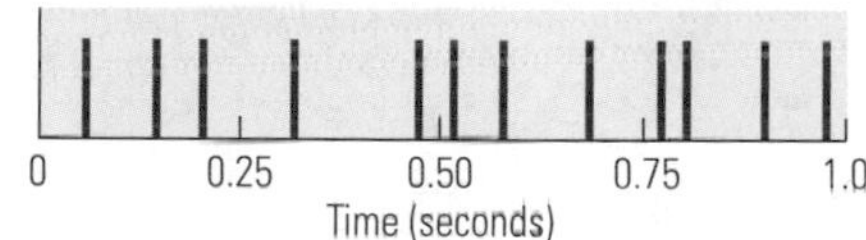


**(B)** Excitation

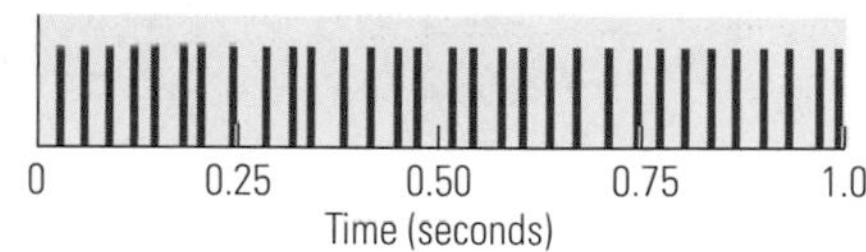


**(C)** Inhibition

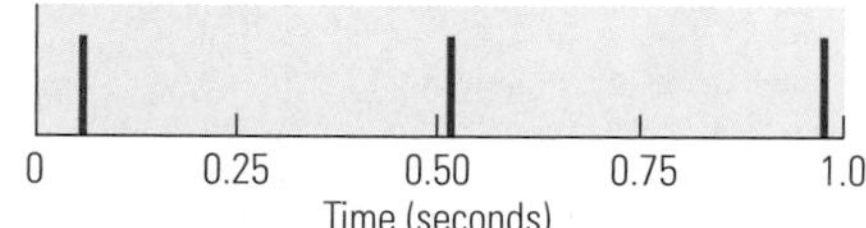


**Figure 8-25**

**(A)** In this illustration of the baseline firing rate of a neuron, each action potential is represented by a spike. In a 1-second time period, there were 12 spikes. **(B)** Excitation is indicated by an increase in firing rate over baseline. **(C)** Inhibition is indicated by a decrease in firing rate under baseline. When visually responsive neurons encounter a particular stimulus in their visual fields, they may show either excitation or inhibition.

### Seeing Shape

Imagine that we have placed a microelectrode near a neuron in the visual system and are using that electrode to record changes in the neuron's membrane potential. This neuron occasionally fires spontaneously, producing action potentials with each discharge. Let us assume that the neuron discharges, on the average, once every 0.08 second. Each action potential is brief, on the order of 1 millisecond. If we plotted action potentials over a minute, we would see only spikes in the record because the action potentials are so brief. (Refer to Figure 4-12 for an illustration of this effect.) Figure 8-25 is a single-cell recording in which there are 12 spikes. If the firing rate of this cell increases, we will see more spikes; if the firing rate decreases, we will see fewer spikes. The increase in firing represents excitation of the cell, whereas the decrease represents inhibition. Excitation and inhibition, as you know, are the principal mechanisms of information transfer in the nervous system.

Now suppose we present some type of stimulus to the neuron through its connections to the retina. For instance, we might place before the eye a straight line positioned at a 45° angle. If the cell were to respond to this stimulus, it could do so by either increasing or decreasing its firing rate. In either case, we would conclude that the cell is creating information about the line. Note that the same cell could show excitation to one stimulus and inhibition to another stimulus. For instance, the cell could be excited by lines oriented 45° to the left and inhibited by lines oriented 45° to the right. Similarly, the cell could be excited by stimulation in one part of its receptive field (such as the center) and inhibited by stimulation in another part (such as the periphery). Finally, we might find that the cell's response to a particular stimulus is selective. For instance, the cell might fire when the stimulus is presented with food but not fire (be inhibited) when the same stimulus is presented alone. In each of these cases, the cell is sensitive to specific characteristics of the visual world.

Now we are ready to move from a hypothetical example to what visual neurons actually do when they process information about shape. Neurons at each level of the visual system have distinctly different characteristics and functions. Our goal is not to look at each neuron type, but rather to consider generally how some typical neurons at each level differ from one another in their contributions to processing shape. For this purpose, we will focus on neurons in three areas: those in the ganglion-cell layer of the retina, those in the primary visual cortex, and those in the temporal cortex.

## PROCESSING IN RETINAL GANGLION CELLS

Cells in the retina do not actually see shapes. Shapes are constructed by the cortex from the information that ganglion cells pass on about events in their receptive fields. Keep in mind that the receptive fields of ganglion cells are very small dots. Each ganglion cell responds only to the presence or absence of light in its receptive field, not to shape.

The receptive field of a ganglion cell has a concentric circle arrangement, as illustrated in Figure 8-26. For some of these cells, a spot of light falling in the central circle of the receptive field causes the cell to be excited, whereas a spot of light falling in the periphery of the receptive field causes the cell to be inhibited. A spot of light falling across the entire receptive field causes a weak increase in the cell's rate of firing. This type of cell is called an *on-center cell.* Other ganglion cells have an opposite arrangement, with light in the center of the receptive field causing inhibition, light in the surround causing excitation, and light across the entire field producing weak inhibition. These cells are called *off-center cells.* The on–off arrangement of ganglion-cell receptive fields allows these cells to be especially responsive to very small spots of light.

This description of ganglion-cell receptive fields might mislead you into thinking that they form a mosaic of nonoverlapping little circles on the retina. In fact, neighboring retinal ganglion cells receive their inputs from an overlapping set of receptors. As a result, their receptive fields overlap, as illustrated in Figure 8-27. In this way, a small spot of light shining on the retina is likely to produce activity in many ganglion cells, including both on-center and off-center cells.

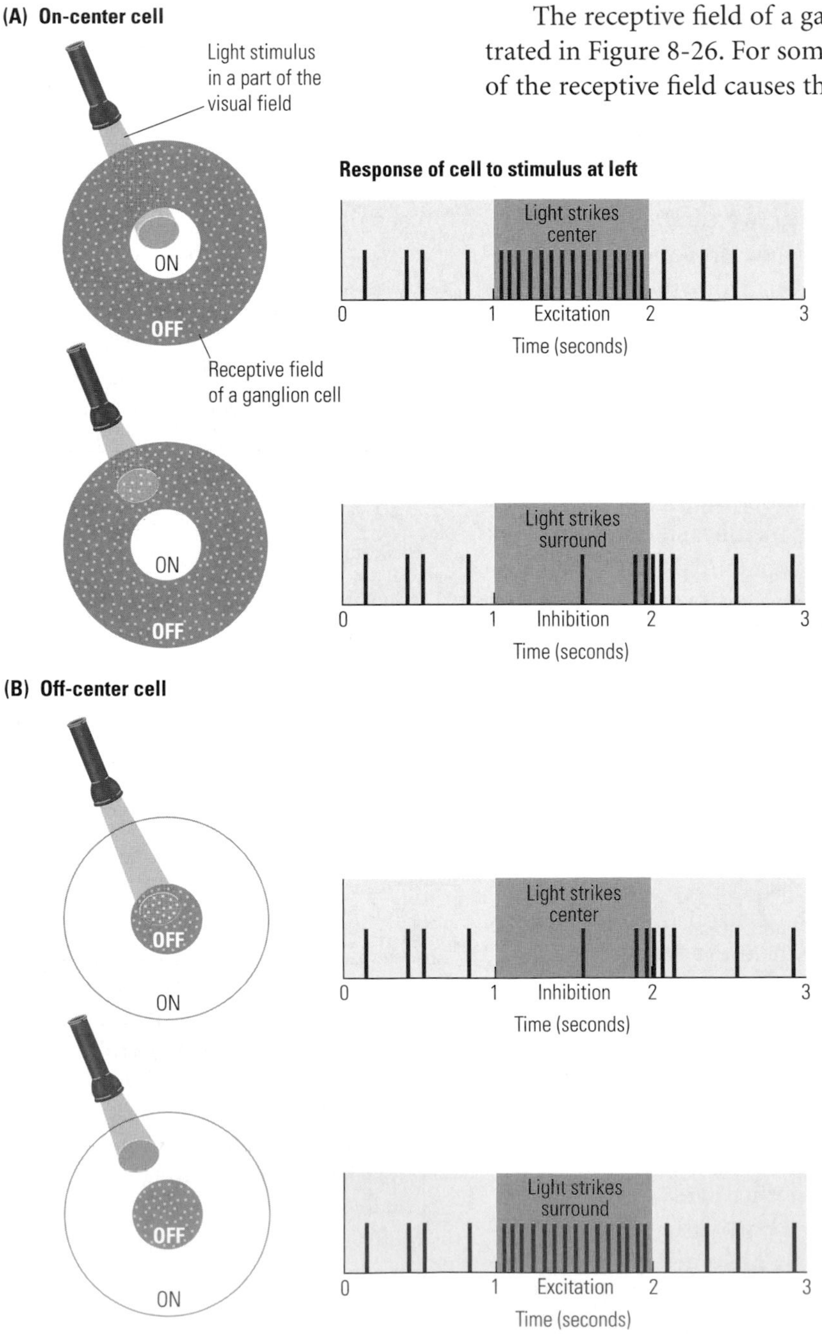

**Figure 8-26**

**(A)** The receptive field of a retinal ganglion cell with an on-center and off-surround. A spot of light placed on the center causes excitation in the neuron, whereas a spot of light in the surround causes inhibition. When the light is turned off in the surround region, there is a decrease in firing. A light that is in both the center and the surround would produce little reaction from the cell. **(B)** The receptive field of a retinal ganglion cell with an off-center and on-surround. Light in the center produces inhibition, whereas light on the surround produces excitation.

How can on-center and off-center ganglion cells tell the brain anything about shape? The answer is that a ganglion cell is able to tell the brain about the amount of light hitting a certain spot on the retina as compared with the average amount of light falling on the surrounding retinal region. This comparison is known as **luminance contrast.** To understand how this mechanism tells the brain about shape, consider the hypothetical population of on-center ganglion cells in Figure 8-28. Their receptive fields are distributed across the retinal image of a light–dark edge. Some of the ganglion cells have receptive fields in the dark area, others have receptive fields in the light area, and still others have fields that straddle the edge of the light. The ganglion cells with receptive fields in the dark or light areas are least affected because they experience either no stimulation or stimulation of *both* the excitatory and the inhibitory regions of their receptive fields. The ganglion cells most affected by the stimulus are those lying along the edge. Ganglion cell B is inhibited because the light falls mostly on its inhibitory surround, and ganglion cell D is excited because its entire excitatory center is stimulated but only part of its inhibitory surround is. Consequently, information transmitted from retinal ganglion cells to the visual areas in the brain does not give equal weight to all regions of the visual field. Rather, it emphasizes regions containing differences in luminance. Areas with differences in luminance are found along edges. So retinal ganglion cells are really sending signals about edges, and edges are what form shapes.

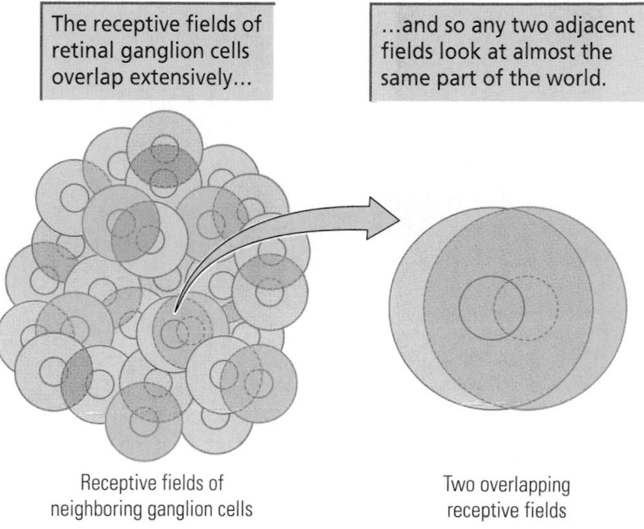

The receptive fields of retinal ganglion cells overlap extensively...
...and so any two adjacent fields look at almost the same part of the world.
Receptive fields of neighboring ganglion cells
Two overlapping receptive fields

**Figure 8-27**

The receptive fields of neighboring retinal ganglion cells usually overlap. The smallest light that is likely to hit the retina will therefore affect many ganglion cells.

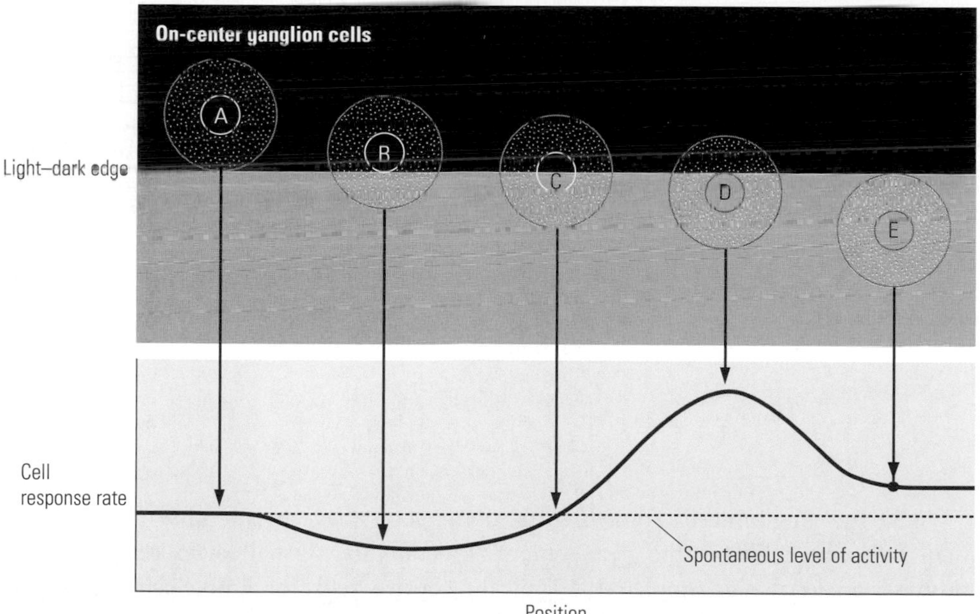


**Figure 8-28**

Responses of a hypothetical population of on-center ganglion cells whose receptive fields (A–E) are distributed across a light–dark edge. The activity of the cells along the edge is most affected relative to those away from the edge.

Adapted from *Neuroscience* (p. 195), edited by D. Purves, G. J. Augustine, D. Fitzpatrick, L. C. Katz, A.-S. LaMantia, and J. O. McNamara, 1997, Sunderland, MA: Sinauer.

Visit the area on the eye in the Visual System module of your CD to learn more about ganglion, on-center, and off-center cells.

## PROCESSING IN THE PRIMARY VISUAL CORTEX

Now let us consider cells in region V1, the primary visual cortex. As you know, the neurons in region V1 receive their visual inputs from LGN cells, which in turn receive theirs from retinal ganglion cells. Because each V1 cell receives input from multiple retinal ganglion cells, the receptive fields of the V1 neurons are much larger than those of neurons in the retina. Consequently, the V1 cells respond to stimuli more complex than simply "light on" or "light off." In particular, these cells are maximally excited by bars of light oriented in a particular direction, rather than by spots of light. These cells are therefore called *orientation detectors.*

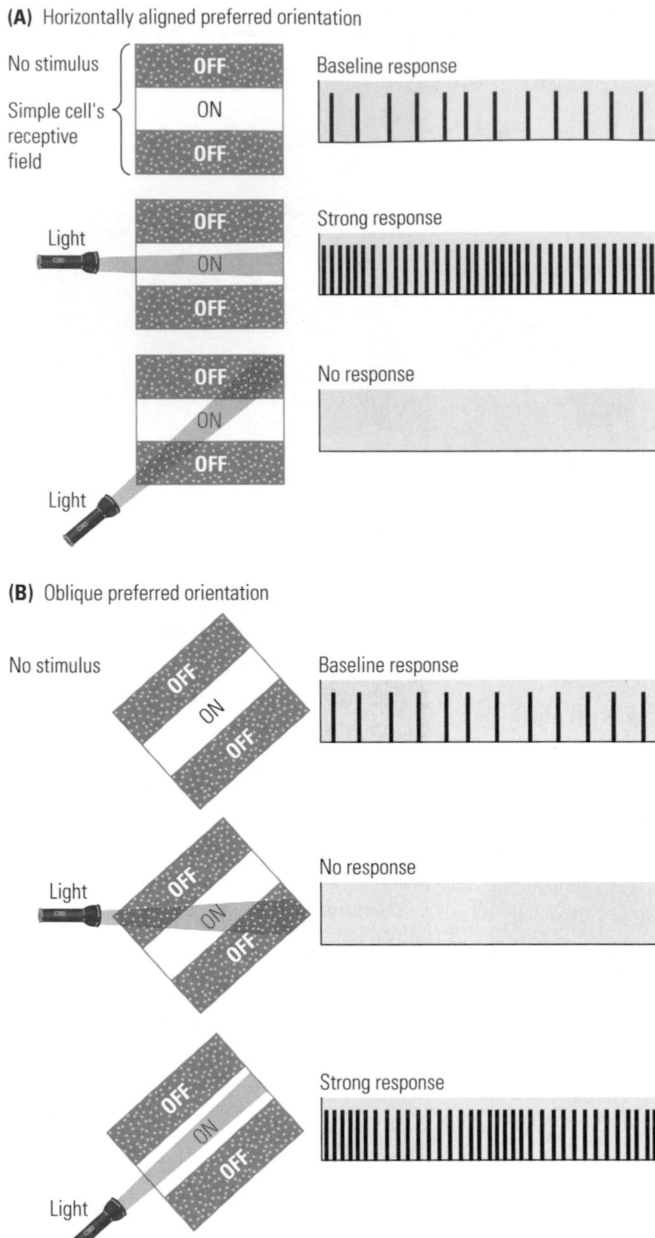


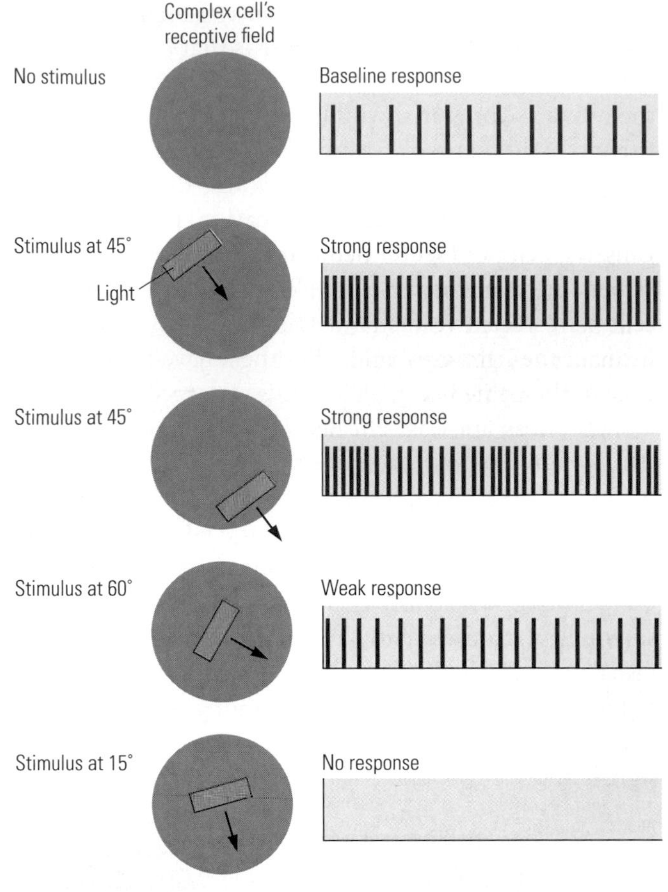


**Figure 8-30**

The receptive field (circle) of a complex cell in the visual cortex. Complex cells respond to bars of light that move across the field at a particular angle. Unlike a simple cell, a complex cell does *not* show an OFF response; rather, it shows the same response throughout the field. The cell responds best when the bar is at a particular orientation, and its response is reduced or does not occur at other orientations of the bar.

**Figure 8-29**

Typical receptive fields for simple visual cortex cells. Simple cells respond to a bar of light in a particular orientation, such as horizontal **(A)** or oblique **(B)**. The position of the bar in the visual field is important, because the cell responds with either an ON or an OFF to light in adjacent regions of the visual field.

Like the ganglion cells, some orientation detectors have an on–off arrangement in their receptive fields but the arrangement is rectangular. Visual cortex cells with this property are known as **simple cells.** Typical receptive fields for simple cells in the primary visual cortex are shown in Figure 8-29.

Simple cells are not the only kind of orientation detector in the primary visual cortex; there are several functionally distinct types of neurons in region V1. For instance, in addition to the simple cells, there are cells that are maximally excited by bars of light moving in a particular direction through the visual field. These cells are known as **complex cells.** They have receptive fields such as those in Figure 8-30. Another type of V1 cell, known as a **hypercomplex cell,** like a complex cell, is maximally responsive to moving bars, but a hypercomplex cell also has a strong inhibitory area at one end of its receptive field. As illustrated in Figure 8-31, a bar of light landing on the right side of the receptive field excites the cell, but if the bar lands on the inhibitory area to the left, the cell's firing is inhibited.

Note that each class of V1 neurons responds to bars of light in some way, yet this response results from input originating in retinal ganglion cells that respond maximally not to bars but to spots of light. How does this conversion from responding to spots to responding to bars take place? An example will help explain the process. Imagine that a thin bar of light falls on the retina. This bar of light will strike the receptive fields of perhaps dozens of retinal ganglion cells. If the input to a V1 neuron is from a group of ganglion cells that happen to be aligned in a row, as in Figure 8-32, then that V1 neuron will be activated (or inhibited) only when a bar of light hitting the retina strikes that particular row of ganglion cells. If the bar of light is at a slightly different angle, only some of the retinal ganglion cells in the row will be activated, and so the V1 neuron will be excited only weakly.

Figure 8-32 illustrates the connection between light striking the retina in a certain pattern and activation of a simple cell in the primary visual cortex, one that responds to a bar of light in a particular orientation. Using the same logic, we can also diagram the retinal receptive fields of complex or hypercomplex V1 neurons. Try this as an exercise yourself by making drawings like the one in Figure 8-32.

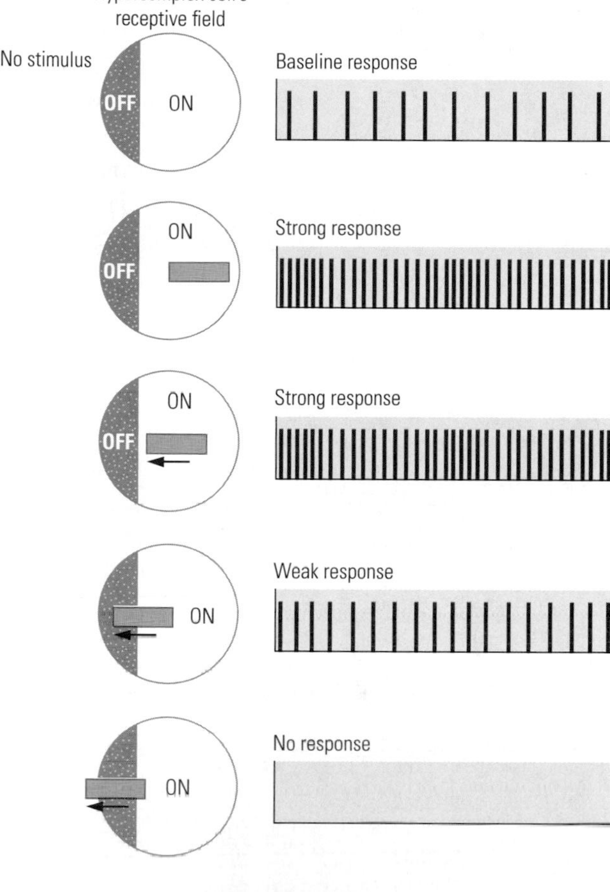


**Figure 8-31**

The receptive field of a hypercomplex cell. A hypercomplex cell responds to a bar of light in a particular orientation (for example, horizontal) anywhere in the ON part of its receptive field. If the bar extends into the inhibitory area (OFF), the response is inhibited.

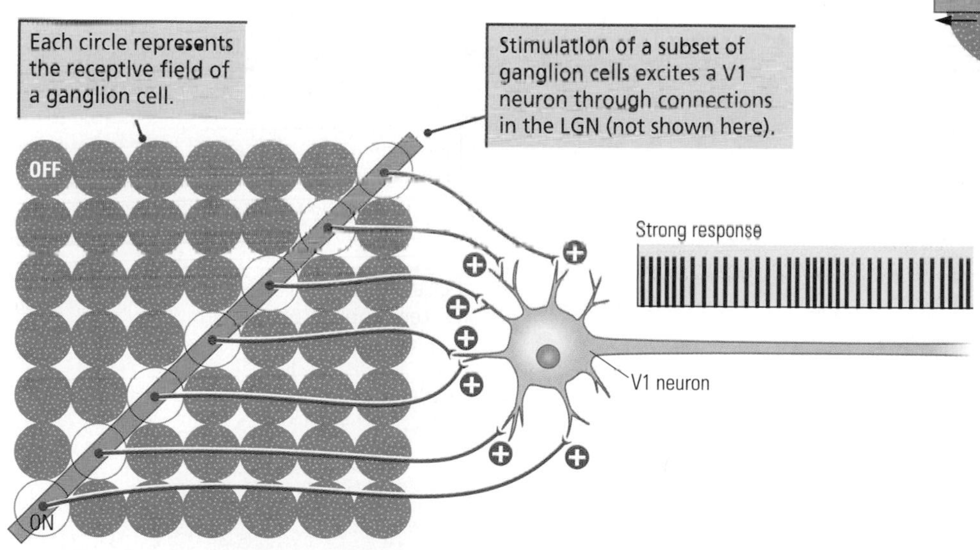


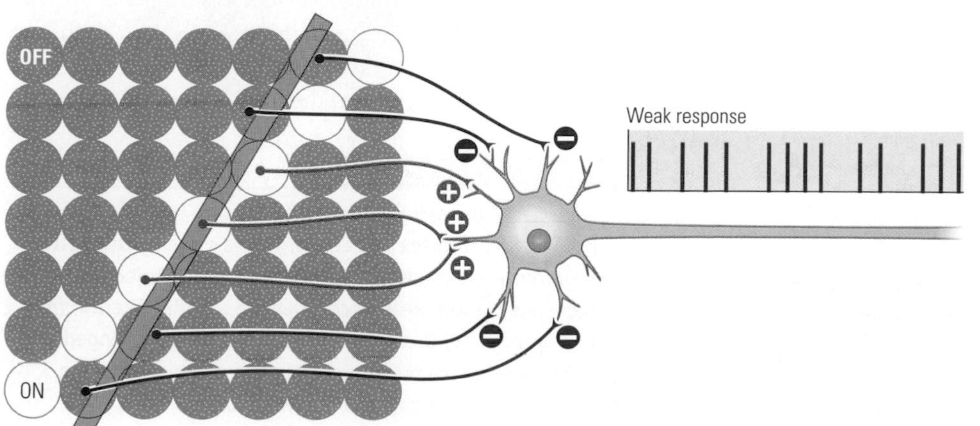


**Figure 8-32**

In this diagram illustrating how a V1 cell can respond to a row of ganglion cells in a particular orientation, the left-hand side illustrates two patches of retina. Each circle represents the receptive field of a retinal ganglion cell. The bar of light activates a row of ganglion cells, each of which is connected, through the LGN, to a V1 neuron. The activity of this neuron will be most affected by a bar of light at a 45° angle.

A characteristic of cortical structure is that the cells are organized into functional columns. Figure 8-33 shows such a column, a 0.5-millimeter-diameter strip of cortex that includes neurons and their connections. The pattern of connectivity in a column is vertical: inputs arrive in layer IV and then connect with cells in the other layers. The neurons within a column have similar functions. For example, Figure 8-34 shows that neurons within the same column respond to lines oriented in the same direction. Adjacent columns house cells that are responsive to different line orientations. Figure 8-34 also shows the columns of input coming from each eye, as discussed earlier.

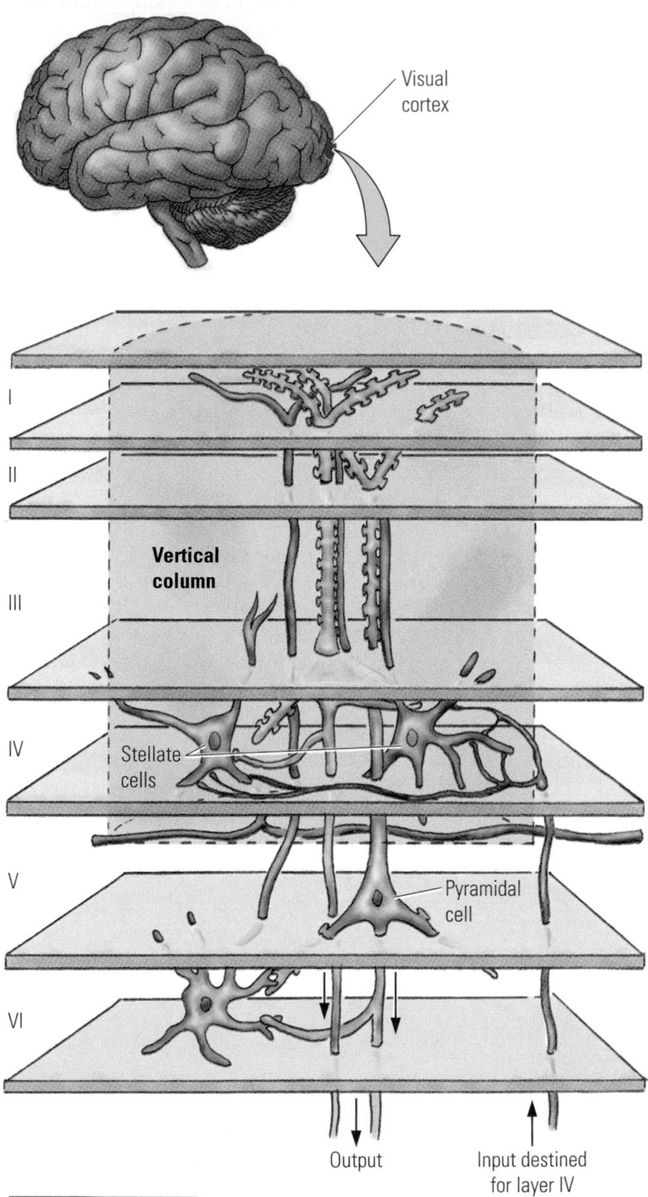


**Figure 8-33**

A stereoscopic view of a neural circuit in a column in the visual cortex. The sensory inputs terminate on stellate cells in layer IV. These stellate cells synapse in layers III and V with pyramidal cells in the same vertical column of tissue. Thus the flow of information is vertical. The axons of the pyramidal cells leave the column to join with other columns or with other structures.

Adapted from "The 'Module-Concept' in Cerebral Architecture," by J. Szentagothai, 1975, *Brain Research, 95*, p. 490.

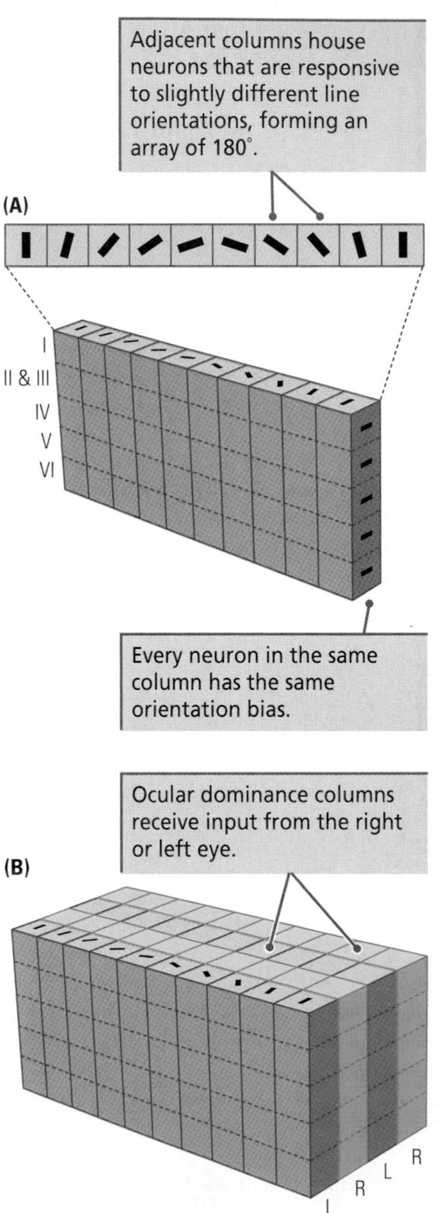


**Figure 8-34**

A model of the organization of functional columns in the primary visual cortex. **(A)** Cells with the same orientation preference are found throughout a column. Adjacent columns have orientation preferences that are slightly different from one another. **(B)** Ocular dominance columns are arranged at right angles to the orientation columns, producing a three-dimensional organization of the visual cortex.

These columns are called **ocular dominance columns.** So not only does the visual cortex have columns housing neurons that are similar in their orientation sensitivity (orientation columns), it also has ocular dominance columns with input from one or the other eye.

**Ocular dominance column.** A functional column in the visual cortex maximally responsive to information coming from one eye.

## PROCESSING IN THE TEMPORAL CORTEX

Finally, let us consider neurons along the ventral stream in region TE of the temporal lobe (see page 294). Rather than being responsive to spots or bars of light, these neurons are maximally excited by complex visual stimuli, such as faces or hands. Such neurons can be remarkably specific in their responsiveness. They may be responsive to particular faces seen head-on, to faces viewed in profile, to the posture of the head, or even to particular facial expressions.

How far does this specialized responsiveness extend? Would it be practical to have visual neurons in the temporal cortex specialized to respond to every conceivable feature of objects? Keiji Tanaka (1993) approached this question by presenting monkeys with many three-dimensional representations of animals and plants to find stimuli that were effective in activating particular neurons of the inferior temporal cortex. Having identified stimuli that were especially effective, such as faces or hands, he then wondered which specific features of those stimuli were critical to stimulating the neurons. Tanaka found that most neurons in area TE required rather complex features for their activation. These features included a combination of characteristics such as orientation, size, color, and texture. Furthermore, neurons with similar, although slightly different, responsiveness to particular features tended to cluster together in columns, as shown in Figure 8-35.

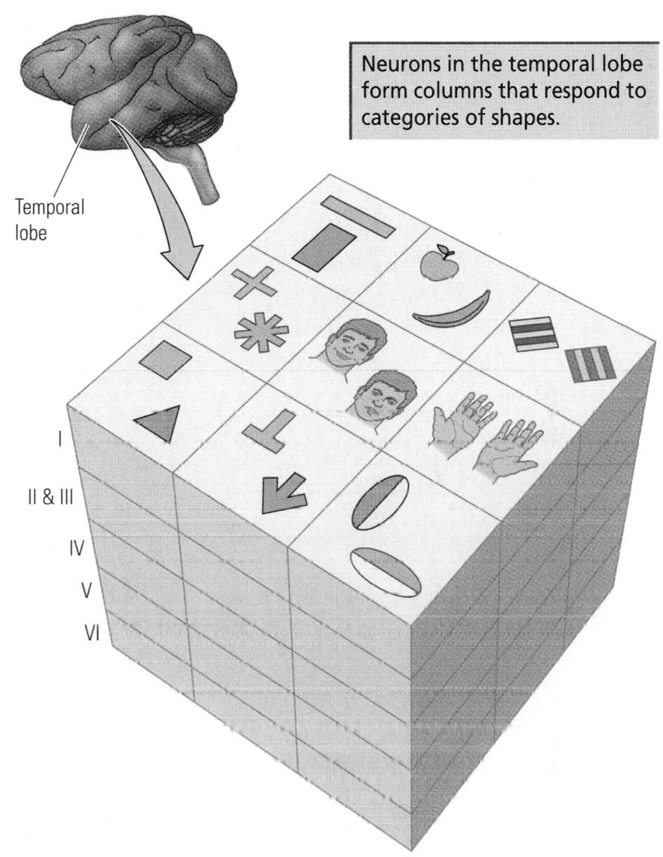
Neurons in the temporal lobe form columns that respond to categories of shapes.
Temporal lobe
I
II & III
IV
V
VI

**Figure 8-35**

The columnar organization of area TE. Neurons with similar but slightly different pattern selectivity cluster in vertical columns, perpendicular to the cortical surface.

Apparently, then, an object is not represented in the temporal cortex by the activity of a single neuron. Rather, objects are represented by the activity of many neurons with slightly varying stimulus specificity that are grouped together in a column. This finding is important because it provides an explanation for what is called **stimulus equivalence**—the tendency to see something as remaining the same object despite being viewed from different orientations. Think of how the representation of objects by multiple neurons in a column can produce stimulus equivalence. If each neuron in the column module varies slightly in regard to the features to which it responds but the effective stimuli largely overlap, the effect of small changes in incoming visual images will be minimized and we will tend to keep perceiving an object as the same thing.

Another remarkable feature of neurons of the inferior temporal cortex in monkeys is that the stimulus specificity of these neurons is altered by experience. If monkeys are trained to discriminate particular shapes to obtain a food reward, not only do they improve their discriminatory ability, but neurons in the temporal lobe also modify their preferred stimuli to fire maximally to some of the stimuli used in training. This result shows that the temporal lobe's role in visual processing is not determined genetically but is instead subject to experience, even in adults.

We can speculate that this experience-dependent characteristic evolved because it allows the visual system to adapt to different demands in a changing visual environment. Think of how different the demands on your visual recognition abilities are when you move from a dense forest to a treeless plain to a highly complex city street. The visual neurons of your temporal cortex can adapt to these differences. In addition, experience-dependent visual neurons ensure that people can identify visual stimuli that were never encountered as the human brain evolved.

Note that the preferred stimuli of neurons in the primary visual cortex are *not* modified by experience, which implies that the stimulus preferences of V1 neurons are genetically programmed. In any case, the functions of the V1 neurons provide the building blocks for the more complex and flexible characteristics of the inferior temporal cortex neurons.

## Seeing Color

Go to the area on the eye in the module on the Visual System on your CD. Review the process of color vision and move the wavelength to different locations so that you can note the receptor ratios involved in processing them.

Scientists have long wondered how people are able to see a world so rich in color. One explanation is the **trichromatic theory** of color vision. This theory has its roots in the Renaissance, when artists discovered that they could obtain the entire range of colors in the visual world by mixing only three colors of paint. These three colors came to be called the primary colors. Although people at the time did not understand the basis of this three-color (trichromatic) mixing, we now know that it is a property of the cones in the retina. Light of different wavelengths stimulates the three different types of cone receptors in different ways, and the ratio of the activity of these three receptor types creates our impression of different colors.

Here is an example of how the process works. If you look at Figure 8-7, you can see that light at 500 nanometers excites short-wavelength receptors to about 30 percent of their maximum, medium-wavelength receptors to about 65 percent of their maximum, and long-wavelength receptors to about 40 percent of their maximum. In contrast, a light at 600 nanometers excites these receptors to about 0, 25, and 75 percent of maximum, respectively. According to the trichromatic theory, the color that we see—in this case, blue green at 500 nanometers and orange at 600 nanometers—is determined by the relative responses of the different cone types. If all three cone types are equally active, we see white.

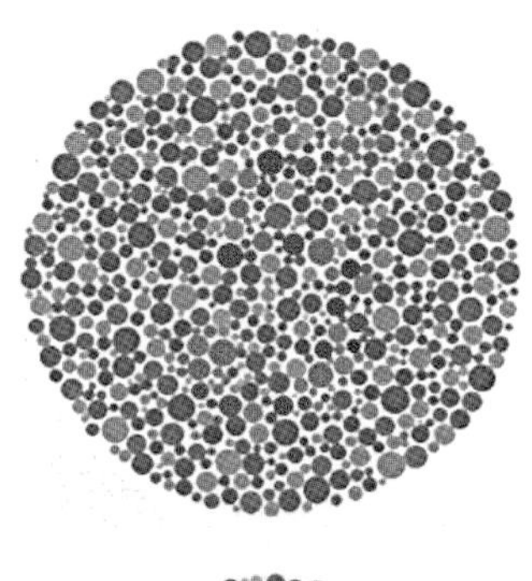

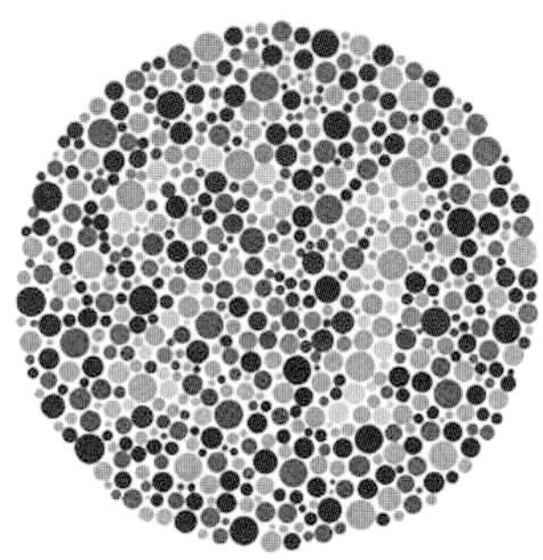

Individuals with deficiencies in red-green color perception have difficulty seeing the numbers within the circles.

The trichromatic theory predicts that, if we lacked one type of cone, we could not create as many colors as we can with three types of cone receptors. This is exactly what happens when a person is born with only two cone types. The colors that the person is unable to create depend on which receptor type is missing. The most common deficiency, as mentioned earlier in this chapter, is red-green color blindness, which afflicts about 5 percent of males and 0.5 percent of females. It is caused by the absence of either the medium-wavelength or the long-wavelength receptor. If a person is missing two types of cones, he or she cannot create any color, as the trichromatic theory also predicts.

Notice that the mere presence of cones in an animal's retina does not mean that the animal has color vision. It simply means that the animal has photoreceptors that are particularly sensitive to light. Many animals lack color vision as we know it, but the only animal known to have no cones at all is a fish, the skate.

**Trichromatic theory.** An explanation of color vision that is based on the coding of three basic colors: red, green, and blue.

**Opponent-process theory.** An explanation of color vision that emphasizes the importance of the opposition of pairs of colors: red versus green and blue versus yellow.

As helpful as the trichromatic theory is in explaining color blindness, it cannot explain everything about human color vision—for example, the sense that there are four "basic" colors (red, green, yellow, and blue) instead of three. A curious property of these four fundamental colors is that they seem to be linked as two pairs of opposites, one pair being red and green and the other pair being yellow and blue. Why do we call these pairs of colors opposites? You can see why by staring at one or more of these colors for about a minute and then looking at a white surface. For instance, try staring first at the red and blue box in Figure 8-36 and then at the white box next to it. When you shift your gaze to the white surface, you will experience a color afterimage

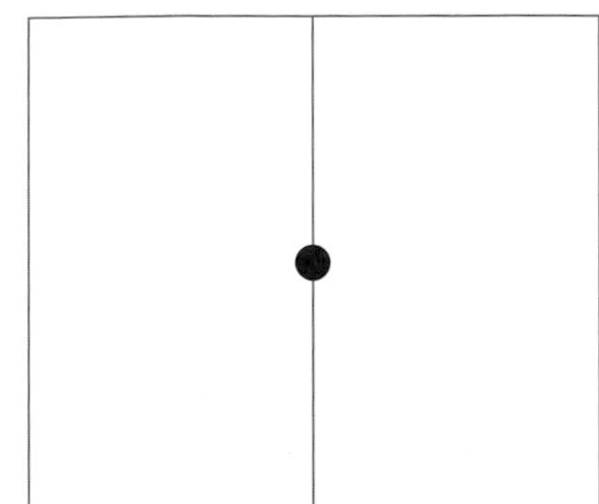

**Figure 8-36**

Stare at the rectangle on the left for about 30 seconds. Then stare at the white box. You will experience an afterimage of green on the red side and yellow on the blue side.

in the color opposites of red and blue—that is, green and yellow. Conversely, if you stare at a green and yellow box and then shift to white, you will see a red and blue afterimage. These observations are not easily explained by the trichromatic theory.

In 1874, Ewald Hering, a German physiologist, proposed the so-called **opponent-process theory** as a way of explaining human color vision that could also account for color afterimages. He argued that color vision is mediated by opponent processes in the retina. Remember that retinal ganglion cells have an on–off/center–surround organization. That is, stimulation to the center of the neuron's receptive field is either excitatory (in some cells) or inhibitory (in other cells), whereas stimulation to the periphery of the receptive field has the opposite effect. You can probably guess how this arrangement could be used to create color opponent-process cells. If excitation is produced by one wavelength of light and inhibition by another, we could create cells that are excited by red and inhibited by green (or vice versa), as well as cells that are excited by blue and inhibited by yellow (or vice versa). Red–green and blue–yellow would therefore be linked to each other as color opposites, just as the opponent-process theory says.

In fact, about 60 percent of human retinal ganglion cells are color-sensitive in this way, with the center being responsive to one wavelength and the surround to another. The most common pairing, shown in Figure 8-37, is medium-wavelength (green) versus long-wavelength (red), but there are also blue versus yellow cells. Most likely, the reason for having opponent-process cells is to enhance the relatively small differences in spectral absorption of the three types of cones.

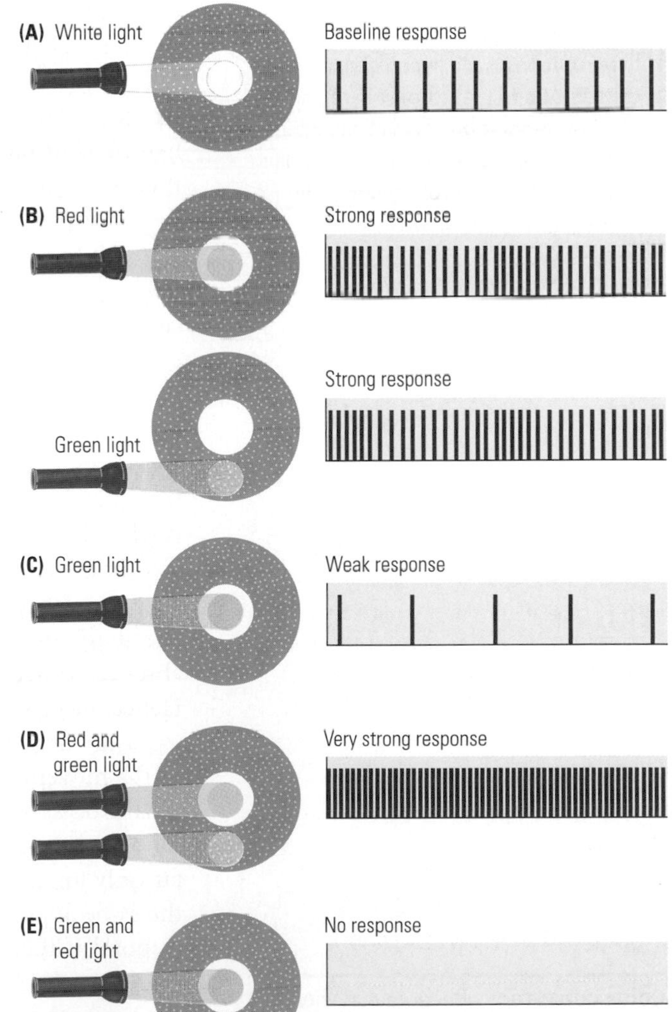


**Figure 8-37**

The opponent-color contrast cell illustrated here responds weakly to a small spot of white light in its center **(A)** because red and green cones absorb white light to similar extents, and so their inputs cancel out. The cell responds strongly to a spot of red light in its center **(B)**, as well as to red's paired wavelength, green, in the periphery. It is inhibited by a small spot of green in its center **(C)**. The cell responds very strongly to simultaneous illumination of the center with red and the surround with green **(D)** and is completely inhibited by the simultaneous illumination of the center with green and the surround with red **(E)**.

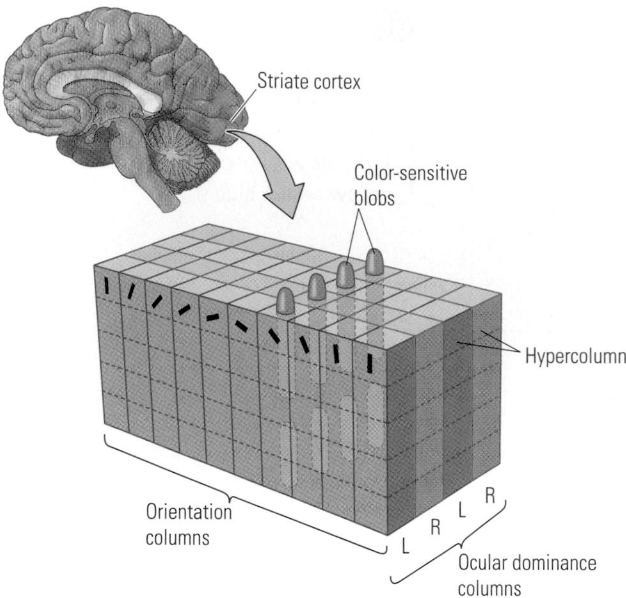


**Figure 8-38**

A module of striate cortex showing the orientation columns, ocular dominance columns, and color-sensitive blobs. The module is composed of two hypercolumns. Each hypercolumn consists of a full set (shown in red and blue) of orientation columns spanning 180° of preferred angle as well as a pair of blobs. All cells in the hypercolumn share the same receptive field.

Cortical neurons in region V1 also respond to color in an opponent-process manner reminiscent of retinal ganglion cells. Recall that color inputs in the primary visual cortex go to the blobs that appear in sections stained for cytochrome oxidase. These blobs are where the color-sensitive cells are found. But how are the color-sensitive cells in the blobs organized relative to the columns of orientation-sensitive cells and the ocular dominance columns? Figure 8-38 illustrates the solution. The color-sensitive cells in the blobs are inserted amid the orientation and ocular dominance columns. In this way, the primary visual cortex appears to be organized into modules that include ocular dominance and orientation columns as well as blobs. You can think of it as being composed of several thousand modules, each analyzing color and contour for a particular region of the visual world. This organization allows the primary visual cortex to perform several functions concurrently.

What about neurons of the visual system beyond region V1? How do they process color? You have already learned that cells in region V4 respond to color, but, in contrast with the cells in region V1, these V4 cells do not respond to particular wavelengths. Rather, they are responsive to different perceived colors, with the center of the field being excited by a certain color and the surround being inhibited.

There has been much speculation about the function of these cells. One idea is that they are important for **color constancy,** which is the property of color perception whereby colors appear to remain the same relative to one another despite changes in light. For instance, if you were to look at a bowl of fruit through light-green glasses, the fruit would take on a greenish tinge, but bananas would still look yellow relative to red apples. If you removed all the fruit except the bananas and looked at them through the tinted glasses, they would appear green because their color would not be relative to any other. Monkeys with V4 lesions lose color constancy, even though they can discriminate different wavelengths.

## Neural Activity in the Dorsal Stream

A striking characteristic of many cells in the visual areas of the parietal cortex is that they are virtually silent to visual stimulation when a person is under anesthesia. This is true of neurons in the posterior parietal regions of the dorsal stream, in contrast to cells in the temporal cortex, which do respond to visual stimulation even when a person is anesthetized. The silence on the part of posterior parietal cortex neurons under anesthesia makes sense if their role is to process visual information for action. In the absence of action when a person is unconscious, there is no need for processing. Hence the cells are totally quiescent.

Cells in the dorsal stream are of many types, their details varying with the nature of the movement in which a particular cell is taking part. One interesting category of cells processes the visual appearance of an object to be grasped. For instance, if a monkey is going to pick up an apple, these cells respond even when the monkey is so far only looking at the apple. The cells do not respond when the monkey encounters the same apple in a situation where no movement is to be made. Curiously, these cells respond if the monkey merely watches another monkey making movements to pick up the apple. Apparently, the cells have some sort of "understanding" of what is happening in the external world. But that understanding is always related to *action* with respect to visually perceived objects. These cells are what led David Milner and Mel Goodale (1995) to conclude that the dorsal stream is really a "how" visual system.

**Color constancy.** Phenomena whereby the perceived color of an object tends to remain constant, regardless of changes in illumination.

## In Review

The brain perceives color, form, and motion on the basis of information provided by retinal ganglion cells. In regard to seeing shapes, each ganglion cell tells the brain about the amount of light hitting a certain spot on the retina compared with light hitting surrounding regions. Because these luminance contrasts are located along the edges of shapes, ganglion cells send inputs to the brain that are the starting points for shape analysis. Neurons in the primary visual cortex then respond to more complex properties of shapes, especially bars of light oriented in a certain direction. A V1 neuron's particular response pattern depends on the spatial arrangement of the ganglion cells to which it is connected. Visual analysis is completed in the temporal lobes, where neurons respond to complex visual stimuli, such as faces.

Color analysis also begins in the retina, when light strikes the cone receptors that are connected to ganglion cells. According to the trichromatic theory, light of different wavelengths stimulates the three different types of cones in different ways, and the ratio of the activity of these three receptor types creates our impression of different colors. Color vision is also mediated by opponent processes in the retina, whereby ganglion cells are excited by one wavelength of light and inhibited by another. This arrangement produces two pairs of what seem to be color opposites and can account for red-versus-green and yellow-versus-blue color afterimages.

The activity of neurons in the dorsal stream is quite different from that of neurons in the ventral stream. In the dorsal stream's parietal cortex, the cells are of many types, but all respond to visual information only when movement of the body is to take place.

# THE VISUAL BRAIN IN ACTION

Anatomical and physiological studies of brain systems leave one key question unanswered: How do all the cells in these systems act together to produce a particular function? One way to answer this question is to evaluate what happens when parts of the visual system are dysfunctional. Then we can see how these parts contribute to the workings of the whole. We will use this strategy to examine the neuropsychology of vision—the study of the visual brain in action.

## Injury to the Visual Pathway Leading to the Cortex

Let us begin by seeing what happens when various parts of the visual pathway leading from the eye to the cortex are injured. For instance, destruction of the retina or optic nerve of one eye produces *monocular blindness*, the loss of sight in that eye. Partial destruction of the retina or optic nerve produces a partial loss of sight in one eye, with the loss restricted to the region of the visual field that has severed its connections to the brain. Injuries to the visual pathway beyond the eye also produce blindness. For example, complete cuts of the optic tract, the LGN, or region V1 of the cortex result in **homonymous hemianopia,** which is blindness of one entire side of the visual field, as shown in Figure 8-39A. We already encountered this syndrome in D. B., who had a lesion in region V1. Should a lesion in one of these areas be partial, as is often the case, the result is **quadrantanopia:** destruction of only a part of the visual field. This condition is illustrated in Figure 8-39B.

**Homonymous hemianopia.** Blindness of an entire left or right visual field.

**Quadrantanopia.** Blindness of one quadrant of the visual field.

Figure 8-39C shows that small lesions in the occipital lobe often produce small blind spots, known as **scotomas,** in the visual field. Curiously, people are often totally unaware of scotomas for several reasons, one being tiny, involuntary eye movements called *nystagmus,* which we make almost constantly. Because of this usually constant eye motion, a scotoma moves about the visual field, allowing the brain to perceive all the information in that field. If the eyes are temporarily held still, the visual system actually compensates for a scotoma by "completing" the people and objects in the visual world—filling in the hole, so to speak. The result is a seemingly normal set of perceptions.

The visual system may cover up a scotoma so successfully that its presence can be demonstrated to the patient only by "tricking" the visual system. This can be done by placing an object entirely within the scotoma and, without allowing the patient to shift gaze, asking what the object is. If the patient reports seeing nothing, the examiner moves the object out of the scotoma so that it suddenly "appears" in the intact region of the visual field, thus demonstrating the existence of a blind area. This is similar to the technique used to demonstrate the presence of the blind spot that is due to the optic disc. When a person is looking at an object with only one eye, the brain compensates for this scotoma in the same way as it does for the optic-disc blind spot. As a result, the person does not notice the scotoma.

As you may have deduced by now, the type of blindness that a person suffers gives clues about where in the visual pathway the cause of the problem lies. If there is a loss of vision in one eye only, the problem must be in that eye or its optic nerve; but if there is loss of vision in both eyes, the problem is most likely in the brain. Many people have difficulty understanding why a person with

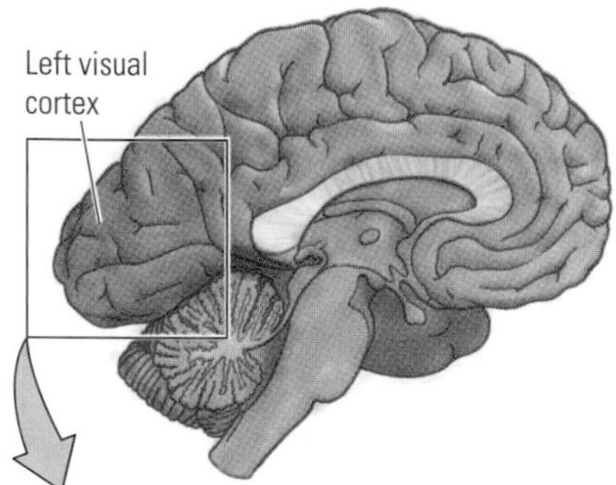

**(A)** Hemianopia

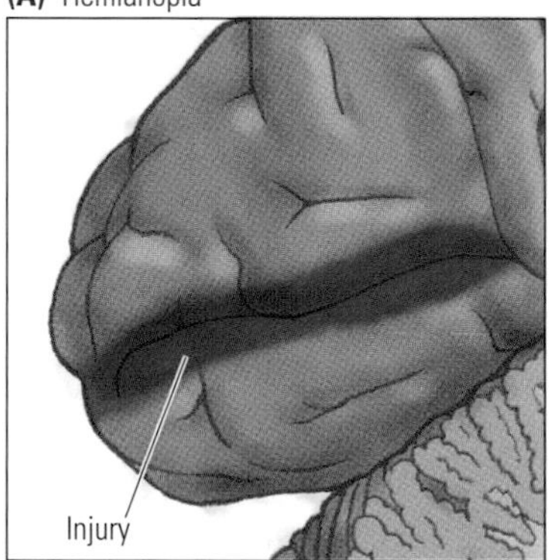


Left visual field

Right visual field

**(B)** Quadrantanopia

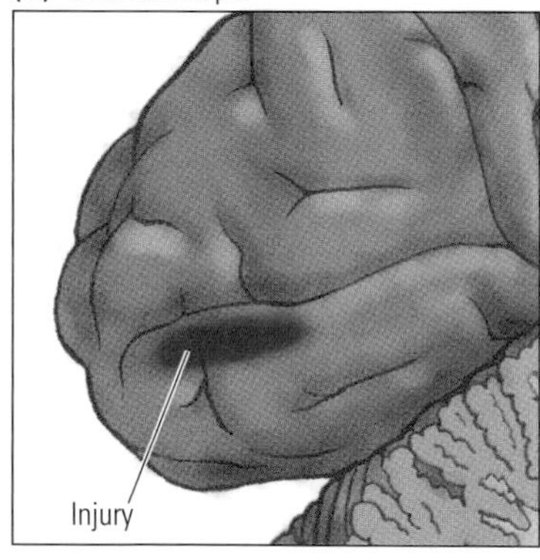

**(C)** Scotoma

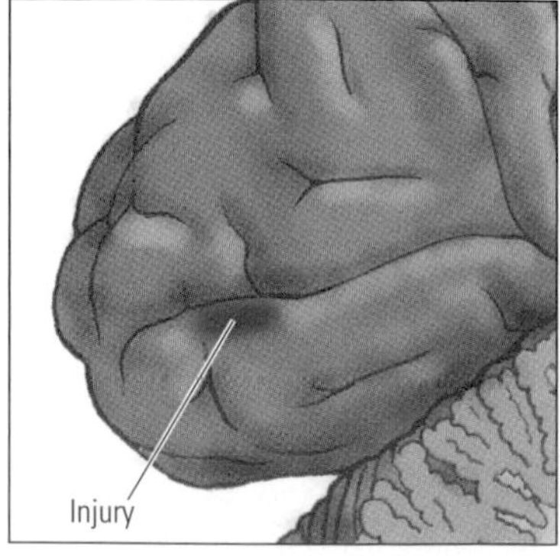

Jim Pickerell/Stock Connection/PictureQuest

**Figure 8-39**

The consequences of lesions in layer V1. The shaded areas indicate the regions of visual loss. **(A)** The effect of a complete lesion of V1 in the left hemisphere is hemianopia affecting the right visual field. **(B)** A large lesion of the lower lip of the calcarine fissure produces quadrantanopia that affects most of the upper-right visual quadrant. **(C)** A smaller lesion of the lower lip of the calcarine fissure results in a smaller scotoma.

damage to the visual cortex has difficulty with both eyes. They fail to remember that it is the visual field, not the eye, that is represented in the brain.

Beyond region V1, the nature of visual loss caused by injury is considerably more complex. It is also very different in the ventral and dorsal streams. We therefore look at each of these pathways separately.

**Scotoma.** Small blind spot in the visual field caused by a small lesion, an epileptic focus, or migraines of the visual cortex.

**Visual-form agnosia.** The inability to recognize objects or drawings of objects.

## Injury to the "What" Pathway

While taking a shower, D. F., a 35-year-old woman, suffered carbon monoxide poisoning from a faulty gas-fueled water heater. Although carbon monoxide poisoning can cause several kinds of neurological damage, as discussed in "Carbon Monoxide Poisoning" on page 313, the result in D. F. was an extensive lesion of the lateral occipital region, including cortical tissue in the ventral visual pathway. The principal deficit that D. F. experienced was a severe inability to recognize objects, real or drawn, which is known as **visual-form agnosia** (see Farah, 1990). (*Agnosia* literally means "not knowing," so a person with an agnosia has essentially no knowledge about some perceptual phenomenon.) A visual-form agnosia is an inability to recognize visual forms, whereas a color agnosia is an inability to recognize colors, and a face agnosia is an inability to recognize faces. Not only was D. F. unable to recognize objects, especially line drawings of objects, she could not estimate their size or their orientation; nor could she copy drawings of objects. Yet, interestingly, as Figure 8-40 illustrates, even though D. F. could not copy drawings of objects, she could draw reasonable facsimiles of objects from memory. But, when doing so, she did not recognize what she was drawing. D. F. clearly had a lesion that interfered with her ventral stream "what" pathway.

Visit the area on the higher-order visual cortex in the Visual System module of your CD to watch video clips from patients with damage to their visual pathways.

It is remarkable that, despite her inability to identify objects or to estimate their size and orientation, D. F. still retained the capacity to appropriately shape her hand when reaching out to grasp something. This capacity is illustrated in Figure 8-1. Mel Goodale, David Milner, and their research colleagues (1991) have studied D. F. extensively for the past few years, and they have devised a way to demonstrate D. F.'s skill at reaching for objects. Figure 8-41 shows the grasp patterns of a control subject (S. H.) when she picks up something irregularly shaped. S. H. grasps the object along one of two different axes that makes it easiest to pick up. When D. F. is presented with the same task, she is as good as S. H. at placing her index finger and thumb on appropriately opposed "grasp" points. Clearly, D. F. remains able to use the structural features

David Milner Mel Goodale

**Figure 8-40**

Examples of the inability of D. F. to recognize and copy line drawings. She was not able to recognize either of the two drawings on the left. Nor, as the middle column shows, was she able to make recognizable copies of those drawings. She was, however, able to draw reasonable renditions from memory, although, when she was later shown her drawings, she had no idea what they were.

Adapted from *The Visual Brain in Action* (p. 127), by A. D. Milner and M. A. Goodale, 1995, Oxford: Oxford University Press.

of objects to control her visually guided grasping movements, even though she is unable to "perceive" these same features. This result demonstrates that we are consciously aware of only a small part of the sensory processing that goes on in the brain.

D. F.'s lesion is quite far posterior in the ventral visual pathway. Lesions that are located more anteriorly produce other types of deficits, depending on the exact location. For example, J. I., whose case has been described by Oliver Sacks and Robert Wasserman (1987), was an artist who became color-blind owing to a cortical lesion presumed to be in region V4. His principal symptom was an inability to distinguish any colors whatsoever, yet his vision appeared otherwise unaffected. Similarly, L. M., a woman described by J. Zihl and his colleagues (1983), lost her ability to detect movement after suffering a lesion presumed to be in region V5. In her case, objects either vanished when they moved or appeared frozen despite their movement. L. M. had particular difficulty pouring tea into a cup, because the fluid appeared to be frozen in

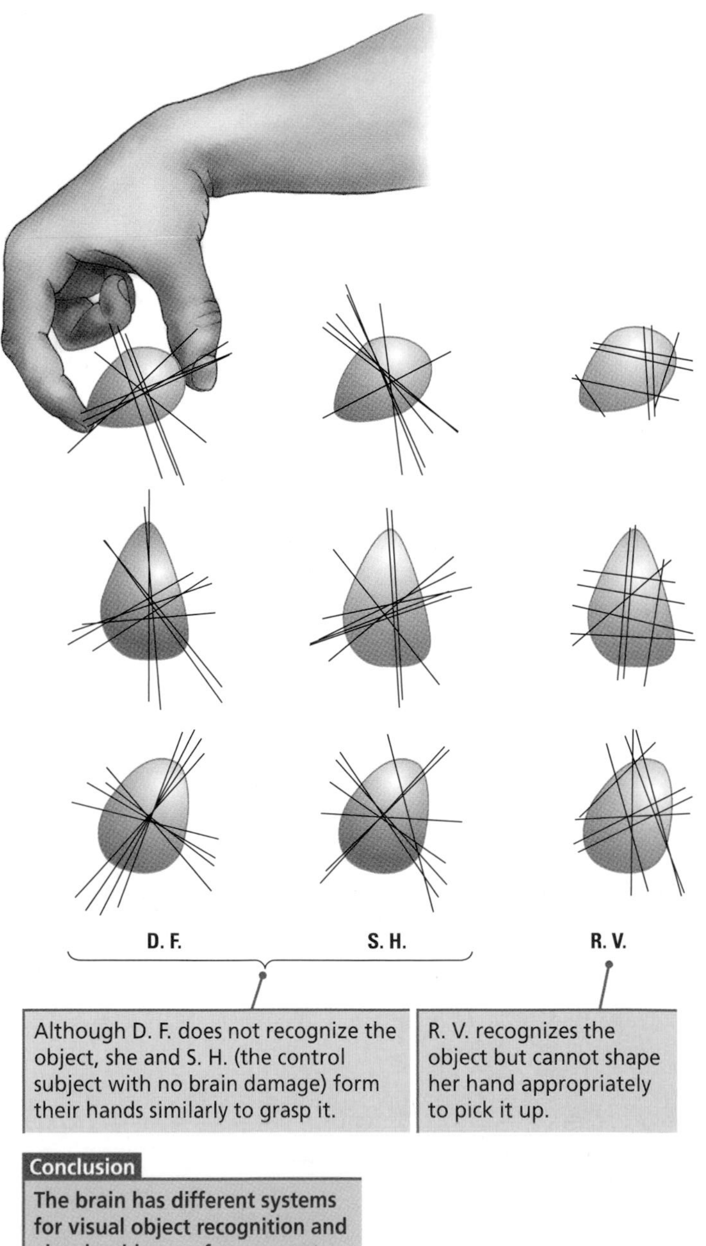

D. F.
S. H.
R. V.
Although D. F. does not recognize the object, she and S. H. (the control subject with no brain damage) form their hands similarly to grasp it.
R. V. recognizes the object but cannot shape her hand appropriately to pick it up.
Conclusion
The brain has different systems for visual object recognition and visual guidance of movement.


**Figure 8-41**

Representative "grasping" axes involving three different shapes for patient D. F., who has visual-form agnosia, a control subject S. H., and patient R. V., who suffered bilateral occipital parietal damage. Each line passes through the points where the index finger and thumb first made contact with the perimeter of the shape on individual trials in which the subjects were instructed to pick up the shape. Notice that D. F., who is unable to discriminate between any of these shapes when they are presented as pairs in a same–different task, places her finger and thumb on appropriately opposed points on either side of the shape. In contrast, R. V. chose very unstable grasp points, and the grasp lines often do not pass through the center of mass of the object. Thus, even though D. F. cannot "perceive" the shape of the object, she is able to use information about shape to control the posture and position of her fingers as she picks up the object. In contrast, R. V. can perceive the shape of the object but cannot control her movements in relation to it.

Adapted from *The Visual Brain in Action* [p. 132], by A. D. Milner and M. A. Goodale, 1995, Oxford: Oxford University Press.

## Focus on Disorders

### Carbon Monoxide Poisoning

As described in the text, D. F. had a lesion of the dorsal stream that resulted from accidental carbon monoxide (CO) poisoning. While D. F. was showering, she was overcome by carbon monoxide fumes from a faulty space heater. It is unclear how long she was exposed to the carbon monoxide, but when her roommate found her, the shower water was cold. Brain damage from carbon monoxide poisoning is usually caused either by a faulty gas heater or by motor vehicle exhaust fumes. The gas is absorbed by the blood, resulting in swelling and bleeding of the lungs and anoxia (a loss of oxygen) in the brain. The cerebral cortex, hippocampus, cerebellum, and striatum are especially sensitive to CO-induced anoxia.

A curious characteristic of carbon monoxide poisoning is that only a small proportion of people who succumb to it have permanent neurological symptoms, and, among those who do have them, the symptoms are highly variable. The most common symptoms are cortical blindness and various forms of agnosia, as seen in D. F. In addition, many of the victims suffer language difficulties.

The peculiarities of the language difficulties are shown clearly in a young woman whose case was described by Norman Geschwind. Geschwind studied this patient for 9 years after her accidental poisoning; she required complete nursing care during this time. She never uttered spontaneous speech and did not comprehend spoken language. Nonetheless, she could repeat with perfect accuracy sentences that had just been said to her. She could also complete certain well-known phrases. For example, if she heard "Roses are red," she would say "Roses are red, violets are blue, sugar is sweet, and so are you." Even odder was her ability to learn new songs. She did not appear to understand the content of the songs; yet, with only a few repetitions of a new song, she would begin to sing along with it and, eventually, she could sing the song spontaneously, making no errors in either words or melody.

Postmortem examination of this woman's brain, shown here, found that, although she had extensive damage to the parietal and temporal lobes, her speech areas were intact. Geschwind proposed that she could not comprehend speech because the words that she heard did not arouse associations in other parts of her cortex. She could, however, repeat sentences because the internal connections of the speech regions were undamaged. Geschwind did not comment on whether this woman suffered from agnosia, but it seems likely that she did. The difficulty would be in diagnosing agnosia in a person who is unable to communicate.

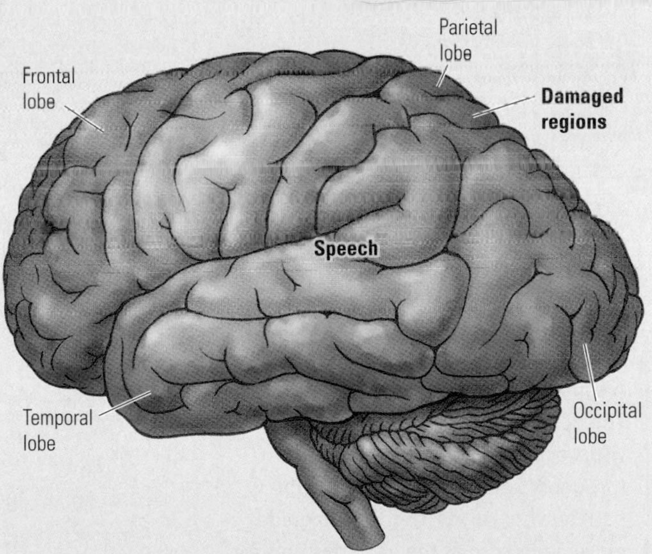


Areas damaged by carbon monoxide poisoning are shown in red in this postmortem diagram of the brain of Geschwind's patient.

mid-air. Yet she could read and write and recognize objects, and she appeared to have normal form vision—that is, until objects moved.

These various cases demonstrate that cortical injuries in the ventral stream all somehow interfere with the determination of "what" things are or are like. In each case, the symptoms are somewhat different, however, which is thought to be indicative of damage to different subregions or substreams of the ventral visual pathway.

**Optic ataxia.** Deficit in the visual control of reaching and other movements.

## Injury to the "How" Pathway

In 1909, R. Balint described a bilateral parietal lesion that was associated with rather peculiar visual symptoms. The patient had full visual fields and could recognize, use, and name objects, pictures, and colors normally. But he had a severe deficit in visually guided reaching, even though he could still make accurate movements directed toward his own body (presumably guided by tactile or proprioceptive feedback from his joints). Balint called this syndrome **optic ataxia.**

Since Balint's time, there have many descriptions of optic ataxia associated with parietal injury. Mel Goodale has studied several such patients, one of whom is a woman identified as R. V. In contrast with patient D. F. with her visual-form agnosia, R. V. had normal perception of line drawings, objects, and so on, but she could not guide her hand to reach for objects. Figure 8-41 shows that when R. V. was asked to pick up the same irregularly shaped objects that D. F. could grasp normally, she often failed to place her fingers on the appropriate grasp points, even though she could distinguish the objects easily. In other words, although her perception of the features of an object was normal for the task of describing that object, her perception was not normal for the task of visually guiding her hand to reach for the object.

To summarize, people with damage to the parietal cortex in the dorsal visual stream can "see" perfectly well, yet they cannot accurately guide their movements on the basis of visual information. This is the function of the dorsal stream. In contrast, people with damage to the ventral stream cannot "see" objects, because the perception of objects is a ventral-stream function. Yet these same people can guide their movements to objects on the basis of visual information. The first kind of patient, like R. V., has an intact ventral stream that analyzes the visual characteristics of objects. The second kind of patient, like D. F., has an intact dorsal stream that visually directs movements. By comparing the two types of cases, we can infer the visual functions of the dorsal and ventral streams.

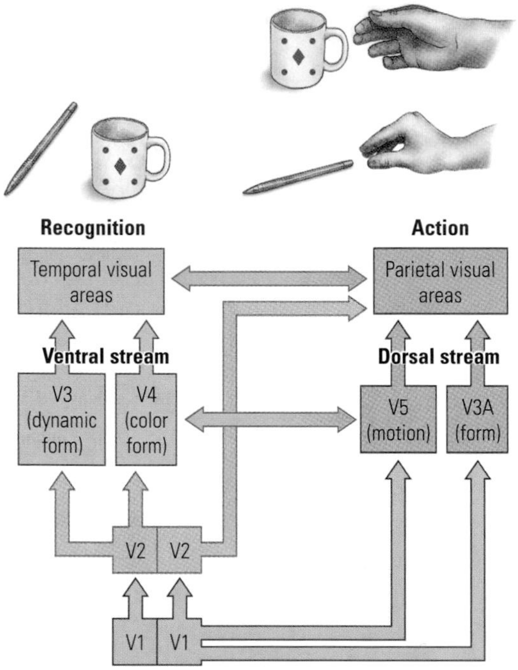

**Figure 8-42**

A summary of the two visual streams. The dorsal stream, which takes part in visual action, begins in V1 and flows through V5 and V3A to the posterior parietal visual areas. Its role is to guide movements such as the hand postures for grasping a mug or pen as illustrated. The ventral stream, which takes part in object recognition, begins in V1 and flows through V2 to V3 and V4 to the temporal visual areas. Its job is to identify things such as objects in our visual world. The double-headed arrows show that information flows back and forth between the dorsal and ventral streams.

### In Review

As Figure 8-42 shows, there are two relatively independent streams of visual processing: the dorsal and ventral streams. Our visual experience is largely a result of visual processing in the ventral stream, but much of our visually guided behavior is a result of activity in the dorsal stream. An important lesson here is that we are conscious of only a small amount of what the brain actually does, even though we usually have the impression of being in control of all our thoughts and behaviors. Apparently, this impression of "free will" is partly an illusion.

## SUMMARY

We began this chapter with D. B.'s surprising ability to locate lights in the blind side of his visual field. This ability makes clear that our sensory world is not unitary, despite what our conscious experience suggests. To understand the nature of sensory experience, and vision in particular, we dissected the visual system into its parts. Our next task was to identify what the cells in the different parts do. Finally, we examined the way in which the parts work together to produce vision for action in the world. We can now answer some basic questions about the visual system's organization.

1. *How does the brain transform light energy into our impression of the visual world?* Like all sensory systems, vision begins with receptors that convert sensory energy (such as light waves) into neural activity. The visual receptors (rods and cones) are located in the retina at the back of the eye. The rods and cones are structurally and functionally different. Rods are sensitive to dim light, whereas cones are sensitive to bright light and are responsible for color vision. There are three types of cones, each of which is maximally sensitive to a different wavelength of light. They are often referred to as blue, green, and red cones. The name refers not to the color of light that the cone sees but rather to the wavelength of light to which it is *maximally sensitive.*
2. *How does visual information get from receptors in the retina to the brain?* Retinal ganglion cells receive input from photoreceptors through bipolar cells, and the axons of the ganglion cells send their axons out of the eye to form the optic nerve. There are two categories of ganglion cells, P and M, each of which sends a different kind of message to the brain. The P cells receive input mostly from cones and convey information about color and fine detail. The M cells receive input from rods and convey information about light but not color. The optic nerve forms two distinct routes into the brain: the geniculostriate and tectopulvinar pathways. The geniculostriate pathway synapses first in the lateral geniculate nucleus of the thalamus and then in the primary visual cortex. The tectopulvinar pathway synapses first in the superior colliculus of the midbrain's tectum, then in the pulvinar of the thalamus, and finally in the visual cortex.
3. *What are the pathways for visual information within the cortex?* There are a number of visual regions in the occipital cortex. Regions V1 and V2 carry out multiple functions, whereas the remaining regions (V3, V3A, V4, and V5) have more specialized functions. Visual information flows from the thalamus to V1 and V2 and then divides to form two distinctly different pathways, which are referred to as the dorsal and ventral streams. The dorsal stream is concerned with the visual guidance of movements, whereas the ventral stream is concerned with the perception of objects.
4. *How are neurons in the visual system organized?* Neurons at each step in the visual pathways produce distinctly different forms of neural activity. The sum of the activity in all regions produces our visual experience. Like all cortical regions, the cortex in the visual regions is organized into functional columns. Each column is a functional unit that is about 0.5 millimeter in diameter and extends the depth of the cortex. Columns in the visual system are specialized for processes such as analyzing lines of a particular orientation.
5. *How does the visual system see shapes?* Neurons in the ventral stream are selective for different characteristics of shapes. For example, cells in the visual cortex are maximally responsive to lines of different orientations, whereas cells in the inferior temporal cortex are responsive to different shapes, which in some cases appear to be abstract and in other cases have forms such as hands or faces.
6. *How does the visual system see colors?* Cones in the retina are maximally responsive to different wavelengths, roughly corresponding to the perception of green, blue, and red. Retinal ganglion cells are opponent-process cells and have a center–surround organization such that cells are excited by one hue and inhibited by another (for example, red versus green; blue versus yellow). Color-sensitive cells in the primary visual cortex, which are located in the blobs, also have opponent-process properties. Cells in region V4 also respond to color, but they do

not respond to particular wavelengths. Rather, they respond to our perceived colors, which are influenced by the brightness of the world and the color of nearby objects.

7. *What happens when the visual system is damaged?* If the eye or optic nerve is injured, there is a complete or partial loss of vision in one eye. When the visual information enters the brain, information from the left and right visual fields goes to the right and left sides of the brain, respectively. As a result, damage to visual areas on one side of the brain results in a visual disturbance in both eyes. Specific visual functions are localized to different regions of the brain, so localized damage to a particular region results in the loss of a particular function. For example, damage to region V4 produces a loss of color constancy, whereas damage to regions in the parietal cortex produces an inability to shape the hand appropriately to grasp objects.

**neuroscience interactive**

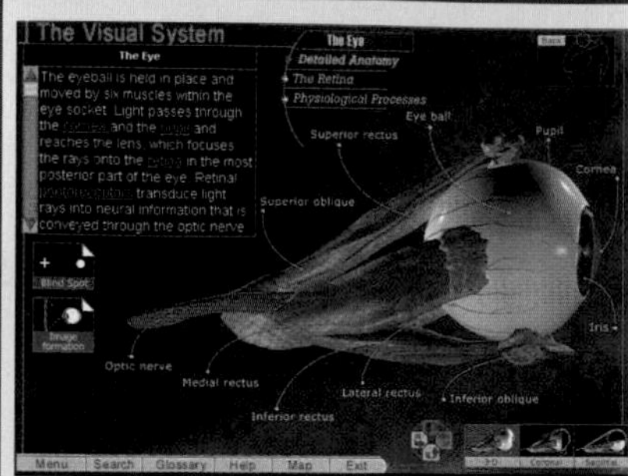


There are many resources available for expanding your learning on line:

- **www.worthpublishers.com/kolb/chapter8**

Try some self-tests to reinforce your mastery of the material. Look at some of the news updates reflecting current research on the brain. You'll also be able to link to other sites which will reinforce what you've learned.

On your CD-ROM you'll be able to quiz yourself on your comprehension of the chapter. The module on the Visual System includes a three-dimensional model of the eye, illustrations of the substructures of the eye and the visual cortex, video clips of patients with visual disorders, and interactive activities to explore how the visual field and color vision are created.

## KEY TERMS

blind spot, p. 282
blob, p. 293
color constancy, p. 308
cone, p. 284
cortical column, p. 292
extrastriate (secondary) cortex, p. 292
fovea, p. 284
geniculostriate system, p. 288
homonymous hemianopia, p. 309
ocular dominance column, p. 305
opponent-process theory, p. 307
optic ataxia, p. 314
optic chiasm, p. 288
primary visual cortex, p. 292
quadrantanopia, p. 309
receptive field, p. 295
retina, p. 281
retinal ganglion cell, p. 287
rod, p. 284
scotoma, p. 310
striate cortex, p. 288
tectopulvinar system, p. 289
trichromatic theory, p. 306
visual field, p. 295
visual-form agnosia, p. 311

## REVIEW QUESTIONS

1. Describe the pathways that visual information follows through the brain.
2. Describe how the M and P cells differ and how they give rise to distinctly different pathways that eventually form the dorsal and ventral visual streams.
3. How do cells in the different levels of the visual system code different types of information?
4. Summarize what you believe to be the one major point of this chapter.

## FOR FURTHER THOUGHT

How does the visual system create a visual world? What differences between people and members of other species would contribute to different impressions of visual reality?

## RECOMMENDED READING

Hubel, D. H. (1988) *Eye, brain, and vision*. New York: Scientific American Library. This book, written by a Nobel laureate for work on vision, is a general survey of how the visual system is organized. Like the other books in the Scientific American Library series, this one has beautiful illustrations that bring the visual system to life.

Milner, A. D., & Goodale, M. A. (1995). *The visual brain in action*. Oxford: Oxford University Press. Milner and Goodale have revolutionized our thinking of how the sensory systems are organized. This little book is a beautiful survey of neuropsychological and neurophysiological studies of the visual system.

Posner, M. I., & Raichle, M. E. (1997). *Images of the mind*. New York: Scientific American Library. This award-winning book is an introduction to the study of cognitive neuroscience, with an emphasis on visual cognitive neuroscience.

Weizkrantz, L. (1986). *Blindsight: A case study and implications*. Oxford: Oxford University Press. Weizkrantz's book about a single patient describes one of the most important case studies in neuropsychology. This book forced investigators to reconsider preconceived notions not only about how sensory systems work, but also about ideas such as consciousness.

Zeki, S. (1993). *A vision of the brain*. Oxford: Blackwell Scientific. Not only is Zeki's book a discussion of how he believes the visual system works, but it also has much broader implications for cortical functioning in general. Zeki is not afraid to be controversial, and the book does not disappoint.

CHAPTER

# 9

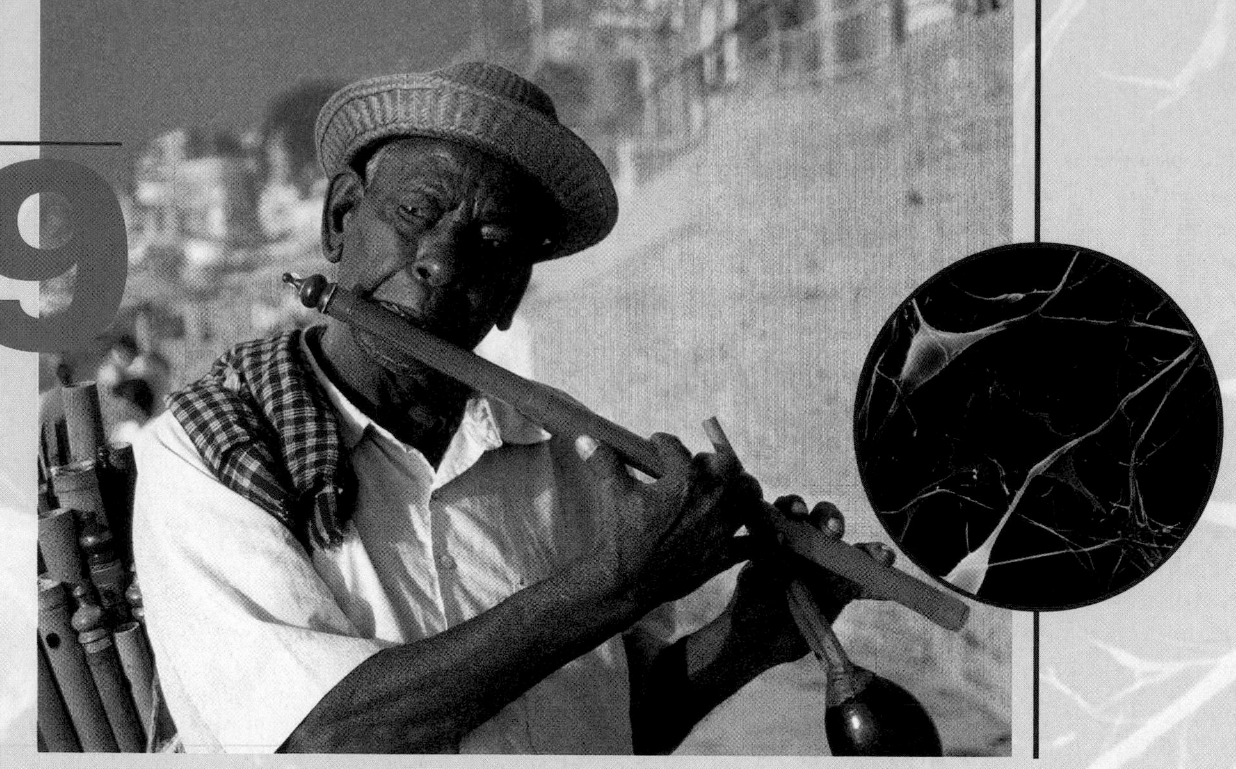

# How Do We Hear, Speak, and Make Music?



Barbara Haynor/Tony Stone
Micrograph: Dr. Dennis Kunkel/Phototake

In 1995, Ivan Turk, a paleontologist at the Slovenian Academy of Sciences in Ljubljana, excavated a cave in northern Slovenia that Neanderthals once used as a hunting camp. Neanderthals have long fascinated researchers, in part because they are considered to be the last truly "primitive" members of the genus *Homo*. Neanderthals (*Homo neanderthalensis*) originated approximately 230,000 years ago and disappeared some 200,000 years later. During that time, they coexisted with early modern humans (*Homo sapiens*), whom they resembled in many ways. In some locations, the two groups may have even shared resources and tools. But researchers had assumed that Neanderthal culture was significantly less developed than that of early modern humans. Although the Neanderthals did bury their dead with artifacts, which implies that they may have held spiritual beliefs, there is no evidence that they made cave paintings, as *Homo sapiens* did beginning near the end of the Neanderthal era. Perhaps even more important, some skeletal analyses suggest that, whatever language ability Neanderthals had, they were far less fluent than the *Homo sapiens* who lived at the same time.

This view of the Neanderthals as culturally "primitive" is what made one of Turk's discoveries so surprising and intriguing. Buried in the cave among a cache of stone tools was the leg bone of a young bear that looked as if it had been fashioned into a flute. As shown in Figure 9-1, the bone had holes aligned along one of its sides that could not have been made by gnawing animals. The holes were spaced unevenly, resembling the holes on a modern flute. But this flute was at least 43,000 years old—perhaps as old as 82,000 years. All the evidence suggested that Neanderthals, not modern humans, had made the instrument. Was music, then, a creation not just of *Homo sapiens* but of *Homo neanderthalensis,* too?

To help find out, Bob Fink, a musicologist, analyzed the flute for its musical capabilities. He found that a scale could be played on the flute, similar to our do-re-mi scale; but relative to the scale most familiar to us, one of the notes was slightly off. That note is called a "blue note" in jazz and is found in scales throughout Africa and India.

The similarity between the Neanderthal musical scale and one of our modern musical scales encourages us to speculate about the brain that made this ancient flute. The human brain has a specialized region in the right temporal lobe for analyzing music, and the Neanderthal flute suggests that its maker had this region, too. Furthermore, in the modern human brain, the specialization for analyzing music in the right temporal lobe is complemented by a specialization for analyzing speech

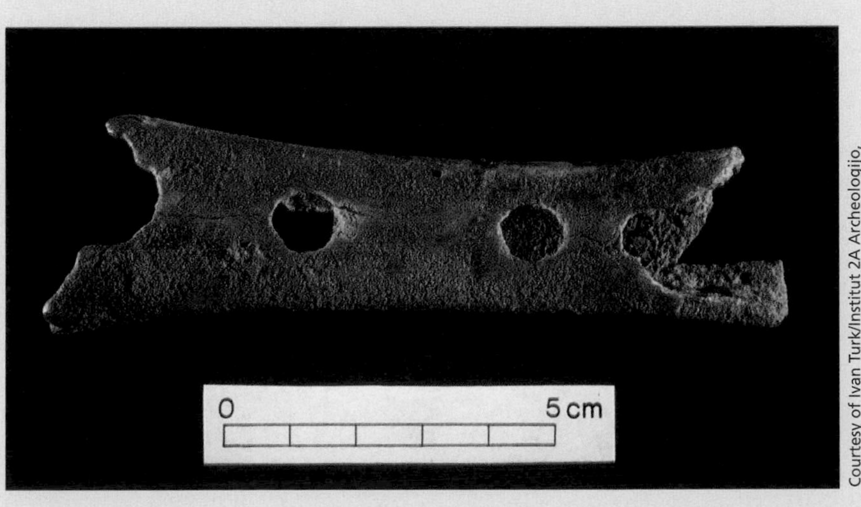


**Figure 9-1**
A piece of bear femur found in the cemented sediment on the ancient floor of a cave in Slovenia, apparently used by Neanderthals as a hunting camp. The alignment of the holes suggests that they were made not by gnawing animals but by ancient people. An analysis of the distances between the holes indicates that they match those of a modern-day flute, which suggests that Neanderthals made music.

sounds in the left temporal lobe. We are therefore left to wonder if the evolutionary development of music and language may have been simultaneous. In other words, early in human evolution, the left temporal lobe may have become specialized for analyzing speech sounds while the right temporal lobe became specialized for analyzing musical sounds. If this is so, then perhaps the Neanderthals had the beginnings of a left-hemisphere specialization for language in addition to the start of a right-hemisphere specialization for music. Consequently, they may have had both more language skills and more cultural development than formerly assumed.

Spoken language and musical ability are not just linked as complementary systems in the brain. They are also linked conceptually because both are based on the use of sound. So, to understand how humans engage in each of these behaviors, we must first examine the nature of sound and how the human ear and nervous system are structured to detect it. We then ask how the human brain is designed to analyze both language and music. Finally, we look at two examples of how other species use auditory stimuli for specific functions: communication through song by birds and navigation through sonar by bats.

## AN INTRODUCTION TO SOUND

**Hertz.** A measure of frequency; one hertz is equal to one cycle per second.

Sound is a creation of the brain and does not exist without it, as you learned in Chapter 8. When a tree falls in the forest, it makes no sound unless someone is there to hear it. What a falling tree makes are merely changes in air pressure. These pressure changes take the form of waves generated by vibrating air molecules.

One way to produce these so-called *sound waves* is to strike a tuning fork. The vibrating prongs of the fork displace the adjacent air molecules. Figure 9-2 shows that, as one prong moves to the left, it compresses (makes more dense) the air molecules to the left of it and rarefies (makes less dense) the air molecules to the right of it. The opposite happens when the prong moves to the right. This displacement of air molecules causes waves of changing air pressure to emanate from the fork. These waves are sound waves.

We can represent the waves of changing air pressure emanating from the tuning fork by plotting air-molecule density against time at a single point at the right-hand side of the fork. Such a graph is shown at the top of Figure 9-3. The bottom graph in

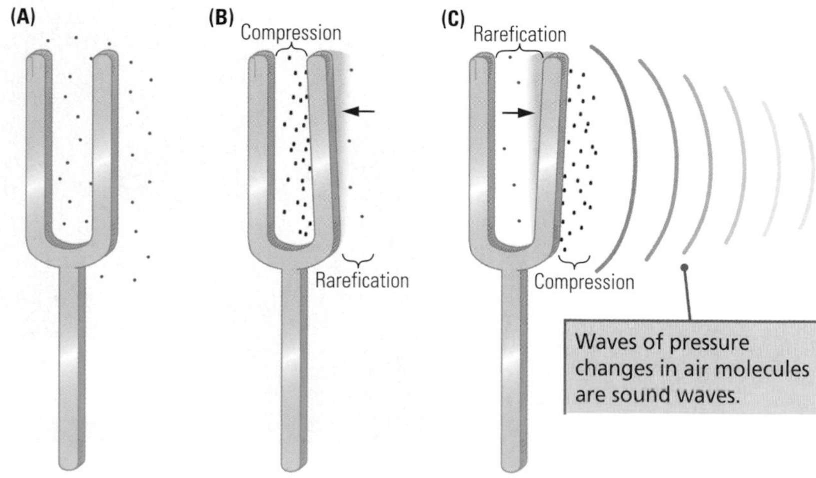


**Figure 9-2**

How a tuning fork produces sound. **(A)** When the fork is still, the air molecules are distributed randomly around it. **(B)** The right arm of the fork moves to the left, causing the air to be compressed on the leading edge and rarefied on the trailing edge. **(C)** The arm moves to the right, compressing the air to the right and rarefying the air to the left.

Figure 9-3 shows how the right-hand prong of the fork moves to create the air-pressure changes associated with a single cycle. A *cycle* is one complete peak or valley on the graph—that is, the change from one maximum or minimum air-pressure level to the next.

**Figure 9-3**

Air molecule density plotted against time at a particular point to the right of the tuning fork. The resulting cyclical wave is referred to as a sine wave.

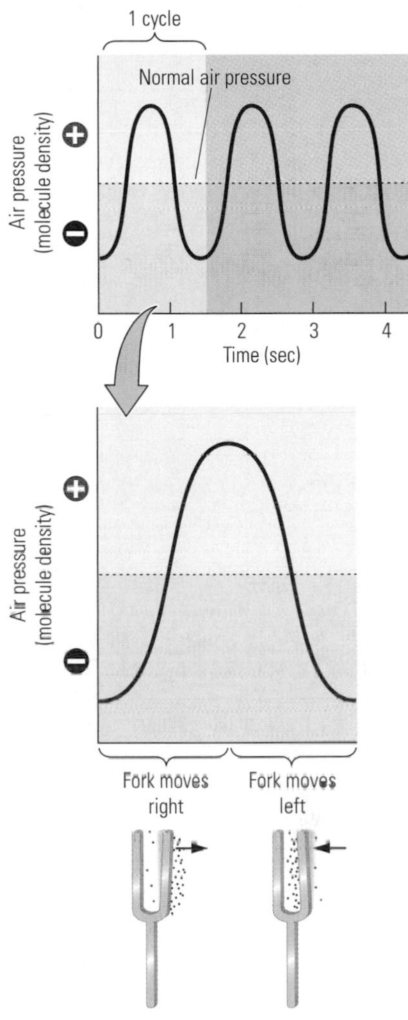


## The Basic Qualities of Sound Waves

The sound waves produced by the displacement of air have three qualities: frequency, amplitude, and complexity. These properties are summarized in Figure 9-4. The auditory system analyzes each of these properties separately, just as the visual system analyzes color and form separately. After examining these three properties of sound in some detail, we will consider how we perceive sounds and interpret them as language and music.

### SOUND FREQUENCY

Although sound travels at a fixed speed of 1100 feet per second, sound waves vary in the rate at which they vibrate, called their frequency. More precisely, **frequency** refers to the number of cycles of a wave that are completed in a given amount of time. Sound-wave frequencies are measured in units of cycles per second called **hertz** (Hz), named after the German physicist Heinrich Rudolph Hertz. One hertz is one cycle per second; 50 hertz is 50 cycles per second; 6000 hertz is 6000 cycles per second; 20,000 hertz is 20,000 cycles per second; and so on. Figure 9-4 shows that sounds that we perceive as being low in *pitch* have low frequencies (few cycles per second), whereas sounds that we perceive as being high in pitch have high frequencies (many cycles per second).

Just as we can perceive light of only certain wavelengths, we can perceive sounds in only a limited range of frequencies. For humans, this range is from about 20 to 20,000 hertz. Like humans, many animals produce some form of sound to communicate, which means that they must have auditory systems designed to interpret their

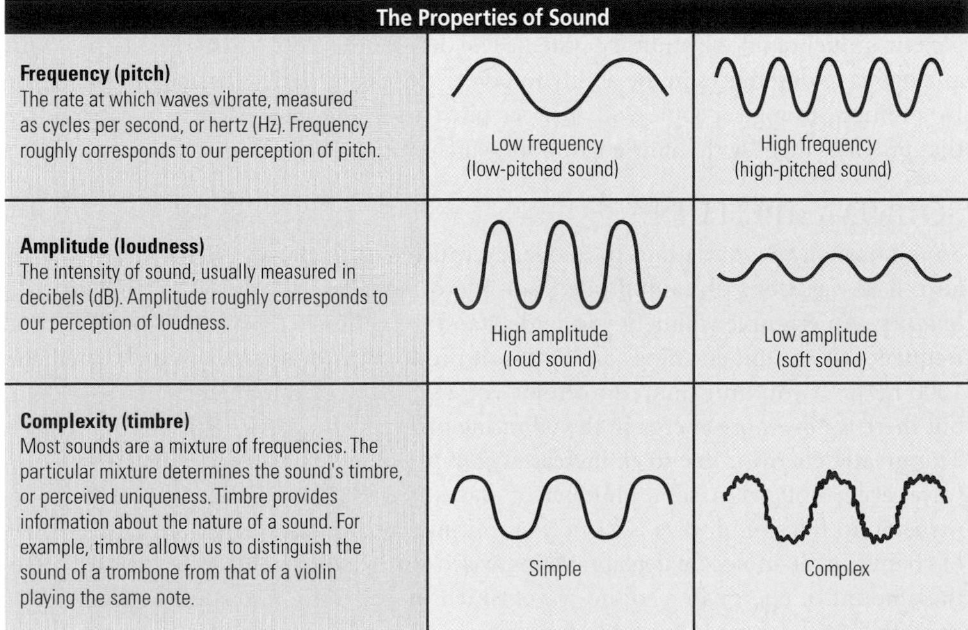

| The Properties of Sound | | |
|---|---|---|
| **Frequency (pitch)** The rate at which waves vibrate, measured as cycles per second, or hertz (Hz). Frequency roughly corresponds to our perception of pitch. | Low frequency (low-pitched sound) | High frequency (high-pitched sound) |
| **Amplitude (loudness)** The intensity of sound, usually measured in decibels (dB). Amplitude roughly corresponds to our perception of loudness. | High amplitude (loud sound) | Low amplitude (soft sound) |
| **Complexity (timbre)** Most sounds are a mixture of frequencies. The particular mixture determines the sound's timbre, or perceived uniqueness. Timbre provides information about the nature of a sound. For example, timbre allows us to distinguish the sound of a trombone from that of a violin playing the same note. | Simple | Complex |

**Figure 9-4**

Sound has three physical dimensions: frequency, amplitude, and complexity. These dimensions correspond to the perceptual dimensions of pitch, loudness, and timbre.

species-typical sounds. After all, there is no point in making complicated songs or calls if other members of the species cannot hear them. The ranges of sound frequencies that different species use vary quite extensively. Figure 9-5 shows that some species (such as frogs and birds) have rather narrow ranges, whereas others (such as whales and humans) have broad ranges. Some species use extremely high frequencies, whereas others use low ones (compare bats and fish, for instance). It is quite an achievement for the auditory systems of whales and dolphins to be able to respond to sounds of such widely varying frequencies. The characteristics of these different frequencies allow them to be used in different ways. For example, very-low-frequency sound waves travel long distances in water, so whales produce them as a form of underwater communication over miles of distance. In contrast, high-frequency sounds create echoes and form the basis of sonar, so dolphins produce them in bursts, listening for the echoes that bounce back from objects and help the dolphins to locate fish.

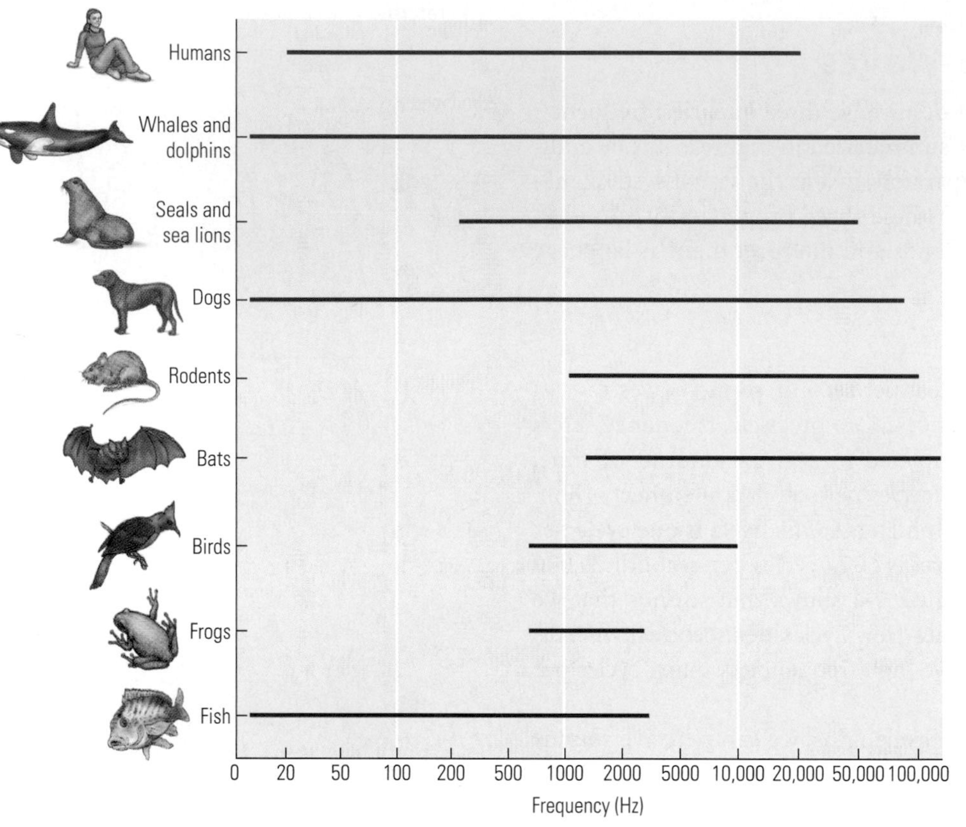


**Figure 9-5**

Hearing ranges of different animals. Frogs hear only a very narrow range of frequencies, whereas whales and dolphins have an extensive range. Although the human range of hearing is fairly broad, peaking at about 20,000 hertz, humans are unable to perceive many of the sounds that other animals can both make and hear.

As stated earlier, we hear differences in the frequency of sound waves as differences in pitch. Consequently, each note in the musical scale must have a different frequency because each has a different pitch. Middle C on the piano, for instance, has a frequency of 264 hertz. Although most people can discriminate between one musical note and another, some people are able to name any note (A, B flat, C sharp, and so forth) that they hear. This ability is referred to as *perfect pitch*, or *absolute pitch*. People with perfect pitch are more likely than not to have a family member who also has perfect pitch, suggesting that the ability is caused by some genetic influence on the auditory system. The difference in the auditory system may be analogous to differences in the ability to perceive the color red, discussed in Chapter 8. In addition, though, people with perfect pitch probably have early musical training that provides them with knowledge about which pitch goes with which note.

## SOUND AMPLITUDE

Sound not only has variations in frequency, causing differences in perceived pitch, but also has variations in amplitude, causing differences in perceived *intensity*, or *loudness*. An example will help you understand the difference between amplitude and frequency. If you hit a tuning fork lightly, it produces a tone with a frequency of, say, 1000 hertz. If you hit it more forcefully, you still produce a frequency of 1000 hertz, but there is now more energy in the vibrating prong, so it moves farther left and right. This greater energy is due to an increased *quantity* of air molecules compacted in each wave, even though the same number of waves is created every second. The new dimension to the sound wave is its new **amplitude,** a term that refers to the magnitude of change in air-molecule density. An increased compaction of air molecules increases the amount of energy in a sound wave, which makes the sound seem louder—more amplified. Differences in sound amplitude can be graphically illustrated by increasing the height of a sound wave, as shown in Figure 9-4.

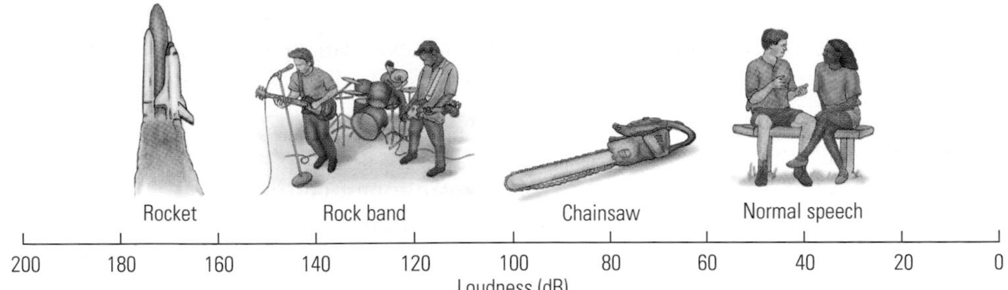


Sound amplitude is usually measured in *decibels* (dB), which describe the strength of a sound relative to a standard reference intensity. Sounds greater than about 70 decibels we perceive as loud, whereas those less than about 20 decibels we perceive as quiet. Normal speech sounds are about 40 decibels.

Because the human nervous system is sensitive to weak sounds, it is literally "blown away" by extremely strong ones. It is common for people to damage their hearing by exposure to very loud sounds (such as rifle fire at close range) or even by prolonged exposure to sounds that are only relatively loud (such as rock music in concert). As a rule of thumb, sounds louder than 100 decibels are likely to damage our hearing, especially if they are prolonged. Some bands, especially heavy-metal groups, routinely play music higher than 120 decibels and sometimes as high as 135 decibels. One researcher (Drake-Lee, 1992) found that rock musicians had a significant loss of sensitivity to sound, especially at about 6000 hertz. After a typical 90-minute concert, this loss was temporarily far worse—as much as a 40-fold increase in sound pressure was needed to reach a musician's hearing threshold.

## SOUND COMPLEXITY

Sounds with a single frequency are **pure tones**, but most sounds are not single frequencies. Most sounds are made up of combinations of frequencies and so are called **complex tones.** A complex tone is a sound with a basic waveform that is repeated periodically, but a complex tone is more complicated than a pure tone. Complex tones contain at least two pure tones and often many more.

To better understand the nature of a complex tone, consider the sound of a clarinet playing a steady note. Figure 9-6 (top) represents the sound wave that the clarinet produces. Notice that this wave has a more complex pattern than those of the simple waves described earlier: even when a single note is played, the clarinet is making a complex tone, not a pure tone. Using a technique known as Fourier analysis, we can break this complex tone into its many component pure tones, as shown in Figure 9-6 (bottom). The *fundamental frequency* is the rate at which the basic pattern of the complex waveform is repeated. *Overtones* are higher-frequency waves that are multiples of the fundamental frequency. Different musical instruments produce overtones of different amplitudes. For the clarinet in Figure 9-6, wave 5 is of low amplitude, whereas wave 2 is of high amplitude.

Christian Ducasse/Gamma-Liaison

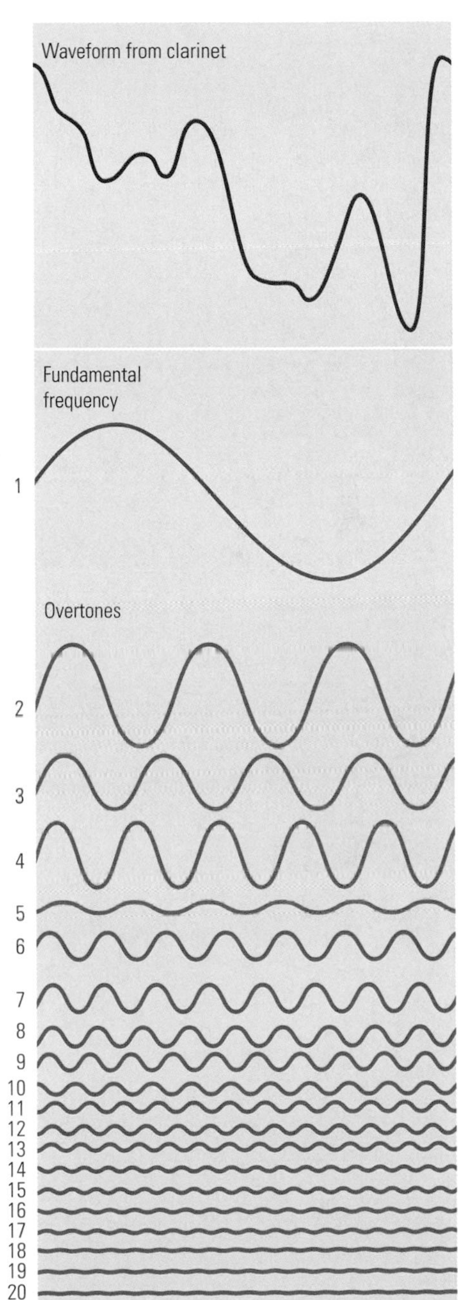


**Figure 9-6**

The shape of a complex sound wave from Don Byron's clarinet (*top*) and the component frequencies—the fundamental frequency (*middle*) and overtones (*bottom*)—that make up the complex sound wave.

Stereo Review, copyright 1977 by Diamandis Communications Inc.

Pure tones can be combined into complex tones in an almost infinite variety of ways. In addition to musical instruments, other examples of complex tone sources are the human voice, birdsong, and certain machines having rhythmic or repetitive mechanisms that give rise to buzzing or humming sounds. A key feature of complex tones, besides being made up of two or more pure tones, is some sort of periodicity, or repetition of the fundamental frequency. Sounds that are aperiodic, or random, are known as *noise*.

## The Perception of Sound

The auditory system's task is to convert the air-pressure changes associated with sound waves into neural activity that travels to the brain. This task is accomplished through a series of steps to be described shortly. The critical point here is that waves of air-pressure changes are transformed into neural activity, which we then perceive as sounds. Remember that the waves themselves make no sounds. The sounds that we hear are only a product of the brain.

To better understand the relation between energy waves and sound perceptions, consider this analogy. When you toss a pebble into a pond, waves emanate from the point where the pebble enters the water. These waves produce no audible sound. But what would happen if your skin were able to convert the action of the waves in the water into neural activity that stimulated your auditory system? When you placed your hand into the rippling water, you would "hear" the waves, and, when you removed your hand, the "sound" would stop. The pebble hitting the water is much like a falling tree, and the waves that emanate from the pebble's point of entry are like the air-pressure waves that emanate from the place where the tree strikes the ground. The frequency of the waves determines the pitch of the sound heard by the brain, whereas the size (amplitude) of the waves determines the sound's loudness.

Our sensitivity to sound waves is extraordinary. At the threshold of hearing, we can detect the displacement of air molecules of about 10 picometers ($10^{-11}$ meter). We are rarely in an environment where we can detect such a small air-pressure change, because there is usually too much background noise. A very quiet rural setting is probably as close as we ever get to an environment suited to testing the acuteness of our hearing. So, the next time you visit the countryside, take note of the sounds that you can hear. If there is no sound competition, you can often hear a single car engine literally miles away.

In addition to detecting very small changes in air pressure, the auditory system is also very adept at simultaneously perceiving different sounds. As you sit reading this chapter, you are able to differentiate all sorts of sounds around you, such as traffic on the street, people talking next door, your computer's fan humming, and footsteps in the hall. Similarly, as you listen to music, you are able to detect the sounds of different instruments and voices. You can perceive different sounds simultaneously because the different frequencies of air-pressure change associated with each sound stimulate different neurons in your auditory system.

The perception of sounds is only the beginning of your auditory experience. Your brain interprets sounds to obtain information about events in your environment, and it analyzes a sound's meaning. These processes are clearly illustrated in your use of sound to communicate with other people through both language and music.

## Language and Music as Sounds

Language and music differ from other auditory inputs in several fundamental ways. First, both speech and musical sounds convey special meaning. The analysis of meaning in sound is considerably more complex than simply the detection of a sound's presence. To analyze speech and musical sounds for meaning, the brain has had to develop special systems. As you learned at the beginning of this chapter, these special systems lie in the left and right temporal lobes, respectively.

Another characteristic that distinguishes speech and musical sounds from other auditory inputs is the speed at which a series of these sounds arrives at our auditory receptors. Nonspeech and nonmusical noise is perceived as a buzz that occurs at a rate of about 5 segments per second. (A sound segment is a distinct unit of sound.) Normal speech is faster than this, on the order of 8 to 10 segments per second, and we are capable of understanding speech at rates of nearly 30 segments per second. Speech perception at these higher rates is truly amazing, because the speed of input far exceeds the auditory system's ability to transmit all the speech as separate pieces of information. Experience in listening to a particular language helps the brain to analyze rapid speech, which is one reason why unfamiliar languages often sound so incredibly fast when you hear them spoken. Your brain does not know where the foreign words end and begin, making them seem to run together in a rapid-fire stream.

A unique characteristic of our perception of speech sounds is our tendency to hear the variations of a sound as identical sounds, even though the sound varies considerably from one context to another. For instance, the English letter "d" is pronounced differently in the words "deep," "deck," and "duke," yet a listener perceives the pronunciations to be the same "d" sound. The auditory system must therefore have a mechanism for categorizing sounds as being the same despite small differences in pronunciation. This mechanism, moreover, must be affected by experience, because different languages categorize speech sounds differently. A major obstacle to mastering a foreign language is the difficulty of learning the categories of sound that are treated as equivalent.

Like other types of sounds, musical sounds differ from one another in the properties that we perceive them to have. One property is *loudness,* which refers to the magnitude of the sound as judged by a given person. Loudness, as you know, is related to the amplitude of a sound, which is measured in decibels, but it is also a subjective factor. What is "very loud" music for one person may be only "moderately loud" for another, whereas music that seems "soft" to one listener may not seem soft at all to someone else.

Another property of musical sounds is *pitch,* which refers to the position of each sound on a musical scale as judged by the particular listener. Although pitch is clearly related to the frequency of a sound, there is more to it than that. Consider the note middle C as played on a piano. This note can be described as a pattern of sound frequencies, as is the clarinet note in Figure 9-6. Like the note on the clarinet, any musical note is defined by its fundamental frequency, which is the lowest frequency of the sound pattern, or the rate at which the overall pattern is repeated. For middle C, the fundamental frequency is 264 hertz. The sound waves, as measured by a spectrograph, are shown in Figure 9-7. An important feature of our brain's analysis of music is that middle C is perceived as being the same note regardless of whether it is played on a piano or a guitar, even though the sound is very different on different instruments. The right temporal lobe has a special function in extracting pitch from sound, whether the sound is in speech or music. In speech, pitch contributes to perceived "tone" of voice, which is known as **prosody.**

A final property of musical sound is its *quality,* which refers to the characteristics that distinguish a particular sound from all others of similar pitch and loudness. For example, we can easily distinguish the sound of a violin from that of a trombone even though the same note is being played on both instruments at the same loudness. We can do so because the two sounds differ in quality. The French word *timbre* (pronounced ***tam** brah*) is normally used to describe this characteristic of sound.

**Prosody.** Melody or tone of voice.

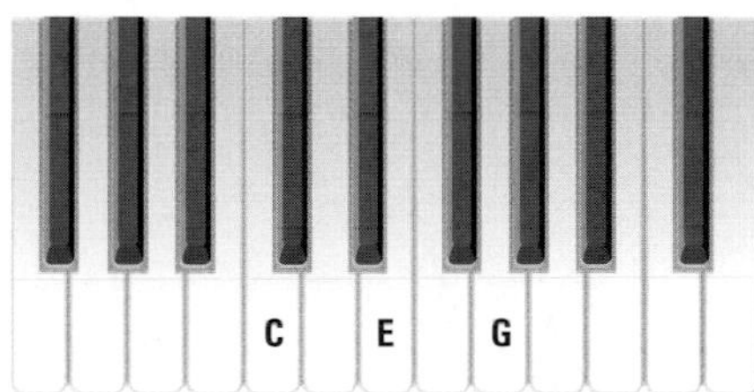


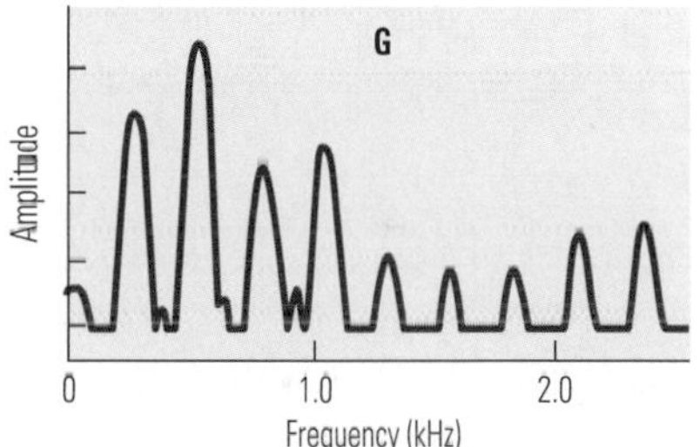


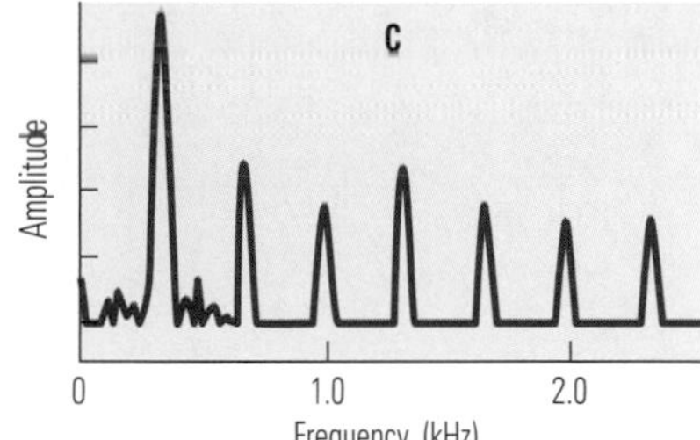


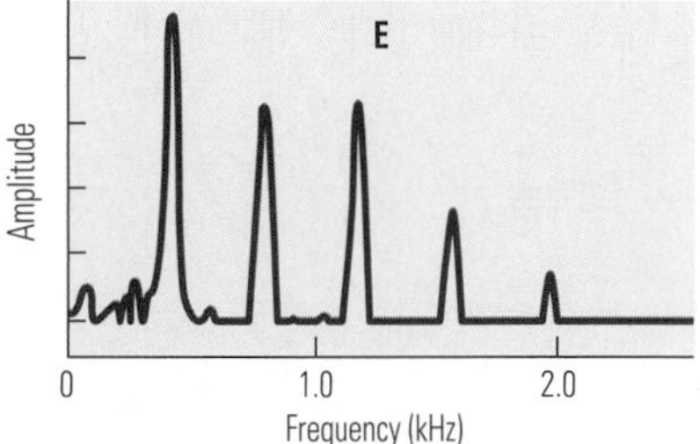


**Figure 9-7**

The shapes of the sound waves of C, E, and G as played on a piano and recorded on a spectrograph. The first wave in each of these graphs is the fundamental frequency, and the secondary waves are the over tones.

Courtesy of D. Rendall.

## In Review

Sound, the stimulus for the auditory system, is produced by changes in air pressure, which form complex waves that are converted into neural activity in the ear. Sound waves have three key qualities: frequency, amplitude, and complexity. Frequency is the rate at which the waves vibrate and roughly corresponds to perceived pitch. Amplitude is the magnitude of change in air-molecule density that the wave undergoes and roughly corresponds to perceived loudness. Complexity refers to the particular mixture of frequencies that create a sound's perceived uniqueness, or timbre. Combinations of these qualities allow the auditory system to comprehend sounds as complex as language and music. Our next task is to explain how this analysis of sound is accomplished. We begin by tracing the pathway taken by sound through the brain.

# THE ANATOMY OF THE AUDITORY SYSTEM

The ear collects sound waves from the surrounding world and converts them into neural activity, which then begins a long route through the brainstem to the auditory cortex. Before we can trace the journey from the ear to the cortex, we need to ask what the auditory system is designed to do. Because sound has the properties of frequency, amplitude, and complexity, we can assume that the auditory system is structured to code these properties. In addition, most animals can tell where a sound comes from, so there must be some mechanism for locating sounds in space. Finally, many animals, including humans, not only analyze sounds for their meanings but also make sounds themselves. Because the sounds that they produce are often the same as the ones that they hear, we can infer that the systems for sound production and analysis must be closely related. In humans, the development of sound-processing systems for both language and music led to the development of specialized cortical regions, especially in the temporal lobes. In fact, a major difference between the human and the monkey cortex is a marked expansion of auditory areas in humans.

## The Ear

The ear is a masterpiece of engineering that consists of three sections: the outer, middle, and inner ear, all illustrated in Figure 9-8. The outer ear consists of both the *pinna,* the funnel-like external structure made of cartilage and flesh, and the *external ear canal,* which extends a short distance from the pinna inside the head. The pinna is designed to catch the waves of air pressure in the surrounding environment and deflect them into the external ear canal. This canal amplifies the waves somewhat and directs them to the *eardrum* at its inner end. When sound waves strike the eardrum, it vibrates, the rate of vibration varying with the frequency of the waves.

On the inner side of the eardrum is the middle ear, an air-filled chamber that contains three small bones, or **ossicles,** connected to one another in a series. These three small bones (the smallest bones in the human body) are called the *hammer,* the *anvil,* and the *stirrup* because of their distinctive shapes. The ossicles attach the eardrum to the *oval window,* an opening in the bony casing of the **cochlea,** which is the inner-ear structure that contains the auditory receptors. When sound waves cause the eardrum to vibrate, those vibrations are transmitted to the ossicles. The ossicles, in turn, produce a leverlike action that conveys and amplifies the vibrations onto the membrane that covers the cochlea's oval window.

**Basilar membrane.** The receptor surface in the cochlea that transduces sound waves into neural activity.

As Figure 9-8 shows, the cochlea coils around itself and looks a bit like the shell of a snail. (The name *cochlea* derives from the Latin word for "snail.") Inside its bony exterior, the cochlea is hollow, as the cross-sectional drawing reveals. The compartments of this hollow interior are filled with fluid, and floating in the middle of the fluid is a thin membrane called the **basilar membrane.** Embedded in a part of the basilar membrane are **hair cells,** which are the auditory receptors. These hair cells and their supporting cells are collectively called the **organ of Corti.** The tips of the hair cells have little filaments, known as *cilia,* and the cilia of the outer hair cells are embedded in an overlying membrane, called the **tectorial membrane.**

The movement of the cilia converts sound waves into neural activity. Pressure from the stirrup on the oval window starts the process by causing movement of the cochlear fluid. This movement is made possible by a second membranous window in the cochlea (the *round window*), which bulges outward as the stirrup presses inward on the

**Figure 9-8**

The ear comprises three major anatomical parts: the outer, middle, and inner ears. Sound is gathered by the outer ear, transduced from air pressure into mechanical energy in the middle ear, and transduced into neural activity by the cochlea in the inner ear. The hair cells of the cochlea are the receptor cells. The cilia of the hair cells are displaced by movements of the basilar membrane, leading to changes in membrane potential of the hair cells. The hair cells connect with the auditory nerve.

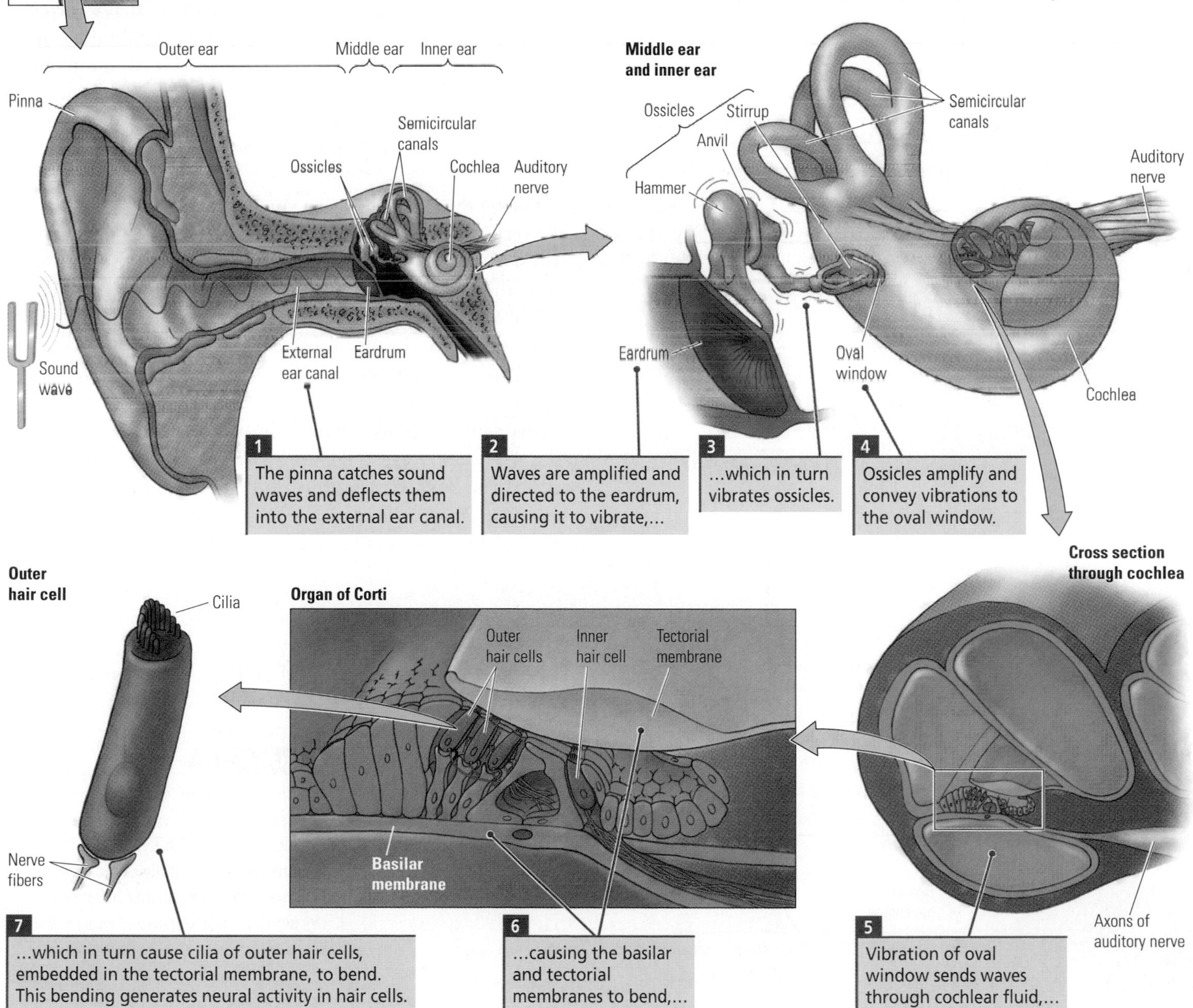

Outer ear
Middle ear
Inner ear
Pinna
Semicircular canals
Ossicles
Cochlea
Auditory nerve
Sound wave
External ear canal
Eardrum
Middle ear and inner ear
Ossicles
Stirrup
Anvil
Hammer
Semicircular canals
Auditory nerve
Eardrum
Oval window
Cochlea
1 The pinna catches sound waves and deflects them into the external ear canal.
2 Waves are amplified and directed to the eardrum, causing it to vibrate,...
3 ...which in turn vibrates ossicles.
4 Ossicles amplify and convey vibrations to the oval window.
Cross section through cochlea
Outer hair cell
Cilia
Organ of Corti
Outer hair cells
Inner hair cell
Tectorial membrane
Basilar membrane
Nerve fibers
Axons of auditory nerve
7 ...which in turn cause cilia of outer hair cells, embedded in the tectorial membrane, to bend. This bending generates neural activity in hair cells.
6 ...causing the basilar and tectorial membranes to bend,...
5 Vibration of oval window sends waves through cochlear fluid,...

oval window. In a chain reaction, the movement of the cochlear fluid causes movements of the basilar and tectorial membranes, which in turn bend the cilia in one direction or another.

The structure and function of the basilar membrane are easier to visualize if the cochlea is uncoiled and laid flat, as in Figure 9-9. When the oval window vibrates in response to the vibrations of the ossicles, it generates waves that travel through the fluid of the cochlea. The waves cause the basilar and tectorial membranes to bend, and, when the membranes bend, the cilia of the hair cells are stimulated. This stimulation generates action potentials in the hair cells.

The key question is how this arrangement can code for the various properties of sound. In the late 1800s, German physiologist Hermann von Helmholtz proposed that sounds of different frequencies cause different parts of the basilar membrane to resonate. Von Helmholtz was not precisely correct. Actually, *all* parts of the basilar membrane bend in response to incoming waves of any frequency. The key is where on the basilar membrane the *peak* displacement takes place.

George von Békésy (1899–1972)

This solution to the coding puzzle was not determined until 1960, when George von Békésy was able to observe the basilar membrane directly and see that a traveling wave moves along it all the way from the oval window to the membrane's apex. Békésy placed little grains along the basilar membrane and watched them jump in different places with different frequencies of incoming waves. Faster wave frequencies caused maximum peaks of displacement near the base of the basilar membrane, whereas slower wave frequencies caused maximum displacement peaks near the membrane's apex.

As a rough analogy, consider what happens when you shake a rope. If you shake it very quickly, the waves are very small and remain close to the part of the rope that you are holding. But, if you shake the rope slowly with a larger movement, the waves reach their peak farther along the rope. The key point is that, although both rapid and slow shakes of the rope produce movement along the rope's entire length, the maximum displacement of the rope is found at one end or the other, depending on whether the wave movements are rapid or slow.

This same response pattern is true of the basilar membrane. All sounds cause some displacement along the entire length of the basilar membrane, but the amount of displacement at any point varies with the frequency of the sound. In the human cochlea, the basilar membrane near the oval window

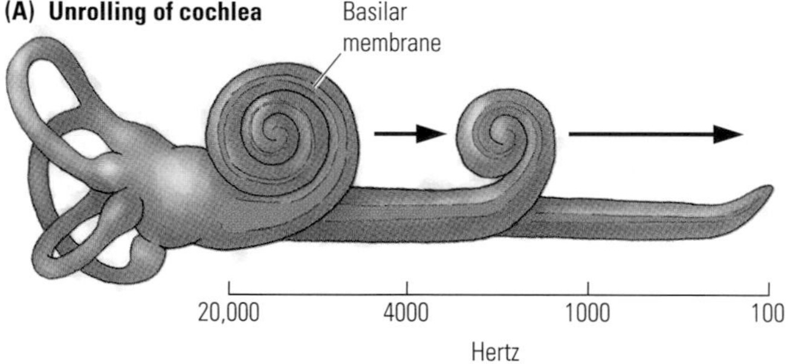
(A) Unrolling of cochlea
Basilar membrane
20,000
4000
1000
100
Hertz

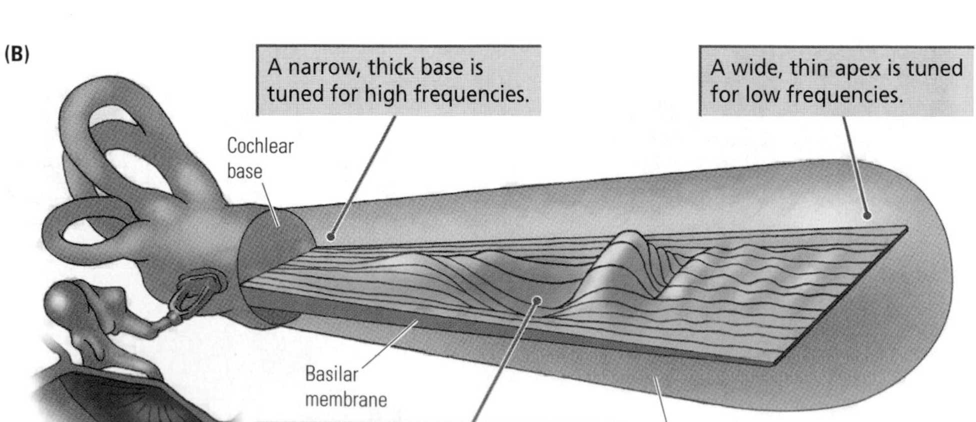
(B)
A narrow, thick base is tuned for high frequencies.
A wide, thin apex is tuned for low frequencies.
Cochlear base
Basilar membrane
Sound waves at medium frequencies cause peak bending of the basilar membrane at this point.
"Unrolled" cochlea

**Figure 9-9**

**(A)** Anatomy of the cochlea, which is being unrolled. The numbers are the frequencies to which the basilar membrane is maximally responsive. **(B)** The basilar membrane has been unrolled. A traveling wave moves along the basilar membrane, producing its maximal displacement of the membrane as it approaches the apex.

is maximally affected by frequencies as high as about 20,000 hertz, whereas the most effective frequencies at the membrane's apex are less than 100 hertz. Intermediate frequencies maximally displace points on the basilar membrane between its two ends, as shown in Figure 9-9. When a wave of a certain frequency travels down the basilar membrane, hair cells at the point of peak displacement are stimulated, resulting in a maximal neural response in those cells. An incoming signal composed of many frequencies causes several different points along the basilar membrane to vibrate and excites hair cells at all these points.

Not surprisingly, the basilar membrane is much more sensitive to changes in frequency than our rope is. This greater sensitivity is achieved because the basilar membrane is not the same thickness along its entire length. Instead, it is narrow and thick near the oval window and wider and thinner at its opposite end. The combination of varying width and thickness enhances the effect of small differences in frequency on the basilar membrane. As a result, the cochlea can code small differences in frequency.

## The Auditory Receptors

As you know, hair cells are what ultimately transform sound waves into neural activity. Figure 9-8 shows the structure of a hair cell, and Figure 9-10 illustrates how it functions to generate an action potential. There are two sets of hair cells: *inner hair cells* and *outer hair cells*. The human cochlea has 3500 inner hair cells and 12,000 outer hair cells, which is a small total number considering how many different sounds we can hear. As is also shown in Figure 9-10, the tips of the cilia of outer hair cells are attached to the overlying tectorial membrane, but the cilia of the inner hair cells do not touch the tectorial membrane. Nevertheless, the movement of the basilar and tectorial membranes causes the cochlear fluid to flow past the cilia of the inner hair cells, bending them back and forth. The inner hair cells are the auditory receptors. Animals with intact outer hair cells but no inner hair cells are effectively deaf. The outer hair cells function simply to sharpen the resolving power of the cochlea by contracting or relaxing and thereby changing the stiffness of the tectorial membrane.

One puzzle is how this function of the outer hair cells is controlled. How do these cells know when they need to contract or relax? The answer seems to be that the outer hair cells, through connections with axons in the auditory nerve, send some type of

**Figure 9-10**

Transduction of movement into neural activity is mediated by the hair cells. Movement of the basilar membrane creates a shearing force that bends the cilia, leading to the opening or closing of calcium channels in the hair cell. The influx of calcium ions leads to the release of transmitter by the hair cell, which stimulates an action potential in the cochlear (or auditory) nerve.

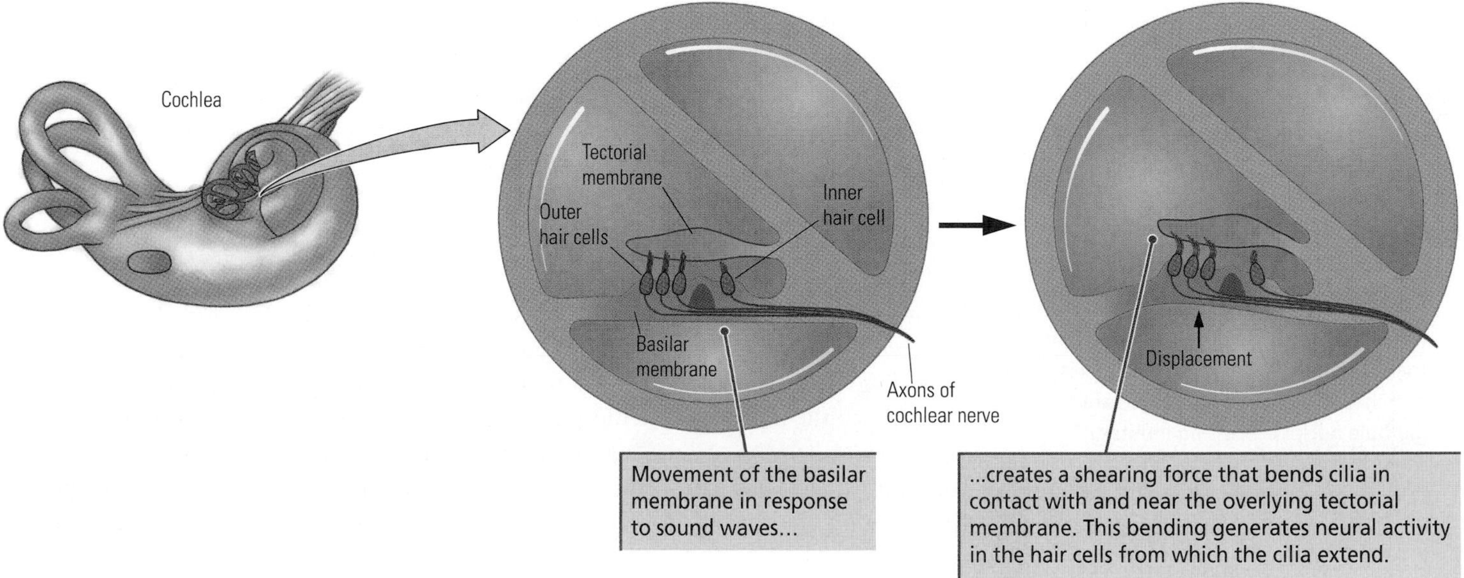
Cochlea
Tectorial membrane
Outer hair cells
Inner hair cell
Basilar membrane
Axons of cochlear nerve
Displacement
Movement of the basilar membrane in response to sound waves...
...creates a shearing force that bends cilia in contact with and near the overlying tectorial membrane. This bending generates neural activity in the hair cells from which the cilia extend.

message to the brainstem auditory areas. These areas then send a message back to the outer hairs, causing appropriate alterations of tension on the tectorial membrane. In this way, the brain helps the receptors create an auditory world.

A final question remains about the workings of hair cells: How does movement of their cilia generate neural activity? The answer is that movement of the cilia causes a change in polarization of the hair cell. Look at Figure 9-8 again and notice that the cilia of a hair cell differ in height. Movement of the cilia in the direction of the tallest cilia results in depolarization, which in turn opens calcium channels and leads to the release of transmitter onto the dendrites of the cells that form the auditory nerve. Movement in the direction of the shortest cilia results in hyperpolarization and a corresponding decrease in transmitter release. Hair cells are amazingly sensitive to the movement of their cilia. A movement sufficient to allow sound detection is only about 0.3 nanometer, or about the diameter of a large atom.

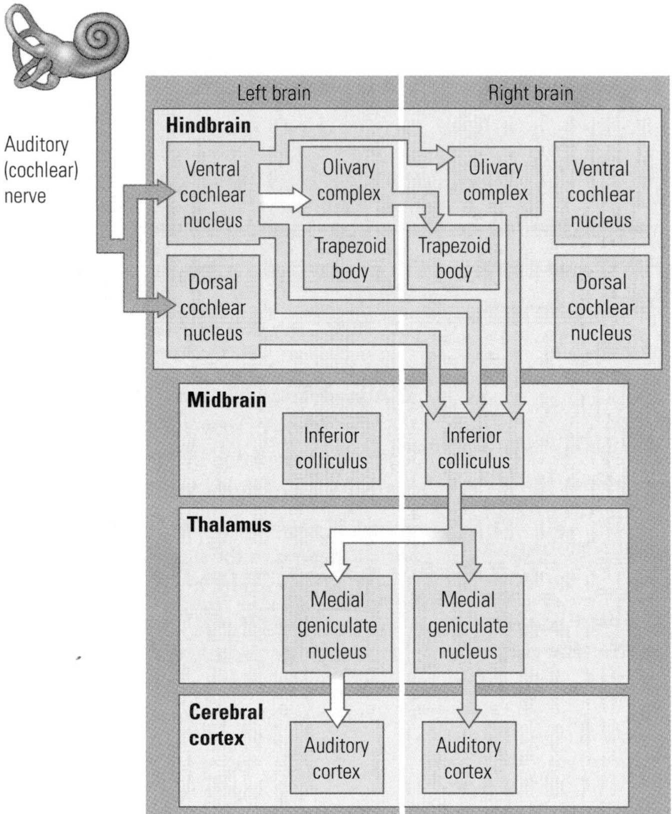


**Figure 9-11**

The primary route of auditory information from the cochlear nucleus through the hindbrain to the midbrain to the cortex. Three major points are evident: (1) the auditory inputs cross to the opposite side in the hindbrain; (2) there is recrossing of information, so that information from the ear reaches both hemispheres; and (3) there are multiple nuclei processing inputs en route to the cortex.

## The Auditory Pathways

Hair cells in the organ of Corti synapse with neighboring bipolar cells, the axons of which form the **cochlear** (auditory) **nerve,** which in turn forms part of the eighth cranial nerve. Each bipolar cell receives information from only one inner hair cell. This arrangement contrasts with inputs to retinal ganglion cells, which you learned about in Chapter 8. Whereas ganglion cells in the eye receive inputs from many receptor cells, bipolar cells in the ear receive input from but a single receptor.

The cochlear-nerve axons enter the brainstem at the level of the medulla and synapse in the *cochlear nucleus,* which has two subdivisions (the ventral and dorsal). Two other nearby structures in the brainstem, the **superior olivary complex** (superior olive) and the **trapezoid body,** each receive connections from the cochlear nucleus, as shown in Figure 9-11. The projections from the cochlear nucleus connect with cells on the same side of the brain as well as with cells on the opposite side. This arrangement mixes the inputs from the two ears to form the perception of a single sound. The cochlear nucleus and the superior olive both send projections to the **inferior colliculus** at the top of the midbrain. Two distinct pathways emerge from the inferior colliculus, coursing to the **medial geniculate nucleus,** which lies in the thalamus. The ventral region of the medial geniculate nucleus projects to the primary auditory cortex (known as A1), whereas the dorsal region projects to the auditory cortical regions adjacent to A1.

## The Auditory Cortex

In the human cortex, area A1 is within **Heschl's gyrus** and is surrounded by other secondary cortical areas, as shown in Figure 9-12. The secondary cortex lying behind Heschl's gyrus is called the **planum temporale** (meaning "temporal plane"). In right-handed people, the planum temporale is larger on the left side of the brain than it is on the right, whereas Heschl's gyrus is larger on the right side than on the left. The cortex of the left planum forms a speech zone, known as **Wernicke's area** (the **posterior speech zone**), whereas the cortex of the right Heschl's gyrus has a special role in

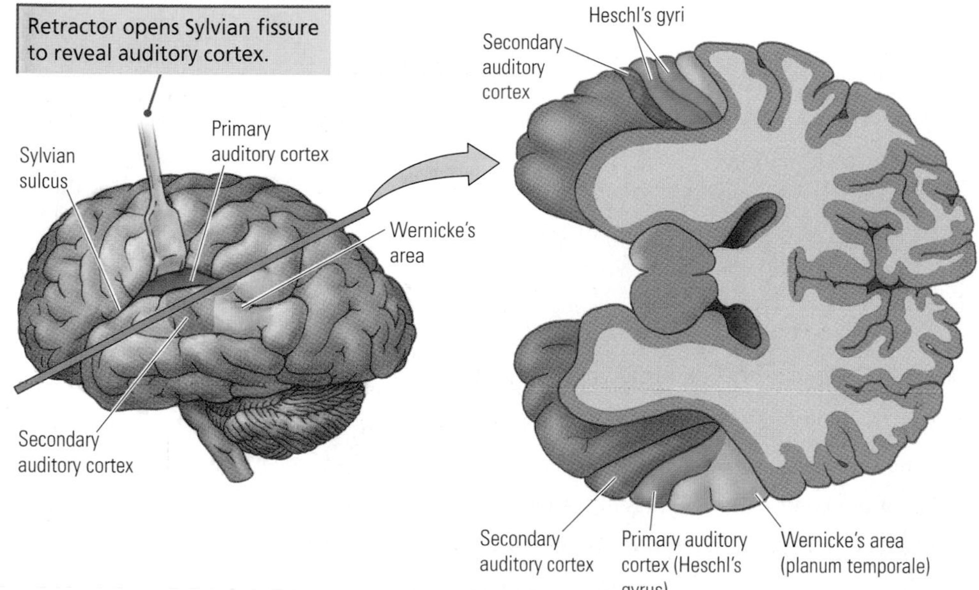


**Figure 9-12**

The human auditory cortex areas. (*Left*) Diagram of the left hemisphere of the brain showing the primary auditory cortex and the adjacent secondary regions. (*Right*) The posterior auditory cortex forms the posterior speech zone (Wernicke's area), which is larger on the left. Heschl's gyrus is larger on the right.

the analysis of music. These differences mean that the auditory cortex is anatomically and functionally asymmetrical, a property called *cerebral asymmetry*. Although cerebral asymmetry is not unique to the auditory system, it is most obvious here because the auditory analysis of language takes place only in the left hemisphere. Most left-handed people (about 70 percent) have the same anatomical asymmetries as those of right-handers, an indication that language organization is not related to hand preference. The remaining 30 percent of left-handers fall into two distinct groups: about half have an organization opposite that of right-handers; the other half have some type of idiosyncratic bilateral representation of language in which some language functions are in one hemisphere and others are in the other hemisphere.

The localization of language on the left side of the brain is often referred to as the **lateralization** of language. As a rule of thumb, if one hemisphere is specialized for one type of analysis, such as language, the other hemisphere has some type of complementary function, which in regard to audition appears to be music. We will return to the lateralization of language later in this chapter and again in Chapter 14.

In Chapter 8, you learned that there are two distinct visual pathways through the cortex: the temporal stream for object recognition and the dorsal stream for the visual control of movement. A similar distinction exists in the auditory cortex (Romanski et al., 1999). Just as we can identify objects by their sound characteristics, we can direct our movements by sound. The role of sound in guiding movement is less familiar to sight-dominated people than it is to people who are blind. Nevertheless, it exists in us all. Imagine waking up in the dark and reaching to pick up a ringing telephone or to turn off an alarm clock. Your hand will automatically form the appropriate shape needed to carry out these movements just on the basis of the sound that you have heard. That sound is guiding your movements much as a visual image can guide them. Although relatively little is known about the auditory pathways in the cortex, one pathway appears to continue through the temporal lobe, much like the ventral visual pathway, and plays a role in identifying auditory stimuli. A second auditory pathway apparently goes to the posterior parietal region, where it forms a type of dorsal pathway for the auditory control of movement.

In the overview of the brain area in the Central Nervous System module of your CD, investigate cortical anatomy and the four lobes.

**Heschl's gyrus.** The primary auditory cortex found in the temporal lobes.

**Wernicke's area.** A region in the posterior part of the left temporal lobe that regulates the comprehension of language; sometimes referred to as the posterior speech zone.

**Tonotopic representation.** A representation of the auditory world in which sounds are located in a systematic fashion in a procession from lower to higher frequencies.

**Tuning curve.** A curve representing the maximum sensitivity of a neuron to a range of auditory frequencies. Each hair cell is maximally responsive to a particular frequency, but it also responds to nearby frequencies, although the sound must be louder for the cell to respond.

## In Review

Changes in air pressure are converted into neural activity by hair cells in the inner-ear structure called the cochlea. Incoming sound waves vibrate the eardrum, which in turn vibrates the tiny bones of the middle ear, the innermost one of which presses on the cochlea's oval window and sets in motion the cochlear fluid. The motion of this fluid displaces the basilar membrane, causing cilia on the hair cells to bend and generate action potentials. The frequencies of incoming sound waves are largely coded by the places on the basilar membrane that are most displaced by the incoming sound waves. The axons of bipolar cells of the cochlea form the auditory (cochlear) nerve, which enters the brain at the medulla and synapses on cells in the cochlear nucleus. The neurons of the cochlear nucleus and associated regions in the medulla then begin a pathway on each side of the brain that courses to the midbrain (inferior colliculus), the thalamus (medial geniculate nucleus), and the cortex. In the brains of right-handed people, the auditory cortex on the left and right are asymmetrical, with the planum temporale being larger on the left and Heschl's gyrus being larger on the right. This anatomical asymmetry is correlated to a functional asymmetry: the left temporal cortex analyzes language-related sounds, whereas the right temporal cortex analyzes music-related ones. Most left-handed people have a similar arrangement, although about 30 percent of left-handers have a different pattern.

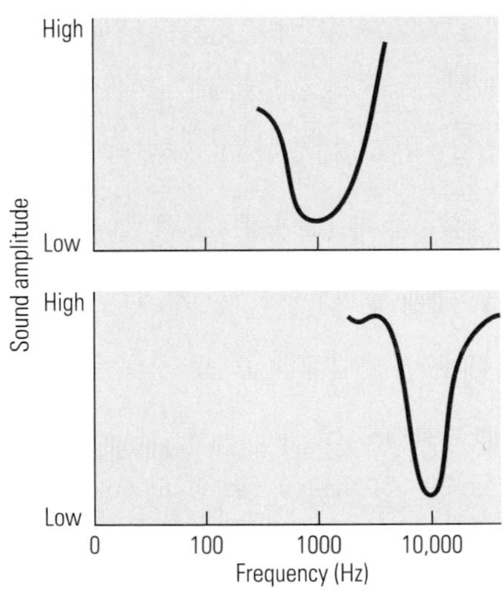


**Figure 9-13** The frequency tuning curves of two different axons in the cochlear nerve. Each graph plots the frequency against the amplitude of the sound required to increase the firing rate of the neuron. The lowest point on each graph is the frequency to which that cell is most sensitive. The upper tuning curve is centered on 1000 hertz, whereas the lower tuning curve is centered on 10,000 hertz.

# NEURAL ACTIVITY AND HEARING

We now turn to the ways in which the activities of neurons in the auditory system create our perception of sounds. Neurons at different levels in this system serve different functions. To get an idea of what the individual cells do, we will consider how the auditory system codes for pitch, loudness, location, and pattern.

## Hearing Pitch

Recall that our perception of pitch corresponds to the property of sound called frequency, which is measured in cycles per second, or hertz. Cells in the cochlea code frequency by their location on the basilar membrane. The cilia of hair cells at the base of the cochlea are maximally displaced by high-frequency sounds, and those at the apex are displaced the most by sounds of low frequency. This arrangement is referred to as a **tonotopic representation** (literally meaning "tone place"). Because axons of the bipolar cells that form the cochlear nerve are each connected to only one hair cell, they contain information about the place on the basilar membrane being stimulated.

If we record from single fibers in the cochlear nerve, we find that, although each axon transmits information about only a small part of the auditory spectrum, the cells do respond to a range of frequencies. In other words, each hair cell is maximally responsive to a particular frequency, but it also responds to nearby frequencies, even though the sound must be louder for these nearby frequencies to generate a response. This range of responses to different frequencies at different amplitudes can be plotted to form a **tuning curve,** like those in Figure 9-13. Such a curve is reminiscent of the curves in Figure 8-7, which show the responsiveness of cones in the retina to different wavelengths of light. Each cone is maximally sensitive to a particular wavelength of light, but it still responds somewhat to nearby wavelengths.

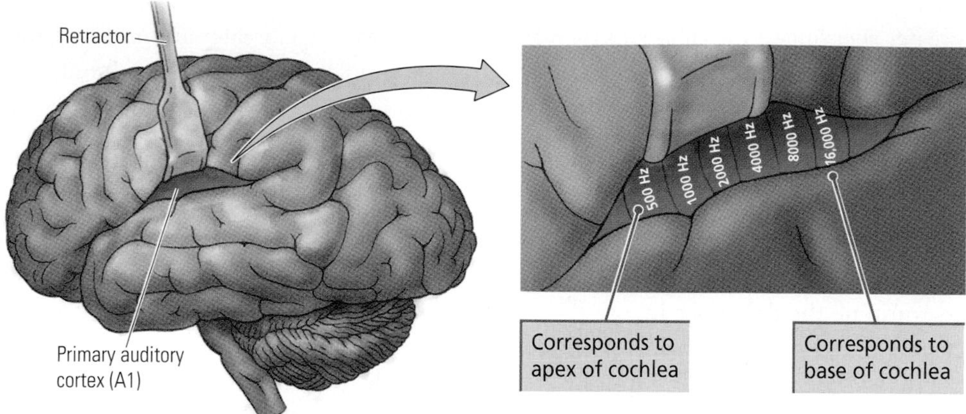


**Figure 9-14**

The tonotopic representation of the primary auditory cortex, or region A1. The anterior end of A1 represents the apex of the cochlea and hence low-frequency sounds, whereas the posterior end represents the base of the cochlea and hence high-frequency sounds. Because the auditory cortex is buried in the Sylvian fissure, a retractor is used to open the fissure to reveal the auditory cortex.

The axons of the bipolar cells in the cochlea project to the cochlear nucleus in an orderly manner. The axons entering from the base of the cochlea connect with one location, those entering from the middle connect to another location, and those entering from the apex connect to yet another place. As a result, the tonotopic representation of the basilar membrane is reproduced in the cochlear nucleus. This systematic representation is maintained throughout the auditory pathways and can be found in cortical region A1—the primary auditory cortex. Figure 9-14 shows the distribution of projections from the base and apex of the cochlea across A1. Similar tonotopic maps can be constructed for each level of the auditory system.

The systematic organization of tonotopic maps has enabled the development of **cochlear implants**—electronic devices surgically inserted in the inner ear to allow deaf people to hear (see Loeb, 1990). A miniature microphone-like processor detects the component frequencies of incoming sounds and sends them to the appropriate place on the basilar membrane through tiny wires. The nervous system does not distinguish between stimulation coming from this artificial device and stimulation coming through the ear. As long as appropriate signals go to the correct locations on the basilar membrane, the brain will "hear." Cochlear implants work very well, even allowing the deaf to detect the fluctuating pitches of speech. Their success provides corroborating evidence for the tonotopic representation of pitch in the basilar membrane.

Cochlear implants bypass the normal route for hearing by processing incoming sounds and sending them directly to the correct locations on the basilar membrane.

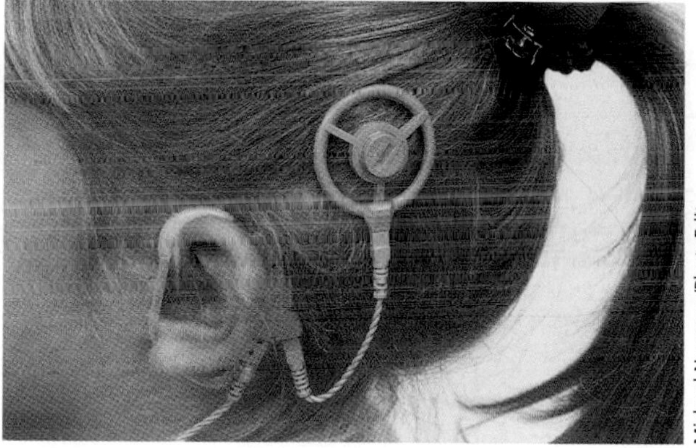

Michael Newman/PhotoEdit

One minor difficulty with the tonotopic theory of frequency detection is that the cochlea does not use this mechanism at the very apex of the basilar membrane, where hair cells, as well as the bipolar cells to which they are connected, respond to frequencies below about 200 hertz. At this location, *all* the cells respond to movement of the basilar membrane, but they do so in proportion to the frequency of the incoming wave. Higher rates of firing signal a relatively higher frequency, whereas lower rates of firing signal a lower frequency. Why the cochlea uses a different system to differentiate pitches within this range of very-low-frequency sounds is not clear. The reason probably has to do with the physical limitations of the basilar membrane. Although discriminating among low-frequency sounds is not important to humans, animals such as elephants and whales depend on these frequencies for their communication. Most likely they have more neurons at this end of the basilar membrane than do people.

Learn more about the development of the cochlear implant on the Web site at **www.worthpublishers.com/kolb/chapter9.**

## Detecting Loudness

The simplest way for cochlear cells to indicate sound intensity is to fire at a higher rate when sounds are louder, which is exactly what happens. More-intense air-pressure changes produce more-intense vibrations of the basilar membrane and therefore

**Cochlear implant.** An electronic device that is implanted surgically into the inner ear to transduce sound waves into neural activity and allow deaf people to hear.

greater shearing of the cilia. This increased shearing leads to a greater amount of transmitter released onto bipolar cells. As a result, the bipolar axons fire more frequently, telling the auditory system that the sound is louder.

## Detecting Location

The fact that each cochlear nerve synapses on both sides of the brain provides mechanisms for determining the source of a sound. One such mechanism is for brain cells to compute the difference in a sound's arrival time at the two ears. Figure 9-15 shows how a sound originating on the left reaches the left ear slightly before it reaches the right ear. Such differences in arrival time need not be large to be detected. If two sounds presented through earphones are separated by as little as 10 microseconds, the listener will perceive that a single sound came from the leading ear. This computation of left-ear–right-ear arrival times is carried out in the medial part of the superior olivary complex. Because these cells receive inputs from each ear, they are able to compare exactly when the signal from each ear reaches them.

Extra distance that sound must travel to reach the right ear.

**Figure 9-15**

Sounds that originate on the left side of the body reach the left ear slightly before they reach the right ear, providing information about the location of the sound source. The difference in arrival time is subtle and, although the auditory system can use this information to localize sound, it is able to fuse the two sounds perceptually so that we hear but a single, clear sound.

As the source of a sound moves from the side of the head toward the middle, a person has greater and greater difficulty locating the source of the sound. The reason is that the difference in arrival time becomes smaller and smaller until there is no difference at all. When no difference exists, we can infer that the sound is either directly in front of us or directly behind us. To tell which it is, we move our heads, making the sound strike one of the ears sooner. We have a similar problem distinguishing between sounds directly above and below us. Again, we solve the problem by tilting our heads, thus causing the sound to strike one ear before the other.

Another way in which the auditory system can tell the location of the source of a sound has to do not with the difference in arrival times of a sound at the two ears, but instead with the sound's relative loudness on the left or the right. The basis of this mechanism is that higher-frequency sounds do not easily bend around the head, so the head acts as an obstacle to them. As a result, higher-frequency sounds on one side of the head are louder on that side than on the other. This difference is detected in the lateral part of the superior olivary complex and the trapezoid body. For sounds coming from directly in front or behind or from directly above or below, the same problem of differentiation exists, requiring the same solution of tilting or turning the head.

Although head tilting and turning are effective aids in localizing sounds, doing so takes time. The time needed is not usually important for humans, but it is important for certain other animals, such as owls, that hunt by using sound. Owls need to know the location of a sound simultaneously in at least two directions (left and below, for example, or right and above). The owl's solution is to have ears that are slightly displaced in the vertical direction so that sounds from above strike one ear sooner, whereas sounds from below strike the other ear sooner. This solution, shown in Figure 9-16, allows owls to hunt entirely by sound in the dark, which is bad news for mice.

## Detecting Sound Patterns

Music and language are good examples of sound patterns that we can recognize. Because the right and left temporal lobes have roles in music and language, respectively, we can guess that neurons in the right and left temporal cortex take part in analyzing

Art Wolfe/Tony Stone

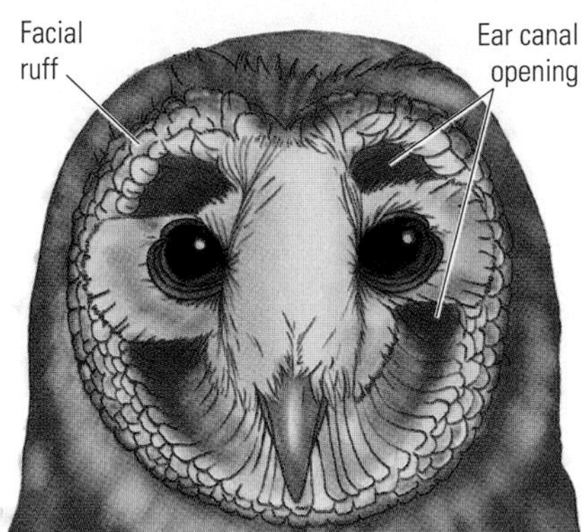


**Figure 9-16**

In this photograph of a barn owl catching a mouse in the dark, the owl has aligned its talons with the body axis of the mouse. The drawing above depicts the facial structure of the barn owl. The face is formed by rows of tightly packed feathers, called the facial ruff, that extend from the relatively narrow skull. The external ears are troughs formed by the part of the ruff that runs down the length of the face to join below the beak. The ruff collects sounds and funnels them into ear-canal openings. The owl's left ear is more sensitive to low-frequency sounds from the left, and the right ear is more sensitive to low-frequency sounds from the right. With sounds of high frequency, however, the right ear is more sensitive to those coming from above, because the ear canal is lower on the right and the trough is tilted up. The ear canal is higher on the left side and the trough is tilted down. Therefore, the left ear is more sensitive to sounds coming from below. For an owl, then, differences in perceived loudness can yield clues to the elevation of a source of sounds as well as to its horizontal direction.

Drawing adapted from "The Hearing of the Barn Owl," by E. I. Knudsen, 1981, *Scientific American, 245*(6), p. 115.

patterns in these two kinds of auditory experience. Studying the activities of these neurons in humans is not easy, however. Most of the knowledge that we have comes from studies of how individual neurons respond in nonhuman primates. For instance, Peter Winter and Hans Funkenstein (1971) found that neurons in the auditory cortex of the squirrel monkey are specifically responsive to squirrel monkey vocalizations. More recently, Joseph Rauschecker and his colleagues (1995) discovered that neurons in the secondary auditory areas of rhesus monkeys are more responsive to mixtures of sounds than to pure tones. Other researchers also have shown that the removal of the temporal auditory cortex abolishes the ability to discriminate the vocalizations made by other members of the species (Heffner and Heffner, 1990). Interestingly, discrimination of species-typical vocalizations in monkeys seems more severely disrupted by injury to the left temporal cortex than to the right. This finding implies that there may be a functional asymmetry for the analysis of complex auditory material in nonhuman primates, too.

## In Review

Neurons in the cochlea form a tonotopic map that codes for a sound's frequencies. Such tonotopic maps of sound stimuli are maintained throughout the auditory system. The same cells in the cochlea that code for different frequencies of sound can also code for differences in sound amplitude by varying their firing rate, depending on a sound's loudness. Detecting the location of a sound is a function of neurons in the superior olive and trapezoid body of the brainstem. These neurons perform this role by computing differences in sound arrival time and loudness in the two ears. Understanding the meaning of sounds such as music and language requires pattern recognition, which is performed by cortical neurons.

## THE ANATOMY OF LANGUAGE AND MUSIC

This chapter began with the story of the Neanderthal flute. The fact that Neanderthals made this instrument implies that they not only could process musical sounds but also could produce music. In the modern human brain, musical ability in general is largely a right-hemisphere specialization that forms a complementary system with language ability, which is largely localized in the left hemisphere. No one knows whether these two complementary systems evolved together in the brain, but it is certainly very possible that they did. If so, the Neanderthals, in addition to having the beginnings of music, must have had some form of language.

In the modern human brain, both language and music abilities are highly developed. Although little is known about how language and music are processed at the cellular level, electrical-stimulation and blood-flow studies have been sources of important insights into the regions of the cortex in which they are processed. We will investigate such studies next, starting with those that focus on how the brain processes language.

## Processing Language

There are more than 4000 human languages in the world today, and probably many others have gone extinct in past millennia. Researchers have wondered whether the brain has a single system for understanding and producing *any* language, regardless of its structure, or whether very different languages, such as English and Japanese, are processed in different ways. To answer this question, it helps to analyze languages to determine just how similar they are, despite their various differences in vocabulary and grammar.

### THE UNIFORMITY OF LANGUAGE

Foreign languages often seem impossibly complex to those who are unfamiliar with them. Their sounds alone may seem odd and difficult to make. If you are a native speaker of English, for instance, Asian languages, such as Japanese, probably sound peculiarly tonal to you, whereas European languages, such as German or Dutch, may sound heavily guttural. Even within related languages, such as English and French, there are marked differences in grammatical rules that can make the foreign language challenging to learn. Yet, as real as these linguistic differences may be, it turns out that they are superficial. The similarities in human languages, although not immediately apparent, are actually far more fundamental than their differences.

Noam Chomsky is usually credited with being the first linguist to stress the similarities over the differences in how human languages are structured. In a series of books and papers written in the past 40 years, he made a very sweeping claim, as have researchers such as Steven Pinker (1997) more recently. They argue that all languages have common structural characteristics because of a genetically determined constraint on the nature of human language. When this idea was first proposed in the 1960s, it was greeted with some skepticism. Since then, however, it has become clear that it is probably correct.

An obvious piece of evidence in favor of a genetic basis of human language is the fact that language is universal in human populations. All people everywhere use language. Furthermore, the complexity of language is not related to the complexity of a group's culture. The languages of technologically primitive peoples are every bit as complex and elegant as the languages of industrialized cultures. Old English is not inferior to modern English; it is just different. Humans, apparently, have a built-in capacity for creating and using language.

Another piece of evidence in favor of a genetic basis of human language is the fact that language is learned early in life and seemingly without effort. At about 12 months of age, children everywhere start to speak words. By 18 months, they are combining words, and, by age 3 years, they have a rich language capability. Perhaps the most amazing thing about language development is that children are not specifically taught the structure of their language. As toddlers, they are not painstakingly instructed in the rules of grammar. In fact, their early grammatical errors—for example, sentences such as "I goed to the zoo"—are seldom even corrected by adults. Yet children master language rapidly just the same. They also go through a series of stages of language acquisition that are remarkably similar across cultures. Indeed, the process of language acquisition plays an important role in Chomsky's theory of the innateness of language.

This is not to say that language development is not also influenced by experience. At the most basic level, children learn the language that they hear spoken. In an English household, they learn English; in a Japanese home, they learn Japanese. They also pick up the vocabulary of the people around them, which can vary from one speaker of a language to another. Furthermore, children go through a sensitive period of language acquisition, probably from about 1 to 6 years of age. If they are not exposed to language during this period, their language skills are severely compromised (see Chapter 7).

A third piece of evidence in favor of a genetic basis of language is the fact that all languages have many basic structural elements in common. Granted, every language has its own particular rules of grammar that specify exactly how the various parts of speech are to be positioned in a sentence, how words are to be inflected to convey different meanings, and so forth. But there are also overarching rules of grammar that apply to all human languages. For instance, all languages have the parts of speech that we call subjects, verbs, and direct objects. Consider the sentence "Jane ate the apple." "Jane" is the subject, "ate" is the verb, and "apple" is the direct object. The location of these three words in the sentence is not specified by any universal rule of grammar. Their positioning is a matter of the particular language spoken. In English, the order is subject, verb, object; in Japanese, the order is subject, object, verb; in Gaelic, the order is verb, subject, object. Nonetheless, all languages have these three classes of words.

The existence of basic structural elements in all human languages can be seen in the phenomenon of *creolization*—the development of a new language from what was formerly a very rudimentary pidgin language. This process took place in the seventeenth-century Americas, when slave traders and the owners of colonial plantations brought together people from various African villages who lacked a common language. Because the new slaves needed to communicate, they quickly created a simplified pidgin language that was based on whatever language the plantation owners spoke, be it English, French, Spanish, or Portuguese. The pidgin language had a crude syntax (word order), but it lacked a real grammar. The children of the slaves who spoke this pidgin language were brought up by caretakers who spoke only pidgin to them. Yet, surprisingly, these children did not learn the pidgin too. Rather, within a generation, they had created their own language, complete with a genuine grammar. Clearly, the pidgin was not a learnable language for children. The innate biology of their language-control systems shaped the development of a new language that was similar in basic structure to all other human languages. All creolized languages seem to evolve in a similar way, even though they are unrelated. This phenomenon can happen only if there is a significant innate component to language development.

Paul Broca (1824–1880)

Look at the area of the brain involved in language on the three-dimensional brain model on your CD located in the brain overview section in the module on the Central Nervous System.

## THE LOCALIZATION OF LANGUAGE IN THE BRAIN

The universality of language's basic structure set researchers on a search for a set of innate brain regions that underlie language use. By the late nineteenth century, it had become clear that language functions were at least partly localized—not just within the left hemisphere, but to specific areas there. Clues to this localization began in the early part of the nineteenth century, when neurologists observed patients with frontal-lobe injuries who suffered language difficulties. It was not until 1861, however, that Paul Broca examined a patient who had entirely lost his ability to speak except to say "tan" and to utter an oath. The man died shortly thereafter and Broca examined his brain, finding a fresh injury of the left frontal lobe. On the basis of this case and several subsequent cases, Broca concluded that language functions are localized in the left frontal lobe in a region just in front of the central fissure. This region, which is shown in Figure 9-17, soon became known as **Broca's area,** and the syndrome that results from damage to it became known as **Broca's aphasia.** A person with Broca's aphasia is unable to speak despite normal language comprehension and an intact vocal apparatus. The discovery of Broca's area was significant because it initiated the idea that the left and right hemispheres might have different functions.

Other neurologists at the time believed that Broca's area might be only one left-hemisphere region that controls language. In particular, neurologists suspected a relation between hearing and speech. Proving this suspicion to be correct, Karl Wernicke later described patients who had difficulty comprehending language after injury to the posterior region of the left temporal lobe. This region subsequently became known as Wernicke's area (the speech zone referred to earlier; see Figure 9-12), and the syndrome associated with damage to it became known as **Wernicke's aphasia.** People who suffer Wernicke's aphasia can speak fluently, but their language is confused and makes little sense, as if they have no idea of what they are saying.

Wernicke went on to propose a model for how the two language areas of the left hemisphere interact to produce speech. He theorized that images of words are encoded by their sound and stored in Wernicke's area. When we hear a word that

**Figure 9-17**

Wernicke's model of the neurology of language, showing the regions of the cortex involved. In this model, words are believed to be understood in Wernicke's area as summarized in **(A).** Words are produced through the connection that the arcuate fasciculus makes between Wernicke's area and Broca's area as summarized in **(B).**

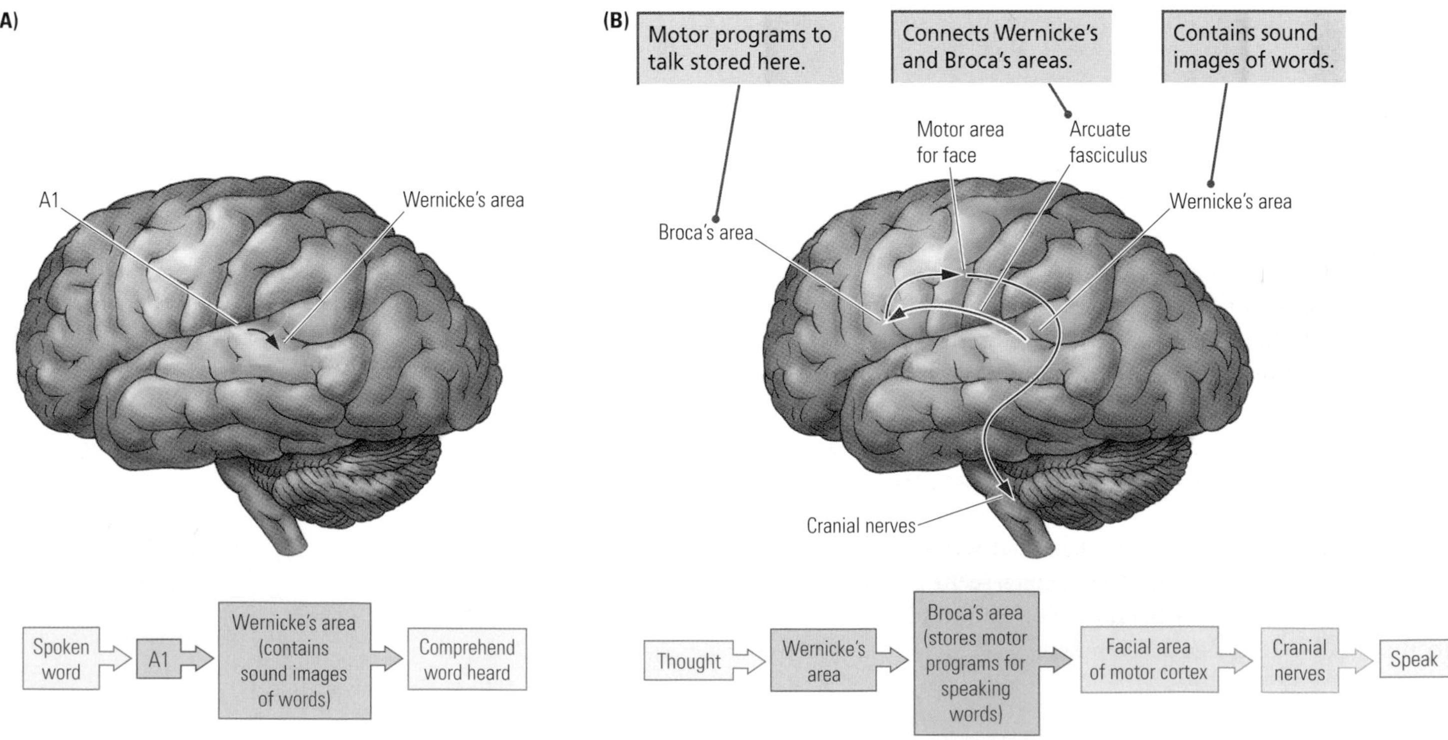

matches one of those sound images, we recognize the word, which is how Wernicke's area contributes to speech comprehension. To *speak* words, Broca's area must come into play, because the motor program to produce each word is stored in this area. Messages are sent to Broca's area from Wernicke's area through a pathway known as the arcuate fasciculus, which connects the two regions. Broca's area in turn controls the articulation of the words by the vocal apparatus.

Wernicke's model provided a simple explanation for the existence of two major language areas in the brain and for the contribution of each area to the control of language. One difficulty, however, was that the model was based on postmortem examinations of patients with brain lesions that were often extensive. Not until the pioneering studies of Wilder Penfield, begun in the 1930s, were the language areas of the left hemisphere clearly and accurately mapped.

**Broca's area.** Just in front of the motor representation in the left hemisphere, the region that functions to produce the movements needed for language; sometimes referred to as the anterior speech area.

**Broca's aphasia.** The inability to speak fluently despite the presence of normal comprehension and intact vocal mechanisms.

**Wernicke's aphasia.** An inability to understand or to produce meaningful language even though the production of words is still intact.

## AUDITORY AND SPEECH ZONES MAPPED BY BRAIN STIMULATION

Neurosurgeon Wilder Penfield took advantage of the chance to map auditory and language areas of the brain when operating on patients undergoing elective surgery to treat intractable epilepsy (see "Epilepsy" on page 144). The goal of this surgery is to remove abnormal tissues that cause the epileptic discharges. A major problem for the surgeon is to ensure that critical regions that serve important functions such as language are spared from injury. To determine the location of these regions, Penfield used a tiny electrical current to stimulate the surface of the brain. By monitoring the response of the patient to stimulation in different locations, Penfield could map brain functions.

Figure 9-18 shows what happens in such surgery. Typically, two neurosurgeons perform the operation, and a neurologist analyzes the electroencephalogram in an adjacent room. Because patients are awake during the procedure, the effects of brain stimulation in specific regions can be determined in detail. Penfield placed little numbers on different parts of the brain's surface where the patient noted that stimulation had produced some noticeable effect.

When Penfield stimulated the auditory cortex, patients often reported hearing various sounds, such as a ringing sound like that of a doorbell, a buzzing noise, or a sound like that of birds chirping. This result is consistent with those of later studies of single-cell recordings from the auditory cortex in nonhuman primates. As mentioned earlier, findings in these later studies showed that the auditory cortex has a role in pattern recognition. Penfield also found that stimulation in A1 seemed to produce simple tones, ringing sounds, and so forth, whereas stimulation in the adjacent auditory cortex was more apt to cause some interpretation of a sound, such as ascribing it to a familiar source such as a cricket. There was no difference in the effects of stimulation of the left or right auditory cortex, and the patients heard no words when the brain was stimulated. Sometimes, however, stimulation of the auditory cortex produced effects other than the perception of sounds. Stimulation of one area, for example, might cause a patient to experience a sense of deafness, whereas stimulation of another area might produce a distortion of sounds actually being heard. As one patient exclaimed after a certain region had been stimulated, "All that you said was mixed up!"

Penfield was most interested in the effects of brain stimulation not on simple sound processing but on language. He mapped language areas in two ways. First, he stimulated different regions of the cortex while the patient was in the process of speaking. He expected that the electrical current might disrupt the ongoing speech by effectively "short-circuiting" the brain. In fact, this disruption did happen. The disruption of speech took several forms, such as slurred speech, confusion of words, or

**Figure 9-18**

(A) Neurosurgery performed on an awake epileptic patient. The patient is fully conscious, lying on his right side, with the left hemisphere of his brain exposed. He is kept comfortable with local anesthesia. In the background, the neurologist is studying the electroencephalogram being recorded from the patient's cortex, which will help in identifying the eleptogenic focus. The anesthetist is observing the effects of electrical stimulation of the cortex. **(B)** A drawing of the entire skull overlies a photograph of the patient's exposed brain at surgery. The numbered tickets identify the points that the surgeon (Wilder Penfield) stimulated. The application of a stimulating electrode at points 26, 27, and 28 produced interference with speech. Point 26 is presumably in Broca's area, 27 is in the face area, and 28 is in Wernicke's area in this patient.

**(A)**

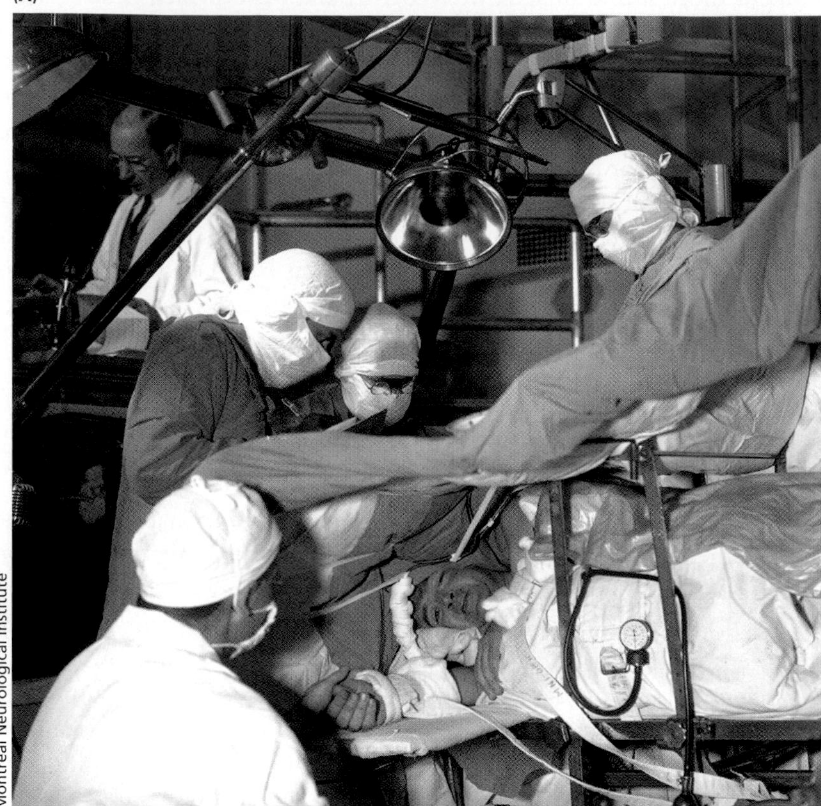


**(B)**

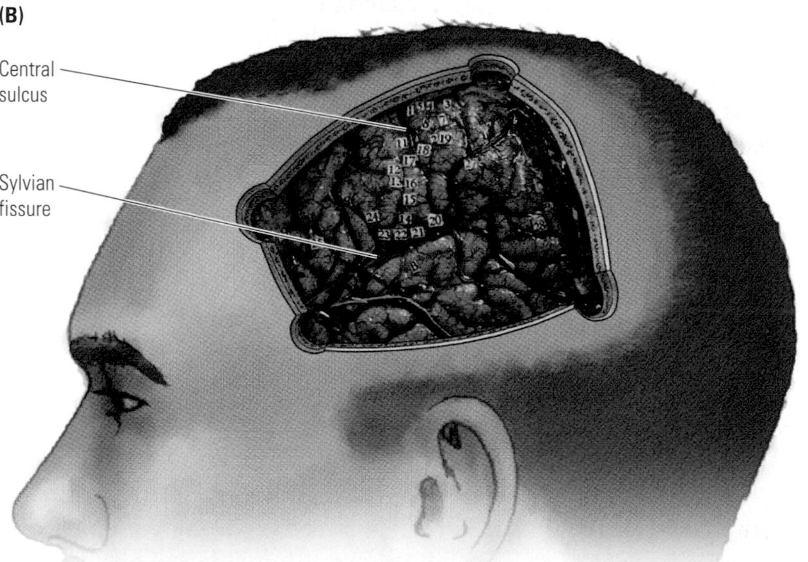


Click on the Web site at **www.worthpublishers.com/kolb/chapter9** for current research on aphasia.

**Aphasia.** The inability to speak despite the presence of normal comprehension and intact vocal mechanisms.

**Supplementary speech area.** A region on the dorsal surface of the left frontal lobe that takes part in the production of speech.

difficulty in finding the right word. Such disruptions of speech are referred to as **aphasia,** which is a general term for any inability to comprehend or produce language. Electrical stimulation could also completely stop ongoing speech, a reaction that Penfield called *speech arrest.* Stimulation of regions well removed from the speech areas had no effect on ongoing speech, with the exception of regions of the motor cortex that control movements of the face. This exception makes sense because facial movement is required for talking.

The second way that Penfield mapped language areas in the brain was to stimulate the cortex when a patient was *not* speaking to see if he could cause the person to utter some kind of speech sound. Penfield did not expect to trigger coherent speech, because the stimulation was not physiologically normal and so probably would not produce actual words or word combinations. This expectation was borne out. Stimulation of a region now known as the **supplementary speech area** produced a sustained vowel cry, such as "Oh" or "Eee." Stimulation of the facial areas in the motor cortex and the somatosensory cortex also produced some vocalization because of their relation to movements of the mouth and tongue. Stimulation outside these speech-related zones produced no such effects. Figure 9-19 shows the areas of the left hemisphere that Penfield found were in some way engaged in processing language. Clearly, much of the left hemisphere takes part in this function.

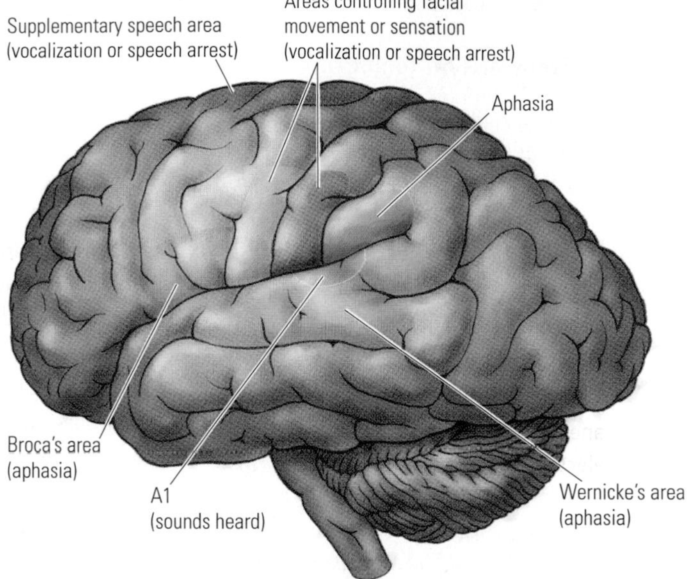


**Figure 9-19**

This map, based on Penfield and Rasmussen's extensive study of patients who had surgery for the relief of intractable epilepsy, summarizes areas in which stimulation may interfere with speech or produce vocalization in the left hemisphere.

Adapted from *Speech and Brain Mechanisms* (p. 201), by W. Penfield and L. Roberts, 1956, London: Oxford University Press.

In summary, Penfield and later researchers used electrical stimulation to identify four important cortical regions that control language. Two classic regions—Broca's area and Wernicke's area—are in the left hemisphere. Interestingly, although Broca's area has traditionally been thought of as the site of speech production and Wernicke's area as the site of language comprehension, electrical stimulation of either region disrupts both processes. Located on both sides of the brain are the other two major regions of language use: the supplementary speech area and the facial regions of the motor and somatosensory cortex. Although the effects on speech vary, depending on which of these four regions is stimulated, stimulation of any of them disrupts speech in some way. Not surprisingly, damage to each of these areas produces some form of aphasia, as described below in "Left-Hemisphere Dysfunction: The Story of Susan S."

Focus on Disorders

## Left-Hemisphere Dysfunction: The Story of Susan S.

Susan S. was a 25-year-old college graduate and mother of two who suffered from epilepsy. When she had a seizure, which was almost every day, she would lose consciousness for a short period, during which she would often engage in repetitive behaviors, such as rocking back and forth. Such psychomotor seizures can usually be controlled by medication, but the drugs were ineffective for Susan. The attacks were very disruptive to her life because they prevented her from driving a car and restricted the types of jobs that she could hold. So Susan decided to undergo neurosurgery to remove the region of abnormal brain tissue that was causing the seizures. This kind of surgery has a very high success rate. In her case, it entailed the removal of a part of the left temporal lobe, including most of the cortex in front of the auditory areas. Although this may seem to be a substantial amount of the brain to cut away, the excised tissue is usually abnormal, so any negative consequences are typically minor.

After her surgery, Susan did well for a few days, but then she suffered unexpected and unusual complications, which led to the death of the remainder of her left temporal lobe, including the auditory cortex and Wernicke's area. As a result, she was no longer able to understand language, except for responding to the sound of her name, and she could say only one phrase: "I love you." She was also unable to read, showing no sign that she could even recognize her own name in writing.

As we, the authors of this book, attempted to find ways to communicate with Susan, we tried humming nursery rhymes to her. She immediately recognized them and could say the words. We also discovered that she could sing. Although she was not ready for a concert performance, her singing skill was well within the normal range and she had a considerable repertoire of songs. She did not seem able to learn new songs, however, and she did not understand us if we "sang messages" to her. Apparently, Susan's repertoire of songs and her singing ability were stored and controlled independently of her language system.

**Positron emission tomography (PET).** A technique whereby changes in blood flow can be detected by measuring changes in the uptake of compounds such as oxygen or glucose.

Go to the CD area on PET in the Research Methods module for a three-dimensional model of a PET camera and samples of PET scans.

## THE AUDITORY CORTEX MAPPED BY POSITRON EMISSION TOMOGRAPHY

More recently, to analyze how the brain processes language, researchers have used a procedure known as **positron emission tomography (PET)** to study the metabolic activity of brain cells. Positron emission tomography is based on an idea that is surprisingly old. In the late 1800s, Angelo Mosso noticed pulsations in the living brain that kept pace with the heartbeat. Mosso was fascinated by this observation and believed that the pulsations were related to changes in blood flow in the brain. He later noticed that the pulsations appeared to be linked to mental activity. For example, when a subject was asked to perform a simple calculation, there was an immediate increase in brain pulsations and, presumably, in blood flow. But to demonstrate a relation between mental activity and blood flow within the brain, a more quantifiable measure than just visual observation would have to be used.

Various procedures for measuring blood flow in the brain were devised in the first 75 years of the twentieth century, one of which is described in "Arteriovenous Malformations." But not until the development of PET in the 1970s could blood flow in the brain of a human subject be measured safely and precisely (Posner and Raichle, 1997). This technique confirmed Mosso's observations.

A PET camera, like the one shown in Figure 9-20, is a doughnut-shaped array of radiation detectors that encircles a subject's head. A small amount of water, containing radioactive molecules to label it, is injected into the bloodstream. The person injected with these molecules is in no danger, because the molecules are very unstable

**Figure 9-20**

A subject lying in a PET scanner, the operation of which is diagrammed at center. A scan is shown at the far right. Brightly colored areas (yellow and red) are regions of high blood flow.

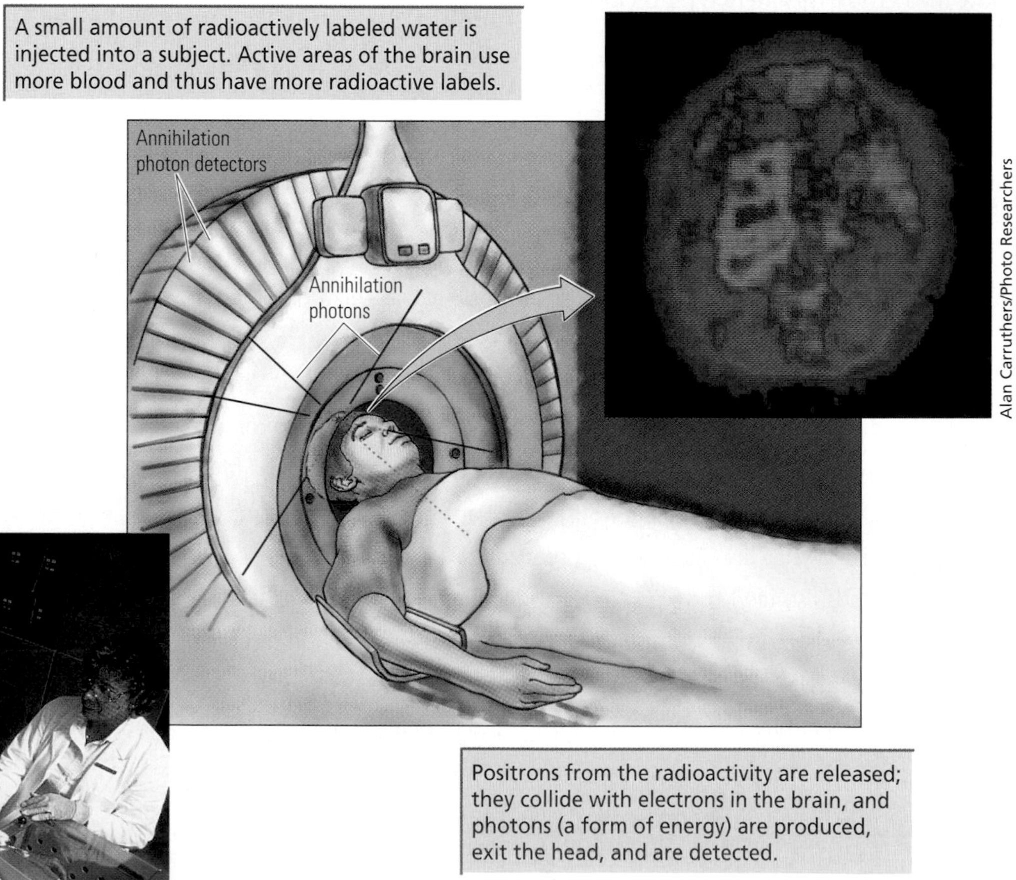

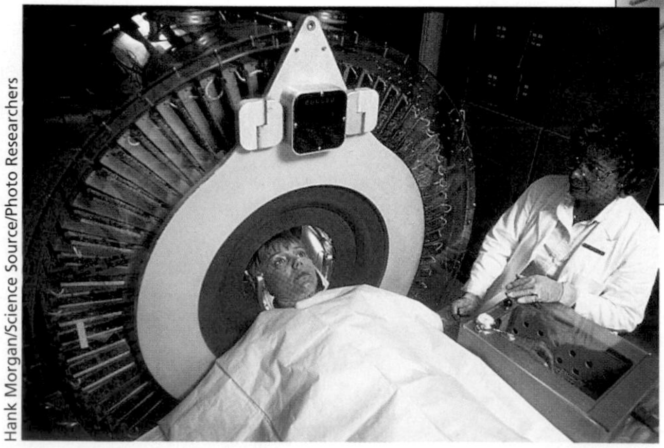

A small amount of radioactively labeled water is injected into a subject. Active areas of the brain use more blood and thus have more radioactive labels.
Annihilation photon detectors
Annihilation photons
Positrons from the radioactivity are released; they collide with electrons in the brain, and photons (a form of energy) are produced, exit the head, and are detected.
Alan Carruthers/Photo Researchers
Hank Morgan/Science Source/Photo Researchers

Focus on Disorders

## Arteriovenous Malformations

An arteriovenous malformation (also called an AV malformation or an angioma) consists of a mass of enlarged and tortuous cortical blood vessels that form congenitally. AV malformations are quite common, accounting for as many as 5 percent of all cases of cerebrovascular disease. Although these malformations may be benign, they often interfere with the functioning of the underlying brain and can produce epileptic seizures. The only treatment is to remove the malformation. This procedure carries significant risk, however, because the brain may be injured in the process.

Walter K. was diagnosed with an AV malformation when he was 26 years old. He had consulted a physician because of increasingly severe headaches, and a neurological examination had revealed an AV malformation over his occipital lobe. A surgeon attempted to remove the malformation, but the surgery did not go well; Walter was left with a defect in the bone overlying his visual cortex. This bone defect made it possible to listen to the blood flow through the malformation.

Dr. John Fulton noticed that when Walter suddenly began to use his eyes after being in the dark, there was a prompt increase in the noise (known as a bruit) associated with blood flow. Fulton documented his observations by recording the sounds of the bruit while Walter performed visual experiments. For example, if Walter had his eyes closed and then opened them to read a newspaper, there was a noticeable increase in blood flow through the occipital lobe. If the lights went out, the noise of the blood flow subsided. Merely shining light into Walter's eyes had no effect; nor was there an effect when he smelled vanilla or strained to listen to faint sounds. Apparently, the bruit and its associated blood flow were triggered by mental effort related to vision. To be able to reach this conclusion was remarkable, given that Fulton used only a stethoscope and a simple recording device for his study. Modern instrumentation, such as that of positron emission tomography, has shown that Fulton's conclusion was correct.

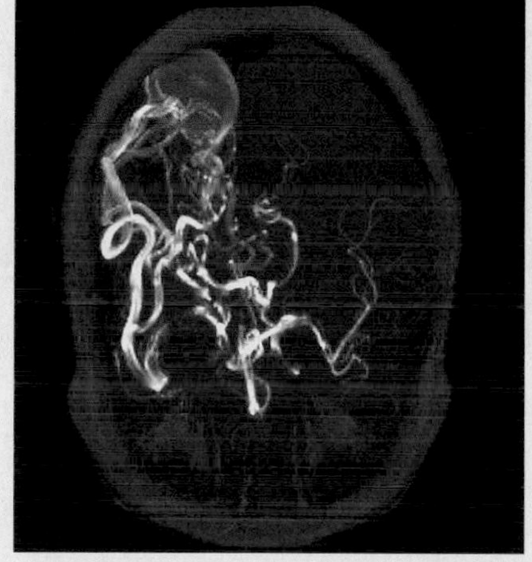

Simon Fraser/Royal Victoria Infirmary, Newcastle Upon Tyne/Science Photo Library/Photo Researchers

An MRI angiogram of an 18-year-old female with an AV malformation. The abnormal cerebral blood vessels (in white) formed a balloon-like structure (the blue area at lower right) that caused the death of the brain tissue around it.

and break down in just a few minutes. The radioactive molecules, such as the radioactive isotope oxygen-15 ($^{15}O$), release tiny positively charged particles known as positrons. These particles are emitted from an atom that is unstable because it is deficient in neutrons. The positrons are attracted to the negative charge of electrons in the brain, and the subsequent collision of these two particles leads to both of them being annihilated, thus creating energy. This energy, which is in the form of photons, leaves the head at the speed of light and is detected by the PET camera. The photons exit the head in exactly opposite directions at the same speed, so it is possible to identify where the source of the photons is.

How does this system enable the measurement of blood flow in the brain? The answer is that the unstable radioactive molecules accumulate in the brain in direct proportion to the rate of local blood flow. Local blood flow, in turn, reflects neural activity because potassium ions released from stimulated neurons dilate adjacent blood

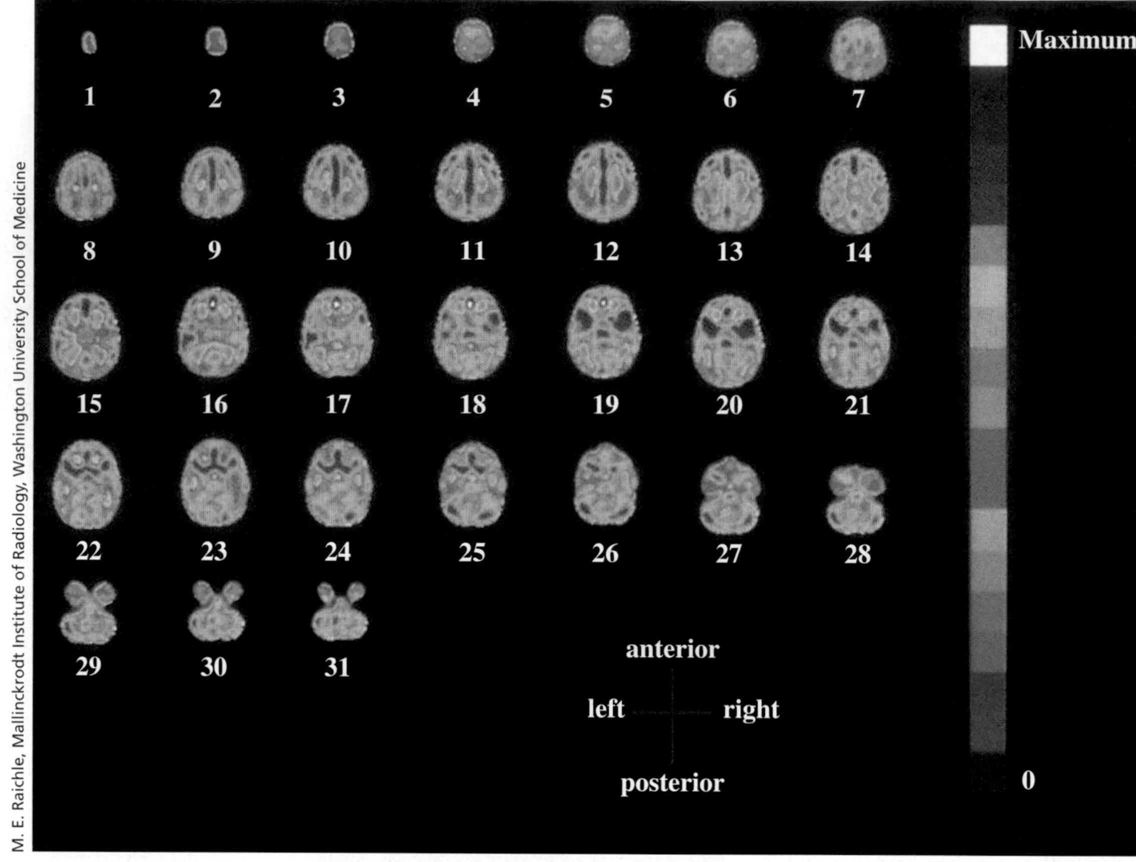


**Figure 9-21**

The PET images of blood flow obtained from a single subject while that subject was resting quietly with eyes closed. Each scan represents a horizontal plane, or section, from the top (1) to the bottom (31) of the brain.

vessels. The greater the blood flow, the higher the radiation counts recorded by the PET camera. With the use of sophisticated computer imaging, it is possible to create a map of the brain, like the one in Figure 9-21, which shows where the blood flow is highest.

Even though the distribution of blood is not uniform in Figure 9-21, it is still difficult to conclude very much from such a map. So PET researchers who are studying the link between blood flow and mental activity resort to a statistical trick. They take the pattern of blood flow when the subject is engaged in the experimental task and subtract from it the blood-flow pattern when the brain is in a carefully selected control state (such as when the person is lying quietly with eyes closed). As illustrated in Figure 9-22, this subtraction provides an image of the change in blood flow in the two states. The change can be averaged across subjects to yield an average image difference, revealing which areas of the brain are selectively active.

What happens when PET is used while subjects listen to sounds? Although there are many PET studies of auditory stimulation, a series conducted by Robert Zatorre and his colleagues (1992, 1995) serves as a good example. These researchers hypothesized that simple auditory stimulation, such as bursts of noise, would be analyzed by area A1, whereas more complex auditory stimulation, such as speech syllables, would be analyzed in adjacent secondary auditory areas. The researchers also hypothesized that performance of a speech-sound-discrimination task would selectively activate left-hemisphere regions. This is exactly what they found. Figure 9-23 shows that the primary auditory cortex experienced increased activity in response to noise bursts, whereas secondary auditory areas were activated by speech syllables. Both types of stimuli produced responses in both hemispheres, but there was greater activation in

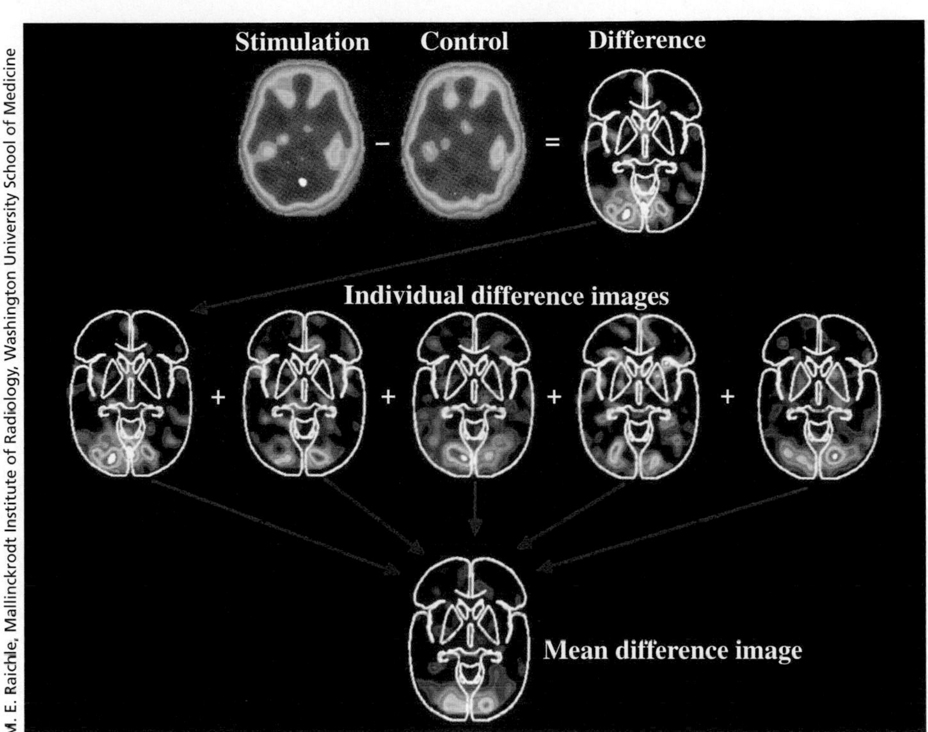


**Figure 9-22**

The procedure of subtraction. In the upper row of scans, the control condition (in this case, resting while looking at a static fixation point) is subtracted from the experimental condition of looking at a flickering checkerboard. The subtraction produces a somewhat different image for each of the five subjects shown in the middle row, but all show increased blood flow in the occipital region. The images are averaged to produce the image at the bottom.

the left hemisphere for the speech syllables. These results imply that auditory area A1 analyzes all incoming auditory signals, speech and nonspeech, whereas the secondary auditory areas are responsible for some higher-order signal processing required for the analysis of language sounds.

As Figure 9-23C shows, the speech-sound-discrimination task yielded an intriguing additional result: during this task, there was also activation of Broca's area in the left hemisphere. The involvement of this region in the frontal lobe during auditory analysis may seem surprising. In Wernicke's model, Broca's area is considered the place where the motor programs needed to *produce* words are stored. It is not normally a region thought of as the site of speech-sound discrimination. A possible explanation is that, to determine that the "g" in "bag" and "pig" is the same speech sound, the auditory stimulus must be related to how that sound is actually articulated. That is, the speech-sound perception requires a match with the motor behaviors associated with making that sound. This role for Broca's area in speech analysis is seen in further studies in which people are asked to determine if a stimulus is a word

**Figure 9-23**

Selective cortical areas are activated in different language-related tasks. **(A)** Passively listening to noise bursts activates the primary auditory cortex. **(B)** Listening to words activates the posterior speech area. **(C)** Making a phonetic discrimination activates the frontal region, including Broca's area.

**(A) Listening to bursts of noise**

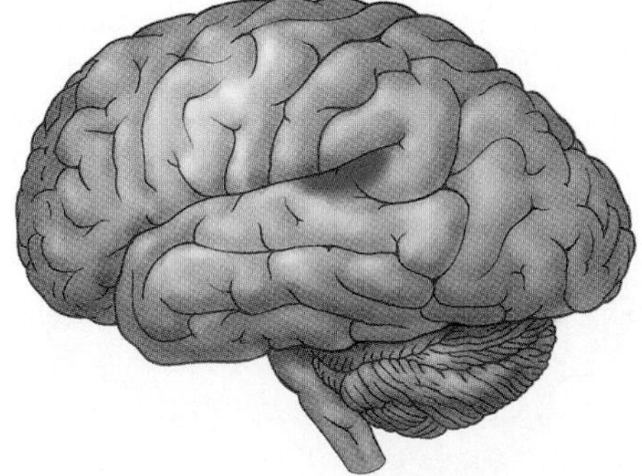

**(B) Listening to words**

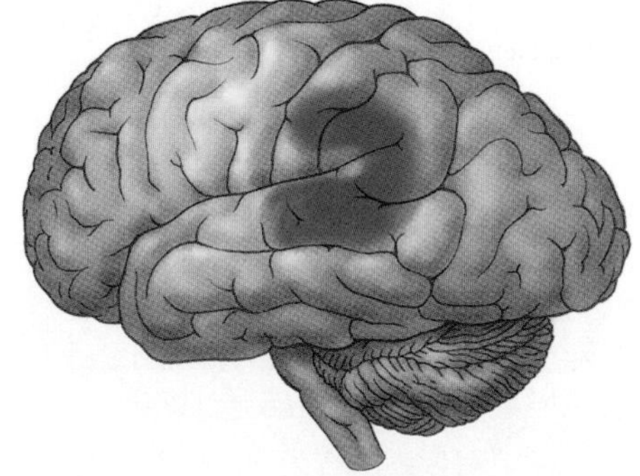

**(C) Discriminating speech sounds**

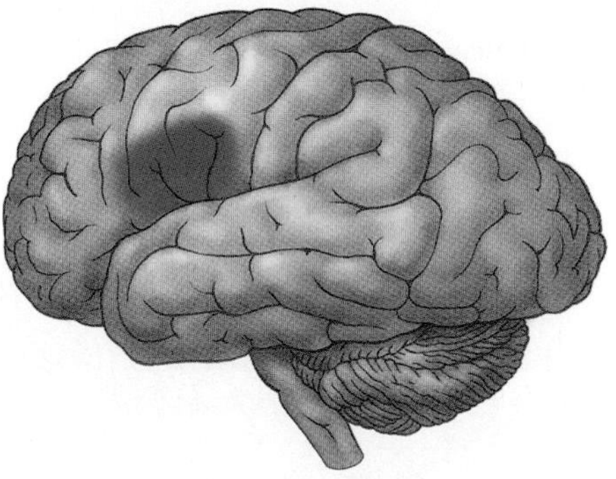

or a nonword (for example, "tid" versus "tin" or "gan" versus "tan"). In this case, information about how the words are articulated is irrelevant, and Broca's area would not need to be recruited. It is not.

## Processing Music

Although Penfield did not study the effect of brain stimulation on musical analysis, there are many studies of musical processing in brain-damaged patients. "Cerebral Aneurysms: The Story of C. N." describes one of them. Collectively, the results of these studies confirm that musical processing is in fact largely a right-hemisphere specialization, just as language processing is largely a left-hemisphere one.

Maurice Ravel (1875–1937)

An excellent example of right-hemisphere predominance for the processing of music is seen in a famous patient—composer Maurice Ravel (1875–1937). Ravel suffered a left-hemisphere stroke and developed aphasia while at the peak of his career. Yet many of Ravel's musical skills remained intact after the stroke because they were localized to the right hemisphere. For instance, he could still recognize melodies, pick up tiny mistakes in music that he heard being played, and even judge the tuning of pianos. Interestingly, however, not all his musical skills were preserved. Skills that had to do with music production were among those that were destroyed. For instance, Ravel could no longer recognize written music, play the piano, or compose. This dissociation of music perception and music production is curious. Apparently, the left hemisphere plays at least some role in certain aspects of music processing, especially those that have to do with the "making" of music.

To find out more about how the brain carries out the perceptual side of music processing, Zatorre and his colleagues (1994) conducted PET studies. When subjects listened simply to bursts of noise, Heschl's gyrus became activated, but this was not the case when the subjects listened to melodies. As shown in Figure 9-24, the perception of melodies triggered major activation in the right-hemisphere auditory cortex lying in front of Heschl's gyrus, as well as minor activation in the same region of the left hemisphere. In another test, subjects listened to the same melodies but this time were asked to indicate whether the pitch of the second note was higher or lower than that of the first note. During this task, which requires short-term memory of what has just been heard, blood flow in the right frontal lobe increased. As with language, then, the frontal lobe plays a role in auditory analysis when short-term memory is used.

As noted earlier, the capacity for language appears to be innate. Sandra Trehab and her colleagues (1999) showed that this may be true for music as well. For example, infants show learning preferences for musical scales versus random notes. Furthermore, like adults, children are very sensitive to musical errors, presumably because they are biased for perceiving regularity in rhythms. Thus, it appears that, at birth, the brain is prepared for both music and language and, presumably, selectively attends to these types of auditory signals.

**Figure 9-24**

Selective cortical areas activated in different music-related tasks. **(A)** Passively listening to noise bursts activates Heschl's gyrus. **(B)** Listening to melodies activates the primary auditory cortex. **(C)** Making relative pitch judgments about two notes of each melody activates a right frontal lobe area.

**(A) Listening to bursts of noise**

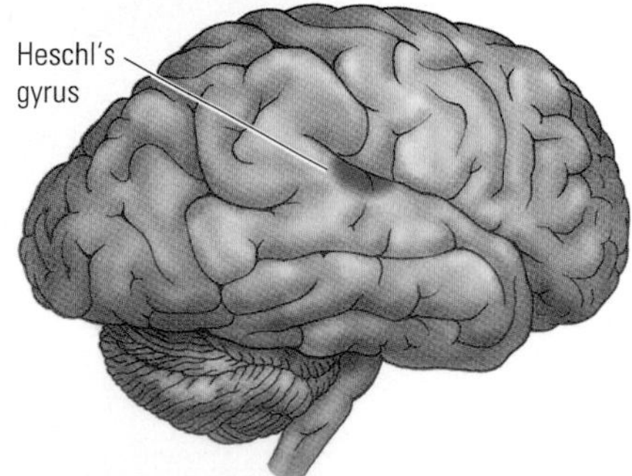

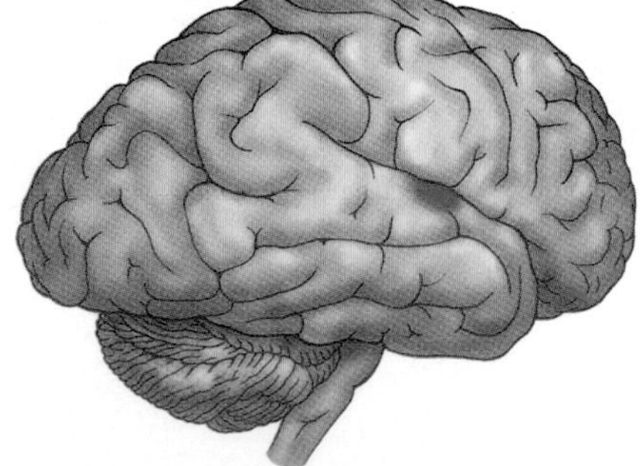

**(C) Comparing pitches**

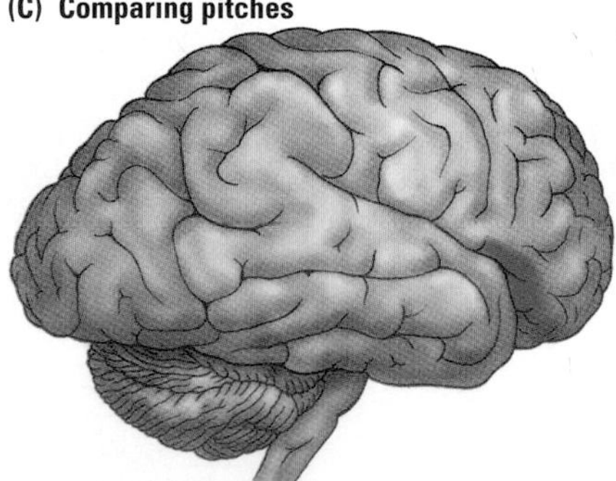

Focus on Disorders

## Cerebral Aneurysms: The Story of C. N.

C. N. is a 35-year-old nurse whose case was described by Isabelle Peretz and her colleagues (1994). In December 1986, C. N. suddenly developed severe neck pain and headache. A neurological examination revealed an aneurysm in the middle cerebral artery on the right side of her brain. An *aneurysm* is a bulge in a blood vessel wall caused by a weakening of the tissue, much like the bulge that appears in a bicycle tube at a spot that is no longer strong. Aneurysms in a cerebral artery are dangerous because, if they burst, severe bleeding and subsequent brain damage result.

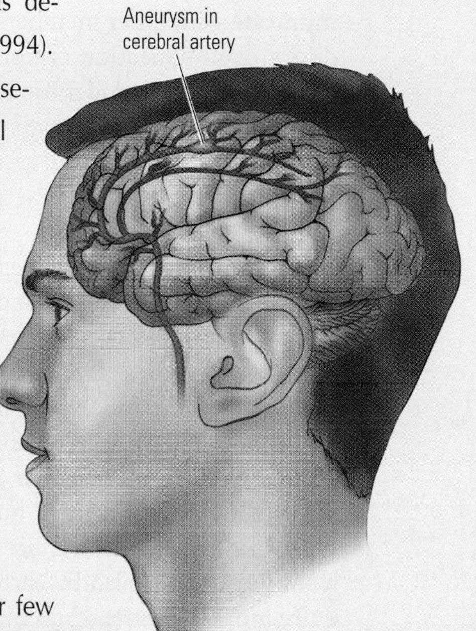

In February 1987, C. N.'s aneurysm was surgically repaired, and she appeared to suffer few adverse effects. However, postoperative brain imaging revealed that a new aneurysm had formed in the same location but on the opposite side of the brain. This second aneurysm was repaired 2 weeks later. After her surgery, C. N. had temporary difficulty finding the right word when she spoke, but, more important, her perception of music was deranged. She could no longer sing, nor could she recognize familiar tunes. In fact, singers sounded to her as if they were talking instead of singing. But C. N. could still dance to music. Because her music-related symptoms did not go away, she was given a brain scan. It revealed damage along the Sylvian fissure in both temporal lobes. The damage did not include the primary auditory cortex, nor did it include any part of the posterior speech zone. For these reasons, C. N. could still recognize nonmusical sounds and showed no evidence of language disturbance. Apparently, nonmusical sounds and speech sounds are analyzed in separate parts of the brain from music.

## In Review

The auditory system has a complementary specialization in the cortex: left for language-related analyses and right for music-related ones. This asymmetry, however, appears to be relative, because there is good evidence that the left hemisphere plays a role in some aspects of music-related behaviors and that the right hemisphere has some language capabilities. The results of both electrical-stimulation and PET studies have shown that the left hemisphere contains several language-related areas. For instance, Wernicke's area identifies speech syllables and words, representations of which are stored in that location. Broca's area matches speech sounds to the motor programs necessary to articulate them, and, in this way, it plays a role in discriminating closely related speech sounds. The auditory cortex of the right hemisphere plays a major part in the comprehension of music.

# AUDITORY COMMUNICATION IN NONHUMAN SPECIES

Many animals use sounds to aid their survival. Some, as we do, use sounds to communicate with other members of their species. Here we consider just two types of auditory communication in nonhumans: birdsong and bat echolocation. Each of these types provides a model for understanding different aspects of brain–behavior relations involving the auditory system.

## Birdsong

There are about 8500 living species of birds, of which about half are considered songbirds. Birdsong has many functions, including attracting mates (usually by males), demarcating territories, and announcing location or even mere presence. Although birds of the same species all have a similar song, the details of that song vary markedly from region to region, much as dialects of the same human language vary. Figure 9-25 includes sound spectrograms for the songs of male white-crowned sparrows that live in three different localities near San Francisco. Notice how the songs of birds are nearly identical in a single region but quite different from region to region. These regional differences are due to the fact that song development in young birds is influenced not just by genes but also by early experience and learning. In fact, young birds can acquire more elaborate songs than can other members of their species if the young birds have a good tutor (Marler, 1991).

There are some broad similarities between birdsong and human language. For instance, if a young bird is not exposed to any songs until it is a juvenile and then listens to recordings of the songs of different species, there is a general preference for the song of the bird's own species. This preference must mean that there is some kind of species-specific song template in the brain of each species and that the details of this template are modified by experience. In a similar way, humans seem to have a basic structural template for language that is programmed into the brain, and a variety of specific grammatical forms are added to this template.

Another broad similarity between birdsong and human language is the great diversity of each. Among birds, this diversity can be seen in the sheer number of songs that a species possesses. Species such as the white-crowned sparrow have but a single song, whereas others such as the marsh wren have as many as 150 songs. The number of syllables in birdsong also varies greatly, ranging from 30 for the canary to about 2000 for the brown thrasher. In a similar way, even though all modern human languages are equally complex grammatically, they vary significantly in the type and number of elements that they employ. For instance, the number of meaningful speech sounds in human languages ranges from about 15 (for some Polynesian languages) to about 100 (for some dialects spoken in the Caucasus Mountains).

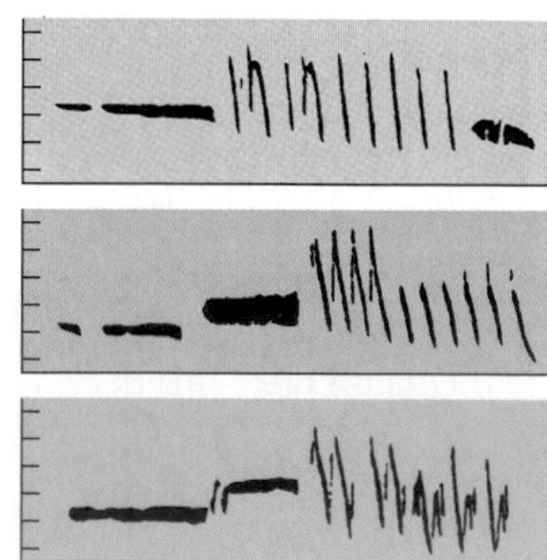

**Figure 9-25**

Sound spectrograms of three male white-crowned sparrows whose songs were recorded in three separate localities (Point Reyes in Marin County, Berkeley, and Sunset Beach) around San Francisco Bay. The sound spectrograms of males found in any one place are very similar but differ from those of males in other regions. Thus, birds raised in different regions have different dialects.

Adapted from P. Marler, "The instinct to learn." In S. Carey & R. German (Eds.). *The Epigenesis of mind: Essays on biology and cognition.* Hillsdale, NJ: Lawrence Erlbaum, 1991, p. 39.

A final broad similarity between birdsong and human language lies in how they develop. In many bird species, song development is heavily influenced by experience during a so-called sensitive period, just as it is in humans, as you learned in Chapter 7. Birds also go through stages in song development, just as humans go through stages in language development. Early in life, birds make noises that attract the attention of their parents, usually for feeding, and human babies, too, emit cries, often to signal hunger. When a bird is older and often ready to leave the nest, it begins to make noises that Charles Darwin compared to the prespeech babbling of human infants. These noises, called *subsong,* are variable in structure and low in volume, and they are often produced as the bird appears to doze. Presumably, subsong, like human babbling, is a type of practice for the later development of adult communication. As a young bird matures, it starts to produce sound patterns that contain recognizable bits of the adult song. Finally, the adult song emerges. In most species, the adult song remains remarkably stable, although a few species, such as canaries, can develop a new song every year.

The neural control of birdsong has been a topic of intense research, partly because it provides an excellent model of changes in the brain that accompany learning and partly because it can be a source of insight into how sex hormones influence behavior. Fernando Nottebohm and his colleagues first identified the major structures controlling birdsong in the late 1970s. These structures are illustrated in Figure 9-26. The largest are the *higher vocal control center* (HVC) and the *nucleus robustus archistriatalis* (RA). The axons of the HVC connect to the RA, which in turn sends axons to the 12th cranial nerve. This nerve controls the muscles of the syrinx, the structure that actually produces the song.

The HVC and RA have several important characteristics. First, they are asymmetrical in some species, with the structures in the left hemisphere being larger than those in the right hemisphere. In many cases, this asymmetry is similar to the lateralized control of language in humans: if the left-hemisphere pathways are damaged, the birds stop singing, but similar injury in the right hemisphere has no effect on song. Second, birdsong structures are sexually dimorphic. That is, they are much larger in males than in females. In canaries, they are five times as large in the male bird. This sexual difference is due to the hormone testosterone in males. Injection of testosterone into female birds causes the song-controlling nuclei to increase in size. Third, the size of the birdsong nuclei is related to singing skill. For instance, unusually talented singers among male canaries tend to have larger HVCs and RAs than do less-

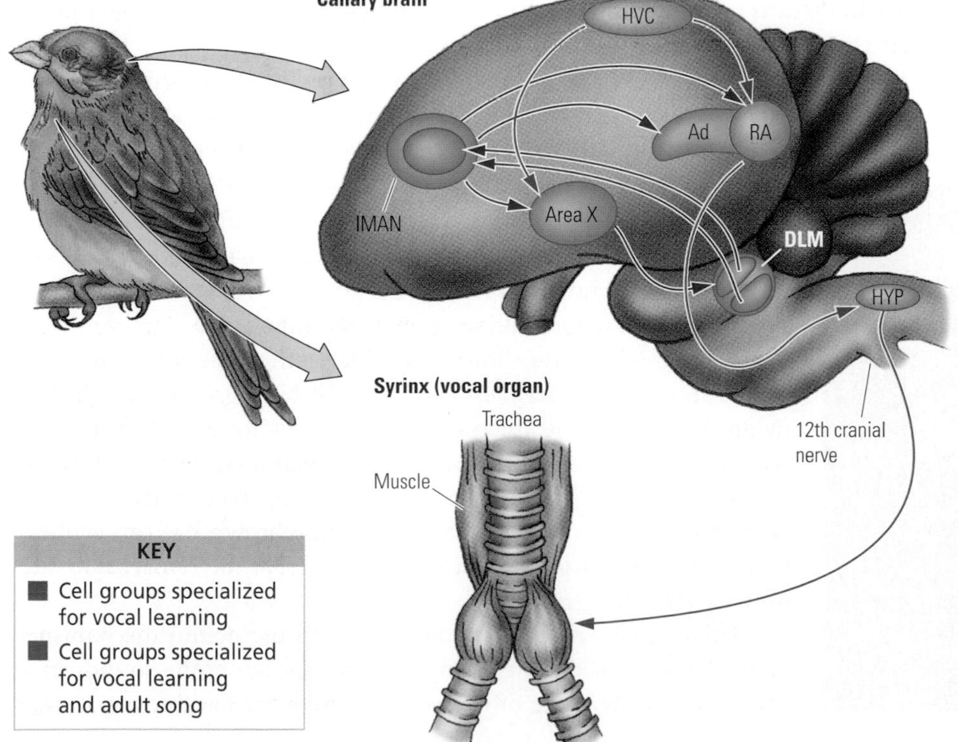


**Figure 9-26**

This side view of the canary brain shows several nuclei that control song learning, the two critical ones being the HVC (higher vocal control center) and the nucleus robustus archistriatalis (RA). These areas are necessary both for adult singing and for learning the song. Other regions necessary for learning the song during development but not required for the adult song include the dorsal archistriatum (Ad), the lateral magnocellular nucleus of the anterior neostriatum (IMAN), area X of the avian striatum, and the medial dorsolateral nucleus of the thalamus (DLM).

**Echolocation.** The ability to identify and locate an object by sound that bounces off the object.

gifted singers. Finally, the HVC and RA contain not only cells that produce birdsong but also cells responsive to hearing song, especially the song of a bird's own species. The same structures therefore play a role in both song production and song perception—comparable to the overlapping roles of Broca's and Wernicke's areas in language perception and production.

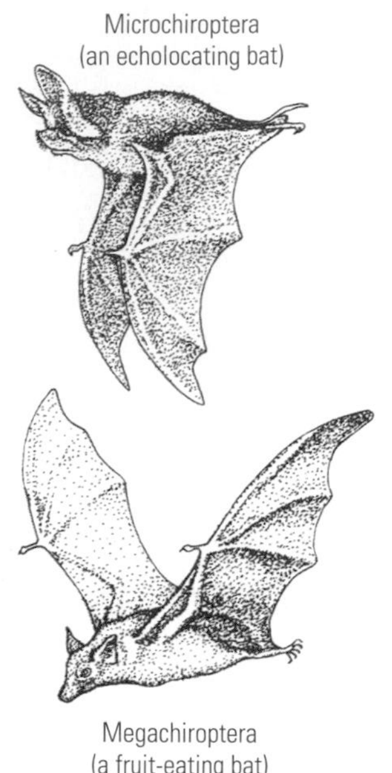


## Echolocation in Bats

Next to rodents, bats are the most numerous order of mammals. There are two general groups of bats, known as suborders. One suborder consists of the smaller echolocating bats (Microchiroptera); the other comprises the larger fruit-eating and flower-visiting bats (Megachiroptera), sometimes called flying foxes. The echolocating bats interest us here because they use sound as a means of navigation.

There are 680 species of echolocating bats, most of which feed on insects. Some of the others live on blood (vampire bats), and some catch frogs, lizards, fishes, birds, and small mammals. These bats use echolocation for two purposes: for flying in the dark and for detecting and pursuing prey. The auditory system of bats is specialized for both tasks.

**Echolocation** allows bats not only to locate targets in the dark but also to analyze the features of targets, as well as features of the environment in general. Through echolocation, a bat identifies prey, navigates through the leaves of trees, and locates surfaces suitable to land on. Perhaps a term analogous to *visualization*, such as "audification," would be more appropriate.

How, exactly, does echolocation work? The answer is, Rather like radar. The larynx of a bat emits bursts of ultrasonic sound that bounce off objects and return to the bat's ears, allowing the animal to tell what is in the surrounding environment. The bat, in other words, navigates by the echoes that it hears, differentiating among the different characteristics of those echoes. Objects that are moving, such as insects, have a moving echo. Smooth objects give a different echo from that of rough objects, and so on. A key component of this echolocation system is the analysis of differences in the return times of echoes. Close objects return echoes sooner than more distant objects do, and there are minute differences in return times, depending on the texture of an object's surface.

**Figure 9-27**

A bat with a 40-centimeter wingspan can navigate through a 14-by-14-centimeter mesh made of 80-micrometer nylon thread while flying in total darkness. The sonar of the bat is capable of creating an accurate map of the world that is based entirely on auditory information.

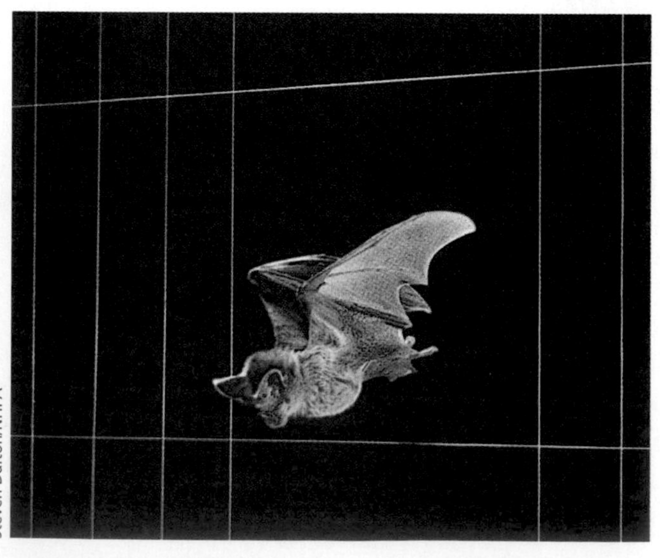
Steven Dalton/NHPA

A bat's cries are of short duration (from 0.3 to 200 milliseconds) and high frequency (from 12,000 to 200,000 hertz), mostly at too high a frequency for the human ear to detect. Different bat species produce sounds of different frequency, with the particular frequency used depending on the animal's ecology. For instance, bats that catch prey in the open use different frequencies from those used by bats that catch insects in foliage and from those used by bats that hunt for prey on the ground.

The echolocation abilities of bats are impressive. The results of laboratory studies have shown that a bat with a 40-centimeter wing span can fly in total darkness through a 14-by-14-centimeter grid of nylon threads only 80 micrometers thick, as shown in Figure 9-27. Bats in the wild can be trained to catch small food particles thrown up into the air in the dark. These echolocating skills make the bat a very efficient hunter. For instance, the little brown bat can capture very small flying insects, such as mosquitoes, at the remarkable rate of two per second.

There has been considerable interest in the neural mechanisms of the bat echolocation system. Each bat species emits sounds in a relatively narrow range of frequencies, and a bat's auditory pathway has cells specifically tuned to echoes in the frequency range of its species. For example, the mustached bat sends out sounds ranging from 60,000 to 62,000 hertz, and its auditory system has a *cochlear fovea* (a maximally sensitive area in the organ of Corti) that corresponds to that frequency range. In this way, more neurons are dedicated to the frequency range used for echolocation than to any other range of frequencies. Analogously, our visual system dedicates more neurons to the retina's fovea, the area responsible for our most detailed vision. In the cortex of the bat's brain, there are several distinct areas for processing complex echo-related inputs. For instance, one area computes the distance of given targets from the animal, whereas another area computes the velocity of a moving target. This neural system makes the bat exquisitely adapted for nighttime navigation.

## In Review

The analysis of birdsong has identified several important principles of auditory functioning. One principle is that specialized structures in the brain produce and perceive vocal stimuli. Another is that these structures are influenced by early experience. Third, an innate template imposes an important constraint on the nature of the songs that a bird produces and perceives. These principles underlying birdsong are similar to those observed in human language and reinforce the idea that many characteristics of human language may be innate. Insect-eating bats have evolved a different use of sound from that of birds. Such bats employ high-frequency sounds as a type of sonar that allows them to fly in the dark and to catch insects. An echolocating bat's auditory world is much richer than ours because it contains information about the shape and velocity of objects—information that our visual system provides.

## SUMMARY

1. *What is the nature of the stimulus that the brain perceives as sound?* The stimulus for the auditory system is change in air pressure. The ear transduces changes in air pressure into what we perceive as sound. Sound has three fundamental physical qualities: frequency, amplitude, and complexity. Perceptually, these qualities translate into pitch, loudness, and timbre.
2. *How does the nervous system transform changes in air pressure into our impression of sounds?* Sound waves are transformed into perceptions of sound through a combination of mechanical and neural activities. The auditory receptor apparatus is the cochlea, located in the inner ear. The auditory receptors themselves are hair cells that are found on the basilar membrane. Changes in air pressure are conveyed in a chain reaction from the eardrum to the bones of the middle ear to the oval window of the cochlea and the cochlear fluid that lies behind it. Movements of the cochlear fluid produce movements in specific regions of the basilar membrane, leading to changes in the activity of the hair cells. The basilar membrane has a tonotopic organization. High-frequency sounds maximally stimulate hair cells at one of its ends, whereas low-frequency sounds maximally stimulate hair cells at the other end. In this way, cochlear neurons code for the various frequencies of sounds. The tonotopic organization of sound analysis is found at all levels of the auditory system. The auditory system also detects both sound amplitude and sound location. Sound amplitude is coded by the firing rate of cochlear neurons, with loud sounds producing higher firing rates than soft sounds do.

**neuroscience interactive**

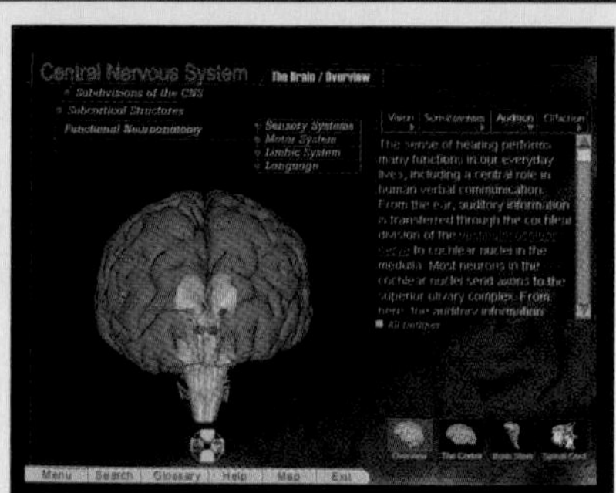

There are many resources available for expanding your learning on line:

- **www.worthpublishers.com/kolb/chapter9**

Try some self-tests to reinforce your mastery of the material. Look at some of the updates reflecting current research on the brain. You'll also be able to link to other sites which will reinforce what you've learned.

- **www.nad.org**

Link to the National Association of the Deaf and learn about living with deafness.

- **www.aphasia.org**

Do more research about aphasia at the site for the National Aphasia Association.

On your CD-ROM you'll be able to quiz yourself on your comprehension of the chapter. The module on the Central Nervous System also provides important review of the auditory pathways and cortical anatomy important for understanding this chapter.

Sound location is detected by structures in the brainstem that compute differences in the arrival times and the loudness of a sound in the two ears.

3. *How does auditory information get from the receptors to the brain?* The hair cells of the cochlea synapse with bipolar neurons that form the cochlear nerve, which in turn forms part of the eighth cranial nerve. The cochlear nerve takes auditory information to three structures in the hindbrain: the cochlear nucleus, the olivary complex, and trapezoid body. Cells in these areas are sensitive to differences in sound intensity and sound arrival time in the two ears. In this way, they enable the location of a sound to be determined. The auditory pathway continues from the hindbrain areas to the inferior colliculus of the midbrain, then to the medial geniculate nucleus in the thalamus, and finally to the auditory cortex. Cells in the cortex are responsive to specific categories of sound, such as sounds used in communication by a given species.
4. *How does the brain understand language and music?* Despite their differences in speech sounds and grammar, all human languages have the same basic structure. This fundamental similarity implies that the brain possesses a basic template for creating language. The auditory areas of the cortex in the left hemisphere play a special role in analyzing language-related information, whereas those in the right hemisphere play a special role in analyzing music-related information. Studies have revealed several language-processing areas in the left hemisphere. For instance, Wernicke's area identifies speech syllables and words and so is critically engaged in speech comprehension. Broca's area matches speech sounds to the motor programs necessary to make them and so plays a major role in speech production. Broca's area also discriminates between closely related speech sounds. The primary auditory cortex of the right hemisphere plays a critical role in comprehending music. The right temporal lobe analyzes the musical qualities of speech, known as prosody.
5. *How does brain organization relate to the unique auditory worlds of other species?* Nonhuman species often use auditory analysis in specialized behaviors. One example is birdsong. Songbirds have regions of the brain that are specialized for producing and comprehending song. In many species, these regions are lateralized to the left hemisphere, just as the language areas are lateralized to the left hemisphere in humans. There are also striking similarities between the development of song in birds and the development of language in humans, as well as similarities in the neural mechanisms underlying both the production and the perception of song and language. Another example of the use of sound in nonhuman species is the auditory control of movements. Both owls and bats use auditory information to guide movement in the dark. These animals can fly and catch prey at night by using only auditory information. Bats have the added ability to produce a type of sonar that allows them to create an auditory map of the objects in their world. This type of sensory reality we can only try to imagine.

## KEY TERMS

aphasia, p. 340
basilar membrane, p. 327
Broca's aphasia, p. 338
Broca's area, p. 338
cochlear implant, p. 333
echolocation, p. 350
Heschl's gyrus, p. 330
hertz, p. 321
positron emission tomography (PET), p. 342
prosody, p. 325
supplementary speech area, p. 341
tonotopic representation, p. 332
tuning curve, p. 332
Wernicke's aphasia, p. 338
Wernicke's area, p. 330

## REVIEW QUESTIONS

1. What are the three principal qualities of sound, and how does the auditory system code them?
2. How does the auditory system code the location of a sound?
3. Why do all human languages have the same basic structure?
4. How is language perception organized in the brain?
5. How is blood flow measured in the brain, and what does it tell us about brain function?
6. Give a simple neurobiological explanation of how we understand and produce language.
7. What can we learn from birdsong that is relevant to human auditory function?

## FOR FURTHER THOUGHT

1. Different species have different ranges of hearing. Why would this be adaptive?
2. What is special about language and music?

## RECOMMENDED READING

Drake-Lee, A. B. (1992). Beyond music: Auditory temporary threshold shift in rock musicians after a heavy metal concert. *Journal of the Royal Society of Medicine, 85,* 617–619. Have you ever wondered what listening to loud music might be doing to your hearing? This paper looks at the effects of hearing loud music at a rock concert on hearing thresholds in the musicians. What is important to remember is that the musicians are standing beside the speakers, so those in the front rows are likely to hear even louder music.

Gazzaniga, M. S. (1992). *Nature's mind.* New York: Basic Books. Michael Gazzaniga is an eminent cognitive neuroscientist who has an easy writing style. He has written several popular books, such as *Nature's Mind,* each of which is chock full of interesting ideas about how the brain works. This book is a pleasure to read and introduces the reader to Gazzaniga's ideas about why the brain is asymmetrically organized and what the fundamental differences between the hemispheres might be.

Luria, A. R. (1972). *The man with a shattered world.* Chicago: Regnery. Alexander Luria wrote many neuropsychology books in his long career, but this one is perhaps the most interesting and accessible to the nonspecialist. This book describes the effect of a bullet wound to the head of a university student who was recruited to defend Leningrad in World War II. The book has many anecdotes, often humorous, that show how the young man's mental world was severely altered by this traumatic experience. Reading this book can be a source of insight into what it is like to cope with brain damage.

Pinker, S. (1997). *How the mind works.* New York: Norton. Stephen Pinker gives us a provocative look at theories of how brain activity produces mental events. For those interested in cognitive neuroscience, this book is a good introduction to questions we might ask in everyday life. For example, why does a face look more attractive with makeup? Or, why is the thought of eating worms disgusting?

CHAPTER

# 10

# How Does the Brain Produce Movement?



Kevork Djansezian/AP Photo

Micrograph: Dr. David Scott/Phototake

Kamala is a female Indian elephant that lives at the zoo in Calgary, Canada. Her trunk, which is really just a greatly extended upper lip and nose, consists of about 2000 fused muscles. A pair of nostrils runs its length, and fingerlike projections are located at its tip. The skin of the trunk is soft and supple and is covered sparsely with sensory hairs. Like all elephants, Kamala uses her trunk for many purposes. It can gather food, scratch an ear, rub an itchy eye, or caress a baby. It can also be used to explore. Kamala raises it to sniff the wind, lowers it to examine the ground for scents, and sometimes even pokes it into another elephant's mouth to investigate the food there. She, like other elephants, can inhale as much as 4 liters of water into her trunk, which she can then place in her mouth to drink or squirt over her body to bathe. She can also inhale dust or mud for bathing. Kamala's trunk is a potential weapon, too. She can flick it as a threat, lash out with it in aggression, and throw missiles with it. Her trunk is both immensely strong and very agile. With it, Kamala can lift objects as large as an elephant calf, sometimes uprooting entire trees, yet this same trunk can grasp a single peanut from the palm of a proffered hand.

In one way, however, Kamala uses this versatile trunk very unusually for an elephant (Onodera & Hicks, 1999). She is one of only a few elephants in the world that paints with its trunk (Figure 10-1). Like many artists, she paints when it suits her, but nevertheless she has commemorated many important zoo events, such as the arrival of new species to the zoo. An elephant artist is not as far-fetched as the idea may at first seem. Other elephants, both in the wild and in captivity, pick up small stones and sticks and draw in the dust with them. But Kamala has gone well beyond this simple doodling. When given paints and a brush, she began to produce works of art, many of which have been sold to art collectors. Kamala, in fact, has achieved an international reputation as an artist.

A defining feature of animals is their ability to move. As the example of Kamala illustrates, even very skilled movements are not limited to humans. Although we humans display the most skilled motor control of all animals, members of many species have highly dexterous movements. This chapter explores how the brain produces movement. We begin by considering how the control of movement is organized. Then, we examine the various contributions of the neocortex, the brainstem, and the spinal cord to movement. Of particular interest is how neurons of the motor cortex take part in producing skilled movements. Next, we investigate how the basal ganglia and the cerebellum help to fine-tune our control of movement. Finally, we turn to the role of the somatosensory system. Although other senses, such as vision, play a part in enabling movement, body senses play a special role, as you will soon discover.

The Calgary Zoological Society

The Calgary Zoological Society

**Figure 10-1**
Kamala (her name means "lotus flower") was born in 1975 in Sri Lanka's Yala National Park and orphaned shortly thereafter. She was adopted by the Calgary, Alberta, Zoological Society. Elephants were first observed to paint with sticks or rocks in the dust, and some have become accomplished artists when given paints and a brush. Kamala began painting as part of an environmental enrichment program, and her paintings are widely sold to collectors.

## THE HIERARCHICAL CONTROL OF MOVEMENT

When Kamala paints a picture, her behaviors are sequentially organized. First, she looks at her canvas and her selection of paints; then, she considers what she wants to paint; and, finally, she executes her painting. These sequentially organized behaviors are dictated by the hierarchical organization of Kamala's nervous system. The major components of this nervous system hierarchy are the neocortex, the brainstem, and the spinal cord. All contribute to controlling the behaviors required to produce her artwork.

In the same way, your hierarchically organized nervous system controls every movement that you make. Figure 10-2 shows the sequence of steps taken when the human nervous system directs a hand to pick up a coffee mug. The visual system must first inspect the cup to determine what part of it should be grasped. This information is then relayed from the visual cortex to cortical motor regions, which plan and initiate the movement, sending instructions to the part of the spinal cord that controls the muscles of the arm and hand. As the handle of the cup is grasped, information from sensory receptors in the fingers travels to the spinal cord, and from there messages are sent to sensory regions of the cortex that control touch. The sensory cortex, in turn, in-

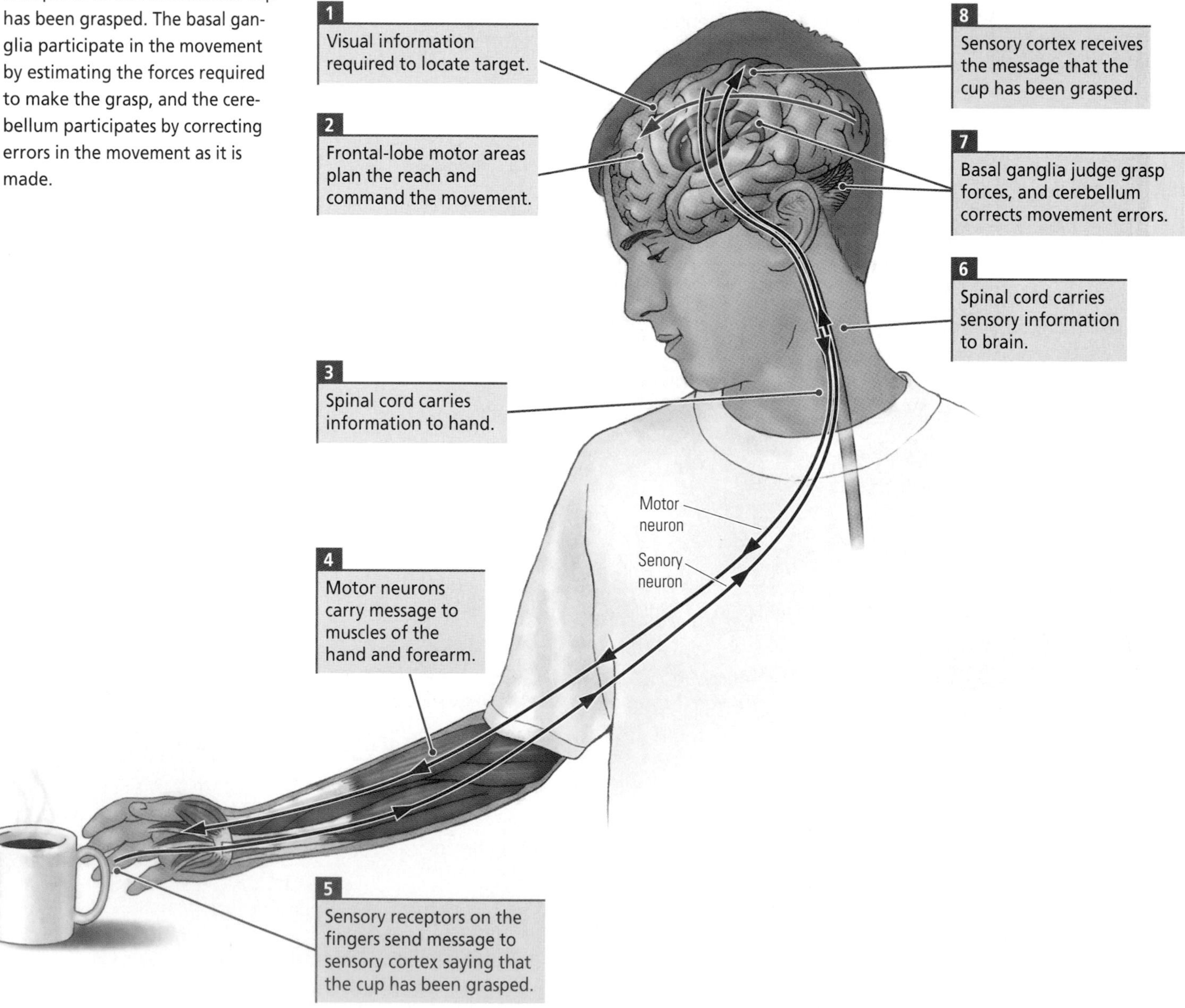
1
Visual information required to locate target.
2
Frontal-lobe motor areas plan the reach and command the movement.
3
Spinal cord carries information to hand.
4
Motor neurons carry message to muscles of the hand and forearm.
5
Sensory receptors on the fingers send message to sensory cortex saying that the cup has been grasped.
6
Spinal cord carries sensory information to brain.
7
Basal ganglia judge grasp forces, and cerebellum corrects movement errors.
8
Sensory cortex receives the message that the cup has been grasped.
Motor neuron
Senory neuron

**Figure 10-2**

The brain tells the hand to reach, and the hand tells the brain that it has succeeded. Movements such as reaching for a cup require the participation of wide areas of the nervous system. The motor regions of the frontal lobe formulate the plan and command the movements required to reach for the cup. The message to the muscles is carried by pathways from the frontal lobe to the spinal cord. Motor neurons of the spinal cord carry the message to the muscles of the hand and arm. Sensory information from the visual system is required to direct the hand to the cup, and sensory information from sensory receptors in the hand is required to confirm that the cup has been grasped. The basal ganglia participate in the movement by estimating the forces required to make the grasp, and the cerebellum participates by correcting errors in the movement as it is made.

forms the motor cortex that the cup is now being held. Other regions of the brain also participate in controlling the movement, such as the basal ganglia, which help to produce the appropriate amount of force, and the cerebellum, which helps to regulate timing and corrects any errors in movement. Although at this point you probably will not remember all these various steps in controlling a movement, refer to Figure 10-2 when you reach the end of this chapter as a way of reviewing what you have learned. The important concept to remember right now is simply the hierarchical organization of the entire system.

The idea that the nervous system is hierarchically organized originated with the English neurologist John Hughlings-Jackson. He thought of the nervous system as being organized into a number of layers, with successively higher levels controlling more complex aspects of behavior by acting through the lower levels. The three major levels in Hughlings-Jackson's model are the same as those just mentioned for Kamala: the forebrain, the brainstem, and the spinal cord. Hughlings-Jackson also proposed that, within these divisions, further levels of organization could be found.

Hughlings-Jackson adopted the concept of hierarchical organization from evolutionary theory. He knew that the chordate nervous system had evolved in a series of steps: the spinal cord had developed in worms; the brainstem in fish, amphibians, and reptiles; and the forebrain in birds and mammals. Because each level of the nervous system had developed at different times, Hughlings-Jackson assumed that each must have some functional independence. Consequently, if higher levels of the nervous system were damaged, the result would be regression to the simpler behaviors of "lower" animals, a phenomenon that Hughlings-Jackson called **dissolution.** The brain-damaged person would still possess a repertoire of behaviors, but they would be more typical of animals that had not yet evolved the destroyed brain structure.

A hierarchically organized structure such as the mammalian nervous system, however, does not operate piece by piece. It functions as a whole, with the higher regions working through and influencing the actions of the lower ones. In the control of movement, many parts of the nervous system participate, with some regions engaged in sensory control, others in planning and commanding the movement, and still others in actually carrying the action out. To understand how all these various regions work together to produce even a simple movement, we will consider the major components of the hierarchy one by one, starting at the top with the forebrain.

## The Forebrain and Movement Initiation

Complex movements, such as painting a work of art, include many components. For instance, your perceptions of what is appearing on the canvas must be closely coordinated with the brush strokes that your hand makes to achieve the desired effect. The same high degree of control is necessary for many other complex behaviors. Consider playing basketball. At every moment, decisions must be made and actions must be performed. Dribble, pass, and shoot are different categories of movement, and each can be carried out in numerous ways. Good players choose among the categories effortlessly and execute the movements seemingly without thought.

One explanation of how we control movements that was popular in the 1930s centers on the concept of feedback. It holds that, after we perform an action, we wait for feedback about how well that action has succeeded, and then we make the next movement accordingly. But Karl Lashley (1951), in an article titled "The Problem of Serial Order in Behavior," found fault with this explanation. Lashley argued that movements such as those required for playing the piano were performed too quickly to rely on feedback about one movement shaping the next movement. The time required to receive feedback about the first movement, combined with the time needed to develop a

**Dissolution.** The condition whereby disease or damage in the highest levels of the brain would produce not just loss of function, but a repertory of simpler behaviors as seen in animals that have not evolved that particular brain structure.

**Motor sequence.** A sequence of movements preprogrammed by the brain and produced as a unit.

plan for the subsequent movement and send a corresponding message to muscles, was simply too long to permit piano playing. Lashley suggested that movements must be performed as **motor sequences,** with one sequence being held in readiness while an ongoing sequence was being completed. According to this view, all complex behaviors, including playing the piano, painting pictures, and playing basketball, would require the selection and execution of multiple sequences of movements. As one sequence is being executed, the next sequence is being prepared so that the second can follow the first smoothly. Interestingly, Lashley's view seems to be borne out in how we execute speech. When people use complex sequences of words, they are more likely to pause and make "umm" and "ahh" sounds, suggesting that it is taking them more time than usual to organize their word sequences.

The frontal lobe of each hemisphere is responsible for planning and initiating sequences of behavior. The frontal lobe is divided into a number of different regions, including the three illustrated in Figure 10-3. From front to back, they are the *prefrontal cortex,* the *premotor cortex,* and the *primary motor cortex.*

A function of the prefrontal cortex is to plan complex behaviors. Such plans might be deciding to get up at a certain hour to arrive at work on time, deciding to stop at the library to return a book that is due, or deciding what kind of picture to paint for an art class. The prefrontal cortex does not specify the precise movements that should be made. It simply specifies the goal toward which movements should be directed.

To bring a plan to completion, the prefrontal cortex sends instructions to the premotor cortex, which produces complex sequences of movement appropriate to the task. If the premotor cortex is damaged, such sequences cannot be coordinated and the goal cannot be accomplished. For example, the monkey in Figure 10-4 has a lesion in the dorsal part of its premotor cortex. It has been given the task of extracting a piece of food wedged in a hole in a table (Brinkman, 1984). If it simply pushes the food with a finger, the food will drop to the floor and be lost. The monkey has to catch the food by holding a palm beneath the hole as the food is being pushed out. This animal is unable to make the two complementary movements together. It can push the food with a finger and extend an open palm, but it cannot coordinate these actions of its two hands.

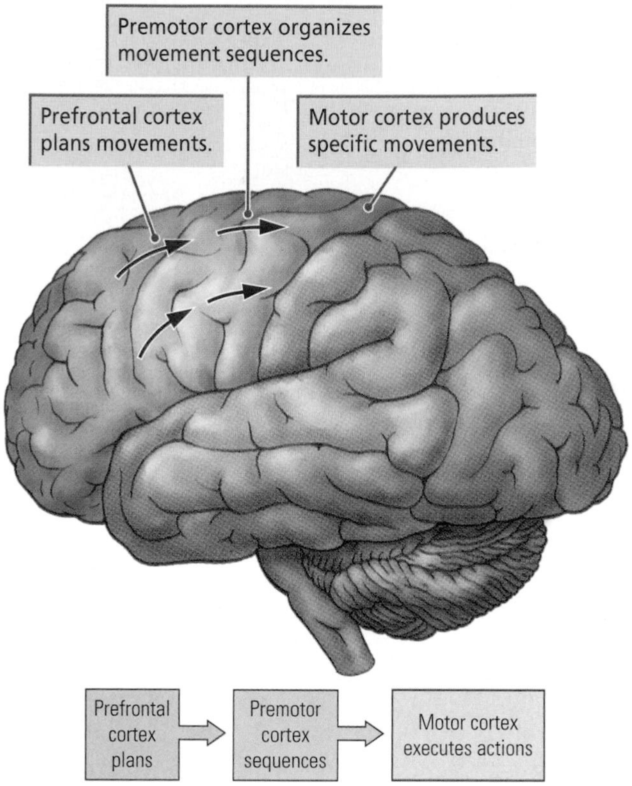

Premotor cortex organizes movement sequences.
Prefrontal cortex plans movements.
Motor cortex produces specific movements.
Prefrontal cortex plans → Premotor cortex sequences → Motor cortex executes actions

**Figure 10-3**

The prefrontal cortex of the frontal lobe plans movements. The premotor cortex organizes sequences of movements. The motor cortex executes specific movements. Information flow is from prefrontal to premotor cortex and then to motor cortex.

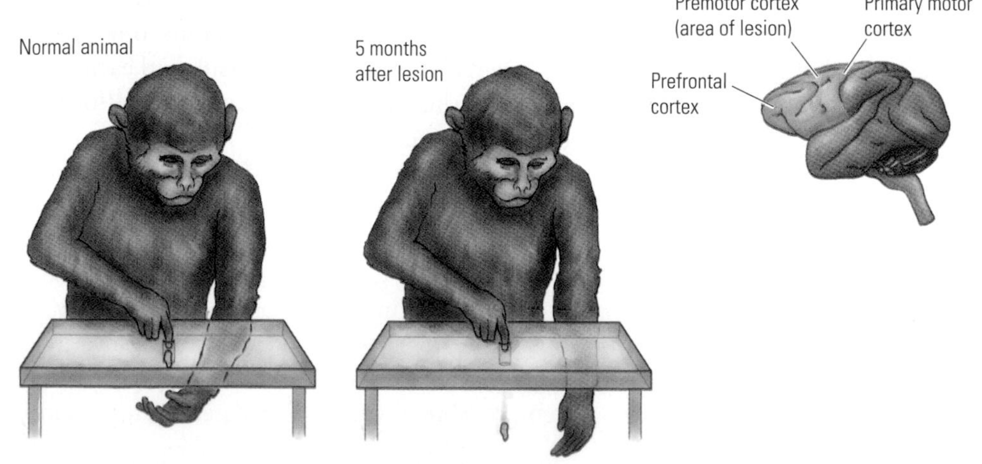


**Figure 10-4**

A unilateral lesion in the premotor cortex impairs performance by a monkey on a task requiring both hands. The normal monkey can push the peanut out of a hole with one hand and catch it in the other, but the experimental monkey is unable to do so.

Adapted from "Supplementary Motor Area of the Monkey's Cerebral Cortex: Short - and Long-Term Effects After Unilateral Ablation and the Effects of Subsequent Callosal Section," by C. Brinkman, 1984, *Journal of Neuroscience, 4,* p. 925.

Although the premotor cortex organizes movements, it does not specify the details of how each movement is to be carried out. Specifying the details is the responsibility of the primary motor cortex. The primary motor cortex is responsible for executing skilled movements. Its role can be seen by considering some of the movements that we use to pick up objects, illustrated in Figure 10-5. In using the pincer grip, we hold an object between the thumb and index finger. This grip not only allows small objects to be picked up easily, but also allows whatever is held to be used with considerable skill. In contrast, in using the power grasp (Figure 10-5B), we hold an object much less dexterously, by simply closing all of the fingers around it. Clearly, the pincer grip is a more demanding movement because the two fingers must be placed precisely on the object. People with damage to the primary motor cortex have difficulty correctly shaping their fingers to perform the pincer grip and so use the power grasp instead (Jeannerod, 1988).

(A)

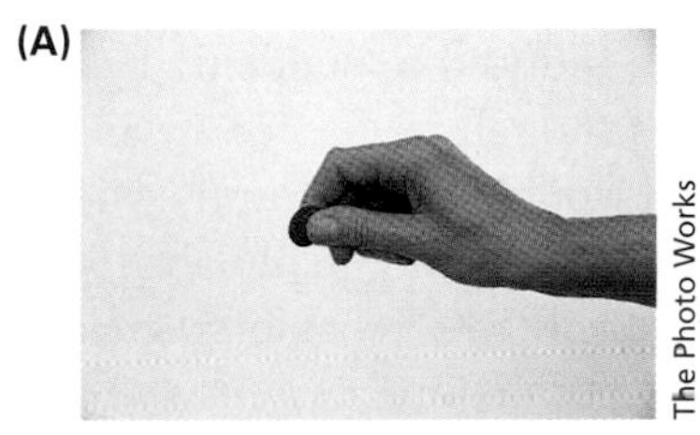


(B)

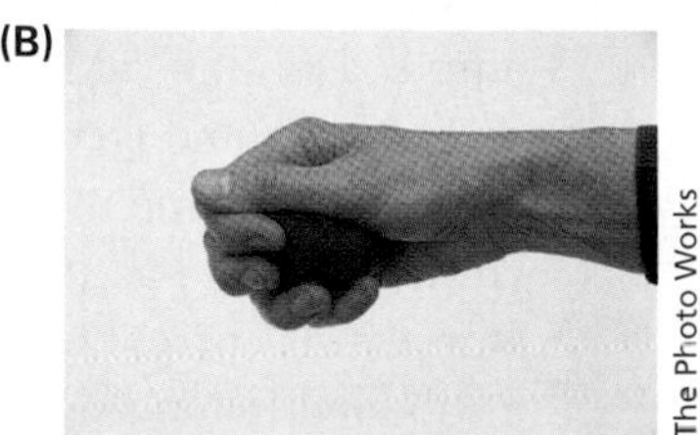


**Figure 10-5**

**(A)** In a pincer grip, an object is held between the thumb and index finger. **(B)** In a power grasp, also called a whole-hand grip, an object is held against the palm of the hand with the digits.

In summary, the frontal cortex executes precise movements, as well as planning them and coordinating different body parts to carry them out. The various regions of the frontal cortex that perform these functions are hierarchically related. After the prefrontal cortex has formulated a plan of action, it instructs the premotor cortex to organize the appropriate sequence of behaviors.

The hierarchical organization of frontal-lobe areas in producing movements is supported by studies of cerebral blood flow, which serves as an indicator of neural activity. Figure 10-6 shows the regions of the brain that were active when subjects in one such study were performing different tasks (Roland, 1993). When the subjects were tapping a finger, increases in blood flow were limited to the primary motor cortex. When the subjects were executing a sequence of finger movements, blood flow also increased in the premotor cortex. And when the subjects were using a finger to trace their way through a maze, a task that requires coordination of movements in relation to a goal, blood flow increased in the prefrontal cortex, too. Notice that blood flow did not increase throughout the entire frontal lobe as the subjects were performing these tasks. Blood flow increased only in those regions taking part in the required movements.

**Figure 10-6**

Blood flow increases in the cerebral cortex depend on the motor task that the subject performs. The pattern of activation supports the idea that simple motor movements are mainly controlled by the motor cortex, movements requiring sequencing are additionally controlled by the premotor cortex, and movements requiring planning are controlled by other cortical areas, including the prefrontal cortex and regions of the parietal and temporal cortex.

Adapted from *Brain Activation* (p. 63), by P. E. Roland, 1993, New York: Wiley-Liss.

(A)

Blood flow increased in the hand area of the primary somatosensory and primary motor cortex when subjects used a finger to push a lever.

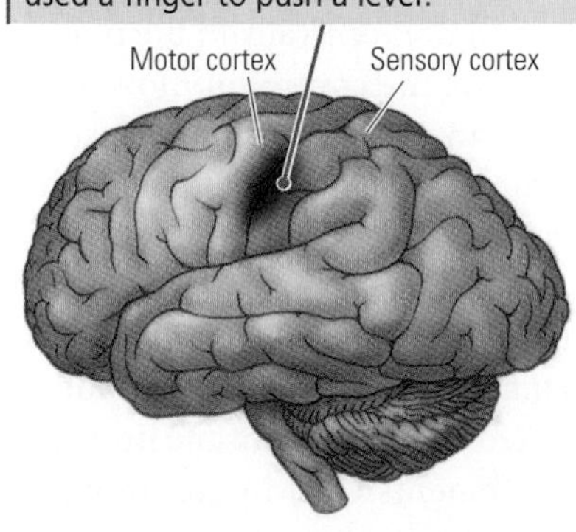


(B)

Blood flow increased in the premotor cortex when subjects performed a sequence of movements.

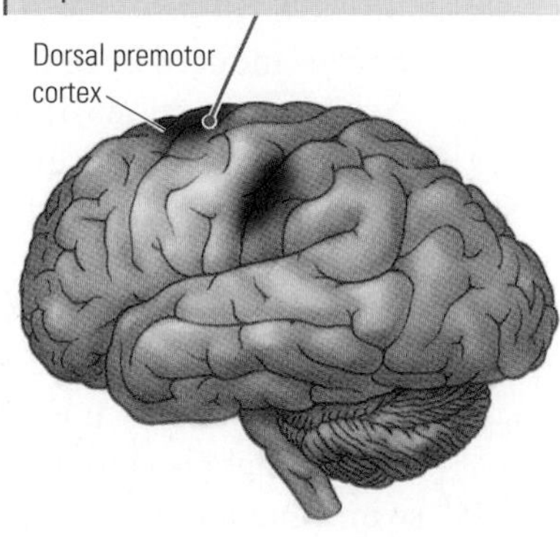


(C)

Blood flow increased in the prefrontal and temporal cortex when subjects used a finger to find a route through a maze.

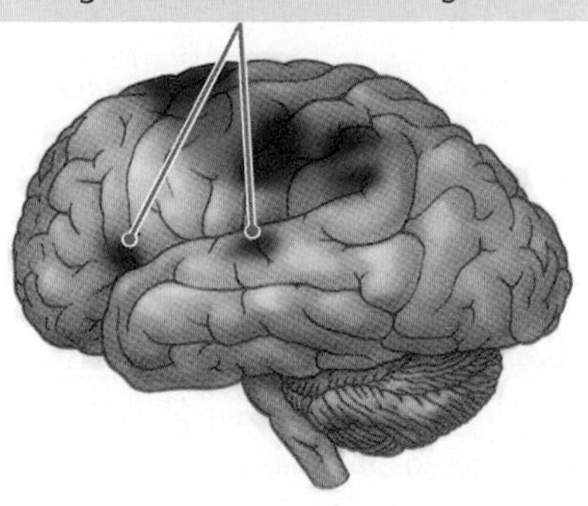

EXPERIMENT
Question: What are the effects of brainstem stimulation under different conditions?
Procedures
Results
Stimulating electrode in brainstem
Electrical stimulation alone produces restless behavior.
Electrical stimulation and the presence of a fist produces slight threat.
Electrical stimulation in the presence of a stuffed polecat (a type of weasel) produces vigorous threat.
Continued electrical stimulation in the presence of the stuffed polecat produces flight and screeching.
Conclusion
Stimulation of some brainstem sites produces behavior that depends on context, suggesting that an important function of the brainstem is to produce appropriate species-typical behavior.


**Figure 10-7**

Electrical stimulation of the brainstem of a chicken elicits species-typical adaptive behavior.

Adapted from *The Collected Papers of Erich von Holst* (p. 121), translated by R. Martin, 1973, Coral Gables, FL: University of Miami Press.

## The Brainstem and Species-Typical Movement

Species-typical behaviors are actions displayed by every member of a species, such as the pecking of a robin, the hissing of a cat, or the breaching of a whale. In a series of studies, Swiss neuroscientist Walter Hess (1957) found that the brainstem controls species-typical behaviors. Hess developed the technique of implanting electrodes into the brains of cats and other animals and cementing them in place. These electrodes could then be attached to stimulating leads in the freely moving animal, without causing the animal much discomfort. By stimulating the brainstem, Hess was able to elicit almost every innate movement that the animal might be expected to make. For example, a resting cat could be induced to suddenly leap up with an arched back and erect hair as though frightened by an approaching dog. The movements elicited would begin abruptly when the stimulating current was turned on and end equally abruptly when the stimulating current was turned off. The behaviors were performed in a subdued manner when the stimulating current was low, but they increased in vigor as the stimulating current was turned up. The actions varied, depending on the site that was stimulated. Stimulation of some sites produced turning of the head, others produced walking or running, and still others elicited displays of aggression or fear, and so on. The reaction of the animal toward a particular stimulus could be modified accordingly. For instance, when shown a stuffed toy, a cat would respond to electrical stimulation of some sites by stalking the toy, whereas it would respond to stimulation of other sites with fear and withdrawal behavior.

Hess's experiments have been confirmed and expanded by other researchers using many different kinds of animals. For instance, Figure 10-7 shows the effects of brainstem stimulation on a chicken under various conditions (von Holst, 1973). Notice how the site stimulated interacts with both the presence of an object to react to and the length of stimulation. With stimulation of a certain site alone, the chicken displays only restless behavior. But, when a fist is displayed, the same stimulation elicits slight threatening behavior. When the object displayed is then switched from a fist to a stuffed polecat, the chicken responds with vigorous threats. Finally, with continued stimulation in the presence of the polecat, the chicken flees, screeching. Experiments such as these show that an important function of the brainstem is to produce species-typical behavior. Hess's experiments also gave rise to a sizable science fiction literature in which "mind control" induced by brain stimulation figures centrally in the plot.

Other functions of the brainstem are the control of movements used in eating and drinking and the control of movements used in sexual behavior. Animals can be induced to display these behaviors when certain areas of the brainstem are stimulated. An animal can even be induced to eat nonfood objects, such as chips of wood, if the part of the brainstem that triggers eating is sufficiently stimulated. The brainstem is also important for posture, for the ability to stand upright and to make coordinated movements of the limbs, for swimming and walking, and for movements used in grooming the fur and making nests.

Grooming provides an example of a particularly complex movement pattern that is coordinated mainly by the brainstem (Berridge, 1989). When grooming, a rat sits back on its haunches, licks its paws, wipes its nose with its paws, then wipes its paws across its face, and finally turns to lick the fur on its body. These movements are always performed in the same order. The next time you dry off after a shower or swimming, note the "grooming sequence" that you use. This human grooming sequence is very similar to the one that rats use.

The effects of damage to regions of the brainstem that organize sequences of movement can be seen in a person with cerebral palsy. A disorder primarily of motor function, **cerebral palsy** is caused by brain trauma. The trauma usually occurs during fetal development or birth, but it can sometimes happen in early infancy, as it did in the case of E. S., whom we examined (see "Cerebral Palsy" on page 248).

> E. S. suffered a cold and infection when he was about 6 months old. Subsequently, he had a great deal of difficulty in making movements. As he grew up, his hands and legs were almost useless, and his speech was extremely difficult to understand. For most of his childhood, he was considered retarded and was sent to a special school. When he was 13 years old, the school bought a computer and one of his teachers attempted to teach him to use it by pushing the keys with a pencil that he held in his mouth. Within a few weeks, the teacher realized that E. S. was extremely intelligent and could communicate and complete school assignments on his computer. He was eventually given a motorized wheelchair that he could control with finger movements of his right hand. With the assistance of his computer and wheelchair, he soon became almost self-sufficient and eventually attended college, where he achieved excellent grades and became a student leader. On graduation with a major in psychology, he became a social worker and worked with children who suffered from cerebral palsy.

Clearly, a brain injury such as that causing cerebral palsy can be extremely damaging to movement, while leaving sensory abilities and cognitive capacities unimpaired. Damage to the brainstem can also cause changes in cognitive function, such as occurs in autism (see "Autism" on pages 362–363).

**Cerebral palsy.** A group of brain disorders that result from brain damage acquired perinatally.

**Paraplegia.** Paralysis of the legs due to spinal-cord injury.

Photofest

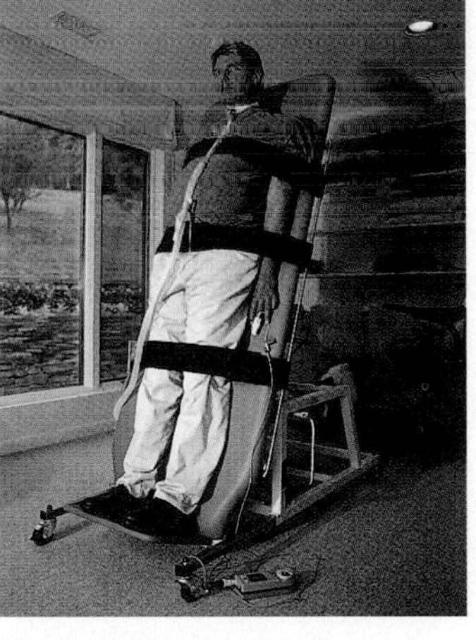
Ted Thai/*Time* magazine

**Figure 10-8**

Christopher Reeve portrayed Superman, as illustrated in this 1980 *Superman II* photograph. As a result of a fall from his jumping horse in 1995 in which he suffered damage at the C1–C2 level of the spinal cord, he has little movement below his neck. He is now active in raising money for spinal-cord research, and he still acts in movies.

## The Spinal Cord and Movement Execution

On Memorial Day weekend in 1995, Christopher Reeve, a well-known actor who portrayed Superman, was thrown from his horse at the third jump of a riding competition in Culpeper, Virginia. Reeve's spinal cord was severed at the C1–C2 level, near the upper end of the spinal cord. This injury left his brain intact and functioning and the rest of his spinal cord intact and functioning, too, but his brain and spinal cord were no longer connected. As a result, other than movements of his head and slight movement in his shoulders, Reeve's body was completely paralyzed. He was even unable to breathe without assistance. Whereas only a few decades ago such a severe injury would have been fatal, modern and timely medical treatment allowed Reeve to survive. Reeve capitalized on his celebrity status to campaign for disabled people, fighting to prevent lifetime caps on compensation for spinal-cord injuries and raising money for spinal-cord research. As a result of this research, Reeve hopes to someday walk again.

In view of the complex behaviors that the brain produces, the spinal cord is sometimes considered simply a pathway for conveying information between the brain and the rest of the body. It does serve this function. If the spinal cord is severed, a person loses sensation and voluntary movements below the cut. If the cut is relatively low, the paralysis and loss of sensation are in the legs and lower body. This condition, called **paraplegia,** is described in "Paraplegia" on page 364. If a cut is higher on the spinal

## Focus on Disorders

### Autism

Hi! I'm Chris Slater, a 17-year-old guy from Rice Lake, WI. I have High Functioning Autism. My page has been put up so I can teach people about autism, and to help anyone with any question about autism. When I was younger, I had the same characteristics as any other person with autism. Today, I'm very active. I have many friends, some have autism; some don't. I love to play Magic: The Gathering, a collectible card game, and some of my friends without autism play it also. I love to play golf, but I never play alone! What made this possible was that I was "educated" about people that don't have autism. What I mean by that is that I learned how they interact, and how they present themselves. I feel that every person with autism can, in fact, make it in this world—if they can learn how to socialize! (*http://slater.autistics.org/*)

Leo Kanner and Hans Asperger first used the term *autism* in the 1940s to describe children who suffered from a severe set of symptoms, including greatly impaired social interaction, a bizarre and narrow range of interests, and marked abnormalities in language and communication. Although some of these children were classified as mentally retarded, others had their intellectual functioning preserved. Because these children seemed to live in their own self-created worlds, the condition was named autism, from the Greek *autos,* meaning "self."

An estimated 1 of every 500 people has autism. Although it knows no racial, ethnic, or social boundaries, autism is four times as prevalent in boys as in girls. Many autistic children are noticeably different from birth. To avoid physical contact, these babies arch their backs and pull away from their caregivers or they become limp when held. But approximately one-third of autistic children develop normally until somewhere between 1 and 3 years of age. Then the autistic symptoms emerge.

One common characteristic of autism is a failure to interact socially with other people. Some autistic children do not relate to other people on any level. The attachments that they do form are to inanimate objects, not to other human beings. Another common characteristic of autism is an extreme insistence on sameness. Autistic children vehemently resist even small modifications to their surroundings or their daily routines. Objects must always be placed in exactly the same locations, and tasks must always be carried out in precisely the same ways. One possible reason for this insistence on sameness may be an inability to understand and cope with novel situations. Autistic children also have marked impairments in their language development. Many do not speak at all, and others repeat words aimlessly with little attempt to communicate or convey meaning. These children also exhibit what seem like endlessly repetitive body movements, such as rocking, spinning, or flapping the hands. In some cases, they may engage as well in aggressive or self-injurious behavior. The severity of these symptoms varies. Some autistic people are severely impaired, whereas others, like Chris Slater, can learn to function quite well. Still others may have exceptional abilities in certain areas, including music, art, and mathematics.

As might be expected of a disorder with as many symptoms as those of autism, anatomical studies reveal abnormal structures and cells in a number of brain regions, including

cord, as in Christopher Reeve's spinal cord, paralysis and loss of sensation can include the arms as well as the legs, a condition called **quadriplegia.**

In addition to its role in transmitting messages to and from the brain, the spinal cord is capable of producing many movements without any brain involvement. Movements that depend on the spinal cord alone are collectively called *spinal-cord reflexes.* Some of these reflexes entail the movement of limbs. For example, a light touch to the surface of the foot causes the leg to extend reflexively to contact the object that is touching it. This reflex aids the leg in contacting the ground to bear weight in walking. Other limb reflexes consist of withdrawal. For instance, a noxious stimulus applied to a hand causes the whole arm to reflexively pull back, thereby avoiding the injurious object.

Spinal circuits can also produce more complex movements than the simple ones just described. An example is the stepping movement in walking. If body weight is supported while the feet are in contact with a conveyor belt, the legs "walk" reflexively to

Visit the Web site at **www.worthpublishers.com/kolb/chapter10** for up-to-the-minute links to current research on spinal cord injury.

**Quadriplegia.** Paralysis of the legs and arms due to spinal-cord injury.

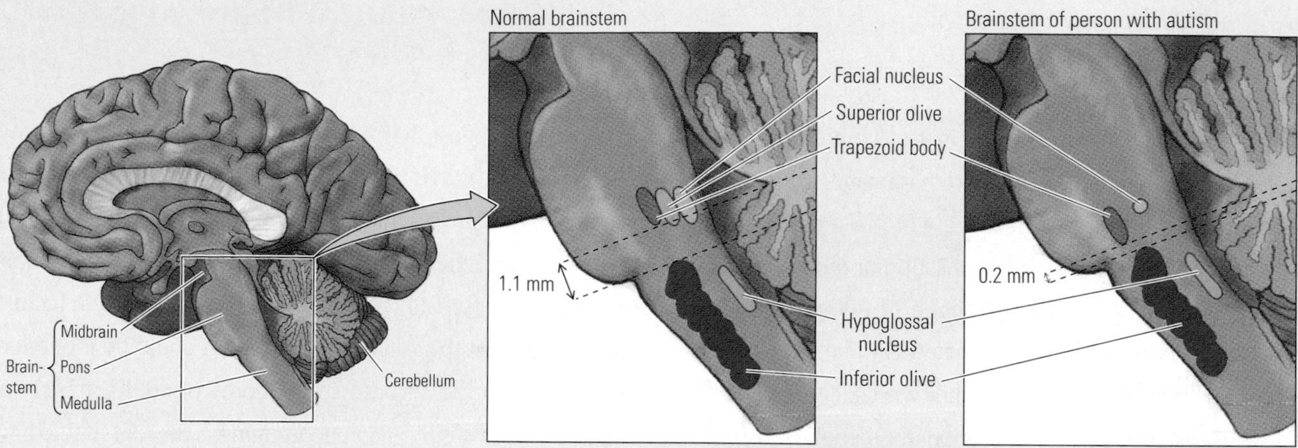


the limbic system and the cerebellum. Brain scans have indicated that the cerebellum may be smaller in people with autism than in control subjects.

The cause or causes of the neurological traits that give rise to autism are not yet understood. There is some indication of a genetic influence because both members of identical twins are more likely than those of fraternal twins to develop autism. There is also evidence that a virus can trigger the disorder. For instance, women have an increased risk of giving birth to an autistic child if they are exposed to rubella (German measles) in the first trimester of pregnancy. There is also a suspicion that autism can be caused by industrial toxins, but the evidence for this possibility is uncertain.

Patricia Roder (2000) suggests that one cause of autism may be an abnormality in the HOSA1 gene that plays a central role in the development of the brainstem. She has found that an area of the brainstem in the caudal part of the pons is small in autistic people, as the accompanying drawing shows. Several nuclei in this area, including the nucleus that controls facial muscles, are either small or missing, which may lead to subtle facial abnormalities.

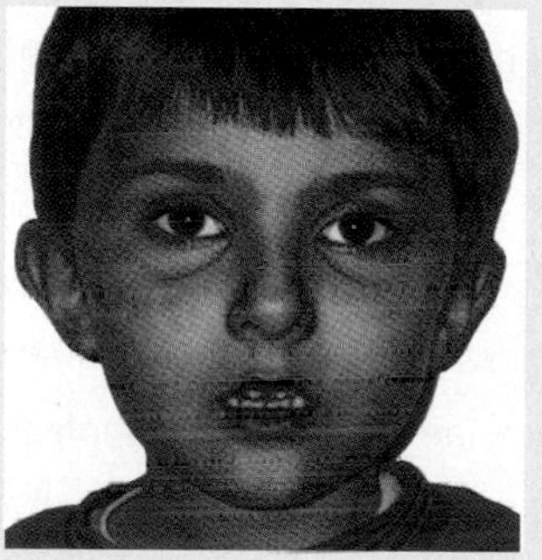

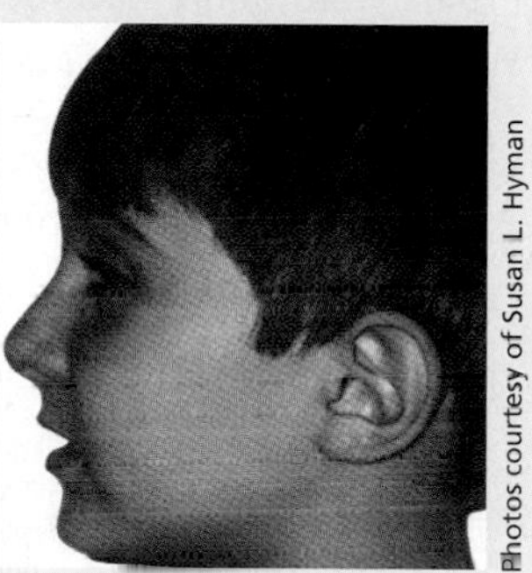

Photos courtesy of Susan L. Hyman

**(Upper)** Autism's effects include changes to the brainstem in which the posterior part of the pons is reduced in size. Several nuclei in this region, including the facial nucleus, superior olive, and trapezoid body, are smaller than normal. **(Lower)** A child with autism is normal in appearance but may have some physical anomalies characteristic of the disorder. The corners of the mouth may be low compared with the upper lip, the tops of the ears may flop over (*left*), and the ears may be a bit lower than normal and have an almost square shape (*right*).

keep up with the belt. Each leg has its own neural circuit that allows it to step. When the limb is moved backward on the conveyor belt, causing the foot to lose support, the limb reflexively lifts off the belt and swings forward underneath the body. As the foot then touches the surface of the belt again, tactile receptors initiate the reflex that causes the leg to push against the surface and support the body's weight. In this way, several spinal reflexes work together to produce the complex movement of walking. Because this walking is reflexive, even a newborn baby will display it when held in the correct position on a conveyor belt.

One of the more complex reflexes that can be observed in other spinal animals is the **scratch reflex.** Here an animal reflexively scratches a part of its body in response to a tickle. The complexity of this reflex is revealed in the accuracy of the movement. Without direction from the brain, the tip of a limb, usually a hind limb, can be correctly directed to the part of the body that is irritated.

Scratch reflex

**Scratch reflex.** A reflex by which the hind limb removes a stimulus from the surface of the body.

Focus on Disorders

## Paraplegia

Each year about 11,000 people in the United States and 1000 people in Canada suffer direct damage to the spinal cord. Often in these cases the spinal cord is completely severed, leaving the victim with no sensation or movement from the site of the cut downward. Although 12,000 people annually incurring spinal-cord injury may seem like a large number, it is small relative to the number who suffer other kinds of nervous system damage. Consequently, some of those with spinal-cord injury have become very active in campaigning for public awareness of their condition and for research into possible treatments for it.

Currently, two people who are especially active in this campaign are Christopher Reeve, the actor who once played Superman, and Rick Hansen, a Canadian. Hansen was an athletic teenager when he became a paraplegic as the result of a lower thoracic spinal injury in 1975. Twelve years later, to raise public awareness of the potential of people with disabilities, Rick wheeled himself 40,000 kilometers around the world, generating more than $24 million for the Man in Motion Legacy Trust Fund. To date, this fund has contributed more than $100 million in support of spinal-cord research, rehabilitation, wheelchair sports, and public-awareness programs. Rick Hansen is currently executive director of the Rick Hansen Institute at the University of British Columbia, which provides leadership and support for initiatives in the field of disability, with a special focus on spinal-cord injury.

Research to find treatments for spinal-cord damage is a frustrating field. A severed spinal cord, like a severed electrical cord, entails just a single cut that leaves the machinery on both sides of it intact. If only the cut could somehow be bridged, sensory and motor function might be restored. But the solution is not so easy. Several factors prevent nerve fibers from growing across a cut in a spinal cord. These factors include the formation of scar tissue, the lack of a blood supply, the absence of appropriate growth factors to stimulate growth, and the fact that normal tissue at the edge of the cut actively repels regrowth. Can these obstacles somehow be overcome?

Studies suggest that it may be possible to induce neural fibers to grow across a spinal-cord cut. For instance, if the spinal cord in chicks and other baby animals is cut in the first 2 weeks of life, the spinal cord regrows and apparently normal function returns. Presumably, if the mix of growth factors that enables this spinal-cord regeneration could be identified and applied to the severed spinal cords of adults, the same regrowth could result. Also encouraging is the fact that, when a nerve fiber in the peripheral nervous system is cut, it regrows no matter how old the injured person is. The Schwann cells that form the severed axon's myelin are thought to produce the chemical environment that facilitates this regrowth. This finding has led to experiments in which Schwann cells are implanted into a cut spinal cord. The results have been positive, although no cure has been effected. Other investigators have built little bridges across a severed spinal cord and also have obtained some encouraging evidence of regrowth. Rats that had been unable to move their legs regained postural support and were able to step after receiving this treatment. From a theoretical and experimental perspective, obtaining spinal-cord regeneration and recovery seems an achievable goal.

Rick Hansen on the Man in Motion Tour.

In humans and other animals with a severed spinal cord, spinal reflexes still function, even though the spinal cord is cut off from communication with the brain. As a result, there may be spontaneous movements or spasms in the paralyzed limbs. But the brain can no longer guide the timing of these reflexes. Consequently, reflexes related to bladder and bowel control may need to be artificially stimulated by caregivers.

### In Review

The motor system is organized hierarchically. The forebrain, especially the frontal lobe, is responsible for selecting plans of action, coordinating body parts to carry out those plans, and executing precise movements. The brainstem, in contrast, is responsible for species-typical movements, for actions related to survival such as eating, drinking, and sexual behavior, and for posture and walking. Finally, in addition to being a pathway between the brain and the rest of the body, the spinal cord is independently responsible for reflexive movements. Although lower-level functions in this hierarchical system can continue in the absence of higher-level ones, the higher levels are what provide voluntary control over movements. Consequently, when the brain is disconnected from the spinal cord, there is no way to control movement at will.

## THE ORGANIZATION OF THE MOTOR SYSTEM

If we compare how Kamala paints a picture with her trunk with how human artists do so with their hands, it may seem remarkable that such different behavioral strategies could be used to achieve the same goal. The use of different body parts for skilled movements is widespread among animals. For instance, dolphins and seals are adept at using their noses to carry and manipulate objects, and many other animals, including domestic dogs, accomplish the same end by using their mouths. Among birds, the beak is often specially designed for getting food, for building nests, and sometimes even for making and using tools. Tails also are useful appendages. Some marsupials and some species of New World primates can pick up and carry objects with them. Among horses, the lips are dexterous enough to manipulate things. Using its lips, a horse can select a single blade of grass of the type that it prefers from a patch of vegetation. Although humans tend to rely primarily on their hands for manipulating objects, they can still learn to handle things with other body parts, such as the mouth or a foot, if they have to. Some people without arms have become extremely proficient at using a foot for writing or for painting, for example.

Link to the area on the organization of the motor system in the module on Control of Movement on your CD for a review of the organization of movement and motor systems.

What are the properties of the motor system that allow such versatility in carrying out skilled movements? In the next section, we will find the answer to this question by examining the organization of the motor cortex and its descending pathways to the brainstem and spinal cord, which in turn connects with the muscles of the body. We will then consider how the electrical activity of neurons executes skilled movements. Finally, we will look at some differences in the motor cortices of different animal species that may be related to their specialized movement abilities.

### The Motor Cortex

In 1870, two Prussian physicians, Gustav Fritsch and Eduard Hitzig, electrically stimulated the neocortex of an anesthetized dog and produced movements of the mouth, limbs, and paws on the opposite side of the dog's body. This was the first direct evidence that the neocortex could control movement. Later researchers confirmed the finding by using a variety of animals as subjects, including primates such as monkeys.

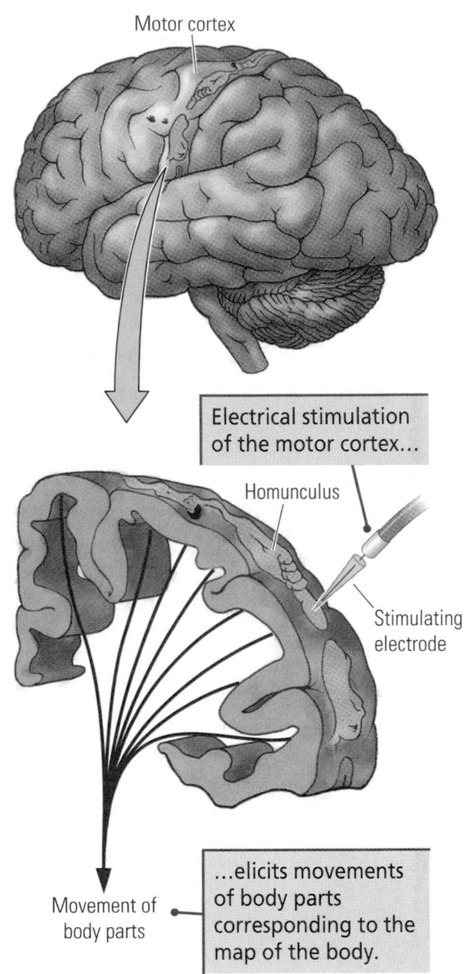


**Figure 10-9**

Penfield's homunculus. Electrical stimulation, in conscious human patients, of the motor cortex (precentral gyrus, or Brodmann's area 4) elicits movement of the body parts corresponding to the map of the body. Movements are topographically organized so that stimulation of the dorsal medial regions of the cortex produces movements in the lower limbs, and stimulation in ventral regions of the cortex produces movements in the upper body, hands, and face.

Go to the area on the primary motor cortex in the module on the Control of Movement on your CD for a more detailed analysis of the motor homunculus. Notice the exaggerated body parts associated with fine motor control.

Then, in the 1950s, Wilder Penfield used electrical stimulation to map the cortex of conscious human patients who were about to undergo neurosurgery. (See the discussion of Penfield's techniques in Chapter 9.) He and his colleagues found that movements were triggered mainly in response to stimulation of the primary motor cortex (also known as *Brodmann's area 4* or the *precentral gyrus*). Penfield summarized his results by drawing cartoons of body parts to represent the areas of the primary motor cortex that produce movement in those parts. The result was a **homunculus** (little person) that could be spread out across the motor cortex, as illustrated in Figure 10-9. Because the body is symmetrical, an equivalent motor homunculus is represented in the cortex of each hemisphere. Penfield also identified another, smaller motor homunculus in the dorsal premotor area of each frontal lobe, a region sometimes referred to as the supplementary motor cortex.

The most striking feature of the motor homunculus is the disproportionate relative sizes of its body parts compared with the relative sizes of actual parts of the body. This distinctive feature is even more clearly illustrated in some of the artistic renditions of the homunculus that other scientists have made, one of which is shown in Figure 10-10. As you can see, the homunculus has very large hands with an especially large thumb. It also has very large lips and a large tongue. In contrast, the trunk, arms, and legs, which constitute most of the area of a real body, are much smaller in relative size. These size distortions illustrate the fact that large parts of the motor cortex regulate the hands, fingers, lips, and tongue, giving us precise motor control over these body parts. Areas of the body over which we have much less motor control have a much smaller representation in the motor cortex.

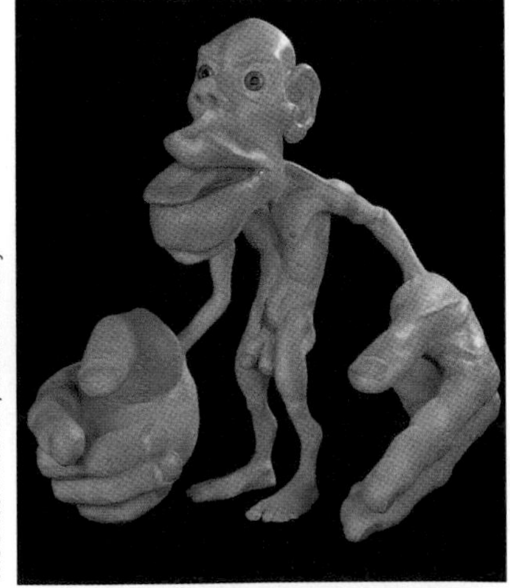
The British Museum, Natural History

**Figure 10-10**

An artistic representation of the cortical homunculus illustrates the disproportionate areas of the sensory and motor cortex that control different parts of the body.

Another distinctive feature of the homunculus when it is laid out across the motor cortex is that the body parts are arranged somewhat differently than in an actual body. For instance, the area of the cortex that produces eye movements is located in front of the homunculus's head. The head is oriented with the chin up and the forehead down, with the tongue located below the forehead. But such details aside, the homunculus is still a useful concept for understanding the **topographic organization** (functional layout) of the primary motor cortex. It shows at a glance that relatively larger areas of the brain control the parts of the body that are able to make the most skilled movements.

The discovery of the topographical representation of the motor cortex suggested how movements might be produced. Information from other regions of the neocortex could be sent to the motor homunculus, and neurons in the appropriate part of the homunculus could then execute the movements called for. If finger movements are needed, for example, messages could be sent to the finger area of the motor cortex, triggering the required activity there. If this model of how the motor system works is correct, damage to any part of the homunculus would result in loss of movement in the corresponding part of the body.

Although the general idea underlying this model is right, more detailed mapping of the motor cortex and more detailed studies of the effects of damage to it indicate that the picture is a bit more complex. When researchers investigated the motor cortex in nonhuman primates, with the use of smaller electrodes than those used by Penfield to examine his patients, they discovered as many as 10 motor homunculi (Galea & Darian-Smith, 1994). As many as 4 representations of the body may exist in the primary motor cortex, and a number of other representations may be found in the premotor cortex. What each of these different homunculi does is still unclear. Perhaps each is responsible for a particular class of movements. Whatever the functions turn out to be, they will have to be determined by future research.

**Homunculus.** The representation of the human body in the sensory or motor cortex; also any topographical representation of the body by a neural area.

**Topographic organization.** A neural spatial representation of the body or areas of the sensory world perceived by a sensory organ.

## The Corticospinal Tracts

The main pathways from the motor cortex to the brainstem and spinal cord are called the **corticospinal tracts.** (The term *corticospinal* indicates that these tracts begin in the neocortex and terminate in the spinal cord.) The axons of the corticospinal tracts originate mainly in layer-V pyramidal cells of the motor cortex, although axons also come from the premotor cortex and sensory cortex. The axons from the motor cortex descend into the brainstem, sending collaterals to a few brainstem nuclei and eventually emerging on the brainstem's ventral surface, where they form a large bump on each side of that surface. These bumps, known as **pyramids,** give the corticospinal tracts their alternate name, the **pyramidal tracts.** At this point, some of the axons descending from the left hemisphere cross over to the right side of the brainstem, and some of the axons descending from the right hemisphere cross over to the left side of the brainstem. The rest of the axons stay on their original sides. This division produces two corticospinal tracts entering each side of the spinal cord. Figure 10-11 illustrates the division of axons for the tract originating in the left-hemisphere cortex. The dual tracts on each side of the brainstem then descend into the spinal cord.

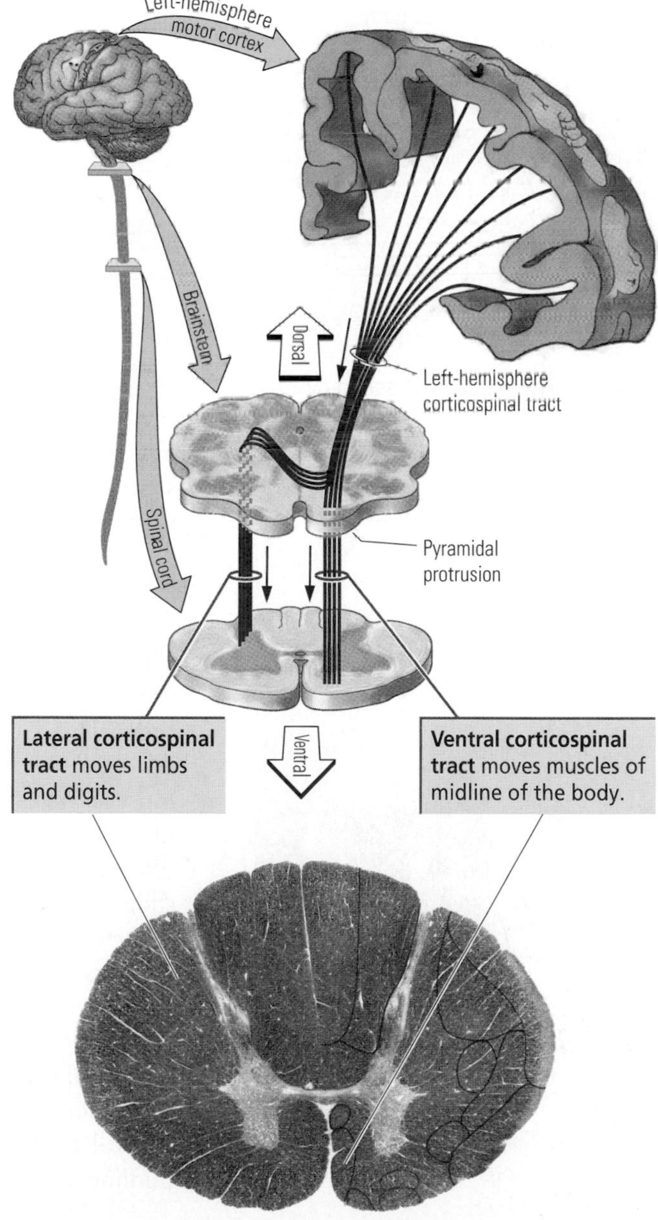


**Figure 10-11**

The corticospinal (from cortex to spinal cord) tracts descend from the motor cortex to the brainstem. Their location in the lower brainstem produces a protrusion (a pyramid) on the ventral surface of the brain. A tract from each hemisphere (only that from the left hemisphere is shown) divides into a lateral spinothalamic tract, which crosses the midline to the other side of the spinal cord, and a ventral spinothalamic tract, which remains on the same side. Fibers in the lateral spinothalamic tract are represented by the limbs and digits of the cortical homunculus and are destined to move muscles of the limbs and digits. Fibers of the ventral spinothalamic tract are represented by the midline of the homunculus's body and are destined to move muscles of the midline of the body.

Photo of spinal cord reproduced from *The Human Brain: Dissections of the Real Brain* by T. H. Williams, N. Gluhbegovic, and J. Jew, on CD-ROM. Published by Brain University, brain-university.com 2000.

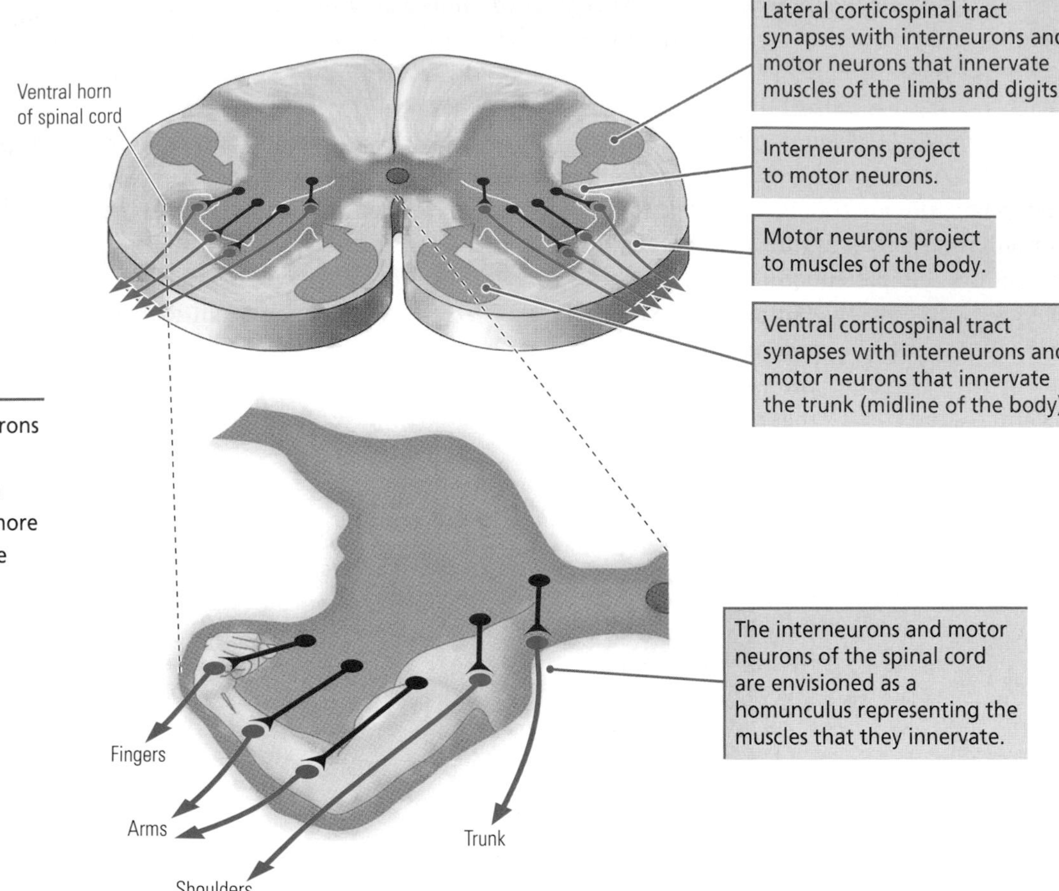
Ventral horn
of spinal cord
Lateral corticospinal tract synapses with interneurons and motor neurons that innervate muscles of the limbs and digits.
Interneurons project to motor neurons.
Motor neurons project to muscles of the body.
Ventral corticospinal tract synapses with interneurons and motor neurons that innervate the trunk (midline of the body).
The interneurons and motor neurons of the spinal cord are envisioned as a homunculus representing the muscles that they innervate.
Fingers
Arms
Shoulders
Trunk

**Figure 10-12**

The interneurons and the motor neurons of the ventral spinal cord are topographically arranged so that the more lateral neurons innervate the more distal parts of the limbs and the more medial neurons innervate the more proximal muscles of the body.

Click on the area on descending motor tracts in the module on the Control of Movement on your CD for a visual overview of the corticospinal tracts.

In looking at the cross section of the spinal cord in Figure 10-12, you can see the location of the two tracts on each side. Those fibers that cross to the opposite side of the brainstem descend the spinal cord in a lateral position, giving them the name **lateral corticospinal tract.** Those fibers that remain on their original side of the brainstem continue down the spinal cord in a ventral position, giving them the name **ventral corticospinal tract.**

## The Motor Neurons

The spinal-cord motor neurons that connect to muscles are located in the spinal cord's ventral horns. Interneurons lie just medial to the motor neurons and project onto them. The fibers from the corticospinal tracts make synaptic connections with both the interneurons and the motor neurons, but all nervous system commands to the muscles are carried by the motor neurons. Figure 10-12 shows that the more laterally located motor neurons project to muscles that control the fingers and hands, whereas intermediately located motor neurons project to muscles that control the arms and shoulders. The most medially located motor neurons project to muscles that control the trunk. The lateral corticospinal tract axons connect mainly with the lateral motor neurons, and the ventral corticospinal tract axons connect mainly to the medial motor neurons.

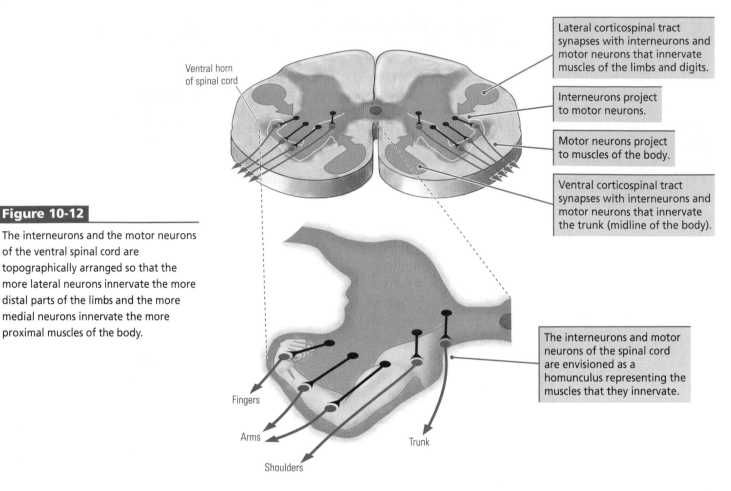

To picture how the motor homunculus in the cortex is related to motor neurons in the spinal cord, imagine placing your right index finger on the index-finger region of the motor homunculus on the left side of the brain and then following the axons of the cortical neurons downward. Your route takes you through the brainstem, across its midline, and down the lateral corticospinal tract, ending on interneurons and motor neurons in the most lateral region of the spinal cord's right ventral horn—the horn on the opposite side of the nervous system from which you began. If you next follow the axons of these motor neurons, you will find that they synapse with muscles that move the index finger on that same right-hand side of the body. (By the way, the neurons that your brain is using to carry out this task are the same neurons whose pathway you are tracing.) If you repeat the procedure but this time trace the pathway from the trunk of the motor homunculus on the left side of the brain, you will follow the same route through the upper part of the brainstem. However, you will not cross over to the brainstem's opposite side. Instead, you will descend into the spinal cord on the same side of the nervous system as that on which you began (the left side), eventually ending up in the most medially located interneurons and motor neurons of that side's ventral horn. Finally, if you follow the axons of these motor neurons, you will end up at their synapses with muscles that move the trunk on the left side of the body.

This imaginary exercise should help you to remember the routes taken by the axons of the motor system. The limb regions of the motor homunculus contribute most of their fibers to the lateral corticospinal tract. Because these fibers have crossed over to the opposite side of the brainstem, they activate motor neurons that move the arm, hand, leg, and foot on *the opposite side of the body*. In contrast, the trunk regions of the motor homunculus contribute their fibers to the ventral corticospinal tract and, because these fibers do not cross over at the brainstem, they activate motor neurons that move the trunk on *the same side of the body*. In short, the neurons of the motor homunculus in the left-hemisphere cortex control the trunk on the body's left side and the limbs on the body's right side. Similarly, neurons of the motor homunculus in the right-hemisphere cortex control the trunk on the body's right side and the limbs on the body's left side (Kuypers, 1981).

This description of motor-system pathways descending from the brain is a simplified one. There are actually about 26 pathways, including the corticospinal tracts. The other pathways carry instructions from the brainstem, such as information related to posture and balance, and control the autonomic nervous system. For all of these functions, however, the motor neurons are the final common path.

## The Control of Muscles

The muscles with which spinal-cord motor neurons synapse control movement of the body. For example, the biceps and triceps of the upper arm control movement of the lower arm. Limb muscles are arranged in pairs, as shown in Figure 10-13. One member of a pair, the extensor, extends the limb away from the trunk. The other member of the pair, the flexor, moves the limb toward the trunk. Connections between the interneurons and motor neurons of the spinal cord ensure that the muscles work together so that, when one muscle contracts, the other relaxes. As you know, the neurotransmitter at the motor neuron– muscle junction is acetylcholine.

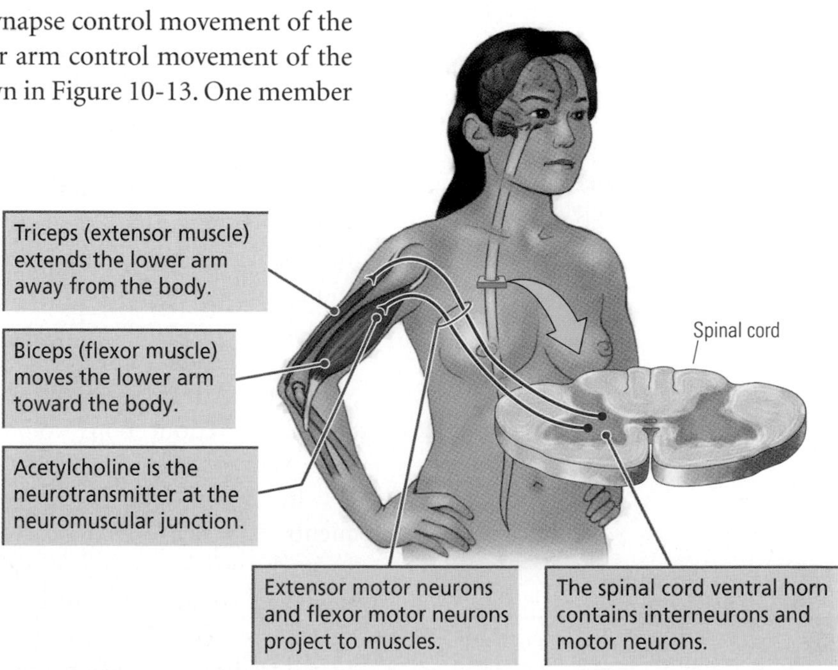
Triceps (extensor muscle) extends the lower arm away from the body.
Biceps (flexor muscle) moves the lower arm toward the body.
Acetylcholine is the neurotransmitter at the neuromuscular junction.
Spinal cord
Extensor motor neurons and flexor motor neurons project to muscles.
The spinal cord ventral horn contains interneurons and motor neurons.

**Figure 10-13**

Motor neurons of the ventral horn of the spinal cord project to extensor muscles (which move limbs away from the body) and flexor muscles (which move limbs toward the body).

## In Review

The motor cortex is topographically organized as a homunculus in which parts of the body that are capable of the most skilled movements (especially the mouth, fingers, and thumb) are regulated by relatively larger cortical regions. Instructions regarding movement travel from the motor cortex through the corticospinal tracts to interneurons and motor neurons in the ventral horn of the spinal cord. The ventral corticospinal tracts carry instructions for trunk movements, whereas the lateral corticospinal tracts carry instructions for arm and finger movements. The axons of motor neurons in the spinal cord then carry instructions to muscles.

# THE MOTOR CORTEX AND SKILLED MOVEMENTS

Baseball pitcher winding up

There is remarkable similarity in the way that people perform skilled movements. For instance, most people who reach for a small paperclip on a desk do so with the hand rotated so that the fingers are on the top and the thumb is on the side. They also use the pincer grip to hold the clip—that is, they grasp it between the thumb and index finger. These movements could be learned by watching other people use them, but we have no recollection of having, as children, spent any time observing and mastering such movement patterns. In fact, at about 12 months of age, babies simply spontaneously begin to use the pincer grip to pick up tiny objects such as breadcrumbs. Most other primates use this same grip pattern. All of the evidence therefore suggests that this skilled movement and many others are not learned but, instead, are innate. They are encoded in the neural connections of the motor cortex as basic patterns of movement that are common to the particular species. These patterns are known as **synergies.** In this section, we will see how neurons produce such synergies. We will also see how the motor cortices of other species produce skilled movements in these species, including the highly dexterous movements of an elephant's trunk.

## Investigating Neural Control of Skilled Movements

Visit the area on control of movement in the module on the Control of Movement in your CD for more detail on the role of the central nervous system.

Apostolos Georgopoulos and his coworkers (1999) investigated the neural control of movement by recording from neurons in the motor cortices of monkeys that had been trained to make specific finger movements. They expected that, when a thumb or a certain finger moved, only the area of the motor cortex that represented that particular digit would be active. But this is not what happened. When one finger moved, not only were neurons in that finger's area of the motor cortex active, but so were neurons in the cortical areas of other fingers. Apparently, the entire hand's representation in the motor cortex participates even in simple acts, such as moving one finger. Although at first this finding may seem surprising, it makes intuitive sense. After all, to move one finger, some effort must be exerted to keep the other fingers still. There must be connections between all of the participating neurons to allow them to act in concert. These same connections would be necessary for sequential movements of the fingers, such as those used in playing the piano or painting a work of art.

In another study designed to investigate how the motor cortex controls movements, E. V. Evarts (1968) used the simple procedure illustrated in Figure 10-14. He trained a monkey to flex its wrist in order to move a bar to which weights of different heaviness could be attached. An electrode implanted in the wrist region of the motor cortex recorded the activity of neurons there. Evarts discovered that these neurons began to discharge even before the monkey flexed its wrist. Apparently, they took part

**Synergy.** A pattern of movement that is coded by the motor cortex.

in planning the movement as well as initiating it. The neurons also continued to discharge as the wrist moved, confirming that they played a role in producing the movement. Finally, the neurons discharged at a higher rate when the bar was loaded with a weight. This finding showed that motor-cortex neurons increase the force of a movement by increasing their rate of firing.

Evarts's experiment also revealed that the motor cortex has a role in specifying the direction of a movement. The neurons of the motor-cortex wrist area discharged when the monkey flexed its wrist inward but not when the wrist was extended back to its starting position. These on–off responses of the neurons, depending on whether the

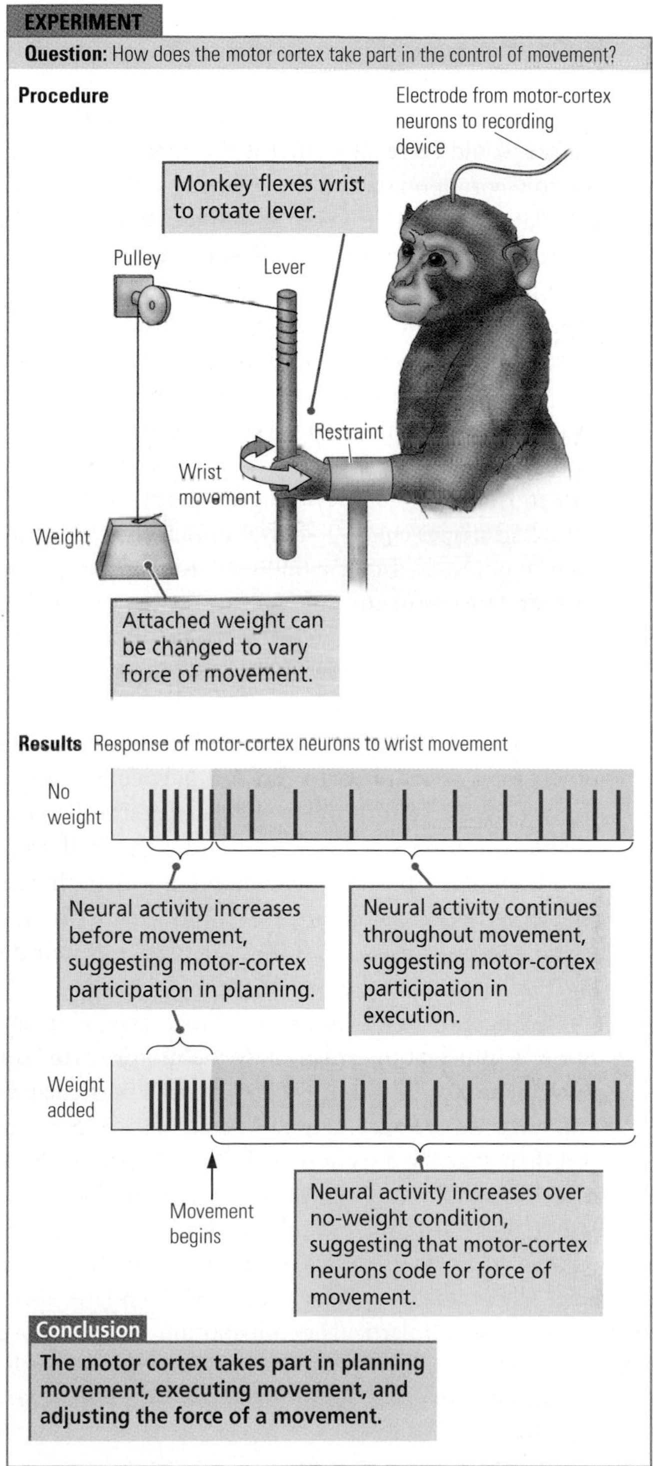

EXPERIMENT
Question: How does the motor cortex take part in the control of movement?
Procedure
Electrode from motor-cortex neurons to recording device
Monkey flexes wrist to rotate lever.
Pulley
Lever
Restraint
Wrist movement
Weight
Attached weight can be changed to vary force of movement.
Results Response of motor-cortex neurons to wrist movement
No weight
Neural activity increases before movement, suggesting motor-cortex participation in planning.
Neural activity continues throughout movement, suggesting motor-cortex participation in execution.
Weight added
Movement begins
Neural activity increases over no-weight condition, suggesting that motor-cortex neurons code for force of movement.
Conclusion
The motor cortex takes part in planning movement, executing movement, and adjusting the force of a movement.


**Figure 10-14**

This experiment demonstrates that motor-cortex neurons take part in planning movements, executing movements, and regulating movement force and duration.

Adapted from "Relation of Pyramidal Tract Activity to Force Exerted During Voluntary Movement," by E. V. Evarts, 1968, *Journal of Neurophysiology, 31,* p. 15.

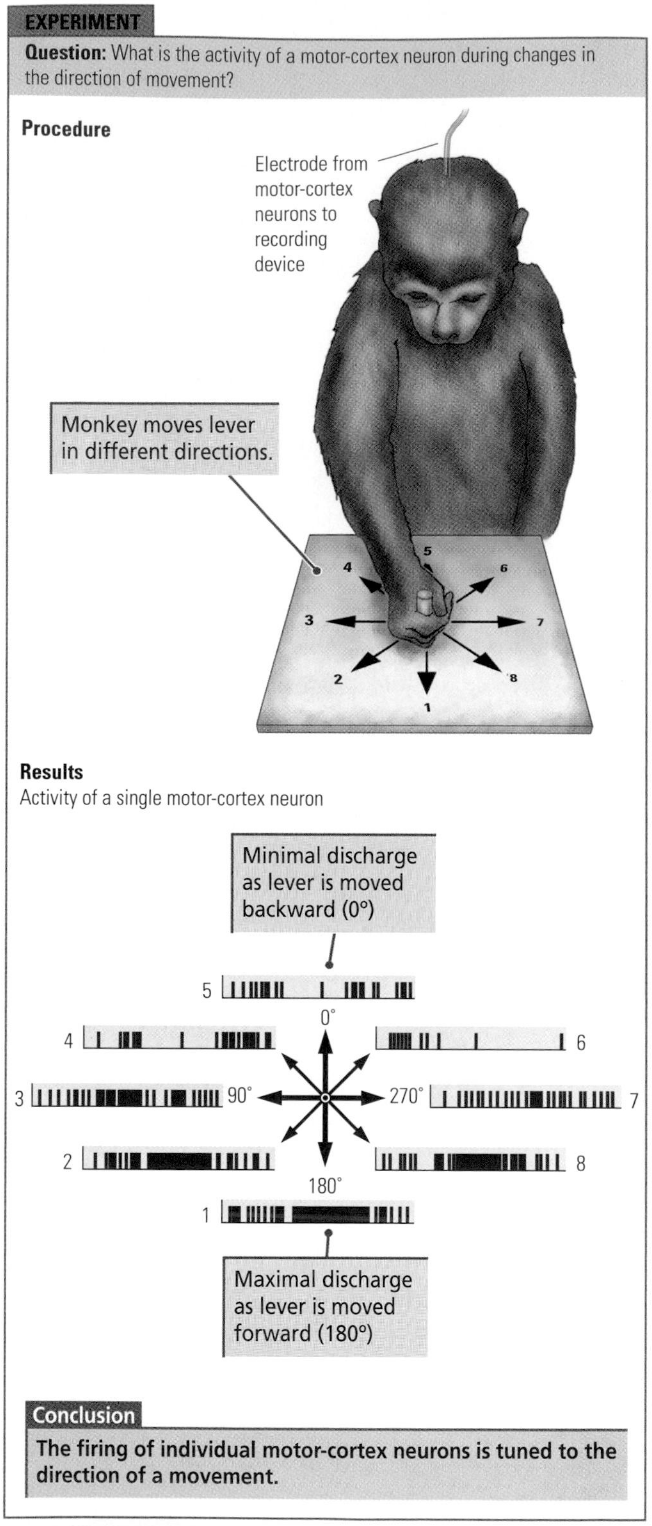

**EXPERIMENT**

**Question:** What is the activity of a motor-cortex neuron during changes in the direction of movement?

**Procedure**

Electrode from motor-cortex neurons to recording device

Monkey moves lever in different directions.

**Results**

Activity of a single motor-cortex neuron

Minimal discharge as lever is moved backward (0°)

Maximal discharge as lever is moved forward (180°)

**Conclusion**

**The firing of individual motor-cortex neurons is tuned to the direction of a movement.**

**Figure 10-15**

Individual motor-cortex neurons are maximally responsive to movements in a particular direction.

Adapted from "On the Relations Between the Direction of Two-Dimensional Arm Movements and Cell Discharge in Primate Motor Cortex," by A. P. Georgopoulos, J. F. Kalaska, R. Caminiti, and J. T. Massey, 1982, *Journal of Neuroscience, 2,* p. 1530.

flexor or extensor muscle is being used, are a simple way of coding the direction in which the wrist is moving.

Georgopoulos (1993) and his coworkers used a method similar to that of Evarts to further examine the coding of movement direction. They trained monkeys to move a lever in different directions across the surface of a table. Recording from single cells in the arm region of the motor cortex, they found that each cell was maximally active when the monkey moved its arm in a particular direction. Figure 10-15 summarizes the results. As the monkey's arm moved in directions other than the one to which a particular cell maximally responded, the cell would decrease its activity in proportion to the displacement from the "preferred" direction. For example, if a neuron discharged maximally as the arm moved directly forward, its discharge would be halved if the arm moved to one side, and discharge would cease altogether if the arm moved backward. According to Georgopoulos and his coworkers, the motor cortex seems to calculate both the direction and the distance of movements. Each neuron in a large population of motor-cortex neurons could participate in producing a particular movement, just as other studies have suggested. But the discharge rate of a particular neuron would depend on that movement's direction.

Georgopoulos proposed a different hypothesis from that of Evarts about how the motor cortex exerts control over movement. Both researchers believe that motor-cortex neurons plan and execute movements, but they disagree about what those plans and execution strategies entail. To better understand the difference between their hypotheses, imagine that you are preparing to throw a ball to a catcher. Does your throw require calculating which muscles to use and how much force to apply to each one? This is Evarts's position. It is based on his findings about how neurons of the motor cortex change their rates of discharge in response not only to which muscle is needed (flexor or extensor, for instance), but also to how much force is required to make a particular movement. Alternatively, perhaps your throw to the catcher simply requires determining the location at which you want the ball to arrive. This is Georgopoulos's position. He maintains that the cortex needs to specify only the spatial target of a movement—that is, its basic direction. Other brain structures, such as the brainstem and spinal cord, will look after the details of the throw.

Georgopoulos's hypothesis is very appealing in its simplicity. But is it sufficient to explain how the motor cortex controls a skilled movement? When you move an arm in a particular direction, many arm muscles are very active, whereas others are less active. When you then alter the direction of the movement, most of the same arm muscles remain active, but the force produced by each muscle changes, with some becoming less active and others more active. Recording from a single neuron associated with a single muscle might give the impression that the neuron is coding the movement's directional target, but the neuron might also be coding the force associated with the muscle's particular contribution to that movement. Exactly what the code entails is still not understood. The directional hypothesis and the force hypothesis are both topics of current debate in the study of how the motor cortex controls movement (Fetz, 1992).

## The Control of Skilled Movements in Other Species

Humans are far from the only species making skilled movements. Kamala, the elephant, as you know, paints works of art with her trunk, and primates other than humans are very skillful with their hands, as we are. What is it about the motor cortex in other species that enables these skilled movement patterns?

Studies of a wide range of animals show that the motor cortex is organized to correspond to the skilled movements of a species. Just as in humans, larger parts of the motor cortex regulate body parts that carry out these movements. Figure 10-16 shows the human homunculus and comparable cartoon figures for four other animals—the rabbit, cat, monkey, and elephant. As you can see, rabbits have a large motor-cortex representation for the head and mouth, cats for the mouth and front claws, and monkeys for the hands, feet, and digits. Although no one has mapped the motor cortex of an elephant, it is likely that elephants have a disproportionately large area of motor cortex regulating the trunk.

How did these specialized representations of the motor cortex evolve? One possibility is that they were constructed from the outside inward (Woolsey & Wann, 1976). Chance mutations caused an increase in the number of muscles in a particular part of the body, which led to more motor neurons in the spinal cord. This increase in motor neurons, in turn, led to an increase in the area of the motor cortex controlling those spinal-cord motor neurons. Finally, the larger motor-cortex representation, along with an increased possibility of making connections between these cortical neurons, led to a capacity for making new and more complex movements.

Let us apply this scenario to the development of the elephant's trunk. First, chance mutations led to the expansion of muscles in the elephant's lip and nose and the spinal-cord motor neurons needed to move them. These developments were retained because they were useful for feeding. The area of the motor cortex then expanded to represent the new muscles of the trunk.

**Figure 10-16**

The difference in the size of the motor-cortex representation of different body parts in several species of animals suggests that the size of the cortical area regulating a body part corresponds to the skill required to move that body part. The representation for the elephant is only surmised.

Adapted from *Principles of Neural Science* (3rd ed., p. 373), by E. R. Kandel, J. H. Schwartz, and T. M. Jessel, 1991, New York: Elsevier.

## How Motor-Cortex Damage Affects Skilled Movements

In the 1940s, when scientists were first producing maps of the motor cortex, a number of researchers got slightly different results when they repeated the mapping procedures on the same subjects. These findings led to a debate. Some scientists held that the map of the motor cortex was capable of changing—that areas controlling particular body parts might not always stay in exactly the same place and retain exactly the same dimensions. But other researchers felt that this view was unlikely. They argued that, given the enormous specificity of topographic maps of the motor cortex, these maps must surely be quite stable. If they appeared to change, it must be because the relatively large electrodes used for stimulating and recording from cortical neurons must be producing inexact results. As the mapping procedures improved, however, and as smaller and smaller electrodes were used, it became clear that these maps can indeed change. They can change as a result of sensory or motor learning (a topic to be explored in Chapter 13), and they can change when part of the motor cortex is damaged, as the following example shows.

A study by Randy Nudo and his coworkers (1996), summarized in Figure 10-17, illustrates change in a map of the motor cortex that is due to cortical damage. These

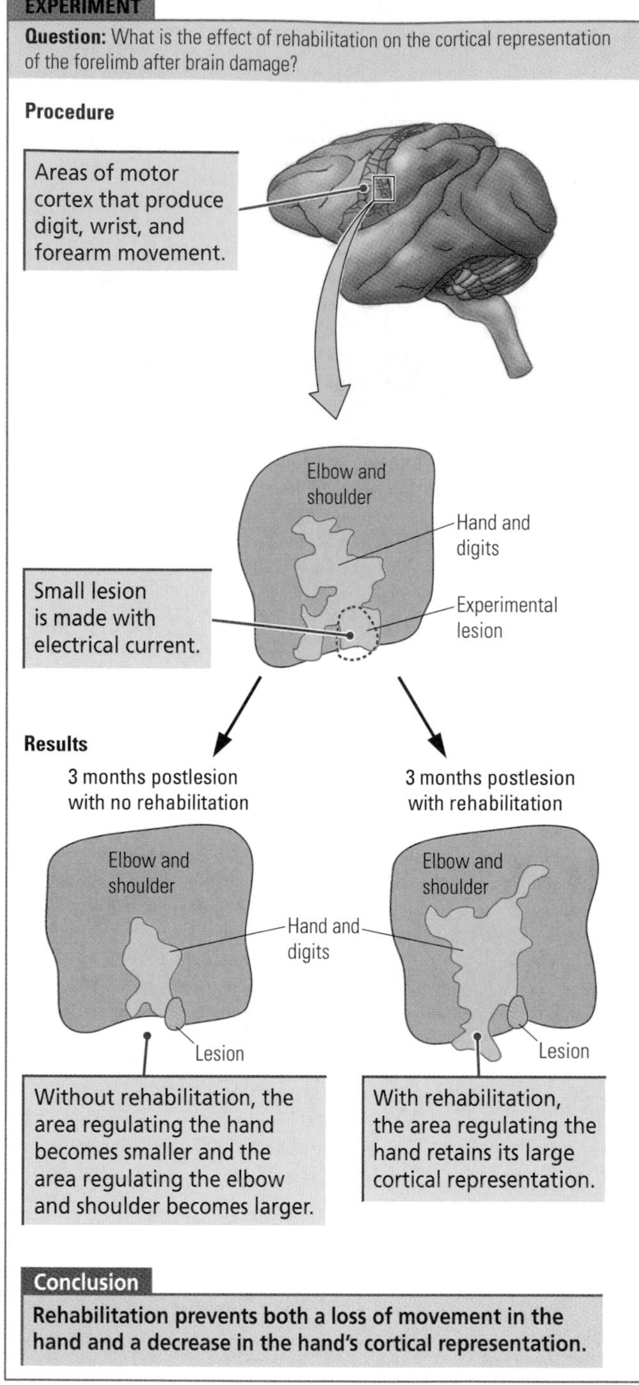

EXPERIMENT
Question: What is the effect of rehabilitation on the cortical representation of the forelimb after brain damage?
Procedure
Areas of motor cortex that produce digit, wrist, and forearm movement.
Elbow and shoulder
Hand and digits
Small lesion is made with electrical current.
Experimental lesion
Results
3 months postlesion with no rehabilitation
3 months postlesion with rehabilitation
Elbow and shoulder
Hand and digits
Elbow and shoulder
Lesion
Lesion
Without rehabilitation, the area regulating the hand becomes smaller and the area regulating the elbow and shoulder becomes larger.
With rehabilitation, the area regulating the hand retains its large cortical representation.
Conclusion
Rehabilitation prevents both a loss of movement in the hand and a decrease in the hand's cortical representation.


**Figure 10-17**

Effect of experience on the cortical representation of the forelimb in the motor cortex of a monkey after brain damage. Weak electrical stimulation shows the areas of the cortex that produce digit, wrist, and forearm movements in a monkey before a small lesion is made with a larger electrical current through the electrode. The area that receives the lesion is indicated by the dashed lines. In the monkey that was not forced to use its affected limb, the area of cortex representing the hand has become smaller and the area of motor cortex representing the elbow and shoulder has become larger. In a monkey that was forced to use the affected limb because the good limb was bound, the hand area retains its large cortical representation.

Adapted from "Neural Substrates for the Effects of Rehabilitative Training on Motor Recovery After Ischemic Infarct," by R. J. Nudo, B. M. Wise, F. SiFuentes, and G. W. Milliken, 1996, *Science, 272,* p. 1793.

researchers mapped the motor cortices of monkeys to identify the hand and digit areas. They then surgically removed a small part of the digit area. After the surgery, the monkeys used the affected hand much less, relying mainly on the good hand. Three months later, the researchers examined the monkeys. They found that the animals were unable to produce many movements of the lower arm, including the wrist, the hand, and the digits surrounding the area with the lesion. They also discovered that much of the area representing the hand and lower arm was gone from the cortical map. The shoulder, upper arm, and elbow areas had spread to take up what had formerly been space representing the hand and digits. Figure 10-17 (Results, left) shows this topographic change.

The experimenters wondered whether the change could have been prevented had they forced the monkeys to use the affected arm. To find out, they used the same procedure on other monkeys, except that, during the postsurgery period, they made the animals rely on the bad arm by binding the good arm in a sling. Three months later, when the experimenters reexamined the motor maps of these monkeys, they found that the hand and digit area retained its large size, even though there was no neural activity in the spot with the lesion. Nevertheless, the monkeys had gained some function in the digits that had formerly been connected to the damaged spot. Apparently, the remaining digit area of the cortex was now controlling the movement of these fingers.

The motor-cortex reorganization that Nudo and his colleagues observed probably explains some kinds of recovery from brain damage observed in humans. For instance, Paul Bucy and his coworkers (1964) studied a man who had had the corticospinal tract cut on one side of his nervous system to stop involuntary movement of his muscles. During the first 24 hours after the surgery, the side of his body contralateral to the cut was completely flaccid, and he was unable to make any movements on that side. (The impairment was on the side of the body opposite that of the cut because the corticospinal tract crossed to the other side just below the location of the cut.) Then gradually there was some recovery of function. By the 10th day after the surgery, the patient could stand alone and walk with assistance. By the 24th day, he could walk unaided. Within 7 months, he could move his feet, hands, fingers, and toes with only slight impairment.

The explanation of this man's remarkable recovery is twofold. First, when the man died about 2½ years later, an autopsy revealed that approximately 17 percent of the corticospinal fibers were intact in the tract that had been cut. Apparently, the remaining corticospinal fibers were able to take over much of the function formerly served by the entire pathway. Second, extensive reorganization likely took place in the map of the man's motor cortex, so many cortical regions could use the fibers that had remained intact to send messages to motor neurons in the spinal cord.

## In Review

Basic patterns of movement that are common to a particular species are organized in the motor cortex as synergies. The discharge patterns of motor-cortex neurons suggest that these neurons take part in planning and initiating movements, as well as in carrying movements out. The discharge rate of these neurons is related both to the force of muscle contraction and to the direction of a movement. The topographic map of the motor cortex in a particular species is related to the species' body parts that are capable of making the most skillful movements. The relation between neurons in the motor cortex and the movement of specific muscles is not fixed. Considerable change can take place in the cortical motor map after injury to the motor cortex.

# THE BASAL GANGLIA AND THE CEREBELLUM

The main evidence that the basal ganglia and the cerebellum have motor functions is that damage to either structure impairs movement. Both structures also have extensive connections with the motor cortex, further suggesting their participation in movement. After an overview of the anatomy of the basal ganglia and cerebellum, we will look at some of the symptoms that arise after they are damaged. Then we will consider some experiments that illustrate the roles that they might play in controlling movement.

Investigate the area on control of movement in the module on Control of Movement in the CD. Look for details on what happens when there is damage to these regions.

## The Basal Ganglia and Movement Force

The basal ganglia are a collection of nuclei in the forebrain that make connections with the motor cortex and with the midbrain. As shown in Figure 10-18, a prominent structure in the basal ganglia is the *caudate putamen,* a large cluster of nuclei located beneath the frontal cortex. Part of the caudate extends as a "tail" into the temporal lobe, ending in the amygdala.

The basal ganglia receive inputs from two main sources. First, all areas of the neocortex and limbic cortex, including the motor cortex, project to the basal ganglia. Second, there is a dopaminergic projection to the basal ganglia from the substantia nigra, a cluster of darkly pigmented cells of the midbrain. The basal ganglia project back to both the motor cortex and the substantia nigra.

Two different, and in many ways opposite, kinds of movement disorders result from basal ganglia damage. If cells of the caudate putamen are damaged, unwanted choreiform (writhing and twitching) movements occur. For example, Huntington's chorea, in which caudate putamen cells are destroyed, is characterized by involuntary and exaggerated movements. Other examples of involuntary movements related to caudate putamen damage are the unwanted tics

**Figure 10-18** The basal ganglia consist of the caudate putamen, the tail of the caudate nucleus, and the amygdala. The caudate putamen makes reciprocal connections with the substantia nigra. It also receives input from most regions of the cortex and sends input into the frontal lobes via the thalamus.

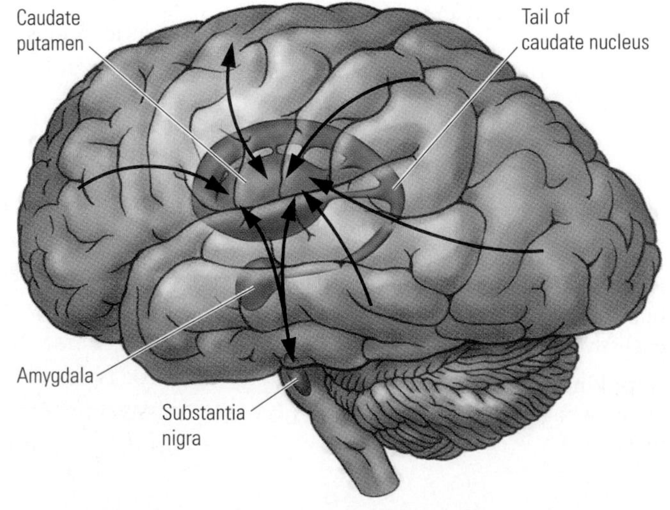

Focus on Disorders

## Tourette's Syndrome

The neurological disorder known as Tourette's syndrome (TS) was first described in 1885 by Georges Gilles de la Tourette, a young French neurologist and friend of Sigmund Freud. Here is how Tourette described the symptoms as they appeared in Madame de D., one of his own patients:

> Madame de D., presently age 26, at the age of 7 was afflicted by convulsive movements of the hands and arms. These abnormal movements occurred above all when the child tried to write, causing her to crudely reproduce the letters she was trying to trace. After each spasm, the movements of the hand became more regular and better controlled until another convulsive movement would again interrupt her work. She was felt to be suffering from over-excitement and mischief, and because the movements became more and more frequent, she was subject to reprimand and punishment. Soon it became clear that these movements were indeed involuntary and convulsive in nature. The movements involved the shoulders, the neck, and the face, and resulted in contortions and extraordinary grimaces. As the disease progressed, and the spasms spread to involve her voice and speech, the young lady made strange screams and said words that made no sense. (Friedhoff & Chase, 1982)

Tourette's syndrome has an incidence of less than 1 per 1000 people. It is found in all racial groups and seems to be hereditary. The average age of onset is between 2 and 25 years. The most frequent symptoms are involuntary tics and involuntary complex movements, such as hitting, lunging, or jumping. People with the syndrome may also suddenly emit cries and other vocalizations or inexplicably utter words that do not make sense in the context, including swear words. TS is not associated with any other disorders, although much milder cases of tics may be related to it.

TS is thought to be due to an abnormality of the basal ganglia, especially the right basal ganglia. It is an example of one of the hyperkinetic disorders that can result from basal ganglia dysfunction. The symptoms of TS can be controlled with haloperidol, which blocks dopamine synapses in the basal ganglia.

Many people with TS function quite well, coping successfully with their symptoms. There are people with Tourette's syndrome in all walks of life, even surgeons who must perform delicate operations. With the existence of the Tourette's Society in the past 20 years, public awareness of the disorder has increased. Children with TS are now less likely to be diagnosed as having a psychiatric condition, being hyperactive, or being troublemakers.

and vocalizations peculiar to Tourette's syndrome, which is discussed in "Tourette's Syndrome" above. In addition to causing involuntary movements, called **hyperkinetic symptoms,** damage to the basal ganglia can result in a loss of motor ability, called **hypokinetic symptoms.** One such hypokinetic disorder, Parkinson's disease, was discussed in preceding chapters. It is caused by the loss of dopamine cells in the substantia nigra and is characterized by an inability to produce normal movements. The two different kinds of symptoms that arise subsequent to basal ganglia damage—hyperkinetic and hypokinetic symptoms—suggest that a major function of these nuclei is to modulate movement.

Steven Keele and Richard Ivry (1991) tried to relate the two different kinds of basal ganglia symptoms by suggesting that the underlying function of the basal ganglia is to generate the force required for each particular movement. According to this idea, some types of basal ganglia damage cause errors of too much force and so result in excessive movement, whereas other types of damage cause errors of too little force and so result in insufficient movement. Keele and Ivry tested their hypothesis by giving

**Hyperkinetic symptom.** A symptom of brain damage that involves involuntary excessive movements.

**Hypokinetic symptom.** A symptom of brain damage that involves a paucity of movement.

healthy subjects as well as patients with various kinds of basal ganglia disorders a task that tested their ability to exert appropriate amounts of force. The subjects viewed a line on a television screen; by pushing a button with varying amounts of force, they could produce a second line to match the length of the first. After a number of practice trials, the subjects were then asked to press the button with the appropriate amount of force even when the first line was no longer visible as a guide. In contrast to control subjects, patients with basal ganglia disorders were unable to reliably do so. The force that they exerted was usually too little or too much, resulting in a line too short or too long.

What neural pathways enable the basal ganglia to modulate the force of movements? Basal ganglia circuits are quite complex, but one theory holds that there are two pathways through which the activity of the motor cortex is affected: an inhibitory pathway and an excitatory pathway (Alexander & Crutcher, 1990). Both these pathways converge on an area of the basal ganglia called the internal part of the **globus pallidus** ($GP_i$), as shown in Figure 10-19. The $GP_i$ in turn projects to the thalamus (more specifically, to the ventral thalamic nucleus), and the thalamus projects to the motor cortex. The thalamic projection modulates the size or force of a movement that the cortex produces, but the thalamic projection is influenced by the $GP_i$. The $GP_i$ is thought of as acting like the volume dial on a radio because its output determines whether a movement will be weak or strong.

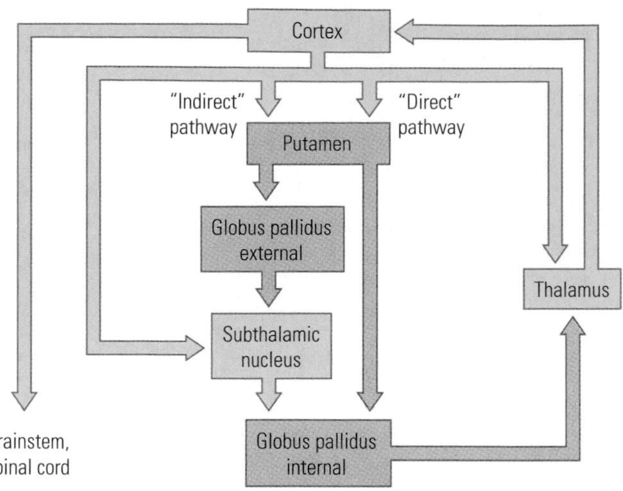


**Figure 10-19**

Two pathways in the basal ganglia modulate cortically produced movements. Green indicates the parts of the pathways that are excitatory, and red indicates the parts that are inhibitory. The indirect pathway has an excitatory effect on the internal part of the globus pallidus, whereas the direct pathway has an inhibitory effect on it. If inhibition dominates, the thalamus is shut down and the cortex is unable to produce movement. If excitation predominates, the thalamus can become overactive, thus amplifying movement.

Adapted from "Functional Architecture of Basal Ganglia Circuits: Neural Substrates of Parallel Processing," by R. E. Alexander and M. D. Crutcher, 1990, *Trends in Neuroscience, 13,* p. 269.

The inputs to the $GP_i$ are shown in red and green in Figure 10-19 to illustrate how they affect movement. If activity in the inhibitory pathway (red) is high relative to that in the excitatory pathway (green), inhibition of the $GP_i$ will predominate and the thalamus will be free to excite the cortex, thus amplifying movement. If, on the other hand, activity in the excitatory pathway is high relative to that in the inhibitory pathway, excitation of the $GP_i$ will predominate and the thalamus will be inhibited, thus reducing input to the cortex and decreasing the force of movements.

The idea that the $GP_i$ acts like a volume control over movement is currently receiving a great deal of attention. If the $GP_i$ is surgically destroyed in Parkinson patients, muscular rigidity is reduced and the ability to make normal movements is improved. Also consistent with this "volume hypothesis," recordings made from cells of the globus pallidus show that they are excessively active in people with Parkinson's disease.

## The Cerebellum and Movement Skill

In referring to the amount of practice required to play a musical instrument, musicians have a saying: "Miss a day of practice and you're OK; miss two days and you notice; miss three days and the world notices." Apparently, some change must take place in the brain when practice of a motor skill is neglected. The cerebellum may be the part of the motor system that is affected. Whether the skill is playing a musical instrument, pitching a baseball, or typing on a computer keyboard, the cerebellum is critical for acquiring and maintaining motor skills.

The cerebellum, a large and conspicuous part of the motor system, sits on top of the brainstem and is clearly visible just behind the cerebral cortex. The cerebellum is divided into two hemispheres, as is the cerebral cortex. A small lobe called the **flocculus** projects from its ventral surface. Despite the cerebellum's relatively small size, it contains about one-half of all the neurons of the nervous system.

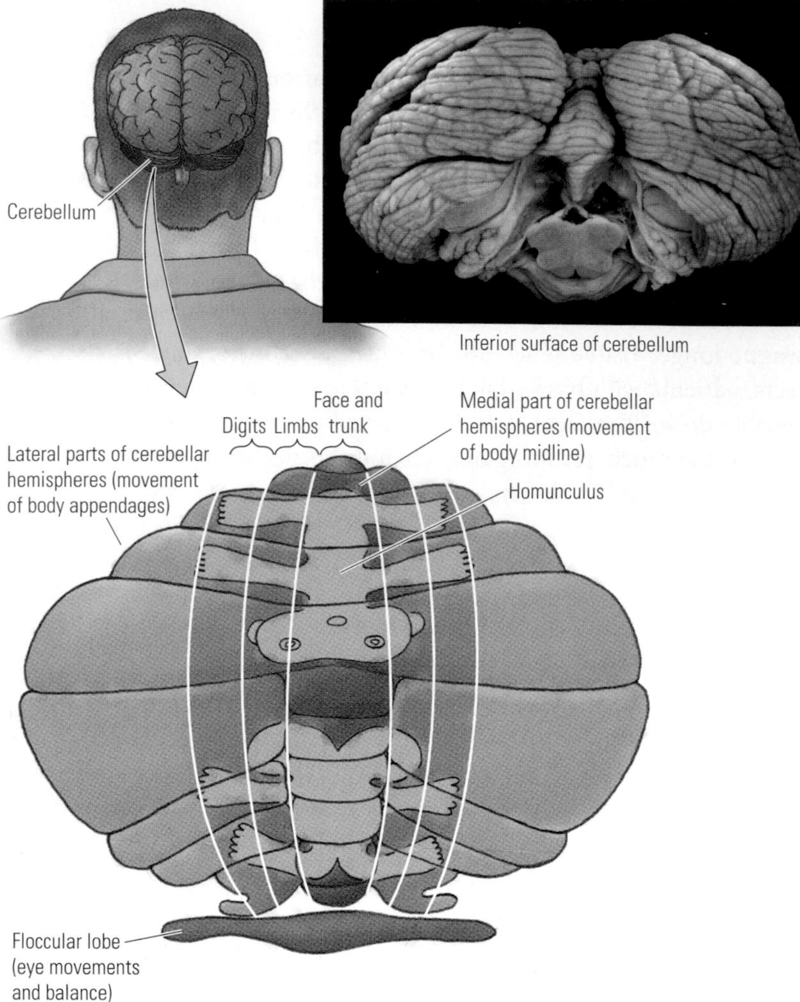


**Figure 10-20**

The cerebellum consists of the cerebellar hemispheres and the flocculus. The hemispheres control body movements, and the flocculus controls balance. The cerebellum is topographically organized, with its more medial parts representing the midline of the body and its more lateral parts representing the limbs and digits.

Photo of cerebellum reproduced from *The Human Brain: Dissections of the Real Brain* by T. H. Williams, N. Gluhbegovic, and J. Jew, on CD-ROM. Published by Brain University, brain-university.com 2000.

As Figure 10-20 shows, the cerebellum can be divided into several regions, each of which specializes in a different aspect of motor control. The flocculus receives projections from the vestibular system, which will be described shortly, and takes part in the control of balance and eye movements. Many of its projections go to the spinal cord and to the motor nuclei that control eye movements. The hemispheres of the cerebellum can be subdivided as shown by the white lines in the drawing. The most medial part controls the face and the midline of the body. The more lateral parts are connected to areas of the motor cortex and are associated with movements of the limbs, hands, feet, and digits. The pathways from the hemispheres project to nuclei of the cerebellum, which in turn project to other brain regions, including the motor cortex.

To summarize the cerebellum's topographic organization, the midline of the homunculus is represented in the central part of the cerebellum, whereas the limbs and digits are represented in the cerebellum's lateral parts. Tumors or damage to midline areas of the cerebellum disrupt balance, eye movements, upright posture, and walking but do not substantially disrupt other movements such as reaching, grasping, and using the fingers. For example, a person with medial damage to the cerebellum may, when lying down, show few symptoms. Damage to lateral parts of the cerebellum disrupts arm, hand, and finger movements much more than movements of the body's trunk.

Attempts to understand how the cerebellum controls movements have centered on two major ideas: (1) that the cerebellum plays a role in the timing of movements and (2) that the cerebellum maintains movement accuracy. Keele and Ivry support the first of these two ideas. They suggest that the underlying impairment in disorders of the cerebellum is a loss of timing. According to them, the cerebellum acts like a clock or pacemaker to ensure that both movements and perceptions are appropriately timed. In a motor test of timing, subjects were asked to tap a finger to keep time with a metronome. After a number of taps, the metronome was turned off and the subjects were to continue to tap with the same beat. Those with damage to the cerebellum, especially to the lateral cerebellum, were impaired on the task. In a perceptual test of timing, subjects were presented with two pairs of tones. The silent period between the first two tones was always the same length, whereas the silent period between the second two tones changed from trial to trial. The subjects had to tell whether the second silent period was longer or shorter than the first. Those with damage to the cerebellum were also impaired on this task. Apparently, the cerebellum can act like a clock to time perceptions as well as movements.

Not all researchers believe that the cerebellum's major contribution to controlling movements is one of timing, however. Tom Thach and his coworkers (1992) argue that the primary role of the cerebellum is to help make the adjustments needed to keep movements accurate. They gathered evidence in support of this view by having subjects throw darts at a target, as shown in Figure 10-21. After a number of throws, the subjects put on glasses containing wedge-shaped prisms that displaced the apparent location of the target to the left. Then when the subjects threw a dart, it landed to the left of the intended target. All subjects showed this initial distortion in aim. But then came an important difference. When normal subjects saw the dart miss the mark, they adjusted each successive throw until reasonable accuracy was restored. In contrast, subjects with damage to the cerebellum could not correct for this error. They kept missing the target far to the left time after time. Next the subjects removed the prism glasses and threw a few more darts. Again, another significant difference emerged. The first dart thrown by each normal subject was much too far to the right (owing to the previous adjustment that the subject had learned to make), but soon each adjusted once again until his or her former accuracy was regained. In contrast, subjects with damage to the cerebellum showed no aftereffects from having worn the prisms, as if they had never compensated for the glasses to begin with. This experiment suggests that many movements that we make—whether throwing a dart, hitting a ball with a bat, writing neatly, or painting a work of art—depend on moment-to-moment learning and adjustments that are made by the cerebellum.

To better understand how the cerebellum improves motor skills by making required adjustments to movements, imagine throwing a dart yourself. Suppose you aim at the bull's eye, throw the dart, and find that it misses the board completely. You then aim again, this time adjusting your throw to correct for the original error. Notice that there are actually two versions of your action: (1) the movement that you intended to make and (2) the actual movement as recorded by sensory receptors in your arm and shoulder. If the intended movement is successfully carried out, you need make no correction on your next try. But, if you miss, an adjustment is called for. One way in which the adjustment might be made is through the

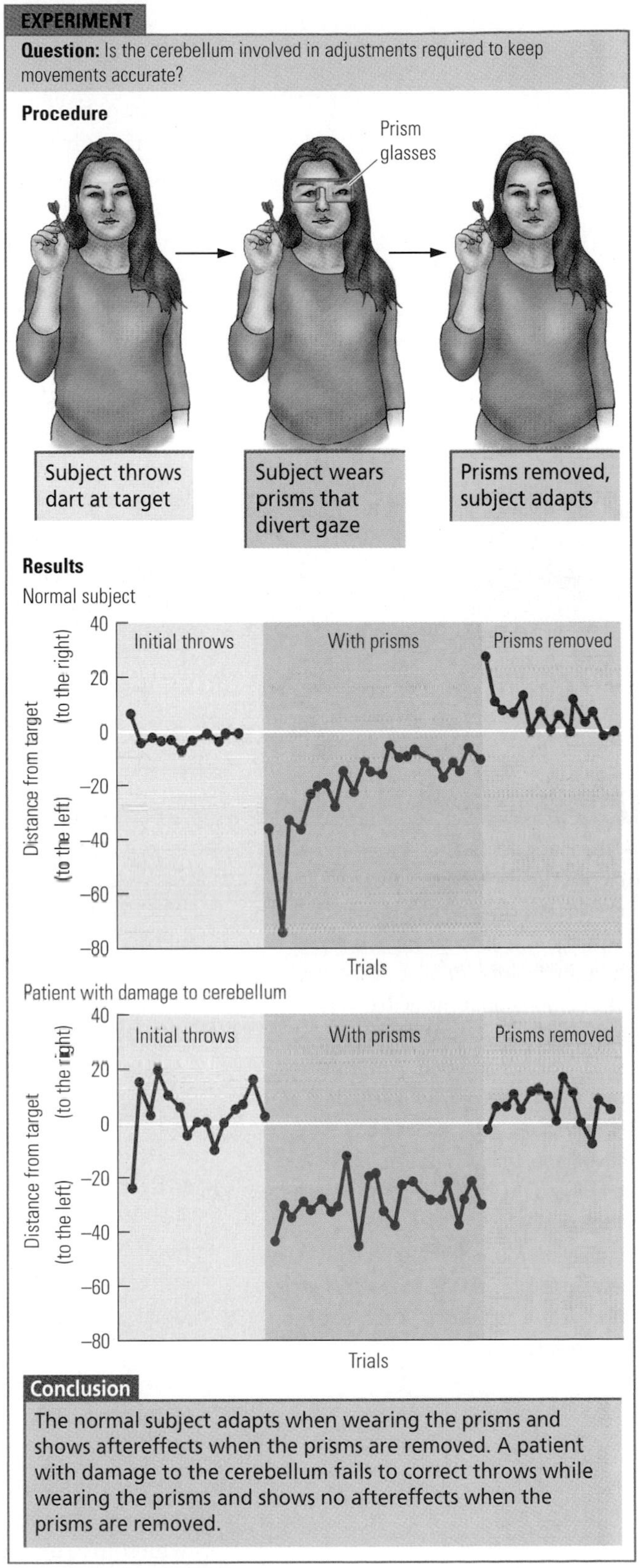

**EXPERIMENT**

**Question:** Is the cerebellum involved in adjustments required to keep movements accurate?

**Procedure**

Prism glasses

Subject throws dart at target

Subject wears prisms that divert gaze

Prisms removed, subject adapts

**Results**

Normal subject

Initial throws | With prisms | Prisms removed

Distance from target (to the left) (to the right)

40, 20, 0, −20, −40, −60, −80

Trials

Patient with damage to cerebellum

Initial throws | With prisms | Prisms removed

Distance from target (to the left) (to the right)

40, 20, 0, −20, −40, −60, −80

Trials

**Conclusion**

The normal subject adapts when wearing the prisms and shows aftereffects when the prisms are removed. A patient with damage to the cerebellum fails to correct throws while wearing the prisms and shows no aftereffects when the prisms are removed.

**Figure 10-21**

This experiment demonstrates that the cerebellum is required to adapt movements to compensate for visual displacement produced by prisms that divert gaze.

Adapted from "The Cerebellum and the Adaptive Coordination of Movement," by W. T. Thach, H. P. Goodkin, and J. G. Keating, 1992, *Annual Review of Neuroscience, 15,* p. 429.

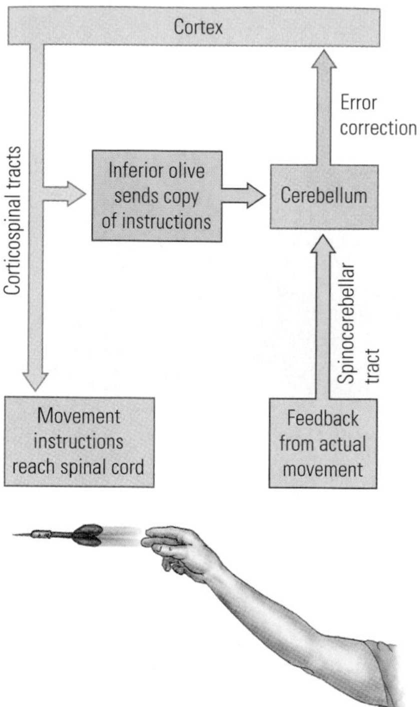


**Figure 10-22**

A feedback circuit allows the cerebellum to correct movements. The cerebellum receives information about the instructions sent to motor neurons through the inferior olive. It receives information about the actual movement through the spinocerebellar tract (a sensory pathway carrying information from the spinal cord to the cerebellum that provides information about movements that have been made). By comparing the message for the intended movement with the movement that was actually performed, the cerebellum can send an error message to the cortex to improve the accuracy of a subsequent movement.

circuit shown in Figure 10-22. The cortex sends instructions to the spinal cord to throw a dart at the target. A copy of the same instructions is sent to the cerebellum through the inferior olive. When you then throw the dart, the sensory receptors in your arm and shoulder code the actual movement that you make and send a message about it to the cerebellum. The cerebellum now has information about both versions of the movement: what you intended to do and what you actually did. The cerebellum can now calculate the error and tell the cortex how it should correct the movement. When you next throw a dart, you incorporate that correction into your throw.

## In Review

The basal ganglia contribute to motor control by adjusting the force associated with each movement. Consequently, damage to the basal ganglia results either in unwanted involuntary movements (too much force being exerted) or in such rigidity that movements are difficult to perform (too little force being exerted). The cerebellum contributes to the control of movement by improving movement skill. One way in which it may do so is by keeping track of the timing of movements. Another way is by making adjustments in movements to maintain their accuracy. In the latter case, the cerebellum compares an intended movement with an actual movement and calculates any necessary corrections.

## THE ORGANIZATION OF THE SOMATOSENSORY SYSTEM

The somatosensory system tells us what the body is up to by providing information about bodily sensations, such as touch, temperature, pain, position in space, movement of the joints, and so forth. In addition to helping us learn about the world, the somatosensory system allows us to distinguish what the world does *to us* from what we do *to it*. For example, when someone pushes you sideways, your somatosensory system tells you that you have been pushed. Similarly, if you lunge to the side yourself, your somatosensory system tells you that you did the moving.

Although, in this book, the visual system and the auditory system are treated in separate chapters, here we explore the somatosensory system and the motor system in a single chapter. The reason is that somatosensation has a closer relation to movement than the other senses do. If we lose sight or hearing or even both, we are still able to move around, and the same is true of other animals. For instance, fish that inhabit deep, dark caves cannot see at all, yet they are able to move about normally. And animals, such as the butterfly, that cannot hear can still move very well. If an animal were to lose its body senses, however, its movements would quickly become so impaired that it would not be able to survive. Some aspects of somatosensation are absolutely essential to movement, so the two topics are covered together.

In considering the motor system, we started at the cortex and followed the motor pathways to the spinal cord. This route makes sense because it follows the direction in which instructions regarding movements flow. As we explore the somatosensory system, we will proceed in the opposite direction, because it is the direction in which sensory information flows. We will start at sensory receptors in various parts of the body and follow sensory pathways to the cortex.

The somatosensory system is unique among sensory systems because it is distributed throughout the entire body; it is not just localized in the head as are vision, hearing, taste, and smell. Somatosensory receptors are found in all parts of the body, and neurons from these receptors carry information to the spinal cord. Within the spinal cord, two somatosensory pathways project to the brain and, eventually, to the so-

Review the somatosensory system in the brain overview section in the Central Nervous System module on your CD.

matosensory cortex. One part of the somatosensory system, the vestibular system, is confined to a single organ, however. The vestibular system, located in the middle ear, contributes to our sense of movement and balance. In the following sections, we will look at the anatomy of the different parts of the somatosensory system and at examples of how each contributes to movement.

**Glabrous skin.** Skin that does not have hair follicles but contains larger numbers of sensory receptors than do other skin areas.

## Somatosensory Receptors and Sensory Perception

Our bodies are covered with sensory receptors. They are attached to body hairs. They are located in both surface layers and deeper layers of the skin. They are embedded in muscles, tendons, and joints. Some consist simply of the ending of a sensory neuron dendrite. On others, the dendrite is covered by a special capsule or it is attached by a sheath of connective tissue to adjacent tissue.

The density of sensory receptors varies greatly in different parts of the body, not only in the skin, but in the muscles, tendons, and joints as well. The variation in density is one reason why different parts of the body are more or less sensitive to somatosensory stimulation. Parts of the body that are very sensitive to touch or capable of fine movements—including the hands, feet, lips, and eyes—have many more somatosensory receptors than other body parts do. Sensitivity to different somatosensory stimuli is also a function of the kinds of receptors that are found in a particular region.

Figure 10-23 includes examples of somatosensory receptors located in the skin. Humans have two kinds of skin, **hairy skin** (shown in Figure 10-23) and **glabrous skin**

**Figure 10-23**

The perceptions derived from the body senses depend on different receptors located in different parts of the skin, muscles, joints, and tendons.

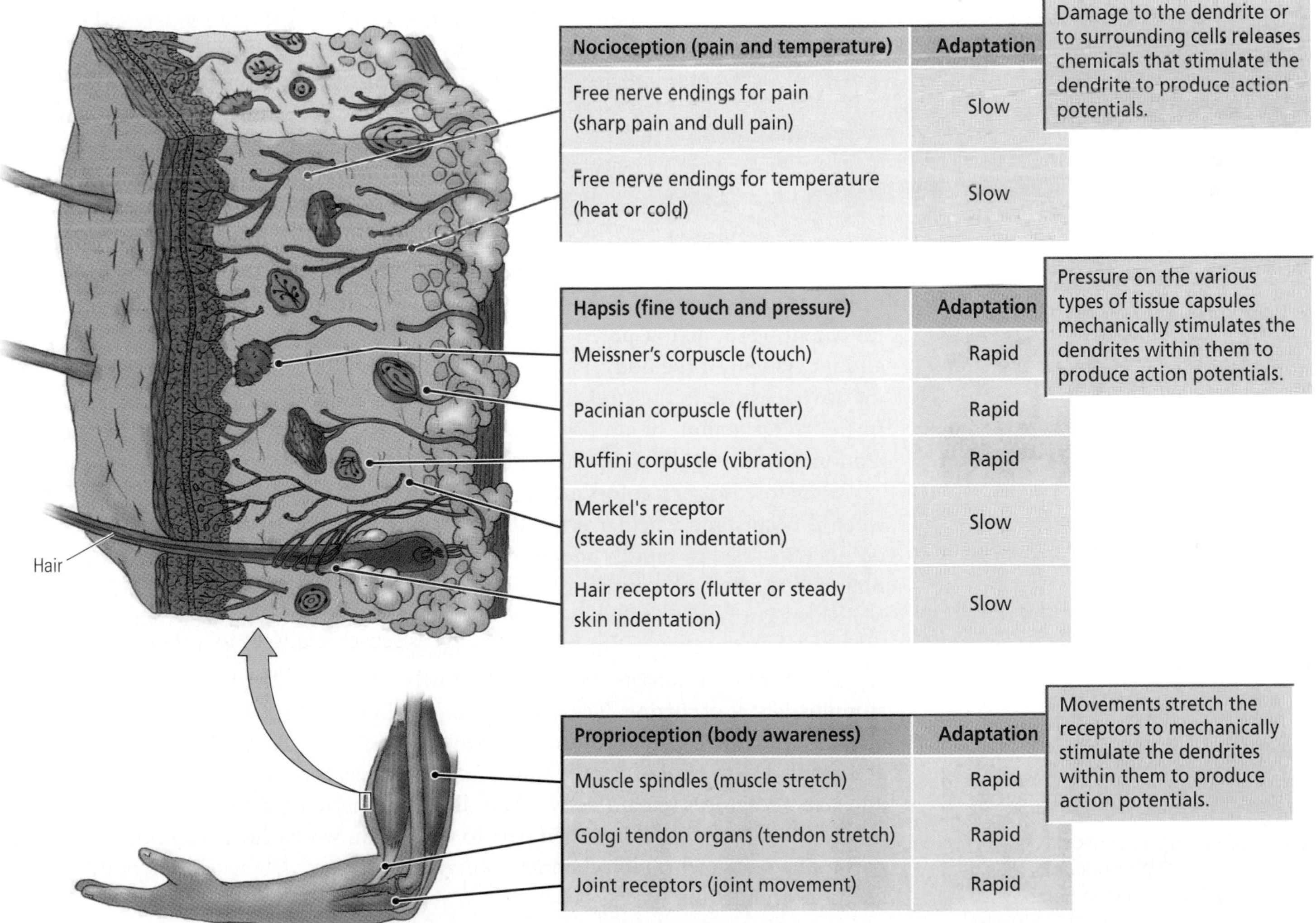


| Nocioception (pain and temperature) | Adaptation |
|---|---|
| Free nerve endings for pain (sharp pain and dull pain) | Slow |
| Free nerve endings for temperature (heat or cold) | Slow |

Damage to the dendrite or to surrounding cells releases chemicals that stimulate the dendrite to produce action potentials.

| Hapsis (fine touch and pressure) | Adaptation |
|---|---|
| Meissner's corpuscle (touch) | Rapid |
| Pacinian corpuscle (flutter) | Rapid |
| Ruffini corpuscle (vibration) | Rapid |
| Merkel's receptor (steady skin indentation) | Slow |
| Hair receptors (flutter or steady skin indentation) | Slow |

Pressure on the various types of tissue capsules mechanically stimulates the dendrites within them to produce action potentials.

| Proprioception (body awareness) | Adaptation |
|---|---|
| Muscle spindles (muscle stretch) | Rapid |
| Golgi tendon organs (tendon stretch) | Rapid |
| Joint receptors (joint movement) | Rapid |

Movements stretch the receptors to mechanically stimulate the dendrites within them to produce action potentials.

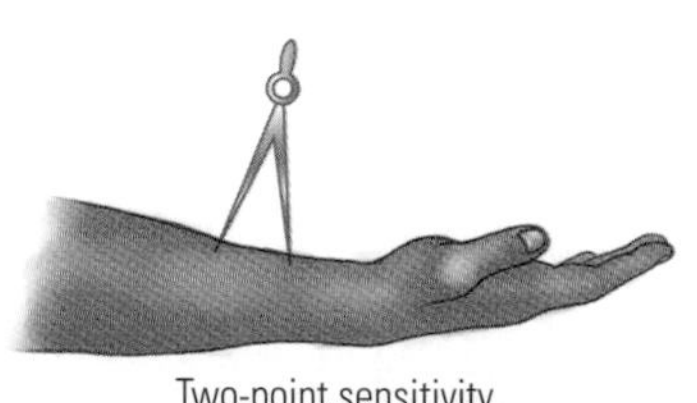
Two-point sensitivity

(which is hairless). Glabrous skin, which includes the skin on the hands, lips, and tongue, is much more richly endowed with receptors than hairy skin is, which makes it exquisitely sensitive to a wide range of stimuli. The need for sensitivity in glabrous skin is due to the fact that it covers the parts of the body with which we explore objects.

The touch sensitivity of skin is often measured with a two-point sensitivity test. This test consists of touching the skin with two sharp points simultaneously and observing how close together they can be placed while still being detected as two points rather than one. On glabrous skin, we can detect the two points when they are as close as 3 millimeters apart. On hairy skin, in contrast, two-point sensitivity is much less. The two points seem to merge into one below a separation distance ranging from 2 to 5 centimeters, depending on exactly which part of the body is tested. You can confirm these differences in sensitivity on your own body by touching two sharp pencil points to a palm and to a forearm, varying the distances that you hold the points apart. Be sure not to look as you touch each surface.

Although there may be as many as 20 or more kinds of somatosensory receptors in the human body, they can be classified into three groups, depending on the type of perception that they enable. These three types of perception, as listed in Table 10-1, are *nociception, hapsis,* and *proprioception.* **Nociception** is the perception of pain and temperature. Nociceptors consist of free nerve endings. When these endings are damaged or irritated, they secrete chemicals, usually peptides, that stimulate the nerve to produce an action potential. The action potential then conveys a message about pain or temperature to the central nervous system. **Hapsis** is the perception of objects that we grasp and manipulate or that contact the body. It is also called the perception of fine touch and pressure. Haptic receptors are found in both superficial layers and deep layers of the skin and are attached to body hairs as well. A haptic receptor consists of a dendrite encased in a capsule of tissue. Mechanical stimulation of the capsule activates special channels on the dendrite, which in turn initiate an action potential. Differences in the tissue forming the capsule determine the kinds of mechanical energy conducted through it to the nerve. For example, pressure that squeezes the capsule of a Pacinian corpuscle is the necessary stimulus for initiating an action potential. **Proprioception** is the perception of the location and movement of the body. Proprioceptors, which also are encapsulated nerve endings, are sensitive to the stretch of muscles and tendons and the movement of joints. In the Golgi tendon organ, for instance, an action potential is triggered when the tendon moves, stretching the receptor attached to it.

**Table 10-1 Somatosensory Receptors**

| |
|---|
| **Nociception** (pain and temperature) |
| Free nerve endings for pain (sharp pain and dull pain) |
| Free nerve endings for temperature (heat or cold) |
| **Hapsis** (fine touch and pressure) |
| Meissner's corpuscle (touch) |
| Pacinian corpuscle (flutter) |
| Ruffini corpuscle (vibration) |
| Merkel's receptor (steady skin indentation) |
| Hair receptors (flutter or steady skin indentation) |
| **Proprioception** (body awareness) |
| Muscle spindles (muscle stretch) |
| Golgi tendon organs (tendon stretch) |
| Joint receptors (joint movement) |

Somatosensory receptors are specialized to tell two things about a sensory event: when it occurs and whether it is still occurring. Information about when a stimulus occurs is handled by **rapidly adapting receptors.** These receptors respond to the beginning and the end of a stimulus and produce only brief bursts of action potentials. Meissner's corpuscles (which respond to touch), Pacinian corpuscles (which respond to fluttering sensations), and Ruffini corpuscles (which respond to vibration) are all rapidly adapting receptors. In contrast, **slowly adapting receptors** detect whether a stimulus is still occurring. These receptors continue to respond as long as a sensory event is present. For instance, after you have put on an article of clothing and become accustomed to the feel of it, only slowly adapting receptors (such as Merkel's receptors and hair receptors) remain active. The difference between a rapidly adapting and a slowly adapting receptor is due in part to the way in which each is stimulated and in part to the way in which ion channels in the membrane of the dendrite respond to mechanical stimulation.

**Nociception.** The perception of pain and temperature.

**Hapsis.** The perceptual ability to discriminate objects on the basis of touch.

**Proprioception.** Perception of the position and movement of the body, limbs, and head.

**Rapidly adapting receptor.** A body sensory receptor that responds briefly to the onset of a stimulus on the body.

**Slowly adapting receptor.** A body sensory receptor that responds as long as a sensory stimulus is on the body.

## Dorsal-Root Ganglion Neurons

The dendrites that form somatosensory receptors belong to *dorsal-root ganglion neurons*. A dorsal-root ganglion neuron contains a single long dendrite, only the tip of which is responsive to sensory stimulation. This dendrite is continuous with the neuron's axon because the cell body is off to one side. The cell body, as the name of this neuron implies, is located in one of the dorsal-root ganglions that lie just beside the spinal cord. Each segment of the spinal cord has one dorsal-root ganglion on each of its sides. The axons of the dorsal-root ganglion neurons enter the spinal cord, forming the spinal cord's dorsal roots. In the spinal cord, these axons may synapse with other neurons or continue to the brain, as shown in Figure 10-24.

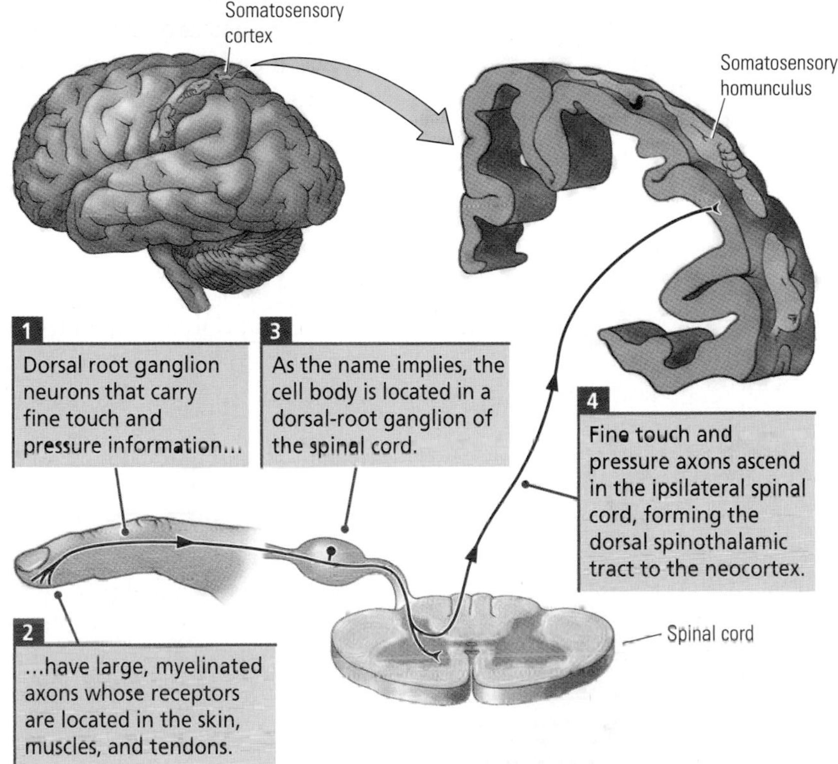
Somatosensory cortex
Somatosensory homunculus
1
Dorsal root ganglion neurons that carry fine touch and pressure information...
3
As the name implies, the cell body is located in a dorsal-root ganglion of the spinal cord.
4
Fine touch and pressure axons ascend in the ipsilateral spinal cord, forming the dorsal spinothalamic tract to the neocortex.
2
...have large, myelinated axons whose receptors are located in the skin, muscles, and tendons.
Spinal cord

**Figure 10-24** Somatosensory Information is carried from the body to the central nervous system by dorsal-root ganglion neurons. The dendrite and axon of the ganglion neuron are contiguous and carry sensory information from the skin, muscles, and tendons. Fine touch and pressure information is carried by large myelinated axons, and pain and temperature information is carried by smaller unmyelinated axons. The large axons travel up the spinal cord to the brain in the dorsal columns, whereas the small axons synapse with neurons whose axons cross the spinal cord and ascend on the other side.

The axons of dorsal-root ganglion neurons vary in diameter and myelination. These structural features are related to the kind of information that the neurons carry. Proprioceptive (location and movement) information and haptic (touch and pressure) information are carried by dorsal-root ganglion neurons that have large, well-myelinated axons. Nociceptive (pain and temperature) information is carried by dorsal-root ganglion neurons that have smaller axons with little myelination. Because of their size and myelination, the larger neurons carry information much more quickly than the smaller neurons do. One explanation of why proprioceptive and haptic neurons are designed to carry messages quickly is that their information requires rapid responses. For instance, the nervous system must react to moment-to-moment changes in posture and to the equally rapid sensory changes that take place as we explore an object with our hands. In contrast, when the body is injured or cold, such rapid responding is not as essential, because these forms of stimulation usually continue for quite some time.

What happens when dorsal-root ganglion neurons are damaged? A clue comes from a visit to the dentist. If you have ever had a tooth "frozen" for dental work, you have experienced the very strange effect of losing sensation on one side of your face. Not only do you lose pain perception, you also lose the ability to move your facial muscles properly, making it difficult to talk, eat, and smile. So, even though the anesthetic is blocking only sensory nerves, your movement ability is affected, too.

In much the same way, damage to sensory nerves affects both sensory perceptions and motor abilities. For instance, John Rothwell and his coworkers (1982) described a patient, G. O., who was **deafferented** (lost sensory fibers) by a disease that destroyed sensory neurons. G. O. had no somatosensory input from his hands. He could not, for example, feel when his hand was holding something. However, G. O. could still accurately produce a range of finger movements, and he could outline figures in the air even with his eyes closed. He could also move his thumb accurately through different distances and at different speeds, judge weights, and match forces by using his thumb. Nevertheless, his hands were relatively useless to him in daily life. Although he was able to drive his old car, he was unable to learn to drive a new one. He was also unable to write, to fasten shirt buttons, or to hold a cup. He could begin movements quite normally, but, as he proceeded, the movement patterns gradually fell apart, ending in

**Deafferented.** Refers to loss of incoming sensory input usually due to damage to sensory fibers; also refers to loss of any afferent input to a structure.

failure. Part of his difficulties lay in maintaining muscle force for any length of time. When he tried to carry a suitcase, he would quickly drop it unless he continually looked down to confirm that it was there. Clearly, although G. O. had damage only to his sensory neurons, he suffered severe motor disability as well, including the inability to learn new motor skills.

Oliver Sacks

Abnormalities in movement also result from more selective damage to sensory neurons, such as damage to neurons that carry proprioceptive information about body location and movement. Neurologist Oliver Sacks (1998) gives a dramatic example in his description of a patient, named Christina, who suffered damage to proprioceptive sensory fibers throughout her body after taking megadoses of vitamin B6. Christina was left with very little ability to control her movements and spent most of each day lying prone. Here is how she describes what a loss of proprioception means:

> "What I must do then," she said slowly, "is use vision, use my eyes, in every situation where I used—what do you call it?—proprioception before. I've already noticed," she added, musingly, "that I may lose my arms. I think they are in one place, and I find they're in another. This proprioception is like the eyes of the body, the way the body sees itself. And if it goes, as it's gone with me, *it's like the body's blind.* My body can't see itself if it's lost its eyes, right? So I have to watch it—be its eyes." (Sacks, 1998, p. 46)

Clearly, although Christina's motor system is intact, she is almost completely immobilized without a sense of where her body is in space and what her body is doing. She tries to use her eyes to compensate for loss of proprioception, but visual monitoring is less than satisfactory. Just imagine what it would be like to have to look at each of your limbs in order to move them to appropriate locations, which is why proprioception is so essential for movement (Cole, 1995).

## The Somatosensory Pathways to the Brain

As the axons of somatosensory neurons enter the spinal cord, they divide, forming two pathways to the brain. The haptic-proprioceptive axons ascend the spinal cord on the same side of the body from which they have entered, whereas nocioceptive fibers synapse with neurons whose axons cross to the other side of the spinal cord before ascending to the brain. Figure 10-24 shows the first of these two routes through the spinal cord, whereas Figure 10-25 shows the second.

The haptic-proprioceptive axons form the **dorsal spinothalamic tract.** These axons synapse in the **dorsal-column nuclei** located at the base of the brain. Axons of neurons in the dorsal-column nuclei then cross over to the other side of the brainstem and ascend through the brainstem as part of a pathway called the **medial lemniscus.** These axons synapse in the **ventrolateral thalamus.** The neurons of the ventrolateral thalamus send most of their axons to the somatosensory cortex, but some axons go to the motor cortex.

The nocioceptive axons, as already stated, take a different route to the brain. They synapse with neurons in the dorsal part of the spinal cord's gray matter. These neurons, in turn, send their axons to the other side of the spinal cord, where they form the **ventral spinothalamic tract.** This tract joins the medial lemniscus in the brainstem to continue on to the ventrolateral thalamus. Some of the thalamic neurons receiving input from ventral spinothalamic tract axons also send their axons to the somatosensory cortex.

Because somatosensory information is conveyed by two separate pathways in the spinal cord, unilateral damage in the spinal cord results in distinctive sensory losses to both sides of the body below the site of injury. As is illustrated in Figure 10-26, there is loss of hapsis and proprioception on the side of the body on which the damage oc-

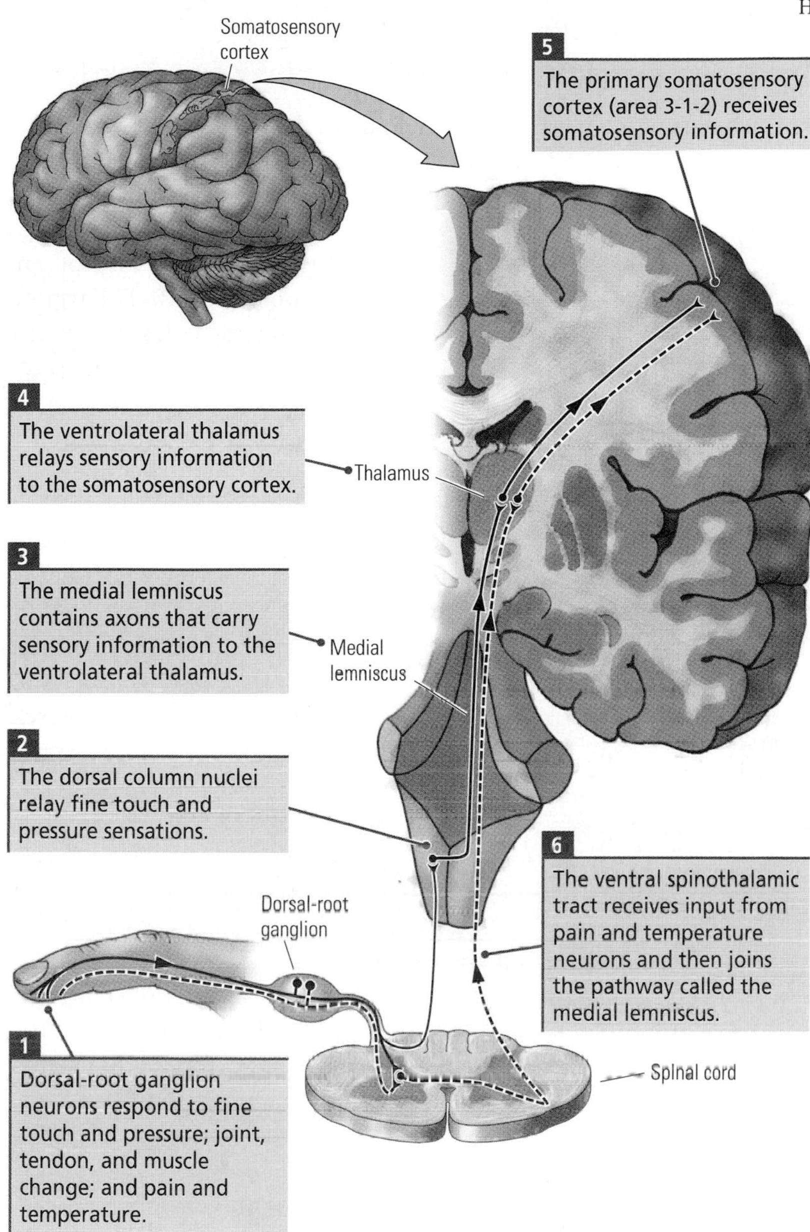
Somatosensory cortex
5
The primary somatosensory cortex (area 3-1-2) receives somatosensory information.
4
The ventrolateral thalamus relays sensory information to the somatosensory cortex.
Thalamus
3
The medial lemniscus contains axons that carry sensory information to the ventrolateral thalamus.
Medial lemniscus
2
The dorsal column nuclei relay fine touch and pressure sensations.
6
The ventral spinothalamic tract receives input from pain and temperature neurons and then joins the pathway called the medial lemniscus.
Dorsal-root ganglion
1
Dorsal-root ganglion neurons respond to fine touch and pressure; joint, tendon, and muscle change; and pain and temperature.
Spinal cord

**Figure 10-25**

Somatosensory pathways to the brain diverge as dorsal-column neurons enter the spinal cord. Fine touch and pressure axons ascend in the dorsal column of the spinal cord, forming the dorsal spinothalamic tract. The axons synapse in the dorsal-column nuclei of the brainstem. Dorsal-column nucleus neurons cross the brainstem and ascend to synapse with ventrolateral thalamic neurons. The thalamic neurons project to the primary somatosensory cortex (area 3-1-2). Pain and temperature axons synapse with neurons as they enter the spinal cord. The pain and temperature axons cross the midline and ascend to the ventrolateral thalamus as the ventral spinothalamic tract. Both pathways form the medial lemniscus as they ascend through the brainstem.

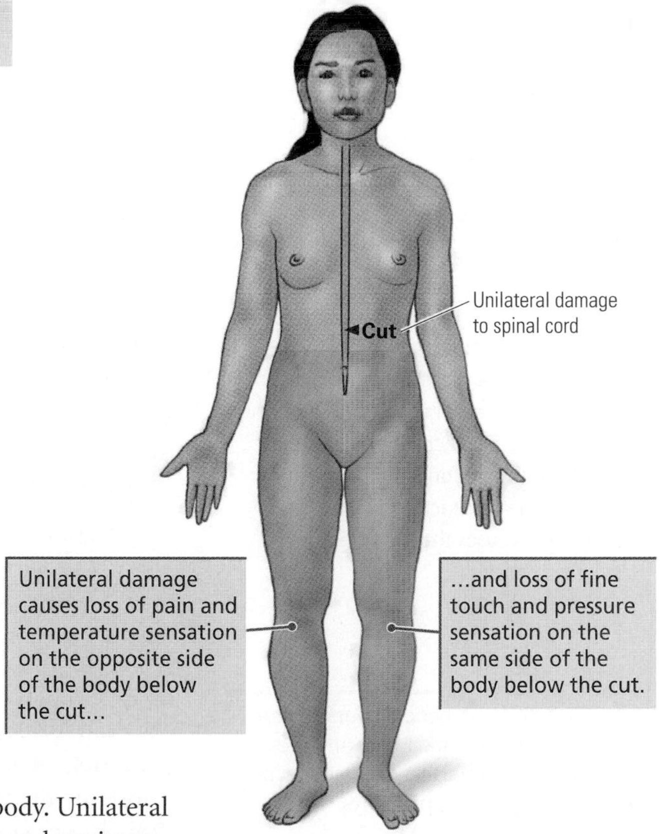

Cut

Unilateral damage to spinal cord

Unilateral damage causes loss of pain and temperature sensation on the opposite side of the body below the cut...

...and loss of fine touch and pressure sensation on the same side of the body below the cut.

**Figure 10-26**

Unilateral damage to the spinal cord has different effects on fine touch and pressure versus pain and temperature sensations. Because fine touch and pressure information is conducted to the brain ipsilaterally through the dorsal spinothalamic tract, fine touch and pressure sensations are lost below the level of damage ipsilateral to the damage. Because pain and temperature information is conducted to the thalamus contralaterally through the ventral spinothalamic tract, pain and temperature sensations are lost below the level of damage contralateral to the damage.

curred, and there is a loss of nocioception on the opposite side of the body. Unilateral damage in the brainstem or the thalamus affects hapsis, proprioception, and nocioception equally, because the pathway for hapsis and proprioception and that for nocioception lie in close proximity.

Go to the area on the CD on the spinal reflexes in the Control of Movement module for more illustrations of the spinal cord and the spinal reflexes.

## Spinal-Cord Responses to Somatosensory Input

Spinal-cord somatosensory axons, even those ascending in the dorsal columns, give off collaterals that synapse with interneurons and motor neurons on both sides of the spinal cord. The circuits made between sensory receptors and muscles through these connections mediate spinal reflexes. The simplest of these reflexes consists of a single synapse between a sensory neuron and a motor neuron. Figure 10-27 illustrates such a **monosynaptic reflex.** It concerns the quadriceps muscle of the thigh, which is anchored to the leg bone by the patellar tendon. When this tendon is tapped with a small hammer, the quadriceps muscle is stretched, activating the stretch-sensitive sensory receptors embedded in it. The sensory receptors then send a signal to the spinal cord through sensory neurons that synapse with motor neurons projecting back to the same thigh muscle. The discharge from the motor neurons stimulates the muscle, causing it to contract to resist the stretch. Because the tap is brief, the stimulation is over before the motor message arrives, so the muscle contracts even though it is no longer stretched. This contraction pulls the leg up, thereby producing the reflexive knee jerk.

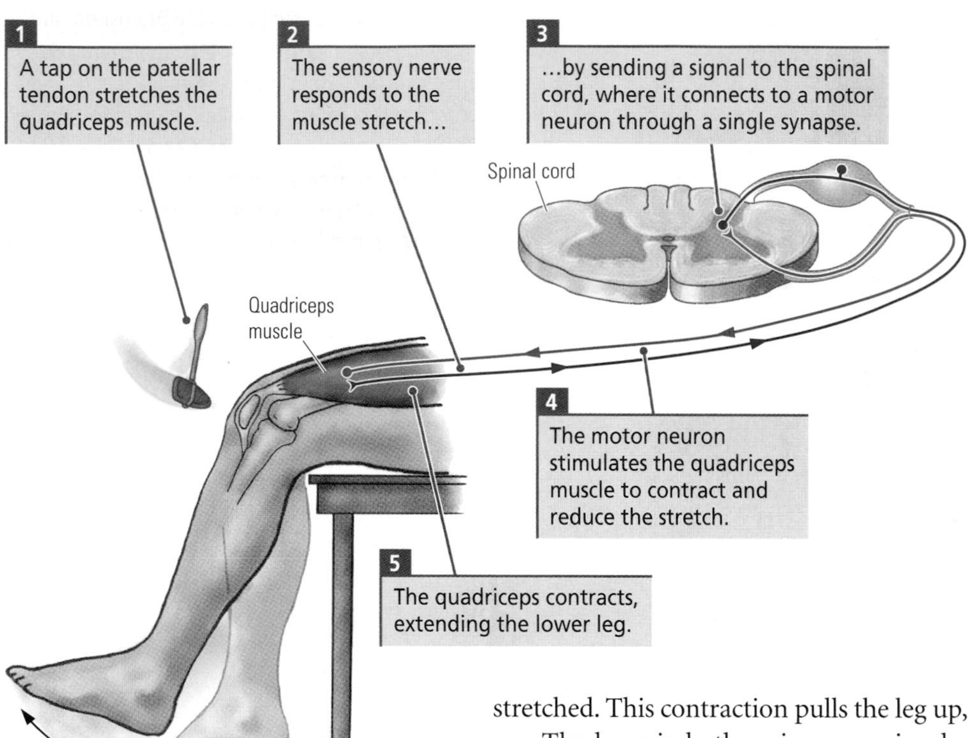

1
A tap on the patellar tendon stretches the quadriceps muscle.
2
The sensory nerve responds to the muscle stretch...
3
...by sending a signal to the spinal cord, where it connects to a motor neuron through a single synapse.
Spinal cord
Quadriceps muscle
4
The motor neuron stimulates the quadriceps muscle to contract and reduce the stretch.
5
The quadriceps contracts, extending the lower leg.
Extension


**Figure 10-27** The "knee-jerk," or stretch, reflex produced by a light tap on the patellar tendon. The subject is seated on a table so that the lower leg hangs free. The tap on the patellar tendon stretches the quadriceps muscle to which it is attached. Stretch receptors in the muscle send a brief burst of action potentials to the spinal cord to activate the motor neuron to the quadriceps by a single synapse. The contraction of the quadriceps causes the lower leg to extend.

The knee jerk, then, is a very simple reflex, with monosynaptic connections between single sensory neurons and single motor neurons. Somatosensory axons from other receptors, especially those of the skin, make much more complex connections with both interneurons and motor neurons. These multisynaptic connections are responsible for more complex reflexes that include many muscles on both sides of the body.

Circuits in the spinal cord also allow haptic-proprioceptive and nocioceptive pathways to interact. Such interactions may be responsible for our very puzzling and variable responses to pain. For example, people who are engaged in combat or intense athletic competition may receive a serious injury to the body but start to feel the pain only much later. For example, a friend of the authors, F. V., who was attacked by a grizzly bear while hiking, received 200 stitches to repair the bites that he received. When friends asked if it hurt to be bitten by a grizzly bear, he surprisingly answered no. As he explained it:

> I had read the week before about someone who was killed and eaten by a grizzly bear. So I was thinking that this bear was going to eat me unless I got away. I did not have time for pain. I was fighting for my life. It was not until the next day that I started feeling pain and fear.

Pain is also puzzling in the variety of ways in which it can be lessened. Treatments for pain include opioid drugs (such as morphine), acupuncture (which entails the rapid vibration of needles embedded in the skin), and even simply rubbing the area surrounding the injury. To explain how pain can be suppressed in so many different ways, Ronald Melzack and Patrick Wall (1965) proposed a gate theory of pain. They argued that activity in the haptic-proprioceptive pathway can inhibit the pain pathway in the spinal cord through collaterals to spinal-cord interneurons. This **pain gate,** as it is

**Pain gate.** A hypothetical neural circuit in which activity in fine touch and pressure pathways diminishes the activity in pain and temperature pathways.

**Referred pain.** Pain felt on the surface of the body that is actually due to pain in one of the internal organs of the body.

called, is illustrated in Figure 10-28. Notice that both the haptic-proprioceptive fibers and the nocioceptive fibers synapse with the interneuron. Collaterals from the haptic-proprioceptive pathway excite the interneuron, whereas collaterals from the nocioceptive pathway inhibit the interneuron. The interneuron, in turn, inhibits the neuron that relays pain information to the brain. Consequently, when the haptic-proprioceptive pathway is active, the pain gate partly closes, reducing the sensation of pain.

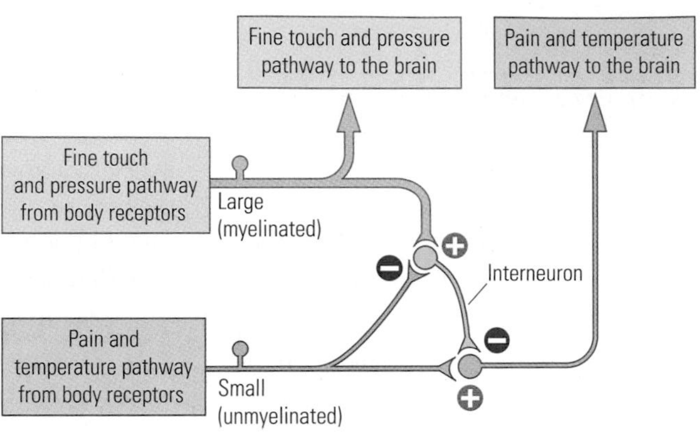


**Figure 10-28**

A pain gate. An interneuron in the spinal cord receives excitatory input from the fine touch and pressure pathway and inhibitor input from the pain and temperature pathway. The relative activity of the interneuron then determines whether pain and temperature information is sent to the brain. For example, if the fine touch and pressure pathway is active, it will excite the interneuron, which will in turn inhibit the second-order neurons in the pain and temperature pathway.

Adapted from *The Puzzle of Pain* (p. 154), by R. Melzack, 1973, New York: Basic Books.

The gate theory can help explain how different treatments for pain work. For instance, when you stub your toe, you feel pain because the pain pathway to the brain is open. If you then rub the toe, activating the haptic-proprioceptive pathway, the flow of information in the pain pathway is reduced because the pain gate partly closes, which relieves the pain sensation. Similarly, acupuncture may have its pain-relieving effects because the vibrating needles used in this treatment selectively activate haptic and proprioceptive fibers, closing the pain gate. Interestingly, the interneurons in the pain gate may use opioid peptides as a neurotransmitter. If so, the gate theory can also explain how natural and endogenous opiods reduce pain.

The gate theory even suggests an explanation for the painlike sensation of "pins and needles" that we feel after sitting too long in one position. Loss of oxygen from reduced blood flow may first deactivate the large myelinated axons that carry touch and pressure information, leaving the small unmyelinated fibers that carry pain and temperature messages unaffected. As a result, "ungated" sensory information flows in the pain and temperature pathway, leading to the curious pins and needles sensation.

Melzack and Wall propose that pain gates may be located in the brainstem and cortex in addition to the spinal cord. These additional gates could help explain how other approaches to pain relief work. For example, researchers have found that feelings of severe pain can be lessened when people have a chance to shift their attention from the pain to other stimuli. Dentists have long used this pain-reducing technique by giving their patients something soothing to listen to while undergoing painful work on their teeth. This influence of attention on pain sensations may work through a cortical pain gate. Electrical stimulation in a number of sites in the brainstem also can reduce pain, perhaps by closing brainstem pain gates. Another way in which pain perceptions might be lessened is through descending pathways from the forebrain and the brainstem to the spinal-cord pain gate.

Many internal organs of the body, including the heart, the kidneys, and the blood vessels, have pain receptors, but the ganglion neurons carrying information from these receptors do not have their own pathway to the brain. Instead, these ganglion neurons synapse with spinal-cord neurons that receive nocioceptive information from the body's surface. Consequently, the neurons in the spinal cord that relay pain and temperature messages to the brain receive two sets of signals: one from the body's surface and one from internal organs. These neurons cannot distinguish between these two sets of signals; nor can we. As a result, pain in body organs is often felt as pain from the surface of the body. Such pain is called **referred pain.** For example, the pain in the heart associated with a heart attack is felt as pain in the shoulder and upper arm. Similarly, pain in the stomach is felt as pain in the midline of the trunk, whereas pain in the kidneys is felt as pain in the lower back, and pain in blood vessels in the head is felt as diffuse pain that we call a headache. Figure 10-29 illustrates the referred pain felt in a heart attack.

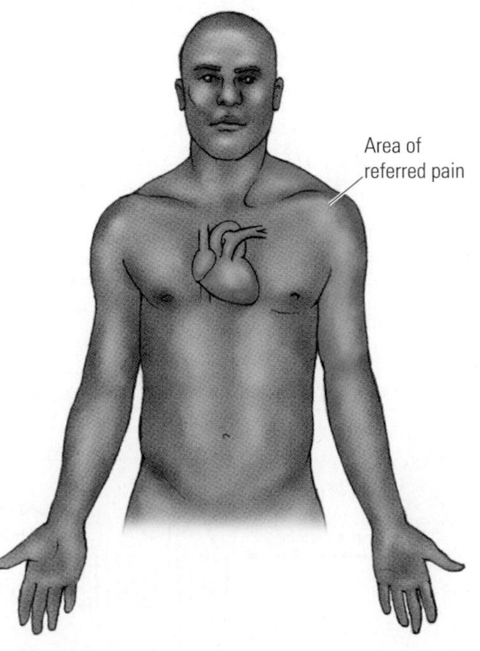


**Figure 10-29**

In a heart attack, pain can be felt in the shoulder and upper arm.

## The Vestibular System and Balance

**Vestibular system.** A set of receptors in the middle ear that indicate position and movement of the head.

The **vestibular system,** also a part of the somatosensory system, consists of two organs, one located in each middle ear. As Figure 10-30 shows, each vestibular organ is made up of two groups of receptors: the **semicircular canals,** of which there are three, and the **otolith organs,** which consist of the **utricle** and the **saccule.** These vestibular receptors do two jobs. First, they tell us the position of the body in relation to gravity. Second, they signal changes in the direction and the speed of movements.

You can see in Figure 10-30 that the semicircular canals are oriented in three different planes: two vertical planes that are perpendicular to each other and one horizontal plane. Each canal furnishes information about movement in its particular plane. The semicircular canals are filled with a fluid called *endolymph.* Immersed in the endolymph is a set of hair cells very much like the hair cells on the arm. When the head moves, the endolymph also moves, splashing against the hair cells and bending the hairs. The force of the hairs bending is converted into action potentials that are sent over ganglion cells to the brain. The axons from these hair cells are normally quite active, but bending the hairs in one direction increases their activity, whereas bending the hairs in the other direction decreases it. Typically, when the head turns in one direction, the message on the side of the body to which the turn is made is an increase in neural firing, whereas the message on the body's opposite side is a decrease in firing.

The utricle and saccule are located just beneath the semicircular canals. They also contain hair cells, but their hair cells are embedded in a gelatin-like substance that contains small crystals of calcium carbonate know as **otoconia.** When the head is tilted, the gelatin and otoconia press against the hair cells, bending the hairs. When the hairs bend, the mechanical action produces action potentials in their neurons. In this way, the neurons' axons convey messages about the position of the head in space.

The receptors in the vestibular system tell us about our location relative to gravity, about acceleration and deceleration of our movements, and about changes in movement direction. They also allow us to ignore the otherwise very destabilizing influence that our movements might have on us. For example, when

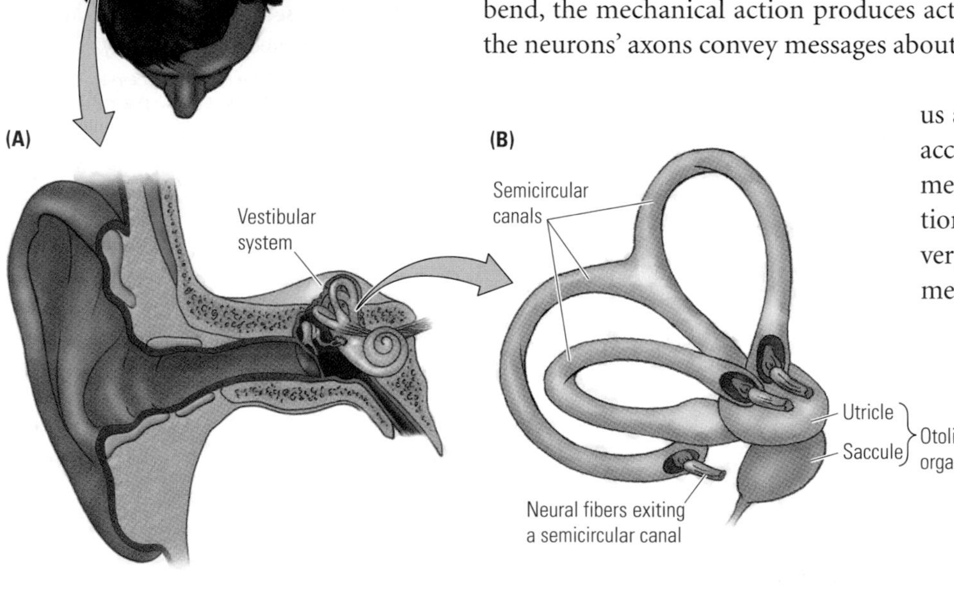


**Figure 10-30**

**(A)** The vestibular system. **(B)** The vestibular system consists of the three semicircular canals and the utricle and saccule. The receptors in the vestibular system are sensitive to movement of the head and to gravity. **(C)** Hair-cell receptors are located in the semicircular canals and in the utricle and the saccule. A vestibular neuron is normally active, and its activity increases if its hair-cell receptors are bent in one direction, but it decreases if the hair-cell receptors are bent in the opposite direction.

you are standing on a bus, even slight movements of the vehicle could potentially throw you off balance, but they do not. Similarly, when you make movements yourself, you easily avoid tipping over, despite the constant shifting of your body weight. Your vestibular system enables you to keep from tipping over.

Here is an experiment that you can perform to illustrate the role of vestibular receptors in helping you to compensate for your own movements. If you hold your hand in front of you and shake it, your hand appears blurry. But, if you shake your head instead of your hand, the hand remains in focus. Compensatory signals from your vestibular system allow you to see the hand as stable even though you are moving around.

## In Review

Body senses contribute to the perception of hapsis (touch and pressure), proprioception (location and movement), and nocioception (temperature and pain). Haptic-proprioceptive information is carried by the dorsal spinothalamic tract, whereas nocioceptive information is carried by the ventral spinothalamic tract. The two systems interact in the spinal cord to regulate the perception of pain by a pain gate. Another part of the somatosensory system, the vestibular system, signals information about head position and movement.

## EXPLORING THE SOMATOSENSORY CORTEX

We have yet to explore a major part of the somatosensory system—the somatosensory cortex. As illustrated in Figure 10-31, there are two main somatosensory cortex areas. The primary somatosensory cortex is the area that receives projections from the thalamus. It consists of Brodmann's areas 3-1-2 (all shaded red, below). This area begins the process of constructing perceptions from somatosensory information. It mainly consists of the postcentral gyrus just behind the central fissure, which means that the primary somatosensory cortex is adjacent to the primary motor cortex. The secondary somatosensory cortex (Brodmann's areas 5 and 7, shaded orange and yellow, below) is located in the parietal lobe just behind the primary somatosensory cortex.

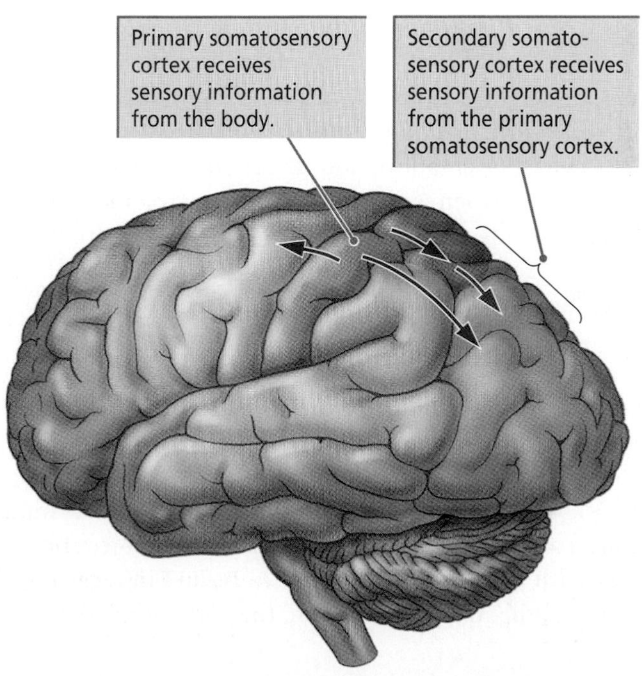

Primary somatosensory cortex receives sensory information from the body.
Secondary somatosensory cortex receives sensory information from the primary somatosensory cortex.

**Figure 10-31**

Locations of the primary and the secondary somatosensory cortex. Information in the primary somatosensory cortex is sent to the secondary somatosensory cortex. Stimulation of the primary somatosensory cortex produces sensations that are referred to appropriate body parts. As is the motor cortex, the primary somatosensory cortex is organized as a homunculus, with a large area representing body parts that are highly sensitive.

## The Somatosensory Homunculus

In his studies of human patients undergoing brain surgery, Wilder Penfield electrically stimulated the somatosensory cortex and recorded the patients' responses. Stimulation at some sites elicited sensations in the foot, whereas stimulation of other sites produced sensations in a hand, the body, or the face. By mapping these responses, Penfield was able to construct a somatosensory homunculus in the cortex. This homunculus looks very similar to the motor homunculus in that the areas of the body that are most sensitive to sensory stimulation are accorded a relatively larger area of somatosensory cortex.

Using slightly different recording techniques in monkeys, John Kaas (1987) stimulated sensory receptors on the body and recorded the activity of cells in the sensory cortex. He found that the somatosensory cortex is actually composed of four representations of the body, each associated with a certain class of sensory receptors. In a progression across the cortex from front to back, as shown in Figure 10-32, area 3a cells are responsive to muscle receptors, area 3b cells are responsive to skin receptors, area 1 cells are responsive to rapidly adapting skin receptors, and area 2 cells are responsive to deep tissue pressure and joint receptors. In other studies, Hiroshi Asanuma (1989) and his coworkers found still another sensory representation in the motor cortex (area 4) in which cells responded to muscle and joint receptors.

Research by Vernon Mountcastle (1978) showed that cells in the somatosensory cortex are arranged in functional columns running from layer I to layer VI, similar to columns found in the visual cortex. Every cell in a column responds to a single class of receptors. Some columns of cells are activated by rapidly adapting skin receptors, others by slowly adapting skin receptors, still others by pressure receptors, and so forth. All neurons in a column receive information from the same local area of skin. In this way, neurons lying within a column seem to provide an elementary functional module of the somatosensory cortex.

Single-cell recordings in the sensory cortex suggest a hierarchical organization, with basic sensations being combined to form more complex perceptions. This combining of information occurs as areas 3a and 3b project onto area 1, which in turn projects onto area 2. With each successive relay of information, both the size of the pertinent receptive fields and the synthesis of somatosensory modalities increase. For example, whereas a cell in area 3a or 3b may respond to activity in only a certain area on a certain finger, cells in area 1 may respond to similar information from a number of different fingers. At the next level of synthesis, cells in area 2 may respond to stimulation in a number of different locations on a number of different fingers, as well as to stimulation from different kinds of receptors. Thus, area 2 contains neurons that are responsive to movement, orientation, and direction of movement, all of which are properties that we perceive when we hold an object in our hands and manipulate it.

That the different kinds of somatosensory information are both separated and combined in the cortex raises the question of why both segregation and synthesis are needed. One reason why sensory information remains segregated at the level of the cortex could be that we often need to distinguish between different kinds of sensory stimuli coming from different kinds of sources. For example, we need to be able to tell the difference between tactile stimulation on the surface of the skin, which is usually produced by some external agent, and stimulation coming from muscles, tendons, and joints, which is likely produced by our own movements. Yet, at the same time, we also often need to know about the combined sensory properties of a stimulus. For instance, when we manipulate an object, it is useful to "know" the object both in regard to its sensory properties, such as temperature and texture, and in regard to the movements that we make as we handle it. For this reason, the cortex provides for somatosensory synthesis, too.

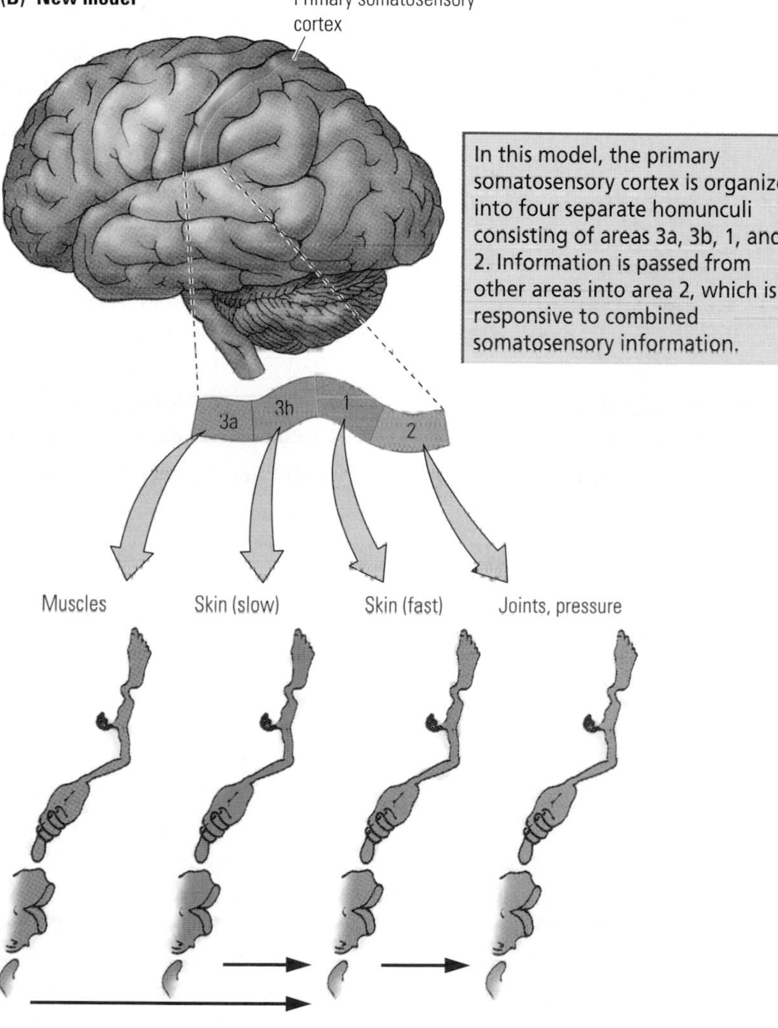
(A) Original model
Primary somatosensory cortex
In this model, the primary somatosensory cortex is organized as a single homunculus with large areas representing body parts that are very sensitive to sensory stimulation.
(B) New model
Primary somatosensory cortex
In this model, the primary somatosensory cortex is organized into four separate homunculi consisting of areas 3a, 3b, 1, and 2. Information is passed from other areas into area 2, which is responsive to combined somatosensory information.
3a
3b
1
2
Muscles
Skin (slow)
Skin (fast)
Joints, pressure

**Figure 10-32**

A comparison of two models of the somatosensory cortex organization: **(A)** a single-homunculus model and **(B)** a four-homunculi model, which is based on the stimulation of sensory receptors on the body surface and recording from the somatosensory cortex. In the model in (B), four separate homunculi are obtained in the primary somatosensory cortex. Neurons in area 3a are responsive to muscle length, neurons in area 3b are responsive to slowly adapting receptors in the skin, neurons in area 1 are responsive to rapidly adapting skin receptors, and neurons in area 2 are responsive to joint and pressure sensations. Information is passed from the other areas into area 2, in which neurons that are responsive to a number of kinds of somatosensory information (multimodal neurons) are found.

## The Effects of Damage to the Somatosensory Cortex

Damage to the primary somatosensory cortex impairs the ability to make even simple sensory discriminations and movements, as was clearly demonstrated in a study by Suzanne Corkin and her coworkers (1970), who examined patients with cortical lesions that included most of area 3-1-2 in one hemisphere. The researchers mapped the

Suzanne Corkin

sensory cortices of these patients before they underwent elective surgery for removal of a carefully defined piece of that cortex, including the hand area. The patients' sensory and motor skills in both hands were tested on three different occasions: before the surgery, shortly after the surgery, and almost a year afterward. The tests included pressure sensitivity, two-point touch discrimination, position sense (reporting the direction in which a finger was being moved), and haptic sense (using touch to identify objects, such as a pencil, a penny, eyeglasses, and so forth). For all the sensory abilities tested, the surgical lesions produced a severe and seemingly permanent deficit in the contralateral hand. Sensory thresholds, proprioception, and hapsis were all greatly impaired. The results of other studies in both humans and animals have shown that damage to the somatosensory cortex also impairs simple movements. For example, limb use in reaching for an object is impaired, as is the ability to shape the hand to hold an object (Leonard et al., 1991).

Interestingly, the somatosensory cortex can dramatically reorganize itself after the cutting of sensory fibers (deafferentation). In 1991, Tim Pons and his coworkers reported a dramatic change in the somatosensory maps of monkeys that had had the ganglion cells for one arm deafferented a number of years earlier. The researchers had wanted to develop an animal model of damage to sensory nerves that could be a source of insight into human injuries, but they were interrupted by a legal dispute with an animal advocacy group. Years later, as the health of the animals declined, a court injunction allowed the mapping experiment to be conducted. Pons and his coworkers discovered that the area of the somatosensory cortex that had previously represented the arm no longer did so. Light touches on the lower face of a monkey now activated cells in what had previously been the cortical arm region. As illustrated in Figure 10-33, the face area had expanded by as much as 10 to 14 millimeters, virtually doubling its original size by entering the arm area. This massive change was completely unexpected. The stimuli–response patterns associated with the new expanded facial area of the cortex appeared indistinguishable from those associated with the original facial area. Furthermore, the trunk area, which bounded the other side of the cortical arm area, did not expand into the vacated arm area.

What could account for this expansion of the face area into the arm area? One possibility is that axons grew across the cortex from the face area into the arm area, but no evidence supports this possibility. It is also possible that the thalamic neurons representing the face area projected axon collaterals to the cortical neurons representing the arm area. These collaterals might be preexisting or they might be new growths subsequent to deafferentation. There is evidence for preexisting collaterals that are not normally active, but these collaterals would probably not be able to extend far enough to account for all of the cortical reorganization. A third possibility is that, within the dorsal columns, face-area neurons projected collaterals to arm-area neurons. These neurons are close together, so the collaterals need travel only a millimeter or so. Whatever the mechanism, the very dramatic cortical reorganization observed in this study eventually had far-reaching consequences for understanding other remarkable phenomena. We will return to this story in Chapter 13, which looks at how the brain changes in response to experience.

## The Somatosensory Cortex and Complex Movement

This chapter began with a description of the remarkable painting skills of Kamala. To accomplish this task, Kamala first needs to have some idea of what she wants to paint. She must then execute the movements required to apply paint to her canvas, and she must also use somatosensory information to confirm that she has produced the move-

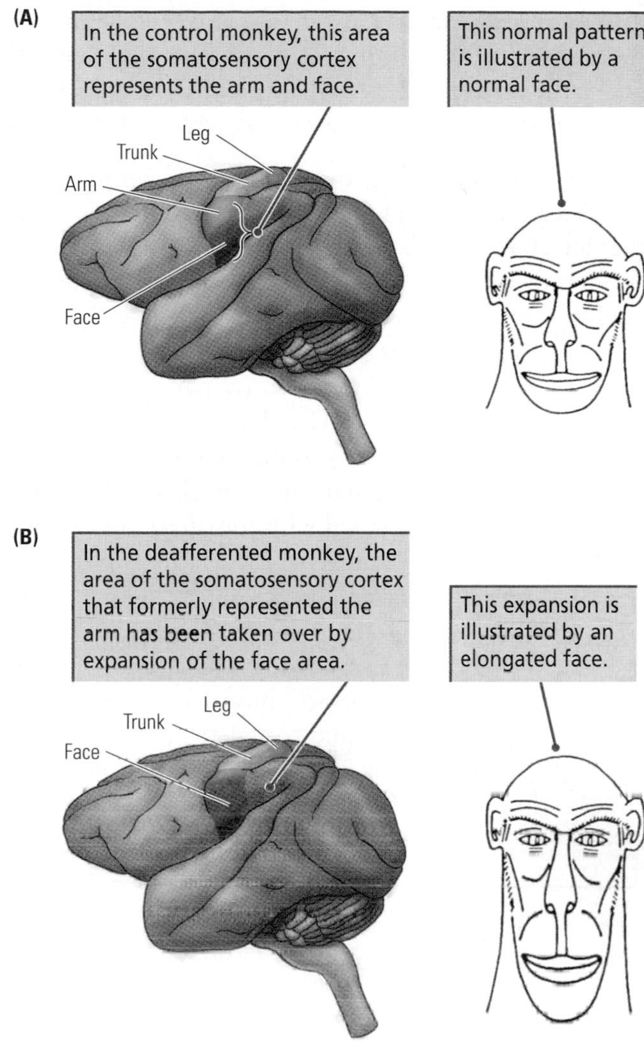

(A)
In the control monkey, this area of the somatosensory cortex represents the arm and face.
This normal pattern is illustrated by a normal face.
Leg
Trunk
Arm
Face
(B)
In the deafferented monkey, the area of the somatosensory cortex that formerly represented the arm has been taken over by expansion of the face area.
This expansion is illustrated by an elongated face.
Leg
Trunk
Face


**Figure 10-33**

Somatosensory cortex of a control monkey **(A)** and a monkey that had received arm deafferentation **(B)**. In the deafferented monkey, the area of sensory cortex that had formerly represented the hand and arm area of the body now represents the face. Thus, the area that represents the face is greatly expanded, as illustrated by the elongated face to the right. The face representations are shown right side up for simplicity. Electrical recordings show that only the lower face area has expanded into the arm and hand region.

Adapted from "Massive Cortical Reorganization After Sensory Deafferentation in Adult Macaques," by T. P. Pons, P. E. Garraghty, A. K. Ommaya, J. H. Kaas, and M. Miskin, 1991, *Science, 252,* p. 1858.

ments that she intended. So to paint, or to perform virtually any other complex movement, the motor system and the somatosensory system must closely interact. In this final section of the chapter, we explore that interaction.

The secondary somatosensory cortex plays an important role in confirming which movements have already taken place and in deciding which movements should follow. Damage to the secondary somatosensory cortex does not disrupt the plans for making movements, but it does disrupt how the movements are performed, leaving them fragmented and confused. The inability to complete a plan of action accurately is called **apraxia** (from the Greek words for "not" and "action"). The following example highlights the symptoms of apraxia:

> A woman with a biparietal lesion (that is, a lesion in both sides of the secondary somatosensory cortex) had worked for years as a fish-filleter. With the development of her symptoms, she began to experience difficulty in carrying on with her job. She did not seem to know what to do with her knife. She would stick the point in the head of a fish, start the first stroke, and then come to a stop. In her own mind she knew how to fillet fish, but yet she could not execute the maneuver. The foreman accused her of being drunk and sent her home for mutilating fish.
>
> The same patient also showed another unusual phenomenon that might possibly be apraxic in nature. She could never finish an undertaking. She

**Apraxia.** An inability to make voluntary movements in the absence of paralysis or other motor or sensory impairment, especially an inability to make proper use of an object.

would begin a job, drop it, start another, abandon that one, and within a short while would have four or five uncompleted tasks on her hands. This would cause her to do such inappropriate actions as putting the sugar bowl in the refrigerator, and the coffeepot inside the oven. (Critchley, 1953, pp. 158–159)

How does an intact secondary somatosensory cortex contribute to the organization of movement? Recall from Chapter 8 that visual information influences movement through the dorsal and ventral streams. The dorsal stream, working without conscious awareness, provides vision for action, as when we use the visual form of a cup to shape a hand so as to grasp that cup. The ventral stream, in contrast, works with conscious awareness and provides the vision needed to identify objects. As Figure 10-34 illustrates, the secondary somatosensory cortex participates in both these visual streams. The dorsal visual stream projects to the secondary somatosensory cortex and then to the prefrontal cortex. In this way, visual information is integrated with somatosensory information to produce movements that are appropriately shaped and directed for their targets. Much less is known about how the secondary somatosensory cortex contributes to the ventral stream, but it is likely that somatosensory information about the identity of objects and completed movements is relayed by the ventral stream to the prefrontal cortex. The prefrontal cortex can then select the actions that should follow those that are already completed.

Information from the secondary somatosensory cortex contributes to the dorsal stream by shaping hand movements directed to targets.
Secondary somatosensory cortex
Dorsal stream
Visual cortex
Ventral stream
Information from the secondary somatosensory cortex contributes to the ventral stream by providing information about object size and shape.

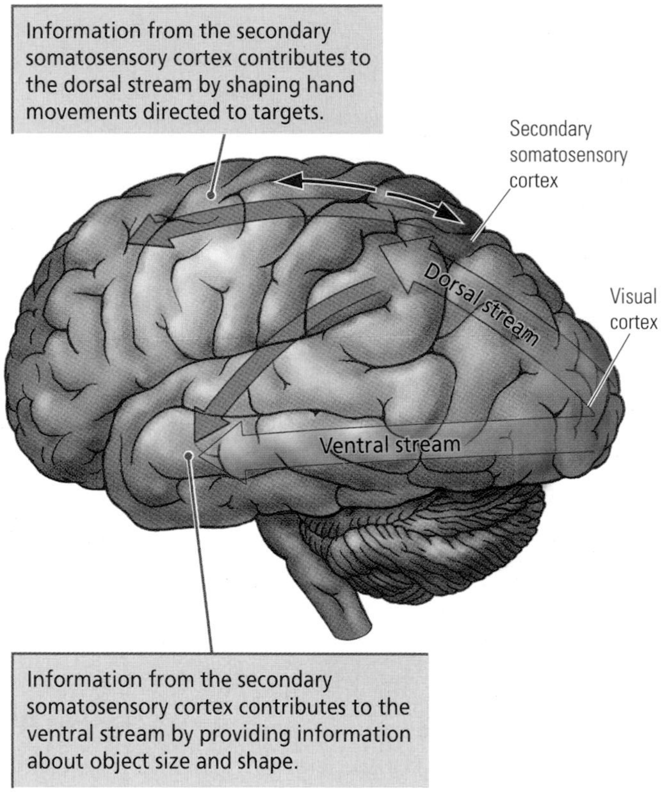

**Figure 10-34** The somatosensory cortex contributes to information flow in dorsal and ventral streams.

A close interrelation between the somatosensory system and the motor system exists at all levels of the nervous system. It can be seen in the spinal cord, where sensory information contributes to spinal reflexes. It can also be seen in the brainstem, where various species-specific behaviors, such as attack, withdrawal, and grooming, require both appropriate patterns of movement and appropriate sensory information. The close interrelation is found as well at the level of the neocortex, where skilled movements elicited by the motor regions of the frontal lobes require information about actions that have just taken place and about objects that have been or could be manipulated. In short, an interaction between the motor cortex, which decides what should be done, and the sensory cortex, which knows what has been done, is central to how the brain produces movement.

## In Review

The primary somatosensory cortex is arranged as a series of homunculi, each of which represents a different body sense. This area of the cortex provides information to the secondary somatosensory cortex, which in turn contributes to the dorsal and ventral streams. Damage to the secondary somatosensory cortex produces apraxia, an inability to complete a series of movements. A person with this condition has trouble knowing both what action has just been completed and what action should follow in a movement sequence.

## SUMMARY

1. *How is the motor system organized?* The organization of movement is hierarchical, with almost all of the brain contributing to it in some way. The forebrain plans, organizes, and initiates movements, whereas the brainstem coordinates regulatory functions, such as eating and drinking, and controls neural mechanisms that maintain posture and produce locomotion. Many reflexes are organized at the level of the spinal cord and occur without any involvement of the brain.
2. *How is the motor cortex organized?* Maps produced by stimulating the motor cortex show that it is organized topographically as a homunculus, with parts of the body capable of fine movements associated with larger regions of motor cortex. There are two pathways from the motor cortex to the spinal cord, the lateral corticospinal tract and the ventral corticospinal tract. The lateral corticospinal tract consists of axons from the digit, hand, and arm regions of the motor cortex. The tract synapses with spinal interneurons and motor neurons located laterally in the spinal cord, on the side of the cord opposite the side of the brain on which the corticospinal tract started. The ventral corticospinal tract consists of axons from the trunk region of the motor cortex. This tract synapses with interneurons and motor neurons located medially in the spinal cord, on the same side of the cord as the side of the brain on which the corticospinal tract started. Interneurons and motor neurons of the spinal cord also are topographically organized, with more laterally located motor neurons projecting to digit, hand, and arm muscles and more medially located motor neurons projecting to trunk muscles.
3. *How do motor-cortex neurons produce movement?* Movements are organized as synergies, or movement patterns. Motor neurons initiate movement, produce movement, control the force of movement, and indicate movement direction. Different species of animals have topographic maps in which areas of the body capable of the most-skilled movements have the largest motor-cortex representation. Disuse of a limb, such as that which might follow motor-cortex injury, results in shrinkage of that limb's representation in the motor cortex. This shrinkage of motor-cortex representation can be prevented, however, if the limb can be somehow forced into use.
4. *How do the basal ganglia and the cerebellum contribute to controlling movement?* Damage to the basal ganglia or to the cerebellum results in abnormalities of movement. This result tells us that both these brain structures somehow participate in movement control. The results of experimental studies suggest that the basal ganglia regulate the force of movements whereas the cerebellum plays a role in movement timing and in maintaining the accuracy of movements.
5. *How is the somatosensory system organized?* The somatosensory system is distributed throughout the entire body and consists of more than 20 types of specialized receptors, each of which is sensitive to a particular form of mechanical energy. Each somatosensory receptor projecting from skin, muscles, tendons, or joints is associated with a dorsal-root ganglion neuron that carries the sensory information into the brain. Fibers carrying proprioceptive (location and movement) information and haptic (touch and pressure) information ascend the spinal cord as the dorsal spinothalamic tract. These fibers synapse in the dorsal-column nuclei at the base of the brain, at which point axons cross over to the other side of the brainstem to form the medial lemniscus, which ascends to the ventrolateral thalamus. Most of the ventrolateral thalamus cells project to the somatosensory cortex. Nocioceptive (pain and temperature) dorsal-root ganglion neurons synapse on entering the spinal cord. Their relay neurons cross the spinal cord to ascend to the thalamus as the ventral spinothalamic tract. Because there are two somatosensory

**neuroscience interactive**

There are many resources available for expanding your learning on line:

- **www.worthpublishers.com/kolb/chapter10**

Try some self-tests to reinforce your mastery of the material. Look at some of the updates reflecting current research on the brain. You'll also be able to link to other sites which will reinforce what you've learned.

- **www.circleoffriends.org**

Go to this site to learn more about current research on spinal cord injury.

- **tsa.mgh.harvard.edu**

Learn more about this misunderstood disorder at the home page of the Tourette's Syndrome Association.

On your CD-ROM you'll be able to quiz yourself on your comprehension of the chapter. The module in your CD on Control of Movement offers interactive illustrations to reinforce your understanding of key concepts.

pathways that take somewhat different routes, unilateral spinal-cord damage impairs proprioception and hapsis ipsilaterally below the site of injury and nocioception contralaterally below the site.

6. *How is somatosensory information represented in the neocortex?* The somatosensory system is represented topographically as a homunculus in the primary somatosensory region of the parietal cortex (area 3-1-2) such that the most sensitive parts of the body are accorded the largest regions of neocortex. A number of homunculi represent different sensory modalities, and these regions are hierarchically organized. If sensory input from a part of the body is cut off from the cortex by damage to sensory fibers, adjacent functional regions of the sensory cortex can expand into the now-unoccupied region.
7. *How are the somatosensory system and the motor system interrelated?* The somatosensory system and the motor system are interrelated at all levels of the nervous system. At the level of the spinal cord, sensory information contributes to motor reflexes; in the brainstem, sensory information contributes to complex regulatory movements. At the level of the neocortex, sensory information is used to record just-completed movements, as well as to represent the sizes and shapes of objects. The somatosensory cortex contributes to the dorsal visual stream to direct hand movements to targets. The somatosensory cortex also contributes to the ventral visual stream to create representations of external objects.

## KEY TERMS

apraxia, p. 393
cerebral palsy, p. 361
deafferented, p. 383
dissolution, p. 357
glabrous skin, p. 381
hapsis, p. 382
homunculus, p. 366
hyperkinetic symptom, p. 376
hypokinetic symptom, p. 376
motor sequence, p. 358
nocioception, p. 382
pain gate, p. 386
paraplegia, p. 361
proprioception, p. 382
quadriplegia, p. 362
rapidly adapting receptor, p. 382
referred pain, p. 387
scratch reflex, p. 363
slowly adapting receptor, p. 382
synergy, p. 370
topographic organization, p. 366
vestibular system, p. 388

## REVIEW QUESTIONS

1. How are the somatosensory system and the motor system related?
2. Describe the pathways that convey somatosensory information to the brain.
3. Describe the pathways that convey motor instructions to the spinal cord.
4. What are the contributions of the cortex, the basal ganglia, and the cerebellum to movement?
5. Describe two theories of how our motor cortex moves a hand to a target to grasp it.
6. Describe the changes that the somatosensory cortex and the motor cortex might undergo in response to injury to the cortex or to a limb.

## FOR FURTHER THOUGHT

1. Why is the somatosensory system so much more intimately linked to movement than the other sensory systems are?
2. Why might the dorsal and ventral streams be separate systems for controlling hand movements?

## RECOMMENDED READING

Asanuma, H. (1989). *The motor cortex.* New York: Raven Press. An excellent summary of the motor system by a scientist who made important advances in studying the role of the motor cortex in behavior.

Cole, J. (1995). *Pride and a daily marathon.* London: MIT Press. At the age of 19 Ian Waterman was struck down by a rare neurological condition that deprived him of joint position and proprioception. This is the story of how he gradually adapted to his strange condition by using vision and elaborate tricks to monitor his every movement and regain his life.

Melzack, R. (1973). *The puzzle of pain.* New York: Basic Books. For ages, physicians and scientists have attempted with little success to understand and control pain. Here one of the world's leading researchers in the field of pain theory and treatment presents a totally readable book to unravel the mystery of pain.

Sacks, O. (1974). *Awakenings.* New York: Vintage Books. This prize-winning book presents a fascinating account of one of the mysteries of the motor system, how the great flu of the 1920s produced the Parkinsonism that developed as the aftermath of the "sleeping sickness." This story presents wonderful insights into the function of the motor system.

Porter, R., & Lemon, R. (1993). *Corticospinal function and voluntary movement.* Oxford: Clarendon Press. This book tells the story of the human brain's great pathway, the corticospinal tract.

CHAPTER

# 11

# What Causes Behavior?



Michael Grecco/Stock Boston/Picture Quest
Micrograph: Dr. Dennis Kunkel/Phototake

We first met Roger, a 25-year-old man, in the admissions ward of a large mental hospital. Roger approached us and asked if we had any snacks. We had chewing gum, which he accepted eagerly. We thought little about this encounter until 10 minutes later when we noticed that Roger was eating the flowers from the vase on a table. A nurse took the flowers away but said little to Roger. Later, as we wandered about the ward, we encountered a worker replacing linoleum floor tiles. Roger was watching the worker and, as he did, he dipped his finger into the pot of gluing compound and licked the glue from his finger, as if he were sampling honey from a jar. When we asked Roger what he was doing, he said that he was really hungry and that this stuff was not too bad. It reminded him of peanut butter. One of us tasted the glue and concluded not only that it did not taste like peanut butter, but that it actually tasted awful. Roger was undeterred. We alerted a nurse, who quickly removed him from the glue. Later, we saw him eating another bouquet of flowers. Subsequent neurological testing revealed that Roger had a tumor that had invaded the hypothalamus at the base of his brain. He was indeed hungry all the time and could likely consume more than 20,000 calories a day if allowed to.

Roger was not the only person whom we met in the ward. John was on a spying mission to determine how the government had acquired a deficit. He was convinced that the government was hiding gold in the hospital's door handles and hinges, even though the hardware was clearly made of brass. John was diagnosed as schizophrenic. We asked another man, Ralph, why he had been hospitalized. He said that it was because he had written a letter to his mother. It turned out that he had written on his arm with a razor blade rather than on paper with a pen. His arm was badly cut and heavily bandaged. Ralph had been high on "angel dust" during the letter-writing incident and even a week later, when we saw him, he was still disturbed. Joyce, another person whom we met, had tried to commit suicide. She was severely depressed about the death of her child and had also been abused by her husband. She could not face returning home. Finally, there was Allan, who had tried to kill his estranged wife. He could not tell us why he had done it. He said that he had a lot of trouble with his emotions and would sometimes "fly off the handle" for no apparent reason. He was hoping that counseling could help him get back together with his wife and children.

All the people whom we met in the ward had one thing in common. They all engaged in behavior that most of us would consider abnormal. But what were the causes of their abnormal thoughts, feelings, and actions? Consider Roger. Roger really was extremely hungry and craved something to eat. His choice of foods, however, seemed bizarre. But, if you were literally starving and no other food was available, might you try eating something strange? Many people would. Roger, however, was not starving by normal standards, because he ate regular meals. Evidently, though, his brain *thought* that he was starving. So, to understand Roger's behavior, we might ask why he felt so hungry or, more generally, why anyone feels hunger and a motivation to eat? Questions such as this one focus on the underlying reasons for **motivated behavior**—that is, behavior in humans and other animals that seems purposeful and goal directed. Explaining motivated behavior is the major task in this chapter.

We begin by exploring possible causes of the many kinds of behavior in which human beings and other animals may engage. Our exploration will lead us to the conclusion that the actions of neural circuits and hormones are of primary importance in explaining behavior. We then study the anatomical structures responsible for motivated behaviors, focusing on the hypothalamus, the limbic system, and the frontal lobes. Next, we look at examples of motivated behavior—feeding, sexual activity, and emotion—to learn in more detail how the brain controls each one. Finally, we consider the topic of reward, which also plays a key role in explaining motivated behaviors.

## IDENTIFYING THE CAUSES OF BEHAVIOR

We may think that the most obvious explanation for why we behave as we do is simply that we want to. This explanation assumes that we act out of free will—that we always have a choice to do one thing or another. But free will is not a likely cause of behavior. Would you say that Roger had free will regarding his appetite and food preferences? Probably not. Roger seemed compelled to eat whatever he could find, driven by a ravenous hunger. In this case, the nervous system has produced behavior that is not an act of free will. If it can produce one such behavior, it can likely produce many others. Free will therefore does not adequately explain why we act as we do.

If free will is not a satisfactory explanation of behavior, what explanation is? One possibility is the brain's inherent need for environmental stimulation. This need was first demonstrated in the early 1950s by psychologists Donald Hebb and Woodburn Heron and their colleagues (Hebb, 1955; Heron, 1957). They argued that people are motivated to interact with their environments to maintain at least a minimum level of brain stimulation, and they conducted a fascinating series of experiments that supported this view.

### Behavior and the Maintenance of Brain Stimulation

Hebb and his coworkers studied the effects of depriving people of nearly all sensory input—a state called **sensory deprivation.** They wanted to see how well-fed, physically comfortable college students who were paid handsomely for their time would react if they did nothing, saw nothing, and heard or touched very little for 24 hours a day. Figure 11-1 shows the setting for this experiment. Each man lay on a bed in a small sound-proofed room with his ears enveloped by a hollowed-out pillow that muffled the monotonous hums of a nearby fan and air conditioner. Cardboard tubes covered

**Figure 11-1**

In an environmental cubicle for sensory deprivation, the subject lies on a bed 24 hours a day, with time out only for meals and visiting the bathroom. The room is always dimly lit. A translucent plastic visor restricts visual input; a U-shaped pillow and the noise of a fan and air conditioner limit the subject's auditory experience. In the experiment depicted here, the subject is wired for EEG recordings. The subject's sense of touch is restricted by cotton gloves and long cardboard cuffs.

Adapted from "The Pathology of Boredom," by W. Heron, 1957, *Scientific American, 197*(4), p. 52.

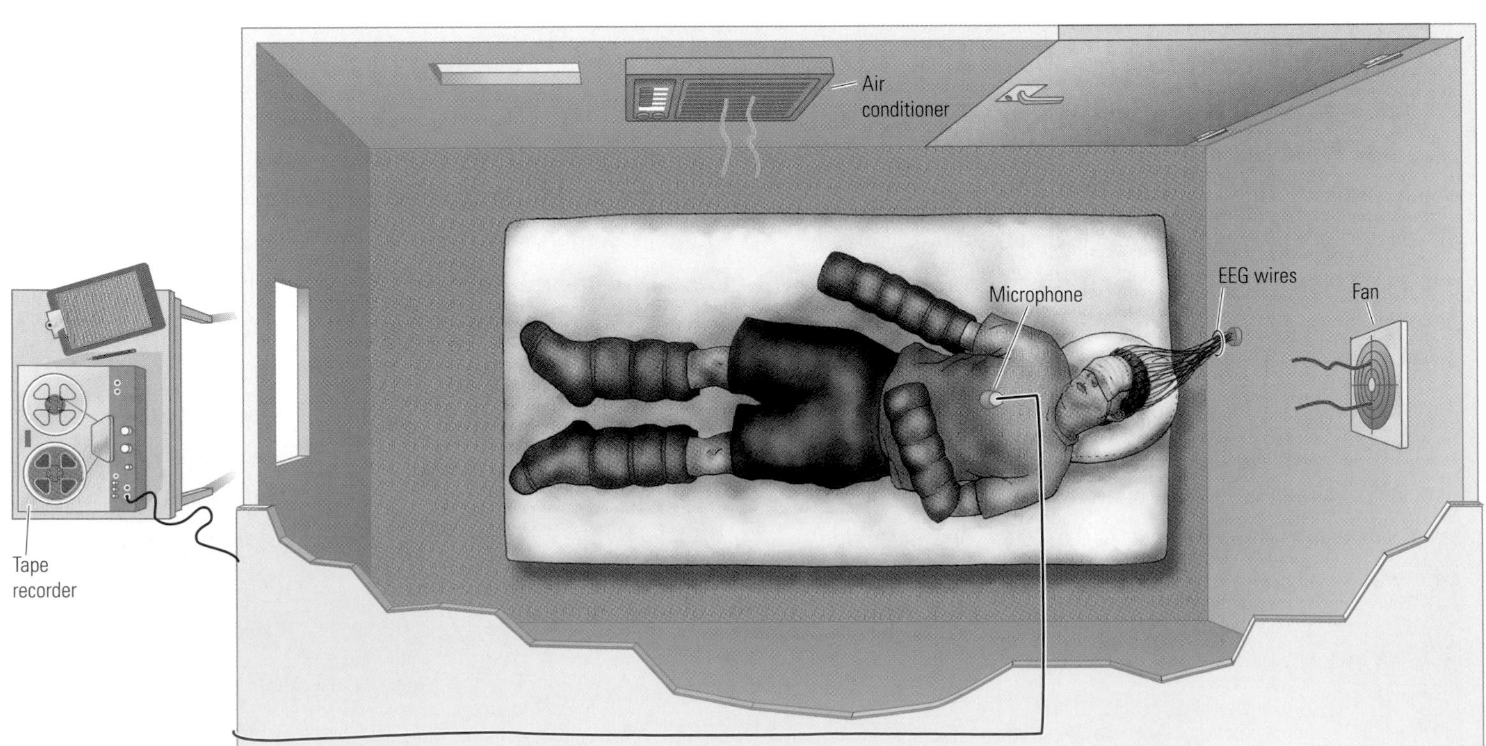

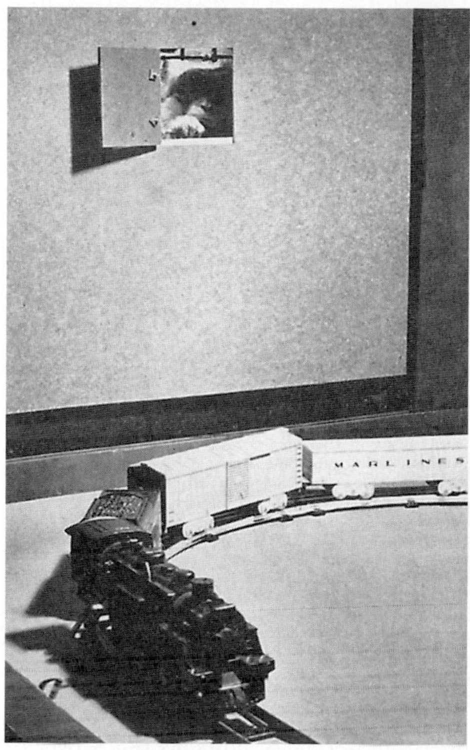

University of Wisconsin

**Figure 11-2**

Monkeys quickly learn to solve puzzles or do other tricks to gain access to a door that looks out into an adjacent room. A toy train is a strong visual incentive for the monkey peeking through the door, whereas a bowl of fruit is less rewarding.

Adapted from "Persistence of Visual Exploration in Monkeys," by R. A. Butler and H. F. Harlow, 1954, *Journal of Comparative and Physiological Psychology, 47,* p. 260.

his hands and arms, cutting off his sense of touch, and a translucent visor covered his eyes, blurring the visual world. The subjects were given food on request and access to bathroom facilities. Otherwise, they were asked simply to enjoy the peace and quiet. For doing so, they would receive $20 a day, which was about four times what a student at the time could earn even for a hard day's labor.

Wouldn't you think the subjects would be quite happy to contribute to scientific knowledge in such a painless way? In fact, they were far from happy. Most subjects were content for perhaps 4 to 8 hours, but then they became increasingly distressed. They developed a need for stimulation of almost any kind. In one version of the experiment, the subjects could listen, on request, to a talk for 6-year-old children on the dangers of alcohol. Some of them requested to hear it 20 times a day. Few subjects lasted more than 24 hours in these conditions.

The results of such studies are curious. After all, the subjects' basic needs were being met, except perhaps the need for sexual gratification. (But Hebb assumed that, at the risk of insulting their virility, most of the young men in his study were accustomed to stretches of at least 3 or 4 days without engaging in sexual activity.) So what was the cause of the subjects' distress? Why did they find sensory deprivation so aversive? The answer, Hebb and his colleagues concluded, must be that the brain has an inherent need for stimulation.

Psychologists Robert Butler and Harry Harlow (1954) came to a similar conclusion through a series of experiments that they conducted at about the same time that Hebb conducted his sensory-deprivation studies. Butler placed rhesus monkeys in a dimly lit room with a small door that could be opened to view an adjoining room. As shown in Figure 11-2, the researchers could vary the stimuli in the adjoining room so that the monkeys could view different objects or animals each time they opened the door. Monkeys in these conditions spent a lot of time opening the door and viewing whatever was on display, such as toy trains in action. The monkeys were even willing to perform various tasks just for an opportunity to look through the door. The greater the amount of time during which they were deprived of a chance to look, the more time they spent looking when finally given the opportunity. These experiments, taken together with those of Hebb and his colleagues, show that one of the reasons that we engage in behavior is to stimulate the brain. In the absence of stimulation, the brain seeks ways to increase it.

## Drives and Behavior

Surely stimulation of the brain is not the only reason for behavior. Consider the behavior of a typical pet cat living in a house or apartment. It awakes in the morning, stretches, wanders to its feeding place, and has a drink of water and some food. Then it sits and cleans itself. Next, it wanders around and spots its favorite toy mouse, which it pounces on and throws in the air. It may pounce and throw again and again for a number of minutes. Eventually, seemingly bored with the toy, it wanders about looking for attention. It sits on its owner's lap, starts to purr, and falls asleep. Shortly thereafter, it gets up and walks away, passes its food and mouse toy, and meows. It explores the apartment, sniffing here and there, before napping in a sunbeam. On waking, the cat returns to the food bowl, eats heartily, bats once at the toy in passing, and searches for its wool ball, which it chases for a while. Later, it stares out the window and eventually settles down for a long sleep.

This cat's seemingly unremarkable actions provide several clues to the causes of behavior. First, the cat's response to a particular stimulus is not the same each time. Both the food and the toy mouse elicit behavior on some occasions but not on others. Second, the strength of the cat's behaviors varies. For instance, the mouse toy stimulates vigorous behavior at one time and none at another. Third, the cat engages not only in behaviors that satisfy obvious biological needs (eating, drinking, sleeping), but also in behaviors that are not so obviously necessary (playing, affection seeking, exploring). These same patterns of behavior are not atypical of dogs or even of people. People can be amused by a puzzle or a book at one moment and completely bored by it soon thereafter. They also respond to a certain object or situation vigorously on some occasions and half-heartedly on others. And they engage in many behaviors that do not seem to have any obvious function, such as tapping their toes to music. What generates all these different kinds of behavior?

As psychologists and biologists began to ponder the causes of behavior in the 1930s, they concluded that there must be some sort of internal energy that drives it. This internal energizing factor had many names, including instincts and **drives.** (Actually, instincts and drives are not identical concepts, but for our purposes it does not matter.) The concept of drives gave rise to what became known as drive theories of behavior. Drive theorists assumed that, because animals perform many different behaviors, they must have many different drives. There must be a sexual drive, a curiosity drive, a hunger drive, a thirst drive, and so on. According to drive theories, an animal engages in a particular behavior because its drive for it is high, and it ceases engaging in that behavior because its drive for it becomes low. Our cat, for example, played vigorously with the toy mouse when its play drive was high and ceased playing when its play drive diminished to zero.

Notice how drive theory suggests that the brain is somehow storing energy for behavior. That energy builds up until it reaches a level where it is released in action, thereby becoming a cause of behavior. Ethologists (scientists who study animal behavior) offer an interesting analogy to describe this process. They compare behavior caused by drives to the flushing of a toilet. When the water reservoir of a toilet is full, depressing the handle leads to a "whoosh" of water that, once begun, cannot be

**Drive.** A hypothetical state of arousal that motivates an organism to engage in a particular behavior.

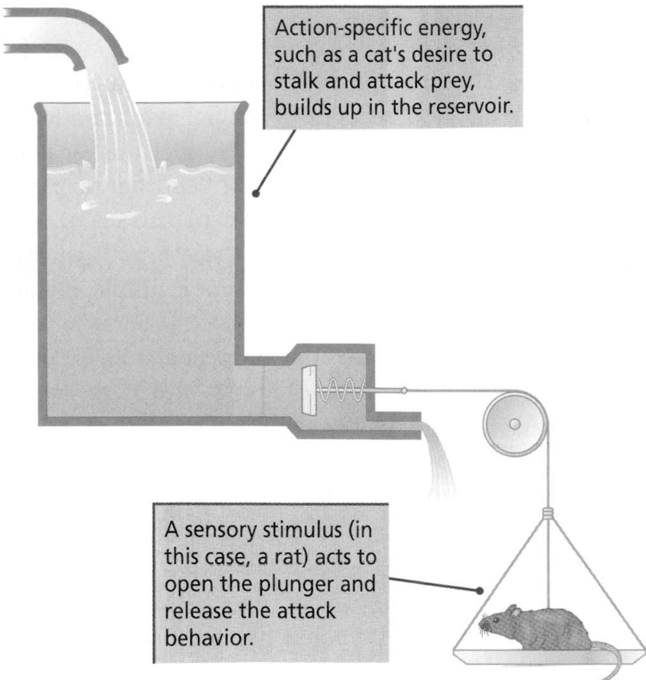

Action-specific energy, such as a cat's desire to stalk and attack prey, builds up in the reservoir.
A sensory stimulus (in this case, a rat) acts to open the plunger and release the attack behavior.

**Figure 11-3**

The flush model of motivation. According to drive theories, there is a store of action-specific energy that, once released, flows out and produces behavior. The greater the store of energy, the longer the behavior persists. If there is no energy, there is no behavior. Each type of behavior is assumed to have its own store of energy.

stopped. When the reservoir is only partly full, depressing the handle still produces a flush, but a less vigorous one. If the reservoir is empty, no amount of handle pressing will cause the toilet to flush. Applying this analogy to our cat with the toy mouse, the cat will play vigorously if the play reservoir is full, less vigorously if it is partly full, and not at all if the reservoir is empty.

The **flush model** makes several assumptions about a drive-induced behavior (Figure 11-3). First, it assumes that the behavior, once started, will continue until all the energy for it in the reservoir is gone. Our cat keeps playing, although with decreasing vigor, until all the energy held in reserve for play is depleted. The flush model also assumes separate stores of energy for different behaviors. For instance, cats have a drive to play, and they have a drive to kill. Engaging in one of these behaviors does not reduce the energy stored for the other. That is presumably why a cat may play with a mouse that it has caught for many minutes before finally killing it. The cat will pounce and attack the mouse repeatedly until all of its energy for play is used up, and only then will it proceed to the next drive-induced behavior.

The flush model can be applied to many different kinds of actions and seems to make some intuitive sense. We do seem to behave as if there were a store of energy for various behaviors. For instance, males of most mammalian species typically have a refractory period subsequent to sexual intercourse when they no longer have interest in (or possibly energy for) sexual behavior. Later, the interest or energy returns. It is as though there was a pent-up sexual urge that, once satisfied, vanishes for a time, awaiting a new energy buildup.

## Neural Circuits and Behavior

The problem with drive theories of behavior becomes clear when we try to relate drives to brain activity. It was once assumed that physiologists would quickly discover how the brain executes drives. Unfortunately, however, researchers were unable to establish a link between drives and brain activity. As they searched inside the brain for drives, they found instead that behavioral change correlates with changes in hormones and cellular activity. For example, researchers studying sexual drive found that a man's frequency of copulation is correlated with his levels of male hormones, called androgens.

Unusually high androgen levels are related to very high sexual interest, whereas abnormally low androgen levels are linked to low sexual interest or perhaps no interest at all. With knowledge of this correlation between sexual behavior and male hormones, the concept of sexual drive no longer seemed needed. Rather than searching for a sexual drive, researchers now sought to explain the action of androgens on neural circuits.

This type of analysis provides more powerful explanations of behavior than does simply invoking the concept of drives. It allows us to say exactly what particular events in the brain can trigger a certain kind of behavior. For example, if an electrode is used to stimulate the brain cells activated by androgens, sexual behavior can be induced. In fact, such brain stimulation can produce amazing sexual activity in male rats, sometimes allowing 50 ejaculations over a couple of hours. Clearly, the activity of neurons is responsible for the behavior, rather than some hidden energy reservoir as is presumed in drive theories.

The idea that there is a neural basis for behavior has wide applications. For instance, we can say that Roger had such a voracious and indiscriminate appetite either because his brain circuits that initiated eating were excessively active or because his circuits that terminated eating were inactive. Similarly, we can say that Hebb's subjects were highly upset by sensory deprivation because their neural circuits that responded to sensory inputs were forced to be abnormally underactive. So the main reason why a particular thought, feeling, or action occurs lies in what is going on in brain circuits.

## Why Do Cats Kill Birds?

Although neural circuits have some plasticity when they form during development, they are not so easily changed later in life. It therefore follows that behaviors that are caused by these neural circuits also are going to be hard to modify. The killing of prey by cats is a good example.

One of the frustrating things about being a cat owner is that even well-fed cats kill birds—often lots of birds. Most people are not too bothered when their cats kill mice, because they view mice as a nuisance. But birds are a different matter because people enjoy watching birds in their yards and gardens. Many cat owners wonder why their pets keep killing birds. To provide an answer, we can look to the activities of neural circuits in the brain. Cats must have a circuit that controls prey killing. When this circuit is active, a cat makes an appropriate kill. Viewed in an evolutionary context, it makes sense for cats to have such a circuit because, in the days when cats were not owned by doting human beings, they did not have food dishes that were regularly being filled.

Why does this prey-killing circuit become active when a cat does not need food? One explanation is that, to secure survival, the activity of circuits such as the prey-killing circuit have become rewarding in some way—they make the cat "feel good." As a result, the cat is likely to engage in the pleasure-producing behavior often, which helps to guarantee that it will usually not go hungry. In the wild, after all, a cat that did not like killing would probably be a dead cat. This idea of behaviors such as prey killing being rewarding was first proposed by Steve Glickman and Bernard Schiff in the early 1960s. Because it is important to our understanding of the causes of behavior, we will return to it at the end of this chapter when we consider reward.

Killing behavior by cats is innate, not learned. It is triggered automatically in the presence of the right stimulus. The innateness of killing in cats is demonstrated by a cat named Hunter, who was found abandoned when she was a tiny kitten. Her mother had apparently perished. Hunter was bottle fed and raised without a mother cat to "teach" her to hunt. She did not need an education in hunting. She got her name from her innate and deadly skill at catching mice and other small prey. The prey-killing circuits in her brainstem worked without training. They no doubt were influenced by practice, however, because Hunter became more proficient at killing as she grew older. But the ultimate underlying cause of the behavior is a neural circuit that, when activated, produces stalking and killing responses.

**Innate releasing mechanism (IRM).** A hypothetical mechanism that detects specific sensory stimuli and directs the organism to take a particular action.

## In Review

Free will is not an adequate explanation of behavior, because the nervous system can produce behaviors over which an organism has no choice. Researchers have investigated several other possible causes of behavior, including the apparent need of the brain to maintain at least a minimum level of stimulation and the idea that there are internal energizing factors called drives that build up and are released in behavior. A more powerful way to explain behavior, however, is to search inside the brain for the hormone actions and neural circuits that control how we think, act, and feel.

# EVOLUTIONARY AND ENVIRONMENTAL FACTORS

What factors influence the brain-circuit activity that in turn produces behaviors? For instance, why does the sight of a bird or a mouse trigger stalking and killing in a cat? Or why does the female human form stimulate sexual interest in men? We can address such questions at two levels: one evolutionary, the other environmental.

## Evolutionary Influences on Behavior

The evolutionary explanation hinges on the concept of **innate releasing mechanisms (IRMs).** The meaning of this concept is best understood by analyzing its parts. The term *innate* means that these mechanisms are present from birth, rather than being acquired through experience. Innate also implies that the mechanisms have proved adaptive for the species and therefore have been maintained in the species' genome. The term *releasing* in the concept of IRMs means that the mechanisms act as triggers to set free behaviors for which there are internal programs. Thus, innate releasing mechanisms are the activators for innate and adaptive responses that aid in an animal's survival by helping it to successfully feed, reproduce, escape from its predators, and so forth.

Let us return to our cat as an example. The brain of a cat must have a built-in mechanism that triggers appropriate stalking and killing in response to stimuli such as a bird or a mouse. Similarly, a cat must also have a built-in mechanism that triggers appropriate mating behavior in the presence of a suitable cat of the opposite sex. Although not all of a cat's behaviors are due to IRMs, you can probably think of other innate releasing mechanisms that cats possess, such as arching and hissing when encountering a threat. For all these IRMs, the animal's brain must have a set of norms against which it can match stimuli in order to trigger an appropriate response.

The existence of such innate, internalized norms is suggested in the following experiment. One of us (B. K.) and Arthur Nonneman allowed 6-week-old kittens to play in a room and become familiar with it. After this adjustment period, we introduced a two-dimensional image of an adult cat in a "Halloween posture," as shown in Figure 11-4. The kittens responded with raised fur, an arched back, and a baring of teeth, seeming threatened by the image of the adult. Some even hissed at the model. These kittens had no experience with any adult cat except their mother, and there was no reason to believe that she had ever shown them this behavior. Rather, there must have

(A)

(B)

**Figure 11-4**

A "Halloween cat" stimulates a similar posture in other cats. This posture appears at about 6 weeks of age in kittens who have never seen such a posture before. The "Picasso" cat shown below doesn't evoke any response at all.

been some sort of template of this posture prewired in the kitten brain. When the kittens saw the model that matched the preexisting template, a threat response was automatically triggered. This innate triggering mechanism is an IRM.

The concept of an IRM also applies to humans. In one study, Tiffany Field and her colleagues (1982) had an adult display to young infants various exaggerated facial expressions, such as happiness, sadness, and surprise. As Figure 11-5 shows, the babies responded with very much the same expressions. These infants were too young to be intentionally imitating the adult faces. Rather, the responses must have been due to an IRM. The babies must have had an innate ability to match these facial expressions to internal templates, which in turn triggered some prewired program to reproduce the expressions in their own faces. Such an ability would have adaptive value if these facial expressions serve as important social signals for humans. Evidence for a prewired motor program related to facial expressions also comes from the study of congenitally blind children. These children spontaneously produce the very same facial expressions that sighted people do, even though they have never seen them in others.

**Figure 11-5**

Facial expressions made by young infants in response to expressions made by the experimenter.

From "Discrimination and Imitation of Facial Expression by Neonates," by T. M. Field, R. Woodson, R. Greenberg, and D. Cohen, 1982, *Science, 218*, p. 180.

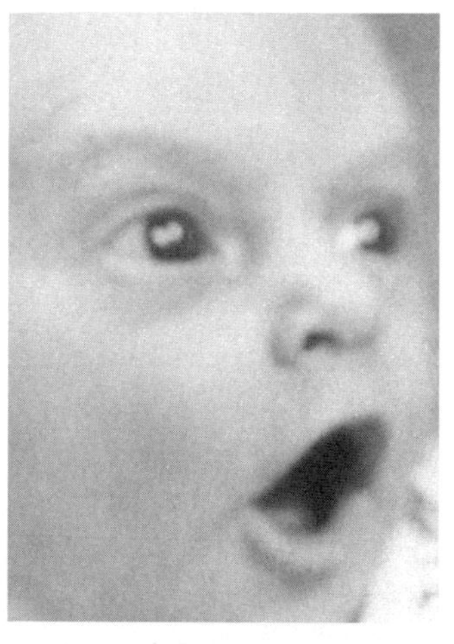

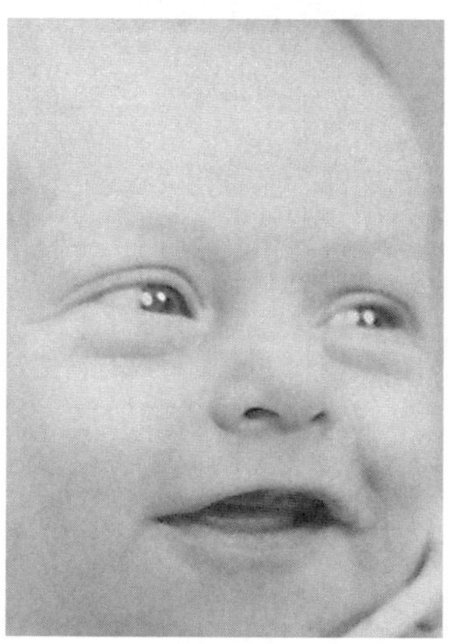

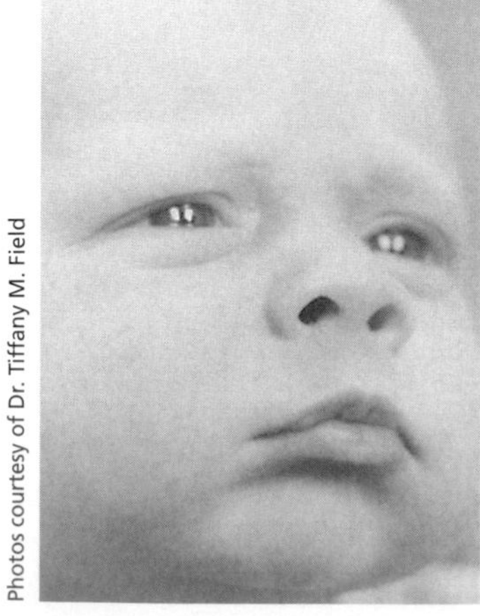
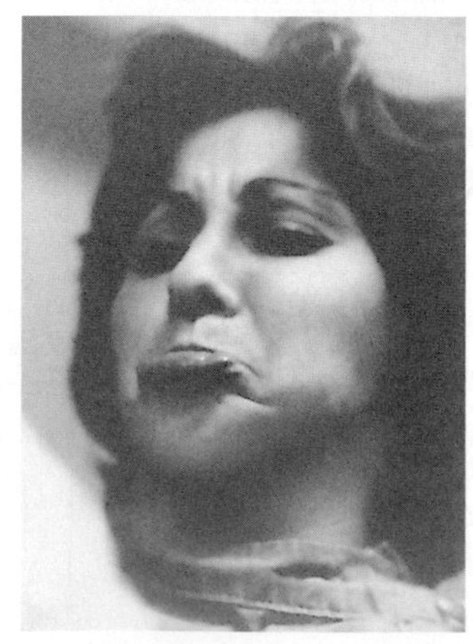

Photos courtesy of Dr. Tiffany M. Field

Although IRMs such as those just described are prewired into the brain, they can be modified by experience. For instance, Hunter's stalking skills were not inherited fully developed at birth but rather matured functionally as she grew older. The same is true of many human IRMs, such as those for responding to sexually arousing stimuli. Different cultures may emphasize different sexual stimuli, and, even within a single culture, there is variation in what different people find sexually stimulating. Nonetheless, some human attributes are universally found to have sexually arousing value. An example is the hip-to-waist ratio of human females for most human males. This ratio is probably part of an IRM.

The concept of the IRM can be related to the Darwinian view of how the nervous system evolves. According to this view, natural selection favors behaviors that prove adaptive for an organism, and these behaviors are passed on to future generations. Because behavior patterns are produced by the activity of neurons in the brain, the natural selection of specific behaviors is really the selection of particular brain circuits. Animals that survive long enough to reproduce and have healthy offspring are more likely to pass on the genes for making their brain circuits than are animals with traits that make them less likely to survive and successfully reproduce. Thus, cats with brain circuits that made them adept at stalking prey or responding fiercely to threats were more likely to survive and produce many offspring, passing on those adaptive brain circuits and behaviors to their young. In this way, the behaviors became widespread in the species through time.

Although the Darwinian view seems straightforward when considering how cats evolved brain circuits for stalking prey or responding to threats, it is less so when applied to many complex human behaviors. For instance, why have humans evolved the behavior of killing other members of their species? At first glance, this behavior would seem counterproductive to the survival of humans, so why has it endured?

Some insights come from a field of study called **evolutionary psychology,** which seeks to apply evolutionary ideas to help understand the causes of human behavior.

Consider how evolutionary psychologists account for homicide. When two men fight a duel, one common-sense explanation might be that they are fighting to maintain status or self-esteem. But evolutionary psychologists would look at a duel differently, asking why a behavior pattern that risks people's lives is sustained in a population. Evolutionary psychologists assume that any behavior, including dueling, exists because the neural circuits producing it have been favored through natural selection. In this case, men who fought and won duels passed on their genes to future generations, whereas those who lost duels did not. Through time, therefore, the traits associated with successful dueling—strength, aggression, agility—became more prevalent among humans, and so, too, did dueling itself.

Martin Daly and Margot Wilson (1988) extended this type of analysis to further account for homicide. In their view, homicide may endure in our society despite its severe punishment because it is related to behaviors that were adaptive in the human past. Suppose, for example, that natural selection favored sexually jealous males who effectively intimidated their rivals and bullied their mates so as to guarantee their own paternity of any offspring produced by their mates. As a result, male jealousy would become a prevalent motive for interpersonal violence, including homicide. Note that, in this view, homicide itself does not help a man produce more children. But men who are apt to commit homicides are more likely to engage in other behaviors (bullying and intimidation) that improve their reproductive fitness. Homicide therefore is related to adaptive traits that have been selected through millennia.

The evolutionary psychology view is introduced here not to account for all human behavior and perhaps not even to account for homicide; rather, it demonstrates that evolutionary theory can generate hypotheses about how natural selection might have shaped the brain and behavior. In this way, evolutionary psychology can sometimes provide an additional and intriguing perspective on the neurological bases of behavior.

Visit the Web site at **www.worthpublishers.com/kolb/chapter11** to learn more about evolutionary psychology.

## Environmental Influences on Behavior

Many psychologists, especially B. F. Skinner, have emphasized learning as a cause of behavior. No one would question that we modify our behavior as we learn, but Skinner went much further. He believed that behaviors are selected by environmental factors. His argument is simple. Certain kinds of events function as rewards, called **reinforcers,** and, when such an event follows a particular response, similar responses are more likely to occur again. Skinner further argued that reinforcement can be manipulated so as to encourage the display of complex forms of behavior.

B. F. Skinner (1904–1990)

The power of experiences to shape behavior by pairing stimuli and rewards is typified by one of Skinner's experiments. A pigeon is placed in a box that has a small disc on one wall (the stimulus). If the pigeon pecks at the disc (the response), a food tray opens and the pigeon can feed (the reinforcement, or reward). A pigeon quickly learns the association between the stimulus and the rewarded behavior, especially if the disc has a small spot on it. It pecks at the spot, and within minutes it has mastered the behavior needed to receive a reward. Now the reward requirement can be made more complex. The pigeon might be required to turn 360° before pecking the disc to gain the reward. The pigeon can learn this movement, too. Other contingencies might then be added, making the behavioral requirements even more complex. For instance, the pigeon might be trained to turn in a clockwise circle if the disc is green, to turn in a counterclockwise circle if the disc is red, and to scratch at the floor if the disc is yellow. If you suddenly came upon this complex behavior in a pigeon, you would probably be astounded. But, if you understood the experience that had shaped the bird's behavior,

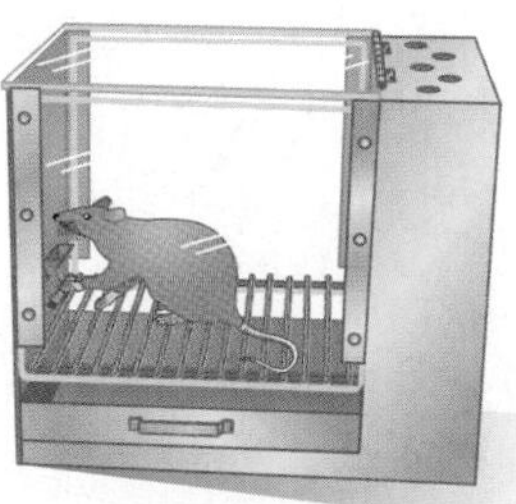

Skinner box

you would understand the cause. The rewards offered to the pigeon altered its behavior so that its responses were controlled by the color of the disc on the wall.

Skinner extended this type of analysis to include all sorts of behaviors that, at first, do not appear to be easily explained. For instance, he argued that various phobias could be accounted for by understanding a person's reinforcement history. An example is someone who was once terrified by a turbulent ride on a plane thereafter avoiding air travel and manifesting a phobia of flying. The avoidance of flying is rewarding because it lowers the person's anxiety level, and so the phobic behavior is maintained. Skinner also argued against the commonly held view that much of human behavior is under our own control. From Skinner's perspective, free will is only an illusion, because behavior is controlled by the environment through our experiences.

Although the intent is not to debate the pros and cons of Skinner's ideas here, we *can* conclude that many complex behaviors are learned. It is also true that learning takes place in a brain that has been selected for evolutionary adaptations. This combination of learning and inherited brain circuits can lead to some surprising results. A case in point can again be seen in pigeons.

Although a pigeon in a Skinner box can quickly learn to peck a disc to receive a bit of food, it cannot learn to peck a disc to escape from a mild electric shock to its feet. Why not? After all, the same simple pecking behavior is being rewarded. But apparently, the pigeon's brain is not prewired for this second kind of association. The bird is prepared to make the first association but not prepared to make the second, which makes adaptive sense. For a pigeon, pecking is a behavior that in a natural environment is widely linked with obtaining food, so learning associations between pecking and food come easily to a pigeon. In contrast, learning to peck to prevent electric shock is not part of the brain circuitry with which a pigeon is born; so mastering this association does not come easily to the bird.

The selective nature of the behavior–consequence associations that animals are able to learn was first shown in 1966 by psychologist John Garcia. He observed that farmers in the western United States are constantly shooting at coyotes for attacking lambs; yet, despite the painful consequences, the coyotes never seem to learn to stop killing lambs in favor of safer prey. The reason, Garcia speculated, is that a coyote's brain is not prewired to make this kind of association. So Garcia proposed an alternative to deter coyotes from killing lambs—one that uses an association that a coyote's brain is prepared to make. This association is the connection between eating something that makes one sick and avoiding that food in the future. So Garcia gave the coyotes a poisoned lamb carcass, which made them sick but did not kill them. With only one pairing of lamb and illness, most coyotes learned not to eat sheep for the rest of their lives.

Many humans have similarly acquired food aversions because the taste of a certain food—especially a novel one—was subsequently paired with illness. This **learned taste aversion** is acquired even when the food that was eaten is in fact unrelated to the later illness. As long as the taste and the nausea are paired in time, the brain is prewired to make a connection between them. For instance, one author of this book ate his first Caesar salad the night before coming down with a stomach flu. A year later, he was offered another Caesar salad and, to his amazement, felt ill just at the smell of it. Even though his earlier illness had not been due to the salad, he had formed an association between the novel flavor and illness. This kind of strong and rapid associative learning makes adaptive sense. Having a brain that is prepared to make a connection between a novel taste and subsequent illness will help an animal avoid poisonous foods and so aid in its survival. Interestingly, a curious aspect of taste-aversion learning is that we are not even aware of having formed the association until we encounter the taste again.

The fact that the nervous system is often prepared to make certain associations but not to make others has led to the concept of **preparedness** in learning theories. This concept can help account for some quite complex behaviors. For example, if two rats are paired in a small box and exposed to a mild electric shock, they will immediately fight with one another, even though neither was responsible for the shock. Apparently, the brain is prepared to make associations between injury and nearby objects or other animals. Perhaps you have occasionally felt your own temper flare toward someone who was near you when you were accidentally hurt or in pain for some reason unrelated to that person. The extent to which we might extend this idea to explain human behaviors such as bigotry and racism is an interesting topic for debate. But the important point here is that environmental events are working on a brain that is prewired to make certain types of associations.

## Purpose in Behavior: To Know a Fly

A pitfall in studying the causes of behavior is to infer purposefulness from an organism's actions. In other words, we have a tendency to assume that behavior is intentional. The problems in making this assumption are illustrated in a wonderful little book titled *To Know a Fly*, written by Vincent Dethier.

When a fly lands on a kitchen table, it wanders about, occasionally stomping its feet. Eventually, it finds a bit of food and sticks its proboscis (a trunklike extension) into the food and eats. The fly may then walk to a nearby place and begin to groom by rubbing its legs together quickly. Finally, it spends a long period motionless. If you observed a fly engaged in these behaviors, it might appear that it was initially searching for food because it was hungry. When it found food, you might assume that it gorged itself until it was satisfied, and then it cleaned up and rested. In short, the fly's behavior might seem to you to have some purposefulness or intention. Dethier studied flies for years to understand what a fly is actually doing when it engages in these kinds of behaviors.

His findings had little to do with purpose or intention. First, when a fly wanders about a table, it is not deliberately searching; it is tasting things that it walks on. As Figure 11-6 shows, a fly's taste receptors are on its feet, rather than in its mouth as in humans. So tasting is automatic when a fly walks. An adult fly's nervous system has a built-in preference for sweet tastes and aversions to sour, salty, or bitter flavors. Therefore, when a fly encounters something sweet, it automatically lowers its proboscis and eats. A fly must also drink, and the proboscis is used to drink as well. So, on some occasions, a fly will find water instead of food and will drink instead of eat.

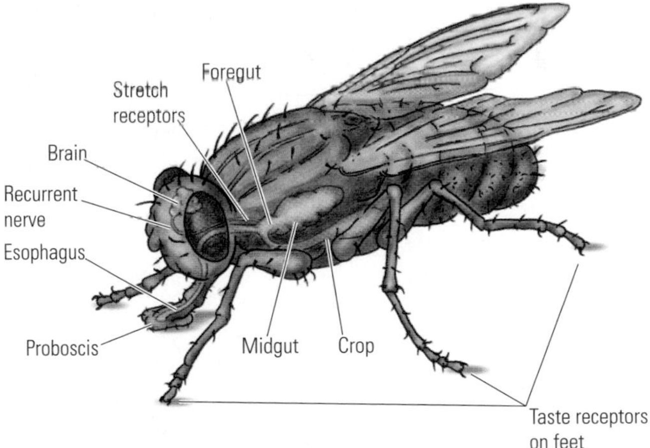


**Figure 11-6** This schematic representation of the feeding system of the fly shows food being taken in via the proboscis, after which it passes through the esophagus to the gut. Stretch receptors at the entrance to the gut determine when the esophagus is full. A nerve (the recurrent nerve) connects with the brain to signal cessation of eating.

The taste preferences of a fly are interesting. When humans are given very sweet foods, they normally eat less of them than foods that are not as sweet. In contrast, the sweeter the food is, the more a fly will consume. This taste preference can be measured by comparing how much a fly drinks of sugar solutions with different concentrations. The fly has a lower preference for weak sugar solutions and drinks less of them than very strong solutions. The fly's preference for sweet tastes is so great that it will choose food that tastes very sweet over food that is less sweet but nutritionally better. For instance, when given a choice between regular glucose and an exceptionally sweet sugar called fucose that a fly cannot digest, the fly will always choose the fucose, presumably because it tastes better to a fly. In fact, if given the opportunity to do so, a fly will literally die of starvation by eating nothing but fucose, even though nutritious glucose is available only centimeters away.

What causes a fly to stop eating? A logical possibility is that the amount of sugar in its blood rises to some threshold level. If this possibility were correct, injecting glucose into the circulatory system of a fly would prevent the fly from eating. But it is not what happens. Blood-glucose level has no effect on a fly's feeding. Furthermore, injecting food into the animal's stomach or intestine has no effect either. So what is left? The upper part of the digestive tract. It turns out that flies have a nerve (the recurrent nerve) that extends from the neck to the brain and carries information about whether there is any food in the esophagus. If this nerve is cut, the fly is chronically "hungry" and never stops eating. Such flies become so full and fat that their feet no longer reach the ground, and they become so heavy that they cannot fly.

So what have we learned about the fly? The main message is that, even though a fly appears to act with a "purpose in mind," it actually has very simple mechanisms controlling its behavior—mechanisms that are not remotely related to our concept of thought. A fly eats because its esophagus is devoid of food, and it stops when its esophagus has some food in it. When the nerve connecting the esophagus to the brain is cut, a fly will keep on eating even though the food is flattening its internal organs against the sides of its body. Hunger is simply the activity of the nerve, not some drive concerning intention. Clearly, we should not assume that a behavior has a conscious purpose just because it appears to have one. Behavior can have very subtle causes that do not include purpose, which raises the question, How we know that any behavior is purposeful? That question turns out to be difficult to answer.

## In Review

Behavior is a result of both evolutionary and environmental selection, as well as an interaction of these two forces. The brain of a species is prewired to produce certain behaviors in response to specific sensory stimuli. The brain is also prewired to learn associations between certain environmental events. These prewired circuits have been selected by evolution. In addition, behaviors can be selected by an individual organism's own unique history of experiences. In searching for the causes of behavior, then, we must be aware that behaviors can have multiple causes, which can vary from one behavior to another.

# TYPES OF MOTIVATED BEHAVIOR

*Motivation* is a term that is commonly used to describe what appears to be purpose underlying behavior, especially in humans. It is used in that sense here but with the caution that, like drives, motivations are not something that we can point to in the brain. Rather, **motivations** are inferences that we make about why someone engages in a particular behavior. We seek mates, food, sensory stimulation, and so forth because of brain activity, but it is convenient to talk about such behavior as being "motivated." There are two general classes of motivated behaviors: regulatory and nonregulatory. In this section, we explore each of these classes before exploring the brain structures taking part in motivated behaviors.

## Regulatory Behaviors

*Regulatory behaviors* are behaviors that are controlled by a **homeostatic mechanism**—that is, by a mechanism that works to keep certain body functions within a narrow, fixed range. To understand how a homeostatic mechanism operates, consider a thermostat in a house that is set at 18°C, like the one in Figure 11-7. When the temperature

**Homeostatic mechanism.** A mechanism that keeps certain body functions within a narrow, fixed range.

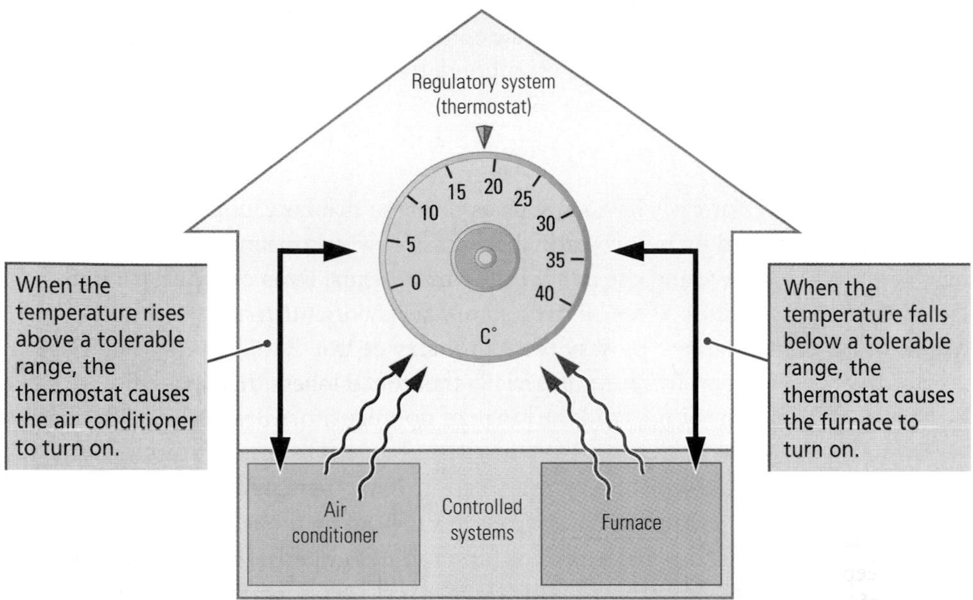


**Figure 11-7**

How a thermostat controls the temperature inside a house. An analogous mechanism could control body temperature.

falls below a certain tolerable range (say, to 16°C), the thermostat causes the furnace to go on. When the temperature rises above a certain tolerable level (say, to 20°C), the thermostat causes the air conditioner to go on.

The human body temperature is controlled in a somewhat similar manner by a "thermostat" in the hypothalamus. The internal temperature is held at about 37°C. Even slight variations in body temperature cause us to engage in various behaviors to regain this setpoint. For example, when the body temperature drops slightly, neural circuits that increase temperature are turned on. These neural circuits might induce an involuntary response such as shivering or a seemingly voluntary behavior such as moving closer to a heat source. Conversely, if body temperature rises slightly, we sweat or move to a cooler place. Similar mechanisms control many other body processes, including the amount of water in the body, the balance of dietary nutrients, and the level of blood sugar. The control of many of these homeostatic systems is quite complex, requiring both neural and hormonal mechanisms. However, in some way, all the body's homeostatic systems include the activity of the hypothalamus.

| Some regulatory behaviors |
|---|
| Temperature regulation |
| Eating and drinking |
| Salt consumption |
| Waste elimination |

Although there is obviously no thermostat in the hypothalamus, it is still able to act as if it had one. To understand how, imagine that specific cells are especially sensitive to temperature. When they are cool, they become very active; when they are warm, they become less active. These cells could function as a thermostat, telling the body when it is too cool or too warm. A similar set of cells could serve as a "glucostat," controlling the level of sugar in the blood, or as a "waterstat," controlling the amount of $H_2O$ in the body. In fact, the body's real homeostatic mechanisms are slightly more complex than this imagined one, but they work in accord with the same general principle.

Plug in the CD to examine the hypothalamus in three dimensions in the module on the Central Nervous System in the subsection on subcortical structures.

Why have we evolved mechanisms to hold conditions such as temperature constant? One reason is that, because the body, including the brain, is a chemical "soup" in which thousands of chemical reactions are taking place all of the time, constant temperature becomes critical. When temperature rises, even by such a small amount as 2 Celsius degrees, the rates at which chemical reactions take place change. Such changes might be tolerable, within certain limits, if all the reaction times changed to the same extent. But they do not do so. Consequently, an increase of 2 degrees might increase one reaction by 10 percent and another by only 2 percent. Such uneven changes would wreak havoc with finely tuned body processes such as metabolism and the workings of neurons. A similar logic applies to maintaining other body systems in a constant state. For instance, cells require certain concentrations of water, salt, or glucose to function properly. If those concentrations were to fluctuate wildly, there would be a gross disturbance of metabolic balance and a subsequent biological disaster.

## Nonregulatory Behaviors

| Some nonregulatory behaviors |
|---|
| Sexual behavior |
| Parental behavior |
| Aggression |
| Food preference |
| Curiosity |
| Reading |

In contrast with regulatory behaviors, such as eating or drinking, **nonregulatory behaviors** are not controlled by homeostatic mechanisms, which means that nonregulatory behaviors include everything else that we do—from sexual intercourse, to parenting, to curiosity-driven activities. Some nonregulatory behaviors, such as sexual intercourse, entail the hypothalamus, but most of them probably do not. Rather, such behaviors entail a variety of forebrain structures, especially the frontal lobes. Presumably, as the forebrain evolved to a larger size, so did the range of nonregulatory behaviors.

Most nonregulatory behaviors are strongly influenced by external stimuli. As a result, sensory systems must play some role in controlling them. For example, the sexual behavior of most male mammals is strongly influenced by the odor that receptive females emit. If the olfactory system is not functioning properly, we can expect abnormalities in sexual behavior. We will return to the topic of sexual behavior later in this chapter when we investigate it as an example of how a nonregulatory behavior is controlled. But first we will look at the brain structures taking part in motivated behaviors—both nonregulatory and regulatory ones.

### In Review

Human behaviors are often thought of as being motivated, or possessing purpose. Two general classes of motivated behaviors are regulatory and nonregulatory ones. A regulatory behavior is controlled by a homeostatic mechanism that works to keep a certain aspect of body function within a narrow, fixed range. Nonregulatory behaviors consist of everything else that we do. Many nonregulatory behaviors are partly controlled by external stimuli that serve as cues.

# THE ANATOMY OF MOTIVATED BEHAVIOR

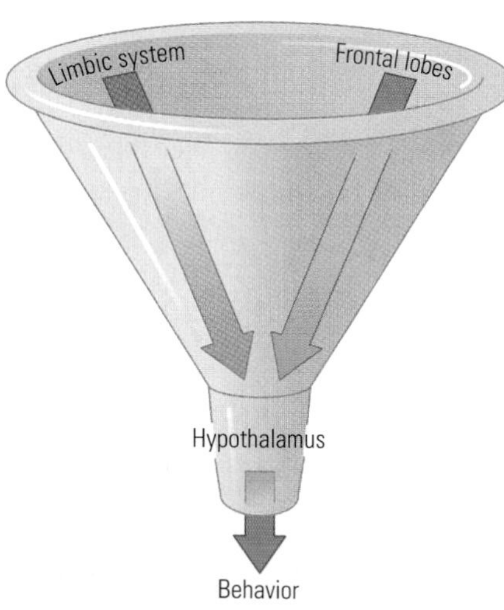


**Figure 11-8**

In this funnel model of control of motivated behaviors, inputs from the frontal lobes and limbic system are funneled through the hypothalamus, which controls the brainstem circuits to produce the behavioral patterns.

Although the circuits that control both regulatory and nonregulatory behaviors include regions at all levels of the brain, the critical structures are the hypothalamus and the associated pituitary gland, the limbic system, and the frontal lobes. In this section, we investigate the anatomical and functional organization of these major structures. As we do so, we should bear in mind that these structures are functionally interrelated. The hypothalamus receives much of its input from the limbic system and the frontal lobes, as illustrated in Figure 11-8, in which the hypothalamus is shown as the neck of a funnel, with the limbic system and the frontal lobes forming the rim. The limbic and frontal regions project to the hypothalamus, which houses many of the basic circuits and homeostatic mechanisms for controlling behavior. To produce behavior, the hypothalamus then sends axons to other brainstem circuits. Thus, although the hypothalamus plays a central role in the control of motivated behavior, it receives its instructions from the limbic system and the frontal lobes.

## The Role of the Hypothalamus

As stated earlier in regard to regulatory behaviors, one function of the hypothalamus is to produce constancy in our internal environment. It does so by acting on both the endocrine system and the autonomic nervous system (see Chapter 2). The hypothalamus also influences the selection of behaviors by the rest of the brain, especially by the limbic system. In these ways, the hypothalamus, although it constitutes less than 1 percent of the human brain's volume, controls an amazing variety of behaviors, ranging from heart rate to feeding to sexual activity.

## HYPOTHALAMIC INVOLVEMENT IN HORMONE SECRETIONS

A principal function of the hypothalamus is to control the **pituitary gland,** which is attached to the hypothalamus by a stalk, known as the **infundibulum,** that lies just behind the optic chiasm (see Figure 2-17). The optic nerves cross to form the optic chiasm right in front of the hypothalamus, and the optic tracts are just lateral to it. The location of the optic chiasm makes it susceptible to pressure from commonly occurring tumors or swelling of the pituitary gland. As a result, one of the first symptoms of pituitary disease is often a change in vision, such as a shrinking of the visual field.

The hypothalamus can be divided into three regions: the lateral, the medial, and the periventricular, as illustrated in Figure 11-9B. The lateral region is composed both of nuclei and of tracts running up and down the brain, connecting the lower brainstem to the forebrain. The principal tract, shown in Figure 11-10, is the **medial forebrain bundle** (MFB), which connects structures of the brainstem with various parts of the limbic

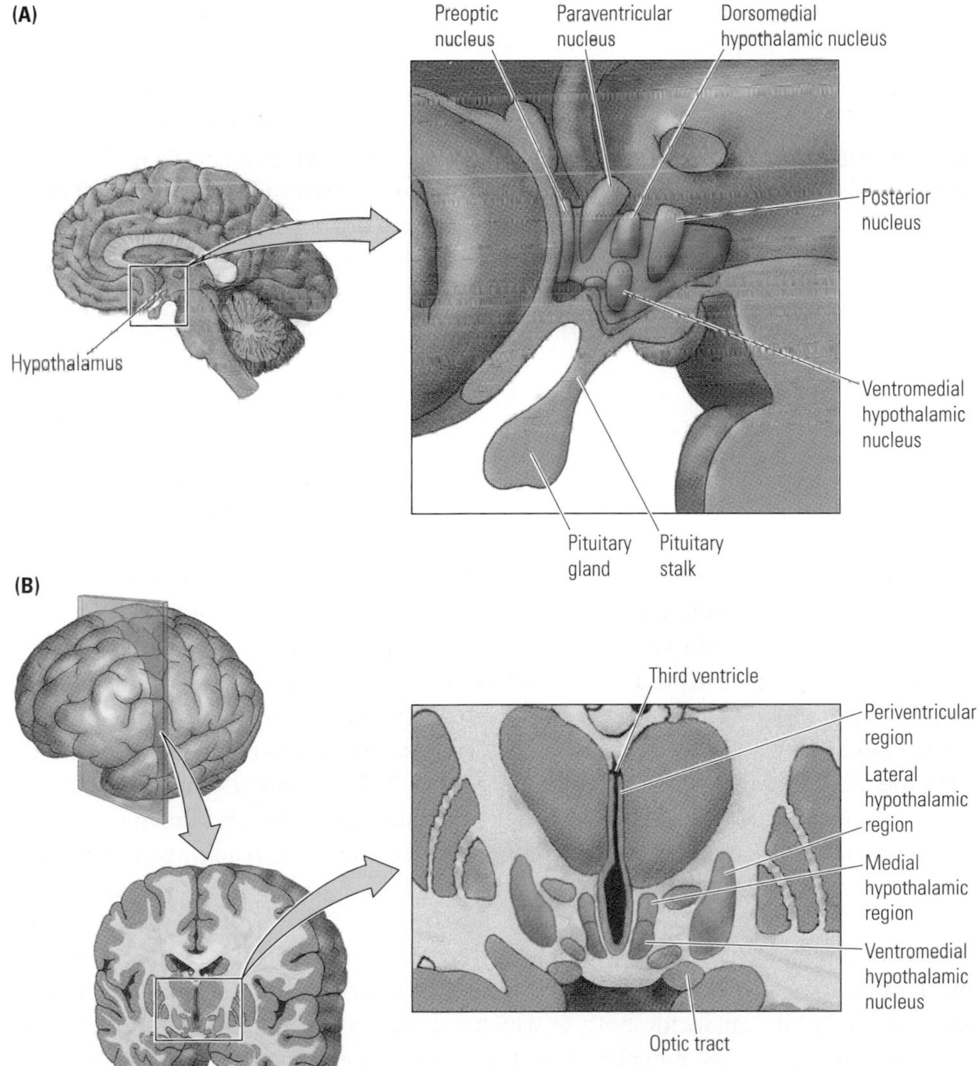


**Figure 11-9** The location and structure of the hypothalamus: **(A)** a medial view showing the relation between the hypothalamus and the rest of the brain; **(B)** a frontal section, taken at the plane indicated. The relation between the hypothalamus and the third ventricle can be seen. There are three principal hypothalamic regions: the lateral, medial, and periventricular regions.

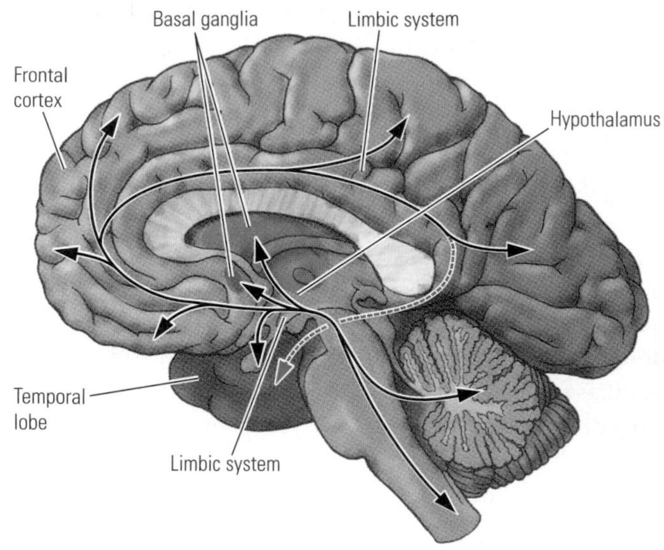


**Figure 11-10**

The medial forebrain bundle is a major pathway for fibers connecting various parts of the limbic system with the brainstem. Major components of the MFB are the ascending projections that run from the brainstem to the basal ganglia and frontal cortex.

system. Fibers that ascend from the dopamine- and noradrenaline-containing cells of the lower brainstem form a significant part of the MFB. Recall from Chapter 6 that dopamine is important in our experience of reward. Thus, the dopamine-containing fibers of the MFB contribute to the control of many motivated behaviors, including eating and sexual behaviors.

Each nucleus of the hypothalamus is anatomically distinct, but most have multiple functions. These multiple functions are due, in part, to the fact that the cells in different nuclei contain various peptide transmitters, each of which plays a role in different behaviors. For instance, the transmitters in the cells in the paraventricular nucleus may be vasopressin, oxytocin, or various combinations of other peptides (such as enkephalin and neurotensin). The production of these various peptides is related to the specialized relation between the hypothalamus and the pituitary.

The pituitary consists of two distinct glands, the anterior pituitary and the posterior pituitary, as shown in Figure 11-11. The posterior pituitary is composed of neural tissue and is essentially a continuation of the hypothalamus. Neurons in the hypothalamus make peptides (for example, oxytocin and vasopressin) that are transported down their axons to terminals lying in the posterior pituitary. If these neurons become active, they send action potentials to the terminals, causing the terminals to release the peptides that are stored there. But rather than affecting another neuron, as occurs at most synapses, these peptides are picked up by capillaries in the posterior pituitary's rich vascular bed. From there, they enter the body's bloodstream. The blood then carries the peptides to distant targets, where they have their effects. For example, vasopressin affects water resorption by the kidneys, and oxytocin controls both uterine contractions and the ejection of milk by mammary glands in the breasts.

The anterior pituitary is composed of glandular tissue that synthesizes various hormones, the major ones being listed in Figure 11-11. The hypothalamus controls the release of these anterior pituitary hormones by producing chemicals known as **releasing hormones.** Produced by hypothalamic cell bodies, releasing hormones are secreted into tiny blood vessels, or capillaries, that transport them to the anterior pituitary, as Figure 11-11 shows. A releasing hormone can either stimulate or inhibit the release of an anterior pituitary hormone. For example, the hormone prolactin is produced by the anterior pituitary, but its release is controlled by a prolactin-releasing factor and a prolactin release–inhibiting factor, both of which are made in the hypothalamus. The release of hormones by the anterior pituitary in turn provides a means by which the brain can control what is taking place in many other parts of the body.

**Releasing hormones.** Peptides that are released by the hypothalamus and act to increase or decrease the release of hormones from the anterior pituitary.

**Figure 11-11**

The location and organization of the hypothalamus and pituitary gland in the human brain. The pituitary has two divisions: the anterior and posterior. The anterior pituitary is connected to the hypothalamus by a system of blood vessels that carry hormones from the hypothalamus to the pituitary. The posterior pituitary receives input from axons of hypothalamic neurons. Both regions of the pituitary respond to hypothalamic input by producing hormones that travel in the bloodstream to stimulate target organs.

Pituitary gland

1 Hormones are synthesized here and sent to axon terminals in the posterior pituitary.

3 Releasing hormones are synthesized here and secreted into capillaries that carry them to the anterior pituitary.

Hypothalamus

Capillaries

Blood in

Blood in

Axon terminals

Anterior pituitary

Posterior pituitary

Blood out

Blood out (carrying posterior pituitary hormones)

4 Releasing hormones then leave the capillaries and act on hormone-secreting anterior pituitary cells.

2 Hormones released by axon terminals in the posterior pituitary are picked up by capillaries and carried into the bloodstream.

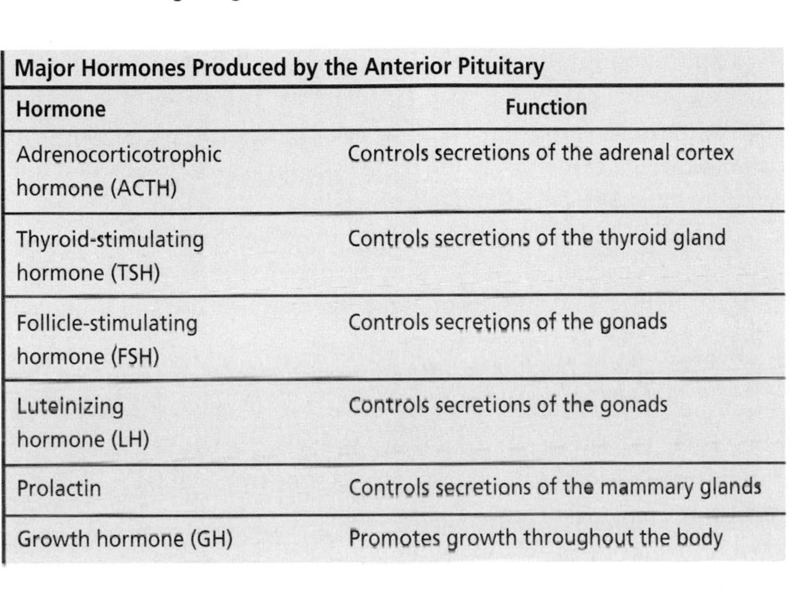

**Major Hormones Produced by the Anterior Pituitary**

| Hormone | Function |
|---|---|
| Adrenocorticotrophic hormone (ACTH) | Controls secretions of the adrenal cortex |
| Thyroid-stimulating hormone (TSH) | Controls secretions of the thyroid gland |
| Follicle-stimulating hormone (FSH) | Controls secretions of the gonads |
| Luteinizing hormone (LH) | Controls secretions of the gonads |
| Prolactin | Controls secretions of the mammary glands |
| Growth hormone (GH) | Promotes growth throughout the body |

There are three controls over hypothalamic hormone-related activity. First, as illustrated in Figure 11-12A, the hypothalamus has a feedback mechanism to maintain a fairly constant circulating level of certain hormones. For example, when the level of thyroid hormone is low, the hypothalamus releases thyroid-stimulating hormone-releasing hormone (also called TSH-releasing hormone). The TSH-releasing hormone stimulates the anterior pituitary to release thyroid-stimulating hormone, which then acts on the thyroid gland to secrete more thyroid hormone. There must, however, be some control over how much thyroid hormone is secreted, and so the hypothalamus has receptors to detect the level of thyroid hormone. When that level rises, the hypothalamus lessens its secretion of TSH-releasing hormone. This type of system, known as a **feedback mechanism,** is essentially a form of homeostatic control. The hypothalamus initiates a cascade of events that result in the secretion of hormones, but it pays attention to how much hormone is released and, when a certain level is reached, it stops its hormone-stimulating signals.

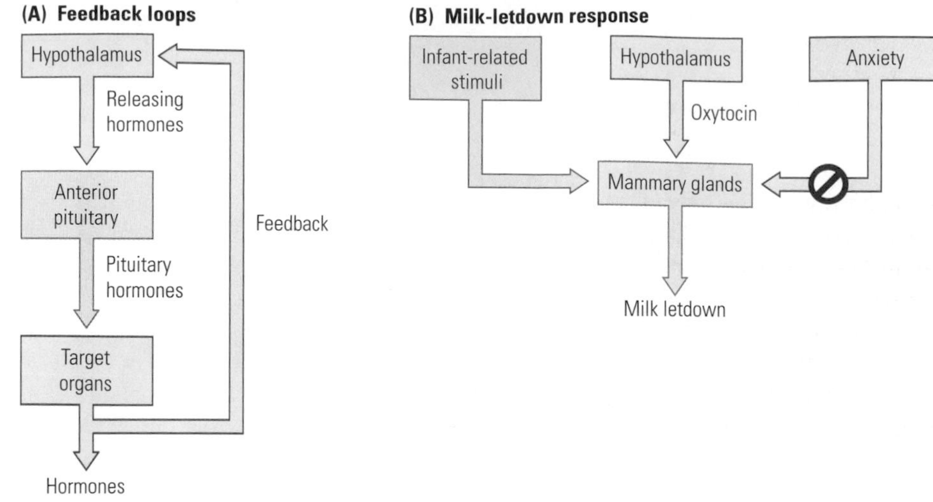


**Figure 11-12**

**(A)** The hormone-controlling feedback loops from the hypothalamus to the pituitary and its target organs. The hypothalamus releases hormones, which stimulate the anterior pituitary to release its hormones, which stimulate target organs such as the thyroid or adrenal gland to release their hormones. Those hormones act, in turn, to influence the hypothalamus to decrease its secretion of the releasing hormone. **(B)** Oxytocin stimulates the mammary glands to release milk. This release is enhanced by infant-related stimuli and inhibited by maternal anxiety.

A second type of control over hormone-related activities of the hypothalamus requires regulation by other brain structures, such as the limbic system and the frontal lobes. Figure 11-12B diagrams this type of control in relation to the effects of oxytocin released from the paraventricular nucleus of the hypothalamus. As stated earlier, one function of oxytocin is to stimulate cells of the mammary glands to release milk. As an infant suckles the breast, the tactile stimulation causes hypothalamic cells to release oxytocin, which stimulates milk letdown. In this way, the oxytocin cells participate in a fairly simple reflex that is both neural and hormonal. Other stimuli also can influence the release of oxytocin, however, and this is where control by other brain structures comes in. For example, the sight, sound, or even thought of her baby can trigger a lactating mother to eject milk. Conversely, feelings of anxiety in a lactating woman can inhibit milk ejection. These excitatory and inhibitory influences exerted by cognitive activity imply that the cortex can influence paraventricular neurons. In fact, there are projections from the frontal lobes to the hypothalamus that could perform this role.

The third way that the hormone-related activities of the hypothalamus are controlled is by the brain's responses to experience. In response to experience, neurons in the hypothalamus undergo structural and biochemical changes just as cells in other brain regions do. In other words, hypothalamic neurons are like neurons elsewhere in the brain in that they can be changed by prolonged demands placed on them. Such changes in hypothalamic neurons can affect the output of hormones. For instance, when a woman is lactating, the cells producing oxytocin increase in size in order to promote oxytocin release that meets the demands of a growing infant. Through this control, which is mediated by experience, the baby is provided with sufficient milk over time.

## HYPOTHALAMIC INVOLVEMENT IN GENERATING BEHAVIOR

So far, we have considered the role of the hypothalamus in controlling hormone systems, but equally important is its role in generating behavior. This function was first demonstrated by studies in which stimulating electrodes were placed into the hypothalami of various animals, ranging from chickens to rats and cats. When a small electric current was delivered through a wire, an animal suddenly engaged in a complex behavior, including eating and drinking, digging, and displaying fear, attack, predatory, or reproductive behavior. The particular behavior depended on which of many sites in the hypothalamus was stimulated. All of the behaviors were smooth, well integrated, and indistinguishable from normally occurring ones. Furthermore, all were goal directed.

The onset and termination of these behaviors depended entirely on the hypothalamic stimulation. For example, if an electrode in a certain location elicited feeding be-

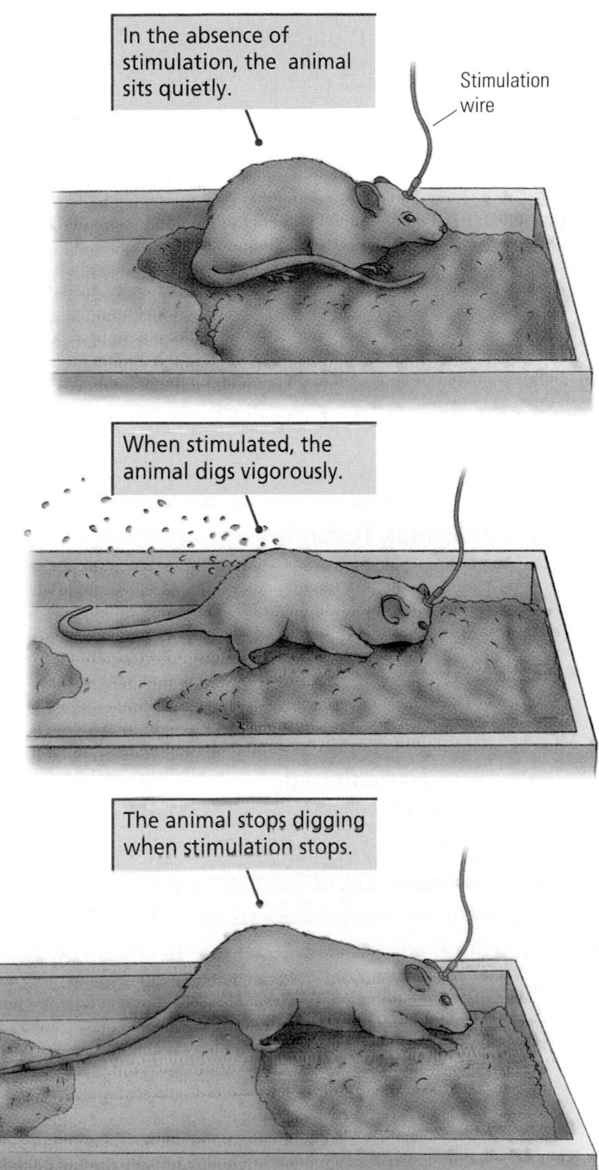
In the absence of stimulation, the animal sits quietly.
Stimulation wire
When stimulated, the animal digs vigorously.
The animal stops digging when stimulation stops.

**Figure 11-13**

When rats receive electrical stimulation of the hypothalamus, they produce goal-directed behaviors. This rat is stimulated to dig when and only when the electricity is turned on. When there is no current (*top*), the animal sits quietly. If the current is turned on (*middle*), the animal digs vigorously into the sawdust. When the current is turned off (*bottom*) or if the sawdust is removed (not shown), there is no digging.

havior, the animal would eat as soon as the stimulation was turned on and would continue to eat until the stimulation was turned off. If the food was removed, however, the animal would neither eat nor engage in other behaviors such as drinking. Figure 11-13 illustrates the effect of stimulation at a site that elicits digging. When there is no current, the animal sits quietly. When the current is turned on, the animal digs into the sawdust vigorously; when the current is turned off, the animal stops digging. If the sawdust is removed, there also is no digging.

There are two important additional characteristics of the behaviors generated by hypothalamic stimulation. First, all of these behaviors are related to the survival of the animal and the species. Second, animals apparently find the stimulation of these behaviors pleasant, as suggested by the fact that they willingly expend effort, such as pressing a bar, to trigger the stimulation. Recall that cats kill birds and mice because the act of stalking and killing prey is rewarding to them. Similarly, we can hypothesize that animals eat because eating is rewarding, drink because drinking is rewarding, mate because mating is rewarding, and so forth.

## The Role of the Limbic System

We now turn our attention to parts of the brain that interact with the hypothalamus in generating motivated behaviors. These parts, known collectively as the **limbic system,** evolved as a ring of structures around the brainstem in early amphibians and reptiles. Paul Broca was impressed by this evolutionary development and called these structures the limbic lobe (from the Latin word *limbus,* meaning "border" or "hem"). The structures of the limbic lobe are actually a primitive cortex. In mammals, they are the cortex in the cingulate gyrus and the hippocampal formation, as shown in Figure 11-14. The **hippocampal formation** includes the **hippocampus,** which is a cortical structure, and the cortex adjacent to it, which is referred to as *parahippocampal cortex.*

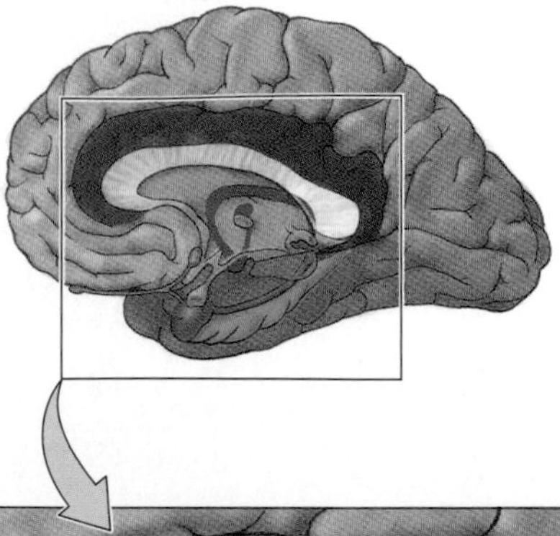

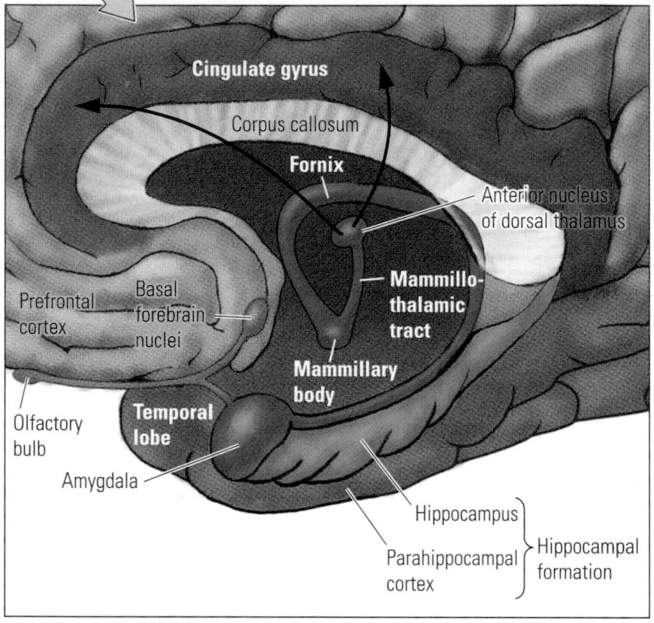

**Figure 11-14**

The limbic lobe consists of the cingulate gyrus and hippocampal formation (the hippocampus and parahippocampal cortex), the amygdala, the mammillothalamic tract, and the anterior thalamus, which can be seen to encircle the brainstem.

### THE ORGANIZATION OF THE LIMBIC CIRCUIT

As anatomists began to study the limbic lobe structures, it became evident that there are connections between these structures and the hypothalamus. It also became apparent that the limbic lobe has a role in emotion. For instance, James Papez observed that people with rabies had radical abnormalities in their emotional behavior, and postmortems of them showed that the rabies had selectively attacked the hippocampus. (The definitive proof of rabies is still a postmortem examination of the hippocampus.) On the basis of this finding, Papez concluded that the limbic lobe and associated subcortical structures provide the neural basis of emotion. He proposed a circuit, now known as the **Papez circuit,** whereby emotion could reach consciousness, presumably in the cerebral cortex. Papez's limbic circuit concept (also called the limbic system) was expanded by Paul MacLean in 1949 to include the amygdala and prefrontal cortex as well. Figure 11-14 shows that the amygdala lies adjacent to the hippocampus in the temporal lobe, with the prefrontal cortex lying just anterior. (We will consider the prefrontal cortex in more detail shortly.)

Figure 11-15B schematically illustrates the limbic circuit. The hippocampus, amygdala, and prefrontal cortex all connect with the hypothalamus. The mammillary nucleus of the hypothalamus connects to the anterior thalamus, which in turn connects with the cingulate cortex, which completes the circuit by connecting with the hippocampal formation, amygdala, and prefrontal cortex. Compare this anatomical arrangement with the funnel in Figure 11-15C, which shows the hypothalamus as the spout leading to motivated behavior.

There is now little doubt that most structures of the limbic system take part in emotional behaviors, especially the amygdala and hypothalamus, but most limbic structures have other functions, too. Structures of the limbic system are now known to play an important role in various motivated behaviors, especially feeding and sexual activity. The critical structures for such behaviors, as well as emotion, are the amygdala and the hypothalamus. Having already considered the hypothalamus, we now turn to the amygdala.

### THE AMYGDALA

The **amygdala** (from the Greek word for "almond") is shown in Figure 11-14, just anterior to the hippocampus. It consists of three principal subdivisions: the corticomedial area, the basolateral area, and the central area. Like the hypothalamus, the amygdala receives inputs from all of the sensory systems. But, in contrast with the neurons of the hypothalamus, those of the amygdala require more-complex stimuli (such

Visit the CD to see the hippocampus and the amygdala in three dimensions in the subsection on subcortical structures in the module on the Central Nervous System.

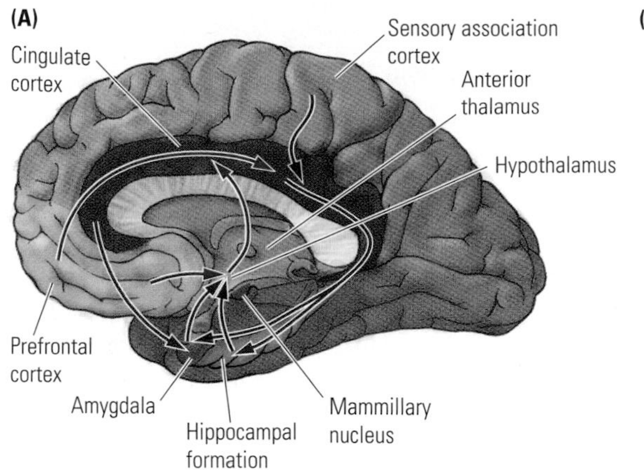


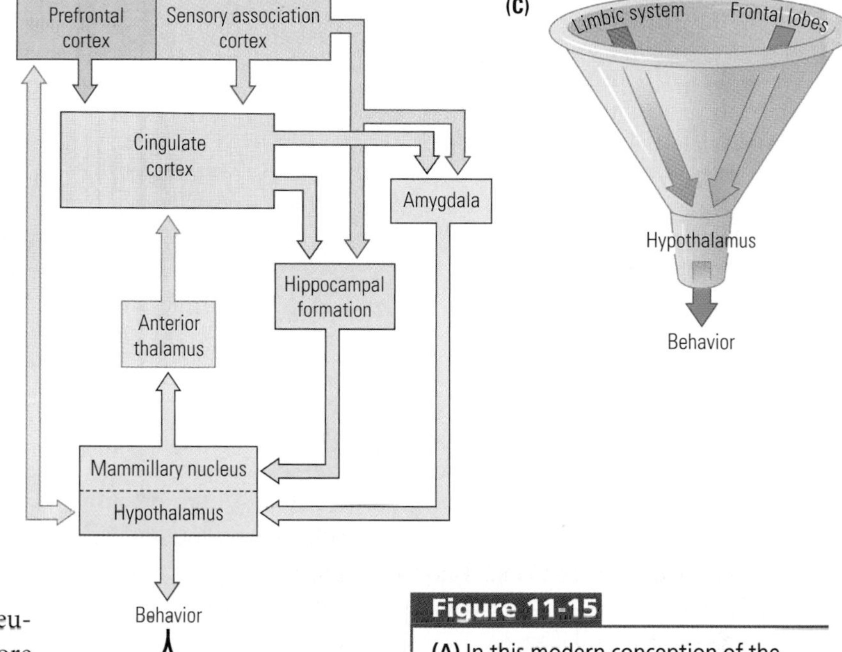


**Figure 11-15**

**(A)** In this modern conception of the limbic system, an interconnected network of structures controls emotional expression. The main structures include the cingulate cortex, the hippocampal formation (hippocampus and adjacent parahippocampal cortex), the amygdala with its extensive connections to the hypothalamus and cortex, the mammillary body of the hypothalamus, and the prefrontal cortex. **(B)** A schematic representation of the major connections of the limbic system. The prefrontal and sensory regions connect with the cingulate cortex, hippocampal formation, and amygdala. The last two structures connect with the hypothalamus, which in turn connects with the cingulate cortex through the thalamus. **(C)** A reminder that parts A and B can be conceptualized as a funnel of outputs through the hypothalamus.

as faces) to be excited. In addition, many amygdala neurons are multimodal, meaning that they respond to more than one sensory modality. In fact, some neurons in the amygdala respond to sight, sound, touch, taste, *and* smell stimuli. These cells must create a rather complex image of the sensory world.

The amygdala sends connections primarily to the hypothalamus and the brainstem, where it influences neural activity associated with emotions and species-typical behavior. For example, when the amygdalae of epileptic patients are electrically stimulated before brain surgery, the patients become fearful and anxious. We observed a woman who responded with increased respiration and heart rate, saying that she felt as if something bad was going to happen, although she could not specify what. Amygdala stimulation can also induce eating and drinking. We observed a man who drank water every time the stimulation was turned on. (There happened to be a pitcher of water on the table next to him.) Within 20 minutes, he had consumed about 2 liters of water. When asked if he was thirsty, he said "No, not really. I just feel like drinking." The amygdala's role in eating can be seen in patients with lesions in the amygdala. These patients may be much less discriminating in their food choices, eating foods that were previously unpalatable to them. Such lesions may also give rise to hypersexuality.

## The Role of the Frontal Lobes

The amygdala is also intimately connected with the functioning of the frontal lobes. These lobes constitute all of the cortical tissue in front of the central sulcus. This large area is made up of several functionally distinct cortical regions. Figure 11-16 shows that the three main regions are the motor cortex, the premotor cortex, and the prefrontal cortex. As you learned in Chapter 10, the motor cortex controls fine movements, especially of the fingers, hands, toes, feet, tongue, and face. The premotor cortex, in contrast, does not participate in the details of movements, but rather in the selection of sequences of movement that are called for. For instance, a resting dog may get up in response to its owner's call, which serves as an environmental cue for a series of movements that is processed by one region of the premotor cortex. Or a dog may get up for no apparent reason and wander about the yard, which is a sequence of actions in response to an internal cue, this time processed by a different region of the premotor cortex. Finally, the **prefrontal cortex** (which literally means "in front of the

**Prefrontal cortex.** The cortex lying in front of the motor and premotor cortex of the frontal lobe; the prefrontal cortex is particularly large in the human brain.

**Figure 11-16**

Lateral view of the gross subdivisions of the frontal lobe, including the motor, premotor, and prefrontal regions. The prefrontal region has two main areas, referred to as the dorsolateral and inferior prefrontal regions. One subregion of the inferior prefrontal cortex is the orbital cortex, which lies directly behind the eyes.

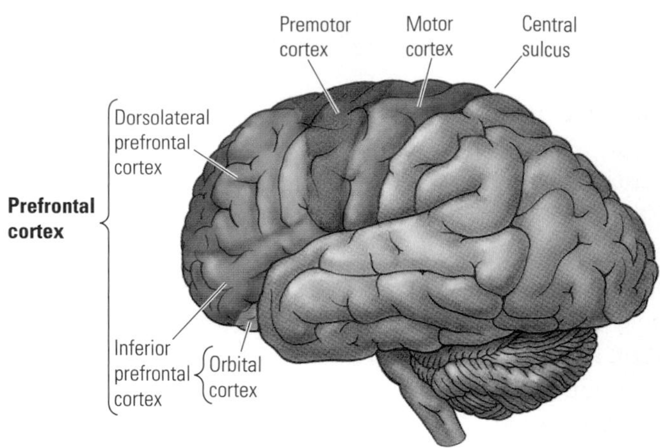


Click on the area on the Central Nervous System on your CD to see a model and sections of the frontal lobes.

front") is anterior to the premotor cortex. It is made up of two primary areas: the dorsolateral region and the inferior region. As stated in Chapter 10, the prefrontal cortex plays a role in specifying the goals toward which movement should be directed. In this role, it controls the processes by which we select movements that are appropriate for the particular time and place. This selection may be cued by internal information (such as memory and emotions) or it may be made in response to context (that is, environmental information).

Like the amygdala, the frontal lobes, and particularly the prefrontal cortex, receive highly processed information from all of the sensory areas. Many of the neurons in the prefrontal cortex are also multimodal, just like those in the amygdala. As shown in Figure 11-17, the prefrontal cortex receives connections from the amygdala, the dorsal medial thalamus, the posterior parietal (sensory association) cortex, and the dopaminergic cells of the ventral tegmental area. The dopaminergic input plays an important role in regulating how prefrontal neurons react to stimuli, including emotional ones. Abnormalities in this dopaminergic projection may account for some conditions, such as certain forms of schizophrenia, in which people have little emotional reaction to normally arousing stimuli.

Figure 11-17 also shows the areas to which the prefrontal cortex sends connections. The inferior prefrontal region projects axons to the amygdala and the hypothalamus in particular. These axons provide a route for influencing the autonomic system, which controls changes in blood pressure, respiration, and so forth. The dorsolateral prefrontal region sends its connections primarily to the posterior parietal cortex, the cingulate cortex, the basal ganglia, and the premotor cortex. These connections pro-

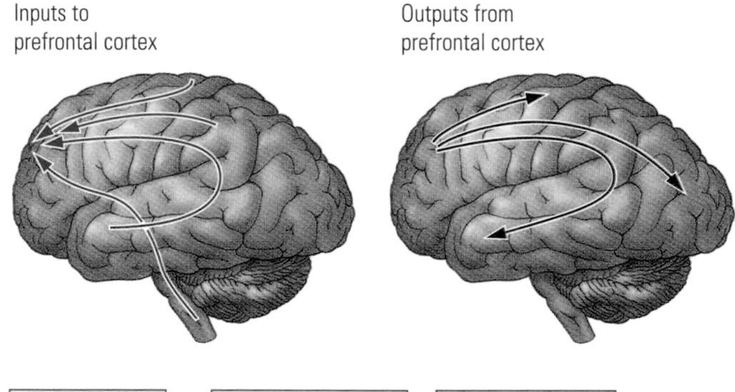


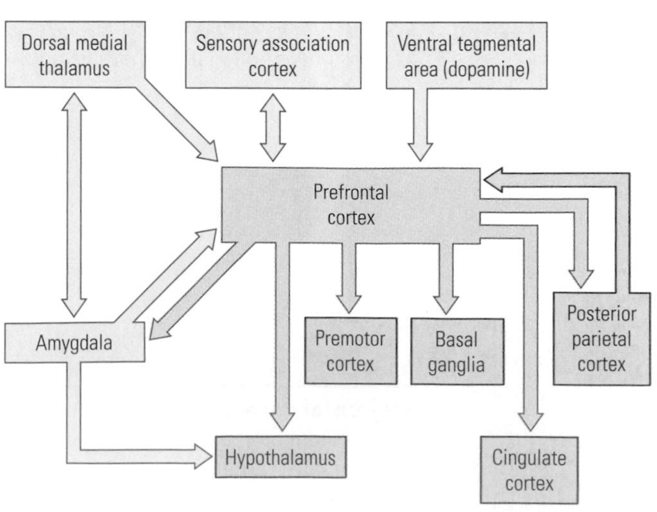


**Figure 11-17**

The prefrontal cortex receives inputs from all of the sensory systems, the amygdala, the dorsal medial thalamus, and the dopamine-rich cells of the ventral tegmentum. The prefrontal cortex sends connections to the amygdala, premotor cortex, basal ganglia, posterior parietal cortex, and hypothalamus.

vide a route for influencing movement as well as certain memory functions to be considered in Chapter 13.

As already stated, the prefrontal cortex takes part in the selection of behaviors appropriate to the particular time and place. This selection may be cued by internal information or it may be made in response to the environmental context. Disruption to this selection function can be seen in people with injury to the dorsolateral frontal lobe. They become overly dependent on environmental cues to determine their behavior. Like small children, they become totally distracted by what they see or hear. As a result, they are unable to focus on the task at hand. We have all experienced this kind of loss of concentration to some extent, but, for a frontal-lobe patient, the problem is exaggerated and persistent. Because the person becomes so absorbed in irrelevant stimuli, he or she is unable to act on internalized information most of the time.

J. C. is a good example. He had bilateral damage to the dorsolateral prefrontal cortex as a result of having a tumor removed. J. C. would lie in bed most of the day fixated on television programs. He was aware of his wife's opinion of this behavior, but only the opening of the garage door when she returned home from work in the evening would stimulate him into action. Getting out of bed was controlled by this specific environmental cue and, without it, he seemed to lack motivation. Television completely distracted him from acting on internal knowledge of what he should be doing.

Adapting behavior appropriately to the environmental context also is a function of the prefrontal cortex. Most people readily change their behavior to match the situation at hand. We behave in one way with our parents, in another with our friends, in another with our children, and in another with our coworkers. Each set of people creates a different context, and we shift our behaviors accordingly. Our tone of voice, our use of slang or profanities, and the content of our conversations are quite different in different contexts. Even among our peers, we act differently, depending on who is present. We may be relaxed in the presence of some people and be ill at ease in the presence of others. It is therefore no accident that the size of the frontal lobes is related to the sociability of a species' behavior. Social behavior is extremely rich in contextual information.

The control of behavior in context requires detailed sensory information, which is conveyed from all of the sensory regions to the frontal lobes. This sensory input includes not only information from the external world, but internal information from the autonomic nervous system as well. People with damage to the inferior prefrontal cortex, which is relatively common in closed head injuries, have difficulty adapting their behavior according to the context, especially the social context. Consequently, they are known to make social gaffes.

In summary, the role of the frontal lobes in selecting behaviors is important in considering behavioral causes. The frontal lobes act much like a composer, but, instead of selecting notes and instruments, they select our actions. Not surprisingly, the frontal lobes are sometimes described as housing **executive functions,** a concept that we will return to in Chapter 14 in considering the frontal lobe's role in planning.

## In Review

The hypothalamus, the limbic system, and the frontal lobes house the circuitry for controlling motivated behaviors. The hypothalamus provides the simplest control, which is largely homeostatic. The limbic system creates emotion, whereas the frontal lobes generate behavior at the right time and place, taking factors such as external events and internal information into account. We now turn to examples of how these circuits interact to control representative regulatory and nonregulatory behaviors.

## THE CONTROL OF A REGULATORY BEHAVIOR: FEEDING

Feeding includes behaviors that are central to our existence. An obvious reason is that we must eat and drink to live. But there is more to feeding behavior than sustenance alone. We also derive great pleasure from eating and drinking. In fact, for many people, these behaviors are a focus of daily life, around which they schedule their social activities, such as business meetings and get-togethers with family and friends. In this section, we focus mainly on the control of eating in humans, but we also consider how our intake of fluids is controlled.

### Controlling Eating

Link to the Web site at **www.worthpublishers.com/kolb/chapter11** to learn more about eating disorders.

For many people, control over eating is a source of much frustration and grief. An estimated 50 percent of the North American population is overweight, with 30 to 40 percent being sufficiently obese for their weight to constitute a medical problem. About half of the population has dieted at some point in their lives, and, at any given time, at least 25 percent report that they are currently on a diet. In a culture that is so obsessed with slimness, there are also eating disorders. An example is **anorexia nervosa,** a disorder in which people (especially adolescent girls) intentionally starve themselves to become exceedingly thin.

The control of feeding in humans is not as simple as it is in flies. The human control system for feeding has multiple inputs. These inputs come from three major sources: the digestive system, the hypothalamus, and cognitive factors, such as thoughts about food. We begin our consideration of feeding by looking at controls related to the digestive system.

#### THE DIGESTIVE SYSTEM AND THE CONTROL OF EATING

The digestive system, illustrated in Figure 11-18, begins with the mouth and ends with the anus. Food travels from the oral cavity to the stomach through the esophagus. The stomach, which is a storage reservoir, secretes both hydrochloric acid, which starts to break food into small particles, and pepsin, which breaks down proteins into amino acids. The partly broken down food then moves to the upper part of the intestine through the duodenum, where digestive enzymes produced in the gall bladder and pancreas further break down the food to allow the absorption of amino acids and simple sugars into the bloodstream. Most of the remaining water and electrolytes in food are absorbed by the large intestine, and the waste passes out of the body through the anus.

The digestive system produces three types of compounds for the body: lipids (fats), amino acids (the building blocks of proteins), and glucose (sugar). Each is a specialized form of energy reserve. Because we require varying amounts of these reserves, depending on what we are doing, the body has detector cells to keep track of the level of each in the bloodstream.

Glucose is the body's primary form of energy and is virtually the only energy source for the brain. Because the brain requires glucose even when the digestive tract is empty, the liver acts as a short-term reservoir of sugar, which is stored there as glycogen. When blood-sugar

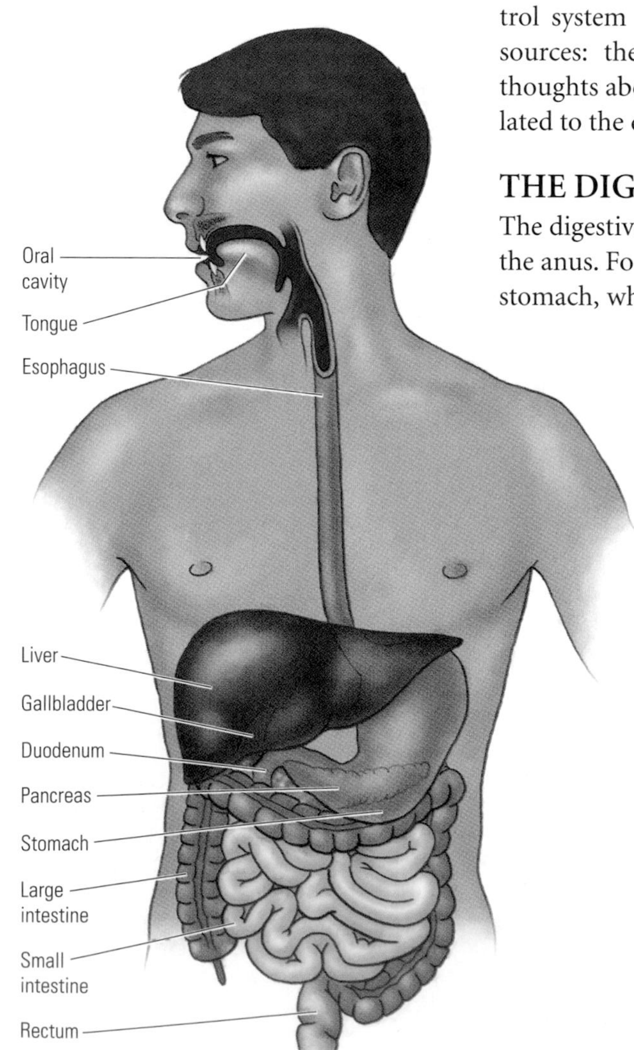


**Figure 11-18**
The digestive system.

levels fall, such as when we are sleeping, detector cells tell the liver to release glucose.

Thus the digestive system functions mainly to break down food, and the body needs to be apprised of how well this breakdown is proceeding. Feedback mechanisms provide such information. When food reaches the intestines, it interacts with receptors there to trigger the release of at least 10 different peptides, including one known as **cholecystokinin** (CCK). The released peptides inform the brain (and perhaps other organs in the digestive system) about the nature and quality of the food in the gastrointestinal tract. The level of CCK appears to play a role in satiety, or the feeling of having eaten enough. For example, if CCK is infused into the hypothalamus of an animal, the animal's appetite diminishes.

## THE HYPOTHALAMUS AND THE CONTROL OF EATING

Feeding behavior is influenced by hormones including insulin, growth hormone, and sex steroids. These hormones act to stimulate and inhibit feeding, and they aid in the conversion of nutrients into fat and the conversion of fat into glucose. Not surprisingly, the hypothalamus, which controls hormone systems, is the key brain structure in feeding. Investigation into the role of the hypothalamus in the control of feeding began in the early 1950s, when researchers discovered that damage to the **lateral hypothalamus** in rats caused the animals to stop eating, a symptom known as **aphagia.** In contrast, damage to another region of the hypothalamus, the **ventromedial hypothalamus** (VMH), caused the animals to overeat, a symptom known as **hyperphagia.** A VMH-lesioned rat that overate to the point of obesity is shown in Figure 11-19. At about the same time, researchers also found that electrical stimulation of the lateral hypothalamus elicited feeding, whereas stimulation of the ventromedial hypothalamus inhibited feeding. The opposing effects of injury and stimulation to these two hypothalamic regions led to the idea that the lateral hypothalamus signals "eating on," whereas the ventromedial hypothalamus signals "eating off."

This model quickly proved to be too simple, however. The lateral hypothalamus contains not only cell bodies but also fiber bundles passing through it, and damage to either can produce aphagia. Similarly, damage to fibers passing through the ventromedial hypothalamus often causes injury as well to the paraventricular nucleus of the hypothalamus. And damage to the paraventricular nucleus alone is now known to produce hyperphagia. Clearly, then, there is more to the hypothalamus's role in the control of feeding than the activities of the lateral and ventromedial hypothalamus alone.

In the 50 years since the first studies on the hypothalamus's role in feeding, researchers have learned that damage to the lateral and ventromedial hypothalamus and to the paraventricular nucleus has multiple effects. These effects include changes in hormone levels (especially that of insulin), in sensory reactivity (the taste and attractiveness of food is altered), in glucose and lipid levels in the blood, and in metabolic rate. The general role of the hypothalamus is to act as a sensor for the levels of lipids, glucose, hormones, and various peptides. For example, there are hypothalamic neurons that sense the level of glucose (so-called glucostatic neurons) as well as

**EXPERIMENT**

**Question:** Does the hypothalamus play a role in eating?

**Procedure**

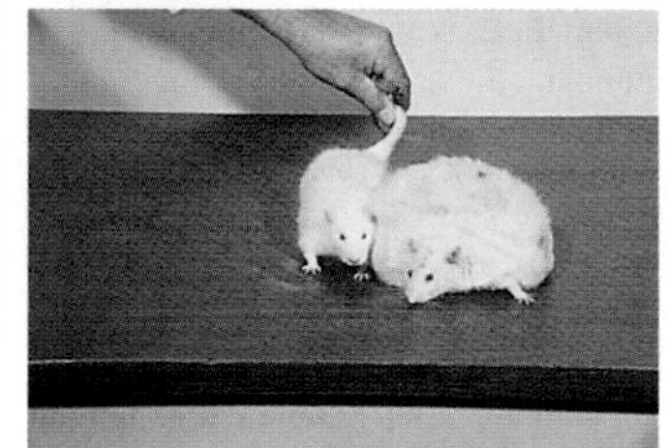

The ventromedial hypothalamus (VMH) of the rat on the right was damaged and her body weight was monitored for a year. Her sister on the left is normal.

**Results:** Lesioned rat brain — Brain of sister of lesioned rat

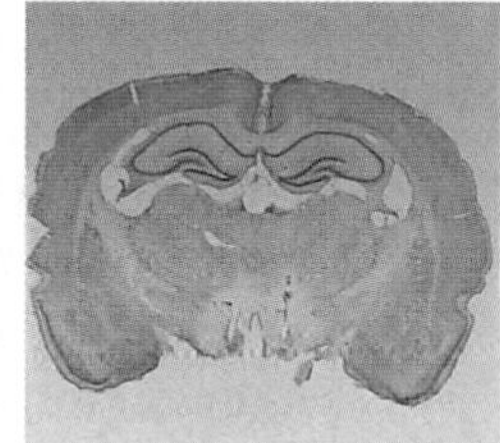

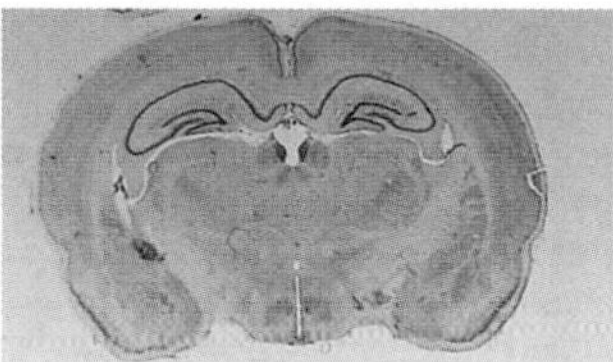

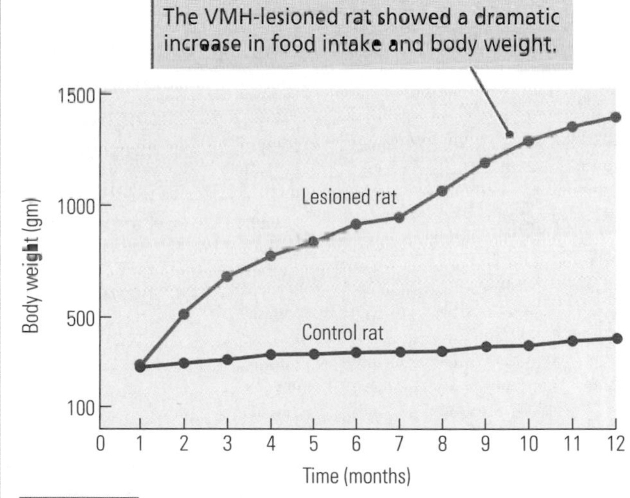


**Conclusion**

**The VMH plays a role in controlling the cessation of eating. Damage to the VMH results in prolonged and dramatic weight gain.**

**Figure 11-19**

A rat that received a VMH lesion became hyperphagic and consequently obese. The VMH rat weighs more than a kilogram, whereas her sister weighs 340 grams.

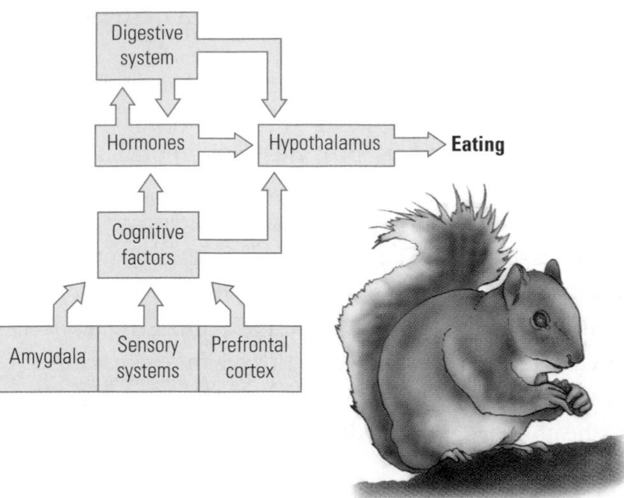


**Figure 11-20** A simple model of the control of feeding behavior.

hypothalamic neurons that sense the level of lipids (so-called lipostatic neurons). The sum of the activity of all such hypothalamic neurons creates a very complex homeostat controlling feeding. Figure 11-20 shows that this homeostat receives inputs from three sources: from the digestive system (such as information about blood-glucose levels), from hormone systems (such as information about the level of CCK), and from parts of the brain that process cognitive factors. We turn to these cognitive factors next.

### COGNITIVE FACTORS AND THE CONTROL OF EATING

Cognitive factors are especially important for the control of eating in humans. For example, just thinking about a favorite food is often enough to make us feel hungry. The cognitive aspect to feeding includes not only the images of food that we pull from memory, but also external sensory information, especially food-related sights and smells. In addition, there are facts that we learn that are related to feeding, such as learned taste aversions, discussed earlier.

The neural control of cognitive factors probably originates in multiple brain regions. Two structures are clearly important: the amygdala and the inferior prefrontal cortex. Damage to the amygdala alters food preferences and abolishes taste-aversion learning. These effects are probably related to the amygdala's efferent connections to the hypothalamus. The role of the inferior prefrontal cortex is more difficult to pin down, but rats and monkeys with damage to the orbital cortex lose weight, in part because they eat less. In our experience, humans with orbital injuries are invariably slim, but we know of no formal studies on their eating habits. The inferior prefrontal cortex receives projections from the olfactory bulb, and cells in this region do respond to smells. Because odors influence the taste of foods, it seems likely that damage to the inferior prefrontal cortex decreases eating because of diminished responses to food odor and perhaps to taste.

An additional cognitive factor in the control of eating is the pleasure that we derive from this activity, especially from eating foods with certain tastes, such as chocolate. What pleasure is and how the brain produces it are topics discussed at the end of this chapter in the context of reward. At this point, simply keep in mind that pleasure and its absence are cognitive factors in the control of eating.

## Controlling Drinking

About 70 percent of the human body is composed of water. This water contains a range of chemicals that are used in the hundreds of chemical reactions in bodily functions. The body has mechanisms to control water levels (and hence chemical concentrations) within rather narrow limits. These mechanisms are essential because the rate of a chemical reaction is partly determined by how concentrated the supplies of participating chemicals are.

As with eating, we drink for many reasons. Some beverages (such as coffee, wine, beer, and soda) we consume as part of social activities or just because they taste good. Sometimes we drink water to help wash down a meal or to intensify the flavor of dry foods. On a hot day, we drink water because we are thirsty, presumably because we have lost significant moisture through sweating and evaporation.

Although we think of thirst as a single phenomenon, there are actually two kinds of thirst. One type, called **osmotic thirst,** results from an increase in the concentrations of chemicals, known as solutes, in the body fluids. The other type, called **hypovolemic thirst,** results from a loss of overall fluid volume. Here we consider each kind of thirst briefly.

## OSMOTIC THIRST

The solutes found inside and outside cells in the body have an ideal concentration for the body's chemical reactions. This concentration requires a kind of homeostat, much like the one for body temperature. Deviations from the ideal solute concentration activate systems to reestablish that concentration. Consider what happens when we eat salty foods, such as potato chips. The salt (NaCl) spreads through the blood and enters the extracellular fluid that fills the spaces between our cells. This produces a shift away from the ideal solute concentration. Receptors in the hypothalamus along the third ventricle detect the altered solute concentration and relay this message to various hypothalamic areas that, in turn, stimulate us to drink in response to osmotic thirst. In addition, other messages are sent to the kidneys to reduce water excretion.

## HYPOVOLEMIC THIRST

Unlike osmotic thirst, hypovolemic thirst arises when the total volume of body fluids declines, motivating us to drink more and replenish their supplies. In contrast with osmotic thirst, however, hypovolemic thirst encourages us to drink something other than pure water, because pure water would dilute the solute concentration in the blood. Rather, we prefer to drink beverages that contain salts. Hypovolemic thirst and its satiation are controlled by a hypothalamic circuit other than the one that controls osmotic thirst. When fluid volume drops, the kidneys send a hormone signal (angiotensin) that stimulates midline hypothalamic neurons. These neurons, in turn, stimulate drinking.

### In Review

The hypothalamus is the principal brain structure in the control of eating. Three of its regions—the lateral hypothalamus, the ventromedial hypothalamus, and the paraventricular nucleus—play especially important roles. Neurons of the hypothalamus act as sensors to detect the levels of glucose, lipids, and peptides in the blood. Neural control of the cognitive factors in eating probably includes multiple brain regions. The brain also motivates us to drink whenever solutes in the blood deviate from ideal levels or whenever there is a significant drop in the body's volume of fluids. In either case, receptors detect the shifts, and neurons in the hypothalamus stimulate the experience of thirst.

# THE CONTROL OF A NONREGULATORY BEHAVIOR: SEXUAL ACTIVITY

Unlike feeding, which we must repeatedly do to survive, sexual behavior (aside from procreation) is not essential for survival. Yet sexual activity is of enormous psychological importance to us. Sexual themes repeatedly appear in our art, literature, and films. They also bombard us in the advertising that we create to help sell products. Indeed, in Sigmund Freud's psychodynamic theory of human behavior, sexual drives were central. Such significance makes it all the more important to understand how human sexual behavior is controlled. The answer lies in both gonadal hormones and brain circuits.

## The Effects of Sex Hormones on the Brain

In Chapter 7, we encountered the influence of gonadal hormones on the brain when we considered how a male's Y chromosome controls the differentiation of embryonic gonad tissue into testes, which in turn secrete testosterone. The testosterone masculinizes both the sex organs and the brain during development. This process is referred to as an **organizing effect** of gonadal hormones. A major organizing effect that gonadal hormones have on the brain is in the hypothalamus, especially the preoptic area of the medial hypothalamus. But there are also organizing effects in other nervous system regions, notably the amygdala, the prefrontal cortex, and the spinal cord.

The creation of these sex-related differences in the nervous system makes sense behaviorally. After all, animal courtship rituals differ between the sexes, as do copulatory behaviors, with females engaging in sexually receptive responses and males in mounting ones. The production of these sex differences in behaviors depends on the action of gonadal hormones on the brain both during development and during adulthood. The actions of hormones on the adult brain are referred to as **activating effects,** in contrast with the developmental organizing effects. Here we consider organizing and activating effects separately.

### THE ORGANIZING EFFECTS OF HORMONES

During fetal development, a male's testes produce male hormones, which, as you know, are called androgens. In the developing rat (the species in which the organizing effects of gonadal hormones have been most extensively studied), androgens are produced during the last week of fetal development and the first week after birth. The androgens produced at this time greatly alter both neural structures and later behavior. For example, the hypothalamus and prefrontal cortex of a male rat differ structurally both from those of female rats and from those of males that were not exposed to androgens during their development. Furthermore, in adulthood, males with little exposure to the androgen testosterone during development behave like genetic female rats. If given estrogen and progesterone, they become sexually "receptive" and display typical female behaviors when mounted by males. Male rats that are castrated in adulthood do not act in this way.

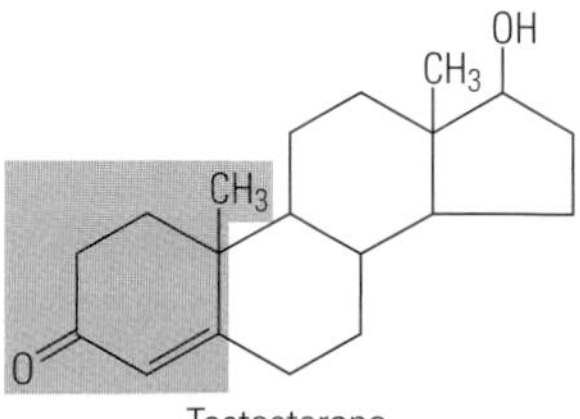

Testosterone

Estradiol

Differential development of brain areas in the two sexes, referred to as **sexual dimorphism,** arises from a complex series of steps. Cells in the brain produce aromatase, an enzyme that converts testosterone into estradiol, which is one of the female sex hormones called estrogens. Therefore a female hormone, estradiol, actually masculinizes a male brain. Females are not masculinized by the presence of estrogens in their bodies, because the fetuses of both sexes produce a liver enzyme *(alpha fetoprotein)* that binds to estrogen, rendering it incapable of entering neurons. Testosterone is unaffected by alpha fetoprotein, so it enters neurons and is converted into estradiol.

The organizing effects of testosterone are clearly illustrated in the preoptic area of the hypothalamus, which plays a critical role in the copulatory behavior of male rats. Comparing this area in males and females, Roger Gorski and his colleagues found a nucleus there that was about five times larger in the males (Gorski, 1984). Significantly, the sexual dimorphism of the preoptic area can be altered by manipulating gonadal hormones during development. Castration of males at birth leads to a smaller preoptic area, whereas treating infant females with testosterone increases the preoptic area's size.

**Sexual dimorphism.** The process whereby gonadal hormones act on the brain to produce a distinctly female or male brain.

The organizing effects of gonadal hormones are more difficult to study in humans. The work of John Money and Anke Ehrhardt (1972), however, revealed an important role of these hormones in human development (see "Androgen Insensitivity Syndrome and the Androgenital Syndrome" on page 428).

## THE ACTIVATING EFFECTS OF HORMONES

The sexual behavior of both males and females also depends on the actions that gonadal hormones have on the *adult* brain. In most vertebrate species, female sexual behavior varies in the course of an estrous cycle in which the levels of hormones that the ovaries produce fluctuate. The rat's estrous cycle is about 4 days long, with sexual receptivity being only in the few hours during which the production of the ovarian hormones estrogen and progesterone peaks. These ovarian hormones alter brain activity, which in turn alters behavior. Furthermore, in females, various chemicals are released after mating, and these chemicals inhibit further mating behavior.

The **activating effect** of ovarian hormones can be seen clearly in cells of the hippocampus. Figure 11-21 compares hippocampal pyramidal neurons taken from a female rat at two points in her estrous cycle: one when estrogen levels are high and the other when they are low. When estrogen levels are high, there are more dendritic spines and, presumably, more synapses. These neural differences during the estrous cycle are all the more remarkable when we consider that cells in the female hippocampus are continually changing their connections to other cells every 4 days throughout the animal's adulthood.

In males, testosterone activates sexual behavior in two distinctly different ways. First, the actions of testosterone on the amygdala are related to the motivation to seek sexual activity. Second, the actions of testosterone on the hypothalamus are needed to produce copulatory behavior. In the next section, we look at both these processes.

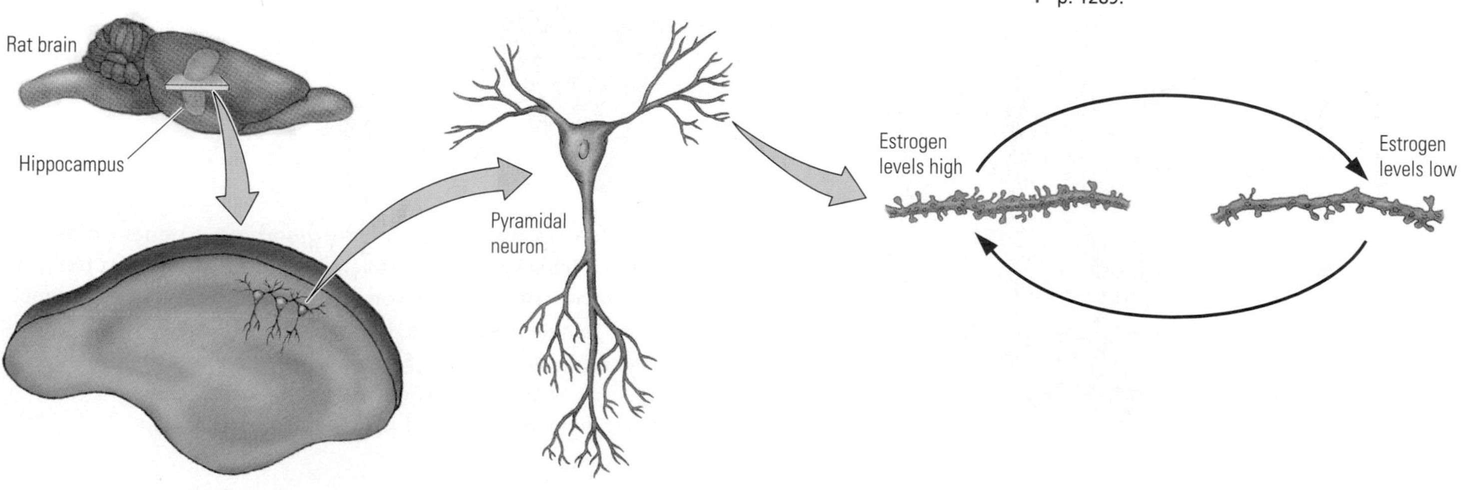


**Figure 11-21**

Dendrites of hippocampal pyramidal neurons at high and low levels of estrogen in the rat's (4-day) estrous cycle. There are many fewer dendritic spines during the low period.

Adapted from "Naturally Occurring Fluctuation in Dendritic Spine Density on Adult Hippocampal Pyramidal Neurons," by C. S. Woolley, E. Gould, M. Frankfurt, and B. McEwen, 1990, *Journal of Neuroscience, 10,* p. 1289.

Focus on Disorders

## Androgen Insensitivity Syndrome and the Androgenital Syndrome

After the testes of a male fetus have formed, sexual development depends on the actions of testicular hormones. This dependence is made extremely clear by studying people with *androgen insensitivity syndrome.* In this syndrome, an XY (male) fetus produces androgens, but the body is not able to respond to them. Such a genetic male therefore develops a female appearance, or phenotype, as shown in the photograph below. Because their estrogen receptors are not affected by the syndrome, these people are still responsive to estrogen produced both by the adrenal gland and by the testes. As a result, they develop female secondary sexual characteristics during puberty, even without additional hormone treatment. A person with androgen insensitivity syndrome is therefore a genetic male who appears to be female.

If there is no Y chromosome to induce the growth of testes, a fetus develops ovaries and becomes a female. In some cases, however, the female fetus is exposed to androgens, producing a syndrome known both as *congenital adrenal hyperplasia* and as the *androgenital syndrome.* This exposure to androgens can occur if the adrenal glands of either the mother or the infant produce an excessive amount of these hormones. The effects vary, depending on when the androgens are produced and how much exposure there is. In extreme cases, an enlarged clitoris develops that can be mistaken for a small penis. In less severe cases, there is no gross abnormality in genital structure, but there is a behavioral effect: these girls show a high degree of tomboyishness. In early childhood, they identify with boys and prefer boys' clothes and boys' toys and games. One explanation for this behavioral effect is that the developing brain is masculinized, thus changing later behavior.

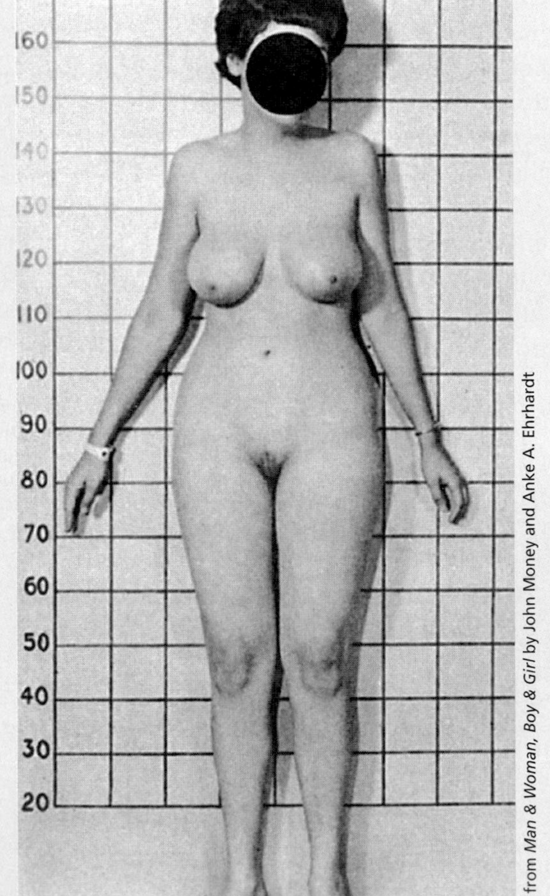


Reprinted from *Man & Woman, Boy & Girl* by John Money and Anke A. Ehrhardt

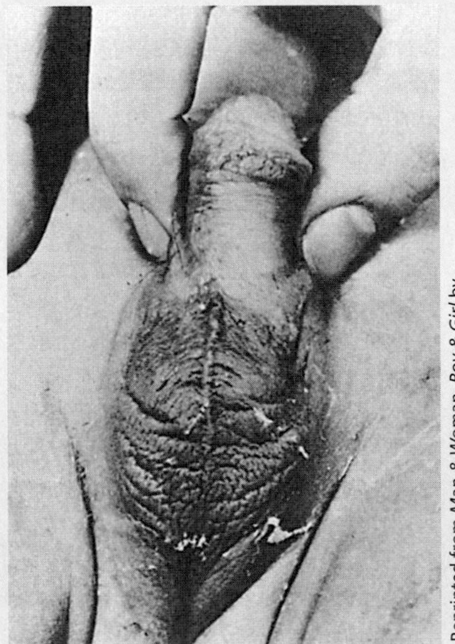

Reprinted from *Man & Woman, Boy & Girl* by John Money and Anke A. Ehrhardt

(*Left*) In androgen insensitivity syndrome, a genetic male (XY) is insensitive to gonadally produced androgens but remains sensitive to estrogens, leading to the development of a female phenotype. (*Right*) In congenital adrenal hyperplasia, a genetic female (XX) is exposed to adrenal gland-produced androgens embryonically, leading to the partial development of male external genitalia.

## The Hypothalamus and the Amygdala in Sexual Behavior

The hypothalamus is the critical structure controlling copulatory behaviors in both males and females. The ventromedial hypothalamus controls the female mating posture, which in quadrapedal animals is called **lordosis** and consists of an arching of the back and an elevation of the rump while the animal otherwise remains quite still. Damage to the ventromedial hypothalamus abolishes lordosis. The role of the VMH is probably twofold: it controls the neural circuit that produces lordosis, and it influences hormonal changes in the female during coitus.

In males, the neural control of sexual behavior is somewhat more complex. The medial preoptic area, which is larger in males than in females, controls copulation. Damage to the medial preoptic area greatly disrupts mating performance, whereas electrical stimulation of this area activates mating, provided that testosterone is circulating in the bloodstream. Curiously, however, although destruction of the medial preoptic area stops males from mating, they continue to show interest in receptive females. For instance, monkeys with lesions in the medial preoptic area will not mate with receptive females, but they will masturbate while watching them from across the room.

Barry Everitt (1990) studied this phenomenon in an ingenious way. He designed an apparatus, shown in Figure 11-22, that allowed male rats to press a bar to deliver receptive females. After males were trained in the use of this apparatus, lesions were made in their medial preoptic areas. Immediately, their sexual behavior changed. They would still press the bar to obtain access to females, but they would no longer mate with them. Apparently, the medial preoptic area controls mating, but it does not control sexual motivation. The brain structure controlling sexual motivation appears to be the amygdala. When Everitt trained male rats in his apparatus and then made lesions in their amygdalae, they would no longer press the bar to gain access to receptive females, but they would mate with receptive females that were provided to them.

Courtesy of Barry J. Everitt

**Figure 11-22**

In an experiment to study sexual motivation and mating, a male rat is required to press the bar 10 times to gain access to a receptive female who "drops in" through a trap door. The copulatory behavior of the male rat illustrates mating behavior, whereas the bar-pressing for access to a female rat illustrates sexual motivation.

Adapted from "Sexual Motivation: A Neural and Behavioral Analysis of the Mechanisms Underlying Appetitive and Copulatory Responses of Male Rats," by B. J. Everitt, 1990, *Neuroscience and Biobehavioral Reviews, 14,* p. 227.

In summary, the hypothalamus controls copulatory behavior in both males and females. In males, the amygdala influences sexual motivation, and it may do the same among females of species in which sexual activity is not tied to fluctuations in ovarian hormones, which includes the human species. In other words, it is likely that the amygdala plays a key role in sexual motivation for human females as well as males.

## Sexual Orientation, Sexual Identity, and Brain Organization

An interesting question about human sexual behavior has to do with sexual orientation—a person's sexual attraction to the opposite sex or to the same sex. Is there a neural basis for sexual orientation? Although research to answer this question has been limited in scope, it now appears that differences in the structure of the hypothalamus may form a basis not only for sexual orientation, but also for a person's sexual identity—the feeling that one is either male or female.

Like rats, humans have sex-related differences in the structure of the hypothalamus. According to Dick Swaab and his colleagues (Swaab & Hofman, 1995), the preoptic area of male humans can have twice as many neurons as does that of females, and a region known as the bed nucleus of the stria terminalis is 2.5 times as large in males. Similarly, a hypothalamic region known as INAH3 is two times as large in males, and a region known as the suprachiasmatic nucleus (SCN) contains twice as many cells in males as in females.

One hypothesis regarding homosexual men is that they should have a hypothalamus that is more similar to the norm for females than for males. This hypothesis turns out to be incorrect, however. First, there is no difference in the size of the preoptic area of heterosexual and homosexual men. Second, the SCN is twice as large in homosexual men as in heterosexual men. Some evidence suggests a role of the SCN in sexual behavior in both male and female rats, and there is strong evidence that manipulating gonadal hormones alters the structure of the SCN. In contrast with the larger SCN in homosexual men, the INAH3 is twice as large in the heterosexual brain as in the homosexual brain. These findings suggest that homosexual men form, in effect, a "third sex" because their hypothalami differ from those of either females or heterosexual males (Swaab & Hofman, 1995).

In contrast with homosexuals, transsexuals are people who feel strongly that they have been born the wrong sex. Their desire to be the opposite sex can be so strong that they are willing to undergo sex-change surgery. Little is known about the causes of transsexuality, but it is generally assumed to result from a disturbed interaction between brain development and circulating hormones. Swaab and Hofman (1995) found that the bed nucleus of the stria terminalis was female sized in a small group of five male-to-female transsexuals. This finding suggests the possibility of a biological basis for transsexuality. We must, however, be wary of drawing cause-and-effect conclusions, especially in such a small sample of people.

If differences in brain organization do exist in people with nontraditional sexual orientations and sex identities, what might give rise to these brain differences? Dean Hamer and his colleagues (1993) studied the incidence of homosexuality in the families of 114 homosexual men. There was a higher-than-average incidence of male homosexuality on the maternal side of the men's families but not on the paternal side. This maternal–paternal difference is most easily explained if a gene on the mother's X chromosome is implicated. Further investigation revealed that a large percentage of homosexual brothers had in common one small area at the tip of the X chromosome (known as area Xq28). This finding suggests that at least one subtype of male sexual orientation may be genetically influenced.

We must be cautious in drawing this conclusion, however. William Byne (1994) argued that, even if certain configurations of genes and neurotransmitters are found to be correlated with homosexuality, these correlations do not mean that these configurations cause the homosexual orientation. After all, genes specify proteins, not sexual behavior. Conceivably, particular sequences of DNA might cause the brain to be wired in ways that lead to a particular sexual orientation. But it is equally possible that these genes could influence the development of certain personality traits that in turn influence the way in which social experiences contribute to learning a certain sexual orientation. Clearly, establishing the cause-and-effect connections is not an easy task.

## Cognitive Influences on Sexual Behavior

People think about "sex." People dream about "sex." People make plans about "sex." These behaviors may include activity in the amygdala or the hypothalamus, but they must certainly also include the cortex. This is not to say that the cortex is essential for sexual motivation and copulation. In studies of rats whose entire cortices have been removed, both males and females still engage in sexual activity, although the males are somewhat clumsy. Nevertheless, the cortex must play a role in certain aspects of sexual behavior. For instance, imagery about sexual activity must include activity in the ventral visual pathway of the cortex. And thinking about and planning for sexual activity must require the participation of the frontal lobes.

As you might expect, these aspects of sexual behavior are not easily studied in rats, and they remain uncharted waters in humans. However, changes in the sexual behavior of people with frontal-lobe injury are well documented. An example is J. P.'s case, described in "Agenesis of the Frontal Lobes—J. P.'s Case" on page 432. Although J. P. displayed a loss of inhibition about sexual behavior, frontal-lobe damage is just as likely to produce a loss of sexual interest (libido). The wife of a man who, 5 years earlier, had had a small tumor removed from the medial frontal region complained that she and her husband had since had no sexual contact whatsoever. He was simply not interested, even though they were both still in their 20s. The husband said that he no longer had sexual fantasies or sexual dreams and, although he still loved his wife, he did not have any sexual urges toward her or anyone else. Cases like these clearly indicate that the human cortex has an important role in controlling sexual behaviors, even though the exact nature of that role is still poorly understood.

### In Review

Sexual behavior is controlled by a combination of gonadal hormones, the neurons of the hypothalamus and limbic system, and cognitive factors. The hypothalamus controls the details of copulation in both males and females, whereas the motivation for sexual behavior is controlled by the amygdala. In contrast with feeding behavior, the neural control of sexual behavior is affected by the organizational actions of hormones during development. These hormones influence the size of subregions and the structure of cells in the hypothalamus, as well as in the cerebral hemispheres. These anatomical differences presumably account for some of the differences in sexual behavior between males and females and between individual persons.

Focus on Disorders

## Agenesis of the Frontal Lobes—J. P.'s Case

The role of the frontal lobes in behavior is perhaps best understood by looking at J. P.'s case, described in detail by Stafford Ackerly (1964). J. P., who was born in December 1912, was a problem from early childhood. For instance, as a child, he developed the habit of wandering. Policemen would find him miles from home, as he had no fear of being lost. Severe whippings by his father did not deter him. J. P.'s behavioral problems continued as he grew older, and, by adolescence, he was constantly in trouble. Yet J. P. also had a good side. When he started school, his first-grade teacher was so impressed with his polite manners that she began writing a letter to his parents to compliment them on having such a well-mannered child who was such a good influence in the class. As she composed the letter, she looked up to find J. P. exposing himself to the class and masturbating. This contradiction of polite manners and odd behavior characterized J. P.'s conduct throughout his life. At one moment, he was charming and, at the next, he was engaged in socially unacceptable behavior. He developed no close friendships with people of either sex, in large part because of his repeated incidents of public masturbation, stealing, excessive boastfulness, and wandering. He was a person of normal intelligence who seemed unaffected by the consequences of his behavior. The police officers, teachers, and neighbors felt that he was willfully behaving in an asocial manner and blamed his parents for not enforcing strict enough discipline. Perhaps as a result, it was not until he was 19 years old that J. P.'s true condition was detected.

To prevent J. P. from serving a prison term for repeated automobile theft, a lawyer suggested that J. P. undergo psychiatric evaluation. When he was examined by a psychiatrist, who ordered a brain scan, J. P. was found to lack a right frontal lobe; his left frontal lobe was about 50 percent of normal size. It is almost certain that he simply never developed frontal lobes. The failure of a structure to develop is known as *agenesis;* J. P. had agenesis of the frontal lobes. His case offers an unusual opportunity to study the role of the frontal lobes in the motivation of behavior.

Clearly, J. P. lacked the "bag of mental tricks" that most people use to come to terms with the world. Normally, behavior is affected both by its past consequences and by current environmental input. J. P. did not seem to be influenced much by either of these factors. As a result, the world was simply too much for him. He always acted childlike and was unable to formulate plans for the future or to inhibit many of his behaviors. He acted on impulse. At home, he was prone to aggressive outbursts about small matters, especially with regard to his mother. Curiously, he seemed completely unaware of his life situation. Even though the rest of his brain was working fairly well (his IQ was normal and his language skills were very good), the functional parts of his brain were unable to compensate for the absence of the frontal lobes.

## EMOTION

Why we behave in a certain way is clearly influenced by our subjective feelings about things, events, and people. We call these subjective feelings emotions and can readily list examples of them—anger, fear, sadness, jealousy, embarrassment, joy. Even though we all know what emotions are, the concept of emotion is difficult to define because emotion is not tangible; rather it is an inferred state. It is easier to identify how emotions are expressed than to say exactly what emotions are. The expression of emotions includes physiological changes, such as changes in heart rate, blood pressure, and hormone secretions. It also includes certain motor responses, especially movements of the facial muscles to produce facial expression.

The importance of emotion to our everyday lives cannot be underestimated. Emotion is the inspiration for artistic expression ranging from poetry to filmmaking to painting. Indeed, one reason that many people enjoy the arts is that they evoke emotions. We can therefore conclude that people find certain emotions pleasant. On the other hand, severe and prolonged negative emotions, especially anxiety and depression, can cause psychiatric disorders. Because so much of human life revolves around emotions, an understanding of them is central to understanding our humanness.

To explore the neural control of emotions, we must first specify the types of behavior that we want to explain. Think of any significant emotional experience that you have had. Perhaps you had a serious disagreement with a close friend or endured a harrowing escape from danger. A common characteristic of such experiences is that they include autonomic responses such as rapid breathing, sweating, and dry mouth. They may also entail strong subjective feelings that we often label, such as feelings of anger or fear. Finally, emotions typically entail thoughts or plans related to the experience, which may take the form of replaying conversations and events in your mind or anticipating what you might say or do under similar circumstances in the future. These three types of experiences suggest the influence of different neural systems. The autonomic component must include the hypothalamus and associated structures. The feelings are more difficult to localize but clearly include the amygdala and probably parts of the frontal lobes. And, finally, the cognitions are likely to be cortical.

## What Stimulates an Emotion?

What is the relation between our cognitive experience of an emotion and the physiological changes associated with it? One view is that the physiological changes (such as trembling and rapid heartbeat) come first, and the brain then interprets these changes as an emotion of some kind. This perspective implies that the brain (most likely the cortex) creates a cognitive response to autonomic information. That response varies with the context in which the autonomic arousal occurs. For example, if we are frightened by a movie, we experience a weaker, more short-lived emotion than if we are frightened by a real-life encounter with a gang of muggers. Variations of this perspective have gone by many names, beginning with the *James-Lange theory*. All assume that the brain concocts a story to explain bodily reactions.

Two lines of evidence support the James-Lange theory and similar points of view. One is that the same autonomic responses can accompany different emotions. In other words, particular emotions are not tied to their own unique autonomic changes. This leaves room for interpreting what a particular pattern of arousal means, even though particular physiological changes may suggest only a limited range of possibilities. (The physiological changes experienced during fear and happiness are unlikely to be confused with one another, for instance.) The second line of evidence supporting the view that physiological changes are the starting point for emotions comes from people with reduced information about their own autonomic arousal, owing to spinal-cord injury, for example. Such people suffer a decrease in perceived emotion, the severity of which depends on how much sensory input they have lost. Figure 11-23 illustrates this relation. It shows that people with the greatest loss of sensory input, which occurs with injuries at the uppermost end of the spinal cord, also have the greatest loss of emotional intensity. In contrast, people with low spinal injuries retain most of their visceral input and have essentially normal emotional reactions.

Antonio Damasio (1999) emphasized an important additional aspect of the link between emotion and cognitive factors in his

**Figure 11-23**

Spinal injury reduces the experience of emotion. The extent of emotional loss is greatest when the lesion is high on the spine.

Adapted from *Principles of Behavioral Neuroscience* (p. 339), by J. Beatty, 1995, Dubuque, IA: Brown & Benchmark.

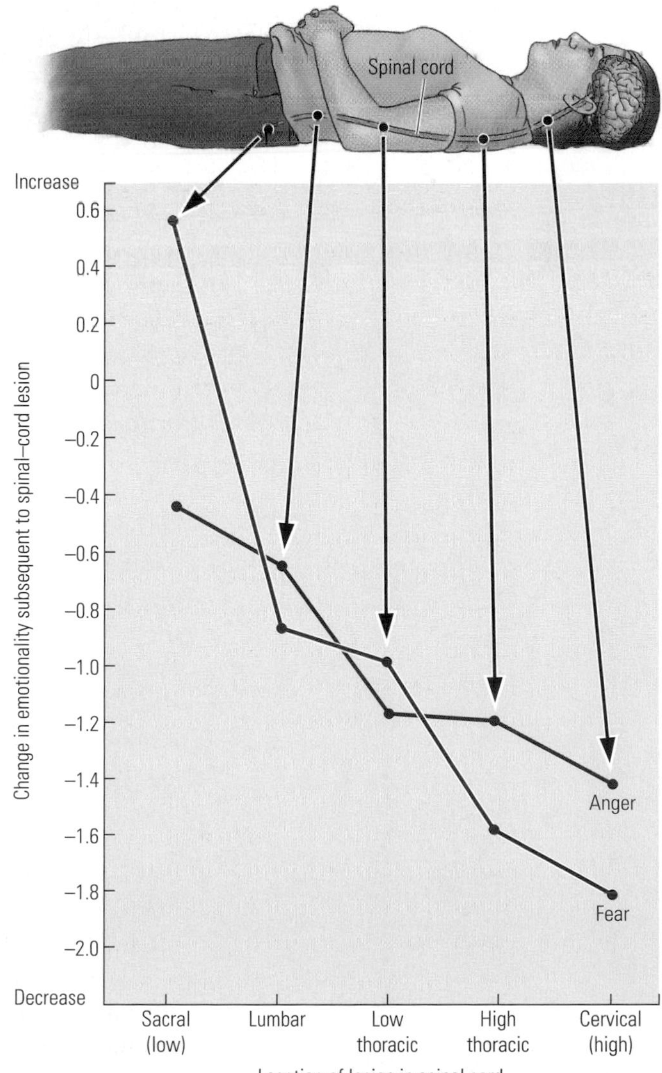

**Somatic marker hypothesis.** A hypothesis positing that "marker" signals arising from emotions and feelings act to guide behavior and decision making, usually in an unconscious process.

**Kluver-Bucy syndrome.** A behavioral syndrome, characterized especially by hypersexuality, that results from bilateral injury to the temporal lobe.

**somatic marker hypothesis.** When Damasio studied patients with frontal-lobe injuries, he was struck by how they could be highly rational in analyzing the world yet still make decidedly irrational social and personal decisions. The explanation, he argued, is that the reasoning of people with frontal-lobe injury is no longer affected, either consciously or unconsciously, by the neural machinery that underlies emotion. Cut off from critical emotional input, many social and personal decisions are therefore rather poor.

To account for these observations, Damasio proposed that emotions are responses induced by either internal or external stimuli not normally attended to consciously. For example, if you encounter a bear as you walk down the street, the stimulus is processed rapidly without conscious appraisal. In other words, a sensory representation of the bear in the visual cortex is transmitted directly to brain structures, such as the amygdala, that initiate an emotional response. This emotional response includes actions on structures in the forebrain and brainstem and ultimately on the autonomic nervous system. As mentioned earlier, the amygdala has connections to the frontal lobes, so the emotional response can influence the frontal lobes' appraisal of the world. However, if the frontal lobes were injured, the emotional information would be excluded from the cognitive processing, so the quality of emotion-related appraisals would suffer.

To summarize, Damasio's somatic marker hypothesis proposes how emotions are normally linked to a person's thoughts, decisions, and actions. In a typical emotional state, certain regions of the brain send messages to many other brain areas and to most of the rest of the body by hormones and the autonomic nervous system. These messages produce a global change in the organism's state, and this altered state influences behavior, usually in a nonconscious way.

## The Amygdala and Emotional Behavior

In addition to controlling certain species-typical behaviors, the amygdala influences emotion (Davis, 1992). The role of the amygdala can be seen most clearly in monkeys whose amygdalae have been removed. In 1939, Heinrich Kluver and Paul Bucy reported an extraordinary result, now known as the **Kluver-Bucy syndrome,** that followed removal of the amygdalae and anterior temporal cortices of monkeys. The principal symptoms include: (1) tameness and loss of fear; (2) indiscriminate dietary behavior (eating many types of previously rejected foods); (3) greatly increased autoerotic, homosexual, and heterosexual activity, with inappropriate object choice (for example, sexual mounting of chairs); (4) a tendency to attend to and react to every visual stimulus; (5) a tendency to examine all objects by mouth; and (6) visual agnosia. The last symptom is due to damage to the ventral visual stream in the temporal lobe, but the others are related to the amygdala damage. The tameness and loss of fear after amygdalectomy is especially striking. Monkeys that normally show a strong aversion to stimuli such as snakes show no fear of them whatsoever. In fact, amygdalectomized monkeys may pick up live snakes and even put them in their mouths.

Although the Kluver-Bucy syndrome is not common in humans, because bilateral temporal lobectomies are rare, symptoms of the syndrome can be seen in people with certain forms of brain infection known as encephalitis. In some cases, an encephalitis that is centered on the base of the brain can damage both temporal lobes and produce many of the Kluver-Bucy symptoms, including especially indiscriminate sexual behavior and the tendency to examine objects by mouth.

The role of the amygdala in Kluver-Bucy syndrome points to the central role of the amygdala in emotion. So does electrical stimulation of the amygdala, which produces an autonomic response (such as increased blood pressure and arousal) as well as a feeling of fear. Although this production of fear by the brain may seem odd, fear is important to species survival. To improve their chances of surviving, most organisms must minimize their contact with dangerous animals, objects, and places and maximize their contact with things that are safe.

The awareness of danger and safety has both an innate and a learned component, as Joe LeDoux (1996) emphasized. The innate component is the automatic processing of species-relevant sensory information, specifically sensory inputs from the visual, auditory, and olfactory systems. The importance of olfactory inputs is not so obvious to humans, whose senses are dominated by vision. But, for other animals, olfactory cues often predominate, and there is a major input of olfactory information directly into the amygdala. Thus, a rat that has never encountered a ferret shows an immediate fear response to the odor of ferret. Other novel odors (such as peppermint or coffee) do not produce an innate fear reaction. The innate response triggers an autonomic activation that stimulates conscious awareness of danger. In contrast, the learned component of fear consists of the avoidance of specific animals, places, and objects that the organism has come to associate with danger. The organism is not born with this avoidance behavior prewired. In a similar way, animals learn to increase contact with environmental stimuli that they associate with positive outcomes, such as food or sexual activity or, in the laboratory, drugs. Damage to the amygdala interferes with all of these behaviors. The animal loses not only its innate fears, but also its acquired fears and preferences for certain environmental stimuli.

To summarize, the amygdala is required for species survival. It influences autonomic and hormonal responses through its connections to the hypothalamus. It influences our conscious awareness of the positive and negative consequences of events and objects through its connections to the prefrontal cortex.

**Psychosurgery.** A neurosurgical intervention to destroy brain areas or sever connections between areas with the intent of modifying disturbances of behavior.

## The Prefrontal Cortex and Emotional Behavior

About the same time that Kluver and Bucy began studying their monkeys, Carlyle Jacobsen was studying the effects of frontal lobotomy on the cognitive capacities of two chimpanzees. A frontal lobotomy consists of inserting a sharp instrument into the frontal lobes and moving it back and forth to destroy a substantial amount of brain tissue. In 1935, Jacobsen reported that one of the chimps subjected to this procedure, which had been particularly neurotic before the surgery, became more relaxed after it. Incredibly, a leading Portuguese neurologist named Egas Moniz seized on this observation as a treatment for behavioral disorders in humans, and the frontal lobotomy was initiated as the first form of **psychosurgery.** The procedure is illustrated in Figure 11-24.

The use of psychosurgery, which refers to any neurosurgical technique intended to alter behavior, grew rapidly in the 1950s. In North America alone, nearly 40,000 people received frontal lobotomies as a treatment for psychiatric disorders. Not until the 1960s was there any systematic research into the effects of frontal lesions on social and emotional behavior, by which time the frontal lobotomy had virtually vanished as a "treatment." There is now little doubt that prefrontal lesions in various species, including humans, have severe effects on social and emotional behavior.

Agnes is a case in point. We met Agnes at the psychiatric hospital where we met Roger and the other people described at the beginning of this chapter. Agnes was not a patient but rather was visiting one of the nurses. Agnes had, however, once been a patient. She was a 57-year-old woman who had been subjected to a procedure known as a **frontal leukotomy** because her husband felt that she was too gregarious. Evidently, as an oil tycoon, he felt that her "loose lips" were a detriment to his business dealings. He convinced two psychiatrists that she would benefit from the surgical procedure and her life was changed forever.

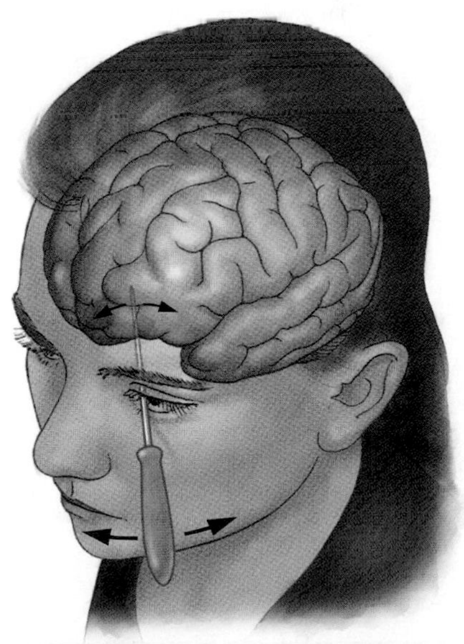

**Figure 11-24**

In the procedure for a transorbital leukotomy, a leukotome is inserted through the bone of the eye socket and the inferior frontal cortex is disconnected from the rest of the brain.

Learn more about the history of the frontal leukotomy and other psychosurgeries at the Web site at **www.worthpublishers.com/kolb/chapter11**

To perform a leukotomy, a surgeon uses a special knife called a leukotome to sever the connections of a region of the inferior frontal cortex, including especially the orbital cortex (see Figure 11-16). The first thing that we noticed about Agnes was that she exhibited no outward sign of emotion. She had virtually no facial expression. In our conversations with her, however, we quickly discovered that she had considerable insight into the changes in her brought about by the leukotomy. In particular, she indicated that she no longer had any feelings about things or most people, although, curiously, she was attached to her dog. She said that she often just felt empty, much like a zombie. Her only moment of real happiness in the 30 years since her operation was the sudden death of her husband, whom she blamed for ruining her life. Unfortunately, Agnes had squandered her dead husband's considerable wealth because of her inability to plan or organize, which we have seen is another symptom of prefrontal injury.

The orbital region of the inferior prefrontal area has direct connections with the amygdala and hypothalamus. Stimulation of this area can produce autonomic responses, and, as we saw in Agnes, damage to this area can produce severe personality change characterized by apathy and loss of initiative or drive. The orbital cortex is likely responsible for the conscious awareness of emotional states that are produced by the rest of the limbic system, especially the amygdala.

Agnes's loss of facial expression is also fairly typical of frontal-lobe damage. In fact, people with frontal-lobe injuries or those who suffer from schizophrenia are usually impaired both at producing and perceiving facial expressions, including a wide range of expressions found in all human cultures—happiness, sadness, fear, anger, disgust, and surprise (Kolb & Taylor, 2000). It is difficult to imagine how such people can function effectively in our highly social world without being able to recognize the emotions of others. Although facial expression is a key part of recognizing emotion, so is tone of voice, or **prosody.** Frontal-lobe patients are devoid of prosody both in their own conversations and in understanding the prosody of others.

The lost ability to comprehend emotional expression in both faces and language partly explains the apathy of frontal-lobe patients. In some ways, they are similar to spinal-cord patients who have lost autonomic feedback and so can no longer feel the arousal associated with emotion. Frontal-lobe patients can no longer either read emotion in other people's faces and voices or experience it in their own. Some psychologists have proposed that our own facial expressions may provide us with important clues to the emotions that we are feeling. This idea has been demonstrated in experiments reviewed by Pamela Adelmann and Robert Zajonc (1989). In one such study, people were required to contract their facial muscles in ways that produced happy and angry expressions without even realizing what expressions they were displaying. Then they viewed a series of slides and reported how the slides made them feel. They said that they felt happier when they were inadvertently making a happy face and angrier when the face that they were making was one of anger. Frontal-lobe patients presumably would have no such feedback from their own facial expressions, which could be a reason why their emotional experiences are dampened.

## Emotional Disorders

A highly disruptive emotional disorder is **depression,** characterized by abnormal regulation of the feelings of sadness and happiness. A depressed person feels severely despondent for a prolonged period of time. Depression is common in our modern world, with a prevalence of nearly 10 percent in the population (see "Depression" on page 206). This disorder has a genetic component. Not only does it run in families, but it also frequently tends to be found in both members of a pair of identical twins. The genetic component in depression implies a biological abnormality, but the cause remains unknown.

**Depression.** A condition characterized by an abnormal regulation of the feelings of sadness and happiness.

**Anxiety Disorder.** A psychological disorder characterized by persistently high levels of anxiety or by maladaptive behaviors that reduce anxiety.

**Table 11-1 Types of Antidepressant Medications**

| Drug type | Action | Examples |
|---|---|---|
| Tricyclic antidepressants | Block reuptake of serotonin and noradrenaline | Imipramine |
| MAO inhibitors | Block activity of monoamine oxidase | Iproniazid |
| Serotonin reuptake inhibitors (SRIs) | Block reuptake of serotonin | Fluoxetine (Prozac)<br>Sertraline (Zoloft)<br>Paroxetine (Paxil) |

The strongest evidence supporting a biological cause of depression comes from the fact that about 70 percent of depressed people can be treated with one of several antidepressant drugs. This success rate has made antidepressants among the most widely prescribed classes of drugs in the world. As summarized in Table 11-1, antidepressants act on synapses (especially noradrenaline- and serotonin-containing synapses) by increasing the amount of available transmitter at them. The major projections of noradrenaline- and serotonin-containing cells to the limbic system imply that the activity of limbic regions, including the prefrontal cortex, is abnormal in depression.

Excessive anxiety is another common emotional problem. In fact, **anxiety disorders** are estimated to affect from 15 to 35 percent of the population. Symptoms include persistent fears and worries in the absence of any direct threat, usually accompanied by various physiological stress reactions, such as rapid heartbeat, nausea, and breathing difficulty. As with depression, the cause of anxiety disorders is not known, but the effectiveness of drug treatments implies a biological basis.

The most widely prescribed **anxiolytic** (antianxiety) **drugs** are the **benzodiazepines,** such as Valium, Librium, and Xanax. These drugs are thought to be effective because of their agonistic action on the $GABA_A$ receptor. Although $GABA_A$ receptors are found throughout the brain, the amygdala has an especially high concentration of them. Infusion of benzodiazepines into the amygdala blocks fear, suggesting that the amygdala may be the site of their action.

Why would the brain have a mechanism for benzodiazepine action? It certainly did not evolve to allow us to take Valium. Probably this mechanism is part of a system that both increases and reduces anxiety levels. The mechanism for raising anxiety seems to entail a compound known as diazepam-binding inhibitor. This compound appears to bind antagonistically with the $GABA_A$ receptor, resulting in greater anxiety. There are times when such an increase in anxiety is beneficial, especially if we are drowsy and need to be alert to deal with some kind of crisis. Impairment of this mechanism or the one that reduces anxiety can cause serious emotional problems, such as the development of anxiety disorders (see "Anxiety and Affective Disorders" on page 438.)

## In Review

The experience of an emotion includes autonomic responses (such as sweating and rapid heartbeat), subjective feelings (such as fear), and thoughts about the emotion-arousing situation. The autonomic responses result from the activity of the hypothalamus and related structures. The production of feelings probably includes both the amygdala and the orbitofrontal cortex. Emotional thoughts are likely the result of activity throughout the cerebral hemispheres. Various psychologists have proposed that, when the body experiences an autonomic reaction and intense feelings, the brain concocts a story to explain those experiences. Abnormalities in the neural circuits controlling the production of emotion are responsible for the most pervasive psychiatric disorders—namely, depression and anxiety disorders.

Focus on Disorders

## Anxiety and Affective Disorders

It is normal for animals to become anxious at times, especially when they are in obvious danger. But anxiety disorders are different. They are characterized by intense feelings of fear or anxiety that are not appropriate for the circumstances. People with an anxiety disorder have persistent and unrealistic worries about impending misfortunes. They also tend to suffer multiple physical symptoms attributable to hyperactivity of the sympathetic nervous system.

G. B.'s case is a good example. He was a 36-year-old man with two college degrees who began to experience severe spells that were initially diagnosed as some type of heart condition. He would begin to breathe heavily, sweat, experience heart palpitations, and sometimes suffer pains in his chest and arms. During these attacks, he was unable to communicate coherently and would lie helpless on the floor until an ambulance arrived to take him to the emergency room. Extensive medical testing and multiple attacks over a period of about 2 years eventually led to the diagnosis of *generalized anxiety disorder.* Like most of the 5 percent of the population who suffer an anxiety disorder at some point in their lives, G. B. was unaware that he was overly anxious.

It is difficult to determine the cause of generalized anxiety attacks, but one likely explanation is that they are related to the cumulative effect of general stress. Although G. B. appeared outwardly calm most of the time, he had been a prodemocracy activist in communist Poland, which was a dangerous position in which to be. Because of the dangers, he and his family eventually had to escape from Poland to Turkey, and from there they went to Canada. G. B. may have had continuing worries about the repercussions of his political activities—worries (and stress) that eventually expressed themselves as generalized anxiety attacks.

There are several types of anxiety disorders. The most common and least disabling are *phobias.* A phobia pertains to a clearly defined dreaded object (such as spiders or snakes) or some greatly feared situation (such as enclosed spaces or crowds). Most people have mild aversions to some types of stimuli. Such an aversion becomes a phobia only when a person's feelings toward a disliked stimulus lead to overwhelming fear and anxiety. The incidence of disabling phobias is surprisingly high, being estimated to affect at least one in ten people. For most people with a phobia, the emotional reaction can be controlled by avoiding what they dread.

A third common type of anxiety disorder is *panic disorder,* which has an estimated incidence on the order of 3 percent of the population. The symptoms of panic disorder include recurrent attacks of intense terror that come on without warning and without any apparent relation to external circumstances. Panic attacks usually last only a few minutes, but the experience is always terrifying. There is sudden activation of the sympathetic nervous system, leading to sweating, a wildly beating heart, and trembling. Although panic attacks may occur only occasionally, the victim's dread of another episode may be continual. Consequently, many people with panic disorders also have agoraphobia, a fear of public places or situations in which help might not be available. This phobia makes some sense because a person with a panic disorder may feel particularly vulnerable to having an attack in a public place.

Freud believed that anxiety disorders were psychological in origin and treatable with talking therapies in which people confronted their fears. But it is now known that anxiety disorders have a clear biological link. These disorders are most effectively treated with benzodiazepines, of which diazepam (Valium) is the best known. Alprazolam (Xanax) is the most commonly prescribed drug for panic attacks. Benzodiazepines act by augmenting GABA's inhibitory effect and are believed to exert a major influence on neurons in the amygdala.

## REWARD

As you know, survival for most animals depends on their minimizing contact with certain stimuli and maximizing contact with others. Contact is minimized when an animal experiences fear or anxiety, but sometimes an animal *avoids* a stimulus that is not fear arousing. Why? And why do animals *maintain* contact with other stimuli? A simple answer is that animals maintain contact with stimuli that they find rewarding in some way and ignore or avoid stimuli that they find neutral or aversive. According to this view, reward is a mechanism that evolved to help increase the adaptive fitness of both individual animals and species.

But what exactly is reward? One rather circular definition is that reward is the activity of neural circuits that function to maintain an animal's contact with certain environmental stimuli, either now or in the future. Presumably, there must be something about the activity of these circuits that an animal perceives as pleasant. This pleasantness would explain why reward can help maintain not only adaptive behaviors such as feeding and sexual activity, but also potentially nonadaptive behaviors such as drug addiction. After all, evolution would not have prepared the brain for the eventual development of psychoactive drugs.

The first clue to the presence of a reward system in the brain came with an accidental discovery by James Olds and Peter Milner in 1954. They found that rats would perform behaviors, such as pressing a bar, to administer a brief burst of electrical stimulation to specific sites in their brains. This phenomenon is called **intracranial self-stimulation** or **brain-stimulation reward.** Typically, rats will press a lever hundreds or even thousands of times per hour to obtain this brain stimulation, stopping only when they are exhausted. Why would animals engage in such a behavior when it has absolutely no value to the survival of either themselves or their species? The simplest explanation is that the brain stimulation is activating the system underlying reward (Wise, 1996).

After nearly 50 years of research on brain-stimulation reward, we now know that there are dozens of sites in the brain that will maintain self-stimulation. Significantly, however, there are some regions, including the lateral hypothalamus and medial forebrain bundle, that are especially effective. Stimulation there activates fibers that form the ascending pathways from dopamine-producing cells of the midbrain tegmentum, shown in Figure 11-25. This pathway, which is known as the mesolimbic dopamine pathway, sends dopamine-containing terminals to various sites, including especially the nucleus accumbens (a large structure located adjacent to the striatum) and the prefrontal cortex.

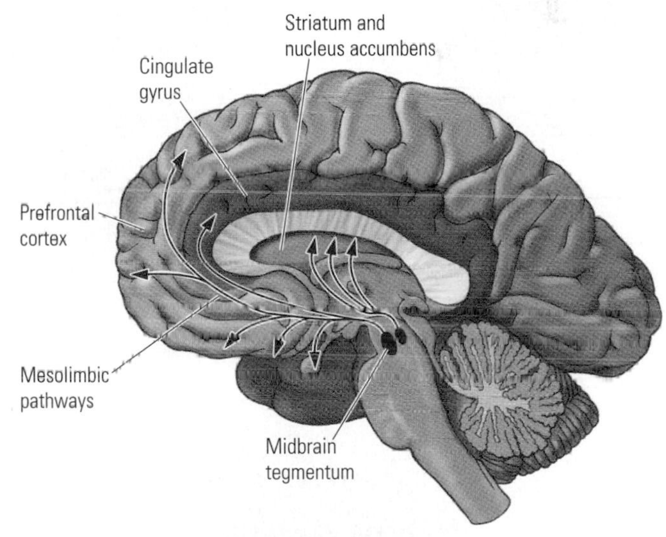


**Figure 11-25**

The mesolimbic dopamine system. The nucleus accumbens is a critical structure in the reward system.

There are several reasons for believing that the mesolimbic dopamine system is central to circuits mediating reward. First, there is a marked increase in dopamine release when animals are engaged in intracranial self-stimulation. Second, drugs that enhance dopamine release increase self-stimulation, whereas drugs that decrease dopamine release decrease self-stimulation. It seems that the amount of dopamine released somehow determines how rewarding an event is. Third, when animals engage in behaviors such as feeding or sexual activity, the release of dopamine rapidly increases in places such as the nucleus accumbens. Finally, highly addictive drugs such as nicotine and cocaine increase the level of dopamine in the nucleus accumbens. Even opiates appear to have at least some of their actions through the dopamine system. Animals quickly learn to press a bar to obtain an injection of opiates directly into the midbrain tegmentum or the nucleus accumbens. The same animals do not work to obtain the opiates if the dopaminergic neurons of the mesolimbic system are inactivated. Apparently, then, animals engage in behaviors that increase dopamine release.

Visit the CD and watch a video showing self-stimulation in a rat in the area on electrical stimulation in the module on Research Methods.

Note, however, that dopamine is not the only reward compound in the brain. For example, Rainer Spanagel and Friedbert Weiss (1999) stressed that drugs can be rewarding in the absence of dopamine, and Keith Trujillo and his colleagues (1993) found that the reinforcing actions of opiates occur through activation of both

**Incentive.** An environmental stimulus that motivates behavior.

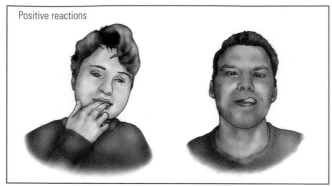

dopaminergic and nondopaminergic systems. These findings suggest the existence of more than one reward-related system in the brain.

In Chapter 6, we encountered the idea that reward has multiple parts in our consideration of Robinson and Berridge's (1993) incentive-sensitization theory of addiction. These researchers proposed that reward contains separable psychological components, corresponding roughly to "wanting" (which is often called **incentive**) and "liking" (which is equivalent to an evaluation of pleasure). This idea can be applied to why we increase contact with a stimulus such as chocolate. There are two independent factors at work: our desire to have the chocolate (wanting) and the pleasurable effect of the chocolate on us (liking). This distinction is important. If we maintain contact with a certain stimulus because dopamine is released, the question becomes whether the dopamine plays a role in the wanting or the liking aspect of the behavior. Robinson and Berridge proposed that wanting and liking processes are mediated by separable neural systems and that dopamine is the transmitter in wanting. Liking, they hypothesize, entails opioid and benzodiazepine–GABA systems.

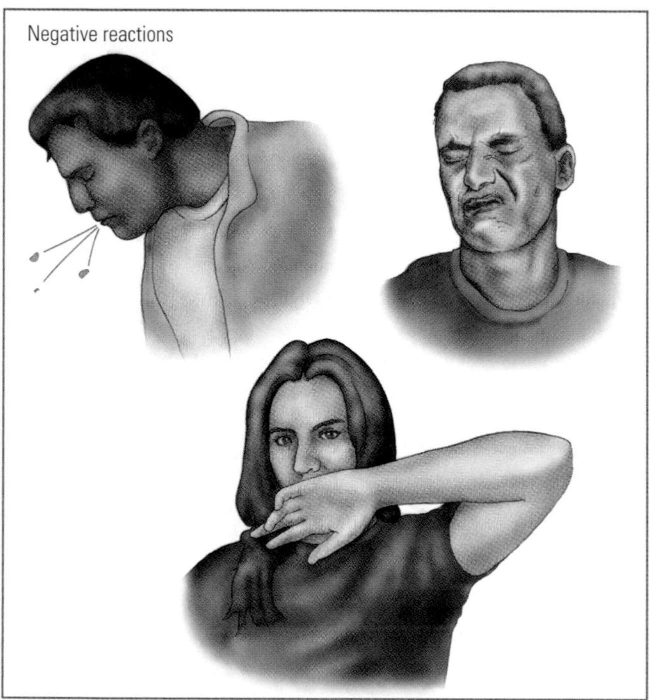


**Figure 11-26**

Human reactions to taste. Positive (hedonic) reactions are elicited by sucrose and other palatable tastes. Hedonic reactions include licking the fingers and licking the lips. Negative (aversive) reactions are elicited by quinine and other nonpalatable tastes. Aversive reactions include spitting, making a face of distaste, and wiping the mouth with the back of the hand.

Adapted from "Food Reward: Brain Substrates of Wanting and Liking," by K. C. Berridge, 1996, *Neuroscience and Biobehavioral Reviews, 20,* p. 6.

According to Robinson and Berridge, wanting and liking are normally two aspects of the same process, so rewards are usually wanted and liked to the same degree. However, it is possible, under certain circumstances, for wanting and liking to change independently. Consider rats with lesions of the ascending dopaminergic pathway to the forebrain. These rats do not eat. Is it simply that they do not desire to eat (a loss of wanting) or has food become aversive to them (a loss of liking for it)? To find out which factor is at work, the animals' facial expressions and body movements in response to food can be observed to see how liking is affected. After all, when animals are given various foods to taste, they produce different facial and body reactions, depending on whether they perceive the food as pleasant or aversive. For example, when a normal person tastes something sweet, he or she usually responds by licking the fingers or the lips, as shown in Figure 11-26. In contrast, if the taste is unpleasantly salty, the reaction is often spitting, grimacing, or wiping the mouth with the back of the hand. Rats, too, show distinctive positive and negative responses to pleasant and unpleasant tastes. So, by watching these responses when food is squirted into the mouth of a rat that otherwise refuses to eat, we can tell to what extent a loss of liking for food is a factor in the animal's food rejection. Interestingly, rats that do not eat after receiving lesions to the dopamine pathway act as though they still like food.

Now consider a rat with a self-stimulation electrode in the lateral hypothalamus. A rat with such an electrode will often eat heartily while the stimulation is on. The obvious inference is that the food must taste good—presumably even better than it does usually. But what if we squirt food into the rat's mouth and observe its behavior when the stimulation is on versus when it is off? If the brain stimulation primes eating by evoking pleasurable sensations, we would expect that the animal would be more positive in its facial and body reactions toward foods when the stimulation is turned on. In fact, the opposite is found. During stimulation, rats react more aversively to tastes such as sugar and salt than when stimulation is off. Apparently, the stimulation increases wanting but not liking.

In conclusion, experiments of this sort have shown that what appears to be a single event—reward—is actually composed of at least two independent processes. Just as our visual system independently processes "what" and "how" information in two separate streams, our reward system appears to include independent processes of wanting and liking. Reward is not a single phenomenon any more than the processes of perception or memory are.

## In Review

Reward refers to the effect that events have on the behavior of animals. Reward acts on the activity of neural circuits that function to maintain contact with certain environmental stimuli now or in the future, through either liking or wanting subsystems. The challenges are to separate the neural subsystems taking part in reward and to account for how the rewarding effects of environmental events influence these subsystems.

## SUMMARY

1. *What controls the types of behaviors in which animals will engage at any given time?* Animals engage in behavior for multiple reasons. These reasons range from a need for the brain to have sensory stimulation to the activity of hormones to the activity of dopamine cells in the brainstem.

   The neural circuits controlling species-typical behaviors such as mouse killing by cats are organized in the brainstem. There is an evolutionary advantage for the activity of these circuits to be rewarding. If animals did not want to engage in these behaviors, their species would become extinct.

   Behavior is also controlled by its consequences. These consequences may affect the evolution of the species or the behavior of an individual animal. Behaviors that are selected by evolution are often triggered by innate releasing mechanisms. Behaviors that are selected only in an individual animal are shaped by that animal's environment and are learned.
2. *What is motivation?* Motivation is a shorthand term referring to the cause of what appears to be purposeful behavior in animals. There are two distinctly different types of motivated behaviors: regulatory and nonregulatory. Regulatory behaviors (homeostatic behaviors) maintain some body system in balance, such as body temperature. Nonregulatory behaviors are those that are not controlled by a homeostatic mechanism and are not reflexive.
3. *What are the principal neural structures in motivated behavior?* The principal neural structures that initiate motivated behaviors are the hypothalamus, the pituitary gland, the amygdala, the ascending projections from the dopamine and noradrenaline cell bodies in the lower brainstem, and the frontal lobe.
4. *What is the difference between the neural control of regulatory behaviors and that of nonregulatory behaviors?* Feeding is an example of a regulatory behavior. It is controlled by the digestive system, hormonal systems, the hypothalamus, and cognitive factors that presumably are controlled by the cerebral cortex. Sexual activity is an example of a nonregulatory behavior. Copulatory behavior is controlled by the hypothalamus (the ventromedial hypothalamus in females and the preoptic area in males). Motivation for sexual behavior is controlled by the amygdala.
5. *What is emotion and how is it produced by the brain?* Emotion, which is a common experience but difficult to define, is believed to be a mental state concocted by the brain to account for bodily reactions to sensory events. The hypothalamus, the amygdala, and the prefrontal cortex are the key structures in emotion. Impairment

**neuroscience interactive**

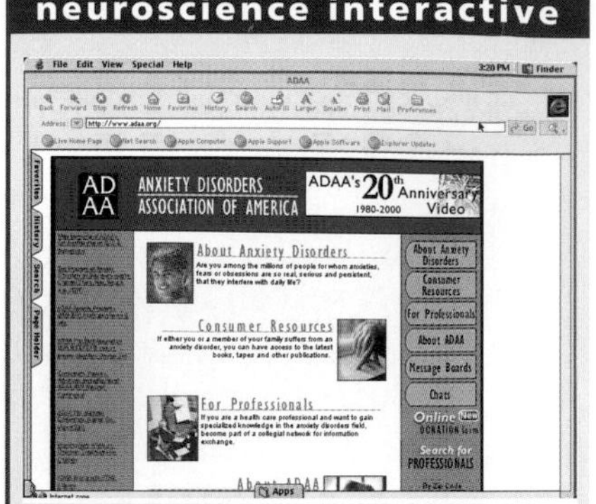


There are many resources available for expanding your learning on-line:

■ **www.worthpublishers.com/kolb/chapter11**
Try some self-tests to reinforce your mastery of the material. Look at some of the updates reflecting current research on the brain. You'll also be able to link to other sites which will reinforce what you've learned.

■ **www.adaa.org**
Link to this site to learn more about anxiety disorders.

■ **www.aabainc.org**
Learn more about the research and treatment of anorexia nervosa and bulimia at this site for the American Anorexia and Bulimia Association.

On your CD-ROM you can review some of the anatomical structures that are important to understanding what causes behaviors in the module on the Central Nervous System.

in the workings of these structures is related to a variety of disorders, including depression and anxiety disorders.

6. *Why do we find certain experiences rewarding?* Survival depends on maximizing contact with some environmental stimuli and minimizing contact with others. One mechanism to control this differential contact is called reward. Two independent features of reward are wanting and liking. The wanting component is thought to be controlled by dopaminergic systems, whereas the liking component is thought to be controlled by opiate–benzodiazepine systems.

## KEY TERMS

anxiety disorder, p. 437
depression, p. 436
drives, p. 402
homeostatic mechanism, p. 410
incentive, p. 440
innate releasing mechanism (IRM), p. 405
Kluver-Bucy syndrome, p. 434
prefrontal cortex, p. 419
psychosurgery, p. 435
releasing hormone, p. 414
sexual dimorphism, p. 426
somatic marker hypothesis, p. 434

## REVIEW QUESTIONS

1. What are some causes of behavior?
2. Compare the evolutionary and environmental influences on behavior.
3. What are the key structures controlling motivated behavior? How does each of them contribute to this control?
4. Contrast the organizing and activating effects of hormones.
5. Contrast the roles of the hypothalamus and the amygdala in sexual behavior and sexual motivation.

## FOR FURTHER THOUGHT

1. Why do cats kill birds? Use the same logic to account for a specific human behavior.
2. How could a concept such as preparedness explain racism?
3. What can you infer about brain and behavior relations from the finding that stimulation of the hypothalamus elicits complex behaviors such as feeding, digging, and sexual activity?
4. What are the social and moral implications of evidence that sexual orientation is associated with brain organization?

## RECOMMENDED READING

Barondes, S. H. (1993). *Molecules and mental illness.* New York: Scientific American Library. A very readable summary of the neurochemical bases of various forms of psychiatric disease. The Scientific American Library series has excellent illustrations and is written for an educated lay audience.

Becker, J. B., Breedlove, S. M., & Crews, D. (2000). *Behavioral endocrinology.* Cambridge, MA: MIT Press. What is behavioral endocrinology and why study it? This book provides the answers. It is a broad survey of the effects of hormones on the behavior of humans and other animals. The topics range from sexual behavior to cognitive and motor behaviors.

Damasio, A. R. (1999). *The feeling of what happens: Body and emotion in the making of consciousness.* New York: Harcourt Brace. Damasio argues that emotions are curious adaptations that are part and parcel of the neural machinery that we have evolved for our survival. Damasio's ideas have developed from his study of people with frontal-lobe injuries who have abnormal emotional control and a parallel abnormality in other cognitive activities. This interesting book has influenced thinking about the role of emotion in the brain's daily activities.

Eibl-Eibesfeldt, I. (1989). *Human ethology*. New York: Aldine de Gruyter. One of the first human ethologists has written a thorough book in which he summarizes what is known about the species-typical behavior of people. This book provides a wealth of photographic examples of human behaviors that are genetically programmed and found throughout the world's cultures.

Lane, R. D., & Nadel, L. (Eds.). (2000). *Cognitive neuroscience of emotion.* New York: Oxford University Press. This book is a showcase for the newly emerging ideas of the cognitive neuroscience of emotion. The chapters range from heavily theoretical accounts to strongly empirical ones, but all focus on the role of emotion in cognition.

Robinson, T. E., & Berridge, K. C. (1993). The neural basis of drug craving: An incentive-sensitization theory of addiction. *Brain Research Reviews, 18,* 247–291. The Robinson-Berridge theory of drug addiction and craving is a thorough analysis of the evidence that wanting and liking drugs are two different things that likely have different neural bases.

Woods, S. C., Seeley, R. J., Porte, D., & Schwartz, M. W. (1998). Signals that regulate food intake and energy homeostasis. *Science, 280,* 1378–1382. Obesity is an increasingly prevalent and important health problem. Naturally, those who wish to lose weight are hoping that a magic bullet will be found to treat obesity. This article is one in a special issue of *Science* that looks at the regulation of body weight. The authors review the signals that tell us when to eat (or not) and conclude that a single magic bullet is unlikely but that treatments aimed at multiple targets may be realistic.

CHAPTER

# 12

# Why Do We Sleep?



Bob Thomas/Tony Stone
Micrograph: Dr. Dennis Kunkel/Phototake

The polar bear, or sea bear (*Ursus maritimus),* has an amazing life style (Figure 12-1). As winter begins in the Arctic and the days become shorter, the bears congregate to prepare for their migration north onto the pack ice. Some bears travel thousands of kilometers. In the continuous darkness of the Arctic winter, the bears hunt seals, walrus, and whales. While the bears are on the ice, they take time to sleep; but their sleep cannot be called either nighttime or daytime sleep, because their world is continuously dark. At the same time as the bears are preparing to go out onto the ice, many other Arctic animals are escaping winter. Arctic terns fly 15,000 kilometers to Antarctica, where it is summer. Lemmings, mice, and ground squirrels cannot travel long distances; these rodents spend the winter in burrows in a sleeplike state called hibernation. When summer comes again, the birds return and the rodents emerge from their burrows. The sea bears return from the ice, dig beds in the earth, and spend the summer in sleep.

The behavior of the sea bears is remarkable to us in two ways. First, we are *diurnal* animals (from the Latin *diaes,* meaning "by day"): we are active in the daylight, and we sleep when it is dark. Our recent evolutionary history places early humans in Africa at latitudes where day and night are almost equal in length. Because we are adapted for daylight vision and have difficulty seeing anything at night, we prefer to avoid darkness. Therefore, it seems strange to us that an animal would seek out and flourish in darkness. Second, as diurnal animals, we obtain our food in daylight and we sleep for about 8 hours each night. Our sleep is characterized by a decline in body temperature and a loss of awareness of our surroundings. The sea bears sleep in the winter, as mentioned, but they will spend the entire summer in a condition of shallow **torpor**—a condition resembling sleep except that the decline in body temperature is greater than that during sleep. Their torpor appears to be voluntary because, if they have access to food throughout the year, they do not enter torpor. It is hard to imagine that we could voluntarily spend all summer in a sleeplike condition.

Despite the very great differences between our behavior and the behavior of sea bears, the environmental pressure to which they and we respond is similar. Our behaviors are adaptations that maximize our ability to obtain food and minimize the loss of energy stores that we obtain from food. In other words, we are active during the day because that is when we can obtain food, and we are inactive at night to conserve body resources. Bears hunt all winter to build up fat supplies, and they enter torpor so that they can extend the period during which they can live on those fat stores. *Hibernation* is a strategy that rodents use to extend fat supplies for as long as possible. It is similar to shallow torpor except that body temperature declines are so extreme that the animals expend almost no energy. The *migratory behavior* of birds is also a strategy used to maximize food acquisition and minimize energy loss, except the objective is achieved by moving to a habitat where food is abundant.

There is one other way in which we are similar to sea bears, rodents, and birds. Our behaviors are not simply responses to the immediate changes that are taking place in our respective environments. We anticipate and prepare for the environmental changes that will result in food abundance or food shortages. The sea bears are clearly prepared to go out on the ice well in advance of its formation because they walk along the Arctic shores for weeks before the ice forms; they also leave the ice before it melts. The birds migrate before food resources are depleted and winter sets in. Rodents gorge themselves, build nests, and store food in their burrows before winter arrives. We retire to

David Myers/Tony Stone

**Figure 12-1**

In winter polar bears migrate to the Arctic ice, where they hunt in darkness and periodically sleep.

sleeping sites in preparation for sleep, and we frequently get up before it is fully light to prepare for our daily activities. Because we, along with other animals, appear to have warning of impending winter or impending changes in the day–night cycle, there must be signals to which we all respond. In this chapter, we will seek answers to the following questions related to biological rhythms and sleep: How is our behavior modified to cope with the day–night cycle? Why have we chosen sleep as a strategy for waiting out the night? What neural mechanisms regulate sleep and waking, and what disorders develop when those mechanisms are disrupted?

## A CLOCK FOR ALL SEASONS

To anticipate daily and seasonal changes, we have biological clocks that respond to cues in our environment. In this section, we will consider the cues that guide our behavior. Because environmental cues themselves are not always consistent, we will examine the role of biological clocks in interpreting environmental cues in an intelligent way. We will also discover how our internal biological clocks adjust our behavior to maintain our schedules.

### The Origins of Biological Rhythms

The daily and the seasonal changes displayed by animals are called *biological rhythms*. These rhythms are in turn related to the rhythmic cycle of days and seasons produced by the earth's rotation on its axis and the earth's progression around the sun (Figure 12-2). The earth rotates on its axis once every 24 hours, producing a 24-hour cycle of day and night. The axis of the earth is inclined slightly, and so, as the earth orbits the sun, the North Pole is tilted slightly toward the sun for part of the year and is tilted slightly away from the sun for the rest of the year. When inclined toward the sun, the Southern Hemisphere experiences summer and gets more direct sunshine for more hours each day and the climate is warmer. At the same time, the Northern Hemisphere, inclined away from the sun, receives less direct sunlight, making the days shorter and

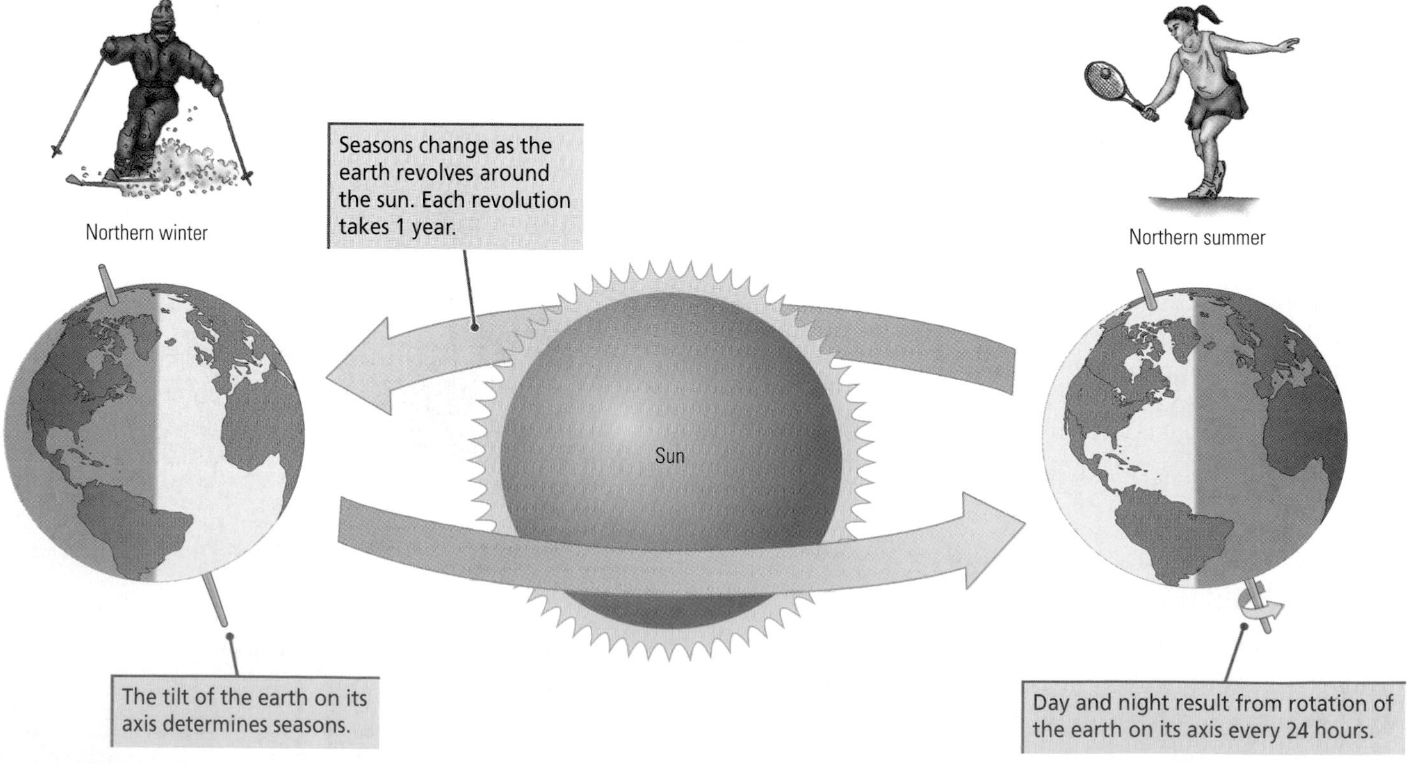
Northern winter
Seasons change as the earth revolves around the sun. Each revolution takes 1 year.
Northern summer
Sun
The tilt of the earth on its axis determines seasons.
Day and night result from rotation of the earth on its axis every 24 hours.

**Figure 12-2**

Daily light–dark changes are produced by the daily rotation of the earth on its axis in which each part of the earth faces the sun for part of the rotation cycle (daytime) and faces away from the sun for the other part (nighttime). Seasonal changes in amount of daylight are related to the annual movement of the earth around the sun. Because the axis of the earth is tilted, one pole points toward the sun for part of the year (summertime) and away for the other part of the year (wintertime).

the climate colder. Tropical regions, being near the equator, undergo little climatic change as the earth progresses around the sun.

Because of the seasonal differences in polar and equatorial regions, animals living near the poles are relatively more affected by seasonal changes and animals living near the equator are relatively more affected by day-and-night changes. In addition, the seasonal and daily changes may have combined effects on organisms, inasmuch as the onset and duration of daily changes depend on the season and latitude. Animals living in the polar regions also have to cope with greater fluctuations in daily temperature, light, and food availability than do animals living near the equator.

We humans are equatorial animals in that our behavior is governed more by daily cycles than by seasonal cycles. Our behavior is dominated by a rhythm of daylight activity and nocturnal sleep. Not only does human waking and sleep behavior cycle daily, so also do pulse rate, blood pressure, body temperature, rate of cell division, blood cell count, alertness, urine composition, metabolic rate, sexual drive, and responsiveness to medications. But humans are not unique in this respect. Plants display rhythmic behavior, as exemplified by species in which leaves or flowers open during the day and close at night. Even unicellular algae and fungi display rhythmic behaviors related to the passage of the day. Some animals, including lizards and crabs, change color in a rhythmic pattern. The Florida chameleon, for example, turns green at night, whereas its color matches that of its environment during the day. In short, almost every organism displays changes of some sort that are related to daily or seasonal changes.

## Biological Clocks

If the behavior of animals were affected only by seasonal and daily changes, the neural mechanisms that account for changes in behavior would be much simpler to study than they are. That is, behavior would be driven by external cues, which would be easy to identify, and, accordingly, the central processes that respond to those cues also would be easy to identify. That something else is required was first recognized in 1729 by French geologist Jean Jacques D'Ortous de Mairan (see Raven et al., 1992). In an experiment similar to that illustrated in Figure 12-3, De Mairan isolated a plant from daily light and dark cues and from temperature cues and noted that the rhythmic movements of its leaves continued. What concerned de Marain's followers was the possibility that some undetected external cue stimulated the rhythmical behavior of the plant. Such cues could include changes in gravity, changes in electromagnetic fields,

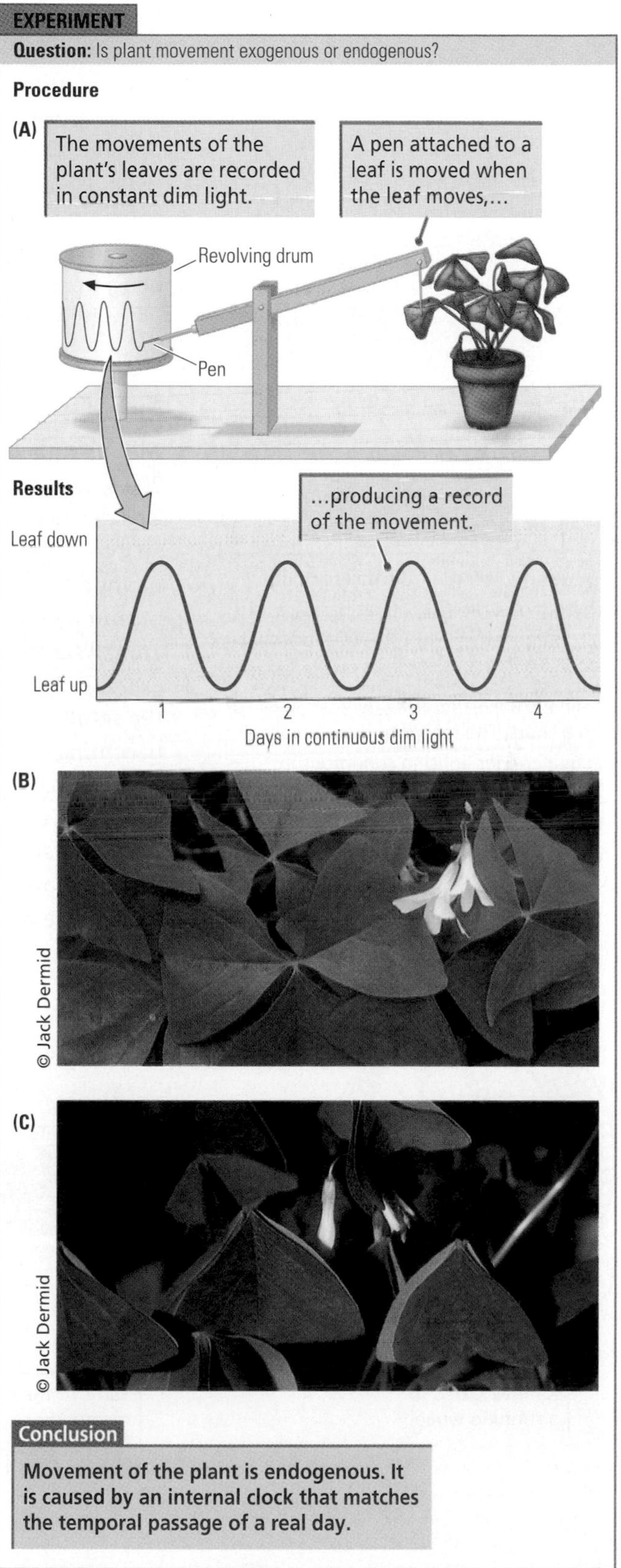

EXPERIMENT
Question: Is plant movement exogenous or endogenous?
Procedure
(A)
The movements of the plant's leaves are recorded in constant dim light.
A pen attached to a leaf is moved when the leaf moves,...
Revolving drum
Pen
Results
...producing a record of the movement.
Leaf down
Leaf up
1
2
3
4
Days in continuous dim light
(B)
© Jack Dermid
(C)
© Jack Dermid
Conclusion
Movement of the plant is endogenous. It is caused by an internal clock that matches the temporal passage of a real day.


**Figure 12-3**

**(A)** An experimental setup for demonstrating a daily rhythm in wood sorrel. A pen attached to a leaf moves when the leaf moves, producing a record of the leaf's movement on a revolving drum. The plant **(B)** opens its leaves during the day and **(C)** closes them at night. The rhythmical activity recorded when the plant is kept in dim light demonstrates that the movement of the leaves is endogenous.

and even changes in the intensity of rays from outer space. Nevertheless, it eventually became clear from further experiments that the daily fluctuations were endogenous—that is, they came from within the plant. As we will learn in the following sections, experiments show that most organisms have an **internal clock** that matches the temporal passage of a real day.

A wristwatch or a wall clock enables you to plan and schedule your time. Your internal clock performs these functions, too. A clock allows an animal to anticipate an event: it can migrate before it gets cold rather than waiting until it gets cold. A clock allows an animal to mate at the correct time of the year. A clock allows animals to arrive at the same place at the same time if they are to mate or to begin a migration. Most important, a clock allows an animal to know that if daylight lasts for about 12 hours today, it will last for about 12 hours tomorrow. We can only speculate about how plants and animals evolved internal clocks. Perhaps if behavior were simply driven by external cues, an animal could be tricked into displaying maladaptive behavior. This happens, for example, when plant bulbs begin to grow during a January thaw only to be killed by a subsequent cold spell.

## Biological Rhythms

Although the existence of endogenous biological clocks was demonstrated more than 200 years ago, rhythmic behaviors were not studied extensively until quite recently. The detailed study of rhythms had to await the development of procedures that could analyze ongoing behavior over a long period of time. Behavioral analysis requires a method for counting behavioral events and a method for displaying those events in a meaningful way. For example, the behavior of a rodent can be measured by giving the animal access to a running wheel, such as that illustrated in Figure 12-4, in which it can exercise. A chart recorder or a computer records each turn of the wheel and displays the result on a chart. Because rodents are nocturnal, sleeping during light hours and becoming active during dark hours, their wheel-running activity takes place in the dark. If each day's activity is plotted under the preceding day's activity in a column, we can observe a pattern of activity over a period of time. Various details of the record can then be examined, including when the animal was active and how active it was. One of the most important pieces of information that can be obtained from an activity record is the cycle of activity. The time required for a complete cycle of activity to occur is

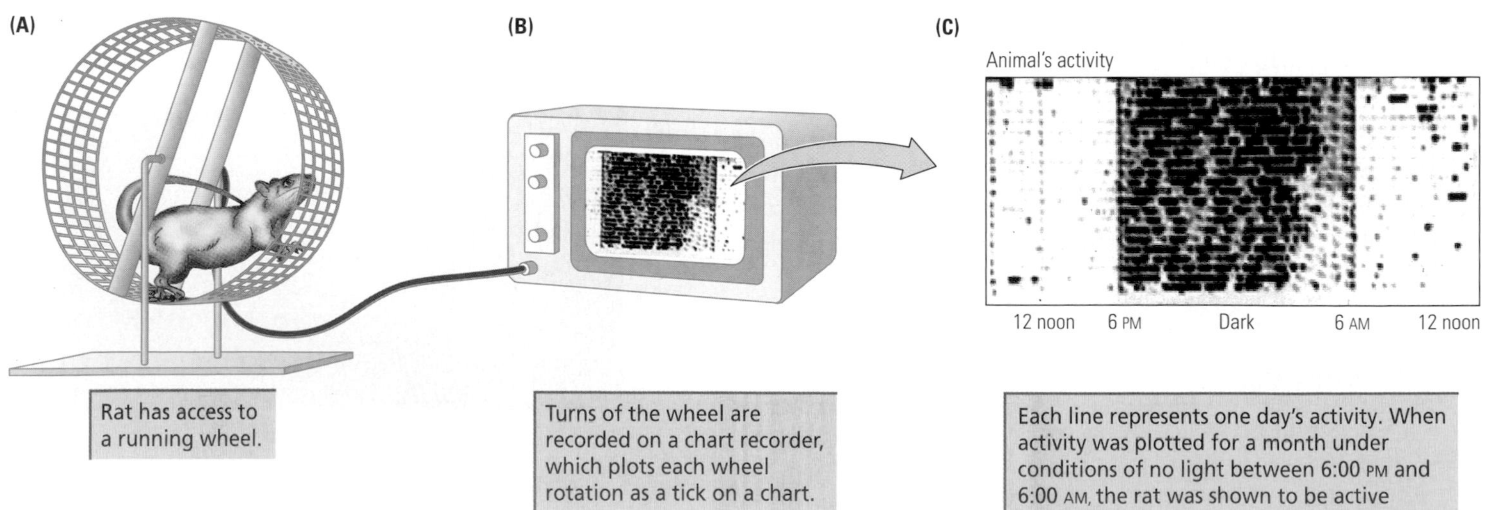

(A)
(B)
(C)
Animal's activity
12 noon
6 PM
Dark
6 AM
12 noon
Rat has access to a running wheel.
Turns of the wheel are recorded on a chart recorder, which plots each wheel rotation as a tick on a chart.
Each line represents one day's activity. When activity was plotted for a month under conditions of no light between 6:00 PM and 6:00 AM, the rat was shown to be active during dark hours of the day–night cycle.


**Figure 12-4**

Creating a record of the daily activity rhythm of a rat. **(A)** The rat has access to a running wheel. **(B)** Turns of the wheel are recorded on a chart. **(C)** The record of each day's activity of a single rat is pasted on a chart. The record of the animal's activity under lighting conditions in which the lights were turned off at 6:00 PM and on at 6:00 AM shows that the animal is active during the dark hours of the day–night cycle.

Adapted from *Biological Clocks in Medicine and Psychiatry* (pp. 12–15), by C. P. Richter, 1965, Springfield, IL: Charles C. Thomas.

called a *period.* The period of activity of most rodents is about 24 hours in an environment in which the lights go on and off with regularity. Our own sleep–wake period also is about 24 hours. Many other kinds of behaviors, however, have periods that are more or less than 24 hours.

The results of studies of different species of animals and of different aspects of behavior in a specific animal indicate that a surprisingly large number of biological clocks have varying periods. Two kinds of rhythms typical of most animals are **circannual rhythms** (Latin *circa*, "about," plus *annual*, "yearly"), of which the migratory cycles of sea bears and Arctic terns are examples, and **circadian rhythms** (Latin *circa*, "about," plus *dies*, "daily"), which are the day–night rhythms found in almost all animals and cellular processes. These are not the only kinds of rhythms, however. **Ultradian** (Latin *ultra*, "smaller than") **rhythms** are those that have a period of less than one day. Our eating behavior, which occurs about every 90 minutes to 2 hours, including snacks, is an example of an ultradian rhythm. Rodents, although active throughout the night, are most active at the beginning and end of the dark period. Many sea-dwelling animals have rhythms that are about 12 hours, which match the twice-daily changes in tides produced by the pull of the moon on the earth and its oceans. Therefore, an ultradian rhythm is embedded within their circadian rhythm. Our eye-blink rate, our heart rate, and even the rhythmic action potentials of some of our neurons are other examples of ultradian rhythms. There are also rhythms that have periods of more than a day and less than a year, which are called **infradian** (*infra* meaning "within a year") **rhythms.** The menstrual cycle of female humans, which has a period of about 28 days, is an example of an infradian rhythm. The term *lunatic* (from the Latin for "moon") was once used to describe people with mental illness, on the mistaken notion that madness was influenced by the cyclic appearance of a full moon.

In this chapter, we will focus on the circadian rhythm, which is central to our sleep–waking behavior. Note, however, that the fact that a behavior appears to be rhythmic does not mean that it is produced by a clock. There is evidence that sea bears will remain on the ice as long as the ice pack and food supplies last, and many migrating birds will postpone their migrations as long as they have a food supply. Therefore, it is necessary to demonstrate experimentally that a rhythmic behavior is produced by a biological clock. A definitive experiment to support the conclusion that the sea bear does have a clock would be methodologically difficult to conduct, but such demonstrations are not difficult to make with other animals, including ourselves.

**Circadian rhythm.** An event that occurs with a rhythmic cycle once each day.

| Biological rhythm | Time frame | Example |
|---|---|---|
| Circannual | Yearly | Migratory cycles of birds |
| Infradian | Less than a year | Human menstrual cycle |
| Circadian | Daily | Human sleep cycle |
| Ultradian | Less than a day | Human eating cycles |

## Free-Running Rhythms

To determine if a rhythm is produced by a biological clock, researchers must design a test in which they remove all external cues. If light is assumed to be a major cue, there are three ways to set up the experiment: a test can be given in continuous light, it can be given in continuous dark, or the selection of light–dark can be left to the subject.

That the human sleep–waking rhythm is governed by a biological clock was first demonstrated by Jurgen Aschoff and Rutger Weber (see Kleitman, 1965), who allowed subjects to select their light–dark cycle. The experimenters placed individual subjects in an underground bunker in which there were no cues to signal when day began or ended. Thus, the subjects selected the periods when their lights were on or off, when they were active, and when they slept. In short, they selected their own day and night length. By measuring ongoing behavior and recording sleeping periods with sensors on the beds, Aschoff and Weber found that the subjects continued to show daily sleep-activity rhythms. This finding demonstrated that humans have an endogenous biological clock that governs sleep–waking behavior.

**Figure 12-5**

A free-running rhythm in a human subject. The record for days 1–3 shows the daily sleep period under normal day–night conditions. Days 4–20 show the free-running rhythm that developed while the subject was isolated in a bunker and allowed to control day and night length. The daily activity rhythm shifts from 24 hours to 25.9 hours. On days 21–25, the rhythm frequency returns to 24 hours when the subject is again exposed to a normal light and dark cycle.
Adapted from *Sleep* (p. 33), by J. A. Hobson, 1989, New York: Scientific American Library.

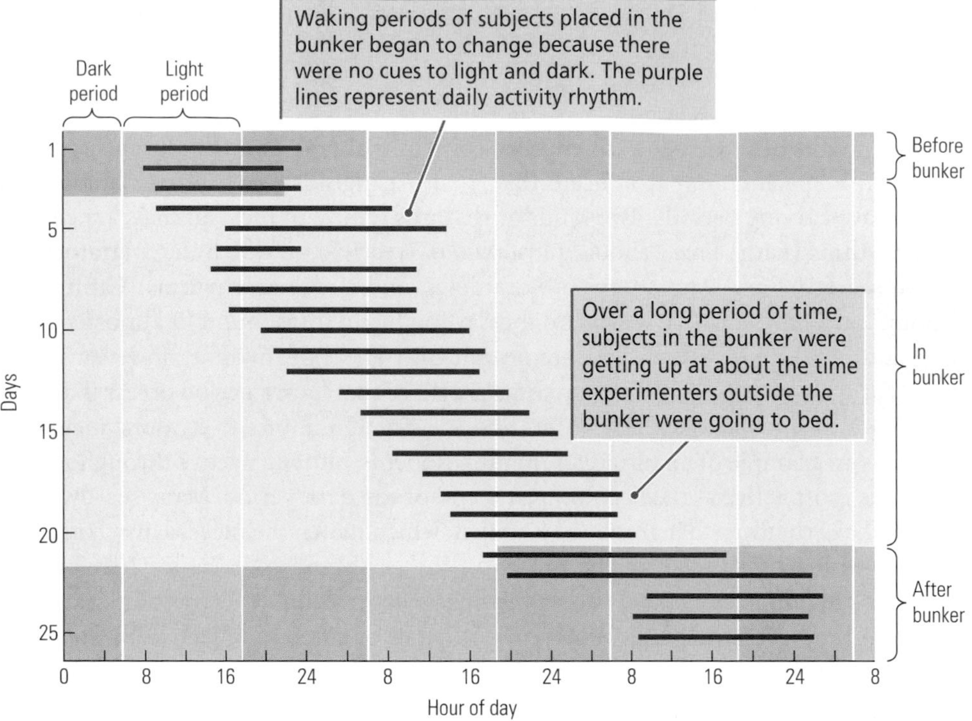
Waking periods of subjects placed in the bunker began to change because there were no cues to light and dark. The purple lines represent daily activity rhythm.
Dark period
Light period
Before bunker
In bunker
After bunker
Over a long period of time, subjects in the bunker were getting up at about the time experimenters outside the bunker were going to bed.
Days
1
5
10
15
20
25
0
8
16
24
8
16
24
8
16
24
8
Hour of day

Figure 12-5 shows, however, that the rhythms recorded by Aschoff and Weber were rather peculiar when compared with the rhythms before and after isolation. Although the period of the sleep–wake cycle of Aschoff and Weber's subjects approximated a normal rhythm of 24 hours before and after the test, during the test it progressively deviated away from clock time. Rather than being 24 hours, the period of the rhythm in the bunker was about 25 to 27 hours, depending on the subject. The subjects were choosing to go to bed from 1 to 2 hours later every night. A shift by an hour or so of sleeping time is not remarkable for a few days, but its cumulative effect over a longer period of time was quite dramatic: soon the subjects were getting up at about the time the experimenters outside the bunker were going to bed. Clearly, the subjects were displaying their own personal rhythms. A rhythm that runs at a frequency of the body's own devising when environmental cues are absent is called a **free-running rhythm.**

The period of free-running rhythms depends on the way in which external cues are removed. When hamsters, a nocturnal species, are tested in constant darkness, their free-running periods are a little shorter than 24 hours; when they are tested in constant light, their free-running periods are a little longer than 24 hours. This test dependency in hamsters is typical of nocturnal animals. As Figure 12-6 shows, the opposite free-running periods are typical of diurnal animals (Binkley, 1990). When sparrows, which are diurnal birds, are tested in constant dark, their free-running periods are a little longer than 24 hours; when they are tested in constant light, their free-running periods are a little shorter than 24 hours. It is not clear why periods change in different lighting conditions, but a rule of thumb is that animals will expand and contract their sleep periods as the sleep-related lighting period expands or contracts. If you understand this point, you can predict how artificial lighting influences human circadian periods, and you can offer an explanation of why Aschoff and Weber's subjects displayed periods that were longer than 24 hours. Endogenous rhythmicity is not the only factor that contributes to circadian periods, however. An endogenous rhythm that is just a little slow or a little fast would be useless, so there must also be a mechanism for setting rhythms so that they correspond to environmental events.

**Free-running rhythm.** A rhythm of the body's own devising in the absence of all external cues.

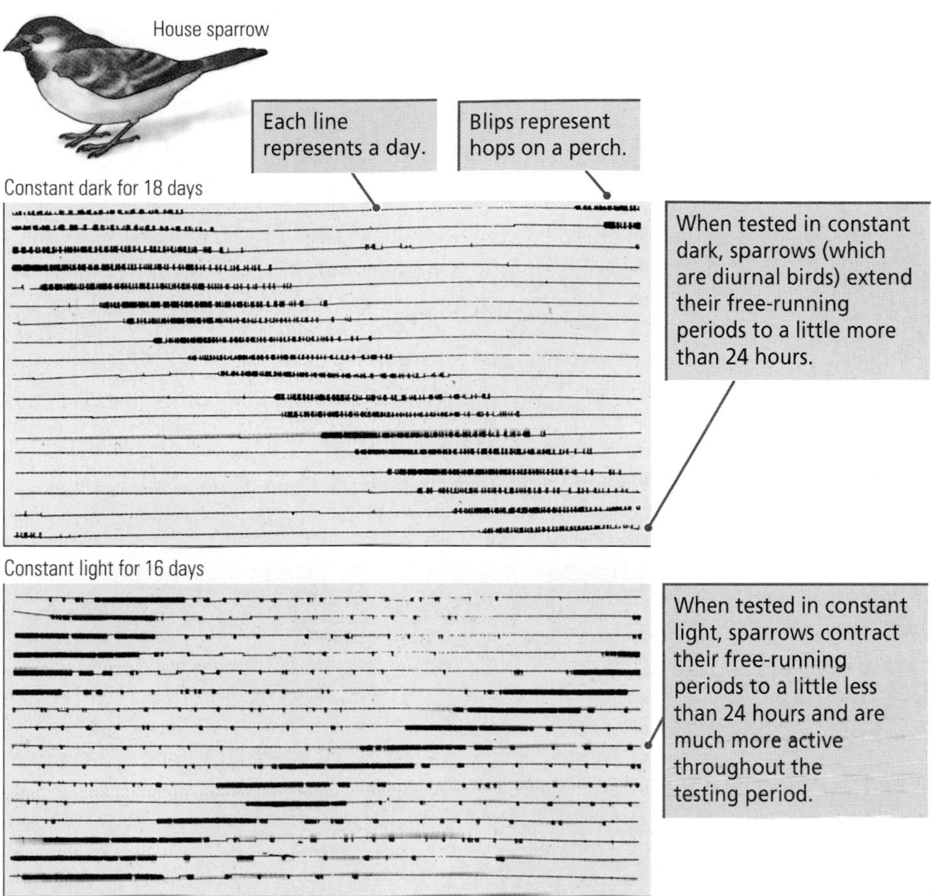
House sparrow
Each line represents a day.
Blips represent hops on a perch.
Constant dark for 18 days
When tested in constant dark, sparrows (which are diurnal birds) extend their free-running periods to a little more than 24 hours.
Constant light for 16 days
When tested in constant light, sparrows contract their free-running periods to a little less than 24 hours and are much more active throughout the testing period.

**Figure 12-6**

The upper event record shows a house sparrow's free-running rhythm in constant dark (the thicker segments of each link on the record represent the bird's movements on a perch). The lower record shows a sparrow's free-running rhythm in constant light. The differences in a sparrow's responses to constant dark and constant light are characteristic of the free-running rhythms of diurnal animals.

Adapted from *The Clockwork Sparrow* (p. 16), by S. Binkley, 1990, Englewood Cliffs, NJ: Prentice Hall.

## Zeitgebers

Because Aschoff and Weber's subjects had a sleep–wake cycle of 24 hours before and after they entered the experiment and because hamsters usually have a 24-hour rhythm, we might wonder how normal rhythms are maintained. There must be some way that the biological clock is kept to a time that matches changes in the day–night cycle. If a biological clock is like a slightly defective wristwatch that runs either too slow or too fast, it will eventually provide times that are inaccurate by hours and so become useless. If we reset the wristwatch each day, however—say, when we awaken—it would then provide useful information even though it is not perfectly accurate. There must be an equivalent way of resetting an errant biological clock. In experiments to determine how clocks are set, researchers have found that cues such as sunrise and sunset, eating times, and other activities can all set the circadian clock. Normally, light is the most potent stimulus for setting a biological clock. Aschoff and Weber called such cues ***Zeitgebers*** (the German word for "time givers"). When a clock is reset by a zeitgeber, it is said to be **entrained.** The importance of light in entraining circadian rhythms is explained in "Seasonal Affective Disorder" on page 452.

Biological clocks can be reset each day so that they accurately correspond to the season. Remember that, in polar regions, the time of onset and the length of day and night are changing as the seasons progress. To adjust to these changes, an animal needs to anticipate daylight as well as have a good idea of how long the day will last. A biological clock that is reset each day tells an animal that daylight will begin tomorrow at approximately the same time that it began today and that tomorrow will last approximately as long as today did. This information is very useful when we consider

**Zeitgeber.** An environmental event that entrains biological rhythms; a "time giver."

**Entrain.** To make one event occur within the same period as another event occurs; literally, to get on a train.

## Focus on Disorders

## Seasonal Affective Disorder

| | |
|---|---|
| Sadness | Later waking |
| Anxiety | Increased sleep time |
| Irritability | Interrupted, not refreshing sleep |
| Decreased physical activity | Daytime drowsiness |
| Increased appetite | Decreased libido |
| Carbohydrate craving | Menstrual difficulties |
| Increased weight | Work difficulties |
| Earlier sleep onset | Interpersonal difficulties |

The symptoms listed above are those observed in more than 66 percent of people who report depression during the winter months in northern latitudes, a condition called *seasonal affective disorder (SAD)*. One explanation of seasonal affective disorder is that the light phase of the circadian rhythm is too short to entrain the circadian rhythms. Consequently, a person's rhythm likely becomes a free-running rhythm. Because people vary in the duration of the phase of their free-running rhythms, some people may be phase retarded, with sleep time coming earlier each day, or phase delayed, with sleep time coming later each day, in relation to the actual day–night cycle. In a diurnal species, the perception of longer nights by the circadian pacemaker most likely results in pressure for increased sleep duration which, if not satisfied, results in cumulative sleep deprivation.

One treatment for SAD is to entrain the circadian rhythm. The basic idea is to increase the short winter photoperiod by exposing a person to artificial bright light (at least 2500 lux; usual room lighting is not thought to be sufficiently bright). Typically, a person undergoing phototherapy for SAD sits in front of a bank of bright lights. Some investigators recommend the exposure in the morning, others recommend it in the evening, and still others recommend bracketing the day with morning and evening exposure. Investigators consistently report that light is capable of ameliorating depression.

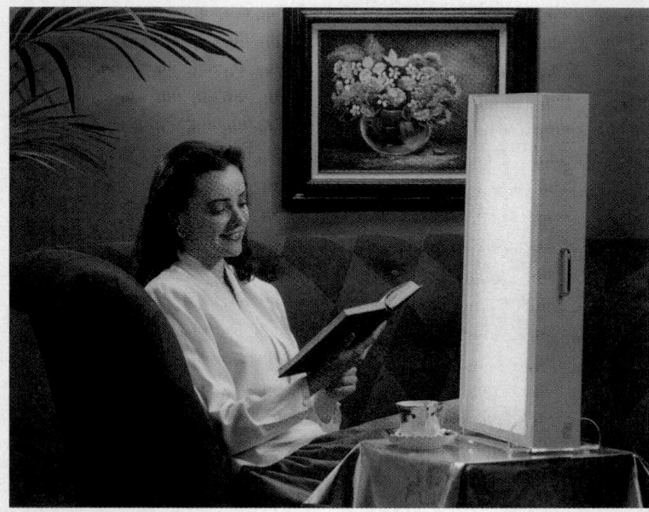

**Exposure to a bright light each winter morning entrains the circadian rhythm.**

Courtesy of Bio-Light by Enviro-Med, 800-222-3296, www.bio-light.com

that, in higher latitudes, daylight begins very early in the morning in summer and very late in the morning in winter.

When should the clock be reset? Zeitgebers work best when they are given near the beginning of the light segment of the cycle. The very potent entraining effect of zeitgebers is illustrated by laboratory studies of Syrian hamsters, perhaps one of the most compulsive animals with respect to timekeeping. When given access to running wheels, hamsters exercise during the night segment of the laboratory day–night cycle. A single brief flash of light is an effective zeitgeber for entraining their biological clocks. (If a hamster happens to blink during this zeitgeber, the light will still penetrate its closed eyelids and entrain its biological clock.) Considering the somewhat less compulsive behavior displayed by some of us, we should shudder at the way that we entrain our own clocks when we stay up late in artificial light, sleep late some days, and get up early by using an alarm clock on other days. Such inconsistent behavior with respect to the human biological clock has been associated with job-related fatigue and accidents.

Hamster

Entrainment also works best if the adjustment to the clock is not too large. People who do shift work are often subject to huge adjustments, especially when they work the graveyard shift (11:00 PM to 8:00 AM), the period when they would normally sleep. Studies show that such a change is difficult to adapt to and is very stressful. Adaptations to shift work are better if workers work the evening shift (3:00 PM to 11:00 PM) before beginning the graveyard shift. Traveling from North America to Europe or Asia also demands a large and difficult time adjustment. For example, travelers flying east from New York to Paris will be beginning their first European day just when their biological clocks are prepared for sleep (Figure 12-7). The difference between a person's circadian rhythm and the daylight cycle in a new environment can produce a feeling of disorientation called "jet lag," referring to jet travel as the cause of such a large, rapid difference. The west-to-east flyer generally has a more difficult adjustment than does the east-to-west traveler, who needs to stay up only a little longer than normal.

**Figure 12-7**

Jet lag is a disruption in the entrainment of a person's biological clock that may be brought on by jet travel. The disorientation is likely to be more pronounced in west-to-east travel, as from New York to Paris, because the disruption in the person's circadian rhythm is more dramatic. On the return journey, the traveler's biological clock has a much easier adjustment to make.

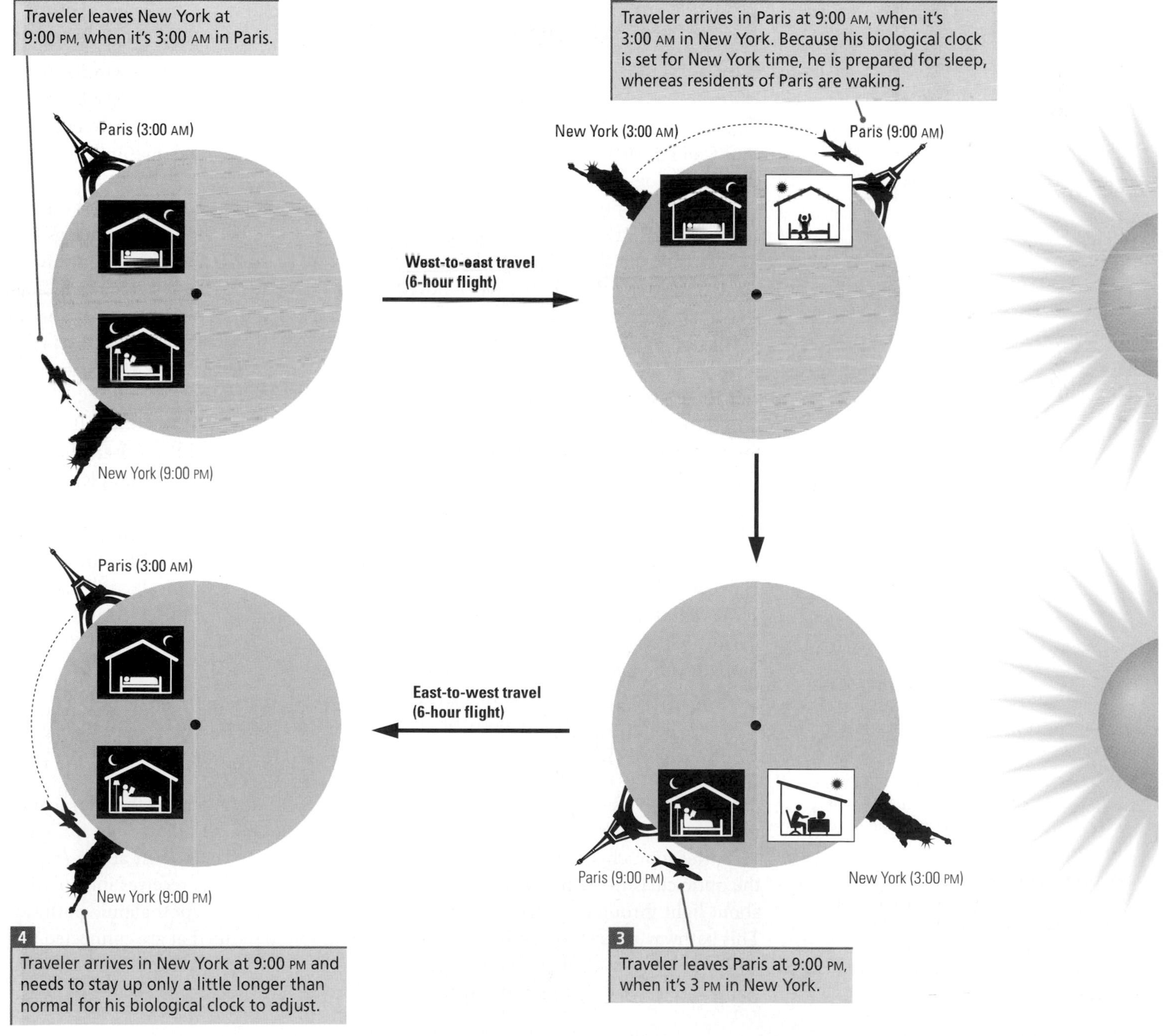
1
Traveler leaves New York at 9:00 PM, when it's 3:00 AM in Paris.
Paris (3:00 AM)
New York (9:00 PM)
West-to-east travel (6-hour flight)
2
Traveler arrives in Paris at 9:00 AM, when it's 3:00 AM in New York. Because his biological clock is set for New York time, he is prepared for sleep, whereas residents of Paris are waking.
New York (3:00 AM)
Paris (9:00 AM)
Paris (3:00 AM)
East-to-west travel (6-hour flight)
New York (9:00 PM)
Paris (9:00 PM)
New York (3:00 PM)
4
Traveler arrives in New York at 9:00 PM and needs to stay up only a little longer than normal for his biological clock to adjust.
3
Traveler leaves Paris at 9:00 PM, when it's 3 PM in New York.

## In Review

Many behaviors occur in a rhythmic pattern in relation to time of year or time of day. These rhythmic behaviors are called biological rhythms: the behaviors having a yearly cycle are called circannual rhythms, and the behaviors having a daily cycle are called circadian rhythms. Biological rhythms are timed by regions of the nervous system that serve as biological clocks to time most of our circadian rhythms, especially our sleep–wake cycles. Although biological clocks keep fairly good time, their periods may be slightly shorter or longer than a 24-hour day unless they are reset each day. Their spontaneous periods are called free-running rhythms. The environmental cues that reset the biological clock are called zeitgebers.

## THE NEURAL BASIS OF THE BIOLOGICAL CLOCK

Curt Richter (1965) was the first person to attempt to locate biological clocks in the brain. In the 1930s, he captured wild rats and tested them in activity wheels; he found that the animals ran, ate, and drank when the lights were off and were relatively quiescent when the lights were on. Richter's hypothesis was that the rats' rhythmic behavior and the biological clock that was responsible for rhythmicity were separate.

Richter proposed that observable behavior was analogous to the hands of a real clock and was driven by a biological clockwork that was analogous to the springs and wheel inside the clock. The clockwork moved the clock hands and would continue to keep time even if the hands were removed. In other words, he thought that the biological clock acted as a **pacemaker** to instruct other neural structures when they should produce the behaviors for which they were responsible. Thus, behaviors such as running, eating, drinking, and changes in body temperature occur when the pacemaker tells their relevant neural areas that it is time to begin. In support of this idea, Richter found that drugs and changes in body temperature could abolish rhythmic behavior for a number of days, but when the behavior resumed, it occurred at precisely the right time. If an animal was drugged or cooled to decrease its activity, for example, its biological clock still kept the correct time, as indicated by the animal's increased activity when it was warmed up. Many subsequent experiments have confirmed that the timekeeping of the biological clock is resistant to changes in temperature. This finding explains why hibernating animals, whose temperature falls so dramatically, still wake up at the right time in the spring. The finding also demonstrates that the clock and the behavior that it generates are separate, because the biological clock can keep time even though paced behavior does not take place.

Richter further proposed that the biological clock is localized in the brain, rather than being a property of all body or all brain cells. By inserting an electrode into the brain to damage brain tissue with electric current, he found that animals lost their circadian rhythms after damage to the hypothalamus. Subsequently, by making much more discrete lesions, experimenters have shown that a region called the **suprachiasmatic nucleus** is a biological clock (Ralph & Lehman, 1991). As illustrated in Figure 12-8, the suprachiasmatic nucleus is located in the hypothalamus, just above *(supra)* the optic chiasm—hence its name. The suprachiasmatic nucleus receives information about light through its own special visual pathway, the **retinohypothalamic pathway.** This pathway consists of a subset of cone receptors in the retina that are connected to a subset of optic-tract fibers and use glutamate as their primary neurotransmitter. Light signals are carried by this pathway to the suprachiasmatic nucleus to excite and to en-

**Pacemaker.** A structure that times or determines the period of activity of another structure or an event.

**Suprachiasmatic nucleus.** A nucleus, located just above the optic chiasm, that is the main pacemaker of circadian rhythms.

**Retinohypothalamic pathway.** A pathway from a subset of cone receptors in the retina to the suprachiasmatic nucleus that allows light to entrain the rhythmic activity of the suprachiasmatic nucleus.

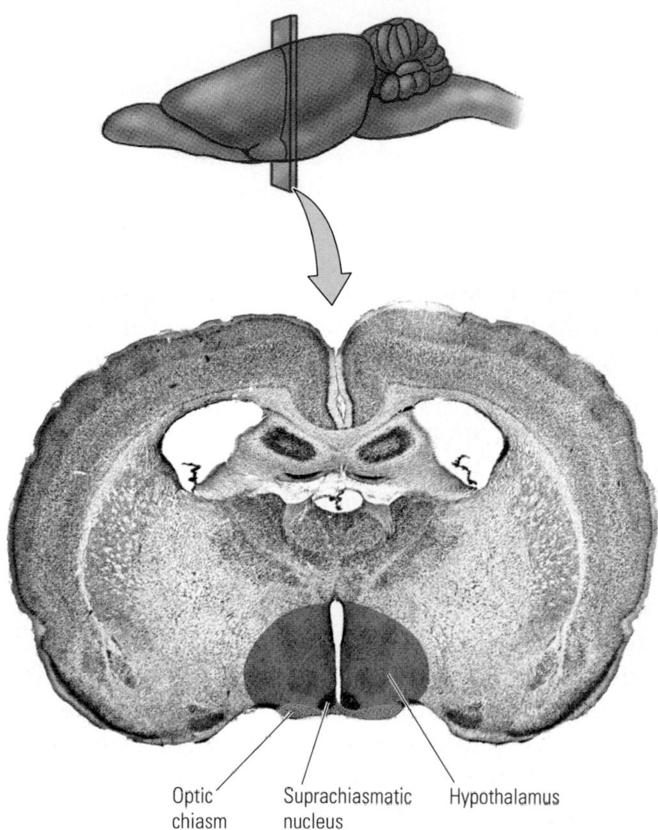


**Figure 12-8**

*(Top)* A lateral view of the rat brain. *(Bottom)* A coronal section through the brain at the level of the optic chiasm, showing the location of the suprachiasmatic nuclei within the hypothalamus and just above the optic chiasm.

train the suprachiasmatic nucleus. Visual fibers carrying information about rhythms also go to an area of the thalamus called the intergeniculate leaflet, but we will limit our consideration of rhythms to the role of the suprachiasmatic nucleus.

Scientists have found another pacemaker in the retina and a third one in the pineal gland. Some behaviors may be paced by widely distributed pacemaker brain cells. Among the other possible pacemakers, the pineal gland has received the most study. It acts as a pacemaker in some species of birds. It is excited by light that enters the brain not through the visual system but through the skull. When the heads of such birds are painted black, the pineal gland's pacemaker activities are blocked. Because the pineal gland can respond directly to light, it has been called the "third eye." In most animals, however, the suprachiasmatic nucleus is the main pacemaker.

## Suprachiasmatic Rhythms in a Dish

Further evidence for the role of the suprachiasmatic nucleus in circadian rhythms comes from a remarkable series of experiments demonstrating that the neurons of the nucleus have intrinsic rhythmic activity (Earnest et al., 1999). Following up on Richter's original experiments, investigators have found that if the suprachiasmatic nuclei are selectively lesioned in rodents, the animals still eat, drink, exercise, and sleep a normal amount, but at haphazard times. By itself, disorganized behavior does not definitively demonstrate that the suprachiasmatic nucleus is the clock that gives instructions about when these activities should take place. The suprachiasmatic nucleus could just be a way station between receptors in the eye and a clock located elsewhere in the brain.

Three other lines of evidence do show, however, that the suprachiasmatic nucleus is indeed the biological clock. First, the metabolic activity of the suprachiasmatic nucleus is higher during the light period of the day–night cycle than it is during the dark period of the cycle. If 2-deoxyglucose—a form of glucose that is taken up by metabolically active cells but is not used by them and cannot escape from them—is tagged with a radioactive label, then cells that are more active will subsequently give off more radioactivity. When 2-deoxyglucose is injected into rodents, its accumulation by the suprachiasmatic nucleus should be relative to the animal's daily rhythm if the neurons in the nucleus are responsible for the rhythm. More tracer is found in the suprachiasmatic nucleus after injections given in the light period of the light–dark cycle than after injections given in the dark period. This experiment demonstrates that suprachiasmatic cells have rhythmic metabolic activity, with their active period correlated with the light period of the light–dark cycle. Other regions of the brain do not show an equivalent rhythmic metabolic pattern; the suprachiasmatic nucleus is special in this respect. Second, recording electrodes placed in the suprachiasmatic nucleus show that neurons in this region are more active during the light period of the cycle than during the dark period, confirming that each neuron has a rhythmic pattern of electrical activity. Third, if all the pathways into and out of the suprachiasmatic nucleus are cut, the neurons of the suprachiasmatic nucleus maintain their rhythmic electrical activity. Together, these experiments show that the suprachiasmatic neurons have a rhythmic pattern of activity that is intrinsic and not a response to rhythmic driving by some other brain structure or to changes in an animal's behavior.

After scientists had demonstrated that the suprachiasmatic nucleus was rhythmically active, the question of how that rhythmicity was generated became central. When the suprachiasmatic nucleus was removed from the brain, maintained in a laboratory dish, and subjected to electrical recording, the neurons were found to maintain their rhythmic activity. Furthermore, if the neurons were isolated from one another, each one was rhythmic. Individual cells did seem to have slightly different rhythms, however. This cellular individuality suggests either that, collectively, the cells express average rhythm or that the suprachiasmatic nucleus has components that are able to produce rhythms with different periods, or both.

## Immortal Time

How do suprachiasmatic cells develop their rhythmic activity? One possibility is that the endogenous rhythm is learned. That is, the cells may initially have no rhythm but, after they receive their first exposure to rhythmic stimulation from environmental zeitgebers, they become rhythmic. A number of studies show, however, that rhythmicity is not learned but is genetically specified.

One way of examining whether rhythmicity is learned is to maintain animals from birth in an environment in which there are no zeitgebers. In experiments in which animals are raised in constant darkness, the animals' behavior still becomes rhythmic. It is possible that the animals' fetal suprachiasmatic cells acquired rhythmicity from the mother, but, in experiments in which animals have been maintained without entraining cues for a number of generations, each generation continues to have rhythmic behavior. Even if the mother has received a lesion of the suprachiasmatic nucleus so that her behavior is not rhythmic, the behavior of the offspring is rhythmic. Thus, it seems that rhythmicity is not learned.

A line of evidence supporting the idea that suprachiasmatic cells are genetically programmed for rhythmicity comes from studies performed in Canada by Martin Ralph and his coworkers with the use of transplantation techniques (Ralph & Lehman, 1991). The general design of the experiments is illustrated in Figure 12-9. First, hamsters are tested in constant dim light or in constant dark, to establish their free-running rhythm. They then receive a suprachiasmatic lesion, followed by another test to show that the lesion has abolished their rhythmicity. Finally, the hamsters receive transplants of suprachiasmatic cells obtained from hamster embryos. About 60 days later, the hamsters again show rhythmic activity, demonstrating that the transplanted cells have become integrated into the host brain and are responsible for reestablishing rhythmic behavior.

In further experiments, Ralph and his coworkers identified and selectively bred hamsters that had a 20-hour rhythm. They named the gene that was responsible for the short rhythm *tau*. If they destroyed the suprachiasmatic nucleus in a genetically normal hamster with a 24-hour period and then transplanted cells from a fetal 20-hour hamster into the cavity, the former 24-hour hamster exhibited the 20-hour period of the *tau* hamster.

David Earnest and his coworkers (1999) carried the transplantation methodology one step further. They harvested cells from the rat suprachiasmatic nucleus and used them to produce an immortalized cell line. By treating each generation of cells with 2-deoxyglucose, they were able to demonstrate that the cells' rhythm was passed on from one generation of cells to the next. The transplantation of cells from the immortal cell line into rats that had received suprachiasmatic lesions restored the circadian rhythm in the rats. Thus, the time encoded by the suprachiasmatic neurons is immortal in that it is passed from one hamster generation to the next or from one cultured suprachiasmatic neuron to the next.

Considerable research is being directed toward determining what genes control the ticking of the circadian clock. Because a single suprachiasmatic neuron displays a circadian rhythm, the timing device must be in the neuron itself, possibly entailing an increase and decrease of one or more proteins made by the cell. Just as the back-and-forth swing of a pendulum makes a grandfather clock tick, the increase and decrease in the amount of the protein makes the cell tick once each day. According to this notion, a protein is made until it crests at a certain level, at which point it inhibits its own production; when its level falls to a critical point, production again rises. In turn, the electrical activity of the cell is linked to protein oscillation, allowing the cell to control other cells during a part of the oscillation. The actual way that the oscillation is produced is a little more complex than this description suggests. Studies on mutant and knockout mice suggest that at least a half dozen genes and the proteins that they produce form two interlocking loops to produce the circadian rhythm of suprachiasmatic cells in mammals (Shearman et al., 2000). Although the mechanism has not yet been worked out, the excitation of suprachiasmatic cells through the retinohypothalamic pathway can presumably degrade one of the proteins to entrain the sequence of biochemical steps in the interlocking loops.

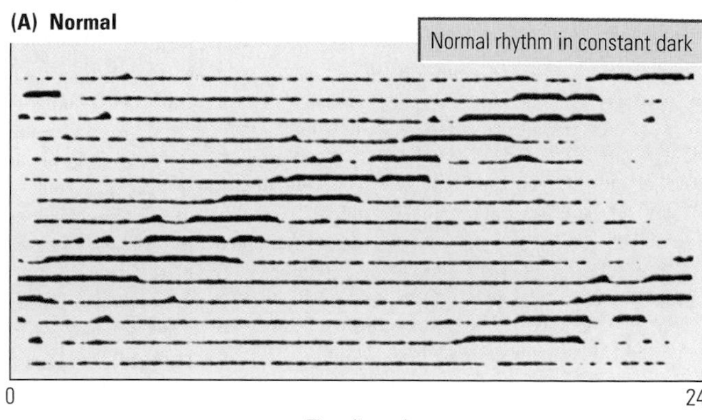


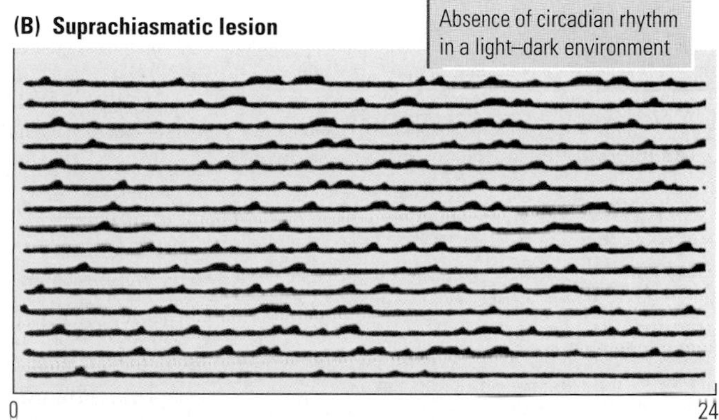


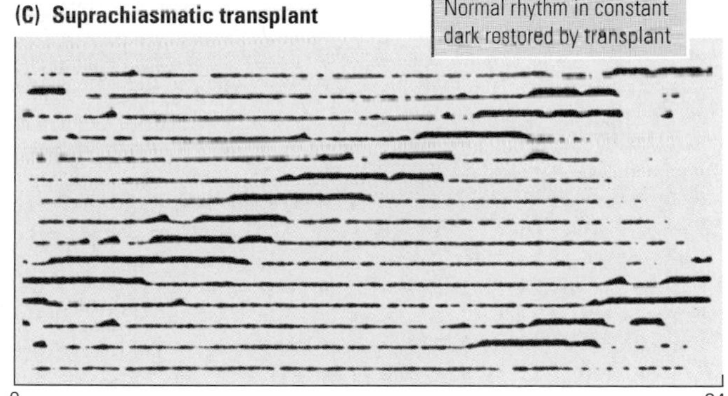


**Figure 12-9**

Recordings showing that hamsters' circadian rhythms are restored by neural transplantation: **(A)** free-running rhythm in constant dark; **(B)** rhythmic behavior eliminated after the suprachiasmatic nucleus has been lesioned; **(C)** circadian rhythm restored after transplant.

Adapted from "Transplantation: A New Tool in the Analysis of the Mammalian Hypothalamic Circadian Pacemaker," by M. R. Ralph and M. N. Lehman, 1991, *Trends in Neurosciences, 14*, p. 363.

## Pacemaking

The suprachiasmatic nucleus is of itself not responsible for directly producing behavior. For example, after the suprachiasmatic nucleus is damaged, the behavioral activities of drinking, eating, and sleep and wakefulness still occur. They no longer occur at appropriate times, however. One proposal for how the suprachiasmatic nucleus controls behavior is illustrated in Figure 12-10. In this model, light entrains the suprachiasmatic nucleus, and the pacemaker in turn drives a number of "slave" oscillators. Each slave oscillator is responsible for the rhythmic occurrence of one behavior. In other words, drinking and eating, body temperature, and sleep and wakefulness are each produced by a separate slave oscillator.

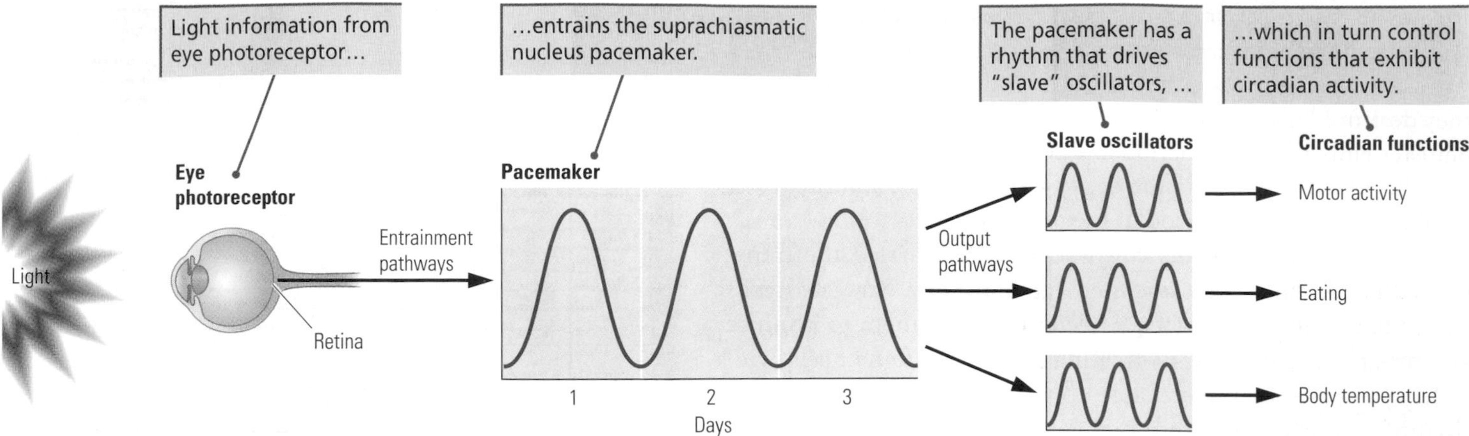


**Figure 12-10**

A model of the organization of the circadian timing system.

Russel Reiter (1980) showed that the suprachiasmatic circadian pacemaker may also be responsible for some circannual behaviors. Hamsters are summertime, or long-day, breeders. As the days lengthen in springtime, the gonads of male hamsters grow and release hormones that stimulate the males' sexual behavior. As the days shorten in the winter, the gonads shrink, the amount of the hormones that the gonads produce decreases, and the males stop being interested in sexual behavior. As Figure 12-11 shows, when melatonin secretion by the pineal gland during a period of a day is low, gonads enlarge; when melatonin secretion during a period of a day is high, gonads shrink. The control that the pineal gland exerts over the gonads is, in turn, controlled by the suprachiasmatic nucleus. Over a rather indirect pathway that need not concern us here, the suprachiasmatic nucleus drives the pineal gland as a slave oscillator. During the daylight period of the circadian cycle, melatonin secretion by the pineal gland is inhibited by the suprachiasmatic nucleus. Thus, as the days become shorter, the period of inhibition becomes shorter and thus the period during which melatonin is released becomes longer. When the period of daylight is shorter than 12 hours, melatonin release becomes sufficiently long to inhibit the hamster's gonads so that they shrink. In animals, such as sheep and deer, that are short-day breeders and mate in the fall and early winter, melatonin also influences the testes. Its effect on reproductive behavior in these species is the reverse of that in the hamster: reproductive activities begin as melatonin release increases.

The origins of many biological rhythms are not yet understood. In his 1965 book titled *Biological Clocks in Medicine and Psychiatry*, Curt Richter summarized a lifetime

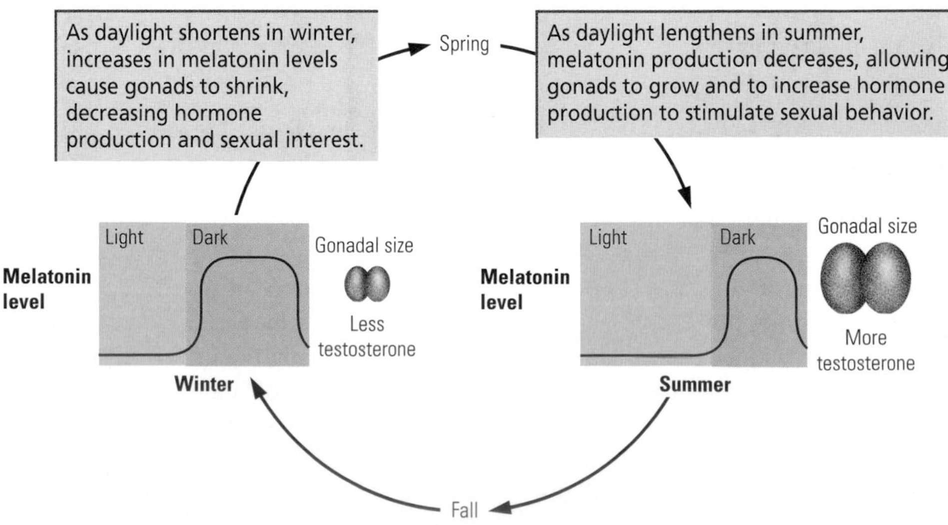


**Figure 12-11**

The circadian pacemaker of the hamster controls circannual sexual activity. In winter, as daylight shortens and night lengthens, there is an increase in total nighttime melatonin secretion, which in turn inhibits testicular growth.

Adapted from "The Pineal and Its Hormones in the Control of Reproduction in Mammals," by R. J. Reiter, 1980, *Endocrinology Review, 1*, p. 120.

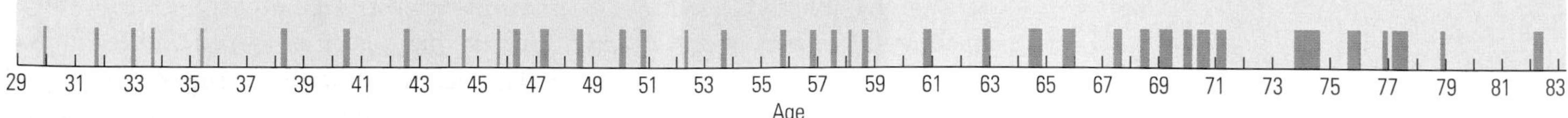


**Figure 12-12**

The attacks of mental illness displayed by the English writer Mary Lamb appear to have had a cyclical component. Such observations would be difficult to obtain today, because the drugs used to treat psychiatric disorders can mask abnormal rhythms.

Adapted from *Biological Clocks in Medicine and Psychiatry* (p. 92), by C. P. Richter, 1965, Springfield, IL: Charles C Thomas.

of recording various normal and abnormal rhythms. Richter recorded rhythmic activity in many bodily functions—including body temperature, hormone levels, eating, and drinking—that were associated but not *in phase,* or perfectly coordinated, with the sleep–wake cycle. He suggested that rhythms with similar periods but different phases might be controlled by different clocks. For example, although body temperature is generally low during sleep, the fact that it does not correlate perfectly with sleep suggests that the two are paced by different biological clocks. Richter also reviewed evidence of peripheral clocks—clocks that are not controlled by the brain. One such example was a patient whose knee swelled up every few days. The person was an accomplished athlete, and the managers of the rugby team for which he played measured the phase of knee swelling and scheduled matches for periods when his knee was functioning normally. Richter hypothesized that many physical and behavioral disorders might be caused by "shocks," either physical or environmental, that upset the timing of biological clocks. Richter's legacy includes a rich line of research that examines the relation between various kinds of illness and biological clocks. For example, the record of psychotic attacks suffered by the English writer Mary Lamb, illustrated in Figure 12-12, is one of many rhythmic records that Richter thought represented the action of a biological clock.

In the next section, we will consider some of the events of sleeping and waking behavior and the neural mechanisms that control them. Understanding circadian rhythms is important for understanding sleeping and waking. If the circadian pacemaker function of the suprachiasmatic nucleus is disrupted, then sleep will be disrupted. Consequently, many sleep disorders may be due not to the mechanisms that control sleep but to a malfunction of the pacemaker.

## In Review

A number of nuclei in the brain serve as biological clocks, including the suprachiasmatic nucleus of the hypothalamus and the pineal gland of the thalamus. Damage to the suprachiasmatic nucleus disrupts the rhythm of daily behaviors. We know that the timing produced by the suprachiasmatic nucleus is a product of its cells because, if removed and cultured in a dish, the cells continue their rhythmic behavior and even pass on their rhythms to offspring cells cultured in a dish. If such cells are transplanted back into a brain from which the suprachiasmatic nucleus has been removed, they restore the animal's rhythmic behavior.

# SLEEP STAGES AND DREAMS

Most people are awake during the day and asleep at night. Both of these behavioral states, which we call *waking* and *sleeping,* are more complex than suggested by our daily experiences. Waking behavior encompasses some periods in which we sit relatively still, other periods when we are still but mentally active, and still other periods when we are physically active. Each of these different conditions is associated with different neural activity. Our sleep behavior is similarly variable in that it consists of periods of resting, napping, long bouts of sleep, and various sleep-related events including snoring, dreaming, thrashing about, and even sleepwalking. Each of these conditions, too, is associated with different neural activity. This section describes some of the behavioral events of waking and sleeping and some of the neural processes that underlie them.

We will begin with the measurement of sleep and waking behavior. A crude measure is to have people record in a diary when they are awake and when they are asleep. Such measures show that there is considerable variation in sleep–waking behavior. People do sleep more when they are young than when they are old. Most people sleep about 7 to 8 hours per night, but some people sleep much more or less than that. There are recorded cases of people who even sleep for less than 1 hour each day. Some people nap for a brief period in the daytime, and others never nap. For example, one of the authors of this textbook can close his eyes and nap almost anytime, including during important lectures, while riding in a car, and even while riding on a ski lift. The other author never naps and finds his colleague's behavior amazing. Benjamin Franklin is credited with the statement, "Early to bed and early to rise makes a man healthy, wealthy, and wise," but measures of sleep behavior indicate that the correlation does not actually exist. Apparently, variations in sleeping time are quite normal.

Experimental studies in which sleep behavior is measured by observing sleeping subjects indicate that diaries are not always accurate. Many people who complain that they have insomnia and are unable to sleep are found, when their sleep is observed, to sleep a normal amount. Many others who report that they sleep a normal amount but are always tired are observed to have such disturbed sleep that they can be described as sleeping hardly at all. Even direct observations of one person by another are not completely accurate, however. We are remarkable dissemblers. We frequently pretend to be more awake than we are or more asleep than we are. Many legal cases revolve around the "state of consciousness" of a car operator or a worker involved in an accident, attesting to the difficulty of determining whether someone is awake or asleep. It is even more difficult to determine sleep–waking behavior in other animals. After examining how sleep can be objectively measured, we will turn to the stages of sleep and dreams.

## Measuring Sleep

Reliable measures of sleep and waking behavior can be obtained by recording the electrical activity of the brain and body with a polygraph, a machine that graphs many biological events (*poly* meaning "many"). Figure 12-13 illustrates a typical polygraph setup and some commonly used measures. Electrodes are pasted onto a number of standard locations on the skull's surface for an electroencephalogram (EEG, a record of brain-wave activity), onto muscles of the neck for an electromyogram (EMG, a record of muscle activity), and above the eyes for an electrooculogram (EOG, a record of eye movements). A thermometer also may be used, to measure body temperature. Together, these measures provide a comprehensive description of sleep–waking states.

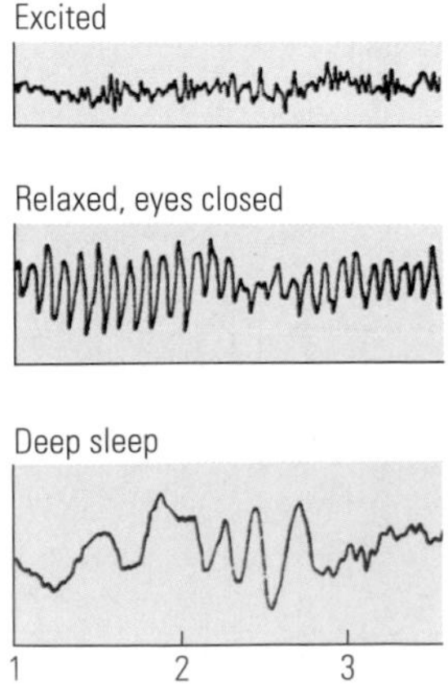


The EEG record is the primary measure of sleep states. The electroencephalograph records patterns from different parts of the brain; we will look at the patterns of the neocortex. When a person is awake, the EEG of the neocortex consists of small-amplitude waves with a fast frequency. This pattern of activity is usually referred to as fast activity, activated EEG, or waking EEG—or, more formally, as a **beta rhythm** (which means that the rhythm of the waves has a frequency, or period, ranging from 15 to 30 hertz, or times per second). When a person becomes drowsy, the fast-wave activity of the neocortex changes in two ways: (1) the amplitude (height) of the waves becomes greater, and (2) the frequency (period) of the waves becomes slower. Usually the two changes occur together. When subjects relax and close their eyes, they may produce a

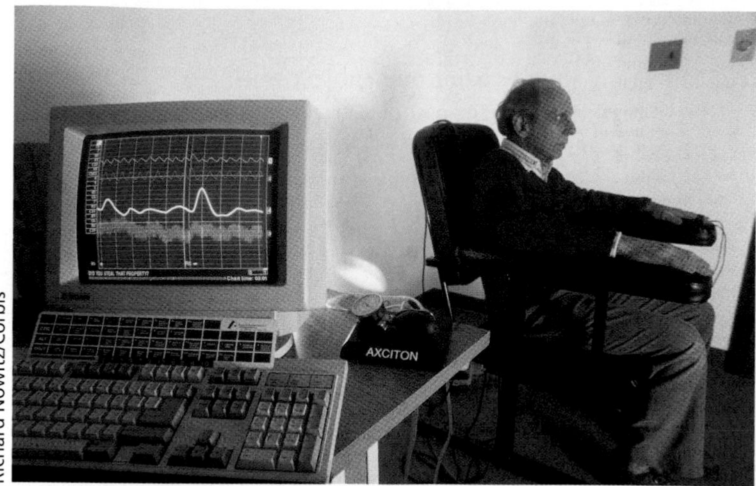

Richard Nowitz/Corbis

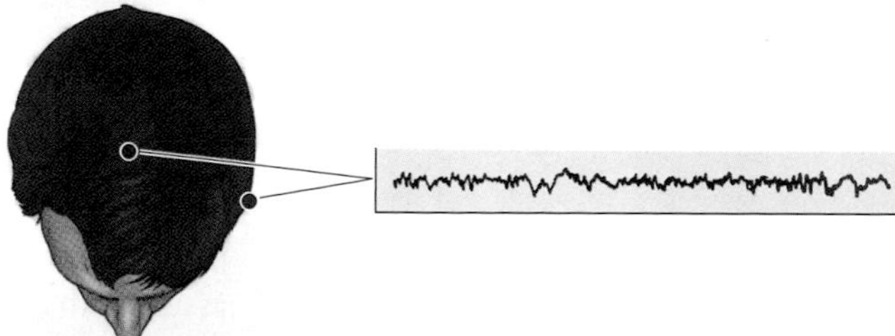


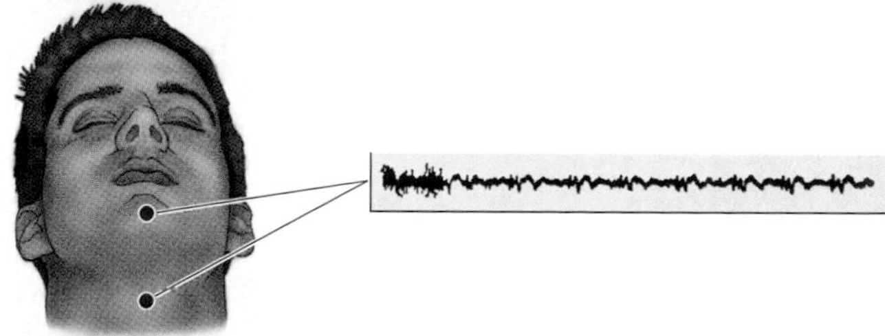


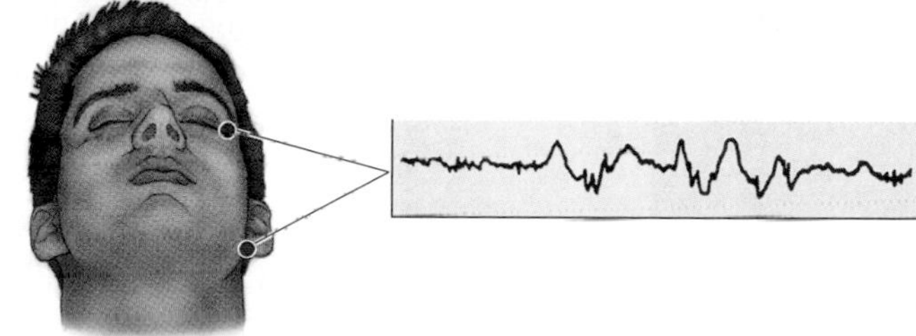


**Figure 12-13**

The setup for a polygraph recording. The electronic equipment in the foreground records the various readings from the electrodes attached to the subject. **(A)** Electroencephalogram made from a point on the skull relative to a neutral point on the ear. **(B)** Electromyogram made between two muscles, such as those on the chin and throat. **(C)** Electrooculogram made between the eye and a neutral point on the ear.

particular rhythmic pattern called an **alpha rhythm** (large waves whose rhythms have a frequency ranging from 7 to 11 hertz). As subjects go to sleep, they produce slower, larger EEG waves known as slow-wave activity, resting activity, or sleeplike activity—or, more formally, as **delta rhythms** (waves with a frequency of 1 to 3 hertz). The relation of EEG patterns to behavior is correlational, not causative; that is, the waves are not producing the behavior, nor is the behavior producing the waves. That accepted, a rule of thumb is that fast-wave activity is associated with waking behavior, and slow-wave activity is associated with sleeping behavior.

Visit the section on the EEG in the Research Methods module of your CD to learn more about the EEG and the stages of sleep and waking.

Observers of sleep have long known that sleep consists of segments in which a sleeper is relatively still and segments in which twitching movements of the mouth, fingers, and toes occur. These two different aspects of sleep are readily observable in household pets and bed partners. In 1955 Eugene Aserinsky and Nathaniel Kleitman (see Dement, 1972), working at the University of Chicago, discovered that the twitching periods were also associated with rapid eye movements, or REMs, in which the eyes can be observed flickering back and forth behind the sleeper's closed eyelids. More remarkably, they discovered that, during REMs, the neocortical EEG record displays a fast-wave pattern. That is, the EEG record suggested that the subjects were awake, even though Aserinsky and Kleitman were able to confirm that the subjects really were asleep.

This phase of sleep, in which fast-wave activity occurs in association with REMs, was designated as **REM sleep.** The other phase of sleep, associated with slowing of the EEG, is called **NREM** ( for non-REM) **sleep** and sometimes **slow-wave sleep.** With these distinctions in mind, we can turn now to the EEG patterns associated with a typical night's sleep.

## A Typical Night's Sleep

Figure 12-14 is a record of brain activity from one subject during a typical night's sleep. Figure 12-14A displays the EEG patterns associated with waking and with sleep. Sleep is divided into four stages on the basis of EEG records. Notice that the main change characterizing these stages is that the EEG waves become larger and slower in a progression from stage 1 sleep through stage 4 sleep. The designation of these stages assumes that the sleeper moves from relatively shallow sleep in stage 1 to deeper sleep in stage 4.

Figure 12-14B illustrates graphically when these different stages of sleep occur and how long they last in the course of a night's sleep. Notice that the depth of sleep changes several times. The subject gradually descends from a waking state to stage 4 sleep in about one-half hour, stays in stage 4 sleep for about one-half hour, and then ascends to stage 1 sleep. This sequence lasts approximately 90 minutes and is typically repeated four times, except that, as the night progresses, the stages of sleep associated with the slowest EEG patterns are less frequent.

As already mentioned, the EEG of stage 1 sleep is similar to the EEG of waking, but the subject is asleep. The oculograph indicates that the subject's eyes are moving during stage 1, meaning that it is REM sleep. Therefore, the duration of the different stages of sleep roughly divides a night's sleep into two parts, the first dominated by NREM sleep and the second dominated by REM sleep. Body temperature is lowest (about 1.5 degrees below a normal temperature of 37.7°C) during the first part of a night's sleep and rises during the second part. Self-reports of subjects who are awakened from sleep at different times suggest that stage 4, the deepest sleep, occurs early. Subjects are difficult to awaken at this time and act groggy when disturbed. When subjects are awakened in the second half of sleep, they appear more alert and attentive.

In considering a "typical" night's sleep, we should bear in mind that the behavior of individual people is very variable and most variations are not abnormal. Adults typically sleep about 8 hours with about 2 of those hours spent in REM, but some people sleep less than 8 hours and others sleep more. A person's sleep patterns may also vary at different times of life. The time that we spend asleep increases during growth spurts and in conjunction with physical exertion. Sleep durations also increase for women

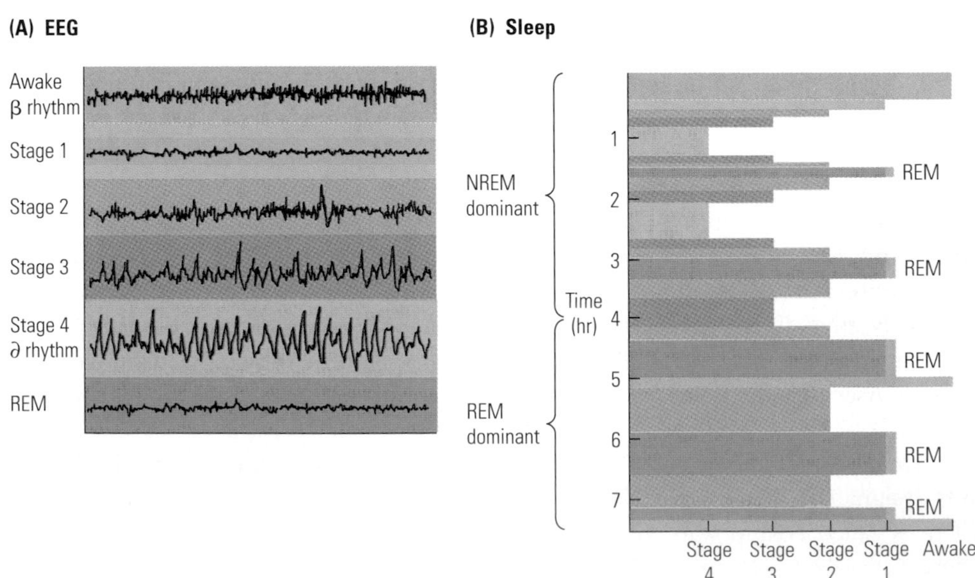


**Figure 12-14**

**(A)** Electroencephalographic patterns associated with waking and four stages of sleep. Stage 1 has the same EEG pattern as REM sleep, and stages 2 to 4 are called NREM sleep. **(B)** In a typical night's sleep, a person undergoes a number of sleep-state changes. NREM sleep dominates the early sleep hours, and REM sleep dominates the later sleep hours. The depth of sleep is indicated by the relative lengths of the bars, and the duration of each stage of sleep is indicated by the thicknesses of the bars. The time spent in REM sleep is indicated by dark purple bars.

Adapted from "Sleep and Dreaming," by D. D. Kelley, in E. R. Kandel, J. H. Schwartz, and T. M. Jessell (Eds.), *Principles of Neuroscience,* 1991, New York: Elsevier, p. 794.

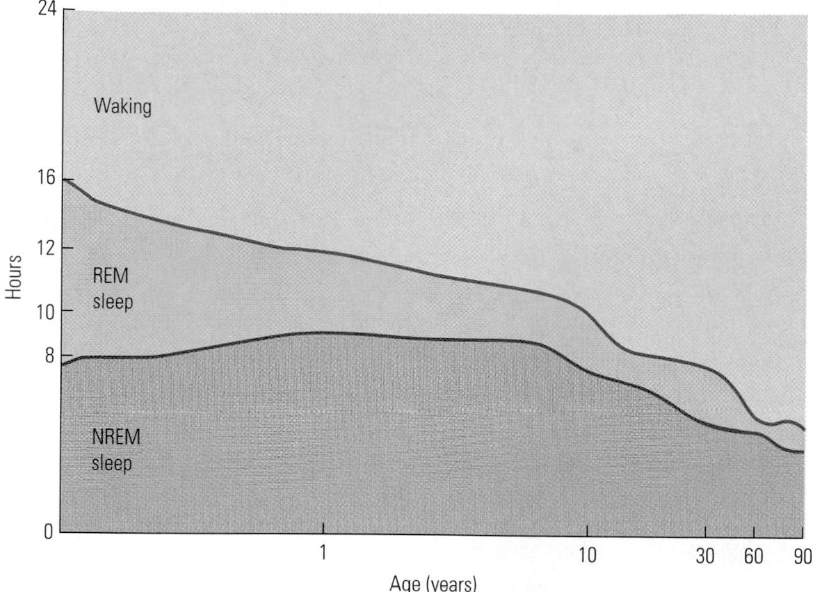


**Figure 12-15**

The amount of time that humans spend sleeping decreases with age. The amount of REM sleep is especially high in the first few years of life.

Adapted from "Ontogenetic Development of the Human Sleep-Dream Cycle," by H. P. Roffward, J. Muzio, and W. C. Dement (1966), *Science, 152*.

during pregnancy. The time that is spent in different stages of sleep changes dramatically over the life span. As is illustrated in Figure 12-15, most people sleep less as they grow older. Furthermore, in the first 2 years of life, REM sleep makes up nearly half of sleep time, but it declines proportionately until, in middle age, it constitutes little more than 10 percent of sleep time.

Another aspect of "typical" patterns of sleep has to do with the fact that we modern humans, because much of our time is spent indoors, are exposed to less outdoor light than our ancestors were. This difference is important because outdoor light is much brighter than indoor light, and bright light may be necessary for setting our circadian rhythms. Therefore, we cannot really be sure if our patterns of sleep would be the same as those of people living in "natural" environments. Some scientists have commented on the fact that we are the only primates to take all of our sleep in one block. They speculate that if we were exposed to natural light, we might divide our sleep into two parts, an early evening part and an early morning part, with a period of waking in between.

## NREM Sleep

Although many people may think that sleep is an inactive period, a remarkable range of activities take place during sleep (see "Restless Legs Syndrome" on page 464). During NREM sleep, body temperature declines, heart rate decreases, blood flow decreases, we perspire and lose body weight owing to water loss, and our levels of growth hormone increase. It was once thought that we do not dream during NREM sleep, but recent studies show that, when subjects are aroused from NREM sleep, they do report dreams. NREM sleep is also the time during which we toss and turn in bed, pull on the covers, and engage in other movements. If we talk in our sleep, we will do so during NREM sleep. If we make flailing movements of the limbs, such as banging with an arm or kicking with a foot, we will usually do so in NREM sleep. Some people even get up and walk during sleep, and this "sleepwalking" is thought to occur in NREM sleep. Children may experience brief, very frightening dreams called night terrors, which also occur in NREM sleep. All these conditions are inconsistent with a period that is often described as quiet and inactive.

To learn more about night terrors, visit the Web site at **www.worthpublishers.com/kolb/chapter12.**

Focus on Disorders

## Restless Legs Syndrome

I've always been a fairly untalented sleeper. Even as a child, it would take me some time to fall asleep, and I would often roll around searching for a comfortable position before going under. But my real difficulties with sleeping did not manifest themselves until early adulthood. By that time, my father had been diagnosed with Restless Legs Syndrome (RLS) and I was suffering the same symptoms.

Initially, my symptoms consisted of a mild tingling in my legs. It caused me to be fidgety and made it hard to fall asleep. Eventually, I went through a number of days without much sleep and reached a point where I simply could not function. I went to a doctor who prescribed a small course of sleeping medication (a benzodiazepine). I was able to get good sleep and my sleep cycle seemed to get back on track. Over the next decade I had periodic bouts of tingling in my legs which caused me to be fidgety and interfered with sleep. As time passed, the bouts occurred with increasing frequency and the symptoms became more noticeable and uncomfortable. I would simply suffer through these bouts, sleeping poorly and paying the consequences, or I would seek medical help. Being a student, I did not have a regular doctor. Unfortunately, most physicians I met did not know about RLS, and thought I was "drug seeking" or merely stressed out. I received a variety of patronizing responses and found these experiences insulting and demeaning. It would have been easy to give up and try to deal with it on my own, but because of my father's diagnosis, I knew the true source of the problem and was determined to get help.

When I took my current position, I started seeing a doctor on a regular basis. By this time, my sleep was being seriously affected by RLS. The sensations in my legs were something like a combination of an ache in my muscles (much like one gets after exercising) and an electrical, tingling sensation. They would be briefly relieved with movement, such as stretching, rubbing, contracting my muscles, or changing position, but would return within seconds. In fact, my wife says my cycle is about 13 to 15 seconds between movements. I do this either when awake or during sleep. Trying not to move greatly increases the discomfort—much like trying to not scratch a very bad itch. The symptoms get worse in the evening and at night. Most nights, I have trouble falling asleep. Other nights, I wake up after an hour or so and then have trouble going back under.

Now my doctor takes me seriously. We exchanged research articles and thoroughly discussed treatment options. As part of this process, my wife met with my physician to relate her experiences. I was stunned to learn how severely my RLS was interfering with her sleep. I think she was being compassionate and not complaining so I wouldn't feel any more upset than I already was about my sleeping difficulties. My doctor started me on a regular course of sleeping medication (again, a benzodiazepine) and encouraged me to stay on it. This was a life-changing event. For the first time in my adult life, I was getting good sleep on a regular basis. My wife and I also got separate beds.

On the down side, RLS is a chronic and progressive condition. Over the years I've had to slowly increase dosages, switch to new medicines, and am now on two medications. I have always communicated openly and honestly with my physician, and we have worked together to monitor issues such as tolerance and medication dosages. I have gone for consultation with a neurologist experienced with RLS. I still get good sleep, but I have had to make many significant adjustments.

## REM Sleep and Dreaming

REM sleep is no less exciting and remarkable than NREM sleep. During REM sleep, our eyes move and our toes, fingers, and mouths twitch, and males have penile erections. Still, we are paralyzed, as indicated by the absence of muscle activity on an EMG. You can get an idea of what REM sleep is like by observing a cat or dog. At the onset of REM sleep, the animal usually subsides into a sprawled posture as the paralysis of its

I am very up front about the fact that I have RLS. In fact, whenever I teach the topic of sleep and sleep disorders in my brain and behavior classes, I always make some time to talk about my experiences with RLS. Occasionally, students approach me with their own difficulties, and I try to provide them with information and resources.

—Stuart Hall, Ph.D., University of Montana

*Restless legs syndrome* (RLS) is a sleep disorder in which a person experiences unpleasant sensations in the legs described as creeping, crawling, tingling, pulling, or pain. The sensations are usually in the calf area but may be felt anywhere from the thigh to the ankle. One or both legs may be affected; for some people, the sensations are also felt in the arms. People with RLS describe an irresistible urge to move the legs when the sensations occur. Many people with RLS have a related sleep disorder called *periodic limb movement in sleep* (PLMS). It is characterized by involuntary jerking or bending leg movements in sleep that typically occur every 10 to 60 seconds. Some people experience hundreds of such movements per night, which can wake them, disturb their sleep, and annoy bed partners. People with these disorders get less sleep at night and may feel sleepy during the day.

Bill Aron/PhotoEdit

Insomnia like that shown in this time-lapse photograph is a frequent consequence of restless legs syndrome, a sleep disorder characterized by painful sensations in the legs.

These symptoms affect both sexes, and symptoms can begin at any time but are more severe among older people. Young people who experience symptoms are sometimes thought to have "growing pains" or may be considered hyperactive because they cannot easily sit still in school. There is no laboratory test for these disorders, and a doctor cannot detect anything abnormal in a physical examination. In mild cases of the disorders, massage, exercise, stretching, and hot baths may be helpful. For more severe cases, patients can restrict their intake of caffeine, take benzodiazepines to help them get to sleep, and take L-dopa, a drug that is also used to treat Parkinson's disease. These treatments reduce symptoms, but at present there is no cure for the condition.

muscles sets in. Figure 12-16 illustrates the sleep postures of a horse. Horses can sleep while standing up by locking their knee joints, and they can sleep while lying down with their heads held slightly up. At these times, they are in NREM sleep; when they are completely sprawled out, they are in REM sleep. During REM sleep, animals' limbs twitch visibly, and, if you look carefully at the face of a dog or cat, you will also see the skin of the snout twitch and the eyes move behind the eyelids. It might seem strange

Courtesy of Ian Whishaw

Courtesy of Ian Whishaw

Courtesy of Ian Whishaw

**Figure 12-16**

Horses usually seek an open, sunny area in which to take brief periods of sleep. Ian's horse, Lady Jones, illustrates three sleep postures. At top left she displays NREM sleep, standing with legs locked and head down, and at top right she displays NREM sleep lying down with head up. At bottom left she is in REM sleep, in which all posture and muscle tone is lost.

that an animal that is paralyzed can make small twitching movements, but the neural pathways that mediate these twitches are presumably spared the paralysis. One explanation for the twitching movements of the eyes, face, and distal parts of the limbs is that such movements may help to maintain blood flow in those parts of the body. An additional change resulting from the absence of muscle activity during REM sleep is that mechanisms that regulate body temperature stop working and body temperature moves toward room temperature. The sleeper may wake up from REM sleep feeling cold or hot, depending on the temperature of the room.

The most remarkable aspect of REM sleep was discovered by William Dement and Nathaniel Kleitman in 1957 (Dement, 1972). When subjects were awakened from REM sleep, they reported that they had been having vivid dreams. In contrast, subjects aroused from NREM sleep were much less likely to report that they had been dreaming, and the dreams that they did report were much less vivid.

The technique of electrical recording from a sleeping subject in a sleep laboratory made it possible to subject dreams to experimental analysis, and such studies provided some objective answers to a number of interesting questions concerning dreaming. The first question that studies of dreaming answered was, How often do people dream? Reports by people on their dreaming behavior had previously suggested that dreaming was quite variable, with some people reporting that they dreamed frequently and others reporting that they never dreamed. Waking subjects up during periods of REM showed that everyone dreams, that they dream a number of times each night, and that dreams last longer as a sleep session progresses. Those who claimed not to dream were presumably forgetting their dreams. Perhaps people who forget their dreams do so because they do not wake up during or immediately after a dream, thus allowing a subsequent NREM sleep session to erase the memory of the dream.

Another interesting question that objective measures answered was, How long do dreams last? There had been suggestions that dreams last but an instant. By waking people up at different intervals after the onset of a REM period and matching the reported dream content to the previous duration of REM sleep, researchers were able to show that dreams appear to take place in real time. That is, an action that a person performed in a dream lasts about as long as it would take to perform while awake.

## What Do We Dream About?

The study of dreaming in sleep laboratories also allowed researchers to study the content of dreams. Past explanations of dreaming have ranged from messages from the gods to indigestion. The first modern treatment of dreams was described by the founder of psychoanalysis, Sigmund Freud, in *The Interpretation of Dreams,* published in 1900. Freud reviewed the early literature on dreams, described a methodology for studying dreams, and provided a theory to explain their meaning. We will briefly consider Freud's theory inasmuch as it remains popular in psychoanalysis and in the arts.

Click on the Web site to investigate more about research on dreams at **www.worthpublishers.com/kolb/chapter12.**

Freud suggested that the function of dreams was the symbolic fulfillment of unconscious wishes. His theory of personality was that people have both a conscious and an unconscious. Freud proposed that the unconscious contains unacknowledged desires and wishes, many of which are sexual. He further proposed that dreams have two levels of meaning. The *manifest content* of a dream consists of a series of often bizarre images and actions that are only loosely connected. The *latent content* of the dream contains its true meaning, which, when interpreted by a psychoanalyst, provides a coherent account of the dreamer's unconscious wishes.

Freud provided a method for interpreting symbols and reconstructing the latent content of dreams. For example, he pointed out that a dream usually began with an incident from the previous day, incorporated childhood experiences, and included ongoing unfulfilled wishes. He also identified a number of types of dreams, such as those that dealt with childhood events, anxiety, and wish fulfillment. The content of the dream was important to Freud and other psychoanalysts in clinical practice because, when interpreted, dreams were a source of insight into a patient's problems.

Other psychoanalysts, unhappy with Freud's emphasis on sexual desire, developed their own methods of interpretation. Carl Jung, another psychoanalyst and contemporary of Freud, for example, proposed that the symbolism of dreams signified distant human memories that were encoded in the brain but had long since been lost to conscious awareness. Jung proposed that dreams allowed a dreamer to relive the history of the human race. As more theories of dream interpretation developed, their central weakness became apparent: it was difficult, if not impossible, to know which interpretation was correct.

The dream research of Freud and his contemporaries was impeded by their reliance on a subject's memory of a dream and by the fact that many of their subjects were patients. This unquestionably resulted in the selection of the unusual by both the patient and the analyst. Now that researchers study dreams more objectively by waking subjects and questioning them, one might think that the meaning of dreams might be better understood. Certainly, knowledge of the content of dreams has improved. Research suggests that most dreams are about events that happened quite recently and concern ongoing problems. Colors of objects, symbols, and emotional content most often relate to events taking place in a person's recent waking period. Calvin Hall documented more than 10,000 dreams of normal people and found that more than 64 percent were associated with sadness, anxiety, or anger. Only about 18 percent were happy. Hostile acts against the dreamer outnumbered friendly acts by more than two to one. Surprisingly, in light of Freud's theory, only about 1 percent of dreams included sexual feelings or acts.

Contemporary dream theories fall into two groups—continuity and discontinuity theories. Continuity theories propose that as we pass from waking into NREM and then into REM sleep, we continue to ruminate and worry (that is, daydream), but the worrying becomes more bizarre as we lose conscious control over our thoughts. Discontinuity theories propose that both the content and the neural basis of ruminating of NREM dreams and of REM dreams are different. Two discontinuity theories that represent opposing views of the meaning of REM dreams are described next.

J. Allen Hobson (1989) proposed what he calls the *activation-synthesis hypothesis* of dreaming. According to this view, during a dream the cortex is bombarded by signals from the brainstem, and these signals produce the pattern of waking (or activated) EEG. The cortex, in response to this excitation, generates images, actions, and emotion from personal memory stores. In the absence of external verification, these dream events are fragmented and bizarre and reveal nothing more than that the cortex has been activated. According to the activation-synthesis hypothesis, dreams are nevertheless personal in that a person's memories and experiences are activated, but they have no meaning. So, for example, the following dream, with its bizarre, delusional, and fragmented elements, would be representative of images that are synthesized to accompany brain activation. According to this hypothesis, any meaning that the dream might seem to have is created by the dreamer after the fact, as was perhaps done by the middle-aged dreamer who recounted this dream:

> I found myself walking in a jungle. Everything was green and fresh and I felt refreshed and content. After some time I encountered a girl whom I did not know. The most remarkable thing about her was her eyes, which had an almost gold color. I was really struck by her eyes not only because of their unique color but also because of their expression. I tried to make out other details of her face and body but her eyes were so dominating that was all I could see. Eventually, however, I noticed that she was dressed in a white robe and was standing very still with her hands at her side. I then noticed that she was in a compound with wire around it. I became concerned that she was a prisoner. Soon, I noticed other people dressed in white robes and they were also standing still or walking slowly without swinging their arms. It was really apparent that they were all prisoners. At this time I was standing by the fence that enclosed them, and I was starting to feel more concerned. Suddenly it dawned on me that I was in the compound and when I looked down at myself I found that I was dressed in a white robe as well. I remember that I suddenly became quite frightened and woke up when I realized that I was exactly like everyone else. The reason that I remembered this dream is the very striking way in which my emotions seemed to be going from contentment, to concern, to fear as the dream progressed. I think that this dream reflected my desire in the 1970's to maintain my individuality. (Recounted by A. W.)

Anttio Revonsuo (2000) of Finland agrees with Hobson about the content of dreams but uses content analysis to argue that dreams are biologically important in that they lead to enhanced performance in dealing with threatening life events. In his *evolutionary hypothesis of dreams,* Revonsuo argues that this enhanced performance would have been especially important for early humans, whose environment included frequent dangerous events that constituted extreme threats to their reproductive success. He notes that dreams are highly organized and are significantly biased toward threatening images (as, for example, in the preceding dream). People seldom dream about reading, writing, and calculating, even though these behaviors may occupy much of their day. The threatening events of dreams are the same ones that are threatening in real life (Figure 12-17). For example, animals and strange men who could be characterized as "enemies" figure prominently in dreams. Revonsuo notes that there is overwhelming evidence that dream content incorporates the current emotional problems of the dreamer. He also reviews evidence to suggest that depressed dreamers who dream about their focal problems are better adjusted than those who do not. Revonsuo also notes that recurrent dreams and nightmares generally begin in childhood, when a

Erich Lessing/Art Resource

**Figure 12-17**

The terrifying visions that may persist even after awakening from a frightening dream are represented in this painting titled *The Night,* by the Swiss artist Ferdinand Hodler.

*The Night,* by Ferdinand Hodler (1853–1918), oil on canvas, 116 x 299 cm., Kunstmuseum, Berne, Switzerland.

person is most vulnerable, and are associated with anxiety, threats, and pursuit. In them, the dreamer is usually watching, hiding, or running away. Revonsuo therefore proposes that the experience of dealing with threats in dreams is adaptive because it can be applied to dealing with real-life threats. To illustrate, a student provided the following account of a dream from childhood that she had dreamed subsequently a few times:

> When I was five years old, I had a dream that at the time frightened me but that I now find somewhat amusing. It took place in the skating rink of my small hometown. There was no ice in the rink, but instead the floor consisted of sod. The women, my mother included, were working in the concession booth, and the men were in the arena, dressed in their work clothes. I was among the children of the town who were lined up in the lobby of the rink. None of the children, including myself, knew why we were lined up. The adults were summoning the children two at a time. I decided to take a peek through the window, and this is what I saw. There was a large circus-ride type metal chair that was connected to a pulley, which would raise the chair to about 20 feet into the air. The seat would be lowered and two children at a time would be placed in it. A noose was then placed around the neck of each and the chair was again raised. Once the chair reached its greatest height, the bottom would drop out of the chair and the children would be hanged (I did not see this but I thought that is what happened to them). At this point, I turned to a friend and said, "Here, Ursula, you can go ahead of me" and I went to my mother and told her what was going on. She smiled as if I were just being difficult and told me that I was to get back in the line. At this point I thought, "Forget it," and I found a place to hide underneath the big wooden bleachers in the lobby. It was dark and I could hear everyone out looking for me. (Recounted by N. W.)

When asked what she thought this dream meant, this student said that she really did not know. When told that it could be an anxiety dream, something common in children, that might represent an activity that she considered stressful, such as competing in figure skating and failing, she said that she did not think that was it. She volunteered, however, that her community's skating rink was natural ice and that it was bitterly cold whenever there was enough ice to go skating. When she had to skate, her feet got cold and her mother almost had to lift her up and drag her out onto the ice. Being dropped out of the chair may have been a symbolic representation of being pushed out onto the ice. Elements of the dream did represent what went on at the skating rink. Men did prepare the ice and the women did run a confection booth, and she did resist being sent out to skate. The recurrence of the dream could be due to the conflict that she felt about having to do something that exposed her to the cold and her solution in hiding.

## In Review

The average length of a night's sleep is from 7 to 8 hours, but some people sleep much less or much more. Sleep is divided into four stages on the basis of the EEG record. The first three stages are characterized by progressive slowing of the EEG record, whereas the fourth stage is characterized by a waking EEG record. Because rapid eye movements accompany stage 4 sleep, it is called REM sleep; the other three stages are grouped together as NREM sleep. There are about four REM sleep periods each night, with each period getting longer as sleep progresses. REM sleep is also marked by muscle paralysis and dreams that are more vivid than those of NREM sleep. There are various interpretations of the function of dreams. The activation-synthesis hypothesis suggests that they are simply a by-product of the brain's activity and so have no meaning, whereas the evolutionary hypothesis suggests that dreams help people to work out solutions to threatening problems and events.

## THEORIES OF SLEEP

The simplest question that we can ask about sleep is, Why do we sleep? Any satisfactory explanation has a lot to account for. As we have seen, sleep is complex, consisting as it does of at least four stages. Sleep also seems to have within it a rhythmic component lasting about 90 minutes in which the EEG gradually slows and then speeds up again. Finally, in one of these stages, the sleeping brain has a waking EEG, the motor system is paralyzed except for twitching movements, and people have more vivid dreams than those in other stages of sleep. An adequate theory of sleep must account for all these phenomena. This section summarizes four theories of why we sleep.

### Sleep as a Passive Process

One of the earliest theories views sleep as a passive process that takes place as a result of a decrease in sensory stimulation. According to the theory, as evening approaches, there are fewer stimuli to maintain alertness, so sleep sets in. This theory does not account for the complexity of sleep, nor is it supported by direct experimental investigations. It predicts that if subjects are deprived of all stimulation they will go to sleep. Experiments reveal, however, that when subjects are isolated in bedrooms, they spend less, not more, time asleep. These results do not support the idea that sleep sets in because there is nothing to do.

Shimir Amir Jane Stewart

Although the passive-process theory of sleep originally did not consider biological rhythms as a contributing factor to sleep, what we now know about biological rhythms provides some support for a weak version of this idea. Shimir Amir and Jane Stewart (1996) showed that initially neutral stimuli can be conditioned to be zeitgebers, which entrain more regular circadian rhythms and thus more regular periods of sleep. In other words, the activities that we engage in before we sleep and after we wake up will become zeitgebers by being associated with light–dark changes. Therefore, exposure to darkness and quiet in the evening and to light and other kinds of stimulation in the morning is one way of synchronizing biological rhythms.

## Sleep as a Biological Adaptation

The biological theory of sleep holds that it is an adaptive behavior that is influenced by the many ways in which a species adapts to its environment. First, sleep is designed as an energy-conserving strategy to cope with times when food is scarce. In other words, each animal species gathers food at optimal times and conserves energy the rest of the time. If the nutrient value of the food that a species eats is high, it can spend less time foraging and more time sleeping. Second, an animal species' behavior is influenced by whether the species is predator or prey. If an animal is a predator, it can sleep at its ease; if it is a prey, its sleep time is reduced because it must remain alert as much as possible. Third, an animal that is strictly nocturnal or diurnal will likely also sleep when it cannot travel easily. Dement has stated this idea as follows: "We sleep to keep from bumping into things in the dark" (Figure 12-18).

The sleep patterns of most animal species are consistent with the adaptive theory. Figure 12-19 illustrates the average sleep time of a number of common mammals. Because herbivores—including donkeys, horses, and cows—consume food that is poor in nutrients, they have to spend a long time collecting enough food to sustain themselves, which reduces their sleep time. Because they are also prey, their sleep time is further reduced as they watch for predators. Carnivores, including domestic cats and dogs, eat nutrient-rich foods and usually consume most of a day's or even a week's food at a single meal. Thus, because they do not need to eat constantly and because by resting they can conserve energy, carnivores spend a great deal of time each day sleeping. The behavior of some animals does appear odd, however. Opossums, which spend much of their time asleep, may have specialized in energy conservation as a survival strategy. We humans are average in our sleep time, which is presumably indicative of an evolutionary pattern in which food gathering was not an overwhelming preoccupation and predation was not a major concern.

Lynn Hoffman/Photo Researchers

**Figure 12-18**

Biological theories of sleep suggest that sleep is an energy-conserving strategy and also serves other functions, such as staying safe during the night.

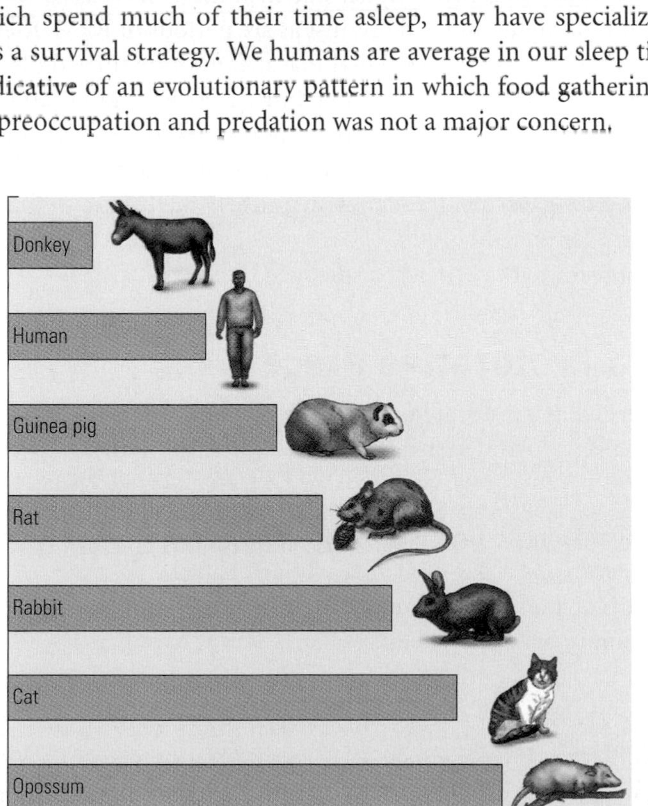


**Figure 12-19**

The average amount of time spent sleeping each day by different animal species. Sleep time is affected both by the amount of time required to obtain food and by the risk of predation.

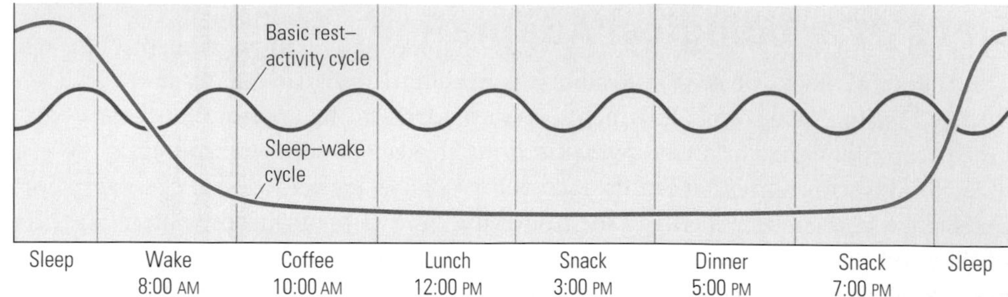


**Figure 12-20**

Our behavior is dominated by a basic rest–activity cycle (red) in which our activity level changes in the course of the day and by an NREM–REM sleep cycle (purple) in the course of the night.

Sleep can contribute to energy conservation in a number of ways. Inactivity is a way of conserving energy because energy is not being expended in moving the body or supporting posture. The brain is a major user of energy, so switching off the brain during sleep—especially NREM sleep—is another good way to conserve energy. The drop in body temperature that typically accompanies sleep also contributes to energy conservation.

A good theory of sleep must explain not only sleep but also NREM and REM sleep. Before the discovery of REM sleep, Kleitman had suggested that animals, including humans, have a **basic rest–activity cycle** (BRAC) that has a period of about 90 minutes (see Dement, 1972). He based his hypothesis on the observation that human infants have frequent feeding periods between which they sleep. As is illustrated in Figure 12-20, the behavior of adult humans also suggests that activity and rest are organized into temporal packets. School classes, work periods, meal times, coffee breaks, and snack times appear to be divided into intervals of 90 minutes or so. The later discovery that REM sleep occurs at intervals of about 90 minutes added support to Kleitman's hypothesis, because the REM periods could be considered to be a continuation into sleep of the 90-minute BRAC cycle. The hypothesis now assumes that periods of eating are periods of high brain activity, just as are periods of REM. Kleitman proposes that the BRAC rhythm is so fundamental that it cannot be turned off. Accordingly, in order for a night's sleep to be uninterrupted by periodic waking (and perhaps snacking), the body is paralyzed and only the brain is allowed to be active. In other words, to use an analogy, rather than turning off the engine of an automobile stopped at a red light, the driver disengages the transmission and sets the brakes so that the car cannot move. Although Kleitman's hypothesis has not been subjected to serious experimentation, it does not seem to be seriously challenged by any competing explanation.

## Sleep as a Restorative Process

The idea that sleep has a restorative function is widely held among poets, philosophers, and the public, as illustrated by Macbeth's description of sleep in Shakespeare's *Macbeth*:

> Sleep that knits up the ravell'd sleave of care,
> The death of each day's life, sore labour's bath,
> Balm of hurt minds, great nature's second course,
> Chief nourisher in life's feast.

It is also an idea that we can understand from a personal perspective. Toward the end of the day, we become tired, and when we awaken from sleep, we are refreshed. If we do not get enough sleep, we often become irritable. Nevertheless, fatigue and alertness may simply be aspects of the circadian rhythm and have nothing at all to do with wear and tear on the body or depletion of essential bodily resources. To evaluate whether sleep is essential for one or another bodily process, many studies of sleep deprivation have been conducted. The studies fall into three types: total sleep deprivation, deprivation of slow-wave sleep, and deprivation of REM sleep.

**Microsleep.** A brief period of sleep lasting a second or so.

Sleep-deprivation studies have not identified any function for which sleep is essential. One well-known case study on sleep deprivation described by Dement illustrates this point. In 1965, as part of a science-fair project, a student named Randy Gardner planned to break the world record of 260 hours (almost 11 days) of consecutive wakefulness with the help of two classmates, who would keep him awake. Gardner did break the record, then slept for 14 hours and reported no ill effects. The world record now stands at a little more than 18 days. A number of reviews of sleep-deprivation research are consistent in concluding that, at least for these limited periods of sleep deprivation, no marked physiological alterations ensue.

Although sleep deprivation does not seem to have adverse physiological consequences, it is associated with poor cognitive performance. The decreases in performance contribute to many accidents at work and on the road. The sleep-deprivation deficit does not manifest itself in an inability to do a task, because sleep-deprived subjects can perform even very complex tasks. Rather, the deficit is revealed when sustained attention is required and when a task is repetitive or boring. Even short periods of sleep deprivation, amounting to the loss of a few hours of sleep, can increase errors on tasks requiring sustained attention. A confounding factor in cognitive performance is that sleep-deprived subjects will take **microsleeps,** which are brief sleeps lasting a few seconds. During microsleep, subjects may remain sitting or standing, but their eyelids droop briefly and they become less responsive to external stimuli. Many people who have driven a car while tired have experienced a microsleep and awakened just in time to prevent themselves from driving off the road.

Some studies have focused on the selective contributions of REM sleep. To deprive a subject of REM sleep, researchers allow subjects to sleep but awaken them as they start to go into REM sleep. REM-sleep deprivation has two effects. First, subjects show an increased tendency to go into REM sleep in subsequent sleep sessions, so awakenings must become more and more frequent. Second, subsequent to REM deprivation, subjects experience "REM rebound," showing more than the usual amount of REM sleep in the first available sleep session. Some early REM-deprivation studies reported that subjects could begin to hallucinate and display other abnormalities in behavior, but these reports have not been confirmed.

Two kinds of observations, however, suggest that there are no adverse effects of prolonged or even complete deprivation of REM sleep. Virtually all antidepressant drugs, including MAO inhibitors, tricyclic antidepressants, and selective serotonin reuptake inhibitors, suppress REM sleep either partly or completely. In fact, the clinical effectiveness of these drugs may derive from their REM-depressant effects (Vogel et al., 1990). There are no reports, however, of adverse consequences of prolonged REM deprivation as a consequence of antidepressant drug treatments. A number of cases have been reported of people who have suffered lower brainstem damage that results in a complete loss of REM sleep. Some of these people suffer from a condition termed the "locked-in" syndrome: they are fully conscious, alert, and responsive but are quadriplegic and mute. O. N. Markand and M. L. Dyken (1976) reported that REM sleep was completely absent in five of seven patients with locked-in syndrome without apparent ill effects. I. Osorio and R. B. Daroff (1980) also described patients who had more selective lesions that abolished REM but left them ambulatory and verbally communicative; they lived quite satisfactorily without REM sleep.

## Sleep and Memory Storage

Two groups of experiments have proposed that dreams play a role in solidifying and organizing events so that we can remember them. One group proposes that dreams in NREM sleep store events in memory, whereas researchers in the other group propose that dreams in REM sleep fulfill this function.

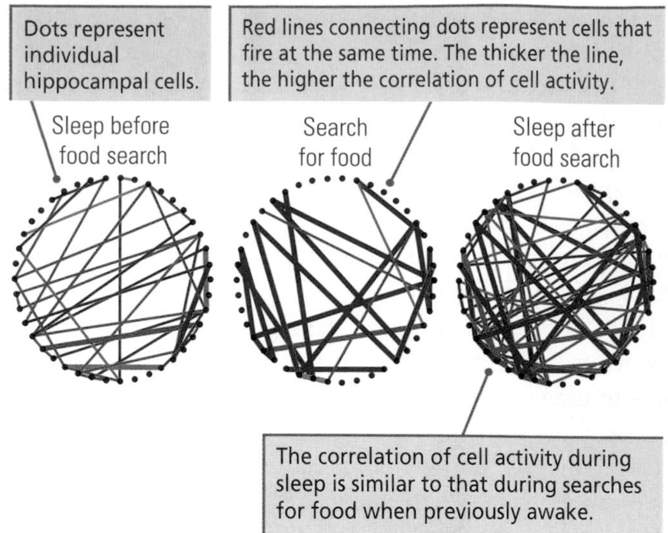

Dots represent individual hippocampal cells.
Red lines connecting dots represent cells that fire at the same time. The thicker the line, the higher the correlation of cell activity.
Sleep before food search
Search for food
Sleep after food search
The correlation of cell activity during sleep is similar to that during searches for food when previously awake.

**Figure 12-21**

Are waking events replayed in sleep? The activity of hippocampal cells suggests that rats dream about previous experiences. The dots on the periphery of the circle represent 42 hippocampal cells that were recorded at the same time under three conditions: (1) a session of slow-wave sleep before a food-searching task, (2) the food-searching task, and (3) during slow-wave sleep after the food-searching task. The red lines connecting cells indicate cells whose discharge occurred at the same time. There were no strong correlations between cells during the slow-wave sleep that preceded the food-searching task, but the correlations between cells during the food search and during the subsequent slow-wave sleep were similar.

Adapted from "Reactivation of Hippocampal Ensemble Memories During Sleep," by M. A. Wilson and B. L. McNaughton, 1994, *Science, 165,* p. 678.

To examine whether rats "dream" about their experiences, Matthew Wilson and Bruce McNaughton (1994) made use of the finding that many hippocampal cells fire when a rat is in a certain location in an environment. These cells, called place cells, are relatively inactive until the rat passes through a particular place in its environment, whether it spontaneously walks through that place or is carried through it by the experimenter. The experimenters trained rats to look for food in a circular container or to search for food on a four-arm maze. Recordings were made from as many as 100 place cells at the same time in three conditions: during slow-wave sleep, during a session in the food-searching task, and during slow-wave sleep after a session in the food-searching task. The experimenters then used computer methodology to look for cells whose discharge was correlated—that is, cells that discharged at the same time. As is illustrated in Figure 12-21, the activity of only a few cells was strongly correlated in the sleep session that preceded the food-searching task. During food searching, quite a number of cells discharged at the same time as a rat visited different locations in the apparatus. In the sleep session that followed the food-searching experience, correlations that were remarkably similar to those observed during food searching were observed. In short, the rats appeared to be dreaming about their previous food-searching experience. In addition to demonstrating that rats dream, Wilson and McNaughton propose that dreaming during slow-wave sleep helps to store the memory of the previous food-searching experience, so that, if given the opportunity, the animal would know where to look for the food. This group also proposes that REM sleep may be important for storing memories (Poe et al., 2000), but we will look at an example from a study on human subjects that demonstrates this possibility.

To determine whether humans dream about their experiences, Pierre Maquet and his coworkers in Belgium trained subjects on a serial reaction task and observed regional blood flow in the brain with PET scans during training and during REM sleep on the subsequent night (Maquet et al., 2000). The subjects faced a computer screen on which were six positional markers. The subjects were to push one of six keys when a corresponding positional marker was illuminated. The subjects did not know that the sequence in which the positional markers were illuminated was predetermined. Consequently, as training progressed, the subjects indicated that they were learning because their reaction time improved on trials on which one positional marker was correlated with a preceding marker. On the PET scan measures of brain activation, a similar pattern of neocortical activation was found during task acquisition and during REM sleep (Figure 12-22). On the basis of this result, Maquet and coworkers suggest,

**(A)** Reaction-time task

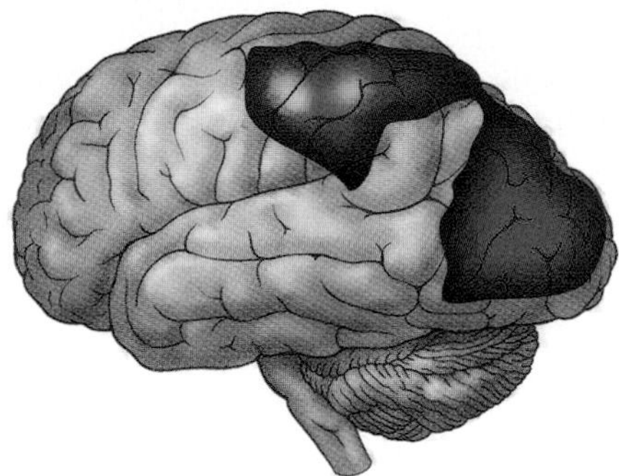

Subjects are trained on a reaction-time task, and brain activity is recorded with PET.

**(B)** REM sleep that night

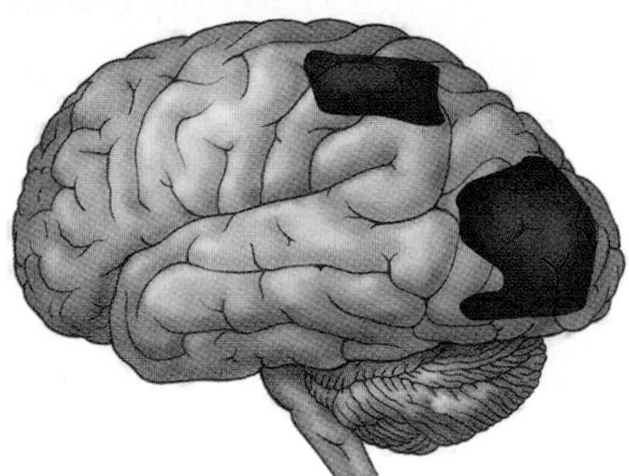

Subjects display a similar pattern of brain activity during subsequent REM sleep.

**Figure 12-22**

Do we store memories during REM sleep? **(A)** Regional blood flow in the brain as measured by PET during learning on a reaction-time task. **(B)** A very similar pattern of blood flow during REM sleep on the subsequent night suggests that subjects were dreaming about their learning experience.
Adapted from "Experience Dependent Changes in Cerebral Activation During Human REM Sleep," by P. Maquet et al., 1998, *Nature Neuroscience, 3,* p. 832.

first, that the subjects were dreaming about their learning experience and, second, that the replay while dreaming strengthened the memory of the task.

The interpretation of dreaming given to these two experiments is quite different from the psychoanalytical and activation-synthesis interpretations of dreaming. The conclusion from both of these studies is that dreams, whether in slow-wave sleep or in REM sleep, in rats or in humans, are important for storing memories. This is a rich area of study, with additional experimental support. Substantial evidence suggests both that sleep increases after a session of learning and that memory improves after a sleep session. Other research shows that sleep deprivation impairs memory formation.

The results of some natural experiments raise questions about the memory-storing functions of sleep. There are many documented cases of people who sleep less than a couple of hours each day yet remain active and healthy. These cases raise the question of why most people need much longer periods of sleep. Many people who take minor tranquilizers as a way of improving sleep have changes in sleep without corresponding complaints about learning. Although the drugs do improve the onset and duration of sleep, they also suppress stage 4 sleep, a result that raises questions about the importance of stage 4 for memory. P. Lavie and coworkers (1984) reported the case of a 33-year-old man who suffered a head injury at age 20 and subsequently displayed little REM sleep, as documented in sleep-recording sessions in a sleep laboratory. The lack of REM sleep did not appear to cause serious effects: the subject completed high school, attended law school, and subsequently practiced law. Human infants spend a great deal of time sleeping in their first year or so, but they remember nothing of this period of life. Finally, the sloth is one of nature's great sleepers but is not noted to be among its great learners. In conclusion, we can say that memory-storing theories of sleep are extremely interesting, and it is certainly possible that, just as sleep appears to contribute to well-being, it may also contribute to memory.

Sloth

## In Review

Several theories have been put forward to explain why we sleep. The biological theory, that sleep is an adaptive strategy for conserving energy during times when food resources are hard to obtain, has replaced the passive theory, that sleep results from lack of sensory stimulation. Scientists are examining the ideas that sleep is a restorative process and that sleep has a role in storing and sorting memory, but so far the evidence in favor of these ideas is not strong.

## THE NEURAL BASIS OF SLEEP

Granted that we do not yet know for sure *why* we sleep, is there any firm evidence of *how* we fall asleep? An early popular idea held that the body secretes a chemical that induces sleep and that can be removed only by sleeping. This idea is the basis for the "sleeping potion" featured in many stories. The hormone melatonin, which is secreted from the pineal gland during the dark phase of the light–dark cycle, causes sleepiness and is taken as an aid for sleep, so it might be thought to be the sleep-producing substance. Sleep, however, survives removal of the pineal gland. Thus, melatonin, and many other chemical substances, may only contribute to sleep, not cause it. If any chemical actually regulates sleep, it has not yet been identified. In fact, experimenters who have studied sleep in various species of animals have obtained evidence that sleep is *not* produced by a compound circulating in the bloodstream. When dolphins and birds sleep, only one hemisphere sleeps at a time. This ability presumably allows an animal's other hemisphere to remain behaviorally alert. Because any blood-borne substance would affect both hemispheres, this finding suggests that sleep is not caused by a chemical that circulates in the bloodstream. This observation also strongly suggests that sleep is produced by the action of some region within each hemisphere.

In this section, we consider two points about the neural basis of sleep. First, we examine evidence that sleep is produced by activity in a region of the brainstem. Second, we look at evidence that the various events associated with sleep, including events associated with REM and NREM sleep, are controlled by a number of different brainstem nuclei.

### The Reticular Activating System and Sleep

A dramatic experiment and a clever hypothesis by Giuseppe Moruzzi and Horace Magoun (1949) provide the beginnings of an answer to the question of which areas of the brain regulate sleep. Moruzzi and Magoun were recording the cortical EEG from anesthetized cats while electrically stimulating the cats' brainstems. They discovered that, in response to the electrical stimulation, the large, slow cortical EEG typical of the condition of anesthesia was dramatically replaced by the low-voltage, fast-wave EEG typical of waking. The waking pattern of EEG activity outlasted the period of stimulation, demonstrating that it was produced by the activity of neurons in the region of the stimulating electrode. During the "waking period," the cat did not become behaviorally aroused because it was anesthetized, but its cortical EEG appeared to indicate that it was awake. This pattern of EEG is referred to as a *desynchronized EEG,* meaning that the large, synchronized waves of sleep were replaced by low-voltage, fast activity. Subsequent experiments by Moruzzi and Magoun and by others showed that desynchronized EEG could be induced from a large area running through the center of the brainstem. Anatomically, this area of the brainstem is composed of a mixture of nuclei and fibers forming a *reticulum* (from the Latin word *rete*, meaning "net"). Moruzzi and Magoun named this brainstem area the *reticular activating system (RAS)* and proposed that this area of the brain is responsible for sleep–waking behavior. The location of the RAS is illustrated in Figure 12-23.

We know that if someone disturbs us when we are asleep, we usually wake up. To explain how sensory stimulation and the RAS are related, Moruzzi and Magoun proposed that sensory pathways entering the brainstem have collateral axons that synapse with neurons in the RAS. They proposed that sensory stimulation is conveyed to RAS neurons by these collaterals, and then RAS neurons produce the desynchronized EEG by axons that project to the cortex. Subsequent experiments with sleeping cats showed that stimulation would produce waking EEG activity and behavioral arousal in the animals just as if they had been provided with sensory stimulation to wake them up.

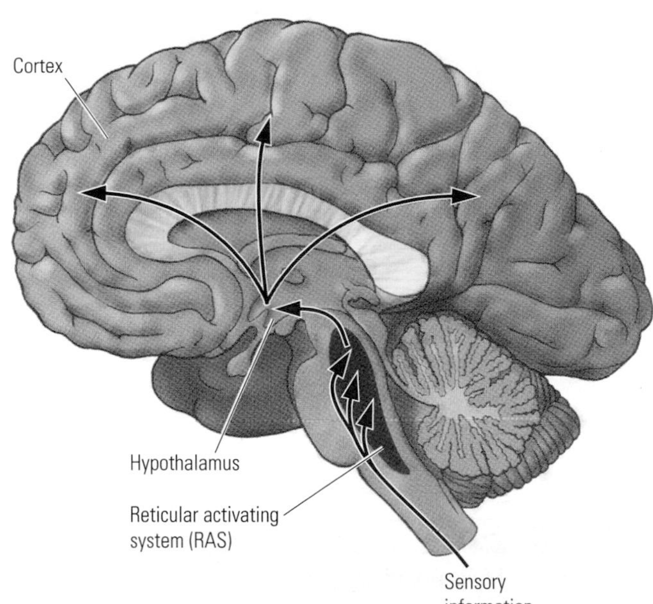


**Figure 12-23**

The reticular activating system is a region in the middle of the brain characterized by a mixture of cells and fiber pathways. Stimulation of the RAS produces a waking EEG, whereas damage to it produces a slow-wave, sleeplike EEG.

Moruzzi and Magoun further proposed that the cortex sends axons to the RAS, providing a route for people to stimulate their own reticular activating systems in order to stay awake. In sum, both sensory stimulation and conscious effort could activate the RAS to maintain waking.

Two other lines of experimental evidence support the idea that the RAS is responsible for desynchronized EEG. Because it was possible that Moruzzi and Magoun had stimulated various sensory pathways passing through the brainstem, it was necessary to demonstrate that brainstem neurons and not sensory pathway stimulation produced the waking EEG. When experimenters cut the brainstem just behind the RAS, thereby severing incoming sensory pathways, RAS stimulation still produced a desynchronized EEG. This result strengthened the argument that RAS neurons, not sensory pathways running through the region, are responsible for producing a desynchronized EEG. Furthermore, if the cut was made through the brainstem just in front of the RAS, the desynchronized EEG activity no longer occurred in response to electrical stimulation of the RAS. Together these experiments demonstrated that RAS neurons acting through axons projecting to the cortex produce the waking EEG.

A different line of evidence obtained from humans who have suffered brainstem injury supports this conclusion. Damage that affects the RAS results in **coma**, a state of deep unconsciousness resembling sleep. In a well-publicized case, a 21-year-old woman named Karen Ann Quinlan (Quinlan & Quinlan, 1977), after taking a minor tranquilizer and having a few drinks at a birthday party, sustained RAS damage that put her in a coma. She was hospitalized, placed on a respirator to support breathing, and fed by tubes. Her family fought a protracted legal battle to have her removed from life support, which was finally won before the Supreme Court of New Jersey. Even after being removed from life support, however, Quinlan lived for 10 more years in a perpetual coma.

Despite substantial evidence that the RAS has a role in sleep–waking behavior, attempts to localize sleep to a particular structure or group of neurons within the RAS have not been successful. Many studies have demonstrated that discrete lesions at various locations within the RAS can produce periods of sleep that last for days; but, with care, animals in the laboratory and human brain-injured patients recover from these acute symptoms. These findings suggest that sleep–waking behavior is due to the activity of a diffuse network of fibers and cells rather than being regulated by a single nucleus. As described in the next section, there are at least two routes through which patterns of a waking EEG are produced.

## The Neural Basis of the EEG Changes Associated with Waking

A series of experiments performed on rats by Case Vanderwolf and his coworkers suggest that two brain structures are responsible for producing the waking EEG of the neocortex (Vanderwolf, 1988). Figure 12-24 illustrates the location of these structures, both of which are ascending neural pathways (described in Chapter 6).

One of the structures, the basal forebrain, contains large cholinergic cells whose axons project diffusely to the neocortex. When these cells secrete acetylcholine from their terminals, they stimulate neocortical neurons that then change their activity pattern to produce a waking EEG. The other structure, the median raphé, contains serotonin neurons whose axons also project diffusely to the neocortex. When these cells secrete serotonin (5-HT) from their terminals, they also stimulate neocortical cells to

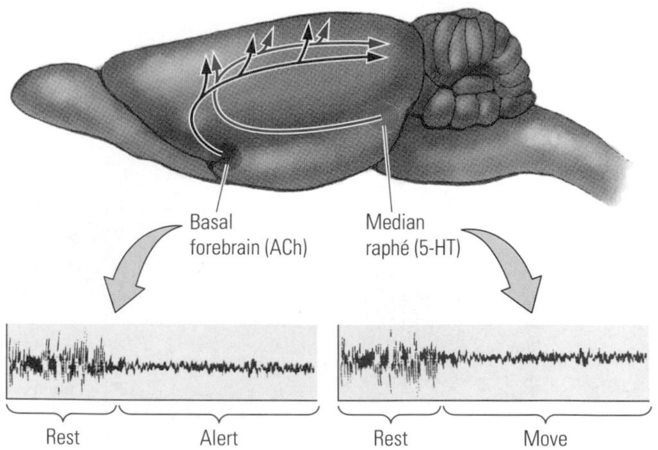


**Figure 12-24**

The cells of two ascending systems are responsible for an activated (beta) EEG in the rat. Basal forebrain acetylcholine (ACh) cells produce an activated EEG pattern when a rat is alert but immobile. The serotonergic raphé cells of the midbrain produce an activated EEG pattern when the rat moves.

produce a waking EEG. Although both pathways produce a very similar pattern of EEG activity, the relations of the two types of desynchronized EEG to behavior are different. If the activity of the cholinergic projection is blocked with drugs or with lesions to the cells of the basal forebrain, the normal waking EEG that should be recorded from an immobile rat is replaced by EEG activity resembling that of NREM sleep. If the rat walks or is otherwise active, a waking EEG is obtained from the neocortex. These findings suggest that the cholinergic EEG is responsible for the waking EEG when the rat is still and alert, whereas serotonergic activation is additionally responsible for the waking EEG when the animal moves.

It is important to note that neither the basal forebrain system nor the median raphé system is responsible for behavior. In fact, if both structures are pharmacologically or surgically destroyed, a rat can still stand and walk around. Its neocortical EEG, however, resembles that of a sleeping animal. As long as one of the systems is producing a waking EEG, rats can learn simple tasks. If both systems are destroyed, however, an animal, although still able to walk around, is no longer able to learn or display intelligent behavior. In a sense, the cortex is like a house in which the lights are powered by two separate power sources: both power sources must fail for the house to be left in darkness.

We do not know if the basal forebrain and median raphé produce the same two desynchronized patterns of EEG activity in humans as they do in rats, but it is likely that they do. Consequently, it is likely that, when we are alert, the cholinergic neurons are active and, when we move, the serotonin neurons are additionally active. You may have had the experience, when you felt sleepy in a class or behind the wheel of a car, of being able to wake yourself up by moving around a little—shaking your head or stretching. Presumably, your arousal level decreased as your cholinergic neurons became inactive; but, when you moved, your serotonergic neurons became active and restored your level of arousal. When we enter sleep, both cholinergic and serotonergic neurons become less active, allowing slow waves to appear in the cortical record.

## The Neural Basis of REM Sleep

When we were looking at evidence related to the function of REM sleep, we considered a number of clinical cases in which people who had suffered brainstem damage no longer displayed REM sleep. This observation suggests that REM sleep is produced by the action of a neural area that is distinct from the RAS, which produces NREM sleep.

Barbara Jones

Barbara Jones (1993) and her colleagues described a group of cholinergic neurons known as the **peribrachial area,** which appears to be implicated in REM sleep. This area is located in the dorsal part of the brainstem just anterior to the cerebellum. Jones selectively destroyed these cells by injecting the neurotoxin kainic acid onto them and found that REM sleep in her experimental animal subjects was drastically reduced. This result suggested that the peribrachial area is responsible for producing REM sleep and REM-related behaviors. The peribrachial area extends into a more ventrally located nucleus called the **medial pontine reticular formation** (MPRF). Lesions of the MPRF also abolish REM sleep, and injections of cholinergic agonists (drugs that act like acetylcholine) into the MPRF induce REM sleep. Thus, both the peribrachial area and the MPRF, illustrated in Figure 12-25, take part in the production of REM sleep.

If these two brain areas are responsible for producing REM sleep, how do other events related to REM sleep take place? Such events include: (1) an EEG pattern similar to the waking EEG pattern; (2) eye movements, or REMs; (3) sharp EEG spikes recorded from the pons, the lateral geniculate nucleus, and the visual cortex, called

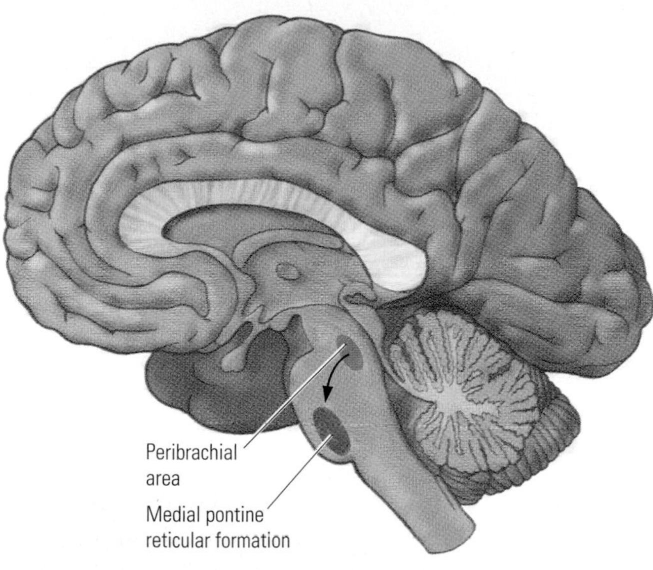


**Figure 12-25**

The location of the two brainstem structures responsible for REM sleep. Damage to either area will reduce or abolish REM sleep.

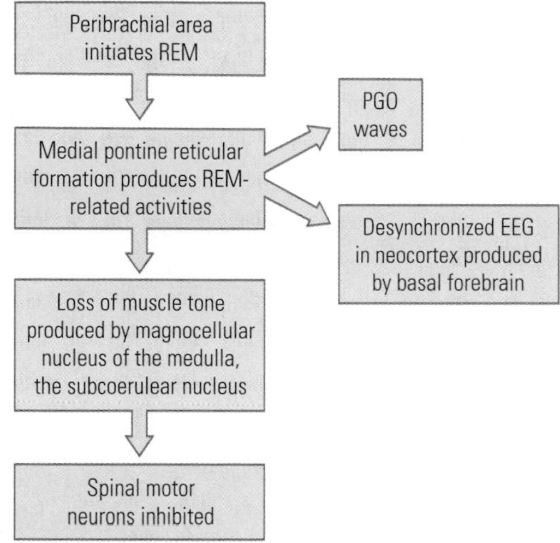


**Figure 12-26**

The neural control of events related to REM sleep.

PGO (pons, geniculate, occipital) waves after the structures in which they are found; and (4) **atonia,** an absence of muscle tone due to the inhibition of motor neurons. These REM-related activities are likely to be found in humans, although, at present, PGO waves have not been confirmed in humans.

One explanation of how other REM-related activities take place is illustrated in Figure 12-26. The MPRF sends projections to basal forebrain cholinergic neurons to activate them and so produce the activated EEG of the cortex. Then the peribrachial area excites the PGO pathway to produce PGO waves and eye movements. Finally, the atonia of REM sleep is produced by the MPRF through a pathway that sends input to the **subcoerulear nucleus,** located just behind it. The subcoerulear nucleus excites the **magnocellular nucleus of the medulla,** which sends projections to the spinal motor neurons to inhibit them so that paralysis is achieved during the REM-sleep period.

French researcher Michael Jouvet (1972) observed that cats with lesions in the subcoerulear nucleus displayed a remarkable behavior when they entered REM sleep. Rather than losing muscle tone and stretching out in the paralysis that typically accompanies REM sleep, they stood up, looked around, and made movements of catching an imaginary mouse or running from an imaginary threat. If cats dream about catching mice or dream about escaping from a threat, then it appeared that these cats were acting out their dreams.

## In Review

Separate neural regions are responsible for sleep. The reticular activating system (RAS) in the central region of the brainstem is responsible for NREM sleep, whereas the peribrachial area and the medial pontine reticular formation (MPRF) are responsible for REM sleep. The last two areas, through pathways to the neocortex and spinal cord, are responsible for producing the waking EEG and the muscular paralysis that are associated with REM sleep.

## SLEEP DISORDERS

Disturbances of sleep are annoying and result in impaired performance during the following day. Some people suffer from sleep disorders almost every night that leave them chronically tired and unproductive. Some people are also visited by unwanted attacks of sleep in the daytime. In this section, we will consider abnormalities of sleep—some related to NREM sleep and others related to REM sleep.

### Disorders of NREM Sleep

The two most common sleep disorders are **insomnia,** the inability to sleep, and **narcolepsy** (from the Greek *narco*, "a stupor," and *lepsy*, "to be seized"), falling asleep at inconvenient times. They are considered disorders of slow-wave sleep. About 15 percent of people complain of ongoing sleep problems; an additional 20 percent complain of occasional sleep problems. As people age, the incidence of complaints about problems with sleep increases. Insomnia and narcolepsy are related, as anyone who has stayed up late at night can confirm: a short night's sleep is often accompanied by a tendency to fall asleep at inconvenient times the next day.

Our understanding of insomnia is complicated by a large variation in how much time people spend asleep. Some short sleepers may think that they should sleep more, and some long sleepers may think that they should sleep less; yet, for each, the sleeping pattern may be appropriate. It is also possible that, for some people, circadian rhythms are disrupted by subtle life-style choices. Staying up late may set a person's circadian rhythm forward, encouraging a cascade of late sleep followed by still later staying up.

Some sleep problems are brought on by shift work or by international travel. Institutions that use shift workers attempt to schedule shifts so that they disrupt sleep patterns as little as possible, usually by having workers change to shifts forward in time rather than backward. Disruptions caused by international travel are an inconvenience for the occasional traveler, but, for airline crews who travel regularly, especially on west-to-east flights, light–dark changes and time-zone changes can seriously disrupt sleep. Other common causes of sleep disorders are stress, long hours of work, and irregular life styles. Even worrying about insomnia is thought to play a major role in about 15 percent of insomnia cases.

Sleep disorders are a complicating factor in other conditions, including depression, a condition in which people may sleep too much or too little. Anxiety and depression may account for about 35 percent of insomnias. There are also quantitative differences in the sleep of depressed patients, because they enter REM sleep very quickly. It is possible, however, that entering REM sleep quickly is secondarily related to sleep deprivation, rather than being related directly to depression, because people who are sleep deprived also enter REM very quickly. Irregular sleeping patterns are also common in schizophrenia.

Insomnia may be brought on by sedative-hypnotic drugs, including seconal, sodium amytal, and many minor tranquilizers. These "sleeping pills" do help people get to sleep, but they cause additional problems. People may sleep under one of these drugs, but they are likely to feel groggy and tired the next day, which defeats the purpose of taking the drug. In addition, people develop tolerance to these medications, become dependent on them, and display rebound insomnia when they stop taking them. A person may increase the dose of the drug each time the drug fails to produce the desired effect. The syndrome in which patients unsuccessfully attempt to sleep by increasing their dosage of a drug is called **drug-dependency insomnia.**

Like many other people, you may have had the experience of being suddenly overcome with an urge to sleep at an inconvenient time, such as while attending a lecture.

**Narcolepsy.** A sleep disorder in which a person falls asleep at inappropriate times of the day.

**Drug-dependency insomnia.** A condition that results from continuous use of "sleeping pills" in which a person becomes tolerant of the drug while the drug also results in deprivation of either REM or NREM sleep, leading the person to increase the drug dosage.

For some people, such experiences with narcolepsy are common and disruptive. J. S., a junior in college, sat in the front row of the classroom for his course on the brain; within a few minutes of the beginning of each class, he dropped off to sleep. The instructor became concerned about his abilities as a lecturer, but one day he heard another instructor describe the sleeping behavior of a student who turned out to be J. S. The instructor then asked J. S. to stay after class to discuss his sleeping behavior. J. S. reported that sleeping in classes was a chronic problem. Not only did he sleep in class, but he fell asleep whenever he tried to study. He even fell asleep at the dinner table and in other inappropriate locations. His sleeping problem had made it a challenge to get through high school and was making it very difficult for him to pass his college courses.

About 1 percent of people suffer from narcolepsy, which takes a surprising number of forms. J. S. had a form of narcolepsy in which he fell asleep while sitting still, and his sleeping bouts consisted of brief bouts of NREM sleep lasting from 5 to 10 minutes. This pattern was very similar to napping and to dropping off to sleep in class after a late night, but it was distinguishable as narcolepsy by its frequency and by the disruptive effect that it had on his academic career. J. S. eventually discussed his problem with his physician and received a prescription for Ritalin, an amphetamine-like drug that stimulates dopamine transmission (see Chapter 6), which proved very helpful.

Link to the Web site at **www.worthpublishers.com/kolb/chapter12** to learn more about narcolepsy.

Some people who suffer from daytime sleepiness attend a sleep clinic to get help in sleeping better at night. Studies of narcoleptic people in sleep clinics have resulted in one surprising discovery concerning the causes of narcolepsy. "Sleep Apnea," on page 482, describes a person who had to wake up in order to breathe; his *sleep apnea* left him extremely tired and caused him to nod off in the daytime.

## Disorders of REM Sleep

Recall from the description of REM sleep that it is associated with muscular atonia and dreaming. REM-sleep atonia can occur when a person is not asleep, as in the case of L. M., a college senior who, after hearing a lecture on narcoleptic disorders, recounted the following experience. She had just gone to sleep when her roommate came into their room. She woke up and intended to ask her roommate if she wanted to go skating the next morning, but found herself completely unable to speak. She tried to turn her head to follow her roommate's movements across the room but found that she was paralyzed. She had the terrifying feeling that some kind of monstrous creature was hiding in the bathroom waiting for her roommate. She tried to cry out but could produce only harsh, gurgling noises. Her roommate knocked her out of her paralysis by hitting her with a pillow.

This form of narcolepsy, called **sleep paralysis,** is extremely common. In informal class surveys, almost a third of students state that they have had such an experience. The atonia is typically accompanied by an unpleasant feeling of dread or fear. It seems likely that, in sleep paralysis, a person has entered REM sleep and atonia has occurred, but the person remains partly conscious or has partly awakened.

The atonia of REM sleep may also occur while a person is awake; this form is called **cataplexy** (from the Greek *cata,* "to fall," and *plexus,* "seized"). In cataplexy, an awake, alert person suddenly loses all muscle tone and falls to the floor. These attacks are frequently reported to be triggered by excitement or laughing. Suddenly, the jaw drops, the head sinks, the arms go limp, the legs buckle, and the person falls down. The collapse can be so sudden that there is a real risk of injury. While in an atonic condition, the person may see imaginary creatures or hear imaginary voices. These hallucinations are called **hypnogogic** (Greek *hypno,* "sleep," and *agogic,* "leading into") hallucinations. People who fall into a state of cataplexy with hypnogogic hallucinations give every appearance of having fallen into REM sleep while remaining conscious.

**Sleep paralysis.** An inability to move owing to the brain's inhibition of motor neurons.

**Cataplexy.** A condition in which a person collapses owing to the loss of all muscle activity or tone.

**Hypnogogic.** Referring to a hallucinogenic or dreamlike event at the beginning of sleep.

Focus on Disorders

## Sleep Apnea

The first time I went to a doctor for my insomnia, I was twenty-five—that was about thirty years ago. I explained to the doctor that I couldn't sleep; I had trouble falling asleep, I woke up many, many times during the night, and I was tired and sleepy all day long. As I explained my problem to him, he smiled and nodded. Inwardly, this attitude infuriated me—he couldn't possibly understand what I was going through. He asked me one or two questions: Had any close friend or relative died recently? Was I having any trouble in my job or at home? When I answered no, he shrugged his shoulders and reached for his prescription pad. Since that first occasion I have seen I don't know how many doctors, but none could help me. I've been given hundreds of different pills—to put me to sleep at night, to keep me awake in the daytime, to calm me down, to pep me up—have even been psychoanalyzed. But still I cannot sleep at night. (In Dement, 1992, p. 73).

This patient went to the Stanford University Sleep Disorders Clinic in 1972. He had recording electrodes attached so that brain, muscle, eye, and breathing activity could be recorded while he slept. The experimenters were amazed to find that he had to wake up to breathe. They observed that he would go for more than a minute and a half without breathing, wake up and gasp for breath, and then return to sleep, at which time the sequence was repeated. This condition is called sleep apnea (*a*, "not," and *pnea*, "breathing"). It may be produced by a central problem, such as a weak command to the respiratory muscles, or it may be obstructive, caused by collapse of the upper airway. When people suffering from sleep apnea stop breathing, they either wake up completely and have difficulty getting back to sleep or they make repeated partial awakenings throughout the night to gasp for breath.

Because sufferers are apparently unaware of their sleep apnea, it must be diagnosed by someone who watches them sleep. Sleep apnea affects all ages and both sexes, and 30 percent of people older than 65 years of age may have some form of it. Sleep apnea is thought to be more common among people who are overweight and who snore, conditions in which air flow is restricted. Surgery to expand the upper airway, weight loss, and face masks that deliver negative pressure to open the airway are all treatments for sleep apnea. Sleep apnea may also be related to sudden infant death syndrome, or crib death, in which otherwise healthy infants inexplicably die in their sleep.

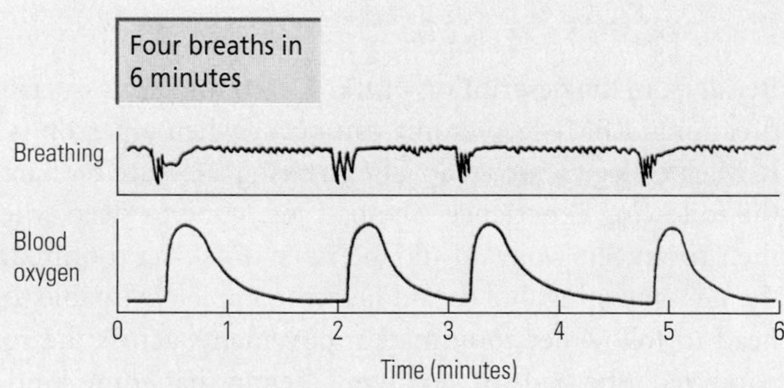


A 6-minute record of two measures taken from a person with sleep apnea, taken when the person was in REM sleep. The breathing record shows points at which the person inhaled. The record of blood oxygen shows that blood oxygen increased after each breath and then continued to fall until another breath was taken. This person breathed only 4 times in the 6-minute period; a normal sleeper would breathe more than 60 times in the same interval.

Conditions in which REM-sleep atonia occurs frequently may have a genetic basis. In 1970, William Dement was given a litter of Doberman pinscher dogs and, later, a litter of Labrador retrievers, all of whom had cataplexy. The disease is transmitted as a recessive trait; so, to develop the disease, a dog must inherit the trait from both its mother and its father. The descendants of those dogs provide animal models for investigating the neural basis of the disease as well as its treatment. When a dog is excited, such as when it is running for a piece of food, it may suddenly collapse, as is illustrated in Figure 12-27. Jerome Siegel (2000) investigated the cause of narcolepsy in dogs and found that neurons in the subcoerulear nucleus become inactive and neurons in the magnocellular nucleus of the medulla become active during attacks of cataplexy, just as they do during REM sleep. For some reason, the neurons responsible for paralysis during REM were producing cataplexy during waking. On the basis of anatomical examinations of the brains of narcoleptic dogs, Siegel suggested that the death of neurons in the amygdala and adjacent forebrain areas occurs as a one-time event just before the onset of the disease early in life. Presumably, the loss of these neurons somehow results in the loss of inhibition in the brainstem areas that produce paralysis. It is important to note that, although a genetic basis for cataplexy has been identified in dogs, there is as yet no evidence that all cases of human cataplexy are genetic. Like some forms of narcolepsy, cataplexy is treatable with Ritalin.

Recall Jouvet's experiment, in which he reported that cats with lesions to the subcoerulear region of the brainstem entered REM sleep without the accompanying atonia and apparently acted out their dreams. A similar condition has been reported in people and may either have a genetic basis or be caused by

**Figure 12-27**

Dog and man with narcolepsy having an attack of cataplexy, with complete loss of muscle tone, while awake and conscious. In both, the attack causes the head to droop and the back and legs to sag, and it can progress to a complete loss of muscle tone. Cataplexy is distinct from the sleep attacks that afflict most narcoleptics in that people hear and remember what is said around them and dogs can track a moving object with their eyes.

James Aronovsky (dog sequence), Joel Deutsch (human sequence), Slim Films.

brain damage. The condition has been named *REM without atonia.* The behavior of people who have REM without atonia suggests that they are acting out their dreams. The following two accounts are those of a 67-year-old patient described by Carlos Schenck and his coworkers (1986):

> I was on a motorcycle going down the highway when another motorcyclist comes up alongside me and tries to ram me with his motorcycle. Well, I decided I'm going to kick his motorcycle away and at that point my wife woke me up and said, "What in heavens are you doing to me?" because I was kicking the hell out of her.

> I had a dream where someone was shooting at me with a rifle and it was in a field that had ridges in it, so I decided to crawl behind a ridge—and I then had a gun too—and I look over the ridge so when he showed up I would shoot back at him and when I came to [i.e., awakened] I was kneeling alongside the bed with my arms extended like I was holding the rifle up and ready to shoot.

In both of these dreams, the patient had vivid pictorial images, but he heard nothing and he felt afraid. Although a large number of patients who have had such experiences have been described, most are elderly and suffer from brain injury or other brain-related disorders. REM without atonia can be treated with benzodiazepines, which block REM sleep.

## Sleep and Consciousness

Many scientists interested in the neural basis of consciousness study sleep and sleep-related disorders because the many different kinds of waking and sleep conditions suggest that consciousness is not a unitary condition, either neurally or behaviorally. Rather, there are a variety of "states of consciousness," some of which can occur simultaneously. René Descartes, whose theory of mind was described in Chapter 1, conceived of his idea of a mind through a dream. He dreamed that he was interpreting the dream as it occurred. Later, when awake, he reasoned that, if he could think and analyze a dream while asleep, the mind must be able to function during both waking and sleep. Therefore it must be independent of the body that underwent sleep and waking transitions.

More recent research is a source of additional insight into consciousness. For example, what we colloquially refer to as waking comprises at least two different states, one in which there is alert consciousness and one in which there are movement and consciousness. People attempting to go to sleep or attempting to stay awake appear to realize that they can take advantage of these different conditions to achieve their objective. People who are tired and wish to fall asleep usually seek out a dark, quiet room, where they lie still. In doing so, they are removing themselves from a condition of "moving consciousness." People who want to stay awake, especially if they are tired, can apparently do so as long as they keep moving. By walking around and otherwise remaining active, they can stay awake indefinitely.

Similarly, sleep consists of a number of NREM conditions and a REM-sleep condition. People in both NREM sleep and REM sleep are at least in some sense conscious when they dream. Dream consciousness can also occur in conjunction with waking consciousness, as witnessed by reports that people who fall into a state of cataplexy are conscious of being awake while experiencing the visual and emotional features of dreams when they have hypnogogic hallucinations.

Besides being a source of insight into the neural basis of consciousness, the study of sleep states and events may help to explain some psychiatric and drug-induced conditions. For example, among the symptoms of schizophrenia are visual and auditory hallucinations. Are these dream events that occur unexpectedly during waking? Many people who take hallucinogenic drugs such as LSD report that they have visual hallucinations. Does the drug initiate the visual features of dreams? People who have panic attacks suffer from very real fright that has no obvious cause. Are they experiencing the fear attacks that commonly occur during sleep paralysis and cataplexy? The answers to these questions are incomplete, but the similarities in symptoms between some waking and some sleep conditions do suggest that some waking disturbances may be sleep events that occur during waking.

## In Review

Disorders of NREM sleep include insomnia, in which a person has difficulty falling asleep at night, and narcolepsy, in which a person falls asleep involuntarily in the daytime. Treating insomnia with sleeping pills, usually sedative hypnotics, may cause drug-dependent insomnia, in which progressively higher doses must be taken to achieve sleep. Disorders of REM sleep include sleep paralysis, in which a person awakes but is paralyzed and experiences a sense of fear, and cataplexy, in which a person may lose muscle tone and collapse in the daytime. Cataplexy may be associated with hypnogogic hallucinations, in which a person experiences dreams while paralyzed but awake.

## SUMMARY

1. *What are biological rhythms?* Biological rhythms are cyclic patterns of behavior of varying length that are displayed by animals, plants, and even single-celled organisms. Mammals display a number of biological rhythms including circadian, or daily, rhythms and circannual, or yearly, rhythms. In the absence of environmental cues, circadian rhythms are free running, lasting a little more or a little less than their usual period of 24 hours, depending on the individual or the environmental conditions. Cues that reset a biological clock to a 24-hour rhythm are called zeitgebers.
2. *What is a biological clock?* A biological clock is a neural structure responsible for producing rhythmic behavior. There are a number of biological clocks in the brain, including the suprachiasmatic nucleus and the pineal gland. The suprachiasmatic nucleus is the mammalian biological clock responsible for circadian rhythms, and it has its own free-running rhythm with a period that is a little more or a little less than 24 hours. Stimuli from the environment such as sunrise and sunset entrain the free-running rhythm so that its period is 24 hours.
3. *How does a biological clock keep time?* Neurons of the suprachiasmatic nucleus have an activity rhythm in which they are active in the daytime and inactive at night. These neurons display their rhythmicity when disconnected from other brain structures, when removed from the brain and cultured in a dish, and after being cultured for a number of generations in a dish. When reimplanted into a brain without a suprachiasmatic nucleus, they restore the animal's circadian rhythms. The different aspects of circadian rhythms of neurons, including their period, are under genetic control.
4. *How is sleep measured?* Sleep events are measured by recording the brain's activity to produce an electroencephalogram, or EEG; muscular activity to produce an electromyogram, or EMG; and eye movements to produce an electrooculogram,

**neuroscience interactive**

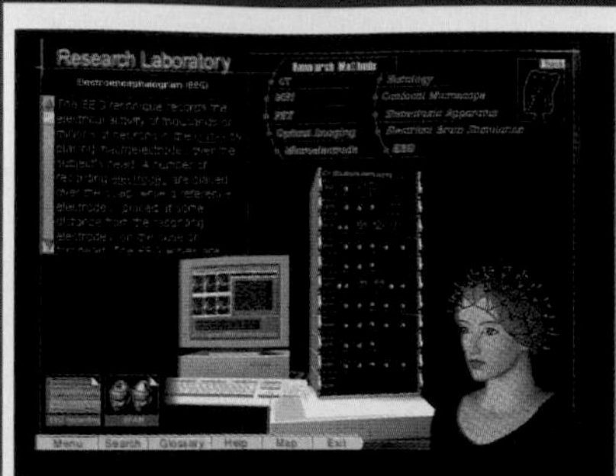

There are many resources available for expanding your learning on line:

■ **www.worthpublishers.com/kolb/chapter12**
Try some self-tests to reinforce your mastery of the material. Look at some of the updates reflecting current research on the brain. You'll also be able to link to other sites which will reinforce what you've learned.

■ **www.rls.org**
Link to this site to learn more about restless legs syndrome and current research to help people suffering from this disorder.

■ **www.sleepfoundation.org**
The headquarters of the National Sleep Foundation can be a fascinating starting point for investigation about sleep disorders and normal sleep patterns.

On your CD-ROM you can review some of the research methods useful to understanding sleep in the three-dimensional research lab.

or EOG. A typical night's sleep consists of four stages, as indicated by physiological measures, which take place in a number of cycles in the course of the night. During one stage of sleep, the EEG has a waking pattern and, because the sleeper displays rapid eye movements, this stage is called REM sleep. The other stages of sleep, in which the EEG has a slower rhythm, are called non-REM (NREM) sleep. NREM-sleep and REM-sleep intervals alternate four or five times each night; the duration of NREM sleep is longer in the early part of sleep, whereas the duration of REM sleep is longer in the later part of sleep.

5. *What events are associated with REM sleep?* A sleeper in slow-wave sleep has muscle tone, may toss and turn, and has dreams that are not especially vivid. A sleeper in REM sleep has no muscle tone and so is paralyzed, and has vivid dreams whose duration coincides with the duration of the REM period. There are several hypotheses about why we dream. The activation-synthesis hypothesis proposes that dreams are not meaningful and are only a by-product of the brain's state of excitation during REM. The evolutionary hypothesis suggests that dreams evolved as a mechanism to cope with real threats and fears posed by the environment.
6. *Why do we sleep?* There are several theories of sleep, including the propositions that sleep results from the absence of sensory stimulation, that it is a biological adaptation that conserves energy resources, and that it is a restorative process that fixes wear and tear in the brain. Sleep may also organize and store each day's memories.
7. *What is the neural basis of sleep?* Separate neural regions of the brain are responsible for NREM and REM sleep. The reticular activating system (RAS) located in the central area of the brainstem is responsible for NREM sleep. If it is stimulated, a sleeper awakes; if it is damaged, a person may enter a condition of coma. The peribrachial area and the medial pontine reticular formation of the brainstem are responsible for REM sleep. If these areas are damaged, REM sleep may no longer occur. Pathways from these areas project to the cortex to produce the cortical activation of REM and to the brainstem to produce the muscular paralysis of REM.
8. *What disorders are associated with sleep?* There are several disorders of NREM sleep, including insomnia, the inability to sleep at night, and narcolepsy, inconveniently falling asleep in the daytime. The administration of sedative hypnotics to induce sleep may induce drug-dependency insomnia, a sleep disorder in which progressively larger doses of the drug are required to produce sleep. Disorders of REM sleep include sleep paralysis, in which a person awakens but remains paralyzed and sometimes feels fear and dread. Cataplexy is a disorder in which an awake person collapses into a state of paralysis. At the same time, the person may remain awake and have hypnogogic hallucinations similar to dreaming while awake.

## KEY TERMS

cataplexy, p. 481
circadian rhythm, p. 449
drug-dependency insomnia, p. 480
entrain, p. 451
free-running rhythm, p. 450
hypnogogic, p. 481
microsleep, p. 473
narcolepsy, p. 480
pacemaker, p. 454
retinohypothalamic pathway, p. 454
sleep paralysis, p. 481
suprachiasmatic nucleus, p. 454
zeitgeber, p. 451

## REVIEW QUESTIONS

1. Why are circadian and circannual rhythms such prominent rhythms in mammals?
2. Describe some of the details of the circadian clock that allow it to be easily studied.
3. In what ways are NREM sleep and REM sleep organized differently in the brain?
4. Describe the various theories of sleep.
5. What are some of the most common sleep disorders, and what are their causes and treatments?

## FOR FURTHER THOUGHT

What ways can you suggest to combine the different theories of why we sleep into a unified theory?

## RECOMMENDED READING

Dement, W. C. (1972). *Some must watch while some must sleep*. New York: Norton. This short book is written in an engaging style for the beginning student of sleep. Nevertheless, instructors and even experts in sleep find it to be an excellent introduction by one of the pioneers of sleep research.

Hobson, J. (1989). *Sleep*. New York: Scientific American Library. This book covers most of the main ideas that have developed from research into sleep. It also covers areas of psychology, ethology, neuroscience, and molecular biology, and it provides an overview of the disorders of sleep. Hobson presents his own theory of dreams, the theory of activation synthesis.

Kleitman, N. (1965). *Sleep and wakefulness*. Chicago: University of Chicago Press. This book is an exhaustive description of research into sleep and covers all the major findings produced by the first decades of sleep research.

CHAPTER

13

# How Do We Learn from Experience?



Dimitri Messinis/AP Photo
Micrograph: Oliver Meckes/Ottawa/Photo Researchers

Donna was born on June 14, 1933. Her memory of the period from 1933 to 1937 is sketchy, but those who knew her as a baby report that she was like most other infants. At first, she could not talk, walk, or use a toilet. Indeed, she did not even seem to recognize her father, although her mother seemed more familiar to her. Like all children, Donna grew quickly, and in no time she was using and understanding simple language and could recognize many people by sight almost instantly. Donna began taking dancing lessons when she was four and was a "natural." By the time she finished high school she had the training and skill necessary for a career as a dancer with a major dance company. She remembers vividly the day that she was chosen to play a leading role in *The Nutcracker*. She had marveled at the costumes as she watched the popular Christmas ballet as a child, and now she was to be dancing in those costumes!

Donna's part in *The Nutcracker* had an even greater impact on her life when she met a man at a party after the last performance. He had seen her dance and took the opportunity to tell her how much he had enjoyed it. He was a young assistant professor of paleontology who studied dinosaur eggs in Montana. She was swept off her feet, and they married in 1958. Although her career as a dancer was soon interrupted by the births of two children, Donna never lost interest in dancing. In 1968, once both her children were in school, she began dancing again with a local company. To her amazement, she still could perform most of the movements, although she was rusty on the classic dances that she had once memorized so meticulously. Nonetheless, she quickly relearned. In retrospect, she should not have been so surprised, as she had always had an excellent memory.

One evening in 1990, while on a bicycle ride, Donna was struck by a drunk driver. Although she was wearing a helmet, she suffered a closed head injury that put her in a coma for several weeks. As she regained consciousness, she was confused and had difficulty in talking and in understanding others. Her memory was very poor; she had spatial disorientation and often got lost; she had various motor disturbances; and she had difficulty recognizing anyone but her family and closest friends.

Over the ensuing 10 months, Donna regained most of her motor abilities and language skills, and her spatial abilities improved significantly. Nonetheless, she was short-tempered and easily frustrated by the slowness of her recovery, symptoms that are typical of people with closed head injuries. She suffered periods of depression. She also found herself prone to inexplicable surges of panic when doing simple things. On one occasion early in her rehabilitation, she was shopping in a large supermarket and became overwhelmed by the number of salad dressing choices. She ran from the store, and it was only after she sat outside and calmed herself that she could go back inside to continue shopping.

Two years later, Donna was dancing once again, but she now found it very difficult to learn new steps. Her emotions were still unstable, which was a strain on her family, but her episodes of frustration and temper outbursts became much less frequent. A year later, they were gone and her life was not obviously different from that of other 57-year-old women. She did have some cognitive changes that persisted, however. She seemed unable to remember the names or faces of new people she met and was unable to concentrate if there were distractions such as a television or radio playing in the background. She could not dance as she had before her injury, although she did work at it diligently. Her balance on sudden turns gave her the most difficulty; rather than risk falling, she retired from her life's first love.

Donna's experiences demonstrate one of the most intriguing and important properties of the human brain: its capacity for continuously changing its structure, and ultimately its function, throughout a lifetime. This capacity to change, which is known as **brain plasticity,** allows the brain to respond to changes in the environment or within the organism. In describing the events of Donna's life, we can see several types of behavioral change that must be correlated with different plastic changes in the brain. First, during her early childhood, Donna's brain changed dramatically in structure as she learned about the world and how to respond to it. She had to learn to use language, to distinguish different faces, to walk, to ride a bicycle, to read, to dance, and so on. Because her brain is solely responsible for her behavior, her brain somehow changed to reflect her experiences and new abilities. When Donna reached puberty, her body changed and so did her thoughts. Her dreams often had sexual content; because dreams are a product of the brain, there must have been some change in her brain activity for her dreams to change so dramatically. When Donna returned to dancing after a 10-year break, she found that she had retained much of her skill, even though she had not practiced at all. In this case the brain saved the earlier changes. After her accident, Donna had to "relearn" how to talk, to walk, and so on. In actual fact, she did not go through the same process of learning that she had experienced as a baby, but something in her brain had to change in order to allow her to regain her lost abilities. That change must have had some limits, however, because she never did recover her memory or her ability to learn new dances.

One lesson of the story of Donna is that although we tend to look at the brain as a relatively static structure that controls our behavior, the brain changes throughout our lifetime, and it is these changes that allow us to modify our behavior. If we reflect upon our own lives, we can easily compile a list of the experiences that must change our brains. A typical list would include the profound changes in brain and behavior during development that we discussed in Chapter 7, as well as the acquisition of culture, preferences for certain foods or beverages or art or other experiences, the ability to cope with the progressive loss of brain cells during the aging process, and, for many people (including Donna), the capacity to accommodate to neurological injury or disease. One common characteristic of all these examples is that they include what we would typically describe as some form of learning. Understanding how the brain supports learning is one of the fundamental questions of neuroscience.

The analysis of learning and the brain can be approached on several levels:

1. We can ask questions about the nature of learning. For example, is all learning the same, or are there different types of learning?
2. If there are different types of learning, then we might expect that there would be separate brain circuits related to the different types. In Chapter 5, we noted that synapses change with events such as those observed in long-term enhancement, but such changes could occur anywhere in the brain. The bigger question is just where such changes might occur when we learn specific types of information.
3. We can investigate the nature of the neural changes that support learning. One way to do this is to describe the changes in neurons when they are exposed to specific sensory experiences. Another is to look at the neural changes that accompany various forms of brain plasticity, such as recovery from brain injury or addiction to drugs.

These three approaches to the study of learning are presented in this chapter. The overriding goal, however, is to generalize beyond learning in order to understand the nature of behavior and the changing brain.

## WHAT ARE LEARNING AND MEMORY?

**Learning** is a relatively permanent change in an organism's behavior as a result of experience. **Memory** refers to the ability to recall or recognize previous experience. Memory thus implies a mental representation of the previous experience. This mental representation is sometimes referred to as a *memory trace*, and it is presumed that a memory trace reflects some type of change in the brain. Note that what we know about the process of learning and the formation of memories is inferred from changes in behavior, not observed directly. The study of learning and memory therefore requires the creation of behavioral measures to evaluate such behavioral changes. We begin our discussion of the nature of learning by looking at the ways in which animals are studied in the laboratory. We then look at what general types of learning can be identified from such studies.

**Brain plasticity.** The ability of the brain to change its structure in response to experience, drugs, hormones, or injury.

**Learning.** A relatively permanent change in an organism's behavior as a result of experience.

**Memory.** The ability to recall or recognize previous experience.

## Studying Memory in the Laboratory

One of the challenges for psychologists studying memory in laboratory animals (or people) is to get the subjects to reveal what they can remember. Because laboratory animals do not talk, investigators must devise ways for a subject to show its knowledge. Different species can "talk" to us in different ways, so the choice of test must be matched to the capabilities of the species. In the study of rodents, mazes or swimming pools are typically used because rodents live in tunnels and around water. Studies of monkeys have taken advantage of the monkeys' sharp vision and avid curiosity by requiring them to look under objects for food or at television monitors. When birds are the subjects, it is common to use natural behaviors such as singing. And for human subjects there is a tendency to use paper-and-pencil tests. The result is that psychologists have devised hundreds of different tests in the past century and, in doing so, have shown that there are many types of learning and memory, each of which appears to have its own neural circuitry. Let us consider some examples of how animals can be trained to "talk."

**Pavlovian conditioning.** A learning procedure whereby a neutral stimulus (such as a tone) comes to elicit a response because of its repeated pairing with some event (such as the delivery of food); also called classical conditioning or respondent conditioning.

### PAVLOVIAN CONDITIONING

At the beginning of the twentieth century, two very different traditions of studying learning and memory emerged. The Russian physiologist Ivan Pavlov discovered that when a food reward accompanied some stimulus, such as a tone, dogs learned to associate the stimulus with the food. Then, whenever they heard the tone, they would salivate even though no food was present. This type of learning has many names, including **Pavlovian conditioning**, *respondent conditioning*, and *classical conditioning*, and its characteristics have been documented by many studies. A key feature of Pavlovian conditioning is that animals learn the association between two stimuli (such as the presentation of the food and the tone) and tell us they have learned it by giving the same response (such as salivation) to both stimuli. Pet owners are familiar with this type of learning: to a cat or dog, the sound of a can opener is a clear stimulus for food. Experimentally, two forms of Pavlovian conditioning are commonly used today: eye-blink conditioning and fear conditioning. These have proved especially useful because they are associated with neural circuits in discrete brain regions.

**Eye-blink conditioning** has been used to study Pavlovian learning in rabbits and people (Figure 13-1). In these studies, a tone (or some other stimulus) is associated with a painless puff of air to the eye of the subject. The tone, which is known as the **conditioned stimulus** (CS), comes to elicit a blink that is initially produced by the air puff, which is known as the **unconditioned response** (UCR), because it is the normal reaction to a puff of air. Thus, the subject tells us that it has learned that the signal stimulus predicts the puff by blinking in response to the signal alone—a **conditioned response** (CR). This form of learning is mediated by circuits in the cerebellum. The cerebellum does not have special circuits just for eye-blink conditioning, which is an artificial situation. Rather, the cerebellum has circuits designed to pair various motor responses with environmental events. The eye-blink conditioning experiments simply take advantage of this predisposition.

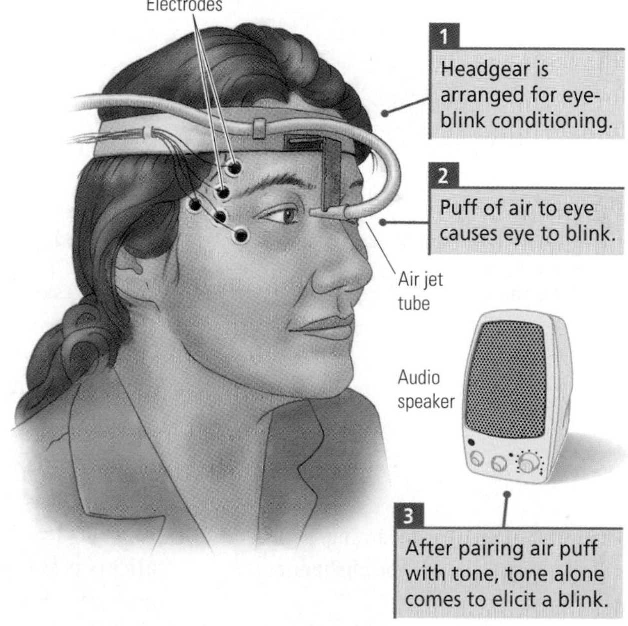
Electrodes
1
Headgear is arranged for eye-blink conditioning.
2
Puff of air to eye causes eye to blink.
Air jet tube
Audio speaker
3
After pairing air puff with tone, tone alone comes to elicit a blink.

**Figure 13-1**

A subject wearing headgear arranged for eye-blink conditioning. The apparatus delivers a puff of air to the eye, which causes the subject to blink. When the air puff is paired with a tone, the subject learns the association and subsequently blinks to the tone alone. This form of learning is mediated by circuits in the cerebellum.

EXPERIMENT

**Question:** Does an animal learn the association between emotional experience and environmental stimuli?

**Procedure and results**

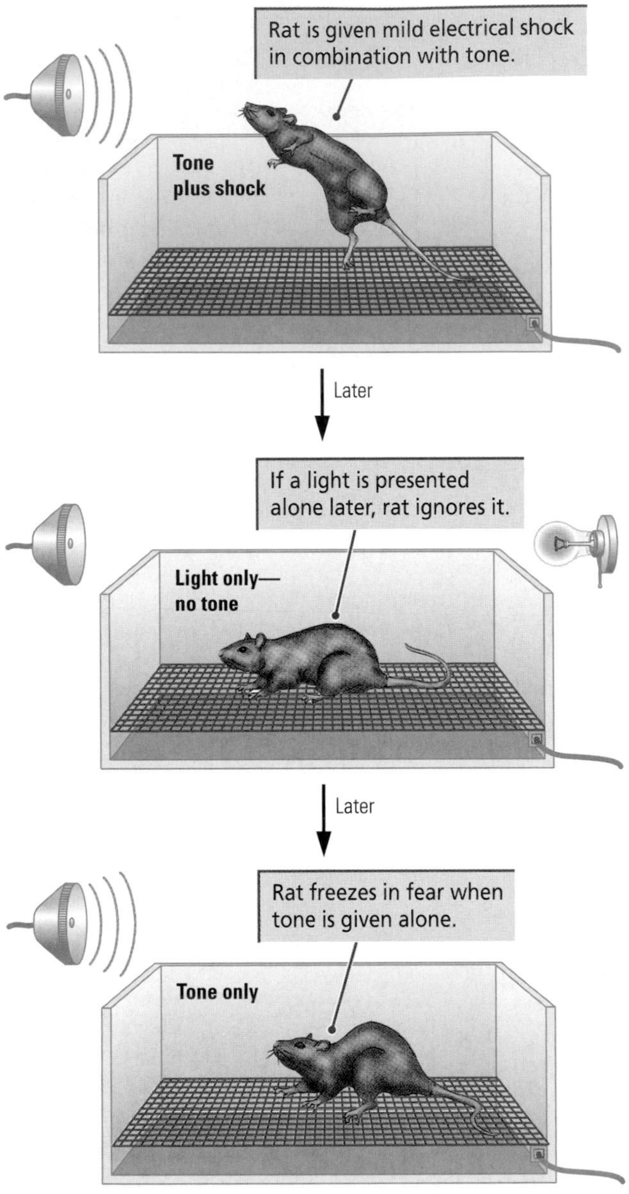

Rat is given mild electrical shock in combination with tone.

Tone plus shock

Later

If a light is presented alone later, rat ignores it.

Light only—no tone

Later

Rat freezes in fear when tone is given alone.

Tone only

Conclusion

**The rat has learned an association between the tone and the shock, which produces a fear response. Circuits that include the amygdala are involved in this learning process.**

**Figure 13-2**

An example of a conditioned emotional response. A rat is given a mild electric shock in combination with a tone (*top*). If a light is presented alone later, the animal ignores it (*center*). When the tone is presented alone later, the rat freezes in fear because it has learned an association between the tone and a shock (*bottom*). The amygdala and associated circuits play a key role in this form of conditioning.

In **fear conditioning,** a noxious stimulus is used to elicit fear. A rat or other animal is placed in a box that has a grid floor through which a mild but noxious electric current can be passed. As shown in Figure 13-2, a tone (the CS) is presented just before a brief, unexpected, mild electric shock. (This shock is roughly equivalent to the static-electrical shock we get when we rub our feet on a carpet and then touch a metal object or another person.) When the tone is later presented without the shock, the animal will act as though afraid. For example, it may become motionless and may urinate in anticipation of the shock. Presentation of a novel stimulus, such as a light, in the same environment has little effect on the animal. Thus, the animal tells us that it has learned the association between the tone and the shock. Circuits of the amygdala, rather than the cerebellum, mediate fear conditioning. Although both eye-blink and fear conditioning are Pavlovian, different parts of the brain mediate the learning.

## INSTRUMENTAL CONDITIONING

The second tradition of studying learning and memory was begun in the United States by Edward Thorndike (1898). Thorndike was interested in how animals solved problems. In one famous series of experiments, Thorndike placed cats in a box with a plate of fish outside it (Figure 13-3). The only way for a hungry cat to get to the fish was to figure out how to get out of the box. The solution was to press on a lever, which activated a system of pulleys that opened the box's door. The cat gradually learned that its actions had consequences: on the initial trial, the cat would touch the releasing mechanism only by chance as it restlessly paced inside the box. The cat apparently learned that something it did opened the door, and it would tend to repeat the behaviors that had occurred just prior to the door opening. After a few trials, the cat would take just seconds to get the door open so it could devour the fish.

Later studies by B. F. Skinner (e.g., 1938) used a similar strategy to train rats to press bars or pigeons to peck keys to obtain food. Many animals will learn to bar press or key peck if they are simply placed into the apparatus and allowed to discover the response necessary to obtain the reward, just as Thorndike's cats learned to escape the boxes. This type of learning is referred to as **instrumental conditioning** or *operant conditioning*. The subject indicates that it has learned the association between its actions and the consequences by increasing the speed at which it can perform the task. The variety of such instrumental associations is staggering, as we are constantly learning the association between our behavior and its consequences. It should be no surprise, therefore, that instrumental learning is

For a simulation on learning, go to the Web site at **www.worthpublishers.com/kolb/chapter13**

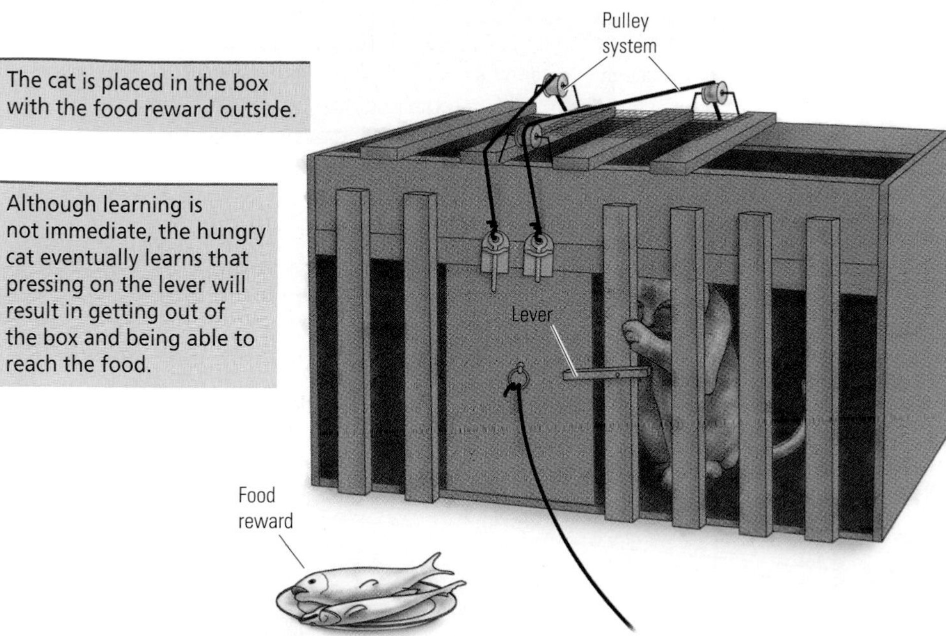

The cat is placed in the box with the food reward outside.
Although learning is not immediate, the hungry cat eventually learns that pressing on the lever will result in getting out of the box and being able to reach the food.
Pulley system
Lever
Food reward

**Figure 13-3**

An example of the puzzle box used by Thorndike to study learning in cats. The task is for the cat to open the door to get to the fish reward.

not localized to any particular circuit in the brain. The circuits needed vary with the actual requirements of the task, as is demonstrated by the following examples.

Richard Morris devised a task in 1980 that has become popular in research in learning and memory. He placed rats in a large swimming pool in which there was an escape platform that was invisible to the rats because it was just under the water's surface. (Figure 13-4A shows the setup.) The task for the rat was to discover that there was an escape and then to figure out where the platform was. In one version of the test, which is illustrated in Figure 13-4B, the only available cues were distal ones—that is, external to the pool. Because no single cue would identify the location of the platform, the rats had to learn the relationship between several cues in the room and the platform's location. This obviously requires **visuospatial learning,** or the use of visual information to identify an object's spatial location. Rats normally learn the Morris task in just a few trials such that when placed anywhere in the pool, they can swim directly to the hidden platform. We can infer that a rat that is able to swim but is unable to learn this task has some disturbance in the neural circuits underlying visuospatial learning,

In a variation of the task, once rats are trained to find the platform, the location of the platform is changed (Figure 13-4C). The platform is moved to a new position every day; the rats must find the platform on the first trial in the pool and then go to that location for the remainder of that day's trials. In this case, the rats' task is to learn not only the platform's location with respect to the visual world but also its new location each day. Rats quickly learn this puzzle and form what is known as a learning set. A **learning set** is an understanding of how a problem can be solved through the use of a rule that can be applied in many different situations. In the current example, the rule is that the successful solution (finding the platform) requires a shift in strategy when the old strategy fails. Well-trained animals need only a single trial to learn the platform's location each day and will swim flawlessly to that location on subsequent trials. This type of task, in which the rat must keep track of a specific piece of information on a given day, places demands on the brain that are clearly different from the simpler Morris version, in which the learning is gradual, much like that in Thorndike's cats.

**Fear conditioning.** The learning of an association between a neutral stimulus and and a noxious event such as a shock.

**Instrumental conditioning.** A learning procedure in which the consequences (such as obtaining a reward) of a particular behavior (such as pressing a bar) increase or decrease the probability of the behavior occurring again; also called operant conditioning.

**Learning set.** An understanding of how a problem can be solved with a rule that can be applied in many different situations.

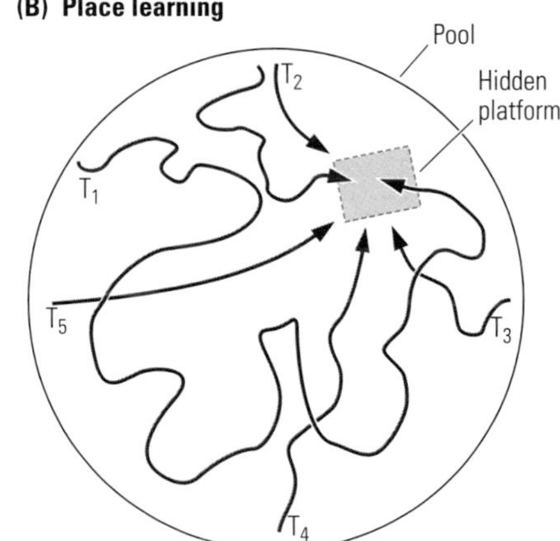


**(C) Matching-to-place learning**

$T_1$

$T_2$

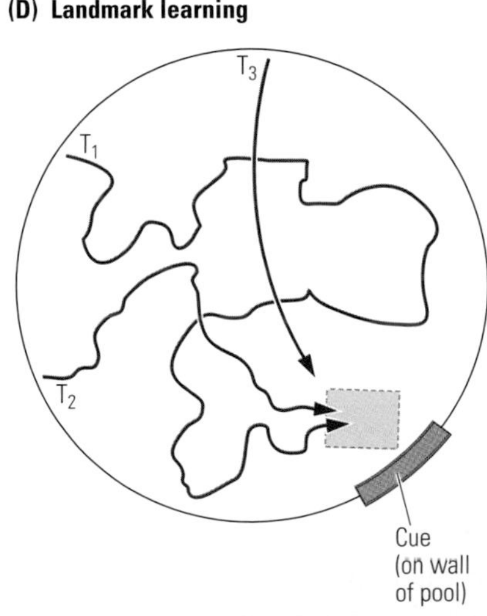


**Figure 13-4**

Three different visuospatial learning tasks in a swimming pool for rats. **(A)** The general arrangement of the pool. **(B)** In a place-learning task (Morris, 1981), a rat is put into the pool at various starting locations. The animal must learn the location of a hidden platform, which can be done only by considering the configuration of visual cues in the room—windows, wall decorations, potted plants, and the like. **(C)** In a matching-to-place task (Whishaw, 1989), the rat is again put in the pool at random locations, but in this case the hidden platform is in a new location each test day. The animal must learn that the location where it finds the platform on the first trial of each day is the location of the platform for all that day's trials. **(D)** In a landmark-learning task (Kolb & Walkey, 1987), the rat is required to ignore the room cues and to learn that the cue on the wall of the pool signals the location of the platform. The platform and cue are moved on each trial so that the animal is penalized for trying to use room cues to solve the problem. The red lines in **(B)**, **(C)**, and **(D)** mark the rat's swimming path on each trial (T).

In yet another variation, a cue can be placed on the wall of the pool (Figure 13-4D). The rat's task is to learn that the cue, and only the cue, indicates the approximate location of the platform. In this case, the platform moves on every trial but always maintains the same relationship to the cue, which also moves. The brain therefore is learning that all the distal cues are irrelevant and only the local cue is relevant. This is a very different task, and, once again, different neural circuitry is required to solve it.

**Implicit memory.** Memory in which subjects can demonstrate knowledge but cannot explicitly retrieve the information.

**Explicit memory.** Memory in which subjects can retrieve an item and indicate that they know the item they have retrieved is the correct item (that is, conscious memory).

## Two Types of Memory

Humans present a different challenge to the study of memory because so much of our learning is verbal. Psychologists have been studying human memory since the mid-1800s, and cognitive psychologists have developed sophisticated measures of learning and memory for neuropsychological investigations. Two such measures will help us distinguish between two types of memory in humans. In one kind of task, subjects are given a list of words to read, such as *spring, winter, car*, and *boat.* Another group of subjects reads a list consisting of the words *trip, tumble, run,* and *sun.* All the subjects are then asked to define a series of words, one of which is *fall.* The word *fall* has multiple meanings, including the season and a tumble. People who have just read the word list containing names of seasons are likely to give the "season" meaning, whereas those who have read the second list will give the "tumble" meaning. Obviously, some form of unconscious (and unintentional) learning takes place as the subjects read the word lists.

This word-list task is a measure of **implicit memory.** People with **amnesia,** which is a partial or total loss of memory, perform normally on such tests of implicit memory. The amnesic person has no recollection of having read the word list, yet acts as though some neural circuit has been influenced by the list. Thus, there is a dissociation between the memory of the unconscious (or implicit) learning and the conscious recollection of training, which is referred to as **explicit memory**. This implicit–explicit distinction is not restricted to verbal learning but is true of visual learning and motor learning tasks as well. For example, subjects can be shown an incomplete sketch, such as the top panel of the Gollin figure test shown in Figure 13-5, and asked what it is. They are unlikely to be able to identify the image, so they are presented with a succession of more nearly complete sketches until they can identify the picture. When control subjects and amnesics are later shown the same sketch, both groups are able to identify the figure sooner than they could the first time. Even though the amnesic subjects may not recall having seen the sketches before, they behave as though they had.

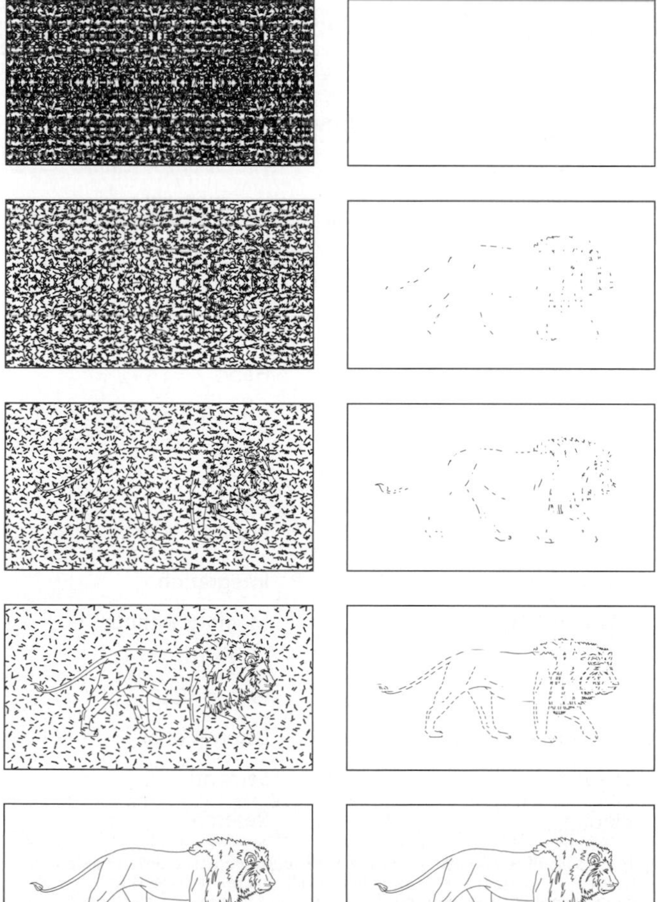

**Figure 13-5**

The Gollin figure test. Subjects are shown a series of drawings in sequence, from least to most clear, and asked to identify the object. It is impossible to identify the object from the first sketch, and most people must see several of the panels before they can identify the figure. On a retention test some time later, however, subjects identify the image sooner than they did on the first test, indicating some form of memory for the image. Amnesic subjects also show improvement on this test, even though they do not recall having done the test before.

**Figure 13-6**

The pursuit-rotor task. The subject must keep the stylus in contact with the metal disc that is moving in a circular pattern on a turntable, which is also moving in a circular pattern. Although the task is difficult, most people show significant improvement after a brief period of training. When given a second test at some later time, both normal subjects and amnesics show retention of the task. The amnesics typically do not recall having ever done the task before.

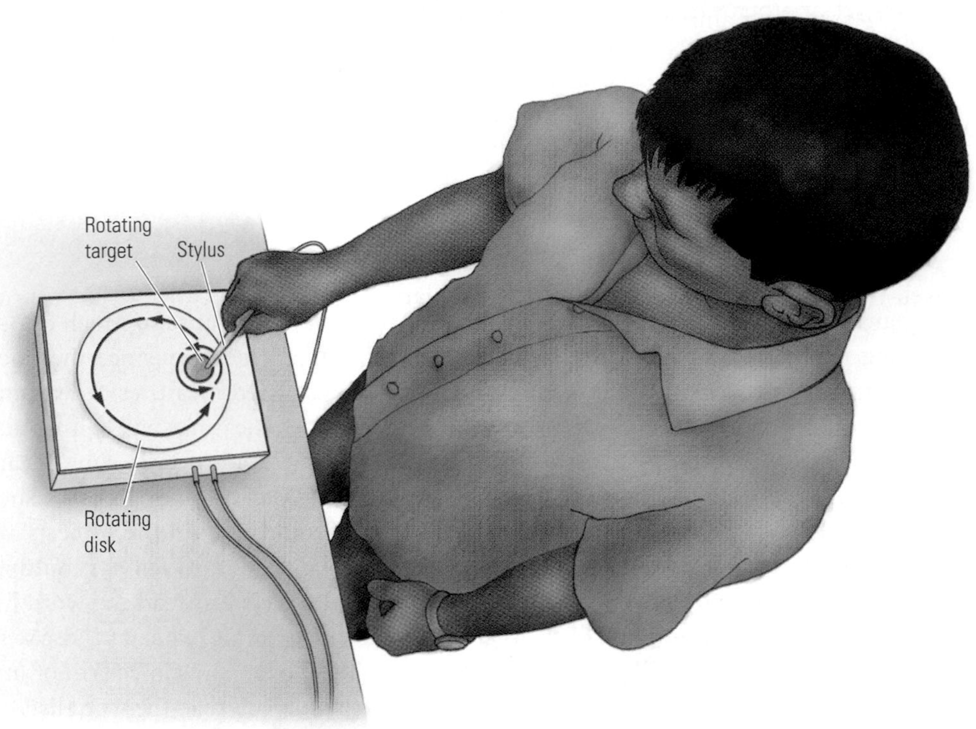


A second kind of measure reveals implicit learning of motor skills. For instance, a person can be taught some form of motor skill, such as the pursuit-rotor task shown in Figure 13-6. A small metal disc moves in a circular pattern on a turntable that is also moving. The task is to hold a stylus on the small disc as it spins. This task is not as easy as it looks, especially when the turntable is moving quickly. Nonetheless, with an hour's practice people become reasonably proficient. If they are presented with the same task a week later, both normal subjects and amnesics will take less time to perform the task. Here, too, the amnesics will fail to recall having ever done the task before. We can see, therefore, that the distinction between tests of implicit and explicit memory is consistent and must provide some key to how the brain stores information.

**Table 13-1 Terms Describing Two Kinds of Memory**

| Term for conscious memory | Term for unconscious memory |
|---|---|
| Explicit | Implicit |
| Declarative | Procedural |
| Fact | Skill |
| Memory | Habit |
| Knowing that | Knowing how |
| Locale | Taxon |
| Cognitive mediation | Semantic |
| Conscious recollection | Skills |
| Elaboration | Integration |
| Memory with record | Memory without record |
| Autobiographical | Perceptual |
| Representational | Dispositional |
| Episodic | Semantic |
| Working | Reference |

These pairs of terms have been used by various theorists to differentiate two forms of memory. This list is intended to help you relate other discussions of memory that you may encounter to the one in this book, which favors the explicit–implicit distinction.

The distinction between implicit and explicit memory is just one way in which psychologists have categorized different memory processes. Many researchers prefer to distinguish between **declarative memory**, which refers to the specific contents of specific experiences, and **procedural memory**, which is memory of how to do something. Although some theorists may make subtle distinctions between the implicit–explicit and declarative–procedural dichotomies, there is really little practical difference and, in our view, the explicit–implicit dichotomy is the simplest one to understand. Table 13-1 lists other commonly used dichotomies, with the general distinction being that one type of memory requires the recollection of specific information whereas the other type refers to knowledge of which we are not consciously aware. We can include Pavlov's classical conditioning, Thorndike's instrumental learning, and Skinner's operant learning in this analysis, too, as they can all be considered types of implicit learning.

Nonspeaking animals can display explicit memory. One of us owned a cat that loved to play with a little ball. One day the ball was temporarily put on a shelf to keep it away from an inquisitive 1-year-old boy. For weeks afterward the cat would sit and stare at the location where the ball had been placed. This is an explicit memory.

Animals also display explicit memory when they learn psychological tasks. Recall that in one variant of the Morris task, rats were given a new platform location on each day of training. The task therefore was to go to the platform's last location. This is an explicit piece of information, which can be demonstrably forgotten. Suppose that a well-trained rat is given one trial with the platform at a new location, and then not given a second trial for an hour, a day, 3 days, or a week. The rat has no difficulty with a delay of an hour or even a day. Some rats are flawless at 3 days, but most have forgotten the location by the time a week has elapsed. Instead, they swim around looking for the platform, which illustrates their implicit memory of the learning set, or the "rules of the game"—namely, that there is a platform and that it can be found with a certain type of search strategy.

## What Makes Explicit and Implicit Memory Different?

One reason that explicit and implicit memories differ is that each type of memory is housed in a different set of neural structures. Another reason they differ is that the information is processed differently. Implicit information is encoded in very much the same way as it is perceived. This can be described as data-driven, or "bottom-up," processing. The idea is that information enters the brain by the sensory receptors and is then processed in a series of subcortical and cortical regions. For example, recall from Chapter 8 that visual information about an object goes from the visual receptors (the "bottom") to the lateral geniculate nucleus, the occipital cortex, and then the temporal lobe via the temporal stream where the object is recognized.

Explicit memory, in contrast, depends on conceptually driven, or "top-down," processing, in which the subject reorganizes the data. For example, if we were searching for a particular object such as our keys, we would ignore other objects. This is referred to as top-down because circuits in the temporal lobe (the "top") form an image that influences how incoming information is processed, which in turn greatly influences the recall of information later. Because a person has a relatively passive role in encoding implicit memory, he or she will have difficulty recalling the memory spontaneously but will recall the memory more easily when primed by the original stimulus or some feature of it. Because a person plays an active role in processing information explicitly, the internal cues that were used in processing can also be used to initiate spontaneous recall.

Studies of eyewitness testimony demonstrate the active nature of explicit memory (e.g., Loftus, 1997). In a typical experiment, people are shown a video clip of an accident in which a car collides with another car stopped at an intersection. One group of subjects is asked to estimate how fast the car was going when it "smashed" into the other car. A second group is asked how fast the car was going when it "bumped" into the other car. Later questioning indicates that the memory of how fast the first car was moving is biased by the instruction: subjects looking for "smashing" cars estimate faster speeds than those looking for "bumping" cars. In other words, the instruction causes the information to be processed differently. In both cases, the subjects were certain that their memories were accurate.

Other experiments also show that implicit memory is fallible, too. For example, subjects are read the following list of words: *sweet, chocolate, shoe, table, candy, horse,*

To test your own memory, go to the Web site at **www.worthpublishers.com/kolb/chapter13**

*car, cake, coffee, wall, book, cookie, hat.* After a delay of a few minutes, the subjects hear another list of words that includes some of the words from the first list and some that are new. Subjects are asked to identify which words were present on the first list and to indicate how certain they are of the identification. One of the words on the second list is *sugar*. Most subjects indicate not just that *sugar* was on the first list but that they are *certain* that it was. Of course, it was not. This type of demonstration is intriguing, for it shows the ease with which we can form "false memories" and defend their veracity with certainty.

Although memories can be distinguished generally as implicit or explicit, the brain does not process all implicit or all explicit memories in the same way. Memories can be divided according to categories that are different from those listed in Table 13-1. For example, we can make a distinction between memories for different types of sensory information. We have seen that visual and auditory information is processed by different neural areas, so it is reasonable to assume that auditory memories are stored in different brain regions from those in which visual memories are stored. We can also make a distinction between information stored in so-called *short-term memory* and information held for a longer time in *long-term memory.* In short-term memory, information—such as the phone number of a restaurant that we have just looked up in the Yellow Pages—is held in memory only briefly, for a few minutes at most, and then is discarded. In long-term memory, information—such as a close friend's name—is held in memory indefinitely, perhaps for a lifetime. The frontal lobe plays an important role in temporary memory, whereas the temporal lobe plays a central role in long-term storage of verbal information. The crucial point is that no single place in the nervous system can be identified as the location for memory or learning. Virtually the entire nervous system can be changed with experience, but different experiences change different parts. One challenge for the experimentalist is to devise ways of manipulating experience in order to demonstrate change in different parts of the brain.

Accepting the idea that every part of the brain can learn influences our view of the nature of the neural circuits that mediate memory. For example, we could expect that areas that process information also house the memory of that information. Areas that process visual information likely will house visual memory. Because the temporal lobe has specialized regions for processing color, shape, and other visual information regarding an object's characteristics, we can predict that the memory for the visual attributes of objects will be stored separately. This prediction has been confirmed by a series of PET studies by Alex Martin and colleagues (1995) at the U.S. National Institutes of Mental Health.

In one of these studies, subjects were shown black-and-white line drawings of objects and asked to generate words denoting either colors or actions of the objects. The idea was that the processing of color and motion of objects is carried out in different locations in the temporal lobe, and thus the activity associated with the memories of color or motion might also be dissociated. In fact, just such a dissociation was demonstrated. Figure 13-7 shows that recall of colors activated a region next to the area controlling color perception, whereas recall of movement activated an area next to the area controlling the perception of motion. This distribution of activation shows not only that object memory is at least partly located in the temporal lobe but also that it is found in regions associated with the original perception of the objects.

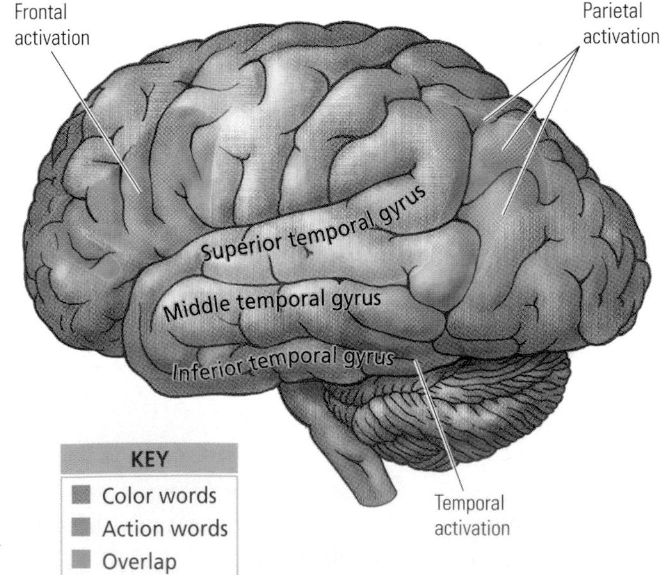


**Figure 13-7**

A lateral view of the left hemisphere showing regions of increased blood flow when subjects generated color words (red) and action words (blue) in describing the visual characteristics of objects shown to them in static, black-and-white drawings. Purple indicates areas of overlap. The red region extends under the lateral portion of the temporal lobe. The generation of color words selectively activated a region in the ventral temporal lobe, just anterior to the area normally taking part in the perception of color, whereas generation of action words activated a region in the middle temporal gyrus, just anterior to the area involved in the perception of motion. These data suggest that object knowledge is organized as a distributed system in which the attributes of an object are stored close to the regions of the cortex that mediate perception of those attributes. There is also activation in the parietal lobe, which is likely related to the movements associated with actions, and in the frontal lobe, which is related to the spontaneous generation of behavior.

Adapted from "Discrete Cortical Regions Associated with Knowledge of Color and Knowledge of Action," by A. Martin, J.V. Haxby, F.M. Lalonde, C.L. Wiggs, and L.G. Ungerleider, 1995, *Science, 270,* p. 104.

## In Review

Learning is a process that results in a relatively permanent change in behavior. There are multiple forms of learning. The primary distinction can be made between Pavlovian conditioning, in which some environmental stimulus (such as a tone) is paired with a reward, and operant conditioning, in which a response (such as pushing a button) is paired with a reward. The demands on the nervous system are different in the two types of learning, so we can expect that the regions of the brain related to each learning form will be different.

Memory is the ability to recall or recognize previous experience; this implies the existence of a memory trace, or a mental representation of a previous experience. There are many forms of memory, each related to mental representations in different parts of the brain. One useful distinction is between implicit memory, in which information is unconsciously learned, and explicit memory, which is a memory for specific information. The mental representations of these forms of memory are held in different regions of the brain, as we shall see.

**Figure 13-8**

H.M.'s brain viewed from below, with the lesion highlighted. The right side of the brain has been left intact to show the relative location of the medial temporal structures. Because the lesion runs along the wall of the medial temporal lobe, it can be seen in several cross sections of the brain. **(A)**, **(B)**, and **(C)** depict such sections of H.M.'s brain. The drawings are based on an MRI scan of H.M.'s brain.

Adapted from "H.M.'s Medial Temporal Lobe Lesion: Findings from Magnetic Resonance Imaging," by S. Corkin, D.G. Amaral, R.G. Gonzalez , K.A. Johnson, B.T. Hyman, 1997, *Journal of Neuroscience*, 17.



(A)

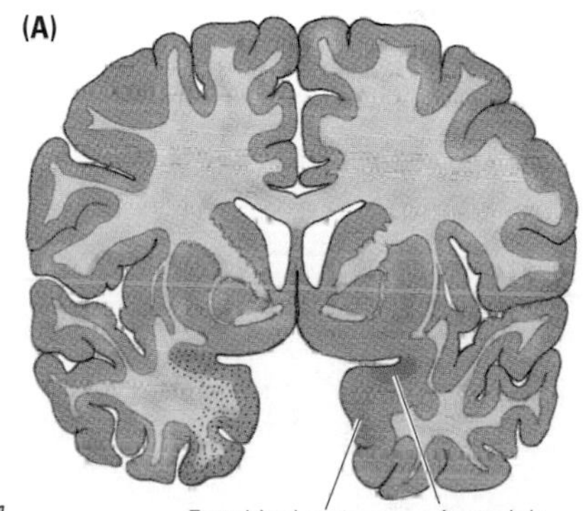


(B)

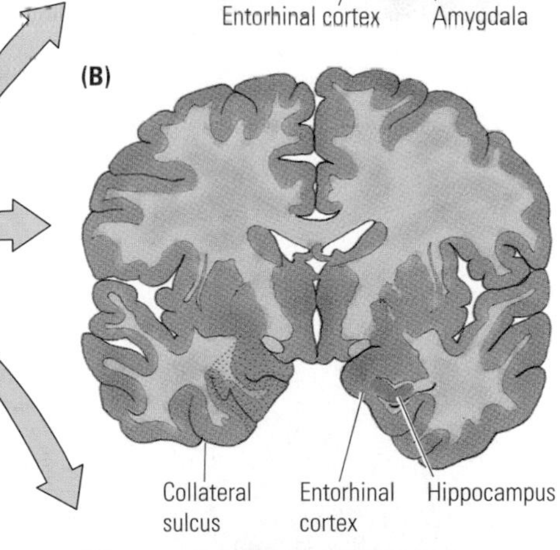


(C)

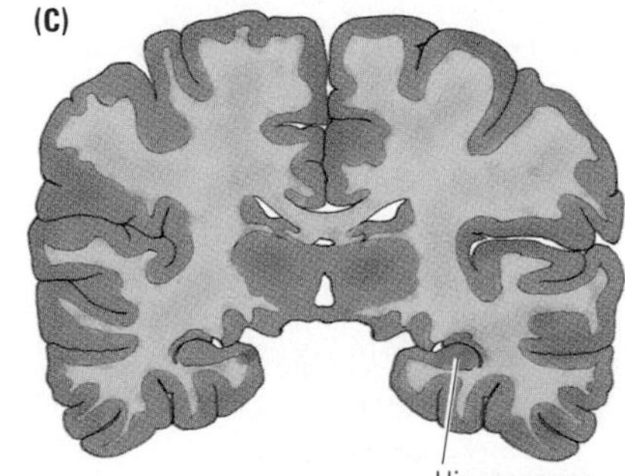


## DISSOCIATING MEMORY CIRCUITS

Beginning in the 1920s and continuing until the early 1950s, the American psychologist Karl Lashley looked for the neural circuits underlying memory for the solutions to mazes learned by laboratory rats and monkeys. Lashley's working hypothesis was that memories must be represented in the perceptual and motor circuitry used to learn solutions to problems. He believed that if he removed bits of this circuitry or made knife cuts that disconnected it, amnesia should result. In fact, however, neither procedure produced amnesia. What Lashley found was that the severity of the memory disturbance was related to the size of the injury rather than to its location. In 1951, after 30 years of searching, Lashley concluded that he had failed to find the location of the memory trace, although he did believe that he knew where it was *not* located (Lashley, 1960).

Ironically, it was just two years later that William Scoville made a serendipitous discovery that had not been predicted by Lashley's studies. On August 23, 1953, Scoville performed a bilateral medial temporal lobe resection on a young man who became known as Case H.M. H.M. had severe epilepsy that was not controlled by medication. Like Wilder Penfield (see Chapter 9), Scoville was a neurosurgeon who was attempting to rid people of seizures by removing the abnormal brain tissue that was causing them. H.M.'s seizures were originating in the medial temporal region, which includes the amygdala, hippocampal formation, and associated cortical structures, so Scoville removed them, first from one hemisphere and later from the other. As shown in Figure 13-8, the removal included the anterior portion of the hippocampus, the amygdala, and the adjacent cortex. The behavioral symptoms that Scoville noted after the second surgery were completely unexpected, so he invited

Brenda Milner, one of Penfield's associates, to study H.M. Milner and her colleagues have studied H.M. for nearly 50 years, making him the most studied case in neuroscience (e.g. Milner, Corkin, & Teuber, 1968).

H.M.'s most remarkable symptom is severe amnesia: he is unable to recall anything that has happened since his surgery in 1953. H.M. still has an above-average I.Q. (118 on the Wechsler Adult Intelligence Scale), and he performs normally on perceptual tests. Furthermore, his recall of events from his childhood and school days is intact. Socially, H.M. is well mannered, and he can engage in sophisticated conversations. However, he cannot recall events that have just happened. H.M. has no explicit memory. In one study by Suzanne Corkin, H.M. was given a tray of hospital food, which he ate. A few minutes later he was given another tray. He did not recall having eaten the first meal and proceeded to eat another. A third tray was brought, and this time he ate only the dessert, complaining that he did not seem to be very hungry.

To understand the implications and severity of H.M.'s condition, one need only consider a few events in his postsurgical life. His father died, but H.M. continued to ask where his father was, only to experience anew the grief of hearing that his father had passed away. (Eventually H.M. stopped asking about his father, suggesting that some type of learning had occurred.) Similarly, when in the hospital he typically asks, with many apologies, if the nurses can tell him where he is and how he came to be there. He remarked on one occasion, "Every day is alone in itself, whatever enjoyment I've had, and whatever sorrow I've had." His experience is that of a person who perceives his surroundings but cannot comprehend the situation he is in because he does not remember what has gone before.

Formal tests of H.M.'s memory show what one would expect: he cannot recall specific information just presented. In contrast, his implicit memory performance is nearly intact. He performs normally on tests like the pursuit-rotor or incomplete-figure tasks described earlier. Whatever systems are required for implicit memory must therefore be intact, but those systems crucial to explicit memory are gone or dysfunctional. Another case, similar to that of H.M., is discussed in "Patient Boswell's Amnesia."

There are probably several reasons why Lashley did not find a syndrome like that shown by H.M. Most important, Lashley was not using tests of explicit memory, so his animal subjects would not have shown H.M.'s deficits. Rather, Lashley's tests were mostly measures of implicit memory, which H.M. has no problems with. The following case illustrates that Lashley probably should have been looking in the basal ganglia for deficits revealed by his tests.

J.K. was born on June 28, 1914. He was above average in intelligence and worked as a petroleum engineer for 45 years. In his mid-70s he began to show symptoms of Parkinson's disease, and at about age 78 he started to have memory difficulties. (Recall that in Parkinson's disease, the projections from the dopaminergic cells of the brainstem to the basal ganglia die.) Curiously, J.K.'s memory disturbance was related to tasks that he had done all his life. On one occasion, he stood at the door of his bedroom frustrated by his inability to recall how to turn on the lights. He remarked, "I must be crazy. I've done this all my life and now I can't remember how to do it!" On another occasion, he was seen trying to turn the radio off with the TV remote control. This time he explained, "I don't recall how to turn off the radio so I thought I would try this thing!" J.K. clearly had a deficit in implicit memory. In contrast, he was aware of daily events and could recall explicit events as well as most men his age can. He could still speak intelligently on issues of the day that he had just read about. Once when we visited him, one of us entered the room first and he immediately asked where the other was, even though it had been 2 weeks since we had told him we would be coming to visit. This intact long-term memory is very different from the situation of H.M., who

Focus on Disorders

## Patient Boswell's Amnesia

Boswell is a man who, at the age of 48, developed a brain infection known as herpes simplex encephalitis. Prior to his illness, Boswell had 13 years of schooling and had worked for nearly 30 years in the newspaper advertising business. By all accounts, he was successful in his profession and was a normal, well-adjusted person. Boswell recovered from the acute symptoms of the disease, which included seizures and a 3-day coma. His postdisease intelligence was low average, probably reflecting the neurological damage caused by the disease. Nonetheless, his speech and language remained normal in every respect, and he suffered no defects of sensory perception or of movement. But Boswell was left with a profound amnesic syndrome. If he hears a short paragraph and is asked to describe the main points of the paragraph, he routinely gets scores of zero. He can only guess the day's date and is unable even to guess what year it is. When asked what city he is in, he simply guesses. He does know his place of birth, and he can correctly recall his birth date about half the time. In sum, Boswell has a profound amnesia for events both prior to and since his encephalitis. Boswell does show implicit memory, however, on tests such as the pursuit-rotor task (see Figure 13-6).

Boswell has been extensively investigated by Damasio and his colleagues (1989), and his brain pathology is now well documented. The critical damage is a bilateral destruction of the medial temporal regions and a loss of the basal forebrain and the posterior part of the orbital frontal cortex. In addition, Boswell has lost the tissue known as the insular cortex, which is found in the Sylvian fissure. In contrast, his sensory and motor cortices are intact, as are his basal ganglia. Boswell's injury is thus more extensive than H.M.'s. Like H.M., he has a loss of new memories, but, unlike H.M., he also has a severe loss of access to old information, probably because of his insular and prefrontal injuries. Nonetheless, again like H.M., Boswell has an intact procedural memory, a fact that illustrates the dissociation between neural circuits underlying explicit and implicit forms of memory.

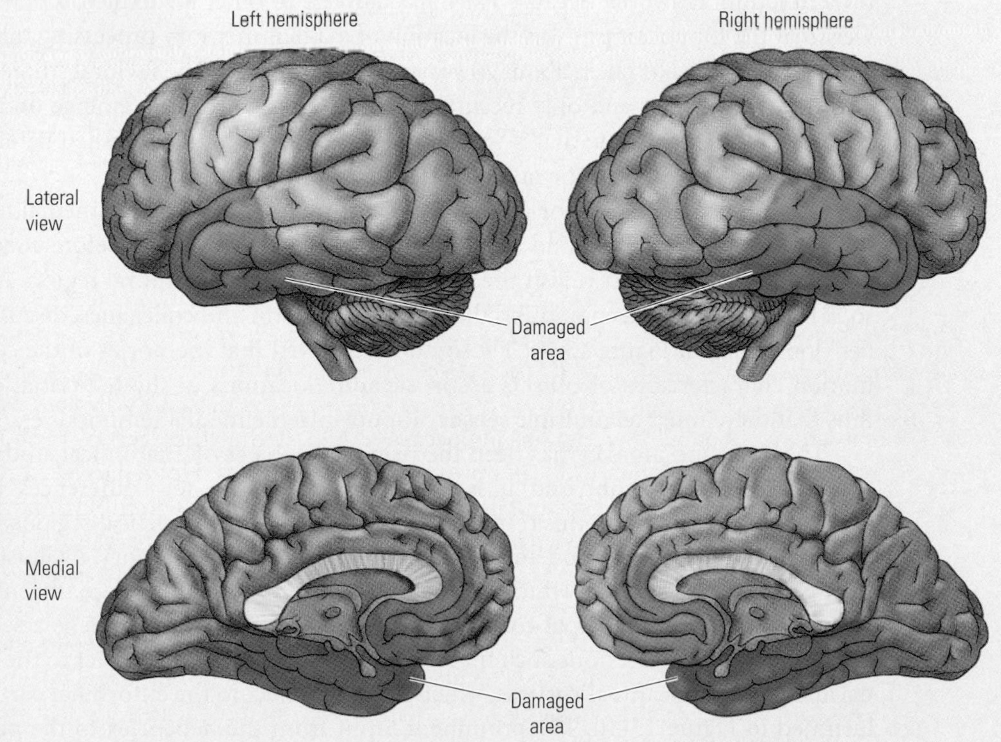


After a herpes simplex encephalitis infection, patient Boswell suffers profound amnesia and has difficulty remembering events before and after his illness. This model highlights the areas of damage in the medial temporal region, the basal forebrain, and the posterior orbital frontal cortex.

would not have remembered that anybody was coming, even 5 minutes after being told. Because Parkinson's disease primarily affects the basal ganglia, J.K.'s deficit in implicit memory was likely related to his basal ganglia dysfunction.

## In Review

In identifying the circuits responsible for memory, it is important to separate explicit memory from implicit memory. Explicit memory relies on the anterior portion of the hippocampus, the amygdala, and the adjacent cortex. These areas were damaged in H.M.'s brain, so he had no explicit memory. An implicit memory deficit indicates deterioration of the basal ganglia characteristic of Parkinson's disease, as seen in patients such as J.K.

# NEURAL SYSTEMS UNDERLYING EXPLICIT AND IMPLICIT MEMORIES

Laboratory studies, largely on rats and monkeys, have shown that the symptoms of patients such as H.M. and J.K. can be reproduced in animals by injuring the medial temporal region and basal ganglia, respectively. Other structures, most notably in the frontal and temporal lobes, have also been found to play roles in certain types of explicit memory. We consider the systems for explicit and implicit memory separately.

## A Neural Circuit for Explicit Memories

The dramatic amnesic syndrome discovered in H.M. in the 1950s led investigators to focus on the hippocampus, which at the time was a large anatomical structure looking for a function. However, because H.M. has damage to other structures, too, the initial view that the hippocampus was the location of explicit memory processing turned out to be incorrect. It has taken about 20 years of anatomical and behavioral studies to sort out the complexities, and only recently has a consensus begun to emerge on a theory for explicit memory. Note that if you consult books or reviews published before about 1995, the explanation may be quite different (see Gazzaniga, 2000).

The prime candidates for a role in explicit memory include the medial temporal region, the frontal cortex, and structures closely related to them. Before considering the model, we must first revisit the anatomy of the medial temporal region. As we do so, it is important to keep in mind the studies by Martin and colleagues, discussed earlier (look again at Figure 13-7). Those studies showed that memories of the color and motion characteristics of objects are in separate locations in the temporal lobe and thus that there must be multiple sensory inputs into the medial temporal region.

The macaque monkey has been the principal subject of anatomical study on the medial temporal region, and it is likely that there are few differences between macaques and humans in this respect. Three medial temporal cortical regions, in addition to the hippocampus and amygdala, take part in explicit memory. As illustrated in Figure 13-9, these regions, which lie adjacent to the hippocampus, are the **entorhinal cortex**, the **parahippocampal cortex**, and the **perirhinal cortex.** There is a sequential arrangement of connections such that the other cortical regions project to the perirhinal and parahippocampal cortices, which in turn project to the entorhinal cortex, as illustrated in Figure 13-10. The prominent input from the neocortex to the perirhinal region is from the visual regions of the ventral stream coursing through the temporal

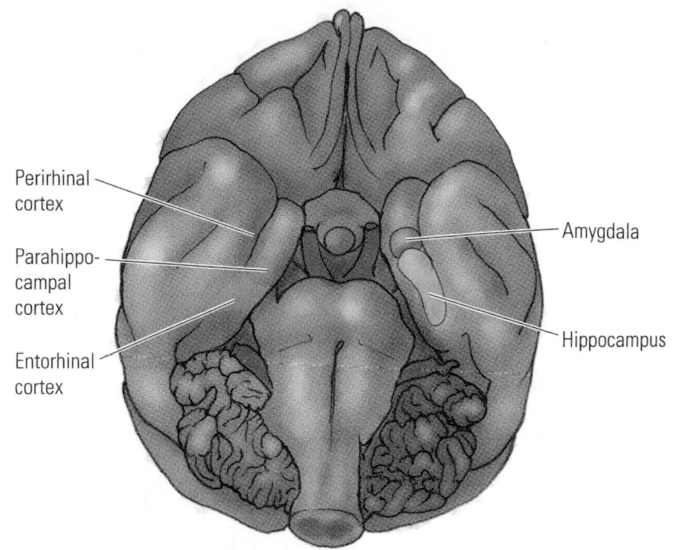


**Figure 13-9**

A rhesus monkey brain viewed from below, showing the medial temporal regions. On the left, three medial temporal cortical areas are shown: the perirhinal cortex (gray), the parahippocampal cortex (red), and the entorhinal cortex (green). Each of these regions plays a distinct role in processing sensory information for memory storage. On the right, the hippocampus (turquoise) and amygdala (purple) are illustrated. These last two structures are not directly visible from the surface of the brain because they lie beneath the medial temporal cortical regions illustrated on the left. Note that although these cortical and subcortical structures are illustrated on different sides of the brain, all of them are present on both sides of the brain.

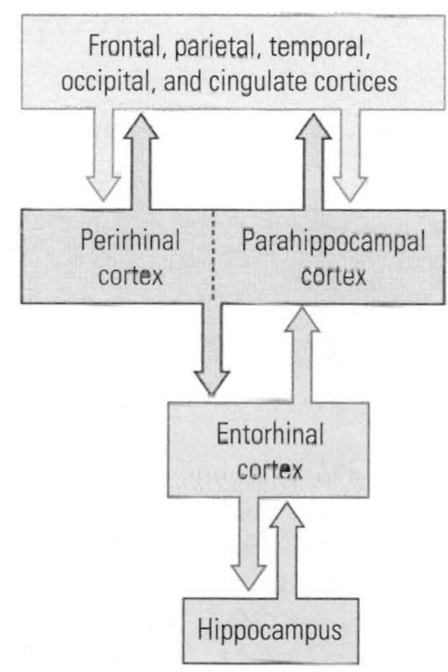


**Figure 13-10**

Connections among the medial temporal regions. Input from the sensory cortex flows to the parahippocampal and perirhinal regions, then to the entorhinal cortex, and, finally, to the hippocampus. The flow of sensory information is from the sensory regions to the medial temporal regions, and it then feeds back from the medial temporal regions to the sensory regions.

lobe. The perirhinal region is thus a prime candidate for visual object memory. Similarly, the parahippocampal region has a strong input from regions of the parietal cortex believed to take part in visuospatial processing. Thus, the parahippocampal region likely has a role in visuospatial memory. Because both the perirhinal and parahippocampal regions project to the entorhinal cortex, this region is likely to participate in more integrative forms of memory. Indeed, it is the entorhinal cortex that first shows cell death in **Alzheimer's disease,** which is a form of dementia characterized by severe deficits in explicit memory. (For a more detailed discussion, see "Alzheimer's Disease" on page 504.)

We are now left with a conundrum. If the hippocampus is not the key structure in explicit memory, yet is the recipient of the entorhinal connections, what does it do? The answer is that the hippocampus is probably engaged primarily in processes requiring the memory for places, such as the recall of the location of an object. This idea was first advanced by John O'Keefe and Lynn Nadel in 1978. Certainly, both laboratory animals and human patients with selective hippocampal injury have severe deficits in various forms of spatial memory. For example, rats with hippocampal damage have great difficulty solving spatial navigation tasks such as those shown in Figure 13-4.

Focus on Disorders

## Alzheimer's Disease

It was noted in the 1880s that the brain undergoes atrophy with aging, but the reason was not really understood until the German physician Alois Alzheimer published a landmark study in 1906. Alzheimer reported on a 51-year-old woman for whom he described a set of behavioral symptoms and associated neuropathology. In particular, the woman was demented and had various abnormalities in the cellular structure of the cerebral cortex, including both the neocortex and the limbic cortex. An estimated 1 million people now are affected by Alzheimer's disease in the United States, although the only certain diagnostic test is postmortem examination of cerebral tissue. The disease progresses slowly, and many people with Alzheimer's disease probably die from other causes before the cognitive symptoms become incapacitating. We knew of a physics professor who continued to work until he was nearly 80 years old, at which time he succumbed to a heart attack. Postmortem examination of his brain revealed significant Alzheimer's pathology. His slipping memory had been attributed by his colleagues to a case of "old-timer's disease."

The cause of Alzheimer's disease remains unknown, although it has been variously attributed to genetic predisposition, abnormal levels of trace elements, immune reactions, and slow viruses. Two principal neuronal changes occur in Alzheimer's disease. First, there is a loss of cholinergic cells in the basal forebrain. One type of treatment for Alzheimer's, therefore, is to provide medication to increase cholinergic levels in the forebrain. An example is Cognex, which is the trade name for tacrine hydrochloride, a cholinergic agonist that appears to provide temporary relief from the progression of the disease.

The second pathology is the development of neuritic plaques in the cerebral cortex. The plaques consist of a central core of homogeneous protein material known as amyloid, surrounded by degenerative cellular fragments. The cortical plaques are not distributed evenly throughout the cortex but are concentrated especially in the temporal-lobe areas related to memory. Cortical neurons begin to deteriorate as the cholinergic loss and plaques develop, as illustrated here. The first cells to die are in the entorhinal cortex, and significant memory disturbance ensues.

(A)

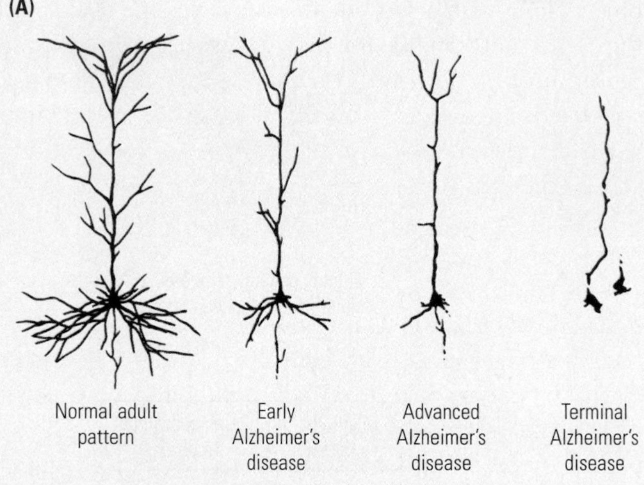


(B)

Cecil Fox/Science Source/Photo Researchers

As Alzheimer's disease progresses, neurons begin to deteriorate. (*Top*) These cortical pyramidal cells illustrate the progression of the disease. (*Bottom*) The neuritic plaque often found in the cerebral cortices of Alzheimer's patients. The plaque, which is the dark spot in the center of the image, is surrounded by the residue of degenerated cells. Part (A) drawn from Golgi-stained sections. After "Age-Related Changes in the Human Forebrain," by A. Scheibel, *Neuroscience Research Program Bulletin,* 1982, *20,* pp. 577–83.

Similarly, monkeys with hippocampal lesions have difficulty learning the location of objects. This can be demonstrated in tasks such as those illustrated in Figure 13-11. Monkeys are trained to displace objects to obtain a food reward (Figure 13-11A). Once they have learned how to do this, they are given one of two tasks. In the first task, shown in Figure 13-11B, known as a *visual-recognition task*, the animal displaces a sample object to obtain a food reward. After a short delay, the animal is presented with two objects, one of which is novel. The task is to learn that the novel object must be displaced in order to obtain a food reward. This is a test of explicit visual object memory. In the second task, shown in Figure 13-11C, the monkey is shown one object, which is displaced for a food reward. Then the monkey is shown the same object along with a second, identical one. The task is to learn that the object that is in the same position as it was in the initial presentation must be displaced. Monkeys with hippocampal lesions are selectively impaired at this object-position task. (Monkeys with perirhinal lesions are impaired at the object-recognition task.)

From these studies on the hippocampus, we would predict that animals with especially good spatial memories should have bigger hippocampi than do species with poorer spatial memories. David Sherry and his colleagues (1992) tested this hypothesis in birds. Many birds will take food items, such as sunflower seeds, and hide them for later consumption. Some birds can find hundreds of items that they have cached. To evaluate whether the hippocampus plays a role in this activity, Sherry and his coworkers measured hippocampal size in bird species that are closely related but only one of which is a food cacher. As shown in Figure 13-12, the hippocampal formation is larger in birds that cache food than in birds that do not. In fact, the hippocampus of food-storing birds is more than twice as large as expected for birds of their brain size and body weight. Sherry found a similar relationship when he compared different species of food-storing rodents. Rodents such as Merrian's kangaroo rat, which stores food in various places around its territory, have larger hippocampi than do rodents such as the bannertail kangaroo rat, which stores food only in its burrow. Hippocampal size in both birds and mammals appears to be related to the cognitive demands of foraging and food storing, which are highly spatial activities.

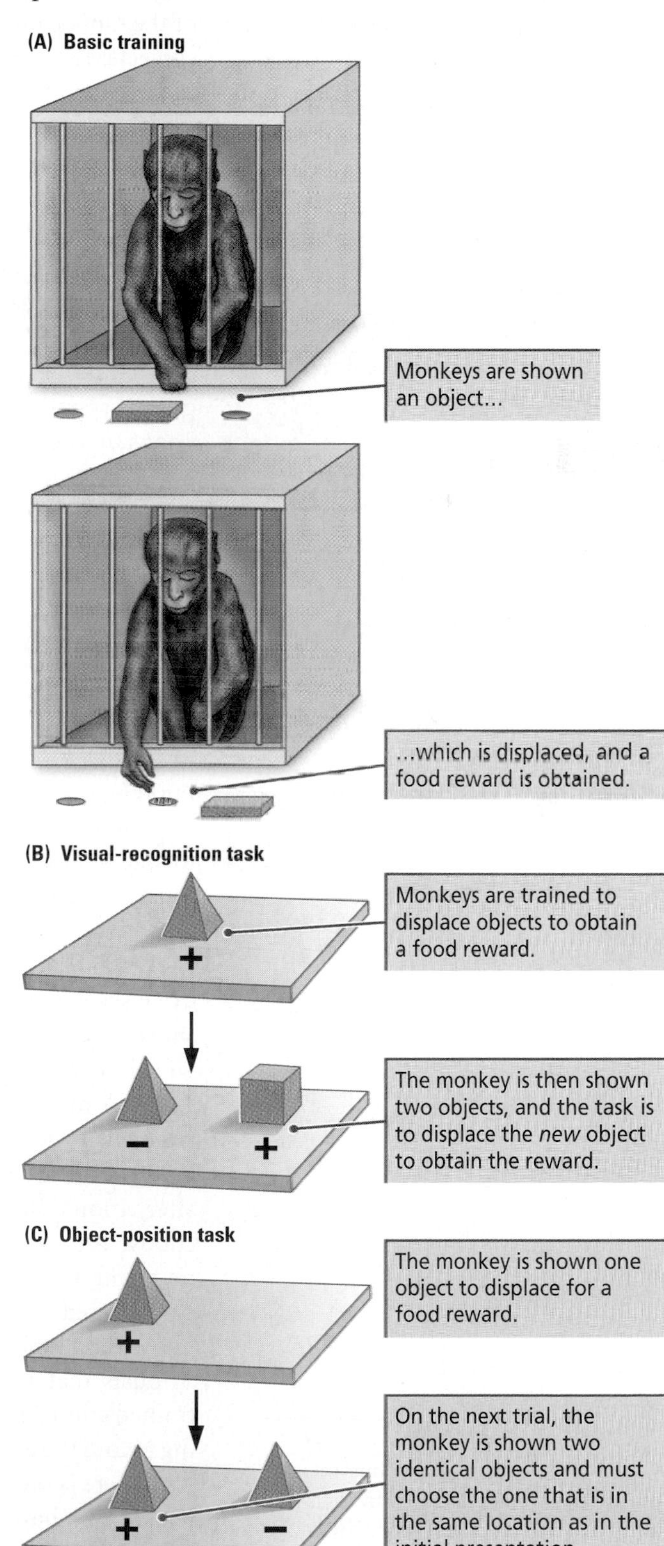
(A) Basic training
Monkeys are shown an object...
...which is displaced, and a food reward is obtained.
(B) Visual-recognition task
Monkeys are trained to displace objects to obtain a food reward.
+
–
+
The monkey is then shown two objects, and the task is to displace the *new* object to obtain the reward.
(C) Object-position task
The monkey is shown one object to displace for a food reward.
+
+
–
On the next trial, the monkey is shown two identical objects and must choose the one that is in the same location as in the initial presentation.

**Figure 13-11**

Two memory tasks for monkeys. **(A)** The monkey is shown an object, which is displaced to obtain a food reward. **(B)** A visual-recognition task. After a brief delay, the monkey is shown two objects and the task is to displace the novel object to obtain the reward. The monkey must retain the explicit information regarding which object was just seen. **(C)** An object-position task. The monkey is shown one object, which is displaced for a food reward. The monkey is then shown the same object plus a second, identical object. The task is to choose the object that is in the same location as in the first presentation. The + and – indicate whether the object is (+) or is not (–) associated with food.

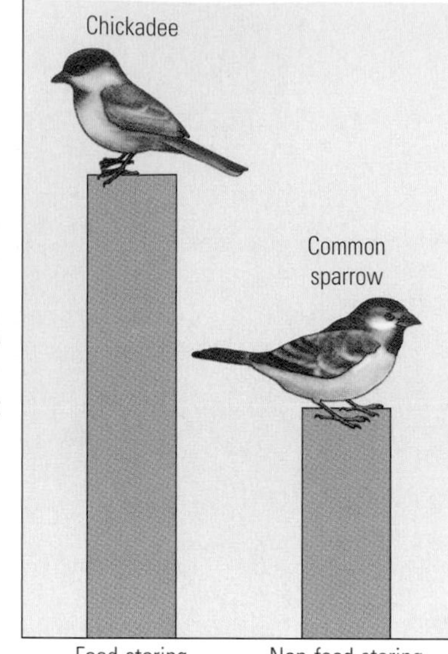


**Figure 13-12**

The volume of the hippocampus relative to the volume of the forebrain in three food-storing and ten non-food-storing families of passerine birds. The hippocampus of food-storing birds, such as the black-capped chickadee, is about twice as large as the hippocampus of non-food-storing birds, such as the sparrow.

Data from "Spatial Memory and Adaptive Specialization of the Hippocampus," by D.F. Sherry, L.F. Jacobs, and S.J.C. Gaulin, 1992, *Trends in Neuroscience, 15,* pp. 298–303.

One prediction that we might make from the Sherry experiments is that people who have jobs with high spatial demands might have large hippocampi. Taxi drivers in London fit this category. In order to qualify for a cab driver's license in London, candidates must pass an extensive exam in which they must demonstrate that they know the location of every street in that huge and ancient city. Eleanor Maguire and her colleagues (2000), using magnetic resonance imaging (MRI), found the posterior region of the hippocampus in London taxi drivers to be significantly larger than in the control subjects. This finding presumably explains why this select group is able to pass a spatial memory test that most of us would fail miserably.

One key feature of the medial temporal pathway of explicit memory is that it is reciprocal. That is, the connections from the neocortex run to the entorhinal cortex and then back to the neocortex. These reciprocal connections have two benefits. First, the signals that the medial temporal regions send back to the cortical sensory regions keep the sensory experience alive in the brain. This means that the neural record of an experience outlasts the actual experience. Second, the pathway back to the cortex means that the neocortex is kept apprised of information being processed in the medial temporal regions. We shall see that such feedback does not happen in the basal ganglia systems taking part in implicit memory, which may help to explain the unconscious nature of implicit memory.

Although we have focused on the role of the medial temporal regions, other structures are also important in explicit memory. People with frontal-lobe injuries are not amnesic like H.M. or J.K., but they do have difficulties with memory for the temporal order of events. Imagine that you are shown a series of photographs and asked to remember them. A few minutes later, you are asked whether you recognize two photographs and, if so, to indicate which one you saw first. H.M. would not remember the photographs. People with frontal-lobe injuries would recall seeing the photographs but would have difficulty recalling which one they had seen most recently. The role of the frontal lobe in explicit memory is clearly more subtle than that of the medial temporal lobe. But just what is that role?

All the sensory systems in the brain send information to the frontal lobe, as do the medial temporal regions. This information is not used for direct sensory analysis, so it must have some other purpose. In general, it appears that the frontal lobe has a role in many forms of short-term memory. Over the past 30 years, Joaquin Fuster (e.g., Fuster et al., 2000) has studied single-cell activity in the frontal lobe during short-term memory tasks. For example, if monkeys are shown an object that they must remember for a short time before being allowed to make a response, neurons in the prefrontal cortex will show a sustained firing during the delay. Consider the tests illustrated in Figure 13-13. A monkey is shown a light, which is the cue, and then must make a response after a delay. In the delayed-response task, the monkey is shown two lights in the choice test and must choose the one that is in the same location as the cue. In the delayed-alternation task, the monkey is again shown two lights in the choice tests but now must choose the light that is *not* in the same location as the cue. Finally, in the delayed-matching-to-sample task, the monkey is shown, say, a red light, and then after a delay is shown a red and a green light. The task is to choose the red light. Fuster has found that in each task, there are cells in the prefrontal cortex that will fire throughout the delay. Animals that have not learned the task show no such cell activity. Curiously, if a trained animal makes an error, the activity of the cells reflects it: the cells stop responding before the error occurs. In a real sense, the cell has "forgotten" the cue.

**Korsakoff's syndrome.** A permanent loss of the ability to learn new information (anterograde amnesia) caused by diencephalic damage resulting from chronic alcoholism or malnutrition that produces a vitamin $B_1$ deficiency.

There is one form of explicit memory disturbance that we have not yet described. People who have chronically abused alcohol develop a disorder known as **Korsakoff's syndrome.** Such people have severe deficits in explicit memory and, in some cases, implicit memory as well. This syndrome is caused by a thiamine (vitamin $B_1$) deficiency

Orange juice reward
In these tests, a monkey is shown a light, which is the cue, and then it makes a response after a delay.

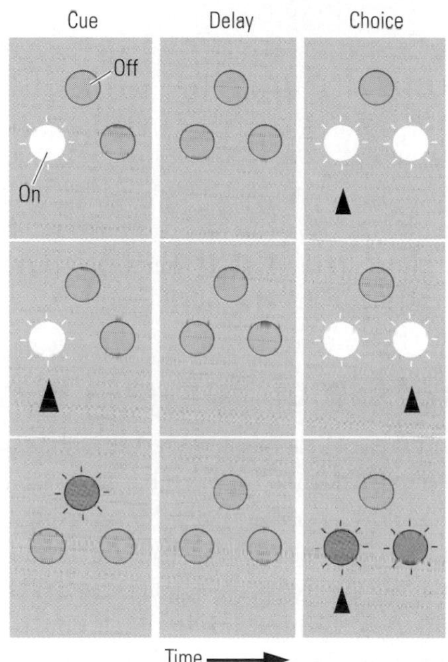
Cue
Delay
Choice
Off
On
Delayed response task: The monkey must choose the light that is in the same location as the cue.
Delayed alternation task: The monkey must choose the light that is not in the same location as the cue.
Delayed matching-to-sample task: The monkey must choose the light that is the same color as the cue.
Time

**Figure 13-13**

(*Top*) A monkey performing a short-term memory task. A disc lights up and the animal responds by pressing the disc in order to get a fruit juice reward. After a delay, the two lower discs are illuminated. The monkey must press the appropriate disc to obtain a reward. (The correct disc varies, depending on the requirements of the task.) (*Bottom*) Three different short-term delay tasks. The correct disc is indicated by the arrow in each case.

Adapted from *Memory in the Cerebral Cortex*, p. 178, by J. Fuster, 1995, Cambridge, MA: MIT Press.

that results from poor nutrition and the fact that alcohol inhibits the body's ability to absorb vitamin $B_1$. The effect of the $B_1$ deficiency is to produce cell death in the medial part of the diencephalon, including the medial thalamus and mammillary bodies of the hypothalamus. In addition, 80 percent of Korsakoff patients have atrophy (loss of cells) of the frontal lobes. The memory disturbance is probably so severe in many Korsakoff patients because the damage includes not only the frontal lobe but medial temporal structures as well. (This syndrome is discussed further in "Korsakoff's Syndrome" on page 509.)

Mort Mishkin and his colleagues (Mishkin, 1982; Murray, 2000) at the U.S. National Institutes of Mental Health have proposed a circuit for explicit memory that incorporates the evidence from both humans and laboratory animals with injuries to the temporal and frontal lobes. Figure 13-14 presents a modified version of the Mishkin model that includes not only the frontal and temporal lobes but also the medial thalamus, which is implicated in Korsakoff's syndrome, as well as the ascending systems from the basal forebrain, which are implicated in Alzheimer's disease. The sensory neocortical areas send their connections to the medial temporal regions, which are in turn connected to the medial thalamus and prefrontal cortex. The basal forebrain structures are hypothesized to play a role in the maintenance of appropriate levels of activity in the forebrain structures so that they can process information. The

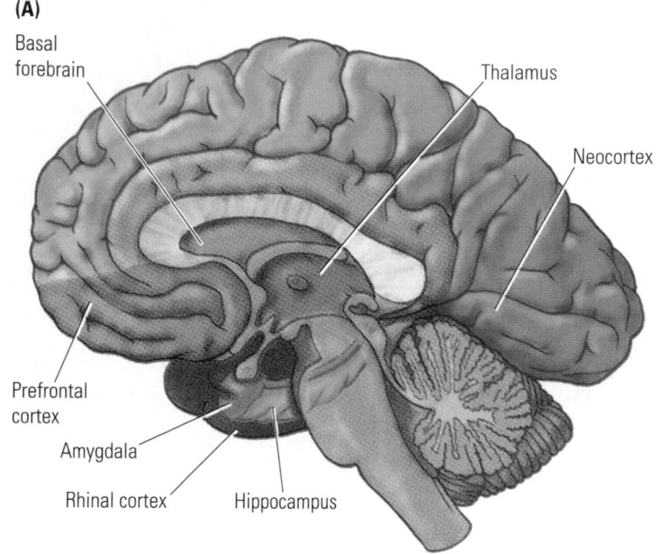


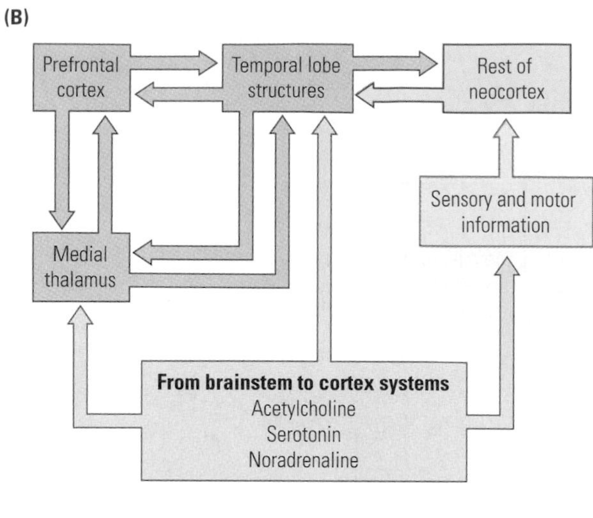


**Figure 13-14**

A neural circuit proposed for explicit memory. **(A)** The general anatomical areas of explicit memory. **(B)** A circuit diagram showing the flow of information through the circuits. Information flow begins with inputs from the sensory and motor systems, which themselves are not considered part of the circuit.

temporal-lobe structures are hypothesized to be central to the formation of long-term explicit memories, whereas the prefrontal cortex is central to the maintenance of temporary (short-term) explicit memories as well as memory for the recency (that is, the chronological order) of explicit events.

## A Neural Circuit for Implicit Memories

Mishkin and his colleagues (1982, 1997) have also proposed a circuit for implicit memories, hypothesizing that the basal ganglia are central to implicit memory. As Figure 13-15 shows, the basal ganglia receive input from the entire cortex. The basal ganglia send projections to the ventral thalamus and then to the premotor cortex. The basal ganglia also receive projections from cells in the substantia nigra. These projections contain the neurotransmitter dopamine, which is widely and densely distributed to the basal ganglia. Dopamine appears to be necessary for circuits in the basal ganglia to function, so it may indirectly participate in implicit memory formation.

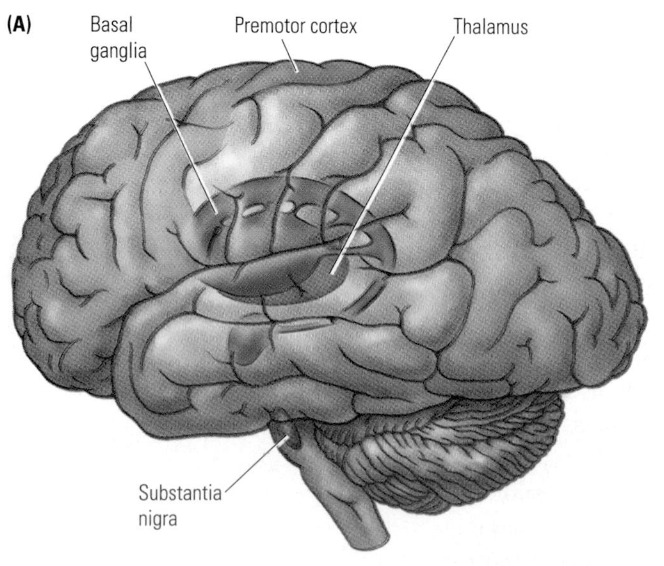


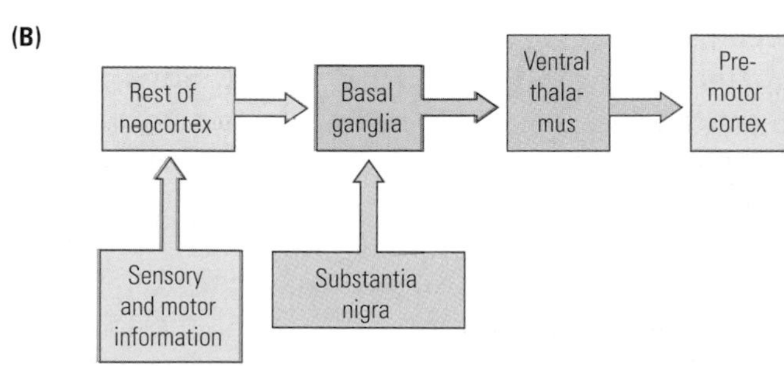


**Figure 13-15**

A neural circuit proposed for implicit memory. **(A)** The general anatomical areas involved in implicit memory. **(B)** A circuit diagram showing the flow of information through the circuits. Information flow begins with inputs from the sensory and motor systems, which themselves are not considered part of the circuit.

Focus on Disorders

## Korsakoff's Syndrome

Long-term alcoholism, especially when accompanied by malnutrition, has long been known to produce defects of memory. Joe R. was a 62-year-old man who was hospitalized because his family complained that his memory had become abysmal. His intelligence was in the average range, and he had no obvious sensory or motor difficulties. Nevertheless, he was unable to say why he was in the hospital and usually stated that he was actually in a hotel. When asked what he had done the previous night, he typically would say that he "went to the Legion for a few beers with the boys." Although he had, in fact, been in the hospital, it was a sensible response because that is what he had done on most nights over the previous 30 years. Joe R.was not certain what he had done for a living but believed that he had been a butcher. In fact, he had been a truck driver for a local delivery firm. His son was a butcher, however, so once again his story was related to something in his life. His memory for immediate events was little better. On one occasion, we asked him to remember having met us, and then we left the room. Upon our return 2 or 3 minutes later, he had no recollection of having ever met us or of having taken psychological tests administered by us.

Joe R. had Korsakoff's syndrome, a condition named after Sergei Korsakoff, a Russian physician who in the 1880s first called attention to a syndrome that accompanies chronic alcoholism. The most obvious symptom is severe loss of memory, including amnesia for both information learned in the past (retrograde amnesia) and information learned since the onset of the memory disturbance (anterograde amnesia). One unique characteristic of the amnesic syndrome in Korsakoff patients is that they tend to make up stories about past events, rather than admit that they do not remember. Like those of Joe R., however, these stories are generally plausible because they are based on actual experiences.

Curiously, Korsakoff patients have little insight into their memory disturbance and are generally indifferent to suggestions that they have a memory problem. In fact, such patients are generally apathetic to things going on around them. Joe R. was often seen watching television when the set was not turned on.

The cause of Korsakoff's syndrome is a thiamine (vitamin $B_1$) deficiency resulting from prolonged intake of large quantities of alcohol. Joe R. had a long history of drinking a 26-ounce bottle of rum every day, in addition to a "few beers with the boys." The thiamine deficiency results in the death of cells in the midline diencephalon, including especially the medial regions of the thalamus and the mammillary bodies of the hypothalamus. The majority of Korsakoff patients also show cortical atrophy, especially in the frontal lobe. Once the Korsakoff symptoms appear, which can happen quite suddenly, prognosis is poor. Only about 20 percent of patients show much recovery after a year on a vitamin $B_1$–enriched diet. Joe R. has shown no recovery after several years and will spend the rest of his life in a hospital setting.

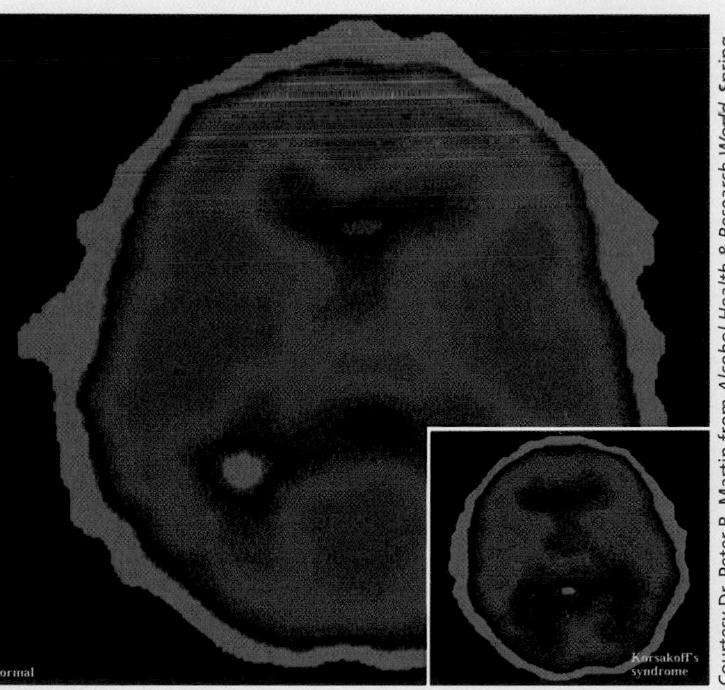


Courtesy Dr. Peter R. Martin from *Alcohol Health & Research World*, Spring 1985, 9, cover.

These PET scans from a normal patient (the larger image) and a patient suffering from Korsakoff's syndrome (the inset) demonstrate reduced activity in the frontal lobe of the diseased brain. (The frontal lobes of the brains shown are at the bottom center of each photo.) Red and yellow represent areas of high metabolic activity versus the lower level of activity in the darker areas.

The connection from the cortex to the basal ganglia in the implicit memory system is unidirectional. Thus, most of the neocortex receives no direct information regarding the activities of the basal ganglia. Mishkin believes that this accounts for the unconscious nature of implicit memories. In order for memories to be conscious, there must be direct feedback to the neocortical regions involved. (Recall that in the explicit memory system, the medial temporal regions send connections back to the neocortical regions.)

Review the locations of the basal ganglia on the CD-ROM in the module on the Central Nervous System.

Mishkin's model shows why people with dysfunction of the basal ganglia, as in Parkinson's disease, have deficits in implicit memory, whereas people with injuries to the frontal or temporal lobes have relatively good implicit memories, even though they may have profound disturbances of explicit memory. In fact, some people with Alzheimer's disease are able to play games expertly even though they have no recollection of having played them before. Daniel Schacter (1983) wrote of a golfer with Alzheimer's disease who retained his ability to play golf, despite some impairment of his explicit knowledge of the events of having played a round, as indexed by his inability to find shots or to remember his strokes on each hole. This man's medial temporal system was severely compromised by the disease, but his basal ganglia were unaffected.

## A Neural Circuit for Emotional Memories

We have not yet considered a third type of memory, which we can label *emotional memory.* It is not altogether clear whether emotional memories are implicit or explicit; in fact, it seems that they could be both. Certainly, people can react with fear to specific stimuli that they can identify; we have seen that they can also have fear of situations for which they do not seem to have specific memories. Indeed, one common pathology is a panic disorder in which people show marked anxiety but cannot identify a specific cause. For this reason, we see emotional memory as a special form of memory. This form of memory also has a unique anatomical component, namely the amygdala, which we discussed in detail in Chapter 11, where we noted that the amygdala seems to be responsible for our feelings of anxiety toward stimuli that by themselves would not normally produce fear. The amygdala has connections to systems that control autonomic functions (for example, blood pressure and heart rate) as well as connections to the hypothalamus and its control of hormonal systems.

Emotional memory has been studied most thoroughly by pairing noxious stimuli, such as foot shock, with a tone (see Figure 13-2). Michael Davis (1992) and Joseph LeDoux (1995) used this type of experiment to demonstrate that the amygdala is critical to this form of memory. Damage to the amygdala abolishes emotional memory but has little effect on implicit or explicit memory. The amygdala has close connections with the medial temporal cortical structures, as well as the rest of the cortex, and it sends projections to structures involved in the production of autonomic responses, namely the hypothalamus and central gray of the brainstem (Figure 13-16). In addition, the amygdala is connected to the implicit system via its connections with the basal ganglia.

Fear is not the only type of emotional memory that is coded by the amygdala. A study of severely demented patients by Bob Sainsbury and Marjorie Coristine (1986) nicely illustrates this point. The patients were believed to have severe cortical abnormalities but intact amygdalar functioning. The researchers first established that the ability of these patients to recognize photographs of close relatives was severely impaired. The patients then were shown four photographs, one of which depicted a relative (either a sibling or a child) who had visited in the past 2 weeks. The task was to identify the person that they liked better than the others. Although the subjects were unaware that they knew anyone in the group of photographs, they consistently pre-

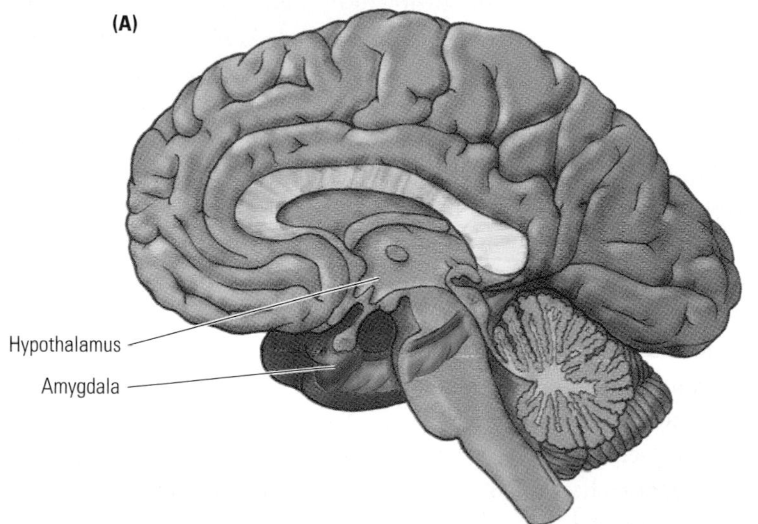


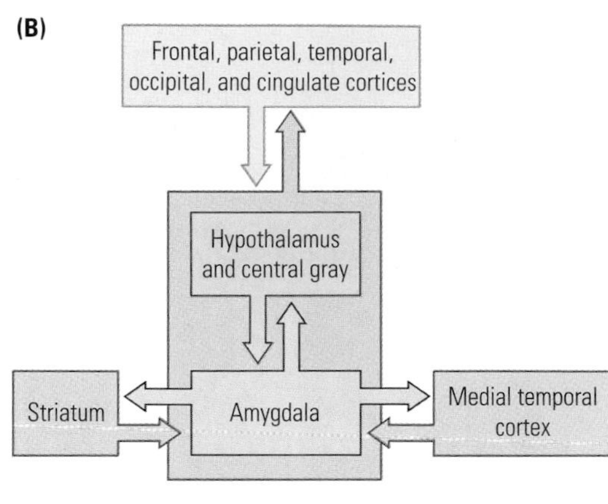


**Figure 13-16**

**(A)** The key structure in emotional memory is the amygdala. **(B)** A circuit diagram showing the flow of information in emotional memory.

ferred the photographs of their relatives. This result suggests that although the explicit, and probably implicit, memory of the relative was gone, each patient still had an emotional memory that guided his or her preference.

## In Review

Certain neural structures and circuits are associated with different types of learning and memory. One system, consisting of the prefrontal cortex and the medial temporal lobe and regions related to them, is the likely neural location of explicit memory. A second system, consisting of the basal ganglia and neocortex, forms the neural basis for implicit memory. A third system, which includes the amygdala and its associated structures, forms the neural basis for emotional memory. Presumably, when we learn different types of information, changes take place in synapses in these systems, and these changes produce our memory of the experience. We now turn to the question of what these synaptic changes might be.

# THE STRUCTURAL BASIS OF BRAIN PLASTICITY

We have seen that there are different types of memory and that different brain circuits underlie each memory type. Our next task is to consider how the neurons in these circuits change to store the memories. The consensus among neuroscientists is that the changes occur at the synapse, in part because that is where neurons influence one another. This idea is not new, dating back to 1928, when the Spanish anatomist Santiago Ramón y Cajal suggested that the process of learning might produce prolonged morphological changes in the efficiency of the synapses activated in the learning process. This idea turned out to be easier to propose than to study. The major challenge that researchers still encounter as they investigate Cajal's suggestion is that they have to know where in the brain to look for synaptic changes that might be correlated with memory for a specific stimulus. This task is formidable. Imagine trying to find the exact location of the neurons responsible for storing your grandmother's name. We would have a similar problem in finding the neurons responsible for the memory of an object as a monkey performs the visual-recognition task illustrated in Figure 13-11.

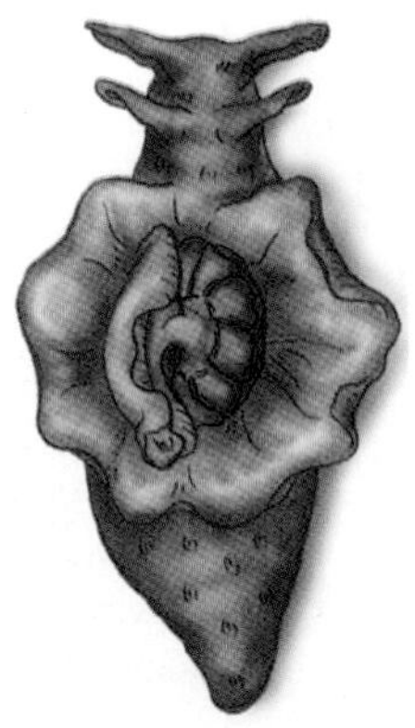

*Aplysia*

Investigators have approached the problem of identifying synaptic change in two distinctly different ways. The first is to study relatively simple neural systems. Recall from Chapter 5 that the study of *Aplysia* revealed that changes occur in the properties of the synapse when animals learn the association between a noxious stimulus and a cue signaling the onset of the stimulus. Similarly, we saw that synaptic changes occur in hippocampal slices in which long-term enhancement (LTE) is induced. The identification of synaptic change is possible in *Aplysia* and LTE because we know where in the nervous system to look. But we have little information about where to look for memory-storing synapses in mammals.

Accordingly, a second approach to finding the neural correlates of memory aims to determine that synaptic changes are correlated with memory in the mammalian brain. The next step is to localize the synaptic changes to specific neural pathways. Then the task is to analyze the nature of the synaptic changes themselves.

The goal of this section of the chapter is to describe the studies that have identified the presence of synaptic changes correlated with various types of experience. We first consider the general research strategy. We then look at the gross neural changes correlated with different forms of experience, ranging from living in specific environments, to learning specific tasks or having specific experiences, to the chronic administration of trophic factors, hormones, and addictive drugs. We shall see that the general synaptic organization of the brain is modified in a strikingly similar manner with each of these quite diverse forms of experience.

## Measuring Synaptic Change

In principle, experience could alter the brain in either of two ways: by modifying existing circuitry or by creating novel circuitry. In actuality, the brain uses both of these strategies.

### MODIFYING EXISTING CIRCUITS

The simplest way to look for synaptic change is to look for gross changes in the morphology of dendrites. Dendrites are essentially extensions of the neuron membrane that are present to allow more space for synapses. Because complex neurons, such as pyramidal cells, have 95 percent of their synapses on the dendrites, measurement of the changes in dendritic extent can be used to infer synaptic change. Cells that have few or no dendrites have limited space for inputs, whereas cells with complex dendritic structure have space for tens of thousands of inputs. More dendrites mean more connections, and fewer dendrites mean fewer connections. Change in dendritic structure, therefore, implies change in synaptic organization.

A striking feature of dendrites is that their shape is highly changeable. Dale Purves and his colleagues (Purves & Voyvodic, 1987) labeled cells in the dorsal-root ganglia of living mice with a special dye that allowed them to visualize the cells' dendrites. As shown in Figure 13-17, when they examined the same cells at intervals ranging from a few days to weeks, they identified obvious qualitative changes in dendritic extent. We can assume that new dendritic branches have new synapses and that lost branches mean lost synapses. One obvious lesson from the Purves studies is that the morphology of neurons is not static. Instead, neurons change their morphology in response to their changing experiences. Researchers can take advantage of this changeability as they search for

**Figure 13-17**

Reconstructions of portions of the dendrites of three mouse superior cervical ganglion cells observed at an interval of 3 months. Changes in both the extension and retraction of particular dendritic branches are evident.

Adapted from "Imaging Mammalian Nerve Cells and Their Connections over Time in Living Animals," by D. Purves and J.T. Voyvodic, *Trends in Neuroscience*, 1987, *10*, p. 400.

Labeled with dye

88–90 days later

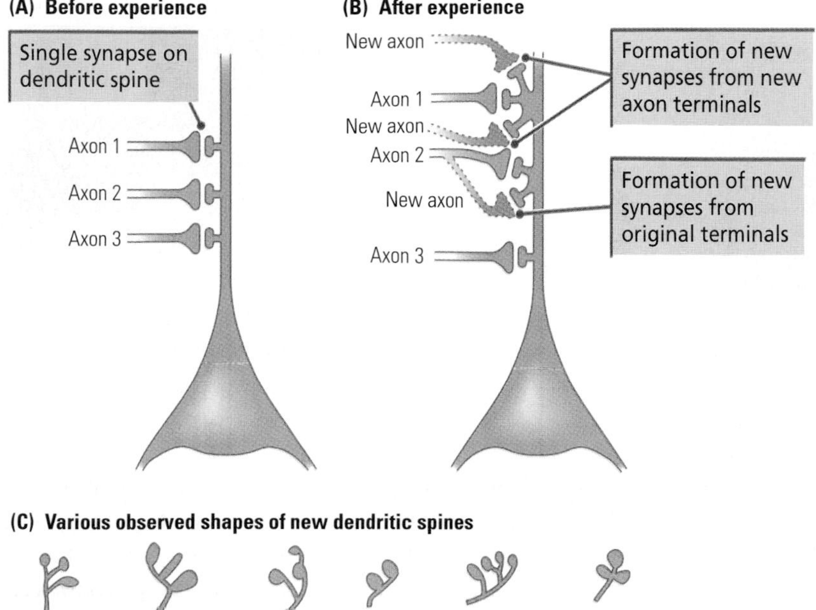


**Figure 13-18**

**(A)** Three inputs to a dendrite of a pyramidal cell. Each axon forms a synapse with a different dendritic spine. **(B)** The formation of multiple spine heads. The original axons may divide and innervate two spine heads, or new axons (dotted outlines) may innervate the new spine heads. **(C)** Drawings of multiple spine heads, showing that single dendritic spines may have multiple synapses.

neural correlates of memory by studying the changes in dendritic morphology that are correlated with specific experiences, such as the learning of some task.

What do changes in dendritic morphology actually reveal? Let us consider the case in which a given neuron generates more synaptic space. The new synapses that are formed can be either additional synapses between neurons that were already connected with the neuron in question or synapses between neurons that were not previously connected. Examples of these distinctly different synapse types are illustrated in Figure 13-18. New synapses can result either from the growth of new axon terminals or from the formation of synapses along axons as they pass by dendrites. In both cases, however, the formation of new synapses reflects changes in the local circuitry of a region and not the development of new connections between distant parts of the brain. Forming new connections between widely separated brain regions would be very difficult in a fully grown brain because of the dense plexus of cells, fibers, and blood vessels that lies in the way. Thus, the growth of new synapses indicates modifications to basic circuits that are already in the brain. This point has an important implication for the location of synaptic changes underlying memory. During development, the brain forms circuits to process sensory information and to produce behavior. These circuits are most likely to be modified to form memories, just as we saw in the Martin study discussed earlier.

## CREATING NOVEL CIRCUITS

Prior to the mid-1990s, it was generally assumed that the mammalian brain did not make new neurons in adulthood. The unexpected discovery in the 1970s that the brains of songbirds such as canaries grow new neurons to produce songs during the mating season led researchers to reconsider the possibility that the adult mammalian brain, too, might be capable of generating new neurons. This possibility can be tested directly by injecting animals with a compound that is taken up by cells when they divide to produce new cells, including neurons. When such a compound, bromodeoxyuridine (BrdU), is injected into adult rats, dividing cells incorporate it into their DNA. During later analysis, a specific stain can be used to identify the new neurons. Figure 13-19 shows such an analysis in the olfactory bulb and hippocampus.

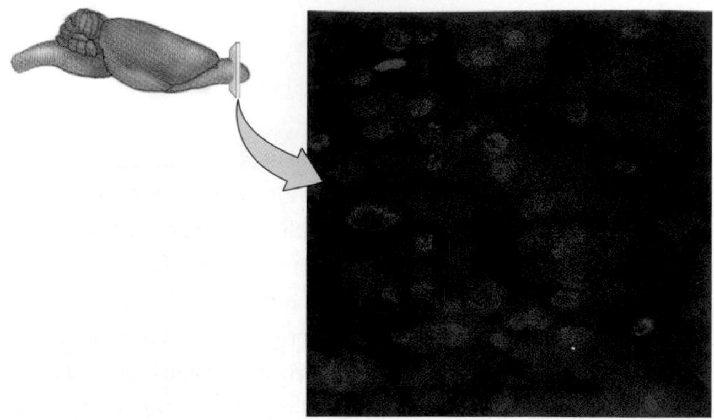

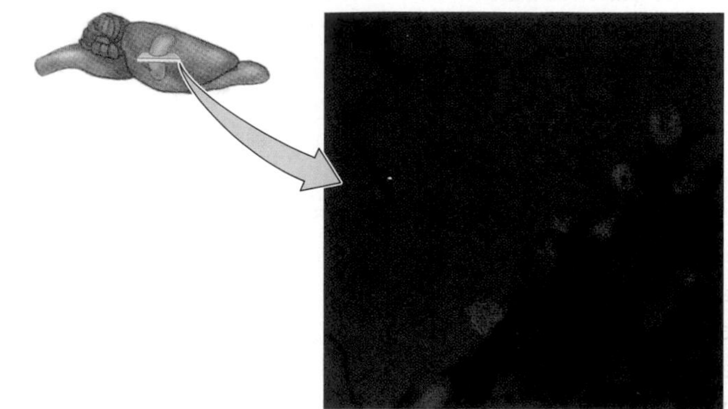

**Figure 13-19**

Confocal microscope photographs: cells stained red with an antibody to neurons called NeuN are neurons; cells stained green with an antibody to bromodeoxyuridine (BrdU) are new cells; cells stained yellow are positive for both red and green and are new neurons. *(Left)* Olfactory bulb. *(Right)* Hippocampus.

This technique has now yielded considerable evidence that the mammalian brain, including the primate brain, can generate neurons destined for the olfactory bulb, hippocampal formation, and even the neocortex of the frontal and temporal lobes (Eriksson et al., 1998; Gould et al., 1999). The reason for this generation is not yet clear; it may function to enhance brain plasticity, particularly with respect to processes underlying learning and memory. For example, Elizabeth Gould and her colleagues (1999) showed that the generation of new neurons in the hippocampus is enhanced when animals learn explicit memory tasks such as the Morris water task (see Figure 13-4). Furthermore, as we shall see, the generation of these new neurons appears to be increased by experience.

## Enriched Experience and Plasticity

One way to stimulate the brain is to house animals in environments that provide some form of generalized sensory or motor experience. We described such an experiment in Chapter 7: Donald Hebb took laboratory rats home and let them have the run of his kitchen. After an interval, Hebb compared the enriched rats with a second group of rats that had remained in cages in his laboratory at McGill University, training both groups to solve various mazes. When the enriched animals performed better, Hebb concluded that one effect of the enriched experience was to enhance later learning. This important conclusion laid the foundation for the initiation of Head Start in the United States, a program to provide academic experiences for disadvantaged preschool-aged children.

When subsequent investigators have worked with rats, they have opted for a more constrained enrichment procedure that uses some type of "enriched enclosure." For example, in our own studies, we place groups of six rats in enclosures. These enclosures give animals a rich social experience as well as extensive sensory and motor experience.

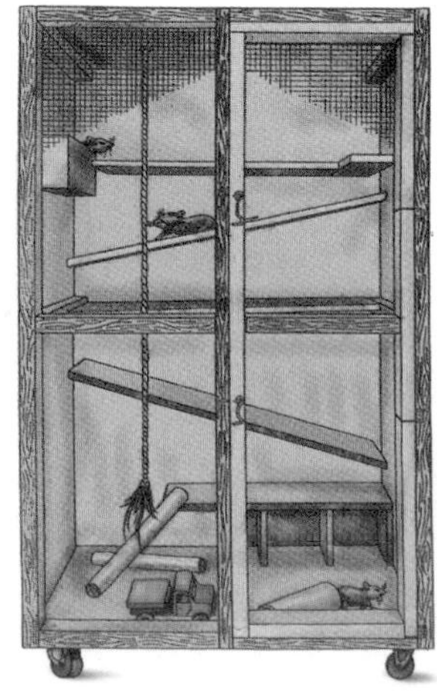

Enriched rat enclosure

The most obvious consequence of such experience is an increase in brain weight that may be on the order of 10 percent relative to cage-reared animals, even though the enriched rats typically weigh less, in part because they get more exercise. The key question is, What is responsible for the increased brain weight? A comprehensive series of studies by Anita Sirevaag and Bill Greenough (1988) used light- and electron-microscopic techniques to analyze 36 different aspects of cortical synaptic, cellular, and vascular morphology in rats raised either in cages or in complex environments. The simple conclusion was that there is a coordinated change not only in the extent of dendrites but also in glial, vascular, and metabolic processes in response to differential experiences (see Figure 13-20). Animals with enriched experience have not only more synapses per neuron but also more astrocytic material, more blood capillaries, and higher mitochondrial volume. (Higher mitochondrial volume means greater metabolic activity.) It is therefore clear that when the brain changes in response to experience, the expected neural changes occur, but there are also adjustments in the metabolic requirements of the larger neurons.

Gerd Kempermann and his colleagues (1998) sought to determine whether experience altered the number of neurons in the brain. To test this idea, they compared the generation of neurons in the hippocampus of mice housed in complex environments with that of mice reared in laboratory cages. They located the number of new neurons by injecting the animals with BrdU several times in the course of their complex housing experience. The BrdU was incorporated into new neurons that were generated in the brain during the experiment. When they later looked at the hippocampus, they found more new neurons in the complex-housed rats than in the cage-housed rats. Although the investigators did not look in other parts of the brain, such as the olfactory bulb, it is reasonable to expect that similar changes may have taken place in other structures. This result is exciting because it implies that experience not only can alter existing circuitry but also can influence the generation of new neurons, and thus new circuitry.

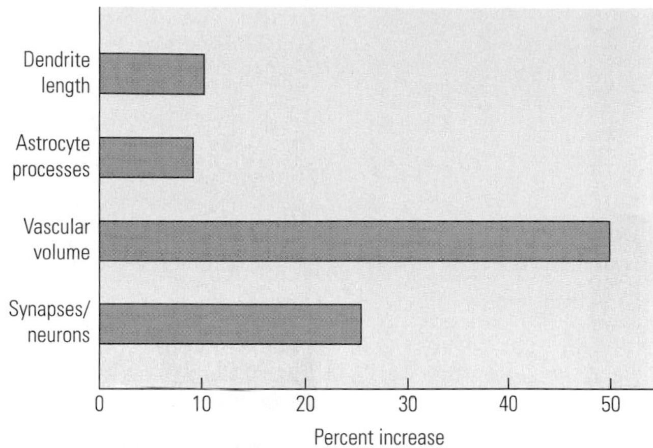


**Figure 13-20**

A schematic summary of some of the changes that take place in the cortex in response to experience. Note that such changes are found not only in neurons but also in astrocytes and vasculature.

Based on data from "Differential Rearing Effects on Rat Visual Cortex Synapses. I. Synaptic and Neuronal Density and Synapses per Neuron," by A. Turner & W. T. Greenough, *Brain Research,* 1985, *329,* 195–203; "Differential Rearing Effects on Rat Visual Cortex Synapses, III, Neuronal and Glial Nuclei," by A. M. Slrevaag and W. T. Greenough, *Brain Research,* 1987, *424,* 320–332; and "Experience-Dependent Changes in Dendritic Arbor and Spine Density in Neocortex Vary with Age and Sex," by R. Gibb, G. Garny, and B. Kolb, *Neurobiology of Learning and Memory,* 2001.

## Sensory or Motor Training and Plasticity

The studies showing neuronal change in animals housed in complex environments demonstrate that large areas of the brain can be changed with such experience. This finding leads us to ask whether specific experiences would produce synaptic changes in localized cerebral regions. One way to approach this question is to give animals specific experiences and then to see how their brains have been changed by the experiences. Another way is to look at the brains of people who have had a lifetime of some particular experience. We will consider each of these research strategies separately.

### MANIPULATING EXPERIENCE EXPERIMENTALLY

Perhaps the most convincing study of this sort was done by Fen-Lei Chang and Bill Greenough (1982). They took advantage of the fact that the visual pathways of the laboratory rat are about 90 percent crossed. That is, about 90 percent of the connections from the left eye to the cortex project via the right lateral geniculate nucleus to the right hemisphere, and vice versa for the right eye. Chang and Greenough placed a patch over one eye of each rat and then trained the animals in a maze. The visual cortex of only one eye would receive input about the maze, but the auditory, olfactory, tactile, and motor regions of both hemispheres would be equally active as the animals explored the maze. (Chang and Greenough also severed the corpus callosum so that the two hemispheres could not communicate and share information about the world.) Comparison of the neurons in the two hemispheres revealed that those in the visual cortex of the trained hemisphere had more extensive dendrites. The researchers concluded that some feature associated with the reception, processing, or storage of visual input from training was responsible for the formation of new synapses because the hemispheres did not differ in other respects.

Complementary studies have been conducted in monkeys by Randy Nudo and his colleagues. In the discussions of both the sensory and motor systems (Chapters 8–10), you learned that the sensory and motor worlds are represented by cortical maps. For example, in the motor system there are maps of the body that represent discrete muscles and movements (see Figure 10-17). In the course of mapping the motor cortex of monkeys, Nudo and his colleagues (1997) noted striking individual differences in the topography of the maps. They speculated that the individual map variability might reflect each animal's experiences up to the time in life at which the cortical map was derived. To test this idea directly, they trained one group of monkeys to retrieve food pellets from a small food well while another group retrieved them from a substantially larger well, as illustrated in Figure 13-21. Monkeys in the two groups were matched for number of finger flexions, which totaled about 12,000 for the entire study. No systematic changes were seen in motor hand maps in the monkeys retrieving food pellets from the large well, but those animals retrieving pellets from the small well showed robust changes that were presumably due to the more demanding motor requirements of the small-well condition.

Most studies demonstrating plasticity in the motor cortex have been performed on laboratory animals in which the cortex has been mapped by microelectrode stimulation. Now the development of new imaging techniques, such as transmagnetic stimulation and functional magnetic resonance imaging (fMRI), has made it possible to show parallel results in humans who have special motor skills. For example, there is an increased cortical representation of the fingers of the left hand in musicians who play string instruments and an increased cortical representation of the reading finger in Braille readers. Thus, the functional organization of the motor cortex is altered by skilled use in humans. It can also be altered by chronic injury. Jon Kaas (2000) showed that when the sensory nerves from one limb are severed in monkeys, large-scale changes in the somatosensory maps ensue. In particular, in the absence of input, the relevant part of the cortex no longer responds to stimulation of the limb, which is not surprising. But this cortex does not remain inactive. Rather, the denervated cortex begins to respond to input from other parts of the body. The region that once would have responded to the hand now responds to stimulation on the

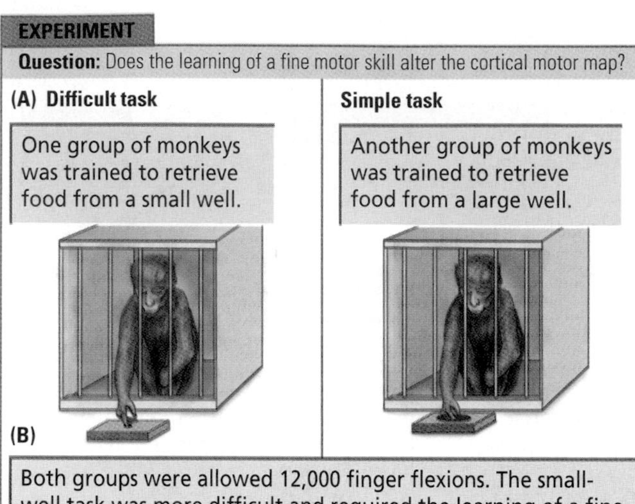

EXPERIMENT
Question: Does the learning of a fine motor skill alter the cortical motor map?
(A) Difficult task
Simple task
One group of monkeys was trained to retrieve food from a small well.
Another group of monkeys was trained to retrieve food from a large well.
(B)
Both groups were allowed 12,000 finger flexions. The small-well task was more difficult and required the learning of a fine motor skill in order to match performance of the simpler task.
Retrievals per day
0 200 400 600 800 1000 1200
Day of training
0 2 4 6 8 10 12 14 16
(C)
The motor representation of digit, wrist, and arm was mapped.
KEY
Digit
Wrist/forearm
Digit, wrist, and forearm
Conclusion
There is a larger digit representation in the brain of the animal with the more difficult task, reflecting the neuronal changes necessary for the acquired skill.


**Figure 13-21**

Differential effects of motor-skill acquisition and motor use on functional organization of the squirrel monkey motor cortex. **(A)** Training procedures consisted of retrieving small banana-flavored pellets from either a small or large well. The monkey is able to insert the entire hand into the large well but can insert only one or two fingers into the smaller well. **(B)** The monkeys trained on the small well improved with practice (making fewer finger flexions per food retrieval) over the course of training. In order to control for mere motor activity, the researchers trained both groups until they made 12,000 finger flexions. **(C)** Maps of forelimb movements were produced by microelectrode stimulation of the cortex. The maps showed systematic changes in the animals trained with the small, but not the large, well. This experiment demonstrated that the functional topography of the motor cortex is shaped by learning new motor skills, not simply by repetitive motor use.

Adapted from "Adaptive Plasticity in Primate Motor Cortex as a Consequence of Behavioral Experience and Neuronal Injury," by R.J. Nudo, E.J. Plautz, and G.W. Milliken, *Seminars in Neuroscience*, 1997, *9*, p. 20.

face, whose area is normally adjacent to the hand area. Similar results can be found in the cortical maps of people who have had limbs amputated. For example, Vilayanur Ramachandran (1993) found that when the face of a limb amputee is brushed lightly with a cotton swab, there is a sensation of the amputated hand being touched. Figure 13-22 illustrates the rough map of the hand that Ramachandran was actually able to chart on the face. The likely explanation is that the face area has expanded to occupy the denervated limb cortex, but the brain has circuits that still "believe" that the activity of this cortex represents input from the limb. This may explain the "phantom limb" pain often experienced by amputees.

The idea that experience can alter cortical maps can be demonstrated with other types of experience. For example, if animals are trained to make certain digit movements over and over again, the cortical representation of those digits expands at the expense of the remaining areas. Similarly, if animals are trained extensively to discriminate among different sensory stimuli such as tones, the cortical areas responding to those stimuli are increased in size. We can speculate that one of the effects of musical training is to alter the motor representations of the digits used to play different instruments or to alter the auditory representations of specific sound frequencies. This is essentially a form of memory, and the underlying synaptic changes are likely to occur on the appropriate sensory or motor cortical maps.

## EXPERIENCE-DEPENDENT CHANGE IN THE HUMAN BRAIN

We saw from the Ramachandran amputee study that the human brain appears to change with altered experience. This study did not directly examine neuronal change, however; neuronal change was inferred from behavior. The only way to directly examine synaptic change is to look directly at brain tissue. It is obviously not practical to manipulate experiences experimentally in people and then examine their brains. It is possible to examine the brains of people who died from nonneurological causes and then to relate the structure of their cortical neurons to their experience.

One way to test this idea is to look for a relationship between neuronal structure and education. Arnold Scheibel and his colleagues conducted many such studies in the past decade (Jacobs & Scheibel, 1993; Jacobs, Scholl, & Scheibel, 1993). In one study, they found a relationship between the size of the dendrites in a cortical language area (Wernicke's area) and the amount of education. The cortical neurons from the brains of deceased people with a college education had more dendritic branches than did those from people with a high school education, which, in turn, had more dendritic material than did those from people with less than a high school education. Of course, it may be that people who have larger dendrites in their neurons are more likely to go to college, but that possibility is not easy to test.

Another way to look at the relationship between human brain structure and behavior is to correlate the functional abilities of people with neuronal structure. For example, one might expect to find differences in language-related areas between people with high and low verbal abilities. This experiment is difficult to do, however, because it presupposes behavioral measures taken prior to death, and such measures are not normally available. However, Scheibel and his colleagues took advantage of the now well-documented observation that, on average, females have superior verbal abilities to males. When they examined the structure of neurons in Wernicke's area, they found that females have more extensive dendritic branching than males do. Furthermore, in a subsequent study, they found that this sex difference was present as early as age nine, suggesting that such sex differences emerge within the first decade. In fact, it is known that young girls do tend to have significantly better verbal skills than young boys do.

Finally, these investigators approached the link between experience and neuronal morphology in a slightly different way. They began with two hypotheses. First, they suggested that there is a relationship between the complexity of dendritic branching

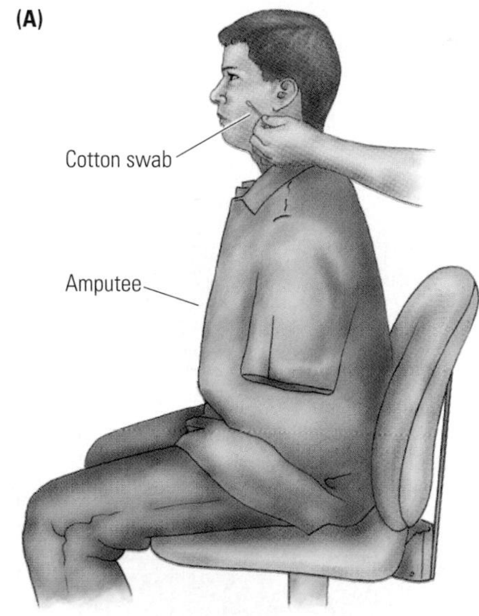


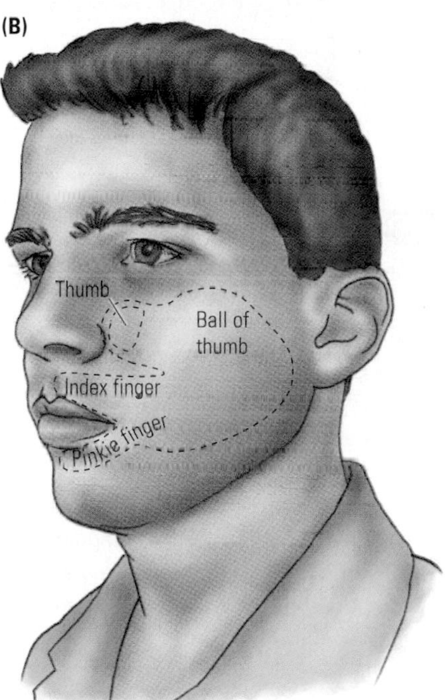


**Figure 13-22**

When the face of an amputee is stroked lightly with a cotton swab **(A)**, there is an experience of the missing hand being lightly touched. **(B)** This hand experience forms a representation on the face. As in the normal map of the somatosensory cortex, the thumb is disproportionately large.

Adapted from "Behavioral and Magnetoencephalographic Correlates of Plasticity in the Adult Human Brain," by V.S. Ramachandran, 1993, *Proceedings of the National Academy of Sciences, USA, 90.*

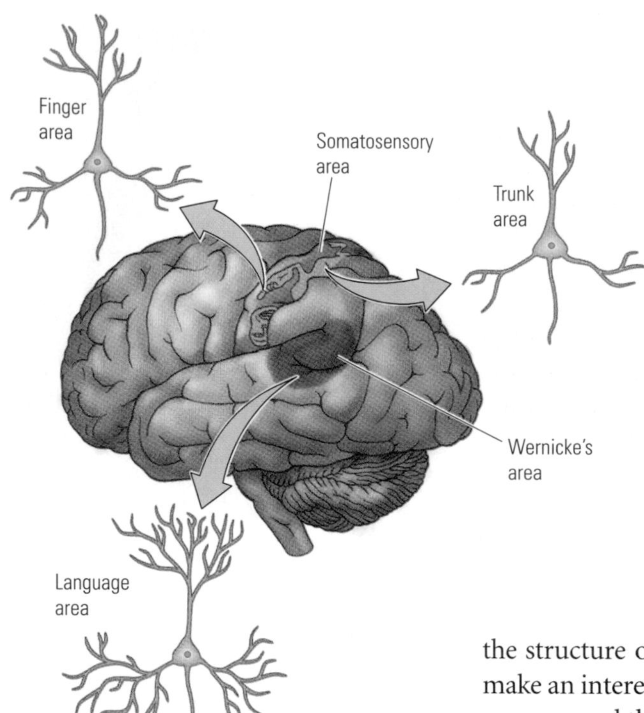


**Figure 13-23**

An illustration of Scheibel's hypothesis that cell complexity is related to the computational demands required for the cell. Cells that represent the trunk area of the body have relatively less computational demand than that required for cells representing the finger region. In turn, cells engaged in more cognitive functions (such as language, as in Wernicke's area) would have greater computational demands than those engaged in finger functions.

and the nature of the computational tasks performed by a brain area. To test this hypothesis, they examined the dendritic structure of neurons in different cortical regions that involved different computational tasks. For example, when they compared the structure of neurons corresponding to the somatosensory representation of the trunk with those for the fingers, they found the latter to have more complex cells. They reasoned that the somatosensory inputs from receptive fields on the chest wall would constitute less of a computational challenge to cortical neurons than would those from the fingers and that the neurons representing the chest would therefore be less complex. This hypothesis was shown to be correct (see Figure 13-23). Similarly, when they compared the cells in the finger area with those in the supramarginal gyrus (SMG), a region of the parietal lobe that is associated with higher cognitive processes (that is, thinking), they found the SMG neurons to be more complex.

The second hypothesis was that dendritic branching in all regions is subject to experience-dependent change. As a result, they hypothesized that predominant life experience (for example, occupation) should alter the structure of dendrites. Although they did not test this hypothesis directly, they did make an interesting observation. In their study comparing cells in the trunk area, the finger area, and the SMG, they found curious individual differences. For example, especially large differences in trunk and finger neurons were found in the brains of people who had a high level of finger dexterity maintained over long periods of time (for example, typists). In contrast, no difference between trunk and finger was found in a sales representative. One would not expect a good deal of specialized finger use in this occupation, which would mean less complex demands on the finger neurons.

In summary, although the studies showing a relationship between experience and neural structure in humans are correlative studies, rather than actual experiments, their findings are consistent with those observed in studies of other species. We are thus led to the general conclusion that specific experiences can produce localized changes in the synaptic organization of the brain. It seems likely that such changes form the structural basis of memory.

## Plasticity, Hormones, Trophic Factors, and Drugs

Articles in newspapers and popular magazines often report that drugs can damage your brain. Some drugs certainly do act as toxins and can selectively kill brain regions, but a more realistic mode of action of drugs is to *change* the brain. Although not many studies have looked at drug-induced morphological changes, there is evidence that some compounds can profoundly change the synaptic organization of the brain. These compounds include hormones, neurotrophic factors, and psychoactive drugs. We will briefly consider each of these kinds of substances.

### HORMONES

We have seen in earlier chapters that the levels of circulating hormones play a critical role both in determining the structure of the brain and in eliciting certain behaviors in adulthood. Although it was once believed that the structural effects of hormones were expressed only during development, it is now generally agreed that even adult neurons can respond to hormonal manipulations with dramatic structural changes. We will consider the actions of two types of hormones, the gonadal hormones and the glucocorticoids, which are stress-related hormones.

We encountered the gonadal hormones in Chapters 7 and 11. Research has established that there are differences in the structure of neurons in the cortices of male versus

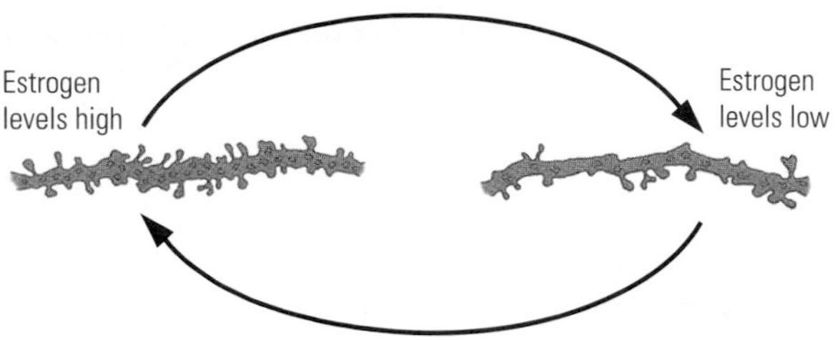


**Figure 13-24**

Sections of dendrites from times of high and low levels of estrogen during the rat's 4-day estrous cycle. There are many more dendritic spines during the period of high estrogen.

Adapted from "Naturally Occurring Fluctuation in Dendritic Spine Density on Adult Hippocampal Pyramidal Neurons," by C.S. Woolley, E. Gould, M. Frankfurt, and B.S. McEwen, 1990, *Journal of Neuroscience, 10,* p. 4038.

female rats and that these differences depend on gonadal hormones. What is more surprising, perhaps, is that gonadal hormones continue to influence cell structure and behavior in adulthood. Elizabeth Hampson and Doreen Kimura (1988) showed that the performance of women on various cognitive tasks changes throughout the menstrual cycle as the estrogen level goes up and down. This fluctuation in estrogen level appears to alter the structure of neurons and astrocytes in the neocortex and hippocampus, which likely accounts for at least part of the behavioral fluctuation. Figure 13-24 illustrates changes in the dendritic spines of female rats at different phases of their 4-day estrous cycle. As the estrogen level rises, the number of synapses rises; as the estrogen level drops, the number of synapses declines. Curiously, the influence of estrogen on cell structure may be different in the hippocampus and neocortex. Jane Stewart has found, for example, that when the ovaries of middle-aged female rats are removed, estrogen levels drop sharply, producing an increase in the number of spines on pyramidal cells throughout the neocortex but a decrease in spine density in the hippocampus (Stewart & Kolb, 1994). It is not immediately obvious how these synaptic changes might influence processes such as memory, but it is a reasonable question—especially because menopausal women also experience sharp drops in estrogen levels and a corresponding decline in verbal memory ability. This question is also relevant to middle-aged men, who show a slow decline in testosterone levels that is correlated with a drop in spatial ability. Rats that are gonadectomized in adulthood show an increase in cortical spine density, much like the ovariectomized females, although we do not know how this change is related to spatial behavior. Nonetheless, it is reasonable to suppose that testosterone levels might influence spatial memory.

When the body is stressed, the pituitary gland produces adrenocorticotrophic hormone (ACTH), which stimulates the adrenal cortex to produce hormones known as **glucocorticoids.** Glucocorticoids have many actions on the body, including the brain. Robert Sapolsky (1992) proposed that glucocorticoids can sometimes be neurotoxic. In particular, he has found that with prolonged stress, cells in the hippocampus appear to be killed by glucocorticoids. Elizabeth Gould and her colleagues (1998) showed that even relatively brief periods of stress can reduce the number of new granule cells produced in the hippocampus in monkeys, presumably through the actions of stress-related hormones. Evidence of neuron death and reduced neuron generation in the hippocampus has obvious implications for the behavior of animals, especially for processes like memory.

In sum, hormones can alter the synaptic organization of the brain and even the number of neurons in the brain. Little is known today about the behavioral consequences of such changes, but it is likely that hormones can alter the course of plastic changes in the brain.

## NEUROTROPHIC FACTORS

**Neurotrophic factors** are a group of compounds that act to reorganize neural circuits. These compounds are listed in Table 13-2. The first neurotrophic factor was discovered in the peripheral nervous system more than 30 years ago; it is known as **nerve growth factor (NGF).** NGF is trophic (that is, having to do with the process of nutrition) in

**Glucocorticoid.** One of a group of hormones, secreted in times of stress, that are important in protein and carbohydrate metabolism.

**Neurotrophic factors.** A group of compounds that act to promote the growth and survival of neurons.

**Table 13-2 Molecules Exhibiting Neurotrophic Activities**

| |
|---|
| Proteins initially characterized as neurotrophic factors |
| Nerve growth factor (NGF) |
| Brain-derived neurotrophic factor (BDNF) |
| Neurotrophin-3 (NT-3) |
| Ciliary neurotrophic factor (CNTF) |
| Growth factors with neurotrophic activity |
| Fibroblast growth factor, acidic (aFGF or FGF-1) |
| Fibroblast growth factor, basic (bFGF or FGF-2) |
| Epidermal growth factor (EGF) |
| Insulin-like growth factor (ILGF) |
| Transforming growth factor (TGF) |
| Lymphokines (interleukin 1, 3, 6 or IL-1, IL-3, IL-6) |
| Protease nexin I, II |
| Cholinergic neuronal differentiation factor |

the sense that it stimulates neurons to grow dendrites and synapses, and in some cases it promotes the survival of neurons. Trophic factors are produced in the brain, by both neurons and glia. Trophic factors can affect neurons both through cell-membrane receptors and by actually entering the neuron to act internally on its operation. For example, trophic factors may be released postsynaptically to act as signals that can influence the presynaptic cell. Recall from Chapter 5 that the Hebb synapse is hypothesized to have just such a mechanism.

Experience stimulates the production of trophic factors, so neurotrophic factors have been proposed as agents of synaptic change. For example, brain-derived neurotrophic factor (BDNF) is increased when animals solve specific problems such as mazes. This finding has led to speculation that the release of BDNF may enhance plastic changes, such as the growth of dendrites and synapses. Unfortunately, although many researchers would like to conclude that BDNF has a role in learning, this conclusion does not necessarily follow. The behavior of animals when they solve mazes is different from their behavior when they remain in cages, so we must first demonstrate that changes in BDNF, NGF, or any other trophic factor are actually related to the formation of new synapses. Nevertheless, if we assume that trophic factors do act as agents of synaptic change, then we should be able to use the presence of increased trophic factor activity during learning as a marker of where to look for changed synapses associated with learning and memory.

## PSYCHOACTIVE DRUGS

Many people commonly take stimulant drugs like caffeine, and some use more psychoactively stimulating drugs like nicotine, amphetamine, or cocaine. The long-term consequences of abusing psychoactive drugs are now well documented, but the question of why the drugs cause these problems remains to be solved. One explanation for the behavioral changes associated with chronic psychoactive drug abuse is that the brain is changed by the drugs. One experimental demonstration of these changes is known as **drug-induced behavioral sensitization,** often referred to as just *behavioral sensitization*. Behavioral sensitization is the progressive increase in the behavioral actions of a drug that occur after repeated administration of that drug, even when the amount given in each dose does not change. Behavioral sensitization occurs with most psychoactive drugs, including amphetamine, cocaine, morphine, and nicotine. In Chapter 5, we saw that *Aplysia* became more sensitive to a stimulus after repeated ex-

**Drug-induced behavioral sensitization.** The phenomenon whereby there is an escalating behavioral response to repeated administration of a psychomotor stimulant such as amphetamine, cocaine, or nicotine.

posure to it. Psychoactive drugs appear to have a parallel action: they lead to increased behavioral sensitivity to their actions. For example, a rat given a small dose of amphetamine may show an increase in activity. When the rat is given the same dose of amphetamine on subsequent occasions, the increase in activity is progressively larger. If no drug is given for weeks or even months, and then the drug is given in the same dose as before, behavioral sensitization continues to occur, which means that some type of long-lasting change must occur in the brain in response to the drug. Behavioral sensitization can therefore be viewed as a form of memory for a particular drug.

The parallel between drug-induced behavioral sensitization and other forms of memory leads us to ask if the changes in the brain after behavioral sensitization are similar to those found after other forms of learning. They are. For example, there is evidence of increased numbers of receptors at synapses and of more synapses in sensitized animals. In a series of studies, Terry Robinson and his colleagues have found a dramatic increase in dendritic growth and spine density in rats that were sensitized to amphetamine or cocaine relative to rats that received injections of a saline solution (Robinson & Kolb, 1999). Figure 13-25 compares the effects of amphetamine and saline treatments on cells in the nucleus accumbens. It can be seen that neurons in the amphetamine-treated brains have more dendritic branches and increased spine density. These plastic changes were not found throughout the brain, however. Rather, they were localized to such regions as the prefrontal cortex and nucleus accumbens, both of which receive a large dopamine projection. Recall from Chapters 6 and 11 that dopamine is believed to play a significant role in the rewarding properties of drugs.

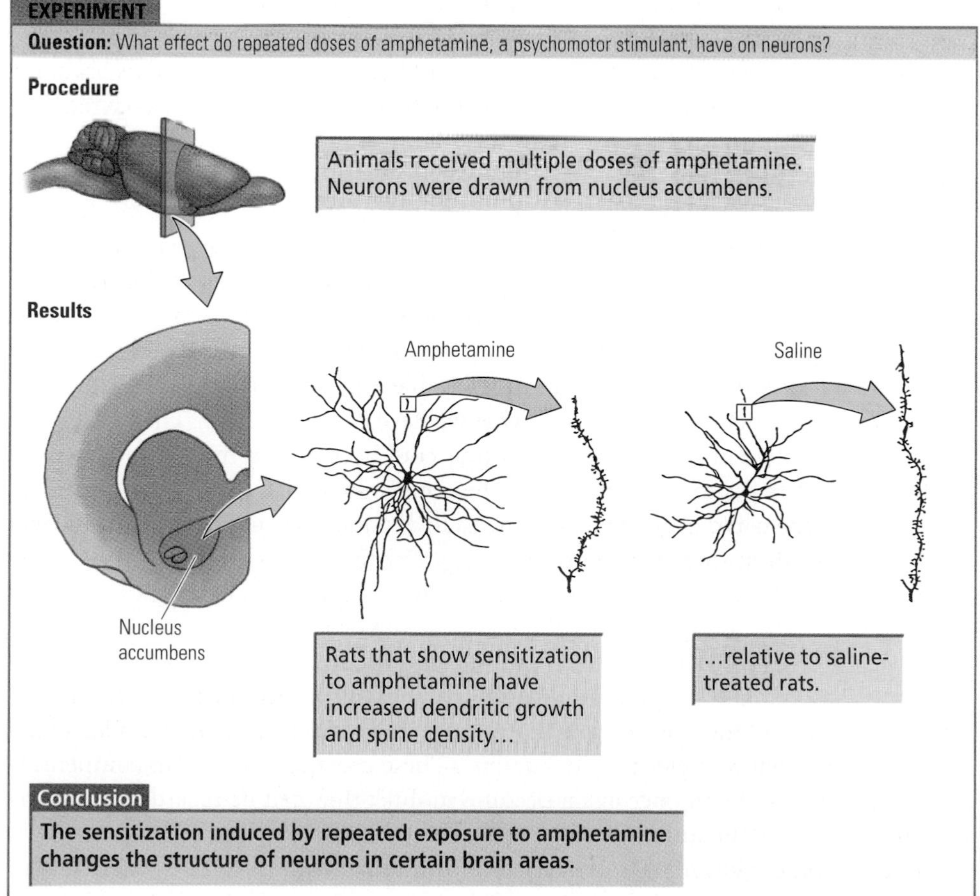

EXPERIMENT
Question: What effect do repeated doses of amphetamine, a psychomotor stimulant, have on neurons?
Procedure
Animals received multiple doses of amphetamine. Neurons were drawn from nucleus accumbens.
Results
Amphetamine
Saline
Nucleus accumbens
Rats that show sensitization to amphetamine have increased dendritic growth and spine density...
...relative to saline-treated rats.
Conclusion
The sensitization induced by repeated exposure to amphetamine changes the structure of neurons in certain brain areas.


**Figure 13-25**

Neurons in the nucleus accumbens of saline- and amphetamine-treated rats. Rats that show sensitization to amphetamine (or cocaine) experience increased dendritic growth and increased spine density relative to saline-treated rats. Repeated exposure to psychoactive stimulant drugs thus alters the structure of cells in the brain.

Adapted from "Persistent Structural Adaptations in Nucleus Accumbens and Prefrontal Cortex Neurons Produced by Prior Experience with Amphetamine," by T.E. Robinson and B. Kolb, 1997, *Journal of Neuroscience, 17,* p. 8495.

## In Review

We have seen that experience produces plastic changes in the brain, including the growth of dendrites, the formation of synapses, and the production of new neurons. Further, like environmental stimulation, it appears that hormones, neurotrophic factors, and psychoactive drugs can produce long-lasting effects on brain morphology that are strikingly similar to those observed when animals show evidence of memory for sensory events. These changes in morphology include not only changes in synaptic organization, as inferred from the dendritic analyses, but also changes in the neuron numbers, at least in the hippocampus. Thus, the neural changes that correlate with memory are similar to those observed in other situations of behavioral change.

We can infer that the nervous system appears to be conservative in its use of mechanisms related to behavioral change. This is an important message, because it implies that if we wish to change the brain, as after injury or disease, then we should look for treatments that will produce the types of neural changes that we have found to be related to memory and other forms of behavioral change. Recall that Donna showed significant recovery from her head injury; it is reasonable to ask whether that recovery was related to neuronal change. This question is the next, and last, one to be considered in this chapter.

# RECOVERY FROM BRAIN INJURY

In this chapter's introductory story, Donna showed some, albeit incomplete, recovery of function after a brain injury. Partial recovery of function is common after brain injury, and the average person would probably say that the process of recovery requires that the injured person relearn lost skills, whether walking, talking, or use of the fingers. But what exactly does recovery entail? After all, a person with a brain injury or brain disease has lost neurons, so the brain may be missing critical structures that are needed for learning. Recall, for example, that H.M. has shown no recovery of his lost memory capacities, even after 50 years of practice in trying to remember information. The requisite neuron structures are no longer there, so relearning is simply not possible. In H.M.'s case, the only solution would be to replace his lost medial temporal structures, a procedure that at present is not feasible. But other people, such as Donna, do show some recovery. On the basis of what we have described in this chapter, we can identify three different ways in which Donna could recover from brain injury: she could learn new ways to solve problems, she could reorganize the brain to do more with less, and she could generate new neurons to produce new neural circuits. We will briefly examine these three possibilities.

## The Three-Legged Cat Solution

The simplest solution to recovery from brain injury is to compensate for the injury in a manner that we call the "three-legged cat solution." Consider cats that lose a leg to accident (and subsequent veterinary treatment). These cats quickly learn to compensate for the missing limb and once again become mobile; they can be regarded as having shown recovery of function. The limb is still gone, of course, but the behavior has changed in compensation. A similar explanation can account for many instances of apparent recovery of function after brain injury. Imagine a right-handed person who has a stroke that leads to loss of use of the right hand and arm. Unable to write with the affected limb, she switches to her left hand. This type of behavioral compensation is presumably associated with some sort of change in the brain. After all, if a person learns to use the opposite hand to write, some changes in the nervous system must underlie this new skill.

## The New-Circuit Solution

A second way to recover from brain damage is for the brain to change its neural connections to overcome the neural loss. This is most easily accomplished by processes that are similar to those we considered for other forms of plasticity. That is, the brain forms new connections that allow it to "do more with less." Although this would seem to be a logical change in the brain, such changes appear to be fairly small. As a result, there is relatively modest recovery in most instances of brain injury, *unless there is some form of intervention*. Stated differently, recovery from brain damage can be increased significantly if the individual engages in some form of behavioral or pharmacological therapy. Thus, the therapy must play a role in stimulating the brain to make new connections and to do more with less.

Behavioral therapy, such as speech therapy or physiotherapy, presumably increases brain activity, which facilitates the neural changes. In a pharmacological intervention, the patient takes a drug that is known to influence brain plasticity. An example is NGF. When NGF is given to animals with strokes that damaged the motor cortex, there is an improvement in motor functions, such as reaching with the forelimb to obtain food (Figure 13-26). The behavioral changes are correlated with a dramatic increase in dendritic branching and spine density in the remaining, intact motor regions. The morphological changes are correlated with improved motor functions, such as reaching with the forelimb to obtain food, as illustrated in Figure 13-21 (Kolb et al., 1997). Recovery is by no means complete, but this is not surprising because brain tissue is still missing.

In principle, we might expect that any drug that stimulates the growth of new connections would help people recover from brain injury. There is one important constraint, however. The neural growth must be in regions of the brain that could influence a particular lost function. For example, if a drug stimulated growth of synapses on cells in the visual cortex, we would not expect to find enhanced recovery of hand use. The visual neurons play no direct role in moving the hand. Rather, we would need a drug that stimulated the growth of synapses on neurons that could control hand use, such as neurons in the premotor or prefrontal cortex. We saw earlier that amphetamine has this action, so we might predict that amphetamine would stimulate motor recovery. This possibility is now undergoing clinical trials.

Bryan Kolb

## The Lost-Neuron-Replacement Solution

The idea that brain tissue could be transplanted from one animal to another goes back to the beginning of the twentieth century. There is now good evidence that tissue from embryonic brains can be transplanted and will grow and form some connections in the new brain. Unfortunately, in contrast to transplanted hearts or livers, transplanted brain tissue functions poorly. The procedure seems most suited to conditions in which a small number of functional cells are required, such as in the replacement of dopamine-producing cells in Parkinson's disease. In fact, dopamine-producing cells have been surgically transplanted into the striatum of at least 50 Parkinson patients to date. Although the disease has not been reversed, some patients, especially the younger ones, have shown functional gains that justify the procedure. Nonetheless, the fact that the embryonic tissue is taken from human fetuses raises serious ethical issues that will not be easily resolved.

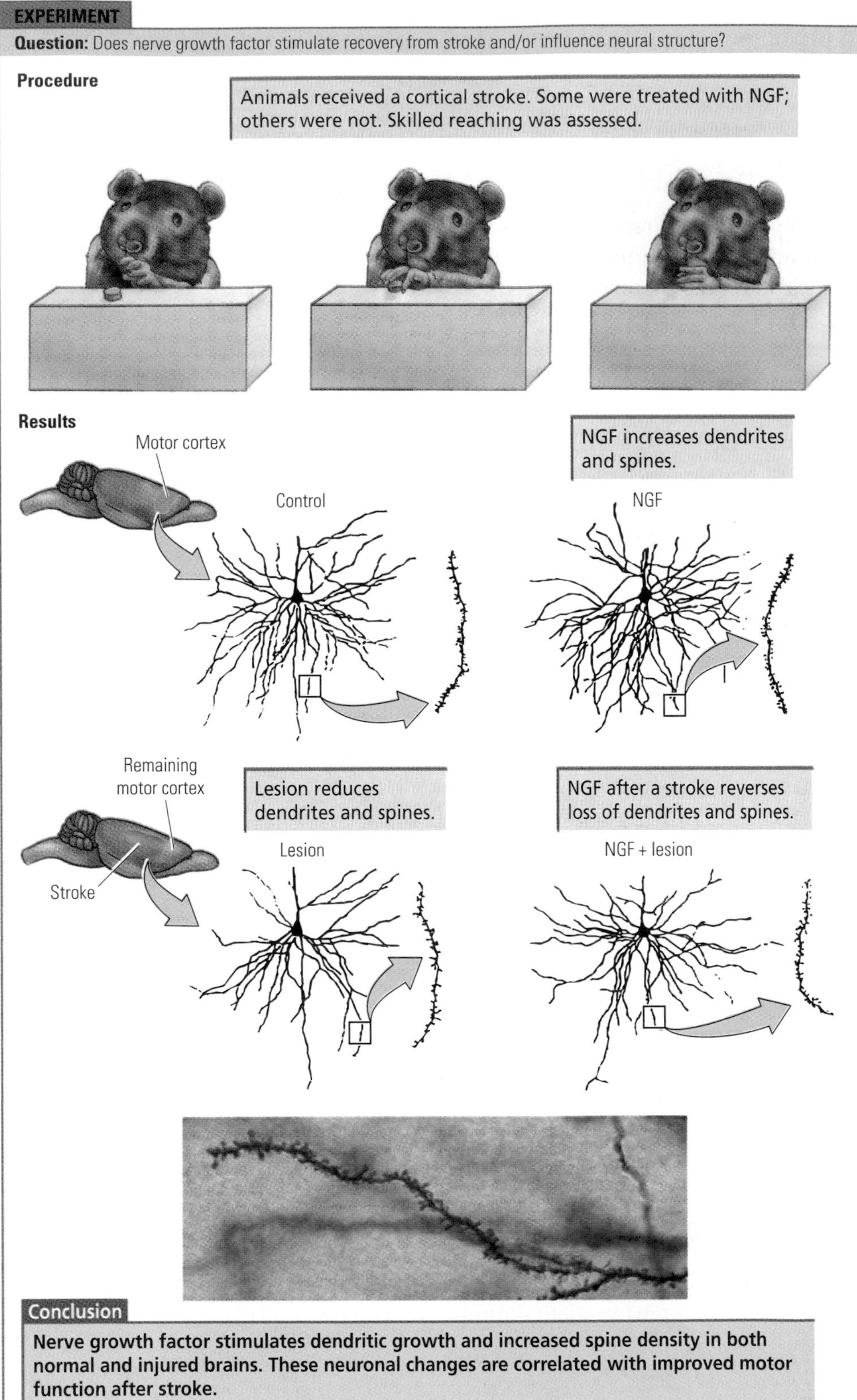

EXPERIMENT
Question: Does nerve growth factor stimulate recovery from stroke and/or influence neural structure?
Procedure
Animals received a cortical stroke. Some were treated with NGF; others were not. Skilled reaching was assessed.
Results
Motor cortex
Control
NGF increases dendrites and spines.
NGF
Remaining motor cortex
Stroke
Lesion reduces dendrites and spines.
Lesion
NGF after a stroke reverses loss of dendrites and spines.
NGF + lesion
Conclusion
Nerve growth factor stimulates dendritic growth and increased spine density in both normal and injured brains. These neuronal changes are correlated with improved motor function after stroke.

**Figure 13-26**

In the reaching task shown, rats must make skilled forelimb movements to obtain a food reward. Rats treated with NGF after motor-cortex injury show better performance on this task than do rats that receive no treatment. The cells from the NGF-treated rats show a marked increase in both dendritic branching and spine density. This plastic change is hypothesized to be responsible for the partial functional recovery in the rats treated with NGF.

Adapted from "Nerve Growth Factor Treatment Prevents Dendritic Atrophy and Promotes Recovery of Function After Cortical Injury," by B. Kolb, S. Cote, A. Ribeiro-da-Silva, and A.C. Cuello, 1997, *Neuroscience, 76,* p. 1146.

There is a second way to replace lost neurons. We saw earlier that experience can induce the brain to generate new neurons, so we know that the brain is capable of making neurons in adulthood. The challenge is to get the brain to do it after an injury. The first breakthrough in this research was made by Brent Reynolds and Sam Weiss

(1992). Cells lining the ventricle of adult mice were removed and placed in a culture medium. The researchers demonstrated that if the right trophic factors are added, the cells begin to divide and can produce new neurons and glia. Furthermore, if the trophic factors—particularly **epidermal growth factor** (EGF)—are infused into the ventricle of a living animal, the subventricular zone generates cells that migrate into the striatum and eventually differentiate into neurons and glia.

In principle, it ought to be possible to use trophic factors to stimulate the subventricular zone to generate new cells in the injured brain. If these new cells were to migrate to the site of injury and essentially to regenerate the lost area, then it might be possible to restore at least some of the lost functions. It seems unlikely that all lost behaviors could be restored, however, because the new neurons would have to establish the same connections with the rest of the brain that the lost neurons once had. This would be a daunting task, because the connections would have to be formed in an adult brain that already had billions of connections. Nonetheless, there is at least reason to hope that such a treatment might someday be feasible.

There may be another way to use trophic factors to stimulate neurogenesis and enhance recovery. Recall that regions such as the hippocampus and olfactory bulb normally produce new neurons in adulthood and that the number of neurons in these areas can be influenced by experience. It is possible, therefore, that we could stimulate the generation of new neurons in intact regions of the injured brains and that these neurons could help the brain develop new circuits to restore partial functioning. Thus, experience and trophic factors are likely to be used in studies of recovery from brain injury in the coming years.

## In Review

Learning to recover from brain injury poses a special problem, because the brain may lose large areas of neurons and their associated functions. There are three ways to compensate for the loss of neurons: learn new ways to solve problems, reorganize the brain to do more with less, and replace the lost neurons. Although complete recovery is not currently practical, it is possible to use all three strategies to enhance recovery from injury. Moreover, it is likely that rehabilitation programs will begin to look at the possibility of combining these three ways to further enhance recovery. In each case, however, recovery entails taking advantage of the brain's capacity to change.

## SUMMARY

Donna's experience with brain injury illustrates the brain's ability to change its structure and function throughout a lifetime. The discussion leads to the following questions.

1. *How does the brain learn and remember?* There are two distinctly different forms of learning and memory, which may be referred to as implicit and explicit memory. The neural circuits underlying these forms of memory are distinctly different: the system for explicit memory involves medial temporal structures; the system for implicit memory includes the basal ganglia. There are multiple subsystems within the explicit and implicit systems, with different ones controlling different forms of memory. A third form of memory is emotional memory, which has characteristics of both implicit and explicit memory. The neural circuits for emotional memory are unique in that they include the amygdala.

**neuroscience interactive**

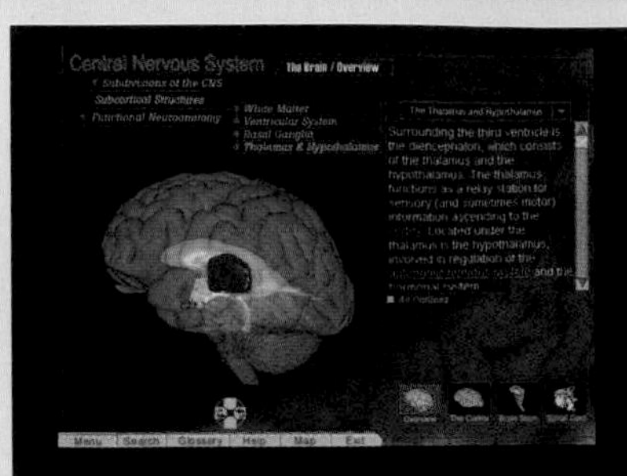

There are many resources available for expanding your learning on line:

■ **www.worthpublishers.com/kolb/chapter13**
Try some self-tests to reinforce your mastery of the material. Look at some of the updates on current research. You'll also be able to link to other sites which will reinforce what you've learned.

■ **www.alz.org**
Learn more about what happens when memory function deteriorates in Alzheimer's disease.

On your CD-ROM you can review the brain anatomy that underlies learning and memory in the module on the Central Nervous System.

2. *What changes take place in the brain in response to experience?* The brain has the capacity for structural change, which is presumed to underlie functional change. The brain changes in two fundamental ways. First, changes occur in existing neural circuits. Second, novel neural circuits are formed, both by forming new connections among existing neurons and by generating new neurons.
3. *What stimulates plastic change in the brain?* The key to brain plasticity is neural activity. Through such activity, synapses are formed and changed. Neural activity can be induced by general or specific experience, as well as by electrical or chemical stimulation of the brain. Chemical stimulation may range from hormones to neurotrophic compounds to psychoactive drugs. Much of the brain is capable of plastic change with experience. Different experiences lead to changes in different neural systems.
4. *How might brain plasticity stimulate recovery from injury?* There are plastic changes after brain injury that parallel those seen when the brain changes with experience. Changes related to recovery do not always occur spontaneously, however, and must be stimulated either by behavioral training or by the stimulating effects of psychoactive drugs or neurotrophic factors. The key to stimulating recovery from brain injury is to produce an increase in the plastic changes underlying the recovery.

## KEY TERMS

brain plasticity, p. 489
drug-induced behavioral sensitization, p. 520
explicit memory, p. 495
fear conditioning, p. 492
glucocorticoid, p. 519
implicit memory, p. 495
instrumental conditioning, p. 492
Korsakoff's syndrome, p. 506
learning, p. 490
learning set, p. 493
memory, p. 490
neurotrophic factors, p. 519
Pavlovian conditioning, p. 491

## REVIEW QUESTIONS

1. How does experience change the brain?
2. What are the critical differences between the studies of learning conducted by Pavlov and those conducted by Thorndike?
3. Distinguish among explicit, implicit, and emotional memory; what are the circuits for each?
4. What is the structural basis of brain plasticity, and what are various methods for studying its relation to behavior?
5. Why do changes in sensory representations occur after amputation of a limb?
6. What mechanisms might account for recovery from brain injury?

## FOR FURTHER THOUGHT

1. Imagine that a person has a stroke and loses a large portion of the left hemisphere, rendering him unable to speak. Imagine further that a treatment has been devised in which new neurons can be generated to replace the lost brain regions. What would be the behavioral consequences of this brain regeneration? Would the person be the same as he was before the stroke? (Hint: The new cells would have no experiences.)
2. How do we learn from experience?

## RECOMMENDED READING


Florence, S.L., Jain, N., & Kaas, J.H. (1997). Plasticity of somatosensory cortex in primates. *Seminars in Neuroscience, 9,* 3–12. Jon Kaas and his colleagues are leaders in the study of brain plasticity. This very readable review introduces the reader to the exciting discoveries that Kaas and his colleagues are making in the study of cortical plasticity in monkeys.

Fuster, J.M. (1995). *Memory in the cerebral cortex.* Cambridge, MA: MIT Press. Joaquin Fuster has summarized the evidence on how the cortex codes information for storage and retrieval, and he presents a cogent theory of how the cortex allows us to learn and to remember.

Gazzaniga, M.S. (Ed.). (2000). *The new cognitive neurosciences.* Cambridge, MA: MIT Press. This edited book spans the entire field of cognitive neuroscience. There is something for everyone in this broad and well-written collection of chapters.

Hebb, D. O. (1949). *The organization of behavior.* New York: Wiley. Although this book was written 50 years ago, it remains the clearest introduction to the fundamental questions about how the brain can learn.

Kolb, B., & Whishaw, I.Q. (1998). Brain plasticity and behavior. *Annual Review of Psychology, 49,* 43–64. The authors provide a general review of the field of brain plasticity and behavior. Any student writing a paper on this topic would do well to start with this paper and its extensive bibliography.

Sapolsky, R.M. (1992). *Stress, the aging brain, and the mechanisms of neuron death.* Cambridge, MA: MIT Press. Robert Sapolsky is one of the leading researchers and theorists interested in the rôle of hormones and brain function. This very readable text not only introduces the reader to the basic facts but also provides a provocative broth of ideas.

Squire, L. (1987). *Memory and brain.* New York: Oxford University Press. Larry Squire is perhaps the most visible cognitive neuroscientist studying brain mechanisms underlying memory. This monograph is the best single volume describing what is known about the organization of the brain and memory.

CHAPTER

14

# How Does the Brain Think?



Paul Chesley/Tony Stone
Micrograph: Carolina Biological Supply/Phototake

A fundamental characteristic of intelligent animals is that they think. But how does the brain think, and where does thinking take place? We begin to answer these questions by examining thought in an intelligent nonhuman animal—an African gray parrot named Alex, shown in Figure 14-1. Irene Pepperberg (e.g., 1990, 1999) has been studying Alex's ability to think and use language. A typical session with Alex and Pepperberg might proceed like this (Mukerjee, 1996): Pepperberg shows Alex a tray with four corks. "How many?" she asks. "Four," Alex replies. She then shows him a metal key and a green plastic one.

"What toy?"

"Key."

"How many?"

"Two."

"What's different?"

"Color."

Alex does not just have a vocabulary; the words have meaning to him. He can correctly apply English labels to numerous colors (red, green, blue, yellow, gray, purple, orange), shapes (two-, three-, four-, five-, six-corner), and materials (cork, wood, rawhide, rock, paper, chalk, wool). He can also label various items made of metal (chain, key, grate, tray, toy truck), wood (clothespin, block), and plastic or paper (cup, box). Most surprising of all, he can use words to identify, request, and refuse items and to respond to questions about abstract ideas, such as the color, shape, material, relative size, and quantity of more than 100 different objects.

Wm. Munoz

**Figure 14-1**
Alex, an African gray parrot, and Irene Pepperberg, along with items of various shapes and colors, which Alex can count, describe, and answer questions about.

Alex's thinking is often quite complex. Suppose he is presented with a tray that contains these seven items: a circular rose-colored piece of rawhide, a piece of purple wool, a three-corner purple key, a four-corner yellow piece of rawhide, a five-corner orange piece of rawhide, a six-corner purple piece of rawhide, and a purple metal box. If he is then asked, "What shape is the purple hide?" he will answer correctly, "Six-corner." To come up with this answer, Alex has to do several things. He must comprehend the question, locate the correct object of the correct color, determine the answer to the question about that object's shape, and encode his answer into an appropriate verbal response. This is not easy to do. After all, there are four pieces of rawhide and three purple objects, so Alex cannot respond to just one attribute. He has to mentally combine the concepts of rawhide and purple and find the object that possesses them both. Then he has to figure out the object's shape. Clearly, considerable mental processing is required, but Alex succeeds at such tasks time and again.

Alex also demonstrates that he understands what he is saying. For example, if he requests one object and is presented with another, he is likely to say no and repeat his original request. In fact, when given incorrect objects on numerous occasions in formal testing, he said no and repeated his request 72 percent of the time, said no without repeating his request 18 percent of the time, and made a new request the other 10 percent of the time. This suggests that Alex's requests lead to an expectation in his mind. He knows what he is asking for, and he anticipates getting it.

Alex's cognitive abilities are unexpected in a bird. We all know that parrots can talk, but most of us assume that there is no real thought behind their words. Alex proves otherwise. Over the past 30 years, there has been great interest in the intellectual capacities of chimpanzees and dolphins, but Alex has a mental life that appears to be as rich as that of those two large-brained mammals.

The fact that birds like Alex are capable of forms of "thought" is a clue to what the neural basis of thinking might be. At first, it seems logical to presume that thinking, which humans are so good at, must reflect some special property of our massive neocortex. But birds do not possess a neocortex. Instead of the cortex that developed in mammalian brains, birds evolved specific brain nuclei that function much like the layers of the cortex do. (See Figure 1-12 for a comparison of the parrot and human brains.) This different organization of the forebrain in birds versus mammals implies that thinking must be an activity of complex neural circuits and not of some particular region in the brain.

The idea of neural circuits was the essence of Donald Hebb's concept of the **cell assembly.** Hebb proposed that networks of neurons (cell assemblies) could represent objects or ideas, and it was the interplay between those networks that resulted in complex mental activity. Of course, as you have seen in the last few chapters, connections among neurons are not random, but rather are organized into systems (the visual, auditory, and motor systems, for instance) and subsystems (such as the dorsal and ventral streams of vision). Thinking, therefore, must reflect the activity of many different systems, which in the mammalian brain are in the cortex.

This chapter examines the organization of the neural systems and subsystems that are involved in thinking. Our first task is to define the mental processes that we wish to study. What, in other words, do we mean by thought? We then consider the cortical regions that play the major roles in thinking. You have encountered all these regions before in the course of studying vision, audition, and movement. Here we examine how these same regions may function to produce thought. One characteristic of how the cortex is organized to produce thought is that fundamentally different types of thinking are carried out in the left and right cerebral hemispheres. As a result, this chapter also explores the asymmetrical organization of the brain. Another distinguishing feature of human thought is that there are individual differences in the ways that people think. We consider several sources of these differences, including those related to sex and to what we call intelligence. Finally, we address the issue of consciousness and how it may relate to the neural control of thought.

## THE NATURE OF THOUGHT

The study of thought, language, memory, emotion, and motivation is tricky because these mental processes cannot be seen. They can only be inferred from behavior and are best thought of as **psychological constructs.** A psychological construct is an idea that results from a set of impressions. The mind *constructs* the idea as being real, even though it is not a tangible thing. Thought is a psychological construct that is built out of the impression that people are constantly monitoring events and behaviors in their minds. We have the impression that people are good or bad at forming these things we call thoughts, even though thoughts do not really exist as things. We run into trouble, however, when we try to locate constructs like thought or memory in the brain. The fact that we have English words for these constructs does not mean that the brain is organized around them. Indeed, it is not.

For instance, you saw in Chapter 13 that although people talk about memory as a unitary thing, the brain does not treat memory as something unitary that is localized in one particular place. In fact, there are many forms of memory, each of which is treated differently by quite widely distributed brain circuits. Thus, this psychological construct of memory that we think of as being a single thing turns out not to be unitary at all.

**Psychological construct.** An idea, resulting from a set of impressions, that some mental ability exists as an entity; examples include memory, language, and emotion.

Even though it is risky to make assumptions about psychological constructs like memory and thought, we should certainly not give up searching for how the brain produces them. Assuming a neurological basis for psychological constructs has perils, but this does not mean that we should fail to consider brain locations for these constructs. After all, thought, memory, emotion, motivation, and other constructs are the most interesting activities that the brain performs.

Psychologists typically use the term **cognition** to describe the processes involved in thought. The term *cognition* literally means "knowing." It refers to the processes by which we come to know about the world. For behavioral neuroscientists, cognition usually entails the ability to attend to stimuli, whether external or internal, to identify these stimuli, and to plan meaningful responses to them. External stimuli are those that stimulate neural activity in our sensory receptors. Internal stimuli include cues from the autonomic nervous system as well as from neural processes related to constructs such as memory and motivation.

## Characteristics of Human Thought

It is widely believed that human cognition has unique characteristics. But in what ways, exactly, is it unique? Many may answer that human thought is verbal, whereas the thought of other animals is nonverbal. Language is presumed to give humans an edge in thinking, and in some ways it does. For one thing, language provides the brain with a way to categorize information, allowing us to easily group together objects, actions, and events that have factors in common. In addition, language provides a means of organizing time, especially future time. It enables us to plan our behavior around time (such as "Monday at 3:00 PM") in ways that nonverbal animals cannot. But perhaps most important of all, human language has **syntax**—a set of rules about how words should be put together to create meaningful utterances. Thus, syntax is an aspect of the grammar, or correct usage, of a language. Linguists argue that although other animals, such as chimpanzees, can use and recognize a large number of sounds (about three dozen for chimps), they do not arrange these sounds in different orders to produce new meanings. Because of this lack of syntax, chimpanzee language is literal and inflexible. Human language, in contrast, has enormous flexibility, which enables us to talk about virtually any topic, even highly abstract ones. In this way, our thinking is carried beyond a rigid here and now.

The importance of syntax to human thinking is illustrated by Oliver Sacks's description of an 11-year-old deaf boy named Joseph who was raised without sign language for his first 10 years, and so was never exposed to syntax. According to Sacks:

> Joseph saw, distinguished, used; he had no problems with perceptual categorization or generalization, but he could not, it seemed, go much beyond this, hold abstract ideas in mind, reflect, play, plan. He seemed completely literal—unable to juggle images or hypotheses or possibilities, unable to enter an imaginative or figurative realm. . . . He seemed, like an animal, or an infant, to be stuck in the present, to be confined to literal and immediate perception. . . . (Sacks, 1989, p. 40)

As we said in Chapter 9, language, including syntax, develops innately in children because the brain is programmed to use words in a form of universal grammar. However, in the absence of words—either spoken or signed—there can be no development of grammar. And without the flexibility of language that grammar allows, there can also be no "higher-level" thought. Without syntactic language, thought is stuck in the world of concrete, here-and-now perceptions. Syntactic language, in other words,

**Syntax.** The way in which words are put together, following the rules of grammar, to form phrases, clauses, or sentences; proposed to be a unique characteristic of human language.

influences the very nature of our thinking. We will return to this idea when we consider the differences between the thought processes of the left and right hemispheres.

In addition to arranging words in syntactical patterns, the human brain appears to have a passion for stringing together events, movements, and thoughts. For example, we combine notes into melodies, movements into dances, and images into movies. We design elaborate rules for games. It seems reasonable to conclude that the human brain is organized to structure events, movements, and thoughts into chains. Grammar is merely one example of this innate human way of thinking about the world.

We do not know how this propensity to string things together evolved, but one possibility is that there was natural selection for stringing movements together. Stringing movements together into sequences can be highly adaptive. For instance, it would allow for building houses or weaving fibers into cloth. William Calvin (1996) proposed that the most important motor sequences to ancient humans were those used in hunting. Throwing a rock or a spear at a moving target is a complex act that requires much planning. Sudden ballistic movements, such as throwing, last less than an eighth of a second and cannot be corrected by feedback. The brain has to plan every detail of these movements and then spit them out as a smooth-flowing sequence. A modern-day quarterback does this when he throws a football to a receiver who is running a zigzag pattern to elude a defender. A skilled quarterback can hit the target on virtually every throw, stringing his movements together rapidly in a continuous sequence with no pauses or gaps. This skill is unique to humans. Although chimpanzees can throw objects, they do not do so accurately. No chimpanzee would be able to learn to throw a ball so that it hit a moving target.

The human predisposition to sequence movements may have encouraged our development of language. Spoken language, after all, is a sequence of movements of the tongue and mouth. Viewed in this way, the development of language is a by-product of a brain that was already predisposed to operate by stringing movements, events, or even ideas together.

One critical characteristic of human motor sequencing is that we are able to create novel sequences with ease. We constantly produce new sentences, and composers and choreographers earn a living creating new sequences in music and dance. Creating novel sequences of movements or thoughts is a function of the frontal lobes. People with damaged frontal lobes have difficulty generating novel solutions to problems, and they are described as lacking imagination. As you know, the frontal lobes are critical to the organization of behavior; it turns out that they are critical to the organization of thinking as well. One of the major differences between the human brain and the brains of other primates is the size of the frontal lobes.

## The Neural Unit of Thought

What exactly goes on within the brain to produce what we call thinking? In our discussion of Alex, we concluded that thinking must result from the activity of complex neural circuits rather than being the property of some particular region in the brain. One way to identify the role of neural circuits is to consider the behavior of individual neurons in cognitive activity.

William Newsome and his colleagues (1995) took this approach by training monkeys to identify the presence of apparent motion in a set of moving dots on a TV screen. Figure 14-2 shows their procedure. The researchers varied the difficulty of the task by manipulating the number of dots that moved in the same direction. For instance, if all the dots are made to move in the same direction, it is very easy to perceive the whole array of dots as moving in that direction. If only a small percentage of the dots are made to move in the same direction, however, perceiving apparent motion in that direction is much more difficult. In fact, a threshold number of dots moving together is required to create apparent motion. If the number of dots moving in the same direction is too small, the viewer gets an impression of random movement. Apparently, on the basis of the proportion of dots moving in the same direction, the brain decides whether or not dots are moving in a consistent direction.

Once the monkeys were trained in the task, the investigators recorded from single neurons in visual area V5, which contains cells that are sensitive to movement in a preferred direction. Consider a neuron that is sensitive to motion in the vertical direction. Such a neuron responds with a vigorous burst of action potentials when there is vertical movement in its receptive field. But just as the observer has a threshold for the perception of coherent motion in one direction, so too does the neuron. In other words, if at some point random activity of the dots increases to a level at which it obscures movement in a neuron's preferred direction, that neuron will stop responding because it does not detect any consistent pattern. So the question becomes: How does the activity of any given neuron correlate with the perceptual threshold for apparent motion? On the one hand, if our perception of apparent motion results from the summed activity of many dozens, or even thousands, of neurons, there should be little correlation between the activity of any one neuron and that perception. On the other hand, if our perception of apparent motion is influenced by individual neurons, then there should be a strong correlation between the activity of a single cell and that perception.

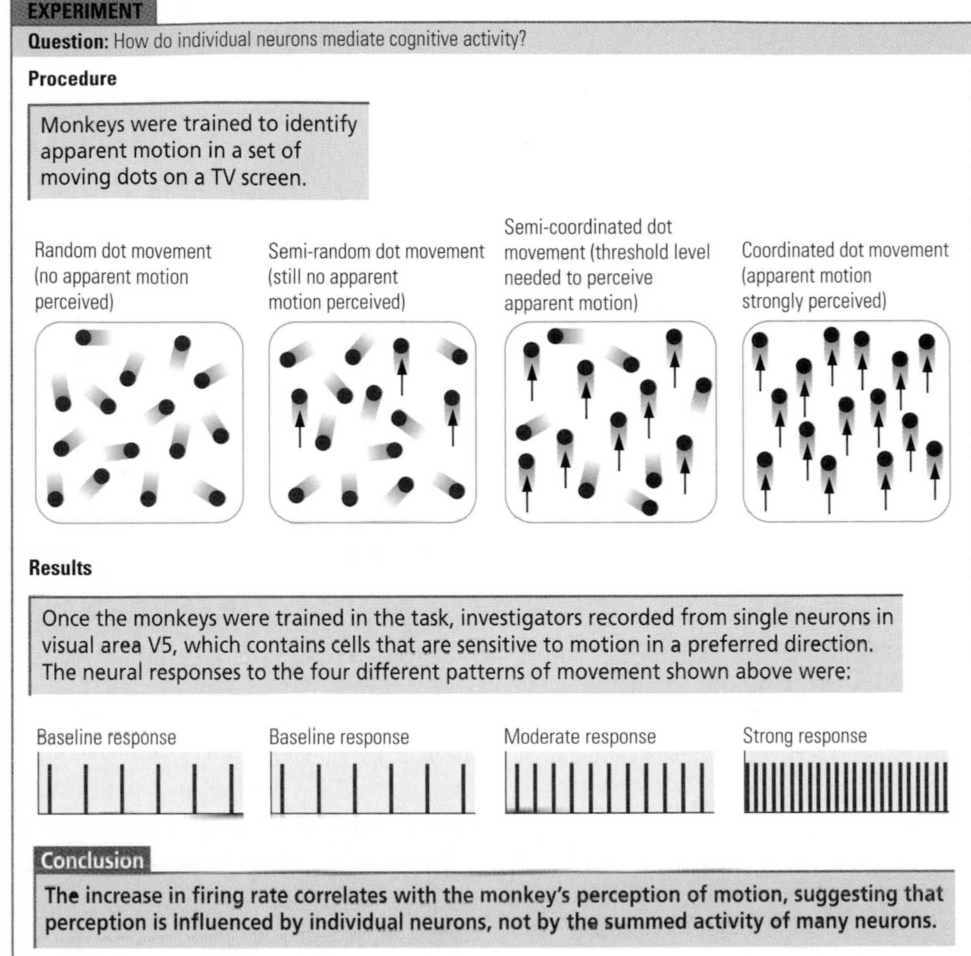

EXPERIMENT
Question: How do individual neurons mediate cognitive activity?
Procedure
Monkeys were trained to identify apparent motion in a set of moving dots on a TV screen.
Random dot movement (no apparent motion perceived)
Semi-random dot movement (still no apparent motion perceived)
Semi-coordinated dot movement (threshold level needed to perceive apparent motion)
Coordinated dot movement (apparent motion strongly perceived)
Results
Once the monkeys were trained in the task, investigators recorded from single neurons in visual area V5, which contains cells that are sensitive to motion in a preferred direction. The neural responses to the four different patterns of movement shown above were:
Baseline response
Baseline response
Moderate response
Strong response
Conclusion
The increase in firing rate correlates with the monkey's perception of motion, suggesting that perception is influenced by individual neurons, not by the summed activity of many neurons.


**Figure 14-2**

A representation of the visual stimuli employed in Newsome's experiments. The stimuli were patterns of dots that moved either randomly, semi-randomly, in a semi-coordinated manner, or all in the same direction. A reasonable degree of coordination in dot movement was needed for a monkey to perceive apparent motion. The threshold for detecting apparent motion by individual cells correlated with the monkey's subjective perception of motion, suggesting that individual cells mediate this perception.

The results of the experiment were unequivocal: the sensitivity of individual neurons was very similar to the perceptual sensitivity of the monkeys to apparent motion. In other words, if individual neurons failed to respond to the stimulus, the monkeys behaved as if they did not perceive any apparent motion. This is a curious finding. Given the large number of V5 neurons, one would think that perceptual decisions are based upon the responses of a large pool of neurons. But this experiment showed that individual cortical neurons can influence perception.

Still, there must be some way of converging the inputs of individual neurons to arrive at a consensus. This convergence of inputs can be explained by Hebb's idea of a cell assembly—an ensemble of neurons that represents a complex concept. In this case, the ensemble of neurons represents a sensory event (apparent motion), which the activity of the ensemble detects. Such ensembles of neurons could be distributed over fairly large regions of the brain, or they could be confined to smaller areas, such as cortical columns. Cognitive scientists have developed computer models of these circuits and have demonstrated that they are capable of sophisticated statistical computations with reasonably high efficiency. The performance of other complex tasks, such as Alex the parrot's detection of an object's color, are also believed to involve ensembles of neurons. These ensembles (or cell assemblies) provide the basis for cognition. Different ensembles combine together, much like words in language, to produce coherent thoughts.

What is the contribution of individual neurons to a cell assembly? Each neuron acts as a computational unit. In the moving-dots experiment, we saw that even one solitary neuron was capable of deciding on its own when to fire when its summed inputs indicated that movement was occurring. Neurons are the only elements in the brain that combine evidence and make decisions. They are the foundation of thought and cognitive processes. It is the combination of these individual neurons into novel neural networks that produces complex representations, such as ideas.

### In Review

Thought is the act of attending to, identifying, and making meaningful responses to stimuli. Many animals, probably including all mammals and birds, are capable of this type of mental activity. Human thought is characterized by the ability to generate strings of ideas, many of which are novel. The basic unit of thought is the neuron. The cell assembly is the vehicle by which neurons can interact to influence behavior and to produce cognitive processes. Our next problem is to determine where the cell assemblies for various complex cognitive processes are located in the human brain.

## COGNITION AND THE ASSOCIATION CORTEX

In Chapters 8 to 10, we discussed the regions of the cortex responsible for deciphering inputs from sensory receptors and for executing movements. These regions together occupy about a third of the cortex. The remaining cortex is located in the frontal, temporal, and parietal lobes (see Figure 14-3) and is often referred to as the **association cortex.** It functions to produce cognition.

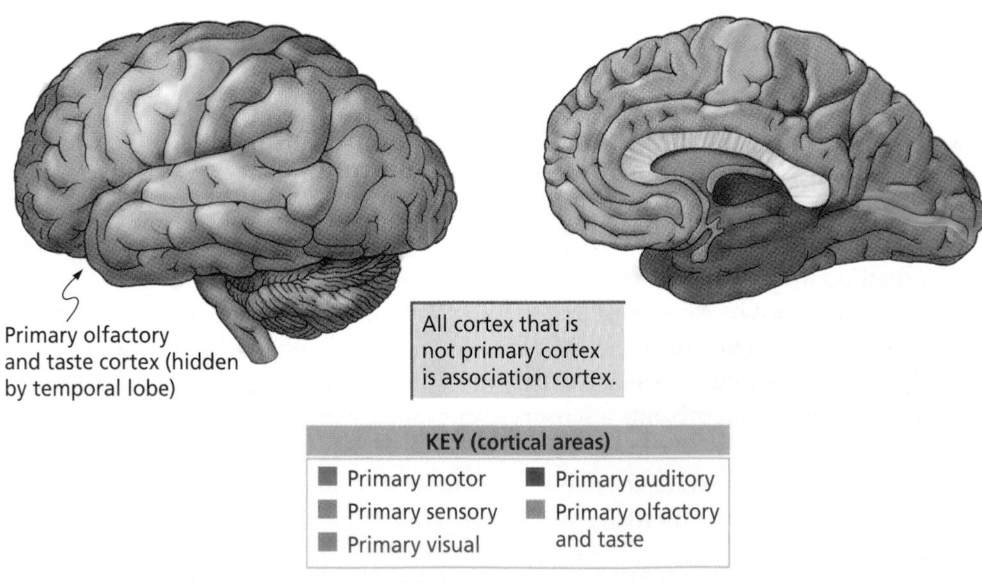


**Figure 14-3**

Lateral and medial views of the left hemisphere, showing the primary motor areas and the primary areas for receiving inputs from the five senses. All remaining cortical areas are collectively referred to as association cortex.

One fundamental difference between the association cortex and the primary sensory and motor cortex is that the association cortex has a distinctive pattern of connections. Recall that a major source of input to all cortical areas is the thalamus. The primary sensory cortex receives inputs from thalamic areas that receive information from the sense organs. In contrast, the association cortex receives its inputs from regions of the thalamus that receive their inputs from other regions of the cortex. As a result, the inputs to the association cortex have been highly processed before they get to the association regions. This information must therefore be fundamentally different from the information reaching the primary sensory and motor cortex. The association regions contain knowledge, either about our external or internal world or about movements. In order to appreciate the types of knowledge that the association areas contain, we will consider different forms of cognitive behavior and then trace these behaviors to different parts of the association cortex.

**Association cortex.** Neocortex that is outside the primary sensory or motor cortex; it functions to produce cognition.

Review the locations of these regions on the CD in the module on the Central Nervous System.

## Knowledge About Objects

Imagine looking at a cardboard milk carton sitting on a counter directly in front of you. What do you see? Now imagine moving the carton off to one side. What do you see now? Next tilt the carton toward you at a 45° angle. Again, what do you see? Probably you answered that you saw the same thing in each situation: a white rectangular object with colored lettering on it. Intuitively, you probably feel that the brain must "see" the object much as you have perceived it. As you learned in Chapter 8, however, the brain's "seeing" is more compartmentalized than your perceptions. This is revealed in people who suffer damage to different regions of the occipital cortex. They often lose one particular aspect of visual perception. For instance, those with damage to visual area V4 can no longer perceive color, while those with damage to area V5 can no longer see movement (when the milk carton moves, it becomes invisible to them). Moreover, your perception of the milk carton's rectangular shape is not always a completely accurate interpretation of the forms that your visual system is processing. When the carton is tipped toward you, you still perceive it as rectangular, even though it is no longer presenting a rectangular shape to your eyes. Your brain has somehow ignored the change in information about shape that your retinas have sent it and concluded that this is still the same milk carton.

This example demonstrates many properties of visual perception. But there is more to your processing of the milk carton than merely determining its physical characteristics. For example, you know what a milk carton is, what it contains, and where you can get one. This knowledge about milk cartons that you have acquired is represented in the temporal association cortex that forms the ventral stream of visual processing. If the temporal association regions are destroyed, a person loses visual knowledge not only about milk cartons but also about all other objects. Like D. F., whose case is discussed in Chapter 8, the person becomes agnosic.

Knowledge about objects includes even more than simply knowing what they are and what they are used for. Two cases described by Martha Farah (1995) illustrate this point nicely. Case 1 was unable to localize visual stimuli in space and to describe the location of familiar objects from memory. He was, however, good at both identifying objects and at describing their appearance from memory. In other words, Case 1 could both perceive and imagine objects, but he could not perceive or imagine their location. Case 2 was the opposite of Case 1. Case 2 could localize objects and describe their locations from memory, but he could not identify objects or describe them from memory. Case 1 had a lesion in the parietal association cortex, whereas Case 2's lesion was in the temporal association cortex. Knowledge about objects is thus found in more than one location, depending on the nature of the knowledge. Knowledge of *what* things are is temporal, whereas knowledge of *where* things are is parietal.

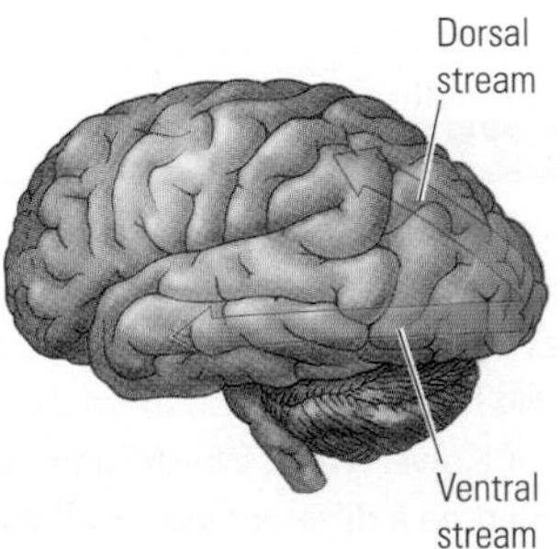

## Spatial Cognition

The location of objects is just one aspect of what we know about space. *Spatial cognition* refers to a whole range of mental functions that vary from navigational ability (the ability to go from point A to point B) to the mental manipulation of complex visual arrays, as illustrated in Figure 14-4. For example, imagine traveling to an unfamiliar park for a walk. As you walk about the park, you need to proceed in an organized, systematic way. You do not want to go around and around in circles. You also need to be able to find your way back to your bus stop. These abilities require a representation of the physical environment in your mind's eye.

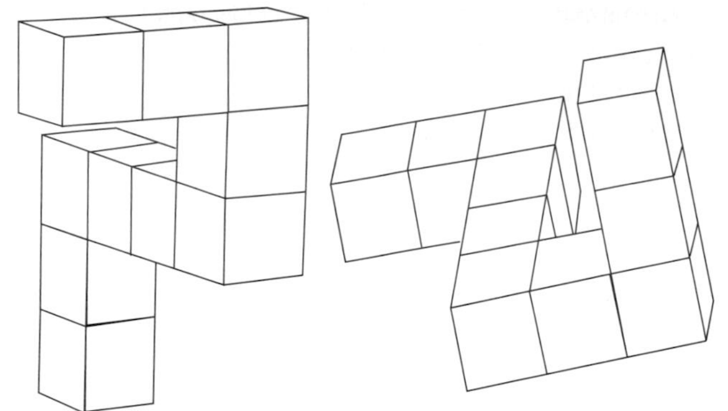

**Figure 14-4**

These two figures are the same, but they have different orientations in space. Researchers test spatial cognition by giving subjects a pair of stimuli, such as those shown, and asking if the shapes are the same or different.

Now let's presume that at some time during the walk, you are uncertain where you are (a common problem). One solution is to create a mental image of your route, complete with various landmarks and turns. It is a small step from mentally manipulating these kinds of navigational landmarks and movements to manipulating other kinds of images in your mind. It therefore seems likely that the ability to mentally manipulate visual images arose from the ability to navigate in space.

The evolution of skill at mentally manipulating things is also closely tied to the evolution of physical movements. In the course of evolution, it seems likely that animals first moved by using whole-body movements (such as the swimming motion of a fish), then developed coordinated limb movements (quadrupedal walking), and finally became capable of discrete limb movements, such as the reaching movements of human arms. As the guidance strategies for controlling movements became more sophisticated, cognitive abilities probably increased as well to support those guidance systems. It seems unlikely that more sophisticated cognitive abilities evolved on their own. For instance, why would a fish be able to manipulate an object in its mind that it could not manipulate in the real world? In contrast, a human who can manipulate objects by hand might be expected to be able to imagine such manipulations. After all, we are constantly observing our hands manipulate things, so we must have many mental representations of such activity. Once the brain can process the manipulation of objects that are physically present, it seems a small step to picturing the manipulation of objects that are only imagined. This ability enables us to solve problems like the one in Figure 14-5. The task is to mentally manipulate the cube at the left to determine which of cubes *a, b,* and *c* could result from those manipulations. The ability to carry out such manipulations of an object in the mind's eye probably flows from the ability to manipulate tangible objects with the hands.

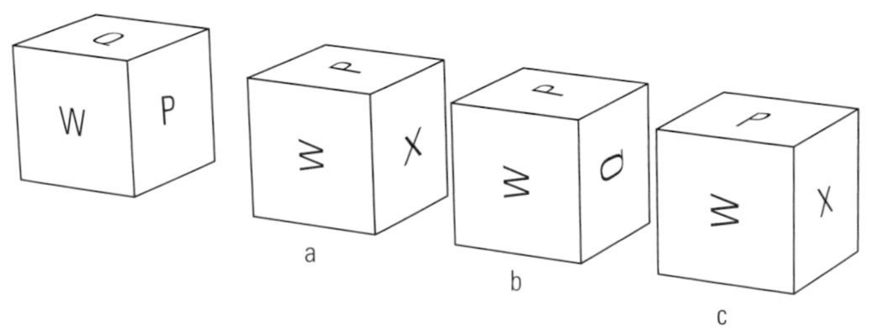


**Figure 14-5**

A sample test item used to measure spatial orientation. Compare the three cubes on the right with the one on the left. No letter appears on more than one face of a given cube. Which cube—*a, b,* or *c*—could be a different view of the cube on the left? (The correct answer is *a*.)

Which parts of the brain take part in the various aspects of spatial cognition? Some clues related to spatial navigation come from the study of how children develop navigational skills. People navigate by using several kinds of information to guide them. They may take note of single cues or landmarks (a pine tree, a park bench), they may keep track of their movements (turned left, walked 30 meters), and they may relate observed landmarks to their own movements (turned right *at* the bench), thus creating a spatial representation known as a *place response*. Research shows a progressive change in the type of navigational information that children use at different ages. In one study, Linda Acredolo (1976) brought children into a small, nondescript room that had a door at one end, a window at the other end, and a table along one wall. The children were walked to a corner of the table and blindfolded. While blindfolded, they were walked in a circuitous route back to the door; then the blindfold was removed and they were asked to return to the point at which they had been blindfolded. Unbeknownst to the children, the table had sometimes been moved. If children used a place response, they returned to the correct place, even though the table had been moved. If children used a cue or landmark response, they walked directly to the table, regardless of where it was positioned. And if children used a movement response, they turned in the direction in which they had originally turned when first entering the room. Acredolo found that 3-year-olds tend to use a movement response, whereas children a few years older used a cue or landmark response, and by age 7 children had begun to use a place response to find the correct location. This developmental progression probably mimics the evolutionary progression of spatial cognition. Because the cortex develops so late in children, it is likely that the cortex controls the more sophisticated place response in spatial navigation.

Research has also provided clues to the brain regions involved in other aspects of spatial cognition. For instance, we saw in Chapter 8 that the dorsal stream in the parietal lobes plays a central role in the control of vision for action. Discrete limb movements are made to points in space, so it is reasonable to suppose that the development of the dorsal stream may have provided a neural basis for such spatial cognitive skills as the mental rotation of objects. In fact, people with damage to the parietal association regions, especially in the right hemisphere, have deficits in the processing of complex spatial information, both in the real world and in their imaginations.

If we trace the evolutionary development of the human brain, we find that the parietal association regions expanded considerably more in humans than in other primates. This expanded brain region functions, in part, to perform complex spatial operations such as those we have been discussing. Humans have a capacity for constructing things that far exceeds that of our nearest relative, the chimpanzee. A long leap of logic may be required in making the assertion, but perhaps our increased capacity for building and manipulating objects played an important role in the development of our spatial cognitive abilities.

## Attention

Imagine going to a football game where you intend to meet some friends. You search for them as you meander through the crowd in the stadium. Suddenly, you hear the distinctive laugh of one friend, and you turn to scan in that direction. You see your group and rush to join it. This common experience demonstrates the nature of attention. Even when you are bombarded by sounds, smells, feelings, and sights, you can still detect a familiar laugh or spot a familiar face. In other words, you can direct your attention.

More than 100 years ago, William James (1890) defined *attention* this way: "It is the taking possession by the mind in clear and vivid form of one out of what seem several simultaneous objects or trains of thought." James's definition goes beyond our example of locating friends in a crowd, for he notes that we can attend selectively to thoughts as well as to sensory stimuli. Who hasn't at some time been so preoccupied with a thought as to exclude all else from mind? Attention can be directed inward as well as outward.

Like the neural basis of many other mental processes, the neural basis of attention is particularly difficult to study. However, research on monkeys has identified neurons in the cortex and midbrain that show enhanced firing rates to particular locations or visual stimuli to which the animals have been trained to attend. Significantly, *the same stimulus* can activate a neuron at one time but not at another, depending on the monkey's learned focus of attention.

In the study shown in Figure 14-6, James Moran and Robert Desimone (1985) trained monkeys to hold a bar while they gazed at a fixation point on a screen. A sample stimulus (for instance, a vertical red bar) appeared briefly at one location in the visual field, followed about 500 milliseconds later by a test stimulus at the same location.

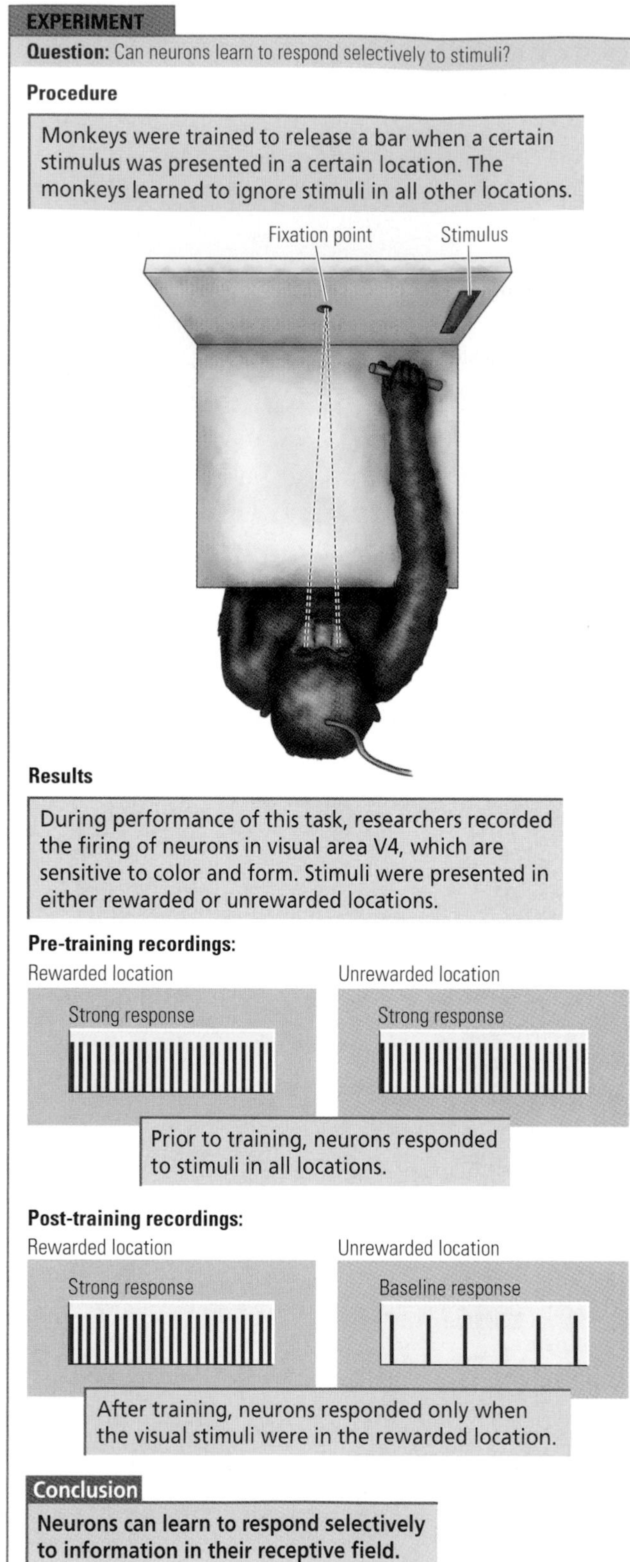

EXPERIMENT
Question: Can neurons learn to respond selectively to stimuli?
Procedure
Monkeys were trained to release a bar when a certain stimulus was presented in a certain location. The monkeys learned to ignore stimuli in all other locations.
Fixation point
Stimulus
Results
During performance of this task, researchers recorded the firing of neurons in visual area V4, which are sensitive to color and form. Stimuli were presented in either rewarded or unrewarded locations.
Pre-training recordings:
Rewarded location
Unrewarded location
Strong response
Strong response
Prior to training, neurons responded to stimuli in all locations.
Post-training recordings:
Rewarded location
Unrewarded location
Strong response
Baseline response
After training, neurons responded only when the visual stimuli were in the rewarded location.
Conclusion
Neurons can learn to respond selectively to information in their receptive field.


**Figure 14-6**

A monkey performing an attentional task. The monkey is trained to respond only to a particular stimulus in a particular location. Recordings from visual neurons in the monkey's brain show that even though a given neuron would normally respond to a stimulus in many locations, the neuron can be trained to attend selectively to information in a specific region of its receptive field.

When the test stimulus was identical to the initial sample stimulus, the animal was rewarded if it immediately released the bar that it held in its hand. Each animal was trained to attend to stimuli presented in one particular area of the visual field and to ignore stimuli in any other area. In this way, the same visual stimulus could be presented to different regions of a neuron's receptive field in order to test whether the cell's response varied with stimulus location.

As the animals performed the task, the researchers recorded the firing of neurons in visual area V4. Neurons in area V4 are sensitive to color and form, with different neurons responding to different combinations of these two variables (for instance, a red vertical bar or a green horizontal bar). Visual stimuli were presented either in the correct location for a reward or in an incorrect location for no reward. Neurons responded only when a visual stimulus was in the correct location, even though *the same stimulus* was presented in the incorrect location. Prior to training, the neurons responded to all stimuli in both locations. This finding tells us that the ability to attend to specific parts of the sensory world is a property of single neurons. Once again we see that the neuron is the computational unit of cognition.

It is likely that attention is a property of neurons throughout the brain but that some regions play a more central role than others. The frontal lobes, for instance, play a very important part. People with frontal-lobe injuries tend to become overly focused on environmental stimuli. They seem to selectively direct their attention to an excessive degree. Studies of these people suggest that the frontal association cortex is critically involved in the ability to flexibly direct attention where it is needed. Indeed, the formation of plans, which you know to be a frontal-lobe function, *requires* this ability. In addition, the parietal association cortex plays a key role in other aspects of attention. This role is perhaps best illustrated by studying the attention deficit referred to as neglect.

**Neglect** is a condition in which a person ignores sensory information that should be considered important. Usually the condition affects only one side of the body, in which case it is called **contralateral neglect.** Figure 14-7 shows an example of contralateral neglect in a dog that would eat food only from the right side of its dish. Neglect is a fascinating symptom because it often entails no damage to sensory pathways. Rather, the problem is a failure of attention.

**Contralateral neglect.** Neglect of a part of the body or world on the side opposite (that is, contralateral) to a brain injury.

People with damage to the parietal association cortex of the right hemisphere may have particularly severe neglect of objects or events in the left side of their world. For example, one man dressed only the right side of his body, shaved only the right side of his face, and read only the right side of a page (if you can call that reading). He was capable of moving his left limbs spontaneously, but when asked to raise both his arms, he would raise only his right one. When pressed, he could be induced to raise the left one, but then he would quickly drop it to his side again.

**Extinction.** A term used in neurology to refer to the neglect of information on one side of the body when it is presented simultaneously with similar information on the other side of the body.

As people with contralateral neglect begin to recover, they show another interesting symptom known as extinction. **Extinction** refers to the neglect of information on one side of the body when it is presented simultaneously with similar information on the other side of the body. Figure 14-8 shows a common clinical test for extinction. The patient is asked to keep his or her eyes fixed on the examiner's face and to report objects presented in one or both sides of the visual field. When presented with a single object to one side or the other, the patient orients to the appropriate side of the visual field, so we know that he or she cannot be blind on either side. But now suppose that two forks are presented, one on the left and one on the right. Curiously, the patient ignores the fork on the left and reports only that there is one on the right. When asked about the left side, the patient is quite certain that nothing appeared there and that only one fork was presented, on the right.

Dennis O'Brien

**Figure 14-7**

Contralateral neglect in a dog. This dog, which had a brain tumor, would eat only the food in the right side of its dish and would ignore food in the left side.

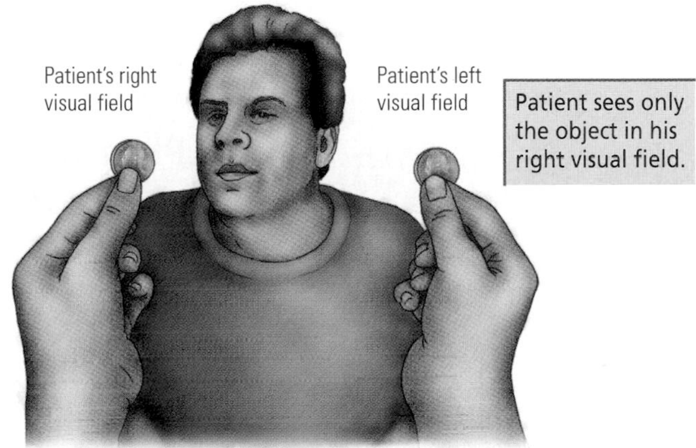
When shown two identical objects
Patient's right visual field
Patient's left visual field
Patient sees only the object in his right visual field.

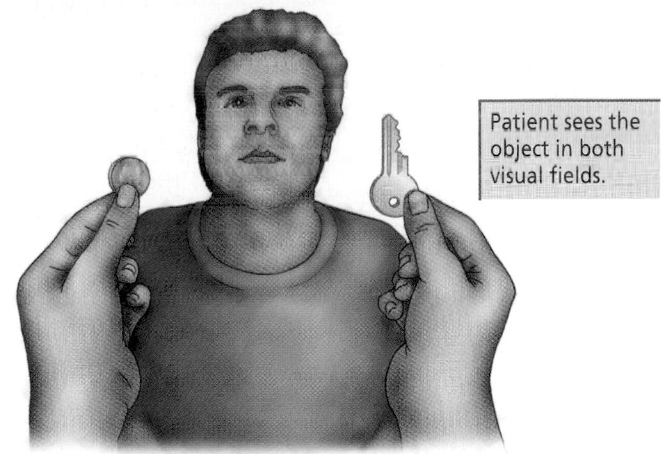
When shown two different objects
Patient sees the object in both visual fields.

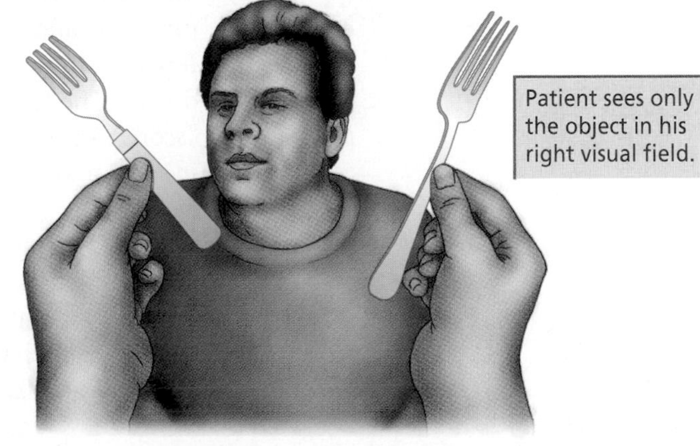
When shown two kinds of an object
Patient sees only the object in his right visual field.

**Figure 14-8**

Testing for extinction in a stroke patient who shows neglect. The patient responds differently depending on whether objects in the left and right visual fields are similar or different. When shown two different objects (a key and a coin), he quickly reports both objects. But when shown two identical objects (coins), he does not notice the one in his left field. Similarly when shown two kinds of forks *(bottom)* in two different orientations, there is still extinction of the fork in the neglected (left) field.

Perhaps the most curious aspect of neglect is that people with it fail to pay attention not only to one side of the physical world around them but also to one side of the world that they represent in their minds. We studied one woman who had complete neglect for everything on her left side. She complained that she could not use her kitchen because she could never remember the location of anything on her left. We asked her to imagine standing at the kitchen door and to describe what was in the various drawers on her right and left. She could not recall anything on her left. We then asked her to imagine walking to the end of the kitchen and turning around. We now asked her what was on her right, which had previously been on her left. She broke into a big smile and tears ran down her face as she realized that she now knew what was on that side of the room. All she had to do was reorient her body in her mind's eye. She later wrote and thanked us for changing her life, for she was now able to cook again! Clearly, neglect can be in the mind as well as in the real world.

## Planning

Imagine the following scenario. It is Friday noon and one of your friends proposes that you go to a nearby city for the weekend to attend a concert. She will pick you up at 6:00 PM and you will drive there together. Because you are completely unprepared for this invitation, and you are going to be busy until 4:00, you must rush home right after 4:00 and get organized. En route you stop at a fast food restaurant so that you won't be hungry on the 2-hour drive. You also need money, so you zoom to the nearest ATM. When you get home, you grab various pieces of clothing appropriate for the concert and the trip. You also pack your toiletries. You somehow manage to get ready by 6:00, when your friend arrives.

Although the task of getting ready in a hurry may make us a bit harried, most of us can manage to do it, but people with frontal-lobe injury cannot. To learn why, let's consider what is involved in the task. First, you have to plan your behavior, which requires selecting from many options. What things do you need to take with you? Money? Then which bank machine is closest and what is the quickest route to get there? Do you also need something to eat? Then what is the fastest way to get food on a Friday afternoon? Second, in view of your time constraint, you have to ignore irrelevant stimuli. For instance, if you pass a sign advertising a sale in your favorite music store, you have to ignore it and persist with the task at hand. Third, you have to keep track of what you have done already. This is especially important during your packing. You do not want to forget items or to pack the same item twice. You do not want to take four pairs of shoes and no toothbrush, for example.

The general requirements of this task can be described as the temporal (or time) organization of behavior. You are planning what you need to do and when you need to do it. This is the general function of the frontal lobes. But note that, in order to perform this task, you also need to recognize objects (an occipital- and temporal-lobe function) and to make appropriate movements with respect to them (a parietal-lobe function). You can therefore think of the frontal lobes as acting like an orchestra conductor. The frontal lobes make and read some sort of motor plan (a kind of motor "score," analogous to the musical score of a conductor) in order to organize behavior in space and time. People with frontal-lobe injuries are simply unable to organize their behavior.

Performance on the Wisconsin Card Sorting Task provides a nice example of the kinds of deficits that frontal-lobe injury creates. Figure 14-9 shows the test materials. The subject is presented with the four stimulus cards arrayed at the top. These cards bear designs that differ in color, form, and number of elements, thus creating three possible sorting categories to be used in the task. The subject must sort a deck of cards into piles in front of the various stimulus cards, depending upon what sorting category is called for. The correct sorting category is never stated. The subject is told afterward whether the choice he or she has made is correct or incorrect. For example, in one trial, the first correct sorting category is color. Then, once the subject has sorted a number of cards by color, the correct solution switches without warning to form. Once the subject has started to sort by form, the correct solution again changes unexpectedly, this time to the number of items on each card. The sorting rule later becomes color again, and so on, with each change in rule coming unannounced. Shifting response strategies is particularly difficult for people with frontal-lobe lesions, who may continue responding to the original stimulus (color) for as many as 100 cards until the test ends. They may even comment that they know that color is no longer the correct category, but they continue to sort on the basis of it. As one such person stated: "Form is probably the correct solution now so this [sorting by color] will be wrong, and this will be wrong, and wrong again." Curiously, then, despite knowing what the correct sorting category is, the frontal-lobe patient is unable to shift behavior in response to the new external information.

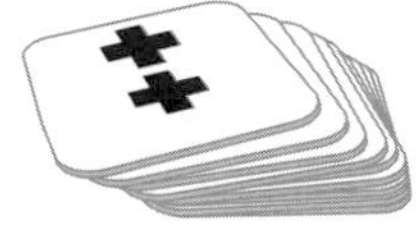

**Figure 14-9**

The Wisconsin Card Sorting Test, showing test materials as presented to the subject. The task is to place each card in the bottom pile under the appropriate card in the top row, sorting by one of three possible categories: color, number, or form. Subjects are never explicitly told what the corrrect sorting category is, only whether their responses are correct or incorrect. Once subjects have begun using one sorting rule, the tester unexpectedly changes to another rule.

## Imitation and Understanding

In all communication—both verbal and nonverbal—it is critical that the sender and receiver have a common understanding of what counts. If a person speaks a word or makes a gesture, it will be effective only if another person interprets it correctly. To accomplish this coordination in communication, the processes of producing and perceiving a message must have some kind of shared representation in the brain of the sender and the receiver. How is this shared representation achieved? How do both the sender and the receiver of a potentially ambiguous gesture, such as a raised hand or a faint smile, come to share an understanding of what that gesture means?

Giacomo Rizzolatti and his colleagues (1998) proposed an answer to this question. They identified neurons in the frontal lobes of monkeys that discharge during the production of active movements of the hand or mouth or both. These neural discharges do not precede the movements but instead occur in synchrony with them. Because it would take time for a neural message to go from a frontal lobe to a hand, we would predict that if these cells are controlling the movements, they will discharge before the movements occur. The cells must therefore be recording that the movement is occurring. In the course of his studies, Rizzolatti also made the remarkable finding that many of these neurons discharge when other monkeys make the same movements. Rizzolatti called these "mirror neurons." **Mirror neurons** do not respond to objects, only to specific observed actions. The researchers proposed that these neurons represent actions, whether one's own or others'. Such neural representations could be used both for imitating others' actions and for understanding the meaning of those actions, thus enabling appropriate responses to them. These neurons therefore provide the link between the sender and the receiver of communication.

Rizzolatti and his colleagues used PET to look for these same neurons in humans. Subjects were asked to watch a movement, to make the same movement, or to imagine the movement. In each case, a region of the lateral frontal lobe in the left hemisphere, including Broca's area, was activated. Taken together with the monkey studies, this finding suggests that primates have a fundamental mechanism for action recognition. People apparently recognize actions made by others because the neural patterns produced when the actions are observed are similar to those produced when they themselves make those same actions. According to Rizzolatti, the human capacity to communicate with words may have resulted from a progressive evolution of the mirror neuron system observed in the monkey brain. After all, the ability to mimic behaviors, such as in dances and song, is central to human culture. The evolution of this capacity was perhaps the precursor to the evolution of language.

One major difference between humans and monkeys is that in humans the mirror neurons are localized to the left hemisphere. Although it is not immediately clear why this is, the existence of a unilateral representation may be significant for understanding how language is organized in the brain. If the abilities to mimic and to understand gestures were present before language developed, and if the neural circuits for these abilities became lateralized, then language would also become lateralized because the system on which it is based already existed in the left hemisphere.

### In Review

The association areas of the cortex contain knowledge about both our external and internal worlds, and they function to produce the many different forms of cognitive behavior in which we engage. As a general rule, the temporal lobes generate knowledge about objects, whereas the parietal lobes and the hippocampus produce various forms of spatial cognition. In addition, there are neurons in both the temporal and the parietal lobes that seem to contribute to our ability to selectively attend to particular sensory information. The frontal lobes function not only to make movements but also to plan movements and to organize our behavior over time. In humans, an area of the left frontal lobe interprets the behavior of others so that the information can be used to plan appropriate actions.

## STUDYING THE HUMAN BRAIN AND COGNITION

Historically, the functions of the association cortex have been inferred largely from the study of neurological patients. In recent years, however, many new technologies have been developed to study cognition in the normal brain. So in addition to traditional neuropsychological studies of brain-damaged patients, researchers now have a rich array of more modern methods to help them analyze the neural correlates of human thought. Here we consider some of these research techniques. Using them to study the neural basis of cognition is often referred to as **cognitive neuroscience.**

### Methods of Cognitive Neuroscience

Beginning in the mid-1800s, physicians like Paul Broca began to make clinical observations about the mental activity of people with specific brain injuries. During the twentieth century, this clinical approach developed into the discipline that is now called **neuropsychology.** Neuropsychological studies involve analyzing the behavioral symptoms of people with circumscribed, usually unilateral brain lesions due to stroke, illness, surgery, or accident. Presumably, if a patient shows impairment on some behavioral test, the damaged area must play a role in that particular behavior. In order to conclude that the area in question has a special function, however, it is also necessary to show that lesions in other parts of the brain do not produce a similar deficit. For example, if a temporal-lobe patient is impaired on a test of verbal memory, we would need to demonstrate that someone with frontal- or parietal-lobe injury does not have a similar impairment. Neuropsychological studies typically compare the effects that injuries to different brain regions have on particular tasks, as illustrated in "Neuropsychological Assessment."

**Cognitive neuroscience.** The study of the neural basis of cognition.

**Neuropsychology.** A general term used to refer to the study of the relationship between brain function and behavior.

Focus on Disorders

## Neuropsychological Assessment

The oldest method of investigating the brain's hemispheric organization is to study the effects of circumscribed unilateral lesions that occur as a result of strokes, surgery, and other injuries and to infer the function of the lesioned area by observing the patient's behavioral deficits. Beginning in the late 1940s and continuing until today, neuropsychologists have devised a battery of neuropsychological tests that are designed to evaluate the functional capacities of different cortical areas, especially association areas. Although "high-tech" procedures such as PET, fMRI, and ERP have also been developed, the "low-tech" behavioral assessment continues to be one of the best and simplest ways to measure cognitive function.

To illustrate the nature and power of neuropsychological assessment, we will compare the test performance of three patients on five of the tests used in a complete neuropsychological assessment. The first two tests are tests of delayed memory—one verbal, the other visual. The patients were read a list of words and two short stories. They were also shown a series of simple drawings. Their task was to repeat the words and stories immediately after hearing them and to draw the simple figures. Then, without warning, they were asked to do so again 30 minutes later. Their performances on these delayed tests yield the delayed verbal and visual memory scores. The third test is one of verbal fluency, in which patients were given 5 minutes to write down as many words as they could think of that start with the letter *s*, excluding both people's names and numbers. The next test is the Wisconsin Card Sorting Test, which assesses abstract reasoning (see Figure 14-9). Finally, the patients were given a reading test. For all these tests, performance was compared with that of a normal control subject.

The first patient, J. N., was a 28-year-old man who had developed a tumor in the anterior and medial part of the left temporal lobe. Preoperative psychological tests showed this man to be of superior intelligence, with his only significant deficits being on tests of verbal memory. When we saw him, one year after surgery that successfully removed the tumor, he had returned to his job as a personnel manager. His intelligence was still superior, but, as the accompanying score summary shows, he was still impaired on the delayed verbal memory test, recalling only about 50 percent as much as the other subjects did.

The second patient, E. B., was a college senior majoring in psychology. An aneurysm in the right temporal lobe had burst, and the anterior part of that lobe had been removed. She was of above-average intelligence and completed her bachelor of arts degree with good grades. Her residual deficit was clearly shown on her delayed visual memory test, where she recalled just a little more than half of what the other subjects did.

**Subjects' Scores**

| Test | Control | J. N. | E. B. | J. W. |
|---|---|---|---|---|
| Delayed verbal memory | 17 | 9* | 16 | 16 |
| Delayed visual memory | 12 | 14 | 8* | 12 |
| Verbal fluency | 62 | 62 | 66 | 35* |
| Card-sorting errors | 9 | 10 | 12 | 56* |
| Reading | 15 | 21 | 22 | 17 |

*An abnormally poor score

Finally, the third patient, J. W., was a 42-year-old police inspector who had a college diploma and was also of above-average intelligence. He had a benign tumor in the left frontal lobe. We saw him 10 years after his surgery, at which time he was still working in the police force, although at a desk job. His verbal fluency was markedly reduced, as was his ability to solve the card-sorting task. His reading skill, however, was unimpaired, which was also true of the other patients.

Two points can be made from these neuropsychological results. First, damage to different parts of the brain produces different symptoms, which allows functions to be localized to different cerebral regions. Second, there is an asymmetry in brain organization. Left-hemisphere damage preferentially affects verbal functions, whereas right-hemisphere damage preferentially affects nonverbal functions.

**Magnetic resonance imaging (MRI).** An imaging procedure in which a computer draws a map from the measured changes in the magnetic resonance of atoms in the brain. MRI allows the production of a structural map of the brain without actually opening the skull.

A second approach to examining human brain function is to measure brain activity in some way and correlate this measurement with the cognitive activity inferred to be taking place at the same time. One method of measuring brain activity is to use electrical recordings, such as the event-related potentials (ERPs) that we discussed in Chapter 4 (see Figures 4-26 and 4-27). Another method is to take advantage of the fact that the electrical currents of neurons generate tiny magnetic fields. With the use of a special recording device known as a SQUID (superconducting quantum interference device), it is possible to record these magnetic fields and to produce a **magnetoencephalogram (MEG).** Like the ERP, the MEG procedure requires that many measurements be taken and averaged.

A third strategy for studying human brain function is to measure brain metabolism, as in a PET scan, described in Chapter 8. A more recent, less invasive alternative is **magnetic resonance imaging (MRI)**, illustrated in Figure 14-10. MRI is based on the principle that atoms behave like spinning bar magnets in the presence of a magnetic field. Normally, atoms are pointed randomly in different directions, but when placed

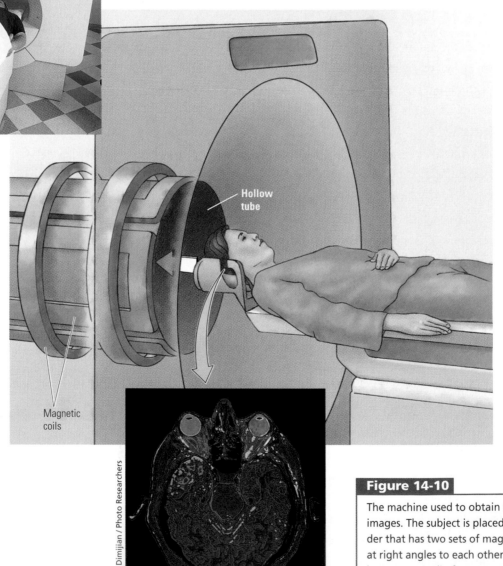

Bob Schatz / Liaison International

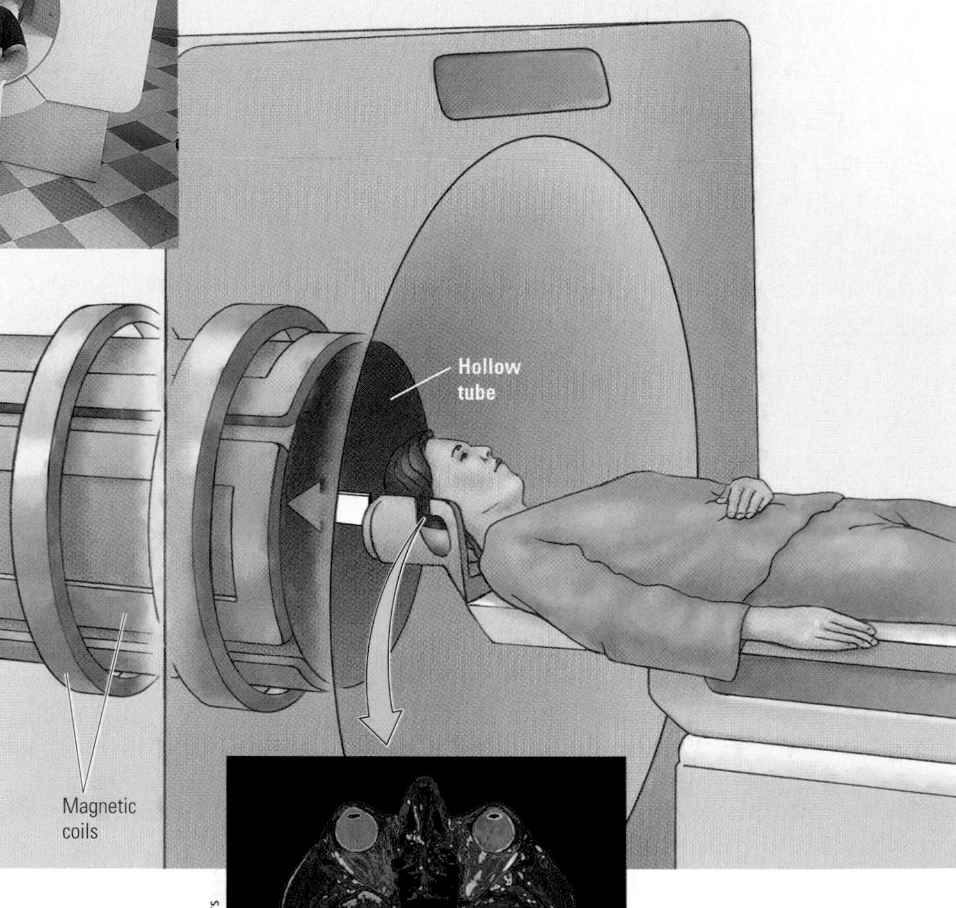


Gregory G. Dimijian / Photo Researchers

**Figure 14-10**

The machine used to obtain magnetic resonance images. The subject is placed in a long metal cylinder that has two sets of magnetic coils arranged at right angles to each other. An additional coil, known as a radio frequency coil, surrounds the head (not shown) and is designed to perturb the the static magnetic fields to produce the MRI.

in a magnetic field, they line up in parallel as they orient themselves with respect to the field's lines of force. In MRI, radio pulses are applied to a brain whose atoms have been aligned in this manner, and the radio pulses form a second magnetic field. This second field causes the spinning atoms to wobble irregularly, thus producing a tiny electric current that the MRI measures. When the currents are recorded, it is possible to make images of the brain that are based on the density of the atoms in different regions. Figure 14-10 shows such an image, which is known as a magnetic resonance image. When a region of the brain is active, the amount of blood flow and oxygen to it increases. A change in the oxygen content of the blood alters the blood's magnetic properties. This alteration, in turn, affects the MRI signal.

**Functional MRI (fMRI).** A type of magnetic resonance imaging that takes advantage of the fact that changes in the distribution of elements such as oxygen alter the magnetic properties of the brain. Because oxygen consumption varies with behavior, it is possible to map and measure changes that are produced by behavior.

In 1990, Segi Ogawa and his colleagues showed that MRI could accurately match these changes in magnetic properties to specific locations in the brain. The resulting images are known as **functional MRIs (fMRIs)**. Figure 14-11 illustrates changes in the fMRI signal in the visual cortex of a person who is being stimulated visually. Manipulation of the characteristics of the stimulus (color, motion, spatial orientation) makes it possible to dissociate the activity of the various visual areas of the occipital lobes (the areas shown in Figure 8-17). In other words, fMRI can show that different visual areas are differentially activated when different types of visual stimuli are presented.

Link to your CD to investigate more about MRI, including scans of the brain, in the module on Research Methods.

In addition to its many advantages, fMRI has some disadvantages. A major advantage over PET is that fMRI allows the anatomical structure of each subject's brain to be

**Figure 14-11**

Functional MRI (fMRI) images showing V1 activation in a normal human brain during visual stimulation. The occipital pole is at the bottom. A baseline acquired in darkness (*far left*) was subtracted from the subsequent images. The subject wore tightly fitting goggles that contained light-emitting diodes that were turned on and off as a rapid sequence of scans was obtained over a period of 270 seconds. The images show prominent activity in the visual cortex when the light is on and rapid cessation of activity when the light is off. The graph (*bottom*) illustrates that the on-line fMRI measure can be quantified.

Adapted from "Dynamic Magnetic Resonance Imaging of Human Brain Activity During Primary Sensory Stimulation," by K. K. Kwong et al., *Proceedings of the National Academy of Sciences (USA), 89,* p. 5678.

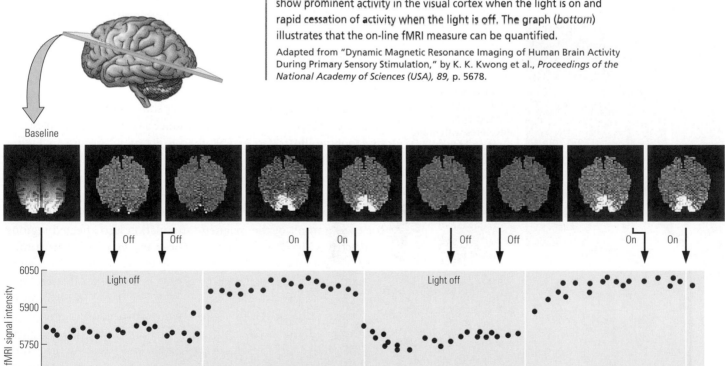

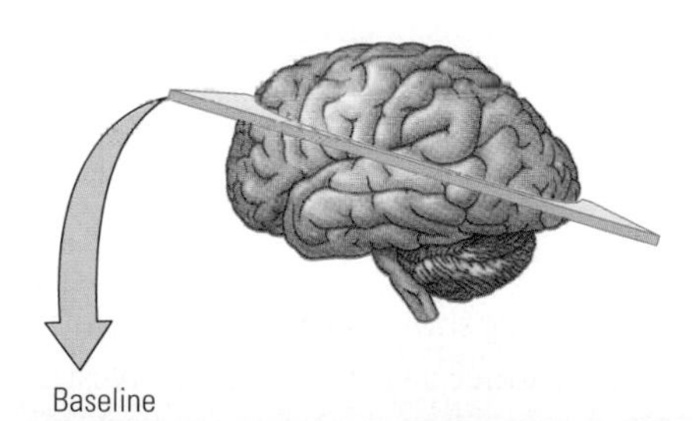

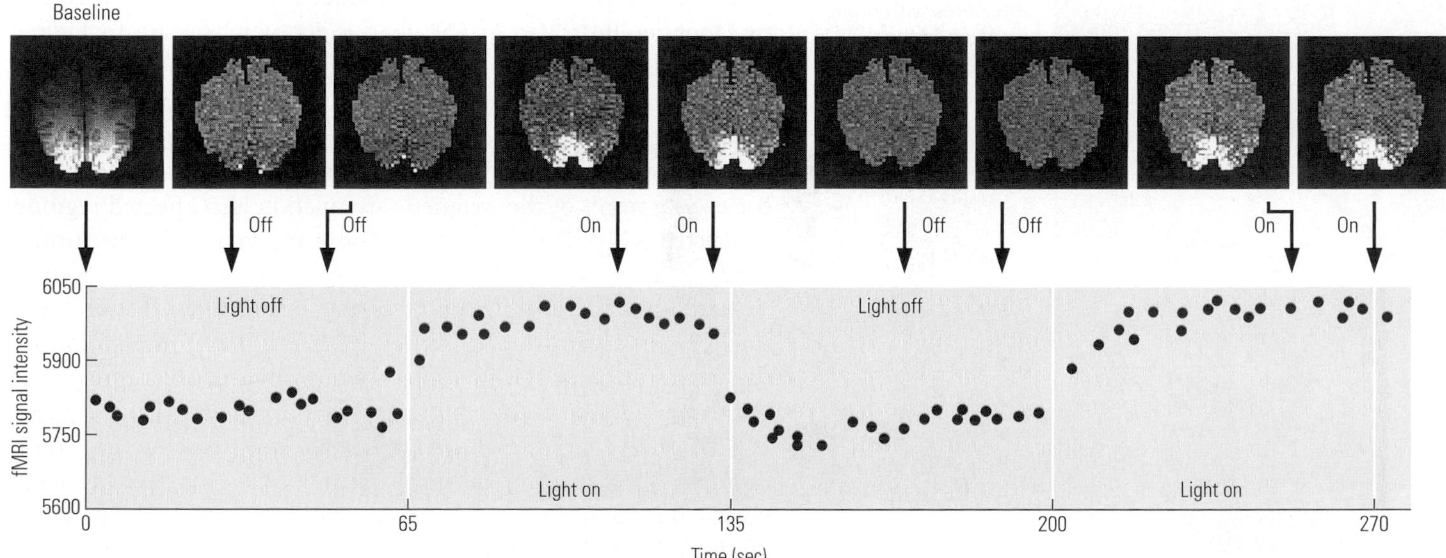

identified, and brain activity can then be related to localized anatomical regions on the brain image. fMRI also has better spatial resolution than does PET. And it is possible to monitor the actual change in the oxygen signal caused by changes in blood flow. On the negative side, however, fMRIs are expensive. The resolution of standard hospital MRIs is generally insufficient for research purposes, so neuroscientists need to buy even more expensive equipment in order to do specialized research. In addition, fMRI can be very difficult for subjects to endure. They are required to lie motionless in a long, noisy tube, an experience that can be quite claustrophobic. The confined space also restricts the types of behavioral experiments that can be performed.

Transcranial magnetic stimulation (TMS) is used to stimulate brain regions near the skull. Researchers like Tomas Paus use MRI, TMS, and PET to locate and to study brain regions in healthy subjects.

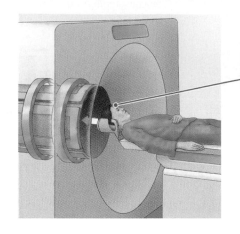

Brain region is located using MRI.

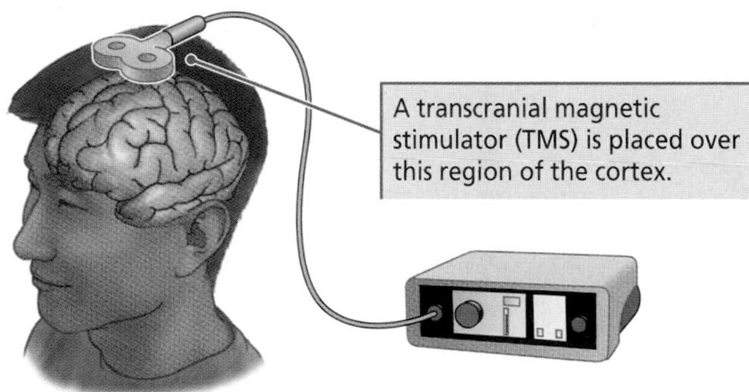

A transcranial magnetic stimulator (TMS) is placed over this region of the cortex.

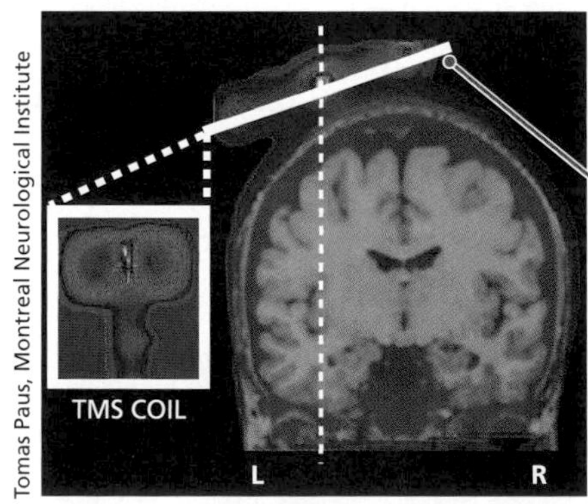


Tomas Paus, Montreal Neurological Institute

The TMS coil, shown here in a composite MRI/PET scan photograph, interferes with brain function in the adjacent area.

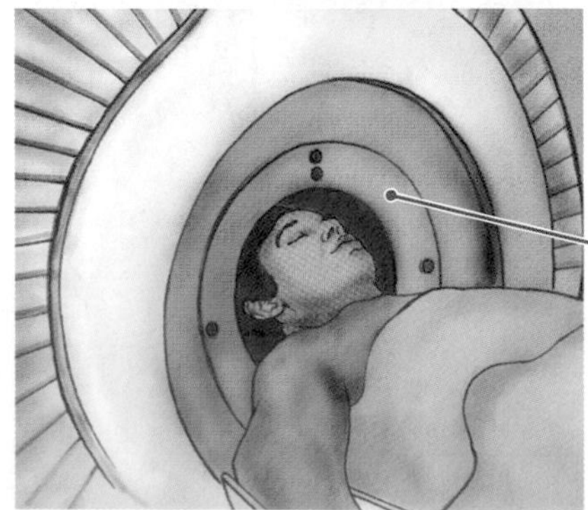

With the TMS in place, the subject is then placed in a PET scanner where cortical activity is monitored.

Yet another way to study human brain function is to disrupt brain activity briefly while a person is performing some task in order to observe the results. You saw in Chapter 9 that Wilder Penfield used this procedure when he electrically stimulated the brains of patients who were about to undergo neurosurgery. Although much has been learned by using the technique, it has a major drawback: it can be carried out only on subjects whose brains are exposed. This requirement makes it impractical as a laboratory research tool.

More recently, a procedure has been developed that can be used on normal subjects. This technique is called **transcranial magnetic stimulation (TMS)**. When a magnetic stimulus is placed next to the skull, there is a disruption of brain function in the region immediately adjacent to the magnet. Thus, by placing a small coil over the skull and using repetitive TMS, one can interfere with the neural activity of the brain regions under the coil. One reason for this interference is a drop in blood flow in the stimulated area, resulting in disturbed functioning. In a typical experiment, a region of brain is located first on an MRI image. When the coordinates of the region are identified, the magnetic coil for TMS is placed.

## The Power of Cognitive Neuroscientific Analysis

Thomas Paus and his colleagues (1997) showed that it is possible to combine TMS, PET, and fMRI to produce a very powerful investigative tool, as illustrated at left, the results of which are in Figure 14-12. Paus first located the motor cortex by using fMRI. Then a magnetic coil was positioned over that region. The subject was next placed in a PET scanner, and PET activity was recorded while magnetic stimulation was applied. The drop in blood flow to the motor cortex as a result of the magnetic stimulation also affected regions connected with the motor cortex. For example, when Paus stimulated the frontal eye fields in the premotor area, he found a decline in blood flow in parietal regions in the dorsal stream that are presumably connected to the frontal eye fields. The combination of these three technologies thus allows a novel procedure for mapping connectivity in the human brain as well as for measuring the effect of TMS on the performance of particular cognitive activities. Studies using TMS to record cognitive activity have not yet been reported, but the technique is powerful and will certainly be used for this purpose in the near future.

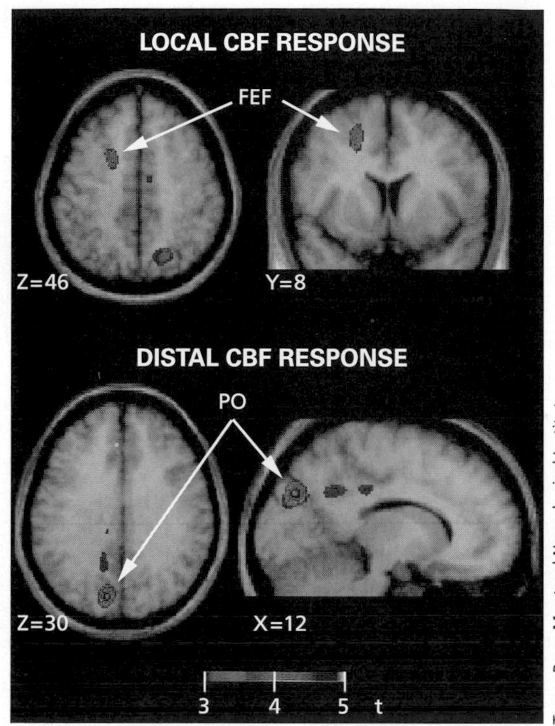


Tomas Paus, Montreal Neurological Institute

**Figure 14-12**

Transcranial magnetic stimulation (TMS) can be used in combination with other imaging techniques, such as PET or fMRI, to study cortical functioning. In this example, TMS was used to stimulate the premotor cortex region that controls eye movements and is called the frontal eye field (FEF). A TMS coil was then positioned over that area. Measurement of cerebral blood flow (CBF), using PET, showed that the TMS altered blood flow, both at the site of stimulation (the local CBF response) and in the parietal-occipital cortex (PO, the distal CBF response), which reveals the connections between the frontal and posterior cortical regions.

Adapted from "Transcranial Magnetic Stimulation During Positron Emission Tomography: A New Method for Studying Connectivity of the Human Cerebral Cortex," by T. Paus, R. Jech, C. J. Thompson, R. Comeau, T. Peters, & A. Evans, 1997, *Journal of Neuroscience, 17,* pp. 3178-3184.

The power of cognitive neuroscientific analysis can also be illustrated in an fMRI study by Dirk Wildgruber and his colleagues (1999). This study was based on the clinical observation that people with damage to the frontal lobe of either hemisphere often have difficulty reversing the serial order of items such as digits, the days of the week, or the months of the year. For instance, when these patients are asked to count or to list the days or months in a forward direction, they do so with ease, but when asked for the same information in reverse order (Sunday, Saturday, Friday, and so on), they have difficulty. It seems that the frontal lobes are active during the reverse-serial-order task but not during the forward task.

In order to evaluate this hypothesis, fMRI was conducted on normal subjects who silently recited the names of the months either forward or backward. Figure 14-13 summarizes the major findings of the study. The top row shows scans from the right and left hemispheres when the subjects were lying quietly for 10 seconds before the task began. The second row shows scans during the first 10 seconds after the verbal instructions to start reciting were given, whereas the third row shows scans during the next 40–50 seconds while the silent recitation was going on. Finally, the fourth row shows scans during the 10 seconds after the subjects were told to stop reciting. Two major results emerge from the study. First, when the subjects heard and analyzed the verbal instructions, increased blood flow to the temporal auditory areas was larger in the left (language-processing) hemisphere than in the right. This activation did not last, however, because the subjects heard nothing new during the task. Second, reciting the months activated the brain differently, depending on whether the recitation was in a forward or backward direction. During the forward recitation, activation was largely restricted to the posterior temporal cortex in the left hemisphere. During the backward recitation, in contrast, there was bilateral activation of the frontal and parietal cortex, although activation was greater on the left side. Clearly, functional magnetic resonance imaging is a highly valuable method for analyzing changes in brain activity as they occur.

Although the major goal of the Wildgruber study was to examine the role of the frontal lobes in serial-ordering tasks, it also showed involvement of the parietal and posterior temporal regions, as well as a left–right asymmetry in cerebral activity. We encountered cerebral asymmetry before, particularly in the discussion of auditory processing of words and music in Chapter 9. In the next section, we consider the differential role of the two hemispheres in thinking.

**Transcranial magnetic stimulation (TMS).** A procedure in which a magnetic coil is placed over the skull to stimulate the underlying brain; can be used either to induce behavior or to disrupt ongoing behavior.

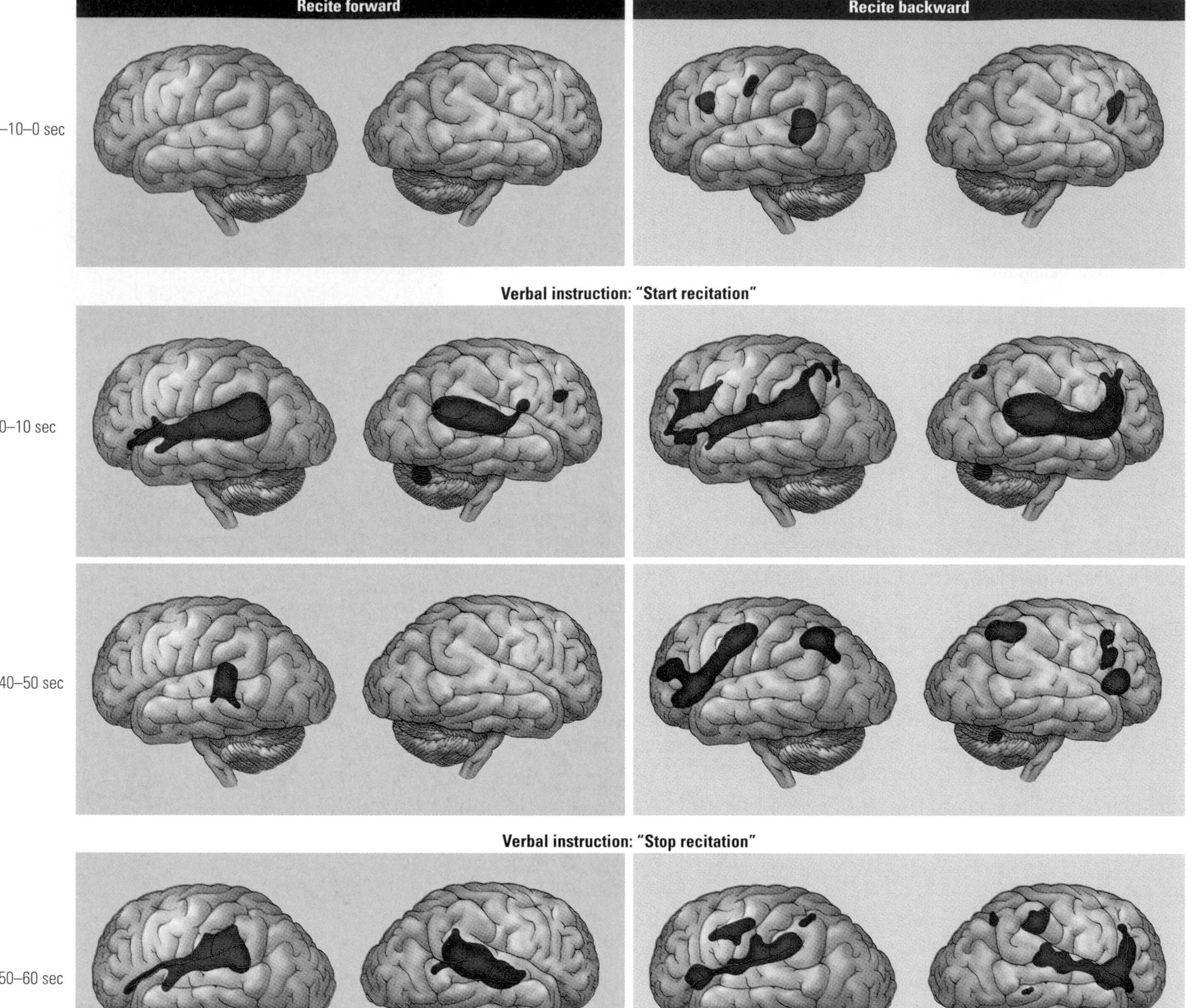


**Figure 14-13**

Summary illustrations of fMRI-measured cerebral activation when subjects were asked to mentally recite the names of the months either forward or in reverse. The top row shows relative fMRI activation in subjects during the 10 seconds preceding the beginning of the task. During this 10-second period there is some fMRI signal in the frontal lobe and posterior temporal region during the "recite backward" condition, possibly because subjects are rehearsing. When the verbal instructions are given, the subjects show activation of the temporal auditory areas bilaterally, with greater activation on the left and greater activation in the frontal lobe in the "recite backward" condition. Once the instructions are completed, activation is seen only in the posterior temporal region during the "recite forward" condition, but in the "recite backward" condition it is also seen in the frontal and posterior parietal regions, especially on the left. Finally, when the subjects hear the instruction to stop, the temporal auditory areas are once again activated.

Adapted from "Dynamic Pattern of Brain Activation During Sequencing of Word Strings Evaluated by fMRI," by D. Wildgruber, U. Kischka, H. Ackermann, U. Klose, and W. Grodd, 1999, *Cognitive Brain Research, 7,* pp. 285–294.

## In Review

Analysis of the behavioral symptoms of brain-injured patients began in the late 1800s. During the twentieth century, this approach developed into the field of neuropsychology. Until the 1990s, neuropsychology was the primary source of insights into how the human brain thinks. In recent years, however, development of sophisticated imaging techniques, including ERP, PET, fMRI, MEG, and TMS, has allowed the study of brain activity while subjects perform various cognitive tasks. By using multiple methods, contemporary researchers can gather converging evidence on the nature of neural activity during human thought.

# CEREBRAL ASYMMETRY IN THINKING

One of the fundamental discoveries of behavioral neuroscience was the finding by Broca and his contemporaries in the mid-1800s that language is lateralized to the left hemisphere. But the implications of this finding were not really appreciated until the 1960s, when Roger Sperry (1968) and his colleagues began to study people who had undergone surgical separation of the two hemispheres as a treatment for intractable epilepsy. It soon became apparent that the two cerebral hemispheres were more specialized in their functions than researchers had previously realized. Popular authors in the 1980s seized on this idea and began to write about "left-brained" and "right-brained" people and how left-brained people's right-hemisphere skills could supposedly be improved by training. Although this type of popularized discussion has declined in recent years, the concept of cerebral asymmetry is still important to understanding how the human brain thinks. So before discussing how the two sides of the brain cooperate in generating cognitive activity, we consider the anatomical differences between the left and right hemispheres.

## Anatomical Asymmetry

When we examined brain asymmetries related to audition in Chapter 9, we explained that the language- and music-related areas of the left and right temporal lobes differed anatomically. In particular, the primary auditory area is larger on the right, whereas the secondary auditory areas are larger on the left. Other regions besides the auditory areas are also asymmetrical. For instance, the posterior parietal cortex of the right hemisphere is larger than the corresponding region of the left hemisphere. Figure 14-14 shows that the Sylvian fissure, which partially separates the temporal and parietal lobes, has a sharper upward course in the right hemisphere relative to the left. The result is that the posterior part of the right temporal lobe is larger than the same region on the left side of the brain. At the same time, the left parietal lobe is larger relative to the right. There are also anatomical asymmetries in the frontal lobes. For example, the region of the sensorimotor cortex representing the face is larger in the left hemisphere than in the right, a difference that presumably reflects the special role of the left hemisphere in talking. Furthermore, the frontal operculum (Broca's area) is organized differently on

**Figure 14-14**

Asymmetry in the size of the parietal cortex of the human brain. The Sylvian fissure in the left hemisphere has a flatter course compared with the Sylvian fissure on the right, which takes a more upward course. As a result, the inferior parietal region is larger on the right than on the left.

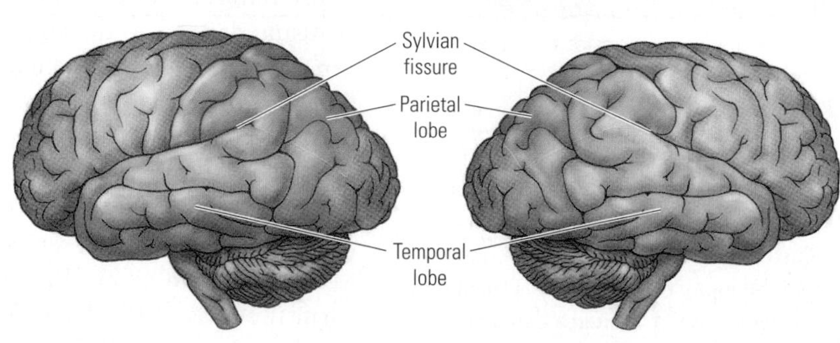

the left and right. The area visible on the surface of the brain is about one-third larger on the right than on the left, whereas the area of cortex buried in the sulci of this region is greater on the left than on the right.

Not only do these gross anatomical differences between the two hemispheres exist, but so too do hemispheric differences in the details of cellular and neurochemical structure. For example, the neurons in Broca's area on the left have larger dendritic fields than do the corresponding neurons on the right. Unfortunately, the discovery of these and other structural asymmetries tells us little about why such differences occur. Presumably, they reflect underlying differences in cognitive processing by the two sides of the brain, but exactly what these processing differences are remains a mystery.

Although many anatomical asymmetries in the human brain are related to language, such asymmetries are not unique to humans. Most, if not all, mammals have brain asymmetries, as do many species of birds. Cerebral asymmetry therefore cannot simply be present for the processing of language. Rather, it is more likely that language evolved after the brain had become asymmetrical. Language simply took advantage of processes that had already been lateralized to the left hemisphere.

**Case G. H.**

Injury to this area of the right hemisphere caused difficulties with copying drawings, assembling puzzles, and finding the way around a familiar city.

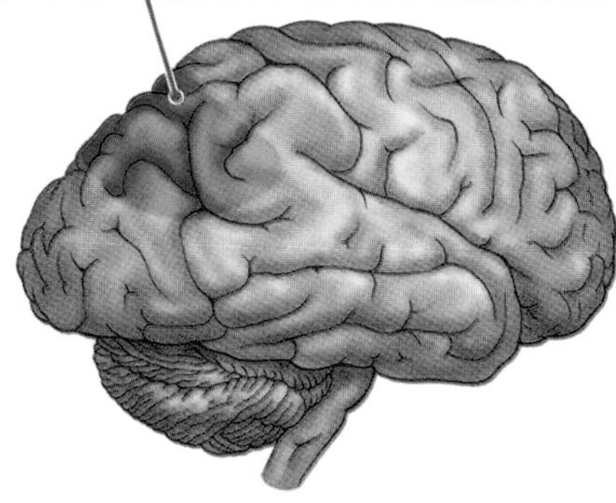

**Case M. M.**

Injury to this area of the left hemisphere caused difficulties with language, copying movements, reading, and generating names of objects or animals.

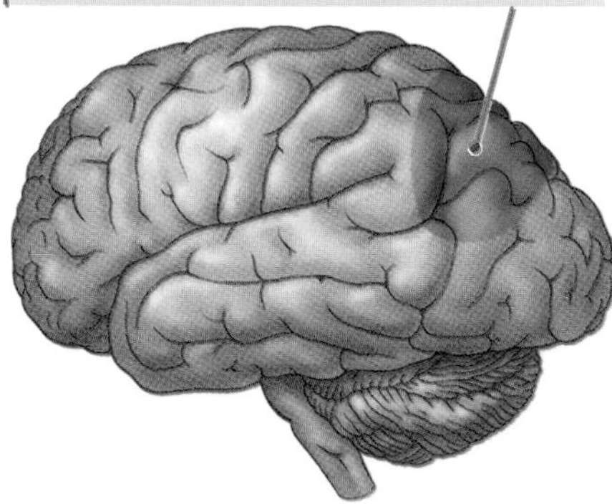

**Figure 14-15**

Brain maps illustrating the region of injury (shaded area) in two people with parietal-lobe injuries. The top brain illustrates Case G. H., who had a right-parietal injury resulting from a childhood accident. Case M. M. had a benign tumor in the left parietal lobe.

## Functional Asymmetry in Neurological Patients

That the two hemispheres of the human brain sometimes specialize in different functions is shown by the study of people with damage to the left or right side of the brain. To see these functional differences clearly, compare the cases of G. H. and M. M.

When G. H. was 5 years old, he went on a hike with his family and was hit on the head by a large rock that rolled off an embankment. He was unconscious for a few minutes and had a severe headache for a few days, but he quickly recovered. By age 18, however, he had started having seizures. Neurosurgical investigation revealed that he had suffered a right posterior parietal injury from the rock accident. Figure 14-15 shows the area affected. Following surgery to remove this area, G. H. had weakness of the left side of his body and showed contralateral neglect. But these symptoms lessened fairly quickly, and a month after the surgery they had completely cleared. Nevertheless, G. H. suffered chronic difficulties in copying drawings, and 4 years later he still performed at about the level of a 6-year-old. He also had trouble assembling puzzles, which he found disappointing because he had enjoyed doing puzzles before his surgery. When asked to do tasks like the one in Figure 14-5, he became very frustrated and refused to continue. Finally, he had difficulty finding his way around the city in which he lived. The general landmarks that he had used to guide his travels before the surgery no longer seemed to work for him. He now has to learn street names and use a verbal strategy to go from one place to another.

M. M.'s difficulties were quite different from those of G. H. M. M. was a 16-year-old girl who had a meningioma, which is a tumor of the brain's protective coverings, the meninges. (See "Brain Tumors," in Chapter 3, page 86.) The tumor was surgically removed, but it had placed considerable pressure on the left parietal region, causing damage to the area shown in Figure 14-15. After the surgery, M. M. experienced a variety of problems. For one thing, she suffered aphasia, or impairment in the use of language, although this condition lessened over time; a year after the surgery, she was able to speak quite fluently. Unfortunately, her other difficulties persisted. In solving arithmetic problems, in reading, and even in simply generating the names of objects or animals, she performed at about the level of a 6-year-old. When asked to copy a series of arm movements, such as those illustrated in Figure 14-16, she had great difficulty. She seemed unable to figure out how to make her arm move as in the example. She had no difficulty in making movements spontaneously, however, which means that she was able to move her limbs. Rather, she had

Series 1

Series 2

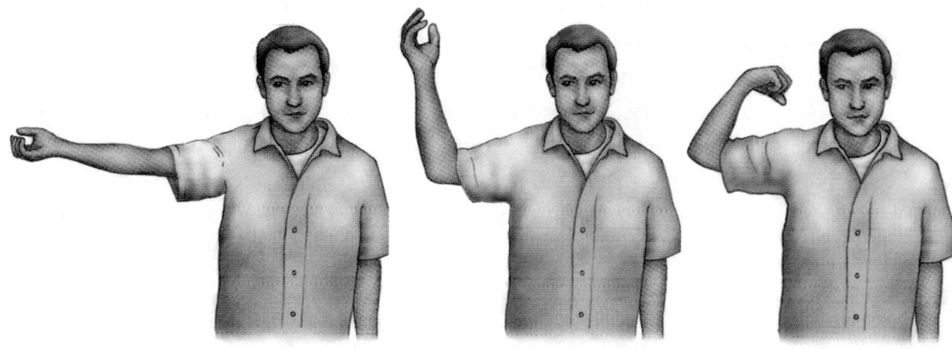

**Figure 14-16**

Illustration of two series of arm movements that are to be copied. Subjects observe the tester perform each sequence and then copy it as accurately as they can. People with left-hemisphere injury, especially in the posterior parietal region, are impaired at copying such movements.

a general impairment in copying movements. This is a symptom of a condition known as **apraxia,** a general impairment in making voluntary movements in the absence of paralysis or a muscular disorder.

What can we learn about brain function by comparing these two patients? Their lesions were in approximately the same location but in opposite hemispheres, and their symptoms were very different. Judging from the difficulties that G. H. had, the right hemisphere plays a role in the control of spatial skills, such as drawing, assembling puzzles, and navigating in space. In contrast, the left hemisphere seems to play some role in the control of language functions, as well as in various cognitive tasks related to schoolwork—namely, reading and arithmetic. In addition, the left hemisphere plays a role in controlling sequences of voluntary movement that is different from the role of the right hemisphere. To some extent, therefore, the left and right hemispheres think about different types of information. The question is whether these differences in function can be observed in a normal brain.

## Functional Asymmetry in the Normal Brain

In the course of studying the auditory capacities of people with temporal-lobe lesions, Doreen Kimura (1967) came upon an unexpected finding in her control subjects. She presented people with two strings of digits, one played into each ear. (This procedure is known as **dichotic listening.**) The subjects' task was to recall as many of the digits as possible. Kimura found that her normal control subjects recalled more digits presented to the right ear than to the left. This result is a bit surprising because the auditory system is repeatedly crossed, beginning in the midbrain. Nonetheless, information coming from the right ear seems to have preferential access to the left (speaking) hemisphere. In a later study, Kimura played two pieces of music, one to each ear (see Kimura, 1973). She then gave subjects a multiple-choice test in which she played four bits of musical selections and asked them to pick out those that they had heard before.

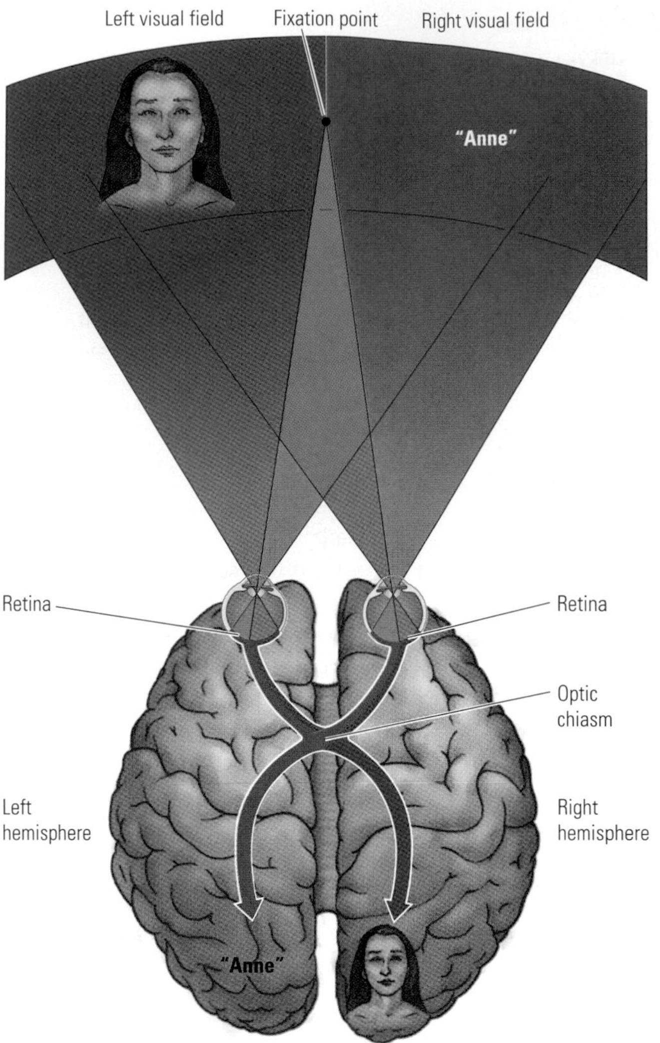


**Figure 14-17**

Visual pathways to the two hemispheres. When fixating at a point, each eye sees both visual fields but sends information about the right visual field only to the left hemisphere and information about the left visual field only to the right hemisphere. Information is shared through the corpus callosum, which allows a complete image to be perceived. If the corpus callosum is cut and if the eyes and head are prevented from moving, each hemisphere can see only half the visual world. In normal subjects given short exposures to stimuli, the left hemisphere is more accurate at perceiving words, whereas the right hemisphere is more accurate at perceiving objects, such as faces.

In this test, she found that normal subjects were more likely to recall the music played to the left ear than that played to the right ear. This result implies that the left ear has preferential access to the right (musical) hemisphere.

The demonstration of this functional asymmetry in the normal brain provoked much interest in the 1970s, leading to demonstrations of functional asymmetries in the visual and tactile systems as well. Consider the visual system. If we fixate on a target, such as a dot, all the information to the left of the dot goes to the right hemisphere and all the information to the right of the dot goes to the left hemisphere, as shown in Figure 14-17. If information is presented for a relatively long time—say, one second—we can easily report what was in each visual field. If, however, the presentation is brief—say, only 40 milliseconds—then the task is considerably harder. This situation allows us to reveal a brain asymmetry. Words presented briefly to the right visual field, and hence sent to the left hemisphere, are more easily reported than are words presented briefly to the left visual field. Similarly, if complex geometric patterns or faces are shown briefly, those presented to the left visual field, and hence sent to the right hemisphere, are more accurately reported than are those presented to the right visual field. Apparently, the two hemispheres are processing information differently. The left hemisphere seems to be biased toward processing language-related information, whereas the right hemisphere seems to be biased toward processing nonverbal, especially spatial, information.

A word of caution is needed. Although asymmetry studies are fascinating, it is not entirely clear what they tell us about the differences between the two hemispheres. They tell us that *something* is different, but it is a long leap to conclude that the two hemispheres house entirely different kinds of skills. Yet this was a common thread in popular writings during the late 1970s and the 1980s, which ignored the fact that the two hemispheres have many functions in common, such as the control of movement in the contralateral hand and the processing of sensory information through the thalamus. Still, there *are* differences in the cognitive operations of the two hemispheres. These differences can be better understood by studying people whose cerebral hemispheres have been surgically separated for medical treatment.

## The Split Brain

Epileptic seizures may begin in a restricted region of one hemisphere and then spread through the fibers of the **corpus callosum** to the corresponding location in the opposite hemisphere. To prevent the spread of seizures that cannot be controlled through medication, neurosurgeons sometimes cut the 200 million nerve fibers of the corpus callosum. The procedure is medically beneficial for many patients, leaving them virtually seizure-free with only minimal effects on their everyday behavior. But in special circumstances, the results of a severed corpus callosum become more readily apparent. This has been demonstrated through extensive psychological testing by Roger Sperry, Michael Gazzaniga, and their colleagues (Sperry, 1968; Gazzaniga, 1970). On close inspection, these **split-brain** patients can be shown to have a unique behavioral syndrome that provides insights into the nature of cerebral asymmetry.

Before discussing the details of split-brain studies, let us make some predictions on the basis of what we already know about cerebral asymmetry. First, we would anticipate that the left hemisphere has language, whereas the right hemisphere does not. Second, we would expect that the right hemisphere might be better at doing certain types of nonverbal tasks, especially those involving visuospatial skills. We might also ask how a severed corpus callosum might affect the way the brain thinks. After all, once the corpus callosum is cut, the two hemispheres have no way to communicate with each other. The left and right hemispheres therefore would be free to think about different things. In a sense, a split-brain patient would have two different brains.

One way to test the cognitive functions of the two hemispheres in a split-brain patient is to take advantage of the fact that information in the left visual field goes to the right hemisphere, whereas information in the right visual field goes to the left hemisphere. Because the corpus callosum is cut in these patients, information presented to one side of the brain has no way of traveling to the other side. It can be processed only in the hemisphere that receives it. Figures 14-18 and 14-19 show some basic testing procedures using this approach. The split-brain subject fixates on the dot in the center of the screen while information is presented to the left or right visual field. The person must make responses with the left hand (controlled by the right hemisphere), with the right hand (controlled by the left hemisphere), or verbally (which is also a left-hemisphere function). In this way, researchers are able to observe what each hemisphere knows and what it is capable of doing.

For instance, a subject might be flashed a picture of some object—say, a spoon—and asked to state what he or she sees. If the picture is presented to the right visual field, the person will answer, "Spoon." If the picture is presented to the left visual field, however, the person will say, "I see nothing." The patient responds in this way for two reasons. First, the right hemisphere (which receives the visual input) does not talk, so it cannot respond verbally, even though it sees the spoon in the left visual field. Second, the left hemisphere does talk but it does not see the spoon, so it answers—quite correctly, from its own perspective—that no picture is present.

Now suppose that the task changes. The picture of a spoon is still presented to the left visual field, but the subject is asked to

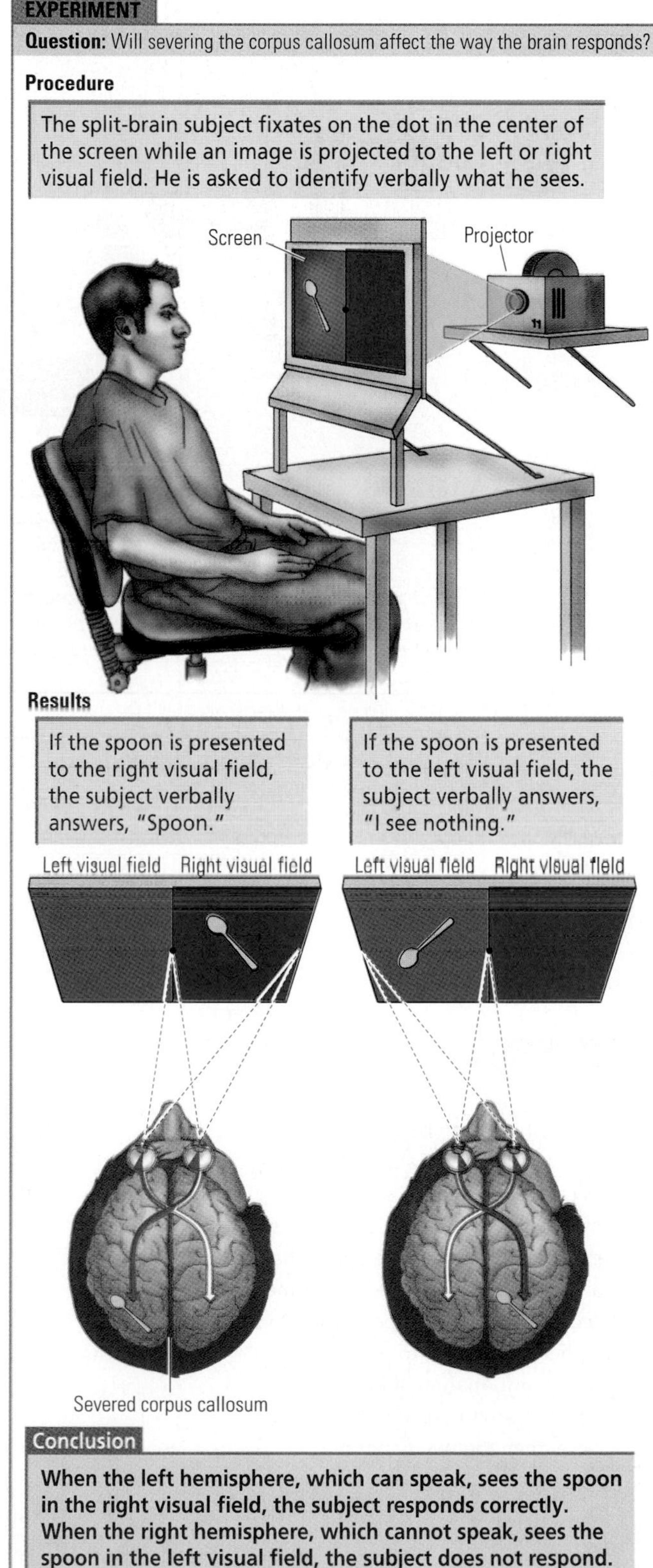

EXPERIMENT
Question: Will severing the corpus callosum affect the way the brain responds?
Procedure
The split-brain subject fixates on the dot in the center of the screen while an image is projected to the left or right visual field. He is asked to identify verbally what he sees.
Screen
Projector
Results
If the spoon is presented to the right visual field, the subject verbally answers, "Spoon."
If the spoon is presented to the left visual field, the subject verbally answers, "I see nothing."
Left visual field
Right visual field
Left visual field
Right visual field
Severed corpus callosum
Conclusion
When the left hemisphere, which can speak, sees the spoon in the right visual field, the subject responds correctly. When the right hemisphere, which cannot speak, sees the spoon in the left visual field, the subject does not respond.


**Figure 14-18** The basic testing arrangement used to lateralize visual information in a split-brain subject. The subject fixates on the dot and an image is projected to the left or right visual field, which goes to one hemisphere or the other. Communication between the hemispheres is prevented because the corpus callosum is severed. Because the right hemisphere cannot speak, it cannot verbally report what it sees in the left visual field.

**EXPERIMENT 1**

**Question:** How can the right hemisphere of a split-brain subject show that it knows information?

**Procedure**

The split-brain subject is asked to use his left hand to pick out the object shown on the screen to the left visual field (right hemisphere).

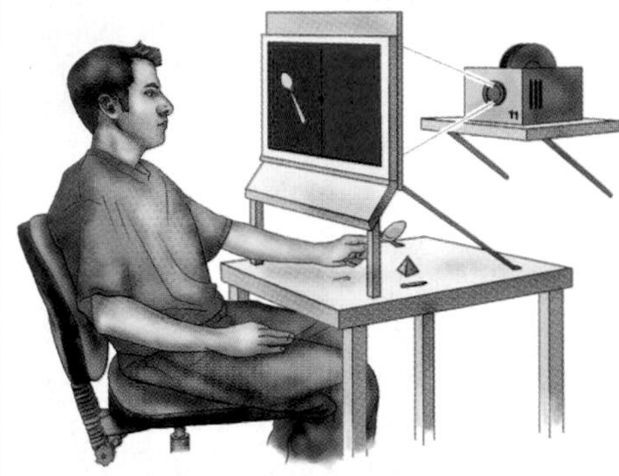

**Results**

The subject chooses the spoon with his left hand because the right hemisphere sees the spoon and controls the left hand. If the right hand is forced to choose, it will do so by chance because no stimulus is shown to the left hemisphere.

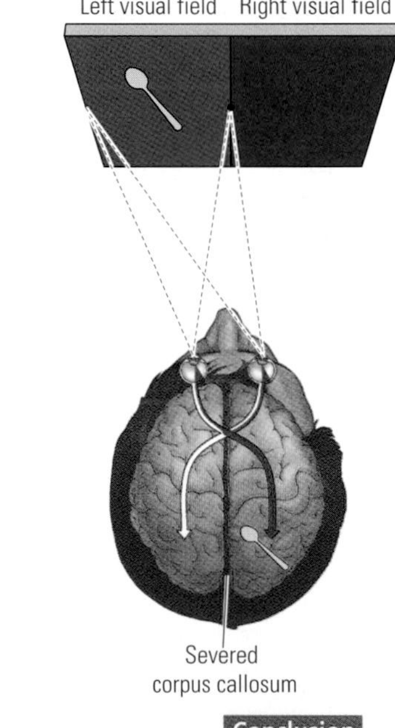


**EXPERIMENT 2**

**Question:** What happens if both hemispheres are asked to respond to competing information?

**Procedure**

Each visual field is shown a different object—a spoon to the left and a pencil to the right. The split-brain subject is asked to use both hands to pick up the object seen.

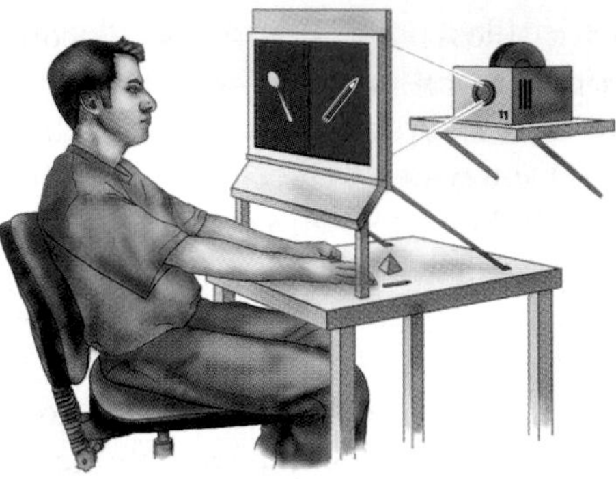

**Results**

In this case, the right and left hands do not agree. They may each pick up a different object, or the right hand may prevent the left hand from performing the task.

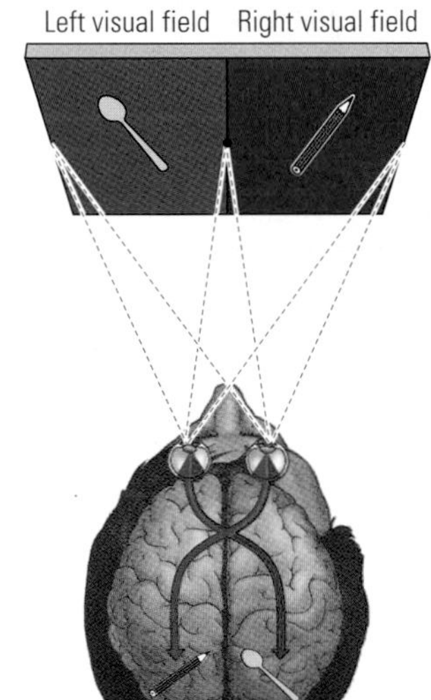


**Conclusion**

**Each hemisphere is capable of responding independently. The left hemisphere may dominate in a competition, even if the response is not verbal.**

**Figure 14-19**

Experiment 1 demonstrates how the right hemisphere can be tested to indicate what it knows about the world. In this case, the response is not verbal but motor, as the subject is asked to use his left hand to pick out the object that he saw in the left visual field. Experiment 2 demonstrates what happens if the two hemispheres are asked to respond to competing information. If both hemispheres are to use a motor response, then the two hands may disagree on the correct answer.

use the left hand to pick out the object shown on the screen. In this case, the left hand, controlled by the right hemisphere, which does see the spoon, readily picks out the correct object. Can the right hand also choose correctly? No, because it is controlled by the left hemisphere, which cannot see a spoon on the left. If the person is forced in this situation to select an object with the right hand, the left hemisphere does so at random.

Now let's consider an interesting twist. Let's show each hemisphere a different object—say, a spoon to the right hemisphere and a pencil to the left. The subject is asked to use both hands to pick out the object seen. The problem here is that the right hand and left hand do not agree. While the left hand tries to pick up the spoon, the right hand tries to pick up the pencil or tries to prevent the left hand from performing the task. This conflict between the hemispheres can be seen in the everyday behavior of some split-brain subjects. One woman, referred to as P. O. V., reported frequent interhemispheric competition for at least 3 years after her surgery. "I open the closet door. I know what I want to wear. But as I reach for something with my right hand, my left comes up and takes something different. I can't put it down if it's in my left hand. I have to call my daughter."

Connect to the Web site at **www.worthpublishers.com/kolb/chapter14** for links to more sites about split-brain patients.

We know from the experiment summarized in Figure 14-19 that the left hemisphere is capable of using language, but what functions does the right hemisphere control? Other split-brain studies have attempted to answer this question. Some of the first insights came from investigations into the visuospatial capacities of the two hands. For example, one split-brain subject was presented with several blocks, each having two red sides, two white sides, and two half-red and half-white sides, as illustrated in Figure 14-20. The task was to arrange the blocks to form patterns identical to those shown on cards. When the subject used his right hand to perform the task, he had great difficulty. His movements were slow and hesitant. In contrast, when he did the task with his left hand, his solutions were not only accurate but quick and decisive. Other studies of split-brain patients have shown that as tasks of this sort become more difficult, the left-hand superiority increases. Normal subjects perform equally well with either hand, indicating the connection between the two hemispheres. But in split-brain subjects the hemispheric connection is severed, so each hemisphere must work on its own. Apparently, the right hemisphere has visuospatial capabilities that the left hemisphere does not.

Once again, however, some caution is needed. Although studies of split-brain patients over the past 30 years have shown that the two hemispheres process information differently, there is more overlap in function between them than was at first suspected. For instance, the right hemisphere does have some language functions, while the left does have some spatial abilities. Nonetheless, the two sides are undoubtedly different. Why does this difference occur?

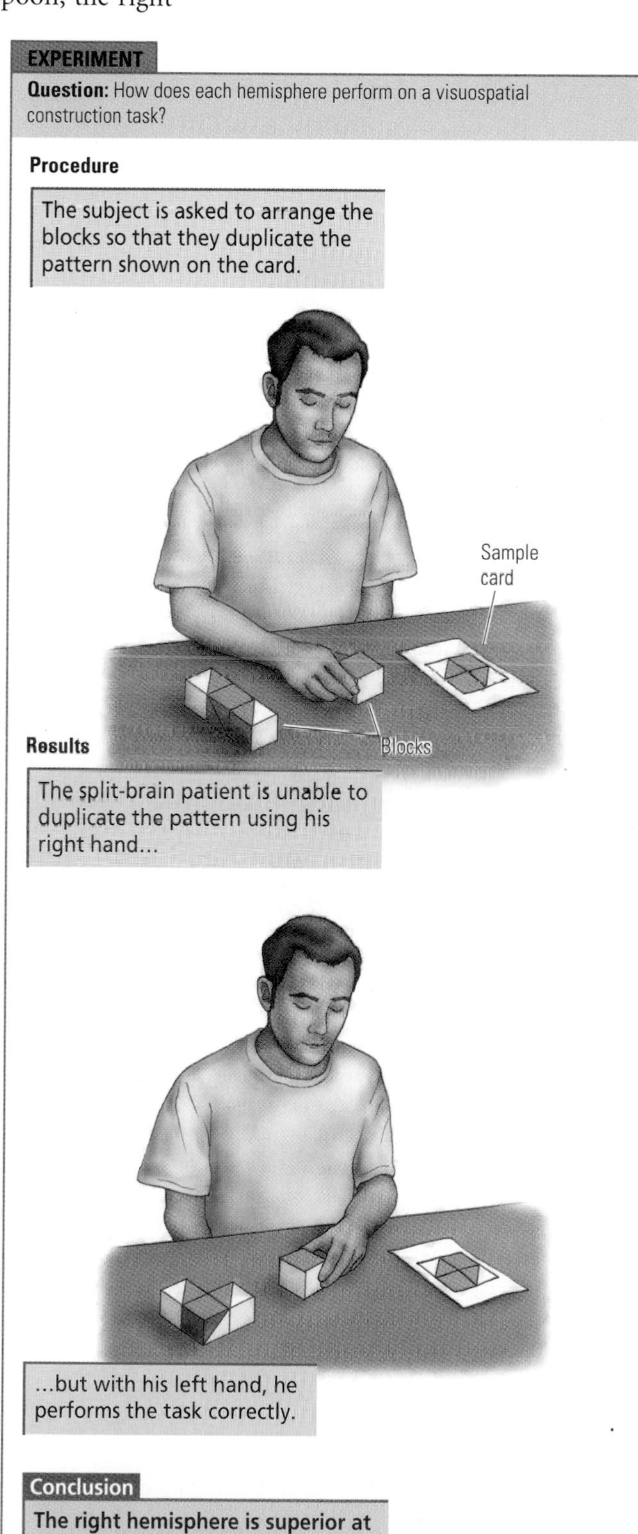

EXPERIMENT
Question: How does each hemisphere perform on a visuospatial construction task?
Procedure
The subject is asked to arrange the blocks so that they duplicate the pattern shown on the card.
Sample card
Blocks
Results
The split-brain patient is unable to duplicate the pattern using his right hand...
...but with his left hand, he performs the task correctly.
Conclusion
The right hemisphere is superior at visuospacial processing.


**Figure 14-20**

The split-brain subject's task is to place the blocks together to form the same pattern as on the sample card. (*Top*) With the right hand (left hemisphere), he is unable to duplicate the pattern. (*Bottom*) With his left hand (right hemisphere), he performs the task correctly.

Adapted from *Cognitive Neuroscience: The Biology of the Mind* (p. 323), by M. S. Gazzaniga, R. B. Ivry, and G. R. Mangun, 1999, New York: Norton.

## Explaining Cerebral Asymmetry

Various theories have been proposed to explain the hemispheric difference. One idea, which dates back to the early 1900s, is that the left hemisphere plays an important role in the control of fine movements. Recall M. M., the patient with left-parietal-lobe damage who suffered apraxia; although that condition subsided, she was left with a chronic difficulty in copying movements. So perhaps one reason the left hemisphere is involved in language is that the production of language requires fine motor movements of the mouth and tongue. Significantly, damage to the language-related areas of the left hemisphere almost always interferes with both language and movement, regardless of whether the person uses oral language or sign language. Reading Braille, however, may not be so affected by left-hemisphere lesions. People use the left hand to read Braille, which is essentially a spatial pattern, so processes related to reading Braille may reside in the right hemisphere.

h ou s e

Braille

Another clue that the left hemisphere's specialization for language may be related to its special role in controlling movements comes from the study of where certain parts of speech are processed in the brain. We said earlier that cognitive systems for representing abstract concepts are likely to be related to systems that produce more concrete behaviors. Consequently, we might expect that the left hemisphere would have a role in forming concepts related to fine movements. Concepts that describe movements are the parts of speech that we call verbs. Interestingly, one fundamental difference between left- and right-hemisphere language abilities is that verbs seem to be processed only in the left hemisphere, whereas nouns are processed in both hemispheres. In other words, not only does the left hemisphere have a special role in controlling the production of actions, but it also controls the production of mental representations of actions in the form of words.

Rotate the hemispheres and investigate the location of language on the CD in the module on the Central Nervous System.

If the left hemisphere excels at language because it is better at controlling fine movements, what is the basis of the right hemisphere's abilities? One idea is that the right hemisphere has a special role in controlling movements in space. In a sense, this role is an elaboration of the functions of the dorsal stream. Once again, we can propose a link between this function at a concrete level and at a more abstract level. If the right hemisphere is producing movements in space, then it is also likely to produce mental images of such movements. We would therefore predict that right-hemisphere patients would be impaired both at the making of spatially guided movements and at thinking about such movements. Significantly, they are.

You should bear in mind that theories about the reasons for hemispheric asymmetry are highly speculative. Our bias is that because the brain is designed to produce movement and to create a sensory reality, the observed asymmetry must be somehow related to these overriding functions. In other words, later-emerging functions, such as language, are likely to be extensions of preexisting functions. The fact that language is represented asymmetrically does not mean that the brain is asymmetrical *because* of language. After all, brains are asymmetrically organized in other species that do not talk.

## The Left Hemisphere, Language, and Thought

We close our discussion of brain asymmetry by considering one other provocative idea. Michael Gazzaniga (1992) proposed that the superior language skills of the left hemisphere are important in understanding the differences in thinking between humans and other animals. He labels the speaking hemisphere the "interpreter." What he means by this is illustrated in the following experiment, using split-brain patients as subjects. Each hemisphere is shown the same two pictures, such as a picture of a match followed by a picture of a piece of wood. A series of other pictures is then shown, and the task is to pick out a third picture that has an inferred relationship with the other two. In our example, the third picture might be of a bonfire. The right hemisphere is incapable of making the inference that a match struck and held to a piece of wood could create a bonfire, whereas the left hemisphere can easily arrive at this interpretation. An analogous task uses words. For example, one or the other hemisphere might be shown the words *pin* and *finger* and then be asked to pick out a third word that is related to the other two. In this case, the correct answer might be *bleed*. The right hemisphere is not able to make this connection. Although it has enough language ability to be able to pick out close synonyms for *pin* and *finger* (*needle* and *thumb*, respectively), it cannot make the inference that pricking a finger with a needle will result in bleeding. Again, the left hemisphere has no difficulty with this task. Apparently, the language capability of the left hemisphere gives it a capacity for interpretation that the right hemisphere lacks. One reason may be that language serves to label and express the computations of other cognitive systems.

Gazzaniga goes even further than this. He suggests that the addition of the language abilities that the left hemisphere possesses makes humans a "believing" species. That is, humans can now make inferences and have beliefs about sensory events. In contrast, Alex, the gray parrot, would not be able to make inferences or hold beliefs about things, because he does not have a system analogous to our left-hemisphere language system. Alex can use language but does not make inferences about sensory events with language. Gazzaniga's idea is certainly intriguing. It implies a fundamental difference in the nature of cerebral asymmetry, and therefore in the nature of cognition, between humans and other animals because of the nature of human language.

### In Review

The two hemispheres process information differently, which means that they think differently. In particular, the right hemisphere plays a role in spatial movements and spatial cognition as well as music. The left hemisphere plays a role in the control of voluntary movement sequences and in language. It has been hypothesized that the addition of verbal mediation to left-hemisphere thinking may confer a fundamental advantage to the left hemisphere because language can label the computations of the brain's various cognitive systems. As a result, the left hemisphere is able to make inferences that the right hemisphere cannot.

## VARIATIONS IN COGNITIVE ORGANIZATION

No two brains are identical. Brains differ in gyral patterns, cytoarchitectonics, vascular patterns, and neurochemistry, among other things. Some of these differences are genetically determined, whereas others reflect plastic changes such as those created by experience and learning. Some brain differences are idiosyncratic, or unique to particular individuals, whereas many other variations are systematic and shared by whole categories of people. In this section, we consider two systematic variations in brain organization, those related to sex and handedness, and one idiosyncratic variation, synesthesia.

### Sex Differences in Cognitive Organization

Popular magazines are rife with the idea that men and women think differently, and there seems to be some scientific basis to this view. Recent texts, such as one by Doreen Kimura (1999), have compiled considerable evidence for the existence of marked sex

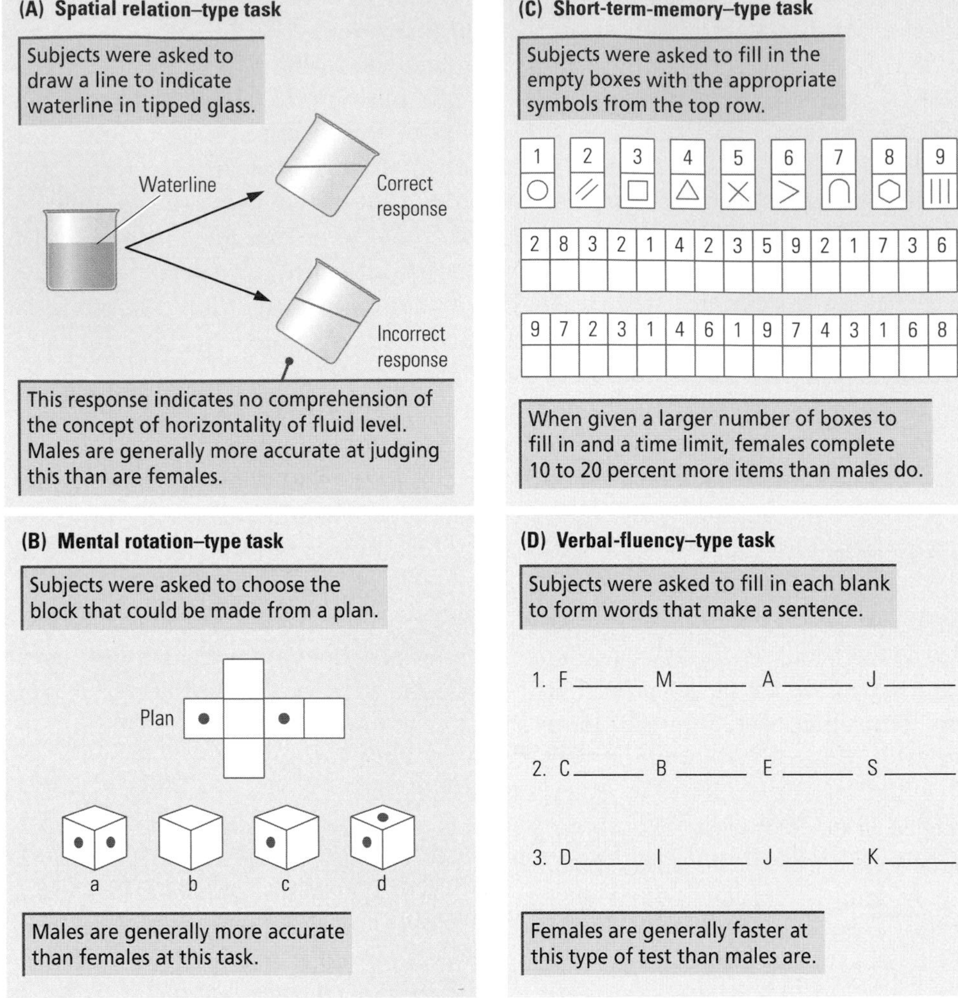

(A) Spatial relation–type task
Subjects were asked to draw a line to indicate waterline in tipped glass.
Waterline
Correct response
Incorrect response
This response indicates no comprehension of the concept of horizontality of fluid level. Males are generally more accurate at judging this than are females.
(B) Mental rotation–type task
Subjects were asked to choose the block that could be made from a plan.
Plan
a
b
c
d
Males are generally more accurate than females at this task.
(C) Short-term-memory–type task
Subjects were asked to fill in the empty boxes with the appropriate symbols from the top row.
1 2 3 4 5 6 7 8 9
2 8 3 2 1 4 2 3 5 9 2 1 7 3 6
9 7 2 3 1 4 6 1 9 7 4 3 1 6 8
When given a larger number of boxes to fill in and a time limit, females complete 10 to 20 percent more items than males do.
(D) Verbal-fluency–type task
Subjects were asked to fill in each blank to form words that make a sentence.
1. F_____ M_____ A _____ J _____
2. C_____ B _____ E _____ S _____
3. D_____ I _____ J _____ K _____
Females are generally faster at this type of test than males are.


**Figure 14-21**

Examples of four types of tasks that reliably show sex-related cognitive differences. **(A)** The drawing at left shows the waterline in a half-full glass. The subjects were asked to draw a line that would indicate the level of water if the same glass were tipped. The illustration at bottom shows the line drawn incorrectly, indicating no comprehension of the concept of horizontality of fluid level. This response was given by about two-thirds of female subjects. **(B)** This task requires the subject to choose the block in the row at the bottom that could be made from the plan shown. Men typically find this task much easier than women. **(C)** In this test, the subject must fill in the empty boxes in the bottom rows with the appropriate symbols from the examples at the top. (This is similar to the digit-symbol task on the Wechsler intelligence tests.) When given a larger number of boxes to fill in and a time limit of 90 seconds, women complete from 10 to 20 percent more items than men do. **(D)** This test of verbal fluency requires the subject to fill in each blank to form words that make a sentence. Women are faster at this type of test than men are.

differences in the way men and women perform on many cognitive tests. For example, paper-and-pencil tests consistently show that, on average, females have better verbal fluency than males do, whereas males do better on tests of spatial reasoning, as illustrated in Figure 14-21. Our focus here is on how such differences relate to the brain.

## THE NEURAL BASIS OF SEX DIFFERENCES

Many investigators have searched without success for gross differences in the structure of the male and female cortex. If such differences exist, they must be subtle. There is stronger indication, however, that gonadal hormones influence the structure of cells in the brain, including cortical cells. For example, the structures of neurons in the prefrontal cortex of rats were found to be influenced by gonadal hormones (Kolb & Stewart, 1991). The cells in one prefrontal region, which is located along the midline, have larger dendritic fields (and presumably more synapses) in males than in females, as shown in Figure 14-22. In contrast, the cells in another frontal region have larger dendritic fields (and presumably more synapses) in females than in males. These sex differences are not found in rats that have had their gonads or ovaries removed at birth. Presumably, sex hormones somehow change the brain's organization and ultimately its cognitive processing.

A second study showed that the presence of gonadal hormones affects the brain not only during early development but also during adulthood. In the course of this study, which focused on how hormones affect recovery from brain damage, the ovaries of middle-aged female rats were removed (Stewart & Kolb, 1994). When the brains of these rats and those of control rats were examined some months later, the rats whose ovaries had been removed had experienced structural changes in their cortical neurons, especially in their prefrontal neurons. Specifically, their cells had grown 30 percent more dendrites and had an increase in spine density relative to the cells in control rats. Clearly, gonadal hormones can affect the neural structure of the brain at any point in an animal's life.

What do these hormonal effects mean in regard to how neurons process information and, ultimately, how the brain thinks? One possibility is that gonadal hormones may influence the way in which experience changes the brain. Evidence in support of this possibility came from a study by Robbin Gibb and her colleagues (in press). They placed male and female rats in complex environments like those described in Chapter 13. After 4 months, they examined the animals' brains and found that there was a sex difference in the effects of experience. Both sexes showed experience-dependent changes in neural structure, but the details of those changes were different. Females exposed to the enriched environment showed a greater increase in dendritic branching, whereas males housed in the same environment showed a greater increase in spine density. In other words, although the brains of both sexes were changed by experience, they were changed *in different ways*, which were presumably mediated by the animals' exposure to different gonadal hormones. These differences in brain changes almost certainly affect cognitive processing in one sex relative to the other, although exactly how is a matter for speculation.

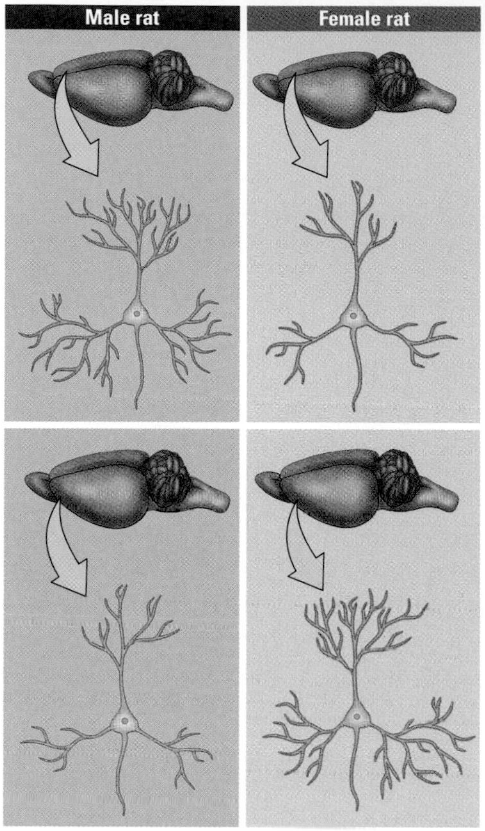

**Figure 14-22** Sex differences in the architecture of neurons in the frontal cortices of male and female rats. The cells in the midline frontal region (shown by arrows in the top two drawings) are more complex in males than in females, whereas the opposite is true of the orbital frontal region (shown by arrows in the bottom two drawings).

Another way to investigate the effects of sex hormones on how neurons process information is to relate differences in hormone exposure to particular human cognitive abilities. This type of study presents obvious problems because we cannot control hormone types and levels in people. We can, however, take advantage of naturally occurring hormone variations within a single sex. This is rather simple to do in females. We can use the age of onset of the first menstrual cycle (known as *menarche*) as a marker for the presence of female gonadal hormones. Because this age varies considerably (from as early as 8 years old to as late as 18), there is ample opportunity to relate the presence of female hormones to cognitive abilities.

In a study by Sharon Rowntree (2000), girls had been recruited at age 8 to take part in a 10-year longitudinal study of the relation between age at menarche and body type. The age at which each started to menstruate was known to within 1 month. At age 16, all the subjects were given tests of verbal fluency (such as writing down in 5 minutes as many words as possible that start with the letter *d*) and of spatial manipulation (such as the one illustrated in Figure 14-5). Rowntree reasoned that if hormones alter cortical neurons, then the age at which the neurons are changed may influence cognitive processing. And this is exactly what she found evidence for, as summarized in Figure 14-23. Specifically, girls who reached menarche earlier (age 12 or younger) were generally better at the verbal tasks than girls who began to menstruate later, whereas girls who reached menarche later were generally better at the spatial tasks. In short, the age at which gonadal hormones affect the brain may be the critical factor in the development of cognitive skills.

This idea was examined in another way by Deborah Waber (1976). She did a retrospective study in which age at puberty was estimated in both boys and girls. She found

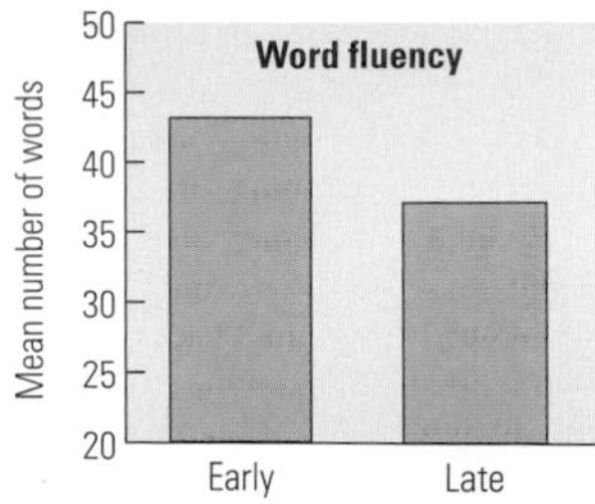


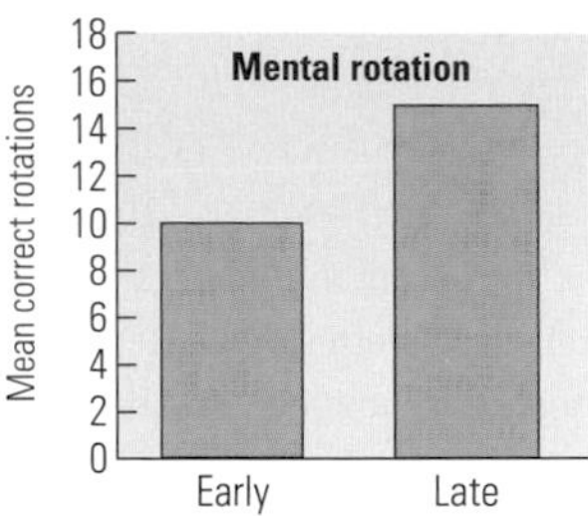


**Figure 14-23**

Girls who reach menarche early (before age 12) have better verbal skills but weaker spatial skills than do girls who reach menarch late (after age 14).

Data courtesy of S. Rowntree, from "Spatial and Verbal Ability in Adult Females Vary with Age at Menses," manuscript in preparation.

that regardless of sex, early-maturing adolescents performed better on tests of verbal than spatial abilities, whereas late-maturing subjects showed the opposite pattern. Waber argued that sex differences in mental abilities reflect differences in the organization of cortical function that are related to differential rates of physical maturation. Because boys usually mature later than girls, they show a different pattern of cognitive skills from that of girls.

The advantage of using same-sex subjects in studies such as these is to reduce the probability that different experiences prior to puberty could account either for the girls' age differences at menarche or for their different cognitive abilities. Rather, it seems more likely that the gonadal hormones of puberty influenced the structure of cortical neurons and, ultimately, cognitive processing. It is possible that the post-pubertal experiences of the girls affected the brains of early maturers differently from those of late maturers, but gonadal hormones would still have played an important mediating role. Interestingly, boys reach puberty later than girls, and boys, on average, do better at spatial tasks and worse on verbal tasks than girls do. Perhaps it is the age at which hormones affect the brain that is the critical factor here.

One additional way to consider the neural basis of sex differences is to look at the effects of cortical injury in men and women. If there are differences in the neural organization of cognitive processing in males and females, there ought to be differences in the effects of cortical injury in the two sexes. In fact, Doreen Kimura (1999) conducted this kind of study and showed that the pattern of cerebral organization within each hemisphere may differ between the sexes. Investigating people who had sustained cortical strokes in adulthood, she tried to match the location and extent of injury in her male and female subjects. She found that although males and females were almost equally likely to be aphasic following left-hemisphere lesions of some kind, males were more likely to be aphasic and apraxic after damage to the left posterior cortex, whereas females were far more likely to be aphasic and apraxic after lesions to the left frontal cortex. These results are summarized in Figure 14-24. They suggest a difference in intrahemispheric organization between the two sexes.

## HOW SEX-RELATED COGNITIVE DIFFERENCES EVOLVED

We have emphasized the role of gonadal hormones to explain sex differences in cognitive function, but we are still left with the question of how these differences arose in the first place. To answer this question, we must look back at human evolution. Ultimately, males and females of a species have virtually all their genes in common. Mothers pass their genes to both sons and daughters, and fathers do the same. The only way in which a gene can affect one sex preferentially is for that gene's activities to be influenced by the animal's gonadal hormones, which in turn are determined by the presence or absence of the Y chromosome. The Y chromosome carries a gene called the testes-determining factor (TDF). This gene stimulates the body to produce testes, which then manufacture androgens, which subsequently influence the activities of other genes.

Like other body organs, the brain is a potential target of natural selection. We should therefore expect to find sex-related differences in the brain whenever the two sexes differ in the adaptive problems that they have faced during the evolutionary history of the species. The degree of aggressive behavior that the brain produces is a good example. Males are more physically aggressive than females in most mammalian species. This trait presumably improved males' reproductive success, causing natural selection for greater aggressiveness in males. Producing higher levels of aggression involves male hormones. We know from studies of nonhuman species that aggression is related directly to the

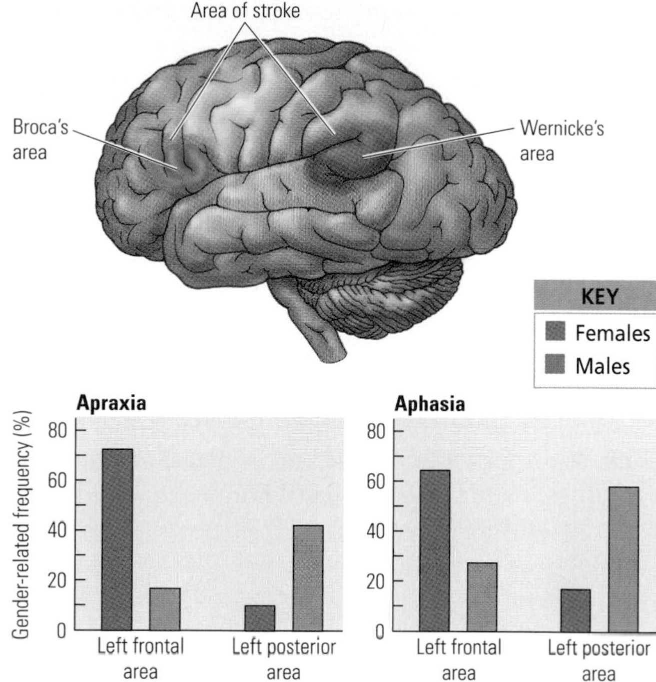


**Figure 14-24**

Evidence for intrahemispheric differences in cortical organization of males and females. Apraxia is associated with frontal damage to the left hemisphere in women and with posterior damage in men. Aphasia occurs most often when damage is to the front of the brain in women but in the rear of the brain in men.

Adapted from *Sex and Cognition,* by D. Kimura, 1999, Cambridge, MA: MIT Press.

presence of androgens and to the effects of these hormones on gene expression both during brain development and later in life. In this case, therefore, natural selection has worked on gonadal hormone levels to favor aggressiveness in males.

Explaining sex-related differences in cognitive processes, such as language or spatial skills, is more speculative than explaining sex-related differences in behaviors, such as aggression. Nevertheless, some hypotheses come to mind. For instance, we can imagine that in the history of mammalian evolution, males have tended to range over larger territories than females have. This behavior requires spatial abilities, so the development of these skills would have been favored in males. Support for this hypothesis comes from comparing spatial problem-solving abilities in males of closely related mammalian species—one in which the males range over large territories versus one in which the males do not have such extensive ranges. For example, pine voles have restricted ranges and no sex-related difference in range, whereas meadow voles have extensive ranges (about 20 times larger than those of pine voles), with the males ranging more widely than the females. When the spatial problem skills of pine voles and meadow voles are compared, meadow voles are far superior. Furthermore, among meadow voles, there is a sex difference in spatial ability that favors males, but no such sex difference exists among pine voles. Recall from Chapter 13 that the hippocampus is implicated in spatial navigation skills. Significantly, the hippocampus is larger in meadow voles than in pine voles, and it is larger in meadow vole males than in females (Gaulin, 1992). A similar logic could help explain sex-related differences in spatial abilities between human males and females.

Explaining sex-related differences in language skills is also speculative. One hypothesis holds that if males were hunters and often away from home, the females left behind in social groups would be favored to develop tools for social interaction, one of which is language. It might also be argued that females were selected for fine motor skills (such as foraging for food and making clothing and baskets). Because of the relationship between language and fine motor skills, enhanced language capacities might have evolved as well in females. Although such speculations are interesting, they are not testable. We will probably never know with certainty why sex-related differences in brain organization developed.

## Handedness and Cognitive Organization

Nearly everyone prefers to use one hand rather than the other for activities such as writing or throwing a ball. Most people prefer to use the right hand. In fact, left-handedness has historically been viewed as somewhat strange. Left-handedness, however, is not rare. The most commonly cited figure is that 10 percent of the human population worldwide is left-handed. This figure represents the number of people who write with the left hand. When other criteria are used to determine left-handedness, estimates range from 10 percent to 30 percent of the population.

Because the left hemisphere controls the right hand, it has generally been assumed that right-handedness is somehow related to the presence of speech in the left hemisphere. If this were so, then language would be located in the right hemispheres of left-handed people. This hypothesis is easily tested, and it turns out to be false. In the course of preparing epileptic patients for surgery to remove the abnormal tissue causing their seizures, Ted Rasmussen and Brenda Milner (1977) injected the left or right hemisphere with a drug known as sodium amobarbital (see "The Sodium Amobarbital Test," below). This drug produces a short-acting anesthesia of the entire hemisphere, making it possible to determine where speech is located. For instance, if a per-

Focus on Disorders

### The Sodium Amobarbital Test

Guy was a 32-year-old lawyer who had a vascular malformation over the region corresponding to the posterior speech zone. The malformation was beginning to cause neurological symptoms, including epilepsy, so the ideal surgical treatment would be removal of the abnormal vessels. The problem was that removing vessels sitting over the posterior speech zone poses a serious risk of permanent aphasia. Because Guy was left-handed, it was possible that he had speech located in the right hemisphere, in which case the surgical risk would be much lower. To avoid inadvertent damage to the speech zones, the surgeon must be certain of their location.

To achieve certainty in doubtful cases, Jun Wada and Ted Rasmussen (1960) pioneered the technique of injecting sodium amobarbital, a barbiturate, into the carotid artery to produce a brief period of anesthesia of the ipsilateral hemisphere. (Injections are now normally made through a catheter inserted into the femoral artery.) This procedure enables an unequivocal localization of speech, because injection into the speech hemisphere results in an arrest of speech lasting as long as several minutes. As speech returns, it is characterized by aphasic errors. Injection into the nonspeaking hemisphere may produce no, or only brief, speech arrest. The amobarbital procedure has the advantage of allowing each hemisphere to be studied separately in the functional absence of the other (anesthetized) hemisphere. Because the period of anesthesia lasts several minutes, it is possible to study a variety of functions, including memory and movement, to determine a hemisphere's capabilities.

The sodium amobarbital test is always performed bilaterally, with the second cerebral hemisphere being injected several days after the first one in order to make sure that there is no residual drug effect. During the brief period of drug action, the patient is given a series of simple tasks involving language, memory, and object recognition. Speech is tested by asking the patient to name some common objects presented in quick succession, to count and to recite the days of the week forward and backward, and to spell simple words.

If the injected hemisphere is nondominant for speech, the patient may continue to carry out the verbal tasks, although there is often a period as long as 30 seconds during which he or she appears confused and is silent but can resume speech with urging. When the injected hemisphere is dominant for speech, the patient typically stops talking and remains completely aphasic until recovery from the anesthesia

son becomes aphasic when the drug is injected into the left hemisphere but not when the drug is injected into the right, then speech must be in that person's left hemisphere. Rasmussen and Milner found that virtually all right-handed people had speech in the left hemisphere, but the reverse was not true for left-handed people. About 70 percent of left-handers also had speech in the left hemisphere. Of the remaining 30 percent, about half had speech in the right hemisphere and half had speech in both hemispheres. Anatomical studies have subsequently shown that left-handers with speech in the left hemisphere have anatomical asymmetries similar to those of right-handers. In contrast, left-handers with speech located in the right hemisphere or in both hemisphere—known as **anomalous speech representation**—have either a reversed anatomical asymmetry or no obvious anatomical asymmetry at all.

**Anomalous speech representation.** A condition in which a person's speech zones are located in the right hemisphere or in both hemispheres.

Sandra Witelson and her colleagues (1991) asked whether there might be any other gross differences in the structure of the brains of right- and left-handers. One possibility is that the connectivity of the cerebral hemispheres may differ. To test this idea, they studied the hand preference of terminally ill subjects on a variety of one-handed tasks. They later did postmortem studies of the brains of these patients, paying particular attention to the size of the corpus callosum. They found that the corpus callosum's cross-sectional area was 11 percent greater in left-handed and ambidextrous

is well along, somewhere in the range of 4 to 10 minutes.

Guy was found to have speech in the left hemisphere. During the test of his left hemisphere, he could not talk. Later, he said that when he was asked about a particular object, he wondered just what that question meant. Once he finally had some vague idea of what it meant, he had no idea of what the answer was or how to say anything. By then he realized that he had been asked all sorts of other questions to which he had also not responded. When asked which objects he had been shown, he said he had no idea. However, when given an array of objects and asked to choose with his left hand, he was able to identify the objects by pointing, because his nonspeaking right hemisphere controlled that hand. In contrast, his speaking left hemisphere had no memory of the objects because it had been asleep.

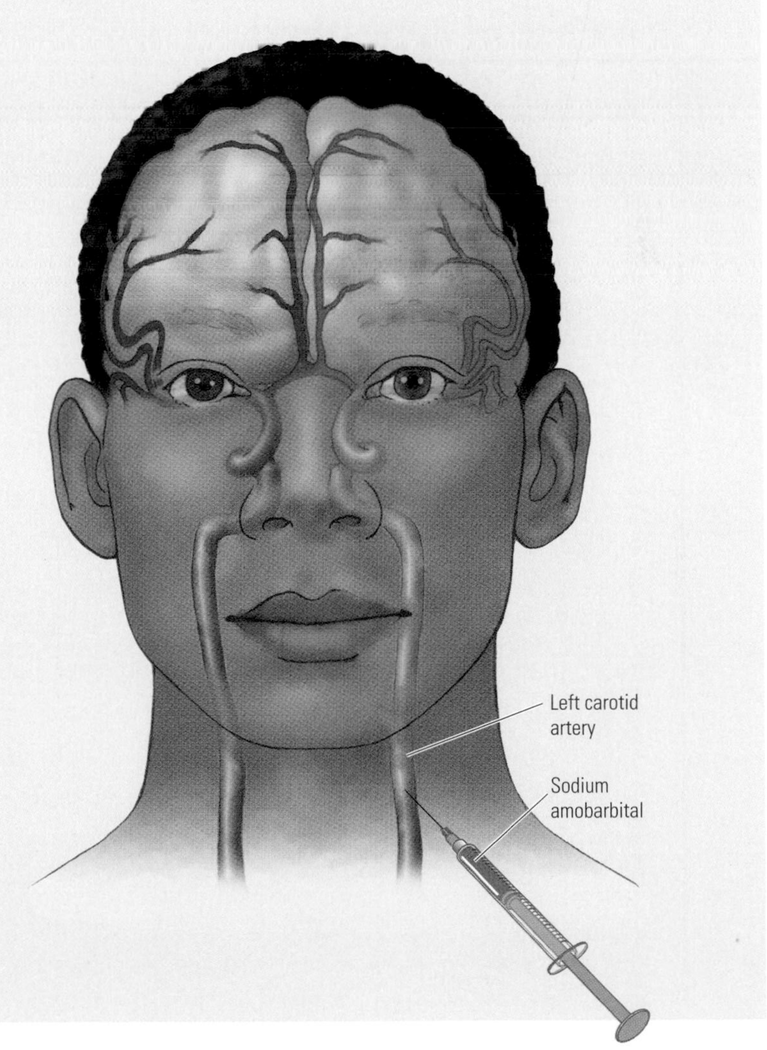


In order to avoid damaging the speech zones of patients about to undergo brain surgery, surgeons inject sodium ambobarbital into the carotid artery. The sodium amobarbital anesthetizes the hemisphere where it is injected (in this case the left), allowing the surgeon to determine if that hemisphere is dominant for speech.

**Synesthesia.** The ability to perceive a stimulus of one sense as a sensation of a different sense, as when sound produces a sensation of color.

(no hand preference) people than in right-handed people. It remains to be seen whether this enlarged callosum is due to a greater number of fibers, thicker fibers, or more myelin. If the larger corpus callosum is due to a greater number of fibers, the difference would be on the order of 25 million more fibers. Presumably, such a difference would have major implications for the organization of cognitive processing in left- and right-handers.

## Synesthesia

**Synesthesia** is the capacity to join sensory experiences across sensory modalities, as discussed in "A Case of Synesthesia.," below. Examples of this rare capacity include the ability to hear colors and to taste shapes. Richard Cytowic (1998) has estimated that the incidence of synesthesia is about 1 in every 25,000 people. Synesthesia runs in families, the most famous case being the family of Russian novelist Vladimir Nabokov. As a toddler, Nabokov complained to his mother that the letter colors on his wooden alphabet blocks were "all wrong." His mother understood what he meant, because she too perceived letters and words in particular colors. Nabokov's son is synesthetic in the same way. Such sensory blendings are difficult for most of us to imagine. We wonder how sounds or letters could possibly produce colors, but there is little doubt that synesthesia exists. Studies of people with this sensory ability show that the same stimuli always elicit the same synesthetic experiences for them.

Experience some simulations of synesthesia on the Web site at **www.worthpublishers.com/kolb/chapter14**

Focus on Disorders

### A Case of Synesthesia

Michael Watson tastes shapes. He first came to the attention of neurologist Richard Cytowic when they were having dinner together. After tasting a sauce he was making for roast chicken, Watson blurted out, "There aren't enough points on the chicken." When Cytowic quizzed him about this strange remark, Watson said that all flavors had shape for him. "I wanted the taste of this chicken to be a pointed shape, but it came out all round. Well, I mean it's nearly spherical. I can't serve this if it doesn't have points" (Cytowic, 1998, p. 4).

Watson has synesthesia, which literally means "feeling together." All his life Watson has experienced the feeling of shape when he tastes or smells food. When he tastes intense flavors he reports an experience of shape that sweeps down his arms to his fingertips. He experiences the feeling of weight, texture, warmth or cold, and shape, just as though he was grasping something. The feelings are not confined to his hands, however. Some taste shapes, like points, are experienced over his whole body. Others are experienced only on the face, back, or shoulders. These impressions are not metaphors, as other people might use when they say that a cheese is "sharp" or that a wine is "textured." Such descriptions make no sense to Watson. He actually feels the shapes.

Cytowic systematically studied Watson to determine whether his feelings of shape were always associated with particular flavors and found that they were. Cytowic devised the set of geometric figures shown here to allow Watson to communicate which shapes he associated with various flavors.

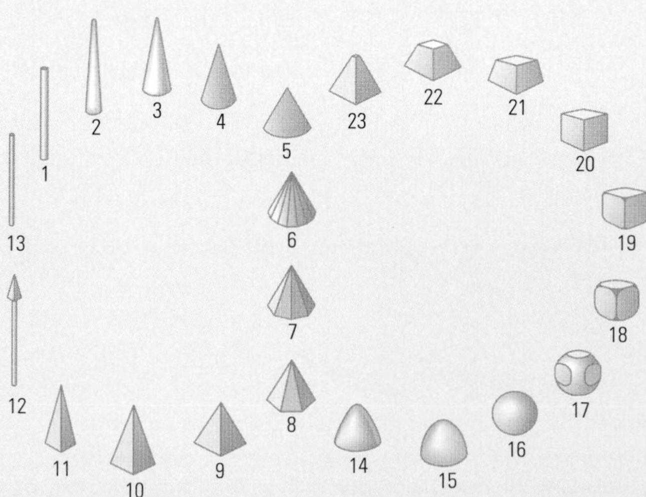


Neurologist Richard Cytowic devised this set of figures to help Michael Watson communicate the shapes he senses when he tastes food.

The most common form of synesthesia is colored hearing. For many synesthetics, this means that they hear both speech and music in color, the experience being a visual melange of colored shapes, movement, and scintillation. The fact that colored hearing is more common than other types of synesthesia is curious. There are five primary senses (vision, hearing, touch, taste, and smell), so in principle there ought to be 10 possible synesthetic pairings. In fact, however, most pairings are in one direction. For instance, whereas synesthetic people may see colors when they hear, they do not hear sounds when they look at colors. Furthermore, some sensory combinations occur rarely, if at all. In particular, it is rare for taste or smell to trigger a synesthetic response.

The neurological basis of synesthesia is difficult to study because each case is so idiosyncratic. Few studies have related synesthesia directly to brain function or brain organization, and it is possible that different people experience synesthesia for different reasons. Various hypotheses have been advanced to account for synesthesia, including: (1) extraordinary connections between the different sensory regions that are related in a particular synesthetic person; (2) increased activity in areas of the frontal lobes that receive inputs from more than one sensory area; and (3) unusual patterns of cerebral activation in response to particular sensory inputs. Whatever the explanation, the brains of synesthetic people clearly think differently about certain types of sensory inputs than the brains of other people do.

### In Review

No two brains are alike, and no two people think the same. Nevertheless, although many individual differences in brain structure and thinking are idiosyncratic, there are also systematic variations, such as those related to sex and handedness. The reasons for these differences in the cerebral organization of thinking are not known; they are undoubtedly related to differences in the synaptic organization of the neural circuits that underlie different types of cognitive processing.

## INTELLIGENCE

Most people would probably say that one of the biggest influences on anyone's thinking ability is intelligence. We consider intelligence easy to identify in people, and even easy to observe in other animals. Yet intelligence is not at all easy to define. Despite years of studying human intelligence, researchers are not yet in agreement as to what intelligence entails. We therefore begin this section by reviewing some theories of intelligence.

### The Concept of General Intelligence

In the 1920s, Charles Spearman proposed that although there may be different kinds of intelligence, there is also some sort of general intelligence, which he called the **"g" factor.** Consider for a moment what a general factor in intelligence might mean for the brain. Presumably, brains with high or low "g" would have some general difference in brain architecture. This difference could not be something as simple as size, because human brain size (which varies from about 1000 to 2000 grams) correlates poorly with intelligence. Another possibility is that "g" is related to some special characteristic of cerebral connectivity or even to the ratio of neurons to glia.

Preliminary studies of Albert Einstein's brain imply that both these characteristics may play important roles. Sandra Witelson and her colleagues (1999) found that, although Einstein's brain was the same size and weight as the average male brain, his

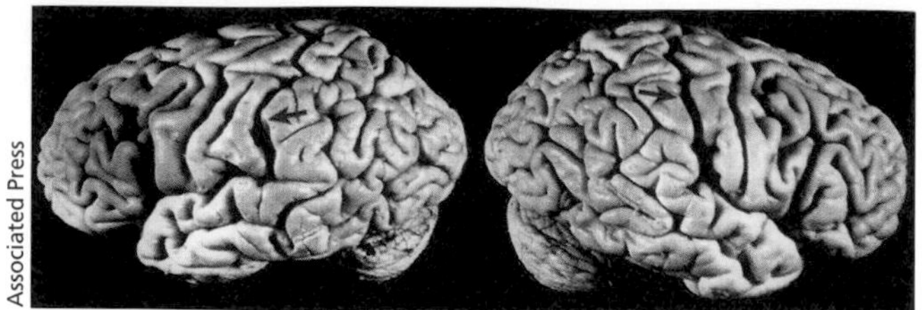

Associated Press

**Figure 14-25**

Photographs of Einstein's brain. The Sylvian fissure (*at arrows*) takes an exaggerated upward course relative to typical brains.

Reprinted with permission of S. Witelson, D. Kigar, T. Harvey, and *The Lancet*, June 19, 1999.

inferior parietal cortex was unusually large, as illustrated in Figure 14-25 (compare these brains to those shown in Figure 14-14). The Sylvian fissure was short in Einstein's brain, and both the left and the right Sylvian fissure had a particularly striking upward deflection. The inferior parietal cortex is known to be involved in mathematical reasoning, so it is tempting to speculate that Einstein's mathematical abilities were related to enlargement of this area. But there may be another important difference in Einstein's brain. Marion Diamond and her colleagues (1985) looked at the glia-to-neuron ratio in Einstein's brain versus the mean for a control population. They found that Einstein's inferior parietal cortex had a higher glia-to-neuron ratio than average, meaning that each of his neurons in this region had an unusually high number of glial cells supporting them. The glia-to-neuron ratio was not unusually high in any other cortical areas of Einstein's brain that these researchers measured. Possibly, then, certain types of intelligence could be related to differences in cell structure in localized regions of the brain. But even if this hypothesis proves to be correct, it still offers little neural evidence in favor of a general factor in intelligence.

One neuropsychological possibility is that "g" is related to language processes in the brain. Recall that language ability qualitatively changes the nature of cognitive processing in humans. So perhaps people with very good language skills also have an advantage in general thinking ability.

## Multiple Intelligences

There have been many other theories of intelligence since Spearman's, but few have considered the brain directly. One exception is a theory proposed by Howard Gardner, a neuropsychologist at Harvard. Gardner (1983) considered the effects of neurological injury on people's behavior. He concluded that there are seven distinctly different forms of intelligence and that each form can be selectively damaged by brain injury. This view that there are multiple kinds of human intelligence should not be surprising, given the many different types of cognitive operations that the human brain is capable of performing.

Gardner's seven categories of intelligence are: linguistic intelligence, musical intelligence, logical-mathematical intelligence, spatial intelligence, bodily-kinesthetic intelligence, intrapersonal intelligence, and interpersonal intelligence. Linguistic and musical intelligence are straightforward concepts, as is logical-mathematical intelligence. Spatial intelligence refers to the spatial abilities that we have discussed in this chapter, especially the ability to navigate in space, as would be required of a hunter or fisherman in a culture that had no modern navigational aids. Bodily-kinesthetic intelligence refers to superior motor abilities, such as those exemplified by skilled athletes and dancers. The two types of "personal" intelligence are less obvious. They refer to operations of the frontal and temporal lobes that are required for success in a highly social environment. The intrapersonal aspect is an awareness of one's own feelings, whereas the extrapersonal aspect is the ability to recognize the feelings of others and to respond appropriately. Gardner's definition of intelligence has the advantage not only of being quite inclusive but also of acknowledging forms of intelligence not typically recognized in industrialized cultures.

One prediction stemming from Gardner's analysis of intelligence is that brains ought to differ in some way when people have more of one form of intelligence and less of another. Logically, we could imagine that if a person were higher in musical intelligence and lower in bodily-kinesthetic intelligence, then the regions of the brain involved in music (especially the temporal lobe) would differ in some fundamental way from the "less efficient" regions involved in kinesthetic intelligence. Unfortunately, we do not know what that difference might be.

## Divergent and Convergent Intelligence

One of the clearest differences between parietal- and temporal-lobe lesions versus lesions to the frontal lobes is in the way they affect performance on standardized intelligence tests. Posterior lesions produce reliable, and often large, decreases in IQ, whereas frontal lesions do not. One thing is puzzling, however. If frontal-lobe damage does not diminish a person's IQ, why do people with this kind of damage often do such "stupid" things? The answer lies in the difference between two kinds of intelligence, referred to as divergent and convergent.

According to J. P. Guilford (1967), traditional intelligence tests measure what is called **convergent thinking**—that is, thinking that applies a person's knowledge and reasoning skills so as to narrow the range of possible solutions to a problem, zeroing in on one correct answer. Typical intelligence test items using vocabulary words, arithmetic problems, puzzles, block designs, and so forth all require convergent thinking. They demand a single correct answer that can be easily scored. There is, however, another type of intelligence that is called **divergent thinking.** Divergent thinking reaches outward from conventional knowledge and reasoning skills to explore new, more unconventional kinds of solutions to problems. With divergent thinking, it is assumed that there is a variety of possible approaches and answers to a question, rather than only one "correct" solution. An example of a task that requires divergent thinking is to list all the possible uses for a coat hanger that you can imagine. Clearly, a person who is very good at divergent thinking might not necessarily be good at convergent thinking, and vice versa.

The distinction between divergent and convergent intelligence is useful because it helps us to understand the effects of brain injury on thought. Frontal-lobe injury is believed to interfere with divergent thinking, rather than with the convergent thinking measured by standardized IQ tests. It is people with damage to the temporal and parietal lobes whose convergent intelligence is often impaired. Injury to the left parietal lobe, in particular, causes devastating impairment of the ability to perform cognitive processes related to academic work. These people may be aphasic, alexic, and apraxic. They often have severe deficits in arithmetic ability. All such impairments would interfere with school performance or, in fact, performance at most jobs. Our patient M. M., discussed earlier, had left-parietal-lobe injury and was unable to return to work. In contrast to people like M. M., people with frontal-lobe injuries seldom have deficits in reading, writing, or arithmetic and show no decrement in standardized IQ tests. The case of C. C. is a good example. He had a meningioma along the midline between the two frontal lobes; extracting it required removal of brain tissue from both hemispheres. C. C. had been a prominent lawyer prior to his surgery; afterward, although he still had a superior IQ and superior memory, he was unable to work, in part because he no longer had any imagination. He could not generate the novel solutions to legal problems that had characterized his career before the surgery. Thus, both M. M. and C. C. suffered problems that prevented them from working, but their problems differed because different kinds of thinking were affected.

## Intelligence, Heredity, Environment, and the Synapse

Another way of categorizing human intelligence was proposed by Donald Hebb. He, too, thought of people as having two forms of intelligence, which he labeled intelligence A and intelligence B. **Intelligence A** refers to innate intellectual potential, which is highly heritable. That is, it has a strong genetic component. **Intelligence B** is observed intelligence, which is influenced by experience as well as other factors, such as disease, injury, or exposure to environmental toxins, especially during development.

**Convergent thinking.** A form of thinking in which there is a search for a single answer to a question (such as 2 + 2 = ?); contrasts with divergent thinking.

**Divergent thinking.** A form of thinking in which there is a search for multiple solutions to a problem (such as, how many different ways can a pen be used?); contrasts with convergent thinking.

Hebb understood that the structure of brain cells can be significantly influenced by experience. In his view (Hebb, 1980), experiences influence brain development, and thus observed intelligence, because they alter the brain's synaptic organization. It follows that people with lower-than-average intelligence A can raise their intelligence B by appropriate postnatal experiences, whereas people with higher-than-average intelligence A can be negatively affected by a poor environment. The task is to identify what is a "good" and a "bad" environment in which to stimulate people to reach their highest potential intelligence.

One implication of Hebb's view of intelligence is that the synaptic organization of the brain plays a key role. This synaptic organization is partly directed by a person's genes, but it is also influenced by experience. Variations in the kinds of experiences to which people are exposed, coupled with variations in genetic patterns, undoubtedly contribute to the individual differences in intelligence that we observe—both quantitative differences (as measured by IQ tests) and qualitative differences (as in Gardner's theory). The effects of experience on intelligence may not simply be due to differences in synaptic organization. Experience changes not only the number of synapses in the brain but also the number of glia. Remember that Einstein's brain was found to have more glia per neuron in the inferior parietal cortex than control brains did. Intelligence, then, may be influenced not only by the way in which synapses are organized but also by glial density.

### In Review

Researchers have proposed many different forms of human intelligence, including Spearman's concept of general intelligence, Gardner's theory of multiple intelligences, Guilford's concepts of convergent and divergent thinking, and Hebb's intelligence A and intelligence B. It is likely that each form of intelligence that humans possess is related to particular structural organizations in the brain. To date, we know little about the structural differences that account for the significant individual variations in intelligence that we observe. Preliminary studies of Einstein's brain suggest some provocative possibilities, however.

## CONSCIOUSNESS

Conscious experience is familiar to all of us, yet it remains a largely mysterious product of the brain. Everyone has an idea of what it means to be conscious, but consciousness is easier to identify than to define. Definitions range from the view that consciousness is merely a reflection of complex processes of thought to more slippery notions that see consciousness as being the subjective experience of awareness or of "the inner self." Despite the difficulty of saying exactly what consciousness is, scientists generally agree that it is a process, not a thing. And consciousness is probably not a single process but a collection of several processes, such as those associated with seeing, talking, thinking, emotion, and so on.

Consciousness is also not always the same. For instance, a person is not necessarily equally conscious at all stages of life. We don't think of a newborn baby as being conscious in the same way that a healthy older child or adult is. Indeed, we might say that part of the process of maturation is becoming fully conscious. Level of consciousness even changes across the span of a day as we pass through various states of drowsiness, sleep, and waking. One trait that characterizes consciousness, then, is its constant variability.

## Why Are We Conscious?

Researchers have wondered why we have the experience we call consciousness. The simplest explanation is that we are conscious because it provides an adaptive advantage. Either our creation of the sensory world or our selection of behavior is enhanced by being conscious. Consider visual consciousness as an example. According to Francis Crick and Christof Koch (1998), an animal such as a frog acts a bit like a zombie when it responds to visual input. Frogs respond to small, preylike objects by snapping, and to large, looming objects by jumping. These responses are controlled by different visual systems and are best thought of as reflexive, rather than conscious. These visual systems work well for the frog. So why do we need to add consciousness? Crick and Koch suggest that reflexive systems are fine when the number of such systems is limited; but as their number grows, reflexive arrangements become inefficient, especially when two or more systems are in conflict. As the amount of information about some event increases, it becomes advantageous to produce a single, complex representation and make it available for a sufficient time to the parts of the brain (such as the frontal lobes) that make a choice among many possible plans of action. This sustained, complex representation is consciousness.

Of course, we must still have the ability to respond quickly and unconsciously when we need to. This ability exists alongside our ability to process information consciously. Recall from our discussion of the visual system in Chapter 8 that we have two visual streams. The ventral stream is conscious, but the dorsal stream, which acts more rapidly, is not. The action of the unconscious, online dorsal stream can be seen in many athletes. To hit a baseball or tennis ball traveling at more than 90 miles per hour requires athletes to swing before they are consciously aware of actually seeing the ball. The conscious awareness of the ball comes just after hitting it.

A series of experiments by Marc Jeannerod and his colleagues (Castiello et al., 1991) showed a similar dissociation between behavior and awareness in normal volunteers as they make grasping movements. Figure 14-26 illustrates the results of a representative experiment. Subjects were required to grasp one of three rods as quickly as possible. The correct target rod on any given trial was indicated by a light on that rod. On some trials, unbeknownst to the subjects, the light jumped from one target to another. Subjects were asked to report if such a jump had occurred. As shown in the figure, although subjects were able to make the trajectory correction, they

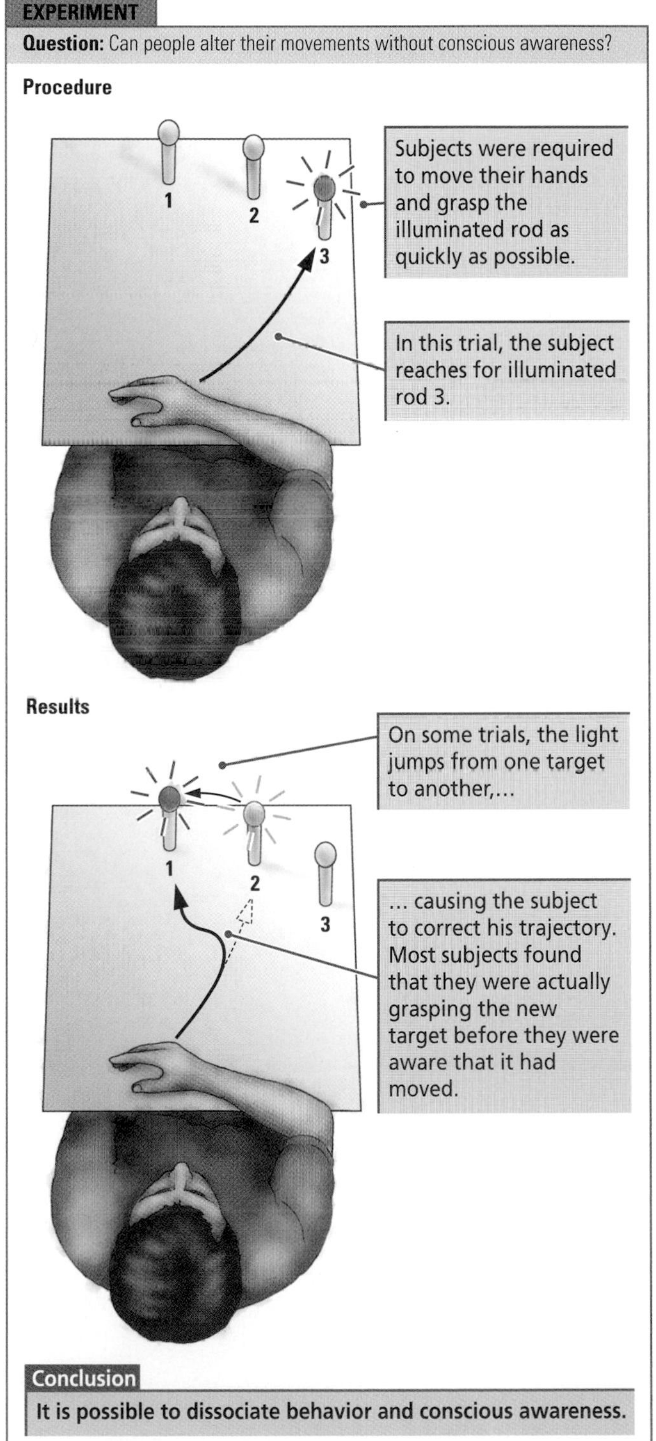

EXPERIMENT
Question: Can people alter their movements without conscious awareness?
Procedure
1
2
3
Subjects were required to move their hands and grasp the illuminated rod as quickly as possible.
In this trial, the subject reaches for illuminated rod 3.
Results
On some trials, the light jumps from one target to another,...
1
2
3
... causing the subject to correct his trajectory. Most subjects found that they were actually grasping the new target before they were aware that it had moved.
Conclusion
It is possible to dissociate behavior and conscious awareness.


**Figure 14-26**

Dissociation of behavior and conscious awareness. When one of the three rods (1, 2, or 3) is illuminated, the subject must grasp that rod with the thumb and index finger as quickly as possible. The paths that the hand follows are indicated by the arrows. On some trials, the light switched from target 2 to either target 1 or target 3. This switch elicited a smooth and rapid movement correction, shown by the solid arrow. Subjects were asked to give a vocal response to indicate that they were aware of the target switch. On some trials, there was a dissociation between motor and vocal responses such that, to their surprise, subjects had already grasped the target some 300 milliseconds before they emitted the vocal response.

Adapted from "The Neural Correlates of Conscious Experience," by C. Frith, R. Perry, and E. Lumer, 1999, *Trends in Cognitive Sciences, 3,* pp. 105–114.

were sometimes actually grasping the correct target before they were aware that the target had changed. Like baseball players, they experienced conscious awareness of the stimulus event only after their movements had taken place. No thought was required to make the movement, just as frogs catch flies without having to think about it.

Such movements are different from those consciously directed toward a specific object, as when we reach into a bowl of jellybeans to select a candy of a certain color. In this case, we must be aware of all the different colors surrounding the color we want. Here the conscious ventral stream is needed to discriminate among and respond differentially to particular stimuli. Consciousness, then, allows us to select behaviors that correspond to an understanding of the nuances of sensory inputs.

## What Is the Neural Basis of Consciousness?

Consciousness must be related in some way to the activity of neural systems in the brain, particularly in the forebrain. One way to investigate these systems is to contrast two kinds of neurological conditions. The first is the condition in which a person lacks conscious awareness about some subset of information, even though he or she processes that information unconsciously. Examples include blindsight (see the case of D. B. in Chapter 8), form agnosia (see D. F.'s case, also in Chapter 8), implicit learning in amnesia (discussed in Chapter 13), and visual neglect (discussed in this chapter). Another example is obsessive-compulsive disorder, in which people persist in some behavior, such as checking to see that the stove is off, even though they have already checked a great many times. All these examples show that stimuli can be highly processed by the brain without entering conscious awareness. These phenomena are quite different from the neurological condition in which people experience conscious awareness of stimuli that are not actually there. Examples include phantom limbs (discussed in Chapter 13) and the hallucinations of schizophrenia. In both these cases, there is consciousness of specific events, such as pain in a missing limb or the perception of voices, even though these events are clearly not "real."

Several conclusions can be drawn from these contrasting examples. First, the representation of a visual object or event is likely to be distributed over many parts of the visual system, and probably over parts of the frontal lobes as well. Damage to different areas not only produces different specific symptoms, such as agnosia or neglect, but can also produce a specific loss of visual consciousness. Second, because visual consciousness can be lost, it follows that there must be parts of the neural circuit that produce this awareness. At the beginning of this chapter, we discussed the idea that the unit of thinking is the neuron. It is unlikely, however, that the neuron can be the unit of conscious experience. Instead, consciousness is presumably a process that somehow emerges from neural circuits, with greater degrees of consciousness being associated with increasingly complex circuitry. This is why it is often suggested that humans, with their more complex brain circuits, have a greater degree of consciousness than other animals do. Thus, simple animals like worms are assumed to have less consciousness (if any) than dogs, which in turn are assumed to have less consciousness than humans. Brain injury may alter self-awareness in humans, as in contralateral neglect, but unless a person is in a coma, he or she still retains some conscious experience.

Some people have argued that language makes a fundamental change in the nature of consciousness. Recall Gazzaniga's belief that the left hemisphere, with its language capabilities, is able to act as an interpreter of stimuli. This ability, he felt, is an important difference between the functions of the two hemispheres. Yet people who are aphasic are not considered to have lost consciousness. In short, although language may alter the nature of our conscious experience, it seems unlikely that any one brain structure can be equated with consciousness. Rather, it makes more sense to view consciousness as a product of all cortical areas, their connections, and their cognitive operations.

We end this chapter on an interesting, if speculative, note. David Chalmers (1995) proposed that consciousness includes not only the information that the brain experiences through its sensory systems but also the information that the brain has stored and, presumably, the information that the brain can imagine. In his view, then, consciousness is the end product of all the brain's cognitive processes. One interesting implication of such a notion is that as the brain changes with experience, so does the state of consciousness. As our sensory experiences become richer and our store of information greater, our consciousness may become more complex. From this perspective, there may indeed be some advantage to growing old.

## In Review

Over the course of human evolution, sensory experience has become increasingly complex as the brain has expanded the analyses that sensory systems perform. It is hypothesized that this informational complexity must be organized in some fashion and that consciousness is a property of the nervous system that emerges as a result. Viewed in this way, consciousness allows the brain to produce a single representation of experience at any given moment and to make a choice among the many different and sometimes conflicting possible plans of action. As our relative brain size has increased during our evolution, so too has our degree of consciousness. But not all behavior needs to be controlled consciously. In fact, it is better that we are able to make rapid movements, such as batting a ball, without conscious thought. In such cases, speed is critical, and it would be impossible to respond quickly enough if there were conscious analysis of the movements.

## SUMMARY

1. *What is thinking?* One of the products of brain activity in both humans and nonhumans is the generation of complex processes that we refer to as thinking or cognition. Various cognitive operations are described by English words such as *language* and *memory.* These operations, however, are not things, but rather psychological constructs. They are merely inferred cognitive operations and are not found in places in the brain. The brain carries out multiple cognitive operations including perception, action for perception, imagery, planning, spatial cognition, and attention. These operations require widespread activity of many cortical areas.
2. *What is the neural basis of cognition?* The unit of cognition is the neuron. The neurons in the association cortex specifically take part in most forms of cognition. Various syndromes result from association cortex injury, including agnosia, apraxia, aphasia, and amnesia. Each of these syndromes reflects the loss or disturbance of a form of cognition.
3. *What is cerebral asymmetry?* The cognitive operations of the brain are organized asymmetrically in the cerebral hemispheres, with the two hemispheres carrying out complementary functions. The most obvious functional difference in the two hemispheres is language, which is normally housed in the left hemisphere. Cerebral asymmetry is manifested in anatomical differences between the two hemispheres and can be inferred from the differential effects of injury to opposite sides of the brain. Asymmetry can also be seen in the normal brain and in the brain that is surgically split for the relief of intractable epilepsy.
4. *What might account for individual differences in cognition?* There are marked differences in the performance of females and males on various cognitive tests, especially on tests of spatial and verbal behavior. Sex differences result from the action

**neuroscience interactive**

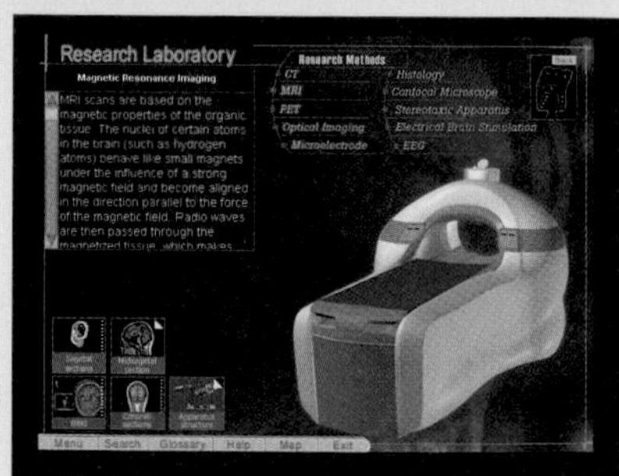

There are many resources available for expanding your learning on line:

■ **www.worthpublishers.com/kolb/chapter14**
Try some self-tests to reinforce your mastery of the material. Look at some of the updates on current research. You'll also be able to link to other sites which will reinforce what you've learned.

■ **www.apraxia-kids.org**
Learn more about apraxia and how it affects children from this Web site from the headquarters of the Childhood Apraxia of Speech Association.

■ **www.web.mit.edu/synesthesia/www/synesthesia.html**
Work through some interactive demonstrations of what it might be like to have synesthesia at this Web site from the Massachusetts Institute of Technology.

On your CD-ROM you can review the brain anatomy that underlies cognition in the module on the Central Nervous System.

of gonadal hormones on the organization of the cerebral cortex, possibly on the formation of the architecture of cortical neurons. It is not only the action of the hormones that is important but also the timing of the hormonal actions. There are also differences in the organization of the cerebral hemispheres in right- and left-handers. Left-handers are not a single group, however, but constitute at least three different groups: one whose members appear to have speech in the left hemisphere, as right-handers do, and two that have anomalous speech representation, either in the right hemisphere or in both hemispheres. The reason for these organizational differences remains unknown.

5. *What is the neural basis of intelligence?* Intelligence is difficult to define. In fact, we find various forms of intelligence among humans within our own culture and in other cultures. There are obvious differences in intelligence across species, as well as within a species. Intelligence is not related to differences in brain size within a species, nor is it related to any obvious gross structural differences between different individuals. It may be related to differences in synaptic organization or to the ratio of glia to neurons.
6. *What methods are used to study how the brain thinks?* Neuropsychological studies, which began in the late 1800s, examine the behavioral capacities of people and laboratory animals with localized brain injuries. The development of different types of brain recording systems, such as EEG, ERP, and MEG, has led to new ways of measuring brain activity while subjects are engaged in various cognitive tasks. Brain metabolism can also be measured by using techniques such as PET and fMRI. An alternative to correlating metabolic activity with behavior is to stimulate the brain during cognitive activity, a technique that disrupts behavior. The original studies by Penfield used direct electrical stimulation, but more recently it has been possible to use transcranial magnetic stimulation to disrupt activity. With the use of multiple methods, it is possible to gather converging evidence on the way the brain thinks.
7. *What is consciousness, and how does it relate to brain organization?* The larger a species' brain is relative to its body size, the more knowledge the brain creates. Consciousness is a property that emerges from the complexity of the nervous system.

## KEY TERMS

anomalous speech representation, p. 563
association cortex, p. 534
cognitive neuroscience, p. 542
contralateral neglect, p. 538
convergent thinking, p. 567
divergent thinking, p. 567
extinction, p. 539
functional MRI (fMRI), p. 545
magnetic resonance imaging (MRI), p. 544
neuropsychology, p. 542
psychological construct, p. 530
synesthesia, p. 564
syntax, p. 531
transcranial magnetic stimulation (TMS), p. 546

## REVIEW QUESTIONS

1. What are the characteristics of thinking? How do these characteristics relate to the brain?
2. Summarize the role of the association cortex in thinking.
3. In what ways is the function of the cerebral hemispheres asymmetrical? In what ways is it symmetrical?
4. Identify the key variations in cerebral asymmetry.
5. How does intelligence relate to brain organization?

## FOR FURTHER THOUGHT

1. Contrast the ideas of syntax, mirror neurons, and the integrative mind with respect to the neural control of thinking.
2. What types of studies are necessary in order to identify a neural basis of consciousness?

## RECOMMENDED READING

Barlow, H. (1995). The neuron doctrine in perception. In M. Gazzaniga (Ed.), *The cognitive neurosciences* (pp. 415–435). Cambridge, MA: MIT Press. Barlow introduces the reader to the fascinating question of what the basic neural unit of cognition might be. He traces the history of thinking about the problem and provides a nice summary of the evidence that the neuron is the basic unit of cognition.

Calvin, W. H. (1996). *How brains think.* New York: Basic Books. This delightful book ties together information from anthropology, evolutionary biology, linguistics, and the neurosciences to deliver an entertaining account of how intelligence evolved and how it may work. This little book would be a wonderful springboard for a group discussion at the undergraduate level and beyond.

Cytowic, R. E. (1998). *The man who tasted shapes.* Cambridge, MA: MIT Press. Cytowic gives us an inside look at the cases that led him to study synesthesia. Reading about "pointed tastes" is better than science fiction, especially for the majority of us who can barely imagine such sensory experiences.

Kimura, D. (1999). *Sex and cognition.* Cambridge, MA: MIT Press. Kimura has written a short yet comprehensive monograph on what is known about sex differences in brain organization and function. She is critical but fair in her analysis of the literature. The book is nicely spiced with ideas about what sex differences in brain organization might mean.

Kolb, B., & Whishaw, I. Q. (1996). *Fundamentals of human neuropsychology,* 4th ed. New York: W.H. Freeman and Company. For those who want to read more about the organization of the human brain and the ways that brain injury alters cognition, this book provides a broad introduction. Indeed, the authors, who incidentally are the authors of the book that you are reading, also provide more extensive discussions of the material that you read in Chapters 8–10, 13 and 14.

CHAPTER

# 15

# What Have We Learned and What Is Its Value?





F. Martinez/PhotoEdit
Micrograph: Dr. Dennis Kunkel/Phototake

We have come a long way through 14 chapters. We have met Fred, D. B., Roger, Donna, Alex the parrot, and Kamala the elephant. We have examined car engines, robots, and prehistoric flutes. We have investigated puffins and sea bears, as well as butterflies and mussels. Each has provided a different lesson about the organization and functioning of the brain. As we reflect on the many topics we have covered, it is time to ask two important questions: What basic concepts about the brain does all this information suggest? And how can we apply what we have learned to the solution of real-life problems?

To answer these two questions, this chapter first retraces our journey through the brain to identify a number of key concepts that summarize the major points of Chapters 1 through 14. Second, it examines ways in which our knowledge about the brain might be used to alleviate some behavioral disorders. To accomplish this second task, we review the nature of behavioral disorders and how they are related to the nervous system. We also discuss in some detail two disorders—schizophrenia and depression—to show how neurobiological information has suggested some causes and treatments. Finally, we look to the future of neuroscience in the twenty-first century.

## CONCEPTS OF BRAIN AND BEHAVIOR

Understanding the basic organization of the brain is only a beginning in understanding how this organ functions. The real task is learning how the brain produces behavior, including thought. In the writing of this book, our discussions of the brain and behavior had to be packaged into separate chapters, each of which covered only a limited amount of information. In fact, however, most of the themes we have introduced span more than a single chapter. Our goal here is to sew those themes together to produce a set of key concepts about brain function and its links to behavior.

### 1. The Brain Has Evolved as an Organ That Creates a Representation of the External World and Produces Behavior in Response to That World (Chapters 1, 2, 8–14).

Most animals with a multicellular brain have a common problem. They must move around in the world in order to eat and to reproduce. These movements, which are controlled by the nervous system, cannot be random. Rather, they must be made in response to the external world where food and mates are found. This external world is also created by the nervous system through inputs from various sensory receptors. An animal's perception of what the external world is like therefore depends on the complexity and organization of its nervous system.

Recall that different animals, such as dogs, bats, and chimpanzees, have developed different "views" of the external world. For a dog, the world is dominated by odors; for a bat, it is largely a world of sounds; and for a chimpanzee, colors are in the forefront of perception. None of these representations of the external world are more "correct" than the others. They are simply different perspectives on what is "out there" to be perceived. Each representation creates a unique picture that suits the behavioral repertoire of the animal species. The behavior of dogs is driven by smells, whether it is the smell of a strange dog, a potential mate, or a possible prey. The flight of bats is guided by auditory information, as when bats use sound to locate insects to eat. And the behavior of chimpanzees is driven by color, the best example being the use of color to spot ripe fruit in trees.

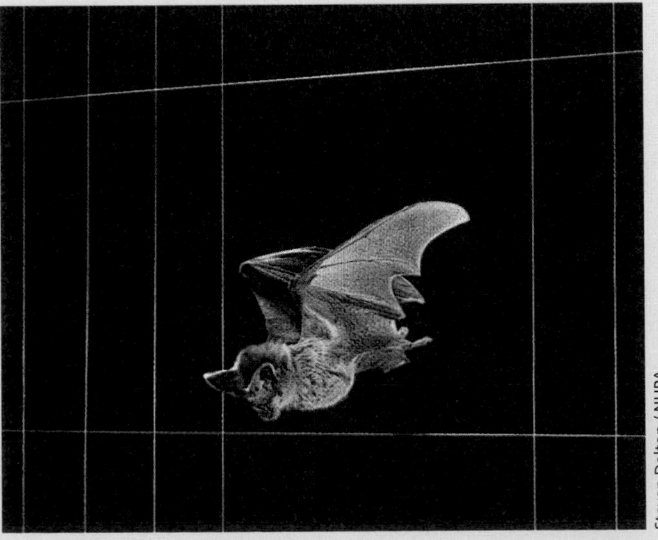
Steven Dalton / NHPA

Even though the world of a bat is created largely through sound, rather than sight, they don't seem to have much trouble getting around. This bat uses its acute sense of hearing and echolocation to ably navigate through this mesh screen. Its nervous system is designed to enable the bat to locate insects and avoid obstacles in the dark.

The brains of these animals do something else as well: they create knowledge about the world. They keep track of where objects are, where food is found, where safe sleeping places are located, and so on. As brains evolved into larger and larger organs, the amount of knowledge processed and stored grew so big that some mechanism for organizing it was needed. One solution to the problem of categorizing information is to create some form of coding system, of which human language is the ultimate example. In essence, the earliest function of language may have been to organize the brain's information. Language, in other words, evolved for the brain to talk to itself. Later, language also provided a way to share knowledge *between* brains. Given the achievements of the human species in all these behavioral functions—representing the world and moving around in it, as well as acquiring and organizing knowledge—it is clear that our brain's evolutionary development has been very successful indeed.

## 2. The Neuron Is the Basic Unit of Anatomy, Physiology, and Cognition (Chapters 1, 4–6, 13, 14).

Review the structure of the neuron in the module on Neural Communication on the CD.

Nerve cells are remarkably similar in all species, no matter where they are found in the nervous system. These cells are the basic unit of information processing, of plasticity, and even of cognition. Drugs, for example, act at the level of individual neurons; and individual neurons are what an animal's experiences change. Individual neurons also communicate with one another to generate sensory perceptions and to produce behaviors. Differences between brains reflect differences in how individual neurons are distributed, organized, and connected.

Although neurons are individual cells, each with a role in behavior, the number of neurons performing similar functions has expanded exponentially as brains have grown larger over the course of evolution. Consider a simple nervous system, such as

The brain integrates and makes decisions about information at several organizational levels.

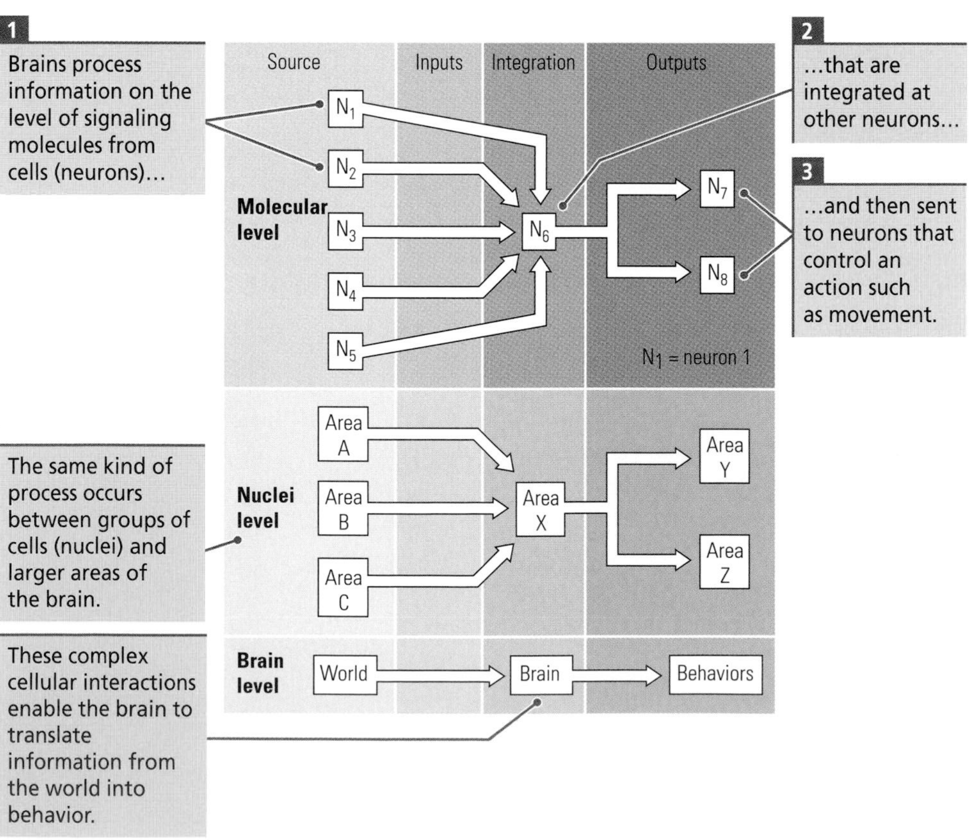

that of the worm *C. elegans*, which consists of 302 neurons, each with a specific job. If one neuron dies or becomes dysfunctional, the entire system is affected. In contrast, the death of one neuron is not a problem in the human brain, which has 80 billion neurons. As brains have evolved to be larger and much harder to build to an exact blueprint, nature's solution has been to create extra neurons that duplicate the function of other neurons. The strategy is to shed unused and unnecessary neurons, sculpting the brain to the organism's current needs and experiences. This strategy not only avoids dependence on the survival of each individual neuron; it also allows great flexibility in adapting to specific environmental conditions. The organism can put its energy into maintaining neurons that are required in its daily life, and allowing unneeded neurons to die does not result in the loss of any essential mental or behavioral function.

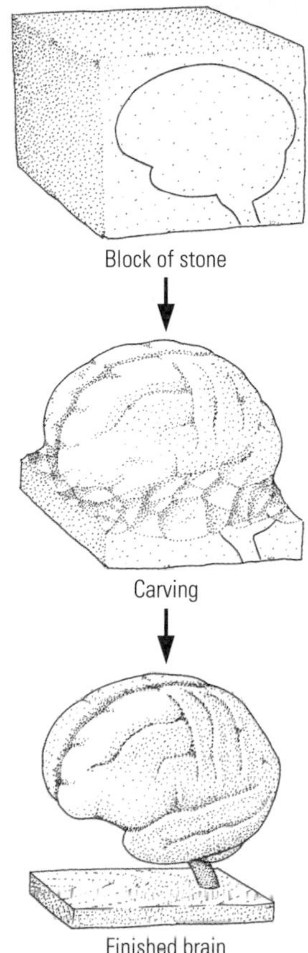


Our brains are created with lots of extra neurons so that we can customize our brains to do exactly what we need them to do. The unneeded neurons can be discarded, just like the residue from making a sculpture out of a block of stone.

### 3. The Synapse Is the Key Site of Neural Communication and Learning (Chapters 4–6, 13).

The three basic parts of the neuron are the cell body, the dendrites, and the axon, including the axon terminal (Figure 15-1). The cell body acts as the factory of the neuron, producing the proteins and energy required for the cell's operation. The dendrites, which are essentially extensions of the cell body's surface, allow a neuron to collect information from other cells, whereas the axon provides a pathway for passing along that information. Although the dendrites and axon both handle messages, the business site for communication is the synapse (Figure 15-2). Synapses are most often between an axon terminal of one cell and a dendrite, cell body, or axon of another cell. The primary mode of communication across most synapses is chemical. The chemical either alters channels on the receiving (postsynaptic) neuron or initiates postsynaptic events through second messengers.

Synaptic activity can be influenced in several ways. The most direct route is either to increase or decrease the amount of chemical transmitter released into the synaptic cleft or to enhance or attenuate that chemical's action on its postsynaptic receptor. This is the primary route of action of most drugs. There are less direct routes, too. One effect of repeated exposure to drugs is either to change characteristics of the postsynaptic membrane (such as the number of receptor sites on it) or to alter the number of synapses. The number of synapses may be increased by adding new synapses to the existing neurons, or the synaptic space may be increased by adding more dendritic material. Changes in receptors or in the number of synapses are likely involved in processes

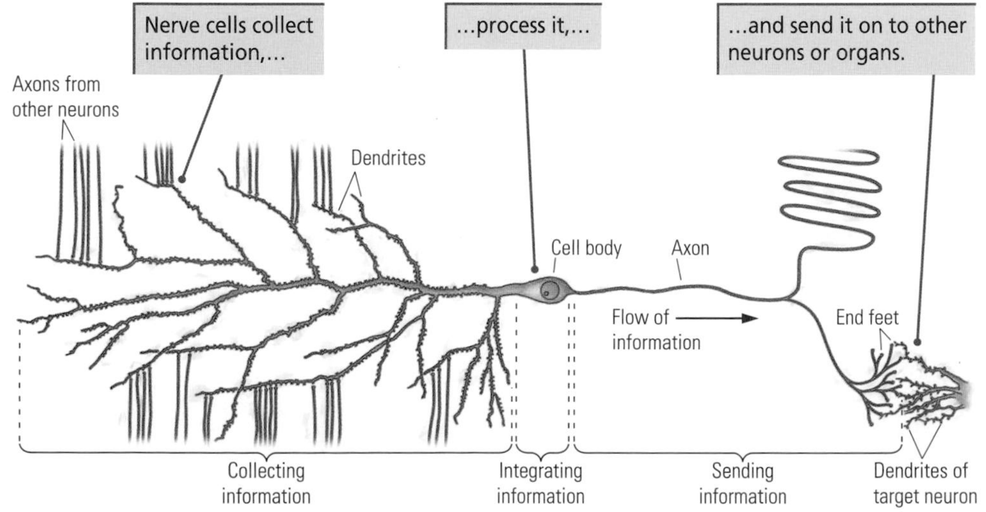


**Figure 15-1**

A neuron is made up of dendrites, which collect information from other cells; an axon, which communicates this information to other neurons; and a cell body, which provides the energy required to keep the operation going.

**Figure 15-2**

The synapse is the site where communication happens between neurons. Most often, synapses occur between the axon terminal of one cell and a dendrite, cell body, or axon of another cell.

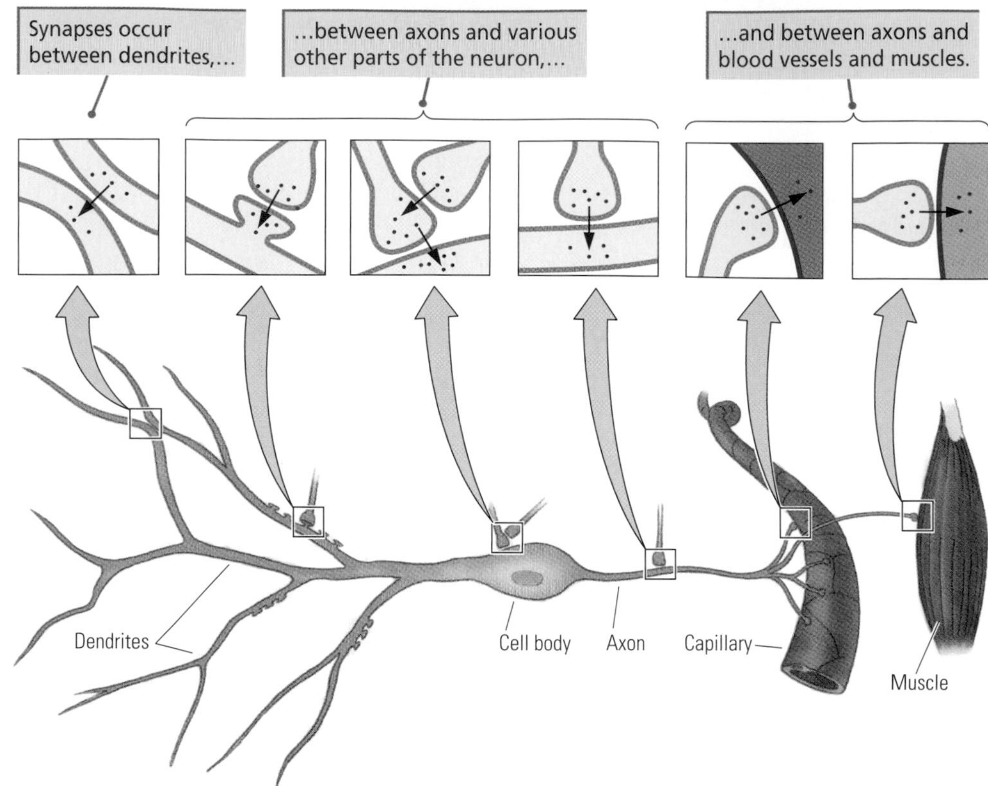


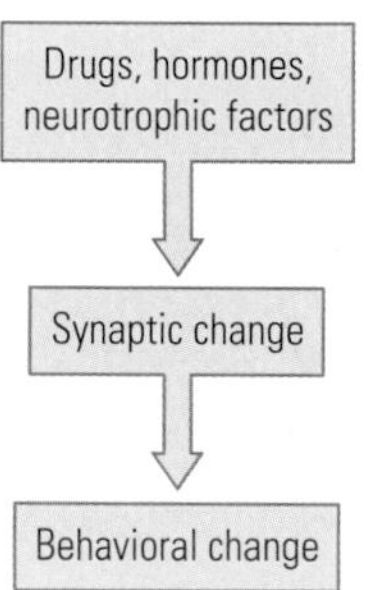


such as learning and drug addiction. Indeed, synaptic change is required for virtually any behavioral change, whether the change is related to learning, to development and aging, or to recovery from brain injury. Because synaptic change is the key to behavioral change, it follows that factors that enhance or diminish synaptic change (such as neurotrophic factors, drugs, hormones, or experiences) will stimulate or retard behavioral change. Many new treatments for behavioral disorders are designed to maximize synaptic change.

### 4. Neural Development Depends on the Influences of Both Genes and Experience (Chapters 7, 13).

Development is not governed by a strict genetic code. Although developmental stages are initiated by genetic instructions, the details of development are strongly influenced by experience (Figure 15-3). Experience does not just mean things that happen in the outside world. It encompasses internal events, too, including the presence of hormones and other chemicals, as well as disease and injury. Because experiential factors can influence the messages that genes produce and because genes, in turn, can influence an organism's developmental environment, it is hard to determine the relative contributions that genes and environment make to development. The complex interaction of genes and environment continues throughout life, influencing how we learn, behave, and think even into old age.

### 5. Consciousness Organizes the Information That Enters the Brain, the Knowledge That the Brain Creates, and the Behavior That the Brain Produces (Chapters 8, 14).

Presumably, consciousness provides an adaptive advantage when a large amount of information must be processed before we decide how to behave in a particular situation. But behaviors that depend on conscious processing are slower than those that are done automatically. As a result, conscious analysis is usually applied to tasks where speed is

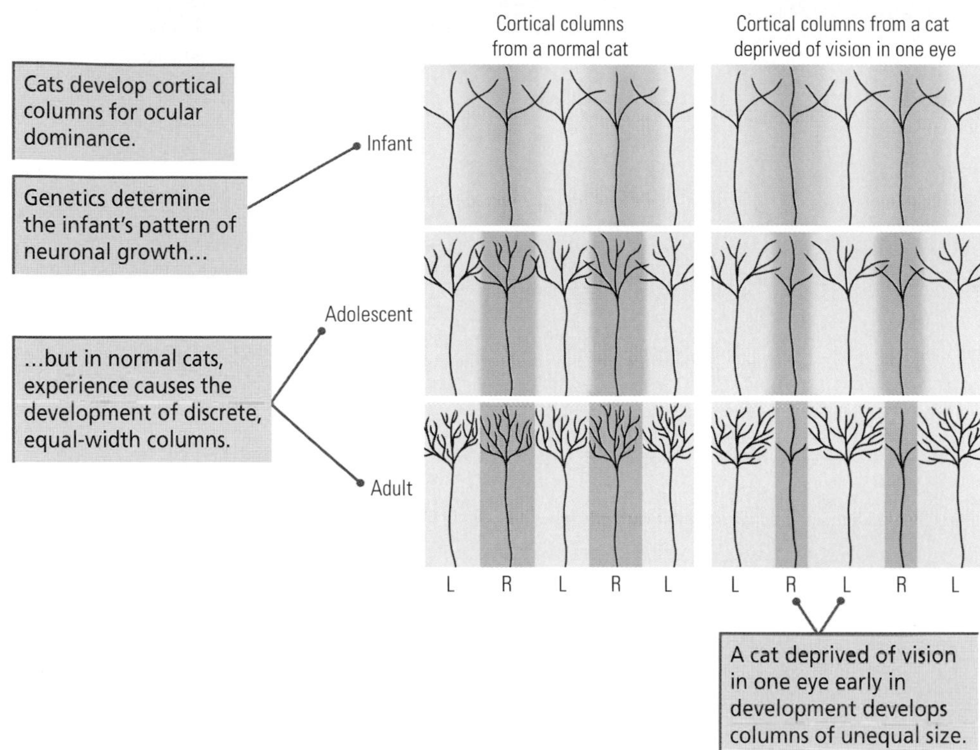
Cortical columns from a normal cat
Cortical columns from a cat deprived of vision in one eye
Cats develop cortical columns for ocular dominance.
Genetics determine the infant's pattern of neuronal growth...
Infant
Adolescent
...but in normal cats, experience causes the development of discrete, equal-width columns.
Adult
L R L R L
L R L R L
A cat deprived of vision in one eye early in development develops columns of unequal size.

**Figure 15-3**

This experiment shows the joint contributions of genetics and experience to development. In early development, a cat was deprived of vision in one eye. While the pattern of neural growth, determined by genetics, was normal, the cat's cortical dominance columns are abnormal, showing the impact of experience.

not really critical, such as discriminating between the various colors of socks in a drawer. In contrast, movements that must be done rapidly, such as swinging a baseball bat at a ball (Figure 15-4), are usually done without conscious control. As you learned in the discussion of the ventral and dorsal streams of the visual system (Chapter 8), the distinction between conscious and unconscious processing is fundamental to the difference between thinking about objects and moving in relation to objects. Very likely, the conscious processing of sensory information was enhanced by the emergence of language, which, as we said earlier, may have evolved in part to categorize information.

Matthew Stockman / Allsport

**Figure 15-4**

Sometimes processing happens so quickly that we cannot be aware of it. The ball coming out of the pitcher's hand will be traveling too fast for Mark McGwire to consciously see it, but he may still be able to get a hit.

## 6. Functions Are Both Localized and Distributed to Specific Regions of the Brain (Chapters 7–14).

Sensory information, knowledge, and the control of movement are all represented at multiple levels in the nervous system, beginning at the spinal cord and ending in the association cortex (Figure 15-5). These multiple levels of representation imply that functions can be localized to specific regions in the brain. In fact, you have seen such localization of function; the segregation of sensory and motor functions is just one example. Even though certain functions are relatively localized in the brain, there are parallel and distributed systems that participate in almost any complex behavior. Localization, in other words, is a relative concept because the brain is also organized into functional networks. Parallel pathways take part even in what seem to be single functions, the clearest example being the visual control of movement versus the visual identification of information.

A key issue in studying the brain is the extent to which functions can be thought to reside in specific locations. A fundamental difficulty in localizing functions begins with the problem of defining what a function is. Consider motivation. In Chapter 11, we used the psychological construct of motivation as a shorthand way to describe the processes that initiate various behaviors. But motivated behavior ranges from basic

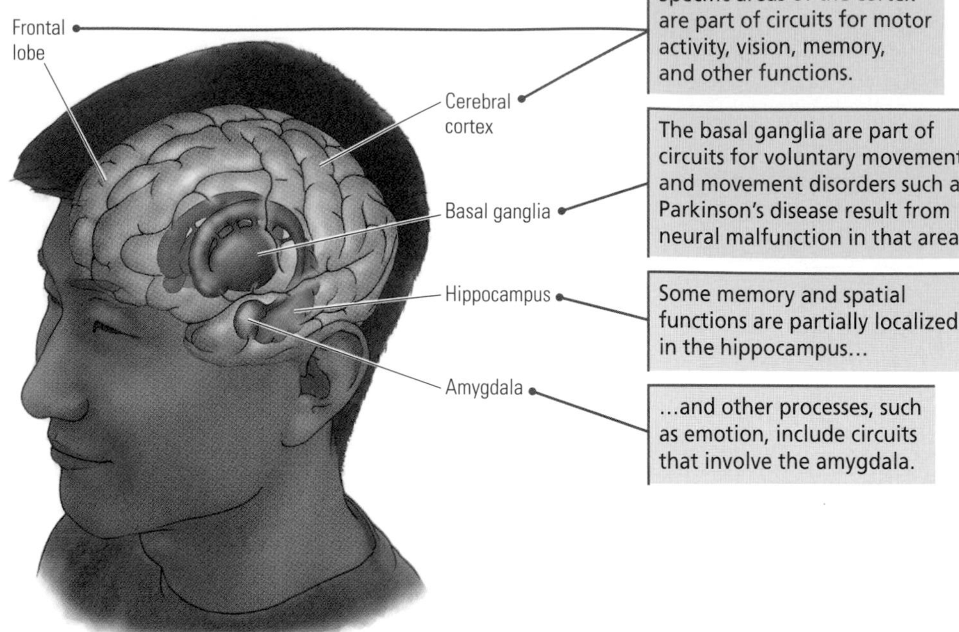

Frontal lobe
Cerebral cortex
Basal ganglia
Hippocampus
Amygdala
Specific areas of the cortex are part of circuits for motor activity, vision, memory, and other functions.
The basal ganglia are part of circuits for voluntary movement, and movement disorders such as Parkinson's disease result from neural malfunction in that area.
Some memory and spatial functions are partially localized in the hippocampus...
...and other processes, such as emotion, include circuits that involve the amygdala.

**Figure 15-5**

Functions are localized in specific parts of the brain, but different aspects of a function, such as memory, may be localized in more than one area.

Rotate the brain and investigate brain anatomy in the module on the Central Nervous System on the CD.

needs, such as maintaining a constant body temperature, to lusting after an abstract concept, such as money. The neural systems underlying such disparate behaviors are clearly going to be segregated from each other. Even when we looked at sexual behavior, which seems to be a single function, we saw that there are two distinctly different components: wanting sex and engaging in sex. These two types of behaviors are organized by different neural pathways. Apparently, the function that we call sexual behavior has many aspects, and these reside in widely separated areas of the brain.

A similar analysis may be applied to most other behaviors, a prime example being memory. Memories are often extremely rich in detail and may include sensory material, feelings, words, and much more. As we saw in Chapter 13, there are many types of memory processing, including the implicit–explicit distinction. Like sexual behavior, then, memory is not located in one place. Specific memory functions, such as facial memory, may be located in discrete neural regions, but the behavior that we call memory is distributed throughout vast areas of the brain.

One implication of the concept of localized and distributed functions is that damage to a small area of the brain produces focal symptoms, but it takes massive brain damage to destroy a function completely. For instance, a relatively small injury can destroy some aspect of memory, but it takes a very widespread injury to destroy *all* memory capability. Thus, a brain-injured person may be amnesic for the explicit recall of new information, but he or she can still recall a lot of explicit information from the past and may retain *implicit* recall of new information.

### 7. Brain Organization Segregates Sensory Information That Is Used for Action and for Knowledge (Such as Object Recognition) (Chapters 2, 8, 9, 10).

The brain is organized around the law of Bell and Magendie, which states that there is a clear demarcation between the control of sensory and motor functions. For instance, in the spinal cord, the dorsal roots and their associated pathways are sensory in function, whereas the ventral roots and their associated pathways are motor in function. Similarly, in the cortex, layer IV is the sensory layer, whereas layers V and VI are the motor layers.

A distinction between motor and sensory functions also exists in a more abstract sense. For example, we have emphasized the difference between vision for the purpose of moving to grasp objects and vision for the purpose of knowing about objects. It is likely that each sensory modality has a separate system for action and for knowledge. The action systems consist of the posterior parietal regions and the associated connections to the frontal motor areas, whereas the knowledge systems consist of the anterior temporal regions and the associated medial temporal and prefrontal regions. The difference between these two systems becomes especially clear in the context of unconscious and conscious activity.

Investigate the sensory systems of the brain in the modules on the Central Nervous System and the Visual System on the CD.

## 8. Both Symmetry and Asymmetry Exist in Brain Anatomy and Function (Chapters 8, 14).

A logical extension of the concept of localization of function is the lateralization of function to a single hemisphere. One reason functions are lateralized may be that it is more efficient to have a single neural network controlling a complex behavior that depends on multiple sources of sensory input, knowledge, or both. For instance, it is hard to imagine language or birdsong being produced by a brain that has bilateral control of the sound-producing apparatus. After all, an organism cannot simultaneously make two different sounds, one produced by each hemisphere. A single control system therefore makes more sense. This concept can easily be applied to other functions as well. For example, although we can move our limbs independently, many of our movements, such as eating or dressing, require limb cooperation. Control of such behaviors clearly necessitates the integration of multiple sources of sensory input and multiple movements. The nervous system has evolved lateralized networks to oversee these functions.

It is tempting to overemphasize the asymmetrical organization of the brain, especially the cerebral hemispheres (for an example of some of the brain's asymmetry, see Figure 15-6). In fact, however, both sides of the brain undertake many, perhaps most, brain functions. Both sides process sensory inputs from all the sensory domains, and both sides produce movements of one side of the body. The brain, in other words, has both symmetrical and asymmetrical organization. Even a function like language, which we think of as lateralized, has both symmetrical and asymmetrical aspects. It is the *output* apparatus for language that must be controlled unilaterally. There is no obvious reason why the receptive aspects of language must be unilaterally controlled, and, in fact, the right hemisphere does have receptive functions, especially for nouns.

The left Sylvian fissure is more horizontal,...
...and the right Sylvian fissure bends upward more.
Sylvian fissure
Parietal lobe
Temporal lobe
Left hemisphere
Right hemisphere
As a result, the parietal lobe is larger on the left...
...and the temporal lobe is larger on the right.

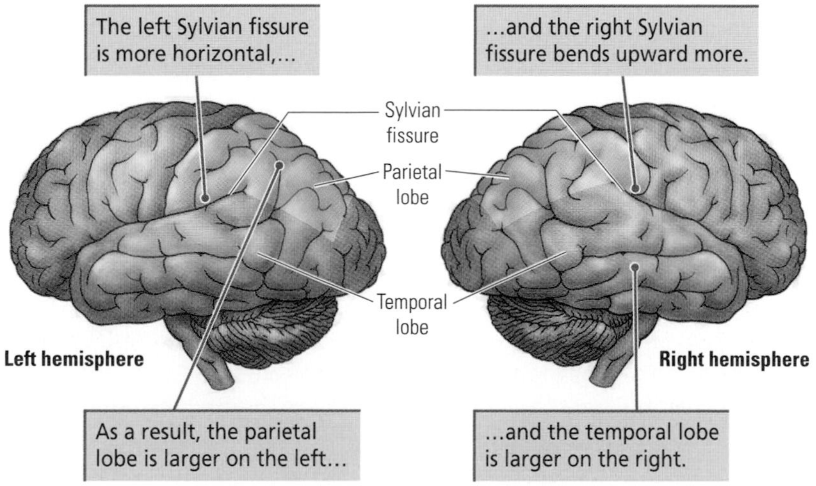

**Figure 15-6**

Although the human brain looks as if it might be identical on the right and the left sides, closer inspection reveals that it is not. The brain's functions, however, are both symmetrical and asymmetrical.

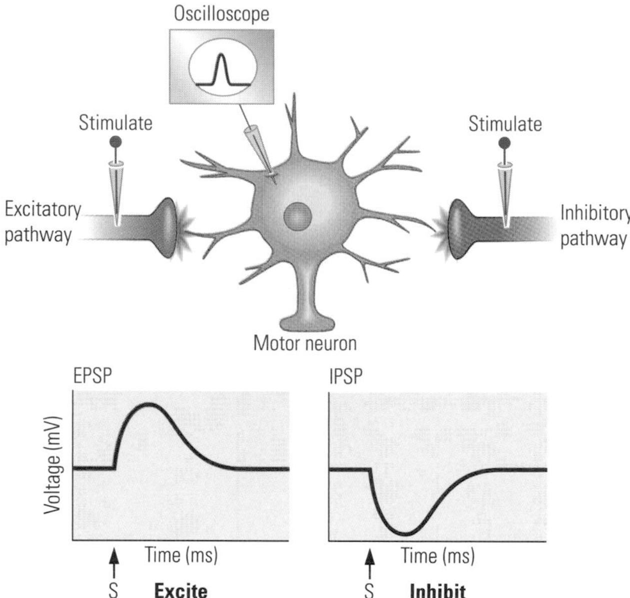


**Figure 15-7**

Neurotransmitters can either excite or inhibit a postsynaptic neuron. The physiological effects of each—depolarization or hyperpolarization—are opposed. Researcher John C. Eccles used this experimental setup to demonstrate that stimulation of a neuron's excitatory pathway produces a membrane depolarization called an EPSP (excitatory postsynaptic potential). Stimulation of the inhibitory pathway produces a membrane hyperpolarization called an IPSP (inhibitory postsynaptic potential).

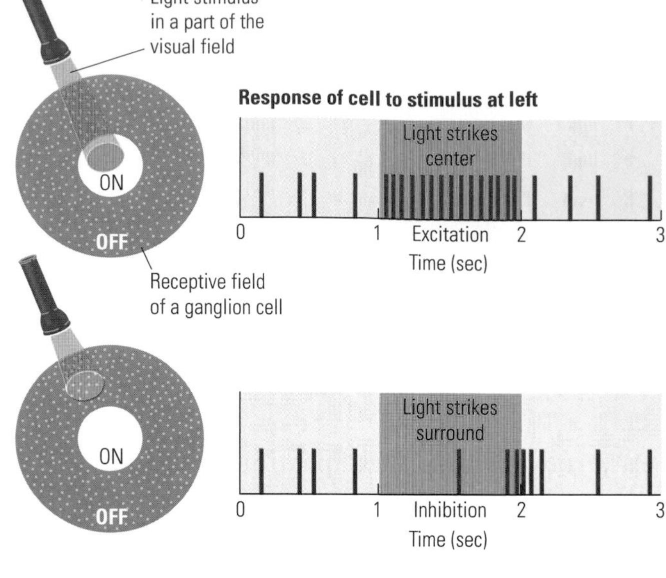


**Figure 15-8**

A single neuron in the visual cortex is receptive to stimulation in part of the visual field. A spot of light in the center causes excitation, but when the light shines elsewhere, the cell is inhibited.

Review the basics of excitation and inhibition in the module on Neural Communication on the CD.

## 9. The Nervous System Operates by a Juxtaposition of Excitation and Inhibition (Chapters 2–6, 8, 10, 11).

An interplay of excitation and inhibition is one of the basic principles of nervous system organization that we listed in Chapter 2. As you have progressed through this book, you have seen that an interplay of excitation and inhibition occurs at many levels of nervous system function. At the level of the cell and its components, single neurons can be either excited or inhibited, and neurotransmitters can act to stimulate or inhibit synaptic activity (Figure 15-7, from Chapter 4). An example is how the activity of single neurons in the visual cortex can be excited or inhibited by stimulation in different parts of the visual field, as shown in Figure 15-8 (from Chapter 8). Beyond the level of the cell, these dual processes continue to apply. For instance, systems in the reticular formation controlling sleep–waking cycles essentially balance the inhibition and activation of forebrain systems (Chapter 12). Similarly, motor control includes the inhibition of some movements while other movements are being activated (Chapter 12), and many diseases can be thought of as disorders of excitatory and inhibitory signals. Huntington's chorea, for example, is the loss of the ability to inhibit choreiform (convulsive) movements, whereas depression represents an inability to activate many kinds of behaviors. Some diseases are characterized by changes in both inhibition and excitation. For instance, Parkinson's disease features both an uncontrollable tremor *and* difficulty in initiating movement, and schizophrenia may feature both flattened emotions *and* sensory hallucinations. The release of behaviors like tremor or hallucinations reflects a loss of inhibition, whereas the absence of behaviors like movement or facial expression represents a loss of excitation. In all these ways, the activity of neurons and neural systems may be viewed as a balance between the forces of inhibition and those of excitation.

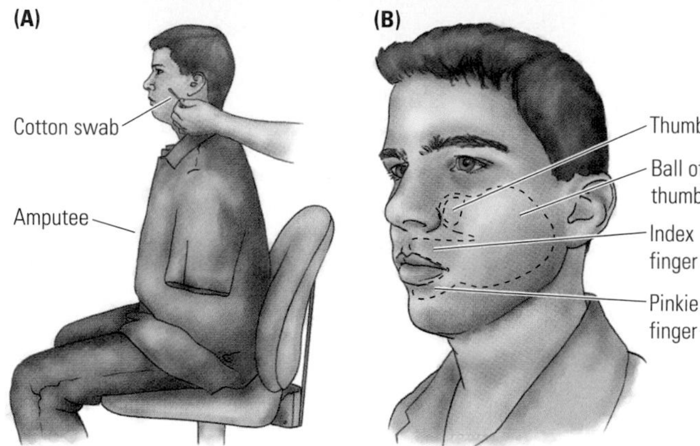


**Figure 15-9**

The brain is extraordinarily flexible. A person who has suffered an arm amputation shows an increase in the representation of the face in the somatosensory cortex. In effect, the representation of the missing hand is transferred onto the face. As a result, when the person's face is lightly touched, as in this drawing, the person feels as if his or her missing hand is being touched.

## 10. Patterns of Neural Organization Are Plastic (Chapters 5, 13).

The brain is plastic in two fundamental ways. First, although we tend to think of regions of the brain as having fixed functions, the brain has a capacity to adapt to different experiences by changing where specific functions are represented. For example, people with an amputated arm were found to have an increase in the representation of the face in the somatosensory cortex, as shown in Figure 15-9 (from Chapter 11). In the absence of the limb, the face becomes more sensitive. Second, the brain is also plastic in the sense that the connections among neurons in a given functional system are constantly changing in response to experience. This type of plasticity is manifested in our capacity for learning and for subsequently recalling learned material (Chapter 13).

There are clearly some limits to the brain's plasticity. Reorganization of sensory representations is constrained by the boundaries of the inputs. For example, the extent of somatosensory representation is limited by the inputs from the somatosensory thalamus. Adjacent regions, which receive input from the motor or visual thalamic nuclei, cannot assume somatosensory functions because they are connected with different receptors. Similarly, although neurons can grow new dendrites in response to experiences, there are limits to how much a given neuron can change and how many connections can be placed on it. Not only are there biophysical limits with respect to how new connections affect membrane potentials; there are metabolic limits too. Neurons, after all, are not designed to have cell bodies a centimeter in diameter.

## 11. Animals Engage in Behaviors for Multiple Reasons (Chapters 11, 12).

One of the most difficult questions to answer is why animals engage in behaviors, especially why they perform particular behaviors at particular times. To address this question, we considered the story of Roger, who seemed to have strange, indiscriminate food preferences. We also considered the housefly and learned that what appeared to be purposeful behavior was really a response to stimuli coming from its feet and esophagus (Figure 15-10). In addition, we looked at why cats kill birds; we considered the annual cycle of polar bears; and we examined ideas about why we sleep and dream. We found it helpful to classify the many different kinds of animal behaviors as either regulatory or nonregulatory. Regulatory behaviors are those that maintain basic body functions, such as maintaining a constant body temperature or generating patterns of sleep and waking. Most regulatory behaviors require very little brain and are largely controlled by the hypothalamus and associated brainstem structures.

It is more difficult to say why we engage in our nonregulatory behaviors. For example, we seek stimulation, finding an absence of sensory input intolerable. We also seek mates, orienting much of our lives around this

**Figure 15-10**

A housefly tastes with its feet. Stretch receptors in its foregut tell it when it is full.

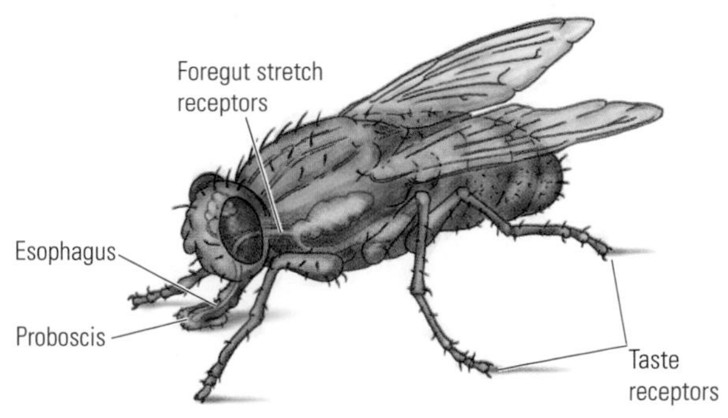

behavior and activities associated with it. In addition, we make plans and organize our behaviors in time. Searching for the reasons for these behaviors led us to investigate the anatomical structures that control each of them.

Although we still do not know much about the reasons for many of our nonregulatory behaviors, we can draw several conclusions. First, behavior is controlled by its consequences. These consequences may shape the behavior of a species or the behavior of an individual organism. Behaviors that are adaptive and brains that are likely to engage in adaptive behaviors are selected in the course of evolution. We learned that cats kill birds because there are neural circuits in the brainstem that control the killing behaviors. Activation of these circuits is presumably rewarding, so, in a sense, animals engage in many behaviors because it feels good to do so. We learned, too, that animals do not need to actually engage in a rewarded behavior to experience this positive feeling. Electrical stimulation of the circuits appears to be just as rewarding (perhaps even more so) than actually using the circuits.

Second, as the brain has expanded in size throughout its evolution, structures in the forebrain have developed to control the activity of brainstem circuits. These developments have probably occurred for two quite different reasons. One is to add complexity to the behaviors being controlled. A second is to ensure that engaging in rewarding behaviors is safe. Sexual activity may feel good, but it will not last long if you are rat and a cat is nearby! The principal forebrain structures involved in the initiation of motivated behaviors are the amygdala and the frontal lobe. Abnormality in these structures is related to a variety of disorders, including schizophrenia and anxiety disorders.

A final conclusion we can draw about the reasons for nonregulatory behaviors is that survival depends on maximizing contact with some environmental stimuli and minimizing contact with others. Reward is one mechanism for controlling this attraction to certain stimuli and avoiding others. There are two independent features of reward: wanting and liking. Wanting is thought to be controlled by dopaminergic systems, while liking is thought to be controlled by opiate–benzodiazepine systems.

## 12. The Study of Brain–Behavior Relationships Is Multidisciplinary (Chapters 1–14).

Studying the link between the brain and behavior involves many methods, ranging from clinical observation to tools of molecular biology. Each method has advantages and disadvantages. In this book, methods have been introduced in the context of specific topics.

One way to summarize the methods of studying brain and behavior is to consider them from the level of the whole organism to the molecular level, as shown in Table 15-1. Behavioral studies by their very nature are investigations of the whole organism. Those conducted by Broca in the nineteenth century were in many ways the starting point of systematic studies of brain–behavior relationships. Later studies of this type used groups of patients or laboratory animals with brain injuries. As the modern science of behavioral analysis developed, more elaborate measures were devised both to analyze mental activity and to relate behavior to brain states. The development of molecular biology has enabled the creation of strains of animals, usually mice, that have either a gene deleted (or inactivated) or a gene inserted. Currently, there is much interest in using this technology both to create animal models of human disorders and to generate treatments for neurobehavioral disorders.

Over the past decade, the development of various brain-imaging techniques has made it possible for changes in brain activity to be measured without direct access to the brain. Although these studies are still in their infancy, they have allowed new insights into the neural organization of cognitive processes. Recall, for example, the dissociation of linguistic and musical abilities both between and within hemispheres that we examined in Chapter 9.

**Table 15-1 Summary of Methods of Studying Brain and Behavior**

| Technique | Chapter in which an example is discussed |
|---|---|
| **Behavioral studies** | |
| Clinical investigations of individual cases | 11 |
| Neurosurgical studies of patients at surgery | 9 |
| Neuropsychological analyses of groups of patients | 14 |
| Neuropsychological analyses of laboratory animals | 13 |
| Ethological studies of behavior | 7 |
| Cognitive psychology and psychophysics | 14 |
| Developmental studies | 7 |
| Behavioral genetics | 7 |
| **Brain imaging** | |
| Positron emission tomography (PET) | 7 |
| Functional magnetic resonance Imaging (fMRI) | 14 |
| **Brain stimulation** | |
| Electrical stimulation | 10 |
| Transmagnetic stimulation | 14 |
| **Brain recording** | |
| Electroencephalography | 5 |
| Magnetoencephalography | 5 |
| Event-related potentials | 5 |
| Long-term enhancement | 5 |
| Single-cell recording | 8 |
| **Brain anatomy** | |
| Cytological measures (i.e., measuring cell morphology) | 3 |
| Histological measures (i.e., measuring cell characteristics) | 3 |
| Tracing neural connections | 4 |
| Synaptic measures | 13 |

Brain-stimulation studies began in the late 1800s, using both humans and laboratory animals as subjects. The early studies of this type involved direct stimulation of the brain with tiny electric currents (Chapter 9); more recently, magnetic stimulation techniques have been developed, which alter brain activity through the skull (Chapter 14). We also saw that brain stimulation can be used to affect the behavior of a freely moving animal (Chapter 11). Recall that animals will press a lever to deliver a mild electric current to certain regions of the brain, especially the medial forebrain bundle.

Brain-recording studies aim to measure the ongoing activity of large areas of the brain (as in EEG or MEG) or to monitor the activity of individual neurons. One important finding of such studies is that brain waves are not so much correlated with mental events as with behavior. Another important discovery is that the behavior of individual neurons is related to perceptions (Chapter 14).

Finally, neuroscience has a rich history of studies in neuroanatomy that began at the turn of the twentieth century with one of the greatest scientists of all time, Santiago Ramón y Cajal (see Chapter 3). Today, we have a vast arsenal of cytological and histological methods. These allow us to characterize details not only of cell structure but also of changes in synapses during periods of brain plasticity.

### 13. Abnormalities in Nervous System Structure, Biochemistry, or Functioning Lead to Abnormal Behavior (Chapters 1–14).

We have encountered disorders of brain and behavior in every chapter of this book, especially in the Focus on Disorders boxes. As summarized in Table 15-2, the variety of abnormalities is wide, including genetic disorders (such as Huntington's chorea), developmental disorders (such as autism), infectious diseases (such as meningitis), nervous system injuries (such as closed head injury), and degenerative conditions (such as Alzheimer's disease). The unifying characteristic of all these disorders is the presence of some underlying nervous system abnormality.

**Table 15-2 Summary of Discussions of Disorders in Chapters 1–14**

| Disorder | Location | Disorder | Location |
|---|---|---|---|
| Addiction | 6 | Insanity | 1* |
| Agenesis of the frontal lobe | 11* | Insomnia | 12 |
| Agnosia | 8 | Korsakoff's syndrome | 13* |
| Alzheimer's disease | 13* | Learning disabilities | 1* |
| Amnesia | 13 | Lou Gehrig's disease | 4* |
| Androgen insensitivity syndrome | 11* | Mania | 15 |
| Androgenital syndrome | 11* | Meningitis | 2* |
| Anencephaly | 7 | Mental retardation | 7 |
| Anxiety disorders | 11* | Migraine | 8* |
| Aphasia | 9 | Missile wound | 1 |
| Arteriovenous malformations | 9* | MPTP poisoning | 5* |
| Autism | 10* | Multiple sclerosis | 3* |
| Bell's palsy | 2* | Myasthenia gravis | 4* |
| Brain tumors | 3* | Myopia | 8* |
| Carbon monoxide poisoning | 8* | Narcolepsy | 12 |
| Cerebral aneurysm | 9* | Panic disorder | 11* |
| Cerebral palsy | 7* | Paraplegia | 10* |
| Closed head injury | 1* | Parkinson's disease | 5* |
| Contralateral neglect | 14 | Phenylketonuria | 15 |
| Demoic acid poisoning | 6 | Presbyopia | 8* |
| Depression | 6, 11* | Psychosis | 6 |
| Down's syndrome | 3 | Restless legs syndrome | 12 |
| Drug-induced psychosis | 6* | Schizophrenia | 6, 7* |
| Encephalitis | 2* | Scotoma | 8 |
| Environmental deprivation | 7* | Seasonal affective disorder | 12* |
| Epilepsy | 4, 9* | Sleep apnea | 12* |
| Fetal alcohol syndrome | 6* | Spinal-cord injury | 10 |
| Fragile X syndrome | 7 | Split-brain syndrome | 14 |
| Frontal leucotomy | 11 | Stroke | 2* |
| Hemianopia | 8 | Synesthesia | 14* |
| Huntington's chorea | 3* | Tay-Sachs disease | 3 |
| Hyperopia | 8* | Tourette's syndrome | 10 |

*Focus on Disorders

Nervous system abnormalities are of many types. They include the congenital absence of neurons or glia, the presence of abnormal neurons or glia, the death of neurons or glia, and neurons or neural connections with unusual structures. Similarly, there may be abnormalities in the biochemical organization or the operation of the nervous system. Such biochemical abnormalities include disordered membrane channels, low or high numbers of receptors, low or high amounts of different molecules (especially transmitters or hormones), and an improper balance of any of these. The long-term prospects for treating behavioral disorders depend on the ability to correct these various structural and biochemical abnormalities.

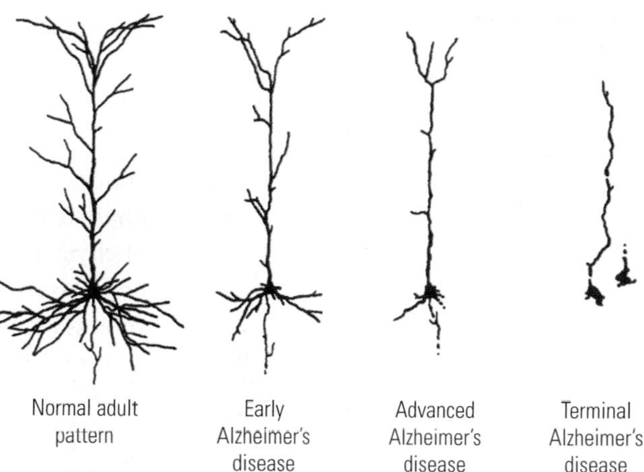


The neurons of patients with Alzheimer's disease degenerate as they experience worsening symptoms, including memory loss and personality change.

Although all behavioral disorders are ultimately related to the nervous system, environmental factors often contribute to them as well. Many social and cultural factors affect how the brain operates to produce behaviors, both normal and abnormal ones. The influence of environmental factors on behavior is illustrated by the simple fact that we behave quite differently in the context of a formal social gathering and in the company of our closest friends. However, we are a long way from understanding exactly how environmental factors can influence brain activity or produce pathological behaviors at specific times and places.

Treatments for behavioral disorders need not be direct biological interventions. Just as the brain can alter behavior, so behavior can alter the brain (Chapter 11). Therefore, treatments for behavioral disorders often focus on key environmental factors that influence how a person acts. As behavior changes in response to these treatments, the brain is affected as well. An example is the treatment of generalized anxiety disorders, as illustrated by the case of G. B. in Chapter 11. Although G. B. required immediate treatment with antianxiety medication, the long-term treatment involved behavioral therapy. His anxiety disorder was not simply a problem of abnormal brain activity. It was also a problem of experiential and social factors that fundamentally altered his perception of the world. We return to this idea shortly.

## In Review

We have identified 13 general concepts that are central to the study of the brain and how it produces thought and behavior. The selection of these concepts is somewhat arbitrary, and additional ones could have been included. For the student, however, the reason for extracting these concepts is just as important as their particular content. Our task is to start to synthesize a large body of information into an integrated theory of how the brain works. Perhaps the overriding message that emerges from this effort is that mental activity results from brain activity, and through research we can eventually understand how this process occurs.

# DISORDERS OF BRAIN AND BEHAVIOR

For most of us, the origins and treatment of abnormal behavior are one of the most fascinating topics in the study of the brain and behavior. Although we have encountered disorders of the brain throughout the preceding 14 chapters, we have not systematically discussed the neural basis of behavioral disorders. This is our next task. We look first at the special challenges inherent in investigating the neurobiology of these disorders. We then examine how such disorders are classified and distributed in the population. Finally, we look at the general causes of behavioral disorders.

**Phenylketonuria (PKU).** A behavioral disorder caused by elevated levels of the amino acid phenylalanine in the blood as a result of a defect in the gene for the enzyme phenylalanine hydroxylase; the major symptom is severe mental retardation.

## Investigating the Neurobiology of Behavioral Disorders

That a single brain abnormality can cause a behavioral disorder, explaining everything about that disorder and its treatment, is nicely illustrated by the condition called **phenylketonuria** (PKU). Babies with PKU have elevated levels of the amino acid phenylalanine in their blood, as a result of a defect in the gene for phenylalanine hydroxylase, an enzyme that breaks down phenylalanine. Left untreated, PKU causes severe mental retardation. Fortunately, PKU can easily be treated just by restricting the dietary intake of phenylalanine. If other behavioral disorders were as simple and well understood as PKU is, research in neuroscience could quickly cure them.

Many disorders do not result from a single abnormality, however, and the causes of most disorders are still largely matters of conjecture. The major problem is that diagnosis is based mainly on behavioral symptoms, and behavioral symptoms give few clues to specific biochemical or structural causes. This problem can be seen in PKU. Table 15-3 lists what is known about PKU at different levels of analysis: genetic, biochemical, histological, neurological, behavioral, and social. The underlying problem in PKU becomes less apparent as we move down the table. In fact, it is not possible to predict from information at the neurological, behavioral, or social levels what the specific biochemical abnormality is. This difficulty has major implications for most behavioral illnesses, because the primary information available *is* at the neurological, behavioral, and social levels. For most diseases, and especially most psychiatric diseases, the pathology is unknown. For PKU, elevated phenylpyruric acid levels in the urine of a single patient was the clue needed to understand the disorder. The task for the future study of most behavioral disorders is to identify the biological markers that will lead to similar understandings.

Knowledge about behavioral disorders is also hampered by diagnostic challenges. By its very nature, most of the diagnostic information that is gathered is about a patient's behavior. This behavioral information comes from both patients and their families. Unfortunately, people are seldom objective observers of their own behavior or that of a loved one. We tend to be selective in noticing and reporting symptoms. If we believe that someone has a memory problem, we often notice memory lapses that we might ordinarily ignore. Furthermore, we are often not specific enough in identifying symptoms. Simply identifying a memory problem is not really helpful. We need to know exactly what type of memory deficit is involved. Loss of memory for words, places, or habits implies a very different underlying pathology.

It is not just patients and their families who make diagnosis difficult. Behavioral information about patients is also interpreted by evaluators who may be general physicians, psychiatrists, neurologists, psychologists, or social workers. Different evaluators have different conceptual biases that shape and filter the questions they ask and the information they gather. Consider the differences among one evaluator who believes that most behavioral disorders are genetic in origin, another who believes that most result from a virus, and a third who believes that many can be

**Table 15-3 Phenylketonuria: A Behavioral Disorder for Which the Neurobiological Pathogenesis Is Known**

| Level of analysis | Information known |
|---|---|
| Genetic | Inborn error of metabolism; autosomal recessive defective gene |
| Biochemical pathogenesis | Impairment in the hydroxylation of phenylalanine to tyrosine, causing elevated blood levels of phenylalanine and its metabolites |
| Histological abnormality | Decreased neuron size and dendritic length, and lowered spine density; abnormal cortical lamination |
| Neurological findings | Severe mental retardation, slow growth, abnormal EEG |
| Behavioral symptoms | For 95 percent of patients, IQ below 50 |
| Social disability | Loss of meaningful, productive life; significant social and economic cost |
| Treatment | Restrict dietary intake of phenylalanine |

Adapted from "Special Challenges in the Investigation of the Neurobiology of Mental Illness," by G. R. Heninger, in *The Neurobiology of Mental Illness* (pp. 89–98), edited by D. S. Charney, E. J. Nestler, and B. S. Bunney, New York: Oxford, 1999.

traced to repressed sexual experiences during childhood. Each will make quite different types of observations and will give very different kinds of diagnostic tests. In principle, this diagnostic problem could apply equally well to nonbehavioral disorders, but the diagnosis of nonbehavioral disorders is not so dependent on behavioral observations made by an evaluator, with all the difficulties that entails.

Even if the problems of diagnosing behavioral disorders were solved, there would still be major obstacles to investigating these disorders. For one thing, the organizational complexity of the nervous system is far greater than that of other body systems. The brain has a wider variety of cell types than does any other organ, and the complex connections among neurons add a whole new dimension to understanding normal and abnormal functioning. As our understanding of brain and behavior has progressed, it has become apparent that there are multiple receptor systems that are used for many different functions. As George Heninger (1999) pointed out, there is as yet no clear demonstration of a single receptor system with a specific relation to a specific behavior. For example, the neurotransmitter GABA affects some 30 percent of the synapses in the brain. When GABA agonists are given to people, multiple effects on behavior become apparent. In fact, it is difficult to administer enough of a benzodiazepine to reduce anxiety to a "normal" level without producing sedative side effects as well. Other receptor systems, such as those involving acetylcholine, NMDA, and serotonin, are equally diffuse, with little specificity between biochemistry and behavior.

Even when the patient has actual lesions of the nervous system, determining the cause of a behavioral disorder may still be difficult. For instance, MRI scans may show that a person with multiple sclerosis has many nervous system lesions, yet the person displays very few symptoms. Similarly, only when the loss of dopamine neurons exceeds something like 60 to 80 percent do we see clinical signs of Parkinson's disease. This is not to suggest that most of our brain cells are not needed. It simply shows that the brain is capable of considerable plasticity and that when diseases are slow in progressing, the brain has a remarkable capacity for adapting.

Just as obvious brain lesions do not always produce behavioral symptoms, so the presence of behavioral symptoms is not always linked to obvious neuropathology. For instance, some people have notable behavioral problems after suffering a closed head injury, yet no obvious signs of brain damage appear on an MRI scan. The pathology may be subtle, such as a drop in dendritic spine density, or so diffuse that it is hard to identify. Thus, given the current diagnostic methods for both behavioral disorders and neuropathology, identifying disorders and their causes is seldom an easy task.

One of the major avenues for investigating the causes of behavioral disorders is the use of animal models. For example, rats with specific lesions of the nigrostriatal dopamine system are used as a model of Parkinson's disease. This model has led to significant advances in our understanding of how specific dopaminergic agonists and cholinergic antagonists act in the treatment of this disorder. One problem with the use of animal models, however, is the oversimplified view they provide of the neurobiology of behavioral abnormalities. The fact that a drug reduces symptoms does not necessarily mean that it is acting on a key biochemical aspect of the pathology. Aspirin can get rid of a headache, but that does not mean that the headache is caused by the receptors on which aspirin acts. Similarly, antipsychotic drugs block dopamine type-2 receptors, but that does not mean that schizophrenia is caused by an abnormality in these receptors. It is quite possible that schizophrenia results from a disturbance in glutamatergic systems and that, for some reason, dopamine antagonists are effective in rectifying the abnormality.

This is not to imply that animal models are unimportant. We have seen throughout this book that they *are* important. But modeling human disorders is a complex task, so caution is needed when you read news stories about studies using animal models that point toward possible cures for human behavioral diseases.

**DSM-IV.** The fourth and most recent edition of the American Psychiatric Association's classification of psychiatric disorders, the *Diagnostic and Statistical Manual of Mental Disorders.*

## Identifying and Classifying Mental Disorders

*Epidemiology* is the study of the distribution and causes of diseases in human populations. A major contribution of epidemiological studies has been to help define and assess behavioral disorders, especially psychiatric disorders. The first set of criteria for diagnoses in psychiatry was developed in 1972. Since that time, two parallel sets of criteria have been developed. One is the World Health Organization's International Classification of Disease (ICD-10 being the most recent version), and the other is the American Psychiatric Association's *Diagnostic and Statistical Manual of Mental Disorders* (**DSM-IV** being the most recent edition). The classification scheme used in DSM-IV is summarized in Table 15-4.

**Table 15-4 Summary of DSM-IV Classification of Abnormal Behaviors**

| Diagnostic category | Core features and examples of specific disorders |
|---|---|
| Disorders usually first diagnosed in infancy, childhood, and adolescence | Tend to emerge and sometimes dissipate before adult life: pervasive developmental disorders (such as autism), learning disorders, attention-deficit hyperactivity disorder, conduct disorder, separation anxiety disorder |
| Delirium, dementia, amnestic, and other cognitive disorders | Dominated by impairment in cognitive functioning: Alzheimer's disease, Huntington's disease |
| Mental disorders due to a general medical condition | Caused primarily by a general medical disorder: mood disorder due to a general medical condition |
| Substance-related disorders | Brought about by the use of substances that affect the central nervous system: alcohol use disorders, opioid use disorders, amphetamine use disorders, cocaine use disorders, hallucinogen use disorders |
| Schizophrenia and other psychotic disorders | Functioning deteriorates toward a state of psychosis, or loss of contact with reality |
| Mood disorders | Severe disturbances of mood resulting in extreme and inappropriate sadness or elation for extended periods of time: major depressive disorder, bipolar disorders |
| Anxiety disorders | Anxiety: generalized anxiety disorder, phobias, panic disorder, obsessive-compulsive disorder, acute stress disorder, posttraumatic stress disorder |
| Somatoform disorders | Physical symptoms that apparently are caused primarily by psychological rather than physiological factors: conversion disorder, somatization disorder, hypochondriasis |
| Factitious disorders | Intentional production or feigning of physical or psychological symptoms |
| Dissociative disorders | Significant changes in consciousness, memory, identity, or perception, without a clear physical cause: dissociative amnesia, dissociative fugue, dissociative identity disorder (multiple personality disorder) |
| Eating disorders | Abnormal patterns of eating that significantly impair functioning: anorexia nervosa, bulimia nervosa |
| Sexual disorders and gender identity disorder | Chronic disruption in sexual functioning, behavior, or preferences: sexual dysfunctions, paraphilias, gender identity disorder |
| Sleep disorders | Chronic sleep problems: primary insomnia, primary hypersomnia, sleep terror disorder, sleepwalking disorder |
| Impulse-control disorders | Chronic inability to resist impulses, drives, or temptations to perform certain acts that are harmful to the self or others: pathological gambling, kleptomania, pyromania, intermittent explosive disorder |
| Adjustment disorders | A maladaptive reaction to a clear stressor, such as divorce or business difficulties, that first occurs within 3 months after the onset of the stressor |
| Other conditions that may be a focus of clinical attention | Conditions or problems that are worth noting because they cause significant impairment, such as relational problems, problems related to abuse or neglect, medication-induced movement disorders, and psychophysiological disorders |

Adapted from *Diagnostic and Statistical Manual of Mental Disorders* (4th ed.), 1994, Washington, DC: American Psychiatric Association.

Any classification of psychiatric disorders is to some extent arbitrary. These classifications unavoidably depend on prevailing cultural views. A good example is the classification of what is considered abnormal sexual behavior. Until 1973, the DSM listed homosexual behavior as pathological. Since then, the DSM has omitted this "disorder." The revision reflects a change in cultural beliefs about how sexual abnormality should be defined.

Recent large-scale surveys of our population have shown a surprisingly high prevalence of psychiatric disorders as currently defined by the DSM-IV. Figure 15-11 summarizes the lifetime rates of psychiatric disorders among people in the United States. Nearly one-half of the sample had met the criteria for a psychiatric disorder at some point in their lives. Of these, only a minority had received treatment of any kind, and an even smaller percentage had received treatment from a mental health specialist. Large-scale surveys of neurological disorders show a similar pattern of prevalence, as summarized in Table 15-5. Looking at Figure 15-11 and Table 15-5, we can only marvel that most people are relatively normal most of the time.

**Figure 15-11**

The distribution of psychiatric disorders in the United States.

Adapted from "Lifetime and 12-Month Prevalence of DSM-III-R Psychiatric Disorders in the United States" by R. C. Kessler, K. A. McGonagle, S. Zhao, D. B. Nelson, M. Hughes, S. Eshleman, H. Wittchen, and K. S. Kendler, 1994, *Archives of General Psychiatry, 51,* pp. 8–19.

**Table 15-5 Prevalence of the Major Neurological and Communicative Disorders in the United States**

| Disorder | Estimated number of cases |
|---|---|
| **Acute disorders (per year)** | |
| Trauma: head and spinal cord | 500,000/yr |
| Stroke | 400,000/yr |
| Infectious disorders | 25,000/yr |
| **Chronic disorders (cumulative survivors)** | |
| Stroke | 2,000,000+ |
| Closed head injury | 10,000,000+ |
| Spinal-cord injury | 500,000 |
| Epilepsy | 2,000,000 |
| Hearing and speech | |
| Deafness | 2,000,000 |
| Partial deafness | 11,600,000 |
| Speech | 8,400,000 |
| Language | 6,600,000 |
| Movement disorders (e.g., Parkinson's, Huntington's, Tourette's) | 800,000 |
| Demyelinating diseases (MS, ALS) | 200,000 |
| Disorders of early life (e.g., cerebral palsy) | 1,000,000 |
| Neuromuscular disorders | 1,000,000 |
| Other neurological disorders (e.g., chronic pain, insomnia, neuro-AIDS) | 9,000,000 |
| Total chronic | 55,100,000 |

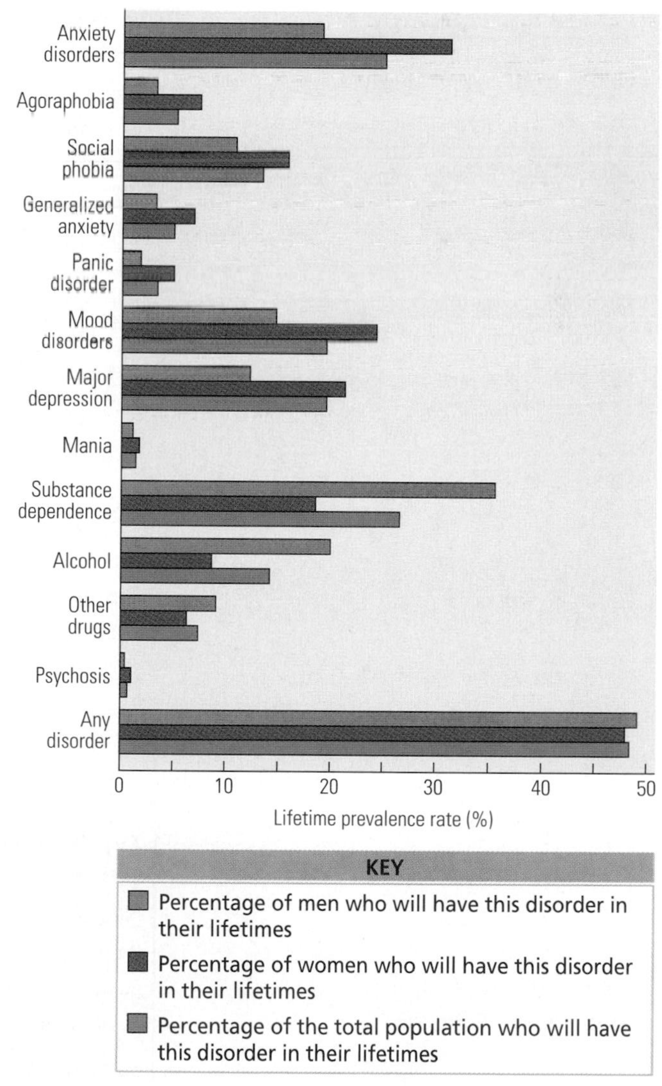

## Causes of Abnormal Behavior

Little is known about the causes of psychiatric disorders. To date, no large-scale neurobiological studies have been done of either postmortem pathology or biochemical pathology in the population at large. Still, clues to the possible causes of these abnormal behaviors are found throughout the preceding 14 chapters. In each case, some abnormality of the brain must be involved. The question is, What is that particular brain abnormality, and why does it occur?

Table 15-6 lists the most likely categories of causes underlying behavioral disorders. The most basic of these causes is a genetic error, such as those responsible for PKU and Tay-Sachs disease. Genetic error is probably linked to some of the other proposed causes, such as hormonal or developmental anomalies. Moreover, genes may be the source not only of anatomical, chemical, or physiological defects, but also of susceptibility to other factors that may cause behavioral problems. For instance, a person may have a genetic predisposition to be vulnerable to stress or infection, which is the immediate cause of some abnormal condition. In other cases, no genetic predisposition is needed, and abnormal behavior arises strictly for environmental reasons. The triggering factor may be poor nutrition or exposure to toxic substances, including naturally occurring toxins, manufactured chemicals, and infectious agents. Other disorders are undoubtedly related to negative experiences. Such experiences range from developmental deprivation, such as the the extreme psychosocial neglect of Romanian orphans in the 1980s and 1990s, to traumas in later life, such as those implicated in anxiety disorders.

**Table 15-6 Causes of Certain Behavioral Disorders**

| Cause | Disorder (chapter in which it is discussed) |
|---|---|
| Genetic error | Tay-Sachs disease (3) |
| Hormonal anomaly | Androgenital syndrome (13) |
| Developmental anomaly | Schizophrenia (7) |
| Infection | Encephalitis (2) |
| Injury | Closed head injury (1) |
| Natural environmental toxins | Shellfish poisoning (4) |
| Manufactured toxins | MPTP poisoning (5) |
| Poor nutrition | Korsakoff's syndrome (13) |
| Stress | Anxiety disorders (11) |
| Negative experience | Developmental delays among Romanian orphans (7) |

### In Review

Neurobiological investigations of behavioral disorders are based on the assumption that there ought to be a direct link between brain abnormalities and disorders in behavior. In most cases, however, this relationship is far from direct. We have seen that discrete biological markers are difficult to identify, except in the most well-studied disorders. Surprisingly, we encounter instances of brain pathology without obvious clinical symptoms and of clinical symptoms without obvious pathology. Epidemiological studies have been used to identify and classify behavioral disorders, but little is known about the relationship between these disorders and specific biological pathologies. Still, it is possible to identify the general causes of behavioral disorders. These causes range from genetic factors to environmental ones, including injuries, toxins, and negative life experiences. It will be some time, however, before a science of brain and behavior can fully explain the disordered mind.

# NEUROBIOLOGY OF SCHIZOPHRENIA AND AFFECTIVE DISORDERS

Schizophrenia and affective disorders provide excellent examples of the challenge of understanding the neurobiology of abnormal behavior. We have encountered both of these disorders several times in the preceding chapters. We revisit them here in an effort to understand their causes. In doing so, we also touch on problems of diagnosis.

## Schizophrenia

It has become clear over the past 20 years that diagnosing, classifying, and understanding schizophrenia is an evolving process that is far from complete. DSM-IV lists six diagnostic symptoms of **schizophrenia:** (1) delusions, or beliefs that distort reality; (2) hallucinations, or distorted perceptions, such as hearing voices; (3) disorganized speech, such as incoherent statements or senselessly rhyming talk; (4) disorganized behavior, or excessively agitated actions; (5) the opposite extreme, excessive immobility (called catatonic behavior); and (6) various "negative" symptoms, such as blunted emotions or loss of interest and drive, all of which are characterized by the absence of some normal response.

One difficulty with the DSM-IV criteria for schizophrenia is that they are more helpful in making clinical diagnoses than they are in relating schizophrenia to brain abnormalities. Timothy Crow addressed this problem by looking for some relationship between brain abnormalities and specific schizophrenic symptoms. He proposed that schizophrenia could be divided into two distinct syndromes, which he labeled type I and type II (Crow, 1980, 1990). Type I schizophrenia is characterized predominantly by "positive" symptoms, meaning those that involve behavioral excesses, such as hallucinations and agitated movements. This type of schizophrenia is also associated with acute onset, good prognosis, and a favorable response to neuroleptics. It likely is due to a dopaminergic dysfunction. Type II schizophrenia, in contrast, is characterized by "negative" symptoms, or those that entail behavioral deficits. It is associated with chronic affliction, poor prognosis, poor response to antipsychotic drugs, cognitive impairments, enlarged ventricles, and cortical atrophy, particularly in the frontal cortex. Crow's analysis had a major impact on clinical thinking about schizophrenia, although one difficulty is that between 20 percent and 30 percent of schizophrenic patients show a pattern of mixed type I and type II symptoms. The type I and type II groupings may actually represent points along a continuum of biological and behavioral manifestations (Andreasen & Olson, 1982).

Another approach to investigating schizophrenia is to de-emphasize diagnostic categories and to focus instead on individual psychotic symptoms. As Alan Breier (1999) stated, a growing number of brain-imaging studies suggest that some of these symptoms may have a neuroanatomical basis. For example, researchers have found abnormalities in the auditory regions of the temporal lobe and in Broca's area among patients with auditory hallucinations (McGuire et al., 1993). Similarly, structural abnormalities

**Schizophrenia.** A behavioral disorder characterized by delusions, hallucinations, disorganized speech, either agitation or immobility, and certain other symptoms, such as blunted emotions.

Hank Morgan / Photo Researchers

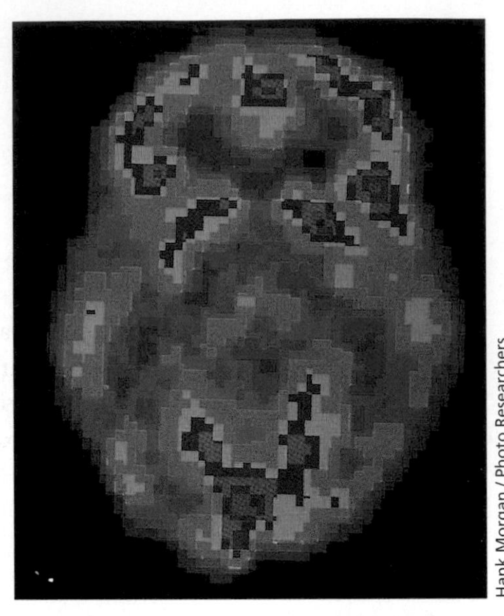

Hank Morgan / Photo Researchers

**Figure 15-12**

The left-hand photo is a PET scan of the brain of a schizophrenic patient; the right-hand photo shows the brain of a person without schizophrenia. Note the abnormally low blood flow in the prefrontal cortex at the top of the photo at left.

in Wernicke's area are often found among patients with thought disorders (Shenton et al., 1992). Another correlation is frequently seen between an abnormally low blood flow in the dorsolateral prefrontal cortex and deficits in executive functions, such as those measured by the Wisconsin Card Sorting Test (for a review, see Berman & Weinberger, 1999). Interestingly, when Daniel Weinberger and Barbara Lipska studied pairs of identical twins in which only one twin had been diagnosed as having schizophrenia, they found that the twin with schizophrenia always had a lower blood flow in the prefrontal cortex while taking this card-sorting test, as shown in Figure 15-12 (Weinberger & Lipska, 1995). Finally, schizophrenics have also been found to have abnormalities in the hippocampus and the entorhinal cortex (Arnold et al., 1997), regions that are both involved in various forms of memory. It is quite possible that deficits in verbal and spatial memory among people with schizophrenia turn out to be correlated with these medial temporal abnormalities.

A final way to approach brain–behavior relationships in schizophrenia is to consider neurochemical correlates. Although dopamine abnormalities are most commonly mentioned, other chemical abnormalities have also been found. Table 15-7 summarizes some of the major neurochemical changes associated with schizophrenia. In particular, there are abnormalities in dopamine and dopamine receptors, glutamate and glutamate receptors, and GABA and GABA binding sites. Considerable variability exists among patients in the extent of each of these abnormalities, however. It is not yet known how these neurochemical variations might relate to the presence or absence of specific symptoms.

To sum up, schizophrenia is a complex disorder. It is associated with both positive and negative symptoms, with abnormalities in brain structure and metabolism (especially in the prefrontal and temporal cortex), and with abnormalities involving dopamine, glutamate, and GABA. Given the complexity of all these behavioral and neurobiological factors, it is not surprising that schizophrenia is so difficult to characterize and to treat.

**Table 15-7 Biochemical Changes Associated with Schizophrenia**

| Biochemical Changes Associated with Schizophrenia |
|---|
| Decreased dopamine metabolites in cerebrospinal fluid |
| Increased striatal $D_2$ receptors |
| Decreased expression of $D_3$ and $D_4$ mRNA in specific cortical regions |
| Decreased cortical glutamate |
| Increased cortical glutamate receptors |
| Decreased glutamate uptake sites in cingulate cortex |
| Decreased mRNA for the synthesis of GABA in prefrontal cortex |
| Increased $GAGA_A$-binding sites in cingulate cortex |

Adapted from "The Neurochemistry of Schizophrenia," by W. Byne, E. Kemegther, L. Jones, V. Harouthunian, & K. L. Davis, in *The Neurobiology of Mental Illness* (p. 242), edited by D. S. Charney, E. J. Nestler, & B. S. Bunney, New York: Oxford, 1999.

## Affective Disorders

Over the past 50 years, researchers have debated whether affective disorders are psychological or biological in origin. It now seems likely that environmental factors such as stress act on the brain to produce biological changes related to people's moods and emotions. These changes are most likely to occur in those with genetic predispositions for them. Although the precise nature of these predispositions is not yet understood, several genes have now been implicated (Sanders et al., 1999).

**Depression.** An affective disorder characterized by prolonged feelings of worthlessness and guilt, disruption of normal eating habits, sleep disturbances, a general slowing of behavior, and frequent thoughts of suicide.

DSM-IV identifies several categories of affective disorders, but the ones of principal interest here are depression and mania. The main symptoms of clinical **depression** are prolonged feelings of worthlessness and guilt, disruption of normal eating habits, sleep disturbances, a general slowing of behavior, and frequent thoughts of suicide. *Mania*, in contrast, is characterized by excessive euphoria, in which the person often formulates grandiose plans and behaves in an uncontrollably hyperactive way. Periods of mania often change, sometimes abruptly, into states of depression and back again, in which case the condition is called *bipolar disorder*. Little is known about the neurobiology of bipolar disorder, so our emphasis here will be on depression.

Clinical studies suggest that monoamine systems, particularly both the norepinephrine and the serotonin systems, have roles in depression. Many monoamine theories of depression have been proposed. To date, however, there is no unifying theory that fully explains either the development of depression in otherwise normal people or the action of the antidepressant medications used to treat depression. For example, it has been known for more than 30 years that antidepressant drugs acutely increase the synaptic levels of norepinephrine (NE) and serotonin (5-HT). This finding led to the idea that depression results from decreased availability of one or both of these transmitters. However, lowering the levels of these transmitters in normal subjects does not produce depression, and although antidepressant medications rapidly (within days) increase the level of NE and 5-HT, it takes weeks for them to start relieving depression. Various explanations for these results have been suggested, but none have been completely satisfactory.

Ronald Duman (1999) reviewed evidence to suggest that antidepressant medications act, at least in part, on signaling pathways, such as on cAMP, in the postsynaptic cell. Furthermore, it appears that neurotrophic factors may affect the action of antidepressants and that neurotrophic factors may underlie the neurobiology of depression. For example, it is known that brain-derived neurotrophic factor, or BDNF (see Chapter 13), is down-regulated by stress and up-regulated by antidepressant medication. Given that BDNF acts to enhance the growth and survival of cortical neurons and synapses, BDNF dysfunction may adversely affect NE and 5-HT systems, through the loss of either neurons or synapses. Antidepressant medication may increase the release of BDNF through its actions on cAMP signal transduction. The key point here is that the cause is most likely not just a simple decrease in transmitter levels. Rather, explaining both the biochemical abnormalities involved in depression and the actions of antidepressants is likely to be far more complex than it seemed 30 years ago.

It is unlikely that depression is related to a single brain structure, especially given that the NE and 5-HT systems are so diffusely distributed. Indeed, neuroimaging studies have shown that depression is accompanied by an increase in blood flow and glucose metabolism in the orbital frontal cortex, the anterior cingulate cortex, and the amygdala. This elevated blood flow drops as the symptoms of depression remit when a patient takes antidepressant medication (Drevets et al., 1999). The involvement of these three structures should not be surprising, given their role in emotional behavior (discussed in Chapter 11).

## In Review

Although significant progress has been made in understanding the neurobiology of schizophrenia and depression, our knowledge of both of these behavioral disorders, as well as most others, is best viewed as work in progress. Schizophrenia is correlated with abnormalities in dopamine, GABA, and glutamate systems. Furthermore, there are structural abnormalities and low blood-glucose utilization in both the prefrontal cortex and the temporal cortex. In contrast, the monoamine systems are abnormal in depression, particularly in signal transduction in postsynaptic cells. And in depression there are abnormally high levels of blood flow and glucose utilization in the prefrontal and anterior cingulate cortex and in the amygdala.

# TREATMENTS OF BRAIN AND BEHAVIORAL DISORDERS

The ultimate clinical problem for behavioral neuroscience is to apply its knowledge to generate treatments that can restore a disordered brain (and mind) to order. This is a daunting challenge, because the first task is so difficult: learning the cause of a particular behavioral disturbance. Few behavioral disorders have as simple a cause as PKU does. Most, like schizophrenia, are extremely complex. Still, it has been possible to develop a variety of more or less effective treatments for a range of behavioral disorders, as summarized in Table 15-8.

**Table 15-8 Summary of Treatments of Brain and Behavior**

| Treatment | Chapter in which an example is discussed |
|---|---|
| **Neurosurgical** | |
| Removal of abnormal tissue (e.g., epilepsy, tumor) | 9 |
| Repair of abnormality (e.g., arteriovenous malformations) | 9 |
| Damage to dysfunctional area (e.g., Parkinson's disease) | 10 |
| Implantation of stimulation electrode (e.g., Parkinson's disease) | 10 |
| Transcranial magnetic stimulation | 14 |
| Implantation of embryonic cells or stem cells to regenerate lost tissue | 13 |
| **Pharmacological** | |
| Drugs to alter neurochemistry | 6 |
| Neurotrophic factors | 13 |
| Antibiotic and/or antiviral agents (e.g., encephalitis) | 2 |
| Nutritional | 11 |
| **Behavioral** | |
| Behavioral training (e.g., speech therapy, cognitive therapy) | 13 |
| Psychotherapy | 15 |

These treatments can be classified into three general categories: neurosurgical, pharmacological, and behavioral. The categories range from very invasive (the skull is opened and some intervention is performed on the brain) to less invasive (a chemical that affects the brain is either ingested or injected) to noninvasive (experience is manipulated, which in turn influences the brain). As you will see, each of these treatments has a specific objective.

## Neurosurgical Treatments

Neurosurgical treatments consist of surgical manipulations of the nervous system with the goal of directly altering it. Historically, such treatments have been largely reparative, as when tumors are removed or arteriovenous malformations are corrected. More recently, however, the medical profession has begun to use neurosurgical approaches aimed at altering brain activity in order to alleviate some behavioral disorder. The activity is altered either by damaging some dysfunctional area of the brain or by stimulating dysfunctional areas with electrodes. The treatment of Parkinson's disease is an example of both these types of neurosurgery. In the first type, an electrode is placed into the motor thalamus and an electric current is used to damage neurons that are responsible for producing the tremor characteristic of Parkinson's. In the second type of treatment, an electrode fixed in place in the putamen is connected to an external electrical stimulator that can be activated to facilitate normal movements.

Another neurosurgical strategy is brand new. In Chapter 7, we saw that the brain develops in a fixed sequence: from cell division to cell differentiation to cell migration to synaptogenesis. If a region of the brain is functioning abnormally or if it is diseased or dead, it should be possible to return this region to the embryonic state and regrow a normal region. Although this technique has a science fiction ring to it, there is reason to believe that it may someday be feasible. We saw in Chapter 11 that in laboratory rats, stem cells can be induced by neurotrophic factors to generate new cells that can migrate to the site of an injury. This process may not be practical in a large brain such as the human brain, but the principle of using stem cells to generate new neurons still holds. Stem cells might be placed directly into a dysfunctional region and then supplied with different growth factors that would be able to stimulate them to generate a functional region.

Where would the stem cells come from? During the 1980s, surgeons experimented with implanting fetal cells into adult brains, but this approach has had limited success. Another idea comes from the discovery that multipotent stem cells in bone marrow appear to be capable of manufacturing neural stem cells. If this proves to be a practical way of generating neural stem cells, it should be possible to take bone marrow cells from a person, place them in a special culture medium to generate thousands or millions of stem cells, and then place these stem cells into the damaged brain. The challenge is to get the cells to differentiate appropriately and develop the correct connections. At present, this is still a formidable obstacle, but it is well within the realm of possibility.

Transplanting cells is today being seriously talked about as a treatment for disorders such as stroke. In fact, Douglas Kondziolka and his colleagues (2000) tried cell transplants with a sample of 12 stroke victims. They harvested progenitor cells from a rare tumor known as a teratocarcinoma. The tumor cells were chemically altered to develop a neuronal phenotype, and then between 2 million and 6 million cells were transplanted into regions around the stroke. The patients were followed for a year, and for 6 of them PET scans showed an increase in metabolic activity in the areas that had received the transplanted cells, indicating that the transplants were having some effect on the host brain. Behavioral analyses also showed some improvement in these patients. This study is only the first of its type and the behavioral outcome was modest, but it does show that such a treatment may be feasible.

The most recent development in the neurosurgical treatment of behavioral disorders is transcranial magnetic stimulation, or TMS (Chapter 14). Although not strictly neurosurgical because it is not invasive, TMS works on a principle similar to that of electrical brain stimulation. That is, cerebral regions are activated by stimulation, although in TMS the stimulation is magnetic and is applied through the skull. To date, the only clinical applications of TMS have been in the treatment of depression, but this technique will probably become far more widely used in the coming decade (Post & Weiss, 1999).

## Pharmacological Treatments

Two developments in the 1950s led to a pharmacological revolution in the treatment of behavioral disorders. First, it was discovered that a drug used to premedicate surgical patients had antipsychotic properties. This finding led to the development of phenothiazines as a treatment for schizophrenia, and over the next 40 years, these drugs became increasingly more selective and effective. Second, a new class of antianxiety drugs was invented, namely the anxiolytics, and medications such as Valium quickly became among the most widely prescribed drugs in the United States. The power of these two classes of drugs to change behavior led to a revolution in the pharmaceutical industry, a revolution that is just now reaping major rewards with the development of so-called atypical drugs, such as Prozac, that hold promise to restore more normal behavior in people with a wide range of behavioral disorders.

The success of L-dopa has also been influential in fostering a pharmacological revolution. As we saw in Chapter 10, L-dopa provided the first treatment for a serious motor disorder, Parkinson's disease. Its effectiveness led to general optimism that drugs might be developed that acted as "magic bullets" to right the chemical imbalances found in Alzheimer's disease and other disorders. We now know that most behavioral disorders cannot be reduced to a single chemical abnormality, so pharmacological treatments will need considerable refinement before they can be seen as a solution to all neurobiological dysfunctions. Nonetheless, for many people, drug treatments have provided relief from a host of mental and motor problems.

Pharmacological treatments have their down sides. These drugs often have significant side effects, and their long-term effects may create new problems. Consider a person who is suffering from depression and receives antidepressant medication. Although the drug may ease the depression, it may produce unwanted side effects, including decreased sexual desire, fatigue, and sleep disturbance. These last two effects may also interfere with cognitive functioning. Thus, although the medication is useful for getting the person out of the depressed state, it may produce other symptoms that are themselves disturbing and may complicate the person's recovery. Furthermore, in cases in which the depression is related to life events, a drug does not provide a person with the behavioral tools needed to cope with an adverse situation. As some psychologists say, "A pill is not a skill."

A second example of the negative side effects that drug treatments may have can be seen in people being treated for schizophrenia with neuroleptics. These drugs act not only on the mesolimbic dopamine system, which is likely to be functioning abnormally in the schizophrenic patient, but also on the nigrostriatal dopaminergic system, which controls movement. It is therefore common for patients who take neuroleptics for a prolonged period to begin having motor disturbances, such as an inability to stop moving the tongue, a symptom known as *tardive dyskinesia*. These movement disorders often persist long after the medication has been stopped. Taking drugs for behavioral disorders, then, does carry some risk. Rather than acting like "magic bullets," these medications can sometimes act like "magic shotguns."

## Behavioral Treatments

If one of your relatives or friends were to have a stroke and become aphasic, you would expect the person to receive speech therapy, which is a form of behavioral treatment for an injured brain. The logic in speech therapy is that by practicing (or relearning) the basic components of speech and language, the patient should be able to regain at least some of the lost function. The same logic can be applied to other types of behavioral disorders, whether they be motor or cognitive. Therapies for cognitive disorders resulting from brain injury or dysfunction aim to retrain people in the fundamental cognitive processes that they have lost. Although this type of therapy appears as logical as speech therapy after a stroke, the difficulty is that such therapy assumes that we know what fundamental elements of cognitive activity are meaningful to the brain. Cognitive scientists are far from understanding these elements well enough to generate optimal therapies. Still, neuropsychologists such as George Prigitano and Catherine Mateer and their respective colleagues are developing neurocognitive programs that are able to improve functional outcomes following closed head injury and stroke (Prigatano, 1986; Sohlberg & Mateer, 1989).

In addition to having disturbances in cognitive activities like language and memory, people may have disturbances in emotional behaviors. In the 1920s, Sigmund Freud developed the idea that talking about such emotional problems enabled people to have insights into their causes that could serve as treatments, too. These "talking cures," as well as other forms of psychological intervention, may be broadly categorized as psychotherapies.

Since Freud's time, many ideas have been put forth about the best type of behavioral therapy for emotional disorders. This topic is well beyond the scope of this chapter. The key point here is that for many disorders, whether they are neurological or psychiatric, medical treatments are ineffective unless people also receive some type of psychotherapy. Indeed, in many cases, the only effective treatment is behavioral therapy.

Consider an example. A 25-year-old woman had a closed head injury in an automobile accident. She had a promising career as a musician, but after the accident she found that she was unable to read music. Not surprisingly, she soon became depressed. Part of her therapy was a requirement that she confront her disabling cognitive loss. Only when she did so was she able to begin to recover from her intense depression. For many people with cognitive impairments resulting from brain disease or injury, the most effective treatment for their state of depression or anxiety is to help them adjust by encouraging them to talk about their difficulties. In fact, group therapy, which provides such encouragement, is standard treatment in brain-injury rehabilitation units. In this regard, Fred Linge, whose case history opens Chapter 1 of this book, has played a major role in establishing support groups for people with head trauma, which serve as a form of group therapy.

You may be thinking that although behavioral therapies may be of some help in treating brain dysfunctions, the real solution must lie in altering the brain and its activities. This may be true, but remember a key fact: because every aspect of behavior is the product of brain activity, it can be argued that behavioral therapies *do* act by changing brain function. That is, not only does altering the brain change our behavior, but altering our behavior also changes the brain. If people can change the way that they think and feel about themselves or some aspect of their lives, this change has occurred because "talking about their problems" has altered the way their brains function. In a sense, then, behavioral therapies can be viewed as "biological interventions." These interventions may sometimes be helped along by drug treatments that make the brain more receptive to change through behavioral therapies. In this way, drug treatments and behavioral therapies may have synergistic effects, each helping the other to be more effective.

## In Review

Therapies for brain and behavioral disorders range from very invasive ones like neurosurgery to moderately invasive ones using drugs and other chemicals to noninvasive cognitive rehabilitation and other behavioral therapies. Today, none of these therapies are completely effective. But as more is learned about the details of brain–behavior relationships, we can anticipate improved recovery from a wide range of behavioral dysfunctions that affect a large portion of the population.

## NEUROSCIENCE IN THE 21ST CENTURY

It is often said that most of what we know about brain function was discovered in the 1990s, the so-called Decade of the Brain. There is some truth to this statement. At the beginning of the 1860s, investigators like John Hughlings-Jackson were just starting to develop a vague idea of how the brain is organized. It was not even known until the 1950s that there were chemical synapses in the brain. With the research technology of recent years, however, many new insights have come to light. For instance, we have now begun to understand the important process of how genes control neural activity. In addition, the development of new imaging techniques like fMRI and ERPs have opened up the normal brain to cognitive neuroscientists, allowing them to investigate brain activity in laboratory subjects. As we reflect on the study of brain and behavior over the past century, we can only marvel at where it is now and how much potential for future discoveries lies just at our doorstep.

Studies of brain and behavior have also begun to capture the public imagination. Whereas such studies were unknown to the general public 20 years ago, today it is hard to pick up a major newspaper without seeing at least weekly accounts of new discoveries and their possible applications. It seems likely that one day we will be able to stimulate processes of repair not only in malfunctioning brains but in injured spinal cords as well. These advances will come about through the efforts of neuroscientists to understand how the brain produces and organizes the mind and, ultimately, behavior. Along the way, we will learn how the brain stores and retrieves information, why we engage in the behaviors we do, and how we are able to read the lines on this page and generate ideas and thoughts. The coming decades will be exciting times for the study of brain and behavior. They offer an opportunity for us to broaden our understanding of what makes us human.

## KEY TERMS

depression, p. 595
DSM-IV, p. 590
phenylketonuria (PKU), p. 588
schizophrenia, p. 593

## REVIEW QUESTIONS

1. What are the difficulties in developing a science of the neurobiology of abnormal behavior?
2. What are the causes of abnormal behavior?
3. What are the treatments for abnormal behavior?

4. What are the methods of studying brain and behavior?
5. In what sense is behavioral therapy a biological intervention?

## FOR FURTHER THOUGHT

Prepare the outline of a lecture to explain to your parents (or grandparents) how the brain works. Remember that you will not be able to assume any knowledge on their part. Your real task is to extract principles that they will understand.

## RECOMMENDED READING

Barondes, S. M. (1993). *Molecules and mental illness.* New York: Scientific American Library. Like the other books in the Scientific American Library, this is a beautifully written and illustrated volume that is easily accessible. It provides a good general discussion of the neurobiology of mental disorders.

Charney, D. S., Nestler, E. J., & Bunney, B. S. (Eds.). (1999). *The neurobiology of mental illness.* New York: Oxford. This is a serious book for those interested in the latest information on the neurobiology of mental illness. Coverage includes the entire spectrum of mental disorders with thorough reference lists and clear discussions.

Sacks, O. (1998). *The man who mistook his wife for a hat: And other clinical tales.* New York: Touchstone. This is a collection of short essays that provide interesting reading about some strange relationships between brain and behavior. Sacks is an excellent writer, and his accounts are not only entertaining but thought provoking as well.

### neuroscience interactive

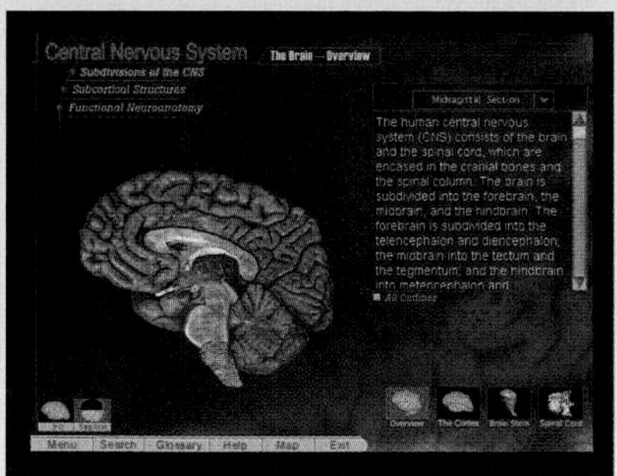


Many resources are available for expanding your learning on-line:

- **www.worthpublishers.com/kolb/chapter15**

Try some self-tests to reinforce your mastery of the material. Look at some of the news updates reflecting current research on the brain. You'll also be able to link to other sites to reinforce what you've learned.

Review the major concepts and anatomical fundamentals in the modules on the Central Nervous System and Neural Communication on the CD.

Appendix

# Why Do Scientists Use Animals in Research?

Definitions

What Are the Arguments in Favor of Using Animals in Research?

What Are the Arguments Against Using Animals in Research?

Legislation and Official Guidelines for the Use of Animals in Research

Policies of Professional Societies on the Use of Animals in Research

Conclusions

In the 1970s, Edward Taub, a scientist at the Institute for Behavioral Research, a private facility in Silver Spring, Maryland, was conducting research on the role that sensory information plays in motor control. Taub was interested in the extent to which the motor system could produce movement in the absence of sensory information. His research was relevant to the question of whether training in humans who had suffered loss of sensory information could be expected to stimulate recovery of function. His studies required cutting the dorsal roots of the spinal cords in monkeys, thus severing the sensory fibers from the arms. The lesion given to the monkeys was analogous to one that would be suffered by a person who had damage to the dorsal cervical roots of the spinal cord, a not uncommon injury.

In 1981, one of Taub's laboratory technicians, Alex Pacheco, accused him of inflicting unnecessary pain on the monkeys and failing to provide them with adequate food and veterinary care. Pacheco convinced the local police to confiscate the animals. In the next several years, an organization called People for the Ethical Treatment of Animals (PETA), cofounded by Pacheco, carried on a legal battle against the Institute for Behavioral Research over the animals' fate. Arguing that humans do not have the moral right to use animals for research purposes, PETA attempted to terminate Taub's Silver Spring experiment. The scientists at the Institute for Behavioral Research sought to continue their research on the grounds that it was conducted according to accepted laboratory standards and that research on animals provides benefits to humans and is legal (Guillermo, 1994).

Whereas the duration of Taub's experiments would have been relatively short, the legal dispute with PETA kept the Silver Spring project and its monkeys in limbo for years. In 1987, a group of scientists led by Mortimer Mishkin, a neuroscientist at the National Institute of Mental Health (NIMH), suggested that the monkeys provided a unique opportunity to look at what happens to parts of the brain that have been deprived of sensory input for a long period of time. The scientists received permission to map the somatosensory cortex of a monkey that was becoming old and would shortly have to be sacrificed because of ill health. They found that the somatosensory cortex had undergone a massive reorganization and that the somatosensory cortex area that previously represented the arm now represented the face (this result is described in Chapter 10).

The face area of the somatosensory cortex had encroached into the arm area over a distance of 10 to 14 millimeters, an order of magnitude greater than what previous studies had suggested might occur (Pons et al., 1991). This result demonstrated that the adult brain is capable of undergoing enormous plastic changes even well into old age. The findings also contributed to an understanding of some aspects of "phantom limbs" experienced by human amputees (discussed in Chapter 14).

The dispute between the scientists and the animal rights group at Silver Spring is not an isolated incident but part of a much larger controversy regarding the experimental use of animals by humans. On one side of the controversy are people who approve of such use of animals; on the other side are people who disapprove, in varying degrees. The debate centers on issues of law, morals, custom, and biology. Because researchers in many branches of science experiment with animals to understand the functions of the body, the brain, and behavior, the issues in this debate are important to them. Because many people benefit from this research, including those who have diseases of the nervous system or nervous system damage, this debate is important to them. And because you, as a student, will encounter many experiments on animals in this book, these issues will also be important to you. In the following sections, we first consider the terminology relevant to this debate. Next, we examine the arguments for and against the use of animals in experimental research. We then consider the legal and administrative rules used by scientific organizations and government bodies to regulate experimentation with laboratory animals and their treatment.

## DEFINITIONS

Inasmuch as this debate centers on animals, let us begin by determining which organisms we consider to be animals. As stated in Chapter 1, the biological definition of an animal includes approximately 1 million species belonging to the 15 phyla of the animal kingdom. When we speak of animal rights, however, we are far more likely to think of monkeys, dogs, and cats than of mice, flatworms, or jellyfish. Thus, we can already glimpse the complexity of the issue: when it comes to animal rights, people have widely divergent views on what they mean by an animal and, by implication, which of the 1 million species of animals should be accorded "rights." As we will see later, scientific organizations and government bodies have focused on higher vertebrates as "animals" for purposes of establishing regulations for their use in research.

It is equally difficult to define the many groups who have an interest in animal welfare. Humane societies are interested in the welfare of pets. The number of pets abandoned or destroyed each year in North America roughly equals the number of animals used for research. These groups promote sterilization of pets, they rescue abandoned pets, and they promote educational programs to improve the welfare of pets. Other groups are interested in the welfare of all animals, including pets, wild animals, and animals used for agriculture and research. They promote the welfare of animals through conservation, they promote education for those who use animals, and they support laws that offer protection to animals from excessive exploitation and abuse. Still other groups are referred to as antivivisectionists, who oppose the use of animals in research, and as "animal rights" groups, who to various extents oppose the use of animals for some or all purposes.

That brings us directly to how we define the "use" of animals. Humans make use of animals in many ways quite apart from scientific experiments. Since prehistoric times, we have hunted animals for food, domesticated them as workers, and raised them not only for meat, but also for milk, eggs, clothing, and shelter. In societies that use animals for food, there are widely divergent practices. For example, people in some societies eat dogs and people in other societies eat horses, whereas these practices are generally not acceptable in North America. Many present-day animal activists oppose hunting or advocate a vegetarian diet. Others oppose all uses of animals. Even though dogs, which were first domesticated more than 12,000 years ago, are used today for herding, for search and rescue, for drug detection, as seeing-eye and hearing companions for the blind and deaf, and as pets, there are groups who oppose such uses. Thus, there are clearly widely divergent attitudes toward the use of animals.

Most of us would agree that animals should not be subjected to needless pain and suffering; but what do we mean by pain and suffering, and what constitutes "needless"? Psychologists have argued that pain and suffering are personal experiences. Because humans have language, we can to some extent describe to one another our experiences. We can surmise on the basis of similar neuroanatomy and outward appearances that other mammals have experiences that might be similar to our own, but we cannot know what they are actually feeling.

As you can see from this brief attempt to define the basic terms of the animal rights debate, the points of view are far-ranging and diverse and the conclusions—here the definitions—very sparse. We would do well to acknowledge at this point that what we are about to consider will yield no simple right or wrong answer.

## WHAT ARE THE ARGUMENTS IN FAVOR OF USING ANIMALS IN RESEARCH?

If paleolithic cave paintings are any indication, humans have observed and studied animals for many thousands of years. Some of the oldest surviving scientific texts were written about animal behavior. The only Nobel Prize ever given for the study of behavior was awarded jointly to three scientists for their studies on animal behavior. As noted in Chapter 1, Descartes made important contributions to the understanding of anatomy and physiology by dissecting animals. When we consider the information contained in this book, we see that the scientific community has acquired much of its knowledge about the nervous system and its relation to behavior through observing, studying, and performing experiments on animals. Many of the students and instructors who use this book learned basic biology by dissecting frogs and administering injections to hatchlings. Most of the treatments for both human and animal diseases originated through studies with animals.

People are also interested in the marvelous abilities that many animals have. We are amazed at the complexity of the songs of birds and whales, the navigational capabilities of migratory geese and butterflies, and the accuracy with which dogs can identify a scent. We humans were mystified that birds can fly and that bats use echolocation until we were able to understand the principles underlying these behaviors and reproduce them mechanically for our own use. Divers and shipbuilders continue to be astonished that sperm whales are able to dive to depths in the ocean that would crush a submarine.

Although people have a wide variety of reasons for wishing to study animals, the arguments in favor of conducting research with animals can be classified into three general categories.

1. **Studying the function and behavior of animals contributes to the health and well-being of animals and humans.**

The benefits to humans of animal research are well documented. Indeed, in a 1989 paper, the American Medical Association (AMA) asserts that research using animals is essential for medical advances. The publication provides a long list of diseases, from the treatment of rabies and anthrax in the 1800s to the development of monoclonal antibodies for cancer at the end of the twentieth century, as examples of the benefits of animal experimentation. The AMA also points out that 54 of 76 Nobel Prizes in medicine were given for discoveries and advances made through the use of experimental animals in research. Looking toward the future, the report states that biomedical research using animals is essential to continued progress in clinical medicine on problems that include AIDS, heart disease, aging, and congenital defects. The AMA's viewpoint is shared by a host of patient groups, including those that advocate for sufferers of Parkinson's disease, Huntington's chorea, multiple sclerosis, Alzheimer's disease, spinal-cord injury, heart disease, and stroke (Feeney, 1987).

There are also many nonmedical ways in which humans benefit from animal research. Farmers, fishermen, and aboriginal groups who have a hunter-gatherer life style depend on thriving animal populations for their livelihoods. In the past century, individual people, governments, and other organizations have become increasingly aware of the economic and ecological value of wildlife as well as domestic animals and have invested in projects designed to preserve animals and their habitats. On an individual level, people who enjoy the company of animals, use them for work, or raise them for food have a keen interest in seeing that their animals are healthy. To attain these goals requires that humans understand the biology and behavior of animals.

Less obvious, perhaps, are the benefits that animals themselves derive from being studied by humans. Biology in general and behavioral neuroscience in particular seek to understand the functions of the body, the functions of the brain, and behavior; the findings are no less applicable to animals than to humans. As already noted, animal research in the 1800s led to the discovery of cures for rabies and anthrax; you may be aware that these diseases are devastating to animals as well as humans. In 1999, a mosquito-borne organism called the West Nile virus was identified as the cause of death of a number of birds in the New York City area; although public concern centered on the health risks to humans, measures to control the virus were also beneficial to birds and other animals susceptible to the disease.

Domestication and captivity also convey benefits to animals. Biologists believe that, if it were not for its domestication, which began in Asia about 12,000 years ago, the horse might be an extinct species today. Selective breeding has made today's horses, dogs, cattle, and other animals healthier than their ancestors were. The world's major zoos, in addition to providing opportunities for the public to observe and learn about animals, are dedicated to developing the best possible habitat, diet, and health care for the animals in their charge. Zoo care has enabled a number of endangered species to survive and even increase their numbers. Animal research in zoos and laboratories has made it possible for farmers and pet owners to buy optimally formulated animal foods and to give their animals advanced veterinary care. Because our lives are connected to the lives of animals in so many ways, the more we humans learn about animal behavior, physiology, genetics, health, and disease, the better we are able to care for the animals with which we interact.

2. **The study of animals can be a source of insight into the evolution of the human body and its functions.**

As described in Chapter 1, all animals, including humans, descend from a common founding ancestor. The study of the anatomy, physiology, genetics, ecology, and behavior of various animals provides the primary information about how evolution occurs and how we humans evolved. A number of branches of science including biology, genetics, psychology, neuroscience, sociology, and anthropology have a primary interest in the evolution of animals and their physical and behavioral traits. The theory of evolution, which proposes that humans descended from an animal lineage through a process of natural selection, is one of the most important theories in all science.

Allied to the study of evolution is the study of the development of behavior. Extremely interesting questions can be answered by combining the two. For example, because development in some respects recapitulates evolution, the study of the development of the brain and behavior can be a source of insight into the neural organization of behavior. In addition, some animals are extremely precocious when born, whereas the maturation of other animals is greatly delayed. The study of rates of maturation can be a source of insight into evolutionary processes that influence brain development and behavior.

3. **Many questions concerning humans cannot be answered by experiments on humans.**

The study of animals is especially important to branches of medical science that deal with genetic bases, including neuroscience and psychology. Specifically, many animals have shorter reproduction cycles than do humans, so that genetic experiments are more feasible. Further, most animals used for research are small and can be kept in laboratories at a reasonable cost.

In regard to ethics—which is where the animal rights debate is centered—it is widely considered morally unacceptable to use humans for certain experiments that can provide answers to important research questions. As mentioned in Chapter 1, in past centuries, experiments on humans, especially the retarded or mentally ill, were justified on the grounds that impaired persons were unable to feel pain in the way that "normal" people do. In the twentieth century, people throughout the world became increasingly intolerant of this kind of justification, and the scientific community developed a stringent code of ethics for experiments on human subjects requiring, among other things, informed consent. Thus, most of today's experiments that are performed on animals cannot be performed on humans and would not otherwise be possible.

Scientists interested in brain function and behavior are especially dependent on animals for such information. Perhaps the earliest study that illustrates the dependence of humans on animals for insights into the function of the nervous system was that performed by François Magendie (Finger, 1994). In 1807, the Scottish anatomist Charles Bell described the dorsal and ventral roots of the spinal cord. He proposed that the dorsal roots subserve motor functions and the ventral roots subserve sensory functions. In adult humans, the roots are fused, making it difficult to conclude anything about their function from studying, say, human spinal-cord-injury victims. However, in 1821, Magendie observed that, in puppies, the dorsal and ventral roots are separate. He was able to selectively cut the roots and determine, contrary to Bell's hypothesis, that the dorsal roots are sensory and the ventral roots are motor. His discovery of the "law of the spinal roots" has been described as the most important discovery in clinical neurology because it allows neurologists to precisely locate an injury to the spinal cord from the symptoms presented by the patient. It also led investigators to search for other locations in the nervous system where sensory and motor functions are separated.

Many other types of experiments must be performed on animals or not at all. Behavioral neuroscientists could not damage a part of the brain of a human as part of a study to determine what that area of the brain does. They could not implant electrodes into the cells of a human brain to study how those cells mediate perceptual, motor, or cognitive functions. Scientists could not experiment with new treatments for diseases on humans. For example, they could not administer a new drug to humans to determine whether it is effective in treating depression, because the consequences of untoward side effects are too risky. Scientists would also not be able to explore cures for the 2000 known genetic diseases that affect the nervous system or explore cures for such common conditions as schizophrenia, Alzheimer's disease, and the behavioral disorders that are secondary to diseases such as AIDS.

## WHAT ARE THE ARGUMENTS AGAINST USING ANIMALS IN RESEARCH?

For as long as animals have been used for scientific study, there has been concern about their use and opposition to it. The American Society for the Prevention of Cruelty to Animals (ASPCA), founded in New York City in 1866, was the first organization in North America with the goal of protecting animals from abuse. Today, however, the ASPCA focuses on rescuing stray animals and does not take an official stand on the question of their use in research. In the early part of the twentieth century, a movement arose against vivisection, the practice of performing surgical operations on living animals to study living organs or the effects of diseases. The Humane Society of the United States, founded in 1954, supports legal sanctions against animal cruelty and worked to pass the Laboratory Animal Welfare Act in 1966. More recently, it established a program of humane alternatives to animal dissection in schools and a goal of eliminating animal pain and distress in laboratories by 2020 (Humane Society of the United States, 2000). PETA, founded in 1980, seeks to ban the use of animals for food, clothing, entertainment, and research. Since the Silver Spring lawsuit mentioned earlier, PETA has engaged in many undercover investigations, lobbying efforts, and court cases to stop uses of animals that violate its views. Many other groups and individual persons also oppose animal use, for widely different reasons and to widely different degrees. This broad variation notwithstanding, the reasons for opposing animal research can be classified as either scientific or philosophical.

### The Scientific Arguments

The scientific arguments discount the validity of the contention that research using animals produces improvements for humans. Some proponents of the scientific argument claim that animals are too different from humans to provide useful biological information about human diseases. Others observe that widespread improvements in human health and longevity have been brought about by improvements in public hygiene and changes in diet and life style. Some also point out that, despite the number of experiments conducted by scientists, there are still many uncured diseases. For example, Ingrid Newkirk, cofounder and president of PETA, said on the *Today* show in 1985: "If [animal experimentation] were such a valuable way to gain knowledge, we should have eternal life by now."

In a 1993 report, H. A. Herzog, Jr., compiled the views of animal rights activists. Among the statements that he collected was the following one. This quotation and others similar to it have been widely used in the animal rights literature and in arguments made by animal rights activists.

> I can't find any substantial data to indicate that anything has been discovered from animals that could not have been gathered from some other source. Thalidomide was a drug that was found to be safe on experimental animals and given to the human population. It was a total disaster. They say that vaccines were discovered from animal research. But the Chinese had vaccines before the time of Christ, and they were not found from animal research. They were discovered from actual clinical trials and human patients (Herzog, 1993).

Herzog also reported that some activists took a blame-the-victim stance toward persons suffering from chronic diseases, particularly illnesses associated with life style and diet. Opponents of experimentation on animals frequently told him that, if people would simply give up eating meat, diseases such as cancer and heart disease would disappear.

Bioethicist Michael W. Fox takes the view that scientific advances create problems of their own for animals and people alike. In a recent book focusing on genetic engineering (M. W. Fox, 1999), he condemns as unethical and unnecessary such advances as cloning, pigs bioengineered to produce human hemoglobin, and transgenic plants that secrete their own insecticides. In Fox's view, all life on earth will eventually suffer from "genetic pollution" as genetically altered animals and other organisms spread their genes throughout the environment.

## The Philosophical Arguments

Two of the several philosophical arguments made against the use of animals in research are the utilitarian argument and the life argument. Both conclude that all use of animals should be ended.

Perhaps the most widely publicized argument against the use of animals is that made by Peter Singer, a professor of philosophy at Princeton University (Singer, 1990). Singer holds that, because animals have in common with humans the capacity to experience pain and suffering, they are worthy of the same degree of moral consideration as is granted to humans. Singer follows the utilitarian philosophy that ethical decisions should be made by adding up all the pleasures and pains that would result from different choices and choosing the option that yields the greatest aggregate pleasure and the least pain. The pleasures and pains of nonhuman animals must be included in this tally. If it were, Singer argues, people would become vegetarians and otherwise adopt a life style that avoids using animals for human purposes. Singer also coined the term *speciesism* to describe a prejudice or attitude of bias in favor of the interests of members of one's own species and against those of members of other species. Thus, Singer argues that, just as one should not be racist or sexist, one should not be speciesist.

Tom Regan, a professor of philosophy at North Carolina State University, also advocates a vegetarian life style but rejects the utilitarian approach (Regan, 1996). Regan argues that there are many ways to sum up pain and pleasure, and one of these ways might include support for the use of animals by humans. For example, most animals used for scientific research do not suffer any pain, and on average a person will suffer approximately 10 years of discomfort and pain in a lifetime. Instead, Regan argues that animals, by virtue of having life, possess an inherent value that is equal to that of humans. Because their lives are equal in importance, one species (humans) does not have the right to end the lives of the other species (animals) for any purpose, including research or food.

In his recent writings, bioethicist Michael A. Fox supports vegetarianism (M. A. Fox, 1999), and he postulates that, if animal experimentation were to stop, the human species would doubtless continue to exist just as it did before such experimentation began, albeit with a diminished life span and quality of life.

In evaluating the arguments against animal use, one might ask about the results of carrying these arguments to their logical extremes. Doing so would require not only universal vegetarianism, but also allowing animals to live naturally and not killing them or harming them under any circumstances. We might conclude that, if this were to happen, there would quickly be chaos. Many industries would cease to operate, and many areas of biological research would cease to acquire new knowledge. Domesticated animals would need to be fed vegetarian diets. Wild and feral animals from gophers to elephants would invade and consume crops planted by humans. Mice, cockroaches, ants, and other creatures would invade human homes.

Some animal rightists have even argued that humans should take responsibility for regulating the conduct of animals in nature, supplying food for predators so that they have no need to kill and eat prey. Because most animals are prey to some animals and predators to other animals, this argument would require regulating and feeding every animal on earth. Given the difficulties that humans have in preserving at-risk species, regulating the behavior of every animal species seems quite impossible. One might also ask whether this animal rights position would require that knowledge gained through animal experimentation should no longer be used. Finally, because anthropologists have found that humans have always used animals for food, to which former life style humans would return is unclear.

## LEGISLATION AND OFFICIAL GUIDELINES FOR THE USE OF ANIMALS IN RESEARCH

Just as the scientific community has established ethical standards for research on human subjects, it has also developed regulations governing experimentation on animals. The governments of most industrialized nations have legislation regulating the use of animals in research; most states and provinces have additional legislation. Universities and other organizations engaged in research also have rules governing animal use. Finally, professional societies to which scientists belong and journals in which scientists publish have rules governing animal use.

For example, in Canada, twenty organizations interested in the care and use of research animals have formed the Canadian Council of Animal Care (see table). The Council is dedicated to enhanced animal care and use through education, voluntary compliance, and codes of ethics. It is organized so that it can flexibly respond to the concerns of both the scientific community and the general public through rapid and frequent amendments to its guidelines. The Council endorses the following principles as guidelines for reviewing protocols for experiments that will use animals:

1. That the use of animals in research, teaching, and testing is acceptable only if it promises to contribute to the understanding of environmental principles or issues, fundamental biological principles, or development of knowledge that can reasonably be expected to benefit humans, animals, or the environment.
2. That optimal standards for animal health and care result in enhanced credibility and reproducibility of experimental results.
3. That acceptance of animal use in science critically depends on maintaining public confidence in the mechanisms and processes used to ensure necessary, humane, and justified animal use.
4. That animals should be used only if the researcher's best efforts to find an alternative have failed. Those using animals should employ the most humane methods on the smallest number of appropriate animals required to obtain valid information.

| Membership in the Canadian Council of Animal Care, a Society Dedicated to Enhanced Animal Care and Use Through Education, Voluntary Compliance, and Codes of Ethics |
|---|
| Agriculture Canada |
| Association of Canadian Faculties of Dentistry |
| Association of Canadian Medical Colleges |
| Association of Universities and Colleges of Canada |
| Canadian Association for Laboratory Animal Medicine |
| Canadian Association for Laboratory Animal Science |
| Canadian Federation of Humane Societies |
| Canadian Society of Zoologists |
| Committee of Chairpersons of Departments of Psychology |
| Confederation of Canadian Faculties of Agriculture and Veterinary Medicine |
| Department of National Defense |
| Environment Canada |
| Fisheries and Oceans Canada |
| Health and Welfare Canada |
| Heart and Stroke Foundation of Canada |
| Medical Research Council |
| National Cancer Institute |
| National Research Council |
| Natural Sciences and Engineering Research Council |
| Pharmaceutical Manufacturer Association of Canada |

Legislation concerning the care and use of laboratory animals in the United States is set forth in the Animal Welfare Act, which includes laws passed by Congress in 1966, 1970, 1976, and 1985. (Legislation in other countries is similar and in some cases more strict.) The Act covers mammals, including rats, mice, and birds, but excludes farm animals that are not used in research. It is administered by the U.S. Department of Agriculture, through inspectors in the Animal and Plant Health Inspection Service, Animal Care. In addition, the Health Research Extension Act (passed in 1986) covers all animal uses conducted or supported by the Public Health Service and applies to any live vertebrate animal used in research, training, or testing. The Office for Protection from Research Risks of the National Institutes of Health administers this Act, which requires that each institution provide acceptable assurance that it meets all minimum regulations and conforms with *The Guide for the Care and Use of Laboratory Animals* (National Research Council, 1996) before conducting any activity that includes animals. The typical method for demonstrating conformance with the *Guide* is to seek voluntary accreditation from the Association for Assessment and Accreditation of Laboratory Animal Care International.

All U.S. universities that are accredited and receive grant support are required to provide adequate treatment for all vertebrates. Reviews and specific protocols for fish, reptiles, mice, dogs, or monkeys to be used in research, teaching, or testing are administered through the same process. Anyone using animals in a U.S. university submits a protocol to that university's institutional Animal Care and Use Committee, composed of researchers, veterinarians, persons who have some knowledge of science, as well as laypeople from the university and the community. Companies that use animals for research are not required to follow this process, but in effect, if they do not, they will be unable to publish the results of their research or obtain regulatory approval for their products.

The U.S. regulations specify that researchers consider alternatives to procedures that may cause more than momentary or slight pain or distress. Most of the attention on alternatives has focused on the use of animals in testing and stems from high public awareness of some tests for pharmacological compounds, especially toxic compounds. The testing of such compounds is now regulated by the National Institute of Environmental Health Sciences.

## POLICIES OF PROFESSIONAL SOCIETIES ON THE USE OF ANIMALS IN RESEARCH

To comply with and reinforce the standards mandated by government bodies, scientific societies, too, have established procedures and policies for ensuring the proper handling of research animals. Most of these organizations hold annual meetings for members so that they may discuss their research findings. Many societies also publish journals that facilitate the dissemination of research results. Both presentations and publication are important to scientists and hence provide means for administering such procedures and policies. Universities and agencies that employ scientists use presentations and publications as evidence of productivity. Granting agencies and councils use evidence of productivity to decide whether to fund a scientist's research. Thus scientists must conform to the procedures and policies to conduct and publish their research.

The Society of Neuroscience is one of the largest professional societies in the world, with more than 20,000 members from many scientific disciplines and many different countries. Presentation at Society meetings and publication in the Society's *Journal of Neuroscience* are governed by its "Policy on the Use of Animals in Neuroscience Research." The Policy requires that research be performed in compliance with the Health Research Extension Act and *The Guide for the Care and Use of Laboratory Animals*. The Society also requires a local committee review of the research that conforms to the following guidelines:

> An important element of the Society Policy is the establishment of a local committee that is charged with reviewing and approving all proposed animal care and use procedures. In addition to scientists experienced in research involving animals and a veterinarian, the membership of this local committee should include an individual who is not affiliated with the member's institution in any other way. In reviewing a proposed use of animals, the committee should evaluate the adequacy of institutional policies, animal husbandry, veterinary care, and the physical plant. Specific attention should be paid to proposed procedures for animal procurement, quarantine and stabilization, separation by species, disease diagnosis and treatment, anesthesia and analgesia, surgery and postsurgical care, and euthanasia. The review committee also should ensure that procedures involving live vertebrate animals are designed and performed with due consideration of their relevance to human or animal health, the advancement of knowledge, or the good of society. This review and approval of a member's use of live vertebrate animals in research by a local committee is an essential component of the Society Policy. (Society for Neuroscience Policies on the Use of Animals and Human Subjects in Neuroscience Research)

From the regulations and laws described in this section, we can see that research in which animal subjects are used is not undertaken without serious consideration for the proper care and handling of the animals.

## CONCLUSIONS

Edward Taub, the researcher mentioned at the beginning of this appendix who conducted research on monkeys at the Institute for Behavioral Research, continued his research at the University of Alabama in Birmingham. On the basis of observations obtained from his monkeys, he developed a therapy for brain injury (Taub & Crago, 1995). His discovery that the cortex was able to reorganize was subsequently applied to humans, leading to the widely acclaimed technique of extremity constraint induced therapy (EXCITe). Through this technique, patients who have lost the use of limbs owing to stroke, spinal-cord injury, or hip fracture work with robots or human therapists to exercise the disabled muscles (Liepert et al., 2000). EXCITe, which promotes enlargement of the muscle-output area in the affected hemisphere as well as greatly improved motor performance of the paretic limb, is one of the most recent examples of a scientific breakthrough that owes its success to experiments with animal subjects.

There is little doubt that the use of animals in research raises important questions. There is also little doubt that attitudes and policies concerning the use of animals in all domains are undergoing constant revision. There was a time when people gave little consideration to the loss of species through extinction, to how domestic animals were housed, or to how scientific experiments were conducted. But there have been changes in all of these areas, and many of the changes now carry the force of law. These changes have been stimulated in large part by improvements in our knowledge of animals, our world, and ourselves. It is also important to note that research on animals is self-limiting: when an answer to a problem has been obtained, the experiment need not be redone.

The debate between groups who support the use of animals in research and groups who oppose their use is often heated and strident. In a 1992 article, Humane Society Vice President for Laboratory Animals Martin L. Stephens argued that it does not need to be so. In his view, the debate has a substantial middle ground, bordered on one side by scientists who are proponents of experimentation and who see no room for improvement in the treatment of laboratory animals and on the other by detractors who see all animal researchers as sadists. In the middle are a great many responsible and reasonable people who, to varying degrees, are willing to work for some reforms and to recognize the value of some animal research.

In his book titled *The Origins of Virtue* (1997), Matt Ridley argues that questions that are posed as moral dilemmas can also be posed as biological ones. As a biological question, the use of animals in scientific research can be addressed as a question of the exploitation by one species (humans) of other species in much the same way that exploitation by nonhuman species of each other can be studied. Presumably, just as human knowledge of other animals and ourselves improves, so too will there be continued improvements in the way in which humans interrelate with other animals.

# Glossary

**absolutely refractory.** Refers to the period in an action potential during which a new action potential cannot be elicited, because of the closing of gate 2 of voltage-sensitive sodium channels.
**acetate.** A molecule that, when combined with choline, forms acetylcholine.
**acetylcholine.** The first neurotransmitter discovered in the peripheral and central nervous systems; also the neurotransmitter that activates skeletal muscles.
**action potential.** A large, brief, reversing change in the voltage of a neuron.
**activating effect of hormones.** The actions of hormones on cells in the adult organism that usually last only while the hormone is present.
**active-transport system.** A pump specialized for the transport of a particular substance across a membrane.
**addiction.** Development of a physical dependence on a drug in addition to abusing it; often associated with tolerance and unpleasant, sometimes dangerous, withdrawal symptoms on cessation of drug use.
**adenine.** One of the bases in a DNA (deoxyribonucleic acid) strand that binds to a base (thymine) in another strand to form double-stranded DNA.
**adrenergic neuron.** A neuron containing epinephrine; the term *adrenergic* derives from the term *adrenaline*.
**afferent.** Conducting toward the central nervous system or toward its higher centers.
**agonist.** A drug that mimics or enhances the effect of a neurotransmitter.
**alcohol myopia.** The behavior displayed after imbibing alcohol in which local and immediate cues become prominent.
**allele.** An alternate form of a gene.
**alpha rhythm.** A rhythmic electroencephalographic waveform with a frequency ranging from 7 to 11 hertz that can be recorded from the scalp of a subject who is resting with closed eyes.
**Alzheimer's disease.** A degenerative brain disorder that first appears as a progressive memory loss and later develops into a generalized dementia. The origin of the disease is unknown, but cholinergic cells in the basal forebrain and cells in the entorhinal cortex appear to degenerate first.
**amblyopia.** A condition in which vision in one eye is reduced as a result of disuse; usually caused by a failure of the two eyes to point in the same direction.
**amino acid.** An organic molecule possessing both a carboxyl group and an amino group. Amino acids are the constituent elements of proteins.
**amnesia.** Partial or total loss of memory.
**amphetamine.** A drug that releases the neurotransmitter dopamine from its synapse and blocks its reuptake into the terminal after use.
**amplitude.** The intensity of a stimulus; in audition, amplitude is roughly equivalent to loudness.
**amygdala.** A collection of nuclei located within the rostral part of the temporal lobe; the amygdala is part of the limb system and has a role in affective behaviors and other species-typical behaviors.
**anencephaly.** Failure of the forebrain to develop.
**anomalous speech representation.** A condition in which a person's speech zones are located in the right hemisphere or in both hemispheres.
**anorexia nervosa.** A condition in which there is an exaggerated concern with being overweight that leads to inadequate food intake and often excessive exercising; can lead to severe weight loss and even starvation.
**antagonist.** A drug that blocks or reduces the effect of a neurotransmitter.
**antianxiety agent.** A type of drug that reduces anxiety; benzodiazepines and sedative-hypnotic agents are of this type.
**anxiety disorder.** A psychological disorder characterized by persistently high levels of anxiety or by maladaptive behaviors that reduce anxiety.
**anxiolytic drugs.** Antianxiety drugs; usually act as GABA (gamma-aminobutyric acid) angonists.
**aphagia.** Failure to eat; may be due to an unwillingness to eat or to motor difficulties, especially with swallowing.
**aphasia.** The inability to speak despite the presence of normal comprehension and intact vocal mechanisms.
**apoptosis.** Cell death that is genetically programmed.
**apraxia.** An inability to make voluntary movements in the absence of paralysis or other motor or sensory impairment, especially an inability to make proper use of an object.
**area postrema.** A nucleus in the brainstem that is sensitive to blood-borne toxins and causes vomiting.
**ascending activating system.** A group of neurons, each of which contains a common neurotransmitter, that have their cell bodies located in a nucleus in the basal forebrain or brainstem and their axons distributed to a wide region of the brain.
**association cortex.** Neocortex that is outside the primary sensory or motor cortex; it functions to produce cognition.
**associative learning.** A form of learning in which two or more unrelated stimuli become associated with each other so that either can elicit the same behavioral response.
**astrocyte.** Present in the central nervous system, a glial cell with a star-shaped appearance; provides structural support to neurons and transports substances between neurons and capillaries.
**atom.** The smallest part of an element that retains the properties of the element.
**atonia.** No tone. Even resting muscles have a certain level of activity, or tone, that can be blocked by inhibiting motor neurons to produce a condition of atonia.
***Australopithecus* (southern ape).** The earliest known humanlike animals, one species of which gave rise to the lineage that led to modern humans.
**autonomic nervous system.** The part of the nervous system that controls the functions of all the parts of the body, with the exception of the skeletal muscles, so that the body, and its organs, is prepared for rest or vigorous activity.
**autoreceptor.** A receptor in the membrane of a neuron that responds to the transmitter that the neuron releases.
**autosomes.** The 22 human chromosomes that do not express traits related to sex.
**axoaxonic synapse.** A synapse between two axons.
**axodendritic synapse.** A synapse between an axon and a dendrite.
**axoextracellular synapse.** A synapse that releases its neurotransmitter chemical into the extracellular space.
**axomuscular synapse.** A synapse between an axon and a muscle.
**axon.** The single fiber of a neuron that carries messages to other neurons.
**axon collateral.** A branch of an axon.
**axon hillock.** The part of the axon that is adjacent to the cell body and is the location where the action potential begins.
**axosecretory synapse.** A synapse between an axon and a blood vessel in which the transmitter substance is passed into the bloodstream as a hormone.
**axosomatic synapse.** A synapse between an axon and the cell body of a neuron.
**axosynaptic synapse.** A synapse between an axon and another synapse.

**barbiturate.** A type of drug that produces sedation and sleep.

**basal ganglia.** A group of structures in the forebrain that are located just beneath the neocortex and have connections to the thalamus and to the midbrain; thought to have motor functions that coordinate the movements of the limbs and the body.

**basic rest–activity cycle (BRAC).** A cycle in humans that has a period of about 90 minutes in which the level of arousal waxes and wanes.

**basilar membrane.** In the cochlea, the receptor surface that transduces sound waves into neural activity.

**behavior.** Any movement or pattern of movement produced by the nervous system.

**benzodiazepine.** A type of drug that reduces anxiety by stimulating the $GABA_A$ (gamma-aminobutyric acid A) receptor; benzodiazepines are also known as minor tranquilizers.

**beta-endorphin.** An endogenous peptide that has actions similar to those of ingested opium.

**beta rhythm.** A rhythmic electroencephalographic waveform with a frequency ranging from 15 to 30 hertz that can be recorded from the scalp of an alert subject or a subject in REM (rapid eye movement) sleep; also called an active or desynchronized pattern.

**bilateral symmetry.** Refers to organs or parts that are present on both sides of the body and very similar in appearance on each side. (For example, the hands are bilaterally symmetrical, whereas the heart is not.)

**bipolar neuron.** A neuron with one axon and one dendrite.

**black widow spider venom.** A poison, produced by the black widow spider, that promotes the release of acetylcholine from the synapse.

**blind spot.** The region of the retina where the axons forming the optic nerve leave the eye and where blood vessels enter; this region has no photoreceptors and is thus "blind."

**blob.** A region in the visual cortex that contains color-sensitive neurons, as revealed by staining for cytochrome oxidase.

**blood–brain barrier.** A barrier formed by tight junctions of capillaries, preventing the passage of most substances from the blood into the brain.

**botulin toxin.** A toxin, associated with food poisoning, that blocks the release of acetylcholine from the synapse. Clinically used to block unwanted activity in muscles.

**brain plasticity.** The ability of the brain to change its structure in response to experience, drugs, hormones, or injury.

**brainstem.** Central structures of the brain including the hindbrain, midbrain, thalamus, and hypothalamus.

**brain-stimulation reward.** A phenomenon in which animals will perform behaviors such as bar pressing in order to turn on electrical stimulation of the brain; also referred to as intracranial self-stimulation behavior.

**Broca's aphasia.** The inability to speak fluently despite the presence of normal comprehension and intact vocal mechanisms.

**Broca's area.** Just in front of the motor representation in the left hemisphere, the region that functions to produce the movements needed for language; sometimes referred to as the anterior speech area.

**calcitonin gene-related peptide (CGRP).** A peptide released by cholinergic end feet that synapse with muscles; the co-release of CGRP increases the force with which a muscle contracts.

**calmodulin.** A protein that, on stimulation by $Ca^{2+}$, plays a role in undocking vesicles containing a neurotransmitter so that the neurotransmitter can be released into the synaptic cleft.

**carbon monoxide (CO).** A gas that acts as a chemical neurotransmitter.

**cataplexy.** A condition in which a person collapses owing to the loss of all muscle activity or tone.

**cell-adhesion molecule (CAM).** A chemical to which specific cells can adhere, thus aiding in migration.

**cell assembly.** A hypothetical group of neurons that become functionally connected because they receive the same sensory inputs. Hebb proposed that cell assemblies were the basis of perception, memory, and thought.

**cell body.** The part of the cell containing the nucleus and other organelles for making proteins.

**cell membrane.** Two layers of phospholipid molecules that surround the cell, separating its contents from the extracellular fluid; membranes that surround components inside the cell also are bilayer.

**cellular tolerance.** A change that takes place in a cell in which the activity of the cell adjusts to the excitatory or inhibitory effects of a drug.

**central nervous system.** The part of the nervous system that is encased in the bones and includes the brain and spinal cord.

**cerebellum.** Major structure of the hindbrain specialized for motor coordination; large in species of animals in which the neocortex is large. In large-brained animals, it may also have a role in the coordination of other mental processes.

**cerebral cortex.** Layer of brain tissue composed of neurons that forms the surface of the brain; the human cerebral cortex contains many folds.

**cerebral palsy.** A group of brain disorders that result from brain damage acquired perinatally.

**cerebrospinal fluid.** A clear solution of sodium chloride and other salts that fills the ventricles inside the brain and circulates around the brain beneath the arachnoid layer in the subarachnoid space.

**cerebrum.** The major structure of the forebrain, consisting of two equal hemispheres (left and right); the most recently evolved part of the central nervous system.

**channel.** An opening in a protein that is embedded in the cell membrane and allows the passage of ions through the cell membrane.

**chemical neurotransmitter.** A chemical that binds to a receptor site of a membrane protein.

**chemical synapse.** When stimulated by an action potential, a synapse that releases a chemical into the synaptic cleft.

**chemoaffinity hypothesis.** The idea that cells or their axons and dendrites are drawn toward a signaling chemical that indicates the correct direction in which to go.

**chimeric animal.** An animal into which a cell from another animal of a different strain or species is inserted at an early stage of development such that the adult contains cells of two different strains or species.

**cholecystokinin (CCK).** A chemical that acts as a neurotransmitter in the brain and as a hormone in the digestive system where it is released by the duodenum to regulate gastric motility and to stimulate the gallbladder to release bile.

**choline.** A natural substance obtained from food and converted into the neurotransmitter acetylcholine.

**cholinergic neuron.** A neuron that contains acetylcholine in its synapses.

**chordates.** Members of the phylum of animals having a notocord; includes the fishes, amphibians, reptiles, birds, and mammals.

**chromosome.** A double-helix structure containing the DNA (deoxyribonucleic acid) of an organism's genes.

**circadian rhythm.** An event that occurs with a rhythmic cycle once each day.

**circannual rhythm.** An event that occurs with a rhythmic cycle once each year.

**cladogram.** A phylogenetic tree that branches repeatedly, suggesting a classification of organisms based on the time sequence in which evolutionary branches arise.

**classical conditioning.** A form of unconscious learning in which a neutral stimulus paired with a stimulus that evokes a behavior also comes to evoke that behavior; also known as Pavlovian conditioning and respondent conditioning.

**cloning.** The creation of an identical twin from the DNA (deoxyribonucleic acid) of a donor animal.

**cocaine.** A drug that is obtained from the coca plant and prevents the reuptake of dopamine in a dopamine synapse.

**cochlea.** Within the inner ear, the coiled structure in which vibrations caused by sound waves are transduced into neural impulses.

**cochlear implant.** An electronic device that is implanted surgically into the inner ear so that it stimulates the basilar membrane to transduce sound waves into neural activity and allow deaf people to hear.

**cochlear nerve.** A branch of the auditory nerve that sends auditory information from the cochlea to the brain.

**codeine.** A synthetic drug that has opioid effects.

**codon.** A triplet of three nucleotides in messenger RNA (ribonucleic acid); directs the placement of a particular amino acid into a polypeptide chain.

**cognition.** The act or process of knowing or coming to know; in psychology, it is used to refer to the processes of thought.

**cognitive neuroscience.** The study of the neural basis of cognition.

**color constancy.** Phenomena whereby the perceived color of an object tends to remain constant, regardless of changes in illumination.

**coma.** A state of deep unconsciousness due to brain injury or disease.

**common ancestor.** An ancestor from which two or more lineages or family groups arise and so is ancestral to both groups.

**common descent.** Refers to individual organisms or families that descend from the same ancestor.

**complex cell.** Type of visual cortex neuron that responds best to a light stimulus of a particular shape in its receptive field.

**complex tone.** A sound whose basic waveform, although repeated periodically, is more complicated than that of a pure tone; a complex tone contains two or more pure-tone components.

**concentration gradient.** The difference in the concentration of a substance between two regions of a container that allows the flow of the substance from an area of high concentration to an area of low concentration.

**conditioned response (CR).** In Pavlovian conditioning, the learned response to a formerly neutral conditioned stimulus (CS).

**conditioned stimulus (CS).** In Pavlovian conditioning, an originally neutral stimulus that, after association with an unconditioned stimulus (UCS), triggers a conditioned response.

**cone.** A photoreceptor specialized for detecting color and producing high visual acuity.

**contralateral neglect.** Neglect of a part of the body or world on the side opposite (that is, contralateral) to a brain injury; also called neglect.

**convergent thinking.** A form of thinking in which there is a search for a single answer to a question (such as $2 + 2 = ?$); contrasts with divergent thinking.

**corpus callosum.** Fiber system connecting the two cerebral hemispheres.

**cortex (neocortex).** Newest layer of the forebrain, forming the outer layer, or "new bark," and composed of about six layers of neurons.

**cortical column.** Unit of cortical organization that represents a vertically organized functional unit.

**corticospinal tract.** A bundle of fibers directly connecting the cerebral cortex to the spinal cord.

**cortisol.** A hormone that prepares the body to cope with stress.

**cranial nerve.** One of a set of nerves that controls sensory and motor functions of the head; includes senses of smell, vision, audition, taste, and touch on the face and head.

**cranial nervous system.** A functional division of the nervous system that refers to the brain and its connections to parts of the head, such as the eyes and ears.

**critical period.** A period in development during which some event has a long-lasting influence on the brain; often referred to as a sensitive period.

**cross-tolerance.** A form of tolerance in which the response to a novel drug is reduced because of tolerance developed in response to a related drug.

**culture.** Behaviors that are learned and passed on from one generation to the next through teaching and learning.

**curare.** A drug, obtained from a South American plant, that blocks the receptors of the acetylcholine synapse.

**current.** The flow of electrons from a region of high negative charge to a region of low negative charge; the flow of various ions across the neuron membrane.

**cyclic adenosine monophosphate (cAMP).** A small molecule that acts as a second messenger in neurons.

**cytoarchitectonic map.** Map of the neocortex based on the organization, structure, and distribution of the cells.

**cytosine.** One of the bases in a DNA (deoxyribonucleic acid) strand that binds to a base (guanine) in another strand to form double-stranded DNA.

**deafferented.** Refers to loss of incoming sensory input usually due to damage to sensory fibers; also refers to loss of any afferent input to a structure.

**declarative memory.** A type of memory illustrated by the ability to recount the details of events, including time, place, and circumstances, in contrast with the ability to perform some act or behavior. Literally, declarative memory refers to the ability to recount what one knows, which is lost in many types of amnesia.

**delta rhythm.** A rhythmic electroencephalographic waveform with a frequency ranging from 0 to 3 hertz that can be recorded from the scalp of a subject who is sleeping.

**dendrite.** A branch of a neuron that consists of an extension of the cell body, thus greatly increasing the area of the cell.

**dendritic spine.** A protrusion of a dendrite that greatly increases the area of the dendrite and is the usual point of dendritic contact with axons.

**dendrodendritic synapse.** A synapse between two dendrites.

**deoxyribonucleic acid (DNA).** A double-stranded, helical nucleic acid molecule capable of replicating and determining the inherited structure of a cell's proteins.

**dependency hypothesis.** A hypothesis of drug addiction that postulates that drug use is maintained to prevent withdrawal symptoms.

**depolarization.** A decrease in the electrical charge across a membrane, usually due to the inward flow of sodium ions.

**depression.** An affective disorder characterized by prolonged feelings of worthlessness and guilt, disruption of normal eating habits, sleep disturbances, a general slowing of behavior, and frequent thoughts of suicide.

**dermatome.** Area of the skin supplied with afferent nerve fibers by a single spinal-cord dorsal root.

**dichotic listening.** A procedure whereby two different auditory stimuli are played simultaneously to each ear.

**diencephalon.** The part of the brain that contains the hypothalamus, thalamus, and epithalamus; thought to coordinate many basic instinctual behaviors including temperature regulation, sexual behavior, and eating.

**diffusion.** The movement of ions from an area of high concentration to an area of low concentration through random motion.

**disinhibition theory.** A theory to explain the effects of alcohol in which intoxication is associated with the loss of moral and social values in favor of instinctual behaviors.

**dissolution.** The process by which a salt or sugar breaks into its constituent parts when placed in water; also the condition whereby disease or damage in the highest levels of the brain would produce not just loss of function, but a repertory of simpler behaviors as seen in animals that have not evolved that particular brain structure.

**divergent thinking.** A form of thinking in which there is a search for multiple solutions to a problem (such as, How many different ways can a pen be used?); contrasts with convergent thinking.

**diving bradycardia.** The slowing or stopping of the heart displayed by most diving animals during immersion in water.

**dominant allele.** Of two alleles of a gene, the allele that is expressed as a behavioral or physical trait.

**domoic acid.** A glutamate analogue that, in small amounts, stimulates glutamate receptors and in higher amounts induces death of the neuron.

**dopamine.** A chemical neurotransmitter released by dopamine neurons.

**dopamine hypothesis of schizophrenia.** A hypothesis proposing that schizophrenic symptoms are due to excess activity of the neurotransmitter dopamine.

**dorsal-column nuclei.** Nuclei in the brainstem that receive fine touch and pressure fibers from the dorsal spinothalamic tract of the spinal cord.

**dorsal spinothalamic tract.** In the dorsal part of the spinal cord, a pathway that carries fine touch and pressure fibers.

**dorsal stream.** A visual processing pathway that orginates in the visual cortex and progresses into the posterior parietal cortex. It controls the visual guidance of movement.

**doubly gated channel.** A membrane channel containing a pore that opens to allow entry of calcium into the cell only when the membrane is simultaneously depolarized and is stimulated by the appropriate neurotransmitter.

**Down's syndrome.** A chromosomal abnormality resulting in mental retardation and other abnormalities, usually caused by an extra chromosome 21.

**$D_2$ receptor.** A receptor for the neurotransmitter dopamine; target for major tranquilizers.

**drive.** A hypothetical state of arousal that motivates an organism to engage in a particular behavior.

**drug.** A substance used to treat physical or mental disorders.

**drug-dependency insomnia.** A condition that results from continuous use of "sleeping pills" in which a person becomes tolerant of the drug while the drug also results in deprivation of either REM (rapid eye movement) or NREM (nonrapid eye movement) sleep, leading the person to increase the drug dosage.

**drug-induced behavioral sensitization.** The phenomenon whereby there is an escalating behavioral response to repeated administration of a psychomotor stimulant such as amphetamine, cocaine, or nicotine.

**DSM-IV.** The fourth and most recent edition of the American Psychiatric Association's classification of psychiatric disorders, the *Diagnostic and Statistical Manual of Mental Disorders.*

**dualism.** A philosophical position that holds that both a nonmaterial mind and the material body contribute to behavior.

**dyskinesia.** Movements that are abnormal or involuntary or both.

**echolocation.** The ability to identify and locate an object by sound that bounces off the object.

**efferent.** Conducting away from the central nervous system.

**electrical potential.** An electrical charge; the ability to do work through the use of stored potential electrical energy.

**electrical stimulation.** The flow of electrical current from the tip of an electrode through brain tissue, resulting in changes in the electrical activity of the tissue.

**electrical synapse.** A synapse in which the presynaptic membrane is fused with the postsynaptic membrane, and so the action potential is passed from one neuron to the next.

**electricity.** The flow of electrons from a body that contains a higher charge to a body that contains a lower charge.

**electrode.** An insulated wire or a salt-filled glass tube that is used to stimulate or record from neurons.

**electroencephalogram (EEG).** Electrical activity that is recorded through the skull or from the brain and represents graded potentials of many neurons.

**electron.** One of three parts of an atom, an electron is a negatively charged particle that moves about the nucleus of an atom.

**element.** A substance that cannot be broken down into another substance; there are 92 natural elements, including hydrogen, sodium, and oxygen.

**emotional memory.** Memory for the affective properties of stimuli or events.

**encephalization quotient (EQ).** A measure of brain size obtained from the ratio of actual brain size to the expected brain size for an animal of a particular body size.

**end foot.** The terminal part of an axon that conveys information to other neurons; also called terminal button.

**endocrine gland.** A gland in the body that makes hormones.

**endoplasmic reticulum.** An extensive membrane that is continuous with the nuclear membrane; parts of the endoplasmic reticulum contain ribosomes for assembling chains of amino acids according to the instructions from messenger RNA (ribonucleic acid).

**endorphin.** An opioid-like substance found in the brain that acts as a neurotransmitter and may be associated with pain or pleasure.

**endothelial cell.** A cell that forms blood vessels.

**end plate.** On a muscle, the receptor–ion complex that is activated by the release of the neurotransmitter acetylcholine from the terminal of a motor neuron.

**entorhinal cortex.** Located on the medial surface of the temporal lobe, the entorhinal cortex provides a major route for neocortical input to the hippocampal formation; often degenerates in Alzheimer's disease.

**entrain.** To make one event take place within the same period as another event takes place. Literally, to get on a train.

**ependymal cell.** A glial cell, found on the walls of the ventricles of the brain, that makes and secretes cerebral spinal fluid.

**epidermal growth factor (EGF).** A neurotrophic factor that acts to stimulate mitosis in stem cells.

**epinephrine (EP).** A neurotransmitter found in the sympathetic nervous system; mobilizes the body for fight or flight.

**event-related potential (ERP).** A change in the slow-wave activity of the brain in response to a sensory stimulus.

**evolutionary psychology.** The study of behavior that uses principles of natural selection to account for human behaviors.

**excitation.** A process that increases the likelihood that neurons will be active.

**excitatory postsynaptic potential (EPSP).** A brief depolarization of a neuron membrane in response to stimulation from a terminal of another neuron, making the neuron more likely to produce an action potential.

**executive function.** Used to describe a brain area's ability to control complex actions. Often used to describe the frontal lobe's role in organizing and planning behavior.

**exocytosis.** The cellular excretion of substances by fusion of their surrounding membrane with the plasma membrane.

**explicit memory.** Memory in which subjects can retrieve an item and indicate that they know that the item they have retrieved is the correct item (that is, conscious memory).

**extinction.** A term used in neurology to refer to the neglect of information on one side of the body when the information is presented simultaneously with similar information on the other side of the body.

**extracellular fluid.** The fluid and its contents that surround a neuron or glial cell.

**extrastriate cortex.** Visual cortical areas outside the striate cortex; also called secondary cortex.

**eye-blink conditioning.** A form of classical conditioning in which a formerly neutral stimulus signals the subsequent arrival of an event that leads to a defensive blinking response. When learning has taken place, the neutral stimulus will elicit the eyeblink in the absence of the noxious stimulus that it predicts.

**fear conditioning.** The learning of an association between a neutral stimulus and a noxious event such as a shock.

**feedback mechanism.** A system in which a neural or hormonal loop regulates the activity of neurons, initiating the neuronal activity or hormone release.

**field potential.** The summed graded potentials of a number of neurons.

**filopod.** A process at the end of a developing axon that reaches out to search for a potential target.

**flocculus.** A part of the cerebellum that receives input from the vestibular receptors in the middle ear.

**flush model.** A hypothetical model of ethologists in which energy for specific behaviors is stored until it reaches a critical level and then is released (flushed) to produce the behavior, much like flushing a toilet releases the stored water.

**forebrain.** The most anterior part of the embryonic brain; contains the basal ganglia and the neocortex and is therefore thought to coordinate advanced cognitive functions such as thinking, planning, and language.

**fovea.** The region at the center of the retina that is specialized for high acuity; its receptive fields are at the center of the eye's visual field.

**free-running rhythm.** A rhythm of the body's own devising in the absence of all external cues.

**frequency.** The number of times that an event is repeated in a given period.

**frontal leukotomy.** A surgical procedure in which nerve fibers to and from the frontal lobe are severed with a special knife called a leukotome (from the Greek *leuko,* meaning "white nerve fibers," and *tome,* meaning "a cutting").

**frontal lobe.** All of the cerebral cortex in front of the central sulcus and beneath the frontal bone.

**functional magnetic resonance imaging (fMRI).** A type of magnetic resonance imaging that takes advantage of the fact that changes in the distribution of elements such as oxygen alter the magnetic properties of the brain. Because oxygen consumption varies with behavior, it is possible to map and measure changes that are produced by behavior.

**$GABA_A$ receptor.** A gamma-aminobutyric acid receptor on which sedative hypnotics and antianxiety drugs act.

**gamma-aminobutyric acid (GABA).** An amino acid neurotransmitter that inhibits neurons.

**ganglion.** A cluster of neurons that are found in a particular part of the body and subserve a particular function.

**gate.** A protein that is embedded in a neural or glial membrane and allows substances to pass through the membrane on some occasions but not on others.

**gene.** A discrete unit of hereditary information located on a chromosome and consisting of DNA (deoxyribonucleic acid); a gene encodes a protein.

**genetic engineering.** An application of genetics directed toward changing physical or behavioral traits by changing genes.

**geniculostriate system.** A system consisting of projections from the retina to the lateral geniculate nucleus to the visual cortex.

**genotype.** The genetic makeup of an organism.

**"g" factor.** A hypothetical form of general intelligence, proposed by Charles Spearman, that can account for individual differences in human intelligence.

**glabrous skin.** Skin that does not have hair follicles but contains larger numbers of sensory receptors than do other skin areas.

**glial cell.** Belongs to one of the two classes of cells of the nervous system; often referred to as a support cell. Glial cells provide insulation, nutrients, and support; they also aid in the repair of neurons.

**glioblast.** A progenitor cell that gives rise to different types of glial cells.

**globus pallidus.** One of the nuclei of the basal ganglia, the globus pallidus plays a role in motor control.

**glucocorticoid.** One of a group of hormones, secreted in times of stress, that are important in protein and carbohydrate metabolism.

**glutamate.** An amino acid neurotransmitter that excites neurons.

**glutamate analogue.** A drug that acts like glutamate on glutamate receptors.

**Golgi body.** A membrane in neurons that provides a membrane covering for proteins manufactured by the cell.

**graded potential.** Hyperpolarization of a membrane or depolarization of the membrane.

**gray matter.** Those areas of the nervous system composed predominantly of cell bodies, leading to a gray appearance.

**growth cone.** The growing tip of an axon.

**growth spurt.** A sudden growth in development that lasts for a finite time.

**guanine.** One of the bases in a DNA (deoxyribonucleic acid) strand that binds to a base (cytosine) in another strand to form double-stranded DNA.

**guanyl nucleotide-binding protein (G protein).** A protein that carries the message from a metabotropic receptor to other receptors or to second messengers.

**gyrus.** A groove in brain matter, usually a groove found in the neocortex or cerebellum.

**habituation.** A form of learning in which a response to a stimulus weakens with repeated stimulus presentations.

**hair cell.** A sensory cell in the cochlea that transduces mechanical displacement into a neural impulse coding the frequency of a sound.

**hairy skin.** Skin that contains hair follicles, in contrast with glabrous skin, which does not.

**hapsis.** The perceptual ability to discriminate objects on the basis of touch.

**head-direction cell.** A neuron in the hippocampus that discharges when an animal faces in a particular direction.

**Hebb synapse.** A synapse that can change with use so that learning takes place.

**hemisphere.** Literally half a sphere, referring to one side of the cerebral cortex or one side of the cerebellum.

**heroin.** A synthetic form of morphine.

**hertz.** A measure of frequency; one hertz is equal to one cycle per second.

**Heschl's gyrus.** The primary auditory cortex found in the temporal lobes.

**heterozygous.** Having two different alleles for the same trait.

**hierarchical organization.** A principle of cerebral organization in which information is processed serially, with each level of processing assumed to elaborate some hypothetical process.

**hindbrain.** The embryonic part of the brain that contains the brainstem and cerebellum; thought to coordinate movements and support movements of walking and posture.

**hippocampal formation.** A general term referring to the hippocampus and a number of associated structures and pathways.

**hippocampus.** A distinctive three-layered cortical structure lying in the medial region of the temporal lobe; plays a role in certain forms of memory and spatial navigation.

**homeostasis.** A process by which the normal balance of metabolic processes is maintained.

**homeostatic mechanism.** A mechanism that keeps certain body functions within a narrow, fixed range.

**hominid.** A general term referring to primates that walk upright, including all forms of humans, living and extinct.

***Homo erectus.*** An extinct hominid that is proposed to be part of the human lineage; its name signifies that it walked upright (erect) on the mistaken notion that its predecessors were stooped.

***Homo habilis.*** An extinct hominid that is proposed to be part of the human lineage; its name signifies that it was a tool user (*habilis,* meaning "handy").

**homonymous hemianopia.** Blindness of an entire left or right visual field.

**homozygous.** Having two identical alleles for a trait.

**homunculus.** The representation of the human body in the sensory or motor cortex; also any topographical representation of the body by a neural area.

**hormone.** A chemical that is released by a gland and circulates in the blood to affect a body target.

**Huntington's chorea.** An autosomal genetic disorder that results in motor and cognitive disturbances and is caused by an increase in the number of CAG (cytosine-adenine-guanine) repeats of chromosome 4.

**hydrocephalus.** A condition in which the flow of ventricular fluid is blocked, causing a buildup of pressure in the brain and swelling of the head that can result in retardation.

**hydrogen bond.** A bond between the positively charged hydrogen of a polar molecule and the negatively charged region of another polar molecule.

**hydrophilic.** Refers to a substance that binds weakly to polar water molecules.

**hydrophobic.** Refers to a substance containing no polar regions that will not bind with polar water molecules.

**hypercomplex cell.** A type of visual cortex neuron that responds best to a precisely limited type of visual stimulus; often a stimulus of a particular size and orientation that moves in one direction.

**hyperkinetic symptom.** A symptom of brain damage that involves involuntary excessive movements.

**hyperphagia.** A disorder in which an animal overeats, leading to significant weight gain.

**hyperpolarization.** An increase in the electrical charge across a membrane, usually due to the inward flow of chloride ions or the outward flow of potassium ions.

**hypnogogic.** Refers to a hallucinogenic or dreamlike event at the beginning of sleep.

**hypokinetic symptom.** A symptom of brain damage that involves a paucity of movement.

**hypothalamus.** A part of the diencephalon that contains many nuclei associated with temperature regulation, eating and drinking, and sexual behavior.

**hypovolemic thirst.** Thirst produced by a reduction in the amount of extracellular fluid.

**implicit memory.** Memory in which subjects can demonstrate knowledge or skill but cannot explicitly retrieve the information.

**imprinting.** Process in which an animal is predisposed to learning an attachment to objects or animals at a critical period in development.

**incentive.** An environmental stimulus that motivates behavior.

**incentive salience.** Refers to cues that, after having been associated with drug use, become sought out.

**incentive-sensitization theory.** A theory that holds that, when a drug has been used in association with certain cues, the cues themselves will elicit desire for the drug.

**inferior colliculus.** A structure on the dorsal surface of the midbrain; used in auditory processing.

**infradian rhythm.** A rhythm with a period of more than a day and less than a year; for example, the female menstrual cycle.

**infundibulum.** Connection between the hypothalamus and pituitary gland.

**inhibition.** A process that decreases the likelihood that neurons will be active.

**inhibitory postsynaptic potential (IPSP).** A brief hyperpolarization of a neuron membrane in response to stimulation from a terminal of another neuron, making the neuron less likely to produce an action potential.

**innate releasing mechanism (IRM).** In built data-processing mechanisms that act like stimulus filters and are interconnected with the motor systems so that specific behaviors are released by specific stimuli. An example is the cat's piloerection in response to another cat's "halloween posture."

**insomnia.** Inability to sleep at the desired time.

**instrumental conditioning.** A learning procedure in which the consequences (such as obtaining a reward) of a particular behavior (such as pressing a bar) increase or decrease the probability of the behavior occurring again; also called operant conditioning.

**insulator.** A substance through which electrons will not flow; for example, rubber or glass.

**intelligence A.** Hebb's term for innate intellectual potential, which is highly heritable. This form of intelligence cannot be measured directly.

**intelligence B.** Hebb's term for our observed intelligence, which is influenced by experience as well as other factors, such as disease, injury, or exposure to environmental toxins, especially during development. This intelligence is measured by intelligence tests.

**internal clock.** A neural structure, such as the suprachiasmatic nucleus, that determines the time at which a behavior will occur.

**internal nervous system.** A functional division of the nervous system that controls the body's internal organs; also called the autonomic nervous system.

**interneuron.** A neuron interposed between a sensory neuron and a motor neuron; thus, in mammals, interneurons constitute most of the neurons of the brain.

**intracellular fluid.** The fluid and its contents found within neurons and glial cells.

**intracranial self-stimulation.** A phenomenon in which animals will perform behaviors such as bar pressing in order to turn on electrical stimulation of the brain; also referred to as brain-stimulation reward.

**ion.** After having been dissolved in water, a part of a molecule that has a charge.

**ionotropic receptor.** A receptor that has two parts: a binding site for a neurotransmitter and a pore that regulates ion flow.

**kainate receptor.** A glutamate receptor that is especially sensitive to the glutamate analogue drug kainic acid.

**Kluver-Bucy syndrome.** A behavioral syndrome, characterized especially by hypersexuality, that results from bilateral injury to the temporal lobe.

**knock-out technology.** A method in genetics in which a gene is deleted from a chromosome or its expression is blocked.

**Korsakoff's syndrome.** A permanent loss of the ability to learn new information (anterograde amnesia), caused by diencephalic damage resulting from chronic alcoholism or malnutrition that produces a vitamin $B_1$ deficiency.

**lateral corticospinal tract.** In the lateral spinal cord, a pathway that carries information instructing movement.

**lateral hypothalamus.** Region of the hypothalamus in which damage impairs eating and drinking and in which animals will intracranially self-stimulate at a very high rate.

**lateralization.** A process whereby functions become located primarily on one side of the brain.

**law of Bell and Magendie.** Named after its cofounders, this law states that the dorsal roots of the spinal cord are sensory and the ventral roots are motor.

**learned taste aversion.** Acquisition of an association between a specific taste (or odor) and illness; leads to an aversion of food objects having that taste.

**learned tolerance.** Experience in performing a behavior under the influence of a drug results in improved performance of the behavior when subsequently under the influence of the drug.

**learning.** A relatively permanent change in an organism's behavior as a result of experience.

**learning set.** An understanding of how a problem can be solved with a rule that can be applied in many different situations.

**Leu-enkephalin.** A peptide neurotransmitter that produces some of the effects of opioid drugs.

**limbic cortex.** Cortical regions within the limbic system; includes both the cingulate cortex and the cortex adjacent to the hippocampus.

**limbic system.** Consists of structures that lie between the neocortex and the brainstem and form a hypothetical functional system that controls affective behavior and certain forms of memory; includes the cingulate cortex and the hippocampus.

**long-term enhancement (LTE).** A change in the amplitude of an excitatory postsynaptic potential that lasts for hours to days in response to stimulation of a synapse; may play a part in learning. Sometimes referred to as long-term or long-lasting potentiation (LTP or LLP).

**long-term memory.** A form of memory in which information is assumed to be stored for longer than about 15 minutes.

**lordosis.** A behavior seen in many four-legged mammals in which a sexually receptive female will arch her back and raise her hindquarters in response to the approach or touch of a male.

**luminance contrast.** The amount of light reflected by an object relative to its surroundings.

**lysergic acid diethylamide (LSD).** A drug that produces visual hallucinations, presumably by influencing the serotonin system.

**lysosome.** A membrane-enclosed bag of enzymes found in cells that is the site of digestion and waste elimination.

**magnetic resonance imaging (MRI).** An imaging procedure in which a computer draws a map from the measured changes in the magnetic resonance of atoms in the brain; allows the production of a structural map of the brain without actually opening the skull.

**magnetoencephalogram (MEG).** A recording of the changes in tiny magnetic fields generated by the brain.

**magnocellular (M) cell.** Large-celled neuron of the visual system that is sensitive to moving stimuli.

**magnocellular nucleus of the medulla.** A part of the brainstem that sends inhibitory impulses to the motor neurons of the spinal cord to produce the paralysis of REM (rapid eye movement) sleep.

**major tranquilizer.** A type of drug that blocks the dopamine-2 ($D_2$) receptor and is used mainly for treating schizophrenia; also called a neuroleptic drug.

**masculinization.** A process by which exposure to androgens alters the brain, rendering it "male-like."

**materialism.** Philosophical position that holds that behavior can be explained as a function of the nervous system without explanatory recourse to the mind.

**medial forebrain bundle (MFB).** A fiber bundle that passes through the lateral hypothalamic area running to and from the forebrain and brainstem.

**medial geniculate nucleus.** The major thalamic region concerned with audition.

**medial lemniscus.** A pathway through the core of the brainstem, the medial lemniscus carries sensory information from the body, including fine touch and pressure, pain, and temperature.

**medial pontine reticular formation.** A brainstem nucleus that is responsible for initiating REM (rapid eye movement) sleep.

**memory.** The ability to recall or recognize previous experience.

**memory trace.** A mental representation of a previous experience.

**meninges.** Three layers of protective tissue—the dura mater, arachnoid, and pia mater—that encase the brain and spinal cord.

**mentalism.** Of the mind; an explanation of behavior as a function of the mind.

**mescaline.** A psychedelic drug extracted from the peyote cactus *(Lophophora williamsii).*

**mesolimbic dopamine system.** Dopamine neurons in the midbrain that project to the nucleus accumbens and to medial parts of the basal ganglia, limbic system, and neocortex.

**messenger RNA (mRNA).** A type of ribonucleic acid synthesized from DNA (deoxyribonucleic acid); attaches to ribosomes to specify the sequences of amino acids that form proteins.

**metabolic tolerance.** Reduced sensitivity to a substance that results from the increased ability of cells to metabolize the substance.

**metabotropic receptor.** This receptor is linked to a G protein (guanyl nucleotide-binding protein) and can affect other receptors or act with second messengers to affect other cellular processes.

**Met-enkephalin.** A peptide neurotransmitter that produces some of the effects of opioid drugs.

**methylene-dioxymethamphetamine (MDMA).** Also called "ecstasy," a widely used synthetic amphetamine.

**mGluR4.** A receptor on the tongue that is sensitive to glutamate.

**microglial cell.** A form of glial cell that scavenges debris in the nervous system.

**microsleep.** A brief period of sleep lasting a second or so.

**midbrain.** Middle part of the embryonic brain that, in the adult, contains circuits for hearing and seeing as well as walking.

**mind.** A nonmaterial entity that is proposed to be responsible for intelligence, attention, awareness, and consciousness.

**mind–body problem.** Problem of how to explain how a nonmaterial mind can command a material body.

**miniature postsynaptic potential.** A small excitatory or inhibitory graded potential, the amplitude of which is related to the number of quanta of neurotransmitter released at the synapse.

**minor tranquilizer.** A sedative hypnotic drug promoted primarily for use in the treatment of anxiety.

**mirror neuron.** A neuron that fires when a monkey observes a specific action being made by another monkey.

**mitochondrion.** An organelle within the cell that provides energy for cell processes.

**molecule.** Two or more atoms held together by chemical bonds.

**monoamine oxidase (MAO) inhibitor.** A chemical that blocks MAO from degrading neurotransmitters such as dopamine, noradrenaline, and serotonin.

**monosynaptic reflex.** A reflex requiring one synapse between sensory input and movement.

**morphine.** A major sedative and pain-relieving drug found in opium, comprising approximately 10 percent of the crude opium extract.

**motivation.** A need or desire that energizes and directs behavior.

**motor nerve.** A collection of nerve fibers that leave the spinal cord and brain and carry commands to muscles to make them contract.

**motor neuron.** A neuron in the central nervous system that sends axons to activate body muscles.

**motor sequence.** A sequence of movements preprogrammed by the brain and produced as a unit.

**multiple sclerosis (MS).** A nervous system disorder that results from the loss of the myelin (glial-cell covering) around neurons.

**mutation.** Alteration of an allele that yields a different version of that allele.

**myelin.** Glial coating that surrounds axons in the central and the peripheral nervous systems.

**nalorphine.** A drug that blocks opioid receptors.

**naloxone.** A chemical that blocks opioid receptors and thus prevents opioid-like drugs from producing their actions; can be used for treating morphine or heroin overdoses.

**narcolepsy.** A sleep disorder in which a person falls asleep at inappropriate times of the day.

**narcotic analgesic drug.** A drug that has sedative and pain-relieving properties.

**natural selection.** Differential success in the reproduction of different phenotypes resulting from the interaction of organisms with their environment. Evolution takes place when natural selection causes changes in relative frequencies of alleles in the gene pool.

**Neanderthal.** A hominid that lived in Europe within the past 30,000 years and is a close relative of modern humans; the name derives from the Neander valley in Germany where the first skeletal remains were found.

**negative pole.** In a battery, the pole with excess electrons.

**neglect.** Neglect of a part of the body or world on the side opposite (that is, contralateral) to a brain injury; also called contralateral neglect.

**neocortex.** Newest layer of the forebrain, forming the outer layer, or "new bark," and composed of about six layers of gray matter.

**neoteny.** A process in which maturation is delayed, and so an adult retains infant characteristics; the idea derived from the observation that newly evolved species resemble the young of their ancestors.

**nerve fiber.** As part of a neuron, a long process that carries information from the neuron to other neurons; also a collection of nerve fibers.

**nerve growth factor (NGF).** A neurotrophic factor that acts to keep neurons alive and to stimulate differentiation of some types of neurons.

**nerve impulse.** Propagation of an action potential on the membrane of an axon.

**nerve tract.** Large collection of axons coursing together within the central nervous system.

**nervous system.** Collective name for all of the neurons in the body.

**netrins.** A class of tropic molecules.

**neural Darwinism.** The idea that the process of cell death and synaptic pruning is not random but is the outcome of competition between neurons for connections and metabolic resources.

**neural plate.** Thickened region of the ectodermal layer that gives rise to the neural tube.

**neural stem cells.** Cells that gives rise to all neurons in the nervous system.

**neural tube.** A structure in the early stage of brain development from which the brain and spinal cord develop.

**neuroblast.** A progenitor cell that gives rise to all the different types of neurons.

**neuroleptic drug.** A type of drug that blocks dopamine-2; also called major tranquilizer.

**neuron.** An information-transmitting cell in the nervous system.

**neuron hypothesis.** The idea that the neuron is the basic unit of brain function.

**neuropeptides.** A class of chemical neurotransmitters manufactured with instructions from a cell's DNA; thus a neuropeptide consists of a chain of amino acids that act as a neurotransmitter.

**neuropsychology.** A general term used to refer to the study of the relation between brain function and behavior.

**neurotrophic factors.** A class of compounds that act to support growth and differentiation in developing neurons and may act to keep certain neurons alive in adulthood.

**neutron.** A large neutrally charged particle found in the nucleus of an atom.

**nicotine.** A natural drug obtained from tobacco leaves that stimulates the nicotine receptors of acetylcholine synapses.

**nicotinic ACh receptor (nAChr).** An ionotropic receptor to which the natural transmitter acetylcholine and the drug nicotine bind to regulate the flow of ions through the receptor pore.

**nitric oxide (NO).** A gas that acts as a chemical neurotransmitter in many cells.

**nocioception.** The perception of pain and temperature.

**node of Ranvier.** The part of an axon that is not covered by myelin.

**nonregulatory behavior.** A behavior that is not required to meet the basic needs of an animal.

**norepinephrine (NE).** A chemical neurotransmitter in the brain, norepinephrine is found in one of the nonspecific ascending systems.

**notochord.** A longitudinal flexible rod located between the gut and the spinal cord in all chordate embryos.

**NREM (nonrapid eye movement) sleep.** All segments of sleep excluding REM sleep.

**nuclear membrane.** Membrane that surrounds the nucleus of a cell.

**nucleotide bases.** A class of molecules that includes adenine, cytosine, guanine, thymine, and uracil. They are constituents of the genetic code. In double-stranded DNA (deoxyribonucleic acid), adenine and thymine (AT) form a complementary pair, as do cytosine and guanine (CG). The same bases are used in RNA (ribonucleic acid), except that uracil replaces thymine.

**nucleus.** A group of cells forming a cluster that can be identified with special stains to form a functional grouping; also the part of a cell that contains the cell's DNA (deoxyribonucleic acid).

**occipital lobe.** The cerebral cortex at the back of the brain and beneath the occipital bone.

**ocular dominance column.** A functional column in the visual cortex maximally responsive to information coming from one eye.

**oligodendroglial cell.** A glial cell in the central nervous system that provides myelin on axons.

**operant conditioning.** A form of learning in which behavior is strengthened if followed by reinforcement or diminished if followed by punishment; also called instrumental conditioning.

**opium.** A crude resinous extract from the opium poppy.

**opponent-process theory.** An explanation of color vision that emphasizes the importance of the opposition of pairs of colors: red versus green and blue versus yellow.

**optic ataxia.** Deficit in the visual control of reaching and other movements.

**optic chiasm.** The junction of the two optic nerves at which the axons from the nasal (inside) halves of the retinas cross to the opposite side of the brain.

**organizing effects of hormones.** Actions of hormones during development in which the hormones alter tissue differentiation; an example is the action of androgens to stimulate the development of male genitalia.

**organ of Corti.** Receptor organ located on the basilar membrane of the cochlea.

**organophosphates.** Chemicals used as fertilizers.

**oscilloscope.** A device that measures the flow of electrons to measure voltage.

**osmotic thirst.** Thirst resulting from cellular dehydration that is produced by an increase in the osmotic pressure of the extracellular fluid relative to the intracellular fluid.

**ossicles.** The bones of the middle ear: the malleus (hammer), incus (anvil), and stapes (stirrup).

**otoconia.** Small crystals of sand in the middle ear that rub against hair cells during movement to provide the stimuli to signal that the head has moved.

**otolith organs.** Bodies in the inner ear that provide vestibular information.

**pacemaker.** A structure that times or determines the period of activity of another structure or an event.

**pain gate.** A hypothetical neural circuit in which activity in fine touch and pressure pathways diminishes the activity in pain and temperature pathways.

**Papez circuit.** Roughly equivalent to the limbic system; Papez proposed that the limbic system and associated structures played a central role in the production of emotions.

**parahippocampal cortex.** Cortex located along the dorsal medial surface of the temporal lobe.

**paralysis.** Loss of sensation and movement due to nervous system injury.

**paraplegia.** Paralysis of the legs due to spinal-cord injury.

**parasympathetic nervous system.** The part of the internal nervous system that acts in opposition to the sympathetic nervous system; for example, reversing the alarm response or stimulating digestion. The rest and digest nervous system.

**parietal lobe.** The cerebral cortex behind the central sulcus and beneath the parietal bone.

**Pavlovian conditioning.** A learning procedure whereby a neutral stimulus (such as a tone) comes to elicit a response because of its repeated pairing with some event (such as the delivery of food); also called classical conditioning or respondent conditioning.

**parvocellular (P) cell.** Small-celled neuron of the visual system that is sensitive to form and color differences.

**peribrachial area.** A nucleus in the brainstem that has a role in producing REM sleep.

**peripheral nerve.** One of a set of nerves that control sensory and motor functions of the body below the head; connects to the spinal cord.

**peripheral nervous system.** Collective name for all of the neurons in the body that are located outside the brain and spinal cord.

**perirhinal cortex.** Cortex lying next to the rhinal fissure on the base of the brain.

**phagocytosis.** Process by which a microglial cell engulfs cellular debris.

**phenylketonuria (PKU).** A behavioral disorder caused by elevated levels of the amino acid phenylalanine in the blood as a result of a defect in the gene for the enzyme phenylalanine hydroxylase; the major symptom is severe mental retardation.

**phenotype.** Behavioral and physical traits of an organism.

**phospholipid.** A molecule consisting of a phosphate head and two tails; phospholipids form cells' membranes.

**physical dependence.** Indicated by the display of withdrawal symptoms on cessation of drug use.

**physostigmine.** A chemical that prevents the breakdown of acetylcholine and thus acts as a cholinergic agonist; can also be used for treating mysthenia gravis.

**pineal gland.** Also called the pineal body, a small endocrine gland on the dorsal surface of the vertebrate forebrain; secretes the hormone melatonin, which regulates body functions related to seasonal day length.

**pituitary gland.** An endocrine gland attached to the bottom of the hypothalamus; its secretions control the activities of many other endocrine glands, and it is known to be associated with biological rhythms.

**planum temporale.** The cortical area just posterior to the primary auditory cortex; normally larger in the left hemisphere and concerned with language processing.

**pleiotropy.** Ability of a single gene to have multiple effects.

**polar molecule.** A molecule with an uneven charge such that one part is negative and the other positive.

**polypeptide.** A molecule in which a number of amino acids are connected by peptide bonds.

**positive pole.** In a battery, the pole to which electrons flow.

**positron emission tomography (PET).** A technique whereby changes in blood flow can be detected by measuring changes in the uptake of compounds such as oxygen or glucose.

**posterior speech zone.** Roughly equivalent to Wernicke's area; concerned with language processing.

**postsynaptic membrane.** A membrane that surrounds the end foot of an axon and thus forms the membrane on one side of a synapse; any membrane on the input (transmitter) side of a synapse.

**prefrontal cortex.** The cortex lying in front of the motor and premotor cortices of the frontal lobe; the prefrontal cortex is particularly large in the human brain.

**preparedness.** Concept used to describe the phenomenon whereby animals appear prewired to make certain types of associations, such as that between taste and illness.

**presynaptic membrane.** A membrane that surrounds a synaptic spine or cell that contains the receptors for a transmitter; any membrane on the output (transmitter) side of a membrane.

**primary visual cortex.** The striate cortex (area 17; V1); it receives input from the lateral geniculate nucleus.

**principle of proper mass.** The idea that complex behavioral functions are produced by a larger brain or brain region than that in which simple behavioral functions are produced; usually used to refer to the idea that the brain size of an animal species is proportional to its behavioral complexity.

**procedural memory.** Memory for certain ways of doing things or for certain movements; this memory system is thought to be independent from declarative memory.

**progenitor cell.** A cell that is derived from a stem cell and acts as a precursor cell that migrates and produces a neuron or glial cell.

**proprioception.** Perception of the position and movement of the body, limbs, and head.

**prosody.** Melody or tone of voice.

**protein.** An organic molecule consisting of a chain of amino acids connected by peptide bonds whose folded and twisted shape allows it to perform various functions.

**proton.** A large positively charged particle found in the nucleus of an atom.

**psilocybin.** A psychedelic drug obtained from the mushroom *Psilocybe mexicana.*

**psyche.** A term often used interchangeably with mind; signifies the total organ that controls behavior.

**psychedelic drug.** A drug that can alter sensory perception.

**psychoactive drug.** A drug that produces behavioral or cognitive changes as a result of its action on the brain.

**psychological construct.** An idea, resulting from a set of impressions, that some mental ability exists as an entity; examples include memory, language, and emotion.

**psychomotor activation.** Increased behavioral and cognitive activity.

**psychosurgery.** A neurosurgical intervention to destroy brain areas or sever connections between brain areas with the intent of modifying disturbances of behavior.

**pulvinar.** A region of the posterior thalamus taking part in visual processing.

**pump.** A protein in the cell membrane that actively transports a substance across the membrane. Also called a transporter.

**pure tone.** A sound made up of a single frequency.

**Purkinje cell.** A distinctive neuron found in the cerebellum.

**pyramid.** A region of the ventral surface of the brainstem at which the corticospinal tracts (pyramidal tracts) cross.

**pyramidal cell.** A distinctive neuron found in the cerebral cortex.

**pyramidal tract.** Another name for corticospinal tract.

**quadrantanopia.** Blindness of one quadrant of the visual field.

**quadriplegia.** Paralysis of the legs and arms due to spinal-cord injury.

**quantum.** A molecule of a neurotransmitter or a sufficient quantity of the neurotransmitter that will produce a just observable change in a cell's membrane voltage.

**radial glial cells.** Cells that form miniature "highways" that provide pathways for migrating neurons to follow to their appropriate destinations.

**radiator hypothesis.** The idea that the development of a new blood flow in early hominids improved brain cooling to such an extent that the brain was able to grow larger.

**rapidly adapting receptor.** A body sensory receptor that responds briefly to the onset of a stimulus on the body.

**rate-limiting factor.** Any enzyme that is in limited supply and so limits the rate at which a chemical can be produced.

**receptive field.** Region of the visual world that stimulates a receptor cell or neuron.

**receptor.** An area on the surface of a protein to which another chemical can bind.

**recessive allele.** An unexpressed allele.

**referred pain.** Pain felt on the surface of the body but actually due to pain in one of the internal organs of the body.

**reinforcer.** In operant conditioning, any event that strengthens the behavior it follows.

**relatively refractory.** Refers to the later phase of an action potential during which increased electrical current is required to produce another action potential; a phase during which potassium channels are still open.

**releasing factor.** A hormone that is produced by the pituitary gland and stimulates endocrine glands to release hormones into the circulatory system.

**releasing hormone.** A peptide that is released by the hypothalamus and acts to increase or decrease the release of hormones from the anterior pituitary.

**REM (rapid eye movement) sleep.** A part of sleep during which rapid eye movements occur; also associated with loss of muscle tone and vivid dreams.

**reproductive function.** Any bodily or behavioral function dedicated to the production of offspring.

**respondent conditioning.** A form of unconscious learning in which an organism learns an association between stimuli; also known as Pavlovian conditioning and classical conditioning.

**resting potential.** The voltage across the cell membrane produced by a greater negative charge on the intracellular side relative to the extracellular side in the absence of stimulation.

**reticular formation (matter).** A part of the midbrain in which nuclei (cell bodies) and fiber pathways (axons) are intermixed, producing a mottled gray and white, or netlike, appearance; associated with sleep–wake behavior and behavioral arousal.

**retina.** Neurons and photoreceptor cells at the back of the eye.

**retinal ganglion cells.** Cells of the retina that give rise to the optic nerve.

**retinohypothalamic pathway.** A pathway from a subset of cone receptors in the retina to the suprachiasmatic nucleus that allows light to entrain the rhythmic activity of the suprachiasmatic nucleus.

**retrograde plasticity factor.** A hypothetical neurotransmitter that carries information from the presynaptic side to the postsynaptic side of the membrane.

**ribonucleic acid (RNA).** A single-stranded nucleic acid molecule whose structure is specified by DNA (deoxyribonucleic acid); required for protein synthesis. There are three kinds of RNA: messenger RNA, ribosomal RNA, and transfer RNA.

**ribosome.** A large complex of enzymes and RNA (ribonucleic acid) molecules that catalyzes reactions in the formation of proteins.

**rod.** A photoreceptor specialized for functioning at low light levels.

**saccule.** A vestibular sac or receptor.

**saltatory conduction.** Propagation of an action potential at successive nodes of Ranvier; saltatory means "jumping" or "dancing."

**schizophrenia.** A behavioral disorder characterized by delusions, hallucinations, disorganized speech, either agitation or immobility, and certain other symptoms, such as blunted emotions.

**Schwann cell.** A glial cell in the peripheral nervous system that forms the myelin on sensory and motor axons.

**scotoma.** Small blind spot in the visual field caused by a small lesion, an epileptic focus, or migraines of the visual cortex.

**scratch reflex.** A reflex by which the hind limb removes a stimulus from the surface of the body.

**secondary visual cortex.** Visual cortical areas outside of the striate cortex; often called extrastriate cortex.

**second-generation antidepressant.** An antidepressant that is thought to be more selective than a first generation antidepressant in its action on serotonin reuptake transporters.

**second messenger.** A chemical that is activated by a neurotransmitter (the first messenger) and carries a message to initiate some biochemical process.

**segmentation.** Refers to animals that can be divided into a number of parts that are similar; also refers to the idea that many animals, including vertebrates, are composed of similarly organized body segments.

**selective serotonin reuptake blocker.** A drug that selectively blocks the reuptake of serotonin into the terminal.

**semicircular canals.** Receptors in the middle ear for head movements.

**sensitization.** A process by which the response to a stimulus increases with repeated presentations of that stimulus; for example, increased behavioral response to the same dose of a drug.

**sensory deprivation.** An experimental setup in which a subject is allowed only restricted sensory input; subjects generally do not like deprivation and may even display hallucinations.

**sensory nerve.** A collection of nerve fibers that carries sensory information from sensory receptors into the spinal cord and brain.

**sensory neuron.** A neuron that carries information from sensory receptors of sensory organs into the nervous system.

**sex chromosomes.** Each person normally has two sex chromosomes; females have two X chromosomes and males have an X and a Y chromosome.

**sexual dimorphism.** Process whereby gonadal hormones act on the brain to produce a distinctly female or male brain.

**short-term memory.** A form of memory in which memory is assumed to be stored for no longer than about 15 minutes.

**simple cell.** Type of visual cortex neuron that is excited by a spot of light in one part of its receptive field and inhibited by a similar spot in another part of the receptive field.

**sleep paralysis.** An inability to move, owing to the brain's inhibition of motor neurons.

**slowly adapting receptor.** A body sensory receptor that responds as long as a sensory stimulus is on the body.

**slow-wave sleep.** Stages of sleep in which the electroencephalogram displays slow waves; also called NREM (nonrapid eye movement) sleep.

**small-molecule transmitters.** A class of neurotransmitters that are manufacured in the synapse from products derived from the diet.

**somatic marker hypothesis.** A hypothesis positing that "marker" signals arising from emotions and feelings act to guide behavior and decision making, usually in an unconscious process.

**spatial summation.** Graded potentials that occur at approximately the same location on a membrane are added together (summate).

**species-typical behavior.** A behavior that is characteristic of all members of a species, such as grooming behavior or courtship behavior.

**spinal cord.** The part of the nervous system that is encased within the vertebrae or spine.

**spinal nervous system.** A functional division of the nervous system that refers to the spinal cord and its connections to and from the body's muscles, as well as its connections from the joints and the skin.

**split brain.** A condition in which the cerebral hemispheres are surgically disconnected by severing the corpus callosum and anterior commissure.

**stellate cell.** A star-shaped neuron found in the central nervous system.

**stimulus equivalence.** Perception of an object as being the same one when it is viewed in different orientations or in changing illumination.

**storage granule.** A membrane-coated structure that contains a number of vesicles containing a neurotransmitter.

**stress.** Events or drugs that produce arousal, excite the fight-or-flight response, and release cortisol from the adrenal gland.

**stress hormone.** A hormone, such as cortisol, that is activated by stress.

**stress response.** Response of the body to stressors; it may be a rapidily mobilized bodily response for avoiding danger or stress or it may be a slower response to repair damage to the body that results from stress.

**stressor.** Any environmental event that activates the stress response.

**stretch-sensitive channel.** On a membrane, a channel that is activated to allow the passage of ions in response to stretching of the membrane; initiates nerve impulses on tactile sensory neurons.

**striate cortex.** The primary visual cortex in the occipital lobe; it has a striped appearance when stained, which gives it this name.

**stroke.** Sudden appearance of neurological symptoms as a result of severe interruption of blood flow.

**subcoerulear nucleus.** One of the areas of the brainstem producing the paralysis of REM (rapid eye movement) sleep.

**subcortical regions.** All of the regions of the brain that are located beneath the neocortex; the term is usually used to distinguish regions of the brain that control basic functions from those regions controlling cognitive functions, which are mediated by the neocortex.

**substance abuse.** Use of a drug for the psychological and behavioral changes that it produces aside from its therapeutic effects.

**substance dependence.** Desire for a drug manifested by frequent use of the drug.

**sulcus.** Small cleft formed by the folding of the cerebral cortex.

**superior olivary complex.** A group of auditory nuclei in the medulla concerned especially with the location of the sources of sounds.

**supplementary speech area.** A region on the dorsal surface of the left frontal lobe that takes part in the production of speech.

**suprachiasmatic nucleus.** A nucleus, located just above the optic chiasm, that is the main pacemaker of circadian rhythms.

**sympathetic nervous system.** The part of the internal nervous system (autonomic nervous system) that arouses the body for action, such as mediating the involuntary response to alarm by increasing heart rate and blood pressure.

**synapse.** The connection between one neuron and another neuron, usually between an end foot of the axon of one neuron and a dendritic spine of the other neuron.

**synaptic cleft.** A small space separating the presynaptic membrane from the postsynaptic membrane.

**synaptic vesicle.** An organelle consisting of a membrane structure containing chemical neurotransmitters.

**synergy.** A pattern of movement that is coded by the motor cortex.

**synesthesia.** Ability to perceive a stimulus of one sense as a sensation of a different sense, as when sound produces a sensation of color.

**syntax.** The way in which words are put together, following the rules of grammar, to form phrases, clauses, or sentences; proposed to be a unique characteristic of human language.

**taxonomy.** The branch of biology concerned with naming and classifying the diverse forms of life.

**Tay-Sachs disease.** An inherited birth defect that appears 4 to 6 months after birth and results in retardation, physical changes, and death at about age 5; caused by the loss of genes that encode the enzyme necessary for breaking down certain fatty substances.

**tectopulvinar system.** A system consisting of projections from the retina to the superior colliculus to the pulvinar (thalamus) to the parietal and temporal visual areas.

**tectorial membrane.** Fibrous sheet overlying the cilia of the hair cells in the cochlea; produces a shearing motion when the basilar membrane is displaced.

**tectum.** The roof of, or area above the ventricle of, the midbrain; its functions are sensory.

**tegmentum.** The floor of, or area below the ventricle of, the midbrain; it has motor functions.

**teleodendrion.** A division of an axon.

**temporal lobe.** The part of the cortex found beneath the temporal bone of the skull.

**temporal summation.** Graded potentials that occur at approximately the same time on a membrane are added together (summate).

**terminal button (end foot).** Terminal part of an axon that conveys information to other neurons.

**testosterone.** A hormone that is secreted from the testes and is responsible for the distinguishing characteristics of the male.

**thalamus.** A part of the diencephalon through which all of the sensory systems project to reach the neocortex and then project, through one region of the neocortex, to relay messages to another region of the forebrain.

**threshold potential.** The voltage level of a neural membrane at which an action potential is triggered by the opening of sodium and potassium voltage-sensitive channels; about –50 millivolts.

**thymine.** One of the bases in a DNA (deoxyribonucleic acid) strand that binds to a base (adenine) in another DNA strand to form double-stranded DNA.

**tight junction.** Cells are usually separated by a small space but, when their membranes are fused, the connection is referred to as a tight junction.

**time out.** Behaviors displayed under the influence of alcohol that are ordinarily contrary to social conventions.

**tolerance.** Decreased response to a drug due to repeated use.

**tonotopic representation.** A representation of the auditory world in which sounds are located in a systematic fashion in a progression from lower to higher frequencies.

**topographic organization.** A neural–spatial representation of the body or areas of the sensory world perceived by a sensory organ.

**topographic representation.** A neural "map" of the external world.

**torpor.** A form of sleep lasting days or weeks that is characterized by a great fall in body temperature.

**transcranial magnetic stimulation (TMS).** A procedure in which a magnetic coil is placed over the skull to stimulate the underlying brain; can be used either to induce behavior or to disrupt ongoing behavior.

**transcription.** Transfer of information from a DNA (deoxyribonucleic acid) molecule to an RNA (ribonucleic acid) molecule.

**transfer RNA (tRNA).** A ribonucleic acid molecule that functions as an interpreter in the translation of nucleic acids into proteins by picking up specific amino acids and recognizing the appropriate codons in the messenger RNA.

**transgenic animal.** An animal that has artificially received a new gene.

**translation.** Transfer of information from an RNA (ribonucleic acid) molecule into a polypeptide, in which the "language" of nucleic acids is translated into that of amino acids.

**transmitter-activated receptor.** In the membrane of a cell, a receptor that has a binding site for a neurotransmitter.

**transmitter-sensitive channel.** A receptor complex that has both a receptor site for a chemical and a pore through which ions can flow.

**transporter.** A protein molecule that pumps substances across a membrane.

**trapezoid body.** A brainstem auditory structure.

**trichromatic theory.** An explanation of color vision based on the coding of three basic colors: red, green, and blue.

**tricyclic antidepressant.** An antidepressant that blocks the serotonin reuptake transporter.

**tropic molecule.** A signaling molecule that attracts or repels growth cones.

**tubules.** A variety of kinds of thin rods of material in cells that provide structure, aid in movement, and serve as highways for the transport of material within a cell.

**tuning curve.** A curve representing the maximum sensitivity of a neuron to a range of auditory frequencies. Each hair cell is maximally responsive to a particular frequency, but it also responds to nearby frequencies, although the sound must be louder for the cell to respond.

**type I synapse.** A synapse that contains an excitatory neurotransmitter that depolarizes the postsynaptic cell.

**type II synapse.** A synapse that contains an inhibitory neurotransmitter that hyperpolarizes the postsynaptic cell.

**ultradian rhythm.** A rhythm that lasts for less than a day; for example, eye blinking.

**unconditioned response (UCR).** In classical conditioning, the unlearned, naturally occurring response to the unconditioned stimulus, such as salivation when food is in the mouth.

**uracil.** One of the bases in RNA (ribonucleic acid); uracil is used in RNA instead of thymine.

**utricle.** A vestibular-system receptor that is sensitive to head movement.

**ventral corticospinal tract.** A pathway from the cortex to the spinal cord carrying instructions for the movement of the trunk; this pathway does not cross over to the opposite side of the brainstem at the pyramidal protrusion.

**ventral spinothalamic tract.** A pathway from the spinal cord to the thalamus carrying information about pain and temperature.

**ventral stream.** A visual processing pathway that orginates in the visual cortex and progresses into the anterior temporal cortex. It controls the visual recognition of objects.

**ventricle.** A cavity of the brain that contains cerebral spinal fluid.

**ventricular zone.** Zone in which stem cells reside that surrounds the ventricles.

**ventrolateral thalamus.** Part of the thalamus that relays information about body senses to the somatosensory cortex.

**ventromedial hypothalamus.** Region of the hypothalamus that plays a role in female sexual behavior and in feeding.

**vertebra.** A single bone, or segment, of the spinal column.

**vestibular system.** A set of receptors in the middle ear that indicates position and movement of the head.

**visual field.** Region of the visual world that is seen by the eyes.

**visual-form agnosia.** Inability to recognize objects or drawings of objects.

**visuospatial learning.** Use of visual information to identify an object's spatial location.

**volt.** A unit of electromotive force, the force that will cause a unit of 1 ampere to flow through a resistor of 1 ohm; the measure of electrical difference across a neuron membrane.

**voltage gradient.** Difference in voltage between two regions that allows a flow of current if the two regions are connected.

**voltage-sensitive ion channel.** In a membrane, a protein channel that opens or closes only at certain membrane voltages.

**voltmeter.** A device that measures voltage.

**Wernicke's aphasia.** An inability to understand or to produce meaningful language even though the production of words is still intact.

**Wernicke's area.** A region in the posterior part of the left temporal lobe that regulates the comprehension of language; sometimes referred to as the posterior speech zone.

**white matter.** Those areas of the nervous system rich in axons, leading to a white appearance because they are coated with myelin.

**wild type.** Refers to a normal phenotype or genotype.

**withdrawal symptom.** A behavior displayed by a user when drug use ends.

**zeitgeber.** An environmental event that entrains biological rhythms; a "time giver."

# References


## Chapter 1

**Benkman, C. W., & Lindholm, A. K.** (1990). The advantages and evolution of morphological novelty. *Nature, 349,* 519–520.

**Blumer, D., & Benson, D. F.** (1975). Personality changes with frontal and temporal lobe lesions. In D. F. Benson & D. Blumer (Eds.), *Psychiatric aspects of neurologic disease* (pp. 151–170). New York: Grune & Stratton.

**Bronson, R. T.** (1979). Brain weight–body weight scaling in dogs and cats. *Brain, Behavior and Evolution, 16,* 227–236.

**Campbell, N. A.** (1996). *Biology.* Menlo Park CA: Benjamin Cummings.

**Coren, S.** (1994). *The intelligence of dogs.* Toronto: The Free Press.

**Darwin, C. (1965).** *The expression of the emotions in man and animals.* Chicago: University of Chicago Press. (Original work published 1872)

**Darwin, C.** (1963). *On the origin of species by means of natural selection, or the preservation of favored races in the struggle for life.* New York: New American Library. (Original work published 1859)

**Dawkins, R.** (1976). *The selfish gene.* Oxford: Oxford University Press.

**Descartes, R.** (1972). *Treatise on man* (T. S. Hall, Trans.). Cambridge, MA: Harvard University Press. (Original work published 1664)

**Eibl-Eibesfeldt, I. (1970).** *Ethology: The biology of behavior.* New York: Holt, Rinehart and Winston.

**Falk, D.** (1990). Brain evolution in *Homo:* The "radiator" theory. *Behavioral and Brain Sciences, 13,* 344–368.

**Goodall, J.** (1986). *The chimpanzees of Gombe.* Cambridge, MA: Harvard University Press.

**Gould, S. J.** (1981). *The mismeasure of man.* New York: Norton.

**Hebb, D. O.** (1949). *The organization of behavior: A neuropsychological theory.* New York: Wiley.

**Jacobsen, E.** (1932). Electrophysiology of mental activities. *American Journal of Psychology, 44,* 677–694.

**Johnson, D., & Blake, E.** (1996). *From Lucy to language.* New York: Simon and Schuster.

**Kolb, B., & Whishaw, I. Q.** (1996). *Fundamentals of human neuropsychology,* New York: W. H. Freeman and Company.

**Linge, F. R.** (1990). Faith, hope, and love: Nontraditional therapy in recovery from serious head injury, a personal account. *Canadian Journal of Psychology, 44,* 116–129.

**Lorenz, K. Z.** (1981). *The foundations of ethology.* New York: Springer Verlag.

**Martin, R. D.** (1990). *Primate origins and evolution: A phylogenetic reconstruction.* Princeton, NJ: Princeton University Press.

**McKinney, M. L.** (1998). The juvenilized ape myth: Our "overdeveloped" brain. *Bioscience, 48,* 109–116.

**Milton, K.** (1993). Diet and primate evolution. *Scientific American, 269*(2), 86–93.

**Murdock, G. P.** (1965). *Culture and society: Twenty-four essays.* Pittsburgh: University of Pittsburg Press.

**Penfield, W., & Roberts, L.** (1959). *Speech and brain mechanisms.* Princeton, NJ: Princeton University Press.

**Terkel, J.** (1995). Cultural transmission in the black rat: Pinecone feeding. *Advances in the Study of Behavior, 24,* 119–154.

**Weiner, J.** (1995). *The beak of the finch.* New York: Vintage.

**Wilson, E. O.** (1980). *Sociobiology.* Cambridge, MA: Belknap Press of Harvard University Press.

## Chapter 2

**Axel, R.** (1995). The molecular logic of smell. *Scientific American, 273*(4), 154–159.

**Brodmann, K.** (1909). *Vergleichende Lokalisationlehr der Grosshirnrinde in ihren Prinzipien dargestellt auf Grund des Zellenbaues.* Leipzig: J. A. Barth.

**Chiu, D., Krieger, D., Villar-Cordova, C., Kasner, S. E., Morgenstern, L. B., Bratina, P. L., Yatsu, F. M., & Grotta, J. C.** (1998). Intravenous tissue plasminogen activator for acute ischemic stroke: Feasibility, safety, and efficacy in the first year of clinical practice. *Stroke, 29,* 18–22.

**Diamond, M. C., Scheibel, A. B., & Elson, L. M.** (1985). *The human brain coloring book.* New York: Barnes & Noble.

**Elliott, H.** (1969). *Textbook of neuroanatomy.* Philadelphia: Lippincott.

**Everett, N. B.** (1965). *Functional neuroanatomy.* Philadelphia: Lea & Febiger.

**Felleman, D. J., & van Essen, D. C.** (1991). Distributed hierarchical processing in the primate cerebral cortex. *Cerebral Cortex, 1,* 1–47.

**Frackowiak, R. S. J., Friston, K. J., Frith, C. D., Dolan, R. J., & Mazziotta, J. C.** (1997). *Human brain function.* New York: Academic Press.

**Hamilton, L. W.** (1976). *Basic limbic system anatomy of the rat.* New York and London: Plenum.

**Heimer, L.** (1995). *The human brain and spinal cord: Functional neuroanatomy and dissection guide* (2d ed.). New York: Springer Verlag.

**Herrick, C. J.** (1926). *Brains of rats and men.* Chicago: University of Chicago Press.

**Jerison, H. J.** (1991). *Brain size and the evolution of mind.* New York: American Museum of Natural History.

**Kandel, E. R., Schwartz, J. H., & Jessell, T. M.** (Eds.). (1995). *Essentials of neural science and behavior.* East Norwalk, CT: Appleton & Lange.

**Luria, A. R.** (1973). *The working brain.* Harmondsworth, UK: Penguin.

**Netter, F. H.** (1962). *The Ciba collection of medical illustrations: Vol 1. Nervous system.* New York: Ciba.

**Papez, J. W.** (1937). A proposed mechanism of emotion. *Archives of Neurology and Psychiatry, 38,* 724–744.

**Penfield, W., & Jasper, H. H.** (1954). *Epilepsy and the functional anatomy of the human brain.* Boston: Little, Brown.

**Purves, D., Augustine, G. J., Fitzpatrick, D., Katz, L. C., LaMantia, A.-S., & McNamara, J. O.** (1997). *Neuroscience.* Sunderland, MA: Sinauer.

**Ranson, S. W., & Clark, S. L.** (1959). *The anatomy of the nervous system.* Philadelphia: Saunders.

**Shepherd, G. M.** (1990). *The synaptic organization of the brain* (3rd ed.). New York: Oxford University Press.

**Truex, R. C., & Carpenter, M. B.** (1969). *Human neuroanatomy.* Baltimore: Williams & Wilkins.

**Zeki, S.** (1993). *A vision of the brain.* London: Blackwell Scientific.

## Chapter 3

**Alberts, B., Bray, D., Lewis, J., Raff, M., Roberts, K., & Watson, J. D.** (1983). *Molecular biology of the cell* (3rd ed.). New York: Garland.

**Balaban, F., Teillet, M. A., & LeDouarin, N.** (1988). Application of the quail-chick chimera system to the study of brain development and behavior. *Science, 241,* 1339–1342.

**Coleman, A.** (1999). Dolly, Polly and other "ollys": Likely impact of cloning technology on biomedical uses of livestock. *Genetic Analysis, 15,* 167–173.

**de Duve, C.** (1996). The birth of complex cells. *Scientific American, 274*(4), 50–57.

**Levitan, I. B., & Kaczmarek, L. K.** (1997). *The neuron: Cell and molecular biology* (2nd ed). Oxford: Oxford University Press.

**Lione, L. A., Carter, R. J., Hunt, M. J., Bates, G. P., Morton, A. J., & Dunnett, S. B.** (1999). Selective discrimination learning impairments in mice expressing the human Huntington's disease mutiation. *Journal of Neuroscience, 19,* 10428–10437.

**Mayford, M., & Kandel, E. R.** (1999). Genetic approaches to memory storage. *Trends in Genetics, 15,* 463–470.

**Nottebohm, F., O'Loughlin, B., Gould, K., Yohay, K., & Alvarez-Buylla, A.** (1994). The life span of new neurons in a song control nucleus of the adult canary brain depends on time of year when these cells are born. *Proceedings of the National Academy of Sciences (USA), 91,* 7849–7853.

**Wahlsten, D., & Ozaki, H. S.** (1994). Defects of the fetal forebrain in acallosal mice. In M. Lassonde & M. A. Jeeves (Eds.), *Callosal agenesis* (pp. 125–132). New York: Plenum.

**Webb, B.** (1996). A cricket robot. *Scientific American, 275*(6), 94–99.

## Chapter 4

**Bartholow, R.** (1874). Experimental investigation into the functions of the human brain. *American Journal of Medical Sciences 67,* 305–313.

**Eccles, J.** (1965). The synapse. *Scientific American, 212*(1), 56–66.

**Hodgkin, A. L., & Huxley, A. F.** (1939). Action potentials recorded from inside nerve fiber. *Nature, 144,* 710–711.

**Penfield, W., & Jasper, H. H.** (1954). *Epilepsy and the functional anatomy of the human brain.* Boston: Little, Brown.

**Posner, M. I., & Raichle, M. E.** (1994). *Images of mind.* New York: W. H. Freeman and Company.

**Ranck, J. B.** (1973). Studies on single neurons in dorsal hippocampal formation and septum in unrestrained rats: I. Behavioral correlates and firing repertoires. *Experimental Neurology, 41,* 461–531.

**Valenstein, E. S.** (1973). *Brain control.* New York: Wiley.

## Chapter 5

**Bailey, C. H., & Chen, M.** (1989). Time course of structural changes at identified sensory neuron synapses during long-term sensitization in *Aplysia. Journal of Neuroscience*, 9, 1774–1780.

**Ballard, A., Tetrud, J. W., & Langston, J. W.** (1985). Permanent human Parkinsonism due to 1-methyl-4-phenyl-1,2,3,6-tetrahydropyridine (MPTP). *Neurology, 35,* 949–956.

**Bliss, T. V. P., & Lomo, T.** (1973). Long lasting potentiation of synaptic transmission in the dentate area of the anesthetized rabbit following stimulation of the perforant path. *Journal of Physiology (London), 232,* 331–356.

**Cooper, J. R., Bloom, F. E., & Roth, R. H.** (1991). *The biochemical basis of neuropharmacology.* New York: Oxford University Press.

**Ehringer, H., & Hornykiewicz, O.** (1960/1974). Distribution of noradrenaline and dopamine (3-hydroxytyramine) in the human brain and their behavior in the presence of disease affecting the extrapyramidal system. In J. Marks (Ed.), *The treatment of Parkinsonism with L-dopa.* (pp. 45–56). Lancaster, UK: MTP Medical and Technical Publishing.

**Engert, F., & Bonhoeffer, T.** (1999). Dendritic spine changes associated with hippocampal long-term synaptic plasticity. *Nature, 399,* 66–70.

**Fischer, M., Kaech, S., Knutti, D., & Matus, A.** (1998). Rapid actin-based plasticity in dendritic spines. *Neuron, 20,* 847–854.

**Galef, B. G., Jr., Attenborough, K. S., & Wishin, E. E.** (1990). Responses of observer rats *(Rattus norvegicus)* to complex, diet-related signals emmitted by demonstrator rats. *Journal of Comparative Psychology, 104,* 11–19.

**Hebb, D. O.** (1949). *The organization of behavior.* New York: Wiley.

**Kandel, E.** (1976). *Cellular basis of behavior.* San Francisco: W. H. Freeman and Company.

**Kandel, E. R., Schwartz, J. H., & T. M. Jessell.** (Eds.). (2000). *Principles of neural science* (4th ed.). New York: McGraw-Hill.

**Parkinson, J.** (1817/1989). An essay on the shaking palsy. In A. D. Morris & F. C. Rose (Eds.), *James Parkinson: His life and times* (pp. 151–175). Boston: Birkhauser.

**Sacks, O.** (1976). *Awakenings.* New York: Doubleday.

**Sulzer, D., Joyce, M. P., Lin, L., Geldwert, D., Haber, S. N., Hatton, T., & Rayport, S.** (1998). Dopamine neurons make glutamatergic synapses in vitro. *Journal of Neuroscience, 18,* 4588–4602.

**Tréatikoff, C.** (1974). Thesis for doctorate in medicine, 1919. In J. Marks (Ed.), *The treatment of Parkinsonism with L-dopa.* (pp. 29–38). Lancaster, UK: MTP Medical and Technical Publishing.

**Ungerstedt, U.** (1971). Adipsia and aphagia after 6-hydroxydopamine induced degeneration of the nigrostriatal dopamine system in the rat brain. *Acta Physiologica (Scandinavia), 82*(Suppl. 367), 95–122.

**Widner, H., Tetrud, J., Rehngrona, S., Snow, B., Brundin, P., Gustavii, B., Bjorklund, A., Lindvall, O., & Langston, W. J.** (1992). Bilateral fetal mesencephalic grafting in two patients with Parkinsonism induced by 1-methyl-4-phenyl-1,2,3,6-tetrahydropyridine (MPTP). *New England Journal of Medicine, 327,* 1556–1563.

## Chapter 6

**Becker, J. B., Breedlove, S. M., & Crews, D.** (1992). *Behavioral endocrinology.* Cambridge, MA: MIT Press.

**Castaneda, E., Becker, J., & Robinson, T. E.** (1988). The long-term effects of repeated amphetamine treatment in vivo on amphetamine, KCl, and electrical stimulation evoked striatal dopamine release in vitro. *Life Sciences, 42,* 2447–2457.

**Comings, D. E., Rosenthal, R. J., Lesieur, H. R., Rugle, L. J., Muhleman, D., Chiu, C., Dietz, G., & Gade, R.** (1996). A study of the dopamine $D_2$ receptor gene in pathological gambling. *Pharmacogenetics, 6,* 223–234.

**Cooper, J. R., Bloom, F. E., & Roth, R. H.** (1998). *The biochemical basis of neuropharmacology.* New York: Oxford University Press.

**Feldman, R. S., Meyer, J. S., & Quenzer, L. F.** (1997). *Principles of neuropsychopharmacology.* Sunderland, MA: Sinauer.

**Fraioli, S., Crombag, H. S., Badiani, A., & Robinson, T. E.** (1999). Susceptibility to amphetamine-induced locomotor sensitization is modulated by environmental stimuli. *Neuropsychopharmacology, 20,* 533–541.

**Hamson, E., & Kimura, D.** (1992). Sex differences and hormonal influences on cognitive function in humans. In J. B. Becker, S. M. Breedlove, & D. Crews (Eds.), *Behavioral endocrinology* (pp. 357–398). Cambridge, MA: MIT Press.

**Hynie, I., & Todd, E. C. D.** (1990). Domoic acid toxicity. *Canada Diseases Weekly Report, 16.*

**Isbell, H., Fraser, H. F., Wikler, R. E., Belleville, R. E., & Eisenman, A. J.** (1955). An experimental study of the etiology of "rum fits" and delirium tremens. *Quarterly Journal of Studies on Alcohol, 16,* 1–35.

**Julien, R. M.** (1995). *A primer of drug action.* New York: W. H. Freeman and Company.

**MacAndrew, C., & Edgerton, R. B.** (1969). *Drunken comportment: A social explanation.* Chicago: Aldine.

**MacDonald, T. K., Zanna, M. P., & Fong, G. T.** (1998). Alcohol and intentions to engage in risky health-related behaviours: Experimental evidence for a casual relationship. In J. Adair & F. Craik (Eds.), *Advances in psychological science: Vol. 2. Developmental, personal, and social aspects* (pp. 12–59). East Sussex, UK: Psychology Press.

**McCann, U. D., Lowe, K. A., & Ricaurte, G. A.** (1997). Long-lasting effects of recreational drugs of abuse on the central nervous system. *The Neurologist, 3,* 399–411.

**Morrow, A. L., Janis, G. C., VanDoren, M. J., Matthews, D. B., Samson, H. H., Janak, P. H., & Grant, K. A.** (1999). Neurosteroids mediate pharmacological effects of ethanol: A new mechanism of ethanol action? *Alcohol and Clinical and Experimental Research, 23,* 1933–1940.

**Olney, J. W., Ho, O. L., & Rhee, V.** (1971). Cytotoxic effects of acidic and sulphur-containing amino acids on the infant mouse central nervous system. *Experimental Brain Research, 14,* 61–67.

**Piazza, P. V., Deminiere, J. M., LeMoal, M., & Simon, H.** (1989). Factors that predict individual vulnerability to amphetamine self-administration. *Science, 29,* 1511–1513.

**Robinson, T. E., & Becker, J. B.** (1986). Enduring changes in brain and behavior produced by chronic amphetamine administration: A review and evaluation of animal models of amphetamine psychosis. *Brain Research Reviews, 11,* 157–198.

**Robinson, T. E., & Berridge, K. C.** (1993). The neural basis of drug craving: An incentive-sensitization theory of addiction. *Brain Research Reviews, 18,* 247–291.

**Sapolsky, R. M.** (1992). *Stress, the aging brain, and the mechanisms of neuron death.* Cambridge, MA: MIT Press.

**Sapolsky, R. M.** (1994). *Why zebras don't get ulcers.* New York: W. H. Freeman and Company.

**Teitelbaum, J. S., Zatorre, R. J., Carpenter, S., Gendron, D., Evans, A. C., Gjedde, A., & Cashman, N. R.** (1990). Neurologic sequelae of domoic acid intoxication due to the ingestion of contaminated mussels. *New England Journal of Medicine, 322,* 1781–1787.

**Wenger, J. R., Tiffany, T. M., Bombardier, C., Nicholls, K., & Woods, S. C.** (1981). Ethanol tolerance in the rat is learned. *Science, 213,* 575–577.

**Whishaw, I. Q., Mittleman, G., & Evenden, J. L.** (1989). Training-dependent decay in performance produced by the neuroleptic *cis*(*Z*)-Flupentixol on spatial navigation by rats in a swimming pool. *Pharmacology, Biochemistry, and Behavior, 32,* 211–220.

## Chapter 7

**Ames, E. W.** (1997). *The development of Romanian orphanage children adopted to Canada* (Final report to Human Resources Development, Canada).

**Bunney, B. G., Potkin, S. G., & Bunney, W. E.** (1997). Neuropathological studies of brain tissue in schizophrenia. *Journal of Psychiatric Research, 31,* 159–173.

**Changeux, J.-P., & Danchin, A.** (1976). Selective stabilization of developing synapses as a mechanism for the specification of neuronal networks. *Nature, 264,* 705–712.

**Curtis, S.** (1978). *Genie: A psycholinguistic study of a modern-day "wild-child."* New York: Academic Press.

**Dawson, G., & Fischer, K. W.** (1994). *Human behavior and the developing brain.* New York: Guilford Press.

**Edelman, G. M.** (1987). *Neural darwinism: The theory of neuronal group selection.* New York: Basic Books.

**Epstein, H. T.** (1979). Correlated brain and intelligence development in humans. In M. E. Hahn, C. Jensen, & B. C. Dudek (Eds.), *Development and evolution of brain size: Behavioral implications* (pp. 111–131). New York: Academic Press.

**Galaburda, A. M., & Christen, Y.** (1997). *Normal and abnormal development of the cortex.* Berlin: Springer Verlag.

**Gershon, E. S., & Rieder, R. O.** (1992). Major disorders of mind and brain. *Scientific American, 267*(3), 126–133.

**Greenough, W. T., & Chang, F. F.** (1988). Plasticity of synapse structure and pattern in the cerebral cortex. In A. Peters and E. G. Jones (Eds.), *Cerebral cortex, Vol. 7: Development and maturation of the cerebral cortex* (pp. 391–440). New York: Plenum.

**Harlow, H. F.** (1971). *Learning to love.* San Francisco: Albion.

**Hebb, D. O.** (1947). The effects of early experience on problem solving at maturity. *American Psychologist, 2,* 737–745.

**Hebb, D. O.** (1949). *The organization of behavior.* New York: Wiley.

**Horn, G., Bradley, P., & McCabe, B. J.** (1985). Changes in the structure of synapses associated with learning. *Journal of Neuroscience, 5,* 3161–3168.

**Huttenlocher, P. R.** (1994). Synaptogenesis in human cerebral cortex. In G. Dawson & K. W. Fischer (Eds.), *Human behavior and the developing brain* (pp. 137–152). New York: Guilford Press.

**Jacobsen, M.** (1991). *Developmental neurobiology* (3rd ed.). New York: Plenum.

**Juraska, J. M.** (1990). The structure of the cerebral cortex: Effects of gender and the environment. In B. Kolb & R. Tees (Eds.), *The cerebral cortex of the rat* (pp. 483–506). Cambridge, MA: MIT Press.

**Kennedy, H., & Dehay, D.** (1993). Cortical specification of men and mice. *Cerebral Cortex, 3,* 171–186.

**Kolb, B., & Fantie, B.** (1997). Development of the child's brain and behavior. In C. R. Reynolds & E. Fletcher-Janzen (Eds.), *Handbook of clinical child neuropsychology* (2nd ed., pp. 17–41). New York: Plenum.

**Kolb, B., Forgie, M., Gibb, R., Gorny, G., & Rowntree, S.** (1998). Age, experience, and the changing brain. *Neuroscience and Biobehavioral Reviews, 22,* 143–159.

**Kolb, B., & Gibb, R.** (1993). Possible anatomical basis of recovery of function after neonatal frontal lesions in rats. *Behavioral Neuroscience, 107,* 799–811.

**Kolb, B., & Whishaw, I. Q.** (1998). Brain plasticity and behavior. *Annual Review of Psychology, 49,* 43–64.

**Kolb, B., Wilson, B., & Taylor, L.** (1992). Developmental changes in the recognition and comprehensional expression: Implications for frontal lobe function. *Brain and Cognition, 20,* 74–84.

**Korsching, S.** (1993). The neurotrophic factor concept: A reexamination. *Journal of Neuroscience, 13,* 2739–2748.

**Kovelman, J. A., & Scheibel, A. B.** (1984). A neurohistologic correlate of schizophrenia. *Biological Psychiatry, 19,* 1601–1621.

**Lenneberg, E. H.** (1967). *Biological foundations of language.* New York: Wiley.

**Levitt, P.** (1995). Experimental approaches that reveal principles of cerebral cortical development. In M. Gazzaniga (Ed.), *The cognitive neurosciences* (pp. 147–163). Cambridge, MA: MIT Press.

**Marin-Padilla, M.** (1988). Early ontogenesis of the human cerebral cortex. In A. Peters & E. G. Jones (Eds.), *Cerebral cortex, Vol. 7: Development and maturation of the cerebral cortex* (pp.1–34). New York: Plenum.

**Marin-Padilla, M.** (1993). Pathogenesis of late-acquired leptomeningeal heterotopias and secondary cortical alterations: A Golgi study. In A. M. Galaburda (Ed.), *Dyslexia and development: Neurobiological aspects of extra-ordinary brains* (pp. 64–88). Cambridge, MA: Harvard University Press.

**Michel, G. F., & Moore, C. L.** (1995). *Developmental psychobiology.* Cambridge, MA: MIT Press.

**Moore, K. L.** (1988). *The developing human: Clinically oriented embryology* (4th ed.). Philadelphia: Saunders.

**Myers, D. G.** (1998). *Psychology* (5th ed.). New York: Worth Publishers.

**Overman, W., Bachevalier, J., Schuhmann, E., & Ryan, P.** (1996). Cognitive gender differences in very young children parallel biologically based cognitive gender differences in monkeys. *Behavioral Neuroscience, 110,* 673–684.

**Overman, W., Bachevalier, J., Turner, M., & Peuster, A.** (1992). Object recognition versus object discrimination: Comparison between human infants and infant monkeys. *Behavioral Neuroscience, 106,* 15–29.

**Piaget, J.** (1952). *The origins of intelligence in children.* New York: Norton.

**Purpura, D. P.** (1974). Dendritic spine "dysgenesis" and mental retardation. *Science, 186,* 1126–1127.

**Purpura, D. P.** (1975). Normal and abnormal development of cerebral cortex in man. *Neurosciences Research Program Bulletin, 20,* 569–577.

**Purves, D., & Lichtman, J. W.** (1985). *Principles of neural development.* Sunderland, MA: Sinauer.

**Rakic, P.** (1995). Corticogenesis in human and nonhuman primates. In M. Gazzaniga (ed.), *The cognitive neurosciences* (pp. 127–145). Cambridge, MA: MIT Press.

**Riesen, A. H.** (1975). *The Developmental neuropsychology of sensory deprivation.* New York: Academic Press.

**Riesen, A. H.** (1982). Effects of environments on development in sensory systems. In W. D. Neff (Ed.), *Contributions to sensory physiology* (Vol. 6, pp. 45–77). New York: Academic Press.

**Rutter, M.** (1998). Developmental catch-up, and deficit, following adoption after severe global early privation. *Journal of Child Psychology and Psychiatry, 39,* 465–476.

**Sherman, S. M., & Spear, P. D.** (1982). Organization of visual pathways in normal and visually deprived cats. *Physiological Reviews, 62,* 738–855.

**Snowdon, D. A.** (1997). Aging and Alzheimer's disease: Lessons from the nun study. *Gerontologist, 37,* 150–156.

**Sperry, R. W.** (1963). Chemoaffinity in the orderly growth of nerve fiber patterns and connections. *Proceedings of the National Academy of Sciences (USA), 50,* 703–710.

**Spreen, O., Tupper, D., Risser, A., Tuokko, H., & Edgell, D.** (1984). *Human developmental neuropsychology.* New York: Oxford University Press.

**Twitchell, T. E.** (1965). The automatic grasping response of infants. *Neuropsychologia, 3,* 247–259.

**Volpe, J. J.** (1987). *Neurology of the newborn* (2nd ed.). Philadelphia: Saunders.

**Weiss, S., Reynolds, B. A., Vescovi, A. L., Morshead, C., Craig, C. G., & van der Kooy, D.** (1996). Is there a neural stem cell in the mammalian forebrain? *Trends in Neurosciences, 19*(9), 387–393.

**Werker, J. F., & Tees, R. C.** (1992). The organization and reorganization of human speech perception. *Annual Review of Neuroscience, 15,* 377–402.

**Wiesel, T. N.** (1982). Postnatal development of the visual cortex and the influence of environment. *Nature, 299,* 583–591.

## Chapter 8

**Balint, R.** (1909). Seelenlähmung des Schauens optiche ataxie, räumlielie Störung der Aufmerksamkeit. *Psychiatry and Neurology, 25,* 51–81.

**Farah, M. J.** (1990). *Visual agnosia.* Cambridge, MA: MIT Press.

**Geschwind, N.** (1972). Language and the brain. *Scientific American, 226*(4): 78–83.

**Goodale, M. A., Milner, D. A., Jakobson, L. S., & Carey, J. D. P.** (1991). A kinematic analysis of reaching and grasping movements in a patient recovering from optic ataxia. *Nature, 349,* 154–156.

**Hubel, D. H.** (1988). *Eye, brain, and vision.* New York: Scientific American Library.

**Kline, D. W.** (1994). Optimizing the visibility of displays for older observers. *Experimental Aging Research, 20,* 11–23.

**Kuffler, S. W.** (1952). Neurons in the retina: Organization, inhibition and excitatory problems. *Cold Spring Harbor Symposia on Quantitative Biology, 17,* 281–292.

**Lashley, K. S.** (1941). Patterns of cerebral integration indicated by the scotomas of migraine. *Archives of Neurology and Psychiatry, 46,* 331–339.

**Merbs, S. L., & Nathans, J.** (1992). Absorption spectra of human cone pigments. *Nature, 356,* 433–435.

**Milner, A. D., & Goodale, M. A.** (1995). *The visual brain in action.* Oxford: Oxford University Press.

**Posner, M. I., & Raichle, M. E.** (1997). *Images of the mind.* New York: Scientific American Library.

**Purves, D., Augustine, G. J., Fitzpatrick, D., Katz, L. C., LaMantia, A.-S., & McNamara, J. O.** (Eds.). *Neuroscience.* Sunderland, MA: Sinauer.

**Sacks, O., & Wasserman, R.** (1987). The case of the colorblind painter. *The New York Review of Books, 34,* 25–33.

**Szentagothai, J.** (1975). The "module-concept" in cerebral cortex architecture. *Brain Research, 95,* 475–496.

**Tanaka, K.** (1993). Neuronal mechanisms of object recognition. *Science, 262,* 685–688.

**Tanaka, K.** (1996). Inferotemporal cortex and object vision. *Annual Review of Neuroscience, 19,* 100–139.

**Weizkrantz, L.** (1986). *Blindsight: A case study and implications.* Oxford: Oxford University Press.

**Winderickx, J., Lindsey, D. T., Sanocki, E., Teller, D. Y., Motulsky, B. G, & Deeb, S. S.** (1992). Polymorphism in red photopigment underlies variation in colour matching. *Nature, 356,* 431–433.

**Wong-Riley, M. T. T., Hevner, R. F., Cutlan, R., Earnest, M., Egan, R., Frost, J., & Nguyen, T.** (1993). Cytochrome oxidase in the human visual cortex: Distribution in the developing and the adult brain. *Visual Neuroscience, 10,* 41–58.

**Zeki, S.** (1993). *A vision of the brain.* Oxford: Blackwell Scientific.

**Zihl, J., von Cramon, D., & Mai, N.** (1983). Selective disturbance of movement vision after bilateral brain damage. *Brain, 106,* 313–340.

## Chapter 9

**Belin, P., Zatorre, R. J., Lafaille, P., & Pike, B.** (2000). Voice-selective areas in the human auditory cortex. *Nature, 403,* 309–312.

**Chomsky, N.** (1965). *Aspects of the theory of syntax.* Cambridge, MA: MIT Press.

**Drake-Lee, A. B.** (1992). Beyond music: Auditory temporary threshold shift in rock musicians after a heavy metal concert. *Journal of the Royal Society of Medicine, 85,* 617–619.

**Fiez, J. A., Raichle, M. E., Balota, D. A., Tallal, P., & Petersen, S. E.** (1996). PET activation of posterior temporal regions during auditory word presentation and verb generation. *Cerebral Cortex, 6,* 1–10.

**Fiez, J. A., Raichle, M. E., Miezin, F. M., & Petersen, S. E.** (1995). PET studies of auditory and phonological processing: Effects of stimulus characteristics and task demands. *Journal of Cognitive Neuroscience, 7,* 357–375.

**Frackowiak, R. S. J., Friston, K. J., Frith, C. D., Dolan, R. J., & Mazziotta, J. C.** (1997). *Human brain function.* San Diego: Academic Press.

**Gazzaniga, M. S.** (1992). *Nature's mind.* New York: Basic Books.

**Heffner, H. E., & Heffner, R. S.** (1990). Role of primate auditory cortex in hearing. In W. C. Stebbins & M. A. Berkeley (Eds.), *Comparative perception: Vol. 2. Complex signals* (pp. 279–310). New York: Wiley.

**Hirsh, I. J.** (1966). Audition. In J. B. Sidowsky (Ed.), *Experimental methods and instrumentation in psychology* (pp.247–272). New York: McGraw-Hill.

**Knudsen, E. I.** (1981). The hearing of the barn owl. *Scientific American, 245*(6), 113–125.

**Lewis, D. B., & Gower, D. M.** (1980). *Biology of communication.* New York: Wiley.

**Loeb, G. E.** (1990). Cochlear prosthetics. *Annual Review of Neuroscience, 13,* 357–371.

**Luria, A. R.** (1972). *The man with a shattered world.* Chicago: Regnery.

**McFarland, D.** (1985). *Animal behaviour.* Bath, UK: Pitman Press.

**Neuweiler, G.** (1990). Auditory adaptations for prey capture in echolocating bats. *Physiological Reviews, 70,* 615–641.

**Penfield, W., & Rasmussen, T.** (1950). *The cerebral cortex of man.* New York: Macmillan.

**Penfield, W., & Roberts, L.** (1959). *Speech and brain mechanisms.* Princeton, NJ: Princeton University Press.

**Peretz, I., Kolinsky, R., Tramo, M., Labrecque, R., Hublet, C., Demeurisse, G., & Belleville, S.** (1994). Functional dissociations following bilateral lesions of auditory cortex. *Brain, 117,* 1283–1301.

**Pinker, S.** (1997). *How the mind works.* New York: Norton.

**Posner, M. I., & Raichle, M. E.** (1997). *Images of mind.* New York: W. H. Freeman and Company.

**Purves, D., Augustine, G. J., Fitzpatrick, D., Katz, L. C., LaMantia, A.-S., & McNamara, J. O.** (1997). *Neuroscience.* Sunderland, MA: Sinauer.

**Rauschecker, J. P., Tian, B., & Hauser, M.** (1995). Processing of complex sounds in the macaque nonprimary auditory cortex. *Science, 268,* 111–114.

**Romanski, L. M., Tian, B., Fritz, J., Mishkin, M., Goldman-Rakic, P. S., & Rauschecker, J. P.** (1999). Dual streams of auditory afferents target multiple domains in the primate prefrontal cortex. *Nature Neuroscience, 2,* 1131–1136.

**Shepherd, G. M.** (1994). *Neurobiology* (3rd ed.). New York: Oxford University Press.

**Trehub, S., Schellenberg, E. G., & Ramenetsky, G. B.** (1999). Infants' and adults' perception of scale structures. *Journal of Experimental Psychology: Human Perception and Performance, 25,* 965–975.

**Winter, P., & Funkenstein, H.** (1971). The auditory cortex of the squirrel monkey: Neuronal discharge patterns to auditory stimuli. *Proceedings of the Third Congress of Primatology, Zurich, 2,* 24–28.

**Yost, W. A.** (1991). Auditory image perception and analysis: The basis for hearing. *Hearing Research, 56,* 8–18.

**Zatorre, R. J., Evans, A. C., & Meyer, E.** (1994). Neural mechanisms underlying melodic perception and memory for pitch. *Journal of Neuroscience, 14,* 1908–1919.

**Zatorre, R. J., Evans, A. C., Meyer, E., & Gjedde, A.** (1992). Lateralization of phonetic and pitch discrimination in speech processing. *Science, 256,* 846–849.

**Zatorre, R. J., Meyer, E., Gjedde, A., & Evans, A. C.** (1995). PET studies of phonetic processing of speech: Review, replication, and reanalysis. *Cerebral Cortex, 6,* 21–30.

## Chapter 10

**Alexander, R. E., & Crutcher, M. D.** (1990). Functional architecture of basal ganglia circuits: Neural substrates of parallel processing. *Trends in Neuroscience, 13,* 266–271.

**Asanuma, H.** (1989). *The motor cortex.* New York: Raven Press.

**Bauman, M. L., & Kemper, T. L.** (1994). *The neurobiology of autism.* Baltimore: Johns Hopkins University Press.

**Berridge, K. C.** (1989). Progressive degradation of serial grooming chains by descending decerebration. *Behavioural Brain Research, 33,* 241–253.

**Brinkman, C.** (1984). Supplementary motor area of the monkey's cerebral cortex: Short- and long-term deficits after unilateral ablation and the effects of subsequent callosal section. *Journal of Neuroscience, 4,* 918–992.

**Bucy, P. C., Keplinger, J. E., & Siqueira, E. B.** (1964). Destruction of the "pyramidal tract" in man. *Journal of Neurosurgery, 21,* 385–398.

**Corkin, S., Milner, B., & Rasmussen, T.** (1970). Somatosensory thresholds. *Archives of Neurology, 23,* 41–58.

**Critchley, M.** (1953). *The parietal lobes.* London: Arnold.

**Evarts, E. V.** (1968). Relation of pyramidal tract activity to force exerted during voluntary movement. *Journal of Neurophysiology, 31,* 14–27.

**Fetz, E. E.** (1992). Are movement parameters recognizably coded in the activity of single neurons? *Behavioral and Brain Sciences, 15,* 679–690.

**Friedhoff, A. J., & Chase, T. N.** (1982). Gilles de la Tourette syndrome. *Advances in Neurology, 35,* 1–17.

**Galea, M. P., & Darian-Smith, I.** (1994). Multiple corticospinal neuron populations in the Macaque monkey are specified by their unique cortical origins, spinal terminations, and connections. *Cerebral Cortex, 4,* 166–194.

**Georgopoulos, A. P., Kalaska, J. F., Caminiti, R., & Massey, J. T.** (1982). On the relations between the direction of two-dimentional arm movements and cell discharge in primate motor cortex. *Journal of Neuroscience, 2,* 1527–1537.

**Georgopoulos, A. P., Pellizzer, G., Poliakov, A. V., & Schieber, M. H.** (1999). Neural coding of finger and wrist movements. *Journal of Computational Neuroscience, 6,* 279–288.

**Georgopoulos, A.P., Taira, M., & Lukashin, A.** (1993). Cognitive neurophysiology of the motor cortex. *Science, 260,* 47–52.

**Hess, W. R.** (1957). *The functional organization of the diencephalon.* London: Grune & Stratton.

**Hughlings-Jackson, J.** (1931). *Selected writings of John Hughlings-Jackson* (Vols. 1 and 2), edited by J. Taylor. London: Hodder.

**Jeannerod, M.** (1988). *The neural and behavioural organization of goal-directed movements.* Oxford: Clarendon Press.

**Kaas, J. H.** (1987). The organization and evolution of neocortex. In S. P. Wise (Ed.), *Higher brain functions* (pp. 237–298). New York: Wiley.

**Kandel, E. R., Schwartz, J. H., & Jessell, T. M.** (Eds.). (2000). *Principles of neural science* (4th ed.). New York: McGraw-Hill.

**Keele, S. W., & Ivry, R.** (1991). Does the cerebellum provide a common computation for diverse tasks? A timing hypothesis. In A. Diamond (Ed.), *The development and neural bases of higher cognitive functions. Annals of the New York Academy of Sciences* (Vol. 608, pp. 197–211). New York: New York Academy of Sciences.

**Kuypers, H. G. J. M.** (1981). Anatomy of descending pathways. In V. B. Brooks (Ed.), *Handbook of Physiology, Vol. VII: The nervous system* (pp. 579–666). Bethesda, MD: American Physiological Society.

**Lashley, K. S.** (1951). The problem of serial order in behavior. In L. A. Jeffress (Ed.), *Cerebral mechanisms and behavior* (pp. 112–136). New York: Wiley.

**Leonard, C. M., Glendinning, D. S., Wilfong, T., Cooper, B. Y., & Vierck, C. J., Jr.** (1991). Alterations of natural hand movements after interruption of fasciculus cuneatus in the macaque. *Somatosensory and Motor Research, 9,* 61–75.

**Melzack, R.** (1973). *The puzzle of pain.* New York: Basic Books.

**Melzack, R., & Wall, P. D.** (1965). Pain mechanisms: A new theory. *Science, 150,* 971–979.

**Mountcastle, V. B.** (1978). An organizing principle for cerebral function: The unit module and the distributed system. In G. M. Edelman & V. B. Mountcastle (Eds.), *The mindful brain* (pp. 7–50). Cambridge, MA: MIT Press.

**Napier, J.** (1980). *Hands.* Princeton NJ: Princeton University Press.

**Nudo, R. J., Wise, B. M., SiFuentes, F., & Milliken, G. W.** (1996). Neural substrates for the effects of rehabilitative training on motor recovery after ischemic infarct. *Science, 272,* 1791–1794.

**Onodera, S., & Hicks, T. P.** (1999). Evolution of the motor system: Why the elehant's trunk works like a human's hand. *The Neuroscientist, 5,* 217–226.

**Penfield, W., & Boldrey, E.** (1958). Somatic motor and sensory representation in the cerebral cortex as studied by electrical stimulation. *Brain, 60,* 389–443.

**Pons, T. P., Garraghty, P. E., Ommaya, A. K., Kaas, J. H., Taum, E., & Mishkin, M.** (1991). Massive cortical reorganization after sensory deafferentation in adult macaques. *Science, 252,* 1857–1860.

**Porter, R., & Lemon, R.** (1993). *Corticospinal function and voluntary movement.* Oxford: Clarendon Press.

**Roder, P. M.** (2000). The early origins of autism. *Scientific American, 282*(2), 56–63.

**Roland, P. E.** (1993). *Brain activation.* New York: Wiley-Liss.

**Rothwell, J. C., Taube, M. M., Day, B. L., Obeso, J. A., Thomas, P. K., & Marsden, C. D.** (1982). Manual motor performance in a deafferented man. *Brain, 105,* 515–542.

**Sacks, O.** (1974). *Awakenings.* New York: Vintage Books.

**Sacks, O. W.** (1998). *The man who mistook his wife for a hat: And other clinical tales.* New York: Touchstone Books.

**Schieber, M. H., & Hibbard, L. S.** (1993). How somatotopic is the motor cortex hand area? *Science, 261,* 489–492.

**Thatch, W. T., Goodkin, H. P., & Keating, J. G.** (1992). The cerebellum and the adaptive coordination of movement. *Annual Reviews of Neuroscience, 15,* 403–442.

**Twitchell, T. E.** (1965). The automatic grasping response of infants. *Neuropsychologia, 3,* 247–259.

**von Holst, E.** (1973). *The collected papers of Erich von Holst* (R. Martin, Trans.). Coral Gables, FL: University of Miami Press.

**Woolsey, T. A., & Wann, J. R.** (1976). Areal changes in mouse cortical barrels following vibrissal damage at different postnatal ages. *Journal of Comparative Neurology, 170,* 53–66.

## Chapter 11

**Ackerly, S. S.** (1964). A case of paranatal bilateral frontal lobe defect observed for thirty years. In J. M. Warren & K. Akert (Eds.), *The frontal granular cortex and behavior* (pp. 192–218). New York: McGraw-Hill.
**Adelmann, P. K., & Zajonc, R. B.** (1989). Facial efferents and the experience of emotion. *Annual Review of Psychology, 40,* 249–280.
**Barondes, S. H.** (1993). *Molecules and mental illness.* New York: Scientific American Library.
**Beatty, J.** (1995). *Principles of behavioral neuroscience.* Dubuque, IA: Brown & Benchmark.
**Becker, J. B., Breedlove, S. M., & Crews, D.** (1992). *Behavioral endocrinology.* Cambridge, MA: MIT Press.
**Berridge, K. C.** (1996). Food reward: Brain substrates of wanting and liking. *Neuroscience and Biobehavioral Reviews, 20,* 1–25.
**Butler, R. A., & Harlow, H. F.** (1954). Persistence of visual exploration in monkeys. *Journal of Comparative and Physiological Psychology, 47,* 257–263.
**Byne, W.** (1994). The biological evidence challenged. *Scientific American, 270*(5), 50–55.
**Daly, M., & Wilson, M.** (1988). *Homicide.* New York: Aldine.
**Damasio, A. R.** (1994). *Descartes' error: Emotion, reason, and the human brain.* New York: Plenum.
**Damasio, A. R.** (1999). *The feeling of what happens: Body and emotion in the making of consciousness.* New York: Harcourt Brace.
**Davis, M.** (1992). The role of the amygdala in fear and anxiety. *Annual Review of Neuroscience, 15,* 353–375.
**Dethier, V. G.** (1962). *To know a fly.* San Francisco: Holden-Day.
**Eibl-Eibesfeldt, I.** (1989). *Human ethology.* New York: Aldine de Gruyter.
**Everitt, B. J.** (1990). Sexual motivation: A neural and behavioral analysis of the mechanisms underlying appetitive and copulatory responses of male rats. *Neuroscience and Biobehavioral Reviews, 14,* 217–232.
**Field, T. M., Woodson, R., Greenberg, R., & Cohen, D.** (1982), Discrimination and imitation of facial expression by neonates. *Science, 218,* 179–181 .
**Garcia, J., & Koelling, R. A.** (1966). Relation of cue to consequences in avoidance learning. *Psychonomic Science, 4,* 123–124.
**Glickman, S. E., & Schiff, B. B.** (1967). A biological theory of reinforcement. *Psychological Review, 74,* 81–109.
**Gorski, R. A.** (1984). Critical role for the medial preoptic area in the sexual differentiation of the brain. *Progress in Brain Research, 61,* 129–146.
**Hamer, D. H., Hu, S., Magnuson, V. L., Hu, N., & Pattatucci, M. L.** (1993). A linkage between DNA markers on the X chromosome and male sexual orientation. *Science, 261,* 321–327.
**Hebb, D. O.** (1955). Drives and the C.N.S. (conceptual nervous system). *Psychological Review, 62,* 243–254.
**Heron, W.** (1957). The pathology of boredom. *Scientific American,* 196(1), 52–56.
**Jacobsen, C. F.** (1936). Studies of cerebral function in primates. *Comparative Psychology Monographs, 13,* 1–68.
**Kluver, H., & Bucy, P. C.** (1939). Preliminary analysis of the temporal lobes in monkeys. *Archives of Neurology and Psychiatry, 42,* 979–1000.
**Kolb, B., & Taylor, L.** (2000). Facial expression, emotion, and hemispheric organization. In L. Nadel R. D. Lane (Eds.), *Emotion and cognitive neuroscience* (pp. 62–83). New York: Oxford University Press.
**Lane, R. D., & Nadel, L.** (Eds.). (2000). *Cognitive neuroscience of emotion.* New York: Oxford University Press.
**LeDoux, J.** (1996). *The emotional brain.* New York: Simon & Schuster.
**MacLean, P. D.** (1949). Psychosomatic disease and the "visceral brain": Recent developments bearing on the Papez theory of emotion. *Psychosomatic Medicine, 11,* 338–353.
**Money, J., & Ehrhardt, A. A.** (1972). *Man and woman, boy and girl.* Baltimore: Johns Hopkins University Press.
**Nieuwenhuys, R., Voogd, J., & van Huijzen, C.** (1981). *The human central nervous system: A synopsis and atlas* (2nd ed.). Berlin: Springer Verlag.
**Olds, J., & Milner, P.** (1954). Positive reinforcement produced by electrical stimulation of septal area and other regions of rat brain. *Journal of Comparative and Physiological Psychology, 47,* 419–427.
**Robinson, T. E., & Berridge, K. C.** (1993). The neural basis of drug craving: An incentive-sensitization theory of addiction. *Brain Research Reviews, 18,* 247–291.
**Skinner, B. F.** (1938). *The Behavior of Organisms.* New York: Appleton-Century-Crofts.
**Spanagel, R., & Weiss, F.** (1999). The dopamine hypothesis of reward: Past and current status. *Trends in Neuroscience, 22,* 521–527.
**Swaab, D. F., Gooren, L. J., & Hofman, M. A.** (1995). Brain research, gender and sexual orientation. *Homosexuality, 28,* 283–301.
**Swaab, D. F., & Hofman, M. A.** (1995). Sexual differentiation of the human hypothalamus in relation to gender and sexual orientation. *Trends in Neurosciences, 18,* 264–270.
**Trujillo, K. A., Herman, J. P., & Schafer, M.-H.** (1993). Drug reward and brain circuitry: Recent advances and future directions. In S. G. Korenman & J. D. Barchas (Eds.), *Biological bases of substance abuse* (pp. 119–142). New York: Oxford University Press.
**Wise, R. A.** (1996). Addictive drugs and brain stimulation reward. *Annual Review of Neuroscience, 19,* 319–340.
**Woods, S. C., Seeley, R. J., Porte, D., & Schwartz, M. W.** (1998). Signals that regulate food intake and energy homeostasis. *Science, 280,* 1378–1382.
**Woolley, C. S., Gould, E., Frankfurt, M., & McEwen, B.** (1990). Naturally occurring fluctuation in dendritic spine density on adult hippocampal pyramidal neurons. *Journal of Neuroscience, 10,* 4035–4039.

## Chapter 12

**Amir, S., & Stewart, J.** (1996). Resetting of the circadian clock by a conditioned stimulus. *Nature, 8,* 542–545.
**Binkley, S.** (1990). *The clockwork sparrow.* Englewood Cliffs, NJ: Prentice Hall.
**Cohen, D. B.** (1979). *Sleep and dreaming: Origins, nature and functions.* Oxford: Pergamon.
**Dement, W. C.** (1972). *Some must watch while some must sleep.* New York: Norton.
**Earnest, D. J., Liang, F. Q., Ratcliff, M., & Cassone, V. M.** (1999). Immortal time: Circadian clock properties of rat suprachiasmatic cell lines. *Science, 283,* 693–695.
**Hobson, J. A.** (1989). *Sleep.* New York: Scientific American Library.
**Jones, B. E.** (1993). The organization of central cholinergic systems and their functional importance in sleep-waking states. *Progress in Brain Research, 98,* 61–71.
**Jouvet, M.** (1972). The role of monoamines and acetylcholine-containing neurons in the regulation of the sleep–waking cycle. *Ergebnisse der Physiologie, 64,* 166–307.
**Kleitman, N.** (1963). *Sleep and wakefulness.* Chicago: University of Chicago Press.
**Lavie, P., Pratt, H., Scharf, B., Peled, R., & Brown, J.** (1984). Localized pontine lesion: Nearly total absence of REM sleep. *Neurology, 34,* 118–120.
**Maquet, P., Laureys, S., Peigneux, P., Fuchs, S., Petiau, C., Phillips, C., Aerts, J., Del Fiore, G., Degueldre, C., Meulemaqns, T., Luxen, A., Franck, G., Van Der Linden, M., Smith, C., & Cleermans, A.** (2000). Experience dependent changes in cerebral activation during human REM sleep. *Nature Neuroscience, 3,* 831–836.
**Markand, O. N., & Dyken, M. L.** (1976). Sleep abnormalities in patients with brain stem lesions. *Neurology, 26,* 769–776.
**Moruzzi, G., & Magoun, H .W.** (1949). Brain stem reticular formation and activation of the EEG. *Electroencephalography and Clinical Neurophysiology, 1,* 455–473.
**Osorio, I., & Daroff, R. B.** (1980). Absence of REM and altered NREM sleep in patients with spinocerebellar degeneration and slow saccades. *Annals of Neurology, 7,* 277–280.
**Quinlan, J., & Quinlan, J.** (1977). *Karen Ann: The Quinlans tell their story.* Toronto: Doubleday.
**Ralph, M.R., & Lehman, M. N.** (1991). Transplantation: A new tool in the analysis of the mammalian hypothalamic circadian pacemaker. *Trends in Neurosciences, 14,* 363–366.
**Raven, P. H., Evert, R. F., & Eichorn, S. E.** (1992). *Biology of plants.* New York: Worth Publishers.
**Revonsuo, A.** (2000). The reinterpretation of dreams: An evolutionary hypothesis of the function of dreaming. *Behavioral and Brain Sciences, 24,* 277–299.
**Reiter, R. J.** (1980). The pineal and its hormones in the control of reproduction in mammals. *Endocrinology Review, 1,* 109–131.
**Richter, C. P.** (1965). *Biological clocks in medicine and psychiatry.* Springfield, IL: Charles C. Thomas.
**Roffward, H. P., Muzio, J., & Dement, W. C.** (1966). Ontogenetic development of the human sleep-dream cycle. *Science, 152,* 604–619.
**Schenck, C. H., Bundlie, S. R., Ettinger, M. G., & Mahowald, M. W.** (1986). Chronic behavioral disorders of human REM sleep: A new category of parasomnia. *Sleep, 9,* 293–308.
**Sherman, L. P., Sriram, S., Weaver, D. R., Maywook, E. S., Chaves, I., Sheng, B., Kume, K., Lee, C. C., van der Horst, G. T. J., Hastings, M. H., and Reppert, S. M.** (2000). Interacting molecular loops in the mammalian circadian clock. *Science, 288,* 1013–1019.
**Siegel, J. S.** (2000). Narcolepsy. *Scientific American, 283*(3), 76–81.
**Vanderwolf, C. H.** (1988). Cerebral activity and behavior: Control by central cholinergic and serotonergic systems. *International Review of Neurobiology, 30,* 225–340.

**Vogel, G. Q., Buffenstein, A., Minter, K., & Hennessey, A.** (1990). Drug effects on REM sleep and on endogenous depression. *Neuroscience and Behavioral Reviews, 14,* 49–63.

**Wilson, M. A., & McNaughton, B. L.** (1994). Reactivation of hippocampal ensemble memories during sleep. *Science, 265,* 676–679.

## Chapter 13

**Chang, F.-L. F., & Greenough, W. T.** ( 1982). Lateralized effects of monocular training on dendritic branching in adult split-brain rats. *Brain Research, 232,* 283–292.

**Corkin, S., Amaral, D. G., Gonzalez, R. G., Johnson, K. A., & Hyman, B. T.** (1997). H. M.'s medial temporal lobe lesion: Findings from magnetic resonance imaging. *Journal of Neuroscience, 17,* 3964–3979.

**Damasio, A. R., Tranel, D., & Damasio, H.** (1989). Amnesia caused by herpes simplex encephalitis, infarctions in basal forebrain, Alzheimer's disease and anoxia/ischemia. In F. Boller & J. Grafman (Eds.), *Handbook of neuropsychology* (Vol. 3, pp. 149–166). New York: Elsevier.

**Davis, M.** (1992). The role of the amygdala in fear and anxiety. *Annual Review of Neuroscience, 15,* 353–375.

**Eriksson, P. S., Perfilieva, E., Bjork-Eriksson, T., Alborn, A. M., Nordborg, C., Peterson, D. A., & Gage, F. H.** (1998). Neurogenesis in the adult human hippocampus. *Nature Medicine, 4,* 1313–1317.

**Florence, S. L., Jain, N., & Kaas, J. H.** (1997). Plasticity of somatosensory cortex in primates. *Seminars in Neuroscience, 9,* 3–12.

**Fuster, J. M.** (1995). *Memory in the cerebral cortex.* Cambridge, MA: MIT Press.

**Fuster, J. M., Bodner, M., & Kroger, J. K.** (2000). Cross-modal and cross-temporal association in neurons of frontal cortex. *Nature, 405,* 347–351.

**Gazzaniga, M. S.** (Ed.). (2000). *The new cognitive neurosciences.* Cambridge, MA: MIT Press.

**Gibb, R., Gorny, G., & Kolb, B.** (2001). Experience-dependent changes in dendritic arbor and spine density in neocortex vary with age and sex. *Neurobiology of Learning and Memory.*

**Gould, E., Tanapat, P., Hastings, N. B., & Shors, T. J.** (1999). Neurogenesis in adulthood: A possible role in learning. *Trends in Cognitive Sciences, 3,* 186–191.

**Gould, E., Tanapat, P., McEwen, B. S., Flugge, G., & Fuchs, E.** (1998). Proliferation of granule cell precursors in the dentate gyrus of adult monkeys is diminished by stress. *Proceedings of the National Academy of Sciences (USA), 95,* 3168–3171.

**Hampson, E., & Kimura, D.** (1988). Reciprocal effects of hormonal fluctuations on human motor and perceptual-spatial skills. *Behavioral Neuroscience, 102,* 456–459.

**Hebb, D. O.** (1947). The effects of early experience on problem solving at maturity. *American Psychologist, 2,* 737–745.

**Hebb, D. O.** (1949). *The organization of behavior.* New York: Wiley.

**Jacobs, B., Schall, M., & Scheibel, A. B.** (1993). A quantitative dendritic analysis of Wernicke's area in humans: II. Gender, hemispheric, and environmental factors. *Journal of Comparative Neurololgy, 327,* 97–111.

**Jacobs, B., & Scheibel, A. B.** (1993). A quantitative dendritic analysis of Wernicke's area in humans: I. Lifespan changes. *Journal of Comparative Neurololgy, 327,* 83–96.

**Kaas, J.** (2000). The reorganization of sensory and motor maps after injury in adult mammals. In M. S. Gazzaniga (Ed.), *The cognitive neurosciences* (pp. 223–236). Cambridge, MA: MIT Press.

**Kempermann, G., Kuhn, H. G., & Gage, F. H.** (1998). Experience-induced neurogenesis in the senescent dentate gyrus. *Journal of Neuroscience, 18,* 3206–3212.

**Kolb, B.** (1999). Towards an ecology of cortical organization: Experience and the changing brain. In J. Grafman & Y. Christen (Eds.), *Neuropsychology: From lab to the clinic* (pp. 17–34). Paris: Springer Verlag.

**Kolb, B., Gorny, G., Cote, S., Ribeiro-da-Silva, & Cuello, A. C.** (1997). Nerve growth factor stimulates growth of cortical pyramidal neurons in young adult rats. *Brain Research, 751,* 289–294.

**Kolb, B., & Walkey, J.** (1987). Behavioral and anatomical studies of the posterior parietal cortex of the rat. *Behavioural Brain Research, 23,* 127–145.

**Kolb, B., & Whishaw, I. Q.** (1998). Brain plasticity and behavior. *Annual Review of Psychology, 49,* 43–64.

**Lashley, K. H.** (1960). In search of the engram. Symposium No. 4 of the Society of Experimental Biology. In F. A. Beach, D. O. Hebb, C. T. Morgan, & H. T. Nissen (Eds.), *The neuropsychology of Lashley* (pp. 478–505). New York: McGraw-Hill. (Reprinted from *Physiological mechanisms of animal behavior,* pp. 454–482, 1951. Cambridge: Cambridge University Press.)

**LeDoux, J. E.** (1995). In search of an emotional system in the brain: Leaping from fear to emotion and consciousness. In M. S. Gazzaniga (Ed.), *The cognitive neurosciences* (pp. 1047–1061). Cambridge, MA: MIT Press.

**Loftus, E. F.** (1997). Creating false memories. *Scientific American, 277*(3), 70–75.

**Maguire, E. A., Gadian, D. G., Johnsrude, I. S., Good, C. D., Ashburner, J., Frackowiak, R. S., & Frith, C. D.** (2000). Navigation-related structural change in the hippocampi of taxi drivers. *Proceedings of the National Academy of Sciences (USA), 97,* 4398–403.

**Martin, A., Haxby, J. V., Lalonde, F. M., Wiggs, C. L., & Ungerleider, L. G.** (1995). Discrete cortical regions associated with knowledge of color and knowledge of action. *Science, 270,* 102–105.

**Milner, B., Corkin, S., & Teuber, H.** (1968). Further analysis of the hippocampal amnesic syndrome: 14 year follow-up study of HM. *Neuropsychologia, 6,* 215–234.

**Mishkin, M.** (1982). A memory system in the brain. *Philosophical Transactions of the Royal Society of London, Biological Sciences, 298,* 83–95.

**Mishkin, M., Suzuki, W. A., Gadian, D. G., & Vargha-Khadem, F.** (1997). Hierarchical organization of cognitive memory. *Philosophical Transactions of the Royal Society of London, Biological Sciences, 352,* 1461–1467.

**Morris, R. G. M.** (1981). Spatial localization does not require the presence of local cues. *Learning and Motivation, 12,* 239–260.

**Murray, E.** (2000). Memory for objects in nonhuman primates. In M. S. Gazzaniga (Ed.), *The new cognitive neurosciences* (pp. 753–763). Cambridge, MA: MIT Press.

**Nudo, R. J., Plautz, E. J., & Milliken, G. W.** (1997). Adaptive plasticity in primate motor cortex as a consequence of behavioral experience and neuronal injury. *Seminars in Neuroscience, 9,* 13–23.

**O'Keefe, J., & Nadel, L.** (1978). *The hippocampus as a spatial map.* New York: Oxford University Press.

**Purves, D., & Voyvodic, J. T.** (1987). Imaging mammalian nerve cells and their connections over time in living animals. *Trends in Neurosciences, 10,* 398–404.

**Ramachandran, V. S.** (1993). Behavioral and magnetoencephalographic correlates of plasticity in the adult human brain. *Proceedings of the National Academy of Sciences (USA), 90,* 10413–10420.

**Ramón y Cajal, S.** (1928). *Degeneration and regeneration of the nervous system.* London: Oxford University Press.

**Reynolds, B., & Weiss, S.** (1992). Generation of neurons and astrocytes from isolated cells of the adult mammalian central nervous system. *Science, 255,* 1707–1710.

**Riesen, A. H., Dickerson, G. P., & Struble, R. G.** (1977). Somatosensory restriction and behavioral development in stumptail monkeys. *Annals of the New York Academy of Sciences, 290,* 285–294.

**Robinson, T. E., & Kolb, B.** (1997). Persistent structural adaptations in nucleus accumbens and prefrontal cortex neurons produced by prior experience with amphetamine. *Journal of Neuroscience, 17,* 8491–8498.

**Robinson, T. E., & Kolb, B.** (1999). Alterations in the morphology of dendrites and dendritic spines in the nucleus accumbens and prefrontal cortex following repeated treatment with amphetamine or cocaine. *European Journal of Neuroscience, 11,* 1598–1604.

**Sainsbury, R. S., & Coristine, M.** (1986). Affective discrimination in moderately to severely demented patients. *Canadian Journal on Aging, 5,* 99–104.

**Sapolsky, R. M.** (1992). *Stress, the aging brain, and the mechanisms of neuron death.* Cambridge, MA: MIT Press.

**Schacter, D. L.** (1983). Amnesia observed: Remembering and forgetting in a natural environment. *Journal of Abnormal Psychology, 92,* 236–242.

**Scheibel, A.** (1982). Age-related changes in the human forebrain. *Neurosciences Research Program Bulletin, 20,* 577–583.

**Sherry, D. F., Jacobs, L. F., & Gaulin, S. J. C.** (1992). Spatial memory and adaptive specialization of the hippocampus. *Trends in Neurosciences, 15,* 298–303.

**Sirevaag, A. M., & Greenough, W. T.** (1987). Differential rearing effects on rat visual cortex synapses: III. Neuronal and glial nuclei, boutons, dendrites, and capillaries. *Brain Research, 424,* 320–332.

**Sirevaag, A. M., & Greenough, W. T.** (1988). A multivariate statistical summary of synaptic plasticity measures in rats exposed to complex, social and individual environments. *Brain Research, 441,* 386–392.

**Skinner, B. F.** (1938). *The behavior of organisms.* New York: Appleton-Century-Crofts.

**Squire, L.** (1987). *Memory and brain.* New York: Oxford University Press.

**Stewart, J., & Kolb, B.** (1994). Dendritic branching in cortical pyramidal cells in response to ovariectomy in adult female rats: Suppression by neonatal exposure to testosterone. *Brain Research, 654,* 149–154.

**Thorndike, E. L.** (1898). Animal intelligence: An experimental study of the associative processes in animals. *Psychological Review Monograph Supplements, 2,* 1–109.

**Turner, A., & Greenough, W. T.** (1985). Differential rearing effects on rat visual cortex synapses: I. Synaptic and neuronal density and synapses per neuron. *Brain Research, 329,* 195–203.

**Whishaw, I. Q.** (1989). Dissociating performance and learning deficits in spatial navigation tasks in rats subjected to cholinergic muscarinic blockade. *Brain Research Bulletin, 23,* 347–358.

**Woolley, C. S., Gould, E., Frankfurt, M., & McEwen, B. S.** (1990). Naturally occurring fluctuation in dendritic spine density on adult hippocampal pyramidal neurons. *Journal of Neuroscience, 10,* 4035–4039.

## Chapter 14

**Acredolo, L. P.** (1976). Frames of reference used by children for orientation in unfamiliar spaces. In G. Moore & R. Gooledge (Eds.), *Environmental knowing* (pp. 165–172). Stroudsburg, PA: Dowden, Hutchinson, and Ross.

**Barlow, H.** (1995). The neuron doctrine in perception. In M. Gazzaniga (Ed.), *The cognitive neurosciences* (pp. 415–435). Cambridge, MA: MIT Press.

**Calvin, W. H.** (1996). *How brains think.* New York: Basic Books.

**Castiello, U., Paulignan, Y., & Jeannerod, M.** (1991). Temporal dissociation of motor responses and subjective awareness. *Brain, 114,* 2639–2655.

**Chalmers, D. J.** (1995). *The conscious mind: In search of a fundamental theory.* Oxford: Oxford University Press.

**Crick, F., & Koch, C.** (1998). Consciousness and neuroscience. *Cerebral Cortex, 8,* 97–107.

**Cytowic, R. E.** (1998). *The man who tasted shapes.* Cambridge, MA: MIT Press.

**Diamond, M. C., Scheibel, A. B., Murphy, G. M., Jr., & Harvey, T.** (1985). On the brain of a scientist: Albert Einstein. *Experimental Neurology, 88,* 198–204.

**Farah, M. J.** (1995). The neural bases of mental imagery. In M. Gazzaniga (Ed.), *The cognitive neurosciences* (pp. 2963–2975). Cambridge, MA: MIT Press.

**Frith, C., Perry, R., & Lumer, E.** (1999). The neural correlates of conscious experience: An experimental framework. *Trends in Cognitive Sciences, 3,* 105–114.

**Gardner, H.** (1983). *Frames of mind.* New York: Basic Books.

**Gaulin, S. J.** (1992). Evolution of sex differences in spatial ability. *Yearbook of Physical Anthropology, 35,* 125–131.

**Gazzaniga, M. S.** (1970). *The bisected brain.* New York: Appleton-Century-Crofts.

**Gazzaniga, M. S.** (1992). *Nature's mind.* New York: Basic Books.

**Gazzaniga, M. S., Ivry, R. B., & Mangun, G. R.** (1999). *Cognitive science: The biology of the mind.* New York: Norton.

**Guilford, J. P.** (1967). *The nature of human intelligence.* New York: McGraw-Hill.

**Hebb, D. O.** (1980). *Essay on mind.* Hillsdale, NJ: Lawrence Erlbaum.

**James, W.** (1890). *Principles of psychology.* New York: Henry Holt.

**Kimura, D.** (1967). Functional asymmetry of the brain in dichotic listening. *Cortex, 3,* 163–178.

**Kimura, D.** (1973). The asymmetry of the human brain. *Scientific American, 228*(3), 70–78.

**Kimura, D.** (1992). Sex differences in the brain. *Scientific American, 367*(3), 119–125.

**Kimura, D.** (1999). *Sex and cognition.* Cambridge, MA: MIT Press.

**Kolb, B., & Stewart, J.** (1991). Sex-related differences in dendritic branching of cells in the prefrontal cortex of rats. *Journal of Neuroendocrinology, 3,* 95–99.

**Kolb, B., & Whishaw, I. Q.** (1996). *Fundamentals of human neuropsychology* (4th ed.). New York: W. H. Freeman and Company.

**Kwong, K. K., Belliveau, J. W., Chesler, D. A., Goldberg, I. E., Weisskiff, R. M., Poncelet, B. P., Kennedy, D. N., Hoppel, B. E., Cohen, M. S., Turner, R., Cheng, H. M., Brady, T. J., & Rosen, B. R.** (1992). Dynamic magnetic resonance imaging of human brain activity druing primary sensory stimulation. *Proceedings of the National Academy of Sciences (USA), 89,* 5675–5679.

**Moran, J., & Desimone, R.** (1985). Selective attention gates visual processing in the extrastriate cortex. *Science, 229,* 782–784.

**Mukerjee, M.** (1996). Interview with a parrot [field note]. *Scientific American, 274* (4), 24.

**Newsome, W. T., Shadlen, M. N., Zohary, E., Britten, K. H., & Movshon, J. A.** (1995). Visual motion: Linking neuronal activity to psychophysical performance. In M. Gazzaniga (Ed.), *The cognitive neurosciences* (pp. 401–414). Cambridge, MA: MIT Press.

**Ogawa, S. J., Lee, L. M., Kay, A. R., & Tank, D W.** (1990). Brain magnetic resonance imaging with contrast dependent on blood oxygenation. *Proceedings of the National Academy of Sciences (USA), 87,* 9868–9872.

**Paus, T., Jech, R., Thompson, C. J., Comeau, R., Peters, T., & Evans, A.** (1997). Transcranial magnetic stimulation during positron emission tomography: A new method for studying connectivity of the human cerebral cortex. *Journal of Neuroscience, 17,* 3178–3184.

**Pepperberg, I. M.** (1990). Some cognitive capacities of an African grey parrot *(Psittacus erithacus).* In P. J. B. Slater, J. S. Rosenblatt, & C. Beer (Eds.), *Advances in the study of behavior* (Vol. 19, pp. 357–409). New York: Academic Press.

**Pepperberg, I. M.** (1992). Proficient performance of a conjunctive, recursive task by an African grey parrot *(Psittacus erithacus). Journal of Comparative Psychology, 106,* 295–305.

**Pepperberg, I. M.** (1999). *The Alex studies.* Cambridge, MA: Harvard University Press.

**Rasmussen, T., & Milner, B.** (1977). The role of early left brain injury in determining lateralization of cerebral speech functions. *Annals of the New York Academy of Sciences, 299,* 355–369.

**Rizzolatti, G., & Arbib, M.A.** (1998). Language within our grasp. *Trends in Neurosciences, 21,* 188–194.

**Rowntree, S.** (2000). Spatial and verbal abilities in adult females vary with age at menses. Manuscript submitted for publication.

**Sacks, O.** (1989). *Seeing voices.* Los Angeles: University of California Press.

**Sperry, R.** (1968). Mental unity following surgical disconnection of the cerebral hemispheres. *Harvey Lectures, 62,* 293–323.

**Stewart, J., & Kolb, B.** (1994). Dendritic branching in cortical pyramidal cells in response to ovariectomy in adult female rats: Suppression by neonatal exposure to testosterone. *Brain Research, 654,* 149–154.

**Waber, D. P.** (1976). Sex differences in cognition: A function of maturation rate? *Science, 192,* 572–574.

**Wada, J., & Rasmussen, T.** (1960). Intracarotid injection of sodium amytal for the lateralization of cerebral speech dominance: Experimental and clinical observations. *Journal of Neurosurgery, 17,* 266–282.

**Warren, D. K., Patterson, D. K., & Pepperberg, I. M.** (1996). Mechanisms of American English vowel production in a grey parrot *(Psittacus erithacus). Auk, 11,* 41–58.

**Wildgruber, D., Kischka, U., Ackermann, H., Klose, U., & Grodd, W.** (1999). Dynamic pattern of brain activation during sequencing of word strings evaluated by fMRI. *Cognitive Brain Research, 7,* 285–294.

**Witelson, S. F., & Goldsmith, C. H.** (1991). The relationship of hand preference to anatomy of the corpus callosum in men. *Brain Research, 545,* 175–182.

**Witelson, S. F., Kigar, D. L., & Harvey, T.** (1999). The exceptional brain of Albert Einstein. *Lancet, 353,* 2149–2153.

## Chapter 15

**American Psychiatric Association.** (1994). *Diagnostic and statistical manual of mental disorders* (4th ed.). Washington, DC: American Psychiatric Association.

**Andreasen, N. C., & Olsen, S. A.** (1982). Negative versus positive symptoms in schizophrenia: Definition and validation. *Archives of General Psychiatry, 39,* 789–794.

**Arnold, S. E., Rushinsky, D. D., & Han, L. Y.** (1997). Further evidence of abnormal cytoarchitecture in the entorhinal cortex in schizophrenia using spatial point analyses. *Biological Psychiatry, 142,* 639–647.

**Barondes, S. M.** (1993). *Molecules and mental illness.* New York: Scientific American Library.

**Berman, K. F., & Weinberger, D. R.** (1999). Neuroimaging studies of schizophrenia. In D. S. Charney, E. J. Nestler, & B. S. Bunney (Eds.), *The neurobiology of mental illness* (pp. 246–257). New York: Oxford University Press.

**Breier, A.** (1999). Diagnostic classification of the psychoses: Historical context and implications for neurobiology. In D. S. Charney, E. J. Nestler, & B. S. Bunney (Eds.), *The neurobiology of mental illness* (pp. 195–202). New York: Oxford University Press.

**Charney, D. S., Nestler, E. J., & Bunney, B. S.** (Eds.). (1999). *The neurobiology of mental illness.* New York: Oxford University Press.

**Crow, T. J.** (1980). Molecular pathology of schizophrenia: More than one disease process? *British Medical Journal, 280,* 66–68.

**Crow, T. J.** (1990). Nature of the genetic contribution to psychotic illness: A continuum viewpoint. *Acta Psychiatrica Scandinavia, 81,* 401–408.

**Drevets, W. C., Gadde, K. M., & Krishnan, K. R.** (1999). Neuroimaging studies of mood disorders. In D. S. Charney, E. J. Nestler, & B. S. Bunney (Eds.), *The neurobiology of mental illness* (pp. 394–418). New York: Oxford University Press.

**Duman, R. S.** (1999). The neurochemistry of mood disorders. In D. S. Charney, E. J. Nestler, & B. S. Bunney (Eds.), *The neurobiology of mental illness* (pp. 333–347). New York: Oxford University Press.

**Heninger, G. R.** (1999). Special challenges in the investigation of the neurobiology of mental illness. In D. S. Charney, E. J. Nestler, & B. S. Bunney (Eds.), *The neurobiology of mental illness* (pp. 89–98). New York: Oxford University Press.

**Kessler, R. C., McGonagle, K. A., Zhao, S., Nelson, C. B., Hughes, M., Eshleman, S., Wittchen, H., & Kendler, K. S.** (1994). Lifetime and 12-month prevalence of DSM-III-R psychiatric disorders in the United States. *Archives of General Psychiatry, 51,* 8–19.

**Kondziolka, D., Wechsler, L., Goldstein, S., Meltzer, C., Thulborn, K. R., Gebel, J., Jannetta, P., DeCesare, S., Elder, E. M., McGrogan, M., Reitman, M. A., & Bynum, L.** (2000). Transplantation of cultured human neuronal cells for patients with stroke. *Neurology, 55,* 565–569.

**McGuire, P. K., Shah, G. M. S., & Murray, R. M.** (1993). Increased blood flow in Broca's area during auditory hallucinations in schizophrenia. *Lancet, 342,* 703–706.

**Merikangas, K. R., & Swendsen, J. D.** (1999). Contributions of epidemiology to the neurobiology of mental illness. In D. S. Charney, E. J. Nestler, & B. S. Bunney (Eds.), *The neurobiology of mental illness* (pp. 100–107). New York: Oxford University Press.

**Post, J. R. M., & Weiss, R. B.** (1999). Neurobiological models of recurrence in mood disorder. In D. S. Charney, E. J. Nestler, & B. S. Bunney (Eds.), *The neurobiology of mental illness* (pp. 365–393). New York: Oxford University Press.

**Prigatano, G.** (1986). *Neuropsychological rehabilitation after brain injury.* Baltimore: Johns Hopkins University Press.

**Sacks, O.** (1998). *The man who mistook his wife for a hat: And other clinical tales.* New York: Touchstone.

**Sanders, A. R., Detera-Wadleigh, & Gershon, E. S.** (1999). Molecular genetics of mood disorders. In D. S. Charney, E. J. Nestler, & B. S. Bunney, *The neurobiology of mental illness* (pp. 299–316). New York: Oxford University Press.

**Shenton, M. E., Kikinis, R., Jolesz, F. A., Pollak, S. D., LeMay, M., Wible, C. G., Hokama, H., Martin, J., Metcalf, D., Colemen, M., & McCarley, R. W.** (1992). Abnormalities of the left temporal lobe and thought disorder in schizophrenia: A quantitative magnetic resonance imaging study. *New England Journal of Medicine, 327,* 604–611.

**Sohlberg, M. M., & Mateer, C.** (1989). *Introduction to cognitive rehabilitation.* New York: Guilford Press.

**Weinberger, D. R., & Lipska, B. K.** (1995). Cortical maldevelopment, antipsychotic drugs and schizophrenia: A search for common ground. *Schizophrenia Research, 16,* 87–110.

## Appendix

**American Medical Association.** (1989). *Use of animals in biomedical research: The challenge and response.* American Medical Association white paper, Chicago.

**Feeney, D. M.** (1987). Human rights and animal welfare. *American Psychologist, 42,* 593–599.

**Finger, S.** (1994). *Origins of neuroscience: A history of explorations into brain function.* New York: Oxford University Press.

**Fox, M. A.** (1986). *The case for animal experimentation: An evolutionary and ethical perspective.* Berkeley: University of California Press.

**Fox, M. A.** (1996). Animal experimentation is not justified. In D. Bender & B. Leone (Eds.), *Animal rights: Opposing viewpoints* (pp. 82–89). San Diego: Greenhaven Press.

**Fox, M. A.** (1999). *Deep vegetarianism.* Philadelphia: Temple University Press.

**Fox, M. W.** (1999). *Beyond evolution.* New York: Lyons Press.

**Guillermo, K. S.** (1994). *Monkey business: The disturbing case that launched the animal rights movement (People for the Ethical Treatment of Animals).* Bethesda, MD: National Press Books.

**Herzog, H. A., Jr.** (1993). The movement is my life: The psychology of animal rights activism. *Journal of Social Issues, 49,* 103–119.

**Humane Society of the United States.** (2000). Animal Research Issues. http://www.hsus.org/about/history.html

**Liepert, J., Bauder, H., Wolfgang, H. R., Miltner, W. H. R., Taub, E., & Weiller, C.** (2000). Treatment-induced cortical reorganization after stroke in humans. *Stroke, 31,* 1210–1216.

**National Research Council.** (1996). *The guide for the care and use of laboratory animals.* Washington, DC: National Research Council.

**Palca, J.** (1991). Famous monkeys provide surprising results. *Science, 254,* 1789.

**Pons, T. P., Garraghty, T. E., Ommaya, A. K., Kaas, J. H., Taub, E., & Mishkin, M.** (1991). Massive cortical reorganization after sensory deafferentation in adult macaques. *Science, 254,* 1857–1860.

**Regan, T.** (1983). *The case for animal rights.* Berkeley: University of California Press.

**Regan T.** (1996). The case for strong animal rights. In D. Bender and B. Leone (Eds.). *Animal rights: Opposing viewpoints* (pp. 34–40). San Diego: Greenhaven Press.

**Ridley, M.** (1997). *The origins of virtue: Human instincts and the evolution of cooperation.* New York: Viking.

**Singer, P.** (1990). *Animal liberation* (2nd ed.). New York: New York Review of Books.

**Stephens, M. L.** (1992). The middle ground. *The Scientist, 6*(17), 12.

**Taub, E., & Crago, J. E.** (1995). Behavioral plasticity following central nervous system damage in monkeys and man. In B. Julesz and I. Kovacs (Eds.), *SFI Studies in the Sciences of Complexity, 23* (pp. 201–215). Redwood City, CA: Addison-Wesley.

# Name Index

Note: Locators in *italics* indicate illustrations.

# Subject Index

Note: Locators in **bold** indicate key terms; locators in *italics* indicate illustrations.